The Almanac of Canadian Politics
Second Edition

Munroe Eagles
James P. Bickerton
Alain-G. Gagnon
Patrick J. Smith

Toronto
Oxford University Press
1995

Oxford University Press
70 Wynford Drive, Don Mills, Ontario M3C 1J9

Oxford New York
Athens Auckland Bangkok Bombay
Calcutta Cape Town Dar es Salaam Delhi
Florence Hong Kong Istanbul Karachi
Kuala Lampur Madras Madrid Melbourne
Mexico City Nairob Paris Singaporre
Taipei Tokyo Toronto

and associated companies in
Berlin Ibadan

Oxford is a trademark of Oxford University Press

Canadian Cataloguing in Publication Data
Eagles, Donald Munroe, 1956-
    The almanac of Canadian politics

2nd ed.
ISBN 0-19-541140-4 (bound)
ISBN 0-19-541141-2 (pbk.)

1. Canada.   Parliament – Election districts –
Statistics.   2. Canada.   Parliament – Elections,
1993 – Statistics.   3. Canada – Population –
Statistics.   I. Title.

JL193.A55 1995   324.971'0648   C95-930981-0

Table of Contents

Dedication

This book is about democratic electoral outcomes. As such, it is as much about the future as the past. The authors dedicate it to the next generation — the inheritors of our democratic traditions.

To

Graeme and Devon;
Neil, Benjamin and Luke;
Vincent;
and Kavan, Erin, Ceilidh, and Liam.

Acknowledgements

The authors would like to gratefully acknowledge support and assistance from various sources over the several years that this revised edition has been in preparation. First of all, we are very grateful to the Social Sciences and Humanities Research Council of Canada (SSHRCC) whose grant (SSHRCC # 410-94-1617) made this work possible. In addition, we all are grateful to the readers and reviewers of our first edition for their helpful comments and suggestions. Elections Canada's Information Division (and particularly John Enright and Sylvie Moncion) have cheerfully and competently handled numerous requests for information. We would also like to thank the many Members of Parliament elected in 1993 for responding to our request for biographical information. We are also grateful to *La Presse* for making the 1992 Constitutional referendum results in Quebec (transposed onto federal electoral district boundaries by Pierre Drouilly) available to us. At Oxford University Press (Canada), Ric Kitowski's and Phyllis Wilson's enthusiastic support and hard work on this project are also gratefully acknowledged.

Each of us would like to express appreciation for assistance and support we have received. Munroe Eagles would like to acknowledge support from the Department of Political Science and the Canadian-American Studies Committee at the State University of New York at Buffalo. Additionally, research by Dan Cohn (Ottawa) and Jeff Jackson (Burlington, Ontario) is gratefully acknowledged.

James P. Bickerton would like to thank the University Council for Research at St Francis Xavier University for financial support. In addition, he was assisted by Robert Currie (Halifax), Kira Mondrus (Saskatoon), Marjorie White (Winnipeg), and Patricia Langlois (St. John's).

Alain-G. Gagnon would like to express his appreciation for the research assistance of Alain Desruisseaux (Montreal), and support provided by McGill University through the Québec Studies Programme.

Patrick J. Smith would like to thank Simon Fraser University for research assistance in the form of work study, SSHRCC Small Grant and Travel Support, and Deb, for her continued support. In addition, he would like to thank particularly Natalie Minunzie and Ken Stewart for their research assistance in support on this volume, and also to acknowledge more specific contributions by Jitesh (Joots) Mistry, Mackenzie Smith, and Bill Souder.

The Authors

Munroe Eagles is an Associate Professor in the Department of Political Science and a Research Scientist with the National Center for Geographic Information and Analysis (NCGIA) at the State University of New York at Buffalo. He is editor of *Spatial and Contextual Models in Political Research* (1995), and has published articles in the *Canadian Journal of Political Science, Canadian Public Policy, European Journal of Political Research*, and the *Political Geography Quarterly*. He has contributed several research studies to the Royal Commission on Electoral Reform and Party Financing, and written several book chapters.

James P. Bickerton is an Associate Professor in the Department of Political Science, St Francis Xavier University, Antigonish, Nova Scotia. He has published extensively on the politics and economy of Atlantic Canada. He is the author of *Nova Scotia, Ottawa, and the Politics of Regional Development* (1990), co-editor of *Canadian Politics* (1990 and 1994), and has contributed articles to *Studies in Political Economy, How Ottawa Spends*, and *Canadian Parties in Transition*, among others.

Alain-G. Gagnon is a Professor of Political Science, and Director of the Québec Studies Programme, at McGill University. He is a prolific writer of books and articles. His publications include *Québec: Beyond the Quiet Revolution* (1990) (with Mary Beth Montcalm), *Allaire, Bélanger, Campeau et les autres* (1991) (with Daniel Latouche), *Québec: State and Society*, 2nd edition (1993), and *Comparative Federalism and Federation: Competing Traditions and Future Directions* (1993) (with Michael Burgess), and *Canadian Parties in Transition* (1996) (with Brian Tanguay).

Patrick J. Smith is an Associate Professor and Past Chair of Political Science at Simon Fraser University. He is currently Director, Institute of Governance Studies at Simon Fraser University. He is co-author of *The Vision and the Game: Making the Canadian Constitution*, co-editor of *Continuities and Discontinuities: The Political Economy of Social Welfare and Labour Market Policy in Canada*; he has articles in *The Canadian Journal of Political Science, International Political Science Review*, and *Canadian Journal of Urban Research* as well as chapters in *Building the Cooperative Commonwealth, The New International Cities Era, Federalism in Canada, Foreign Relations and Federal States*, and *Metropolitan Governance*.

Introduction

Constituencies and the 1993 Canadian General Election

> "There can be few countries in the world in which elections whatever the questions at issue - arouse more fury than in Canada; there can be none in which political contests are entered on with greater gusto. At election-time the public life of the Dominion is to be studied in one of its most curious and characteristic manifestations."
>
> André Siegfried (1907)

This book is the second of our attempts to come to grips with the constituency connection in Canadian electoral politics (Eagles et al., 1991). Although the 295 federal constituencies form crucial components of our democratic structure, most Canadians know relatively little about the political life of ridings other than their own. Even specialists in elections are frequently unfamiliar with basic information sources that can sustain an understanding of electoral forces that manifest themselves at the constituency level. The purpose of this volume is to make available a variety of information on the federal electoral districts, and to present qualitative analysis that we hope will help citizens and scholars alike understand the richness of Canada's political environment. The positive reception given our first work has encouraged us to undertake a second volume in what we hope will become a standard reference work for students of Canadian politics. Whereas our first effort to draw attention to the significant role constituencies play in structuring electoral campaigns and outcomes focused on the 1988 election (and looked back to 1984 as well), this volume extends our work to cover the 1992 Constitutional Referendum vote and the extraordinary 1993 general election. In casting their ballots on these occasions, Canadian voters have given us a fascinating body of raw materials with which to work. While our focus is on the federal ridings themselves, we aggregate the local patterns by province and region in order to provide an interpretation of other political forces that manifest themselves at larger spatial scales. In this introductory section, we briefly describe the 1993 election and outline the contribution we see our work making to the study of Canadian electoral behaviour.

Continuity in Change: The 1993 Canadian General Election

The 35th Canadian General Election was held on Monday, 25 October 1993. At first glance, it suggested an electoral earthquake, a revolution in Canadian politics wrought by the voters: it resulted in the election of 203 out of 295 new Members of Parliament, a 69% turnover in the House of Commons; a Liberal majority of 177 seats, large, but far from the largest in Canadian electoral history, and representing just 41% of the votes cast. More noteworthy than who won, and certainly a more significant aspect of the result, was what happened to the losers: the governing Progressive Conservative Party, which under John A. Macdonald was Canada's founding party and since 1867 one of two national parties in the country, was annihilated - it was virtually eliminated from the House of Commons, dropping 169 seats and 43% of the popular vote in 1988, to just 16% of the votes in 1993, only two parliamentary seats and the loss of official party status for the only time in the party's - or the country's - history. The New Democrats, Canada's traditional social democratic third party was treated almost as harshly by the voters: the 1993 general election produced the lowest share of popular support in the 35 year history of the party; it resulted in just nine seats, three short of the number necessary for official party status in the House. Its popular support shrank to 7% (from 20% and 43 seats in 1988).

The most immediately apparent and striking outcome of the choices made by electors across Canada on the last Monday in October, 1993 was the emergence in Parliament of two new regionally-based parties - the Bloc Québécois from Quebec, as Official Opposition, and the western-based right-wing

Reform Party. These parties replaced the Progressive Conservative and New Democratic parties as the main parliamentary alternatives to the Liberals. The Bloc Québécois, premised on a federal presence for Quebec separatist sentiment, won 54 seats and Official Opposition status for its 49% share of the votes from Quebec; nationally, the Bloc's share of the votes was just 13.5%, lower overall than either Reform or Conservative support, and demonstrating one of the vagaries of our plurality, first-past-the-post electoral system - namely, the advantages of regional concentration of party support. The Bloc had only the fourth highest level of overall voter support across the country, but formed the Official Opposition in Parliament because all of its votes were concentrated in Quebec. Right behind, in seats, was the right-wing Reform Party with 52 MPs elected; Reform's share of the popular vote was 26% in 'TROC' ('the rest of Canada') - Reform did not run candidates in Quebec just as the Bloc did not contest the election outside Quebec - and 18.7% nationally, more than five points ahead of the Bloc. Other minor parties and Independents - such as the National Party, Natural Law, the Greens and Christian Heritage - managed 3.6% of the votes, enough to affect a number of outcomes in individual constituency contests. One independent was elected - in Quebec - as a result of these votes.

Parliamentary results were dramatic and gave every appearance of a significant discontinuity in Canadian politics. A detailed analysis of the results - by constituency, province and region, and by actual party support - however, suggests a more measured conclusion, one with some striking continuities. It is this theme of continuities with discontinuities which informs much of the analysis of the 25 October 1993 Canadian General Election that follows.

Close inspection of the actual results of the 35th Canadian General Election suggests a much less revolutionary conclusion than that indicated by parliamentary victories alone. Indeed, the result accurately reflects Canada's highly regionalized party system and voting behaviour, a long-standing characteristic of national politics. In every region, save perhaps Ontario, the outcome - while not always predictable in terms of party winning - was quite true to form with regard to past patterns of voting behaviour. The popular scholarly and journalistic argument that voting decisions in Canada are largely determined by short-term issues and images belies the high degree of consistency with which Canada's regional electorates have registered their voting preferences, and the continuity of regional political discourses and patterns of competition.

The Atlantic Provinces are the one region of Canada in which the traditional two-party system remains intact. The 1993 General Election did not change this. While the Liberals took 31 of 32 seats in the region, in every constituency it was the Conservatives who placed second. The PCs retained more of their electoral base here than anywhere else in Canada. In Atlantic Canada, Conservatives continue to be the alternative to the governing Liberals both federally and provincially. While the Liberals took 67.3% of the 1993 votes in Newfoundland, the PCs were second with 26.7%. In PEI, the result was 60.1% Liberal and 32% Conservative. In Nova Scotia, even with Reform taking 13.3%, the Conservatives were second to the Liberals with 23.5% to 52%. Equally, in New Brunswick, the PCs won 27.9% support to 56% for the Liberals (and 8.5% for Reform). Part of the Tory losses in Atlantic Canada in 1993 - the worst ever suffered by the party in the region - could be attributed to unfortunate timing, with the federal contest following closely on the heels of three demoralizing provincial elections, all of which had resulted in Conservative defeats.

In Quebec, party politics has always been shaped by nationalist sentiment. Quebeckers also have a long history of homogeneous bloc voting, delivering their support to whatever federal party was most convincing as defender and representative of the province's interests in Ottawa. Throughout most of the twentieth century this was the Liberal Party. After Trudeau's 'constitutional coup' in 1981-82, and the election of Brian Mulroney as Conservative Party leader, Quebec francophones switched their allegiance to the Tories. But the failure of the Meech Lake constitutional accord and the formation of a small sovereignist Bloc Québécois led by former Mulroney Cabinet Minister Lucien Bouchard created a new option for nationalist Quebeckers. For the first time there was a federal party that was complementary to the provincial Parti Québécois, promising to be a 'real' defender and champion of Quebec's interests in

Ottawa. The Bloc quickly displaced the Conservatives in francophone Quebec; the resulting polarization between nationalist and federalist appeals was a simple extension of the past twenty years of provincial politics into the federal arena.

The election result in Ontario in 1993 was perhaps the most surprising; never before had the province elected all of its Members of Parliament (save one) from a single party. Prior to 1993, all three main parties could count on a share of the province's 99 parliamentary seats. This pattern held true in 1988, for example, when Ontario seats were divided more or less evenly between the pro-Free Trade Progressive Conservatives and the anti-Free Trade Liberals and New Democrats. The unusual 1993 result in Ontario (98 Liberals and 1 Reformer) was chiefly a function of the electoral system, the splitting of the Conservative vote between Tory and Reform candidates, and the presence of a highly unpopular NDP provincial government. The collapse of the NDP vote federally in Ontario was very much a result of discontent amongst traditional New Democratic Party supporters provincially: the unpopularity of budgetary choices and the so-called 'Social Contract' by the Rae provincial government meant that the normal party voters switched or stayed home. There was a 67.7% turnout, almost 2% below the national average. When this NDP decline was combined with the distortions of the plurality electoral system and a split in the traditional right wing vote, the result was a distorted bulge of seats to the Liberals. For just 52.9% of the votes, the Liberals took 99% of the seats in Ontario. Reform needed 20.1% support for its one Ontario victory. The PC vote was 17.6% and the NDP 6%. At first glance, Ontario might suggest a straight comparison with Atlantic Canada (where the Liberals also won 97% of the seats). But Ontario clearly presents a different case than the Atlantic region. In Ontario, the Reform Party rather than the Tories finished second, suggesting the possibility of a fundamental shift in political attitudes and the future shape of partisan conflict in the province. In 1993, Reform was second overall in Ontario; it was also in second place in 57 of the 98 constituencies it contested. In only five seats did it place lower than third, usually against a sitting MP. Even in the 35 Ontario seats where Reform placed third, in 23 ridings the margin behind the second place finisher was less than 5%. In an additional seven, the difference was less than 10%. Only in five seats - four with sitting MPs, two New Democrats and two PCs - was the margin more, in each instance within 15% of second place.

In the midwest provinces of Manitoba and Saskatchewan, Tory decline was evident in the 1988 General Election. In Manitoba, the Liberals began their surge in 1988 by taking five Winnipeg seats at the expense of both NDP and Conservative incumbents. The Tories managed to hold half of the province's 14 seats in 1988. In 1993, the Liberals continued their swing, picking up 12 seats. Reform took one - in Lisgar–Marquette - and the NDP held one - Bill Blaikie's seat in Winnipeg Transcona. In the other twelve ridings, Reform placed second in eight - with margins of between 3.3% and 26.5% over the third place finishers. Where Reform placed third or lower, the NDP did better - as in Churchill, where former NDP representative Elijah Harper won for the Liberals, and in Winnipeg's North and North Centre ridings. In Saskatchewan, the rejection of the status quo was less sweeping. The NDP slide was noticeable - from 10 seats (and 44.2% of valid votes cast) in 1988 to five seats (and 26.6% support) in 1993; but the New Democrats were helped locally by the prior election of the Romanow NDP government provincially. The Conservatives held four Saskatchewan seats after the 1988 General Election, for 36.4% of the votes in the province; as elsewhere, their decline was evident in 1993. The Tories' support fell to 11.3% and they lost all four of their Saskatchewan seats. The 1993 vote was fairly evenly split in Saskatchewan (32.1% for the Liberals; 27.2% for the Reform party and 26.6% for the NDP). That produced a fairly even split of the province's 14 parliamentary seats: five for the Liberals, five NDP victories and four seats for Reform. The vote split for second and third place was also divergent. In the four 1993 Reform seats, Liberals placed second in three, the NDP in one. In the five NDP seats, Liberals were second in three, Reform in two, though here margins tended to be closer. In the five Saskatchewan ridings where Liberals won in 1993, the NDP was second in three and Reform in two. Here second and third place differences were somewhat more marked. Conservatives were fourth in 13 of the 14 constituencies. Only in Regina Wascana did a sitting Conservative MP manage third place and even here the PCs were virtually tied with Reform.

Alberta's right-wing, populist traditions were once again evident in the 1993 General Election. Far from being a radical departure from the norm, the swift rise and overwhelming success of the Reform Party (22 out of 26 seats and 52.3% of the total vote) replicated a long-established pattern in the quasi-party politics of the province whereby one dominant party is replaced by another after a set of electoral victories, a feat accomplished through the mass defection of the previously dominant party's supporters to the new dominant party. This is a pattern repeated in both provincial and federal politics in Alberta. It is substantially what occurred with the rise of the United Farmers of Alberta and the Progressives in the 1920s, Social Credit in the 1930s, the Conservatives federally in the 1960s and provincially in the 1970s, and now Reform in the 1990s. The adoption of a radical 'Reform' right wing agenda by provincial Conservative Premier Ralph Klein in the 1990s and the inclination of Federal Reform Leader Preston Manning to eschew provincial politics would appear to support the 'one party dominance' theory at both levels still in Alberta, despite a difference in party labels. Moreover, throughout all but the initial era, there has been a high degree of ideological consistency despite these sea-changes in party support: the Social Credit of the 1930s, the Conservatives of the 1960s and 1970s and the Reform Party of the 1990s has each in turn promised Albertans a 'new conservatism', one which better articulated the frustrations of the province's voters with federal politics and the policies of the governing national parties. Reform Party leader Preston Manning's neoconservative message of smaller government, deficit and debt reduction, provincial equality and undifferentiated Canadianism tapped into a rich vein of voter frustration with the governing Tories in 1993.

For Albertans like Manning, the Mulroney Conservatives appeared focused more on central Canada and particularly Quebec than even the Liberals had been, and - despite their rhetoric - big spenders and taxers as well. Manning even managed to deliver this message wrapped up in some good old Prairie evangelism, paying homage to the populist touchstone of direct democracy to be achieved through tighter control over MPs through the widespread use of initiatives, referenda and recall. Reform won in Alberta on the promise that Albertans would no longer send their MPs to Ottawa only to find them supporting unpopular measures like the GST. In the four seats that were not won by Reform, their candidates took second place, with very small margins between their support and the winners. In each they were considerably ahead of the third placed candidate. Apart from the Reform wave in Alberta, there were other changes in the 1993 election. The Liberals, long ignored in the province, at least in terms of parliamentary seats, found electoral opportunity - they elected four MPs (15.4% of the total and all from Edmonton), the only other party successes in Alberta in 1993. The Liberals managed just under half of the Reform support (25.1%) in the province. More importantly for the Liberals, apart from their four victories, they managed 16 of 22 second place finishes, in each instance placing ahead of third place Conservatives who had for several decades dominated federal politics in Alberta. In each of the other six seats, Liberals were in third place behind Conservatives - generally defeated MPs/Cabinet Ministers - with margins of under 6%. The Conservative vote, at 51.8% in 1988, almost identical to Reform's 1993 support, slipped to 14.6%. They lost all their 25 seats. The lone NDP seat - a first for the party in Alberta - was also lost when New Democratic support bottomed to just 4.1%. The National Party was not far behind with 2.4% of the votes cast by Albertans in 1993.

British Columbia was in one sense the biggest surprise of 1993, but in another sense not. While it did give 24 of its 32 seats to the Alberta-spawned Reform Party, such an 'adoption' had also occurred previously with Social Credit, which was the dominant party in British Columbia provincially for almost four decades beginning in 1952. In 1988 the governing Conservatives took 12 of the federal seats in the province, for 35.3% of the votes. The third party NDP counted on the province as one of its strongholds: in 1988, New Democrats won the support of 37% of B.C.'s voters; for that, they saw 19 MPs elected. B.C. Liberals had grounds for both frustration and hope. In 1988 they managed to hold only one seat - John Turner's Vancouver Quadra - still they had been able to collect the support of over 20% of the province's voters. Reform picked up most of the rest, but that was only 4.9% in 1988. The changes in 1993 in British Columbia were significant. These were suggested by the 1992 constitutional referendum result. Over two-thirds (68%) of the province's voters said 'No' to the Charlottetown Accord. Reform helped ensure a focus for discontent with the federal governing Tories at the end of the Mulroney era and the political honeymoon of the Harcourt New Democrats provincially was over as it began to face a series of hard decisions on issues like resource use that produced mixed, often negative, reactions. Thus both Conservatives and New Democrats became the targets of voter discontent.

The Reform Party - which had opposed the constitutional deal and was in power nowhere - became the primary vehicle for registering this protest in B.C. It was not the only one, however. In 1993, Reform picked up 36.4% of the votes in B.C. The Liberals improved their standing amongst voters in the province to 28.1%. For its 36% vote share, Reform was rewarded with more than double the number (75%) of the parliamentary seats - 24 of the 32 available in B.C. The Liberals managed six seats - all in Greater Vancouver - for their 28% vote, an 18.8% share of the seats. The chief losers in B.C. in 1993 were the New Democrats and the Tories: the NDP dropped 17 of its 19 seats in the province. The NDP's popular vote support fell from 37%, virtually the same as Reform received in 1993, to less than half that - just 15.5%. The B.C. results suggest at least the possibility of a dramatic ideological realignment of the B.C. electorate. In fact, the 1993 result may have been a protest vote against governing parties; in B.C., the NDP had come to be considered a part of the very establishment against whom much of this protest was directed. The emergence of a B.C. Reform Party provincially, against the wishes of federal party leader Preston Manning, does add another dimension to politics in the province. With a resurgent provincial Liberal Party ready to challenge the governing New Democrats also, former Social Credit adherents (the Socreds still exist, if only) have split themselves between Reform and Liberals. Traditionally such splits have helped New Democrats, who seldom manage more than 40% of the votes in B.C., provincially or federally.

The northern territories are perhaps too small in population terms to offer many generalizations, although 1993 did produce some differences. In NWT, the Liberals took two-thirds of the votes (65.4%) and both seats. The Conservatives were second (with 16.2%), while Reform (at 8.4%) and New Democrats (with 7.7%) battled it out for third spot. In Yukon, the new governing Liberals managed only 23.3%. That was good enough for second place, ahead of the Conservatives - with 17.8% - and Reform, in fourth place with 13.1%. National NDP leader Audrey McLaughlin took the riding with 43.3% support.

Overall, the election outcome had several antecedents - in the return of 203 (of 295) new Members of Parliament. It was preceded by several events having an impact on its dramatic outcome. One of the most significant was the series of constitutional crises and accords that followed the 1981 agreement which 'left Quebec out'. The success and subsequent failure of the Meech Lake Accord in 1987 and the agreement on the Charlottetown Accord and the 1992 Constitutional Referendum result - with its rejection - suggested harbingers for the 1993 General Election. In Atlantic Canada, the region's voters were the only ones in the country to vote positively in the constitutional referendum. Though narrowly defeated (51% to 48.5%) in Nova Scotia - the Atlantic province with the highest Reform Party vote in 1993 - the other three provinces registered large 'Yes' votes in the Charlottetown Accord referendum: 63% in Newfoundland, 74% in Prince Edward Island and 61% in New Brunswick. In Quebec, the 'No' vote was 55%; the distribution of the referendum votes amongst the Quebec population prefigured support for the Bloc in the 1993 General Election. In Ontario, the division of partisan loyalties was evident in 1988, reproduced itself in the constitutional referendum. Just as the province had split its support on the free trade issue in the 1988 election, on the Charlottetown Accord, Ontario voters evenly split between Yes and No: 49.9% 'Yes' and 49.6% said 'No'. In the midwest region, both provinces voted 'No'. In Manitoba, opposition to the constitutional changes in the Charlottetown Accord was at 62%; in Saskatchewan, the sentiment was negative but - at 55% 'No' - more evenly split, not unlike the 1993 General Election that followed.

The early warning signal for the Conservatives in Alberta was the 1992 constitutional referendum result in the province. The only party arguing for rejection of the Charlottetown Accord was Reform. When 60% of Alberta's voters said 'No' in 1992, many of the twenty-five sitting Conservative MPs opted for retirement rather than face their electorates in 1993. Those that did seek re-election and those that replaced them were all defeated. In 1992, B.C. voters were the most negative in the country on Charlottetown Accord constitutional amendments. This had as much to do with general political discontent as it did the particulars of constitutional reform. In either event more than two thirds (68%) of B.C.'s voters were on the 'No' side for the referendum. The rising tide of that discontent was reflected throughout all of western Canada to varying degrees; much of it carried over into the 1993 General Election.

In 1993, Canadians elected their fourth consecutive majority government. Since 1980, the single member, simple plurality electoral system has performed as intended, producing majority governments out of minority public support and ensuring comfortable majorities in Parliament for the strongest parties. This recent stability was preceded by a longer period of less stable (though more reflective) governing. From 1957 to 1979, the electoral system and voter choices produced six minority governments and only three majorities in Parliament. Perhaps more significantly, even when majorities have been produced in Parliament, they have as often as not been distorted by the severe regional under-representation of the governing party, for example, the absence of elected Liberals from the West after the party won majorities in 1974 and 1980. The Progressive Conservative majorities of 1984 and 1988 were not as affected by this regional distortion phenomenon; while electoral reform had been on the political agenda between 1979 and 1984, other electoral matters came to replace them during the Mulroney terms. The 1992 report of a Royal Commission on Electoral Reform and Party Financing, appointed in 1989, covered many aspects for 'modernizing' electoral administration and for ensuring response to a variety of Charter-based challenges to aspects of the Canada Elections Act. It did not deal with issues such as the need for an alternative electoral system.

In short, the 1993 election registered an electoral earthquake in Canadian electoral politics, albeit one that exhibited striking continuities with earlier patterns of party support and that produced a majority government led by one of Canada's traditional governing parties. A complex variety of issues, personalities, and local traditions combined to account for this extraordinary result. Whether the new political landscape created by the forces of electoral change will prove enduring is difficult to determine. This volume alerts the reader to the enduring importance of the local dimension in Canadian elections, and provides some background information on the constituency connection in the 1993 federal contest that should assist scholars and citizens alike in coming to intellectual terms with the country's political process.

The Almanac of Canadian Politics

Students of Canadian elections have developed a variety of sophisticated techniques to help understand why Canadians vote the way they do. As in many democracies throughout the world, explanations of voting behaviour and election outcomes have tended to rely upon evidence produced by public opinion surveys. The Canadian National Election Surveys (CNES) have been at the methodological forefront of this tradition of political inquiry (for an excellent review, see Gidengil, 1992). While the information that these surveys (as well as other surveys undertaken either by scholars and/or polling organizations) provide is invaluable in understanding the 'not so simple act of voting', it is our contention that in and of themselves, survey information from randomly sampled individual voters offers an incomplete, and perhaps even distorted, reproduction of an event as complex as an election.

Our contention is *not* that survey research is unreliable or inaccurate; rather, we argue that such analyses ought to be complemented by other methodologies and research traditions if we are to fully appreciate and understand the complexity of an election. One feature that is undervalued in most survey research designs is the fact that a general election in Canada is in significant respects a series of 295 constituency elections held simultaneously. Many of the factors that combine to create a national electoral result reflect the particular distribution of individual riding characteristics across the diverse Canadian landscape. Most surveys are (to paraphrase Allen Barton) 'sociological and political meatgrinders' in that their primary purpose is to randomly select respondents from across the country in order to reflect national trends with maximum fidelity and accuracy. Details concerning local settings and social interactions are discounted, and survey analysts tend to concentrate on the attributes of individuals in constructing explanations as if these relationships were spatially invariant.

Our primary intention, then, is to draw attention to the importance of the constituency dimension of Canadian politics. Even during election contests when electoral districts are most visible, there has been a lamentable tendency to overlook the constituency connection. Election campaigns in Canada have become media spectacles with press coverage resembling 'horserace journalism' focusing on parties as if they were unitary actors (see Fletcher, 1987). Representatives of the mass media follow party leaders on their respective campaign trails. Saturation polling directs our attention to the shifting national or, at best, the regional/provincial standings of the parties. Pressing national issues often dominate the media's election coverage and deflect the voter's view from the local dimension of constituency campaigning.

Yet, while this combination of factors may help explain why we tend to overlook local electoral districts, it also distorts our understanding of elections and political behaviour. Ultimately, all national electoral forces pass through a local constituency filter. We all cast ballots in a single riding, and national party fortunes hinge on its performance across a range of ridings; a federal election in Canada is actually a collection of 295 constituency elections held simultaneously.

There is good reason to expect that the nature of this local filtering of political forces will itself be a highly differentiated process, reflecting the wide geographic variations so often commented upon in Canadian politics. The information presented in this book attests to the wide diversity of constituency contexts. For example, the constituency of Nunatsiaq in Canada's North spans four time zones and covers more territory than most countries in the world, but with only 22,943 residents, however, it is also Canada's least populous riding. At the other extreme, Canada's urban ridings may cover an area of fewer than 20 square kilometres and yet have populations of more than 100,000 voters. On virtually any dimension imaginable (geographic, or socio-economic, for example), constituencies in Canada are extraordinarily diversified.

Political patterns at the constituency level embody and reflect this differentiation. Differences in party organizational strength are similarly both part cause and part consequence of the diversity of these small political worlds. In the end, both the social pressures acting upon and the strategic options confronting a typical voter will vary widely according to the features of their electoral context. In offering this book, then, we hope to enhance appreciation of the importance of this local dimension in Canadian politics.

Secondly, our book is rooted in a concern for the vitality of Canadian democracy. Because the political significance of local settings has frequently been devalued, information bearing on this set of factors has not been made readily available to the average citizen. While several government departments and agencies (notably Elections Canada and Statistics Canada) have gone to considerable trouble to publish basic information for constituencies, much of this information lies underutilized and unappreciated in the "Government Documents" sections of our major libraries. Moreover, much of the information that does exist is in a form that is difficult for the average citizen to digest. Determined citizens who undertake to gather information about their own (or other) ridings confront a bewildering array of indicators. Since most available information is presented in the form of raw numbers, some further processing (if only to compute percentages) is required to render the information meaningful. Occasionally, an enterprising reporter will have performed this function for particular ridings, but this is not often the case. In these circumstances, the costs of informing oneself may appear to be prohibitively high.

By centralizing and consolidating basic information on these electoral environments, we hope to lower the information costs to voters, journalists, and activists alike. We hope also that this book will make an indirect contribution to the academic study of politics. We feel that the practitioners of political science in Canada (with several important exceptions) have also tended to undervalue the significance of the constituency connection. In this we are not alone. In his presidential address to the 1986 convention of the American Political Science Association, for example, Richard Fenno noted: 'We love our constituencies, but we do not study them — not up close, in detail, over time' (1986: 6). Though his intended audience was primarily American, we feel that his comment applies equally well in the Canadian context.

In some measure, then, we see ourselves as responding to Fenno's statement. However, just as there are sound reasons why voters' attention may be deflected from local influences, so too have there been powerful forces directing the attention of most political researchers elsewhere. Without wishing to digress too deeply into a discussion of developments in Canadian social science, we feel that some mention should be made of the intellectual currents that have desensitized the scholarly community to the importance of locale (if only to better guard against them).

The conventions of party discipline in a parliamentary system constitute one of the most obvious institutional factors that diminish the scope for local influences to gain expression directly in the legislative process. In general, we expect that legislators will be motivated by a desire to be re-elected, and therefore act upon their electoral incentive to look after their constituents. In a system where legislators are by and large free agents, unconstrained by the party whip and able to vote according to their conscience or their constituency, the scope for constituency service is reasonably large and unencumbered. But in Canada, parties are among the most highly disciplined in the world and constituency service tends to be limited to 'ombudsman-like' intervention on behalf of specific constituents. In this circumstance, the institutions of parliamentary democracy in Canada may have discouraged political scientists from focusing on local influences in Canadian politics, despite the fact that the impact of these forces outside the legislative arena may be impressive (for an important exception, see Price and Mancuso, 1991).

Somewhat paradoxically, the very politicization of territory in Canada may hold a second clue as to why political scientists have neglected local constituencies. Regional and provincial differences have long been central to any understanding of Canadian politics. 'Regionalism', 'province-building', and 'centre-periphery relationships' are among the terms that have dominated the lexicon of Canadian political scientists for decades. Without denying the importance of the phenomena to which these concepts refer, it seems likely that the very force of provincial and regional factors has retarded the emergence of an appreciation of local factors operating *within* these larger areas.

A small but important body of research demonstrates that Canadian voters are indeed responsive to stimuli emanating from their social interactions and from the characteristics of their local socio-political environments. For example, Richard Johnston has argued that the relationship between religion, social class, and voting varies from province to province, in relation to the proportion of Catholics in the population (Johnston, 1991). William P. Irvine has demonstrated that the propensity of Canadians to vote at elections varies according to the competitive relationship among the parties competing in a riding (Irvine, 1976: 349-50). More generally, Donald Blake has argued that '[t]he socio-economic and political settings associated with the large number of individual contests making up a Canadian national election are clearly important to the fortunes of parties and the actions of voters' (Blake, 1978: 302; see also Eagles, 1990).

These pioneering insights have unfortunately not received much attention in the Canadian context (see Fletcher, 1987; important exceptions can be found in Bell and Fletcher, eds, 1991). We hope that this volume (and its predecessor) will help rectify this situation by providing students of Canadian politics with a reference resource similar to those available in other Anglo-American democracies. Michael Barone's and Grant Ujifusa's regularly updated classic *The Almanac of American Politics* (1994) and Robert Waller's *The Almanac of British Politics* (1991) have quickly become established reference works for students of politics in their respective countries.

In what follows we present a variety of information on the settings within which federal political competition occurs. The information tends to centre on the 1993 federal election campaign, though we hope to capture more deep-seated and enduring features of Canada's political geography. However, since it is often helpful to understand the 1993 result in the context of earlier elections and the 1992 constitutional referendum vote, these campaigns frequently figure in the discussions. Beginning with Atlantic Canada, there is an overview for each region (and in the cases of Quebec, Ontario, Alberta and British

Columbia, a province) in which some of the broader currents of opinion operating beyond the constituency are outlined.

The core of the book, however, consists of profiles of each of Canada's 295 constituencies. These profiles begin with an analytical narrative in which an attempt is made to identify factors that are important for an understanding of the 1993 election's outcome in that setting, but that might not be immediately apparent from the data presented in the standardized grid containing political, campaign finance, ethno-cultural, socio-economic, geographic, and demographic information. We thereby hope to combine some of the advantages of standardization with the interpretative flexibility of less structured and more impressionistic analytical vignettes.

Deciding what to include has been difficult. Our selection of indicators will not satisfy everyone, though we have benefited from the suggestions of several readers of our first edition and have added some new indicators. Appendix Three gives a precise definition of the various measures employed, but a brief introduction may help to clarify the rationale for our choices, and identify the changes we have introduced in this book. For each constituency we present the 1993 election vote shares for each of the three traditional federal parties. This year, we also included a separate tally for the Bloc Québécois (in Quebec) and the Reform Party (outside of Quebec). Votes going to other parties, and to independent candidates, were combined in an 'other' category.

As another indicator of the nature and intensity of party competition in each riding, we include three key pieces of information on local party financing (from Elections Canada, 1995). The number of donors who contribute to local party coffers at election time, and the total value of these donations, are both important indicators of the strength of the local party organization. The Canada Elections Act establishes allowable limits for each party's local campaign expenditures, based on a sliding-scale formula reflecting the number of eligible voters in the riding, deviation from the national average population of districts, and population density (see Appendix Three for the precise definition). Comparing actual party spending on the campaign with the allowable limit indicates the importance attached to the riding by the parties (or its 'winnability'/vulnerability) and provides a measure of the intensity of the local campaign.

Canada's multicultural heritage is difficult to represent adequately in a standardized grid format. We decided to focus attention on the relative size of Canada's two major language groups (English and French as home languages), the percentage of officially bilingual residents, and the percentage of residents using 'other' languages at home. We also include information on the presence and proportionate population size of Canada's aboriginal peoples and of immigrants. In addition to these measures, the 1991 census reported information on the religious composition of electoral districts. Electoral research has established the importance of religion as a determinant of Canadian electoral behaviour (e.g., Johnston, 1991), and we have included information on the proportion of Catholics and Protestants in this edition.

We also include a socio-economic profile that presents various measures of the extent and distribution of wealth in a constituency. Average incomes and dwelling values are self-explanatory. The median income is that level of income which divides households in the constituency into two groups of equal size, half with incomes above the median amount, half with incomes below. Data on the proportion of families classed by Statistics Canada as having 'low incomes' and the proportion of single-family homeowners, attempt to indicate different dimensions of the complex question of constituency affluence.

Unfortunately, it is also difficult to adequately represent the social class structure of constituencies using census data. However, the proportion of the workforce employed in the typically white-collar 'managerial and administrative occupations' and the proportion who have earned university degrees both illustrate important aspects of the class character of ridings. The former is as pure a category as is available to represent the "middle class" (as "controllers of the means of production" in neo-Weberian terms). Given class differentials in access to education, the incidence of university degrees in a population may be taken as an indirect expression of an underlying class structure.

The rate of labour force participation and the level of unemployment are both important indicators of the intensity of local economic activity and the presence or absence of employment opportunities. The proportion of the workforce who are self-employed is also a general barometer of the entrepreneurial climate in a riding. An indicator of the residential stability of a riding is provided by the proportion of residents who report having moved home within the previous five years.

Ridings vary greatly in terms of their economic foundations and primary industries. We therefore include information on the proportion of workers employed in a number of key economic sectors. Full details on the definitions of these sectoral divisions are provided in Appendix Three.

New in this edition are three measures of the homogeneity or heterogeneity of constituency electorates. The first is a 'Herfindahl index' of the homogeneity/heterogeneity of districts in terms of the ethnic origins of their residents. This index is widely used in economics to measure the tendency toward oligopoly in market shares for industrial sectors. While details of the calculation of this measure is given in Appendix Three, the values of this index approach a maximum of 1.00 when all residents are drawn from a single ethnic origin (and approach 0 when residents are distributed in roughly equal proportion across all ethnic origins).

A second 'Herfindahl index' measures the distribution of employment across industrial and economic sectors (again, with values approaching the maximum of 1.00 indicating that employment is almost fully concentrated in one sector, and values nearer to 0 indicating that employment is dispersed roughly equally across all sectors). A third measure of income disparity has been included in the statistical grids - it reflects the difference between median and average family incomes expressed as a percentage of the average family incomes in ridings. In general, the higher the value of this percentage number, the greater is the disparity in the distribution of family incomes in a riding (with zero representing no difference between median and average family incomes). Taken together, these various measures of constituency homogeneity or heterogeneity can assist the reader in ascertaining the extent to which each district approximates a distinctive 'community of interest'.

The size (by area and population) and population density of the riding, together with its origins in terms of the old electoral districts, are given on the data grids. Since constituency boundaries did not change between 1988 and 1993, we have dropped the section dealing with the origins of the districts in terms of pre-1988 districts. Those interested in this information will find it in the first edition. This edition includes a number of maps, both provincial/regional and of each constituency (and its nearest neighbours). We hope these help readers appreciate the local and extra-local context of Canada's electoral districts. We have also included summary information on the Member of Parliament elected for each district in the 1993 election. We are grateful to the many Members who responded to our request for them to verify the information pertaining to their personal background. As in the first edition, we have included a variety of materials in appendices that are designed to enhance the reader's appreciation of constituency competition in Canada. The rankings of constituencies in a number of social and political areas help identify particularly distinctive or interesting settings.

As mentioned above, the narratives attempt to flesh out these data and to draw attention to any unique features of the riding, primarily in the context of the 1993 federal election. However, it is important to point out that the narratives are not intended to constitute a complete account of the election or its outcome; specifically absent is a discussion in each setting of identifiably national or regional/provincial issues. Such factors are discussed in the riding narratives only if their local expression or impact was in some way distinctive.

Because the ridings are diverse the content of the narrative contributions varies considerably. In some parts of the country, for example, political traditions run long and deep. When dealing with such areas, as with Atlantic Canada, our profiles develop this aspect of the setting in somewhat greater detail than elsewhere. In addition to the data presented in the grids, the narratives make extensive use of newspaper or other media accounts of particular riding contests to help interpret and explain the pattern of voting. We are, therefore, heavily indebted to a score of reporters in constructing the riding profiles. While it has been impossible to check all the details of these various media reports, we depend a great deal on the accuracy of a large number of journalists and we have been careful to use only reliable and respected sources.

A variety of appendices are included to help the reader locate constitutencies or candidates, and to appreciate particularly distinctive ridings. In addition, since so much of the media attention in Canadian election campaigns centre on party leaders, and since parties attempt to strategically employ their leader during the campaign through leader tours, we have included a 'campaign calendar' (Appendix Four) that provides a summary of campaign appeareances by the major party leaders.

We have been gratified by the positive reception given to our first edition of this work, and we would like to thank those readers who took the time to write to us with suggestions and criticisms. We have considered these contributions carefully, and have acted on many in this revised edition. We hope to have provided a reasonably useful depiction of the constituency connection in Canadian political life. We fully realize, however, that we will never know as much about any particular riding as those practicing politics within its boundaries. A final caveat concerning the accuracy of our data and interpretations must be given. This has been a large-scale undertaking. In our data grids alone we present over 17,000 separate pieces of information for the constituencies. We have relied on information drawn from a wide variety of sources and, while we have been conscientious in our handling of these materials in a project of this nature inaccuracies are inevitable. While we hope that these will be minor and infrequent, we would appreciate being informed of any that appear. As in the first edition, we invite our readers to forward their suggestions and improvements that might be useful in future revised editions of this work.

REFERENCES

Barone, Michael and Grant Ujifusa, 1994, *The Almanac of American Politics*, Washington: Sunrise Books

Bell, David V. J., and Frederick J. Fletcher, eds, 1991, *Reaching the Voter: Constituency Campaigning in Canada*, Volume 20 of the Research Studies of the Royal Commission on Electoral Reform and Party Financing, Toronto and Ottawa: Dundurn Press and the Minister of Supply and Services Canada

Blake, Donald E., 1978, "Constituency Contexts and Canadian Elections: An Exploratory Study," *Canadian Journal of Political Science*, 11, 2 (June): 279-305

Canada. Elections Canada, 1993, *Official Voting Results, Thirty-Fifth General Election, Synopsis*, Ottawa: Chief Electoral Officer of Canada

Canada. Elections Canada, 1995, *Report of the Chief Electoral Officer Respecting Election Expenses, Thirty-Fifth General Election*, Ottawa: Chief Electoral Officer of Canada

Eagles, Munroe, 1990, "Political Ecology: Local Effects on the Political Behaviour of Canadians," in Alain-G. Gagnon and James P. Bickerton, eds, *Canadian Politics: An Introduction to the Discipline*, Peterborough, ON: Broadview Press, pp. 285-307

Eagles, Munroe, James P. Bickerton, Alain-G. Gagnon, and Patrick J. Smith, 1991, *The Almanac of Canadian Politics*, Peterborough, ON: Broadview Press

Fenno, Richard F., 1986, "Observation, Context, and Sequence in the Study of Politics," *American Political Science Review*, 80,1 (March): 3-15

Fletcher, Frederick J., 1987, "Mass Media and Parliamentary Elections in Canada," *Legislative Studies Ouarterly*, 23, 3 (August): 341-72

Gidengil, Elisabeth, 1992, "Canada Votes: A Quarter Century of Canadian National Election Studies," *Canadian Journal of Political Science*, 25, 2 (June): 219-48

Irvine, William A., 1976, "Testing Explanations of Voting Turnout in Canada," in Ian Budge, Ivor Crewe, Dennis Fairlie, eds, *Party Identification and Beyond: Representations of Voting and Party Competition*, New York: John Wiley and Sons, pp. 335-51

Johnston, Richard, 1991, "The Geography of Class and Religion in Canadian Elections," in Joseph Wearing, ed., *The Ballot and its Message: Voting in Canada*, Toronto: Copp Clark Pitman, pp. 108–35

Price, Richard G., and Maureen Mancuso, 1991, "Ties that Bind: Parliamentary Members and their Constituents," in Robert M. Krause and R. H. Wagenberg, eds, *Introductory Readings in Canadian Government*, Mississauga, ON: Copp Clark Pitman

Statistics Canada, 1993, *Profile of Federal Electoral Districts. Parts A & B*, Ottawa: Canadian Government Publishing Centre, Catalogue 93-335 and 93-336

Waller, Robert M., 1991, *The Almanac of British Politics*, 4th ed., London and New York: Routledge

Canadian Results, 1988 & 1993 Elections, 1992 Referendum[1]

	1988 Election			1993 Election	
	% Vote	Seats	1992	% Vote	Seats
Conservatives	43.0	169		16.0	2
Liberals	31.9	83		41.3	177
NDP	20.4	43		6.9	9
BQ	–	–		13.5	54
Reform	2.1	0		18.7	52
Other/Indep.	2.6	0		6.6	1
Turnout	75.3	–		69.6	–
% Yes (1992)			45.7		
% No (1992)			54.3		

[1] Canada-wide Referendum totals exclude Quebec, since that province administered the Referendum vote (Elections Canada managed the voting in other provinces/territories).

THE ATLANTIC

The Atlantic

Regional Overview

The four provinces that make up Atlantic Canada - Newfoundland, Nova Scotia, New Brunswick, and Prince Edward Island - have the highest unemployment, lowest per capita incomes, and weakest revenue-raising capacities amongst Canadian provinces. Yet there are wide disparities within the region, with some areas experiencing relative prosperity, stability, and growth, while others have experienced economic stagnation or decline. The region's rural areas remain heavily dependent upon resource industries that have tended to supply local residents with insufficient numbers of seasonal jobs. The fishery, which for hundreds of years has provided the economic lifeblood for Newfoundland and numerous coastal communities throughout the rest of the region, is currently in a state of severe and prolonged crisis, brought on by the near extinction of the Atlantic cod and groundfish stocks that once seemed endlessly renewable.

The region as a whole remains heavily dependent upon equalization payments and other fiscal transfers provided by the federal government, a fact which has tended to make the Atlantic provinces supporters of a strong federal government capable of redistributing some of the country's wealth to its poorer regions and citizens. The region's relative economic weakness exaggerates the importance of government expenditures of all sorts, whether social spending, defence spending, or the regional development spending that a series of federal agencies has engaged in for over thirty years. Nowhere is the federal government's deficit-reduction program of spending cuts, privatizations, and downsizing more fraught with the potential for real social and economic hardship than in this region.

The region's populace is the most homogeneous and stable in Canada, comprised overwhelmingly of people of Anglo-Celtic ancestry, with a significant French-speaking minority (the Acadians) centred in New Brunswick. With little immigration since the mid-19th century, local roots and identities run deep and kinship ties are pervasive. This high degree of social integration is aided by geography: surveys suggest that the residents of the region's two island provinces are particularly attached to their provincial identities and the perceived uniqueness of their ways of life. Similar observations could be made with regard to important sub-groups such as the Acadians or perhaps Cape Bretoners.

In the 1988 federal election, the Atlantic region sent twenty Liberals and twelve Conservatives to Ottawa, a reversal of the previous election result. The free trade agreement was the key issue, and Liberal warnings of the dire consequences of the agreement for social programs placed Atlantic Canadian Tories on the defensive throughout the campaign. Prince Edward Island, rural Newfoundland, Cape Breton Island, and Northeast New Brunswick, the poorest areas in the region with the most to lose in the event of any scaling back of federal transfer payments or regional development spending, dealt the incumbent Conservatives their biggest setbacks, returning from their constituencies a full complement of 15 Liberals. Indeed, with the sole exception of the northwest New Brunswick constituency of Madawaska (held by Conservative cabinet minister Bernard Valcourt), the Liberals were able to retrieve all of the ridings that had been traditionally theirs prior to the Tory landslide in 1984. On the other hand, the generally more prosperous and Protestant ridings of anglophone New Brunswick and mainland Nova Scotia returned Conservatives over Liberals by a 2-1 margin.

In 1993, however, even these core Tory seats were lost, and it was the Liberal Party's turn to 'own' the region in an even more impressive fashion than the Tory sweep of 1984. Only one Conservative survived that party's electoral debacle, with the other 31 seats in the region going to the Liberals. In almost every case, the Liberal majority ranged from comfortable to enormous, with some of the largest margins of victory in the country. In only three or four seats could the result be classified as close: the lone Conservative victory by Elsie Wayne in Saint John, largely made possible by a split in the Liberal vote between the official party candidate and a former candidate running as an Independent; the surprise defeat of Conservative Fisheries Minister Ross Reid by homemaker Bonnie Hickey in St John's East (one of the closest results in the country); PC incumbent Greg Thompson's loss to Liberal Harold Culbert in the bedrock Tory riding of Carleton-Charlotte, made possible by a strong showing by the Reform candidate; and Tory minister Bernard Valcourt's loss to Pierrette Ringette-Maltais in Madawaska, despite winning the biggest Conservative vote in Atlantic Canada.

The three defeated Conservative cabinet ministers - Valcourt, Reid, and Peter McCreath in the Nova Scotia riding of South Shore - were replaced by three Liberal ministers after the election: Doug Young re-elected in Acadie–Bathurst became Transport Minister; Dave Dingwall re-elected in Cape Breton East became Minister of Public Works and Minister for the Atlantic Canada Opportunities Agency; and Brian Tobin, re-elected in Humber–St Barbe–Baie Verte, became Minister of Fisheries and Oceans.

The role of third parties has always been small in this region. Throughout its history, Prince Edward Island has sent only Liberals and Tories to Ottawa; New Brunswick hasn't elected a third party candidate in more than 70 years; the 'socialist' coal miners of industrial Cape Breton ended their tradition of electing Nova Scotia's only third party MP in 1979; and Newfoundland, though twice since 1979 electing third party candidates as federal members of parliament (both NDP, neither serving longer than two years), returned traditional party candidates in subsequent elections. In 1993, in many Atlantic Canadian ridings, the NDP was displaced from its customary third place position by the Reform Party. Though Reform was not a factor in Newfoundland, Prince Edward Island, Cape Breton or francophone New Brunswick, it did quite well in a number of other, traditionally-Conservative, Nova Scotia and New Brunswick seats. In no Atlantic Canadian riding, however, did it finish better than third or exceed 20% of the vote.

While the best performance by a Reform candidate in the region was in Halifax West, it was in New Brunswick that the party had hoped to make its Atlantic breakthrough. This is because of the provincial success of the Confederation of Regions Party, which became the province's official opposition in 1991 by running on a program similar in many respects to that of the Reform Party. While CoR planned to contest the 1993 federal election itself, it was hampered by a rift in the national party that led a breakaway faction to establish the Canada Party. CoR subsequently was unable to nominate the 50 candidates necessary to gain official party status, forcing a number of its standard-bearers to run as Independents. This created an opportunity for the Reform Party.

In point of fact, CoR's earlier success in New Brunswick probably harmed rather than enhanced Reform's prospects in that province. In the run-up to the 1993 federal election, the provincial CoR party was going through a very messy and very public disintegration, including defections from the provincial caucus and the embarrassment of two claimants to the position of leader (one inside and one outside the legislature). It seems likely that voter wariness of right-wing populist parties was greatly increased by this negative experience, a conclusion drawn by at least one Reform candidate. Of course, Reform had no chance whatsoever in the province's francophone ridings, where its similarity to the anti-bilingual CoR Party stripped it of any legitimacy in the eyes of voters. No Reform candidate was even nominated in three of these ridings, due to 'lack of voter interest'. Still, the popular vote for Reform in New Brunswick, at 8.5%, allowed it to claim third party status over the NDP, which managed only 4.9% of the vote.

In Nova Scotia, Reform almost doubled the popular vote of the NDP (12.8% to 6.7%), while finishing third in 8 of the 11 provincial seats. In several contests in traditionally-Conservative ridings, Reform was an important factor, indicating that the party may have a future in the province. Still, its appeal remained limited and its hardline message of sharp spending cuts and much smaller government seems poorly designed for a region not averse to government intervention to get the economy rolling again or to ameliorate the effects of chronically high levels of unemployment.

With the addition of Reform and a number of new fringe parties (such as the National Party, the Canada Party, and the Natural Law Party), more candidates ran for office in the region than ever before, and more women candidates than ever before. In part this was due to an effort by the major parties to recruit more women candidates, in part because of the greater number of fringe parties. The result was many more elected women from the region than ever before: 2 of 10 in New Brunswick, 3 of 11 in Nova Scotia, and 2 of 7 in Newfoundland. If still far short of equality, the 22% of the region's MPs who are women nonetheless compares favourably with the national total of 18%.

The overriding issue in the election throughout the region was jobs and the economy. Three years of recession had taken their toll on Atlantic Canadians; through the unremitting economic gloom of deficits and cutbacks, the Liberals' promise of modest job creation through government investment in infrastructure projects was well received. In general, the Liberal policy book - the Red Book - allowed them to present voters with the appearance of a balanced plan of deficit reduction *and* job creation, in contrast with the Conservative campaign's emphasis on leadership style and and the Reform Party's obsession with the deficit. The New Democratic Party's emphasis on cancelling free trade agreements and protecting medicare were not big vote winners in 1993, and seemed driven by the party's ideological agenda. This further contributed to the already evident marginalization of the party.

A number of more specific issues were important in the Atlantic region, as well, though these tended to be tied to the general issue of the economy and job creation. The collapse of the fishery and what to do about it was certainly central to campaign debates in every Newfoundland riding. The Liberals' promise to extend surveillance and custodial management beyond the 200-mile limit to include the nose and tail of the Grand Bank was dismissed by Conservative candidates as illegal, rash, dangerous, unenforceable, and largely irrelevant, but it did give voters the impression that the Liberals would do *something* as opposed to simply waiting with the hope that stocks might recover in a decade or a generation. Another contentious issue in some ridings was the multi-billion dollar contract for new EH-101 helicopters for the military, a 'cadillac' purchase the Liberals promised to cancel if elected. While the Conservatives warned that the cancellation would entail thousands of forgone jobs as well as declining 'search and rescue' and military capabilities, they were unable to muster much outrage or opposition to the Liberals' position even in those ridings that stood to reap direct benefits.

Another factor in the Atlantic region was three provincial elections that preceded the federal by six months or less; all returned Liberal governments to power. In Nova Scotia, the Liberals won a lop-sided majority after 15 years of Tory rule; in P.E.I., the Liberals won every seat but one in the legislature; and in Newfoundland, Clyde Wells' Liberals were returned to power with a slightly improved majority. One negative effect of this on local Conservatives was demoralization and fatigue: re-mobilizing and energizing party workers in the wake of these electoral losses was a difficult task. The downside for Liberal candidates in the federal election was that unpopular provincial policies - a broken campaign promise of 'no new taxes' in Nova Scotia and health care cuts in P.E.I. - could now be used against them. For the most part, however, voter hostility toward provincial Liberal policies appears not to have excessively tarnished their federal counterparts.

The effect on the electorate of two election campaigns in close proximity was also one of fatigue. Interest and tolerance levels were lowered as a result, leading many Liberal candidates to adopt a 'silent running' approach in their campaigns aimed more at not annoying a testy electorate rather than actively winning them over. It was a tactic Conservative candidates, for the most part running from behind from the outset, could ill afford. Polls at the outset of the campaign gave the Liberals a 6% to 10% bulge on the Conservatives in Atlantic Canada and this grew during the campaign. In the final result the Liberals doubled the vote of their traditional rivals, a landslide of immense proportions in a region where the major parties have tended to be fairly evenly matched in classic two-party fashion. Despite this, the Conservatives still did better in this region than any other, and they retain a considerable base of voter support from which to build.

Newfoundland Results, 1988 & 1993 Elections, 1992 Referendum

	1988 Election			1993 Election	
	% Vote	Seats	1992	% Vote	Seats
Conservatives	42.2	2		26.7	0
Liberals	45.0	5		67.3	7
NDP	12.4	0		3.5	0
Reform	–	–		1.0	0
Other/Indep.	0.4	0		1.5	0
Turnout	67.1	–		55.1	–
% Yes (1992)			63.2		
% No (1992)			36.8		

Prince Edward Island Results, 1988 & 1993 Elections, 1992 Referendum

	1988 Election			1993 Election	
	% Vote	Seats	1992	% Vote	Seats
Conservatives	41.5	0		32.0	0
Liberals	49.9	4		60.1	4
NDP	7.5	0		5.2	0
Reform	–	–		1.0	0
Other/Indep.	1.1	0		1.7	0
Turnout	84.9	–		73.2	–
% Yes (1992)			73.9		
% No (1992)			26.1		

Nova Scotia Results, 1988 & 1993 Elections, 1992 Referendum

	1988 Election			1993 Election	
	% Vote	Seats	1992	% Vote	Seats
Conservatives	40.9	5		23.5	0
Liberals	46.5	6		52.0	11
NDP	11.4	0		6.8	0
Reform	–	–		13.3	0
Other/Indep.	1.1	0		6.4	0
Turnout	74.8	–		64.7	–
% Yes (1992)			48.8		
% No (1992)			51.2		

New Brunswick Results, 1988 & 1993 Elections, 1992 Referendum

	1988 Election			1993 Election	
	% Vote	Seats	1992	% Vote	Seats
Conservatives	40.4	5		27.9	1
Liberals	45.4	5		56.0	9
NDP	9.3	0		4.9	0
Reform	–	–		8.5	0
Other/Indep.	4.8	0		2.7	0
Turnout	75.9			69.6	–
% Yes (1992)			61.8		
% No (1992)			38.2		

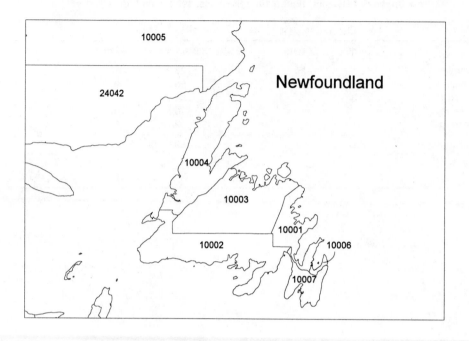

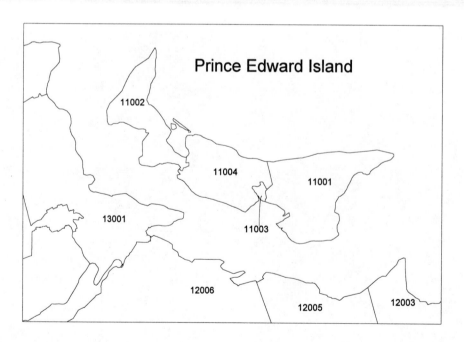

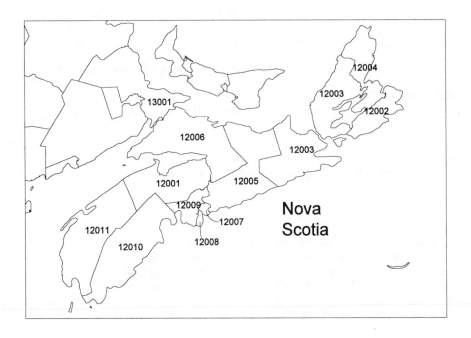

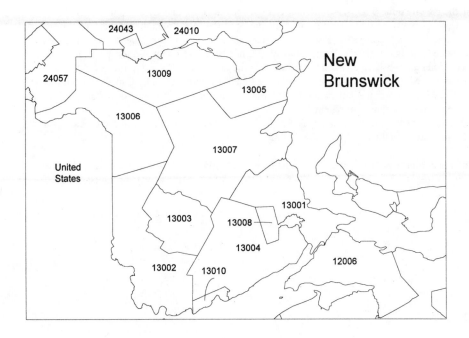

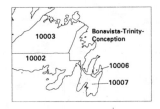

Bonavista–Trinity–Conception

Constituency Number: 10001

One of Canada's poorest ridings, Bonavista–Trinity–Conception in the northwestern part of Newfoundland's Avalon peninsula has the highest unemployment rate in the country (near 40%), one of the lowest average family incomes and the highest level of dependence on government transfers. Including the towns of Bonavista, Clarenville, Carbonear, and Harbour Grace, it is also the most homogeneously English-speaking and Protestant riding in Canada. The main employer is the fishery and its related activities.

This rural riding has been a traditional Liberal stronghold. The seat was held by Liberal Dave Rooney from 1972 to 1984, when it was lost to Conservative Morrisey Johnson, a shipowner and sea captain. In 1988, political neophyte and former naval officer Fred Mifflen regained the seat for the Liberals, winning by a margin of more than 8%. Redistribution could have been a factor in the results: the riding lost communities along Conception Bay to the riding of St John's West; it gained the area of Bonavista North (once part of Liberal MP George Baker's riding of Twillingate) which voted Liberal in 1984 by a plurality of some 1,500 votes.

In 1993, Mifflen was running for re-election against Conservative Charlie Brett, for 17 years a member of the Newfoundland legislature, Clem George for the NDP, and Lynn Tobin for Natural Law. The issues were glaringly obvious: revitalization of the economy, job creation, recovery of the fishery, and preservation of social programs. Fishermen, their families, and area businesses were particularly concerned about their fate after the termination of the northern cod compensation package, a lifeline thrown to Newfoundland fishermen after the collapse of the cod stocks. As a step toward better management of fish stocks, Mifflen advocated the extension of functional jurisdiction by Canada beyond the 200-mile limit to cover the nose and tail of the Grand Bank. But none of the candidates could offer clear solutions to the riding's economic problems.

The election turned out to be a cakewalk for the Liberal incumbent, who won three-quarters of the vote. The Conservative candidate won 21.3% and the New Democrat 2.9%.

Member of Parliament: Fred J. Mifflin; **Party:** Liberal; **Occupation:** Naval admiral (ret.); **Education:** Naval College; **Age:** 56 (February 6, 1938); **Year first elected to the House of Commons:** 1988

10001 Bonavista–Trinity–Conception

A: Political Profile

i) Voting Behaviour

	% 1993	% 1988	Change 1988-93
Conservative	21.3	42.9	-21.6
Liberal	74.8	51.3	23.5
NDP	2.9	5.7	-2.8
Reform	0	0	0
Other	1.1	0	1.1

% Turnout	53.9	Total Ballots (#)	35178
Rejected Ballots (#)	96	% Margin of Victory	53.5
Rural Polls, 1988 (#)	263	Urban Polls, 1988 (#)	14
% Yes - 1992	65.5	% No - 1992	34.1

ii) Campaign Financing

	# of Donations	Total $ Value	% of Limit Spent
Conservative	39	31275	80.5
Liberal	127	50851	79.2
NDP	24	5500	5.5
Reform	0	0	0
Other	3	1184	

B: Ethno-Linguistic Profile

% English Home Language	100	% French Home Language	0
% Official Bilingual	2	% Other Home Language	0
% Catholics	15.9	% Protestants	83.1
% Aboriginal Peoples	0	% Immigrants	0.6

C: Socio-Economic Profile

Average Family Income $	33642	Median Family Income $	29462
% Low Income Families	17.8	Average Home Price $	48244
% Home Owners	89.5	% Unemployment	38.6
% Labour Force Participation	55.7	% Managerial-Administrative	5.6
% Self-Employed	7.3	% University Degrees	3.9
% Movers	18.7		

D: Industrial Profile

% Manufacturing	22.2	% Service Sector	12
% Agriculture	1.1	% Mining	0.4
% Forestry	0.7	% Fishing	5.9
% Government Services	8	% Business Services	1.4

E: Homogeneity Measures

Ethnic Diversity Index	0.97	Religious Homogeneity Index	0.71
Sectoral Concentration Index	0.3	Income Disparity Index	12.4

F: Physical Setting Characteristics

Total Population	88827	Area (km²)	12032
Population Density (pop/km²)	7.4		

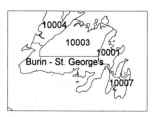

Burin–St George's

Constituency Number: 10002

The second largest riding in area in Atlantic Canada after Labrador, Burin is also one of the most fishing-oriented ridings in the country with more than 100 isolated communities stretching along Newfoundland's south coast, taking in the towns of Stephenville, Burgeo, Grand Bank, Channel-Port aux Basques, and Marystown, site of one of the area's largest employers, the Marystown Shipyard. After Bonavista the poorest riding in Atlantic Canada in terms of average family income and dependence on government transfers, Burin suffers an unemployment rate above 30%.

Burin–St George's was the setting for a political 'dogfight' between Grits and Tories in 1984, and again in 1988. In 1984, low-profile Tory Joe Price defeated the incumbent Liberal Roger Simmons by a scant 299 votes, ending a 35-year Liberal tradition in the constituency. Simmons had been forced to resign from cabinet in 1983 because of a tax evasion scandal. Prior to Simmons' incumbency, the riding had belonged to Don Jamieson, a prominent cabinet minister in the Trudeau governments of the 1970s, who first won the seat for the Liberals in a 1966 by-election and held it for the next 13 years. In 1988, Roger Simmons returned to the political arena to reclaim his old seat for the Liberals. The Liberal cause was aided by the recent redistribution of electoral boundaries, which extended the riding to include the traditionally Liberal Stephenville–Port au Port region. He recaptured the seat by a slim margin of less than a thousand votes.

In 1993, the 53-year-old Simmons was opposed by Progressive Conservative Paul Gallant, a 36-year-old Stephenville businessman, Mark Noseworthy for the NDP, a 22-year-old college student, and Natural Law candidate Michael Rendell. Simmons blamed the fishery crisis on Tory mismanagement and promised better management practices by the Liberals. But he also promised job creation right away, not in the year 2000, when groundfish stocks are expected to have recovered. For his part Gallant charged Simmons with being a part-time MP delivering ineffective representation. In particular, he voiced concern about the future of the Abitibi-Price pulp-and-paper mill and the Marystown Shipyard.

Simmons' political experience helped him to ride the Liberal wave on election night, piling up 80% of the vote. The Tory candidate Gallant barely retained his deposit by getting 15.9%. New Democrat Noseworthy got 2.4%.

Member of Parliament: Roger Simmons; **Party:** Liberal; **Occupation:** Educator; **Education:** EdM, Boston University; **Age:** 55 (June 3, 1939); **Year of first election to the House of Commons:** 1980

10002 Burin–St George's

A: Political Profile

i) Voting Behaviour

	% 1993	% 1988	Change 1988-93
Conservative	15.9	45.6	-29.7
Liberal	80.3	48.4	31.9
NDP	2.4	6	-3.6
Reform	0	0	0
Other	1.4	0	1.4

% Turnout	54.7	Total Ballots (#)	31202
Rejected Ballots (#)	180	% Margin of Victory	64.4
Rural Polls, 1988 (#)	188	Urban Polls, 1988 (#)	50
% Yes - 1992	65.7	% No - 1992	33.6

ii) Campaign Financing

	# of Donations	Total $ Value	% of Limit Spent
Conservative	17	33960	97.2
Liberal	122	34260	40.1
NDP	10	885	1.1
Reform	0	0	0
Other	2	983	

B: Ethno-Linguistic Profile

% English Home Language	99.6	% French Home Language	0.4
% Official Bilingual	3.1	% Other Home Language	0.1
% Catholics	47.7	% Protestants	51.6
% Aboriginal Peoples	1.1	% Immigrants	0.7

C: Socio-Economic Profile

Average Family Income $	33927	Median Family Income $	30068
% Low Income Families	20.8	Average Home Price $	47801
% Home Owners	83.7	% Unemployment	33.3
% Labour Force Participation	57.7	% Managerial-Administrative	5.1
% Self-Employed	7.5	% University Degrees	3.9
% Movers	20.5		

D: Industrial Profile

% Manufacturing	23.3	% Service Sector	12.7
% Agriculture	0.7	% Mining	0.7
% Forestry	1.9	% Fishing	7.1
% Government Services	11.5	% Business Services	1.1

E: Homogeneity Measures

Ethnic Diversity Index	0.84	Religious Homogeneity Index	0.49
Sectoral Concentration Index	0.28	Income Disparity Index	11.4

F: Physical Setting Characteristics

Total Population	79263	Area (km²)	35804
Population Density (pop/km²)	2.2		

Gander–Grand Falls

Constituency Number: 10003

This large, north-central Newfoundland riding has an economy based on the fishery and forest industries. Besides Grand Falls and Gander, it includes the communities of Lewisporte, Springdale, Bishop's Falls and Botwood. The second-most Protestant riding in Canada after Bonavista, Gander was also distinguished in 1993 by having the lowest voter turnout in the country (just ahead of Bonavista). And like the neighbouring Newfoundland ridings of Bonavista, Burin, and Humber–St Barbe–Baie Verte, Gander suffers one of the highest rates of unemployment in Canada (above 30%).

A Liberal stronghold since George Baker won it in 1974, redistribution turned the 1988 contest in this rural Newfoundland seat into a three-way race. Baker had won 48% of the vote in 1984 despite the Tory tide that was sweeping the country. But with the traditionally Liberal northern coast of Trinity Bay shifted to the adjacent riding of Bonavista–Trinity–Conception, victory for the veteran politician was no longer guaranteed. However, despite running a low profile campaign (he was outspent by both the Conservatives and the New Democrats), Baker easily re-took the riding by a margin of almost 9,000 votes.

In 1993, the 50-year-old Baker faced a formidable opponent who was himself a veteran politician of 17 years and a former Newfoundland Premier. Tom Rideout, 45, occupied the Premier's chair briefly after the retirement of Brian Peckford, but lost in the ensuing election to Liberal Clyde Wells. Two other candidates were also contesting in Gander–Grand Falls: inshore fisherman Dennis Whalen for the NDP and Nolan White for Natural Law. All candidates were in agreement on the main issues: first and foremost the fishery, including the future of the compensation package offered fishermen when the cod moratorium was announced and the issue of extending Canadian jurisdiction beyond the 200-mile limit. Baker, a left-leaning Liberal, characteristically took a nationalistic line against foreign fishing and also blasted special tax exemptions for the rich. In the Grand Falls–Windsor area, the main issue was the stability of the paper mill, paper markets, and forest management.

Despite a strong Conservative opponent, Baker had no trouble retaining his seat, winning almost 80% of the vote to Rideout's 19.6%. The NDP attracted less than 2% of voters.

Member of Parliament: George S. Baker; **Party:** Liberal; **Occupation:** Broadcaster; **Education:** Memorial University, University of New Brunswick; **Age:** 52 (1942); **Year first elected to the House of Commons:** 1974

10003 Gander–Grand Falls

A: Political Profile

i) Voting Behaviour

	% 1993	% 1988	Change 1988-93
Conservative	19.6	31.5	-11.9
Liberal	78.1	55.8	22.3
NDP	1.7	12.7	-11
Reform	0	0	0
Other	0.7	0	0.7

% Turnout	52.4	Total Ballots (#)	31076
Rejected Ballots (#)	81	% Margin of Victory	58.5
Rural Polls, 1988 (#)	139	Urban Polls, 1988 (#)	49
% Yes - 1992	65.6	% No - 1992	34

ii) Campaign Financing

	# of Donations	Total $ Value	% of Limit Spent
Conservative	56	28630	65.9*
Liberal	37	27917	50.9
NDP	6	4327	4.5
Reform	0	0	0
Other	3	1066	

B: Ethno-Linguistic Profile

% English Home Language	99.8	% French Home Language	0.1
% Official Bilingual	2.1	% Other Home Language	0.1
% Catholics	17.5	% Protestants	81.1
% Aboriginal Peoples	0.3	% Immigrants	1

C: Socio-Economic Profile

Average Family Income $	36916	Median Family Income $	31533
% Low Income Families	17.3	Average Home Price $	53927
% Home Owners	82.3	% Unemployment	33.2
% Labour Force Participation	56.7	% Managerial-Administrative	6.8
% Self-Employed	7.4	% University Degrees	4.4
% Movers	25.9		

D: Industrial Profile

% Manufacturing	12	% Service Sector	14
% Agriculture	0.9	% Mining	1
% Forestry	4	% Fishing	5.1
% Government Services	11.3	% Business Services	1.6

E: Homogeneity Measures

Ethnic Diversity Index	0.96	Religious Homogeneity Index	0.68
Sectoral Concentration Index	0.36	Income Disparity Index	14.6

F: Physical Setting Characteristics

Total Population	82408	Area (km²)	34307
Population Density (pop/km²)	2.4		

* Tentative value, due to the existence of unpaid campaign expenses.

Humber–St Barbe–Baie Verte

Constituency Number: 10004

Consisting of the northwestern part of Newfoundland, including the Great Northern Peninsula and the Baie Verte Peninsula, the riding takes in the communities of Corner Brook, Deer Lake, Baie Verte and St Anthony. Humber ranks with Bonavista, Burin, and Gander for the worst unemployment rate in Canada, sometimes reaching levels in excess of 50% in the fishing communities on the Northern Peninsula. With the third highest dependence upon fishing in Canada (after Egmont and Cardigan in P.E.I.), the fishery is central to the riding's economy. A pulp and paper mill in Corner Brook makes forest industries important as well, and there is some mining in the Baie Verte region.

Although the traditional Liberal stronghold in the Stephenville–Port au Port area was lost in the last redistribution, the new electoral boundaries still suggested a Liberal advantage in the 1988 election. The incumbent, Liberal Brian Tobin, was first elected to the House of Commons in 1980 at the tender age of 25 by defeating New Democrat MP Fonse Faour. Tobin was re-elected in 1984 with a slim 493-vote majority over his Conservative opponent. In 1988 the chairman of the Liberal caucus in Parliament was challenged by Tory Terry Young, who got some help from Tory cabinet minister and Conservative MP for St John's West, John Crosbie, who announced a multi-million dollar economic aid package for the region in an effort to loosen Tobin's grip on what was considered to be the safest Liberal seat in Newfoundland. Such pre-election 'goodies' failed to help the Tory cause, however, as Tobin took 67% of the vote while racking up the second largest Liberal victory in the country.

In 1993, the popular and now experienced Tobin had the further advantage of appearing to be on the winning side in the election. His opponents were 32-year-old journalist Margaret Ann O'Rourke for the Conservatives, who attempted to paint Tobin as a careerist who had lost touch with the riding's concerns, and 37-year-old postal worker Linda Soper for the New Democrats. The issues in the campaign were familiar - jobs and the fishery crisis - with Tobin promising federal money for job creation through infrastructure projects, while his Tory counterpart emphasized small business and tourism and the New Democrat a national child care program.

Tobin's margin of victory in the election was huge - the fifth-largest anywhere in Canada. He took more than 82% of the vote to O'Rourke's 15.8% and Soper's 2%. Tobin subsequently entered the federal cabinet as Minister for Fisheries and Oceans.

Member of Parliament: Brian Vincent Tobin; **Party:** Liberal; **Occupation:** Broadcaster; **Education:** Memorial University; **Age:** 40 (October 21, 1954); **Year first elected to the House of Commons:** 1980

10004 Humber–St Barbe–Baie Verte

A: Political Profile
i) Voting Behaviour

	% 1993	% 1988	Change 1988-93
Conservative	15.8	29.3	-13.5
Liberal	82.2	67	15.2
NDP	2	3.7	-1.7
Reform	0	0	0
Other	0	0	0

% Turnout	56.9	Total Ballots (#)	32812
Rejected Ballots (#)	115	% Margin of Victory	66.4
Rural Polls, 1988 (#)	159	Urban Polls, 1988 (#)	46
% Yes - 1992	65.3	% No - 1992	34

ii) Campaign Financing

	# of Donations	Total $ Value	% of Limit Spent
Conservative	111	35740	75.2
Liberal	208	100335	85.3
NDP	3	3821	0
Reform	0	0	0
Other	0	0	

B: Ethno-Linguistic Profile

% English Home Language	99.8	% French Home Language	0
% Official Bilingual	2.2	% Other Home Language	0.1
% Catholics	26.9	% Protestants	71.5
% Aboriginal Peoples	0.5	% Immigrants	1

C: Socio-Economic Profile

Average Family Income $	38919	Median Family Income $	34465
% Low Income Families	15.1	Average Home Price $	56400
% Home Owners	82.6	% Unemployment	32.6
% Labour Force Participation	60.7	% Managerial-Administrative	6.9
% Self-Employed	8.1	% University Degrees	5.1
% Movers	23.6		

D: Industrial Profile

% Manufacturing	16.2	% Service Sector	13
% Agriculture	1	% Mining	1.9
% Forestry	3	% Fishing	7.5
% Government Services	8.7	% Business Services	1.4

E: Homogeneity Measures

Ethnic Diversity Index	0.91	Religious Homogeneity Index	0.58
Sectoral Concentration Index	0.32	Income Disparity Index	11.4

F: Physical Setting Characteristics

Total Population	79398	Area (km²)	28352
Population Density (pop/km²)	2.8		

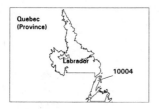

Labrador

Constituency Number: 10005

Labrador, comprised of a huge swath of northern coastline that reaches far back into the interior, is bounded by the province of Quebec on three sides and the north Atlantic on the fourth. Its major communities are Happy Valley-Goose Bay, Labrador City, Wabush, and Churchill Falls. It is the largest riding in Atlantic Canada and the ninth-largest in Canada. The riding also has the highest proportion of aboriginals of any riding in Atlantic Canada, the lowest level of government transfers and the lowest percentage of low-income families in Newfoundland. But it still has an unemployment rate that exceeds 20%. With the second-highest dependence on mining in Canada (after Athabaska), the economy is based on mining and quarrying, as well as fishing and oil exploration industries. Government services make up an important part of the employment base.

Liberal Bill Romkey, known locally as the 'king of Labrador', was first elected to represent the riding in 1972, and has been re-elected in every federal election since. In the course of his political career, the former teacher and superintendent of education served as a cabinet minister under both Pierre Trudeau and John Turner, holding such portfolios as minister of national revenue, minister of state for mines and minister of state for tourism. Challenged for the Labrador seat in 1988 by Conservative Joe Goudie, a Métis from central Labrador and a provincial cabinet minister for seven years, Romkey was returned with a plurality of almost 3000 votes.

In 1993, the 57-year-old Romkey was opposed by Progressive Conservative Wayne Piercey and New Democrat Barry Knight. Both acknowledged that beating Romkey would be difficult. The issues were construction of the Trans-Labrador Highway and other road links and the survival of Labrador's fishing communities. Another sensitive issue was aboriginal land claims. Romkey urged quick settlement of the claims of groups such as the Inuit and Innu, so as not to hold up development and job creation.

The election result saw Romkey carry Labrador for the seventh time, posting 77% of the vote to the Conservative Piercey's 19%. The NDP trailed with 4%.

Member of Parliament: William H. Rompkey; **Party:** Liberal; **Occupation:** Educator; **Education:** MA Memorial University; **Age:** 58 (May 13, 1936); **Year first elected to the House of Commons:** 1972

10005 Labrador

A: Political Profile
i) Voting Behaviour

	% 1993	% 1988	Change 1988-93
Conservative	18.9	33	-14.1
Liberal	77.1	53.5	23.6
NDP	3.9	11.3	-7.4
Reform	0	0	0
Other	0	2.1	-2.1

% Turnout	55.6	Total Ballots (#)	11363
Rejected Ballots (#)	58	% Margin of Victory	58.2
Rural Polls, 1988 (#)	70	Urban Polls, 1988 (#)	0
% Yes - 1992	58.9	% No - 1992	40.5

ii) Campaign Financing

	# of Donations	Total $ Value	% of Limit Spent
Conservative	40	28307	66.5*
Liberal	60	50718	76.4
NDP	22	7261	9.9
Reform	0	0	0
Other	0	0	

B: Ethno-Linguistic Profile

% English Home Language	93.2	% French Home Language	2
% Official Bilingual	7	% Other Home Language	4.8
% Catholics	30.9	% Protestants	66.5
% Aboriginal Peoples	16.8	% Immigrants	2

C: Socio-Economic Profile

Average Family Income $	50854	Median Family Income $	50044
% Low Income Families	12.4	Average Home Price $	46385
% Home Owners	69.7	% Unemployment	22.6
% Labour Force Participation	68.7	% Managerial-Administrative	7.1
% Self-Employed	4.4	% University Degrees	5.4
% Movers	36.9		

D: Industrial Profile

% Manufacturing	3.6	% Service Sector	16.4
% Agriculture	0.2	% Mining	18.6
% Forestry	0.8	% Fishing	4.4
% Government Services	18.1	% Business Services	1.4

E: Homogeneity Measures

Ethnic Diversity Index	0.61	Religious Homogeneity Index	0.53
Sectoral Concentration Index	0.35	Income Disparity Index	1.6

F: Physical Setting Characteristics

Total Population	30379	Area (km²)	310155
Population Density (pop/km²)	0.1		

* Tentative value, due to the existence of unpaid campaign expenses.

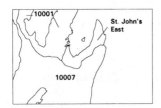

St John's East

Constituency Number: 10006

This predominantly urban riding, geographically the smallest riding in the province, encompasses the western part of the downtown area of the city and Brigus and Cupids in Conception Bay. With the most service-sector based economy in Newfoundland, the Island's lowest unemployment rate, and the second-highest average income (after Labrador), St John's East is Newfoundland's most prosperous and economically stable federal constituency.

In all but nine of the years since Confederation in 1949, this seat has gone to the Conservatives. Veteran Tory James McGrath held the seat for 24 years before he resigned in 1986 to become Newfoundland's lieutenant-governor. The ensuing by-election saw the Tory dynasty come to an abrupt end when New Democrat Jack Harris, a St John's labour lawyer, defeated Tory Tom Hickey and Liberal Steve Neary. In the 1988 election, Harris was opposed by Conservative candidate Ross Reid, a former executive assistant to John Crosbie. While the election revolved around free trade, Reid had to fend off rumours of homosexuality, making his bid an uphill battle from the beginning. Still, he won a convincing 4,200-vote victory, restoring the riding's four-decade-old Tory tradition.

In 1993, Reid entered the election as federal Fisheries Minister against a record number of challengers. The Liberals were running a political neophyte in Bonnie Hickey, a homemaker with an unemployed husband, while the NDP were offering lawyer Bob Buckingham. The other candidates were Bob Tremblett for Christian Heritage, Bill Vetter for the National Party, Len Barron for the Reform Party, and Michael Rayment for Natural Law. Both Reid and Hickey cited unemployment and job creation as the main issues, while Reid as Fisheries Minister was equally focused on the future of the province's cornerstone industry. Reid also refuted the claims of his rivals that the Tories would further cut social programs.

The election result came as a surprise to Reid as well as to the pundits who predicted his re-election. With the smallest margin of victory in Atlantic Canada, Liberal candidate Bonnie Hickey defeated the Tory Minister of Fisheries with 44.2% of the vote to Reid's 42.1%. Third party candidates were clearly a factor in the outcome, with the New Democrat taking 6.4%, the Reform candidate 3%, and the others 4.4%. The low voter turnout may also have been a factor.

Member of Parliament: Bonnie Hickey; **Party:** Liberal; **Occupation:** Travel manager and executive assistant; **Education:** Holy Heart of Mary High School; **Year first elected to the House of Commons:** 1993

10006 St John's East

A: Political Profile
i) Voting Behaviour

	% 1993	% 1988	Change 1988-93
Conservative	42.1	44.1	-2
Liberal	44.2	19.1	25.1
NDP	6.4	35.3	-28.9
Reform	3	0	3
Other	4.4	1.5	2.9

% Turnout	55	Total Ballots (#)	46042
Rejected Ballots (#)	180	% Margin of Victory	2.1
Rural Polls, 1988 (#)	112	Urban Polls, 1988 (#)	119
% Yes - 1992	59.2	% No - 1992	40.4

ii) Campaign Financing

	# of Donations	Total $ Value	% of Limit Spent
Conservative	129	63450	102.5
Liberal	90	37498	47.4
NDP	119	26600	34.7
Reform	15	1470	2.2
Other	49	14066	

B: Ethno-Linguistic Profile

% English Home Language	99.2	% French Home Language	0.2
% Official Bilingual	4.7	% Other Home Language	0.6
% Catholics	49.3	% Protestants	46.5
% Aboriginal Peoples	0.2	% Immigrants	3.1

C: Socio-Economic Profile

Average Family Income $	49905	Median Family Income $	42180
% Low Income Families	17.4	Average Home Price $	7514
% Home Owners	71.9	% Unemployment	17.8
% Labour Force Participation	65	% Managerial-Administrative	12.3
% Self-Employed	5.8	% University Degrees	12.8
% Movers	36.7		

D: Industrial Profile

% Manufacturing	5.9	% Service Sector	13.9
% Agriculture	0.8	% Mining	0.3
% Forestry	0.1	% Fishing	1
% Government Services	15.5	% Business Services	4.6

E: Homogeneity Measures

Ethnic Diversity Index	0.91	Religious Homogeneity Index	0.45
Sectoral Concentration Index	0.52	Income Disparity Index	15.5

F: Physical Setting Characteristics

Total Population	109064	Area (km²)	1148
Population Density (pop/km²)	95		

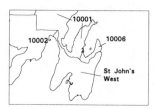

St John's West

Constituency Number: 10007

Covering much of the Avalon peninsula, St John's West is the most populous riding in the province with over half of its voters residing in the urban areas of St John's and Mount Pearl, and on the other side of the peninsula, Placentia. The biggest employers in the urban parts of the riding are government and business services, Memorial University, the retail trade and manufacturing industries. Fishing and fish processing continues to be an important part of the economy of the rest of the peninsula. A 20% unemployment rate makes job creation a major concern.

International Trade Minister John Crosbie was first elected as the MP for St John's West in a 1976 by-election, and was re-elected in the five subsequent federal contests. The St John's lawyer first began his political career as a Liberal in 1966, and held several cabinet portfolios in the Smallwood government. In 1969, after a dispute with the Newfoundland premier, Crosbie crossed the floor of the House of Assembly to lead a Liberal Reform Group, and in 1971 he joined the Tories. Finance minister in the Clark government in 1979, he ran unsuccessfully for the leadership of the federal Conservative party in 1983. In 1984, the Tory cabinet minister trounced his Liberal opponent by almost 25,000 votes, capturing 76% of voter support, one of the largest Conservative majorities in the country. In 1988, as Minister of International Trade, the Tory heavyweight defeated his nearest rival by 12,000 votes.

In 1993, John Crosbie decided to retire from politics, a decision that made the normally safe Tory seat vulnerable. His replacement as candidate was former provincial MHA Loyola Hearn. Running for the second time was Liberal Jean Payne, businesswoman and founding president of the Organization for the Rights of Inshore Fishermen. The other candidates were New Democrat Sharon Walsh, Reformer Dana Tucker, and Guy Harvey for Natural Law. Jobs, the fishery, and the impending closure of the Argentia naval base were the main issues of the campaign.

Payne took the once-safe Tory seat from Hearn by a comfortable 55.1% to 37.6% margin. The New Democrat scored 4% and the Reform candidate 2.4% of the vote. Since his retirement, Crosbie has been named Chancellor of Memorial University.

Member of Parliament: Jean Payne; **Party:** Liberal; **Occupation:** Manager of a personnel consulting and training firm; **Year first elected to the House of Commons:** 1993

10007 St John's West

A: Political Profile
i) Voting Behaviour

	% 1993	% 1988	Change 1988-93
Conservative	37.6	61.5	-23.9
Liberal	55.1	32.5	22.6
NDP	4	5.9	-1.9
Reform	2.4	0	2.4
Other	1	0	1

% Turnout	57.4	Total Ballots (#)	43751
Rejected Ballots (#)	124	% Margin of Victory	17.5
Rural Polls, 1988 (#)	114	Urban Polls, 1988 (#)	127
% Yes - 1992	60.9	% No - 1992	38.5

ii) Campaign Financing

	# of Donations	Total $ Value	% of Limit Spent
Conservative	77	47241	98.9
Liberal	81	45048	81.7
NDP	41	10296	16.1
Reform	10	2161	1.9
Other	2	650	

B: Ethno-Linguistic Profile

% English Home Language	99.6	% French Home Language	0
% Official Bilingual	3.5	% Other Home Language	0.4
% Catholics	60.4	% Protestants	37.7
% Aboriginal Peoples	0.1	% Immigrants	1.6

C: Socio-Economic Profile

Average Family Income $	46040	Median Family Income $	41511
% Low Income Families	15.3	Average Home Price $	84370
% Home Owners	68.9	% Unemployment	20.6
% Labour Force Participation	66.9	% Managerial-Administrative	11.4
% Self-Employed	5.3	% University Degrees	7.7
% Movers	37.9		

D: Industrial Profile

% Manufacturing	10.9	% Service Sector	12.5
% Agriculture	0.8	% Mining	0.3
% Forestry	0.2	% Fishing	2.3
% Government Services	14.3	% Business Services	3.8

E: Homogeneity Measures

Ethnic Diversity Index	0.94	Religious Homogeneity Index	0.5
Sectoral Concentration Index	0.46	Income Disparity Index	9.8

F: Physical Setting Characteristics

Total Population	99135	Area (km²)	7420
Population Density (pop/km²)	13.4		

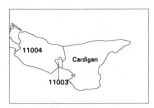

Cardigan

Constituency Number: 11001

A strictly rural riding covering the eastern end of Prince Edward Island, Cardigan is heavily dependent upon fishing and farming-related employment. Indeed, no other riding in all of Canada has a larger proportion of its workforce engaged in fishing; and only one other riding in Atlantic Canada (the adjacent riding of Malpeque) is more dependent upon employment in farming. Tourism is the other major employer. The seasonal nature of these industries translates into high levels of unemployment and dependence on government transfer payments. While all P.E.I. ridings are small, Cardigan has the fewest voters of any in the ten provinces. It also has the second lowest proportion of its population who have changed residence in the last five years. As might be expected from a riding with these characteristics, voter turnout in 1993 was higher than for any other constituency in Atlantic Canada.

Only the Liberals and Conservatives are serious contenders in Cardigan, and the riding has alternated between these two parties. In 1988, the incumbent Progressive Conservative, 40-year-old former provincial cabinet minister Pat Binns, was seeking a second term, having first been elected in 1984 after defeating the incumbent Liberal. While Binn's reputation as a hard-working MP made him the early favourite, a growing backlash against the free trade agreement during the campaign, augmented by the strong intervention of recently elected Premier Joe Ghiz in opposition to the agreement, killed Binn's re-election bid and handed the riding to Liberal Lawrence MacAulay, a seed-potato farmer.

In 1993, MacAulay was bidding for re-election against Tory farmer Wilbur MacDonald, MP for the riding during the 1979 Clark government, and organic farmer and carpenter Reg Phalen for the NDP. With the polls indicating a Liberal sweep in the region, MacAulay ran a low-key campaign with few public appearances. MacDonald tried to counter this 'silent running' approach with calls for more federal jobs for Cardigan and promises to get a food processing operation in the riding. All three candidates participated in a medicare forum to state their positions on threats to the health care system.

On election night MacAulay took almost 62% of the vote for a lop-sided victory over MacDonald, who managed 32.7%. The NDP candidate won 5.7% of the vote.

Member of Parliament: Lawrence A. MacAulay; **Party:** Liberal; **Occupation:** Farmer; **Education:** Morell Regional High School; **Age:** 48 (September 9, 1946); **Year first elected to the House of Commons:** 1988

11001 Cardigan

A: Political Profile

i) Voting Behaviour

	% 1993	% 1988	Change 1988-93
Conservative	32.7	43.9	-11.2
Liberal	61.7	51.6	10.1
NDP	5.7	4.5	1.2
Reform	0	0	0
Other	0	0	0

% Turnout	76.4	Total Ballots (#)	16676
Rejected Ballots (#)	184	% Margin of Victory	29
Rural Polls, 1988 (#)	78	Urban Polls, 1988 (#)	0
% Yes - 1992	70.1	% No - 1992	29.4

ii) Campaign Financing

	# of Donations	Total $ Value	% of Limit Spent
Conservative	174	25915	82.7
Liberal	97	32421	64.4
NDP	41	4805	8.3
Reform	0	0	0
Other	0	0	

B: Ethno-Linguistic Profile

% English Home Language	99.6	% French Home Language	0.2
% Official Bilingual	4.9	% Other Home Language	0.1
% Catholics	50.1	% Protestants	45.4
% Aboriginal Peoples	0.8	% Immigrants	3

C: Socio-Economic Profile

Average Family Income $	42120	Median Family Income $	36409
% Low Income Families	11.4	Average Home Price $	67168
% Home Owners	85.1	% Unemployment	12.5
% Labour Force Participation	69.5	% Managerial-Administrative	8.3
% Self-Employed	14	% University Degrees	5.7
% Movers	24		

D: Industrial Profile

% Manufacturing	16.1	% Service Sector	10.8
% Agriculture	9.9	% Mining	0.1
% Forestry	1	% Fishing	10.9
% Government Services	10.1	% Business Services	1.4

E: Homogeneity Measures

Ethnic Diversity Index	0.76	Religious Homogeneity Index	0.45
Sectoral Concentration Index	0.3	Income Disparity Index	13.6

F: Physical Setting Characteristics

Total Population	30058	Area (km²)	2733
Population Density (pop/km²)	11		

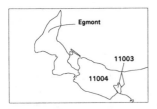

Egmont

Constituency Number: 11002

A rural riding taking in the western end of Prince Edward Island, and including the town of Summerside, Egmont is second only to Cardigan in terms of its dependence upon fishing employment, and regionally follows only Cardigan and Malpeque in terms of the proportion of its workforce employed in farming. Thus dominated by seasonal resource industries and with a high rate of unemployment, one-quarter of family income in the riding comes from government transfer payments, fourth highest in the Atlantic region. The riding's one town, Summerside, was until recently home to CFB Summerside and its 1,300 jobs. The military base was closed in 1989 by the Mulroney Conservatives, a move which made the Tories 'as popular as a potato virus' in P.E.I., even though the town received a handsome offset for the base closure - the new tax-processing centre for the federal sales tax (GST).

Egmont has a strong Liberal history, and in 1984 incumbent Liberal MP George Henderson was able to hold it against the Conservative tide. Henderson did not re-offer in 1988, having accepted a post in the Department of Veterans Affairs. His successor, former school teacher Joe McGuire, who at the time of the election call was an assistant to Liberal Premier Joe Ghiz, easily held Egmont for the Liberals. In 1993, his opponents were two bespectacled and mustachioed Basils: former Summerside mayor Basil Stewart for the Conservatives and machine operator Basil Dumville for the NDP. Stewart, who as mayor had led a delegation to Ottawa to protest the closing of the military base, attempted to score political points against McGuire by noting that McGuire had voted against the GST (and thus, presumably, Summerside's tax-processing centre). Suggesting McGuire was an ineffective MP, too often absent from the House and passive regarding constituency concerns, Stewart claimed his more aggressive approach would be that of 'the Big Voice.' Health care and social program cuts were also prominent campaign issues, as was job creation and federal funding for wharf repairs.

Despite Stewart's attacks on the incumbent, McGuire easily recaptured Egmont, winning 57.6% of the vote to Stewart's 37.6%, while Dumville managed 4.8% for the NDP.

Member of Parliament: Joseph Blair McGuire; **Party:** Liberal; **Occupation:** Teacher; **Education:** BA, St Dunstan's University; **Age:** 50 (June 20, 1944); **Year first elected to the House of Commons:** 1988

11002 Egmont

A: Political Profile

i) Voting Behaviour

	% 1993	% 1988	Change 1988-93
Conservative	37.6	39.4	-1.8
Liberal	57.6	53.1	4.5
NDP	4.8	7.5	-2.7
Reform	0	0	0
Other	0	0	0

% Turnout	74.4	Total Ballots (#)	18730
Rejected Ballots (#)	180	% Margin of Victory	20
Rural Polls, 1988 (#)	73	Urban Polls, 1988 (#)	20
% Yes - 1992	75.5	% No - 1992	24.1

ii) Campaign Financing

	# of Donations	Total $ Value	% of Limit Spent
Conservative	105	28560	71.3
Liberal	80	23663	78.9
NDP	48	4265	9.1
Reform	0	0	0
Other	0	0	

B: Ethno-Linguistic Profile

% English Home Language	92.6	% French Home Language	7.4
% Official Bilingual	17	% Other Home Language	0
% Catholics	55.7	% Protestants	41.8
% Aboriginal Peoples	0.6	% Immigrants	1.7

C: Socio-Economic Profile

Average Family Income $	39873	Median Family Income $	34037
% Low Income Families	12.4	Average Home Price $	60099
% Home Owners	75.5	% Unemployment	17.3
% Labour Force Participation	68.5	% Managerial-Administrative	6.7
% Self-Employed	11.4	% University Degrees	4.8
% Movers	32.2		

D: Industrial Profile

% Manufacturing	12.8	% Service Sector	15.1
% Agriculture	7.7	% Mining	0.9
% Forestry	0.8	% Fishing	9.2
% Government Services	11.1	% Business Services	1.2

E: Homogeneity Measures

Ethnic Diversity Index	0.52	Religious Homogeneity Index	0.48
Sectoral Concentration Index	0.32	Income Disparity Index	14.6

F: Physical Setting Characteristics

Total Population	34266	Area (km²)	1708
Population Density (pop/km²)	20.1		

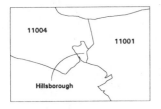

Hillsborough

Constituency Number: 11003

The Island's only urban riding, Hillsborough is comprised of the capital city of Charlottetown and its environs. Government employment, both provincial and federal, forms the core of the constituency's economic base, with the University of Prince Edward Island and the retail service sector additional important components. As a result, Hillsborough is the most prosperous and middle-class of the Island's four constituencies, with a diversified and stable local economy and a relatively well-paid and highly-educated workforce.

Tory since the election of the Diefenbaker government in 1957, Hillsborough was won by Tom McMillan in 1979 and held through the 1980 and 1984 elections. In the 1988 election McMillan, federal Environment Minister at the time, had to cope not only with the free trade issue, but a highly contentious local issue as well: the federal proposal for a fixed link between the Island and the mainland. McMillan was also vulnerable to a familiar accusation faced by cabinet ministers from P.E.I.: that he had lost touch with his constituents. The election outcome in 1988 confirmed McMillan's political vulnerability. With an unusually high percentage of the vote going to third party candidates, McMillan lost by 259 votes to Liberal George Proud, a former MLA and provincial cabinet minister.

In 1993 Proud, Opposition critic for Veterans Affairs (Charlottetown is home to the Department of Veterans Affairs), again faced Tory Tom McMillan (recently returned from a stint as Canadian Consul-General in Boston) and lawyer Dolores Crane for the New Democrats. Teacher Freeman Whitty was contesting for the Reform Party, Dave Patterson for the National Party, university professor Baird Judson for Christian Heritage, and Peter Cameron for Natural Law. Job creation and deficit reduction were important campaign topics, but so were local issues like Liberal accusations that employment at Veterans Affairs would be cut (hotly disputed by the Tories as 'terrorist tactics') and continued protest against the construction of a bridge link to the mainland.

The Liberal juggernaut swept Proud's opponents on election night, decidedly ending the hopes of Tories that the riding would return to its former Conservative leanings. Proud took 60.6% of the vote to McMillan's 26.7%. The NDP held down third place with 5.8% followed by the Reform Party with 3.8%. Other candidates took 3.2% of the vote.

Member of Parliament: George Proud; **Party:** Liberal; **Occupation:** Property supervisor; **Education:** Atlantic Region Labour Education Centre and Labour College of Canada; **Age:** 55 (April 9, 1939); **Year first elected to the House of Commons:** 1988

11003 Hillsborough

A: Political Profile
i) Voting Behaviour

	% 1993	% 1988	Change 1988-93
Conservative	26.7	42.4	-15.7
Liberal	60.6	43.7	16.9
NDP	5.8	9.7	-3.9
Reform	3.8	0	3.8
Other	3.2	4.2	-1

% Turnout	68.7	Total Ballots (#)	19957
Rejected Ballots (#)	185	% Margin of Victory	33.9
Rural Polls, 1988 (#)	22	Urban Polls, 1988 (#)	77
% Yes - 1992	75.9	% No - 1992	23.6

ii) Campaign Financing

	# of Donations	Total $ Value	% of Limit Spent
Conservative	107	29342	94.2
Liberal	233	56014	94.3
NDP	80	13881	24
Reform	38	9303	11.7
Other	28	8177	

B: Ethno-Linguistic Profile

% English Home Language	98.7	% French Home Language	0.6
% Official Bilingual	10.1	% Other Home Language	0.7
% Catholics	48.4	% Protestants	46
% Aboriginal Peoples	0.5	% Immigrants	4.2

C: Socio-Economic Profile

Average Family Income $	48641	Median Family Income $	42813
% Low Income Families	18.6	Average Home Price $	107054
% Home Owners	52	% Unemployment	11.6
% Labour Force Participation	68	% Managerial-Administrative	13.1
% Self-Employed	6.9	% University Degrees	14.6
% Movers	48.7		

D: Industrial Profile

% Manufacturing	4.7	% Service Sector	17.3
% Agriculture	1.8	% Mining	0.1
% Forestry	0.5	% Fishing	0.5
% Government Services	16.6	% Business Services	3.6

E: Homogeneity Measures

Ethnic Diversity Index	0.67	Religious Homogeneity Index	0.42
Sectoral Concentration Index	0.59	Income Disparity Index	12

F: Physical Setting Characteristics

Total Population	33976	Area (km²)	70
Population Density (pop/km²)	485.4		

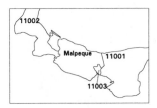

Malpeque

Constituency Number: 11004

The centre portion of Prince Edward Island makes up the constituency of Malpeque. This rural, agricultural riding is the most dependent on farm employment in Atlantic Canada. Not surprisingly, the constituency also has the highest percentage of self-employed in Atlantic Canada. Like Cardigan and Egmont, fishing and tourism are the other important contributors to the local economy.

Malpeque was taken by the Conservatives in their 1984 landslide. MP Mel Gass, however, stepped down before the end of his term to assume the leadership of the provincial PC party shortly after its election loss to the Joe Ghiz-led Liberals in 1986. The 1988 election featured a contest between former provincial cabinet ministers Gordon Lank (for the Conservatives) and Catherine Callbeck (for the Liberals). The results of that election represented one of the largest reversals experienced by the Conservatives in terms of popular vote (a decline of more than 16% over 1984) and one of the biggest turn-arounds for the Liberals, providing Callbeck with a comfortable majority. But like Gass before her, Callbeck stepped down as MP to assume the leadership of the provincial party after the resignation of Premier Joe Ghiz. The Liberal nominee in her stead was Wayne Easter, long-time president of the National Farmers Union and a vocal critic of the Tory-negotiated free trade agreements with the U.S. and Mexico. He was opposed by businessman and former provincial cabinet minister Garth Staples for the Conservatives, organic dairy farmer Karen Fyfe for the NDP, Freddie Gunn for the Christian Heritage Party, and Jeremy Stiles, chair of the P.E.I. Environmental Network, for the Green Party.

The candidates in Malpeque were often faced with complaints from residents about provincial cuts to health care and social services, with Tory candidates blaming the provincial Liberal government and Liberal and NDP candidates citing federal Conservative policies. The fixed link project was also front and centre in the campaign, with Staples calling on Ottawa to get the job-creating project under way.

The election result in Malpeque gave interest group lobbyist Easter the opportunity to work for farmers' rights from within the government caucus. Like other Liberals on the Island he scored an easy victory, winning 60.8% of the vote to Staples' 31.6%. The NDP's Fyfe won 4.4%, with the remaining two candidates splitting 3.2% of the ballots.

Member of Parliament: Arnold Wayne Easter; **Party:** Liberal; **Occupation:** Farmer; **Education:** Dipl.T., Agricultural College of Nova Scotia; **Age:** 45 (June 22, 1949); **Year first elected to the House of Commons:** 1993

11004 Malpeque

A: Political Profile
i) Voting Behaviour

	% 1993	% 1988	Change 1988-93
Conservative	31.6	40.2	-8.6
Liberal	60.8	51.9	8.9
NDP	4.4	7.9	-3.5
Reform	0	0	0
Other	3.2	0	3.2

% Turnout	74.6	Total Ballots (#)	17610
Rejected Ballots (#)	202	% Margin of Victory	29.2
Rural Polls, 1988 (#)	88	Urban Polls, 1988 (#)	0
% Yes - 1992	72.4	% No - 1992	27.1

ii) Campaign Financing

	# of Donations	Total $ Value	% of Limit Spent
Conservative	162	21595	89.9
Liberal	124	29760	69.5
NDP	28	2805	3.5
Reform	0	0	0
Other	10	2950	

B: Ethno-Linguistic Profile

% English Home Language	99.2	% French Home Language	0.5
% Official Bilingual	6.9	% Other Home Language	0.3
% Catholics	34.5	% Protestants	61
% Aboriginal Peoples	0.3	% Immigrants	3.7

C: Socio-Economic Profile

Average Family Income $	42674	Median Family Income $	38420
% Low Income Families	8.6	Average Home Price $	73605
% Home Owners	87.4	% Unemployment	12.1
% Labour Force Participation	70.5	% Managerial-Administrative	10.1
% Self-Employed	14	% University Degrees	8.3
% Movers	32.1		

D: Industrial Profile

% Manufacturing	8.8	% Service Sector	13.6
% Agriculture	14	% Mining	0.1
% Forestry	0.4	% Fishing	2.5
% Government Services	9.8	% Business Services	2.3

E: Homogeneity Measures

Ethnic Diversity Index	0.65	Religious Homogeneity Index	0.49
Sectoral Concentration Index	0.36	Income Disparity Index	10

F: Physical Setting Characteristics

Total Population	31465	Area (km²)	1796
Population Density (pop/km²)	17.5		

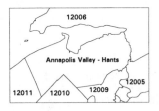

Annapolis Valley–Hants

Constituency Number: 12001

This riding stretches from the military-dominated communities of Kingston and Greenwood through fertile agricultural land as far east as Shubenacadie. Annapolis Valley–Hants is a rural area dotted with small towns like Kentville, Windsor, and the university town of Wolfville (home of Acadia University). It has a healthy mixed economy based on agriculture, manufacturing, and service industries. The constituency is overwhelmingly Protestant and 99% English-speaking, with an unemployment rate below the provincial average.

At the outset of this election, Liberal John Murphy, a soft-spoken psychiatric social worker running for the second time seemed destined to win the Valley for the Liberals after 45 years as a Conservative bastion, during which time a Nowlan had continuously served as the riding's MP. The Liberal candidate had come to within 2,000 votes of winning in 1988, the best Liberal performance in many years. Long-time incumbent Pat Nowlan, who inherited the seat from father George (a former cabinet minister who died in 1965), bolted Tory ranks in 1990 over policy differences with Leader Brian Mulroney. In 1993, he sought re-election as an Independent. Jim White, a 41-year-old Windsor lawyer, was the official candidate of the Conservative Party. Reform candidate John Merriam hoped to do well in this politically conservative riding, as did Christian Heritage candidate Jack Enserink. Like his party, NDP candidate Dick Terfry struggled for votes in 1993. The National Party was represented by Steve Mockford and the Natural Law Party by John Runkle.

The provincial Liberal government's budget announcing new taxes made things more difficult for the Liberal candidate, as did the Liberal promise to scuttle the Conservative plan to purchase expensive new EH-101 helicopters, a lively local issue given the economic importance of CFB Greenwood, located at the western end of the riding. Nowlan and his former riding association sniped at each other during the campaign, with Tories questioning Nowlan's residency and attacking his voting record in the Commons. Both White and Nowlan attacked the Reform Party, fearing its potential to attract otherwise loyal Tory (or Nowlan) voters.

The fracturing of the Conservative vote between the Conservative, Independent, and Reform candidates was sufficient to provide the Liberal Murphy with a comfortable majority. However, the still strong support for long-time incumbent Nowlan translated into the highest 'other' vote in Atlantic Canada. The NDP's Terfry finished a distant fifth, with the three fringe party candidates sharing the remaining votes.

Member of Parliament: John W. Murphy; **Party:** Liberal; **Occupation:** Psychiatric social worker; **Education:** MSW, St Mary's University; **Age:** 57 (August, 26, 1937); **Year first elected to the House of Commons:** 1993

12001 Annapolis Valley–Hants

A: Political Profile
i) Voting Behaviour

	% 1993	% 1988	Change 1988-93
Conservative	20.3	44.2	-23.9
Liberal	39.4	40.1	-0.7
NDP	5	12.5	-7.5
Reform	12.8	0	12.8
Other	22.5	3.2	19.3

% Turnout	62.5	Total Ballots (#)	46544
Rejected Ballots (#)	298	% Margin of Victory	16.9
Rural Polls, 1988 (#)	226	Urban Polls, 1988 (#)	14
% Yes - 1992	45.3	% No - 1992	54.3

ii) Campaign Financing

	# of Donations	Total $ Value	% of Limit Spent
Conservative	147	27461	91.6
Liberal	245	38464	59
NDP	63	6397	8.3
Reform	44	9848	14.9
Other	110	15889	

B: Ethno-Linguistic Profile

% English Home Language	98.5	% French Home Language	0.7
% Official Bilingual	5	% Other Home Language	0.8
% Catholics	17.3	% Protestants	70.9
% Aboriginal Peoples	1.7	% Immigrants	4.2

C: Socio-Economic Profile

Average Family Income $	41178	Median Family Income $	37797
% Low Income Families	13.1	Average Home Price $	78911
% Home Owners	75.1	% Unemployment	11
% Labour Force Participation	64.2	% Managerial-Administrative	8.8
% Self-Employed	9.4	% University Degrees	8.7
% Movers	39.7		

D: Industrial Profile

% Manufacturing	12.7	% Service Sector	14.9
% Agriculture	7.6	% Mining	1
% Forestry	0.8	% Fishing	0.3
% Government Services	11.4	% Business Services	2.6

E: Homogeneity Measures

Ethnic Diversity Index	0.66	Religious Homogeneity Index	0.54
Sectoral Concentration Index	0.36	Income Disparity Index	8.2

F: Physical Setting Characteristics

Total Population	94160	Area (km²)	5433
Population Density (pop/km²)	17.3		

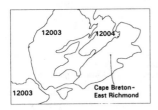

Cape Breton–East Richmond

Constituency Number: 12002

Coal mining, fishing and tourism are important industries in this constituency, with government transfers accounting for one-quarter of personal income. The mining towns of Glace Bay, New Waterford and Dominion once were home to thousands of miners' families who supported the only socialist MP east of Ontario. The long decline of King Coal, however, has been painful for Cape Breton–East Richmond, and now with only one operating mine remaining it has a surfeit of pensioners and an unemployment rate in the 20% range. To add to the riding's considerable economic troubles, the collapse of the fishery has undercut the economic base of rural towns and villages like Louisbourg. In the 1992 Charlottetown Referendum, this riding had the largest 'No' vote in Atlantic Canada.

Incumbent Dave Dingwall, Liberal Party House Leader in Parliament prior to the election, first won election to the House of Commons in 1980 at the age of 27 when he defeated the NDP's Father Andy Hogan by 234 votes. The Conservatives had controlled the riding from 1957 until Hogan's victory in 1974. This marked a return to the riding's association with the political left; from 1944 to 1957, it had been the bailiwick of CCFer Clarie Gillis. Dingwall's margin of victory in 1984 was considerably greater than his initial victory, and in 1988 he piled up a majority of more than 16,000 votes. In 1993, with the tide running to the Liberals, Dingwall was fully expected to repeat by a huge margin. Opposing him was retired union president and former Liberal Sam Boutilier, who was running for the Conservatives, Reform Party candidate Harry Pollett, Joann Lamey for the NDP (a parachuted candidate who was a member of the party's provincial executive), Billy Kennedy for the National Party and the Natural Law Party's Patrick Gilbert, a Halifax resident who did not campaign in the riding.

With Dingwall's re-election virtually assured, the incumbent's prospects for getting into the federal cabinet was a prime topic of speculation for residents of the riding. He had been Chrétien's parliamentary secretary in the early 1980s, a loyal supporter during Chrétien's two leadership bids (1984 and 1990), and was known to be close to the Liberal leader.

Dingwall reduced all of his opponents in 1993 to bit players, electorally speaking, by racking up a majority of 22,000 votes, the third largest margin of victory in Canada. He was subsequently named to the cabinet as Minister of Public Works and Minister Responsible for the Atlantic Canada Opportunities Agency.

Member of Parliament: David Dingwall; **Party:** Liberal; **Occupation:** Lawyer; **Education:** LL.B, Dalhousie University; **Age:** 43 (June 29, 1952); **Year first elected to the House of Commons:** 1980

12002 Cape Breton–East Richmond

A: Political Profile

i) Voting Behaviour

	% 1993	% 1988	Change 1988-93
Conservative	8.6	20.8	-12.2
Liberal	78.3	66.2	12.1
NDP	5.6	13	-7.4
Reform	5.5	0	5.5
Other	1.9	0	1.9

% Turnout	66.4	Total Ballots (#)	32169
Rejected Ballots (#)	259	% Margin of Victory	69.7
Rural Polls, 1988 (#)	95	Urban Polls, 1988 (#)	91
% Yes - 1992	34.7	% No - 1992	65

ii) Campaign Financing

	# of Donations	Total $ Value	% of Limit Spent
Conservative	58	12665	24
Liberal	240	115832	80.7
NDP	0**	0**	0**
Reform	0	0	0
Other	5	337	

B: Ethno-Linguistic Profile

% English Home Language	98.9	% French Home Language	0.7
% Official Bilingual	3.8	% Other Home Language	0.4
% Catholics	66.5	% Protestants	30.9
% Aboriginal Peoples	1	% Immigrants	2

C: Socio-Economic Profile

Average Family Income $	38303	Median Family Income $	34034
% Low Income Families	20.6	Average Home Price $	54440
% Home Owners	80.2	% Unemployment	19.8
% Labour Force Participation	52.5	% Managerial-Administrative	6.7
% Self-Employed	5.8	% University Degrees	5.7
% Movers	25.8		

D: Industrial Profile

% Manufacturing	8	% Service Sector	15.3
% Agriculture	0.5	% Mining	8.1
% Forestry	1	% Fishing	2.7
% Government Services	8.7	% Business Services	2.6

E: Homogeneity Measures

Ethnic Diversity Index	0.69	Religious Homogeneity Index	0.53
Sectoral Concentration Index	0.4	Income Disparity Index	11.1

F: Physical Setting Characteristics

Total Population	61525	Area (km²)	2792
Population Density (pop/km²)	22		

** No return filed.

Cape Breton Highlands–Canso

Constituency Number: 12003

The second largest riding in the Maritimes in area, comprising four counties, Cape Breton Highlands–Canso like the two other Cape Breton ridings suffers from high levels of unemployment and dependence on government transfers as a source of income. The riding itself is dominated by natural resource industries, such as forestry and fishing. Port Hawkesbury hosts the constituency's largest private sector employer, Stora Forest Industries, while Canso and Arichat are fishing ports hit hard by the moratorium on cod fishing. The riding also includes the town of Antigonish, home to St Francis Xavier University.

Traditionally a bastion of Liberal strength, the riding was held by former Deputy Prime Minister and regional political godfather Allan J. MacEachen for a quarter-century before his appointment to the Senate in 1984. It then became the only Cape Breton riding to fall to the Tories in their landslide 1984 victory, returning to the Liberal fold in 1988 with the election of economist and former MacEachen aide Francis LeBlanc. As a Liberal incumbent in an election which the Liberals were favoured to win, the 39-year-old LeBlanc was a heavy favourite to repeat in 1993. He was opposed by 23-year-old Conservative candidate Lewis MacKinnon, a former student union president at St F.X., and Reform candidate Henry VanBerkel, a 50-year-old school vice-principal. There were also two aboriginal challengers, 30-year-old president of the Mi'kmaq Forestry Association Junior Bernard for the NDP and 49-year-old businessman Earl Lafford for the Natural Law Party.

A prominent local issue in the election was an announcement by Stora that an industry-wide recession was forcing it to consider closing its 30-year-old Port Hawkesbury mill, a decision that would choke off a $175 million annual injection into the local economy. All the candidates were forced to address the fears and concerns of constituents regarding this unpleasant prospect, precipitated (according to the company) by new federal environmental laws forcing a major new investment in pollution control. All the candidates, to varying degrees, favoured delaying implementation of environmental regulations at Stora.

Election night saw LeBlanc score a huge victory in a riding that had always mounted credible Conservative opposition to the usually-favoured Liberals. LeBlanc took 64.4% of the vote to MacKinnon's 22.3%, a result MacKinnon blamed on his low profile in the riding due to his late nomination as Conservative candidate. Reform candidate VanBerkel came a fairly distant third, but all the same managed to double the vote of the NDP's Bernard.

Member of Parliament: Francis Gerard LeBlanc; **Party:** Liberal; **Occupation:** Economist; **Education:** MA, Queen's and Laval Universities; **Age:** 41 (December 22, 1953); **Year first elected to the House of Commons:** 1988

12003 Cape Breton Highlands–Canso

A: Political Profile
i) Voting Behaviour

	% 1993	% 1988	Change 1988-93
Conservative	22.3	44	-21.7
Liberal	64.4	50.9	13.5
NDP	3.9	5.1	-1.2
Reform	8.4	0	8.4
Other	1	0	1

% Turnout	71	Total Ballots (#)	35671
Rejected Ballots (#)	391	% Margin of Victory	42.1
Rural Polls, 1988 (#)	171	Urban Polls, 1988 (#)	17
% Yes - 1992	59.1	% No - 1992	40.3

ii) Campaign Financing

	# of Donations	Total $ Value	% of Limit Spent
Conservative	25	21600	41.2
Liberal	241	45961	74.4
NDP	25	3972	3
Reform	24	4730	6.7*
Other	0	0	

B: Ethno-Linguistic Profile

% English Home Language	90.8	% French Home Language	7.9
% Official Bilingual	15.4	% Other Home Language	1.3
% Catholics	69.8	% Protestants	27.1
% Aboriginal Peoples	2.6	% Immigrants	2.6

C: Socio-Economic Profile

Average Family Income $	40745	Median Family Income $	35793
% Low Income Families	12.9	Average Home Price $	57310
% Home Owners	82.3	% Unemployment	17.6
% Labour Force Participation	59.5	% Managerial-Administrative	7.4
% Self-Employed	8.2	% University Degrees	7.9
% Movers	22.8		

D: Industrial Profile

% Manufacturing	14.1	% Service Sector	15.2
% Agriculture	2.7	% Mining	1.2
% Forestry	5.1	% Fishing	4.5
% Government Services	6.8	% Business Services	1.7

E: Homogeneity Measures

Ethnic Diversity Index	0.51	Religious Homogeneity Index	0.55
Sectoral Concentration Index	0.34	Income Disparity Index	12.2

F: Physical Setting Characteristics

Total Population	64761	Area (km²)	11337
Population Density (pop/km²)	5.7		

* Tentative value, due to the existence of unpaid campaign expenses.

Cape Breton–The Sydneys

Constituency Number: 12004

This predominantly urban riding takes in most of industrial Cape Breton, as well as the scenic Cabot Trail and Cape Breton Highlands National Park. It has, like its neighbour Cape Breton–East Richmond, one of the highest unemployment rates in the country. As a result, the constituency is not unlike its Eastern Nova Scotia counterparts in its dependency on government transfers. Steel and coal, tourism, fishing and fish processing, retail and service sector employment form the basis of the riding's economy. Next to Cape Breton East, this riding had the highest 'No' vote in the region in the 1992 Charlottetown Referendum.

The riding was Conservative under Bob Muir in every election from 1957 to 1979, when Liberal Russell MacLellan, a Sydney lawyer, won the seat which he has since retained. In 1988, he won one of the largest Liberal victories in the country. During his fourteen years as an MP prior to the 1993 election, MacLellan had been parliamentary secretary to several ministers and critic for three portfolios.

Running uphill against MacLellan for the Tories was North Sydney native Marlene Lovett, a former dental hygienist turned businesswoman, NDP candidate Bob Hawley, an unemployed fish plant worker, businessman Keith Dingwall for the Reform Party, and Avard Mills of Halifax for Natural Law. MacLellan's opponents focused on the riding's economic problems, with Lovett focusing on creating new business and Dingwall on deficit-reduction. MacLellan also addressed the need for job creation, while distancing himself from the approach of the provincial Liberal administration on this matter.

The election result was unsurprising. None of MacLellan's opponents were able to gain the 15% necessary to retain their deposit. As a solid incumbent riding a Liberal tide nationally, MacLellan received 75.8% of the vote, with his closest rival Lovett getting a mere 11.2%. This lop-sided result gave MacLellan the seventh largest margin of victory in Canada. The NDP's Hawley shaded the Reform candidate for a distant third place finish.

Member of Parliament: Russell G. MacLellan; **Party:** Liberal; **Occupation:** Lawyer; **Education:** LL.B, Dalhousie University; **Age:** 55 (January 16, 1940); **Year first elected to the House of Commons:** 1979

12004 Cape Breton–The Sydneys

A: Political Profile

i) Voting Behaviour

	% 1993	*% 1988*	*Change 1988-93*
Conservative	11.2	28.8	-17.6
Liberal	75.8	63.3	12.5
NDP	6.4	7.9	-1.5
Reform	5.7	0	5.7
Other	0.8	0	0.8

% Turnout	*66.6*	Total Ballots (#)	*33532*
Rejected Ballots (#)	*300*	% Margin of Victory	*64.6*
Rural Polls, 1988 (#)	*58*	Urban Polls, 1988 (#)	*96*
% Yes - 1992	*38.9*	% No - 1992	*60.7*

ii) Campaign Financing

	# of Donations	*Total $ Value*	*% of Limit Spent*
Conservative	83	18297	72.2
Liberal	166	50775	48.4
NDP	0	0	0
Reform	12	1475	1.3*
Other	0	0	

B: Ethno-Linguistic Profile

% English Home Language	*96.6*	% French Home Language	*0.3*
% Official Bilingual	*3.4*	% Other Home Language	*3.1*
% Catholics	*59.8*	% Protestants	*36.8*
% Aboriginal Peoples	*6.5*	% Immigrants	*2.3*

C: Socio-Economic Profile

Average Family Income $	*39253*	Median Family Income $	*34537*
% Low Income Families	*20.1*	Average Home Price $	*60206*
% Home Owners	*70.6*	% Unemployment	*20.1*
% Labour Force Participation	*54.8*	% Managerial-Administrative	*7.6*
% Self-Employed	*5.7*	% University Degrees	*7*
% Movers	*29.1*		

D: Industrial Profile

% Manufacturing	*10.5*	% Service Sector	*16*
% Agriculture	*0.8*	% Mining	*2.7*
% Forestry	*0.8*	% Fishing	*3.1*
% Government Services	*9.5*	% Business Services	*2.4*

E: Homogeneity Measures

Ethnic Diversity Index	*0.66*	Religious Homogeneity Index	*0.48*
Sectoral Concentration Index	*0.42*	Income Disparity Index	*12*

F: Physical Setting Characteristics

Total Population	*66348*	Area (km²)	*3705*
Population Density (pop/km²)	*17.9*		

* Tentative value, due to the existence of unpaid campaign expenses.

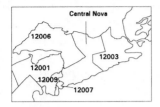

Central Nova

Constituency Number: 12005

A Conservative stronghold since its formation in the 1960s, Central Nova spans Nova Scotia's Eastern and Northumberland shores. Rural industries such as fishing, forestry and agriculture can be found throughout the riding, complemented by a significant manufacturing component centred in Pictou County, comprised of steel fabrication, tire manufacturing, a pulp-and-paper mill, and a shipbuilding yard. As always, economic concerns tended to dominate the agenda in 1993, generated in particular by the cessation of coal-mining in Pictou County following the disastrous 1992 explosion at the Westray mine which killed 27 miners.

Prior to the 1993 election, the riding had been represented for over twenty years by Conservative lawyer Elmer MacKay, but MacKay was not re-offering. A strong Mulroney supporter (he had briefly given up his seat to enable the new Conservative leader to get elected to Parliament), MacKay had served in a number of cabinet portfolios, his last as Minister of Public Works and Minister responsible for the Atlantic Canada Opportunities Agency Act, a key regional patronage post.

MacKay's successor as Conservative candidate in the riding was Ken Streatch, a farmer and former provincial cabinet minister. With no incumbent running and a swing to the Liberals in progress, the once-safe Tory bastion was considered a real battleground in 1993, an assessment that seemed validated by a strong Liberal campaign effort. The Liberal candidate, Stellarton lawyer Roseanne Skoke, had previously gained some local notoriety for her publicly non-conformist stance against reforms in the liturgy of the Catholic Church. Besides this Liberal surge, Conservatives feared the effects of an energetic Reform Party effort, spear-headed by lawyer-candidate Howard MacKinnon. The other contestants were real estate agent Hugh MacKenzie for the NDP, farmer Gerard Horgan for the National Party, and Halifax student Pulkesh Lakhanpal for Natural Law.

The election result confirmed a swing to the Liberals sufficient to elect Skoke with 43.5% of the vote. Her sizeable margin over Conservative candidate Streatch (who gained 32.2% of the total ballot) was somewhat unanticipated, and was undoubtedly aided by the relatively strong Reform Party showing (15.7%). The NDP candidate received 6.5% of the vote for a fourth place finish.

Member of Parliament: Roseanne M. Skoke; **Party:** Liberal; **Occupation:** Lawyer; **Education:** LL.B, Dalhousie University; **Age:** 40 (September 11, 1954); **Year first elected to the House of Commons:** 1993

12005 Central Nova

A: Political Profile

i) Voting Behaviour

	% 1993	% 1988	Change 1988-93
Conservative	32.2	48.6	-16.4
Liberal	43.5	38.4	5.1
NDP	6.5	13	-6.5
Reform	15.7	0	15.7
Other	2.1	0	2.1

% Turnout	68.4	Total Ballots (#)	37894
Rejected Ballots (#)	370	% Margin of Victory	11.3
Rural Polls, 1988 (#)	159	Urban Polls, 1988 (#)	39
% Yes - 1992	47.7	% No - 1992	52

ii) Campaign Financing

	# of Donations	Total $ Value	% of Limit Spent
Conservative	103	28872	93.9
Liberal	287	49558	92.9
NDP	14	2170	4.3
Reform	25	14378	24.7
Other	9	2182	

B: Ethno-Linguistic Profile

% English Home Language	99.4	% French Home Language	0.2
% Official Bilingual	3.9	% Other Home Language	0.3
% Catholics	29.7	% Protestants	63.8
% Aboriginal Peoples	0.8	% Immigrants	2.9

C: Socio-Economic Profile

Average Family Income $	42722	Median Family Income $	38939
% Low Income Families	13.1	Average Home Price $	67322
% Home Owners	81.4	% Unemployment	14
% Labour Force Participation	61.2	% Managerial-Administrative	8.1
% Self-Employed	8	% University Degrees	6.4
% Movers	31.7		

D: Industrial Profile

% Manufacturing	17.8	% Service Sector	12.5
% Agriculture	2.4	% Mining	0.7
% Forestry	1.8	% Fishing	2.6
% Government Services	7.9	% Business Services	2.8

E: Homogeneity Measures

Ethnic Diversity Index	0.7	Religious Homogeneity Index	0.49
Sectoral Concentration Index	0.36	Income Disparity Index	8.9

F: Physical Setting Characteristics

Total Population	74178	Area (km²)	7192
Population Density (pop/km²)	10.3		

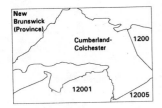

Cumberland–Colchester

Constituency Number: 12006

This mostly rural riding stretches from Shubenacadie in central Nova Scotia to the New Brunswick border in the north. Its two major towns, Truro and Amherst, which anchor the riding at either end, lay claim to several manufacturing establishments ranging from textiles to electronic components. For the most part the rest of the riding depends upon agriculture and other primary industries.

The political history of the riding suggests a strong initial advantage for the Conservatives, who since 1921 failed to carry the riding only twice. Held by Conservative Bob Coates from 1953 to 1985, the legendary Diefenbaker loyalist quit as MP after 11 consecutive victories when his brief stint as Canada's defence minister ended in a political scandal involving an unofficial visit to a West German night club. Coates was replaced by political neophyte Bill Casey, who despite his inexperience was able to ride the coat-tails of his predecessor to victory in 1988. In 1993 the 48-year-old Amherst businessman's main opponents were Truro town councillor Dianne Brushett for the Liberals and businesswoman Audrey Staples for the Reform Party. The other hopefuls were farmer Barbara Jack for the NDP, forestry worker Steve MacLean for Christian Heritage, and Phyllis Hall of Halifax, the Natural Law candidate.

The 1993 campaign was largely devoid of specifically local issues, with the economy and unemployment the dominant concerns. Despite making the best showing of any Conservative candidate in Nova Scotia, Casey was still upset by the Liberal Brushett, who became one of three women elected as Nova Scotia MPs in 1993. Brushett outpolled the incumbent by a 42.6% to 36.6% margin. The Reform Party candidate Staples was a factor in the outcome, placing second to the winner in five polls and third in most of the rest, and finishing with 13.2% of the vote. The traditional third-place finisher, the NDP, this time finished a distant fourth with 5.6%.

Member of Parliament: Dianne Brushett; **Party:** Liberal; **Occupation:** Businesswoman; **Education:** BA, St Mary's University; **Year first elected to the House of Commons:** 1993

12006 Cumberland–Colchester

A: Political Profile
i) Voting Behaviour

	% 1993	% 1988	Change 1988-93
Conservative	36.6	46.2	-9.6
Liberal	42.6	41.6	1
NDP	5.6	9.3	-3.7
Reform	13.2	0	13.2
Other	2.1	2.9	-0.8

% Turnout	68	Total Ballots (#)	43128
Rejected Ballots (#)	284	% Margin of Victory	6
Rural Polls, 1988 (#)	152	Urban Polls, 1988 (#)	92
% Yes - 1992	52.6	% No - 1992	46.9

ii) Campaign Financing

	# of Donations	Total $ Value	% of Limit Spent
Conservative	190	41126	89.2
Liberal	226	42927	92.3
NDP	71	9723	12.4*
Reform	26	9514	25.5
Other	47	6370	

B: Ethno-Linguistic Profile

% English Home Language	99.5	% French Home Language	0.2
% Official Bilingual	4.6	% Other Home Language	0.3
% Catholics	18	% Protestants	73
% Aboriginal Peoples	1.2	% Immigrants	3.4

C: Socio-Economic Profile

Average Family Income $	39179	Median Family Income $	33957
% Low Income Families	15.4	Average Home Price $	64053
% Home Owners	75.7	% Unemployment	15
% Labour Force Participation	60.7	% Managerial-Administrative	8.7
% Self-Employed	9.1	% University Degrees	6.9
% Movers	36.8		

D: Industrial Profile

% Manufacturing	15.3	% Service Sector	13.7
% Agriculture	4.5	% Mining	1.6
% Forestry	2.8	% Fishing	1
% Government Services	9	% Business Services	2.4

E: Homogeneity Measures

Ethnic Diversity Index	0.71	Religious Homogeneity Index	0.56
Sectoral Concentration Index	0.36	Income Disparity Index	13.3

F: Physical Setting Characteristics

Total Population	81967	Area (km²)	8137
Population Density (pop/km²)	10.1		

* Tentative value, due to the existence of unpaid campaign expenses.

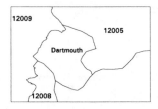

Dartmouth

Constituency Number: 12007

This metropolitan Halifax riding is one of Atlantic Canada's most prosperous and its most mobile, with the region's second lowest unemployment rate and highest percentage of movers. Dartmouth's economy boasts significant manufacturing industries and a high percentage of labour force employment in the public and service sectors. It is also home to CFB Shearwater. The constituency is one of the most racially and culturally diverse in Atlantic Canada, with significant francophone and black populations.

For 23 years prior to 1988, Dartmouth was the bailiwick of the Conservative MP Mike Forrestall. Elected in 1965, Forrestall was defeated in the 'free trade' election by Liberal Ronald MacDonald. Redistribution coupled with rapid population growth and urbanization had deprived the former incumbent of strong Tory polls in adjacent rural areas. MacDonald, a former executive director of the Liberal Party of Nova Scotia who managed a 2,000 vote margin of victory in 1988, was challenged in 1993 by lawyer Judith Gass for the Conservatives, retired broadcaster Orest Ulan for the Reform Party, university professor Marty Zelenietz for the NDP, and Cliff Williams for the National Party. The Natural Law Party was represented by Montrealer Claude Viau.

There was no shortage of issues for the candidates to debate in 1993. The future of social programs and the Quebec question was on the agenda. The importance of military spending to the riding made the government's proposal to spend $5 billion dollars on sophisticated new helicopters - and the Liberal Party's pledge to cancel the contract - an important issue for many residents. An all-candidates debate on racial issues was held in the predominantly black community of Preston.

A lively and at times raucous campaign in Dartmouth did not alter the expected outcome, as incumbent MacDonald was easily re-elected as the riding's Liberal MP. While even MacDonald admitted that the helicopter issue had caused problems for him, the burden of an unpopular Tory government proved too great for local candidates such as Gass. MacDonald racked up 50.8% of the vote, overshadowing the Conservative candidate (23.5%) and a respectable showing by the Reform Party (15.7%). The NDP finished fourth with 7.2% of the vote.

Member of Parliament: Ronald MacDonald; **Party:** Liberal; **Occupation:** Association executive; **Education:** BA, Dalhousie University; **Age:** 40 (June 23, 1955); **Year first elected to the House of Commons:** 1988

12007 Dartmouth

A: Political Profile

i) Voting Behaviour

	% 1993	% 1988	Change 1988-93
Conservative	23.5	41.8	-18.3
Liberal	50.8	46.2	4.6
NDP	7.2	10.9	-3.7
Reform	15.7	0	15.7
Other	2.9	1.2	1.7

% Turnout	59.2	Total Ballots (#)	46611
Rejected Ballots (#)	439	% Margin of Victory	27.3
Rural Polls, 1988 (#)	27	Urban Polls, 1988 (#)	178
% Yes - 1992	49.4	% No - 1992	50.2

ii) Campaign Financing

	# of Donations	Total $ Value	% of Limit Spent
Conservative	123	34966	73.7
Liberal	170	51342	82.3
NDP	70	7261	14.6
Reform	31	4388	9.1
Other	7	461	

B: Ethno-Linguistic Profile

% English Home Language	97.7	% French Home Language	1.4
% Official Bilingual	9	% Other Home Language	0.9
% Catholics	37.9	% Protestants	52.7
% Aboriginal Peoples	0.5	% Immigrants	5.3

C: Socio-Economic Profile

Average Family Income $	49905	Median Family Income $	46206
% Low Income Families	13.8	Average Home Price $	99498
% Home Owners	58.2	% Unemployment	9
% Labour Force Participation	71.5	% Managerial-Administrative	12
% Self-Employed	4.9	% University Degrees	12.5
% Movers	53.7		

D: Industrial Profile

% Manufacturing	6.8	% Service Sector	19.9
% Agriculture	0.3	% Mining	0.5
% Forestry	0.1	% Fishing	0.3
% Government Services	20.9	% Business Services	5.1

E: Homogeneity Measures

Ethnic Diversity Index	0.51	Religious Homogeneity Index	0.42
Sectoral Concentration Index	0.53	Income Disparity Index	7.4

F: Physical Setting Characteristics

Total Population	103105	Area (km²)	237
Population Density (pop/km²)	435		

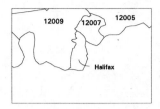

Halifax

Constituency Number: 12008

Nova Scotia's capital city has the region's third lowest unemployment rate and its strongest economy based on a large and diverse service sector (a mix of government, defence, universities, hospitals, business and financial services), manufacturing and port operations. Home to two major universities (Dalhousie and Saint Mary's) and several other institutions of higher learning, the city has an educated, culturally diverse, and mobile population, with the highest proportion of degree-holders, immigrants, and movers in Atlantic Canada.

From 1968 to 1979, Halifax was the home constituency of Conservative party leader Robert Stanfield. With the exception of these years, the riding tended to be a volatile bell-wether for the political tides. Retained by Tory George Cooper in 1979, it was captured by former Liberal Premier Gerald Regan in 1980, only to return to the Tories in 1984. In 1988 Halifax again turned its back on an incumbent cabinet minister (this time Tory Stewart McInnes) to elect Liberal Mary Clancy. In 1993 Clancy, a lawyer and strong feminist, faced nine other candidates in her bid to stop yet another swing of the political pendulum. Trying to re-capture the riding for the Tories was a 59-year-old former provincial MLA, Jim Vaughan. Lynn Jones, one of the few Canadian-born blacks to run federally, was contesting for the NDP and Steve Greene for the Reform Party. Fringe candidates included Vladimir Klonowski for the Green Party, Charles Phillips (head of Nova Scotia's 'No' Campaign in the Charlottetown Referendum) for the National Party, Gilles Bigras for the Natural Law Party, Marxist-Leninist Tony Seed, and Independents Art Canning and Steve Rimek.

Jobs and the deficit were the predominant issues, but as in Dartmouth, the Government's proposal to spend billions on new naval helicopters was a factor in the Halifax campaign, with Clancy opposing the expenditure as extravagant while Tory Vaughan promised hundreds of jobs locally and valuable new expertise for regional aerospace firms Litton and IMP. The federal-provincial Halifax Harbour cleanup project was another much discussed local issue. Throughout the campaign Clancy was dogged by criticism from anti-abortion activists.

The election result wasn't close. Clancy more than doubled the vote total of her Tory opponent, taking 45.9% of the ballot to Vaughan's 20.7%. With 13.4% of the vote, Lynn Jones made the best showing of any NDP candidate east of Ontario, but still lost her deposit and trailed the Reform Party's Steve Greene, who took 14.5% of the vote.

Member of Parliament: Mary Clancy; **Party:** Liberal; **Occupation:** Lawyer; **Education:** LL.M, University of London; **Age:** 47 (January 13, 1948); **Year first elected to the House of Commons:** 1988

12008 Halifax

A: Political Profile
i) Voting Behaviour

	% 1993	% 1988	Change 1988-93
Conservative	20.7	38	-17.3
Liberal	45.9	43	2.9
NDP	13.4	17.7	-4.3
Reform	14.5	0	14.5
Other	5.7	1.3	4.4

% Turnout	58.9	Total Ballots (#)	46894
Rejected Ballots (#)	439	% Margin of Victory	25.2
Rural Polls, 1988 (#)	14	Urban Polls, 1988 (#)	206
% Yes - 1992	54.3	% No - 1992	45.1

ii) Campaign Financing

	# of Donations	Total $ Value	% of Limit Spent
Conservative	60	49679	78.4
Liberal	178	41481	75.1
NDP	244	25393	30.6*
Reform	49	28375	39
Other	15	19465	96.5

B: Ethno-Linguistic Profile

% English Home Language	1	% French Home Language	12.1
% Official Bilingual	2.4	% Other Home Language	3
% Catholics	9.7	% Protestants	44.5
% Aboriginal Peoples	0.8	% Immigrants	9

C: Socio-Economic Profile

Average Family Income $	51780	Median Family Income $	42911
% Low Income Families	21.1	Average Home Price $	137683
% Home Owners	40.9	% Unemployment	9.9
% Labour Force Participation	67.7	% Managerial-Administrative	12
% Self-Employed	6.5	% University Degrees	24.8
% Movers	51.9		

D: Industrial Profile

% Manufacturing	5	% Service Sector	17.1
% Agriculture	0.1	% Mining	0.3
% Forestry	0.1	% Fishing	0.4
% Government Services	15.6	% Business Services	7.4

E: Homogeneity Measures

Ethnic Diversity Index	0.47	Religious Homogeneity Index	0.36
Sectoral Concentration Index	0.64	Income Disparity Index	17.1

F: Physical Setting Characteristics

Total Population	90203	Area (km²)	250
Population Density (pop/km²)	360.8		

* Tentative value, due to the existence of unpaid campaign expenses.

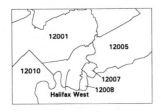

Halifax West

Constituency Number: 12009

Halifax West is the most populous riding in the Maritimes. It consists of the Fairview and Clayton Park areas of Halifax, the surrounding suburbs of Bedford and Sackville, and seashore communities like Peggy's Cove and Lower Prospect in western Halifax County. It is also the richest constituency in Atlantic Canada in terms of average family income, with the region's lowest rate of unemployment and dependence on government transfers and its highest proportion of managers.

Conservative Howard Crosby had represented the riding since 1978, winning his last election by less than 2,000 votes, but was not re-offering in 1993. His replacement on the Tory ticket was Joel Matheson, a former provincial cabinet minister recently defeated in the provincial election of 1993. Running for the Liberals was Geoff Regan, the 33-year-old lawyer son of former provincial Premier and federal cabinet minister Gerald Regan who already had made an unsuccessful run for provincial office in 1988. Thirty-year-old computer analyst Jim Donohue for the Reform Party, National Party candidate Kirby Judge, and Bernard Gormley for Natural Law were also challenging.

As with the other metro constituencies, the EH-101 helicopter purchase was an issue in the campaign, one which pitted jobs against concerns about the deficit. Regan, like his Liberal counterparts, defended the Liberal pledge to axe the purchase in favour of cheaper alternatives. Matheson promised less government interference with business, a halt to tax increases, and more honesty in politics, similar themes to those of the Reform candidate, who stressed as well his differences with the traditional party candidates, particularly the fact that he was not a lawyer.

The election result saw Geoff Regan become the third generation of his family to hold a seat in the House of Commons. He took 46% of the vote to runner-up Joel Matheson's 23.5%. Reformer Jim Donahue came a close third, scoring 19.4% of the vote, the best Reform showing in Atlantic Canada. The NDP candidate placed a distant fourth.

Member of Parliament: Geoffrey Paul Regan; **Party:** Liberal; **Occupation:** Lawyer; **Education:** LL.B, Dalhousie University; **Age:** 35 (November 22, 1959); **Year first elected to the House of Commons:** 1993

12009 Halifax West

A: Political Profile

i) Voting Behaviour

	% 1993	% 1988	Change 1988-93
Conservative	23.5	44.8	-21.3
Liberal	46	38.6	7.4
NDP	8.5	16.3	-7.8
Reform	19.4	0	19.4
Other	2.6	0.4	2.2

% Turnout	63.9	Total Ballots (#)	59354
Rejected Ballots (#)	465	% Margin of Victory	22.5
Rural Polls, 1988 (#)	80	Urban Polls, 1988 (#)	162
% Yes - 1992	51.1	% No - 1992	48.6

ii) Campaign Financing

	# of Donations	Total $ Value	% of Limit Spent
Conservative	91	24385	68.9
Liberal	262	66843	52.2
NDP	131	30918	43
Reform	38	17222	24.1
Other	6	876	

B: Ethno-Linguistic Profile

% English Home Language	97.7	% French Home Language	0.7
% Official Bilingual	8.4	% Other Home Language	1.7
% Catholics	38.8	% Protestants	51.6
% Aboriginal Peoples	0.2	% Immigrants	6

C: Socio-Economic Profile

Average Family Income $	54175	Median Family Income $	49578
% Low Income Families	9.9	Average Home Price $	109987
% Home Owners	70.4	% Unemployment	8.6
% Labour Force Participation	73.2	% Managerial-Administrative	14
% Self-Employed	6.5	% University Degrees	15.1
% Movers	47.7		

D: Industrial Profile

% Manufacturing	7.5	% Service Sector	13.4
% Agriculture	0.6	% Mining	0.2
% Forestry	0.1	% Fishing	0.5
% Government Services	14.1	% Business Services	5.1

E: Homogeneity Measures

Ethnic Diversity Index	0.58	Religious Homogeneity Index	0.42
Sectoral Concentration Index	0.5	Income Disparity Index	8.5

F: Physical Setting Characteristics

Total Population	113013	Area (km²)	1500
Population Density (pop/km²)	75.3		

South Shore

Constituency Number: 12010

This rural and small town riding stretches south from Halifax down the Atlantic shoreline, including the towns of Lunenburg, Bridgewater, Liverpool and Shelburne. Historically it has been dependent on resource industries for employment, especially a rich fishery. Fourth in Canada in terms of fishing as a proportion of its workforce and with a regional high proportion of employment in manufacturing (mainly fish processing, but also pulp and paper and tire manufacture), the South Shore has been heavily impacted by the crisis in the fishery. But parts of the riding closer to Halifax have also benefited from the general prosperity of that city and its environs; as well, they have become a favoured locale for a segment of the urban well-to-do who are relocating to more idyllic (yet still accessible) rural settings. Another fact about the constituency is worthy of note: it has the lowest proportion of Catholics anywhere in Canada.

The South Shore was held by the veteran Conservative Lloyd Crouse for 31 years from 1957 to 1988, a long service in reward for which Crouse would later be named to a term as Lieutenant-Governor of Nova Scotia. Thus it was thought unlikely that Crouse's successor as Tory candidate in 1988 would have any problem retaining the seat. Contrary to expectation, 1988 was a tight two-way race between Tories and Liberals. Many old Conservatives were resentful of the fact that Peter McCreath, a teacher and former broadcaster whose home in Hubbards was just outside the South Shore riding, had defeated three 'local boys' in a hotly contested nomination. The party faithful also openly admitted that Crouse had a personal following even among traditional Liberal supporters. With the help of Crouse who joined him on the campaign trail, McCreath was able to extend the Conservative dynasty, but with a margin of victory which was only slightly more than one thousand votes.

In 1993, the 50-year-old McCreath, a recently-installed Minister of Veterans Affairs, was opposed by 46-year-old lawyer Derek Wells for the Liberals, a long-time party worker who hoped to ride the Liberal tide that in the spring election had given 4 of 5 provincial seats in the constituency to the Liberals. The riding's other candidates were Reform's Ann Matthiasson, Eric Hustvedt for the NDP, National Party hopeful Jim Donahue, and Richard Robertson of Natural Law. While deflecting criticism about recent provincial tax increases, Wells, a cousin of Newfoundland Premier Clyde Wells, argued in the campaign that custodial management of the 200-mile fishing zone should be unilaterally extended another 50 miles to further protect dwindling fish stocks, a position McCreath characterized as 'nonsensical and unrealistic.'

The tide to the Liberals also swept away a long history of Conservative voting in South Shore. The Liberal Wells took 46.9% of the vote to McCreath's 32.6% and Matthiasson's 13.5%. The NDP was bumped into a distant fourth place as it was almost everywhere in Nova Scotia.

Member of Parliament: Derek Wells; **Party:** Liberal; **Occupation:** Lawyer; **Education:** LL.B, Dalhousie University; **Age:** 48 (November 28, 1946); **Year first elected to the House of Commons:** 1993

12010 South Shore

A: Political Profile

i) Voting Behaviour

	% 1993	% 1988	Change 1988-93
Conservative	32.6	46.5	-13.9
Liberal	46.9	42.6	4.3
NDP	5	10.1	-5.1
Reform	13.5	0	13.5
Other	1.9	0.8	1.1

% Turnout	63	Total Ballots (#)	37263
Rejected Ballots (#)	298	% Margin of Victory	14.3
Rural Polls, 1988 (#)	207	Urban Polls, 1988 (#)	16
% Yes - 1992	47.8	% No - 1992	51.8

ii) Campaign Financing

	# of Donations	Total $ Value	% of Limit Spent
Conservative	254	48620	95.4
Liberal	280	45942	85.4
NDP	40	5321	5.2
Reform	70	11715	16.8
Other	0	0	

B: Ethno-Linguistic Profile

% English Home Language	99.6	% French Home Language	0.2
% Official Bilingual	3.9	% Other Home Language	0.2
% Catholics	9.8	% Protestants	79.6
% Aboriginal Peoples	0.8	% Immigrants	3.5

C: Socio-Economic Profile

Average Family Income $	39772	Median Family Income $	35363
% Low Income Families	13.5	Average Home Price $	72746
% Home Owners	82.7	% Unemployment	11.6
% Labour Force Participation	58.5	% Managerial-Administrative	7
% Self-Employed	11.1	% University Degrees	5.7
% Movers	29.6		

D: Industrial Profile

% Manufacturing	23.3	% Service Sector	12.3
% Agriculture	2	% Mining	0.1
% Forestry	1.8	% Fishing	7.5
% Government Services	7.5	% Business Services	2

E: Homogeneity Measures

Ethnic Diversity Index	0.49	Religious Homogeneity Index	0.64
Sectoral Concentration Index	0.32	Income Disparity Index	11.1

F: Physical Setting Characteristics

Total Population	77902	Area (km²)	8625
Population Density (pop/km²)	9		

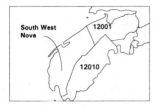

South West Nova

Constituency Number: 12011

South West Nova spans Nova Scotia's Fundy shore, including the towns of Yarmouth, Digby and Middleton. The constituency with the largest French-speaking population in the province (about 25% of the voters are Acadian) and home to the Université Sainte Anne, in 1993 the riding also had a defence base (CFB Cornwallis, since closed), a sizeable agricultural community in Annapolis county, woodland industries, and a number of tourist attractions. The mainstay of the local economy, however, remains the fishing industry, employing more than 25% of the workforce in Yarmouth and Digby counties.

A swing riding held by the Liberals from 1974 to 1984, except for the brief Clark interregnum in 1979, it was captured by the Conservatives in 1984. In the 1988 election, the local fishery, not free trade, was the key issue for the riding's inshore fishermen and small fish plant operators. Incumbent Conservative Gerald Comeau was raked over the proverbial coals about a contentious licensing issue by his main opponent, Coline Campbell, the riding's former Liberal MP. While Campbell emerged the eventual winner in 1988 (by almost the identical margin of Comeau's victory in 1984), she was not re-offering in 1993. In her stead, unilingual retired military photographer Harry Verran of Middleton (the agricultural portion of the riding) was contesting for the Liberals, against former fisheries officer Yvon Thibault for the Conservatives. Louis Mason ran for the Reform Party, Peter Zavitz (as he did in 1988) for the NDP, and Greg Murphy for Natural Law.

While pundits were forecasting that the Liberals would have no trouble retaining the seat, Thibault was pitching his knowledge of the fishery as a key advantage over his Liberal opponent. But he was working against the anger of many Tories with the Conservative government, something Conservative insiders acknowledged was giving a boost to the Reform Party. For his part, Verran promised to learn French while relying on the popularity in his riding of Liberal leader Jean Chrétien. Besides national issues such as jobs, the deficit, and the future of health care, two prominent local issues dominated the campaign: problems in the fishery and the future of CFB Cornwallis in Digby, which the Conservative government had slated for closure.

Election night saw Verran grab 54.8% of the vote to 22.7% for Thibault, a bulge of 12,000 votes. Reformer Matthiasson came third with 15.6% of the ballot, triple the vote of the NDP's Zavitz.

Member of Parliament: Harry Verran; **Party:** Liberal; **Occupation:** Military photographer (retired); **Year first elected to the House of Commons:** 1993

12011 South West Nova

A: Political Profile

i) Voting Behaviour

	% 1993	% 1988	Change 1988-93
Conservative	22.7	41.5	-18.8
Liberal	54.8	50	4.8
NDP	5.6	5.7	-0.1
Reform	15.6	0	15.6
Other	1.4	2.8	-1.4

% Turnout	70.6	Total Ballots (#)	38550
Rejected Ballots (#)	673	% Margin of Victory	32.1
Rural Polls, 1988 (#)	171	Urban Polls, 1988 (#)	22
% Yes - 1992	45.7	% No - 1992	53.4

ii) Campaign Financing

	# of Donations	Total $ Value	% of Limit Spent
Conservative	64	28950	86.6
Liberal	245	55151	85.9
NDP	23	2188	2.8
Reform	59	9340	14.5
Other	0	0	

B: Ethno-Linguistic Profile

% English Home Language	83.6	% French Home Language	16.2
% Official Bilingual	24.3	% Other Home Language	0.1
% Catholics	40.6	% Protestants	51.3
% Aboriginal Peoples	0.6	% Immigrants	3.6

C: Socio-Economic Profile

Average Family Income $	37903	Median Family Income $	32304
% Low Income Families	15	Average Home Price $	64918
% Home Owners	78.6	% Unemployment	13.9
% Labour Force Participation	59.6	% Managerial-Administrative	6.9
% Self-Employed	10.8	% University Degrees	5.5
% Movers	30.6		

D: Industrial Profile

% Manufacturing	16.4	% Service Sector	16
% Agriculture	3.2	% Mining	0.6
% Forestry	1.7	% Fishing	7
% Government Services	11.4	% Business Services	1.5

E: Homogeneity Measures

Ethnic Diversity Index	0.44	Religious Homogeneity Index	0.42
Sectoral Concentration Index	0.33	Income Disparity Index	14.8

F: Physical Setting Characteristics

Total Population	72780	Area (km²)	8653
Population Density (pop/km²)	8.4		

Beauséjour

Constituency Number: 13001

Formerly the riding of Westmoreland–Kent, Beauséjour was created by adding a chunk of the Moncton riding. With an economic base in fishing and fish processing, farming, tourism, wood-cutting plants and industrial parks, Beauséjour runs north and east of Moncton, along the coastline of the Northumberland Strait and along the Nova Scotia border, and includes the university town of Sackville (home of Mount Allison University) and the seaside town of Shediac. In demographic terms, the constituency is split by an invisible line separating the two linguistic communities, with the riding's francophone population almost twice as numerous as the anglophone.

A traditionally Liberal riding, from 1972 to 1984 it was the fiefdom of former Liberal fisheries minister, senator, and now Governor-General, Romeo LeBlanc. In 1984, it was won by businessman Fernand Robichaud, the only New Brunswick Liberal to survive the Tory sweep of that year. In 1988, Robichaud defeated former provincial cabinet minister Omer Leger by a substantial margin to retain the seat for the Liberals. After Jean Chrétien won the Liberal leadership in 1990, Robichaud stepped down to allow Chrétien to contest the by-election and gain a seat in the Commons as MP for Beauséjour.

In 1993, Robichaud was again the Liberal candidate in the riding, Chrétien having shifted his candidature to his old Quebec riding. Running against the heavy favourite was vocational teacher Ian Hamilton for the Conservatives, David Baille for the NDP, Mae Boudreau-Pederson for Christian Heritage, and James Bannister, self-described as 'one of the great educators of this century', for the National Party. The Reform Party did not have a candidate in Beauséjour, due to 'lack of voter interest'. Robichaud ran a campaign emphasizing job creation and protection of social programs, while criticizing the Tory deficit-reduction plan as a job-killer. A prominent local issue was the planned bridge to P.E.I., the effects of which raised concerns for the riding's fishermen and ferry terminal employees.

On election night, Robichaud won a huge victory, taking 76.2% of the vote, leaving the Conservative and NDP candidates with 15.2% and 5.7% respectively.

Member of Parliament: Fernand Robichaud; **Party:** Liberal; **Occupation:** Businessman; **Education:** T.C., Moncton Technical Institute; **Age:** 55 (December 2, 1939); **Year first elected to the House of Commons:** 1984

13001 Beauséjour

A: Political Profile
i) Voting Behaviour

	% 1993	% 1988	Change 1988-93
Conservative	15.2	27.2	-12
Liberal	76.2	58.6	17.6
NDP	5.7	10.2	-4.5
Reform	0	0	0
Other	3	3.9	-0.9

% Turnout	75.3	Total Ballots (#)	40324
Rejected Ballots (#)	774	% Margin of Victory	61
Rural Polls, 1988 (#)	166	Urban Polls, 1988 (#)	0
% Yes - 1992	74.6	% No - 1992	24.7

ii) Campaign Financing

	# of Donations	Total $ Value	% of Limit Spent
Conservative	96	34785	41.9
Liberal	11	59739	50.8
NDP	7	3370	4.2
Reform	0	0	0
Other	21	1644	

B: Ethno-Linguistic Profile

% English Home Language	37.3	% French Home Language	61.1
% Official Bilingual	58.1	% Other Home Language	1.7
% Catholics	74.9	% Protestants	20.8
% Aboriginal Peoples	2.7	% Immigrants	3.3

C: Socio-Economic Profile

Average Family Income $	38922	Median Family Income $	34624
% Low Income Families	13.5	Average Home Price $	60421
% Home Owners	82.4	% Unemployment	18.5
% Labour Force Participation	62.6	% Managerial-Administrative	7.6
% Self-Employed	6.7	% University Degrees	5.6
% Movers	24.9		

D: Industrial Profile

% Manufacturing	17.7	% Service Sector	13.5
% Agriculture	2.4	% Mining	0.5
% Forestry	1.5	% Fishing	2.5
% Government Services	9.3	% Business Services	1.7

E: Homogeneity Measures

Ethnic Diversity Index	0.59	Religious Homogeneity Index	0.59
Sectoral Concentration Index	0.33	Income Disparity Index	11

F: Physical Setting Characteristics

Total Population	68735	Area (km²)	6487
Population Density (pop/km²)	10.6		

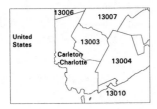

Carleton–Charlotte

Constituency Number: 13002

A large, rural and predominantly Protestant riding of scattered communities, including the towns of Woodstock and St Stephen, New Brunswick's 'fish and chip' constituency stretches half way up the Maine-New Brunswick border from the Bay of Fundy coast to the potato farming country of the St John River Valley. Fishing, farming, forestry, and associated processing industries dominate the local economy.

A Tory riding for 30 years prior to 1988, Carleton–Charlotte had been held by Conservative MP Fred McCain since 1972. His decision not to reoffer in 1988 made the outcome somewhat less predictable than it otherwise might have been. The fact that the Liberals were running Woodstock mayor Harold Culbert, well known in the northern part of the riding for his 12 years in municipal politics, while the Conservatives fielded a relative newcomer in St Stephen, financial advisor Greg Thompson, only added to the uncertainty. In the event, concerns about free trade were not sufficient to topple the Tory dynasty in Carleton–Charlotte. While the Liberals dramatically improved their vote totals over 1984, Conservative Greg Thompson still managed to retain the seat for his party.

The 1993 election had the two major contestants from 1988 facing each other once again. This time the 46-year-old Thompson and 49-year-old Culbert, who had stepped down as Woodstock mayor in 1992, were joined by 24-year-old supply teacher Bill Barteau for the NDP, electrical engineer Greg Wyborn, 37, for the Reform Party, and National Party candidate Richard Shelley, 34. Thompson attempted to portray Liberal job-creation plans as an outdated 'spend, borrow, spend, borrow' approach, while the Conservatives would use improved training to better match job-seekers to available employment. Wyborn emphasized the Reform Party's commitment to allowing individual MPs more independence from party discipline. Barteau and Shelley both argued for fairer corporate taxes and the cancellation of the free trade agreements, while the NDP candidate thought more stringent environmental protection would create jobs as well.

In the second closest race in Atlantic Canada (next to St John's East), incumbent Thompson was edged out by the Liberal Culbert. Thompson blamed a disastrous national campaign and a strong showing by the Reform Party candidate for his downfall. Reformer Wyborn took 11.8% of the ballot, most of them, Thompson thought, stolen from the Conservatives. The NDP and National Party candidates garnered 3% and 1% of the vote respectively.

Member of Parliament: Harold Culbert; **Party:** Liberal; **Occupation:** Hospital administrator; **Year first elected to the House of Commons:** 1993

13002 Carleton–Charlotte

A: Political Profile

i) Voting Behaviour

	% 1993	% 1988	Change 1988-93
Conservative	40.6	47.2	-6.6
Liberal	43.1	41.6	1.5
NDP	3.1	7.7	-4.6
Reform	11.8	0	11.8
Other	1.3	3.5	-2.2

% Turnout	66.2	Total Ballots (#)	32676
Rejected Ballots (#)	269	% Margin of Victory	2.5
Rural Polls, 1988 (#)	165	Urban Polls, 1988 (#)	12
% Yes - 1992	47.5	% No - 1992	52

ii) Campaign Financing

	# of Donations	Total $ Value	% of Limit Spent
Conservative	134	39586	84.0
Liberal	6	25043	54.0
NDP	22	1981	1.7
Reform	18	8494	15.3*
Other	2	149	

B: Ethno-Linguistic Profile

% English Home Language	98.9	% French Home Language	0.8
% Official Bilingual	7.5	% Other Home Language	0.3
% Catholics	16	% Protestants	74.5
% Aboriginal Peoples	0.9	% Immigrants	4.6

C: Socio-Economic Profile

Average Family Income $	39733	Median Family Income $	33792
% Low Income Families	14.5	Average Home Price $	60517
% Home Owners	82.8	% Unemployment	14.4
% Labour Force Participation	61.6	% Managerial-Administrative	8.3
% Self-Employed	10.8	% University Degrees	5.9
% Movers	27.5		

D: Industrial Profile

% Manufacturing	20.8	% Service Sector	12.2
% Agriculture	5.7	% Mining	0.1
% Forestry	3.4	% Fishing	3.9
% Government Services	6.9	% Business Services	2

E: Homogeneity Measures

Ethnic Diversity Index	0.77	Religious Homogeneity Index	0.58
Sectoral Concentration Index	0.31	Income Disparity Index	15

F: Physical Setting Characteristics

Total Population	65293	Area (km²)	11270
Population Density (pop/km²)	5.8		

* Tentative value, due to the existence of unpaid campaign expenses.

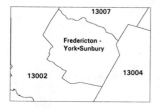

Fredericton–York–Sunbury (formerly Fredericton)

Constituency Number: 13003

This constituency, which takes in New Brunswick's capital city and its environs, boasts a stable economy based on public sector employment - the provincial government, the University of New Brunswick, and a Canadian Forces base - but also on light industry, farming and forestry. Fredericton has relatively low unemployment and a highly-educated population, second only to Halifax in Atlantic Canada in terms of the percentage holding university degrees. It has the highest percentage of its workforce employed in government services in the region, and again is second only to Halifax in the business services category.

This riding was solidly Conservative since 1957 and held since 1972 by PC MP Bob Howie (who carried it by 15,000 votes in 1984). Howie's retirement before the 1988 election gave some hope to Liberal and NDP challengers. This was doused somewhat, however, when the Tories nominated as their candidate well-known businessman J.W. 'Bud' Bird, a former mayor of Fredericton, former provincial cabinet minister, and one of the party's chief organizers in the province. For their candidate the Liberals nominated the acting mayor of Fredericton and a local morning-show radio host, Brad Woodside. Free trade monopolized the bulk of campaign debate for the major parties, with Liberal and NDP candidates decrying the deal and Bird lauding the prospect of a return to pre-Confederation trading patterns. The election result returned Fredericton to the Conservative fold, but with little more than a 1500 vote plurality.

In 1993, five of six provincial seats in this federal riding were held by the anti-bilingual Confederation of Regions Party (CoR, the province's official opposition), giving the 61-year-old incumbent Bird plenty of critics in addition to his traditional opponents. Bird himself staunchly supported official bilingualism, free trade, and the unpopular GST, but was also running on his record of service, his 'good guy' image and his reputation as a hard-working MP. Contesting the election for the Liberals was 37-year-old Andy Scott, a former McKenna aide and provincial intergovernmental affairs bureaucrat. Five other candidates were also contesting. Businessman and Reform Party candidate Jack Lamey focused his attack on the Tory fiscal record and the need for parliamentary reform. The other candidates were high school teacher Pauline MacKenzie for the New Democrats, Steve Gillrie for the Canada Party, Neil Dickie for Natural Law, and Doreen Fraser, Independent.

The election itself proved an easy win for the Liberal Scott, who outpolled the incumbent Bird by a 46.6% to 29.2% margin. Part of this lopsided result can be explained by the strong showing of Reformer Lamey, who took 17.7% of the vote, third best in Atlantic Canada. The NDP was reduced to 5% of the vote, with the other candidates splitting 2%.

Member of Parliament: Andy Scott; **Party:** Liberal; **Occupation:** Assistant Deputy Minister for Intergovernmental Affairs; **Education:** BA, University of New Brunswick; **Age:** 40 (March 16, 1955); **Year first elected to the House of Commons:** 1993

13003 Fredericton–York–Sunbury

A: Political Profile

i) Voting Behaviour

	% 1993	% 1988	Change 1988-93
Conservative	29.2	43	-13.8
Liberal	46.6	39.7	6.9
NDP	5	10.3	-5.3
Reform	17.1	0	17.1
Other	2.1	7	-4.9

% Turnout	63.2	Total Ballots (#)	47014
Rejected Ballots (#)	311	% Margin of Victory	17.4
Rural Polls, 1988 (#)	82	Urban Polls, 1988 (#)	144
% Yes - 1992	48.5	% No - 1992	50.9

ii) Campaign Financing

	# of Donations	Total $ Value	% of Limit Spent
Conservative	188	62759	91.5
Liberal	9	53358	81.2
NDP	131	23655	26.1
Reform	33	9431	23.3
Other	25	3206	

B: Ethno-Linguistic Profile

% English Home Language	94.1	% French Home Language	4.7
% Official Bilingual	16.8	% Other Home Language	1.2
% Catholics	29	% Protestants	59.9
% Aboriginal Peoples	1.7	% Immigrants	5.6

C: Socio-Economic Profile

Average Family Income $	49014	Median Family Income $	44113
% Low Income Families	12.9	Average Home Price $	89642
% Home Owners	68.7	% Unemployment	10.5
% Labour Force Participation	70.7	% Managerial-Administrative	11.6
% Self-Employed	6.4	% University Degrees	16.3
% Movers	45.3		

D: Industrial Profile

% Manufacturing	4.6	% Service Sector	18.9
% Agriculture	2	% Mining	0.2
% Forestry	1.6	% Fishing	0.1
% Government Services	22.8	% Business Services	5.4

E: Homogeneity Measures

Ethnic Diversity Index	0.56	Religious Homogeneity Index	0.45
Sectoral Concentration Index	0.5	Income Disparity Index	10

F: Physical Setting Characteristics

Total Population	91650	Area (km²)	5176
Population Density (pop/km²)	17.7		

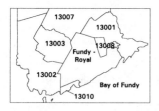

Fundy–Royal

Constituency Number: 13004

A large, mostly rural riding covering a large swath of south-central New Brunswick, Fundy–Royal is home to dairy and beef farming, coal and potash mining, maple sugar and lumber industries, CFB Gagetown, tourism and small business. The constituency is dotted by many small communities, including the towns of Sussex, Minto, Chipman and Gagetown, as well as the communities of the suburban Kennebecasis Valley east of Saint John.

The riding is bedrock Tory country, having returned Conservatives to Parliament since 1917. The incumbent in 1993, businessman Robert Corbett, first won the seat in a by-election in 1978. The riding was changing in the 1980s, however, with an influx of urban commuters into the Kennebecasis Valley area, a development that gave some hope to Liberal and NDP challengers. The incumbent Corbett, though a backbencher, did gain some notoriety for his right-wing views. An advocate of the death penalty, an opponent of bilingualism, and anti-CBC, he was one of nine Tory MPs to break ranks and vote against the government's C-72 bilingualism bill. While the Liberal candidate in 1988 hoped the clean sweep by provincial Liberals one year earlier would provide momentum to his federal campaign, Liberal coat-tails proved to be short on election night. Corbett was still able to coast to a comfortable victory in 1988.

In 1993, Corbett faced one familiar challenger. Colby Fraser, who ran for the Confederation of Regions Party in 1988, was running this time as an Independent because CoR had failed to recruit the 50 candidates necessary to earn official party status. The Liberals were running lawyer Paul Zed, the Reform Party Dan McKeil, and the NDP Mark Connell.

The election result stunned local Conservatives: the riding had gone Liberal for the first time in 75 years, and the result was not even close. Paul Zed took 46.5% of the vote to Corbett's 28.3%. The Tory cause was not helped by the fact that Reformer McKeil received the second highest vote total of any Reform candidate in Atlantic Canada, taking 17.7% of the vote. New Democrat Connell managed 4.8%.

Member of Parliament: Paul Zed; **Party:** Liberal; **Occupation:** Lawyer; **Education:** LL.M, London School of Economics; **Age:** 38 (December 31, 1956); **Year first elected to the House of Commons:** 1993

13004 Fundy–Royal

A: Political Profile
i) Voting Behaviour

	% 1993	% 1988	Change 1988-93
Conservative	28.3	46.7	-18.4
Liberal	46.5	36.3	10.2
NDP	4.8	11	-6.2
Reform	17.7	0	17.7
Other	2.7	6.1	-3.4

% Turnout	70.3	Total Ballots (#)	47304
Rejected Ballots (#)	460	% Margin of Victory	18.2
Rural Polls, 1988 (#)	211	Urban Polls, 1988 (#)	16
% Yes - 1992	45.8	% No - 1992	53.7

ii) Campaign Financing

	# of Donations	Total $ Value	% of Limit Spent
Conservative	161	30562	75.7
Liberal	15	53578	91.3
NDP	2	117	0.2
Reform	39	7758	15.7
Other	25	7087	

B: Ethno-Linguistic Profile

% English Home Language	98.5	% French Home Language	1.3
% Official Bilingual	10.8	% Other Home Language	0.2
% Catholics	26.6	% Protestants	65.7
% Aboriginal Peoples	0.2	% Immigrants	4

C: Socio-Economic Profile

Average Family Income $	46395	Median Family Income $	41223
% Low Income Families	12.5	Average Home Price $	73790
% Home Owners	86	% Unemployment	12
% Labour Force Participation	63.7	% Managerial-Administrative	11.3
% Self-Employed	8.1	% University Degrees	8.3
% Movers	34.4		

D: Industrial Profile

% Manufacturing	13.6	% Service Sector	11
% Agriculture	3.4	% Mining	3.3
% Forestry	2.2	% Fishing	0.4
% Government Services	7.3	% Business Services	3.1

E: Homogeneity Measures

Ethnic Diversity Index	0.71	Religious Homogeneity Index	0.5
Sectoral Concentration Index	0.37	Income Disparity Index	11.1

F: Physical Setting Characteristics

Total Population	89863	Area (km²)	10624
Population Density (pop/km²)	8.5		

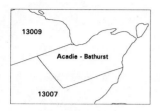

Acadie–Bathurst
(formerly Gloucester)

Constituency Number: 13005

Formerly the riding of Gloucester, Acadie–Bathurst is a rural and small town riding in Northeast New Brunswick whose voters are more or less equally divided amongst four population centres - Tracadie, Caraquet, Shippigan, and Bathurst. The riding's socio-economic profile features low average family incomes, an unemployment rate above 20%, a relatively high contribution to incomes from government transfers, and the lowest percentage of employment derived from government services in Atlantic Canada. It is also the most francophone and most Catholic riding in Atlantic Canada, with the highest 'Yes' vote in the region in the Charlottetown Referendum of 1992. Its economy combines major mining and smelting enterprises, forestry and fishing operations, and a large peat moss industry.

In 1984, this staunchly Liberal constituency elected a Conservative to Parliament for the first time in a century. However, its Tory MP, former Bathurst mayor Roger Clinch, was denied his party's nomination in 1988, losing out to former provincial fisheries minister and popular Acadian political figure Jean Gauvin. The 'Clinch factor' was but one variable in a 'battle of political heavyweights' in Gloucester in 1988. The Liberals ran Doug Young, a former leader of the provincial Liberal party who stepped down as provincial fisheries minister to contest the election. Young defeated Gauvin and returned the riding to its traditional Liberal affiliation.

In 1993, the incumbent Young, who served in Ottawa as Treasury Board and Finance critic, was opposed by two first-time candidates: Luce-Andreé Gauthier, a 41-year-old lawyer and former assistant to Joe Clark, for the Progressive Conservatives, and Kim Gallant, a 30-year-old lab technician and union representative, for the NDP. Job creation was the overriding issue in the campaign, fed by concerns about the problems and ultimately the future of the region's main industries. Young preached the need for infrastructure projects in the region, Gauthier stressed the need for new job training programs, and Gallant argued the need to reduce the riding's dependence on resource industries and 10-weeks-work for unemployment insurance benefits.

With the fluently bilingual Young being touted as a likely cabinet minister in a Liberal government, Acadie-Bathurst voters gave him a resounding vote of confidence. He gathered two-thirds of the riding's votes to 27.6% for Gauthier and 6% for Gallant. Young was subsequently named Minister of Transport in the Chrétien government.

Member of Parliament: M. Douglas Young; **Party:** Liberal; **Occupation:** Lawyer; **Education:** LL.B, University of New Brunswick; **Age:** 54 (September 20, 1940); **Year first elected to the House of Commons:** 1988

13005 Acadie–Bathurst

A: Political Profile
i) Voting Behaviour

	% 1993	% 1988	Change 1988-93
Conservative	27.6	42.7	-15.1
Liberal	66.4	51.7	14.7
NDP	6	5.5	0.5
Reform	0	0	0
Other	0	0	0

% Turnout	75	Total Ballots (#)	41553
Rejected Ballots (#)	1135	% Margin of Victory	38.8
Rural Polls, 1988 (#)	155	Urban Polls, 1988 (#)	32
% Yes - 1992	86.5	% No - 1992	12.9

ii) Campaign Financing

	# of Donations	Total $ Value	% of Limit Spent
Conservative	142	49575	99.8
Liberal	13	50857	85.8
NDP	0	0	0
Reform	0	0	0
Other	0	0	

B: Ethno-Linguistic Profile

% English Home Language	19.4	% French Home Language	80.4
% Official Bilingual	39.2	% Other Home Language	0.1
% Catholics	92.4	% Protestants	6.6
% Aboriginal Peoples	0.3	% Immigrants	0.8

C: Socio-Economic Profile

Average Family Income $	36407	Median Family Income $	31348
% Low Income Families	20.3	Average Home Price $	60277
% Home Owners	79.1	% Unemployment	22.6
% Labour Force Participation	59.5	% Managerial-Administrative	6.8
% Self-Employed	6.5	% University Degrees	5.9
% Movers	24.3		

D: Industrial Profile

% Manufacturing	18.1	% Service Sector	11.6
% Agriculture	1.2	% Mining	5
% Forestry	2.3	% Fishing	4.8
% Government Services	6.6	% Business Services	2.1

E: Homogeneity Measures

Ethnic Diversity Index	0.78	Religious Homogeneity Index	0.84
Sectoral Concentration Index	0.31	Income Disparity Index	13.9

F: Physical Setting Characteristics

Total Population	72351	Area (km²)	4369
Population Density (pop/km²)	16.6		

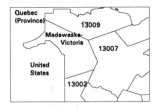

Madawaska–Victoria

Constituency Number: 13006

Tucked into the northwest corner of New Brunswick between Maine and Quebec and including the towns of Edmundston and Grand Falls, Madawaska–Victoria is divided between the predominantly francophone county of Madawaska, which is home to about 60% of the constituency's residents, and the predominantly anglophone county of Victoria. One of the poorest New Brunswick constituencies in terms of average family income, it is also the second most French-speaking riding in Atlantic Canada after Acadie–Bathurst. Not coincidentally, in the 1992 Charlottetown Referendum, it had the second highest 'Yes' vote in the region after Acadie–Bathurst. Agriculture, food processing, pulp and paper, logging and textiles are important components of its economic base.

From 1968 to 1984 the incumbent was Liberal Eymard Corbin. His elevation to the Senate was followed by the loss of the seat to Tory Bernard Valcourt, a young Edmundston lawyer who after his election became the minister of state for tourism and small business, as well as minister of state for Indian affairs and northern development. His popularity within the riding, and his ability to out-spend his opponents by a wide margin, made the prospect of his defeat in 1988 seem unlikely to observers. While Valcourt's Liberal opponent in that election did manage to cut the incumbent's margin to less than 1500 votes, the minister was returned to Parliament for another term.

In 1993 the 41-year-old Valcourt, having survived an alcohol-related motorcycle crash in 1989 and the parliamentary disgrace which followed, went into the election as the most powerful minister in Atlantic Canada, in charge of the Ministry of Human Resources. He faced a feisty Liberal opponent in 37-year-old industrial relations specialist and association director Pierrette Ringuette-Maltais, member of the provincial legislature for Madawaska South since 1987. She blasted proposed reforms to the unemployment insurance system as potentially devastating for the riding. Parise Martin was contesting for the NDP and Kimberly Spikings for the Reform Party.

The result in Madawaska–Victoria was one of the closest in Atlantic Canada. Despite winning the biggest Conservative vote in Atlantic Canada, Valcourt lost to Ringuette-Maltais by a 48.8% to 45.7% margin. Not much was left over for the other candidates, who split the remaining 5.5% of the vote. Valcourt was subsequently (May, 1995) elected leader of the provincial Conservative Party.

Member of Parliament: Pierrette Ringuette-Maltais; **Party:** Liberal; **Occupation:** University lecturer; **Education:** BA, Université de Moncton; **Age:** 39 (December 31, 1955); **Year first elected to the House of Commons:** 1993

13006 Madawaska–Victoria

A: Political Profile
i) Voting Behaviour

	% 1993	% 1988	Change 1988-93
Conservative	45.7	48.2	-2.5
Liberal	48.8	43.8	5
NDP	2.6	8	-5.4
Reform	2.9	0	2.9
Other	0	0	0

% Turnout	75.6	Total Ballots (#)	33643
Rejected Ballots (#)	733	% Margin of Victory	3.1
Rural Polls, 1988 (#)	101	Urban Polls, 1988 (#)	38
% Yes - 1992	81.1	% No - 1992	18.1

ii) Campaign Financing

	# of Donations	Total $ Value	% of Limit Spent
Conservative	189	60774	93
Liberal	211	69261	92
NDP	2	1215	0
Reform	6	2336	2.4
Other	0	0	

B: Ethno-Linguistic Profile

% English Home Language	23.3	% French Home Language	76.4
% Official Bilingual	47	% Other Home Language	0.2
% Catholics	81.2	% Protestants	15.1
% Aboriginal Peoples	0.5	% Immigrants	3.1

C: Socio-Economic Profile

Average Family Income $	37032	Median Family Income $	32629
% Low Income Families	18.6	Average Home Price $	61802
% Home Owners	74.7	% Unemployment	17
% Labour Force Participation	58.8	% Managerial-Administrative	8.1
% Self-Employed	8.4	% University Degrees	7.2
% Movers	28.4		

D: Industrial Profile

% Manufacturing	19.1	% Service Sector	13.2
% Agriculture	5	% Mining	0.1
% Forestry	5.3	% Fishing	0.1
% Government Services	6.7	% Business Services	1.3

E: Homogeneity Measures

Ethnic Diversity Index	0.72	Religious Homogeneity Index	0.67
Sectoral Concentration Index	0.35	Income Disparity Index	11.9

F: Physical Setting Characteristics

Total Population	57340	Area (km²)	8998
Population Density (pop/km²)	6.4		

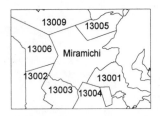

Miramichi

Constituency Number: 13007

This riding in Northeast New Brunswick is dominated by the Miramichi River, its industries and its communities. Newcastle and Chatham at the mouth of the Miramichi River system are the apex for a huge forestry industry and also the riding's only two urban centres. In fact, no other riding in Atlantic Canada has an economy so dependent upon forest industries as Miramichi, supplemented by fishing (both sport and commercial) and government services. The riding also has the highest rate of unemployment in New Brunswick. About a third of its residents are francophone.

A traditionally Liberal riding, Miramichi was held by former school principal Maurice Dionne from 1974-1984, when he was defeated by Bud Jardine, the first Conservative to represent the riding in 50 years. In 1988, Dionne was attempting a comeback against Jardine, who only narrowly won his own nomination battle. The 1988 result reversed that of 1984, returning Dionne to his former seat in Parliament by some 5000 votes. Of note is the fact that the CoR candidate ran third in the constituency, gathering more than 10% of the vote on an anti-bilingualism platform.

In 1993, Dionne was forced to step down as MP and Liberal standard-bearer after being afflicted with Alzheimer's disease. A high-profile nominating convention to name his replacement was won by school principal Charles Hubbard, a first-time political candidate. Trying to recapture the seat for the Tories was Peter Murphy, the mayor of Newcastle. The other candidates were Paul Doyle for the Reform Party, Gordie Allison for the NDP, and 68-year-old Wilmot Ross, a researcher for the CoR Party, for the Canada Party.

On election night, the massive swing to the Liberals was evident in Miramichi as well, with Hubbard collecting more than 60% of the vote. Murphy placed a distant second with 22.8% of the vote, while Reform candidate Doyle took third place with 9.9%, almost double the NDP's 5.1%.

Member of Parliament: Charles Hubbard; **Party:** Liberal; **Occupation:** High school principal; **Education:** MA, University of New Brunswick; **Age:** 54 (October 29, 1940); **Year first elected to the House of Commons:** 1993

13007 Miramichi

A: Political Profile

i) Voting Behaviour

	% 1993	% 1988	Change 1988-93
Conservative	22.8	32.4	-9.6
Liberal	61.1	50.8	10.3
NDP	5.1	6.1	-1
Reform	9.9	0	9.9
Other	1	10.7	-9.7

% Turnout	73.1	Total Ballots (#)	31308
Rejected Ballots (#)	491	% Margin of Victory	38.3
Rural Polls, 1988 (#)	123	Urban Polls, 1988 (#)	31
% Yes - 1992	56.6	% No - 1992	42.7

ii) Campaign Financing

	# of Donations	Total $ Value	% of Limit Spent
Conservative	48	21819	55.3
Liberal	4	24178	71.9*
NDP	21	5628	5
Reform	54	4555	7.5
Other	1	500	

B: Ethno-Linguistic Profile

% English Home Language	72.8	% French Home Language	26.9
% Official Bilingual	26.1	% Other Home Language	0.3
% Catholics	63.9	% Protestants	33.4
% Aboriginal Peoples	1.1	% Immigrants	1.6

C: Socio-Economic Profile

Average Family Income $	38967	Median Family Income $	35214
% Low Income Families	16.8	Average Home Price $	60437
% Home Owners	81.9	% Unemployment	24.5
% Labour Force Participation	59.2	% Managerial-Administrative	6.8
% Self-Employed	5.5	% University Degrees	5.6
% Movers	26		

D: Industrial Profile

% Manufacturing	14.7	% Service Sector	17.3
% Agriculture	1.1	% Mining	1.9
% Forestry	6.8	% Fishing	2.4
% Government Services	11.6	% Business Services	1.6

E: Homogeneity Measures

Ethnic Diversity Index	0.46	Religious Homogeneity Index	0.51
Sectoral Concentration Index	0.32	Income Disparity Index	9.6

F: Physical Setting Characteristics

Total Population	5995	Area (km²)	14944
Population Density (pop/km²)	3.7		

* Tentative value, due to the existence of unpaid campaign expenses.

Moncton

Constituency Number: 13008

This mostly urban constituency in southern New Brunswick is comprised of 5 municipalities and several unincorporated areas centring on the city of Moncton. It is a microcosm of New Brunswick and the country in linguistic terms with a 65:35 English/French population ratio. After Fredericton the most prosperous area of the province, Moncton serves as the transportation and distribution centre for the region, the regional headquarters of a number of federal government departments, and a growth node for the telematics industry. It is also home to the Université de Moncton. Its diverse economic base gives it one of the lowest unemployment rates in the region (after metropolitan Halifax and Fredericton), a high level of business services, and the second highest proportion of managers in Atlantic Canada.

While the riding has a long history of Liberal domination prior to 1968, redistribution had made it a swing riding. In 1988 the incumbent was Conservative MP Dennis Cochrane, a former mayor. Cochrane was first elected to Parliament in 1984, defeating Liberal MP Gary McCauley by more than 15,000 votes. In 1988 he faced his successor in the mayor's office, George Rideout, who was contesting the election for the Liberals. The hottest issue in the campaign was the government's decision to close CN's repair shops in Moncton. The railway workers and their union, seething over the loss of 1200 jobs, conducted an all-out campaign to defeat Cochrane. Another problem for Cochrane was the presence of two right-wing competitors for Conservative votes: the Confederation of Regions Party and Christian Heritage Party. After a hard-fought and at times a nasty campaign, the Liberal candidate Rideout emerged victorious, with a plurality in excess of 6,000 votes.

In 1993, the situation facing the incumbent was very different. Moncton had fared well economically during the previous five years, despite the CN cutbacks, by attracting a number of major national corporations with its bilingual labour force. Rideout, whose parents both served as MPs, faced no focused attack or concerted opposition. Cochrane had assumed the leadership of the provincial Conservative Party. All Rideout had to do was 'ride the wave' of support flowing to the Liberals. His main opponent was a soft-spoken 62-year-old citizenship court judge, Bernadette LeBlanc, for the Conservatives. The other candidates were Gerard Snow for the NDP, Clyde Woodworth for the Reform Party, Ron Openshaw for Natural Law, and Isaac Legère for Christian Heritage.

The election result gave Rideout two-thirds of the vote in Moncton, while the Tory candidate lost her deposit by failing to crack the 15% minimum. The Reform candidate was close behind with 12.4% of the vote. The NDP finished a distant fourth with 4.9%.

Member of Parliament: George Rideout; **Party:** Liberal; **Occupation:** Lawyer; **Education:** LL.L, University of New Brunswick; **Age:** 50 (January 2, 1945); **Year first elected to the House of Commons:** 1988

13008 Moncton

A: Political Profile
i) Voting Behaviour

	% 1993	% 1988	Change 1988-93
Conservative	14.3	34	-19.7
Liberal	66.3	46.9	19.4
NDP	4.9	9.7	-4.8
Reform	12.4	0	12.4
Other	2.1	9.4	-7.3

% Turnout	68.2	Total Ballots (#)	51284
Rejected Ballots (#)	525	% Margin of Victory	52
Rural Polls, 1988 (#)	22	Urban Polls, 1988 (#)	184
% Yes - 1992	60.8	% No - 1992	38.7

ii) Campaign Financing

	# of Donations	Total $ Value	% of Limit Spent
Conservative	115	49362	78.2
Liberal	8	50666	73.9
NDP	63	22519	34.1
Reform	59	10437	20.7
Other	59	5746	

B: Ethno-Linguistic Profile

% English Home Language	74.6	% French Home Language	24.7
% Official Bilingual	40.7	% Other Home Language	0.7
% Catholics	51.7	% Protestants	41.8
% Aboriginal Peoples	0.3	% Immigrants	3.4

C: Socio-Economic Profile

Average Family Income $	47147	Median Family Income $	41543
% Low Income Families	16.1	Average Home Price $	81575
% Home Owners	66.4	% Unemployment	10.9
% Labour Force Participation	65.5	% Managerial-Administrative	13.2
% Self-Employed	6	% University Degrees	11
% Movers	45.2		

D: Industrial Profile

% Manufacturing	7.4	% Service Sector	13.6
% Agriculture	0.9	% Mining	0.3
% Forestry	0.5	% Fishing	0.1
% Government Services	9.7	% Business Services	4.7

E: Homogeneity Measures

Ethnic Diversity Index	0.41	Religious Homogeneity Index	0.44
Sectoral Concentration Index	0.57	Income Disparity Index	11.9

F: Physical Setting Characteristics

Total Population	91759	Area (km^2)	1179
Population Density (pop/km^2)	77.8		

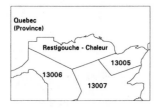

Restigouche–Chaleur

Constituency Number: 13009

This northern New Brunswick riding bordering Quebec's Gaspé Peninsula has a resource-based economy heavily dependent on forestry, mining and resource-linked manufacturing. Its two major urban centres, Dalhousie and Campbellton, are situated at the mouth of the Restigouche River on the Gulf of St Lawrence. More than two-thirds of the riding's residents have French language origins, the third highest percentage in Atlantic Canada and a factor in the riding's high 'Yes' vote in the 1992 Charlottetown Referendum. With an unemployment rate in the 20% range, job creation and the stability of its major industries are major concerns.

Prior to 1984, Restigouche voted Liberal in eight of nine general elections. However, in 1984 the sitting Liberal MP, Maurice Harquail (first elected in a 1975 by-election), was defeated by Conservative Al Girard by a margin of less than 2,000 votes. Girard was favoured by pundits to repeat his 1984 victory for his excellent constituency work. But in something of an upset, given the incumbent's generally high level of popularity, the Liberal candidate Guy Arseneault (who had won the nomination over the former Liberal MP) defeated Girard by close to 3,000 votes.

In 1993, Arsenault, a 41-year-old former high school teacher, was opposed by Tory Bruce MacIntosh, the mayor of Campbellton since 1986, Nancy Quigley for the NDP, and Natural Law candidate Laurent Maltais. As in Beauséjour and Acadie–Bathurst, the Reform Party did not contest the election. The issues were familiar to those of many constituencies: job creation, health services cuts, increasing welfare rolls and the integrity of the social safety net; but especially job creation.

With a national Liberal victory all but assured, Arsenault's victory in Restigouche–Chaleur was not much in question (it had not gone Liberal only once since 1961). He took roughly 70% of the vote in the election, with his Conservative opponent gaining 20%. The NDP received 7% to finish third.

Member of Parliament: Guy H. Arseneault; **Party:** Liberal; **Occupation:** Teacher; **Education:** BEd, St Thomas University; **Age:** 43 (May 11, 1952); **Year first elected to the House of Commons:** 1988

13009 Restigouche–Chaleu

A: Political Profile
i) Voting Behaviour

	% 1993	% 1988	Change 1988-93
Conservative	19.9	40	-20.1
Liberal	70.5	49.4	21.1
NDP	6.9	10.6	-3.7
Reform	0	0	0
Other	2.7	0	2.7

% Turnout	75.1	Total Ballots (#)	30878
Rejected Ballots (#)	1097	% Margin of Victory	50.6
Rural Polls, 1988 (#)	121	Urban Polls, 1988 (#)	38
% Yes - 1992	75.5	% No - 1992	23.3

ii) Campaign Financing

	# of Donations	Total $ Value	% of Limit Spent
Conservative	88	22642	85
Liberal	1	50019	78.3*
NDP	41	15235	16.1
Reform	0	0	0
Other	4	1450	

B: Ethno-Linguistic Profile

% English Home Language	32.5	% French Home Language	67.5
% Official Bilingual	49	% Other Home Language	0.1
% Catholics	88.2	% Protestants	10.3
% Aboriginal Peoples	0.7	% Immigrants	0.9

C: Socio-Economic Profile

Average Family Income $	37809	Median Family Income $	34798
% Low Income Families	18	Average Home Price $	58100
% Home Owners	78.2	% Unemployment	20.6
% Labour Force Participation	59.7	% Managerial-Administrative	7.7
% Self-Employed	5.2	% University Degrees	5.9
% Movers	29.9		

D: Industrial Profile

% Manufacturing	14.2	% Service Sector	15
% Agriculture	1.5	% Mining	2.4
% Forestry	4.1	% Fishing	0.6
% Government Services	7.9	% Business Services	2.2

E: Homogeneity Measures

Ethnic Diversity Index	0.68	Religious Homogeneity Index	0.77
Sectoral Concentration Index	0.4	Income Disparity Index	8

F: Physical Setting Characteristics

Total Population	54510	Area (km²)	9082
Population Density (pop/km²)	6		

* Tentative value, due to the existence of unpaid campaign expenses.

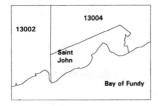

Saint John

Constituency Number: 13010

New Brunswick's 'industrial' city and ocean port, Saint John is home to major shipbuilding and port operations, as well as pulp and paper and oil refining (all part of the Irving family conglomerate). Traditionally a strong Tory riding, the incumbent for Saint John in 1988 was Gerald Merrithew, at the time Minister of Veterans Affairs and Minister responsible for the Atlantic Canada Opportunities Act. A former MLA and provincial cabinet minister between 1972 and 1984, Merrithew went to Ottawa with a massive majority. His hopes for re-election were buoyed by the $6 billion frigate program awarded to Saint John Shipbuilding and Drydock, a program that meant thousands of jobs to the city, including hundreds of sophisticated white-collar jobs, and the transformation of an aging shipyard into a 'world-class' management and construction facility. Besides the frigates, Merrithew could claim another $250 million in federal money for his constituency. On the strength of this record, he was returned to Ottawa for a second term.

Merrithew's decision not to re-offer in 1993 opened the field for a number of newcomers. The most prominent of these was Merrithew's replacement as Tory candidate, popular four-term Saint John mayor Elsie Wayne, whose entry into the race immediately placed all other contenders in an uphill fight. This was true even for the Liberal candidate, Pat Landers, a city councillor and the wife of a former MP. There were six other candidates in Saint John: Shirley Brown for the New Democrats, John Erbs for the Reform Party, Joy Ann Hobson for the National Party, Christopher Collrin for the Natural Law Party, Jim Webb for the Canada Party, and Joe Boyce, a former Liberal candidate who decided to run as an Independent.

On election night, Elsie Wayne became the only Conservative MP elected from Atlantic Canada in 1993. Her 43.3% of the vote was sufficient to give her a comfortable margin over the Liberal Landers, who received 33.6%. The spoiler for Landers was former Liberal Joe Boyce, whose vote total would have more than closed the gap. The Reform candidate finished fourth with 6.3% of the ballot, and the NDP fifth with 4.1%.

Member of Parliament: Elsie Eleanor Wayne; **Party:** Progressive Conservative; **Occupation:** Politician; **Education:** DPA (Hon.) Husson College; LL.D (Hon.) St Thomas University; **Age:** 63 (April 20, 1932); **Year first elected to the House of Commons:** 1993

13010 Saint John

A: Political Profile

i) Voting Behaviour

	% 1993	% 1988	Change 1988-93
Conservative	43.3	43.1	0.2
Liberal	33.6	38.6	-5
NDP	4.1	12.5	-8.4
Reform	6.3	0	6.3
Other	12.7	5.8	6.9

% Turnout	60.3	Total Ballots (#)	35263
Rejected Ballots (#)	353	% Margin of Victory	9.7
Rural Polls, 1988 (#)	11	Urban Polls, 1988 (#)	185
% Yes - 1992	46.3	% No - 1992	53.1

ii) Campaign Financing

	# of Donations	Total $ Value	% of Limit Spent
Conservative	358	63954	77.8
Liberal	6	40697	86.1
NDP	78	21535	40.7*
Reform	55	7220	12.7
Other	81	19507	

B: Ethno-Linguistic Profile

% English Home Language	97.4	% French Home Language	1.8
% Official Bilingual	10	% Other Home Language	0.8
% Catholics	44.1	% Protestants	48.8
% Aboriginal Peoples	0.2	% Immigrants	4.1

C: Socio-Economic Profile

Average Family Income $	42534	Median Family Income $	38483
% Low Income Families	21.6	Average Home Price $	75216
% Home Owners	51.1	% Unemployment	12
% Labour Force Participation	61.7	% Managerial-Administrative	9.6
% Self-Employed	4.1	% University Degrees	7.4
% Movers	46.1		

D: Industrial Profile

% Manufacturing	16.1	% Service Sector	16.2
% Agriculture	0.3	% Mining	0.1
% Forestry	0.5	% Fishing	0.3
% Government Services	7.7	% Business Services	4.3

E: Homogeneity Measures

Ethnic Diversity Index	0.61	Religious Homogeneity Index	0.42
Sectoral Concentration Index	0.48	Income Disparity Index	9.5

F: Physical Setting Characteristics

Total Population	76404	Area (km²)	660
Population Density (pop/km²)	115.8		

* Tentative value, due to the existence of unpaid campaign expenses.

QUEBEC

Quebec

Provincial Overview

The 1993 federal election in Quebec was in line with traditional political behaviour as the province returned an overwhelming number of MPs from the newly-formed Bloc Québécois. This tendency to vote *en bloc* is a particularly well-established tradition in Quebec and has been confirmed several times in previous elections. Quebeckers were supporting a party that was condemned to be on the opposition side since the Bloc Québécois was not running candidates outside the province. Historically, Quebeckers have tended to express homogeneity in voting more than to be associated with the winner on election night. Over the years a pattern was established whereby Quebeckers, anglophones even more so than francophones, tended to favour the Liberal Party.

The last three elections have witnessed a partial break with this historic practice. First, francophone Quebeckers clearly have distanced themselves from the Liberals. This is noteworthy considering that only six times in this century have the Liberals seen their Quebec stronghold escape them: in 1911 during the reciprocity election lost by Liberal Prime Minister Wilfrid Laurier, in 1930 when Quebeckers voted for Conservative R.B. Bennett, in 1958 with the landslide re-election of Conservative John Diefenbaker, and in 1984 and 1988 when Brian Mulroney easily carried the province in the wake of Pierre Trudeau's patriation and amendment (without Quebec's consent) of the Canadian Constitution.

Quebec francophones turned their back on the Liberals following the latter episode, and have not returned to the party since. The level of support for the Liberals among Quebec francophones has continuously dropped from one-third in 1984, to one-fourth in 1988 and down to one-fifth in 1993. The drop has been even sharper in the greater Montreal region where the Liberals claimed only 15% to 20% of the vote. Indeed, Liberals have been largely confined to non-francophone ridings since 1984. Jean Chrétien's lack of popularity among francophone Quebeckers was confirmed during the 1993 campaign. To avoid potentially embarrassing situations, party strategists were reduced to sending Hamilton MP Sheila Copps to campaign in the province. By contrast, the Liberals attracted overwhelming support from both anglophone and allophone (other minority-language speakers) Quebeckers, securing more than 90% of the vote in each case.

Brian Mulroney was able to take advantage of francophone Quebeckers' disaffection toward the Liberal party in 1984 and 1988 by enticing both autonomists and nationalists to trust him when he promised to re-integrate the province into the federal fold 'with honour and enthusiasm'. Following the Meech Lake debacle, Mulroney lost the support of several Quebec MPs, including prominent cabinet minister Lucien Bouchard, who quit the party and later regrouped nationalist forces around the newly-created Bloc Québécois. In an attempt to regain the initiative, Mulroney's Conservatives pursued a new constitutional settlement – the Charlottetown Accord – which was rejected in several parts of the country, including Quebec, where more than 56% of the electorate voted against the deal. The level of rejection in francophone constituencies reached highs of 77% in the nationalist areas of Jonquière and Lac-Saint-Jean, while support in anglophone ridings was as high as 88% in Mont-Royal and 77.2% in Notre-Dame-de-Grâce.

The incidence of language on the 1993 vote needs to be highlighted. For instance, the higher the proportion of francophones the higher the level of support registered by the Bloc Québécois (r=0.66%) while the higher the proportion of anglophones the higher the support for the Liberals (r=0.61%). Only eight ridings did not follow this pattern: Saint-Maurice, Sherbrooke, Beauce, Verdun–Saint-Paul, Hull–Aylmer, Gatineau–La Lièvre, Pontiac–Gatineau–Labelle and Bonaventure–Îles-de-la-Madeleine. Notably, with exception of the particular case of Beauce which elected an Independent, all of these ridings either shared a border with another province or were represented by a 'local hero' or prestigious candidate.

Among the 14 ridings where the percentage of anglophones was higher than 15% (r=0.49%), 12 returned a Liberal candidate, with the two exceptions of La Prairie (BQ) and Brome–Missisquoi (BQ). Liberals also performed better when the proportion of allophones was significant. Hence, among the 15 ridings were the proportion of allophones was higher than 15%, 10 elected Liberal candidates; the exceptions of Laval-Ouest, Bourassa, Ahuntsic, Anjou–Rivière-des-Prairies, and La Prairie all elected Bloc candidates. In the 10 Liberal ridings, the proportion of francophones was less than 66.5%, whereas in the other five cases the proportion of francophones was higher than 66.2%. There was in general a strong negative correlation between support levels for the Liberals and the predominance of francophones in the ridings.

A strong correlation is also evident in the case of constituencies which rejected the Charlottetown Accord and the percentage of vote received by the Bloc Québécois (r=0.887), mirroring the correlation between support for the Accord and vote received by the Liberal party (r=0.85). Only three ridings do not respect this pattern: Saint-Maurice (Liberal Jean Chrétien), Sherbrooke (PC Jean Charest) and Beauce (Independent Gilles Bernier) where the 'No' respectively registered 64.9%, 58.2% and 54.9% and each candidate obtained respectively 54.2%, 52.3%, and 40.2% of the vote.

The lack of popularity of both Liberals and Conservatives in 1993 can essentially be attributed to their handling of the constitutional issue. As noted, since the patriation of the Constitution in 1982, Liberal fortunes have declined precipitously in Quebec and there are few signs of encouragement for them in the 1993 election. Indeed, the Liberals have not been able to obtain more than 35.4% of the popular vote in Quebec at any of the last three elections. In 1984, the Liberals had secured 35.4%, dropped to 30.3% in 1988, and rose slightly to 33.3% in 1993. The number of MPs elected by the Liberals has fluctuated between 17 (1984), 12 (1988) and 19 (1993), giving little comfort to party strategists.

The Liberal Party did maintain and consolidate its grip on the West Island of Montreal, where a significant number of anglophones reside, as well as on the area situated north of Montreal. Of the 19 MPs elected, twelve were elected in the region of Montreal. Interestingly, the Liberals also took ridings situated near neighbouring jurisdictions, whether the United States (Mégantic–Compton–Stanstead), New Brunswick/Prince Edward Island (Bonaventure–Îles-de-la-Madeleine), or Ontario (Hull–Aylmer, Gatineau–La-Lièvre, Pontiac–Gatineau–Labelle). The only exception to this general pattern was the riding of Saint-Maurice where Jean Chrétien was easily elected.

In 1984 and 1988, the Conservatives obtained some of their best results ever in Quebec. Prime Minister Mulroney was able to strengthen his grip on the province over this period, raising his party's seat total from 58 to 63 out of a possibile 75. In 1988, two of the original 1984 seats were lost to Liberals Paul Martin Jr. (Ville-Émard) and Mark Assad (Gatineau–La-Lièvre). In 1993, only one of the 63 seats secured in 1988 remained: Jean Charest, the current leader of the Conservative Party, took 52.4% of the vote in his riding. Overall support for the Conservatives dropped dramatically from 52.7% to 13.5%, taking the party back to its poor pre-1984 performances.

Several Conservative candidates were prevented from contesting the election since they had committed fraud or were facing charges of other wrongdoing. Prime Minister Kim Campbell refused to sign the nomination papers of MP Gilles Bernier (La Beauce), MP Gabriel Fontaine (Lévis), MP Carole Jacques (Mercier), and MP Maurice Tremblay (Lotbinière). Fontaine and Tremblay accepted the decision; Carole Jacques ran as an Independent in Mercier taking 15% of the vote; Gilles Bernier was re-elected in Beauce, this time as an Independent, with 40.5% of the vote. Conservative MP Denis Pronovost did not seek re-election in Saint-Maurice following allegations of sexual harassment.

Most of the seats lost by the Conservatives were snapped up by Bloc Québécois candidates, several of whom ran on Lucien Bouchard´s coat-tails. Bouchard's decision to campaign only in Quebec ensured strong media coverage in each and every region of the province and allowed him to help many less well-known candidates. Bloc Québécois support came from the Conservative Party which lost 39% of its electoral support and from the New Democratic Party which performed poorly, obtaining only 1.5% of the vote after attaining 14.0% in 1988.

The Bloc Québécois program was essentially to represent better Quebec interests in Ottawa, combined with a generally left-leaning approach to social policy. Several Bloc candidates came from or were closely affiliated with one of the four main labour unions (CEQ, QFL, UPA, CSN). In addition, and perhaps more revealingly, several Bloc candidates had been associated with the Parti Québécois. Among these were former PQ minister Francine Lalonde (Mercier), and former MNAs Michel Gauthier (Roberval) and Laurent Lavigne (Beauharnois–Salaberry). Other Bloc candidates had been defeated running under the PQ banner in recent provincial elections: Amin Achem (1989), Maurice Bernier (1985), Maurice Dumas (1981), and Francine Lalonde (1985, 1989). There were also some former PQ political attachés who decided to represent the Bloc Québécois in the federal arena: Stéphane Bergeron and Réal Ménard are two notable cases.

The decimation of the NDP across the country makes the Bloc Québécois the main voice of the social democratic left in the House of Commons. The 1993 federal election was the worst NDP performance in its history. It should be remembered that the NDP had taken a pro-nationalist position in 1988, leading several Parti Québécois party activists to back NDP candidates. After the formation of the Bloc, most nationalists left the NDP to join forces with the new party. In a number of ridings, NDP candidates finished fourth or fifth, oftentimes behind fringe party candidates such as Natural Law. The fact that the political debate in Quebec was dominated by the Constitution was clearly detrimental to NDP candidates.

There were also some controversial nomination battles for the Conservatives, the Liberals, and the Bloc Québécois. For instance, in La Beauce, Conservatives nominated Parti Québécois party activist Jeannine Bourque. In Portneuf, Bloc Québécois leader Lucien Bouchard withdrew the nomination from René Matte following suscipion of wrongdoing. In Roberval, the Bloc leader forced designated candidate Jasmin Dorion to withdraw following revelations of an improper curriculum vitae. Bouchard hand-picked Michel Gauthier who had not even sought the nomination for the party. In Hull–Aylmer, the Liberals experienced the unusual situation of having three Liberals running as candidates. The Liberal leader decided to designate Marcel Massé as official candidate, without any nomination meeting. This led Liberal Tony Cannavino to run as an Independent Liberal and Liberal Pierre Chénier to run under the Conservative banner. In addition, former Liberal Gilles Rocheleau, who quit the party following Jean Chrétien's election as party leader, entered the race for the Bloc Québécois.

Contrary to the 1984 and 1988 federal elections when they tended to assist Mulroney Conservatives, the governing Quebec provincial Liberals for the most part stayed outside the political fray in 1993. As expected, Parti Québécois activists took part in the campaign on the side of Bloc candidates. Profound divergence of views on the wisdom of Quebec nationalists seeking representation in Ottawa were put aside. Several unions also got involved in the election. The Public Service Alliance of Canada targeted several ridings to unseat Conservatives, an objective often accomplished by backing Bloc candidates. The Quebec Teachers' Union (CEQ), Union of Farm Producers (UPA), Quebec Federation of Labour (QFL), and Confederation of National Trade Unions (CSN) all officially supported the Bloc Québécois.

Quebec Results, 1988 & 1993 Elections, 1992 Referendum

	1988 Election		1992 Referendum	1993 Election	
	% Vote	Seats		% Vote	Seats
Conservatives	52.7	63		13.5	1
Liberals	30.3	12		33.3	19
NDP	14.0	0		1.5	0
BQ	–	–		49.3	54
Other/Indep.	2.8	0		2.4	1
Turnout	75.2	–		77.1	–
% Yes (1992)			43.3		
% No (1992)			56.7		

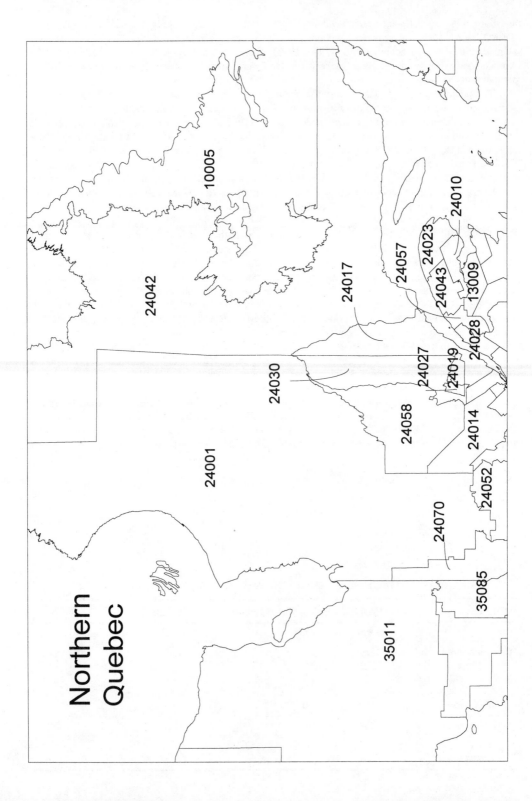

Northern Quebec

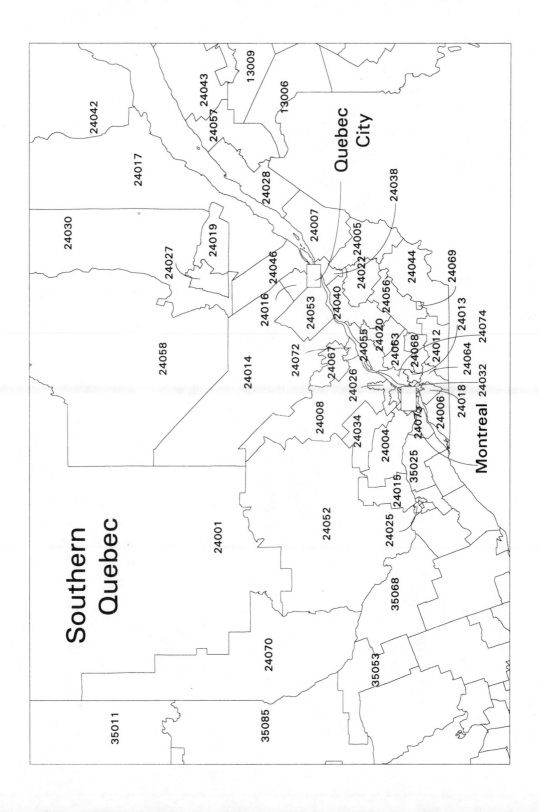

Southern Quebec

Quebec City

Montreal

13009
24043
24057
13006
24042
24017
24028
24038
24030
24019
24007
24022 24005
24044
24069
24027
24046
24016
24053
24040
24056
24013
24058
24014
24072
24055
24020
24063
24068
24012
24074
24067
24026
24064
24032
24008
24034
24004
24073
24006
24018
24052
24025
24015
35025
24001
35068
24070
35053
35011
35085

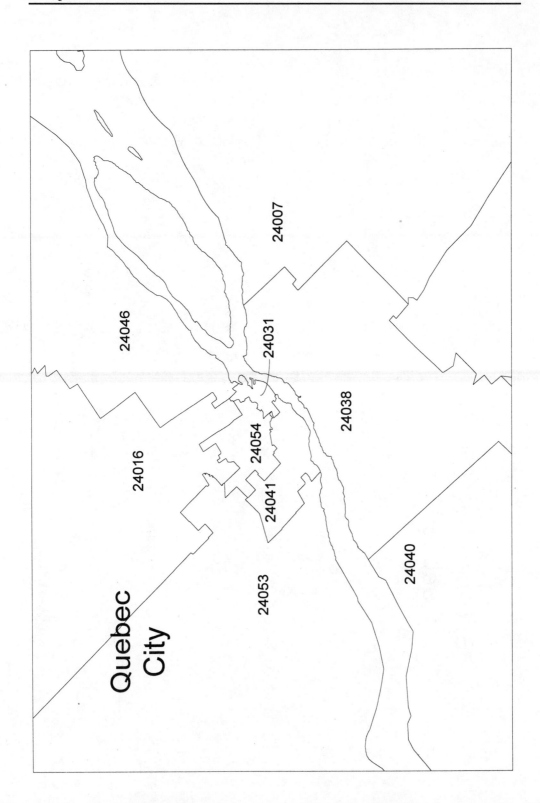

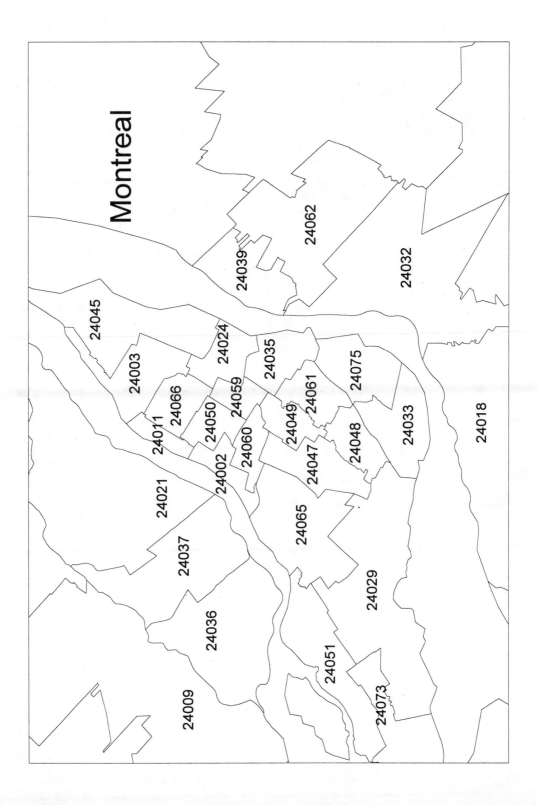

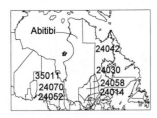

Abitibi

Constituency Number: 24001

The riding of Abitibi, part of the pre-1968 riding of Champlain, is the largest in the province and the third largest in Canada. It begins just south of the town of Val d'Or, and runs north along the Quebec side of James Bay and Hudson Bay to the Hudson Strait. Its 84% francophone population is higher than the provincial average. The aboriginal population is significant with over 13,840 native people, representing 16.3% of the population in the riding. Abitibi's average family income of $45,044 is slightly below the provincial average. Mining occupies 10.4% of the labour force, the second highest proportion in Quebec. Abitibi riding also includes the James Bay mega-project.

The Liberals held the riding from 1935 to 1958 when they lost it to the Conservatives. From 1962 to 1979 it was represented by Gérard Laprise, a *créditiste*. In the 1980 election, René Gingras regained the seat for the Liberals. He was defeated in 1984 by Conservative Guy St-Julien, former head of a James Bay union local who won the riding with a margin of 10,000 votes.

The Liberal candidate in 1988 was Normand Michaud, a local radio and television personality. The NDP ran Gerry Lemoyne, head of the Pulp and Paper Workers' union in western Quebec. For ten years, he had led the union at Domtar in Lebel-sur-Quévillon in the riding. His campaign stressed his opposition to the installation of a PCB treatment plant at Senneterre.

In 1988, St-Julien won a second mandate, with a 12,093 vote margin. Lemoyne finished in second place with 26.3%, the NDP's fourth best showing in Quebec.

Abitibi was one of the rare constituencies where the Conservatives had a chance to elect a member in 1993. St-Julien lost the constituency to Bloc Québécois member Bernard Deshaies, a merchant, attracting support from several nationalist sectors who had voted in favour of St-Julien at the previous two elections. Liberal Lucie Blais was never in the race, confirming a poor showing of the party in francophone constituencies. NDP candidate Louise Cloutier, a teacher, took only 2.3% of valid votes.

Member of Parliament: Bernard Deshaies;**Party:** B.Q.; **Occupation:** Merchant; **Education:** DEC (administration); **Age:** 41 (December 11, 1953) **Year of first election to the House of Commons:** 1993

24001 Abitibi

A: Political Profile
i) Voting Behaviour

	% 1993	% 1988	Change 1988-93
Conservative	35.3	57.6	-22.3
Liberal	16.2	16.2	0
NDP	2.3	26.3	-24
Bloc Québécois	46.2	0	46.2
Other	0	0	0

% Turnout	63.5	Total Ballots (#)	42497
Rejected Ballots (#)	1250	% Margin of Victory	10.9
Rural Polls, 1988 (#)	130	Urban Polls, 1988 (#)	104
% Yes - 1992	35	% No - 1992	65

ii) Campaign Financing

	# of Donations	Total $ Value	% of Limit Spent
Conservative	37	11350	58.8
Liberal	63	28091	28.5
NDP	6	4191	2.6
Bloc Québécois	398	43644	56.8
Other	0	0	

B: Ethno-Linguistic Profile

% English Home Language	2.5	% French Home Language	84
% Official Bilingual	21.9	% Other Home Language	13.5
% Catholics	81.9	% Protestants	15.8
% Aboriginal Peoples	16.3	% Immigrants	1.1

C: Socio-Economic Profile

Average Family Income $	45044	Median Family Income $	41509
% Low Income Families	13.3	Average Home Price $	72424
% Home Owners	55.2	% Unemployment	17.5
% Labour Force Participation	64.7	% Managerial-Administrative	10.2
% Self-Employed	7	% University Degrees	5.5
% Movers	46.1		

D: Industrial Profile

% Manufacturing	10.9	% Service Sector	13.5
% Agriculture	1.7	% Mining	10.4
% Forestry	3.4	% Fishing	0.4
% Government Services	7.4	% Business Services	3.4

E: Homogeneity Measures

Ethnic Diversity Index	0.66	Religious Homogeneity Index	0.68
Sectoral Concentration Index	0.34	Income Disparity Index	7.8

F: Physical Setting Characteristics

Total Population	90165	Area (km^2)	553837
Population Density (pop/km^2)	0.2		

Ahuntsic

Constituency Number: 24002

The riding of Ahuntsic is located in the north central part of the Island of Montreal. It is composed mainly of the old riding of Saint-Michel–Ahuntsic, with parts of four other old ridings included. It constitutes one of the smallest ridings in Canada. At 72% francophone, it is below the Quebec average. Immigrants constitute an important component of the population with close to 23%. There is a strong Italian community of 10,000 people. The riding is generally affluent: the 1991 census estimated the average dwelling cost at $174,000, well above the Quebec average of $110,031, and the average family income of $48,974 is also above the Quebec average. Located on the banks of Rivière-des-Prairies, this riding is populated by middle-income earners and is the home of working class employees who are active mainly in the manufacturing sector. The two most important employers are Hospital Fleury and the CEGEP Ahuntsic.

In 1988, the riding gave the Liberals their most unexpected setback in Quebec on election night. Liberal MP Thérèse Killens had held the riding in 1984 despite the Conservative sweep of Quebec. When she announced she would not seek re-election, the Liberal party's 'Quebec lieutenant', Raymond Garneau, moved over from the riding of Laval-des-Rapides. Garneau, a former chief executive of the Montreal City and District Savings Bank, was Quebec's Finance Minister from 1970-76, before entering federal politics in 1984.

Garneau was expected to win easily over Conservative candidate Nicole Roy-Arcelin, a nurse with no previous political experience, and the NDP's Vincent Guadagnano, a Canada Post trade unionist. Roy-Arcelin won the riding for the Conservatives running a free trade ticket with a 692 margin of victory in 1988. She ran again in 1993 to lose against the Bloc Québécois' Michel Daviault who was her campaign organizer in the previous election. Daviault is a real estate promoter and has been involved in several economic and social development projects in the riding. The Liberals selected high profile candidate Céline Hervieux-Payette, a vice-president of diversification for SNC corporation, and a former federal Liberal minister of State of Fitness and Amateur Sport and minister of State for Youth who went to defeat. As in 1988, Liberals felt this was a safe seat for them. Daviault's victory was most refreshing to the Bloc Québécois considering the large number of immigrants residing in the riding.

Member of Parliament: Michel Daviault; **Party:** B.Q.; **Occupation:** Administrator; **Education:** BA; **Age:** 42 (Nov. 25, 1952); **Year of first election to the House of Commons:** 1993

24002 Ahuntsic

A: Political Profile
i) Voting Behaviour

	% 1993	% 1988	Change 1988-93
Conservative	8.8	42.4	-33.6
Liberal	41.8	41.1	0.7
NDP	1.3	11	-9.7
Bloc Québécois	45.1	0	45.1
Other	3.1	5.5	-2.4

% Turnout	81.9	Total Ballots (#)	51904
Rejected Ballots (#)	1559	% Margin of Victory	6.4
Rural Polls, 1988 (#)	0	Urban Polls, 1988 (#)	209
% Yes - 1992	52.8	% No - 1992	47.2

ii) Campaign Financing

	# of Donations	Total $ Value	% of Limit Spent
Conservative	14	35470	59.7
Liberal	174	87003	87.6
NDP	1	1000	0
Bloc Québécois	215	40362	69.6
Other	10	4329	

B: Ethno-Linguistic Profile

% English Home Language	8	% French Home Language	72
% Official Bilingual	54	% Other Home Language	20
% Catholics	80	% Protestants	5.1
% Aboriginal Peoples	0.3	% Immigrants	23

C: Socio-Economic Profile

Average Family Income $	48974	Median Family Income $	41989
% Low Income Families	24.5	Average Home Price $	174000
% Home Owners	35.7	% Unemployment	12.9
% Labour Force Participation	63.5	% Managerial-Administrative	13.8
% Self-Employed	7.4	% University Degrees	16.3
% Movers	45.6		

D: Industrial Profile

% Manufacturing	18.7	% Service Sector	10.3
% Agriculture	0.3	% Mining	0
% Forestry	0.1	% Fishing	0
% Government Services	6.3	% Business Services	8.5

E: Homogeneity Measures

Ethnic Diversity Index	0.44	Religious Homogeneity Index	0.63
Sectoral Concentration Index	0.46	Income Disparity Index	14.3

F: Physical Setting Characteristics

Total Population	89954	Area (km²)	17
Population Density (pop/km²)	5291.4		

Anjou–Rivière-des-Prairies

Constituency Number: 24003

Anjou–Rivière-des-Prairies is located in the northeast corner of the Island of Montreal. It is composed principally of the city of Anjou. The area is growing rapidly: over 7,000 residences have been built in the riding since 1981, the second highest total in the province. The average family income of $48,388 is above the Quebec average. The riding is 72.8% francophone, below the Quebec average. Nearly one-fifth of the riding's voters are of Italian origin, and there is also a significant Haitian community of a few thousand.

The riding was formed in 1988 when the old ridings of Saint-Léonard–Anjou, Gamelin and Montréal–Mercier were split into Anjou–Rivière-des-Prairies, Saint-Léonard, and Mercier in the electoral redistribution.

The Conservatives fielded Jean Corbeil in the 1988 campaign. Considered a 'star' candidate, Corbeil had served as Mayor of Ville d'Anjou for 15 years, and has been a president of both the Quebec Union of Municipalities and the Canadian Federation of Municipalities. Corbeil was assisted by Quebec Liberal party activists and had Robert Bourassa's benediction in his campaign. Corbeil's campaign was clearly aimed at the riding's francophone majority: in a riding in which nearly 20% of the population are immigrants (double the Quebec average), the Conservative candidate expressed concerns that immigration threatened the distinct character of Quebec, and called for measures to intensify the 'integration' of immigrants.

The Liberals and NDP both ran candidates of Italian origin. Liberal Vincent Arciresi, the owner of a construction company, won a bitterly contested nomination after his opponent Normand Biron withdrew from the race, complaining of Italian influence in the riding association. The dispute led many liberals in the riding to support the Conservative candidate. The NDP ran Vincent Marchione, a Montreal Citizens' Movement activist who works at Louis-Hippolyte Lafontaine, a psychiatric hospital. The Conservatives won a solid victory in the riding, with the Liberal candidate trailing by 10,030 votes.

In 1993, Corbeil ran again but were joined by several newcomers, among them Liberal Normand Biron, an accountant, who has held various positions in companies such as Coopers & Lybrand, Alcan Canada and Mondial Canada and who had lost the nomination to Vincent Arciresi in 1988. Jean Pomerleau who is better known for his connections with the Parti Québécois ran for the Bloc Québécois and won the election getting the third weakest margin of victory in Quebec and the seventh in Canada. Corbeil, a popular politician, embarrassed his party when he demanded two weeks before election day that Prime Minister Campbell retract her statement to the effect that Brian Mulroney was to blame for the Tories' poor campaign strategy.

Member of Parliament: Roger Pomerleau; **Party:** B.Q.; **Occupation:** Carpenter; **Age:** 47 (June 7, 1947); **Year of first election to the House of Commons:** 1993

24003 Anjou–Rivière-des-Prairies

A: Political Profile
i) Voting Behaviour

	% 1993	% 1988	Change 1988-93
Conservative	11.6	51.5	-39.9
Liberal	42.2	32.7	9.5
NDP	1.6	12.6	-11
Bloc Québécois	43.1	0	43.1
Other	1.4	3.2	-1.8

% Turnout	78.9	Total Ballots (#)	62757
Rejected Ballots (#)	2053	% Margin of Victory	2.3
Rural Polls, 1988 (#)	0	Urban Polls, 1988 (#)	228
% Yes - 1992	53.3	% No - 1992	46.7

ii) Campaign Financing

	# of Donations	Total $ Value	% of Limit Spent
Conservative	151	79925	89.7
Liberal	102	32498	64.6
NDP	14	4628	2.9
Bloc Québécois	197	15913	50.7
Other	11	3220	

B: Ethno-Linguistic Profile

% English Home Language	12	% French Home Language	72.8
% Official Bilingual	47.8	% Other Home Language	15.3
% Catholics	89	% Protestants	5.4
% Aboriginal Peoples	0.2	% Immigrants	19.4

C: Socio-Economic Profile

Average Family Income $	48388	Median Family Income $	44847
% Low Income Families	19.8	Average Home Price $	156820
% Home Owners	48.3	% Unemployment	10.8
% Labour Force Participation	68.2	% Managerial-Administrative	13.2
% Self-Employed	6.7	% University Degrees	9.4
% Movers	48.9		

D: Industrial Profile

% Manufacturing	20.5	% Service Sector	11.2
% Agriculture	0.3	% Mining	0.2
% Forestry	0	% Fishing	0
% Government Services	5.8	% Business Services	6.5

E: Homogeneity Measures

Ethnic Diversity Index	0.45	Religious Homogeneity Index	0.76
Sectoral Concentration Index	0.44	Income Disparity Index	7.3

F: Physical Setting Characteristics

Total Population	111128	Area (km²)	46
Population Density (pop/km²)	2415.8		

Argenteuil–Papineau

Constituency Number: 24004

The riding of Argenteuil–Papineau runs along the Ottawa River, northwest of Montreal. The primarily rural riding includes the town of Lachute, the Mohawk territory of Kanesatake (Oka), and the Mirabel airport. Encompassing the Laurentians, Blainville-Deux-Montagnes and Terrebonne, the riding has an impressive potential for tourism. The riding is 87.9% francophone. Argenteuil–Papineau's average family income of $40,873 is 11% below the provincial average.

In 1988, three 'blue' candidates were running against one another. The Conservative incumbent, former real estate administrator Lise Bourgault, had won in 1984 with a plurality of 9,009 votes. Liberal candidate Peter Georgakakos had run as a Conservative in Saint-Denis in 1984, and the NDP's candidate, André Marc Paré, had run provincially for the Union Nationale in Argenteuil in 1985. Paré, an official at the municipal housing office, stressed his opposition to Canada Post 'super mail-boxes'. Georgakakos focused on the issue of local highways. Bourgault held the riding, increasing her margin to 11,988 votes. She received more than double the votes of her Liberal opponent.

In 1993, Lise Bourgault was viewed as one of the rare Conservatives capable of holding their seats but failed abysmally attracting only 22.2% of valid votes. During the campaign she was able to obtain from her government the expropriation of 25 properties to allow families who so desired to leave Oka's disputed territory. The Liberals fielded Jacques Desforges, a thanatologist, who has been involved in the community; he obtained 28.8% of the vote. The Bloc Québécois entered Maurice Dumas, a retired teacher, who has deep connections with the Parti Québécois running for them at the provincial election of 1981. He had acquired some additional political experience in 1966 when he ran for the Rassemblement pour l'indépendance nationale. His sympathies for the left have been constant as demonstrated by his activities in the Quebec teacher union (CEQ) in 1982-1985. In addition, Maurice Dumas was particularly active during the October 26, 1992 referendum, acting as Vice-president for the 'No' committee in Prévost. He won the riding with a plurality of 9,126 votes.

Member of Parliament: Maurice Dumas; **Party:** B.Q.; **Occupation:** Teacher (retired); **Education:** Teaching licence, École normale de Rigaud; **Age:** 67 (1927); **Year of first election to the House of Commons:** 1993

24004 Argenteuil–Papineau

A: Political Profile
i) Voting Behaviour

	% 1993	% 1988	Change 1988-93
Conservative	22.2	56.4	-34.2
Liberal	28.8	27.1	1.7
NDP	1.8	14.1	-12.3
Bloc Québécois	47.3	0	47.3
Other	0	2.3	-2.3

% Turnout	77.4	Total Ballots (#)	51140
Rejected Ballots (#)	1699	% Margin of Victory	18.5
Rural Polls, 1988 (#)	148	Urban Polls, 1988 (#)	41
% Yes - 1992	41.3	% No - 1992	58.7

ii) Campaign Financing

	# of Donations	Total $ Value	% of Limit Spent
Conservative	32	35855	71.5
Liberal	130	20943	58
NDP	8	2354	4
Bloc Québécois	317	15913	34.6
Other	0	0	

B: Ethno-Linguistic Profile

% English Home Language	11.7	% French Home Language	87.9
% Official Bilingual	37.3	% Other Home Language	0.4
% Catholics	86.7	% Protestants	9.7
% Aboriginal Peoples	1.1	% Immigrants	2.6

C: Socio-Economic Profile

Average Family Income $	40873	Median Family Income $	35995
% Low Income Families	15	Average Home Price $	87276
% Home Owners	74.7	% Unemployment	12.9
% Labour Force Participation	62.7	% Managerial-Administrative	11.1
% Self-Employed	13	% University Degrees	5
% Movers	40.8		

D: Industrial Profile

% Manufacturing	18.9	% Service Sector	12.6
% Agriculture	6	% Mining	0.4
% Forestry	0.7	% Fishing	0
% Government Services	5.3	% Business Services	3.6

E: Homogeneity Measures

Ethnic Diversity Index	0.78	Religious Homogeneity Index	0.75
Sectoral Concentration Index	0.35	Income Disparity Index	11.9

F: Physical Setting Characteristics

Total Population	84119	Area (km²)	5169
Population Density (pop/km²)	16.3		

Beauce

Constituency Number: 24005

The riding of Beauce begins 25 kilometres to the south of Quebec City and runs from there down to the Maine border. Four towns are included in the riding: St-Georges, Beauceville, St-Joseph and Ste-Marie. The riding is 99.5% francophone. Beauce is a rural/urban riding: 27.3% of the labour force is involved in the manufacturing sector, the fourth highest proportion in Quebec; yet the riding also has the fifth highest proportion of its labour force involved in agriculture (9.3%). The riding is relatively poor: the average family income of $39,464 is 14% below the Quebec average. The constituency is relatively stable: only 26.2% of families have moved in the past five years, one of the lowest levels in the province. Several companies are present, among them Canam-Manac, Bocenor, MAAX, Culinar, and Procycle.

The constituents of Beauce voted Liberal consistently from 1887 to 1945. But in the following 20 years, the Liberals won only once, ironically enough in 1958, the year of the Diefenbaker sweep. Raoul Poulin represented the riding as an independent from 1949 to 1958. The *créditistes* won the riding in 1962 and 1963, again in 1968, the year of Trudeaumania, and for a final time in 1979. The Liberals regained it in 1965, and again in 1972, holding on to the riding in 1974 - the first time they had won two elections in a row in the riding in three decades.

Normand Lapointe took the seat for the Liberals in 1980, but lost in 1984 when Conservative Gilles Bernier won the riding with a margin of 4,705 votes. Bernier, a former radio announcer for CKRB in St-Georges-de-Beauce, was president of the Quebec party caucus at the time of dissolution.

In 1988, the Liberals ran Pierre-Maurice Vachon, mayor of Ste-Marie de Beauce and a prefect of the regional municipality. Vachon, who like most Liberal candidates was critical of the free trade agreement, was embarrassed in mid-campaign when the Conservative incumbent revealed that a cardboard box factory of which Vachon is part owner was seeking a $3.5 million federal government subsidy to help it increase exports to the U.S. The NDP candidate was Danielle Wolfe. A labour activist, Wolfe was the first woman ever to run in the riding. Bernier won the riding for a second time, with a comfortable 22,571 margin. The 68.7% of the vote received by the Conservatives was their seventh best showing in the country.

In 1993, facing corruption charges (made in June 1990) Bernier was denied the right to run for the Conservatives. Renewing an old practice, Bernier ran as an independent candidate and won the election with a plurality of 2,142 over his closest opponent, Bloc Québécois Jean-Guy Breton. Breton, who received 36.2% of the vote, campaigned in part on the need to renegotiate GATT arrangements. Breton has strong connections with the Parti Québécois and was very active during the October 26, 1992 referendum. The Conservative candidate, Jeannine Bourque, a farmer and union activist with the Union of Farm Producers (UPA) surpised many people when she accepted the nomination due to the fact that she is a strong nationalist, a member of the Parti Québécois and former member of the PQ's national committee.

Member of Parliament: Gilles Bernier; **Party:** Independent; **Occupation:** Member of Parliament; **Education:** Ste-Marie College, Montreal; **Age:** 60 (July 15, 1934); **Year of first election to the House of Commons:** 1984

24005 Beauce

A: Political Profile
i) Voting Behaviour

	% 1993	% 1988	Change 1988-93
Conservative	8.2	68.7	-60.5
Liberal	14.5	25.9	-11.4
NDP	0.7	5.4	-4.7
Bloc Québécois	36.2	0	36.2
Other	40.5	0	40.5

% Turnout	73.1	Total Ballots (#)	51774
Rejected Ballots (#)	1484	% Margin of Victory	62.2
Rural Polls, 1988 (#)	159	Urban Polls, 1988 (#)	69
% Yes - 1992	45.1	% No - 1992	54.9

ii) Campaign Financing

	# of Donations	Total $ Value	% of Limit Spent
Conservative	35	5214	34.1
Liberal	89	19367	28.1
NDP	1	1000	0
Bloc Québécois	301	23408	38.7
Other	293	49825	

B: Ethno-Linguistic Profile

% English Home Language	0.4	% French Home Language	99.5
% Official Bilingual	11.5	% Other Home Language	0
% Catholics	96.8	% Protestants	1.7
% Aboriginal Peoples	0.3	% Immigrants	0.8

C: Socio-Economic Profile

Average Family Income $	39464	Median Family Income $	35511
% Low Income Families	14	Average Home Price $	62929
% Home Owners	75.6	% Unemployment	10.5
% Labour Force Participation	65	% Managerial-Administrative	10.4
% Self-Employed	12.6	% University Degrees	4.5
% Movers	26.2		

D: Industrial Profile

% Manufacturing	27.3	% Service Sector	10.5
% Agriculture	9.3	% Mining	0.2
% Forestry	2.3	% Fishing	0
% Government Services	3.4	% Business Services	1.7

E: Homogeneity Measures

Ethnic Diversity Index	0.95	Religious Homogeneity Index	0.91
Sectoral Concentration Index	0.3	Income Disparity Index	10

F: Physical Setting Characteristics

Total Population	98820	Area (km²)	4829
Population Density (pop/km²)	20.5		

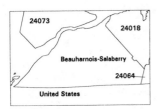

Beauharnois–Salaberry

Constituency Number: 24006

The riding of Beauharnois–Salaberry lies southwest of the Island of Montreal. It is bordered by the St Lawrence river to the northwest, and the United States to the south. The riding is 86.9% francophone. The small anglophone population is concentrated in the rural southern half of the riding. The city of Salaberry-de-Valleyfield is an important centre with 35% of the population. The riding's average family income is $42,929, below the Quebec average. Several manufacturing companies are present: Goodyear, Expo Chemicals, Zinc Electrolytic, and Noranda.

Beauharnois–Salaberry has traditionally been a Liberal riding. Prior to 1984, the Conservatives had won the riding only once since 1908: that was in 1958, the year of the Diefenbaker sweep. Gérald Laniel held the riding for the Liberals from 1962 to 1984, but did not run in the 1984 election. Conservative Jean-Guy Hudon won that race with a margin of 16,000 votes. Hudon, a former Mayor of Beauharnois, served as parliamentary secretary to various ministers in the 1984-1988 Parliament.

In 1988, the Liberal candidate was Linda Julien, a lawyer running for the first time. Her campaign was clearly aimed at anglophone voters in the riding: a Liberal radio advertisement featured the Conservative incumbent speaking English with difficulty.

The NDP ran Daniel Payette, a teacher at a local CEGEP, and the son of well-known Quebeckers André and Lise Payette. Both are television and radio personalities; the latter was a minister in the PQ government from 1976 to 1981.

Pollution was an important issue in the 1988 campaign, with discussions over the possibility of cleaning up the Châteauguay River and the problem of PCBs stored at Allied Chemical in the riding. The free trade debate also had particular importance, as the riding has many industries thought to be vulnerable to the free trade agreement, such as rubber and textiles. The candidates also discussed the problem of transportation links between the riding and Montreal. Hudon once again won the riding easily, receiving more than double the votes of his Liberal opponent.

In 1993, a wind of change was blowing, enticing several new candidates to enter the race. The Liberals came back with Linda Julien who received 31.5% of the vote while the Conservatives had Marie-Andrée Sweeney, a graduate in administration of UQAM, who fell 45 percentage points. The NDP was not able to maintain its strong showing of 1988 and claimed only 2% of the vote. Running on the coat-tails of Lucien Bouchard, Bloc Québécois candidate Laurent Lavigne, a former MNA from 1976 to 1985, obtained the support of 51.4% of the electorate. Lavigne is also a member of the Union of Farm Producers (UPA).

Member of Parliament: Laurent Lavigne; **Party:** B.Q.; **Occupation:** Farmer; **Education:** Welding course and certificate in psycho-pedagogy; **Age:** 59 (Aug. 10, 1935); **Year of first election to the House of Commons:** 1993

24006 Beauharnois–Salaberry

A: Political Profile
i) Voting Behaviour

	% 1993	% 1988	Change 1988-93
Conservative	15.1	58.4	-43.3
Liberal	31.5	26.7	4.8
NDP	2	11.9	-9.9
Bloc Québécois	51.4	0	51.4
Other	0	3	-3

% Turnout	78.7	Total Ballots (#)	52356
Rejected Ballots (#)	2019	% Margin of Victory	19.9
Rural Polls, 1988 (#)	100	Urban Polls, 1988 (#)	85
% Yes - 1992	40.4	% No - 1992	59.6

ii) Campaign Financing

	# of Donations	Total $ Value	% of Limit Spent
Conservative	94	20300	96.8
Liberal	140	40404	93.6
NDP	6	2817	2.8
Bloc Québécois	474	37872	66.9
Other	0	0	

B: Ethno-Linguistic Profile

% English Home Language	12.5	% French Home Language	86.9
% Official Bilingual	36.6	% Other Home Language	0.6
% Catholics	88.1	% Protestants	8.8
% Aboriginal Peoples	0.5	% Immigrants	2.6

C: Socio-Economic Profile

Average Family Income $	42929	Median Family Income $	39116
% Low Income Families	17	Average Home Price $	87429
% Home Owners	66.1	% Unemployment	13.3
% Labour Force Participation	62.2	% Managerial-Administrative	9.8
% Self-Employed	11.1	% University Degrees	4.8
% Movers	38.6		

D: Industrial Profile

% Manufacturing	23.1	% Service Sector	10.8
% Agriculture	8	% Mining	1
% Forestry	0.1	% Fishing	0
% Government Services	3.6	% Business Services	3.2

E: Homogeneity Measures

Ethnic Diversity Index	0.79	Religious Homogeneity Index	0.77
Sectoral Concentration Index	0.33	Income Disparity Index	8.9

F: Physical Setting Characteristics

Total Population	88024	Area (km²)	1950
Population Density (pop/km²)	45.1		

Bellechasse

Constituency Number: 24007

The riding of Bellechasse runs 80 kilometres along the St Lawrence River, beginning just east of Quebec City. It is bordered on the southeast by the State of Maine. The riding is 99.7% francophone and 9.9% of the labour force is involved in agriculture, the highest level in Quebec. The average family income in Bellechasse, $38,258, is 17% below the provincial average. One-fifth of income comes from government transfer payments. Bellechasse has an important rural population embracing Cap-St-Ignace, Lac Etchemin, l'Islet and Dorchester and includes also the town of Montmagny, an important industrial and service centre. The riding is a stable area considering that only 23.9% of families have moved in the past five years, the lowest proportion in Canada. Bellechasse has experienced a decrease in population, dropping from 85,382 in 1981 to 80,187 in 1991.

Bellechasse voted Liberal in every general election from 1917 to 1957, but went Conservative in the Diefenbaker landslide of 1958. It was represented by a Liberal member for only five of the following 22 years (1963-1968). The *créditistes* won the riding in 1962, and held it again from 1968 to 1980. Liberal Alain Garant won Bellechasse in that year, but in 1984 he lost by close to 10,000 votes to the Conservatives' Pierre Blais. Blais, a lawyer who had worked as a professor at Laval University, was appointed Minister of State for Agriculture in 1987. The Liberal candidate in 1988 was Claudette Beaulieu, a teacher. Gilles Papillon sought election for the NDP, and focused on the theme of full employment. Blais won the riding for a second time. With a 16,501 vote margin, he received more than twice the number of votes of his Liberal opponent.

The most recent election witnessed profound political fluctuations. The Conservatives had hoped to keep this riding. Pierre Blais, Minister of Justice, went down to defeat, dropping from 65% to 37.9% of the popular vote but enough to give the Conservatives their second best performance in Quebec (after Sherbrooke) and their sixth in Canada. The Liberals, who came second in 1988, ran newcomer Éric Lemieux, a MBA holder and computer science professor at CEGEP Limoilou, and continued their decline. They attracted only 20%, confirming their lack of popularity among francophone voters. Bloc Québécois François Langlois, a professor of law and political science at CEGEP Lévis-Lauzon, reaped the benefit of the Conservative and Liberal disaffection, and obtained 40.7% of the vote. Langlois was president of the 'No' committee in Bellechasse for the Charlottetown referendum of October 26, 1992. Langlois campaigned on the issue of sovereignty as the best way to create jobs.

Member of Parliament: François Langlois; **Party:** B.Q.; **Occupation:** Lawyer, notary public, professor; **Education:** Doctorate in Constitutional Law, Pacific Western University (USA); **Age:** 46 (Jan. 6, 1948); **Year of first election to the House of Commons:** 1993

24007 Bellechasse

A: Political Profile
i) Voting Behaviour

	% 1993	% 1988	Change 1988-93
Conservative	37.9	65	-27.1
Liberal	20	26.2	-6.2
NDP	1.4	6.5	-5.1
Bloc Québécois	40.7	0	40.7
Other	0	2.4	-2.4

% Turnout	71.4	Total Ballots (#)	42907
Rejected Ballots (#)	1133	% Margin of Victory	2.8
Rural Polls, 1988 (#)	218	Urban Polls, 1988 (#)	33
% Yes - 1992	42.3	% No - 1992	57.7

ii) Campaign Financing

	# of Donations	Total $ Value	% of Limit Spent
Conservative	15	68441	76.5
Liberal	216	31979	84.7
NDP	3	2129	1.2
Bloc Québécois	470	35582	99.9
Other	0	0	

B: Ethno-Linguistic Profile

% English Home Language	0.3	% French Home Language	99.7
% Official Bilingual	9.7	% Other Home Language	0
% Catholics	97.2	% Protestants	1.4
% Aboriginal Peoples	0.2	% Immigrants	0.5

C: Socio-Economic Profile

Average Family Income $	38258	Median Family Income $	33939
% Low Income Families	14.8	Average Home Price $	58723
% Home Owners	76.8	% Unemployment	10.5
% Labour Force Participation	58.7	% Managerial-Administrative	9.9
% Self-Employed	12.8	% University Degrees	4.2
% Movers	23.9		

D: Industrial Profile

% Manufacturing	24.6	% Service Sector	11.6
% Agriculture	9.9	% Mining	0.3
% Forestry	2.5	% Fishing	0.1
% Government Services	4.6	% Business Services	1.7

E: Homogeneity Measures

Ethnic Diversity Index	0.96	Religious Homogeneity Index	0.91
Sectoral Concentration Index	0.33	Income Disparity Index	11.3

F: Physical Setting Characteristics

Total Population	80187	Area (km²)	6330
Population Density (pop/km²)	12.7		

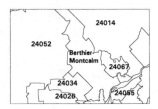

Berthier–Montcalm

Constituency Number: 24008

The riding of Berthier–Montcalm is located north of Montreal. It begins along the St Lawrence River, halfway between Montréal and Trois-Rivières, and forms a narrow strip running 200 kilometres north from there, covering more than 12,000 km². The riding includes the towns of Berthierville, Louiseville, Rawdon, St-Calixte, and St-Gabriel-de-Brandon. The Attikamek reservation of Manawan is part of this riding. The riding is 96.2% francophone. Berthier–Montcalm's average family income of $38,008 is 17% below the Quebec average. Government transfer payments account for nearly one-fifth of total income. 9% of the riding's workforce is concentrated in the agricultural sector, one of the highest proportions in the province.

Since 1921, the voters of the riding have elected members to the opposition side of the House in only the minority elections of 1957, 1963 and 1979. Liberal Antonio Yanakis represented the riding from 1965 until he was crushed in the 1984 election by Conservative Robert de Cotret.

First elected in a 1978 by-election, de Cotret lost his seat in the 1979 general election, after which Joe Clark appointed him to the Senate so that he might serve as Minister of Industry, Trade and Commerce. He tried his hand at electoral politics again in 1984, winning his seat with 70.2% of the vote, the Conservatives' second best result in Quebec. He was appointed President of the Treasury Board in the first Mulroney cabinet, and was later appointed Minister of Regional Industrial Expansion.

In the 1988 campaign, the former Liberal MP Antonio Yanakis ran once again, this time as an independent. The Liberals ran Maurice Roberge, the Mayor of St-Gabriel-de-Brandon. The NDP candidate was insurance broker Pierre Arès. De Cotret won easily, with a margin of 15,746 votes.

The 1993 saw a completely new slate being proposed to the electorate. Following the withdrawal of de Cotret, the Conservatives chose Réal Naud, Mayor of St Gabriel-de-Brandon, who attracted only 8.9% of the vote, a drop of 47.3 percentage points. The Liberals did relatively well in this francophone constituency as its candidate, Madeleine Bélanger, a business woman from Louiseville and a director of the Chamber of Commerce of the regional municipality of Maskinongé, received 27.4% of the vote. The Bloc Québécois was successful in convincing a former provincial (1988-1991) and federal (1988) Liberal organizer in the same riding, Michel Bellehumeur, to run for them. Bellehumeur, a lawyer from Berthierville, played an active role during the October 26, 1992 referendum and acted as a legal adviser for the 'No' committee. Bellehumeur received 60.9% of the vote.

Member of Parliament: Michel Bellehumeur; **Party:** B.Q.; **Occupation:** Lawyer; **Education:** LL.L; **Age:** 31 (Jan. 21, 1963); **Year of first election to the House of Commons:** 1993

24008 Berthier–Montcalm

A: Political Profile
i) Voting Behaviour

	% 1993	% 1988	Change 1988-93
Conservative	8.9	56.2	-47.3
Liberal	27.4	26.1	1.3
NDP	1	11.3	-10.3
Bloc Québécois	60.9	0	60.9
Other	1.9	6.5	-4.6

% Turnout	75.1	Total Ballots (#)	61593
Rejected Ballots (#)	2539	% Margin of Victory	35.4
Rural Polls, 1988 (#)	236	Urban Polls, 1988 (#)	0
% Yes - 1992	34.4	% No - 1992	65.6

ii) Campaign Financing

	# of Donations	Total $ Value	% of Limit Spent
Conservative	89	31035	39.7
Liberal	92	30333	64.3
NDP	1	1882	1.3
Bloc Québécois	639	47192	52.4
Other	13	5565	

B: Ethno-Linguistic Profile

% English Home Language	2.2	% French Home Language	96.2
% Official Bilingual	18.7	% Other Home Language	1.7
% Catholics	94.3	% Protestants	3
% Aboriginal Peoples	1.7	% Immigrants	1.8

C: Socio-Economic Profile

Average Family Income $	38008	Median Family Income $	33866
% Low Income Families	14.9	Average Home Price $	70559
% Home Owners	75.8	% Unemployment	13
% Labour Force Participation	59.3	% Managerial-Administrative	9.7
% Self-Employed	13.4	% University Degrees	3.7
% Movers	38.1		

D: Industrial Profile

% Manufacturing	23.4	% Service Sector	11.4
% Agriculture	9	% Mining	0.2
% Forestry	1.5	% Fishing	0.2
% Government Services	3.9	% Business Services	2.2

E: Homogeneity Measures

Ethnic Diversity Index	0.87	Religious Homogeneity Index	0.87
Sectoral Concentration Index	0.32	Income Disparity Index	10.9

F: Physical Setting Characteristics

Total Population	103766	Area (km²)	12085
Population Density (pop/km²)	8.6		

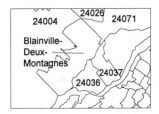

Blainville–Deux-Montagnes

Constituency Number: 24009

Blainville–Deux-Montagnes is located just northwest of Montreal, across the river from Île-Jésus. The riding includes the towns of Blainville, St-Eustache, Ste-Thérèse and Rosemère. The riding is 90.3% francophone and its average family income of $51,570 is 12% above the provincial average. With 145,292 residents, Blainville–Deux-Montagnes is the second most populous riding in Quebec. The two most important employers are General Motors and Kenworth truck company with respectively 3,000 and 850 jobs. In addition to an important manufacturing sector, tourism is viewed as an important area for job creation.

Francis Fox held the seat for the Liberals from 1972 until his defeat in 1984. He represented Argenteuil–Deux-Montagnes from 1972-79. Fox served as Solicitor General from 1976 until he was forced to resign in 1978 after committing a forgery. He re-entered the cabinet as Secretary of State in 1980.

In 1984, Conservative Monique Landry defeated Fox with a margin of 5,131 votes. Landry was appointed Minister for External Relations in 1986, and served as co-president of the 1988 Conservative campaign in Quebec. The Liberal candidate in 1988 was Zsolt Pogany, a notary. Louisette Tremblay-Hinton, a Quebec Federation of Labour unionist, ran for the NDP. Landry easily won a second term, with a margin of 27,023 votes, giving the Conservatives their best result in Quebec that year.

The 1993 election brought serious competitors to Monique Landry. The Liberals fielded Pierre Brien, a Laval University graduate and real estate agent from Ste-Thérèse, who was seeking election for the first time and obtained 23.1% of the vote. Landry's toughest challenge came from the Bloc Québécois candidate, Paul Mercier, mayor of Blainville from 1977 to 1993, who is a retired CEGEP professor. Mercier attracted the support of 59.4% of the electorate, transforming Landry's campaign into a nightmare as she came third in the race, obtaining 14.6% of the vote, a drop of 47.5%. The NDP went from 14.1% to 1.1% of the vote, being outvoted by the Natural Law Party candidate.

Member of Parliament: Paul Mercier; **Party:** B.Q.; **Occupation:** Mayor of Blainville (1977-1993), Administrator; **Education:** Diploma in mathemathics (Belgium); **Age:** 70 (July 26, 1924); **Year of first election to the House of Commons:** 1993

24009 Blainville–Deux-Montagnes

A: Political Profile
i) Voting Behaviour

	% 1993	% 1988	Change 1988-93
Conservative	14.6	62	-47.4
Liberal	23.1	21	2.1
NDP	1.1	14.1	-13
Bloc Québécois	59.4	0	59.4
Other	1.8	2.9	-1.1

% Turnout	79.1	Total Ballots (#)	84430
Rejected Ballots (#)	3276	% Margin of Victory	38.1
Rural Polls, 1988 (#)	0	Urban Polls, 1988 (#)	267
% Yes - 1992	34.7	% No - 1992	65.3

ii) Campaign Financing

	# of Donations	Total $ Value	% of Limit Spent
Conservative	44	106313	95.3
Liberal	84	63338	74.1
NDP	1	1000	0
Bloc Québécois	205	41886	87.1
Other	6	524	

B: Ethno-Linguistic Profile

% English Home Language	7.8	% French Home Language	90.3
% Official Bilingual	42.1	% Other Home Language	1.9
% Catholics	90.4	% Protestants	5
% Aboriginal Peoples	0.7	% Immigrants	4.3

C: Socio-Economic Profile

Average Family Income $	51570	Median Family Income $	48121
% Low Income Families	15.6	Average Home Price $	119684
% Home Owners	68.9	% Unemployment	10.1
% Labour Force Participation	71.5	% Managerial-Administrative	14.5
% Self-Employed	8.4	% University Degrees	8.8
% Movers	51.8		

D: Industrial Profile

% Manufacturing	19.1	% Service Sector	10.9
% Agriculture	1	% Mining	0.2
% Forestry	0.1	% Fishing	0
% Government Services	5.7	% Business Services	5.2

E: Homogeneity Measures

Ethnic Diversity Index	0.77	Religious Homogeneity Index	0.81
Sectoral Concentration Index	0.41	Income Disparity Index	6.7

F: Physical Setting Characteristics

Total Population	145292	Area (km²)	205
Population Density (pop/km²)	708.7		

Bonaventure–Îles-de-la-Madeleine

Constituency Number: 24010

The riding of Bonaventure–Îles-de-la-Madeleine is located on the southern side of the Gaspé Peninsula, stretching from the Matapedia valley to Port-Daniel. It includes the towns of New Richmond and Carleton, and the Madeleine Islands. With 50,295 residents, Bonaventure–Îles-de-la-Madeleine has the smallest population of Quebec ridings and the ninth smallest in Canada. The riding is 87.1% francophone. It is generally poor: the average family income of $38,658 is 16% below the provincial average. The 1991 census estimated unemployment at 22.1%, the second highest level in Quebec. Government transfer payments account for 26.8% of income, the second highest level in Quebec. Fishing occupies 4.7% of the workforce, the highest proportion in the province.

The Conservatives failed to win an election here from 1887 to 1957. The riding reverted to the Liberals in 1962 when it was won by Albert Béchard, who represented the area for 17 years. Rémi Bujold won for the Liberals in 1979 and 1980, but in 1984 he lost by 1,800 votes to the Conservatives' Darryl Gray who held the riding for the two following terms. Gray, a former teacher and farmer, is a native of New Brunswick. Gray held the riding in 1988 with a 6,195 vote margin. The Liberal candidate in 1988 was Lyse Routhier, a former aide to Robert Bourassa. In her campaign, Routhier advocated resumption of the seal hunt. The NDP fielded Germaine Poirier, a health care worker and unionist.

Maintaining the riding's reputation to vote on the side of the new government, Liberal Patrick Gagnon, a graduate of McGill University and an import, export and manufacturing consultant, got 43.6% of the vote. In doing so, the riding was going against the tendency in most francophone ridings in Quebec to give a cold shoulder to Liberal representatives. Bloc Québécois candidate Michel Saint-Pierre, an accountant who has strong links with the Parti Québécois, received 33.5% of the vote. This is the only time in 1993 that a Liberal candidate defeated a Bloc Québécois member in the area east of Trois-Rivières. Coming third in the riding, Gray went to defeat, unable to attract more than 21.5% of the vote. The NDP candidate, Germaine Poirier, saw her 5.9% obtained in 1988 receding to 1.3% of the vote. Job creation was the central issue during the campaign, making the Liberal 'Red Book' a very attractive proposal for the electorate.

Member of Parliament: Patrick Gagnon; **Party:** Liberal; **Occupation:** Consultant;**Education:** BA (Political Science); **Age:** 31; **Year of first election to the House of Commons:** 1993

24010 Bonaventure–Îsles-de-la-Madeleine

A: Political Profile

i) Voting Behaviour

	% 1993	% 1988	Change 1988-93
Conservative	21.5	58.8	-37.3
Liberal	43.6	35.3	8.3
NDP	1.3	5.9	-4.6
Bloc Québécois	33.5	0	33.5
Other	0	0	0

% Turnout	76.5	Total Ballots (#)	28198
Rejected Ballots (#)	655	% Margin of Victory	10.1
Rural Polls, 1988 (#)	154	Urban Polls, 1988 (#)	0
% Yes - 1992	50.6	% No - 1992	49.4

ii) Campaign Financing

	# of Donations	Total $ Value	% of Limit Spent
Conservative	127	28840	70.3*
Liberal	86	33534	71.8
NDP	2	2728	2.4
Bloc Québécois	336	16583	49.9
Other	0	0	

B: Ethno-Linguistic Profile

% English Home Language	12	% French Home Language	87.1
% Official Bilingual	21.4	% Other Home Language	0.9
% Catholics	90.9	% Protestants	8
% Aboriginal Peoples	3	% Immigrants	0.5

C: Socio-Economic Profile

Average Family Income $	38658	Median Family Income $	34287
% Low Income Families	14.5	Average Home Price $	54611
% Home Owners	77.5	% Unemployment	22.1
% Labour Force Participation	59.5	% Managerial-Administrative	7.9
% Self-Employed	7.9	% University Degrees	4.9
% Movers	24.4		

D: Industrial Profile

% Manufacturing	14.1	% Service Sector	14.5
% Agriculture	2	% Mining	1.2
% Forestry	3.8	% Fishing	4.7
% Government Services	6.7	% Business Services	1.7

E: Homogeneity Measures

Ethnic Diversity Index	0.76	Religious Homogeneity Index	0.82
Sectoral Concentration Index	0.33	Income Disparity Index	11.3

F: Physical Setting Characteristics

Total Population	50295	Area (km²)	8155
Population Density (pop/km²)	6.2		

* Tentative value, due to the existence of unpaid campaign expenses.

Bourassa

Constituency Number: 24011

The riding of Bourassa comprises the Town of Montréal-Nord, on the northeast part of the Island of Montreal. It is the fifth smallest riding in Canada. The riding is 78.6% francophone. Roughly one-seventh of the riding's population is of Italian origin, and there is a strong Haitian community approaching 6,000 members. The riding's average family income of $38,605 is 16% below the provincial average. A high proportion of families are in low-income brackets. Manufacturing and services sectors provide more than one third of the jobs in the constituency. Northern Telecom and Beaver Asphalt are among the better known companies.

Historically, the Liberals have performed well in this riding. Heading into the 1988 election, Liberal MP Carlo Rossi had held the riding since 1979, having survived the 1984 Conservative sweep of Quebec with a plurality of 1,518 votes. Many observers considered the ex-policeman to be a low profile MP. The Conservative candidate was Marie Gibeau, a management consultant for Pierre J. Hogue and Associates from 1979 to 1988 and president of the Montreal YWCA. Gibeau was affiliated with the Montreal Citizens' Movement, and received help in her campaign from several people connected with the Parti Québécois and the Quebec Liberal Party. Her chief organizer was a former treasurer of the PQ, and she benefited from the help of a high-level PLQ fund-raiser. The NDP ran Kéder Hyppolite, a Haitian who worked as executive director of an aid service for immigrants. As in 1984, the 1988 riding result was close. Conservative Marie Gibeau edged out the Liberal incumbent by just 820 votes.

As in most places, the Conservatives did not perform well in this riding in 1993, and Gibeau went down to defeat, receiving only 12% of the vote, a drop of 31.4%. The Liberals came close to regaining this historical stronghold with 41.9%. Denis Coderre, a former president of the Quebec Young Liberals of Canada and a host of a French radio public-affairs program on the CKVL station (Verdun), gained recognition for his organizing skills. Coderre received the endorsement of Kéder Hyppolite, a Haitian leader, and defeated NDP candidate at the 1988 general election. Coderre himself had run in the 1988 federal election in Joliette where he obtained 24.8% of the vote. Bloc Québécois candidate Chilean-born Osvaldo Nuñez made a major breakthrough with 42% of the vote, making it the lowest margin of victory in Quebec and the third in Canada. Nuñez's election contributed to give cultural communities a voice in the House of Commons and in the party itself. This victory of Nuñez was most important in providing the Bloc Québécois an entry to the cultural communities. It is assumed that the Haitian community has tended to give its support to Bloc candidates. Nuñez is associated with the Parti Québécois and has been employed as a union adviser by the Quebec Federation of Labour.

Member of Parliament: Osvaldo Nuñez; **Party:** B.Q.; **Occupation:** Unemployment Insurance Commissioner, union adviser (QFL); **Education:** Licence in law studies, licence in industrial relations; **Age:** 56 (Sept. 10, 1938); **Year of first election to the House of Commons:** 1993

24011 Bourassa

A: Political Profile

i) Voting Behaviour

	% 1993	% 1988	Change 1988-93
Conservative	12	43.3	-31.3
Liberal	41.9	41.5	0.4
NDP	2.4	11	-8.6
Bloc Québécois	42	0	42
Other	1.8	4.2	-2.4

% Turnout	77.5	Total Ballots (#)	45046
Rejected Ballots (#)	1615	% Margin of Victory	1.9
Rural Polls, 1988 (#)	0	Urban Polls, 1988 (#)	193
% Yes - 1992	50.5	% No - 1992	49.5

ii) Campaign Financing

	# of Donations	Total $ Value	% of Limit Spent
Conservative	4	60870	84.1
Liberal	81	36493	90.7
NDP	21	14074	20.7
Bloc Québécois	404	29686	58.5
Other	17	1353	

B: Ethno-Linguistic Profile

% English Home Language	7.3	% French Home Language	78.6
% Official Bilingual	39.1	% Other Home Language	14.1
% Catholics	89	% Protestants	5.9
% Aboriginal Peoples	0.6	% Immigrants	18

C: Socio-Economic Profile

Average Family Income $	38605	Median Family Income $	34519
% Low Income Families	31.8	Average Home Price $	157943
% Home Owners	27.5	% Unemployment	16.1
% Labour Force Participation	59.7	% Managerial-Administrative	8
% Self-Employed	5.4	% University Degrees	4.8
% Movers	47.6		

D: Industrial Profile

% Manufacturing	24.6	% Service Sector	12.3
% Agriculture	0.3	% Mining	0.1
% Forestry	0.1	% Fishing	0
% Government Services	5.3	% Business Services	4.6

E: Homogeneity Measures

Ethnic Diversity Index	0.49	Religious Homogeneity Index	0.77
Sectoral Concentration Index	0.39	Income Disparity Index	10.6

F: Physical Setting Characteristics

Total Population	85516	Area (km²)	12
Population Density (pop/km²)	7126.3		

Brome–Missisquoi

Constituency Number: 24012

The riding of Brome–Missisquoi is located to the southeast of Montreal. It borders on the State of Vermont. The riding includes the towns of Bedford, Bromont, Cowansville, Farnham and Magog. The riding is 78.4% francophone, slightly below the provincial average, and 20.6% anglophone. The average family income of $41,612 is 9% below the Quebec average. 26.6% of the riding's work force is occupied in the manufacturing sector, one of the highest levels in Canada. Among the most important companies, one notes IBM enterprises, General Electric, and Dominion Textiles. Hyundai stopped its operations in 1993.

While Brome–Missisquoi was held by the Liberals from 1935 to 1958, it has voted Conservative in eight out of the last eleven general elections. Heward Grafftey won the riding for the Conservatives in the Diefenbaker landslide of 1958, and held it until 1980, with the exception of the 1968-1972 period, when he fell victim to Trudeaumania. Grafftey finally lost the riding in the 1980 election, when he was defeated by Liberal André Bachand. For his part, Bachand lost Brome–Missisquoi in 1984 to Gabrielle Bertrand, widow of former Quebec Premier Jean-Jacques Bertrand and mother of former PQ minister Jean-François Bertrand. Bertrand won the riding for the Conservatives with a 5,985 vote margin. In the 1988 campaign, Bertrand faced Bachand, the Liberal she had defeated in 1984. The NDP candidate was well-known, though not for his political exploits: he was wrestler Paul Vachon. The NDP candidate found the rigours of the political arena tougher than those to which he was accustomed, though he did receive 13.1% of the vote, slightly below the NDP's Quebec average. The Conservatives' Bertrand defeated Bachand for a second time, with a margin of 8,807 votes.

Gabrielle Bertrand did not seek a new mandate at the 1993 election. Francine Vincelette, a business woman, won the nomination but failed to rally all the members of the organization. Vincelette received only 17.2% of the vote. The Liberals recruited Montrealer Joan Kouri, a past president of the Federal Liberal Women Commission, who attracted substantial support with 36.7%. Joan Kouri was supported by former Conservative Heward Grafftey who had joined the Liberals. She obtained an important proportion of the anglophone vote, carrying easily the town of Knowlton. Bloc Québécois Gaston Péloquin, a teacher of English as a second language, ran a campaign focusing on job creation. Péloquin, well connected with the PQ, was involved in the referendum of 1980 on the sovereignty-association side, and in 1992 against the Charlottetown Accord. Péloquin's victory was acquired in Magog where he got 4741 votes to 2922 for Kouri. The margin of victory favoring Péloquin was 1796 votes. This was one of the most impressive showings of the Bloc Québécois in a constituency populated by more than 20% anglophones.

Member of Parliament: Gaston Péloquin; **Party:** B.Q.; **Occupation:** Teacher (English, second language); **Education:** BEd. ; **Age:** 55 (Dec. 11, 1939); **Year of first election to the House of Commons:** 1993

Péloquin died in September 1994. In the February 13, 1995 by-election, Liberal Denis Paradis took the riding with 51.0% of the vote from Bloc Québécois Jean-François Bertrand, son of former Conservative MP Gabrielle Bertrand, with 42.2% of the vote.

24012 Brome–Missisquoi

A: Political Profile
i) Voting Behaviour

	% 1993	% 1988	Change 1988-93
Conservative	17.2	54	-36.8
Liberal	36.7	32.9	3.8
NDP	1.3	13.1	-11.8
Bloc Québécois	40.8	0	40.8
Other	4.3	0	4.3

% Turnout	76.6	Total Ballots (#)	45316
Rejected Ballots (#)	1562	% Margin of Victory	8.4
Rural Polls, 1988 (#)	118	Urban Polls, 1988 (#)	73
% Yes - 1992	52.2	% No - 1992	47.8

ii) Campaign Financing

	# of Donations	Total $ Value	% of Limit Spent
Conservative	111	56073	78
Liberal	199	33873	94.6
NDP	2	1892	0.7
Bloc Québécois	240	33161	80.6
Other	6	1900	

B: Ethno-Linguistic Profile

% English Home Language	20.6	% French Home Language	78.4
% Official Bilingual	41.2	% Other Home Language	0.9
% Catholics	79.9	% Protestants	15.7
% Aboriginal Peoples	0.4	% Immigrants	4.3

C: Socio-Economic Profile

Average Family Income $	41612	Median Family Income $	36080
% Low Income Families	14.4	Average Home Price $	94714
% Home Owners	66.2	% Unemployment	10.8
% Labour Force Participation	63.1	% Managerial-Administrative	12.4
% Self-Employed	13.2	% University Degrees	7.3
% Movers	40.6		

D: Industrial Profile

% Manufacturing	26.6	% Service Sector	12.4
% Agriculture	6.8	% Mining	0.4
% Forestry	0.2	% Fishing	0
% Government Services	4.6	% Business Services	3.7

E: Homogeneity Measures

Ethnic Diversity Index	0.68	Religious Homogeneity Index	0.64
Sectoral Concentration Index	0.35	Income Disparity Index	13.3

F: Physical Setting Characteristics

Total Population	80316	Area (km²)	2916
Population Density (pop/km²)	27.5		

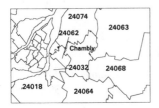

Chambly

Constituency Number: 24013

The riding of Chambly is located southeast of the Island of Montreal. The riding is 90.4% francophone, above the provincial average. It includes the city of Chambly and the towns of Beloeil, Mont St-Hilaire, St-Basile-le-Grand, and St-Bruno. Several of those towns can be defined as bedroom communities. The average family income of $57,450 is well above the Quebec average. Over three-quarters of dwellings are owned by their occupants, the second highest proportion in the province. Chambly's business sector has close links with the American economy, with many firms in the riding holding subcontracts with the U.S. defence industry. High technology companies include Bombardier and ATS Spatial.

The voters of Chambly consistently vote for the goverment party. Since 1896, the riding has elected opposition MPs in only the First World War election of 1917, the minority elections of 1957, 1962, and 1979, and the by-election of September 12, 1990.

Raymond Dupont won the riding for the Liberals in the Trudeau-Clark elections of 1979 and 1980, but he went down to a crushing defeat in 1984, when Richard Grisé won the riding for the Conservatives with a margin of 13,000 votes. Grisé, by profession a life insurance salesman, had not always been a Conservative: he unsuccessfully sought the Liberal nomination in the riding in 1978. Grisé was appointed President of the Privy Council in October 1987.

The 1987 electoral redistribution left the riding with only 50% of its former voters, but was not expected to affect the Conservative margin. In 1988, the NDP's candidate in Chambly, American-born Phil Edmonston, represented one of the party's best hopes in the province. Ex-president of the Automobile Protection Association, Edmonston had won 37% of the vote in a 1977 by-election in Verdun riding. He supports Quebec's Bill 101 and the province's right to use the 'notwithstanding' clause to protect its linguistic identity.

The Liberals ran Bernard Loiselle. A lawyer by profession, he was MP for Chambly from 1974 to 1979 and for neighbouring Verchères from 1979 to 1984. After losing in the 1984 Conservative sweep, Loiselle worked as vice-president for Bell Canada International.

Not surprisingly in the wake of the St-Basile-le-Grand mishap, the environment was an important issue in the 1988 campaign. The issue of transit to Montreal is constantly an issue considering that three quarters of Chambly residents commute to Montreal for work.

Although suspected of conflict of interest and breach of trust, Grisé held the riding in 1988, with a 8,502 vote margin over the NDP's Edmonston. The 31.6% of the vote received by the NDP was the party's second-best result in the province. Later, Grisé was found guilty and was forced to resign. Edmonston won the by-election with 67.5% of the vote, leaving 17.4% to the Liberals and 9.7% to the Conservatives. Edmonston received the support of the PQ at this by-election.

In 1993, Edmonston declined to represent the NDP in part due to his sympathies toward Quebec nationalism and to the decision of Lucien Bouchard to lead the Bloc Québécois in Ottawa. NDP François Côté, a lawyer from Mont St-Hilaire, received only 2.9% of the vote, a drop of 64.6%. The Liberals fielded a star candidate, Jean-Claude Villard, a former deputy minister of International Affairs and assistant deputy minister for Energy in the Quebec government and president of engineering firm SNC-Lavalin International, who obtained only 29.1% of the vote. Conservative candidate Hélène Tremblay, a recruit from Quebec provincial Liberals, attracted only 7.8% of the vote. Public notary Ghislain Lebel, the Bloc candidate, benefited from Lucien Bouchard's popularity and won by a margin of 18,682 votes, receiving 59.7% of the valid votes.

Member of Parliament: Ghislain Lebel; **Party:** B.Q.; **Occupation:** Notary public; **Education:** Licence in law, diploma in notary law; **Age:** 48 (Feb. 17, 1946); **Year of first election to the House of Commons:** 1993

24013 Chambly

A: Political Profile
i) Voting Behaviour

	% 1993	% 1988	Change 1988-93
Conservative	7.8	47	-39.2
Liberal	29.1	19.9	9.2
NDP	2.9	31.5	-28.6
Bloc Québécois	59.7	0	59.7
Other	0.5	1.6	-1.1

% Turnout	82.8	Total Ballots (#)	63726
Rejected Ballots (#)	2605	% Margin of Victory	31.1
Rural Polls, 1988 (#)	16	Urban Polls, 1988 (#)	194
% Yes - 1992	37.6	% No - 1992	62.4

ii) Campaign Financing

	# of Donations	Total $ Value	% of Limit Spent
Conservative	18	7650	35.9*
Liberal	160	60672	78.5
NDP	9	17223	23.2
Bloc Québécois	165	34379	48
Other	0	0	

B: Ethno-Linguistic Profile

% English Home Language	8.9	% French Home Language	90.4
% Official Bilingual	46.6	% Other Home Language	0.7
% Catholics	89.3	% Protestants	5.8
% Aboriginal Peoples	0.4	% Immigrants	4.8

C: Socio-Economic Profile

Average Family Income $	57450	Median Family Income $	52889
% Low Income Families	10.6	Average Home Price $	121030
% Home Owners	78.2	% Unemployment	8.9
% Labour Force Participation	71.7	% Managerial-Administrative	17.5
% Self-Employed	9.2	% University Degrees	12.6
% Movers	43.4		

D: Industrial Profile

% Manufacturing	17.3	% Service Sector	10
% Agriculture	1.2	% Mining	0.2
% Forestry	0.1	% Fishing	0
% Government Services	6.9	% Business Services	6.1

E: Homogeneity Measures

Ethnic Diversity Index	0.8	Religious Homogeneity Index	0.79
Sectoral Concentration Index	0.43	Income Disparity Index	7.9

F: Physical Setting Characteristics

Total Population	103627	Area (km²)	334
Population Density (pop/km²)	310.3		

* Tentative value, due to the existence of unpaid campaign expenses.

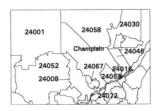

Champlain

Constituency Number: 24014

The riding of Champlain is located northeast of Montreal. It begins along the St Lawrence River just east of Trois-Rivières, and runs northwest from there some 350 kilometres, ending near the Gouin reservoir. The riding includes the town of Cap-de-la-Madeleine, by Trois-Rivières. The riding is 97% francophone. The average family income of $40,785 is 11% below the provincial average. Forest exploitation provides jobs to the riding with companies such as Gérard Crête, Canadian Pacific Forest Products; others include Reynolds Aluminum and Marmen.

Champlain was held by the Liberals throughout the Mackenzie King and Saint-Laurent eras. In 1958, it went Conservative for the first time since 1930. The Liberals recovered the riding in 1962, but in 1968 it was won by *créditiste* candidate René Matte, who held it until 1979. Michel Veillette then represented the riding for the Liberals from 1979 until 1984. Michel Champagne won the riding for the Conservatives in 1984 with a margin of 13,008 votes. Champagne, who lists his profession as 'political analyst,' was 28 years old at the time of his election. The Liberals hoped to unseat Champagne in 1988 with André Burke, a management analyst, who was parachuted into the riding. The NDP ran Jocelyn Crête, a lawyer and former legal advisor to the Parti Québécois. Champagne won the riding again, with a margin of 21,996 votes. The NDP's Crête came in second with 19.1% of the vote, just ahead of the Liberal candidate.

Champagne sought re-election in 1993, coming second with 27% of the vote. He lost to Réjean Lefebvre, mayor of St-Adelphe and past president of the Economic Development Corporation of Mékinac-des-Chenaux, who got 48.8% of the vote with a margin of victory of 10,567 votes. Liberals came back with Michel Veillette who secured only 23.2% of the vote, slightly higher than the average Liberal result in francophone constituencies. NDP candidate André de Billy came fourth with 0.9%, a drop of 18.2% from the 1988 results.

The main issues of the campaign in 1993 were tourism, creation of small and medium enterprises, and protection of the environment with special attention to the ZEC Tawachiche. The environmentalist coalition Mékinac took on challenger Lefebvre several times during the campaign, accusing him of not moving quickly enough to resolve the problem.

Member of Parliament: Réjean Lefebvre; **Party:** B.Q.; **Occupation:** Chief Forestry Worker, businessman, Mayor of Saint-Adelphe (1985-1993); **Education:** Studies at the Institute of Technology, Trois-Rivières; **Age:** 48 (Jan. 6, 1946); **Year of first election to the House of Commons:** 1993

24014 Champlain

A: Political Profile

i) Voting Behaviour

	% 1993	% 1988	Change 1988-93
Conservative	27	64.7	-37.7
Liberal	23.2	16.2	7
NDP	0.9	19.1	-18.2
Bloc Québécois	48.8	0	48.8
Other	0	0	0

% Turnout	78.4	Total Ballots (#)	49989
Rejected Ballots (#)	1553	% Margin of Victory	21.8
Rural Polls, 1988 (#)	69	Urban Polls, 1988 (#)	136
% Yes - 1992	36	% No - 1992	64

ii) Campaign Financing

	# of Donations	Total $ Value	% of Limit Spent
Conservative	56	60810	89.1
Liberal	136	40752	86.4
NDP	0**	0**	0**
Bloc Québécois	615	45587	68.4
Other	0	0	

B: Ethno-Linguistic Profile

% English Home Language	0.7	% French Home Language	97
% Official Bilingual	15.7	% Other Home Language	2.3
% Catholics	96.4	% Protestants	1.9
% Aboriginal Peoples	2.9	% Immigrants	0.8

C: Socio-Economic Profile

Average Family Income $	40785	Median Family Income $	37239
% Low Income Families	17	Average Home Price $	66384
% Home Owners	64.6	% Unemployment	14.4
% Labour Force Participation	60	% Managerial-Administrative	9
% Self-Employed	8.3	% University Degrees	5.1
% Movers	36.5		

D: Industrial Profile

% Manufacturing	22.3	% Service Sector	13.1
% Agriculture	3.8	% Mining	0.2
% Forestry	1.8	% Fishing	0.1
% Government Services	5.6	% Business Services	2.2

E: Homogeneity Measures

Ethnic Diversity Index	0.88	Religious Homogeneity Index	0.91
Sectoral Concentration Index	0.36	Income Disparity Index	8.7

F: Physical Setting Characteristics

Total Population	86168	Area (km²)	32520
Population Density (pop/km²)	2.6		

** No return filed.

Gatineau–La Lièvre
(formerly Chapleau)

Constituency Number: 24015

The riding of Gatineau–La Lièvre is located on the Ottawa River northwest of Montreal. It includes the town of Gatineau, just east of Ottawa-Hull, and Masson and Thurso. The riding is 90.5% francophone. With 128,910 residence, Gatineau–La Lièvre is the third largest in the province in terms of population. The average family income of $51,503 is 12% above the Quebec average. Of the riding's workforce, 22.3% is occupied in government services, the second highest level in Quebec and the tenth highest in Canada. Canadian Pacific Forest Products, tourism, and the service sector are among the other main providers of jobs in the region.

Prior to 1984, the area had been the most consistently Liberal in the province: from 1896 on, when the area formed part of the riding of Wright, the area had only elected Liberals. But Claudy Mailly won the riding for the Conservatives in 1984 with a margin of 8,000 votes over René Cousineau, who had held the riding since 1979. In her 1988 bid for re-election, Mailly was facing Liberal Mark Assad, who had sat in the Quebec National Assembly from 1970 to 1976, and from 1981 until he resigned to run federally. The NDP candidate was Marius Tremblay, a federal NDP organizer. On election night, the riding reverted to its Liberal tradition, and Assad, with his 2,122-vote victory margin, became one of only two Liberals in Quebec to defeat a Conservative incumbent (the other being Paul Martin in Lasalle-Émard).

The Liberals carry the riding in 1993 as voters re-elected Mark Assad who received 55.5% of the vote, and a margin of victory of 14,271 votes, re-establishing the riding as a Liberal stronghold. Conservatives' future went down as Jérôme Falardeau, a businessman and past alderman for the town of Gatineau, achieved a modest 6.3% of the vote. Aylmer Jules Fournier, a PQ liaison officer, a PQ candidate in Pontiac in 1989 and political assistant for Bloc Québécois in 1990-1991, was defeated by 14,271 votes, nonetheless securing 35.3% of the vote. The NDP fielded Elizabeth Holden, a general secretary, who obtained 1.6% of the vote. The principal issues during the campaign were job creation, for the Liberals, while the PQ emphasized economic diversification with the launching of the Société de diversification économique (SDÉ) and integration of federal public service into Quebec civil service in the event of a sovereign Quebec.

Member of Parliament: Mark Assad; **Party:** Liberal; **Occupation:** Manager; **Education:** MA (History), MBA École nationale d'administration publique, Hull; **Age:** 54 (June 14, 1940); **Year of first election to the House of Commons:** 1988

24015 Gatineau–La Lièvre

A: Political Profile
i) Voting Behaviour

	% 1993	% 1988	Change 1988-93
Conservative	6.3	39.4	-33.1
Liberal	55.5	43.3	12.2
NDP	1.6	15.5	-13.9
Bloc Québécois	35.3	0	35.3
Other	1.3	1.9	-0.6

% Turnout	73.8	Total Ballots (#)	72062
Rejected Ballots (#)	1264	% Margin of Victory	20.2
Rural Polls, 1988 (#)	42	Urban Polls, 1988 (#)	209
% Yes - 1992	57.6	% No - 1992	42.4

ii) Campaign Financing

	# of Donations	Total $ Value	% of Limit Spent
Conservative	61	27353	63.9
Liberal	215	37920	89.9
NDP	11	3336	2.5
Bloc Québécois	535	53671	59.7
Other	10	1247	

B: Ethno-Linguistic Profile

% English Home Language	8.2	% French Home Language	90.5
% Official Bilingual	56.2	% Other Home Language	1.4
% Catholics	92	% Protestants	4.4
% Aboriginal Peoples	1.9	% Immigrants	3

C: Socio-Economic Profile

Average Family Income $	51503	Median Family Income $	48584
% Low Income Families	13.9	Average Home Price $	96048
% Home Owners	68.8	% Unemployment	8.5
% Labour Force Participation	72.4	% Managerial-Administrative	13
% Self-Employed	6.4	% University Degrees	8.5
% Movers	49.9		

D: Industrial Profile

% Manufacturing	9	% Service Sector	13.3
% Agriculture	1	% Mining	0.2
% Forestry	0.4	% Fishing	0
% Government Services	22.3	% Business Services	5.1

E: Homogeneity Measures

Ethnic Diversity Index	0.79	Religious Homogeneity Index	0.84
Sectoral Concentration Index	0.45	Income Disparity Index	5.7

F: Physical Setting Characteristics

Total Population	128910	Area (km²)	5102
Population Density (pop/km²)	25.3		

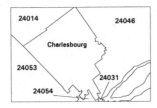

Charlesbourg

Constituency Number: 24016

The riding of Charlesbourg includes parts of Quebec City and the towns of Charlesbourg and Orsainville. The riding is 98.4% francophone. Charlesbourg's average family income of $50,113 is 9% above the provincial average. There is a small aboriginal and anglophone population. With 111,464 residents, Charlesbourg is one of the ten largest ridings in the province. The service sector and government services dominate the employment category. Tourism is important due to the presence of ski facilities at Stoneham and Le Relais.

Conservative Monique Tardif won the 1984 election with a margin of 14,955 votes over the Liberal incumbent, Pierre Bussières, who had represented the area since 1974. Bussières had served as Minister of Revenue in the last Trudeau government.

Denis Courteau, a President of the Canadian Union of Postal Workers, ran for the NDP in the 1988 campaign. The Liberal candidate was Paul Vézina, a former head of the Quebec Bar Association. Vézina stressed the vulnerability of the riding's footwear industry to the free trade agreement. Provincial Liberals campaigned for both Conservatives and Liberals. The organizer for the Conservative incumbent was a long-time Liberal, while Vézina enjoyed support from the Quebec Minister of Transport, Marc-Yvan Côté, who represents the area provincially. Despite her impressive 1984 victory, Tardif did even better this time, with a margin of 19,822 votes.

Tardif ran again in 1993 but could not stop the tidal wave that was to drive her party from all but one Quebec constituency. She came third with 12.6% of the vote, for a drop of 47.5%. Liberal candidate Michel Renaud, a party activist backed again by provincial Liberal Marc-Yvan Côté, entered his first race and got 23.4%. The NDP's well-known candidate Gaston Juneau, union representative with the Public Service Alliance of Canada and employee of the Canadian Union of Postal Workers, saw his party dropping to fifth place with 1.9% of the vote, behind the Natural Law Party. Bloc Québécois Jean-Marc Jacob found fertile ground for his nationalist message and won the riding with 59.4% of the vote, with a margin of 23,385 votes. Jacob was known in the area for his involvement in municipal politics, having served as an alderman in Charlesbourg from 1980 to 1988. He received strong backing from the Public Service Alliance of Canada who wanted to show its strong opposition to the Conservative government.

Member of Parliament: Jean-Marc Jacob; **Party:** B.Q.; **Occupation:** Veterinarian; **Education:** DVM; **Age:** 47 (Feb. 18, 1947); **Year of first election to the House of Commons:** 1993

24016 Charlesbourg

A: Political Profile

i) Voting Behaviour

	% 1993	% 1988	Change 1988-93
Conservative	12.6	60.1	-47.5
Liberal	23.4	26.6	-3.2
NDP	1.9	13.4	-11.5
Bloc Québécois	59.4	0	59.4
Other	2.8	0	2.8

% Turnout	79	Total Ballots (#)	67889
Rejected Ballots (#)	2931	% Margin of Victory	38.8
Rural Polls, 1988 (#)	24	Urban Polls, 1988 (#)	209
% Yes - 1992	34.8	% No - 1992	65.2

ii) Campaign Financing

	# of Donations	Total $ Value	% of Limit Spent
Conservative	92	57806	91
Liberal	79	61136	99.6
NDP	12	5431	4.7
Bloc Québécois	531	35945	95.4
Other	24	3290	

B: Ethno-Linguistic Profile

% English Home Language	1.3	% French Home Language	98.4
% Official Bilingual	26.3	% Other Home Language	0.3
% Catholics	95.3	% Protestants	1.6
% Aboriginal Peoples	0.7	% Immigrants	1.6

C: Socio-Economic Profile

Average Family Income $	50113	Median Family Income $	46822
% Low Income Families	14.6	Average Home Price $	90012
% Home Owners	65.8	% Unemployment	8.5
% Labour Force Participation	69.7	% Managerial-Administrative	13.4
% Self-Employed	6.4	% University Degrees	10.4
% Movers	38.2		

D: Industrial Profile

% Manufacturing	8.7	% Service Sector	14.9
% Agriculture	0.5	% Mining	0.1
% Forestry	0.2	% Fishing	0
% Government Services	18	% Business Services	4.7

E: Homogeneity Measures

Ethnic Diversity Index	0.9	Religious Homogeneity Index	0.9
Sectoral Concentration Index	0.52	Income Disparity Index	6.6

F: Physical Setting Characteristics

Total Population	111464	Area (km²)	1319
Population Density (pop/km²)	84.5		

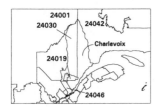

Charlevoix

Constituency Number: 24017

The riding of Charlevoix is located on the north shore of the lower St. Lawrence River, northeast of Quebec City, and runs north to about the 53rd parallel. The towns of Baie-Comeau, Baie-St-Paul, La Malbaie and Tadoussac are the main population centres. The riding is 97.2% francophone. At $42,795, the average family income of Charlevoix is 7% below the provincial average. The 1991 census estimated the unemployment rate at 15.5%, a major improvement from the 1986 census which reported 22.5%.

The Charlevoix area has often bucked trends. Provincially, the area was one of the few to elect a Parti Québécois member in 1970. It also voted 'Yes' in the 1980 referendum on sovereignty-association. No Liberal was elected here in the six elections between 1958 and 1972. The *créditistes* won three elections during that period, while the other three, including the 1968 Trudeaumania election in which Quebec elected only four Conservatives, were won by Conservative Martial Asselin. The Liberals won the seat in 1974. Charles Hamelin won the riding for the Conservatives in 1984, with a margin of 11,000 votes over Liberal incumbent Charles Lapointe. Lapointe had served as Minister of State for External Relations in the last Trudeau government. The 63.6% of the vote Hamelin received in 1984 was the Conservatives' fourth best result in Quebec. Hamelin was not allowed to stand for re-election, however. When the 1987 electoral redistribution moved Baie-Comeau, home town of Brian Mulroney, into Charlevoix from the neighbouring riding of Manicouagan, Hamelin was asked to step aside so that the Prime Minister might run in the riding. Hamelin was given the nomination in Laurier–Sainte-Marie in Montreal, but went down to a predictable defeat against Liberal veteran Jean-Claude Malépart. In the name of running candidates in every riding in the country, the Liberals and NDP both found willing victims to run in Charlevoix. The Liberals ran Martin Cauchon, a 26-year-old Montreal lawyer who had worked for the 'No' side in the 1980 referendum. The NDP candidate was Kenneth Choquette. On election night, Mulroney won the right to represent his third riding in three elections, with a 27,736 vote margin. The 80% of the vote received by the Prime Minister was the Conservatives' best showing in the country.

The election of 1993 brought a major change in public opinion with the Conservatives dropping from 80% to 17.8% of the popular vote. Following the departure of Brian Mulroney, the Conservatives were not able to find a first-rate candidate and invited Gérard Guy, a political adviser for the region, to run. The Liberals fielded André Desgagnés, an information technologist, who came second with 18.8% of the vote. Gérard Asselin, a candidate particularly well-connected with the PQ, presided over the 'Yes' committee at the referendum of 1980 in the region. Asselin ran under the banner of the Bloc Québécois and secured 62% of the vote, with a margin of victory of 16,457 votes. Lucien Bouchard came to visit the riding on several occasions. It is to be noted that the provincial riding of Duplessis with boundaries corresponding largely to the ones for Charlevoix has returned PQ candidate Denis Perron several times to the Quebec National Assembly. The PQ machine intervened throughout the campaign, turning its back on the Conservatives for the first time since 1984.

Member of Parliament: Gérard Asselin; **Party:** B.Q.; **Occupation:** Foreman for metal workers; **Education:** Diploma granted by the École des métiers, Baie-Comeau; **Age:** 44 (Apr. 19, 1950); **Year of first election to the House of Commons:** 1993

24017 Charlevoix

A: Political Profile
i) Voting Behaviour

	% 1993	% 1988	Change 1988-93
Conservative	17.8	80	-62.2
Liberal	18.8	14.2	4.6
NDP	1.4	4.3	-2.9
Bloc Québécois	62	0	62
Other	0	1.4	-1.4

% Turnout	69	Total Ballots (#)	39425
Rejected Ballots (#)	1315	% Margin of Victory	43.2
Rural Polls, 1988 (#)	165	Urban Polls, 1988 (#)	62
% Yes - 1992	32.8	% No - 1992	67.2

ii) Campaign Financing

	# of Donations	Total $ Value	% of Limit Spent
Conservative	117	51216	77.1
Liberal	37	27676	74.5
NDP	2	2200	0
Bloc Québécois	367	47233	71.1
Other	0	0	

B: Ethno-Linguistic Profile

% English Home Language	0.4	% French Home Language	97.2
% Official Bilingual	10.9	% Other Home Language	2.5
% Catholics	97.4	% Protestants	1.1
% Aboriginal Peoples	2.9	% Immigrants	0.5

C: Socio-Economic Profile

Average Family Income $	42795	Median Family Income $	39699
% Low Income Families	15.5	Average Home Price $	65680
% Home Owners	70.6	% Unemployment	15.5
% Labour Force Participation	61.7	% Managerial-Administrative	9.4
% Self-Employed	6	% University Degrees	4.8
% Movers	31.6		

D: Industrial Profile

% Manufacturing	17.6	% Service Sector	16.2
% Agriculture	2.8	% Mining	0.6
% Forestry	3.3	% Fishing	0.2
% Government Services	7.4	% Business Services	1.7

E: Homogeneity Measures

Ethnic Diversity Index	0.88	Religious Homogeneity Index	0.93
Sectoral Concentration Index	0.37	Income Disparity Index	7.2

F: Physical Setting Characteristics

Total Population	79200	Area (km²)	44490
Population Density (pop/km²)	1.8		

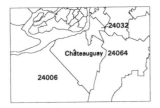

Châteauguay

Constituency Number: 24018

The riding of Châteauguay lies on the south shore of the St Lawrence River and Lac St-Louis, just south of the Island of Montreal. The urban-rural riding includes the Mohawk reservation of Kahnawake and the town of Sherrington. The riding is 82.5% francophone, 15.7% anglophone and has an aboriginal community of 0.7%. The average family income of $48,294 is slightly above the provincial average. 78% of dwellings are owned by their occupants, the fourth highest proportion in Quebec.

Châteauguay is another riding that tends to elect MPs from the government party. Since 1921, it has elected opposition MPs only in the minority elections of 1957, 1962, and 1979. Liberal Ian Watson represented the area from 1963 to 1984. But in the election of 1984 Watson was defeated by 4,005 votes by the Conservative candidate, Spanish-born Ricardo Lopez. Lopez, by profession a lawyer and businessman, served in General Franco's army. He is a controversial MP, who advanced a private member's bill proposing that the unemployment and welfare systems be replaced by work camps. He also proposed that the Mohawks in the riding, along with all other Canadian natives, should be exiled to Labrador. The Liberal candidate in Châteauguay was lawyer Jean-Marc Fournier, who is active in local radio. Fournier stressed the need for development of an industrial park in the riding. The NDP candidate was orchestra conductor Pierre Hétu. As in many south-shore ridings, the problems of transportation between the area and Montreal tend to be viewed as an important local issue. So too was Lopez' record: he was criticized by his Liberal opponent for having missed 70% of the votes in the House of Commons. Despite the charge, Lopez held on to the riding by winning rural polls, increasing his margin to 6,017 votes. The Liberals' Fournier won the town of Châteauguay, where the riding's anglophones are concentrated.

The federal election saw Lopez losing the support of thousands of his supporters, securing only 5,782 votes compared to 22,439 in 1988. The Liberals hoped to unseat Lopez with Kimon Valaskakis, president of the Gamma Institute and economics specialist, who was parachuted into the riding. He came second with 30.3% of the vote. NDP recruited Luc Proulx, an office worker from Westmount, who took 1.4%. Bloc Québécois Maurice Godin, a past PQ candidate and president of the 'No' committee in Châteauguay for the referendum of October 26, 1992, took the riding with 58% of the vote, having obtained a margin of victory of 16,531 votes.

Member of Parliament: Maurice Godin; **Party:** B.Q.; **Occupation:** Chief of division, Hydro-Québec; **Education:** Diploma granted by the École automobile de Montréal; **Age:** 62 (Oct. 21, 1932); **Year of first election to the House of Commons:** 1993

24018 Châteauguay

A: Political Profile

i) Voting Behaviour

	% 1993	% 1988	Change 1988-93
Conservative	9.7	44.8	-35.1
Liberal	30.3	32.8	-2.5
NDP	1.4	16.5	-15.1
Bloc Québécois	58	0	58
Other	0.5	5.9	-5.4

% Turnout	76.5	Total Ballots (#)	61998
Rejected Ballots (#)	2268	% Margin of Victory	28.2
Rural Polls, 1988 (#)	39	Urban Polls, 1988 (#)	168
% Yes - 1992	36.9	% No - 1992	63.1

ii) Campaign Financing

	# of Donations	Total $ Value	% of Limit Spent
Conservative	0**	0**	0**
Liberal	104	44136	100
NDP	1	1000	0
Bloc Québécois	453	25036	40.9
Other	0	0	

B: Ethno-Linguistic Profile

% English Home Language	15.7	% French Home Language	82.5
% Official Bilingual	41.8	% Other Home Language	1.9
% Catholics	88.8	% Protestants	7.9
% Aboriginal Peoples	0.7	% Immigrants	5.3

C: Socio-Economic Profile

Average Family Income $	48294	Median Family Income $	46531
% Low Income Families	10.8	Average Home Price $	97575
% Home Owners	78	% Unemployment	9.9
% Labour Force Participation	70.2	% Managerial-Administrative	12.1
% Self-Employed	7.8	% University Degrees	5.3
% Movers	42.1		

D: Industrial Profile

% Manufacturing	21.7	% Service Sector	11.2
% Agriculture	3.9	% Mining	0.1
% Forestry	0.1	% Fishing	0
% Government Services	4.8	% Business Services	4.2

E: Homogeneity Measures

Ethnic Diversity Index	0.71	Religious Homogeneity Index	0.79
Sectoral Concentration Index	0.37	Income Disparity Index	3.7

F: Physical Setting Characteristics

Total Population	102305	Area (km²)	740
Population Density (pop/km²)	138.3		

** No return filed.

Chicoutimi

Constituency Number: 24019

The riding of Chicoutimi is located along the Saguenay river, northeast of Quebec City, and includes the town of Chicoutimi. There is also the military base of Bagotville.

The riding is 99% francophone. Its average family income of $45,908 approximates the provincial average. Among its main employers, one finds Abitibi-Price and Stone-Consolidated in the forest sector, and Alcan in the sector of aluminum. The level of unemployment is quite high with 13.5% in 1991.

Between 1945 and 1965, the Liberals held Chicoutimi for only one year. An independent represented the area from 1945 to 1957. Briefly represented by a Liberal in 1957, the riding went Conservative in the Diefenbaker landslide of 1958, and then *créditiste* in 1962 and 1963. The Liberals won the riding in 1965, and held it for the next 19 years. Marcel Dionne was MP from 1979 until he lost in 1984 by 11,568 votes to André Harvey, a professor of accounting. The 1988 campaign saw three educators representing the major parties. Against Harvey, the Liberals ran Laval Gauthier while the NDP candidate was Elayoubi Mustapha, a teacher at a local CEGEP. Harvey was re-elected with a margin of 22,652 votes. The 70.4% of the vote he received was the Conservatives' fourth best result in Canada.

In 1993 the story was different for André Harvey who saw his popularity drop sharply, coming second and attracting only 11,126 votes. Liberal Georges Frenette, a professor of economics and administrative sciences at Université du Québec in Chicoutimi, came third with only 10.8% of the vote, confirming the continued decline of the Liberals in the Lac-St-Jean area. Jean Chrétien's lack of popularity in the region hurt the local candidate. The NDP recruited Christine Moore, a political science student parachuted into the region, who obtained 1.2% of the vote compared to 11.2% the party received in 1988. Bloc Québécois Gilbert Fillion, a retired teacher, well-connected in the region and active in municipal politics, received 63.9% of the vote with a margin of victory of 18,385 votes. Fillion had the support of the Public Service Alliance of Canada. The main issues of the campaign were job creation, maintenance of social programs, and regional development. Lucien Bouchard frequently visited the area. Chicoutimi recorded the third highest vote against the 26 October 1992 Charlottetown Accord in Quebec and the eighth in Canada.

Member of Parliament: Gilbert Fillion; **Party:** B.Q.; **Occupation:** Retired professor; **Education:** Diploma in pedagogy, Université Laval; **Age:** 54 (July 27, 1940); **Year of first election to the House of Commons:** 1993

24019 Chicoutimi

A: Political Profile
i) Voting Behaviour

	% 1993	% 1988	Change 1988-93
Conservative	24.1	70.4	-46.3
Liberal	10.8	18.4	-7.6
NDP	1.2	11.2	-10
Bloc Québécois	63.9	0	63.9
Other	0	0	0

% Turnout	72.8	Total Ballots (#)	47360
Rejected Ballots (#)	1175	% Margin of Victory	39.8
Rural Polls, 1988 (#)	29	Urban Polls, 1988 (#)	162
% Yes - 1992	26.7	% No - 1992	73.3

ii) Campaign Financing

	# of Donations	Total $ Value	% of Limit Spent
Conservative	102	56171	93.1
Liberal	32	14321	13.9
NDP	2	2200	0
Bloc Québécois	429	49751	67.4
Other	0	0	

B: Ethno-Linguistic Profile

% English Home Language	0.9	% French Home Language	99
% Official Bilingual	15.4	% Other Home Language	0.1
% Catholics	96.5	% Protestants	1.4
% Aboriginal Peoples	0.6	% Immigrants	0.8

C: Socio-Economic Profile

Average Family Income $	45908	Median Family Income $	42000
% Low Income Families	16.1	Average Home Price $	78463
% Home Owners	57.6	% Unemployment	13.5
% Labour Force Participation	61.1	% Managerial-Administrative	10.6
% Self-Employed	6.2	% University Degrees	9.8
% Movers	40.4		

D: Industrial Profile

% Manufacturing	14.8	% Service Sector	14.9
% Agriculture	1.2	% Mining	0.3
% Forestry	1.6	% Fishing	0.1
% Government Services	9.4	% Business Services	4.4

E: Homogeneity Measures

Ethnic Diversity Index	0.92	Religious Homogeneity Index	0.92
Sectoral Concentration Index	0.42	Income Disparity Index	8.5

F: Physical Setting Characteristics

Total Population	87806	Area (km²)	3503
Population Density (pop/km²)	25.1		

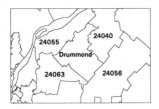

Drummond

Constituency Number: 24020

The riding of Drummond is located east of Montreal. It lies to the south of the riding of Richelieu, and includes the town of Drummondville. The riding is 98.6% francophone. The average family income of $40,044 is 13% below the Quebec average. Of the riding's workforce 26.4% is occupied in the manufacturing sector, one of the highest level in Canada. The service sector provides a major source of income for the riding. Drummond has a significant agricultural base as 6.1% of its residents find their livelihood in this sector.

The Liberals held Drummond from 1887 to 1962, but it has since lost its reputation as a safe seat. It went *créditiste* in 1962, and was recovered for the Liberals by Jean-Luc Pepin in 1963. Pepin held the riding until 1972, when it was lost by just seventy votes to *créditiste* Jean-Marie Boisvert. In 1974, it was Boisvert's turn to lose to Liberal Yvon Pinard by 13 votes. Pinard held the riding until 1984, when he did not seek re-election. Businessman Jean-Guy Guilbault won the riding for the Conservatives in 1984 with a margin of 9,556 votes. In 1988, he was facing lawyer Jean-Claude Lagacé for the Liberals, and Ferdinand Berner for the NDP. Guilbault held the riding with an 8,323 vote margin.

Liberal Bernard Boudreau, a lawyer and mayor of St-Charles-de-Drummond, got 24.1% of the vote, down 10.6% from 1988. Incumbent Jean-Guy Guilbault saw his 1988 majority disappeared as he came third, with 19.8% of the vote. Bloc Québécois Pauline Picard, an administrative assistant, took the riding with 54.9% of the vote. Pauline Picard led the 'No' campaign against the Charlottetown Accord in October 1992 and has also occupied important functions with the Parti Québécois; for instance, she was involved in its national action committee on women's issues. During the nomination process she received the backing of PQ members. She won handily and received the support of prominent local personalities, among them the mayors of Drummondville, Bon-Conseil and Grantham, as well as the regional prefect during the campaign. Picard is the first woman ever elected to represent the riding. Among the issues debated there was the question of waste disposal, with specific reference to American imports of potentially dangerous waste being dumped at St-Nicéphore.

Member of Parliament: Pauline Picard; **Party:** B.Q.; **Occupation:** Administrative assistant; **Education:** Program in administration, psychosocial training in mental health; **Age:** 47 (Apr. 27, 1947); **Year of first election to the House of Commons:** 1993

24020 Drummond

A: Political Profile
i) Voting Behaviour

	% 1993	% 1988	Change 1988-93
Conservative	19.8	53.5	-33.7
Liberal	24.1	34.7	-10.6
NDP	1.2	11.8	-10.6
Bloc Québécois	54.9	0	54.9
Other	0	0	0

% Turnout	76.4	Total Ballots (#)	47439
Rejected Ballots (#)	2016	% Margin of Victory	30.8
Rural Polls, 1988 (#)	65	Urban Polls, 1988 (#)	119
% Yes - 1992	36.5	% No - 1992	63.5

ii) Campaign Financing

	# of Donations	Total $ Value	% of Limit Spent
Conservative	28	42399	98.5
Liberal	79	30564	87.5
NDP	5	3500	0.5
Bloc Québécois	210	28829	50.5
Other	0	0	

B: Ethno-Linguistic Profile

% English Home Language	1	% French Home Language	98.6
% Official Bilingual	18.9	% Other Home Language	0.4
% Catholics	95.2	% Protestants	2.6
% Aboriginal Peoples	0.4	% Immigrants	1.6

C: Socio-Economic Profile

Average Family Income $	40044	Median Family Income $	35361
% Low Income Families	17.1	Average Home Price $	72346
% Home Owners	60.4	% Unemployment	10.6
% Labour Force Participation	64	% Managerial-Administrative	11.7
% Self-Employed	11	% University Degrees	5.9
% Movers	39.9		

D: Industrial Profile

% Manufacturing	26.4	% Service Sector	11.6
% Agriculture	6.1	% Mining	0.3
% Forestry	0.3	% Fishing	0
% Government Services	3.8	% Business Services	2.8

E: Homogeneity Measures

Ethnic Diversity Index	0.92	Religious Homogeneity Index	0.88
Sectoral Concentration Index	0.35	Income Disparity Index	11.7

F: Physical Setting Characteristics

Total Population	84005	Area (km²)	1890
Population Density (pop/km²)	44.4		

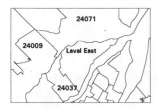

Laval Est (formerly Duvernay)

Constituency Number: 24021

Formerly known as Duvernay, the riding of Laval Est comprises the eastern part of the City of Laval, on Île-Jésus, just north of the Island of Montreal. The riding contains an industrial park, and has an average family income of $54,822, well above the Quebec average. The riding is 89.1% francophone and 5% italophone.

Long considered a Liberal stronghold, Duvernay riding was captured by Conservative Vincent Della Noce in the 1984 election with a plurality of over 11,412 votes. Della Noce, the former president of a gasoline station owners' association, served as parliamentary secretary to various ministers in the 1984-1988 Parliament. In the 1988 campaign, he called for measures to clean up rivers around Laval, and proposed turning the maximum-security Laval Institute into a tourist attraction. The NDP fielded Michel Agnaieff, considered one of their star candidates. Agnaieff, born in Egypt of Russian parents, is an associate president of the party, and director general of the Quebec Corporation of Teachers (CEQ). In a riding with a large percentage of two-income families, the NDP candidate stressed the issue of day-care. He also focused on the problem of public transit between the riding and Montreal. The Liberal Party ran Pierre Amaranian, a Lebanese-Armenian literature professor; he too stressed the issue of day-care. Della Noce again won the riding for the Conservatives, this time with a plurality of over 20,000 votes.

The story was to be quite different for Della Noce in 1993 when he finished third with 18.4% of the vote. During his two mandates in Ottawa Della Noce had become a controversial MP. Liberal Raymonde Folco, president of the Council of Cultural Communities and Immigration of Quebec, got 26.8% of the vote. A longtime community activist and former aide to PQ MNA Jean-Paul Champagne from 1981 to 1985, Maud Debien ran for the Bloc and totalled 31,491 votes, a margin of victory of 12,431 votes. NDP Stéphane Houle, a plumber, took 1.1% of the vote.

Member of Parliament: Maud Debien; **Party:** B.Q.; **Occupation:** Retired; **Education:** Specialized BA in information, studies in communication; **Year of first election to the House of Commons:** 1993

24021 Laval Est

A: Political Profile

i) Voting Behaviour

	% 1993	% 1988	Change 1988-93
Conservative	18.4	60.7	-42.3
Liberal	26.8	22.9	3.9
NDP	1.1	14.8	-13.7
Bloc Québécois	51.9	0	51.9
Other	1.8	1.5	0.3

% Turnout	82.8	Total Ballots (#)	62535
Rejected Ballots (#)	1906	% Margin of Victory	26.9
Rural Polls, 1988 (#)	0	Urban Polls, 1988 (#)	216
% Yes - 1992	42.5	% No - 1992	57.5

ii) Campaign Financing

	# of Donations	Total $ Value	% of Limit Spent
Conservative	88	67093	98.5
Liberal	17	46238	72.6*
NDP	5	2492	1.6
Bloc Québécois	567	42036	69.4
Other	5	666	

B: Ethno-Linguistic Profile

% English Home Language	5.9	% French Home Language	89.1
% Official Bilingual	46.4	% Other Home Language	5
% Catholics	92.9	% Protestants	3.2
% Aboriginal Peoples	0.5	% Immigrants	9.3

C: Socio-Economic Profile

Average Family Income $	54822	Median Family Income $	49885
% Low Income Families	13.5	Average Home Price $	129508
% Home Owners	69.2	% Unemployment	8.8
% Labour Force Participation	68.7	% Managerial-Administrative	15.8
% Self-Employed	8.9	% University Degrees	10.3
% Movers	43		

D: Industrial Profile

% Manufacturing	15.6	% Service Sector	10.1
% Agriculture	0.7	% Mining	0.1
% Forestry	0	% Fishing	0
% Government Services	7.3	% Business Services	6.4

E: Homogeneity Measures

Ethnic Diversity Index	0.68	Religious Homogeneity Index	0.84
Sectoral Concentration Index	0.45	Income Disparity Index	9

F: Physical Setting Characteristics

Total Population	103189	Area (km²)	133
Population Density (pop/km²)	775.9		

* Tentative value, due to the existence of unpaid campaign expenses.

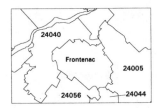

Frontenac

Constituency Number: 24022

The riding of Frontenac is located some 150 kilometres east of Montreal, to the south of the riding of Lotbinière. The riding includes the towns of Thetford Mines, Plessisville, Disraeli and Black Lake, and stretches from East Broughton in the south to Ste-Agathe in the north and from Plessisville to Thetford Mines. The riding is 98.6% francophone. Frontenac's population of 60,799 is the fourth smallest in the province. The average family income of $39,819 is 13% below the provincial average. Just 27.4% of families in the riding have moved in the past five years, the fourth lowest proportion in Quebec. Frontenac has a relatively important manufacturing sector that employs nearly 20% of the population: Metallurgy Frontenac, Foundry Thetford, Bonair trailers are among the most important employers. Jobs are also found in the mining sector, notably in asbestos exploitation and transformation with Asbestos Lab, and Lake Asbestos.

The area was represented by Liberal J.A. Blanchette from 1935 to 1958. In that year it went Conservative, and from 1962 to 1970 it was held by the *créditistes*. From 1970 to 1984, it was represented by Liberal Léopold Corriveau.

In 1984, Corriveau was defeated by Marcel Masse, an administrator with Lavalin, who won for the Conservatives with a margin of 19,092 votes. Masse had previously served for the Union Nationale in the Quebec National Assembly from 1966 to 1973. The 71.3% of the vote he received was the Conservatives' best result in the province. Masse served as Minister of Communications in the first Mulroney cabinet, but he had to leave the cabinet for a time while the RCMP investigated his election expenses. He was appointed Minister of Energy, Mines and Resources in 1986. The Liberal candidate in 1988 was Réal Patry, an administrator working in Sherbrooke. Patry's campaign was weakened by the fact that many local Liberals worked for Masse. The NDP ran Claude L'Heureux, who was parachuted into the riding and did not appear at any public events during the campaign. Masse once again won easily, receiving 73.6% of the vote, the Conservatives' third best result in Canada. He did not seek re-election in 1993 following Charlottetown's failed accord.

1993 brought several new faces on the political scene. The Conservatives found Jean-Claude Nadeau, an administrator, who came third taking 16.3% of the vote. The Liberals were slightly more fortunate with Jean-Guy Jam, a long-time federal and provincial Liberal activist who got 22.5% of the vote. NDP Joseph Bowman, a parachuted Ottawa student, came fourth with 1% of the vote just behind the Green Party candidate, Jean-René Guernon who got 1.1%. Bloc Québécois opted for a long-time committed nationalist, Jean-Guy Chrétien, who had quit the Quebec Liberal Party along with René Lévesque in 1967 to create the Sovereignty-Association Movement. Very involved in his community, Chrétien won easily with a margin of victory of 11,963 votes.

Member of Parliament: Jean-Guy Chrétien; **Party:** B.Q.; **Occupation:** Mayor of Garthby, teacher, farmer; **Education:** BA in pedagogy; **Age:** 48 (1946); **Year of first election to the House of Commons:** 1993

24022 Frontenac

A: Political Profile

i) Voting Behaviour

	% 1993	% 1988	Change 1988-93
Conservative	16.3	73.6	-57.3
Liberal	22.5	19.9	2.6
NDP	1	5.1	-4.1
Bloc Québécois	58.4	0	58.4
Other	1.7	1.5	0.2

% Turnout	78	Total Ballots (#)	34586
Rejected Ballots (#)	1328	% Margin of Victory	37.6
Rural Polls, 1988 (#)	84	Urban Polls, 1988 (#)	84
% Yes - 1992	38.5	% No - 1992	61.5

ii) Campaign Financing

	# of Donations	Total $ Value	% of Limit Spent
Conservative	35	43800	77.9
Liberal	64	6419	24.5
NDP	1	1000	0
Bloc Québécois	448	55539	97.2
Other	0	0	

B: Ethno-Linguistic Profile

% English Home Language	1.2	% French Home Language	98.6
% Official Bilingual	14	% Other Home Language	0.2
% Catholics	96.7	% Protestants	2
% Aboriginal Peoples	0.2	% Immigrants	1.2

C: Socio-Economic Profile

Average Family Income $	39819	Median Family Income $	35313
% Low Income Families	13.9	Average Home Price $	59657
% Home Owners	74.3	% Unemployment	8.8
% Labour Force Participation	60.5	% Managerial-Administrative	9.9
% Self-Employed	13	% University Degrees	4.6
% Movers	27.4		

D: Industrial Profile

% Manufacturing	19.3	% Service Sector	11.5
% Agriculture	8.7	% Mining	5.7
% Forestry	0.9	% Fishing	0
% Government Services	3.4	% Business Services	1.9

E: Homogeneity Measures

Ethnic Diversity Index	0.93	Religious Homogeneity Index	0.88
Sectoral Concentration Index	0.34	Income Disparity Index	11.3

F: Physical Setting Characteristics

Total Population	60799	Area (km^2)	2737
Population Density (pop/km^2)	22.2		

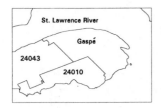

Gaspé

Constituency Number: 24023

The riding of Gaspé comprises the eastern tip of the Gaspé Peninsula. It includes the town of the same name, and the towns of Murdochville, Percé and Ste-Anne-des-Monts. The riding's population of 55,673 is the second smallest in the province. The riding is 93.3% francophone. Gaspé riding is generally poor: the average family income of $35,573 is the seventh lowest in Canada. Government transfer payments represent 28.3% of that income, the highest proportion in Quebec. The 1991 census put the unemployment level at 27.6%, the highest in Quebec. The riding's population is relatively stable: only 24.7% of families have moved in the past five years, the second lowest level in Quebec. Of the riding's workforce 3.8% is involved in fishing, second only to Bonaventure–Îles-de-la-Madeleine in the province. Murdochville Copper Mines is one of the main employers of the region but sensitive to economic vagaries.

Gaspé riding generally went Liberal in the first half of the century. But the Conservatives won the riding three times during the Diefenbaker-Pearson period from 1957 to 1963. Liberal Alexandre Cyr, who had won the riding in 1963 and lost it in 1965, was elected again in 1968 and in the following four elections. But in 1984 he lost to Ste-Anne-des-Monts psychiatrist and president of the local Chamber of Commerce Charles-Eugène Marin, who won the riding for the Conservatives with a margin of 8,913 votes. Marin enjoyed support from Parti Québécois activists in the 1988 campaign. Lawyer Delton Sams of the firm Sams, Dumaresk and Bernatchez, ran a shoe-string campaign for the Liberals, coming second with 34.9% of the vote. Sams had worked as a policy assistant for MP Alexandre Cyr and for Quebec minister of state for fisheries Robert Dutil. The NDP fielded Bertrand Réhel who secured 5.3% of the vote. Marin won the riding for a second time, though his margin was reduced to 6,390 votes.

In 1993 Marin having lost the support of the PQ organization suffered major losses, coming third with only 18.5% of the vote. Liberals again ran Delton Sams who maintained his previous score with 34.6% of the vote. Bloc Québécois Yvan Bernier, a native of Gaspé, and an administrator involved in local community development, was backed by the PQ organization and took the riding with 45.2% of the vote. Yvan Bernier had acquired a reputation as defender of fisherman and lumberjack rights. NDP fielded Montreal Eric Wilson Steedman, a student, who got 0.7% of the vote. Michel Limoges, an administrator, ran for the Green Party and came in fourth place with 1% of the vote. The main issues discussed during the campaign concerned job creation, fisheries and forest development, and the federal deficit.

Member of Parliament: Yvan Bernier; **Party:** B.Q.; **Occupation:** Administrator; **Education:** BA in administration; **Age:** 34 (June 17, 1960); **Year of first election to the House of Commons:** 1993

24023 Gaspé

A: Political Profile

i) Voting Behaviour

	% 1993	% 1988	Change 1988-93
Conservative	18.5	57.3	-38.8
Liberal	34.6	34.9	-0.3
NDP	0.7	5.3	-4.6
Bloc Québécois	45.2	0	45.2
Other	1	2.5	-1.5

% Turnout	70.3	Total Ballots (#)	29758
Rejected Ballots (#)	481	% Margin of Victory	11.6
Rural Polls, 1988 (#)	125	Urban Polls, 1988 (#)	23
% Yes - 1992	40.6	% No - 1992	59.4

ii) Campaign Financing

	# of Donations	Total $ Value	% of Limit Spent
Conservative	93	52619	99.5
Liberal	189	29419	95
NDP	6	2200	0
Bloc Québécois	197	31865	44.9
Other	7	471	

B: Ethno-Linguistic Profile

% English Home Language	6.7	% French Home Language	93.3
% Official Bilingual	15.5	% Other Home Language	0
% Catholics	95	% Protestants	3.9
% Aboriginal Peoples	0.3	% Immigrants	0.3

C: Socio-Economic Profile

Average Family Income $	35573	Median Family Income $	30294
% Low Income Families	23	Average Home Price $	51875
% Home Owners	75.7	% Unemployment	27.6
% Labour Force Participation	56.2	% Managerial-Administrative	7.3
% Self-Employed	6.6	% University Degrees	4
% Movers	24.7		

D: Industrial Profile

% Manufacturing	16.5	% Service Sector	14.6
% Agriculture	1.3	% Mining	2.6
% Forestry	3.4	% Fishing	3.8
% Government Services	9.2	% Business Services	1.4

E: Homogeneity Measures

Ethnic Diversity Index	0.82	Religious Homogeneity Index	0.89
Sectoral Concentration Index	0.33	Income Disparity Index	14.8

F: Physical Setting Characteristics

Total Population	55673	Area (km²)	12268
Population Density (pop/km²)	4.5		

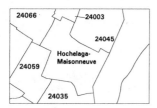

Hochelaga–Maisonneuve

Constituency Number: 24024

One of five ridings on the eastern part of the Island of Montreal, Hochelaga–Maisonneuve runs from the Olympic stadium south to the St Lawrence River. It is a riding of aging industries: ship-building, steel, locomotive works. It is also a riding of aging residences: 40% of dwellings were built before 1946. 18.7% of the riding's dwellings are owned by their occupants, far below the Quebec average of 57.3%. The riding is 90% francophone, and close to a third of families are classified as low-income, one of the highest proportions in the province. The average family income is $37,266, 19% below the Quebec average. It is one of the lowest levels in the country. Low-income families work mainly in the manufacturing sector, notably Nal-Pac (textiles), Standard Paper (wood), and Christie (food). A once-bustling industrial base is showing serious signs of failure with little if any indication of comeback.

In a close 1984 race, Hochelaga–Maisonneuve was won by Conservative Édouard Desrosiers who was dogged by reports that he was under investigation by the RCMP for spending irregularities and potential charges for breach of trust. In early October, the day after a Montreal paper reported that he had been convicted of a hold-up in 1958, he announced that he would not run again. The Conservatives nominated Allan Koury, a local merchant. The Liberal Party was thought to be reserving the riding for Serge Joyal, a former cabinet minister who lost there in 1984. After Joyal decided not to run again, the Liberals chose Serge Laprade, a singer and television personality. The NDP ran Gaétan Nadeau, a lawyer associated with human rights issues. A Montreal Citizens' Movement organizer, he had been elected leader of the provincial wing of the NDP in 1989. Nadeau was reputed to enjoy the support of many local Parti Québécois members in the 1988 campaign. All three candidates stressed issues pertaining to job creation in the riding, and debated the probable impact of the free trade agreement on the riding's industries. The Conservatives held on to the riding, with a 2,078 vote edge over the Liberals. The NDP's Nadeau received 20.7% of the vote, one of only ten NDP candidates in the province to reach the 20% level.

In 1993 Allan Koury sought re-election for the Conservatives and came third, receiving only 8.7% of the vote. In December 1992, Koury's office has been emptied of furniture by a group of unemployed protesting reduction in unemployment benefits and new eligibility requirements. Liberals fielded political rookie Jules Léger, a public notary and senior partner in the Léger & Léger firm, who held 25% of the vote, down 9.2% from the previous election. Bloc Québécois Réal Ménard, a political aide to PQ Louise Harel and a long-time party activist, obtained 61.4% of the vote with a margin of victory of 15,495 votes. Ménard received substantial help from the PQ riding association as 300 volunteers campaigned on his behalf. Hochelaga–Maisonneuve has been a PQ stronghold since the early 1970s. Parachuted wrestler Paul Vachon, after a failed 1988 attempt in Brome-Missisquoi, ran again for the NDP receiving 2.5% of the vote. Due to economic hardship in this area of Montreal, job creation was again the main issue during the campaign.

Member of Parliament: Réal Ménard; **Party:** B.Q.; **Occupation:** Political attaché; **Education:** MA (political science); **Age:** 32 (May 13, 1962); **Year of first election to the House of Commons:** 1993

24024 Hochelaga–Maisonneuve

A: Political Profile
i) Voting Behaviour

	% 1993	% 1988	Change 1988-93
Conservative	8.7	39.3	-30.6
Liberal	25	34.2	-9.2
NDP	2.5	20.7	-18.2
Bloc Québécois	61.4	0	61.4
Other	2.4	5.8	-3.4

% Turnout	74.2	Total Ballots (#)	44502
Rejected Ballots (#)	1857	% Margin of Victory	38.8
Rural Polls, 1988 (#)	0	Urban Polls, 1988 (#)	187
% Yes - 1992	33.6	% No - 1992	66.4

ii) Campaign Financing

	# of Donations	Total $ Value	% of Limit Spent
Conservative	89	29043	82.9
Liberal	44	21565	42
NDP	2	4902	5
Bloc Québécois	480	36336	56.2
Other	8	780	

B: Ethno-Linguistic Profile

% English Home Language	3.7	% French Home Language	90
% Official Bilingual	38.6	% Other Home Language	6.3
% Catholics	86.1	% Protestants	3.5
% Aboriginal Peoples	0.6	% Immigrants	8.9

C: Socio-Economic Profile

Average Family Income $	37266	Median Family Income $	32362
% Low Income Families	37.5	Average Home Price $	142980
% Home Owners	18.7	% Unemployment	16
% Labour Force Participation	57.7	% Managerial-Administrative	11
% Self-Employed	5	% University Degrees	10.6
% Movers	56		

D: Industrial Profile

% Manufacturing	16.3	% Service Sector	14.3
% Agriculture	0.2	% Mining	0.1
% Forestry	0.1	% Fishing	0
% Government Services	7.3	% Business Services	6.9

E: Homogeneity Measures

Ethnic Diversity Index	0.71	Religious Homogeneity Index	0.73
Sectoral Concentration Index	0.5	Income Disparity Index	13.2

F: Physical Setting Characteristics

Total Population	83172	Area (km^2)	15
Population Density (pop/km^2)	5544.8		

Hull–Aylmer

Constituency Number: 24025

The riding of Hull–Aylmer is located across the Ottawa River from Ottawa. The urban riding is 76.6% francophone. The average family income of $52,803 is 15% above the Quebec average. 25.9% of the riding's work force is involved in government services, the highest level in Quebec and the fifth highest level in Canada. E.B. Eddy /Scott Paper company offers job opportunities to the region. A high technology business park has recently been opened.

Hull–Aylmer has voted Liberal since Confederation. Gaston Isabelle, first elected in 1965 after serving one mandate in Gatineau from 1965 to 1968, survived the Conservative sweep of Quebec in 1984 with a margin of 1,495 votes. Isabelle was one of only four non-Montreal Liberals to win in Quebec. When Isabelle decided to retire, the Liberals nominated former Union Nationale Gilles Rocheleau. Rocheleau had served as Mayor of Hull from 1974 to 1980, before being elected to the Quebec National Assembly. When the federal election was called, Rocheleau was provincial Minister of Supply and Services in the Bourassa government. He criticized his former boss's relation to Mulroney when he decided to run, an action that led to defections from the Liberal camp: both his organizer and the head of the Liberal riding association went to work for the Conservative candidate, lawyer and businesswoman Nicole Moreault. Rocheleau wanted to rid Ottawa of *péquistes* in the House of Commons, and to push for free trade although his party opposed it. Despite these divisions, Rocheleau easily defeated Moreault and the NDP's Danielle Lapointe-Vienneau, a teacher. The 49.8% of the vote received by the Liberals was their fourth best result in the province.

In 1993 Liberals ran Rhodes scholar and former Clerk of Privy Council under Joe Clark, Marcel Massé, who has later been deputy secretary of state for External Affairs and president of the Canadian International Development Agency (CIDA). Massé defeated incumbent Gilles Rocheleau, who had left the Liberals to join the Bloc Québécois immediately following the election of Jean Chrétien as leader of the party, with a margin of victory of 13,695 votes. Rocheleau had acquired the reputation of being a loose cannon incapable of team work. Chrétien's decision to designate Massé as the Liberal candidate led policeman Tony Cannavino to run as an independent Liberal; coming third, he received 8.7% of the vote. Another disappointed Liberal, Pierre Chénier, a federal government finance officer, decided to represent the Conservatives and secured 6.2% of the vote. The main issues were job creation, sovereignty, completion of Highway 50 toward Montreal, contraband of cigarettes, and manpower training.

Member of Parliament: Marcel Massé; **Party:** Liberal; **Occupation:** Economist, administrator; **Education:** PhD (Economics); **Age:** 54 (June 23, 1940); **Year of first election to the House of Commons:** 1993

24025 Hull–Aylmer

A: Political Profile
i) Voting Behaviour

	% 1993	% 1988	Change 1988-93
Conservative	6.2	31.9	-25.7
Liberal	53.3	49.8	3.5
NDP	2.6	15.4	-12.8
Bloc Québécois	27.2	0	27.2
Other	10.8	2.9	7.9

% Turnout	77	Total Ballots (#)	53421
Rejected Ballots (#)	873	% Margin of Victory	26.1
Rural Polls, 1988 (#)	0	Urban Polls, 1988 (#)	208
% Yes - 1992	61.4	% No - 1992	38.6

ii) Campaign Financing

	# of Donations	Total $ Value	% of Limit Spent
Conservative	40	20584	86.7
Liberal	303	69000	96.2
NDP	60	14717	22.4
Bloc Québécois	374	37184	67.2
Other	343	35337	

B: Ethno-Linguistic Profile

% English Home Language	19	% French Home Language	76.6
% Official Bilingual	62.6	% Other Home Language	4.4
% Catholics	84.4	% Protestants	6.7
% Aboriginal Peoples	1.8	% Immigrants	8.2

C: Socio-Economic Profile

Average Family Income $	52803	Median Family Income $	48154
% Low Income Families	19.6	Average Home Price $	115006
% Home Owners	47.8	% Unemployment	8.4
% Labour Force Participation	70.5	% Managerial-Administrative	16.1
% Self-Employed	6.7	% University Degrees	16.1
% Movers	53.7		

D: Industrial Profile

% Manufacturing	5	% Service Sector	15.5
% Agriculture	0.6	% Mining	0.1
% Forestry	0.2	% Fishing	0
% Government Services	25.9	% Business Services	7.1

E: Homogeneity Measures

Ethnic Diversity Index	0.63	Religious Homogeneity Index	0.7
Sectoral Concentration Index	0.55	Income Disparity Index	8.8

F: Physical Setting Characteristics

Total Population	92951	Area (km^2)	141
Population Density (pop/km^2)	659.2		

Joliette

Constituency Number: 24026

The riding of Joliette is located just northeast of Montreal. It includes the town of the same name, and the communities of Laurentides and l'Assomption. The riding is 98.8% francophone. Joliette's average family income of $44,138 is slightly below the Quebec average. The manufacturing sector is significant. The town of Joliette has many important companies among which are Scott Paper and the Firestone tire factory.

The Liberals held Joliette from 1917 to 1958. But since then it has been one of the Conservatives' strongest ridings in Quebec: they have won ten of the last twelve general elections there. Roch Lasalle represented the riding from 1968 to 1984. He won his first election in the riding with a plurality of just 172 votes, and was one of only four Conservatives to be elected in Quebec during the year of Trudeaumania. In 1972, Lasalle ran as an Independent, but returned to the Conservative fold two years later. Lasalle served in the ill-fated Clark government of 1979, as Minister of Supply and Services. He resigned in 1981 to lead the Union Nationale, and lost that election in time to return to the House of Commons through the by-election that had been called to replace him. In his final election in 1984, the Conservatives received 73.9% of the vote, their third best result in Quebec. Lasalle resigned from the Cabinet in 1987 following accusations of influence peddling. In 1988, the Conservatives nominated Gaby Larrivée, merchant, prefect of the regional municipality and mayor of Saint-Charles Borromée. Larrivée had first been offered the Liberal nomination. The NDP ran Claude Hétu, a union activist. The Liberal candidate was Denis Coderre, at 25 years old the youngest candidate in the country. A former president of the party's youth commission, Coderre had been openly critical of John Turner's leadership. He had campaigned for the 'Yes' side in the 1980 referendum on sovereignty-association. Free trade was a central issue during the campaign. Larrivée won the riding with a margin of 15,335 votes.

Larrivée ran again in 1993 and came third with 14.8% of the vote. The Liberal Réjean Lefebvre, a local entrepreneur and president of a clothing company, took on the challenge, and secured 16.3% of the vote. Bloc Québécois René Laurin, schoolboard general director and PQ founding member, took 66.3% of the vote, the sixth best results for his party , and secured a margin of victory of 30,953 votes.

Member of Parliament: René Laurin; **Party:** B.Q.; **Occupation:** Director General; **Education:** BSc Comm.; **Age :** 54 (Feb 4, 1940); **Year of first election to the House of Commons :** 1993

24026 Joliette

A: Political Profile
i) Voting Behaviour

	% 1993	% 1988	Change 1988-93
Conservative	14.2	55.1	-40.9
Liberal	16.3	24.8	-8.5
NDP	1.2	14.3	-13.1
Bloc Québécois	66.3	0	66.3
Other	2.1	5.8	-3.7

% Turnout	76.4	Total Ballots (#)	65191
Rejected Ballots (#)	3208	% Margin of Victory	52.1
Rural Polls, 1988 (#)	115	Urban Polls, 1988 (#)	110
% Yes - 1992	28.1	% No - 1992	71.9

ii) Campaign Financing

	# of Donations	Total $ Value	% of Limit Spent
Conservative	319	59122	58.5
Liberal	35	29549	62.4*
NDP	1	1000	0
Bloc Québécois	837	64060	84.4
Other	2	5450	

B: Ethno-Linguistic Profile

% English Home Language	0.9	% French Home Language	98.8
% Official Bilingual	22.1	% Other Home Language	0.3
% Catholics	95.3	% Protestants	2.5
% Aboriginal Peoples	0.6	% Immigrants	1.5

C: Socio-Economic Profile

Average Family Income $	44138	Median Family Income $	40841
% Low Income Families	14	Average Home Price $	90571
% Home Owners	68.2	% Unemployment	10.4
% Labour Force Participation	66.7	% Managerial-Administrative	11.2
% Self-Employed	9.6	% University Degrees	5.3
% Movers	45.5		

D: Industrial Profile

% Manufacturing	20.3	% Service Sector	11
% Agriculture	4	% Mining	0.4
% Forestry	0.1	% Fishing	0
% Government Services	5.7	% Business Services	3.4

E: Homogeneity Measures

Ethnic Diversity Index	0.91	Religious Homogeneity Index	0.87
Sectoral Concentration Index	0.37	Income Disparity Index	7.5

F: Physical Setting Characteristics

Total Population	111863	Area (km²)	894
Population Density (pop/km²)	125.1		

* Tentative value, due to the existence of unpaid campaign expenses.

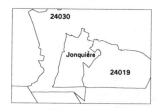

Jonquière

Constituency Number: 24027

The riding of Jonquière, formerly named Lapointe, is located along the Saguenay River, northeast of Quebec City. It includes the towns of Jonquière, Laterrière, and Shipsaw. The riding is 99% francophone. The average family income of $45,006 is slightly below the provincial average. In the aluminum sector, Alcan provides jobs to 4,000 people at Laterrière and 500 at Jonquière. In the forest sector, Abitibi pulp employs more than 300 people in Jonquière.

Prior to 1984, Jonquière had never elected a Conservative. Apart from a period of *créditiste* representation from 1962 to 1968, the riding had been Liberal since its creation in 1947. Gilles Marceau represented the riding from 1968 until his 1984 defeat at the hands of the Conservatives' Jean-Pierre Blackburn, who won with a margin of 4,129 votes. In his bid for re-election in 1988, Blackburn was facing the Liberals' Laval Tremblay, an agronomist and international development consultant. The NDP candidate was lawyer Françoise Gauthier. Blackburn won, with a 14,497 margin over the second place NDP candidate.

In 1993, Blackburn experienced overwhelming opposition from Bloc Québécois candidate André Caron, a guidance counsellor to the CEGEP of Jonquière who has close ties to the PQ and presided over the 'No' Committee in Jonquière to defeat the Charlottetown accord. André Caron got no less than 67.6% of the vote, with a margin of victory of 18,484 votes. Caron also received the support of the Public Service Alliance of Canada who had targeted the riding. The youth wing of the PQ in the region rallied around the Bloc candidate to get the vote out. Jonquière registered the highest score against the 1992 Charlottetown Accord with 77.7%.

Blackburn's participation in the Beaudoin-Dobbie Committee in 1991, following the failure of Meech Lake, did not provide him with the right exposure in this well-known nationalist stronghold. The Liberals nominated businessman Gilles Savard who came third with 12.2% of the vote. Conservative Blackburn came second with 17.9% of the vote compared to 63.6% obtained in 1988. NDP Karl Bélanger, a CEGEP of Jonquière student, received only 1.1.%, a drop of 19.7% from 1988, coming in fourth place after Natural Law's Normand Dufour, a butcher. Main issues of the campaign were regional development, unemployment, and depopulation of the region.

Member of Parliament: André Caron; **Party:** B.Q.; **Occupation:** Guidance counsellor; **Education :** Diploma in careers advising; **Age:** 50 (Dec. 18, 1944); **Year of first election to the House of Commons:** 1993

24027 Jonquière

A: Political Profile

i) Voting Behaviour

	% 1993	% 1988	Change 1988-93
Conservative	17.9	63.6	-45.7
Liberal	12.2	15.6	-3.4
NDP	1.1	20.8	-19.7
Bloc Québécois	67.6	0	67.6
Other	1.2	0	1.2

% Turnout	76.6	Total Ballots (#)	38058
Rejected Ballots (#)	899	% Margin of Victory	50.9
Rural Polls, 1988 (#)	22	Urban Polls, 1988 (#)	118
% Yes - 1992	22.3	% No - 1992	77.7

ii) Campaign Financing

	# of Donations	Total $ Value	% of Limit Spent
Conservative	190	23150	38.7
Liberal	89	37297	62.7
NDP	3	1502	0.8
Bloc Québécois	528	41763	98
Other	10	1033	

B: Ethno-Linguistic Profile

% English Home Language	0.8	% French Home Language	99
% Official Bilingual	14.7	% Other Home Language	0.2
% Catholics	97.5	% Protestants	1.1
% Aboriginal Peoples	0.7	% Immigrants	0.7

C: Socio-Economic Profile

Average Family Income $	45006	Median Family Income $	41781
% Low Income Families	16.8	Average Home Price $	72313
% Home Owners	63.9	% Unemployment	13.5
% Labour Force Participation	59.5	% Managerial-Administrative	9.2
% Self-Employed	4.9	% University Degrees	6.7
% Movers	36.6		

D: Industrial Profile

% Manufacturing	22.9	% Service Sector	14.1
% Agriculture	1	% Mining	0.2
% Forestry	0.6	% Fishing	0.1
% Government Services	8.4	% Business Services	4.4

E: Homogeneity Measures

Ethnic Diversity Index	0.92	Religious Homogeneity Index	0.94
Sectoral Concentration Index	0.37	Income Disparity Index	7.2

F: Physical Setting Characteristics

Total Population	67867	Area (km²)	1926
Population Density (pop/km²)	35.2		

Kamouraska–Rivière-du-Loup

Constituency Number: 24028

The riding of Kamouraska–Rivière-du-Loup runs along the south shore of the St Lawrence River, to the northeast of Quebec City. It is bordered in part on the south by the State of Maine. The riding includes the towns of Ste-Anne-de-la-Pocatière, Pohénégamook, Rivière-du-Loup and Trois-Pistoles. The riding is 99.8% francophone. The riding's average family income of $38,431 is 16% below the provincial average. Government transfer payments account for 21.1% of all income, the fourth highest level in Quebec, with 14.9% unemployment. Among the main job providers, there are pulp and paper manufacturer F. F. Soucy and Bombardier.

The riding dates back to Confederation, but no winner was declared in the 1867 election. The *Canadian Parliamentary Guide* notes that, owing to riots, the returning officer issued no returns that year. By 1887 the riding had become a safe Liberal seat: the party won every election from that year to 1949. Then the riding became a definite òddity for Quebec: it went 26 years without electing a Liberal Party candidate. An Independent Liberal won in 1953, an Independent in 1957, and a Conservative in 1958. *Créditiste* Charles-Eugène Dionne held the riding from 1962 to 1979. Rosaire Gendron won the riding for the Liberals in 1979 and 1980, but did not run again in 1984. Businessman André Plourde won the riding for the Conservatives in that year with a 6,729 vote margin. In 1988, he was opposed by Liberal Gilles Desjardins, an economist and vice-president of Vidéotron Cablevision. But the greatest interest in the riding was sparked by the NDP candidacy of assistant crown prosecutor Maurice Tremblay in Rivière-du-Loup. Tremblay was fired by the Quebec Minister of Justice, Gil Rémillard, after announcing his candidacy, under the terms of a law prohibiting the involvement of prosecutors in politics. Tremblay argued that the law violated the Canadian Charter of Rights and Freedoms, and promised to sue to recover his position should he lose the election. Plourde won the riding for a second time, with a 10,035 vote plurality. The NDP's Tremblay received only 9.9% of the vote, despite the high visibility of his candidacy. Following a judiciary bout, Tremblay was reappointed assistant crown prosecutor.

André Plourde sought re-election in 1993 but came second with 23% of the vote. A conflict with Kim Campbell just before the start of the campaign concerning investment for Gros-Cacouna harbour, a perennial topic at each election in the riding, had led to some pussyfooting regarding the candidacy of Plourde. This time Maurice Tremblay received the Liberal nomination and 21.4% of the vote. Bloc Québécois Paul Crête, a personnel director and secretary at the CEGEP of La Pocatière, defeated Plourde by a margin of 10,459 votes. Crête is also well-known for his involvement in Rural Solidarity, a movement formed to counter population decline in the Eastern Quebec region in the tradition of Operation Dignity of the early 1970s. Among the main issues during the campaign were job creation, a high-speed rail line between Québec and Windsor to be constructed by Bombardier, economic restructuring of traditional sectors, and maintenance of post offices in remote areas.

Member of Parliament: Paul Crête; **Party:** B.Q.; **Occupation:** Personnel director and secretary; **Education:** BSc Admin.; **Age:** 41 (Apr. 8, 1953); **Year of first election to the House of Commons:** 1993

24028 Kamouraska–Rivière-du-Loup

A: Political Profile
i) Voting Behaviour

	% 1993	% 1988	Change 1988-93
Conservative	23	58.5	-35.5
Liberal ˙	21.4	29.7	-8.3
NDP	1.3	9.3	-8
Bloc Québécois	52.9	0	52.9
Other	1.5	2.5	-1

% Turnout	68.8	Total Ballots (#)	36356
Rejected Ballots (#)	1342	% Margin of Victory	31.4
Rural Polls, 1988 (#)	151	Urban Polls, 1988 (#)	43
% Yes - 1992	37.4	% No - 1992	62.6

ii) Campaign Financing

	# of Donations	Total $ Value	% of Limit Spent
Conservative	46	42842	67.6
Liberal	84	33468	62.3*
NDP	2	2200	0
Bloc Québécois	415	34493	59.2
Other	6	1568	

B: Ethno-Linguistic Profile

% English Home Language	0.2	% French Home Language	99.8
% Official Bilingual	9.7	% Other Home Language	0.1
% Catholics	97.4	% Protestants	1
% Aboriginal Peoples	0.1	% Immigrants	0.5

C: Socio-Economic Profile

Average Family Income $	38431	Median Family Income $	33159
% Low Income Families	17.3	Average Home Price $	60409
% Home Owners	71.8	% Unemployment	14.9
% Labour Force Participation	59.2	% Managerial-Administrative	11
% Self-Employed	10.5	% University Degrees	5.8
% Movers	29.6		

D: Industrial Profile

% Manufacturing	12.6	% Service Sector	13.3
% Agriculture	9.3	% Mining	1.6
% Forestry	3.3	% Fishing	0.3
% Government Services	5.1	% Business Services	2.2

E: Homogeneity Measures

Ethnic Diversity Index	0.97	Religious Homogeneity Index	0.91
Sectoral Concentration Index	0.35	Income Disparity Index	13.7

F: Physical Setting Characteristics

Total Population	70605	Area (km²)	5476
Population Density (pop/km²)	12.9		

* Tentative value, due to the existence of unpaid campaign expenses.

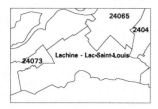

Lachine–Lac-Saint-Louis

Constituency Number: 24029

The riding of Lachine–Lac-Saint-Louis comprises most of the West Island of Montreal, including the towns of Lachine, Dorval, Pointe-Claire and Beaconsfield. The riding was modified in the 1987 redistribution, with the eastern part of Lachine being transferred from Notre-Dame-de-Grâce riding. The primarily residential riding includes Dorval Airport and some high-technology industries. The riding is 57.6% anglophone, the second largest proportion in Quebec. The average family income of $61,969 is the fifth highest in the province. One fifth of the riding's employed constituents are in managerial or administrative occupations, well above the Quebec average of 12.3%. This is the fourth highest proportion in Quebec. Several high technology companies provide significant numbers of jobs: Northern Telecom and Dominion Bridge with more than 1,000 each, and Sandoz Canada and Harris Farinon with approximately 500 each.

In 1984, Robert Layton took the riding for the Conservatives for the first time since the 1958 Diefenbaker sweep, with a plurality of 9,145 votes. A former chairman of the Montreal engineering firm Pringle and Sons, Layton served as Minister of State (Mines) from 1984 to 1986. In September 1988 he was appointed chairman of the party's national caucus. Attempting to recapture the riding, the Liberals ran Victor Drury, national director of the Kidney Foundation of Canada. Drury is the son of Bud Drury, former MP from Westmount and Liberal cabinet minister from 1963 to 1978. The NDP ran Val Udvarhely, who led the union representing Air Canada flight attendants. Not surprisingly in an anglophone riding, all three main candidates called for the 'notwithstanding' clause to be removed from the Constitution. Free trade and fiscal reform took on particular salience in the campaign when the Liberals charged, correctly as it turned out, that Gillette was planning to close its Montreal plant, a move that would cost 700 jobs. Though the plant is actually located in the Mont-Royal riding, many of its workers live in Lachine–Lac-Saint-Louis. Despite these concerns, Layton held on to the riding. His plurality was reduced dramatically, however, to just over 700 votes. Interestingly, Layton won both Beaconsfield, the most anglophone, and Lachine, the most francophone, parts of the riding.

Conservative Bob Layton did not seek re-election and was replaced by Nick Di Tomaso, a consultant and former president of Ultramar Canada, who came third with 8% of the vote. Bloc Québécois parachuted Le Gardeur businessman Guy Amyot who has over the years developed close links with several PQ ridings and who obtained 20.4% of the vote. Clifford Lincoln, a former minister of the Environment in the Quebec government, had resigned his position when Robert Bourassa enacted Bill 178 banning English on commercial signs. After a failed attempt for the Liberals in a by-election in Chambly in 1990, Lincoln received 67.5% of the vote, with an impressive margin of victory of 27,718 votes. NDP Westmount Val Udvarhely ran for the NDP and obtained 1.4% of the vote. Dental surgeon Bill Shaw, a former Union Nationale MNA, ran for the unofficial federal Equality Party, coming fifth with 1.1% of the vote.

Member of Parliament: Clifford Lincoln; **Party:** Liberal; **Occupation:** Consultant; **Education:** F.C.I.Arb.; **Age:** 66 (Sept. 1, 1928); **Year of first election to the House of Commons:** 1993

24029 Lachine–Lac-Saint-Louis

A: Political Profile
i) Voting Behaviour

	% 1993	% 1988	Change 1988-93
Conservative	8	45.4	-37.4
Liberal	67.5	44.1	23.4
NDP	1.4	7.9	-6.5
Bloc Québécois	20.4	0	20.4
Other	2.8	2.7	0.1

% Turnout	84	Total Ballots (#)	59866
Rejected Ballots (#)	963	% Margin of Victory	47.1
Rural Polls, 1988 (#)	0	Urban Polls, 1988 (#)	232
% Yes - 1992	73.2	% No - 1992	26.8

ii) Campaign Financing

	# of Donations	Total $ Value	% of Limit Spent
Conservative	25	40389	89
Liberal	92	58779	80.5
NDP	4	2651	2.2
Bloc Québécois	90	16797	20
Other	49	5637	

B: Ethno-Linguistic Profile

% English Home Language	57.6	% French Home Language	36.6
% Official Bilingual	59.1	% Other Home Language	5.8
% Catholics	59.9	% Protestants	27.3
% Aboriginal Peoples	0.7	% Immigrants	17.1

C: Socio-Economic Profile

Average Family Income $	61969	Median Family Income $	53138
% Low Income Families	14.1	Average Home Price $	160697
% Home Owners	57.8	% Unemployment	9
% Labour Force Participation	65.7	% Managerial-Administrative	19.1
% Self-Employed	7.8	% University Degrees	19.5
% Movers	43.5		

D: Industrial Profile

% Manufacturing	20	% Service Sector	9.5
% Agriculture	0.3	% Mining	0.1
% Forestry	0.1	% Fishing	0
% Government Services	4.2	% Business Services	8

E: Homogeneity Measures

Ethnic Diversity Index	0.31	Religious Homogeneity Index	0.44
Sectoral Concentration Index	0.48	Income Disparity Index	14.3

F: Physical Setting Characteristics

Total Population	99781	Area (km²)	68
Population Density (pop/km²)	1467.4		

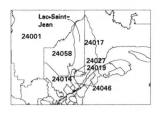

Lac-Saint-Jean

Constituency Number: 24030

The riding of Lac-Saint-Jean is located north of Quebec City. The riding runs some 500 kilometres north from the town of Alma, which is located near the lake that gives the riding its name. The riding is 99.7% francophone and includes the town of Alma. The average family income of $41,576 is 9% below the provincial average. The 1991 census estimated the unemployment rate at 16.5%.

The Lac-Saint-Jean riding was created in 1947. It was held by the Liberals until 1958, and then by the Conservatives and the *Créditistes* for the following ten years. The Liberals recovered the riding in the year of Trudeaumania, and held it until the Mulroney sweep of 1984, when the riding went Conservative for the second time in its history.

The Conservative incumbent in the November 1988 election was Lucien Bouchard, Canadian Ambassador to France from 1985 to 1988, who had won the riding only five months earlier in a tough by-election fight against Pierre Gimaiel who had held the riding for the Liberals from 1980 to 1984. Bouchard, a lawyer and a former member of the Parti Québécois who had decided to join René Lévesque's *Beau risque*, was Secretary of State when the general election was called. The Liberal party could not find a local candidate to oppose Bouchard, and had to parachute in Bertrand Bouchard, a Montreal real estate consultant. The NDP ran Jean Paradis, a CEGEP teacher and former member of the party's national executive committee. Paradis had run in 1984 and in the 1988 by-election. Lucien Bouchard held the riding with a margin of 16,764 votes over the NDP's Paradis. The 66.3% of the vote he received was his party's eighth best result in Canada.

1993 brought some surprises to the Conservative camp with the resignation of minister of Environment Lucien Bouchard that led to the creation of the Bloc Québécois. Bouchard kept the confidence of his constituents, increasing his support to 75.6% of the vote with a margin of victory of 22,086 votes. This was the Bloc's best performance, giving Bouchard the third highest margin of victory in Canada. The Conservatives fielded Denise Falardeau, a teacher, past president of the party and former principal political assistant to Lucien Bouchard, who came third with 8.9% of the vote. Noël Girard, a salesperson involved in community work, ran for the Liberals, seeking election for the first time, and obtained 14.3% of the vote. The NDP asked secretary Marie D. Jalbert, a parachuted candidate from La Beauce, to wear its colours. She got 1.2% of the vote. The Charlottetown Accord was rejected at 77.1%, the second highest opposition score, on 26 October 1992. The failed Meech Lake and Charlottetown attempts to renew the Constitution in ways satisfying to Quebec were central issues during the campaign.

Member of Parliament: Lucien Bouchard; **Party:** B.Q.; **Occupation:** Lawyer and leader of the Bloc Québécois; **Education:** LL.B, Université Laval; **Age:** 56 (Dec. 22, 1938); **Year of first election to the House of Commons:** 1988

24030 Lac-Saint-Jean

A: Political Profile
i) Voting Behaviour

	% 1993	% 1988	Change 1988-93
Conservative	8.9	66.3	-57.4
Liberal	14.3	15.5	-1.2
NDP	1.2	18.2	-17
Bloc Québécois	75.6	0	75.6
Other	0	0	0

% Turnout	76.3	Total Ballots (#)	37260
Rejected Ballots (#)	1186	% Margin of Victory	61.3
Rural Polls, 1988 (#)	101	Urban Polls, 1988 (#)	53
% Yes - 1992	22.9	% No - 1992	77.1

ii) Campaign Financing

	# of Donations	Total $ Value	% of Limit Spent
Conservative	26	8818	41.1
Liberal	77	15590	35.4
NDP	2	2200	0.5
Bloc Québécois	447	39951	48.5
Other	0	0	

B: Ethno-Linguistic Profile

% English Home Language	0.3	% French Home Language	99.7
% Official Bilingual	8.2	% Other Home Language	0
% Catholics	97.3	% Protestants	1.3
% Aboriginal Peoples	0.8	% Immigrants	0.3

C: Socio-Economic Profile

Average Family Income $	41576	Median Family Income $	38325
% Low Income Families	14.1	Average Home Price $	61467
% Home Owners	70.2	% Unemployment	16.5
% Labour Force Participation	60.6	% Managerial-Administrative	9.8
% Self-Employed	8.1	% University Degrees	5.1
% Movers	32.8		

D: Industrial Profile

% Manufacturing	17.3	% Service Sector	11.8
% Agriculture	5.4	% Mining	1
% Forestry	2.8	% Fishing	0
% Government Services	5	% Business Services	3.2

E: Homogeneity Measures

Ethnic Diversity Index	0.94	Religious Homogeneity Index	0.93
Sectoral Concentration Index	0.33	Income Disparity Index	7.8

F: Physical Setting Characteristics

Total Population	69083	Area (km²)	42790
Population Density (pop/km²)	1.6		

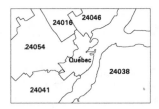

Québec (formerly Langelier)

Constituency Number: 24031

The riding of Québec is located in the heart of Quebec City. Prior to 1968, it was named Quebec-Ouest, and then Langelier. Only since the 1993 election has it been known under its new name, Quebec. It includes the working-class Lower Town and some wealthier neighbourhoods. The riding is 96.5% francophone. Québec's average family income of $39,682 is below the provincial average. Few of the constituents own those dwellings: only 21.7% of dwellings are owned by their occupants, one of the lowest levels in the province. Québec's population is quite mobile: 53.2% of families have moved in the past five years, one of the highest levels in Quebec.

Québec has voted Liberal for most of this century. In 1953 it was one of only four Quebec ridings to go Conservative, something it had previously done only once since 1911. It elected a Conservative again in the Diefenbaker sweep of 1958, and then elected a *créditiste* in 1962 and 1963. The Liberals recovered the riding in 1965, when close Trudeau ally Jean Marchand began a 12-year reign. Gilles Lamontagne, a former Quebec City mayor, succeeded Marchand through a by-election in 1977 and held the riding until 1984, when he declined to run again. Lamontagne held the defence portfolio in the final Trudeau government. In 1984, Conservative Michel Côté won the riding with a 2,868 vote margin. Côté was forced to resign shortly before the dissolution of Parliament, however, after violating conflict of interest guidelines by accepting no-interest loans from a federal government's retailer. The Conservatives then nominated Gilles Loiselle, former delegate-general for the Quebec government to Rome. Loiselle was one of two Conservative candidates in the area targeted for defeat by the Public Service Alliance of Canada. The Liberals were seeking a star candidate for the riding, but had to settle on municipal councillor Marielle Guay-Migneault. The NDP ran social worker Pauline Gingras who enjoyed support from Parti Québécois activists. She stressed the issue of control over the Quebec City port. Loiselle won the riding with a margin of just under 10,000 votes. The NDP received 20.1% of the vote, one of ten ridings in the province in which they reached the 20% plateau.

Quebec was highly disputed in 1993 with both Conservatives and Liberals fielding strong candidates. Star candidate Loiselle sought re-election but finished third with only 13.7% of the vote. Liberal Jean Pelletier, a former Quebec city mayor from 1977 to 1989 and chief of staff for Jean Chrétien as Leader of the Opposition, came second with 27.0% of the vote. Bloc Québécois Christiane Gagnon, a real estate agent, won with a plurality of 13,833 votes. Gagnon had strong connections to the PQ. The popularity of Lucien Bouchard was particularly instrumental in defeating Loiselle and Pelletier, two politicians well known in the riding. Once again the Public Service Alliance of Canada had targeted this riding and supported Bloc Québécois Gagnon without any reserve. Among the main issues were social housing, depollution of Saint-Charles River, and improvements to airport and municipal infrastructures.

Member of Parliament: Christiane Gagnon; **Party:** B.Q.; **Occupation:** Real estate agent; **Education:** Studies in sociology and communications, Université Laval; **Age:** 45 (April 16, 1948); **Year of first election to the House of Commons:** 1993

24031 Québec

A: Political Profile
i) Voting Behaviour

	% 1993	% 1988	Change 1988-93
Conservative	13.7	46.7	-33
Liberal	27	28.2	-1.2
NDP	2	20.1	-18.1
Bloc Québécois	53.8	0	53.8
Other	3.5	5	-1.5

% Turnout	76.4	Total Ballots (#)	53834
Rejected Ballots (#)	2214	% Margin of Victory	30.3
Rural Polls, 1988 (#)	0	Urban Polls, 1988 (#)	216
% Yes - 1992	37.4	% No - 1992	62.6

ii) Campaign Financing

	# of Donations	Total $ Value	% of Limit Spent
Conservative	20	80749	89.8
Liberal	116	86710	86.6
NDP	3	2793	1.5
Bloc Québécois	448	53549	98.7
Other	12	1326	

B: Ethno-Linguistic Profile

% English Home Language	1.5	% French Home Language	96.5
% Official Bilingual	31.5	% Other Home Language	1.9
% Catholics	90.7	% Protestants	1.6
% Aboriginal Peoples	0.5	% Immigrants	3.9

C: Socio-Economic Profile

Average Family Income $	39682	Median Family Income $	31905
% Low Income Families	37	Average Home Price $	95149
% Home Owners	21.7	% Unemployment	13
% Labour Force Participation	56.5	% Managerial-Administrative	12.9
% Self-Employed	6	% University Degrees	16.8
% Movers	53.2		

D: Industrial Profile

% Manufacturing	7	% Service Sector	17.9
% Agriculture	0.4	% Mining	0.1
% Forestry	0.2	% Fishing	0.1
% Government Services	17.2	% Business Services	6.4

E: Homogeneity Measures

Ethnic Diversity Index	0.86	Religious Homogeneity Index	0.79
Sectoral Concentration Index	0.63	Income Disparity Index	19.6

F: Physical Setting Characteristics

Total Population	90045	Area (km²)	25
Population Density (pop/km²)	3601.8		

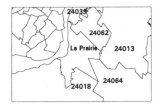

La Prairie

Constituency Number: 24032

The riding of La Prairie is located just across the St Lawrence River from Montreal. It includes the suburbs of Saint-Lambert, Brossard, and La Prairie. The riding is 70.6% francophone, below the Quebec average. La Prairie includes small Chinese, Italian, and black communities. The riding's average family income of $63,058 is third-highest in Quebec. 20.1% of the employed constituents are managers or administrators, compared to the provincial average of 12.3%. This is the highest level in Quebec. Two important employers are Perkins Paper and Plexiglas, who respectively employ 600 and 300 people.

If there is one local issue that seems to have the power to make or break political careers, it is the toll booths operated by the federal government on the Champlain Bridge crossing from Montreal to the south shore. In 1984 Fernand Jourdenais won the riding for the Conservatives with a 1,324 vote margin, after promising that he would abolish the tolls. As a backbencher in Ottawa, he vowed not to seek re-election unless the tolls were removed. The 1988 campaign saw constituents still paying the toll, but Jourdenais nevertheless decided to run again. Jourdenais' Liberal opponent was the man he had defeated in 1984. Pierre Deniger represented the riding from 1979 until his defeat by the Conservatives made him the first Liberal to lose the riding since its creation prior to the 1968 election. A lawyer by profession and president of the Quebec Brewers' Association, Deniger proclaimed himself a supporter of free trade in the campaign. The NDP candidate was Bruce Katz, a high-school teacher of Spanish and English. Apart from the toll issue, the candidates also focused on pollution and the problem of transit to the riding. According to news reports, internal polls in the riding showed the Liberal Deniger with a small lead in the closing days of the campaign. Yet Jourdenais took the riding for a second time, increasing his margin to 11,337 votes.

1993 was not that much different from previous elections. Finally dismantled in May 1990, toll booths were central to Jourdenais' campaign. With the view to being re-elected he promised another bridge to south shore residents. Jourdenais came third with 12.1% suffering, like his party, a major disaffection from the voters. Liberals ran businessman Jacques Saada, a former Protestant school board chairman and past president of the Quebec wing of the Liberal party of Canada, who came second with 42.3% of the vote. Bloc Québécois Richard Bélisle, a rehabilitation counsellor and former city councillor, won the riding with a margin of victory of 476 votes, the second smallest margin in Québec and the sixth in the country. NDP candidate Mohamed Akoum, an information system consultant, took 1.1% of the vote.

Member of Parliament: Richard Bélisle; **Party:** B.Q.; **Occupation:** Rehabilitation counsellor (CSST); **Education:** MBA; **Age:** 48 (B. Jul. 20, 1946); **Year of first election to the House of Commons:** 1993

24032 La Prairie

A: Political Profile
i) Voting Behaviour

	% 1993	% 1988	Change 1988-93
Conservative	12.1	53	-40.9
Liberal	42.3	33.5	8.8
NDP	1.1	10.7	-9.6
Bloc Québécois	43.1	0	43.1
Other	1.4	2.7	-1.3

% Turnout	83.7	Total Ballots (#)	65679
Rejected Ballots (#)	1819	% Margin of Victory	2.2
Rural Polls, 1988 (#)	0	Urban Polls, 1988 (#)	223
% Yes - 1992	53.4	% No - 1992	46.6

ii) Campaign Financing

	# of Donations	Total $ Value	% of Limit Spent
Conservative	16	21152	64.9
Liberal	233	57832	98.8
NDP	4	1311	0.4
Bloc Québécois	372	37516	49.1
Other	6	600	

B: Ethno-Linguistic Profile

% English Home Language	19.6	% French Home Language	70.6
% Official Bilingual	57.1	% Other Home Language	9.7
% Catholics	76.5	% Protestants	9
% Aboriginal Peoples	0.5	% Immigrants	16.8

C: Socio-Economic Profile

Average Family Income $	63058	Median Family Income $	55398
% Low Income Families	12.9	Average Home Price $	149755
% Home Owners	68	% Unemployment	8.6
% Labour Force Participation	71	% Managerial-Administrative	20.1
% Self-Employed	9.1	% University Degrees	19.6
% Movers	47.7		

D: Industrial Profile

% Manufacturing	14.4	% Service Sector	10.1
% Agriculture	0.3	% Mining	0.1
% Forestry	0.1	% Fishing	0
% Government Services	6.3	% Business Services	10

E: Homogeneity Measures

Ethnic Diversity Index	0.5	Religious Homogeneity Index	0.6
Sectoral Concentration Index	0.49	Income Disparity Index	12.1

F: Physical Setting Characteristics

Total Population	111771	Area (km²)	132
Population Density (pop/km²)	846.8		

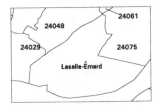

Lasalle–Émard

Constituency Number: 24033

The riding of Lasalle–Émard is located in the southwestern part of the Island of Montreal. It includes the town of Lasalle and part of Ville Émard. The riding is over 32.1% anglophone, one of the higher proportions in Quebec. Immigrants constitute 19% of the riding's population while over 10,000 of the riding's residents are of Italian origin and a significant number are of Haitian origin. Average family income is $43,691, 5% below the Quebec average.

In 1984, Claude Lanthier won the riding for the Conservatives for the first time ever, with a plurality of 3,820 votes. A consulting engineer, Lanthier served as parliamentary secretary to various ministers in the 1984-1988 parliament.

In the 1988 campaign, Lanthier ran up against a Liberal star candidate, Paul Martin Jr, chairman and chief executive officer of Canada Steamship Lines and son of Paul Martin Sr, a former Liberal cabinet minister. Martin, seen as a possible successor to party leader John Turner, was one of the few Liberal candidates supported by Quebec Premier Robert Bourassa in the campaign. The NDP fielded high-school teacher Jean-Claude Bohrer. Environmental issues were important in the campaign, with candidates calling for a clean-up of the polluted Lachine Canal. There was also debate concerning the threat of plant closings in areas neighbouring the riding. Free Trade was a major issue. Martin won the riding for the Liberals by under 1,500 votes. He enjoyed less support in the more francophone parts of the riding.

Paul Martin represented the Liberals again in 1993 and increased his hold on the riding, taking 59.5% of the vote. Martin assumed responsibility for the writing of the Red Book in which the party platform was developed. Martin's popularity has grown in Quebec during the last decade, particularly during the race to become leader of the Liberal party of Canada, when he lost to Jean Chrétien on the first ballot. Bloc Québécois fielded Éric Simon, 23-year-old CEGEP graduate and PQ activist since 1989, who came second with 33.3% of the vote. NDP candidate was Kingston Richard Belzile, an educational consultant, who got 1.4% of the vote. Conservative Johanne Sénécal, a businesswoman, obtained 4.6% of the vote. This was the fourth worst result for the Conservatives in Quebec and the sixth worst in Canada.

Member of Parliament: Paul Martin; **Party:** Liberal; **Occupation:** Businessman, Member of Parliament; **Education:** LL.B, University of Toronto Law School; **Age:** 56 (Aug. 28, 1938); **Year of first election to the House of Commons:** 1988

24033 LaSalle–Émard

A: Political Profile

i) Voting Behaviour

	% 1993	% 1988	Change 1988-93
Conservative	4.6	42.7	-38.1
Liberal	59.5	45.5	14
NDP	1.4	10.6	-9.2
Bloc Québécois	33.3	0	33.3
Other	1.2	1.2	0

% Turnout	81.9	Total Ballots (#)	53238
Rejected Ballots (#)	1364	% Margin of Victory	26.2
Rural Polls, 1988 (#)	0	Urban Polls, 1988 (#)	206
% Yes - 1992	59.8	% No - 1992	40.2

ii) Campaign Financing

	# of Donations	Total $ Value	% of Limit Spent
Conservative	17	53384	95.9
Liberal	116	100674	75
NDP	4	1375	0
Bloc Québécois	131	22183	35.5
Other	0	0	

B: Ethno-Linguistic Profile

% English Home Language	32.1	% French Home Language	55
% Official Bilingual	53.3	% Other Home Language	12.9
% Catholics	77.9	% Protestants	12.8
% Aboriginal Peoples	0.5	% Immigrants	19

C: Socio-Economic Profile

Average Family Income $	43691	Median Family Income $	40684
% Low Income Families	23.6	Average Home Price $	153323
% Home Owners	33.7	% Unemployment	11.1
% Labour Force Participation	65.2	% Managerial-Administrative	10.9
% Self-Employed	5.1	% University Degrees	7.2
% Movers	45.6		

D: Industrial Profile

% Manufacturing	21.7	% Service Sector	13.2
% Agriculture	0.2	% Mining	0.1
% Forestry	0	% Fishing	0
% Government Services	5.1	% Business Services	6.2

E: Homogeneity Measures

Ethnic Diversity Index	0.35	Religious Homogeneity Index	0.62
Sectoral Concentration Index	0.46	Income Disparity Index	6.9

F: Physical Setting Characteristics

Total Population	93542	Area (km²)	20
Population Density (pop/km²)	4677.1		

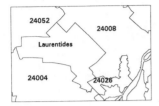

Laurentides

Constituency Number: 24034

The riding of Laurentides is located north of Montreal. It includes the Laurentian resort area. The riding is 96.1% francophone. The average family income of $42,897 is 7% below the provincial average. Government transfer payments provide 15% of the riding income. Manufacturing and service sectors are important job providers. Main employers in the manufacturing sector are Canstar (sport equipment), Phillips Cables and Rolland Paper.

Laurentides was created in the 1987 electoral redistribution, replacing Labelle, one of the oldest constituencies in Quebec. The first MP from Labelle was Henri Bourassa who represented the riding for the Liberals from 1896 to 1908. The Liberals kept the seat without interruption between 1965 and 1984. The Conservatives have not been very fortunate in this riding, electing MPs only for the short periods of 1911-1917, 1949-1953, and 1984-1993. In 1988, bailiff Jacques Vien ran for the Conservatives. The Liberals fielded Serge Paquette, an aide to John Turner, and the NDP candidate was Bill Clay, a research assistant. Vien won the election with a margin of 15,248 votes.

Vien ran again in 1993 and came third with 10.4% of the vote. He had hoped to keep the riding considering that his government had backed a $450 million federal expansion project at Mont-Tremblant ski resort. Liberals ran Michelle Tisseyre, a freelancer and correspondent for *La Presse* and *L'Actualité* and former press secretary and political advisor to First Nations Grand Chief Ovide Mercredi, for 27.1% of the vote. Businesswoman Monique Guay represented the Bloc Québécois, and received 60.7% of the vote, for a margin of victory of 23,171 votes.

Member of Parliament: Monique Guay; **Party:** B.Q.; **Occupation:** Real estate agent; **Education:** Program in administration, Dawson College and McGill University; **Age:** 35 (Oct. 27, 1959); **Year of first election to the House of Commons:** 1993

24034 Laurentides

A: Political Profile
i) Voting Behaviour

	% 1993	% 1988	Change 1988-93
Conservative	10.4	55.2	-44.8
Liberal	27.1	28	-0.9
NDP	1.2	13.8	-12.6
Bloc Québécois	60.7	0	60.7
Other	0.7	3	-2.3

% Turnout	77.3	Total Ballots (#)	71629
Rejected Ballots (#)	2703	% Margin of Victory	34.3
Rural Polls, 1988 (#)	108	Urban Polls, 1988 (#)	150
% Yes - 1992	35.1	% No - 1992	64.9

ii) Campaign Financing

	# of Donations	Total $ Value	% of Limit Spent
Conservative	55	38975	74.6
Liberal	86	53219	99.5
NDP	2	2200	0
Bloc Québécois	386	33438	60.8
Other	0	0	

B: Ethno-Linguistic Profile

% English Home Language	3.6	% French Home Language	96.1
% Official Bilingual	33.9	% Other Home Language	0.3
% Catholics	92.1	% Protestants	3.7
% Aboriginal Peoples	0.7	% Immigrants	2.5

C: Socio-Economic Profile

Average Family Income $	42897	Median Family Income $	37382
% Low Income Families	17	Average Home Price $	102428
% Home Owners	61.5	% Unemployment	14
% Labour Force Participation	64	% Managerial-Administrative	10.6
% Self-Employed	10.6	% University Degrees	6.6
% Movers	49.2		

D: Industrial Profile

% Manufacturing	14.9	% Service Sector	16.2
% Agriculture	1	% Mining	0.4
% Forestry	0.3	% Fishing	0.1
% Government Services	5.9	% Business Services	4

E: Homogeneity Measures

Ethnic Diversity Index	0.86	Religious Homogeneity Index	0.83
Sectoral Concentration Index	0.46	Income Disparity Index	12.9

F: Physical Setting Characteristics

Total Population	115667	Area (km²)	3792
Population Density (pop/km²)	30.5		

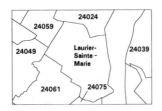

Laurier–Sainte-Marie

Constituency Number: 24035

Laurier–Sainte-Marie includes much of downtown Montreal. The riding was formed in the 1987 redistribution with parts of the old Laurier and Sainte-Marie ridings. The riding is 81.2% francophone, and includes significant Portuguese and Chinese communities. The population is very mobile: 61.8% of families have moved in the past five years, one of the highest proportions in Canada.

With an average family income of $37,053, Laurier–Sainte-Marie is the fifth poorest in the province; 17.3% of income consists of government transfer payments. Over one-third of the riding's residents live in families classified as low-income, the highest proportion in the country. Only 16% of dwellings in the riding are owned by their occupants, the second lowest proportion in Canada.

Liberal Jean-Claude Malépart won the riding of Sainte-Marie in the 1979 election, and survived the 1984 Conservative sweep with a relatively comfortable margin of 2,749 votes. A former worker at Macdonald Tobacco, Malépart was very well-known in the riding, having represented the area provincially in the mid-1970s. In the 1988 campaign Malépart was presented with the challenge of a substantially restructured riding, which left him with under 40% of the voters of his old constituency. Redistribution added the more upscale areas of Plateau Mont-Royal and Old Montreal to the working class areas of Sainte-Marie. It also brought in a gay community estimated as high as 15,000 votes. Redistribution was not expected to help the Conservatives, however: in 1984, the old Laurier riding had given the party its second-worst showing in Quebec. Moreover, the Rhinoceros Party polled 12.1% of the vote in 1984, its best result. The Conservatives originally sought a high-profile candidate for the riding, but settled on Charles Hamelin, the MP from Charlevoix who gave up his riding to Brian Mulroney. The NDP fielded a strong candidate, François Beaulne, former Vice-President of the National Bank and university professor. Beaulne had served as consul of Canada in San Francisco from 1977 to 1980. All three candidates could lay some claim to the support of Parti Québécois sympathizers. Malépart was supported by the PQ Louise Harel. The Conservative campaign was directed by a former PQ organizer. The NDP's Beaulne actively courted the nationalist vote. On election night, Malépart held the riding, increasing his margin to 3,843 votes over the Conservatives. The NDP received 21.6% of the vote, its fifth best showing in the province. Following Malépart's death, a by-election was called for August 1990 and saw the election of the first Bloc Québécois MP, CSN labour organizer Gilles Duceppe. Duceppe received 68% of the vote while Liberal Denis Coderre received 20% and NDP Louise O'Neill took 7%.

In 1993, Gilles Duceppe maintained his grip on the riding with 61.8% of the vote. Former Radio-Canada journalist and former advisor and press secretary to Quebec Deputy Premier Lise Bacon, Robert Desbiens obtained 24.5% of the vote. Coming third was Yvan Routhier, McGill MBA student, who secured 5.3% of the vote.

Member of Parliamen: Gilles Duceppe; **Party:** B.Q.; **Occupation:** Union counsellor, Member of Parliament; **Education:** Studies in political science, Université de Montréal; **Age:** 47 (July 22, 1947); **Year of first election to the House of Commons :** 1990

24035 Laurier–Sainte-Marie

A: Political Profile

i) Voting Behaviour

	% 1993	% 1988	Change 1988-93
Conservative	5.3	29.7	-24.4
Liberal	24.5	39.1	-14.6
NDP	3.1	21.6	-18.5
Bloc Québécois	61.8	0	61.8
Other	5.3	9.7	-4.4

% Turnout	71.3	Total Ballots (#)	42150
Rejected Ballots (#)	1592	% Margin of Victory	42.6
Rural Polls, 1988 (#)	0	Urban Polls, 1988 (#)	198
% Yes - 1992	33.7	% No - 1992	66.3

ii) Campaign Financing

	# of Donations	Total $ Value	% of Limit Spent
Conservative	9	17950	35.1
Liberal	23	51311	77.6*
NDP	8	12135	9.6
Bloc Québécois	288	47845	74.5
Other	51	3137	

B: Ethno-Linguistic Profile

% English Home Language	8.3	% French Home Language	81.2
% Official Bilingual	49.1	% Other Home Language	10.6
% Catholics	77	% Protestants	3.6
% Aboriginal Peoples	0.7	% Immigrants	15.6

C: Socio-Economic Profile

Average Family Income $	37053	Median Family Income $	28988
% Low Income Families	43.7	Average Home Price $	136032
% Home Owners	16	% Unemployment	16.5
% Labour Force Participation	63.7	% Managerial-Administrative	12.4
% Self-Employed	10	% University Degrees	19
% Movers	61.8		

D: Industrial Profile

% Manufacturing	2.4	% Service Sector	17.2
% Agriculture	0.2	% Mining	0.1
% Forestry	0.1	% Fishing	0
% Government Services	6.7	% Business Services	10

E: Homogeneity Measures

Ethnic Diversity Index	0.58	Religious Homogeneity Index	0.58
Sectoral Concentration Index	0.6	Income Disparity Index	21.8

F: Physical Setting Characteristics

Total Population	79378	Area (km²)	18
Population Density (pop/km²)	4409.9		

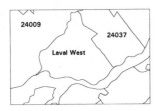

Laval Ouest (formerly Laval)

Constituency Number: 24036

Formerly known as Laval, the riding of Laval Ouest is made up of the western part of the Town of Laval, on Île-Jésus, just north of Montreal. The riding is 68.9% francophone, below the provincial average. The riding includes a Jewish community of 20,605, and a sizeable Greek community. The average family income of $51,700 is well above the provincial average. In this predominantly residential riding, more than three-fourths of dwellings are owned by their occupants. Manufacturing sector is present with companies such as M & R Plastics Inc. and Products MKS.

In 1984, SNC electrical engineer Guy Ricard was elected with a plurality of 7,694 votes. This constituted the first Conservative victory in the riding since the 1958 sweep. Ricard, former Laval city councillor, served as a back-bencher in the 1984-1988 parliament. In the 1987 redistribution, the riding lost a slice at its eastern end, which included several industrial parks. Transposing the 1984 votes to the new boundaries, the Conservative plurality would have been reduced to 5,500 votes. The Liberals fielded Céline Hervieux-Payette, Canada's first Minister of State for Youth. Elected in 1979 in Mercier, Hervieux-Payette was briefly in the Cabinet at the end of the Trudeau reign. But she was excluded from John Turner's short-lived 1984 cabinet, and lost her seat in the election later that year. After her defeat, she worked as a vice-president of the SNC group. In the 1988 campaign, Hervieux-Payette was identified with the anti-Turner forces in the party. Peace activist and physician Paul Cappon contested the riding for the NDP. Playing on Hervieux-Payette's association with the Liberal Party's 'old guard', Cappon accused the Liberal candidate of rejecting the concept of Quebec as a distinct society. Ricard won the contest by 8,039 votes, gaining more support in the francophone parts of the riding.

In 1993, Guy Ricard sought re-election but failed abysmally, receiving only 6.8% of the vote compared to 49.1% in 1988. Bloc Québécois was represented by Michel Leduc, an administrator, who came second with 43% of the vote. Michel Leduc has strong links to the PQ for whom he ran in 1976, 1981, 1985 and 1989, winning only the 1981 campaign. 'Star' candidate Michel Dupuy who served in several diplomatic positions — among them president of the Canadian International Development Agency (CIDA), Ambassador to the United Nations and to France and foreign policy advisor to Opposition leader Jean Chrétien from 1988 to 1993 — took 46.2% of the vote, with a margin of victory of 1,989 votes. Dupuy had run unsuccessfully in Longueuil in 1988, coming second with 22.6% of the vote. As in recent elections in the riding, the question of transit between the riding and Montreal was an important issue. The Liberals focused on the poor highway system serving the riding, while the NDP promised better public transit. Both the Liberals and the Conservatives promised more spending on housing for the poor and elderly. Bloc Québécois echoed the same themes and stated the urgency for Quebec to become sovereign.

Member of Parliament: Michel Dupuy; **Party:** Liberal; **Occupation:** Foreign policy consultant; **Education:** LL.D; **Age :** 64 (January 11, 1930); **Year of first election to the House of Commons:** 1993

24036 Laval Ouest

A: Political Profile
i) Voting Behaviour

	% 1993	% 1988	Change 1988-93
Conservative	6.8	49.1	-42.3
Liberal	46.2	34.4	11.8
NDP	1.1	15.6	-14.5
Bloc Québécois	43	0	43
Other	3	0.9	2.1

% Turnout	79.6	Total Ballots (#)	63290
Rejected Ballots (#)	1765	% Margin of Victory	3.2
Rural Polls, 1988 (#)	0	Urban Polls, 1988 (#)	207
% Yes - 1992	54.3	% No - 1992	45.7

ii) Campaign Financing

	# of Donations	Total $ Value	% of Limit Spent
Conservative	16	5550	96.4
Liberal	54	56206	97.5
NDP	1	2900	4.7
Bloc Québécois	541	39291	72.2
Other	11	9177	

B: Ethno-Linguistic Profile

% English Home Language	16.7	% French Home Language	68.9
% Official Bilingual	51	% Other Home Language	14.4
% Catholics	72	% Protestants	6
% Aboriginal Peoples	0.4	% Immigrants	18.8

C: Socio-Economic Profile

Average Family Income $	51700	Median Family Income $	47575
% Low Income Families	15.5	Average Home Price $	121626
% Home Owners	76.1	% Unemployment	10.5
% Labour Force Participation	70	% Managerial-Administrative	15
% Self-Employed	10.1	% University Degrees	9.8
% Movers	42.1		

D: Industrial Profile

% Manufacturing	19.9	% Service Sector	11.4
% Agriculture	0.7	% Mining	0.1
% Forestry	0	% Fishing	0
% Government Services	4.5	% Business Services	6.3

E: Homogeneity Measures

Ethnic Diversity Index	0.44	Religious Homogeneity Index	0.55
Sectoral Concentration Index	0.45	Income Disparity Index	8

F: Physical Setting Characteristics

Total Population	108671	Area (km²)	74
Population Density (pop/km²)	1468.5		

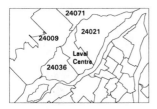

Laval Centre
(formerly Laval-des-Rapides)

Constituency Number: 24037

Formerly known as Laval-des-Rapides, Laval Centre occupies the central part of the city of Laval, on Île-Jésus, just north of Montreal. The riding is 85.2% francophone, somewhat above the Quebec average. There is an Italian community of some 3,000 residents. The average family income of $48,193 is 5% above the provincial average. Several companies involved in medical research are present, among which is the Armand-Frappier Institute. A youth camp introducing the space sciences and research was officially opened late in 1994.

The 1988 campaign in the riding was one of the most confused in the province, as all three parties had difficulties with their candidate nomination processes. Going into the election, the riding was held by the Liberal Party's Quebec lieutenant, Raymond Garneau. However, the 1987 redistribution removed part of the riding that lay on the Island of Montreal, precisely where Garneau's support was concentrated. If 1984 votes are transposed onto the riding's new boundaries, Garneau's 1984 advantage of 2,369 votes is transformed into a Conservative margin of several thousand votes. In response to the redistribution, Garneau decided to seek re-election in the neighbouring riding of Ahuntsic, to which much of his base of support had been transferred. The Liberal Party's electoral commission then blocked the nomination of would-be candidate Mark Bordeleau, allowing François Arsenault, a real-estate administrator, to be nominated in mid-October. The Conservatives, for their part, nominated tabloid publisher Guy Pothier. The party refused to endorse the candidacy, owing to reports that Pothier was to be charged by police for false advertising. The nomination was then offered to lawyer Jacques Tétreault, who accepted on condition that he not have to contest the nomination. Tétreault had served as Mayor of Laval from 1965 to 1973. The NDP nomination went to retired worker John Shatilla. Shatilla had run twice in the neighbouring riding of Duvernay, now known as Laval Est, but that riding's nomination was reserved this time for Michel Agnaieff. The party was apparently not enthusiastic about Shatilla's candidacy in Laval-des-Rapides, as it refused to offer him any material support for the campaign. The Conservatives' second-choice candidate Tétreault won the riding with a large 13,029-vote plurality.

A slate of new candidates emerged in 1993. Conservatives ran lawyer Bruno Fortier who came third, obtaining 8% of the vote. Liberals fielded engineer Guymond Fortin, a past industrial analyst at the Export Development Corporation and the Société de développement industriel du Québec, and now a portfolio manager, who finished second with 33.4% of the vote. This strong showing by the Liberals was one of the rare occasions where the party improved its position in a francophone constituency. Bloc Québécois Madeleine Dalphond-Guiral, a professor with strong PQ affiliations, received 55.2% of the vote, for a margin of victory of 12,431 votes.

Member of Parliament: Madeleine Dalphond-Guiral; **Party:** B.Q.; **Occupation:** Professor; **Education:** BA; **Age :** 56 (1938); **Year of first election to the House of Commons:** 1993

24037 Laval Centre

A: Political Profile
i) Voting Behaviour

	% 1993	% 1988	Change 1988-93
Conservative	8	53.7	-45.7
Liberal	33.4	28.7	4.7
NDP	1.1	14.2	-13.1
Bloc Québécois	55.2	0	55.2
Other	2.3	3.3	-1

% Turnout	79.5	Total Ballots (#)	59203
Rejected Ballots (#)	2200	% Margin of Victory	24.1
Rural Polls, 1988 (#)	0	Urban Polls, 1988 (#)	239
% Yes - 1992	41.7	% No - 1992	58.3

ii) Campaign Financing

	# of Donations	Total $ Value	% of Limit Spent
Conservative	76	47650	64*
Liberal	97	51649	90.9*
NDP	6	2600	0.7
Bloc Québécois	419	33400	61.4
Other	23	5575	

B: Ethno-Linguistic Profile

% English Home Language	7.4	% French Home Language	85.2
% Official Bilingual	47.4	% Other Home Language	7.5
% Catholics	87.1	% Protestants	4.4
% Aboriginal Peoples	0.5	% Immigrants	11.5

C: Socio-Economic Profile

Average Family Income $	48193	Median Family Income $	44285
% Low Income Families	19.1	Average Home Price $	118757
% Home Owners	48	% Unemployment	10.8
% Labour Force Participation	69	% Managerial-Administrative	14.2
% Self-Employed	6.8	% University Degrees	9.7
% Movers	49.5		

D: Industrial Profile

% Manufacturing	16.7	% Service Sector	11.7
% Agriculture	0.4	% Mining	0.1
% Forestry	0	% Fishing	0
% Government Services	6.1	% Business Services	6.3

E: Homogeneity Measures

Ethnic Diversity Index	0.63	Religious Homogeneity Index	0.76
Sectoral Concentration Index	0.46	Income Disparity Index	8.1

F: Physical Setting Characteristics

Total Population	102538	Area (km²)	59
Population Density (pop/km²)	1737.9		

* Tentative value, due to the existence of unpaid campaign expenses.

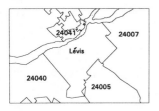

Lévis

Constituency Number: 24038

The riding of Lévis is located on the St Lawrence River, across from Quebec City. It is 99.1% francophone. The average family income of $48,791 is 6% above the provincial average. The riding includes the M.I.L. Davie Shipyard in Lauzon. Other important employers are the Ultramar refinery, Frito-Lay, and Vachon Laboratory (chemicals).

Prior to 1984, Lévis had been held by the Liberals for all but six of the previous 97 years. The Conservatives and the *créditistes* had each won once, the former in 1930 and the latter in 1962. Raynauld Guay held the riding for the Liberals from 1963 until 1981. Gaston Gourde succeeded him in a 1981 by-election, but was crushed three years later when Gabriel Fontaine won Lévis for the Conservatives with a plurality of 15,055 votes, the largest in the Quebec City area. Fontaine served in Ottawa as Deputy Whip. He was supported by the shipbuilders' union, since he helped bring contracts to the shipyard, but he was targeted for defeat by the Public Service Alliance of Canada. The NDP ran one of their stronger candidates in the province: Jean-Paul Harney, a political scientist, won 18.5% of the vote in 1984, the NDP's third best result in the province. Harney had a former head of the Quebec Teachers' Union (CEQ) as his campaign organizer. The Liberal candidate was Denis Sonier, a school principal and municipal councillor. Sonier stressed the issues of keeping the local post office open, and building a new bridge to Quebec City. Not surprisingly given the importance of ship-building to the riding, the issue of nuclear submarines was also quite important. Fontaine won the riding for the second time, with a margin of over 20,671 votes.

Facing corruption charges, Gabriel Fontaine was not allowed to seek re-election for the Conservatives in 1993. Conservatives fielded Serge Léveillé, a sports centre director-general, who received only 14% of the vote. Customer service director for General Trust and former municipal councillor in Saint-Nicholas, Jean-Marc Gagnon represented the Liberals and obtained 21.7% of the vote. Bloc Québécois chose administrator Antoine Dubé who had run for the Parti Nationaliste in Lévis in 1984 and served as political aide to MNA Jean Garon. Dubé won the election handily with 61.5% of the vote, obtaining a margin of victory of 26,203 votes. The main issues were again the M.I.L. Davie Shipyard, and CN job cuts in Charny.

Member of Parliament: Antoine Dubé; **Party:** B.Q.; **Occupation:** Administrator; **Education:** University studies in leisure, social planning, and administration; **Age:** 47 (May 15, 1947); **Year of first election to the House of Commons:** 1993

24038 Lévis

A: Political Profile

i) Voting Behaviour

	% 1993	% 1988	Change 1988-93
Conservative	14	57.4	-43.4
Liberal	21.7	22.2	-0.5
NDP	1.8	19.6	-17.8
Bloc Québécois	61.5	0	61.5
Other	1	0.8	0.2

% Turnout	77.5	Total Ballots (#)	68413
Rejected Ballots (#)	2604	% Margin of Victory	40.8
Rural Polls, 1988 (#)	35	Urban Polls, 1988 (#)	196
% Yes - 1992	30.4	% No - 1992	69.6

ii) Campaign Financing

	# of Donations	Total $ Value	% of Limit Spent
Conservative	144	34849	74.5
Liberal	118	47124	80.5
NDP	2	2200	1.8
Bloc Québécois	316	36517	56.9
Other	0	0	

B: Ethno-Linguistic Profile

% English Home Language	0.7	% French Home Language	99.1
% Official Bilingual	21.5	% Other Home Language	0.2
% Catholics	94.8	% Protestants	1.9
% Aboriginal Peoples	0.2	% Immigrants	1.1

C: Socio-Economic Profile

Average Family Income $	48791	Median Family Income $	45799
% Low Income Families	13.1	Average Home Price $	87129
% Home Owners	68.2	% Unemployment	7.7
% Labour Force Participation	70.2	% Managerial-Administrative	14.5
% Self-Employed	8	% University Degrees	11.4
% Movers	40.8		

D: Industrial Profile

% Manufacturing	13.9	% Service Sector	11.9
% Agriculture	2.5	% Mining	0.2
% Forestry	0.2	% Fishing	0
% Government Services	9.4	% Business Services	4.2

E: Homogeneity Measures

Ethnic Diversity Index	0.92	Religious Homogeneity Index	0.89
Sectoral Concentration Index	0.43	Income Disparity Index	6.1

F: Physical Setting Characteristics

Total Population	117619	Area (km²)	794
Population Density (pop/km²)	148.1		

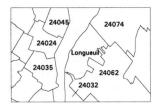

Longueuil

Constituency Number: 24039

The riding of Longueuil is located on the St Lawrence River across from Montreal. The riding is 92.5% francophone. Longueuil's average family income of $45,834 is just below the Quebec average. The riding is highly mobile, with over half of families having moved in the past five years. Economically, Longueuil riding has a significant export sector, including Pratt and Whitney, manufacturer of aircraft engines which provides jobs to approximately 6,000 people. Longueuil is present in the aerospace industry (Heroux Ltd) and in metallurgy.

Prior to 1984, the riding of Longueuil had gone Liberal in nine of eleven general elections since its creation in 1952. The exceptions were 1958 and 1962. In 1984, Conservative Nic Leblanc, former head of an office supplies company, won the riding from Liberal MP Jacques Olivier, with a margin of more than 9,000 votes. Olivier had held the riding since 1972. In an area marked by strong support for the Parti Québécois, Leblanc was helped by PQ organizers in both the 1984 and 1988 campaigns.

The Liberal candidate in Longueuil was considered to be a star: Michel Dupuy was a former ambassador to France and the United Nations, and had also headed the Canadian International Development Agency (CIDA). The NDP candidate was Daniel Senez, a railway union vice-president. Senez stressed the issue of Canada Post super mail-boxes. With a margin of 16,726 votes, Leblanc increased his plurality this time around, winning over twice as many votes as the Liberals' Dupuy.

Following the Meech Lake failure, Nic Leblanc left the Conservatives to become an independent; shortly thereafter, he helped form the Bloc Québécois.

In 1993, the Conservatives ran lawyer Richard Ledoux, a native of Cornwall, Ontario. He was legal advisor for Conservative Marcel Danis at the elections of 1984 and 1988. Ledoux came third with 7.7% of the vote. The Liberals fielded Guy Chartrand, a specialist in Canadian transportation and president of Transport 2000, who received 24.2% of the vote. Sergio Martinez, a professor, represented the NDP and took 1.7% of the vote, a major drop from 1988 when the party had obtained 19.6%. Incumbent Nic Leblanc retained his seat, securing 66% of the vote, with a margin of victory of 24,640 votes.

Member of Parliament: Nic Leblanc; **Party:** B.Q.; **Occupation:** Businessman, Member of Parliament; **Education :** Studies in administration, marketing, and public relations, Université duf Québec et Montréal; **Age:** 53 (Nov. 15, 1941); **Year of first election to the House of Commons:** 1984

24039 Longueuil

A: Political Profile
i) Voting Behaviour

	% 1993	% 1988	Change 1988-93
Conservative	7.7	53.3	-45.6
Liberal	24.2	22.6	1.6
NDP	1.7	19.6	-17.9
Bloc Québécois	66	0	66
Other	0.4	4.5	-4.1

% Turnout	77.4	Total Ballots (#)	61685
Rejected Ballots (#)	2730	% Margin of Victory	42.2
Rural Polls, 1988 (#)	0	Urban Polls, 1988 (#)	225
% Yes - 1992	31.7	% No - 1992	68.3

ii) Campaign Financing

	# of Donations	Total $ Value	% of Limit Spent
Conservative	82	16321	63
Liberal	227	30345	53.4
NDP	6	2450	1.4
Bloc Québécois	338	49165	77.9
Other	0	0	

B: Ethno-Linguistic Profile

% English Home Language	3.4	% French Home Language	92.5
% Official Bilingual	39.8	% Other Home Language	4.2
% Catholics	88.7	% Protestants	3.6
% Aboriginal Peoples	0.6	% Immigrants	8.6

C: Socio-Economic Profile

Average Family Income $	45834	Median Family Income $	40724
% Low Income Families	24	Average Home Price $	124055
% Home Owners	37.7	% Unemployment	12
% Labour Force Participation	68	% Managerial-Administrative	12.2
% Self-Employed	6.4	% University Degrees	10.4
% Movers	56		

D: Industrial Profile

% Manufacturing	17.7	% Service Sector	13.1
% Agriculture	0.4	% Mining	0.1
% Forestry	0	% Fishing	0
% Government Services	6.8	% Business Services	7

E: Homogeneity Measures

Ethnic Diversity Index	0.75	Religious Homogeneity Index	0.78
Sectoral Concentration Index	0.45	Income Disparity Index	11.1

F: Physical Setting Characteristics

Total Population	111847	Area (km²)	45
Population Density (pop/km²)	2485.5		

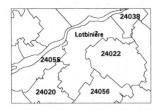

Lotbinière

Constituency Number: 24040

The riding of Lotbinière runs along the south shore of the St Lawrence River, not far east of Quebec City. The riding includes the towns of Victoriaville, Arthabasca, Warwick, and Princeville. The riding is 99.3% francophone. Lotbinière's average family income is 13% below the provincial average, at $39,774. 9.3% of the riding's workforce is involved in agriculture, the third highest level in Quebec. Manufacturing is important to the region's economy with Cascades (pulp and paper), Lactantia (farm products), Sodisco and Mat-Expert (hardware distribution), Vic-West (metallurgy) and Intral (high technology metal).

Lotbinière was held by the Liberals for the first 90 years of Confederation, but it was represented by a Liberal for only five of the following 23 years. R. O'Hurley of the Conservatives held the riding from 1957 to 1963. While the Liberals regained Lotbinière in 1963, they lost it to the *créditistes* in 1968, who held it until 1980. Liberal Jean-Guy Dubois represented the riding from 1980 to 1984, when he was defeated by Maurice Tremblay of the Conservatives, who won with a 2,382 vote margin. In 1988, Tremblay, a lawyer by profession, faced Pierre Lajeunesse of the Liberals. Lajeunesse is a sales representative and municipal councillor for the town of Arthabaska. The NDP ran journalist Richard Lacoursière. Tremblay won the riding for a second time, increasing his margin to 11,518 votes.

In 1993, incumbent Maurice Tremblay received indications that he would not get the support of Prime Minister Kim Campbell due to accusations of wrongdoing. According to press releases, Tremblay was convicted in January 1993 of fraud concerning the use of $5,000 of public money to send members of his riding association (and their spouses) on a trip to Acapulco (Mexico). He has appealed the conviction.

Tremblay decided not to seek re-election. Conservatives were represented this time by Jacques LeSieur, a consultant and special assistant to Conservative MP Maurice Tremblay; he received 15.1% of the vote. Liberals fielded lawyer and Victoriaville municipal councillor Michel Provencher, seeking election for the first time, who came second with 29.7% of the vote. Bloc Québécois Jean Landry, an aerial photographer with connections with the PQ (a founding member) and the CSN, obtained 53.8% of the vote, with a plurality of 12,068 votes. Main issues during the campaign were job creation, universality of social programs, and sovereignty as a means to alleviate regional disparities.

Member of Parliament: Jean Landry; **Party:** B.Q.; **Occupation:** Aerial photographer, cook; **Age:** 46 (Oct. 3, 1948); **Year of first election to the House of Commons:** 1993

24040 Lotbinière

A: Political Profile
i) Voting Behaviour

	% 1993	% 1988	Change 1988-93
Conservative	15.1	52.7	-37.6
Liberal	29.7	29.9	-0.2
NDP	1.4	17.4	-16
Bloc Québécois	53.8	0	53.8
Other	0	0	0

% Turnout	76.5	Total Ballots (#)	52942
Rejected Ballots (#)	2815	% Margin of Victory	24.1
Rural Polls, 1988 (#)	131	Urban Polls, 1988 (#)	103
% Yes - 1992	37.2	% No - 1992	62.8

ii) Campaign Financing

	# of Donations	Total $ Value	% of Limit Spent
Conservative	50	21333	72.4*
Liberal	111	24789	41.8
NDP	1	1000	0
Bloc Québécois	313	25621	50.3
Other	0	0	

B: Ethno-Linguistic Profile

% English Home Language	0.5	% French Home Language	99.3
% Official Bilingual	12.7	% Other Home Language	0.3
% Catholics	96.7	% Protestants	1.7
% Aboriginal Peoples	0.2	% Immigrants	1.2

C: Socio-Economic Profile

Average Family Income $	39774	Median Family Income $	35174
% Low Income Families	14.5	Average Home Price $	67990
% Home Owners	71.3	% Unemployment	10.1
% Labour Force Participation	64.5	% Managerial-Administrative	10.9
% Self-Employed	13.3	% University Degrees	5.1
% Movers	34.2		

D: Industrial Profile

% Manufacturing	24.2	% Service Sector	11.2
% Agriculture	9.3	% Mining	0.2
% Forestry	0.7	% Fishing	0
% Government Services	3.7	% Business Services	2.1

E: Homogeneity Measures

Ethnic Diversity Index	0.94	Religious Homogeneity Index	0.9
Sectoral Concentration Index	0.32	Income Disparity Index	11.6

F: Physical Setting Characteristics

Total Population	94316	Area (km²)	3665
Population Density (pop/km²)	25.7		

* Tentative value, due to the existence of unpaid campaign expenses.

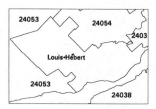

Louis-Hébert

Constituency Number: 24041

The riding of Louis-Hébert includes the affluent western suburbs of Quebec City, Cap-Rouge and Sillery, and the more middle-class suburb of Sainte-Foy. The riding is 96.1% francophone. Its average family income of $62,392 is the fourth highest in Quebec; 28.1% of those fifteen years of age or older have university degrees and 18.8% of the employed constituents are managers or administrators. This is the fifth highest proportion in Quebec. This riding houses several institutions of higher learning, among them Laval University. There is also an important technological park and an international airport.

Louis-Hébert voted Liberal in every general election from 1917 to 1980, with the exception of 1958. Dennis Dawson represented the riding from 1979 until he was defeated in 1984 by Conservative Suzanne Duplessis, who won with a margin of just under 7,000 votes. In the 1988 campaign, Duplessis, a teacher by profession, promised the development of a high-technology industrial park in the riding. She also supported the recriminalization of abortion. The NDP candidate was Pierre Lavigne, affiliated with the École nationale d'administration publique (ÉNAP). The Liberals ran Nicole Duplé, a Laval University lawyer specializing in constitutional law. Duplessis won the riding for a second time, with a margin of just under 21,860 votes.

Suzanne Duplessis tried her chances again for the Conservatives, but could only keep 15.3% of the vote, a drop of 44.5% from the 1988 results. Liberals were trying to reconquer their former stronghold and fielded Margo Brousseau, a Liberal party activist and a lawyer with Arsenault, Moreau, Barakatt & Associates. Brousseau finished second with 25.8% of the vote. Bloc Québécois Philippe Paré, a retired school director, won the riding with a plurality of 18,206 votes, having secured 55.7% of the vote. Natural Law and NDP candidates Michel Nadeau and Karl Adomeit, a student, took respectively 1.5% and 1.3% of the votes. The principal issues of the campaign were economic restructuring and job creation.

Member of Parliament: Philippe Paré; **Party:** B.Q.; **Occupation:** School director, retired; **Education:** BA (pedagogy), licence in careers advising; **Age:** 59 (Aug. 24, 1935);**Year of first election to the House of Commons:** 1993

24041 Louis-Hébert

A: Political Profile
i) Voting Behaviour

	% 1993	% 1988	Change 1988-93
Conservative	15.3	59.8	-44.5
Liberal	25.8	24.8	1
NDP	1.3	13	-11.7
Bloc Québécois	55.7	0	55.7
Other	2	2.4	-0.4

% Turnout	77.2	Total Ballots (#)	62584
Rejected Ballots (#)	1740	% Margin of Victory	31.9
Rural Polls, 1988 (#)	0	Urban Polls, 1988 (#)	236
% Yes - 1992	38	% No - 1992	62

ii) Campaign Financing

	# of Donations	Total $ Value	% of Limit Spent
Conservative	19	31403	57.3
Liberal	83	64448	78.4
NDP	1	1330	0.5
Bloc Québécois	770	49533	95.4
Other	17	14679	

B: Ethno-Linguistic Profile

% English Home Language	2.9	% French Home Language	96.1
% Official Bilingual	44.2	% Other Home Language	1
% Catholics	92.5	% Protestants	1.9
% Aboriginal Peoples	0.2	% Immigrants	4.2

C: Socio-Economic Profile

Average Family Income $	62392	Median Family Income $	54903
% Low Income Families	14.1	Average Home Price $	130051
% Home Owners	54.6	% Unemployment	8.5
% Labour Force Participation	69.2	% Managerial-Administrative	18.8
% Self-Employed	7.2	% University Degrees	28.1
% Movers	45.8		

D: Industrial Profile

% Manufacturing	5.8	% Service Sector	11
% Agriculture	0.7	% Mining	0.1
% Forestry	0.2	% Fishing	0.1
% Government Services	18.6	% Business Services	7.8

E: Homogeneity Measures

Ethnic Diversity Index	0.86	Religious Homogeneity Index	0.85
Sectoral Concentration Index	0.61	Income Disparity Index	12

F: Physical Setting Characteristics

Total Population	97757	Area (km²)	104
Population Density (pop/km²)	940		

Manicouagan

Constituency Number: 24042

The riding of Manicouagan is the second largest in Quebec. It begins along the north shore of the lower St Lawrence River and the Gulf of St Lawrence. It runs from there to the northern extreme of Quebec, along Hudson Strait. The riding includes the towns of Sept-Îles, Port-Cartier, Fermont, and the Inuit community of Kuujjuak. Despite its size, Manicouagan is the province's third smallest riding in terms of population, with just 58,192 residents. The riding is 78.8% francophone and 9.5% anglophone. The riding includes an important proportion of 14.2% of aboriginal people. Manicouagan's average family income of $46,237 is slightly above the provincial average. The 1991 census calculated the unemployment rate to be 18.8%, the fourth highest in Quebec. Manicouagan's 1991 average dwelling value of $56,035 was the fourth lowest in the province. Mining occupies 13.4% of the work force, the highest proportion in Quebec and the sixth highest in Canada. Aluminum smelting (Alouette) is also an important economic agent. This riding is subject to the ups and downs of international markets like few others.

The riding was established in 1947, and prior to 1984 it voted Liberal in all but two elections, those of 1958, when it went Conservative, and 1962, when it elected a *créditiste*. Brian Mulroney, a former president of Iron Ore Canada, won the riding for the Conservatives in 1984, with a margin of 18,568 votes. After Mulroney decided to run in the 1988 campaign in neighbouring Charlevoix due to electoral redistribution, the Conservatives fielded a Liberal: Charles Langlois, card-carrying member of the Quebec Liberal Party. Langlois was the director of a local soft-drink distributor. The Liberals ran Sylvain Garneau, a 26-year-old University of Ottawa political science and management graduate. The NDP candidate was Carol Guay, a union activist who enjoyed some support from Eastern Quebec union leaders, Parti Québécois members and provincial Liberals. There was some doubt during the campaign as to whether the Conservatives would be able to retain the riding. Having the Prime Minister as MP had not saved the area from economic decline: the population of the Sept-Îles area dropped by as much as 30% between 1981 and 1988, while the cities of Schefferville and Gagnonville were becoming ghost towns. In response, the opposition candidates urged voters to elect a member who would 'think Manicouagan'. Despite the economic problems of the area, Langlois won easily for the Conservatives, with a plurality of 10,771 votes.

Langlois represented the Conservatives again in 1993, finishing second with 22.2% of the vote. Liberals parachuted from Montreal Rita Lavoie who took 21.1% of the vote. Similarly NDP fielded Montrealer and 20-year-old student Éric Hébert who secured only 1.7% of the vote. Bernard St-Laurent, a fomer Moisie municipal councillor, won the riding handily with 55% of the vote, and a plurality of 8,847 votes. The main issues were job creation, fishing industry, and development of new infrastructures such as roads, wharfs, and dams (Ste-Marguerite 3).

Member of Parliament: Bernard St-Laurent; **Party:** B.Q.; **Occupation:** Correctional services officer; **Age:** 41 (Dec. 14, 1953); **Year of first election to the House of Common:** 1993

24042 Manicouagan

A: Political Profile

i) Voting Behaviour

	% 1993	% 1988	Change 1988-93
Conservative	22.2	61.7	-39.5
Liberal	21.1	22.9	-1.8
NDP	1.7	14.4	-12.7
Bloc Québécois	55	0	55
Other	0	1	-1

% Turnout	70.2	Total Ballots (#)	27726
Rejected Ballots (#)	698	% Margin of Victory	32.8
Rural Polls, 1988 (#)	71	Urban Polls, 1988 (#)	60
% Yes - 1992	34.4	% No - 1992	65.6

ii) Campaign Financing

	# of Donations	Total $ Value	% of Limit Spent
Conservative	101	28565	95.4*
Liberal	32	16016	21.8
NDP	1	1000	0
Bloc Québécois	396	12669	49.1
Other	0	0	

B: Ethno-Linguistic Profile

% English Home Language	9.5	% French Home Language	78.8
% Official Bilingual	19.4	% Other Home Language	11.8
% Catholics	88	% Protestants	10.4
% Aboriginal Peoples	14.2	% Immigrants	1.2

C: Socio-Economic Profile

Average Family Income $	46237	Median Family Income $	43289
% Low Income Families	14.5	Average Home Price $	56035
% Home Owners	59.4	% Unemployment	18.8
% Labour Force Participation	66.2	% Managerial-Administrative	9.2
% Self-Employed	5.2	% University Degrees	5.2
% Movers	38.3		

D: Industrial Profile

% Manufacturing	7.5	% Service Sector	15
% Agriculture	0.1	% Mining	13.4
% Forestry	0.5	% Fishing	2.6
% Government Services	10	% Business Services	2.3

E: Homogeneity Measures

Ethnic Diversity Index	0.59	Religious Homogeneity Index	0.77
Sectoral Concentration Index	0.33	Income Disparity Index	6.4

F: Physical Setting Characteristics

Total Population	58192	Area (km²)	465680
Population Density (pop/km²)	0.1		

* Tentative value, due to the existence of unpaid campaign expenses.

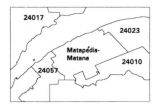

Matapédia–Matane

Constituency Number: 24043

The riding of Matapédia–Matane is located on the northern side of the Gaspé Peninsula. It is bordered on the north by the St Lawrence River and to the south by the State of Maine and the province of New Brunswick. The riding includes the towns of Matane, Mont-Joli, Amqui, Causapscal, and Sayabec. With just 61,942 residents, Matapédia–Matane is Quebec's third smallest riding in terms of population. The riding is 99.6% francophone, the fifth highest level in the country. Its average family income of $36,546 is the lowest in the province. Government transfer payments represent 25.1% of total income, among the highest level in Canada. The 1991 census estimated the riding's unemployment rate at 19.6%, the third highest level in Quebec. Forestry activities occupy 4.9% of the work force, the third highest proportion in Quebec and one of the highest in Canada. Manufacturing sector is present in Matane with Canadian International Paper and Sayabec with Panval Inc. which respectively employ 150 and 225 people.

Since 1921, this riding's MP has sat in opposition only during the 1957 Diefenbaker government and the short-lived 1979 Clark government. Pierre de Bané held the riding for the Liberals from 1968 to 1984, when he did not seek re-election. De Bané held four different portfolios during the last two Trudeau governments, including that of regional economic expansion. In 1984, the Conservative candidate, Jean-Luc Joncas received a margin of just over 6,000 votes. A teacher, Joncas is a former Mayor of Amqui. In 1988, Joncas was opposed by Claude Canuel for the Liberals. Canuel, director of urban services for the town of Matane, was formerly an aide to de Bané. In a region where regional development is always the primary election issue, this background was expected to help Canuel. Montreal businessman Yves Coté was parachuted into the riding for the NDP. Joncas held on to the riding for the Conservatives, though his margin was reduced to 4,378 votes. Coté won 13.4% of the vote for the NDP, the only riding in the Gaspé where the party reached the 10% level.

Joncas sought re-election in 1993 but came third with only 7.7% of the vote, a drop of 42.5%. Matane mayor Maurice Gauthier represented the Liberals, and received 32.6% of the vote. Gauthier was backed by the Public Service Alliance of Canada.

This constituted one of the best showing of the Liberals in francophone constituencies. The NDP parachuted Brossard student Robert McKoy who finished after Natural Law candidate Pierre Gauthier, with 0.7% of the vote. Bloc Québécois candidate was Amqui teacher René Canuel who came first with 57.3% of the vote and a plurality of 7,921 votes. Canuel was appreciated for his commitment to local development and is known to have strong affiliations with the PQ. The main themes were regional development and manpower training.

Member of Parliament: René Canuel; **Party:** B.Q.; **Occupation:** Teacher; **Education:** BA (pedagogy); **Age:** 58 (Oct. 21, 1936); **Year of first election to the House of Commons:** 1993

24043 Matapédia–Matane

A: Political Profile

i) Voting Behaviour

	% 1993	% 1988	Change 1988-93
Conservative	7.7	50.2	-42.5
Liberal	32.6	36.4	-3.8
NDP	0.7	13.4	-12.7
Bloc Québécois	57.3	0	57.3
Other	1.8	0	1.8

% Turnout	71.8	Total Ballots (#)	32595
Rejected Ballots (#)	618	% Margin of Victory	26.5
Rural Polls, 1988 (#)	118	Urban Polls, 1988 (#)	48
% Yes - 1992	33.2	% No - 1992	66.8

ii) Campaign Financing

	# of Donations	Total $ Value	% of Limit Spent
Conservative	45	28604	62.2
Liberal	150	50380	66.5
NDP	1	1000	0
Bloc Québécois	246	28562	56.5
Other	6	1000	

B: Ethno-Linguistic Profile

% English Home Language	0.4	% French Home Language	99.6
% Official Bilingual	8.8	% Other Home Language	0
% Catholics	96.5	% Protestants	2.1
% Aboriginal Peoples	0.6	% Immigrants	0.3

C: Socio-Economic Profile

Average Family Income $	36546	Median Family Income $	31572
% Low Income Families	19.3	Average Home Price $	50897
% Home Owners	70.6	% Unemployment	19.6
% Labour Force Participation	56.2	% Managerial-Administrative	9.5
% Self-Employed	8.9	% University Degrees	4.4
% Movers	30.4		

D: Industrial Profile

% Manufacturing	14.2	% Service Sector	14.5
% Agriculture	6.6	% Mining	0.3
% Forestry	4.9	% Fishing	0.4
% Government Services	6.5	% Business Services	2

E: Homogeneity Measures

Ethnic Diversity Index	0.94	Religious Homogeneity Index	0.91
Sectoral Concentration Index	0.35	Income Disparity Index	13.6

F: Physical Setting Characteristics

Total Population	61942	Area (km²)	10959
Population Density (pop/km²)	5.7		

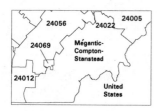

Mégantic–Compton–Stanstead

Constituency Number: 24044

The riding of Mégantic–Compton–Stanstead is located east of Montreal, bordered to the south by the State of Vermont. The riding is 85.6% francophone and 13.9% anglophone. The average family income of $37,307 is 19% below the provincial average. 27.7% of the riding's workforce is employed in the manufacturing sector, the third highest level in the province. The riding includes the towns of Coaticook, East Angus and Lac-Mégantic. Bestar Canada (furniture), Cascades (paper) and Abressa and Taffisa (two Spanish multinationals) are among its main employers. Forestry and farming provide jobs to a group of independent commodity producers.

Claude Tessier held the riding for the Liberals from 1979 to 1984, but lost in the Mulroney sweep of that year to François Gérin, a lawyer who won with a margin of 12,556 votes. In his bid for re-election in 1988, Gérin faced Jean-Guy Landry, a farmer who ran for the Liberals, and teacher Jean-Pierre Walsh of the NDP. Gérin won the riding for a second time, with a slightly reduced margin of victory of 11,680 votes.

François Gérin was the first one to condemn revisions proposed by his party to Meech Lake; he quit the Conservative caucus on May 18, 1990. He later joined forces with Bloc Québécois leader Lucien Bouchard, but did not run in the federal election of October 1993. Conservatives fielded Gilles Goddard, a businessman and former mayor of Ascot Corner, who received 15.7% of the vote. Goddard has strong connections with the provincial Liberals. Liberals ran Compton mayor Eugene Naylor, a farm equipment technician, who finished second with 35.3% of the vote. Bloc Québécois Maurice Bernier, a public servant, took the riding with 44.7% of the vote, and a plurality of 3,612 votes. Bernier had run for the PQ in 1985 and has strong connections to the party. Natural Law teacher Jacqueline Benoît got 2% of the vote. Parachuted NDP teacher Martine Simard, from Laval, came fifth with 1.3%. Central issues during the campaign were railroad transportation, job creation, and creation of small and medium enterprises.

Member of Parliament: Maurice Bernier; **Party:** B.Q.; **Occupation:** Public servant; **Education:** Certificate, psychology of human relations; **Age:** 47 (Mar. 11, 1947); **Year of first election to the House of Commons:** 1993

24044 Mégantic–Compton–Stanstead

A: Political Profile
i) Voting Behaviour

	% 1993	% 1988	Change 1988-93
Conservative	15.7	60.3	-44.6
Liberal	35.3	30	5.3
NDP	1.3	8.3	-7
Bloc Québécois	44.7	0	44.7
Other	3.1	1.4	1.7

% Turnout	73.8	Total Ballots (#)	39762
Rejected Ballots (#)	1267	% Margin of Victory	12.5
Rural Polls, 1988 (#)	146	Urban Polls, 1988 (#)	57
% Yes - 1992	50.5	% No - 1992	49.5

ii) Campaign Financing

	# of Donations	Total $ Value	% of Limit Spent
Conservative	80	30650	93.6
Liberal	223	22999	56
NDP	2	2200	0
Bloc Québécois	288	22358	77
Other	6	486	

B: Ethno-Linguistic Profile

% English Home Language	13.9	% French Home Language	85.6
% Official Bilingual	28.2	% Other Home Language	0.6
% Catholics	84.3	% Protestants	11.7
% Aboriginal Peoples	0.4	% Immigrants	3.2

C: Socio-Economic Profile

Average Family Income $	37307	Median Family Income $	33158
% Low Income Families	16.5	Average Home Price $	71307
% Home Owners	70.8	% Unemployment	10.5
% Labour Force Participation	63	% Managerial-Administrative	10.1
% Self-Employed	13.7	% University Degrees	5.7
% Movers	34.3		

D: Industrial Profile

% Manufacturing	27.7	% Service Sector	12.5
% Agriculture	9	% Mining	0.9
% Forestry	2.4	% Fishing	0.3
% Government Services	4.2	% Business Services	2.3

E: Homogeneity Measures

Ethnic Diversity Index	0.78	Religious Homogeneity Index	0.7
Sectoral Concentration Index	0.31	Income Disparity Index	11.1

F: Physical Setting Characteristics

Total Population	75319	Area (km^2)	6289
Population Density (pop/km^2)	12		

Mercier

Constituency Number: 24045

The riding of Mercier occupies the southeast portion of the Island of Montreal. It contains the town of Montréal-East and part of the Town of Montreal. The riding is highly industrialized, with oil refineries, steel factories, and some high-technology industries. The riding is 91.5% francophone, well above the provincial average. There is a 3,000-strong Italian community. The average family income of $44,065 is slightly below the average for Quebec. This riding has been severely hurt during the last two decades by the closing of several companies, particularly in the sector of oil refineries.

Mercier was created in 1933. In 51 years, the riding was taken by the Conservatives only once: at the time of the Diefenbaker sweep of 1958. Lawyer Carole Jacques won the riding for them in 1984 with a 5,736 vote plurality. The riding was modified in the 1987 redistribution when the old ridings of Saint-Léonard–Anjou and Montréal–Mercier were split into Anjou–Rivière-des-Prairies, Saint-Léonard and Mercier. Transposing the votes cast in the 1984 election to the riding's new boundaries would raise the Conservative margin to 8,000 votes. In 1988, the Liberals ran Luc Chouinard, ex-president of the union at the now-closed Gulf oil refinery. Lawyer André Cordeau contested the election for the NDP. In the 1984 campaign, Cordeau was organizer for Conservative candidate Michel Gravel in the riding of Gamelin. In 1988, Cordeau's chief organizer was a former organizer for then-head of the PQ Pierre-Marc Johnson. A number of local issues were discussed in the campaign, including plant closings, Canada Post's policy of placing super mailboxes in the riding, and Bell Canada's policy of charging long distance rates for phone calls from the riding to some other parts of the Island of Montreal. Jacques held the riding, receiving over twice the votes of the Liberal Chouinard.

Carole Jacques was not allowed to seek re-election under the Tory banner in 1993 due to accusations of possible influence peddling. According to newspapers reports, Jacques received $50,000 from a company who had obtained a lucrative government grant. Jacques ran as an independent and finished third with 15.2% of the vote. Conservatives ran lawyer Gérald Lacoste who finished fourth with 4.2% of the vote. Liberals were represented by party organizer Magda Tadros, an experienced policy adviser and press secretary in Ottawa who came second with 20.1% of the vote. Bloc Québécois Francine Lalonde is a seasoned politician who was appointed Minister responsible for the status of women in the last René Lévesque government; her first two attempts at entering provincial politics were disappointing for her as she lost in both 1985 and 1989. Lalonde, who has developed deep connections with the labour movement, won this working-class riding with 58.9% of the vote, obtaining a plurality of 22,866 votes.

Member of Parliament: Francine Lalonde; **Party:** B.Q.; **Occupation:** Lecturer; **Education:** BA, Licence in history, Université de Montréal; **Age:** 54 (Aug. 24, 1940); **Year of first election to the House of Commons:** 1993

24045 Mercier

A: Political Profile
i) Voting Behaviour

	% 1993	% 1988	Change 1988-93
Conservative	4.2	54.8	-50.6
Liberal	20.1	23	-2.9
NDP	1.2	18.2	-17
Bloc Québécois	58.9	0	58.9
Other	15.8	4	11.8

% Turnout	78.8	Total Ballots (#)	61417
Rejected Ballots (#)	2532	% Margin of Victory	54.6
Rural Polls, 1988 (#)	0	Urban Polls, 1988 (#)	214
% Yes - 1992	33.5	% No - 1992	66.5

ii) Campaign Financing

	# of Donations	Total $ Value	% of Limit Spent
Conservative	145	60910	96
Liberal	99	21924	32*
NDP	1	1000	0
Bloc Québécois	245	47485	90.9
Other	76	55030	

B: Ethno-Linguistic Profile

% English Home Language	3.8	% French Home Language	91.5
% Official Bilingual	35.3	% Other Home Language	4.7
% Catholics	91.2	% Protestants	3.5
% Aboriginal Peoples	0.6	% Immigrants	7

C: Socio-Economic Profile

Average Family Income $	44065	Median Family Income $	41035
% Low Income Families	21.3	Average Home Price $	119030
% Home Owners	42.1	% Unemployment	10.9
% Labour Force Participation	64.5	% Managerial-Administrative	10.2
% Self-Employed	4.6	% University Degrees	5.5
% Movers	48.7		

D: Industrial Profile

% Manufacturing	18.4	% Service Sector	13.9
% Agriculture	0.3	% Mining	0.2
% Forestry	0.1	% Fishing	0
% Government Services	8.2	% Business Services	5.3

E: Homogeneity Measures

Ethnic Diversity Index	0.73	Religious Homogeneity Index	0.78
Sectoral Concentration Index	0.46	Income Disparity Index	6.9

F: Physical Setting Characteristics

Total Population	106721	Area (km²)	55
Population Density (pop/km²)	1940.4		

* Tentative value, due to the existence of unpaid campaign expenses.

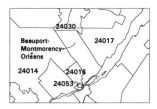

Beauport–Montmorency–Orléans
(formerly Montmorency–Orléans)

Constituency Number: 24046

The riding of Beauport–Montmorency–Orléans runs north from the Island of Orleans in the St Lawrence River, just east of Quebec City, bordering in the north on the ridings of Lac-Saint-Jean and Jonquière. Beauport is the largest town in the riding with 70% of the population. Beauport–Montmorency–Orléans is 99.1% francophone. The average family income of the riding is $45,628, near the Quebec average. The main areas of economic development are concentrated in small manufacturing and tourism.

The voters of Beauport–Montmorency–Orléans tend to elect MPs from the winning party. Since 1921, members from the riding have sat in opposition for just five years. Louis Duclos held the riding for the Liberals from 1974 to 1984, but in the latter year he lost by a margin of 3,527 votes to Anne Blouin of the Conservatives. When Blouin decided not to seek re-election, the party nominated former television journalist Charles DeBlois.

The Liberals hoped to convince Louis Duclos to try to recover his riding, but he declined to seek the nomination, as did Jacques Langlois, Mayor of Beauport. The party settled on the mayor of the small town of Saint-Ferréol-les-Neiges, Robert Paquet.

The NDP ran Éric Gourdeau, a former deputy-minister under René Lévesque (1978-85), Pierre-Marc Johnson, and Robert Bourassa until his resignation in 1986. He was director of the Nouveau-Québec region between 1964 and 1968. Gourdeau attracted much media attention when he spent his campaign planting Norwegian pines in front of homes in the riding. The candidate said he hoped this would stress environmentalism and Norwegian-style full-employment policies. Gourdeau's greening of the riding helped to nearly double the NDP's share of the popular vote, which rose from 8.1% in 1984 to 15.2%. That was still only good enough for third place, and DeBlois held the riding for the Conservatives, with a margin of 19,000 votes, nearly three times the votes of his Liberal opponent.

1993 was to experience major fluctuations in the vote. DeBlois was unable to stop the Bloc Québécois and claimed only 23.1% of the popular vote compared to 60.5% in 1988. The net beneficiary was BQ Michel Guimond, a member of both the Quebec Bar and industrial relations associations, who received 57.7% of the vote. At the time of his nomination, he was in the employ of the firm Caron, Bélanger, Ernst & Young. In 1988, Michel Guimont was ironically DeBlois' official agent. The Liberal candidate, Doris Dawson-Bernard, was not capable of stanching her party's hemorrhage in the region, and saw a further decrease in popularity from 22.9% to 14.4% of the vote. The NDP did not perform well either, dropping from 15.2% to 2.1% as most social democrats joined the BQ. The main issues of the campaign pertained to GATT renegotiations affecting farmers, and jobs in the forest sector at Abitibi-Price (Beaupré) following a decision to put the company up for sale that could lead to a loss of 500 jobs.

Member of Parliament: Michel Guimond; **Party:** B.Q.; **Occupation:** Lawyer; **Education:** LLB, BA in industrial relations; **Age:** 41 (Dec. 26, 1953); **Year of first election to the House of Commons:** 1993

24046 Beauport–Montmorency–Orléans

A: Political Profile
i) Voting Behaviour

	% 1993	% 1988	Change 1988-93
Conservative	23.1	60.5	-37.4
Liberal	14.4	22.9	-8.5
NDP	2.1	15.2	-13.1
Bloc Québécois	57.7	0	57.7
Other	2.6	1.3	1.3

% Turnout	75.5	Total Ballots (#)	57006
Rejected Ballots (#)	2140	% Margin of Victory	37.2
Rural Polls, 1988 (#)	73	Urban Polls, 1988 (#)	127
% Yes - 1992	32.9	% No - 1992	67.1

ii) Campaign Financing

	# of Donations	Total $ Value	% of Limit Spent
Conservative	31	36550	92
Liberal	31	31655	40.5
NDP	4	2728	1.8
Bloc Québécois	253	24413	93.4
Other	7	1004	

B: Ethno-Linguistic Profile

% English Home Language	0.6	% French Home Language	99.1
% Official Bilingual	17.9	% Other Home Language	0.3
% Catholics	96.3	% Protestants	1.4
% Aboriginal Peoples	0.4	% Immigrants	1

C: Socio-Economic Profile

Average Family Income $	45628	Median Family Income $	43607
% Low Income Families	16.3	Average Home Price $	87594
% Home Owners	66.4	% Unemployment	8.6
% Labour Force Participation	66.7	% Managerial-Administrative	12.1
% Self-Employed	6.2	% University Degrees	7.1
% Movers	36.9		

D: Industrial Profile

% Manufacturing	10.3	% Service Sector	14.6
% Agriculture	1.8	% Mining	0.3
% Forestry	0.6	% Fishing	0
% Government Services	12.8	% Business Services	4.1

E: Homogeneity Measures

Ethnic Diversity Index	0.93	Religious Homogeneity Index	0.88
Sectoral Concentration Index	0.5	Income Disparity Index	4.4

F: Physical Setting Characteristics

Total Population	100143	Area (km²)	5418
Population Density (pop/km²)	18.5		

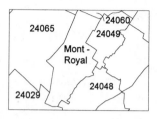

Mont-Royal

Constituency Number: 24047

The riding of Mont-Royal is located in the centre of the Island of Montreal, and includes the towns of Mont-Royal and Hampstead and the city of Côte-Saint-Luc. The riding contains more than 40 ethnic groups, and only 22.6% of the constituents are francophone, the lowest proportion in Quebec. It has the highest proportion of immigrants (41.5%) of any riding in Quebec. Mont-Royal's Jewish community has 51,435 members, representing 55.5% of the population of the riding. The riding is, on average, wealthy and well-educated. Of residents 15 years of age and over, 25.1% have university degrees. The average dwelling value ($291,114 in 1991) is the highest in Quebec while the average family income ($69,899) is the second highest in Quebec. Nearly a fifth of the riding's occupied residents have managerial or administrative jobs. This is the third highest proportion in Quebec. Yet averages can deceive: the riding does contain poorer residents, particularly in the immigrant areas of Snowdon and Côte-des-Neiges.

From 1965 to 1984, Mont-Royal was held by Pierre Elliott Trudeau. After his retirement, Liberal Sheila Finestone, a gerontologist, won the 1984 election with 47.5% of the vote, the party's third best showing in the province. Party critic for communications, Finestone was one of only seven MPs who voted against the Meech Lake accord. In the 1988 campaign, she emphasized issues of housing and pensions. In a riding considered one of the safest Liberal seats in Canada, the Conservatives sacrificed Robert Presser, a 23-year-old computer consultant, who won respect for his in-depth knowledge of the free trade and Meech Lake agreements. The NDP ran lawyer Tariq Alvi. Born in England of Pakistani parents, Alvi worked as a legal researcher with the Centre for Research-Action in race relations. To no-one's surprise, Finestone won the riding again, this time with a 12,753 vote margin. Her 59.9% of the vote represented the Liberals' best showing in Quebec, and sixth best in the country.

Party critic for communications and culture, Sheila Finestone sought re-election for the Liberals in 1993; she finished first with an impressive 82.9% of the vote. This was the best score obtained by the Liberals in Canada in 1993. Bloc Québécois ran 20-year-old student Guillaume Dumas who came second with 7% of the vote. Conservatives ran lawyer Neil Drabkin who obtained 5.8%. Journalist Michael Richard Werbowski secured 1.7% of the vote for the NDP. Independent candidate dental surgeon Harry Polansky, backed by the Equality party, took only 1.1% of the vote. Main issues during the campaign were job creation as well as the economy, language, and the effects of sovereignty on the well-being of the constituents.

Member of Parliament: Sheila Finestone; **Party:** Liberal; **Occupation:** Administrator, Member of Parliament; **Education:** BSc, McGill University; **Age:** 67 (Jan. 28, 1927); **Year of first election to the House of Commons:** 1984

24047 Mont-Royal

A: Political Profile
i) Voting Behaviour

	% 1993	% 1988	Change 1988-93
Conservative	5.8	31.9	-26.1
Liberal	82.9	59.9	23
NDP	1.7	5.4	-3.7
Bloc Québécois	7	0	7
Other	2.7	2.8	-0.1

% Turnout	80.1	Total Ballots (#)	48315
Rejected Ballots (#)	572	% Margin of Victory	75.9
Rural Polls, 1988 (#)	0	Urban Polls, 1988 (#)	190
% Yes - 1992	88.2	% No - 1992	11.8

ii) Campaign Financing

	# of Donations	Total $ Value	% of Limit Spent
Conservative	60	41883	73.5
Liberal	126	61431	89.8
NDP	5	313	0.6
Bloc Québécois	40	11755	15.3
Other	6	4415	

B: Ethno-Linguistic Profile

% English Home Language	56.3	% French Home Language	22.6
% Official Bilingual	54.7	% Other Home Language	21.1
% Catholics	28.6	% Protestants	9.6
% Aboriginal Peoples	0.1	% Immigrants	41.5

C: Socio-Economic Profile

Average Family Income $	69899	Median Family Income $	50391
% Low Income Families	24.6	Average Home Price $	291114
% Home Owners	39.7	% Unemployment	12.4
% Labour Force Participation	60.2	% Managerial-Administrative	19.4
% Self-Employed	15.1	% University Degrees	25.1
% Movers	41.5		

D: Industrial Profile

% Manufacturing	18.2	% Service Sector	10.6
% Agriculture	0.1	% Mining	0
% Forestry	0	% Fishing	0
% Government Services	2.6	% Business Services	11.1

E: Homogeneity Measures

Ethnic Diversity Index	0.36	Religious Homogeneity Index	0.58
Sectoral Concentration Index	0.55	Income Disparity Index	27.9

F: Physical Setting Characteristics

Total Population	94296	Area (km²)	23
Population Density (pop/km²)	4099.8		

Notre-Dame-de-Grâce

Constituency Number: 24048

Located in the centre-south part of the Island of Montreal, the riding of Notre-Dame-de-Grâce contains the towns of Saint-Pierre and Montréal-Ouest, and a western part of the town of Montreal. The riding is 60.3% anglophone, the highest proportion in the province. 29.6% of the riding's residents are immigrants, the fifth-highest proportion in the province. Italophones constitute 5% of the population in this riding. Of the population fifteen years of age or older, 27% have university degrees. The average family income of $54,120 is well above the provincial average, and the average dwelling value of $192,109 is the fifth highest in Quebec. Important employers in the riding include Monsanto (metal products) and Krueger (paper recycling).

The riding has been held since 1965 by Warren Allmand, who had various cabinet posts in the 1970s. Allmand's 1984 victory was a tight race against Montreal Citizens' Movement founder Nick Auf der Maur. The riding was modified somewhat in the 1987 redistribution, with the western part of the riding passing to Lachine–Lac-Saint-Louis riding. Based on 1984 votes, the change improved the Liberal party advantage. In the 1988 campaign, the NDP ran Italian-born Maria Peluso, the president of a refuge for homeless women, and regional director of the Canadian Council for Christians and Jews. The Conservative candidate was Samir Chebeir, a gynaecologist and hospital administrator born in Lebanon. Parachuted into the riding, Chebeir showed little interest in campaigning. On election night, Allmand received almost twice as many votes as his Conservative opponent. The 27.9% of the vote received by the Conservatives was their worst result in Quebec.

In 1993, critic for Immigration Allmand ran again and was elected for his ninth consecutive victory, with a plurality of 22,913 votes over his closest opponent, Bloc Québécois Gilbert Ouellet. The BQ candidate, a retail sales manager, secured only 14.2% of the vote. Conservatives fielded Maeve Quaid, a Trent University professor; she finished third with 6.5% of the vote. NDP ran University of Montreal doctoral candidate Bruce Toombs who secured 3.5% of the vote. Controversial McGill University psychology professor Don Donderi received 1.3%, finishing sixth. Issues raised during the campaign pertained to language policy, affordable housing, and sovereignty. This riding registered the second highest level of support to the Charlottetown Accord in Quebec and the fourth highest in Canada.

Member of Parliament: Warren Allmand; **Party:** Liberal; **Occupation:** Lawyer, Member of Parliament; **Education:** BCL (civil law degree), University of Paris and the Institute of Comparative Law; **Age:** 62 (Sept. 19, 1932); **Year of first election to the House of Commons:** 1965

24048 Notre-Dame-de-Grâce

A: Political Profile
i) Voting Behaviour

	% 1993	% 1988	Change 1988-93
Conservative	6.5	27.9	-21.4
Liberal	70.7	54.6	16.1
NDP	3.5	12.3	-8.8
Bloc Québécois	14.2	0	14.2
Other	5.3	5.3	0

% Turnout	79.8	Total Ballots (#)	41091
Rejected Ballots (#)	583	% Margin of Victory	56.5
Rural Polls, 1988 (#)	0	Urban Polls, 1988 (#)	169
% Yes - 1992	77.2	% No - 1992	22.8

ii) Campaign Financing

	# of Donations	Total $ Value	% of Limit Spent
Conservative	81	19634	55.6
Liberal	112	39256	68.9
NDP	40	6268	10
Bloc Québécois	53	9231	12.7
Other	39	8988	

B: Ethno-Linguistic Profile

% English Home Language	60.3	% French Home Language	25.4
% Official Bilingual	57.3	% Other Home Language	14.3
% Catholics	50.5	% Protestants	22.5
% Aboriginal Peoples	0.3	% Immigrants	29.6

C: Socio-Economic Profile

Average Family Income $	54120	Median Family Income $	43965
% Low Income Families	25.8	Average Home Price $	192109
% Home Owners	31	% Unemployment	12.8
% Labour Force Participation	65	% Managerial-Administrative	15.8
% Self-Employed	10.5	% University Degrees	27
% Movers	47.3		

D: Industrial Profile

% Manufacturing	14.1	% Service Sector	11.9
% Agriculture	0.2	% Mining	0.1
% Forestry	0.1	% Fishing	0
% Government Services	3.7	% Business Services	10.9

E: Homogeneity Measures

Ethnic Diversity Index	0.19	Religious Homogeneity Index	0.34
Sectoral Concentration Index	0.56	Income Disparity Index	18.8

F: Physical Setting Characteristics

Total Population	78703	Area (km²)	15
Population Density (pop/km²)	5246.9		

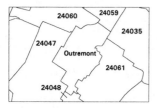

Outremont

Constituency Number: 24049

The riding of Outremont is located in the centre of the Island of Montreal, to the north of Saint-Henri-Westmount. It includes parts of the affluent residential areas of gentry-class Outremont and upper Westmount, Mile End and part of the Côte-des-Neiges immigrant district. The riding is 55.2% francophone, well below the provincial average. There is a Jewish community of over 24,000 people in the riding, and significant Greek and Jamaican communities. About one-third of the riding's constituents were born outside Canada, the fourth highest average in Quebec. Outremont's constituents are well educated: 32.2% of those fifteen years of age and over have university degrees, well above the Quebec average. The average family income for the riding, $54,916, is also well above the provincial average. The riding's 1991 average dwelling value of $259,498 was the third highest in the province. Yet it is a highly mobile riding, 55.9% of families having moved in the past five years.

Since its creation in 1947, Outremont has always voted Liberal. Marc Lalonde held the riding from 1972 to the end of the Trudeau era, a period during which he held six cabinet portfolios in three Trudeau governments. Lucie Pépin won the riding in 1984. Pépin, a former president of the National Advisory Council on the Status of Women, emphasized day-care and programs for immigrant groups in the 1988 campaign. The Conservative candidate in the 1988 campaign was psychology university professor Jean-Pierre Hogue. Hogue, like many Conservative candidates in the Montreal area, promised to work to bring the new space agency to the riding. He enjoyed some support from provincial Liberals. The NDP fielded translator Louise O'Neill in Outremont. O'Neill, a party vice-president in Quebec and an activist in the Montreal Citizens' Movement, promised to focus on the needs of low income residents in the Côte-des-Neiges area. As a pro-choice MP Pépin may have been hurt in the 1988 race by the campaign against her waged by anti-abortion activists. She became the first Liberal ever to lose in Outremont, losing to Hogue by 1,702 votes. The NDP's O'Neill received 20.5% of the vote, one of only ten ridings in the province where the party surpassed the 20% mark.

In 1993, Hogue sought re-election but finished third with only 8.7% of the vote. He was described as an absentee MP during the campaign. Hogue was opposed by Liberal lawyer Martin Cauchon who reconquered this earlier Liberal bastion with 47.1% of the vote. Bloc Québécois economist Jean-Louis Hérivault, backed by the PQ, came second with 37.4% of the vote. NDP psychologist Catherine Kallos got 4.5% of the vote.

Member of Parliament: Martin Cauchon; **Party:** Liberal; **Occupation:** Lawyer; **Education:** LL.M, Master of International Business; **Age:** 32 (Aug. 23, 1962); **Year of first election to the House of Commons:** 1993

24049 Outremont

A: Political Profile

i) Voting Behaviour

	% 1993	% 1988	Change 1988-93
Conservative	8.7	38.4	-29.7
Liberal	47.1	34.7	12.4
NDP	4.5	20.5	-16
Bloc Québécois	37.4	0	37.4
Other	2.4	6.4	-4

% Turnout	78.2	Total Ballots (#)	47432
Rejected Ballots (#)	1317	% Margin of Victory	9.7
Rural Polls, 1988 (#)	0	Urban Polls, 1988 (#)	183
% Yes - 1992	56.4	% No - 1992	43.6

ii) Campaign Financing

	# of Donations	Total $ Value	% of Limit Spent
Conservative	14	64813	97.5
Liberal	55	23491	85.5
NDP	3	3393	4.4
Bloc Québécois	254	54260	97
Other	12	470	

B: Ethno-Linguistic Profile

% English Home Language	21.8	% French Home Language	55.2
% Official Bilingual	58.2	% Other Home Language	23.1
% Catholics	55.5	% Protestants	6.3
% Aboriginal Peoples	0.2	% Immigrants	32.2

C: Socio-Economic Profile

Average Family Income $	54916	Median Family Income $	38001
% Low Income Families	32.6	Average Home Price $	259498
% Home Owners	21.8	% Unemployment	14.4
% Labour Force Participation	66.7	% Managerial-Administrative	15
% Self-Employed	11.3	% University Degrees	32.2
% Movers	55.9		

D: Industrial Profile

% Manufacturing	14.6	% Service Sector	12.8
% Agriculture	0.2	% Mining	0
% Forestry	0.1	% Fishing	0
% Government Services	4.8	% Business Services	11.2

E: Homogeneity Measures

Ethnic Diversity Index	0.3	Religious Homogeneity Index	0.4
Sectoral Concentration Index	0.6	Income Disparity Index	30.8

F: Physical Setting Characteristics

Total Population	94124	Area (km²)	12
Population Density (pop/km²)	7843.7		

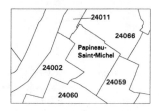

Papineau–Saint-Michel

Constituency Number: 24050

The riding of Papineau–Saint-Michel is located in the northwest portion of the Town of Montreal. It is bordered on the east by Saint-Léonard and to the south by Rosemont. The riding is 65.2% francophone, 8% anglophone. The constituency has a high percentage of immigrants (29.4%) with a strong Italian community of more than 10% of the population. The riding is a relatively poor one. Its average family income of $33,782 is the second lowest in Quebec and the fourth lowest in Canada. 27.1% of the riding's labourforce works in the manufacturing sector, the fifth highest average in Quebec. Over a third of constituents fifteen years of age and over have less than a Grade 9 education.

The riding of Papineau was created in 1947 and has always voted Liberal. André Ouellet has held the riding since his election in a 1967 by-election which was held due to Guy Favreau's resignation as a cabinet minister. Ouellet, a lawyer by profession, held various cabinet posts during the Liberal reign in Ottawa. He barely survived the Conservatives' 1984 sweep of Quebec, holding the riding with a plurality of 701 votes. Ouellet is also associated with the S-31 bill, which was tabled and later withdrawn after political pressures had been exercised, to prevent the Quebec Caisse de dépôt et placement from buying into Canadian Pacific. In the 1988 campaign, Ouellet focused on the issues of low-cost and seniors' housing. The Conservative candidate in the 1988 race was Frank Venneri, a Montreal city councillor elected with the Montreal Citizens' Movement in 1986. Venneri hoped to win the riding with the support of Italian voters, and his campaign literature suggested that he was supported by the Pope. The NDP also ran an Italian candidate, restaurant chef Giovanni Adamo. Ouellet won the 1988 race with a healthy margin of 5,028 votes.

In 1993, André Ouellet regained his seat with a smaller margin of victory of 4,916 votes, for 52% of valid votes. Social worker Daniel Boucher, a former NDP candidate in Anjou and vice-president of the Party in 1992-1993 with affiliation to the Quebec Federation of Labour (QFL), ran for the Bloc Québécois and finished second with 39.2% of the vote. Conservatives fielded Carmen de Pontbriand who took 4.4% of the vote. NDP Gisèle Charlebois, a secretary, secured only 1.8%, compared to the 15.1% the party had obtained in 1988. Among the issues debated were sovereignty, job creation, and lost-cost housing.

Member of Parliament: André Ouellet; **Party:** Liberal; **Occupation:** Lawyer, Member of Parliament; **Education:** LL.L (civil law degree), Université de Sherbrooke; **Age:** 55 (Apr. 6, 1939); **Year of first election to the House of Commons:** 1967

24050 Papineau–Saint-Michel

A: Political Profile
i) Voting Behaviour

	% 1993	% 1988	Change 1988-93
Conservative	4.4	33.2	-28.8
Liberal	52	46	6
NDP	1.8	15.1	-13.3
Bloc Québécois	39.2	0	39.2
Other	2.7	5.7	-3

% Turnout	75.4	Total Ballots (#)	39842
Rejected Ballots (#)	1241	% Margin of Victory	12.8
Rural Polls, 1988 (#)	0	Urban Polls, 1988 (#)	186
% Yes - 1992	55.7	% No - 1992	44.3

ii) Campaign Financing

	# of Donations	Total $ Value	% of Limit Spent
Conservative	17	8084	49.7*
Liberal	219	126969	78.1
NDP	2	2673	0.9
Bloc Québécois	175	19876	35.2
Other	7	855	

B: Ethno-Linguistic Profile

% English Home Language	8	% French Home Language	65.2
% Official Bilingual	38.5	% Other Home Language	26.9
% Catholics	82.1	% Protestants	7.7
% Aboriginal Peoples	0.4	% Immigrants	29.4

C: Socio-Economic Profile

Average Family Income $	33782	Median Family Income $	29465
% Low Income Families	38.8	Average Home Price $	138308
% Home Owners	27	% Unemployment	17.1
% Labour Force Participation	58.3	% Managerial-Administrative	7
% Self-Employed	4.7	% University Degrees	6
% Movers	48.7		

D: Industrial Profile

% Manufacturing	27.1	% Service Sector	15
% Agriculture	0.1	% Mining	0
% Forestry	0	% Fishing	0
% Government Services	4.7	% Business Services	5.3

E: Homogeneity Measures

Ethnic Diversity Index	0.34	Religious Homogeneity Index	0.68
Sectoral Concentration Index	0.41	Income Disparity Index	12.8

F: Physical Setting Characteristics

Total Population	85440	Area (km²)	11
Population Density (pop/km²)	7767.3		

* Tentative value, due to the existence of unpaid campaign expenses.

Pierrefonds–Dollard

Constituency Number: 24051

The riding of Pierrefonds–Dollard occupies the northwest part of the Island of Montreal, and includes the towns of Pierrefonds, Roxboro, Dollard-des-Ormeaux and Sainte-Geneviève. It also includes Île Bizard. The riding is only 34.9% francophone, the third lowest proportion in the province. The riding contains one of Quebec's larger Jewish communities. 18.6% of the riding's workforce occupy managerial and administrative positions, the sixth highest level in Quebec. The average family income of $58,437 is well above the Quebec average. The riding houses several pharmaceutical enterprises.

The riding of Dollard was created in 1952, and prior to 1984 it had always been Liberal. Louis Desmarais was its MP from 1979 to 1984, but he was defeated in the Mulroney landslide of that year by Conservative Gerry Weiner, a pharmacist and ex-Mayor of Dollard. Weiner beat his Liberal opponent by 4,625 votes. Weiner served as a parliamentary secretary to the Minister of Immigration before being appointed Minister for Multiculturalism. The 1987 redistribution of the riding was expected to widen his edge over the Liberals. For their part, the Liberals hoped to recapture the riding with physician Bernard Patry. Patry served 18 years as mayor of Île Bizard, before losing the 1987 election after it came to light that he had made $94,000 from a land flip in his own town. His campaign focused on environmental issues. The NDP ran administrator and finance consultant Pierre Razik. Weiner maintained his 5,288 vote margin in the 1988 campaign.

Liberals again ran Bernard Patry in 1993; he won the riding with a plurality of 29,262 votes. Incumbent Gerry Weiner lost the riding as he could only secure 13.2% of the vote. Bloc Québécois shipmaster (Air Canada) René de Cotret Opzoomer finished second with 10,712 votes or 17.4% of the vote. Community worker Catherine J. Rideout-Érais represented the NDP and obtained 1.4% of the vote. Lionel Albert, a computer analyst, ran unofficially for the Equality party and finished eighth.

Member of Parliament: Bernard Patry; **Party:** Liberal; **Occupation:** General practitioner; **Education:** PhD, Faculty of Medicine, Université de Montréal; **Age:** 51 (Jan. 30, 1943); **Year of first election to the House of Commons:** 1993

24051 Pierrefonds–Dollard

A: Political Profile
i) Voting Behaviour

	% 1993	% 1988	Change 1988-93
Conservative	13.2	49.8	-36.6
Liberal	65	40.2	24.8
NDP	1.4	7	-5.6
Bloc Québécois	17.4	0	17.4
Other	3.1	3	0.1

% Turnout	81	Total Ballots (#)	62439
Rejected Ballots (#)	925	% Margin of Victory	47.6
Rural Polls, 1988 (#)	0	Urban Polls, 1988 (#)	195
% Yes - 1992	76.2	% No - 1992	23.8

ii) Campaign Financing

	# of Donations	Total $ Value	% of Limit Spent
Conservative	71	39837	60*
Liberal	225	50889	54.3*
NDP	2	2317	0.2
Bloc Québécois	158	19684	27.3
Other	29	9961	

B: Ethno-Linguistic Profile

% English Home Language	53.7	% French Home Language	34.9
% Official Bilingual	59.6	% Other Home Language	11.4
% Catholics	56.5	% Protestants	17.4
% Aboriginal Peoples	0.1	% Immigrants	25.8

C: Socio-Economic Profile

Average Family Income $	58437	Median Family Income $	53325
% Low Income Families	13	Average Home Price $	143092
% Home Owners	70.7	% Unemployment	9.9
% Labour Force Participation	73.2	% Managerial-Administrative	18.6
% Self-Employed	8.8	% University Degrees	18.2
% Movers	47.8		

D: Industrial Profile

% Manufacturing	19.9	% Service Sector	9.7
% Agriculture	0.4	% Mining	0.1
% Forestry	0.1	% Fishing	0
% Government Services	3.3	% Business Services	8.3

E: Homogeneity Measures

Ethnic Diversity Index	0.24	Religious Homogeneity Index	0.4
Sectoral Concentration Index	0.49	Income Disparity Index	8.7

F: Physical Setting Characteristics

Total Population	116085	Area (km²)	73
Population Density (pop/km²)	1590.2		

* Tentative value, due to the existence of unpaid campaign expenses.

Pontiac–Gatineau–Labelle

Constituency Number: 24052

The riding of Pontiac–Gatineau–Labelle is located north of Ottawa. The Ottawa River forms much of its southern limit, while to the north it borders on the riding of Témiscamingue. The riding includes the towns of Maniwaki, Mont-Laurier and Low. Pontiac–Gatineau–Labelle is 75.5% francophone, 23.7% anglophone; 4.7% are aboriginals. The average family income of $40,296 is 12% below the provincial average. The forestry sector employs 5.3% of the riding's work force, the second highest proportion in the province and the tenth in Canada. Important local employers in the forest sector are Atlas and CedBec (Gatineau) and Davidson (Pontiac).

MPs from the riding tend to sit on the government side of the House of Commons. Since 1921, the riding has elected members to sit in opposition only in the three minority elections of 1957, 1963 and 1979. Thomas Lefebvre represented the area for the Liberals from 1965 to 1984, but did not run in the 1984 election. Chartered accountant Barry Moore won the riding for the Conservatives in 1984 with a margin of 11,729 votes. In his bid for re-election in 1988 he faced Brian Murphy, a farmer running for the Liberals, and the NDP's John Trent, a professor of political science at University of Ottawa and head of the Council of Canadians. Moore held the riding, his margin slightly reduced to 8,933 votes.

In 1993 Barry Moore sought re-election but received only 21.9% of the vote. Liberals won the riding with life insurer Robert Bertrand. Fort-Coulonge's Bertrand secured the first position with 40.3% of the vote. Bloc Québécois conservation officer and former Sainte-Véronique mayor Claude Radermaker came second with 33.7% of the vote. Radermaker received notable backing from the Labelle sector of the riding. The principal issue during the campaign was job creation.

Member of Parliament: Robert Bertrand; **Party:** Liberal; **Occupation:** Life insurer; **Education:** Studies in science and engineering, financial services and financial planning courses; **Age:** 41; **Year of first election to the House of Commons:** 1993

24052 Pontiac–Gatineau–Labelle

A: Political Profile
i) Voting Behaviour

	% 1993	% 1988	Change 1988-93
Conservative	21.9	53.6	-31.7
Liberal	40.3	30.2	10.1
NDP	1.6	16.2	-14.6
Bloc Québécois	33.7	0	33.7
Other	2.6	0	2.6

% Turnout	72.9	Total Ballots (#)	43769
Rejected Ballots (#)	772	% Margin of Victory	6.6
Rural Polls, 1988 (#)	190	Urban Polls, 1988 (#)	33
% Yes - 1992	52.2	% No - 1992	47.8

ii) Campaign Financing

	# of Donations	Total $ Value	% of Limit Spent
Conservative	134	33925	83.6
Liberal	62	14225	48.4
NDP	0**	0**	0**
Bloc Québécois	389	37153	44.2
Other	49	7364	

B: Ethno-Linguistic Profile

% English Home Language	23.7	% French Home Language	75.5
% Official Bilingual	33.2	% Other Home Language	0.7
% Catholics	84.4	% Protestants	10.8
% Aboriginal Peoples	4.7	% Immigrants	2

C: Socio-Economic Profile

Average Family Income $	40296	Median Family Income $	34391
% Low Income Families	17.3	Average Home Price $	73963
% Home Owners	75.1	% Unemployment	16.6
% Labour Force Participation	61.3	% Managerial-Administrative	10.5
% Self-Employed	11.5	% University Degrees	6.4
% Movers	35.4		

D: Industrial Profile

% Manufacturing	10.4	% Service Sector	13.3
% Agriculture	4.1	% Mining	0.8
% Forestry	5.3	% Fishing	0.2
% Government Services	10.9	% Business Services	2.9

E: Homogeneity Measures

Ethnic Diversity Index	0.65	Religious Homogeneity Index	0.7
Sectoral Concentration Index	0.37	Income Disparity Index	14.7

F: Physical Setting Characteristics

Total Population	80038	Area (km²)	44905
Population Density (pop/km²)	1.8		

** No return filed.

Portneuf

Constituency Number: 24053

The riding of Portneuf is located just northwest of Quebec City. It begins along the St Lawrence River, and runs 70 kilometres northwest from there. The riding includes the town of the same name, and the towns of Donnacona, Saint-Augustin and Val-Bélair. The riding is 98% francophone. Portneuf's average family income of $44,371 is slightly below the provincial average. 11.5% of the riding's workforce hold managerial and administrative positions. Valcartier military base is located in this riding. There are also some industrial parks.

The Liberals won every election here from 1882 to 1957. The Conservatives won the riding in the Diefenbaker landslide of 1958, and from 1962 to 1974 the riding was in *créditiste* hands. The Liberals recovered the riding in 1974. Rolland Dion held the riding for the Liberals from 1979 until he lost by 6,110 votes to industrial designer Conservative Marc Ferland in 1984. In 1988, the Liberals ran Paulin Plamondon, a businessman from Saint-Raymond in the riding. The NDP candidate was Jean-Marie Fiset. Ferland won the riding for a second time, with a margin of 12,838 votes. Ferland received over twice the votes of his Liberal opponent.

In 1993, Marc Ferland sought re-election for the Conservatives, obtaining only 14.8% of the vote. Paulin Plamondon ran again for the Liberals and finished second with 23.1% of the vote. Bloc Québécois Pierre de Savoye, a consultant, got 53.6% of the vote, a margin of victory of 13,683 votes. *Créditiste* MP from 1968 to 1979, writer René Matte who had first obtained the nomination for the Bloc Québécois was disqualified following suspicions of wrongdoing and ran as an independent; he received 5.1% of the vote. NDP fielded John MacFarlane, a sessional lecturer, who finished sixth with 1.4% of the vote. Main issues were job creation and development of small and medium enterprises.

Member of Parliament: Pierre de Savoye; **Party:** B.Q.; **Occupation:** Professor and I.S. consultant; **Education:** BA in education sciences; **Age:** 52 (Nov. 12, 1942); **Year of first election to the House of Common** : 1993

24053 Portneuf

A: Political Profile
i) Voting Behaviour

	% 1993	% 1988	Change 1988-93
Conservative	14.8	57.4	-42.6
Liberal	23.1	26.5	-3.4
NDP	1.4	12.2	-10.8
Bloc Québécois	53.6	0	53.6
Other	7.1	3.9	3.2

% Turnout	72.4	Total Ballots (#)	46649
Rejected Ballots (#)	1778	% Margin of Victory	37.6
Rural Polls, 1988 (#)	105	Urban Polls, 1988 (#)	62
% Yes - 1992	34.5	% No - 1992	65.5

ii) Campaign Financing

	# of Donations	Total $ Value	% of Limit Spent
Conservative	21	6982	79.5
Liberal	46	10273	79.8
NDP	4	1225	0
Bloc Québécois	221	20443	70.3
Other	122	28780	

B: Ethno-Linguistic Profile

% English Home Language	1.8	% French Home Language	98
% Official Bilingual	19.6	% Other Home Language	0.2
% Catholics	96.1	% Protestants	1.6
% Aboriginal Peoples	0.4	% Immigrants	1

C: Socio-Economic Profile

Average Family Income $	44371	Median Family Income $	40897
% Low Income Families	13.4	Average Home Price $	79157
% Home Owners	75.4	% Unemployment	10.5
% Labour Force Participation	64.5	% Managerial-Administrative	11.5
% Self-Employed	8.7	% University Degrees	7.7
% Movers	37		

D: Industrial Profile

% Manufacturing	13.9	% Service Sector	16
% Agriculture	4.5	% Mining	0.5
% Forestry	1.6	% Fishing	0.1
% Government Services	17.4	% Business Services	3.8

E: Homogeneity Measures

Ethnic Diversity Index	0.91	Religious Homogeneity Index	0.9
Sectoral Concentration Index	0.37	Income Disparity Index	7.8

F: Physical Setting Characteristics

Total Population	84947	Area (km²)	3964
Population Density (pop/km²)	21.4		

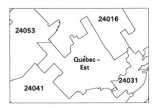

Québec-Est

Constituency Number: 24054

Québec-Est, as the name does not indicate, comprises the western part of Quebec City. The riding includes also the towns of l'Ancienne-Lorette and Vanier. The riding is 98.6% francophone. The average family income of $45,350 approximates the provincial average. The main employer is the Quebec government.

In the 107 years prior to 1984, Québec-Est had been represented by just six members. A by-election ten years after Confederation was won by a 36-year-old lawyer, Wilfrid Laurier. He held the riding until his death in 1919. In that year the riding passed to Ernest Lapointe, who represented it until 1942 for the Liberals. Lapointe was Minister of Justice for a time. Louis Saint-Laurent won a 1942 by-election in the election, and held it until 1957. Québec-Est, home of two Liberal Prime Ministers, voted Conservative in 1958, and *créditiste* in 1962 and 1963. But in 1965 it reverted to the Liberals, being won by Gérard Duquet, who held it until his defeat in 1984. Conservative Marcel Tremblay won the riding in 1984 with a margin of over 5,000 votes. Tremblay entered the 1988 campaign suffering from low public visibility: a public poll showed that only 9% of the riding's voters could name their MP. The 1987 electoral redistribution was expected to help his cause. Rémi Bujold ran for the Liberals. A close confidant of Quebec Premier Robert Bourassa and former MP for the riding of Bonaventure–Îles-de-la-Madeleine, Bujold was chief organizer of the Liberal campaign for the province. Jeanne Lalanne, a community worker, ran for the NDP. Whether or not the voters of Québec-Est knew Marcel Tremblay by name, they were willing to re-elect him in 1988: he won easily, with a margin of 15,761 votes over Bujold.

In 1993, Marcel Tremblay sought a third mandate but could do no better than third place with 11.3% of the vote. Liberals fielded former provincial *créditiste* leader Camil Samson, a populist, who obtained 24.4% of the vote. Samson was backed by provincial Liberals Marc-Yvan Côté, Michel Després, Rémi Poulin and Jean-Guy Lemieux. Camil Samson was campaigning for the 'No' side during the 1980 referendum. Bloc Québécois was represented by Ontario-born writer Jean-Paul Marchand who won the riding with a plurality of 20,443 votes. NDP parachuted Verdun candidate Stéphanie Mitchell who finished in fifth position with 1.7% of the vote. Among the main issues of the campaign were: unemployment insurance reform, creation of small and medium enterprises, and depollution of the Saint-Charles River.

Member of Parliament: Jean-Paul Marchand; **Party:** B.Q.; **Occupation:** Professor; **Education:** PhD (Philosophy); **Age:** 50 (Sept. 13, 1944); **Year of first election to the House of Commons:** 1993

24054 Québec-Est

A: Political Profile
i) Voting Behaviour

	% 1993	% 1988	Change 1988-93
Conservative	11.3	55.7	-44.4
Liberal	24.4	25.9	-1.5
NDP	1.7	14.3	-12.6
Bloc Québécois	59.6	0	59.6
Other	3	4.1	-1.1

% Turnout	75.5	Total Ballots (#)	60599
Rejected Ballots (#)	2548	% Margin of Victory	38.2
Rural Polls, 1988 (#)	0	Urban Polls, 1988 (#)	215
% Yes - 1992	33.7	% No - 1992	66.3

ii) Campaign Financing

	# of Donations	Total $ Value	% of Limit Spent
Conservative	122	54311	78.4*
Liberal	93	71948	99.9
NDP	2	2200	0
Bloc Québécois	106	7119	39.4
Other	11	1568	

B: Ethno-Linguistic Profile

% English Home Language	0.8	% French Home Language	98.6
% Official Bilingual	22.7	% Other Home Language	0.6
% Catholics	95.5	% Protestants	1.4
% Aboriginal Peoples	0.5	% Immigrants	1.7

C: Socio-Economic Profile

Average Family Income $	45350	Median Family Income $	42292
% Low Income Families	20.6	Average Home Price $	91728
% Home Owners	47	% Unemployment	9.5
% Labour Force Participation	67.7	% Managerial-Administrative	12.6
% Self-Employed	5.5	% University Degrees	9.3
% Movers	48.2		

D: Industrial Profile

% Manufacturing	9.1	% Service Sector	15.2
% Agriculture	0.5	% Mining	0.1
% Forestry	0.3	% Fishing	0.1
% Government Services	15.5	% Business Services	4.9

E: Homogeneity Measures

Ethnic Diversity Index	0.91	Religious Homogeneity Index	0.9
Sectoral Concentration Index	0.51	Income Disparity Index	6.7

F: Physical Setting Characteristics

Total Population	102839	Area (km²)	73
Population Density (pop/km²)	1408.8		

* Tentative value, due to the existence of unpaid campaign expenses.

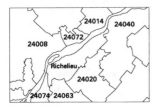

Richelieu

Constituency Number: 24055

The riding of Richelieu runs along the south shore of the St Lawrence River, northeast of Montreal. The riding includes the towns of Sorel, Tracy, Bécancour and Nicolet. The riding is 98.9% francophone. The average family income of $43,003 is 6% below the Quebec average. Norsk Hydro and Sidbec are important employers.

Prior to the 1984 election, Richelieu had not elected a Conservative since 1891. But mathemathics teacher Louis Plamondon won the riding for the Conservatives in 1984 with an ample margin of 13,814 votes over incumbent Jean-Louis Leduc, who had held the riding since 1979. Despite the decision of the Quebec Federation of Labour to back the NDP in the 1988 campaign, Plamondon enjoyed the support of local unions after having presented an anti-scab private members' bill in Ottawa, a bill which died however on the order paper. The Liberals ran businessman Yvon Hébert, while the NDP candidate was Gaston Dupuis, a clerk who also ran in the riding in 1984. Plamondon won the riding with over three times the votes of his Liberal opponent. The 68.9% of the vote received by the Conservatives was their fifth-best result in the country.

Louis Plamondon quit the Conservatives on June 26, 1990 following the failure of Meech Lake and soon thereafter joined the Bloc Québécois. He served as leader of the Bloc Québécois in the House of Commons in 1992-1993.

Bloc Québécois' Plamondon offered another strong performance in 1993, finishing first with 66.5% of the vote with a plurality of 20,625. This was the Bloc Québécois' fifth-best result. Plamondon was facing a charge (April 1993) of soliciting a prostitute as the campaign began but this seems to have had no impact on his electoral performance. Industrialist, and founding president of the Nicolet Caisse d'entraide économique, Michel Biron represented the Liberals and finished second with 23.1% of the vote. Conservatives dropped to third rank with party activist Lorraine Frappier. Issues raised during the campaign dealt with agribusiness (Bécancour), tannery (Pierreville), and compensatory rights.

Member of Parliament: Louis Plamondon;   **Party:**   B.Q.;   **Occupation:**   Businessman, Member of Parliament; **Education:**   BA in pedagogy, Université Laval and Université de Montréal;   **Age:**   51 (July 31, 1943);   **Year of first election to the House of Commons:** 1984

24055 Richelieu

A: Political Profile
i) Voting Behaviour

	% 1993	% 1988	Change 1988-93
Conservative	9.4	68.9	-59.5
Liberal	23.1	19.3	3.8
NDP	0.7	6.8	-6.1
Bloc Québécois	66.5	0	66.5
Other	0.3	5.1	-4.8

% Turnout	81.7	Total Ballots (#)	49318
Rejected Ballots (#)	1878	% Margin of Victory	43.7
Rural Polls, 1988 (#)	65	Urban Polls, 1988 (#)	125
% Yes - 1992	36.1	% No - 1992	63.9

ii) Campaign Financing

	# of Donations	Total $ Value	% of Limit Spent
Conservative	105	45634	80.8
Liberal	28	54381	85.5
NDP	2	2200	0
Bloc Québécois	666	63240	80.6
Other	0	0	

B: Ethno-Linguistic Profile

% English Home Language	0.8	% French Home Language	98.9
% Official Bilingual	17.6	% Other Home Language	0.4
% Catholics	96.6	% Protestants	1.5
% Aboriginal Peoples	0.7	% Immigrants	1.7

C: Socio-Economic Profile

Average Family Income $	43003	Median Family Income $	39552
% Low Income Families	16	Average Home Price $	69500
% Home Owners	68.2	% Unemployment	13.5
% Labour Force Participation	60.5	% Managerial-Administrative	9.5
% Self-Employed	10.6	% University Degrees	5.4
% Movers	33.4		

D: Industrial Profile

% Manufacturing	23.4	% Service Sector	12.6
% Agriculture	6.5	% Mining	0.6
% Forestry	0.2	% Fishing	0.1
% Government Services	4.4	% Business Services	1.8

E: Homogeneity Measures

Ethnic Diversity Index	0.93	Religious Homogeneity Index	0.9
Sectoral Concentration Index	0.34	Income Disparity Index	8

F: Physical Setting Characteristics

Total Population	81957	Area (km²)	1775
Population Density (pop/km²)	46.2		

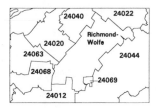

Richmond–Wolfe

Constituency Number: 24056

The riding of Richmond–Wolfe is located some 120 kilometres east of Montreal, near Sherbrooke. The riding includes the towns of Asbestos, Richmond, Rock Forest, Valcourt and Windsor. The riding is 95.6% francophone. The riding's average family income of $41,723 is 9% below the Quebec average. Among the main employers are Bombardier (Valcourt), J. M. Asbestos Co. (Asbestos) and Domtar paper (Windsor).

With the exception of the 1930–1935 Bennett period, Richmond–Wolfe was held by the Liberals from 1896 to 1958. But the party won only two of the following seven elections, those of 1963 and 1965. *Créditiste* Lionel Beaudoin held the riding from 1968 to 1979. In 1979 the riding passed to Liberal Alain Tardif. Tardif, a lawyer by profession, survived the 1984 Conservative landslide with a comfortable margin of 4,234 votes. Richmond–Wolfe was one of only four non-Montreal ridings in the province that stayed Liberal in the sweep. The 51.4% of the vote he received in that election was among the Liberals' best results in Quebec. Liberal Tardif made some headlines when he called for John Turner's resignation. In the 1988 campaign, Tardif stressed the issue of quotas on shoe imports, which affect one of the riding's important industries. The Conservatives sought to unseat Tardif with Yvon Côté, a teacher, municipal councillor and local party organizer in Rock Forest, a town that was added to Richmond–Wolfe from the neighbouring riding of Sherbrooke in the 1987 redistribution. The NDP ran Marc-André Peloquin, a retired teacher and mayor of Kingsbury, a town of some 200 inhabitants. Peloquin had few illusions about his chances: he told supporters 'Don't wish me good luck, wish me a miracle.' Peloquin did not get his miracle, and the NDP failed to receive 10% of the vote. Tardif was unseated by Côté, who won with a margin of 2,638 votes. Main issues during the campaign were acid rain and free trade.

In 1993, Yvon Côté sought re-election but finished second with 23.5% of the vote. Lawyer Gaétan Dumas ran for the Liberals and received 21.5% of the vote. Dumas is involved in community development and has strong connections with provincial Liberals. Bloc Québécois designated Brompton communications advisor Gaston Leroux who took the riding with 52.3% of the vote with a margin of victory of 12,231 votes. Leroux has been involved in several local projects and has gained a strong profile. Retired Marc-André Peloquin again represented the NDP but finished fifth with only 1.1% of the vote, outdone by Natural Law candidate Anne-Marie Marois who secured 1.6% of the vote. The main issues of the campaign were new markets for asbestos and strengthening of small and medium enterprises.

Member of Parliament: Gaston Leroux; **Party:** B.Q.; **Occupation:** Communications advisor, actor; **Education:** Graduate studies in French studies with concentration in marketing; **Age:** 46 (Oct. 1, 1948); **Year of first election to the House of Commons:** 1993

24056 Richmond–Wolfe

A: Political Profile
i) Voting Behaviour

	% 1993	% 1988	Change 1988-93
Conservative	23.5	47.5	-24
Liberal	21.5	41	-19.5
NDP	1.1	9.6	-8.5
Bloc Québécois	52.3	0	52.3
Other	1.6	1.9	-0.3

% Turnout	76.5	Total Ballots (#)	44152
Rejected Ballots (#)	1599	% Margin of Victory	30.4
Rural Polls, 1988 (#)	121	Urban Polls, 1988 (#)	55
% Yes - 1992	39.8	% No - 1992	60.2

ii) Campaign Financing

	# of Donations	Total $ Value	% of Limit Spent
Conservative	45	32468	91.4
Liberal	52	22229	47.8
NDP	4	2017	2.8
Bloc Québécois	374	25815	60.8
Other	3	1053	

B: Ethno-Linguistic Profile

% English Home Language	4.3	% French Home Language	95.6
% Official Bilingual	24.7	% Other Home Language	0.1
% Catholics	92.5	% Protestants	4.6
% Aboriginal Peoples	0.4	% Immigrants	1.6

C: Socio-Economic Profile

Average Family Income $	41723	Median Family Income $	37813
% Low Income Families	12.8	Average Home Price $	72396
% Home Owners	74.8	% Unemployment	10.6
% Labour Force Participation	65.5	% Managerial-Administrative	10.7
% Self-Employed	11.7	% University Degrees	5.9
% Movers	36.1		

D: Industrial Profile

% Manufacturing	24.8	% Service Sector	11
% Agriculture	6.8	% Mining	2
% Forestry	1	% Fishing	0
% Government Services	4.3	% Business Services	2.7

E: Homogeneity Measures

Ethnic Diversity Index	0.89	Religious Homogeneity Index	0.83
Sectoral Concentration Index	0.33	Income Disparity Index	9.4

F: Physical Setting Characteristics

Total Population	79542	Area (km²)	3737
Population Density (pop/km²)	21.3		

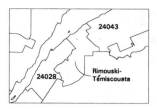

Rimouski–Témiscouata

Constituency Number: 24057

The riding of Rimouski–Témiscouata is located on the southern shore of the lower St Lawrence River. Bordered on the south by the State of Maine, it includes the town of Rimouski. The riding is 99.7% francophone, the second highest level in Canada. The average family income of $41,606 in Rimouski–Témiscouata is 9% below the provincial average, but is the highest in the Bas-Saint-Laurent-Gaspésie region. The economy is essentially based on the service sector, tourism, agriculture, and forest exploitation.

The riding was Liberal from 1917 to 1958, when it went Conservative in the Diefenbaker sweep. The Liberals and the *créditistes* each won four of the following eight elections. In the 1988 campaign, three candidates had at one time or another represented the riding in Ottawa. Incumbent Monique Vézina had won the riding for the Conservatives in 1984 with a comfortable margin of 11,282 votes. Vézina was appointed Minister of External Relations in the first Mulroney cabinet. Altogether, Vézina held five junior portfolios in that government. Éva Côté, the MP defeated by Vézina in 1984, was the Liberal candidate in 1988. The incumbent she had defeated in 1980, Eudore Allard, ran as an independent in 1988. Allard held the riding for Réal Caouette's *créditistes* from 1972 to 1980. The NDP, for their part, ran Pierre Boisjoli, a civil engineer. Vézina won the riding again, with a plurality of 13,228 votes. She received over twice the votes of her Liberal opponent.

In 1993, Conservatives ran Jean Morin, a journalist by profession, who was the political aide to Quebec Liberal ministers André Bourbeau and Robert Middlemiss. Finishing third, Morin received only 12.0% of the vote. Liberal engineer André Reid, a newcomer to politics, obtained 24.7% of the vote. Bloc Québécois ran Suzanne Tremblay, a university professor with deep connections with the PQ. She won the riding with a plurality of 13,541 votes. The Public Service Alliance of Canada backed Tremblay. Principal points of contention during the campaign were modernization of infrastructures, job creation, day-care centres, and depopulation of remote areas.

Member of Parliament: Suzanne Tremblay; **Party:** B.Q.; **Occupation:** Professor; **Education:** MEd (teaching); **Age:** 57 (Jan. 24, 1937); **Year of first election to the House of Commons:** 1993

24057 Rimouski–Témiscouata

A: Political Profile

i) Voting Behaviour

	% 1993	% 1988	Change 1988-93
Conservative	12	62.6	-50.6
Liberal	24.7	27.8	-3.1
NDP	0.9	6.4	-5.5
Bloc Québécois	59.9	0	59.9
Other	2.6	3.2	-0.6

% Turnout	70.8	Total Ballots (#)	39776
Rejected Ballots (#)	1332	% Margin of Victory	37.8
Rural Polls, 1988 (#)	116	Urban Polls, 1988 (#)	71
% Yes - 1992	33	% No - 1992	67

ii) Campaign Financing

	# of Donations	Total $ Value	% of Limit Spent
Conservative	85	21183	59.3
Liberal	89	25216	64.6*
NDP	2	2200	0
Bloc Québécois	432	32260	56.8
Other	33	12760	

B: Ethno-Linguistic Profile

% English Home Language	0.3	% French Home Language	99.7
% Official Bilingual	12.7	% Other Home Language	0.1
% Catholics	96.3	% Protestants	1.5
% Aboriginal Peoples	0.4	% Immigrants	0.7

C: Socio-Economic Profile

Average Family Income $	41606	Median Family Income $	36029
% Low Income Families	17.5	Average Home Price $	63208
% Home Owners	66.8	% Unemployment	14.3
% Labour Force Participation	63	% Managerial-Administrative	11.9
% Self-Employed	8	% University Degrees	8.8
% Movers	35.9		

D: Industrial Profile

% Manufacturing	8.5	% Service Sector	13.2
% Agriculture	4.1	% Mining	0.4
% Forestry	3.9	% Fishing	0.2
% Government Services	7.7	% Business Services	3

E: Homogeneity Measures

Ethnic Diversity Index	0.95	Religious Homogeneity Index	0.91
Sectoral Concentration Index	0.43	Income Disparity Index	13.4

F: Physical Setting Characteristics

Total Population	74485	Area (km²)	6367
Population Density (pop/km²)	11.7		

* Tentative value, due to the existence of unpaid campaign expenses.

Roberval

Constituency Number: 24058

The riding of Roberval is located north-northeast of Quebec City. The riding includes the towns of Roberval on Saint-Jean Lake, Saint-Félicien, Dolbeau, and Chibougamau, farther north. The riding is 98.7% francophone. The riding has also the two aboriginal communities in Pointe-Bleue and Chibougamau. Aboriginal people count for 4.2% of the population. Roberval's average family income of $41,258 is 10% below the Quebec average. The forestry sector employs 7.8% of the riding's workforce, the highest proportion in Quebec and the fourth highest in Canada. The 1991 census estimated the unemployment rate at 18.5%.

Unusual for Quebec, no Liberal represented the area from 1958 to 1980. The Conservatives won the riding in 1958, then lost it to *créditiste* Charles-Arthur Gauthier who held it from 1962 to 1980. Gauthier lost that year to the Liberals' Suzanne Beauchamp-Niquet. Four years later, the Conservatives' Benoît Bouchard won with a comfortable margin of 10,064 votes. Bouchard, a teacher, held four portfolios in the first Mulroney government, including that of Secretary of State. The Liberals parachuted in Martin Cauvier, a merchant. The NDP candidate was Réjean Lalancette, a union activist. Bouchard won re-election, increasing his margin to 22,498 votes. His 76.4% of the vote was the party's second best showing in Canada, surpassed only by Mulroney's result in Charlevoix.

In 1993 there was some surprising moves. First, Bloc Québécois leader Lucien Bouchard forced the Bloc-designated candidate, Jasmin Dorion, to withdraw due to his utilization of an improper curriculum vitae, and designated Roberval schoolboard director Michel Gauthier, a seasoned politician. Gauthier was a PQ backbencher representing the riding of Roberval in the National Assembly from 1981 to 1988. Gauthier took the riding with 60.0% of the vote, and a plurality of 13,246 votes. Liberals ran businessman Aurélien Gill, ex-chief of the Montagnais community of Mashteuiatsh, who finished second with 20.5% of the vote. Dolbeau's mayor from 1981 to 1989, Henri-Paul Brassard came third with 18.1% of the vote. Businessman Brassard ran before under the banners of Quebec provincial Liberals, and the federal Social Credit. NDP ran Montreal student Alain Giguère who took 1.5% of the vote. The main issues during the campaign were unemployment, deficit, protection of the environment and local infrastructures.

Member of Parliament: Michel Gauthier; **Party:** B.Q.; **Occupation:** Administrator; **Education:** MA in school administration; **Age:** 44 (Feb. 18, 1950); **Year of first election to the House of Commons:** 1993

24058 Roberval

A: Political Profile

i) Voting Behaviour

	% 1993	% 1988	Change 1988-93
Conservative	18.1	76.4	-58.3
Liberal	20.5	12.1	8.4
NDP	1.5	9.5	-8
Bloc Québécois	60	0	60
Other	0	2.1	-2.1

% Turnout	70.8	Total Ballots (#)	35121
Rejected Ballots (#)	1584	% Margin of Victory	39.5
Rural Polls, 1988 (#)	75	Urban Polls, 1988 (#)	99
% Yes - 1992	32.6	% No - 1992	67.4

ii) Campaign Financing

	# of Donations	Total $ Value	% of Limit Spent
Conservative	74	43150	86.5
Liberal	142	29809	50.1*
NDP	1	1000	0
Bloc Québécois	224	18385	32.9
Other	0	0	

B: Ethno-Linguistic Profile

% English Home Language	0.4	% French Home Language	98.7
% Official Bilingual	8.9	% Other Home Language	0.8
% Catholics	96.9	% Protestants	1.9
% Aboriginal Peoples	4.2	% Immigrants	0.5

C: Socio-Economic Profile

Average Family Income $	41258	Median Family Income $	38087
% Low Income Families	14.3	Average Home Price $	58197
% Home Owners	68.8	% Unemployment	18.5
% Labour Force Participation	62.6	% Managerial-Administrative	8.2
% Self-Employed	7.9	% University Degrees	4.9
% Movers	33.3		

D: Industrial Profile

% Manufacturing	14.9	% Service Sector	14.3
% Agriculture	4.3	% Mining	3.9
% Forestry	7.8	% Fishing	0.1
% Government Services	5.9	% Business Services	1.7

E: Homogeneity Measures

Ethnic Diversity Index	0.87	Religious Homogeneity Index	0.91
Sectoral Concentration Index	0.34	Income Disparity Index	7.7

F: Physical Setting Characteristics

Total Population	72854	Area (km^2)	67310
Population Density (pop/km^2)	1.1		

* Tentative value, due to the existence of unpaid campaign expenses.

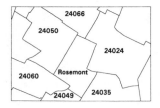

Rosemont

Constituency Number: 24059

The riding of Rosemont is located in the Town of Montreal, just north of the downtown core riding of Laurier–Sainte-Marie. The riding is 86.8% francophone and 4.9% anglophone. The average family income of $37,725 is 18% below the provincial average. Over a third of the riding's residents belong to families classified as low-income, one of the highest levels in the province.

Created in 1947, over time the riding changed its name from Lafontaine to Lafontaine–Rosemont, then to Rosemont. Until 1984 it was represented by just three MPs, all of them Liberals. Georges Lachance, member from 1962 to 1974, was succeeded by his son Claude André who held the riding until he decided not to seek re-election in 1984. That election was won by Suzanne Blais-Grenier for the Conservatives with a 1,305-vote margin. Always a controversial member, she was expelled from the Conservative caucus after alleging the widespread existence of patronage and kickback schemes in the party. In 1988 she sought re-election as an Independent. The 1988 campaign was an interesting one. Eleven candidates ran, the highest number in Quebec. Among the 11 were two sitting MPs, neither of them Conservatives. Opposing the incumbent Blais-Grenier was a second MP, Liberal candidate Jacques Guibault. Guibault had held the Montreal riding of Saint-Jacques since 1968. When Saint-Jacques disappeared in the 1987 redistribution, Guibault, deputy opposition House leader at dissolution, decided to try his luck in Rosemont. The Conservatives sought to unseat the two MPs with Benoît Tremblay. By profession a civil engineer, Tremblay served as city councillor with the Montreal Citizens' Movement. He was also a former provincial assistant deputy minister of Industry, Trade and Commerce in the Parti Québécois, and was considered one of the Conservatives' star candidates. The NDP ran labour lawyer Giuseppe Sciortino, a strong defender of French-language rights, who has strong connections to the PQ. The race was also complicated by the 1987 redistribution, which left the riding with just a third of its former voters. The redistribution was believed to have improved the Conservatives' chances in the riding. The Conservatives' Tremblay won the riding, with a solid margin of 3,918 votes over Guibault. Sciortino took just over 20% of the vote for the NDP. The Conservatives' nemesis Blais-Grenier drew just 4.6% of the vote, narrowly edging out the Rhinoceros candidate for fourth place. The closing of the Gulf Canada refinery was a major issue during the 1988 campaign.

1993 presented a different race. First, Benoît Tremblay had left the Conservatives on June 26 to protest the defeat of Meech Lake, and joined forces with the soon-to-be formed Bloc Québécois. Tremblay won the riding with 63.0% of the vote and a margin of victory of 16,588 votes. Second came Liberal Pierre Bourque, a former race-car driver and businessman, who received 27.5% of the vote. Conservatives fielded communicator Pauline Vincent who had acquired some political experience while working as communication advisor to ministers Perrin Beatty and Monique Landry. Vincent finished third with only 5.4% of the vote, one of the worst results obtained by the Conservatives in Canada. Operator Roger Lamarre represented the NPD, and secured 2.2% of the vote.

Member of Parliament: Benoît Tremblay; **Party:** B.Q.; **Occupation:** Economist; **Education:** MBA, Doctorate in sociology and development, Université de Paris V; **Age:** 46 (Mar. 16, 1948); **Year of first election to the House of Commons :** 1988

24059 Rosemont

A: Political Profile

i) Voting Behaviour

	% 1993	% 1988	Change 1988-93
Conservative	5.4	37.8	-32.4
Liberal	27.5	29.2	-1.7
NDP	2.2	20.2	-18
Bloc Québécois	63	0	63
Other	2	12.5	-10.5

% Turnout	75.4	Total Ballots (#)	48813
Rejected Ballots (#)	2089	% Margin of Victory	37.5
Rural Polls, 1988 (#)	0	Urban Polls, 1988 (#)	224
% Yes - 1992	34.4	% No - 1992	65.6

ii) Campaign Financing

	# of Donations	Total $ Value	% of Limit Spent
Conservative	70	7622	49.3
Liberal	56	33204	60.7*
NDP	3	2507	1.6
Bloc Québécois	681	57130	76.5
Other	8	18829	

B: Ethno-Linguistic Profile

% English Home Language	4.9	% French Home Language	86.8
% Official Bilingual	45.6	% Other Home Language	8.3
% Catholics	85.2	% Protestants	3.2
% Aboriginal Peoples	0.6	% Immigrants	12.4

C: Socio-Economic Profile

Average Family Income $	37725	Median Family Income $	33751
% Low Income Families	33.7	Average Home Price $	126844
% Home Owners	21.5	% Unemployment	14.9
% Labour Force Participation	62.5	% Managerial-Administrative	10.3
% Self-Employed	6.4	% University Degrees	13.9
% Movers	52.8		

D: Industrial Profile

% Manufacturing	15.9	% Service Sector	13.6
% Agriculture	0.3	% Mining	0
% Forestry	0.1	% Fishing	0
% Government Services	7	% Business Services	8.3

E: Homogeneity Measures

Ethnic Diversity Index	0.63	Religious Homogeneity Index	0.72
Sectoral Concentration Index	0.52	Income Disparity Index	10.5

F: Physical Setting Characteristics

Total Population	87257	Area (km²)	8
Population Density (pop/km²)	10907.1		

* Tentative value, due to the existence of unpaid campaign expenses.

Saint-Denis

Constituency Number: 24060

Saint-Denis is located in the northwest corner of the Town of Montreal. The riding is only 49.1% francophone, with an anglophone community of 11.8%, a Greek community of some 11,400 members, and a large Italian community. Over 37% of the riding's constituents were born outside Canada, the third highest percentage in Quebec. The riding is also generally poor: the average family income of $33,076 is the second lowest in Canada. An important percentage of families is classified as low-income. The manufacturing sector employs 27.8% of the riding's workforce, the second highest proportion in Quebec and the seventh highest in Canada. The textile and clothing industries, thought to be vulnerable to free trade, provide employment to an important share of the riding's constituents.

Saint-Denis provides stable employment for its MPs. Since 1921 only four members have represented the riding, all of them Liberal. The latest of these is Marcel Prud'homme. Elected in a 1964 byelection, Prud'homme is the third-longest sitting member of the House. In 1984, despite the Conservative sweep of Quebec, he held the riding with a margin of 6,628 votes. In 1988, Conservative candidate was Madeleine Provost, an executive of the Quebec Ethnic Press Association. Provost received the nomination after the party blocked a Greek candidate. The NDP ran sociologist Jaime Llambias-Wolfe. Director of the Quebec Association of International Development Organizations, Llambias-Wolfe came to Canada in 1973 after the coup in Chile. To no one's surprise, Prud'homme held the riding with a margin of 7,085 votes. The 30.4% of the vote received by the Conservatives was their second-worst showing in Quebec.

In 1993, Liberal Prud'homme did not seek re-election as he was named to the Senate just before the election was called; he was succeeded by parachuted Eleni Bakopanos; she was vice-president of the Quebec Council of Cultural Communities and Immigration. A candidate well-known in the riding, Bakopanos took 52.4% of the vote, easily taking Parc Extension sector. Bakopanos was the first nonfrancophone Liberal to win Saint-Denis. Bloc Québécois manager Gilles Pelchat finished second with 36.6% of the vote; he has strong PQ affiliations. Conservatives fielded teacher Aida Baghjajian, a party activist, who obtained 5.3% of the vote. NDP Josée Panet-Raymond, an administrative assistant, finished fourth with 2.3% of the vote.

Member of Parliament: Eleni Bakopanos; **Party:** Liberal; **Occupation:** Vice-president, Quebec Council of Cultural Communities and Immigration; **Education:** BA (Political Science and History); **Age:** 40 (May 10, 1954); **Year of first election to the House of Commons:** 1993

24060 Saint-Denis

A: Political Profile
i) Voting Behaviour

	% 1993	% 1988	Change 1988-93
Conservative	5.3	30.4	-25.1
Liberal	52.4	47.2	5.2
NDP	2.3	14.6	-12.3
Bloc Québécois	36.6	0	36.6
Other	3.5	7.8	-4.3

% Turnout	79.1	Total Ballots (#)	43150
Rejected Ballots (#)	1393	% Margin of Victory	15.8
Rural Polls, 1988 (#)	0	Urban Polls, 1988 (#)	200
% Yes - 1992	57.5	% No - 1992	42.5

ii) Campaign Financing

	# of Donations	Total $ Value	% of Limit Spent
Conservative	42	23675	86.6*
Liberal	183	57840	81.2
NDP	5	3794	2.4
Bloc Québécois	257	22990	32.8
Other	12	3805	

B: Ethno-Linguistic Profile

% English Home Language	11.8	% French Home Language	49.1
% Official Bilingual	42.9	% Other Home Language	39.1
% Catholics	62	% Protestants	7
% Aboriginal Peoples	0.2	% Immigrants	37.3

C: Socio-Economic Profile

Average Family Income $	33076	Median Family Income $	28789
% Low Income Families	41.3	Average Home Price $	146676
% Home Owners	22.9	% Unemployment	17.8
% Labour Force Participation	61.6	% Managerial-Administrative	8.4
% Self-Employed	5.1	% University Degrees	10.6
% Movers	53.9		

D: Industrial Profile

% Manufacturing	27.8	% Service Sector	16.7
% Agriculture	0.4	% Mining	0
% Forestry	0	% Fishing	0
% Government Services	4.8	% Business Services	6.3

E: Homogeneity Measures

Ethnic Diversity Index	0.28	Religious Homogeneity Index	0.45
Sectoral Concentration Index	0.42	Income Disparity Index	13

F: Physical Setting Characteristics

Total Population	90211	Area (km²)	
Population Density (pop/km²)	10		9021.1

* Tentative value, due to the existence of unpaid campaign expenses.

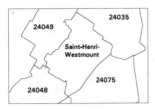

Saint-Henri–Westmount

Constituency Number: 24061

The riding of Saint-Henri–Westmount, which includes the well-to-do Town of Westmount and the poverty-stricken Saint-Henri neighbourhood in southwest Montreal, is the riding of deceptive averages. The average family income of $78,825 is the highest in Quebec and the sixth highest in Canada. Yet a high number of families are classified as low-income. The 1991 average dwelling value of $326,893 is the highest in the province, fourth in the country. Yet only 21% of dwellings are owned by their occupants, one of the lowest levels of ownership in Canada. The riding is 40.2% francophone, one of the lowest levels in the province. Constituents are known to be mobile: 58.2% of families in the riding have moved in the past five years, one of the highest levels in Quebec. 19.5% of the employed constituents are managers or administrators, compared to the provincial average of 12.3%. This is the second highest proportion in Quebec.

Saint-Henri–Westmount has traditionally been a riding for Liberal stars: several of its members from the riding have sat in the cabinet. For more than a decade, it was Donald Johnston, who held the Treasury Board and Economic Development portfolios in the last Trudeau government. Johnston won again in 1984 with a 4,076 margin, a considerable drop from his 18,000-vote margin of 1980. He left the Liberal caucus because of his opposition to his party's support of the Meech Lake accord, and he decided not to seek re-election in 1988. A number of high-profile Liberals reportedly turned down invitations to run in the riding, and the party finally chose David Berger, a lawyer by profession, who had represented the Laurier riding from 1979 until its amalgamation with Sainte-Marie riding in 1987. Berger, Liberal critic for science and technology, was also critical of parts of the Meech Lake accord, in particular the clause recognizing Quebec as a distinct society. The Conservatives also had difficulty securing a star candidate. They settled on financial consultant Keith MacLellan. A retired career diplomat, MacLellan had served as ambassador to various countries. American-born economics professor Ruth Rose contested the riding for the NDP. Berger hung on to the riding for the Liberals, with a margin of 927 votes. He won the Saint-Henri area and the eastern part of the riding that had belonged to his Laurier riding. In the 1989 Quebec provincial election, Berger had supported Equality party Richard Holden which antagonized several Liberal sympathizers.

In 1993, Berger took the riding again, and increased his margin of victory to 17,990 votes. Bloc Québécois Haitian-born Eugénia Romain, a nurse involved in community development, came second with 7,950 votes. Alain Perez, a past general director with SNC-Lavalin, ran for the Conservatives and received 10.7% of the vote. High school teacher Ann Elbourne represented the NDP and finished fourth with 4.0% of the vote. Twelve candidates entered the race. The main theme of the campaign was economic restructuring.

Member of Parliament: David Berger; **Party:** Liberal; **Occupation:** Lawyer; **Education:** BCL, McGill University; **Age:** 44 (Mar. 30, 1950); **Year of first election to the House of Commons:** 1979

In the February 13, 1995 by-election, Liberal Lucienne Robillard, a well-known provincial Liberal who had been defeated on September 12, 1994 by the victory of Parti Québécois, easily won this very safe riding with 75.9% of the vote.

24061 Saint-Henri–Westmount

A: Political Profile

i) Voting Behaviour

	% 1993	% 1988	Change 1988-93
Conservative	10.7	39.3	-28.6
Liberal	61.7	41.6	20.1
NDP	4	13.1	-9.1
Bloc Québécois	18.9	0	18.9
Other	4.7	6	-1.3

% Turnout	74.6	Total Ballots (#)	42896
Rejected Ballots (#)	867	% Margin of Victory	42.8
Rural Polls, 1988 (#)	0	Urban Polls, 1988 (#)	203
% Yes - 1992	70.7	% No - 1992	29.3

ii) Campaign Financing

	# of Donations	Total $ Value	% of Limit Spent
Conservative	92	49793	77.2*
Liberal	150	88498	88.1
NDP	17	3793	4.7
Bloc Québécois	59	11915	20.6
Other	37	24020	

B: Ethno-Linguistic Profile

% English Home Language	47.1	% French Home Language	40.2
% Official Bilingual	60.4	% Other Home Language	12.6
% Catholics	50	% Protestants	17.2
% Aboriginal Peoples	0.5	% Immigrants	26.5

C: Socio-Economic Profile

Average Family Income $	78825	Median Family Income $	45077
% Low Income Families	32.3	Average Home Price $	326893
% Home Owners	21	% Unemployment	12.6
% Labour Force Participation	64.7	% Managerial-Administrative	19.5
% Self-Employed	13.7	% University Degrees	33.2
% Movers	58.2		

D: Industrial Profile

% Manufacturing	12.2	% Service Sector	12.2
% Agriculture	0.3	% Mining	0.1
% Forestry	0.1	% Fishing	0
% Government Services	4	% Business Services	14.2

E: Homogeneity Measures

Ethnic Diversity Index	0.26	Religious Homogeneity Index	0.33
Sectoral Concentration Index	0.58	Income Disparity Index	42.8

F: Physical Setting Characteristics

Total Population	84965	Area (km²)	15
Population Density (pop/km²)	5664.3		

* Tentative value, due to the existence of unpaid campaign expenses.

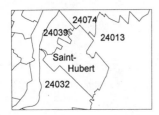

Saint-Hubert

Constituency Number: 24062

The riding of Saint-Hubert is located south of the Island of Montreal, nestled among the ridings of Longueuil, La Prairie, and Chambly. The riding was created in the 1987 electoral redistribution, reflecting the growing population of Quebec's south shore region. Votes cast in 1984 inside the riding's boundaries would have given the Conservatives a plurality of 8,000 votes. Saint-Hubert includes the town of the same name, as well as Greenfield Park and Lemoyne. Its average family income of $47,391 is slightly above the Quebec average. The riding is 80.7% francophone, slightly below the average for Quebec, and is 15.2% anglophone.

The Conservatives' nomination process for the 1988 campaign was somewhat confusing. Lawyer Pierrette Venne was almost acclaimed as candidate in the Rosemont riding when the party asked her to step aside there for Montreal Citizens' Movement activist Benoît Tremblay. The Conservatives' plan to reward Venne for her loyalty by giving her the Saint-Hubert nomination, however, was threatened by Danielle Hervieux, who had already been nominated by acclamation in the riding. Finally, Hervieux gave way to party pressure. Venne's major local issue in the campaign was a proposal to extend Autoroute 30 to Valleyfield. The Liberal candidate, Raymond Dupont, had already been an MP from 1972 to 1984. In 1972, he had wrested the Sainte-Marie riding from Conservative Georges Valade, the only Conservative Montreal MP to have survived Trudeaumania four years earlier. Dupont's victory was one of only two Liberal gains across Canada that year. In 1974, he moved to the south shore riding of Chambly, which he represented until his defeat ten years later. The owner of a construction company, Dupont stressed the need for improvements to the Saint-Hubert airport to attract business to the riding. The NDP candidate was Nicole Desranleau, a nurse in a local health clinic. Desranleau focused on environmental issues. On election night, the Conservatives' Venne won her adopted riding with a margin of 10,364 votes.

Following the failure of Meech Lake, Pierrette Venne joined the Bloc Québécois in August 1993 and decided to run under its banner in 1993. During her time as a Conservative MP, Venne wanted to discuss proposals for a decentralized Canada but failed to receive a positive hearing within the party. Venne won the riding with 56.9% of the vote and a plurality of 15,344 votes. Liberals fielded Angéline Fournier, a political analyst, who obtained 31.9% of the vote. Lawyer Jean Lesage, grandson of Premier Jean Lesage, came third for the Conservatives with only 7.4%. The NDP was represented by Nathalie Rochefort, a student, who took 1.5%, finishing just ahead of Natural Law candidate Jean Cerigo. Among the main themes during the campaign were environmental issues, sovereignty, and job creation.

Member of Parliament: Pierrette Venne; **Party:** B.Q.; **Occupation:** Notary public; **Education:** Diploma in notarial law and licentiate in law, Université de Sherbrooke; **Age:** 49 (Aug. 8, 1945); **Year of first election to the House of Commons:** 1988

24062 Saint-Hubert

A: Political Profile
i) Voting Behaviour

	% 1993	% 1988	Change 1988-93
Conservative	7.4	48.9	-41.5
Liberal	31.9	29.1	2.8
NDP	1.5	18	-16.5
Bloc Québécois	56.9	0	56.9
Other	2.4	4	-1.6

% Turnout	81.5	Total Ballots (#)	63939
Rejected Ballots (#)	2495	% Margin of Victory	27.4
Rural Polls, 1988 (#)	0	Urban Polls, 1988 (#)	213
% Yes - 1992	39.8	% No - 1992	60.2

ii) Campaign Financing

	# of Donations	Total $ Value	% of Limit Spent
Conservative	23	13458	32.6*
Liberal	72	48449	97.6
NDP	0**	0**	0**
Bloc Québécois	309	41533	60.3
Other	12	1842	

B: Ethno-Linguistic Profile

% English Home Language	15.2	% French Home Language	80.7
% Official Bilingual	42.7	% Other Home Language	4
% Catholics	84	% Protestants	9.3
% Aboriginal Peoples	0.6	% Immigrants	9.4

C: Socio-Economic Profile

Average Family Income $	47391	Median Family Income $	45432
% Low Income Families	18.1	Average Home Price $	107436
% Home Owners	62.7	% Unemployment	10.5
% Labour Force Participation	69.7	% Managerial-Administrative	11.6
% Self-Employed	5.7	% University Degrees	7
% Movers	46.6		

D: Industrial Profile

% Manufacturing	18	% Service Sector	12.9
% Agriculture	0.3	% Mining	0
% Forestry	0	% Fishing	0
% Government Services	7.4	% Business Services	5.6

E: Homogeneity Measures

Ethnic Diversity Index	0.64	Religious Homogeneity Index	0.71
Sectoral Concentration Index	0.44	Income Disparity Index	4.1

F: Physical Setting Characteristics

Total Population	115118	Area (km²)	77
Population Density (pop/km²)	1495		

* Tentative value, due to the existence of unpaid campaign expenses.
** No return filed.

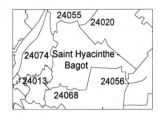

Saint-Hyacinthe–Bagot

Constituency Number: 24063

The riding of Saint-Hyacinthe–Bagot is located to the south of the St Lawrence River, about 40 kilometres east of Montreal. The riding is 99.2% francophone. The average family income of $42,632 is 7% below the Quebec average. 9.3% of the riding's work force is involved in agriculture, the fourth highest proportion in the province.

The riding was a Liberal stronghold: the party held the riding for 70 years prior to 1957. The Conservatives won in that year, and held on for the next 22 years, an unheard-of feat in twentieth-century Quebec. Robert Stanfield's 'Quebec lieutenant', Claude Wagner, represented the riding from 1968 to 1979. Marcel Ostiguy recovered the riding for the Liberals in 1979, and represented it until losing by 1,590 votes to actress and businesswoman Andrée Champagne in 1984. Champagne served as Minister of State for Youth from 1984 until she was dropped from the Cabinet two years later. The Liberal candidate was Michel Gaudette, a recent graduate in international relations at Simon Fraser University in British Columbia. The NDP candidate was Hélène Lortie-Narayana, who had worked in Edmonton as a correspondent for Radio-Canada. Champagne won the riding a second time for the Conservatives, this time with a large plurality of 8,978 votes.

Andrée Champagne sought re-election for the Conservatives in 1993 but finished third with 20.1% of the vote. Champagne's political career was giving signs of being on a descending slope. Liberals were represented by Hélène Riendeau, a public relations officer and political activist with the Quebec provincial Liberals, who came second with 20.7% of the vote. NDP fielded unemployed Luc Chamberland who received 1.7% of the vote. Bloc Québécois ran Yvan Loubier, a former economist with powerful Union of Farm Producers (UPA) connections and one of the main architects of the 1993 party platform. Loubier secured 57.4% of the vote and a margin of victory of 18,890 votes. Loubier gained prominence during the referendum campaign on the Charlottetown Accord when he headed a group of economists for the 'No' side in Quebec. Principal issues of the campaign dealt with the impact of free trade on agricultural products, cost of federalism, and protection of social programs.

Member of Parliament: Yvan Loubier; **Party:** B.Q.; **Occupation:** Economist; **Age:** 35 (Apr. 10, 1959); **Year of first election to the House of Commons:** 1993

24063 Saint-Hyacinthe–Bagot

A: Political Profile
i) Voting Behaviour

	% 1993	% 1988	Change 1988-93
Conservative	20.1	52.6	-32.5
Liberal	20.7	33.9	-13.2
NDP	1.7	13.4	-11.7
Bloc Québécois	57.4	0	57.4
Other	0	0	0

% Turnout	77.3	Total Ballots (#)	51384
Rejected Ballots (#)	2564	% Margin of Victory	36.7
Rural Polls, 1988 (#)	108	Urban Polls, 1988 (#)	88
% Yes - 1992	37.9	% No - 1992	62.1

ii) Campaign Financing

	# of Donations	Total $ Value	% of Limit Spent
Conservative	59	27819	65.9
Liberal	215	27882	62.1
NDP	1	1252	0.4
Bloc Québécois	391	22320	36.4
Other	0	0	

B: Ethno-Linguistic Profile

% English Home Language	0.5	% French Home Language	99.2
% Official Bilingual	18	% Other Home Language	0.3
% Catholics	94.8	% Protestants	2.6
% Aboriginal Peoples	0.4	% Immigrants	1.8

C: Socio-Economic Profile

Average Family Income $	42632	Median Family Income $	37574
% Low Income Families	14.9	Average Home Price $	87209
% Home Owners	60	% Unemployment	9
% Labour Force Participation	66.2	% Managerial-Administrative	11.6
% Self-Employed	12.5	% University Degrees	5.3
% Movers	40.6		

D: Industrial Profile

% Manufacturing	24.6	% Service Sector	10.6
% Agriculture	9.3	% Mining	0.3
% Forestry	0.1	% Fishing	0
% Government Services	4.3	% Business Services	2.7

E: Homogeneity Measures

Ethnic Diversity Index	0.92	Religious Homogeneity Index	0.87
Sectoral Concentration Index	0.34	Income Disparity Index	11.9

F: Physical Setting Characteristics

Total Population	89723	Area (km²)	1652
Population Density (pop/km²)	54.3		

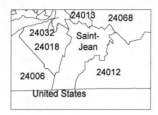

Saint-Jean

Constituency Number: 24064

The riding of Saint-Jean is located forty kilometres southeast of Montreal. It is bordered on the north by the ridings of Saint-Hubert and Chambly, and on the south by the US. The riding includes the towns of Saint-Jean-sur-le-Richelieu, Saint-Luc, Napierville and Iberville. It is 95.8% francophone. The riding's average family income of $44,296 is slightly below the provincial average. The urban/rural riding includes an important Canadian Forces base and a customs office. Saint-Jean is known as a barometer riding.

Until the 1980s, Saint-Jean had voted Liberal since Confederation, with the exception of 1965. Ironically, in that year this Liberal stronghold was one of only eight Quebec ridings to elect a Conservative. André Bissonnette won the riding in 1984 with a wide margin of almost 15,946 votes over Liberal incumbent Paul-André Massé, who had held the riding since 1979. Bissonnette decided not to run in 1988, following the January 1987 Oerlikon scandal, and the nomination went this time to business administrator Clément Couture. The Liberal nomination was bitterly contested. After Gilles Dolbec, the Mayor of Saint-Luc, emerged victorious, his Liberal adversary went to work for the Conservative candidate. The NDP candidate was Rezeq Faraj, a CEGEP teacher. Couture won the riding for the Conservatives with a margin of 13,042 votes.

Clément Couture sought re-election in 1993 but finished in third position with a deceptive 14.6% of the vote. Liberals had high expectations with Saint-Jean mayor and MRC prefect Delbert Deschambault who has been involved in several community projects. For a Liberal running in a dominant francophone riding, Deschambault did relatively well as he finished second and obtained 26.9% of the vote. Bloc Québécois educator Claude Bachand won the riding with 55.9% of the vote and a margin of victory of 15,410 votes. Bachand has strong connections in the riding, especially with the union movement (CSN) and popular groups. NDP parachuted Aylmer Jutta Teigeler, a development consultant, who came fifth with 0.9% of the vote behind the Natural Law candidate, Alain Longpré, who took 1.5% of the vote. Issues raised during the campaign dealt with budget restraints in defence, and the helicopters program.

Member of Parliament: Claude Bachand; **Party:** B.Q.; **Occupation:** Educator; **Education:** Diploma in physical education; **Age:** 43 (Jan. 3, 1951); **Year of first election to the House of Commons:** 1993

24064 Saint-Jean

A: Political Profile

i) Voting Behaviour

	% 1993	% 1988	Change 1988-93
Conservative	14.6	56.3	-41.7
Liberal	26.9	29.8	-2.9
NDP	0.9	11.8	-10.9
Bloc Québécois	55.9	0	55.9
Other	1.7	2.2	-0.5

% Turnout	81.3	Total Ballots (#)	55730
Rejected Ballots (#)	2484	% Margin of Victory	30.7
Rural Polls, 1988 (#)	62	Urban Polls, 1988 (#)	163
% Yes - 1992	37.7	% No - 1992	62.3

ii) Campaign Financing

	# of Donations	Total $ Value	% of Limit Spent
Conservative	17	40200	69.2
Liberal	33	31620	70.9
NDP	2	2200	0
Bloc Québécois	356	29087	47.6
Other	8	1687	

B: Ethno-Linguistic Profile

% English Home Language	3.8	% French Home Language	95.8
% Official Bilingual	34.8	% Other Home Language	0.4
% Catholics	93.5	% Protestants	3.3
% Aboriginal Peoples	0.5	% Immigrants	3.1

C: Socio-Economic Profile

Average Family Income $	44296	Median Family Income $	40144
% Low Income Families	15.1	Average Home Price $	93529
% Home Owners	60.6	% Unemployment	10.4
% Labour Force Participation	67.2	% Managerial-Administrative	12.1
% Self-Employed	8.7	% University Degrees	7.3
% Movers	46.1		

D: Industrial Profile

% Manufacturing	20.6	% Service Sector	15.4
% Agriculture	3.6	% Mining	0.5
% Forestry	0.1	% Fishing	0
% Government Services	10.9	% Business Services	4.1

E: Homogeneity Measures

Ethnic Diversity Index	0.85	Religious Homogeneity Index	0.86
Sectoral Concentration Index	0.37	Income Disparity Index	9.4

F: Physical Setting Characteristics

Total Population	93507	Area (km²)	925
Population Density (pop/km²)	101.1		

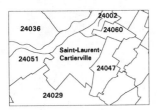

Saint-Laurent–Cartierville
(formerly Saint-Laurent)

Constituency Number: 24065

The riding of Saint-Laurent–Cartierville, formerly known as Saint-Laurent, includes the town of the same name and a northwest portion of the Town of Montreal. It lies just to the east of the West Island ridings of Pierrefonds–Dollard and Lachine–Lac-Saint-Louis. The riding is 43.6% francophone, 28.3% anglophone and has an important immigrant population of 39.4%. Saint-Laurent has the second highest proportion of immigrants in Quebec. This riding has the third highest level in Canada in terms of Jewish presence and the second highest level in Quebec. 56% of residents are classified as bilingual. The average family income of $48.753 is 6% above the Quebec average. The riding is one of the most industrialized in the province, with a large textile sector.

Saint-Laurent–Cartierville replaces the riding of Saint-Laurent which had been created in the 1987 redistribution from portions of the old ridings of Dollard, Saint-Denis and Laval-des-Rapides. Votes cast within the riding in 1984 would give the Liberals a 4,000 vote edge, a factor which led the party to consider the seat a relatively safe one in 1988. As such, they sought to reserve Saint-Laurent for one of their star candidates. It was first thought that 'Quebec lieutenant' Raymond Garneau would run here. When he decided to seek re-election in Ahuntsic, the riding was reserved for party president Michel Robert. But Robert also declined the invitation, and the Liberals turned to insurance broker Shirley Maheu. This decision angered another would-be candidate, William Dery, whose supporters made the national news when they disrupted the Liberals' official launching of their Quebec campaign. Dery eventually gave up his fight for the nomination. Maheu, who worked for the 'No' side in the Quebec referendum of 1980, had been a Saint-Laurent city councillor since 1982. She promised in her campaign to work to bring the new space agency to the riding. The Conservative candidate in Saint-Laurent was Lyse Hubert-Bennett, sales director for an industrial caterer. The NDP ran Sid Ingerman, an economics professor at McGill University and a union consultant. This was Ingerman's fourth attempt at election for the NDP. Apart from free trade, the candidates also stressed housing issues. Though the Conservatives' Hubert-Bennett insisted that free trade would stimulate the riding's industries, voters were apparently sceptical, as they gave the Liberals a 2,131 vote margin.

Maheu, the Official Opposition critic for Multiculturalism and Citizenship, won again for the Liberals in 1993 with 70.1% of the vote. Coming second was Bloc Québécois businessman Amin Hachem who received 18.4% of the vote. Hachem, a native of Lebanon, had been a PQ candidate in Mont-Royal in 1989. Engineer Mark Weiner, the son of Multiculturalism minister Gerry Weiner, represented the Conservatives. Weiner secured only 7.5% of the vote. NDP fielded community worker Francine Poirier who obtained 2.0% of the vote. This riding gave the fourth highest level of support to the Charlottetown Accord in the 1992 referendum in Quebec.

Member of Parliament: Shirley Maheu; **Party:** Liberal; **Occupation:** Insurance broker; **Education:** O'Sullivan Business College; **Age:** 63 (Oct. 7, 1931); **Year of first election to the House of Commons:** 1988

24065 Saint-Laurent–Cartierville

A: Political Profile
i) Voting Behaviour

	% 1993	% 1988	Change 1988-93
Conservative	7.4	41.5	-34.1
Liberal	70.1	46.3	23.8
NDP	2	9.6	-7.6
Bloc Québécois	18.4	0	18.4
Other	2.1	2.7	-0.6

% Turnout	79.8	Total Ballots (#)	46973
Rejected Ballots (#)	1018	% Margin of Victory	51.7
Rural Polls, 1988 (#)	0	Urban Polls, 1988 (#)	200
% Yes - 1992	76	% No - 1992	24

ii) Campaign Financing

	# of Donations	Total $ Value	% of Limit Spent
Conservative	74	28302	50.9*
Liberal	152	48081	65.7
NDP	3	3753	3.6
Bloc Québécois	21	21331	38.8
Other	8	10082	

B: Ethno-Linguistic Profile

% English Home Language	28.3	% French Home Language	43.6
% Official Bilingual	56	% Other Home Language	28.1
% Catholics	51.9	% Protestants	11.7
% Aboriginal Peoples	0.2	% Immigrants	39.4

C: Socio-Economic Profile

Average Family Income $	48753	Median Family Income $	40144
% Low Income Families	28.3	Average Home Price $	190443
% Home Owners	37.3	% Unemployment	14.5
% Labour Force Participation	62.7	% Managerial-Administrative	16.6
% Self-Employed	10.2	% University Degrees	16.9
% Movers	48.9		

D: Industrial Profile

% Manufacturing	22.4	% Service Sector	10.4
% Agriculture	0.3	% Mining	0.1
% Forestry	0	% Fishing	0
% Government Services	3.8	% Business Services	8

E: Homogeneity Measures

Ethnic Diversity Index	0.26	Religious Homogeneity Index	0.38
Sectoral Concentration Index	0.47	Income Disparity Index	17.7

F: Physical Setting Characteristics

Total Population	95015	Area (km²)	50
Population Density (pop/km²)	1900.3		

* Tentative value, due to the existence of unpaid campaign expenses.

Saint-Léonard

Constituency Number: 24066

The riding of Saint-Léonard is located on the eastern portion of the Island of Montreal. It includes the town and suburbs of Saint-Léonard, and part of Montreal edging into the Rosemont riding. The riding is 54.4% francophone, 17.2% anglophone; 29.3% have immigrated to Canada. Over a third of the residents are of Italian origin, the largest concentration of Italians in the province. There is also a significant Haitian community. The 1991 average dwelling value in the riding, $227,109, is among the highest in Quebec. Yet the average family income of $43,434 is 5% below the provincial average.

Saint-Léonard has traditionally voted Liberal. The riding was held by Monique Bégin from 1976 until her retirement in 1984. She held the Health and Welfare portfolio in the last two Trudeau governments. In 1984 she was succeeded by Liberal Alfonso Gagliano who won the riding by 1,245 votes. Born in Sicily, Gagliano is an accountant by profession and a former chairman of a local school board. At dissolution he was party critic for small business and Canada Post, and was head of the Liberals' Quebec caucus. Gagliano's chances for re-election were not hurt by the electoral redistribution. The riding was substantially modified when the old ridings of Saint-Léonard–Anjou and Mercier were split into Anjou–Rivière-des-Prairies, Saint-Léonard, and Mercier. Votes cast in 1984 in the riding's new limits would give the Liberals a plurality of nearly 5,000 votes. The most exciting event in the riding's campaign occurred when NDP candidate Robert Ferland, an AMWAY distributor, had his campaign organizer read his acceptance speech at a nomination meeting attended by 12 people in a local pizzeria. Ferland's organizer, a former *créditiste*, proceeded to declare his candidate's support of free trade and restrictions on abortion, thus rejecting two key planks of his party's platform. Ferland withdrew as a candidate a few days later, and was replaced by Michel Roche, a doctoral student in political science. The Conservatives ran Marc Beaudoin, a lawyer and Montreal city councillor who sat for eight years with Jean Drapeau's Civic Party. He found running with the Conservatives in Montreal more difficult than running as part of the Drapeau machine: he lost the riding to Gagliano by a 5,959 vote margin. The 50.3% of the vote that the Liberals received represented their third best showing in Quebec.

In 1993, all four major party candidates were of Italian extraction. Gagliano sought re-election and won with an impressive margin of victory of 15,920 votes. Whip of the Official Opposition and critic for small business and for Canada Post Corporation, Gagliano kept the confidence of his constituents. Bloc Québécois ran educator Umberto Di Genova who secured 27.4% of the vote. Conservatives' Tomy Tomassi, a political attaché, received 8.5% of the vote. NPD candidate David D'Andrea, a student, finished fourth with 1.2% of the vote.

Member of Parliament: Alfonso Gagliano; **Party:** Liberal; **Occupation:** Certified general accountant; **Education:** CGA, Sir George Williams University; **Age:** 52 (1942); **Year of first election to the House of Commons:** 1984

24066 Saint-Léonard

A: Political Profile

i) Voting Behaviour

	% 1993	% 1988	Change 1988-93
Conservative	8.5	37.2	-28.7
Liberal	61.2	50.3	10.9
NDP	1.2	10.2	-9
Bloc Québécois	27.4	0	27.4
Other	1.8	2.3	-0.5

% Turnout	79.8	Total Ballots (#)	48432
Rejected Ballots (#)	1342	% Margin of Victory	33.8
Rural Polls, 1988 (#)	0	Urban Polls, 1988 (#)	183
% Yes - 1992	66.6	% No - 1992	33.4

ii) Campaign Financing

	# of Donations	Total $ Value	% of Limit Spent
Conservative	46	49750	65.9*
Liberal	61	50793	99.7
NDP	1	1000	0
Bloc Québécois	161	14855	30.4
Other	4	1180	

B: Ethno-Linguistic Profile

% English Home Language	17.2	% French Home Language	54.4
% Official Bilingual	51.4	% Other Home Language	28.5
% Catholics	88.8	% Protestants	4.5
% Aboriginal Peoples	0.2	% Immigrants	29.3

C: Socio-Economic Profile

Average Family Income $	43434	Median Family Income $	39095
% Low Income Families	23.5	Average Home Price $	227109
% Home Owners	31.8	% Unemployment	12.9
% Labour Force Participation	64.5	% Managerial-Administrative	11.1
% Self-Employed	7	% University Degrees	7.8
% Movers	42.7		

D: Industrial Profile

% Manufacturing	23	% Service Sector	12.9
% Agriculture	0.2	% Mining	0.2
% Forestry	0	% Fishing	0
% Government Services	4.7	% Business Services	6

E: Homogeneity Measures

Ethnic Diversity Index	0.38	Religious Homogeneity Index	0.77
Sectoral Concentration Index	0.42	Income Disparity Index	10

F: Physical Setting Characteristics

Total Population	87843	Area (km²)	15
Population Density (pop/km²)	5856.2		

* Tentative value, due to the existence of unpaid campaign expenses.

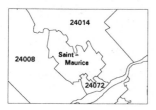

Saint-Maurice

Constituency Number: 24067

The riding of Saint-Maurice is located along the river of the same name, northwest of Trois-Rivières. The riding includes the towns of Shawinigan and Grand-Mère. The riding is 99.2% francophone. The average family income of $38,314 is 16% below the Quebec average. The riding has been experiencing major economic difficulties due to restructuring in the resources sector as well in the chemical industry and textiles. The unemployment figure for 1991 was at 16.6%. Several closures and layoffs have hurt the riding during the two decades: CIL, Dupont, Wabasso, and Shawinigan chemicals, among others.

From 1963 until 1986, Saint-Maurice was the fiefdom of Jean Chrétien. Chrétien easily survived the Mulroney landslide of 1984, winning with a majority of almost 10,000 votes. His 58.9% of the vote in that year was the Liberals' best result in Quebec. After Chrétien went into temporary retirement in 1986, Gilles Grondin won a by-election for the Liberals. He did not seek re-election in 1988, and the chosen candidate, pharmacist Yvon Milette, apparently was not supported by Chrétien. Journalist Denis Pronovost stood for the Conservatives, while the NDP ran Claude Rompré, a teacher. Pronovost won the riding, with a margin of 6,278 votes over the NDP's Rompré. The 30.1% of the vote received by Rompré was the NDP's third best result in Quebec. In this former Liberal stronghold, the Liberal candidate Milette ran a distant third. The issue of depollution of the Saint-Maurice River was an important one during the campaign.

Denis Pronovost did not seek re-election in 1993 following accusation of sexual harassment. Conservatives ran Pauline Daneault, a manager, who finished third with 4.3% of the vote. Claude Rompré ran this time under the banner of the Bloc Québécois and obtained an impressive 40.5% of the vote. Rompré was known to have strong affiliations with the PQ and with the executive of the local NDP as was demonstrated by the defections of both the president and vice-president of the party in favour of the Bloc Québécois candidate. Leader of the Liberal Party Jean Chrétien ran in his former riding and won handily taking 54.1% of the vote. Chrétien is a popular figure in this Quebec riding and has built a strong following over the years. Chrétien has served over the years as Minister of Energy, Mines and Resources, Minister of Finance, Minister of Indian and Northern Affairs, Minister of National Revenue and President of Treasury Board.

Robert Deschamps, a former advisor to the Rhinoceros party, ran for the NDP and received 0.5% just behind parachuted Natural Law candidate, Christian Simard, who received 0.8% of the vote. The Charlottetown Accord was supported by only 35.1%.

Member of Parliament: Jean Chrétien; **Party:** Liberal; **Occupation:** Lawyer and leader of the Liberal Party; **Education:** LL.L; **Age:** 60 (Jan. 11, 1934); **Year of first election to the House of Commons:** 1963

24067 Saint-Maurice

A: Political Profile
i) Voting Behaviour

	% 1993	% 1988	Change 1988-93
Conservative	4.1	45.3	-41.2
Liberal	54.1	24.6	29.5
NDP	0.5	30.1	-29.6
Bloc Québécois	40.5	0	40.5
Other	0.8	0	0.8

% Turnout	83.1	Total Ballots (#)	47622
Rejected Ballots (#)	1009	% Margin of Victory	13.6
Rural Polls, 1988 (#)	58	Urban Polls, 1988 (#)	121
% Yes - 1992	35.1	% No - 1992	64.9

ii) Campaign Financing

	# of Donations	Total $ Value	% of Limit Spent
Conservative	14	7220	53.7
Liberal	96	90768	98.1
NDP	1	1493	0.9
Bloc Québécois	368	41584	86.2
Other	2	1374	

B: Ethno-Linguistic Profile

% English Home Language	0.8	% French Home Language	99.2
% Official Bilingual	16.9	% Other Home Language	0.1
% Catholics	95.3	% Protestants	2.2
% Aboriginal Peoples	0.5	% Immigrants	0.8

C: Socio-Economic Profile

Average Family Income $	38314	Median Family Income $	35299
% Low Income Families	21.3	Average Home Price $	63336
% Home Owners	61.6	% Unemployment	16.6
% Labour Force Participation	54.7	% Managerial-Administrative	8.6
% Self-Employed	7.7	% University Degrees	5.1
% Movers	36.1		

D: Industrial Profile

% Manufacturing	23.7	% Service Sector	12.5
% Agriculture	1.9	% Mining	0.2
% Forestry	1.4	% Fishing	0
% Government Services	9.4	% Business Services	2.8

E: Homogeneity Measures

Ethnic Diversity Index	0.94	Religious Homogeneity Index	0.88
Sectoral Concentration Index	0.36	Income Disparity Index	7.9

F: Physical Setting Characteristics

Total Population	75185	Area (km²)	2315
Population Density (pop/km²)	32.5		

Shefford

Constituency Number: 24068

The riding of Shefford is located seventy kilometres east of Montreal. It includes the towns of Granby and Waterloo. The riding is 96.5% francophone. Its average family income of $43,062 is 6% below the provincial average. Of the riding's workforce 32.9% is employed in the manufacturing sector, the highest proportion in Canada.

Shefford has gone Conservative only twice since Confederation, in 1887 and 1930. Gilbert Rondeau held the riding for the *créditistes* from 1962 to 1965 and again from 1968 to 1979. Lawyer Jean C. Lapierre held the riding for the Liberals from 1979 until his resignation in July 1993, following Jean Chrétien's victory as leader of the Liberal party of Canada, to join the Bloc Québécois. Lapierre served as Minister of State for Youth and for Fitness and Amateur Sport in the short-lived Turner government. Lapierre, who had on occasion indicated his displeasure with John Turner's leadership, was one of only four Liberals in Quebec outside Montreal to survive the 1984 Conservative sweep, holding on to Shefford with a 2,455 vote margin. The 47.5% of the vote he received was the Liberals' fourth best result in the province. The Conservatives hoped to win the riding in 1988 with businesswoman Danielle Côté. The NDP fielded Paul Pearson. Lapierre won once again, with a margin similar to that of 1984. He was the only Quebec Liberal east of Montreal to survive. The 48.2% of the vote received was the Liberals' fifth best showing in Quebec. Lapierre did not seek re-election in 1993.

In 1993 Bloc Québécois Jean H. Leroux had the support of the PQ organization and took the riding with 55.7% of the vote. He won in traditional liberal districts such as Roxton Pond, Saint-Paul and Saint-Césaire but failed to carry Waterloo. Liberals were represented by Granby's Roger Légaré who came second with 29.1% of the vote. Conservatives fielded Jocelyn Compagnat, a corporate director, who received 12.0% of the vote. Having lost the Conservatives' nomination, Denis Loubier ran as an independent and finished in sixth position with 0.5% of the vote. Natural Law and NDP candidates came respectively in fourth and fifth positions with 1.6% and 1.2% of the vote. The main issues during the campaign dealt with decentralization of manpower training, job creation, assistance to small and medium enterprises, and maintenance of the old-age pension.

Member of Parliament: Jean H. Leroux; **Party:** B.Q.; **Occupation:** Teacher; **Education:** BPd (BA in English pedagogy); **Age:** 45 (Feb. 6, 1949); **Year of first election to the House of Commons:** 1993

24068 Shefford

A: Political Profile

i) Voting Behaviour

	% 1993	% 1988	Change 1988-93
Conservative	12	43.2	-31.2
Liberal	29.1	48.2	-19.1
NDP	1.2	8.5	-7.3
Bloc Québécois	55.7	0	55.7
Other	2.1	0	2.1

% Turnout	75.8	Total Ballots (#)	51262
Rejected Ballots (#)	2558	% Margin of Victory	28.7
Rural Polls, 1988 (#)	102	Urban Polls, 1988 (#)	139
% Yes - 1992	39.3	% No - 1992	60.7

ii) Campaign Financing

	# of Donations	Total $ Value	% of Limit Spent
Conservative	189	42605	76*
Liberal	34	24664	69.6
NDP	6	3775	2.3*
Bloc Québécois	471	45791	71.5
Other	1	50	

B: Ethno-Linguistic Profile

% English Home Language	3.2	% French Home Language	96.5
% Official Bilingual	26.9	% Other Home Language	0.3
% Catholics	91.6	% Protestants	4.8
% Aboriginal Peoples	0.6	% Immigrants	2

C: Socio-Economic Profile

Average Family Income $	43062	Median Family Income $	39133
% Low Income Families	14.8	Average Home Price $	88789
% Home Owners	60	% Unemployment	11
% Labour Force Participation	67.5	% Managerial-Administrative	11.8
% Self-Employed	11.7	% University Degrees	5.2
% Movers	46		

D: Industrial Profile

% Manufacturing	32.9	% Service Sector	10.6
% Agriculture	6.9	% Mining	0.1
% Forestry	0	% Fishing	0
% Government Services	3.5	% Business Services	3.3

E: Homogeneity Measures

Ethnic Diversity Index	0.88	Religious Homogeneity Index	0.82
Sectoral Concentration Index	0.35	Income Disparity Index	9.1

F: Physical Setting Characteristics

Total Population	95251	Area (km²)	1367
Population Density (pop/km²)	69.7		

* Tentative value, due to the existence of unpaid campaign expenses.

Sherbrooke

Constituency Number: 24069

The riding of Sherbrooke is centred around the city of the same name, located some 130 kilometres east of Montreal. The riding is 92.8% francophone. The average family income of $42,793 is 7% below the Quebec average. Bishop's and the Université de Sherbrooke are located in the riding. There is a significant manufacturing sector. Berkley Industries and C-MAC are among the most important employers.

Sherbrooke was held by the Liberals from 1911 to 1958. The Conservatives won the elections of 1958 and 1965. From 1962 to 1965 the riding was represented by the *créditistes*. The Liberals recovered the riding in 1968 and held it to the end of the Trudeau period. Irenée Pelletier was MP for Sherbrooke from 1972 until her defeat in 1984 by Jean Charest, a Conservative lawyer. Charest won with a margin of 7,625 votes, and two years later, at the age of 28, he was appointed Minister of State for Youth, the youngest person ever to sit in the cabinet. The Liberals' candidate Dennis Wood ran against free trade, although he had sold his own wallpaper business to an American company. The NDP candidate was Alain Poirier, employed in a documentation centre. Charest won the riding again, increasing his margin to 22,224 votes. Charest had to resign as Minister of State for Youth in 1990 after having tried to influence a judge concerning the selection of athletes. Charest was chosen by Mulroney to prepare a report dealing with Canada's constitutional impasse. He tabled a report which led to the departure of François Gérin, Gilbert Chartrand, and Lucien Bouchard from the caucus. Ironically, Jean Charest was later appointed Minister of Environment, a post occupied previously by Lucien Bouchard.

Charest sought his third consecutive mandate in 1993 and was one of two Conservatives to be elected throughout the country. He received 52.4% of the vote, and saw its margin of victory reduced to 8,210 votes. Charest lost his leadership attempt to Kim Campbell in June 1993; coming second, he was appointed Vice-Prime Minister of Canada. Conservatives obtained their best score in 1993 in this riding. Bloc Québécois ran Guy Boutin, an administrator with deep connections with the sovereigntist movement, who finished second with 37.9% of the vote. Several Bloc Québécois organizers were recruited among Jean Charest's collaborators in the region; Boutin himself was Charest's former campaign manager. Liberals fielded native New Brunswicker and ex-Sherbrooke mayor Jean-Paul Pelletier who obtained a disappointing 7.9% in this former stronghold. Natural Law and NDP candidates received respectively 0.9% and 0.8% of the vote. Among the main issues were transfer of environment technology and job creation.

Member of Parliament: Jean J. Charest; **Party:** P.C.; **Occupation:** Lawyer, Member of Parliament; **Education:** LL.B, Université de Sherbrooke; **Age:** 36 (June 24, 1958); **Year of first election to the House of Commons:** 1984

24069 Sherbrooke

A: Political Profile
i) Voting Behaviour

	% 1993	% 1988	Change 1988-93
Conservative	52.4	63.3	-10.9
Liberal	7.9	22.6	-14.7
NDP	0.8	11.7	-10.9
Bloc Québécois	37.9	0	37.9
Other	1.1	2.4	-1.3

% Turnout	78.1	Total Ballots (#)	58073
Rejected Ballots (#)	1254	% Margin of Victory	14.5
Rural Polls, 1988 (#)	0	Urban Polls, 1988 (#)	233
% Yes - 1992	41.8	% No - 1992	58.2

ii) Campaign Financing

	# of Donations	Total $ Value	% of Limit Spent
Conservative	221	82747	95.2
Liberal	127	30658	45.2
NDP	2	2200	0
Bloc Québécois	218	31665	84.7
Other	14	6940	

B: Ethno-Linguistic Profile

% English Home Language	5.6	% French Home Language	92.8
% Official Bilingual	37.6	% Other Home Language	1.6
% Catholics	89.1	% Protestants	5.1
% Aboriginal Peoples	0.4	% Immigrants	4.2

C: Socio-Economic Profile

Average Family Income $	42793	Median Family Income $	36552
% Low Income Families	23.5	Average Home Price $	94572
% Home Owners	40.4	% Unemployment	11.8
% Labour Force Participation	63.2	% Managerial-Administrative	10.7
% Self-Employed	7.7	% University Degrees	13.1
% Movers	53.7		

D: Industrial Profile

% Manufacturing	15.7	% Service Sector	14.8
% Agriculture	0.8	% Mining	0
% Forestry	0.5	% Fishing	0
% Government Services	6.5	% Business Services	4.8

E: Homogeneity Measures

Ethnic Diversity Index	0.82	Religious Homogeneity Index	0.76
Sectoral Concentration Index	0.51	Income Disparity Index	14.6

F: Physical Setting Characteristics

Total Population	95171	Area (km²)	105
Population Density (pop/km²)	906.4		

Témiscamingue

Constituency Number: 24070

The riding of Témiscamingue is located in western Quebec, bordering on Ontario. It includes the towns of Rouyn-Noranda, and Témiscamingue. The riding is 95.2% francophone. The average family income of $44,484 is slightly below the Quebec average. Mining occupies 9.5% of the work force, the third highest proportion in Quebec. Pulp and paper activities are also important in the riding. Unemployment tends to be particularly high, with 17.1% in 1991.

From 1968 to 1979, Témiscamingue was the riding of *créditiste* Réal Caouette. He was followed by Liberal Henri Tousignant who, in turn, was defeated by 6,591 votes by Conservative Gabriel Desjardins. Desjardins, who has worked as a businessman and professor, served as co-chair of the Official Languages Committee of the House. The NDP's Rémy Trudel was considered one of the party's strongest candidates in the province. The first rector of the Université du Québec in Abitibi-Témiscamingue, Trudel was supported by local Quebec Liberal Party and PQ activists. The Liberals ran lawyer Laurent Guertin, considered out of the running throughout the campaign. Desjardins held the riding with a plurality of 3,483 votes. Trudel took second place for the NDP. The 37.8% of the vote that he received was the party's best showing in Quebec.

Desjardins stood for re-election in 1993 but finished third with 19.3% of the vote. Liberals fielded educator Gilles Héroux, unknown in the riding, who obtained 22.9% of the vote. Bloc Québécois Pierre Brien, an economist trained at the École des Hautes Études Commerciales (HEC) with strong affiliation with the PQ, won the riding with a plurality of 13,292 and 55.7% of the vote. Témiscamingue was the only riding without NDP representation. Former candidate Rémy Trudel, a Bloc sympathizer, has since been elected to Quebec's National Assembly.

Member of Parliament: Pierre Brien; **Party:** B.Q.; **Occupation:** Economist; **Education:** BAA (Diploma in Business Administration, Economics option, HEC); **Age:** 24 (June 22, 1970); **Year of first election to the House of Commons:** 1993

24070 Témiscamingue

A: Political Profile

i) Voting Behaviour

	% 1993	% 1988	Change 1988-93
Conservative	19.3	46.3	-27
Liberal	22.9	14.2	8.7
NDP	0	37.8	-37.8
Bloc Québécois	55.7	0	55.7
Other	2	1.7	0.3

% Turnout	70.7	Total Ballots (#)	41921
Rejected Ballots (#)	1486	% Margin of Victory	34.8
Rural Polls, 1988 (#)	135	Urban Polls, 1988 (#)	84
% Yes - 1992	35.3	% No - 1992	64.7

ii) Campaign Financing

	# of Donations	Total $ Value	% of Limit Spent
Conservative	72	39288	82.2
Liberal	8	22226	34.8*
NDP	0	0	0
Bloc Québécois	433	27615	88
Other	5	700	

B: Ethno-Linguistic Profile

% English Home Language	4.5	% French Home Language	95.2
% Official Bilingual	24.9	% Other Home Language	0.4
% Catholics	95.1	% Protestants	2.4
% Aboriginal Peoples	2.3	% Immigrants	1.3

C: Socio-Economic Profile

Average Family Income $	44484	Median Family Income $	40543
% Low Income Families	14.9	Average Home Price $	70015
% Home Owners	64	% Unemployment	17.1
% Labour Force Participation	63.5	% Managerial-Administrative	10.8
% Self-Employed	7.5	% University Degrees	5.8
% Movers	41.4		

D: Industrial Profile

% Manufacturing	10.8	% Service Sector	12.9
% Agriculture	3.3	% Mining	9.5
% Forestry	3.7	% Fishing	0
% Government Services	6.3	% Business Services	3.1

E: Homogeneity Measures

Ethnic Diversity Index	0.87	Religious Homogeneity Index	0.89
Sectoral Concentration Index	0.34	Income Disparity Index	8.9

F: Physical Setting Characteristics

Total Population	83547	Area (km²)	2645
Population Density (pop/km²)	2.6		

* Tentative value, due to the existence of unpaid campaign expenses.

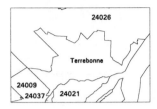

Terrebonne

Constituency Number: 24071

The riding of Terrebonne is located just north of Montreal, across the river from Île-Jésus. Terrebonne includes the towns of Repentigny and Bois-des-Filion and is often viewed as a bedroom community. It is 97.2% francophone. With 152,721 residents, Terrebonne is the most populous riding in the province. The riding is generally well off: the average family income of $51,078 is 11% above the provincial average. Occupants own 78.1% of dwellings in the riding, the third highest proportion in the province and third highest in the country. Manufacturing is important with companies such as Jaymar furniture and Décor Cooper.

Prior to 1984, Terrebonne had voted Liberal in every general election since 1917, with the exception of the 1958 Diefenbaker sweep. Roland Comtois represented the riding from 1968 until he was soundly defeated in 1984. The Conservatives' 1984 candidate, Robert Toupin, won that year with a margin of 24,782 votes. Later, he left the Conservative caucus in 1986 to sit with the NDP, and then finally sat as an independent, a political trajectory that earned him the epithet of the 'chameleon.' Toupin ran in the 1988 campaign as an independent. In that campaign, the Conservatives ran Jean-Marc Robitaille, a realtor and president of local riding association. The Liberal candidate and party activist was Claire Brouillet, niece of the late Pierre Laporte, the Quebec cabinet minister who died in the October crisis. Like others, Brouillet focused on the problem of the Canada Post super mail-boxes. The NDP candidate was Lauraine Vaillancourt, a Quebec Federation of Labour vice-president. Robitaille won with a margin of 22,923 votes. The voters did not entirely turn their backs on their former MP: Robert Toupin received 15.5% of the vote, and came close to edging out the Liberal candidate for second place. His result was the best for any independent candidate in Quebec.

Conservative Jean-Marc Robitaille sought re-election in 1993 and came third with only 11.7% of the vote. Claire Brouillet ran again for the Liberals and received 17.9% the vote. Newcomer Bloc Québécois Benoît Sauvageau, history teacher, won the riding with an impressive 68.9% of the vote, and a plurality of 42,928 votes. This was the Bloc Québécois' second best result in Quebec. NDP fielded teacher Renée-Claude Lorimier who obtained 1.1% of the vote. The principal issues of the campaign were job creation, tourism, and debt and deficit control. The riding had registered the fifth strongest opposition vote to Charlottetown in Quebec.

Member of Parliament: Benoît Sauvageau; **Party:** B.Q.; **Occupation:** Teacher; **Education:** BA in history; **Age:** 31 (Nov. 22, 1963); **Year of first election to the House of Commons:** 1993

24071 Terrebonne

A: Political Profile

i) Voting Behaviour

	% 1993	% 1988	Change 1988-93
Conservative	11.7	52.8	-41.1
Liberal	17.9	18.5	-0.6
NDP	1.1	15.5	-14.4
Bloc Québécois	68.9	0	68.9
Other	0.5	13.2	-12.7

% Turnout	79.1	Total Ballots (#)	88233
Rejected Ballots (#)	3973	% Margin of Victory	51.5
Rural Polls, 1988 (#)	0	Urban Polls, 1988 (#)	272
% Yes - 1992	27	% No - 1992	73

ii) Campaign Financing

	# of Donations	Total $ Value	% of Limit Spent
Conservative	111	34590	89.9
Liberal	204	40794	58.3*
NDP	1	1000	0
Bloc Québécois	705	43564	66
Other	0	0	

B: Ethno-Linguistic Profile

% English Home Language	2.3	% French Home Language	97.2
% Official Bilingual	34.4	% Other Home Language	0.5
% Catholics	94.7	% Protestants	2.5
% Aboriginal Peoples	0.7	% Immigrants	2.4

C: Socio-Economic Profile

Average Family Income $	51078	Median Family Income $	48010
% Low Income Families	13.5	Average Home Price $	109897
% Home Owners	78.1	% Unemployment	9.6
% Labour Force Participation	72.9	% Managerial-Administrative	13.7
% Self-Employed	8.5	% University Degrees	6.9
% Movers	48.9		

D: Industrial Profile

% Manufacturing	17.3	% Service Sector	10.7
% Agriculture	0.7	% Mining	0.2
% Forestry	0	% Fishing	0
% Government Services	6.5	% Business Services	4.9

E: Homogeneity Measures

Ethnic Diversity Index	0.85	Religious Homogeneity Index	0.89
Sectoral Concentration Index	0.41	Income Disparity Index	6

F: Physical Setting Characteristics

Total Population	152721	Area (km²)	300
Population Density (pop/km²)	509.1		

* Tentative value, due to the existence of unpaid campaign expenses.

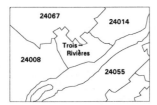

Trois-Rivières

Constituency Number: 24072

The riding of Trois-Rivières includes the town of the same name, as well as the municipalities of Pointe-du-Lac, Saint-Étienne-des-Grès and Yamachiche, and runs west from there along the St Lawrence River. The riding is 98.8% francophone. The average family income of $44,670 is slightly below the provincial average. Important employers are Krueger and Stone Consolidated (sector Wayagamak), Laperrière & Verreault and Niagara Lockport (paper machinery), and Duchesne and Sons (metallurgy).

Trois-Rivières is something of an oddity in Quebec. At the start of the Trudeau era, the Liberals had not won an election there since 1940. Léon Balcer represented the riding for the Conservatives from 1949 to 1965. Balcer's 1949 victory was one of only two for the Conservatives in Quebec that year. Liberal Claude Lajoie won the riding in a 1971 by-election and held it until 1984, when he decided not to seek re-election. Lawyer Pierre H. Vincent won the riding for the Conservatives in 1984 with a margin of 16,627 votes. In his 1988 bid for re-election, Vincent was facing Nicholas Papirakis, a restaurant owner. Though running for the Liberals, Papirakis was something less than a committed member of the Turner team: he had tried unsuccessfully for the Conservative nomination in the riding of Saint-Denis before accepting the Liberal nomination in Trois-Rivières. The NDP candidate was Josée Trudel, a 26-year-old community worker. Vincent won re-election with a margin of 22,643 votes. The 68.9% of the vote he received was the Conservatives' sixth best showing in the country.

Pierre H. Vincent ran again in 1993 but could not withstand the tidal wave against his party. Vincent was offered a ministerial post only in January 1993, nine years after he had entered the Conservatives' caucus. This hurt his chances for re-election. Liberals fielded Jean-Pierre Caron, a former Trois-Rivières city councillor and founding president of the Saint-Maurice River development action committee. Caron finished third with 21.2% of the vote. Bloc Québécois Yves Rocheleau, a development consultant with the Quebec department of Industry, Trade and Technology, easily won the riding with 53.4% of the vote, and a margin of victory of 13,977 votes. NDP parachuted Lachine translator Maryse Choquette who finished behind the Natural Law candidate with only 0.8% of the vote.

Member of Parliament: Yves Rocheleau; **Party:** B.Q.; **Occupation:** Development consultant; **Education:** BA (Administration and History); **Age:** 50 (Oct. 31, 1944); **Year of first election to the House of Commons:** 1993

24072 Trois-Rivières

A: Political Profile

i) Voting Behaviour

	% 1993	% 1988	Change 1988-93
Conservative	23.5	68.9	-45.4
Liberal	21.2	15.8	5.4
NDP	0.8	12.8	-12
Bloc Québécois	53.4	0	53.4
Other	1.1	2.5	-1.4

% Turnout	77.1	Total Ballots (#)	48423
Rejected Ballots (#)	1772	% Margin of Victory	31
Rural Polls, 1988 (#)	27	Urban Polls, 1988 (#)	164
% Yes - 1992	37.2	% No - 1992	62.8

ii) Campaign Financing

	# of Donations	Total $ Value	% of Limit Spent
Conservative	100	75336	98.2
Liberal	82	41094	92.4
NDP	2	2200	0
Bloc Québécois	441	34067	59.3
Other	11	4618	

B: Ethno-Linguistic Profile

% English Home Language	0.9	% French Home Language	98.8
% Official Bilingual	23.7	% Other Home Language	0.3
% Catholics	95.5	% Protestants	1.6
% Aboriginal Peoples	0.7	% Immigrants	1.4

C: Socio-Economic Profile

Average Family Income $	44670	Median Family Income $	39711
% Low Income Families	22.3	Average Home Price $	81728
% Home Owners	49.3	% Unemployment	12.9
% Labour Force Participation	61.1	% Managerial-Administrative	12.5
% Self-Employed	6.7	% University Degrees	10.7
% Movers	46.4		

D: Industrial Profile

% Manufacturing	17.7	% Service Sector	14.3
% Agriculture	1.5	% Mining	0.1
% Forestry	0.3	% Fishing	0
% Government Services	6.5	% Business Services	3.9

E: Homogeneity Measures

Ethnic Diversity Index	0.91	Religious Homogeneity Index	0.89
Sectoral Concentration Index	0.43	Income Disparity Index	11.1

F: Physical Setting Characteristics

Total Population	79784	Area (km²)	383
Population Density (pop/km²)	208.3		

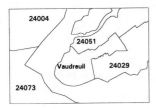

Vaudreuil

Constituency Number: 24073

The riding of Vaudreuil includes the western tip of the Island of Montreal, and runs from there all the way to the Ontario border. The riding is 64.2% francophone, and includes the wealthy anglophone suburbs of Kirkland and Baie d'Urfé, the more working-class areas of Vaudreuil and Dorion, and a large agricultural area in the western part of the riding. Despite the large rural component of the riding, 2.6% of the constituents are farmers. The riding's average family income of $59,161 is well above the Quebec average. Manufacturing is an important provider of jobs: Merck Frosst pharmaceuticals employs approximately 1,000 people, and SPAR aerospace research hires 1,200 employees.

Prior to 1984, Vaudreuil voted Liberal in 23 out of 25 general elections dating back to 1891, the exceptions being 1958 and 1962. Hal Herbert held the riding from 1972 to 1984, but he was soundly defeated in the 1984 election by Conservative Pierre H. Cadieux, who won with a margin of 17,137 votes. Cadieux, a lawyer by profession, was appointed Minister of Labour in 1986. Popular in the area, Cadieux's 1988 candidacy was endorsed by 25 of the riding's 31 mayors. The Liberal riding association, divided over the leadership of John Turner, nominated Jean Blais, a former alderman in Dorion. Blais, an air traffic controller, won the nomination over former MP Hal Herbert. The NDP fielded translator Suzanne Aubertin, associate president of the party's Quebec wing and member of the party's executive. Free trade was a key issue. Late in the campaign, some Montreal newspapers thought that Cadieux would have trouble winning re-election. They were wrong: he won by 13,999 votes, almost double the votes of his Liberal opponent.

In 1993, Cadieux did seek re-election but chose to tender his resignation the day before Kim Campbell called the election. Conservatives were represented by Cadieux's former political aide, Richard Préfontaine who came third with 9.9% of the vote. Bloc Québécois ran Mario Turbide, a community organizer and health worker, who finished second with 38.6% of the vote. Liberals ran Kirkland mayor Nick Discepola who won the riding with 47.8% of the vote and a margin of victory of 6,010 votes. NDP fielded ecological agriculturist Yves Marie Christin who took fourth place with 1.7% of the vote.

Member of Parliament: Nick Discepola; **Party:** Liberal; **Occupation:** Self-employed, Mayor of the Town of Kirkland (1989-1993); **Education:** MBA; **Age:** 44; **Year of first election to the House of Commons:** 1993

24073 Vaudreuil

A: Political Profile

i) Voting Behaviour

	% 1993	% 1988	Change 1988-93
Conservative	9.9	55.7	-45.8
Liberal	47.8	30	17.8
NDP	1.7	11.3	-9.6
Bloc Québécois	38.6	0	38.6
Other	2.1	3	-0.9

% Turnout	82	Total Ballots (#)	67085
Rejected Ballots (#)	1868	% Margin of Victory	9.2
Rural Polls, 1988 (#)	103	Urban Polls, 1988 (#)	116
% Yes - 1992	56.5	% No - 1992	43.5

ii) Campaign Financing

	# of Donations	Total $ Value	% of Limit Spent
Conservative	105	48760	76.3
Liberal	277	80317	82.7
NDP	2	3854	4.5
Bloc Québécois	164	37987	58.5
Other	5	900	

B: Ethno-Linguistic Profile

% English Home Language	33.7	% French Home Language	64.2
% Official Bilingual	54.2	% Other Home Language	2.1
% Catholics	76.9	% Protestants	14.8
% Aboriginal Peoples	0.5	% Immigrants	9.8

C: Socio-Economic Profile

Average Family Income $	59161	Median Family Income $	52496
% Low Income Families	9.4	Average Home Price $	143150
% Home Owners	77.6	% Unemployment	8.1
% Labour Force Participation	71.2	% Managerial-Administrative	17.8
% Self-Employed	10.2	% University Degrees	14
% Movers	46.4		

D: Industrial Profile

% Manufacturing	19	% Service Sector	10.4
% Agriculture	2.6	% Mining	0.2
% Forestry	0.2	% Fishing	0
% Government Services	4.2	% Business Services	6

E: Homogeneity Measures

Ethnic Diversity Index	0.55	Religious Homogeneity Index	0.6
Sectoral Concentration Index	0.43	Income Disparity Index	11.3

F: Physical Setting Characteristics

Total Population	110838	Area (km²)	1070
Population Density (pop/km²)	103.6		

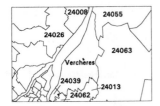

Verchères

Constituency Number: 24074

The riding of Verchères runs along 50 kilometres of the south bank of the St Lawrence River, beginning across from the eastern tip of the Island of Montreal. The riding includes the towns of Boucherville, Contrecoeur, Sainte-Julie, and Varennes. The riding is 97.6% francophone. It is generally wealthy: the average family income of $59,596 is well above the Quebec average; 80.1% of the dwellings in Verchères are owned by their occupants, the highest proportion in Quebec.

Conservative Marcel Danis won Verchères in 1984 with an enormous 19,325 vote-margin over Bernard Loiselle, who had represented the area since 1974. Danis, by profession a lawyer and university professor at Concordia, served as Deputy Speaker in Ottawa. In 1988, he was opposed by Liberal candidate Maurice Lemoine, a lawyer. Former hospital administrator and community worker Maria Jean ran for the NDP. Jean has the unusual political history of being both an ex-Liberal Party activist from the Trudeau years and a Quebec nationalist. Danis increased his plurality this time, to 23,830 votes. The 66.1% of the votes received by the Conservatives was their ninth best result in the country.

Marcel Danis did not seek re-election in 1993. Conservatives fielded lawyer François Leduc, a party activist, who finished third with 9.2% of the vote. Leduc is attached to the Meenan Blaikie law firm. Leduc acquired his experience working for several Liberal MPs, among them John Harvard, Lloyd Axworthy, Derek Lee and Raymond Garneau. Liberals were represented by party activist and legislative assistant Benoît Chiquette who received 21.1% of the vote. NDP parachuted Wakefield industrial hygienist Frances Elbourne who took 1.2% of the vote. Stéphane Bergeron, a political attaché for PQ MNA François Beaulne, won the riding for the Bloc Québécois as he obtained 67.3% of the vote, and received a plurality of 26,501 votes. Bergeron had received a Jean-Charles Bonenfant bursary for a parliamentary internship in Quebec's National Assembly.

Member of Parliamen: Stéphane Bergeron; **Party:** B.Q.; **Occupation:** Political attaché; **Education:** MA (Political Science); **Age:** 29 (Jan. 28, 1965); **Year of first election to the House of Commons:** 1993

24074 Verchères

A: Political Profile
i) Voting Behaviour

	% 1993	% 1988	Change 1988-93
Conservative	9.2	66	-56.8
Liberal	21.1	17.3	3.8
NDP	1.2	13.8	-12.6
Bloc Québécois	67.3	0	67.3
Other	1.1	2.8	-1.7

% Turnout	82.6	Total Ballots (#)	60036
Rejected Ballots (#)	2643	% Margin of Victory	47.3
Rural Polls, 1988 (#)	44	Urban Polls, 1988 (#)	142
% Yes - 1992	31.2	% No - 1992	68.8

ii) Campaign Financing

	# of Donations	Total $ Value	% of Limit Spent
Conservative	65	16850	53.4*
Liberal	85	35930	64.9
NDP	2	2200	0
Bloc Québécois	549	40346	85.3
Other	13	1580	

B: Ethno-Linguistic Profile

% English Home Language	1.9	% French Home Language	97.6
% Official Bilingual	37.7	% Other Home Language	0.5
% Catholics	94.9	% Protestants	2.1
% Aboriginal Peoples	0.3	% Immigrants	2.6

C: Socio-Economic Profile

Average Family Income $	59596	Median Family Income $	54942
% Low Income Families	7.7	Average Home Price $	122016
% Home Owners	80.1	% Unemployment	8.1
% Labour Force Participation	74	% Managerial-Administrative	16.4
% Self-Employed	9.3	% University Degrees	12
% Movers	43		

D: Industrial Profile

% Manufacturing	20.5	% Service Sector	9.9
% Agriculture	2	% Mining	0.4
% Forestry	0	% Fishing	0
% Government Services	6.7	% Business Services	6

E: Homogeneity Measures

Ethnic Diversity Index	0.88	Religious Homogeneity Index	0.89
Sectoral Concentration Index	0.4	Income Disparity Index	7.8

F: Physical Setting Characteristics

Total Population	96594	Area (km²)	840
Population Density (pop/km²)	115		

* Tentative value, due to the existence of unpaid campaign expenses.

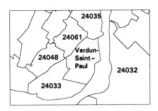

Verdun–Saint-Paul

Constituency Number: 24075

The riding of Verdun–Saint-Paul is located in the centre-south part of the Island of Montreal. It includes the Town of Verdun and part of the Town of Montreal. The riding is 68.5% francophone and 26.3% anglophone. It includes lower income areas such as Verdun and Pointe-Saint-Charles, and the middle class residential area of Île-des-soeurs. Its average family income of $41,639 is 9% below the Quebec average. Jobs are a concern in the riding, with a number of factories having closed or cut back operations in recent years. Imperial Tobacco, AMF Domglass, and Téléglobe provide a significant number of jobs.

The riding was created in 1947. Prior to 1984 it had voted Liberal with the one exception of the 1958 Diefenbaker sweep. An 'ancestor' of the riding, though, also named Verdun, went Conservative in 1935, a year in which the party won only five seats in Quebec. Bryce Mackasey held the riding for most of the 1960s and 1970s. Raymond Savard was MP from 1979 to 1984, but he lost to the Conservatives in the 1984 election. The incumbent in the 1988 campaign was the Conservatives' Gilbert Chartrand. Chartrand ran a bicycle shop before he was elected in 1984 with a margin of 917 votes. Considered a low profile MP, Chartrand spent $25,000 of his own money on advertising in the months before the election to attempt to raise his profile. Furniture store owner Raymond Lavigne represented the Liberals after winning a nomination battle that left local Liberals divided. The NDP ran Alain Tassé, a project manager with the Quebec Housing Association. Chartrand won the riding for a second time, with a much-improved margin of 4,906 votes. His support was concentrated in the more francophone parts of the riding. MP Gilbert Chartrand quit the Conservative caucus on 22 May 1990 in protest of Jean Charest's report on changes to be made to the Meech Lake Accord and sat as an independent before returning to the Conservatives in April 1991.

Chartrand did not seek re-election in 1993. He was replaced by his political assistant from 1983 to 1994, André Martin. Martin finished third with only 8.6% of the vote. Liberal candidate was again Raymond Lavigne who won the riding with a narrow margin of victory of 549 votes on Bloc Québécois 24-year-old bank representative Kim Beaudoin. NDP postal worker Claude Ledoux finished fourth with 1.9% of the vote.

Member of Parliament: Raymond Lavigne; **Party:** Liberal; **Occupation:** Consultant; **Education:** Studies in administration and sales techniques, Université de Montréal; **Age:** 49 (Nov. 16, 1945); **Year of first election to the House of Commons:** 1993

24075 Verdun–Saint-Paul

A: Political Profile

i) Voting Behaviour

	% 1993	% 1988	Change 1988-93
Conservative	8.6	45.3	-36.7
Liberal	43.7	34.3	9.4
NDP	1.9	14.8	-12.9
Bloc Québécois	42.5	0	42.5
Other	3.5	5.6	-2.1

% Turnout	75.5	Total Ballots (#)	46686
Rejected Ballots (#)	1720	% Margin of Victory	2.3
Rural Polls, 1988 (#)	0	Urban Polls, 1988 (#)	188
% Yes - 1992	50.7	% No - 1992	49.3

ii) Campaign Financing

	# of Donations	Total $ Value	% of Limit Spent
Conservative	83	32726	94.1
Liberal	106	26800	66.7
NDP	1	1882	1.6
Bloc Québécois	151	21608	65
Other	9	6200	

B: Ethno-Linguistic Profile

% English Home Language	26.3	% French Home Language	68.5
% Official Bilingual	50.1	% Other Home Language	5.2
% Catholics	79.5	% Protestants	11.3
% Aboriginal Peoples	0.4	% Immigrants	9.6

C: Socio-Economic Profile

Average Family Income $	41639	Median Family Income $	34822
% Low Income Families	34.2	Average Home Price $	140126
% Home Owners	24.6	% Unemployment	13.4
% Labour Force Participation	59	% Managerial-Administrative	13.3
% Self-Employed	6.5	% University Degrees	11.3
% Movers	53.1		

D: Industrial Profile

% Manufacturing	16.7	% Service Sector	13.6
% Agriculture	0.3	% Mining	0.1
% Forestry	0.1	% Fishing	0
% Government Services	5.2	% Business Services	9.7

E: Homogeneity Measures

Ethnic Diversity Index	0.53	Religious Homogeneity Index	0.63
Sectoral Concentration Index	0.51	Income Disparity Index	16.4

F: Physical Setting Characteristics

Total Population	86405	Area (km²)	17
Population Density (pop/km²)	5082.6		

ONTARIO

Ontario

Provincial Overview

Ontario is Canada's heartland province. The province's name is taken from the Iroquois word meaning 'beautiful lakes' or 'beautiful water', an appropriate term for a province in which one-sixth of the area is covered by water. It is the most populous (over ten million residents in 1991, up 10.8% since 1986) and the most affluent of the ten provinces. Geographically, the province is extremely diverse. The northern two-thirds is comprised of the 'Canadian Shield', which is a rugged area scarred by numerous periods of glacial advance and retreat. Southern Ontario, by contrast, is made up of relatively flat or at most gently rolling landscapes. Population is distributed unevenly across this terrain; roughly 90 per cent of the province's residents live in southern Ontario. The combination of the province's central geographic position in Canada, its economic power, its long-standing role in Canadian federalism as a donor province through the equalization grant system, its demographic dominance, and the fact that the national capital is located here, has cultivated among residents a relatively strong sense of Canadian nationalism. Though the vote was close, Ontario was among the four provinces that voted in favour of the Charlottetown Accord in the 1992 referendum.

The economy of Ontario is diverse. Significant resource endowments, both in renewable (hydro-electric power) and non-renewable forms, have ensured that primary industries are important players in the province's economy. The north is sparsely populated, with towns and cities primarily located at transportation junctures on the Great Lakes, or spread out along the Trans-Canada Highway or the railroads. Originally opened up by fur traders who followed the Ottawa River westwards through Lake Nipissing to Lake Superior, the north's economy has been dominated by transportation, resource-extraction and tourism. As such, the region has been somewhat vulnerable to a 'boom-bust' cycle that reflects world commodity market forces. Often harsh living conditions, coupled with a sense of being an internal 'periphery' within Ontario, have engendered a sense of sub-provincial regional identity among residents. Politically, the region is divided into ten ridings (Algoma, Cochrane–Superior, Kenora–Rainy River, Nickel Belt, Nipissing, Sudbury, Thunder Bay–Atikokan, Thunder Bay–Nipigon, Timiskaming, and Timmins–Chapleau).

The southern region combines agricultural land with heavily urbanized settlement patterns. As a whole, the province contains over half of Canada's 'class 1' agricultural land, and virtually all of this is in the south. The 'golden horseshoe', stretching from Oshawa in the east, around the tip of Lake Ontario to Hamilton and St Catharines, is Canada's most heavily urban area. Politically, this densely populated area returns more MPs to the House of Commons (45) than any province except Quebec. At the centre of this prosperous and highly developed urban sub-region, of course, is Toronto, Canada's largest city. The Metro Toronto area itself accounts for 23 ridings. As might be expected, the economy here is highly diversified, with manufacturing, service trades, and agriculture all playing important roles. Proximity to the United States is also significant in this part of the country, particularly so in the past two elections (1988 and 1993) in which international trade agreements figured prominently in the campaigning.

The province's political geography reflects this geographic diversity, prompting some political scientists to distinguish between Northern and Southern Ontario. However, this variety is seemingly belied by the Liberal Party's domination of the 1993 election. Once the dust had settled after the voting on October 25th, a stunning 98 of the province's 99 ridings were represented by Liberal MPs, giving the province an unprecedented level of homogeneity in terms of its partisan representation in the federal government. Could it be that the province's electorate, long noted for its fickle partisan character, was responding *en masse* to a uniform set of political forces that were either province-wide, or perhaps national, in scope?

Doubtless there is something to this interpretation. Voters from sea to sea to sea were discontented and cynical. Many had been drawn to the polls a year earlier to cast a ballot in the constitutional referendum, a vote which was widely interpreted as a repudiation of Canada's political élite. On October 25th, this combination of anger, anti-politician sentiment and perhaps political fatigue produced a low 67.7% turnout rate in Ontario, the lowest level in the province since 1953. The campaign itself seemed to be dominated by a series of issues and images that played themselves out nationally. The Conservatives were struggling with a new leader and an enormously unpopular record as governing party. While there were many reasons for this unpopularity, probably the most important contributing factor was the economic recession that set in as 1989 ended. Not only did the Mulroney administration seem powerless to combat the hard economic times, their GST policy seemed to positively exacerbate the problem. Coming on the heels of the super-heated economy of the mid-to-late 1980s, in which incomes and house prices soared while unemployment levels dropped, this economic turn-around was too much for the governing party to withstand. Kim Campbell's decision to make the deficit a campaigning priority in 1993 arguably seemed insensitive to the plight of those most directly affected by the recession.

A closer look at the Ontario riding-by-riding results contained in the following section suggests that this national focus, while helpful, is incomplete, and that a more nuanced interpretation of the 1993 result may be appropriate. Moreover, 'national' forces assumed a distinctive regional, and even local, expression in Ontario. While the recession was national in scope, it was also different in character from other recent ones. Unlike many earlier recessions, this economic downturn struck deeply into the affluent heart of urban, middle-class Ontario. Downsizing, plant closings, layoffs, managerial restructuring, these were the words that echoed through not only the shop floors but also the corporate boardrooms throughout the province in these years, affecting virtually all but the most well-to-do, either directly or as a prospect. Province-wide, census figures reveal that unemployment levels rose from 6.8% in 1986 to 8.5% in 1991. The recession had not bottomed out in 1991, though, and these levels were probably considerably higher as the election neared. Dropping house values left many in a middle class that had traditionally been insulated from recessionary forces holding mortgages they could no longer afford and with houses that could not be sold. Many laid blame for these developments squarely at the feet of the Conservatives and their Free Trade Agreement (FTA), that had opened up the province's industries to continental economic forces. The North American Free Trade Agreement (NAFTA) subsequently negotiated by the Tories promised more of the same, but this issue did not achieve the prominence in the 1993 campaign that the FTA had in 1988.

As is customary in recessionary times, however, those at the bottom of the economic heap continued to suffer. Signs that this was changing were only just beginning to be seen in the province in the months prior to the 1993 election. For example, the welfare roll in Metro Toronto dropped for the first time in four years in August of 1993 (to a case load of 120,510 cases, down 300 from the preceding month). This economic scenario played havoc with the incumbent Tories' re-election campaign. Nationwide, candidates were forced to justify past government decisions rather than project glorious futures. Scandals, such as the mishandling of the privatization of the Pearson Airport, further hurt the party's image in the province. In Ontario, as election day approached, none of the Tories' 46 seats was considered safe, and most (except for about a dozen seats) were considered unwinnable.

The Tories were not the only party facing difficulties coming into the 1993 campaign. The New Democrats had taken one in every five Ontario votes in 1988, although this produced only ten seats for the party. Following Bob Rae's surprise victory in the September 1990 provincial election, party strategists optimistically developed scenarios for the upcoming federal campaign in which they would target the Liberals and Chrétien and score impressive advances. Although the NDP's collapse was national in scope, it was especially dramatic in Ontario. The massive unpopularity of Rae and his government doubtless contributed to the province-wide 14% drop in support for the party's federal candidates in 1993. Not only did this hurt the party in terms of the average voter, but the activist core of the NDP had become disillusioned by the austere 'social contract' pursued by the provincial administration. Attempting to cope with the swelling numbers of claimants for government transfers at a time of shrinking governmental revenues, Rae's government was forced to cut services. Provisions of the contract that called for re-opening collective agreements were particularly reviled by the labour movement, which interpreted this as an attack on collective bargaining. The feeling of betrayal that accompanied the release of the contract was palpable. As the party's fortunes declined over the campaign, the party targeted a handful of seats for intensive campaigning (Beaches–Woodbine, Trinity–Spadina, for example, where the local electorates are progressive and activist in their orientations). These desperate efforts, ultimately unsuccessful, stressed the need to elect at least some 'left wingers' to the House of Commons, and that dwelt upon the qualities of their local candidates.

For the first time in Ontario, the NDP could not count on a 'protest vote'. Dispirit among the party faithful, of course, left it unable to mount the kind of mobilization effort in getting out the core vote that might have made a difference. Many erstwhile NDP voters probably stayed at home on October 25th (turnout was down about 7% from 1988 in Ontario, and turnout was about 1.5% lower in the 10 seats held by the NDP following the 1988 election than other ridings in the province). It seems highly likely that some of the Liberal Party's 14% gain in popular vote was attributable to migration from this source. NDP candidates all over the province found themselves campaigning against their provincial counterparts, though most fell short of Steven Langdon's (Essex–Windsor) highly public criticism of the Rae administration.

A new dimension was added to party politics in the province when the Reform Party decided to break out of its heartland in western Canada. Preston Manning announced Reform's intention to campaign in Ontario in 1991 and ventured that the party should have particular appeal to the northern Ontario voters who might be tired of being dominated by southern Ontario politicians. Manning made several pre-campaign and campaign swings through the province, speaking to large and enthusiastic audiences, and starting in 1992 local riding associations began popping up around Ontario. Reform found fertile soil in the rural and more 'traditional' anglophone areas of southern and eastern Ontario, and in the tax-weary middle-class suburban areas of the province's cities. In southern Ontario, Reform support seemed to build nicely upon the Christian fundamentalist vote attracted in 1988 by the Christian Heritage Party. Voters seemed to respond positively to Reform's critique of 'big government' and its 'law and order' message.

Ontario was a particular target in Reform's eastward expansion plans, as the party's organizers looked hungrily at the province's large middle class, angry at taxes and government inefficiency, and widely thought to be casting about for an alternative to the Tories. The speed with which the party spread in the province was associated with some growing pains, and the party's haste in setting up its electoral machine in the province arguably cost it some embarrassment. In particular, the Party experienced difficulties in keeping fringe elements from infiltrating its permeable new grassroots organizations, and these produced a series of public relations fiascos surrounding the racist and sexist predispositions of some of its candidates and activists (see Beaches–Woodbine, Burlington, and York Centre profiles, in particular).

These problems notwithstanding, Manning and his strategists sensed opportunity in the 1993 campaign, and he made five high profile campaign swings through the province. The last of these, coming in the final week of the campaign, featured public rallies in several cities (London and Pickering, for examples) that drew thousands of paying supporters. Reform's problem was that its growth through the 1993 campaign left it short of the threshold it needed to achieve a breakthrough for itself. Like many third parties, it was penalized by the single-member plurality electoral system since it seldom had sufficient concentration of support to win a plurality in constituency races. Over the course of the campaign, Manning was aware of this, and aimed his campaign rhetoric squarely at Chrétien and the Liberals. However, this had limited impact. Only in Simcoe Centre was this barrier overcome, and this gave Reform its only seat east of the prairies. While Reform's support in the 1993 was diffuse enough to keep it from electing many candidates, it also was strategically distributed in a manner that hurt the Tories. Besides Simcoe Centre, in 24 ridings across the province the gains made by Reform candidates were probably enough to tip the partisan balance between the Tories and the Liberals (i.e., Reform did better than the margin separating Liberals from Tories). This split of right-wing voters between Reform and the Conservatives, coupled with the collapse of the NDP's vote, together provide a reasonable explanation for much of the Liberal dominance in 1993, even before the party's own strengths are taken into account

The Liberals came into the 1993 campaign with 43 Ontario seats (and the party had attracted slightly more of the popular vote in the province in 1988 than the Tories, despite winning three fewer seats). However, the national party had difficulty paying off its campaign debts from 1988 — for most of 1991, for example, its debt remained constant at about $3.7 million. Financial difficulties aside, the party ran a masterful national campaign, avoiding mistakes and capitalizing on the unpopularity of their traditional rivals. With lots of targets to shoot at during the campaign, and the helpful 'Red Book' outlining the national party's programs, Liberal candidates across the province had little trouble in controlling their local electoral agendas. Such controversy as did afflict the party arose primarily in the nomination process. As in 1988, the mobilization of so-called 'ethnic machines' in 1993 arose some local grumbling about whether 'instant members' ought to be given a vote in nomination meetings. However, it was the national party's policy of reserving the leader's right to nominate local candidates that prompted most ill-will (and a court challenge). In several constituencies in which Chrétien nominated 'star candidates' (Beaches–Woodbine, Etobicoke–Lakeshore, Lincoln, Renfrew–Nipissing–Pembroke, Scarborough–Rouge River, and York Centre), local sensibilities were offended. By election day, however, these wounds had largely healed. Liberal fortunes were directly in the hands of other parties and their strategists. Most obviously, the party benefited enormously from the inroads Reform was making into traditional Tory support.

As might be expected in the context of an election characterized by radical electoral shifts, incumbents did not fare particularly well in the province in 1993. Of the 75 MPs offering for reelection in 1993, 35 were defeated (27 Conservatives, 8 NDP). This number might well have been higher had it not been for the fact that many sitting Members seemed to sense the writing on the wall and resigned before the campaign. There were 24 resignations before the 1993 campaign (19 Conservatives, 3 Liberals, and 2 NDPs), up from a total of 15 prior to the 1988 campaign. Among these retirees were some prominent members of Tory cabinets, including Otto Jelinek (Oakville–Milton), John McDermid (Brampton), Barbara McDougall (St Paul's), Michael Wilson (Etobicoke Centre), Bill Winegard (Guelph–Wellington), and John Wise (Elgin–Norfolk). Among the most prominent Tories going down to defeat in 1993 were Perrin Beatty (Wellington–Grey–Dufferin–Simcoe), Don Blenkarn (Mississauga South), John Bosley (Don Valley West), Paul Dick (Lanark–Carleton), Tom Hockin (London West), Doug Lewis (Simcoe North), Alan Redway (Don Valley East), and Garth Turner (Halton–Peel). In contrast to their counterparts in other parties, obviously Liberal incumbents who stood for re-election in 1993 fared well — all 40 were returned to Ottawa.

In contrast to earlier years, an electoral map illustrating only the winning party in 1993 would not be terribly revealing — 98 of the province's 99 districts would be shaded Liberal red! The only exception would be the tiny piece of Reform green representing their victory in Simcoe Centre. In this respect, the geography of the province is remarkably uniform. However, the geography of seat change is slightly more interesting. While 56 seats changed partisan hands between the 1988 and 1993 elections, only three of the 10 northern seats, and none of the five Ottawa seats, did so. This reflects the Liberal Party's tradition of strength in these areas, a tradition that gave them heavy victories in these regions in 1988. Similarly, in Toronto, where the Liberals have traditionally appealed to the ethnic vote, only 11 of the 23 seats changed partisan hands in the 1988-1993 period. It was rural Ontario, and the affluent, white-collar suburban ridings, where the Reform Party cut inroads into traditional Tory support, that experienced the highest rate of partisan change since 1988.

In sum, while there was considerable evidence in 1993 that national forces were playing themselves out on the Ontario terrain, the precise pattern of competition that produced Ontario's Liberal landslide was geographically differentiated. The profiles that follow document some of the factors mentioned above in greater detail.

Ontario Results, 1988 & 1993 Elections, 1992 Referendum

| | 1988 Election | | | 1993 Election | |
	% Vote	Seats	1992	% Vote	Seats
Conservatives	38.2	46		17.6	0
Liberals	38.9	43		52.9	98
NDP	20.1	10		6.0	0
Reform	–	–		20.1	1
Other/Indep.	2.7	0		3.4	0
Turnout	74.6	–		67.7	–
% Yes (1992)			50.1		
% No (1992)			49.9		

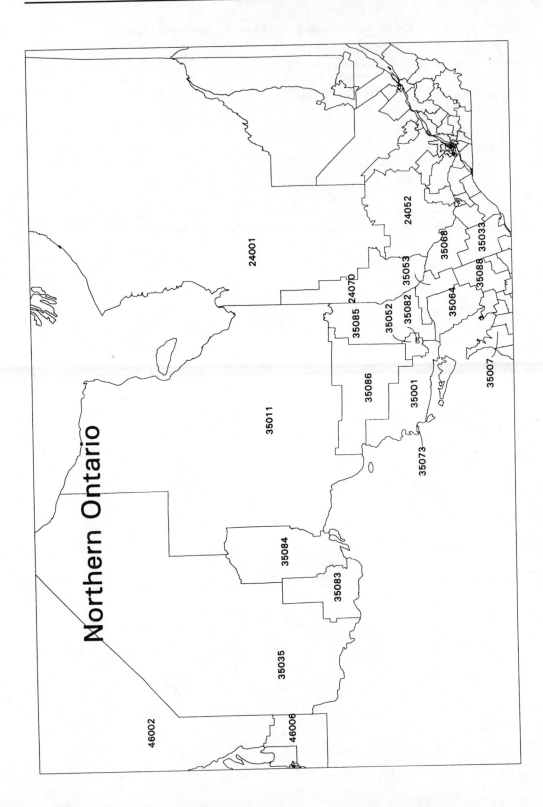

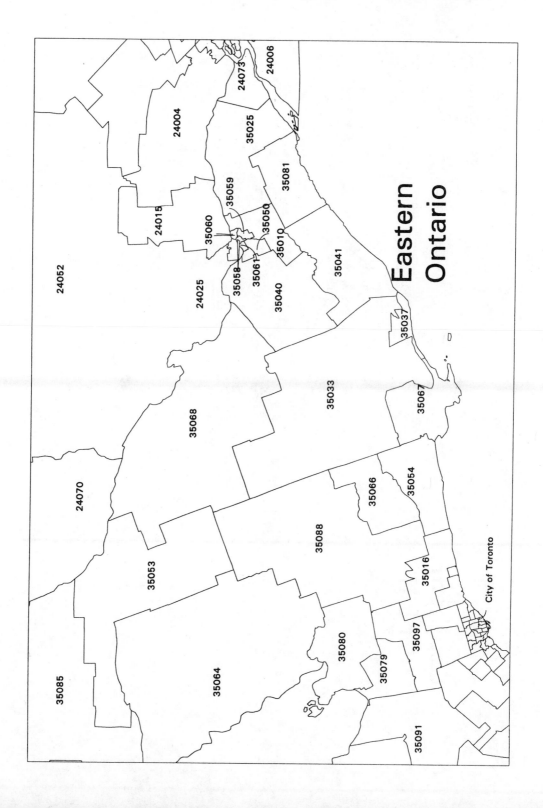

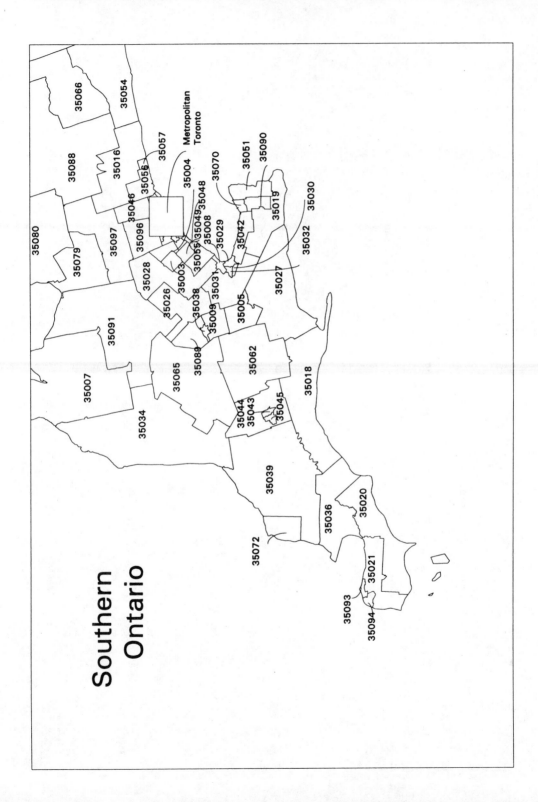

Southern
Ontario

Metropolitan
Toronto

35066
35054
35088
35016
35057
35056
35046
35051
35090
35004
35070
35019
35048
35030
35080
35097
35096
35049 35008
35029
35042
35032
35079
35055
35005
35031
35027
35028
35003
35038
35009
35005
35026
35091
35088
35062
35007
35065
35018
35034
35044
35043
35045
35039
35020
35036
35072
35021
35093
35094

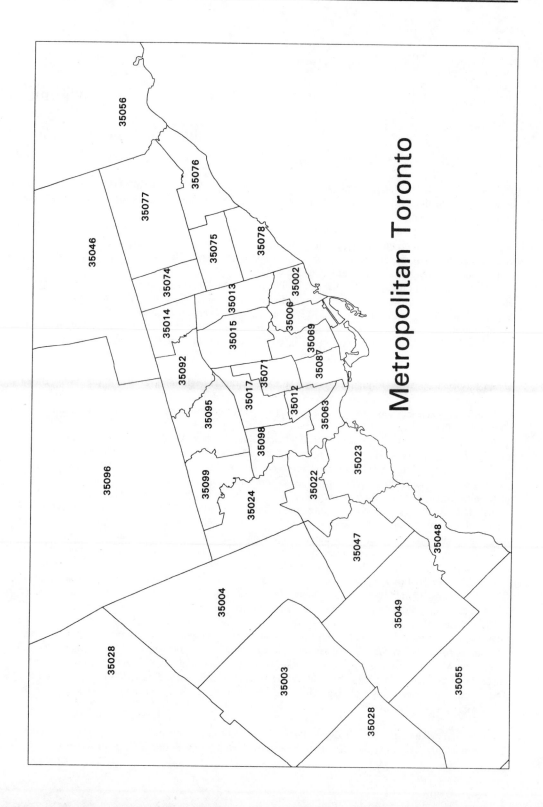

Metropolitan Toronto

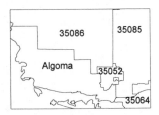

Algoma

Constituency Number: 35001

$\mathbf{A}$lgoma is Ontario's fifth largest riding, taking in most of the North Shore of Lake Huron (excluding the eastern tip and Sault Ste Marie), a good deal of Lake Superior's Eastern Shore and Manitoulin Island. It is sparsely populated, and is home to a variety of resource-based industries, including mining and forestry-based companies. Roughly one in ten residents are members of Canada's aboriginal peoples, making this the third highest concentration in the province. While most (90%) residents are English, roughly seven per cent of the riding's residents speak French as their home language. The 30% voting 'yes' in the 1992 constitutional referendum was the third lowest in Ontario.

A strong Liberal riding, Algoma has been held by the Grits since 1935. It was once represented in the House of Commons by former Prime Minister Lester B. Pearson. Replacing Pearson in 1968 was Dr Maurice Foster, whose retirement in 1993 forced the Liberals to find a new candidate. Foster retired at the top of his game, however; his almost 30% margin of victory in the 1988 contest was the largest of his career.

The Liberals did not travel very far in their search, selecting Brent St Denis (Foster's assistant for a decade). The Tories also nominated a party stalwart, David Mair, a 27-year-old lawyer and special assistant to Mulroney's Minister of Health, Benoit Bouchard. The NDP candidate was Gayle Broad, a community legal aid worker in neighbouring Sault Ste Marie. Though not a resident of the riding, Broad grew up in Algoma and still has a summer property in it. Rounding out the field of major candidates was Ken Leffler, a real estate appraiser, running for Reform, and Bernard Brègaint, a librarian representing the Natural Law Party.

The economy was the big issue of the 1993 campaign: the impact of Free Trade and the NAFTA on the region's heavy manufacturing, the refusal of the Mulroney government to repair the Sault canal, routing traffic through the American locks, forestry and the ability of the forestry industry to export easily to the United States and Europe. Meanwhile cross-border shopping (in Michigan) and smuggling, induced by tax differentials and the strong dollar policy, dented the sales receipts of local retailers. Concerns of the riding's large number of First People figured prominently during the 1993 campaign. Many Native voters felt that the issues of concern to them, including environment, and were being ignored by all the political parties and many predicted that a large number would not even bother voting. The hostility of the electoral process to Native voters was symbolized by an Elections Canada decision to send election promotion kits to a number of reservations. The kits contained the usual posters and promotional material bearing the slogan 'It's your right to vote!' and one new piece of material ... Bingo Daubers! (the thick felt markers Bingo players use to mark their cards). As one Native leader noted 'It's sort of like sending a wallet to a Jewish person and telling them to exercise their right to vote. They shouldn't and wouldn't do that.'

The Liberals' St Denis increased the party's share of the popular vote in 1993, winning 58% of the vote. The Conservatives lost about 12% of their 1988 share. Even though the provincial New Democratic government has extended considerable assistance to the region's industries and displaced workers (Algoma Steel, Saint Mary's Paper and a number of make-work projects) the provincial government was nearly as unpopular in this part of Ontario as elsewhere. The 1993 NDP result was almost 15% lower than in 1988. The largest gains in the riding were registered by the Reform Party, which ended up in second place in the riding with 21.1% of the vote.

Member of Parliament: Brent St Denis; **Party:** Liberal; **Occupation:** Industrial engineer; **Education:** BSc (Engineering); **Age:** 44 (May 27, 1950); **Year first elected to the House of Commons:** 1993

35001 Algoma

A: Political Profile
i) Voting Behaviour

	% 1993	% 1988	Change 1988-93
Conservative	11.5	23.4	-11.9
Liberal	58.1	53.2	4.9
NDP	8.6	23.3	-14.7
Reform	21.1	0	21.1
Other	0.8	0	0.8

% Turnout	66.1	Total Ballots (#)	31556
Rejected Ballots (#)	171	% Margin of Victory	37
Rural Polls, 1988 (#)	138	Urban Polls, 1988 (#)	46
% Yes - 1992	30.3	% No - 1992	69.2

ii) Campaign Financing

	# of Donations	Total $ Value	% of Limit Spent
Conservative	84	22260	70.9*
Liberal	190	27095	61.8
NDP	86	28795	65
Reform	76	9859	22.8
Other	3	750	

B: Ethno-Linguistic Profile

% English Home Language	90.8	% French Home Language	6.6
% Official Bilingual	17.4	% Other Home Language	2.6
% Catholics	42.2	% Protestants	47.5
% Aboriginal Peoples	10.3	% Immigrants	6.8

C: Socio-Economic Profile

Average Family Income $	45469	Median Family Income $	42054
% Low Income Families	12.3	Average Home Price $	84655
% Home Owners	74.7	% Unemployment	11
% Labour Force Participation	60.8	% Managerial-Administrative	8.9
% Self-Employed	9.6	% University Degrees	6.1
% Movers	39.1		

D: Industrial Profile

% Manufacturing	12.1	% Service Sector	13.6
% Agriculture	3	% Mining	9.7
% Forestry	2.9	% Fishing	0.3
% Government Services	8.9	% Business Services	2

E: Homogeneity Measures

Ethnic Diversity Index	0.31	Religious Homogeneity Index	0.41
Sectoral Concentration Index	0.34	Income Disparity Index	7.5

F: Physical Setting Characteristics

Total Population	64447	Area (km²)	36268
Population Density (pop/km²)	1.8		

* Tentative value, due to the existence of unpaid campaign expenses.

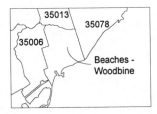

Beaches–Woodbine

Constituency Number: 35002

Beaches–Woodbine is a compact (15 square kilometres) riding that hugs approximately 4 kilometres of the Lake Ontario shoreline in the easternmost part of the City of Toronto. It also includes the southern-most section of the Borough of East York. The riding is home to ethnically-diverse lower and middle-income families. Almost one third are immigrants, drawn from a variety of ethnic backgrounds, and average family incomes are slightly more than $2,500 lower than the provincial norm.

Neil Young held this riding for the NDP for 13 years, but not by particularly large margins. In 1988 his margin of victory was only 861 votes, and the race was closely watched by national media in the 1993 campaign. Given the closeness of the race and the unpopularity of Bob Rae's provincial NDP govern-ment, the race attracted strong candidates. Terry Kelly, a lawyer who was the Liberal candidate and second-place finisher in 1988, decided to take another shot at the seat. However, he had to run as an independent in 1993 as Jean Chrétien personally selected Maria Minna to be the riding Liberal candidate (one of four metro area candidates so appointed). As in other ridings where a 'star' candidate was appointed, the Liberals were internally divided by the nomination process. Minna, a consultant, was selected by Chrétien due to her strong background as an activist in Toronto's large Italian Canadian community. She had previously contested for the Liberal nomination in the 1988 election in the riding of York North, reportedly spending $35,000 in her unsuccessful bid there. Of the six Italian Canadians running in Metro ridings in 1993 for the Liberals, Minna was the only woman. In fact of the 23 Liberals in Metro only two, Minna and Jean Augustine (Etobicoke–Lakeshore) were women. Both were personal appointees of Chrétien.

The 1993 Beaches–Woodbine ballot was crowded by no fewer than 11 candidates' names. In addi-tion to Minna and Kelly (independent), Neil Young, a veteran MP and former business manager, carried the NDP's banner again in 1993. Denise Cole, national secretary of the Conservative Party ran for the Tories. She described herself as a 'black woman of working-class roots' and 'not your stereotypical Tory'. Hugh Prendergast, a senior analyst, represented the Reform Party. John-Frederick Cameron, the Ontario Campaign Manager for the National Party and a resident of Burlington, ran for the National Party. Four minor party candidates rounded out the ballot.

As in most ridings in Metro the issues were the economy and job creation. As elsewhere, the big fight was how this should be accomplished, by further government restraint to improve the environment for business or by positive government action? With prosperous, middle-class, and less advantaged neighbourhoods all crammed together in this riding it cannot be said there was a consensus here on this question. Reform's prospects were probably hurt by revelations in February of 1992 that their local riding association had been infiltrated by a group of white-power advocates (affiliated with the Heritage Front). This prompted the rapidly growing party to review its membership practices.

In the end, the schism in the Liberal party did not hurt Minna and she secured the riding for the Liberals by winning almost 41% of the vote. Young's 18.6% of the vote, though still one of the NDP's eight best finishes in Ontario, was good enough for only a distant second place. Reform's Prendergast finished third with 15.8% of the vote. Kelly and the Tories' Cole were the only other candidates to reach double figures.

Member of Parliament: Maria Minna; **Party:** Liberal; **Occupation:** Businesswoman; **Education:** BA; **Year first elected to the House of Commons:** 1993

35002 Beaches–Woodbine

A: Political Profile
i) Voting Behaviour

	% 1993	% 1988	Change 1988-93
Conservative	10	29.2	-19.2
Liberal	40.7	33.2	7.5
NDP	18.6	35.2	-16.6
Reform	15.8	0	15.8
Other	15	2.3	12.7

% Turnout	66.1	Total Ballots (#)	43780
Rejected Ballots (#)	474	% Margin of Victory	22.1
Rural Polls, 1988 (#)	0	Urban Polls, 1988 (#)	181
% Yes - 1992	53.6	% No - 1992	45.8

ii) Campaign Financing

	# of Donations	Total $ Value	% of Limit Spent
Conservative	196	37210	74.4*
Liberal	180	30193	9.3
NDP	300	49807	73
Reform	28	8735	26
Other	150	19873	

B: Ethno-Linguistic Profile

% English Home Language	82.8	% French Home Language	0.7
% Official Bilingual	9.3	% Other Home Language	16.5
% Catholics	26.2	% Protestants	36.6
% Aboriginal Peoples	0.7	% Immigrants	31.1

C: Socio-Economic Profile

Average Family Income $	53589	Median Family Income $	47091
% Low Income Families	19.6	Average Home Price $	228887
% Home Owners	51.8	% Unemployment	9
% Labour Force Participation	69.7	% Managerial-Administrative	15.9
% Self-Employed	8.3	% University Degrees	16.9
% Movers	47.7		

D: Industrial Profile

% Manufacturing	12.6	% Service Sector	11.7
% Agriculture	0.2	% Mining	0.2
% Forestry	0.1	% Fishing	0
% Government Services	7.3	% Business Services	10.6

E: Homogeneity Measures

Ethnic Diversity Index	0.2	Religious Homogeneity Index	0.28
Sectoral Concentration Index	0.53	Income Disparity Index	12.1

F: Physical Setting Characteristics

Total Population	96142	Area (km²)	15
Population Density (pop/km²)	6409.5		

* Tentative value, due to the existence of unpaid campaign expenses.

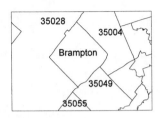

Brampton

Constituency Number: 35003

A mixed urban and rural riding that is growing more urban every year, Brampton might be a classic 'boiling point' riding. The real estate boom which southern Ontario experienced in the late 1980s drove many commuters further out from urban areas and led to a house-building explosion in this part of Ontario. When the slump hit many young families found themselves deep underwater, with unmanageable mortgages and homes essentially unsaleable. Throw in an unemployment rate of almost 8% and ever rising taxation (including the GST and the Tory reduction in benefits to middle-class families) and you have the makings of a middle-class revolt against traditional conservatives similar to that American Kevin Phillips described in *Boiling Point*, his book about the defeat of George Bush and the Republican Party. The riding is home to an important horticulture industry, and also a variety of light manufacturing industries that account for about a quarter of all employment in the district. Brampton's population increased by 37.3% between 1986 and 1991 (the third highest rate of growth in Ontario). Of Brampton's residents, 60% reported moving within the last 5 years—the third highest proportion in Ontario. Demographic changes have left the riding with over 105,000 electors eligible to vote in the 1993 contest, making it Ontario's fifth largest riding.

The riding was created in 1988 from the old Brampton-Georgetown district. Tory cabinet minister John McDermid, who had represented the old riding since 1979, won the seat handily in 1988 with almost a 14,000-vote margin. McDermid's decision to retire prior to the 1993 campaign, coupled with the local economy's weakness, prompted even Tory strategists to admit that the 1993 contest would be a tough one. In particular, the riding electorate seemed to fit the profile of districts in which the Reform Party's strategists were anticipating significant gains (average income slightly above the provincial norm, lower than normal number of low-income voters, and a lot of voters who felt the PCs were too progressive and not conservative enough).

Six candidates competed for the Brampton seat in 1993. Replacing McDermid as the Conservative candidate was Susan Fennell, a two-term regional councillor from Brampton. Colleen Beaumier, a business executive and long-time Liberal campaign worker, ran for the Liberal Party. Ernie McDonald, a school principal, won the Reform Party's nomination. John Morris, a teacher, ran for the NDP. Rounding out the slate were two minor party candidates.

In the end, the local race was not even close. Liberal candidate Colleen Beaumier managed to win an outright majority with 51.7% of the vote. The Conservative vote shrank by over 33 per cent from its 1988 level to 17.8%. The economic recession afflicting southern Ontario, coupled with the taint of controversy surrounding Mulroney's deal to privatize the nearby Pearson airport, doubtless accounted for a substantial part of the collapse in Tory fortunes locally. Much of this support probably contributed to the Reform Party's winning 26.7% of the vote in 1993.

Member of Parliament: Colleen Beaumier; **Party:** Liberal; **Occupation:** Social worker; **Education:** BA; **Year first elected to the House of Commons:** 1993

35003 Brampton

A: Political Profile

i) Voting Behaviour

	% 1993	% 1988	Change 1988-93
Conservative	17.8	51.6	-33.8
Liberal	51.7	24.6	27.1
NDP	2.8	18	-15.2
Reform	26.7	0	26.7
Other	1.1	5.8	-4.7

% Turnout	65.4	Total Ballots (#)	68685
Rejected Ballots (#)	527	% Margin of Victory	25
Rural Polls, 1988 (#)	0	Urban Polls, 1988 (#)	230
% Yes - 1992	52.4	% No - 1992	47.1

ii) Campaign Financing

	# of Donations	Total $ Value	% of Limit Spent
Conservative	104	55530	75.1
Liberal	140	53258	53*
NDP	20	4025	2.1
Reform	63	24626	29
Other	24	3156	

B: Ethno-Linguistic Profile

% English Home Language	86.6	% French Home Language	0.5
% Official Bilingual	6.5	% Other Home Language	12.9
% Catholics	38.5	% Protestants	39.2
% Aboriginal Peoples	0.2	% Immigrants	33.7

C: Socio-Economic Profile

Average Family Income $	61707	Median Family Income $	58447
% Low Income Families	8.5	Average Home Price $	229980
% Home Owners	71.1	% Unemployment	7.7
% Labour Force Participation	78.4	% Managerial-Administrative	14.9
% Self-Employed	6.1	% University Degrees	10.2
% Movers	60		

D: Industrial Profile

% Manufacturing	25.4	% Service Sector	9
% Agriculture	0.9	% Mining	0.2
% Forestry	0.1	% Fishing	0
% Government Services	5.2	% Business Services	7.2

E: Homogeneity Measures

Ethnic Diversity Index	0.19	Religious Homogeneity Index	0.33
Sectoral Concentration Index	0.4	Income Disparity Index	5.3

F: Physical Setting Characteristics

Total Population	166746	Area (km²)	154
Population Density (pop/km²)	1082.8		

* Tentative value, due to the existence of unpaid campaign expenses.

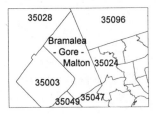

Bramalea–Gore–Malton
(formerly Brampton–Malton)

Constituency Number: 35004

This riding, created in 1988, is located northwest of Metropolitan Toronto. Situated in the rapidly growing commuter belt, the riding's economy includes a variety of light manufacturing (26.7% of employment is in manufacturing) industries and service industries (about a third of all jobs). Almost 16% of residents are non-citizens, and a substantial proportion of the electorate in this riding has ethnic origins in south central Asia. The riding boasts one of the largest Sikh populations in Canada.

In 1988 Conservative candidate Harry Chadwick won this riding by a little over 2,000 votes. However, a combination of the country's general sense of tiredness with the Tory government, inroads made by the Reform Party, and the Pearson International Airport lease, eventually brought about his downfall in 1993. The airport is located in this riding and hence while the issue probably hurt Tory candidates across the 'Golden Horseshoe', it had special salience here. The controversial lease of Terminal 1 and 2 of Pearson International Airport to a company called Pearson Development Corporation appeared to benefit an assortment of 'Friends of Brian'. It was negotiated in secret, with the assistance of two high-priced lobbyists, by a company headed by the former president of the national Progressive Conservative Party. It was concluded over the strenuous reservations of senior civil servants and private consultants from a prestigious international accounting firm. Even the usually pro-privatization *Globe and Mail* found the deal impossible to endorse. Furthermore, the airport deal sparked concerns for the future. Riding residents were concerned that the anticipated lease of runways at Pearson Airport (including contracts to build new ones) would also be conducted without any consultation with the people affected by any expansion, or whose sleep might be disturbed by a decision to extend operating hours on the old ones.

Nine candidates vied to represent Bramalea–Gore–Malton in the 1993 campaign. Chadwick, a former Ford employee and ten-year Brampton city councillor prior to his 1988 federal election victory, returned to campaign for the Tories. Gurbax Malhi, a Mississauga real estate representative, won a tightly contested Liberal nomination. The Liberals' nomination race, reportedly the second largest in Liberal Party history with more than 10,000 new members recruited, featured six contenders, three of whom were Sikh. Darlene Florence, a registered nurse from Bramalea, ran for the Reform Party. Paul Legister, a businessman who had run for the NDP in 1988, carried the party's banner again in 1993. Jack Ardis, an educator from Orangeville, ran for the National Party, while Bill Davies, a Toronto businessman, represented the Natural Law Party. Rounding out the slate were John E. Maxwell, a businessman running as an independent candidate, Bill Emms, a student from Bramalea running for the Greens, and Iqbal Sumbal, a Marxist-Leninist candidate from Toronto.

The national Conservative government's attempt to steer a course slightly more towards that of the Reform party in the field of multiculturalism and immigration probably did not help their chances in this riding. The move was probably just enough to annoy their non-nativeborn supporters but not enough to win back the more right-of-centre voters that they lost to the Reform Party. The eventual victor was the Liberals' Malhi, making him Canada's first Sikh member of Parliament. Malhi benefited from the right-of-centre exodus from the Conservative Party to Reform, and from the simultaneous collapse of the riding's NDP vote (down almost 17.5%), to win a plurality of 5,000 plus votes over Reform's Darlene Florence, who came in second. The incumbent Chadwick had to be content wtih a somewhat distant third place finish, while none of the other candidates broke double figures with their percentage of the vote.

Member of Parliament: Gurbax Singh Malhi; **Party:** Liberal; **Occupation:** Real estate agent; **Education:** BA, Punjab University; **Age:** 45 (October 12, 1949); **Year first elected to the House of Commons:** 1993

35004 Bramalea–Gore–Malton

A: Political Profile
i) Voting Behaviour

	% 1993	% 1988	Change 1988-93
Conservative	19.2	41.5	-22.3
Liberal	43.3	34.4	8.9
NDP	5.1	22.5	-17.4
Reform	29.1	0	29.1
Other	3.4	1.6	1.8

% Turnout	65.1	Total Ballots (#)	41289
Rejected Ballots (#)	431	% Margin of Victory	14.2
Rural Polls, 1988 (#)	0	Urban Polls, 1988 (#)	182
% Yes - 1992	48.2	% No - 1992	51.3

ii) Campaign Financing

	# of Donations	Total $ Value	% of Limit Spent
Conservative	61	41063	61.4
Liberal	36	50268	89
NDP	92	15395	20.6
Reform	161	31013	48.4
Other	40	12919	

B: Ethno-Linguistic Profile

% English Home Language	83	% French Home Language	0.4
% Official Bilingual	5.6	% Other Home Language	16.6
% Catholics	38	% Protestants	36.5
% Aboriginal Peoples	0.2	% Immigrants	39.4

C: Socio-Economic Profile

Average Family Income $	56531	Median Family Income $	53638
% Low Income Families	10.8	Average Home Price $	204538
% Home Owners	73.6	% Unemployment	9
% Labour Force Participation	76.5	% Managerial-Administrative	11.8
% Self-Employed	5.6	% University Degrees	7.5
% Movers	49.7		

D: Industrial Profile

% Manufacturing	26.7	% Service Sector	9.7
% Agriculture	0.7	% Mining	0.1
% Forestry	0	% Fishing	0
% Government Services	4.4	% Business Services	5.9

E: Homogeneity Measures

Ethnic Diversity Index	0.2	Religious Homogeneity Index	0.32
Sectoral Concentration Index	0.39	Income Disparity Index	5.1

F: Physical Setting Characteristics

Total Population	103589	Area (km²)	172
Population Density (pop/km²)	602.3		

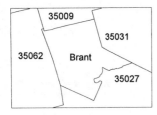

Brant

Constituency Number: 35005

Brant is a southern Ontario riding, located about 40 kilometres west of Hamilton. In addition to some rich agricultural land, it contains the city of Brantford, the seat of Brant county, original home town of hockey superstar Wayne Gretzky, and site of the first Protestant church in Ontario (built in 1785). Unemployment in the region is a couple of percentage points above the national average. Once the home of Massey Ferguson and other heavy industrial enterprises, Brant has been hard hit by plant closings and the general economic downturn. Adding to the area's woes has been the collapse of a number of schemes which were intended to revive the local economy. Most notable among these was a plan to relocate a number of Ontario government offices from Toronto to the area. The plan fell through as a result of the cost-cutting initiated by the NDP provincial government.

The NDP's Derek Blackburn represented Brant in the House of Commons for over 20 years. In 1993, however, he called it quits, thereby throwing the riding up for grabs. His retirement encouraged a large crop of contenders for the open seat. Provincially, much of the territory defined by the riding has a strong Liberal tradition, demonstrated by the long-standing hold that Ontario Liberal Bob Nixon (Provincial Treasurer and Finance Minister in the David Peterson Government and former interim party leader) had over the area's seat in the provincial legislature (Brant–Haldimand). This time the Liberals nominated Jane Stewart, Nixon's daughter, as their candidate. The Reform Party nominated Ken Edmison, a trust company manager from Brantford. Running for the Tories was Mabel Dougherty from Caledonia. Michael E. Smith, an agricultural economist, replaced Blackburn as the NDP's candidate. Four minor party candidates and an independent rounded out the ballot.

Hurt by Blackburn's retirement, and Bob Rae's unpopular provincial government, the NDP's support tumbled 34.6% from the 1988 result to 6.9% (the party's second largest freefall in Ontario). Farmers in the riding, as in the region in general, were concerned by the inflow of subsidized prairie grains replacing local feed crops in area mills and the impact international trade and American protectionism were having on the area. This probably hurt Tory fortunes hardest. In the end, Stewart capitalized on the underlying Liberal partisanship in the area and won an absolute majority in the riding for the Liberals, more than doubling the total vote of her nearest rival, the Reform Party's Edmison.

Member of Parliament: Jane Stewart; **Party:** Liberal; **Occupation:** Human resources consultant; **Education:** BSc. (Hons.); **Year first elected to the House of Commons:** 1993

35005 Brant

A: Political Profile
i) Voting Behaviour

	% 1993	% 1988	Change 1988-93
Conservative	12.2	29.7	-17.5
Liberal	51.5	24.2	27.3
NDP	6.9	41.5	-34.6
Reform	24.7	0	24.7
Other	4.7	4.6	0.1

% Turnout	65.3	Total Ballots (#)	48468
Rejected Ballots (#)	500	% Margin of Victory	26.8
Rural Polls, 1988 (#)	22	Urban Polls, 1988 (#)	170
% Yes - 1992	41	% No - 1992	58.4

ii) Campaign Financing

	# of Donations	Total $ Value	% of Limit Spent
Conservative	142	26792	43*
Liberal	151	31860	65.1
NDP	87	39713	63.3
Reform	192	35329	60.7
Other	58	11396	

B: Ethno-Linguistic Profile

% English Home Language	95.9	% French Home Language	0.2
% Official Bilingual	4.4	% Other Home Language	3.9
% Catholics	25.1	% Protestants	57.8
% Aboriginal Peoples	2	% Immigrants	13.9

C: Socio-Economic Profile

Average Family Income $	49663	Median Family Income $	44464
% Low Income Families	12.5	Average Home Price $	151604
% Home Owners	67	% Unemployment	9.5
% Labour Force Participation	67	% Managerial-Administrative	11.7
% Self-Employed	7.7	% University Degrees	7.4
% Movers	47.5		

D: Industrial Profile

% Manufacturing	24.9	% Service Sector	11.9
% Agriculture	2.6	% Mining	0.2
% Forestry	0.1	% Fishing	0
% Government Services	4.7	% Business Services	4

E: Homogeneity Measures

Ethnic Diversity Index	0.37	Religious Homogeneity Index	0.41
Sectoral Concentration Index	0.42	Income Disparity Index	10.5

F: Physical Setting Characteristics

Total Population	101730	Area (km²)	514
Population Density (pop/km²)	197.9		

* Tentative value, due to the existence of unpaid campaign expenses.

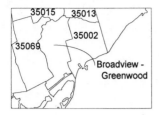

Broadview–Greenwood

Constituency Number: 35006

Broadview–Greenwood is a geographically compact, ethnically diverse, metropolitan Toronto riding. It contains a substantial portion of the Danforth Avenue West Greco-Canadian business district and many Greco-Canadian dominated residential neighbourhoods. There is also a substantial Chinese Canadian community (accounting for approximately 16% of the riding's population in 1991). The area is primarily residential and commercial, but with some light industry. Slightly 'downmarket' by Toronto standards, the district contains a mix of socio-economic backgrounds (average family incomes run about $5 thousand lower than the provincial norm, and almost 1 in 5 residents are classed as 'low income' by Statistics Canada). Like others in Canada's largest city, residents of Broadview–Greenwood were feeling the effects of the recession in 1993. Many of those in the riding who bought and renovated the large homes with majestic views of the downtown core across the Don Valley found themselves in serious difficulties when housing prices crashed during the recession and their homes became worth less than their mortgages, making renewal impossible.

Politically, Broadview–Greenwood had, in the 23 years prior to 1988, been strong NDP territory. However in 1988 the riding narrowly went to the Liberals' Dennis Mills. A one-time policy aide to Pierre Trudeau and formerly a vice-president at Magna International (Canada's largest independent maker of auto parts and components), Mills won over the NDP incumbent in 1988 with approximately a 1,200-vote margin.

The 1993 ballot in Broadview–Greenwood was relatively full. Mills reoffered for the Liberals. Lynne MacDonald, the previous NDP incumbent (1982-1988), former president of the National Action Committee on the Status of Women, and university professor, also returned to contest the riding in 1993. The Tories offered John Papadakis, a municipal councillor, while Frank Meyers, a security administrator, ran for the Reform Party. Barbara Sim, a self-described entrepreneur, ran for the National Party, and Bob Hyman, an office manager, carried the Natural Law Party banner. Three other minor party/independent candidates also contested the seat, but attracted only a handful of votes each.

If the economy and neglect of Metro were the real issues the people of Broadview–Greenwood had little reason not to join the rest of the province in giving the Liberals their sweeping victory by re-electing Mills. The Tories did not finish well in 1988, and saw their support further eroded by the unpopularity of the outgoing administration and the inroads made by Reform. In the end, Mills won a commanding 61.1% of the poll; second-place finisher MacDonald could manage only 14% (and this was enough to make Broadview–Greenwood one of the ten best NDP finishes in Ontario).

Member of Parliament: Dennis Mills; **Party:** Liberal; **Occupation:** Businessperson; **Education:** University of St Thomas; **Age:** 48 (July 19, 1946); **Year first elected to the House of Commons:** 1988

35006 Broadview–Greenwood

A: Political Profile
i) Voting Behaviour

	% 1993	% 1988	Change 1988-93
Conservative	9.3	22.4	-13.1
Liberal	61.1	38.9	22.2
NDP	14	36	-22
Reform	11.3	0	11.3
Other	4.3	2.7	1.6

% Turnout	64.8	Total Ballots (#)	38973
Rejected Ballots (#)	398	% Margin of Victory	47.1
Rural Polls, 1988 (#)	0	Urban Polls, 1988 (#)	171
% Yes - 1992	53.7	% No - 1992	45.4

ii) Campaign Financing

	# of Donations	Total $ Value	% of Limit Spent
Conservative	57	25851	28.1*
Liberal	163	38096	76.8*
NDP	287	48943	79.8
Reform	46	5909	19*
Other	23	5559	

B: Ethno-Linguistic Profile

% English Home Language	69.3	% French Home Language	0.8
% Official Bilingual	9.3	% Other Home Language	29.9
% Catholics	23.3	% Protestants	28.2
% Aboriginal Peoples	0.3	% Immigrants	38.5

C: Socio-Economic Profile

Average Family Income $	51095	Median Family Income $	44041
% Low Income Families	21.8	Average Home Price $	237594
% Home Owners	50.3	% Unemployment	10.4
% Labour Force Participation	68.7	% Managerial-Administrative	15
% Self-Employed	9.2	% University Degrees	18
% Movers	45.7		

D: Industrial Profile

% Manufacturing	13.3	% Service Sector	14.5
% Agriculture	0.2	% Mining	0.2
% Forestry	0	% Fishing	0
% Government Services	6.6	% Business Services	10.7

E: Homogeneity Measures

Ethnic Diversity Index	0.2	Religious Homogeneity Index	0.25
Sectoral Concentration Index	0.54	Income Disparity Index	13.8

F: Physical Setting Characteristics

Total Population	90367	Area (km²)	18
Population Density (pop/km²)	5020.4		

* Tentative value, due to the existence of unpaid campaign expenses.

Bruce–Grey

Constituency Number: 35007

Bruce–Grey is a large, rural constituency on the northern shores of Lake Huron and the southern shore of Georgian Bay. Dividing the riding on a north-south axis is the Niagara Escarpment, a ruggedly beautiful geologic formation that has its northern terminus in this riding's Bruce Peninsula National Park. The riding has a diverse economic base. Fishing and tourism are important along the shoreline; in winter, the area is popular with skiers. Light industry (auto parts and light manufacturing) and farming (dairy, stock, and fruit farming) round out the economic base of Bruce–Grey. Bruce–Grey is among the top 10 most agricultural ridings in the province. Incomes, though not high, are not widely dispersed. Whereas average family incomes run about $11,000 below the norm for ridings (the seventh lowest figure) in the province, only 8.4% of families are classed as 'low income' (the provincial norm is 13.1%). The riding's electorate is distinctly 'WASPish'. With less than .1% of residents reporting French as their home language, Bruce–Grey ranks lowest in the province on this measure. Almost 99% report English as their home language and 71% report their religion as being 'Protestant', making this the third most anglophone and Protestant riding in the province.

Bruce–Grey, exemplifying a 'traditional' Ontario riding, has been Conservative territory, although the Liberals had made inroads by 1988 with its candidate losing the election by a margin of less than 1,000 votes. In 1993 the unpopularity of the governing Conservatives, the growth of Reform in the province, and the retirement of twenty-year incumbent Tory MP Gus Mitges, combined to further open the field.

The Liberal candidate in 1993 was long-time Owen Sound mayor and educator Ovid Jackson. Replacing Mitges as Tory candidate was Stew O'Keeffe, a former teacher and superintendent of schools, and now a financial consultant from Meaford. Alan Aston, a Sauble Beach real estate developer, won the Reform Party's nomination in a riding that seemed to hold particular promise for the party. Cathy Hird, a minister from Chatsworth, offered again for the NDP (she had unsuccessfully contended the seat in 1988). Running for the National Party was Stuart Marwick, an entrepreneur from Chatsworth. Three other minor party candidates rounded out the field, but had neglible impact on the race (none winning more than 1% of the poll).

The big issue locally in the 1993 race was which party and which strategy were most likely to create jobs. Farmers in the riding as in the region in general were concerned by the inflow of subsidized prairie grains replacing local feed crops in area mills. In a riding where government services are a large employer it is not surprising that the Liberal program to help fund local infrastructure was popular. Jackson also promised to use the office of MP to spur local development by setting up a trade directory and conference service, to help local businesses and farmers make contact with one another and discover what goods, products and services are locally produced. Reform certainly had an impact in the riding—in fact, its candidate, Alan Aston, out-polled the Tories' O'Keeffe, in this former PC stronghold.

Jackson's election adds one more name to the unfortunately short list of African-Canadians who have won election to the House of Commons.

Member of Parliament: Ovid L. Jackson; **Party:** Liberal; **Occupation:** Teacher; **Education:** BA; **Age:** 55 (Feb. 3, 1939); **Year first elected to the House of Commons:** 1993

35007 Bruce–Grey

A: Political Profile
i) Voting Behaviour

	% 1993	% 1988	Change 1988-93
Conservative	18.8	40.9	-22.1
Liberal	49.1	38.9	10.2
NDP	4.3	19	-14.7
Reform	24.7	0	24.7
Other	3.1	1.2	1.9

% Turnout	68.5	Total Ballots (#)	52682
Rejected Ballots (#)	333	% Margin of Victory	24.4
Rural Polls, 1988 (#)	156	Urban Polls, 1988 (#)	60
% Yes - 1992	48.4	% No - 1992	50.9

ii) Campaign Financing

	# of Donations	Total $ Value	% of Limit Spent
Conservative	161	34269	98.9
Liberal	320	65228	87.4
NDP	83	13750	18.8
Reform	160	36339	58.9
Other	63	7149	

B: Ethno-Linguistic Profile

% English Home Language	98.8	% French Home Language	0
% Official Bilingual	4.3	% Other Home Language	1.1
% Catholics	16.7	% Protestants	70.8
% Aboriginal Peoples	2.3	% Immigrants	7.2

C: Socio-Economic Profile

Average Family Income $	44922	Median Family Income $	40218
% Low Income Families	10	Average Home Price $	144975
% Home Owners	75.3	% Unemployment	7.9
% Labour Force Participation	65.5	% Managerial-Administrative	10.3
% Self-Employed	15.3	% University Degrees	6.7
% Movers	43.4		

D: Industrial Profile

% Manufacturing	13.8	% Service Sector	12.3
% Agriculture	9.7	% Mining	0.4
% Forestry	0.2	% Fishing	0.1
% Government Services	5.8	% Business Services	3

E: Homogeneity Measures

Ethnic Diversity Index	0.46	Religious Homogeneity Index	0.52
Sectoral Concentration Index	0.38	Income Disparity Index	10.5

F: Physical Setting Characteristics

Total Population	100675	Area (km²)	5997
Population Density (pop/km²)	16.8		

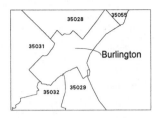

Burlington

Constituency Number: 35008

The constituency of Burlington is nestled east of Hamilton and about 50 kilometres west of Toronto at the head of Lake Ontario. With a more diverse manufacturing base than its neighbouring Hamilton ridings, Burlington is less dependent on heavy industry than its neighbours to the west. Further, many Burlington residents are commuters. Nearly 50 per cent commute to the east toward Metro or to the west toward Hamilton. With family incomes averaging just under $68,000, the riding is one of Ontario's most affluent.

Burlington has traditionally been Conservative territory. Described as a 'Tory titan', Bill Kempling decided to make the term he won in 1988 his last. Having held the riding since its creation in the late 1970s, and having represented one of its predecessors since 1972, his decision was a serious blow to Conservative Party hopes in the riding.

In Kempling's stead, the local Conservative association chose to nominate Mike Kuegle, a 32-year-old lawyer. Kuegle was politically inexperienced. The Liberal challenger was also young. The Grits nominated Paddy Torsney, a 30-year-old public relations executive and former advisor to former Ontario Premier David Peterson. Hugh Ramola, a manager with the Bank of Nova Scotia in Toronto, won the Reform Party nomination. Running for the NDP was Jim Hough, an electronics technician. Two minor party candidates and an independent rounded out the ballot.

The economy in Burlington was a major issue as in other parts of Ontario, and a recession is never good for the incumbent party. In many ways Burlington was a natural Reform riding, in that its middle-class electorate, hard hit by the demise of the real estate boom and resentful of rising taxes associated with the Tory government, was probably looking for an alternative to the right. However, the Reform Party badly mismanaged this opportunity. During a regional all-party debate on crime and criminal justice, NDP Hamilton West candidate Denise Giroux and Reform Hamilton Mountain candidate Craig Chandler were having a heated exchange when Reform's Hugh Ramolla shouted out: 'Hit her, Craig!' Ramolla later apologized for this comment. Subsequently, however, he did himself further damage by explaining that his comment was just a joking way to tell Giroux to 'shut up'. He continued: 'It was clearly done in jest, clear to everyone but Ms Giroux and her feminazis ... Obviously Ms Giroux and her kind don't have a sense of humour.' His opponents in the riding of Burlington and most other candidates across the region did not see the humour in the jest. One asked: 'When is telling someone to hit a woman a joke?' The Reform party took no disciplinary action against Ramolla, other than to warn him to think first, second and third and then and only then make any further jokes. The issue refused to die during the campaign, in part as a consequence of the recent publicity given to violent crimes against women by the trials of Paul Teale and Karla Homolka for the murders of Leslie Mahaffy, Nina DeVilliers and Kristen French in nearby St Catharines. Such insensitivity was clearly hurtful to Reform's prospects in Burlington, and probably elsewhere on the Niagara Peninsula.

In the end, the Liberals' Torsney benefited from the PC-Reform vote split on the right (each party winning about a quarter of the vote) and won the riding by taking 44.3% of the poll. The NDP continued to struggle in this infertile terrain, wining only 2.9% of the vote. None of the other three candidates had any appreciable impact on the result.

Member of Parliament: Patricia A. (Paddy) Torsney; **Party:** Liberal; **Occupation:** Member of Parliament; **Education:** BCom, McGill University; **Age:** 32 (Dec. 19, 1962); **Year first elected to the House of Commons:** 1993

35008 Burlington

A: Political Profile
i) Voting Behaviour

	% 1993	% 1988	Change 1988-93
Conservative	26.3	52.1	-25.8
Liberal	44.3	26.6	17.7
NDP	2.9	16.1	-13.2
Reform	23.3	0	23.3
Other	3.3	5.2	-1.9

% Turnout	71.7	Total Ballots (#)	52109
Rejected Ballots (#)	409	% Margin of Victory	18
Rural Polls, 1988 (#)	0	Urban Polls, 1988 (#)	213
% Yes - 1992	56.6	% No - 1992	43

ii) Campaign Financing

	# of Donations	Total $ Value	% of Limit Spent
Conservative	183	40151	86.8
Liberal	238	42345	66.8
NDP	58	19180	17.5
Reform	201	26646	41.3
Other	92	12615	

B: Ethno-Linguistic Profile

% English Home Language	96	% French Home Language	0.8
% Official Bilingual	9.2	% Other Home Language	3.2
% Catholics	28.5	% Protestants	54.8
% Aboriginal Peoples	0.3	% Immigrants	20.9

C: Socio-Economic Profile

Average Family Income $	67860	Median Family Income $	58471
% Low Income Families	8.9	Average Home Price $	222657
% Home Owners	65.6	% Unemployment	6.7
% Labour Force Participation	71	% Managerial-Administrative	17.6
% Self-Employed	8.1	% University Degrees	14.8
% Movers	43.4		

D: Industrial Profile

% Manufacturing	19.4	% Service Sector	10.3
% Agriculture	0.8	% Mining	0.3
% Forestry	0.1	% Fishing	0
% Government Services	6	% Business Services	7.1

E: Homogeneity Measures

Ethnic Diversity Index	0.33	Religious Homogeneity Index	0.4
Sectoral Concentration Index	0.45	Income Disparity Index	13.8

F: Physical Setting Characteristics

Total Population	93424	Area (km²)	68
Population Density (pop/km²)	1373.9		

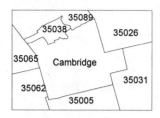

Cambridge

Constituency Number: 35009

Cambridge is a mixed urban and rural riding located about 50 kilometres west of Hamilton. Most of the riding's population is concentrated in the blue collar city of Cambridge that was formed in 1973 by the amalgamation of the communities of Galt, Preston, and Hespeler. With almost one in three workers employed in manufacturing jobs, the riding ranks highest in the province on this measure. Like other communities in Ontario's southwest, Cambridge has been hard hit by the recession. However, as noted, it appears that the economy was in the midst of at least a modest recovery by election time. As an indicator, the week before the election was called it was reported that three local manufacturers had purchased city lands adjacent to their factories (an indication of their plans to expand).

The area has changed partisan colours over time. Traditionally Conservative, the riding went NDP in 1964. In 1979 Chris Speyer won the riding again for the Tories, and held it until his retirement in 1988. Pat Sobeski kept the riding in the Conservative camp in the 1988 election with a 13.6% margin of victory over the second-place NDP candidate

Seven candidates contested the riding in 1993. Sobeski, a former manager for Canada Trust in London, ran again as incumbent. The Liberals nominated Janko Peric, a welder who as a teenager had immigrated to Canada from Croatia. Reg Petersen, a businessman, won the Reform Party's nomination, and was widely expected to mount a serious challenge for the seat, and possibly even win it. Bill McBain, a 'briefing co-ordinator' from Toronto, ran for the NDP. Three minor party candidates rounded out the field.

1993 saw the riding change its partisan stripe once again, this time in favour of the Liberals. The economy and jobs were on voters' minds. Liberal candidate Peric made no secret of the fact that he understood the situation first hand, having himself been out of work for two years in the mid-1980s. Peric benefited from the collapse of the NDP's vote (the party's drop of 22.8% was one of its worst province-wide) and the split of 'small c' conservative support between the Tories (17.3%) and Reform (33.5%). His victory margin of less than 6% was Ontario's third closest finish.

Member of Parliament: Janko Peric; **Party:** Liberal; **Occupation:** Technician; **Education:** Technical School of Zagreb; **Age:** 45 (Feb. 24, 1949); **Year first elected to the House of Commons:** 1993

35009 Cambridge

A: Political Profile

i) Voting Behaviour

	% 1993	% 1988	Change 1988-93
Conservative	17.3	40.4	-23.1
Liberal	39.3	26.8	12.5
NDP	5.3	28.1	-22.8
Reform	33.5	0	33.5
Other	4.6	4.8	-0.2

% Turnout	66.5	Total Ballots (#)	56719
Rejected Ballots (#)	374	% Margin of Victory	5.8
Rural Polls, 1988 (#)	15	Urban Polls, 1988 (#)	177
% Yes - 1992	47.1	% No - 1992	52.4

ii) Campaign Financing

	# of Donations	Total $ Value	% of Limit Spent
Conservative	139	50730	66.5
Liberal	102	28557	52.2*
NDP	145	28701	60.1*
Reform	250	82104	95.4
Other	25	9163	

B: Ethno-Linguistic Profile

% English Home Language	90.8	% French Home Language	0.5
% Official Bilingual	5.3	% Other Home Language	8.7
% Catholics	36.2	% Protestants	49.6
% Aboriginal Peoples	0.3	% Immigrants	21.9

C: Socio-Economic Profile

Average Family Income $	52217	Median Family Income $	48583
% Low Income Families	11.4	Average Home Price $	169633
% Home Owners	66.5	% Unemployment	9.8
% Labour Force Participation	73.7	% Managerial-Administrative	12.1
% Self-Employed	6.3	% University Degrees	7.8
% Movers	51.5		

D: Industrial Profile

% Manufacturing	31.4	% Service Sector	10.4
% Agriculture	1.2	% Mining	0.2
% Forestry	0.1	% Fishing	0
% Government Services	4.3	% Business Services	4.6

E: Homogeneity Measures

Ethnic Diversity Index	0.29	Religious Homogeneity Index	0.38
Sectoral Concentration Index	0.39	Income Disparity Index	7

F: Physical Setting Characteristics

Total Population	125463	Area (km²)	371
Population Density (pop/km²)	338.2		

* Tentative value, due to the existence of unpaid campaign expenses.

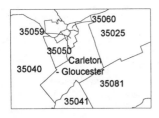

Carleton–Gloucester

Constituency Number: 35010

The riding of Carleton–Gloucester, created just prior to the 1988 election, is located in eastern Ontario just south of Ottawa. A small portion in the northernmost corner borders the Ottawa River (and, beyond that, the province of Quebec). While geographically a predominantly rural riding, most of its residents live in suburban Ottawa communities. Its residents are disproportionately well-educated (with almost twice the provincial average of university graduates) and affluent (average family incomes are over $15,000 higher than the norm for ridings in the province, making this one of the ten most affluent constituencies in Ontario). Almost 20 per cent of residents report French as their home language. Farming, research and development, and electronics are among the riding's main employers. In addition, the suburban Ottawa communities are home to many federal civil servants; the 4.3% of the workforce employed in 'government service' industries rank this riding highest in the province on this measure.

The riding's socio-economic profile suggests that it should be fertile Conservative, or perhaps Reform, soil. Moreover, voters in this riding may be more morally conservative than in other ridings in the region. In the last election many attributed the defeat of PC 'star candidate' Maureen McTeer to her overtly pro-choice views on abortion. McTeer was rumoured to be a potential Tory candidate again in 1993, but this did not transpire. Also the Christian Heritage Party had a respectable local showing in 1988. In some respects, then, the Liberal victory in 1988 might be attributed to idiosyncratic factors. The NDP has found this riding difficult to penetrate.

The Liberal incumbent, Eugene Bellemare, a francophone former high school teacher/adult education administrator and local Gloucester politician, defended the seat in 1993. The Tories nominated Thérèse McKellar, an accountant from Kars. Reform launched its campaign for Ontario here in June 1992 by holding their first nomination meeting. Its local association, with over 750 members, was reputed to be one of the strongest in eastern Ontario. Winning the Reform nomination, against four other candidates, was Ken Binda, a real estate company manager and 46-year-old major who retired from the military in order to stand for election, and run his business. The NDP was represented by Cindy Moriarty, a policy consultant from Orléans, while Shelley Ann Clark, a public servant from Gloucester, ran for the National Party. Four other candidates rounded out the ballot, including one for the Christian Heritage Party, but none was able to attract even 1% of the poll on election day.

The issues in this riding are probably typical of Ottawa-area ridings; the state of the public service, the NAFTA, air connections, and federal restraint. Appointed Liberal critic for the National Capital Commission after his election in 1988, Bellemare was able to 'capitalize' on this local issue. The concentration of French speakers in the riding probably hurt the Reform Party's candidacy, as would the party's anti-Ottawa image. However, press reports suggested that the Liberals took pains not to underestimate Reform's challenge, even sending members to Reform meetings.

Compared to their counterparts in other ridings, voters were engaged in the 1993 campaign — the 75% turnout level in 1993 was the second highest in the province. In the end, Reform's Binda did manage a respectable showing, but finished a distant second, some 34,000 votes behind the Liberals' Bellemare.

Member of Parliament: Eugene Bellemare; **Party:** Liberal; **Occupation:** Administrator; **Education:** MEd, University of Ottawa; **Age:** 64 (April 6, 1932); **Year first elected to the House of Commons:** 1988

35010 Carleton–Gloucester

A: Political Profile

i) Voting Behaviour

	% 1993	% 1988	Change 1988-93
Conservative	15.7	37.3	-21.6
Liberal	61.6	48.1	13.5
NDP	3.7	9.7	-6
Reform	16.4	0	16.4
Other	2.7	4.9	-2.2

% Turnout	75	Total Ballots (#)	76435
Rejected Ballots (#)	410	% Margin of Victory	45.2
Rural Polls, 1988 (#)	72	Urban Polls, 1988 (#)	200
% Yes - 1992	58.6	% No - 1992	40.8

ii) Campaign Financing

	# of Donations	Total $ Value	% of Limit Spent
Conservative	145	33451	54.3*
Liberal	244	56397	88.7
NDP	185	29996	30.7
Reform	148	32785	34.7
Other	36	3184	

B: Ethno-Linguistic Profile

% English Home Language	76	% French Home Language	19.3
% Official Bilingual	42.3	% Other Home Language	4.7
% Catholics	51.9	% Protestants	33.7
% Aboriginal Peoples	0.6	% Immigrants	13.6

C: Socio-Economic Profile

Average Family Income $	71374	Median Family Income $	67138
% Low Income Families	6.2	Average Home Price $	173044
% Home Owners	80.8	% Unemployment	5.4
% Labour Force Participation	79.7	% Managerial-Administrative	20.7
% Self-Employed	7.5	% University Degrees	21.7
% Movers	57		

D: Industrial Profile

% Manufacturing	4	% Service Sector	12.4
% Agriculture	1.6	% Mining	0.1
% Forestry	0.1	% Fishing	0
% Government Services	28.5	% Business Services	7.4

E: Homogeneity Measures

Ethnic Diversity Index	0.26	Religious Homogeneity Index	0.39
Sectoral Concentration Index	0.55	Income Disparity Index	5.9

F: Physical Setting Characteristics

Total Population	134781	Area (km²)	1104
Population Density (pop/km²)	122.1		

*   Tentative value, due to the existence of unpaid campaign expenses.

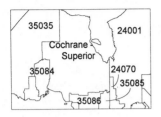

Cochrane–Superior

Constituency Number: 35011

Covering over 350,000 square kilometres in northern Ontario, this riding is the province's largest (and the seventh largest in Canada). Formed in 1933, the constituency stretches northward from the shores of Lake Superior to the shores of Hudson Bay. Most of it is covered by acres of spruce forest and muskeg swamp. Despite its enormous geographic expanse, the riding is the province's third smallest in terms of its eligible electorate. One in five of the riding's residents are members of Canada's aboriginal peoples, making this the second highest concentration of native Canadians in the province. The riding is home to a significant number of francophones (38% report French as their home language) and Catholics (two-thirds of residents); Cochrane–Superior ranks second and third, respectively, on these measures among Ontario's electoral districts. Resource industries dominate this 'Canadian shield' territory; the riding has the highest proportion of forestry workers, and ranks in the top ten in terms of mining and fishing in the province. There is no dominant urban centre in the riding, although Kapuskasing (the name derives from the Cree word for 'branch', since the river of that name is a branch of the Mattagami River) is home to over 11,000. The town, located about 900 kilometres north of Toronto, is known to be one of the snowiest in Canada (there are eight snowmobile dealers!). In 1992 residents of the town demonstrated their determination. At that time, the town made the news for its dramatic (and desperate) move to save its pulp and paper mill, the town's major employer for over 60 years. The mill was threatened with shutdown until about 1,700 of its residents put up a minimum investment of $5,000 to help raise the necessary $15 million to keep it afloat. The antiquated mill faces stiff competition in its bid to remain competitive, and workers have taken pay cuts.

The riding has been solid Liberal territory since its creation. The incumbent MP, Réginald Bélair, had been an assistant for nine years to Keith Penner, and inherited the riding in 1988 with Penner's retirement. Bélair's 4% victory margin in 1988 was hardly overwhelming, however.

In addition to Bélair, who defended the seat for the Liberals, three other candidates offered in the 1993 campaign. Running for the Conservatives was Muriel J. Parent, an administrator from Val Rita. Don Banks, an electrician from Marathon, carried the Reform Party's banner. Jean Paul Lajeunesse, a forestry contractor from Cochrane, ran for the NDP.

In the end, Bélair enjoyed the province-wide Liberal wave and swept to an impressive victory with a margin of 62.6% over his nearest opponent, the Reform candidate Banks. This represented the Liberals' fifth best performance in the province, and generated the province's fourth-largest victory margin.

Member of Parliament: Reginald Bélair; **Party:** Liberal; **Occupation:** Administrator; **Education:** BA, Hearst College; **Age:** 45 (April 6, 1949); **Year first elected to the House of Commons:** 1988

35011 Cochrane–Superior

A: Political Profile

i) Voting Behaviour

	% 1993	% 1988	Change 1988-93
Conservative	9.1	23.6	-14.5
Liberal	72.2	40.2	32
NDP	9	36.2	-27.2
Reform	9.6	0	9.6
Other	0	0	0

% Turnout	62.7	Total Ballots (#)	27335
Rejected Ballots (#)	323	% Margin of Victory	62.6
Rural Polls, 1988 (#)	130	Urban Polls, 1988 (#)	37
% Yes - 1992	49.4	% No - 1992	49.8

ii) Campaign Financing

	# of Donations	Total $ Value	% of Limit Spent
Conservative	64	27455	35.7
Liberal	159	29324	56.1
NDP	0**	0**	0**
Reform	23	3356	2.9
Other	0	0	

B: Ethno-Linguistic Profile

% English Home Language	55.1	% French Home Language	37.6
% Official Bilingual	39	% Other Home Language	7.2
% Catholics	65.8	% Protestants	28.7
% Aboriginal Peoples	20.4	% Immigrants	3.7

C: Socio-Economic Profile

Average Family Income $	51368	Median Family Income $	47549
% Low Income Families	10.4	Average Home Price $	75484
% Home Owners	64.2	% Unemployment	11.9
% Labour Force Participation	65.7	% Managerial-Administrative	6.8
% Self-Employed	5.5	% University Degrees	5.1
% Movers	41.6		

D: Industrial Profile

% Manufacturing	18.6	% Service Sector	14.4
% Agriculture	0.7	% Mining	6.6
% Forestry	5.4	% Fishing	0.2
% Government Services	10.5	% Business Services	1.1

E: Homogeneity Measures

Ethnic Diversity Index	0.35	Religious Homogeneity Index	0.51
Sectoral Concentration Index	0.32	Income Disparity Index	7.4

F: Physical Setting Characteristics

Total Population	63459	Area (km²)	351240
Population Density (pop/km²)	0.2		

** No return filed.

35017
35071
35098 Davenport
35087
35063

Davenport

Constituency Number: 35012

The province's smallest electoral district, Davenport is an ethnically diverse riding of older working-class, established immigrant neighbourhoods in the heart of the metropolitan Toronto area. Interspersed among these neighbourhoods are areas of light industrial and commercial activity. Ethnicity is the distinctive dimension of this riding. Over 50% of the riding's population were born abroad — the highest proportion of immigrants of any riding in Canada. Almost a third of riding residents claim to know Portuguese; a further 16% speak Italian. The riding is very blue-collar. Average family incomes are the province's lowest, over $15,000 below the norm for Ontario ridings. Davenport's unemployment rate of 13.1% ranks the riding among the province's ten highest.

Davenport epitomizes the urban, ethnic riding that has been fertile Liberal ground for many years. The riding's 25-year incumbent, Charles Caccia, is himself an immigrant. During the campaign, he was described by the *Toronto Star* as 'the undisputed granddaddy of federal politics in Metro'. However, in May 1992 Jean Chrétien had to refuse to endorse the nomination papers of Tony Letra, who was planning to challenge Caccia's nomination. Apparently, Letra had pleaded guilty to charges of voters' list tampering in the 1988 Toronto municipal election. Caccia's victory in 1993 was expected, even without the remarkable Liberal sweep province-wide.

Nine candidates emerged to challenge Caccia's hold on Davenport in 1993. John Doherty, a school trustee, ran for the NDP. Michael Jakubcak, an urban planner from Weston, carried the Reform Party banner. Margaret Samuel, a law student, ran for the Conservatives, and Sherelanne Purcell, a teacher, offered for the National Party. Five minor party candidates also stood for election, but none won more than one per cent of the poll on election day.

The local campaign in Davenport reflected national and parochial concerns. A combination of recession, international trade conditions, and trade liberalization cut a swathe through the factories on the western edge of the City of Toronto which employed many of Davenport's residents. The simultaneous slump in the real estate industry also put many of the riding's construction trades workers out of work. Crime and drugs have increasingly become a problem in the riding, especially along the strip of Bloor Street West which runs through the riding. In response residents have undertaken many community strategies including an anti-violence, anti-drug rally just before the election.

Although unlikely to provide congenial campaigning for Conservative candidates, the Tories' record on immigration probably cost the party in settings like Davenport. Specifically, the Conservative government's decision to shift responsibility for immigration to the Public Security Ministry, move cultural policy to the new Heritage Ministry, and leave the Minister of Multiculturalism (Gerry Weiner), as a 'cardboard cut-out minister' angered many, including most of the editors of the Metro's 'non-English' and 'ethnically focused' English language newspapers and media. Some of the editors in this section of the media blamed the reorganization on a Tory attempt to pander to the racists among Reform Party supporters, especially the change in location of the Immigration Department which seemed to equate immigrants with 'gangsters and convicts'.

Caccia's landslide victory (winning just under three quarters of the vote) was the Liberal's third best showing in the province, and produced the third largest victory margin in the province.

Member of Parliament: Charles L. Caccia; **Party**: Liberal; **Occupation**: Businessperson; **Education**: BSc (Forestry Economics), University of Vienna; **Age**: 64 (April 28, 1930); **Year first elected to the House of Commons**: 1968

35012 Davenport

A: Political Profile
i) Voting Behaviour

	% 1993	% 1988	Change 1988-93
Conservative	4.6	18.6	-14
Liberal	73.8	58.9	14.9
NDP	9.2	18.8	-9.6
Reform	7.8	0	7.8
Other	4.6	3.7	0.9

% Turnout	65.2	Total Ballots (#)	27820
Rejected Ballots (#)	418	% Margin of Victory	64.6
Rural Polls, 1988 (#)	0	Urban Polls, 1988 (#)	114
% Yes - 1992	50.7	% No - 1992	47.9

ii) Campaign Financing

	# of Donations	Total $ Value	% of Limit Spent
Conservative	38	6921	13.3
Liberal	146	36648	58.9
NDP	238	34593	59.5
Reform	69	4578	9*
Other	26	3095	

B: Ethno-Linguistic Profile

% English Home Language	45.9	% French Home Language	0.3
% Official Bilingual	6.3	% Other Home Language	53.7
% Catholics	63.9	% Protestants	12.5
% Aboriginal Peoples	0.3	% Immigrants	55.7

C: Socio-Economic Profile

Average Family Income $	40854	Median Family Income $	36973
% Low Income Families	28.1	Average Home Price $	239825
% Home Owners	51.3	% Unemployment	13.1
% Labour Force Participation	65	% Managerial-Administrative	7.7
% Self-Employed	5.7	% University Degrees	8.6
% Movers	44		

D: Industrial Profile

% Manufacturing	18.1	% Service Sector	17.6
% Agriculture	0.3	% Mining	0.1
% Forestry	0	% Fishing	0
% Government Services	4.1	% Business Services	6.3

E: Homogeneity Measures

Ethnic Diversity Index	0.4	Religious Homogeneity Index	0.45
Sectoral Concentration Index	0.45	Income Disparity Index	9.5

F: Physical Setting Characteristics

Total Population	96172	Area (km²)	10
Population Density (pop/km²)	9617.2		

* Tentative value, due to the existence of unpaid campaign expenses.

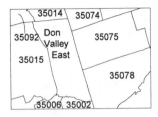

Don Valley East

Constituency Number: 35013

This riding includes neighbourhoods with a wide range of incomes, and a diverse array of housing types, including condominiums, low and high-rise apartments, townhouses and single family dwellings. It is home to a range of established ethnic communities, including one of the largest Greek-speaking populations in Canada. Average family incomes are only slightly below the norm for the province's electoral districts, but 2% more families are classed as 'low income' than is the provincial average. With only just over a third of households owning their own dwellings, the riding ranks seventh lowest on this measure in the province.

Don Valley East is a swing riding, alternating between the Liberals and Conservatives since 1972. Alan Redway, a lawyer, won the riding away from Liberal David Collenette in 1984. He held the riding in 1988 for the Conservatives. Redway was a former mayor of East York and while on the Tory backbenches he became an outspoken critic of the Mulroney government's lack of response to Toronto's housing problems. In 1989 he was named Minister of Housing in Mulroney's government, a job he lost shortly thereafter when he made a joke about having a gun while passing a security gate in an airport!

Nine individuals contested the seat in 1993. Redway attempted to hold the seat for the Tories. David Collenette, a management consultant who had represented the riding on two previous occasions (1974 and 1980), won a tight race for the Liberal nomination in December 1992. In the end, Collenette prevailed by a margin of only 86 votes against Hermes Iordanous, a native of Cyprus, and Yasmin Ratansi, the Liberal's candidate for the riding in the 1988 federal election. Some supporters of Ratansi argued that the nomination meeting had been deliberately delayed so that Collenette could be given a chance to drum up support. Gordon Honsey, a truck driver from North York, ran for the Reform Party. Running for the NDP was Janice Waud Loper, a publishing consultant from Oakville. None of the remaining five minor party candidates managed to win more than one per cent of the vote on election day.

The issue in 1993 here, as everywhere in Metro, was the economy and jobs. The most severely affected by the recession were young families. In the metro area, analyses had suggested that those couples with two partners under 35 years of age had a 1 in 5 chance of living in poverty. If the two partners were under 25 years of age the odds jumped to 2 to 1, and for single parents of any age the odds rose to 4 to 1. On election day, it was Collenette's turn for victory, winning with a comfortable 30% margin over the incumbent.

Member of Parliament: David Michael Collenette; **Party**: Liberal; **Occupation**: Businessperson; **Education:** BA (Hons.); **Age**: 48 (June 24, 1946); **Year first elected to the House of Commons:** 1974

35013 Don Valley East

A: Political Profile
i) Voting Behaviour

	% 1993	% 1988	Change 1988-93
Conservative	23.2	44.7	-21.5
Liberal	53.7	37.9	15.8
NDP	3.8	15.1	-11.3
Reform	16.9	0	16.9
Other	2.4	2.3	0.1

% Turnout	67.5	Total Ballots (#)	40608
Rejected Ballots (#)	327	% Margin of Victory	30.5
Rural Polls, 1988 (#)	0	Urban Polls, 1988 (#)	157
% Yes - 1992	56.2	% No - 1992	43.1

ii) Campaign Financing

	# of Donations	Total $ Value	% of Limit Spent
Conservative	280	46163	78.6
Liberal	167	57382	81
NDP	64	14012	22.4
Reform	74	24826	40.1
Other	7	1595	

B: Ethno-Linguistic Profile

% English Home Language	75.7	% French Home Language	0.6
% Official Bilingual	7.6	% Other Home Language	23.7
% Catholics	27.2	% Protestants	37.8
% Aboriginal Peoples	0.2	% Immigrants	42.8

C: Socio-Economic Profile

Average Family Income $	54541	Median Family Income $	48385
% Low Income Families	18.1	Average Home Price $	251491
% Home Owners	36.6	% Unemployment	10
% Labour Force Participation	68.7	% Managerial-Administrative	15.3
% Self-Employed	6.9	% University Degrees	16
% Movers	47.6		

D: Industrial Profile

% Manufacturing	15.9	% Service Sector	10.8
% Agriculture	0.3	% Mining	0.2
% Forestry	0.1	% Fishing	0
% Government Services	5.9	% Business Services	11.6

E: Homogeneity Measures

Ethnic Diversity Index	0.18	Religious Homogeneity Index	0.28
Sectoral Concentration Index	0.49	Income Disparity Index	11.3

F: Physical Setting Characteristics

Total Population	92287	Area (km²)	23
Population Density (pop/km²)	4012.5		

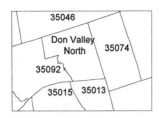

Don Valley North

Constituency Number: 35014

Don Valley North is an urban riding located in the northern section of Metro Toronto (north of Highway 401). Socio-economically and ethnically diverse (it ranks sixth in the province in terms of immigrants and has the second highest proportion of Jews in Ontario), the riding is home to both middle and working-class families, along with some more affluent enclaves. Although average family incomes are approximately $10,000 higher than the norm for the province, incomes are unevenly distributed. With just over 15% of families classed by Statistics Canada as having 'low incomes' in 1991, Don Valley North is at the provincial average on this measure.

A new constituency in the 1988 election, Don Valley North returned Conservative Barbara Greene to the House of Commons in a very close race. Greene, a teacher, single mother, and eleven-year Metro councillor before taking office, turned out to be an outspoken and controversial MP. Despite representing an economically mixed riding, Greene adopted a neo-conservative posture by apparently endorsing a definition of poverty based on a Fraser Institute study written by Professor Chris Sarlo. While Sarlo's study claimed a family of four could survive on $16,400 per annum, Statistics Canada put the poverty level for a single person at $15,000 per annum. Greene acknowledged Sarlo's numbers may be off, but endorsed his general conclusion that poverty practically does not exist in Canada any more, and ventured that unemployment and social inequality, including inequality of opportunity, are not necessarily bad. Greene also ruffled some feathers by venturing that food banks are abused by 'freeloaders'. During the campaign Greene claimed that a Reform government would use the 'notwithstanding' clause in the constitution to deny due process to refugees and immigrants. Meanwhile her own party had moved immigration to the new Ministry of Public Security, perpetrating what was called a 'coup' against immigrants and ethnic Canadians by the editor of Canada's largest Italian newspaper.

Five candidates emerged to challenge Greene in 1993. The Liberal candidate was Sarkis Assadourian who ran a close second (500 votes) to Greene in 1988. Assadourian is an executive director of the Armenian Community Centre (of Metropolitan Toronto) who immigrated to Canada from Syria in 1970. He has a distinguished record of public service and enjoyed the strong support of the riding's Armenian community. The Reform Party ran Peter Cobbold, a business manager, while the NDP offered David Lu, a worker advisor. Rounding out the field were two minor party candidates, neither of whom won more than a handful of votes on election day.

After the dust settled, Don Valley North joined the rest of the province in giving Assadourian and the Liberals the seat with a substantial 40% margin of victory.

Member of Parliament: Sarkis Assadourian; **Party**: Liberal; **Occupation:** Businessperson; **Age:** 46; **Year first elected to the House of Commons**: 1993

35014 Don Valley North

A: Political Profile
i) Voting Behaviour

	% 1993	% 1988	Change 1988-93
Conservative	19.3	43.4	-24.1
Liberal	59.9	41.9	18
NDP	3.7	11.8	-8.1
Reform	16.1	0	16.1
Other	1.1	2.8	-1.7

% Turnout	70.1	Total Ballots (#)	37927
Rejected Ballots (#)	334	% Margin of Victory	40.6
Rural Polls, 1988 (#)	0	Urban Polls, 1988 (#)	165
% Yes - 1992	60.2	% No - 1992	39.2

ii) Campaign Financing

	# of Donations	Total $ Value	% of Limit Spent
Conservative	17	38560	79.8
Liberal	44	40792	65.5
NDP	69	18378	26.4
Reform	61	24887	47.7
Other	3	473	

B: Ethno-Linguistic Profile

% English Home Language	71	% French Home Language	0.4
% Official Bilingual	9.3	% Other Home Language	28.6
% Catholics	24.8	% Protestants	30.6
% Aboriginal Peoples	0.1	% Immigrants	47.7

C: Socio-Economic Profile

Average Family Income $	65126	Median Family Income $	54457
% Low Income Families	15.5	Average Home Price $	284355
% Home Owners	56.4	% Unemployment	8
% Labour Force Participation	69.7	% Managerial-Administrative	19.2
% Self-Employed	10.3	% University Degrees	20.9
% Movers	41.9		

D: Industrial Profile

% Manufacturing	14.6	% Service Sector	8.8
% Agriculture	0.3	% Mining	0.2
% Forestry	0.1	% Fishing	0
% Government Services	5	% Business Services	11.5

E: Homogeneity Measures

Ethnic Diversity Index	0.21	Religious Homogeneity Index	0.27
Sectoral Concentration Index	0.53	Income Disparity Index	16.4

F: Physical Setting Characteristics

Total Population	86913	Area (km²)	20
Population Density (pop/km²)	4345.7		

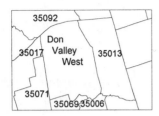

Don Valley West

Constituency Number: 35015

Don Valley West, located adjacent to downtown Toronto east of Yonge Street and south of Highway 401, is one of Canada's most affluent ridings. It contains some of the province's most desirable and most expensive addresses (average home prices are just under half a million dollars!), including the majestic mansions along The Bridle Path. The area also serves as headquarters to a number of corporate offices. There is relatively little public housing, and only 10.5% of the riding's families are classed as 'low income'. Provincially, average family incomes rank second highest (at over $100,000); the median family income is Ontario's highest. The riding has the highest concentration of 'managers and administrators' (the typical upper-echelon white-collar, salaried employees) in Canada, and the second highest proportion of university graduates of Ontario districts. However, the depth of the recession was such that even in such a well-to-do environment, concerns about unemployment (not seen in the area since the 1930s) and hard-to-make mortgage payments were discernible.

As the above description might suggest, the area has been safe Conservative ground. In 1988, John Bosley, a businessman, was elected with a comfortable 16% margin. First elected to the Commons in 1979, Bosley is best remembered as the Speaker of the House of Commons who presided over the anarchy of the first years of the Conservatives' hold on power under Mulroney. Voters in the riding also registered strong support (the third highest level in the province) for the Charlottetown Accord in the 1992 constitutional referendum.

Bosley was challenged in 1993 by eight candidates. Reform sensed an opportunity to appeal to the riding's affluent small-c conservatives, and nominated Julian Pope, a photogenic stockbroker employed in his family's firm. The inroads of Reform in the riding apparently prompted an infuriated Dalton Camp, one of Canada's leading Conservative intellectuals and, many years ago, a candidate for the PCs in this part of Metro, to write a scathing column in the *Toronto Star*. Camp equated Don Valley West's fascination with Reform to the appeals of right-of-centre populist movements in the 1930s. Camp worried that, if the electors of Don Valley West forgot their historical experience with populist reform-minded movements, they could well be doomed to repeat it. Whether Camp's tirade had an impact on the riding will never be known. In addition, the Liberals put up a highly credible candidate in John Godfrey (a former academic and editor of the *Financial Post*, and more recently an executive with a high-tech research agency). Leonard Swartz, a quality engineer, ran for the NDP, and Dorothy Campbell, a retired civil servant, offered for the National Party. Four other minor party candidates rounded out the ballot, but had a neglible impact on the outcome.

Don Valley West was a hotly contended seat in 1993. Even relatively late in the campaign, when the Liberal sweep in the province was clearly visible to pollsters, the Liberal Party's campaign team felt that the Tories might be able to hold this riding. This was not to transpire. On election day, Godfrey polled more votes than the Conservatives and Reform candidates combined, and was returned to power with a comfortable 20% margin. Even so, Bosley's 29% finish was the Tories' fourth-best in the province.

Member of Parliament: John Ferguson Godfrey; **Party:** Liberal; **Occupation:** Economic historian; **Education:** DPhil; **Age:** 52 (December 19, 1942); **Year first elected to the House of Commons:** 1993

35015 Don Valley West

A: Political Profile
i) Voting Behaviour

	% 1993		% 1988	Change 1988-93
Conservative	29.1		53.3	-24.2
Liberal	49.8		36.8	13
NDP	2.7		8.3	-5.6
Reform	15.2		0	15.2
Other	3.3		1.6	1.7

% Turnout	71.5	Total Ballots (#)	52300
Rejected Ballots (#)	318	% Margin of Victory	20.7
Rural Polls, 1988 (#)	0	Urban Polls, 1988 (#)	177
% Yes - 1992	66.3	% No - 1992	33.1

ii) Campaign Financing

	# of Donations	Total $ Value	% of Limit Spent
Conservative	182	45031	73.7
Liberal	246	55601	82
NDP	29	4211	5.4
Reform	74	17070	22.5
Other	16	36063	

B: Ethno-Linguistic Profile

% English Home Language	88.7	% French Home Language	0.8
% Official Bilingual	14.5	% Other Home Language	10.5
% Catholics	21.4	% Protestants	43.9
% Aboriginal Peoples	0.2	% Immigrants	30.1

C: Socio-Economic Profile

Average Family Income $	106136	Median Family Income $	75689
% Low Income Families	10.5	Average Home Price $	480696
% Home Owners	45.6	% Unemployment	5.7
% Labour Force Participation	69.7	% Managerial-Administrative	25
% Self-Employed	15	% University Degrees	35
% Movers	42.4		

D: Industrial Profile

% Manufacturing	9.2	% Service Sector	7.5
% Agriculture	0.3	% Mining	0.4
% Forestry	0.2	% Fishing	0
% Government Services	6.3	% Business Services	16.8

E: Homogeneity Measures

Ethnic Diversity Index	0.23	Religious Homogeneity Index	0.3
Sectoral Concentration Index	0.63	Income Disparity Index	28.7

F: Physical Setting Characteristics

Total Population	95382	Area (km²)	33
Population Density (pop/km²)	2890.4		

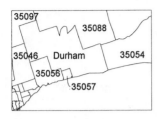

Durham

Constituency Number: 35016

Durham is a mixed urban/rural riding located to the east of Toronto on the shores of Lake Ontario. The riding includes a part of eastern Whitby, and northern Oshawa, and a larger section of the township of Scugog and the municipality of Clarington. Residents are comfortable economically, and Durham is among the province's most quickly growing ridings. Manufacturing is important to the riding's economy, with about 22% of the workforce employed in this sector. In fact, the Durham Region, and especially the neighbouring riding of Oshawa, lives and dies by the fate of General Motors. Even though Oshawa has escaped GM's continent-wide restructuring relatively unscathed, workers both at GM and its contractors were understandably nervous about the economy as they went to the polls in 1993.

The riding has solid Conservative roots. Prior to 1988, it had been held by Tory Allan Lawrence. It was held comfortably for the Conservatives in 1988 by Ross Stevenson, a farmer, ex-Member of the provincial assembly, and former provincial minister of agriculture. However, despite acquiring a reputation for being a party loyalist and a dedicated constituency servant, Stevenson was in trouble from the start of this campaign. His association with the unpopular Tory record, in particular, left him vulnerable to the locally popular Reform challenge mounted by Ian Smyth, a travel consultant from Courtice. Reform showed it would be a force in the area when Preston Manning attracted a crowd of over 4,000 (who paid $5 a head to see him) in nearby Pickering.

Liberal candidate Alex Shepherd, a chartered accountant from Seagrave and former director of a local chamber of commerce, promised to work towards upgrading Durham College to a full university with a concentration on industrial research and development. This was expected to insure that the region's workers and firms constantly had access to leading edge skills and manufacturing processes. The NDP ran Lucy Rybka-Becker, a public servant from Oshawa. Four other minor party candidates rounded out the 1993 ballot.

The result registered a tough three-way race. The split of the right of centre vote between Tory and Reform candidates handed the riding to the Liberals, whose winning 36.8% was the party's third *lowest* performance in the province!

Member of Parliament: Alex Shepherd; **Party**: Liberal; **Occupation**: Accountant; **Education**: BCom, Carleton University; **Age**: 48 (Oct. 13, 1946); **Year first elected to the House of Commons**: 1993

35016 Durham

A: Political Profile
i) Voting Behaviour

	% 1993	% 1988	Change 1988-93
Conservative	24.5	46.5	-22
Liberal	36.8	29.1	7.7
NDP	4.2	20	-15.8
Reform	30.5	0	30.5
Other	4.2	4.5	-0.3

% Turnout	68.7	Total Ballots (#)	61309
Rejected Ballots (#)	417	% Margin of Victory	6.3
Rural Polls, 1988 (#)	117	Urban Polls, 1988 (#)	98
% Yes - 1992	50.2	% No - 1992	49.4

ii) Campaign Financing

	# of Donations	Total $ Value	% of Limit Spent
Conservative	215	46339	68.8
Liberal	179	36671	65.2
NDP	54	12781	15.1
Reform	135	36112	60.5
Other	66	24190	

B: Ethno-Linguistic Profile

% English Home Language	97.3	% French Home Language	0.5
% Official Bilingual	6.1	% Other Home Language	2.2
% Catholics	22.7	% Protestants	61.9
% Aboriginal Peoples	0.4	% Immigrants	14.4

C: Socio-Economic Profile

Average Family Income $	61622	Median Family Income $	56829
% Low Income Families	6.4	Average Home Price $	221521
% Home Owners	75.8	% Unemployment	7.5
% Labour Force Participation	73	% Managerial-Administrative	12.5
% Self-Employed	9	% University Degrees	9
% Movers	52.7		

D: Industrial Profile

% Manufacturing	21.8	% Service Sector	10.2
% Agriculture	4.2	% Mining	0.3
% Forestry	0.1	% Fishing	0
% Government Services	6.2	% Business Services	5.2

E: Homogeneity Measures

Ethnic Diversity Index	0.33	Religious Homogeneity Index	0.45
Sectoral Concentration Index	0.37	Income Disparity Index	7.8

F: Physical Setting Characteristics

Total Population	119575	Area (km^2)	1743
Population Density (pop/km^2)	68.6		

Eglinton–Lawrence

Constituency Number: 35017

Eglinton–Lawrence, a metropolitan Toronto riding, is, to quote Joe Clark, 'a community of communities', with just under half of its population being immigrants. The northeastern section, along the border with the City of Toronto is predominantly Anglo and upper middle class; towards the middle, the complexion changes to middle-upper middle class Jewish. In the centre and north lining both sides of the William Allen Expressway is a sprawling public housing community called Lawrence Heights, that is highly ethnically diverse. African Canadians are also well represented in the southwest of the riding, as are even newer immigrant groups such as Portuguese and people from South East Asia. Finally on the western side of the riding the community is predominantly Italian. Industrial, light manufacturing and wholesaling districts dot the riding on the northwest and towards the southwest. These areas, which gave jobs to many of the new immigrants and less skilled in the riding, were severely affected by the recession, a high dollar (which encouraged cross-border shopping and discouraged exports) and free trade, driving unemployment up in the riding. The construction slump also disproportionately hurt the riding's blue-collar residents.

Reflecting the traditionally solid support of 'urban ethnic' voters, this riding and its predecessors have been traditional Liberal ridings for generations. Once the seat of Liberal cabinet minister Mitchell Sharpe, it was labelled part of the six-riding 'dead zone' for Conservatives in the metro area by a Tory strategist in the 1988 campaign. After successfully challenging incumbent Liberal MP Roland de Corneille for the party's nomination in a bitter contest in 1988, Joseph Volpe went on to win the riding for the party by a comfortable 20% margin. Volpe, an Italian immigrant and high school vice-principal, also had to dodge the debris of the Patti Starr affair, in which through no fault of his own he became involved. Patti Starr was a prominent member of the National Council of Jewish Women, who was convicted of a number of offences under tax and election laws for making improper political donations to provincial and federal Liberal incumbents and candidates. Part of the scandal revolved around a subsidized apartment building erected by the NCJW for the elderly which, unfortunately for Volpe, was constructed in his riding. Starr used funds from the building (some of which was from federal sources) to make the improper contributions to politicians. Volpe, like most other federal and provincial Liberal incumbents, had to do considerable leg work to extricate himself from this quagmire.

Reform's Charles C. Van Tuinen, a millwright, had to run against his party's image as being insensitive to issues of immigration and refugees. His efforts were hampered by the racist and anti-Semitic remarks made by his fellow Reform candidate John Beck in neighbouring York Centre, remarks that prompted Preston Manning to demand Beck's resignation. Mulroney's reforms to the immigration system also hurt the Tories locally. Moreover, the Tory's Marc Monson, a real estate agent, had to justify the failure of the federal government to back a plan to redevelop the Metro convention centre and build a new trade centre in this riding where a number of unemployed construction workers reside. The NDP ran Gael Hepworth, a financial director. Three minor party candidates rounded out the slate, but none exceeded 1% of the poll on election day.

Volpe won easily with 71.6% of the poll and the sixth largest margin of victory in Ontario.

Member of Parliament: Joseph Volpe; **Party**: Liberal; **Occupation**: Educator; **Education**: MEd, University of Toronto; **Age**: 47 (Sept. 21, 1947); **Year first elected to the House of Commons**: 1988

35017 Eglinton–Lawrence

A: Political Profile
i) Voting Behaviour

	% 1993	% 1988	Change 1988-93
Conservative	10.7	30.9	-20.2
Liberal	71.6	51	20.6
NDP	5.2	15.6	-10.4
Reform	10.9	0	10.9
Other	1.7	2.5	-0.8

% Turnout	68.3	Total Ballots (#)	40460
Rejected Ballots (#)	480	% Margin of Victory	60.7
Rural Polls, 1988 (#)	0	Urban Polls, 1988 (#)	157
% Yes - 1992	58.1	% No - 1992	41

ii) Campaign Financing

	# of Donations	Total $ Value	% of Limit Spent
Conservative	32	7199	37
Liberal	307	50639	71.2
NDP	51	15425	22.6
Reform	55	13200	24.9
Other	1	105	

B: Ethno-Linguistic Profile

% English Home Language	69.4	% French Home Language	0.6
% Official Bilingual	7.4	% Other Home Language	30
% Catholics	46.1	% Protestants	22.2
% Aboriginal Peoples	0.2	% Immigrants	46.3

C: Socio-Economic Profile

Average Family Income $	58870	Median Family Income $	46646
% Low Income Families	20.3	Average Home Price $	290768
% Home Owners	52.8	% Unemployment	10.1
% Labour Force Participation	63.6	% Managerial-Administrative	13.2
% Self-Employed	8.7	% University Degrees	14.3
% Movers	40.5		

D: Industrial Profile

% Manufacturing	16.4	% Service Sector	12.9
% Agriculture	0.3	% Mining	0.1
% Forestry	0.1	% Fishing	0
% Government Services	4.9	% Business Services	8.9

E: Homogeneity Measures

Ethnic Diversity Index	0.24	Religious Homogeneity Index	0.33
Sectoral Concentration Index	0.47	Income Disparity Index	20.8

F: Physical Setting Characteristics

Total Population	98094	Area (km²)	23
Population Density (pop/km²)	4265		

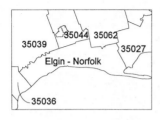

Elgin–Norfolk
(formerly Elgin)

Constituency Number: 35018

Elgin–Norfolk is a richly agricultural and predominantly rural/small town riding that stretches along the north shore of Lake Erie in southwestern Ontario. Fruit, vegetable, and tobacco farming are important to the local economy, and the riding ranks third provincially on the measure of employment in the agricultural sector. Over twenty per cent of the workforce is employed in light manufacturing. The largest population concentration is in the city of St Thomas (pop. about 30,000), the county seat of Elgin. The area is heavily Protestant and anglophone. While not affluent (average family incomes run about $8,000 below the provincial norm), incomes are relatively uniformly distributed. The proportion of families classed as 'low income' is well below the provincial average.

The recession cost the riding a good deal of its manufacturing base and farmers were worried about the impending GATT and NAFTA agreements, not to mention the travails of the tobacco industry, both smuggling and government policy to curb smoking. Writing in September 1993 in the *London Free Press*, St Thomas journalist Sandra Coulson described the situation as follows: 'No one knows what the unemployment rate is here. Statistics Canada lumps us in with Middlesex and Oxford Counties... But the local Canada Employment Centre has counted 4,871 permanent job losses and 18,209 temporary layoffs in the last three years. That's in a total population of just 75,000 in St. Thomas and Elgin.' She went on to note that 'The same centre reports there are big opportunities in door-to-door sales, telephone soliciting, waiting on tables, homemaking, hairdressing, baby-sitting and fast-food delivery.' She advised her readers to confront candidates on the issue and 'go for specifics about what they intended to do'.

This riding has traditionally been a PC stronghold. In the eighteen elections since 1935, Elgin–Norfolk has returned Tories in fourteen of them. Prior to 1988, the riding had been represented for 16 years by Conservative MP and former minister of agriculture John Wise. Wise's resignation in 1988 gave rise to a close race, but eventually the seat was retained for the Conservatives by Ken Monteith.

Monteith, a farmer from Southwold before entering politics, ran again in 1993 for the Tories. He confronted six challengers in the campaign. Gar Knutson, a lawyer and manager of a local business development initiative (funded by a federal program) and community activist from St Thomas, ran for the Liberals. John Van Der Veen, an economist/farmer from Port Stanley, ran for the Reform Party. Bob Habkirk, a paint quality analysis from Aylmer, got the NDP's nomination. Bob Dekraker, a contractor and farmer from South Dorchester ran for the Christian Heritage Party. Two other minor party candidates ran with negligible impact.

The 1993 race was a reasonably tightly contested one. However, this is another riding where a Liberal newcomer stole a traditional Conservative riding from the right of centre parties due to a Tory/Reform vote split. Monteith's 27.5% finish was the Tory's sixth strongest in the province.

Member of Parliament: Gar Knutson; **Party**: Liberal; **Occupation**: Lawyer; **Education**: LL.B; **Year first elected to the House of Commons**: 1993

35018 Elgin–Norfolk

A: Political Profile
i) Voting Behaviour

	% 1993	% 1988	Change 1988-93
Conservative	27.5	38.6	-11.1
Liberal	43.1	34.3	8.8
NDP	5.3	20.8	-15.5
Reform	20.5	0	20.5
Other	3.6	6.2	-2.6

% Turnout	64.7	Total Ballots (#)	40859
Rejected Ballots (#)	349	% Margin of Victory	15.6
Rural Polls, 1988 (#)	118	Urban Polls, 1988 (#)	82
% Yes - 1992	44.2	% No - 1992	55.2

ii) Campaign Financing

	# of Donations	Total $ Value	% of Limit Spent
Conservative	390	47518	92.6
Liberal	122	26917	46.5*
NDP	27	14475	17.8
Reform	42	14903	61.5
Other	82	13566	

B: Ethno-Linguistic Profile

% English Home Language	93.5	% French Home Language	0.2
% Official Bilingual	3.8	% Other Home Language	6.3
% Catholics	20.1	% Protestants	68.4
% Aboriginal Peoples	0.7	% Immigrants	14.1

C: Socio-Economic Profile

Average Family Income $	48237	Median Family Income $	43547
% Low Income Families	10	Average Home Price $	126134
% Home Owners	72.8	% Unemployment	8.6
% Labour Force Participation	69	% Managerial-Administrative	9.1
% Self-Employed	13	% University Degrees	5
% Movers	42.7		

D: Industrial Profile

% Manufacturing	22.3	% Service Sector	10
% Agriculture	15.5	% Mining	0.3
% Forestry	0.2	% Fishing	0.2
% Government Services	4.6	% Business Services	2.8

E: Homogeneity Measures

Ethnic Diversity Index	0.41	Religious Homogeneity Index	0.5
Sectoral Concentration Index	0.33	Income Disparity Index	9.7

F: Physical Setting Characteristics

Total Population	87248	Area (km²)	2574
Population Density (pop/km²)	33.9		

* Tentative value, due to the existence of unpaid campaign expenses.

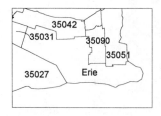

Erie

Constituency Number: 35019

Erie is located along the northern shores at the eastern tip of Lake Erie. It extends from the Canadian-US border town of Fort Erie in the east to the boundary of the Niagara Regional Municipality in the west. The Peace Bridge, joining Fort Erie with Buffalo, New York across the Niagara River, is one of the busiest border crossings between Canada and the United States. The local economy is dominated by agriculture and light industry and manufacturing.

Since 1979, Erie had been represented in the House of Commons by Girve Fretz. The former businessman had to fight off a strong challenge from Liberal candidate Allard Colyn in 1988, winning only by about 800 votes. Fretz retired in 1993, and was replaced for the Conservatives by Bradd Wilson, a car dealer from Port Colborne. The Liberal candidate was John Maloney, a 48-year-old lawyer and long-time Liberal activist also from Port Colborne. Bob Lund, a self-employed construction supervisor from Ridgeway, ran for the Reform Party. The NDP ran Lesley Penwarden, a secretary from St Catharines. Three other minor party candidates rounded out the ballot in 1993.

The 1993 campaign turned on issues of jobs and the economy. This issue took prominence over everything else in the riding and was augmented by concern over trade liberalization (represented by the GATT negotiations and the NAFTA) and the adverse impact on local retailers of cross-border shopping and outright smuggling.

On election day, the lack of an incumbency advantage coupled with a strong local Reform Party performance gave the Liberals' Maloney a comfortable 20% victory margin.

Member of Parliament: John David Maloney; **Party**: Liberal; **Occupation**: Lawyer; **Education**: LL.B; **Age**: 49 (January 5, 1945); **Year first elected to the House of Commons**: 1993

35019 Erie

A: Political Profile

i) Voting Behaviour

	% 1993	% 1988	Change 1988-93
Conservative	14.5	38.5	-24
Liberal	48.7	36.5	12.2
NDP	4.5	20.9	-16.4
Reform	28.9	0	28.9
Other	3.4	4.1	-0.7

% Turnout	70.2	Total Ballots (#)	41007
Rejected Ballots (#)	342	% Margin of Victory	19.8
Rural Polls, 1988 (#)	99	Urban Polls, 1988 (#)	111
% Yes - 1992	37.5	% No - 1992	62

ii) Campaign Financing

	# of Donations	Total $ Value	% of Limit Spent
Conservative	198	48431	65.1
Liberal	174	27548	75.4
NDP	79	12345	14.9
Reform	218	21835	64.4
Other	10	6905	

B: Ethno-Linguistic Profile

% English Home Language	95.3	% French Home Language	1.3
% Official Bilingual	6.8	% Other Home Language	3.4
% Catholics	31.9	% Protestants	57.5
% Aboriginal Peoples	1.3	% Immigrants	15.9

C: Socio-Economic Profile

Average Family Income $	50987	Median Family Income $	45300
% Low Income Families	10.1	Average Home Price $	153404
% Home Owners	79.7	% Unemployment	7.7
% Labour Force Participation	65	% Managerial-Administrative	10.8
% Self-Employed	10.3	% University Degrees	7.2
% Movers	37.8		

D: Industrial Profile

% Manufacturing	22.3	% Service Sector	11.2
% Agriculture	5.9	% Mining	0.5
% Forestry	0.1	% Fishing	0
% Government Services	5.3	% Business Services	4.2

E: Homogeneity Measures

Ethnic Diversity Index	0.28	Religious Homogeneity Index	0.43
Sectoral Concentration Index	0.38	Income Disparity Index	11.2

F: Physical Setting Characteristics

Total Population	81473	Area (km²)	1066
Population Density (pop/km²)	76.4		

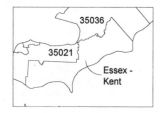

Essex–Kent

Constituency Number: 35020

Essex–Kent is Canada's southernmost riding. It sprawls about 145 kilometres along the northwestern shore of Lake Erie from the middle of Essex County in the west to Kent Bridge in Kent County. The riding is primarily rural, with several urban pockets. Agriculture is one of the mainstays of the area's economy (the riding ranks fifth in the province on agricultural employment). Leamington, for example, is home to Heinz, the food-processing giant, and is known as 'the tomato capital of Canada'. Times have not been good in some sectors of the food-processing industry that is so important to the district. Especially tough was the closure of the Campbell's Soup plant, the impending closure of the Green Giant plant in nearby Tecumseh (Windsor–St Clair) and some other smaller processing plants which not only took away jobs but also buyers for local farmers' crops as well. Light industry and manufacture are also important economic foundations, and some residents, particularly auto workers, commute to jobs in nearby Windsor.

The riding has been held by both Tories and Liberals. A decade-long Liberal hold was broken in 1984, when the Tories' Jim Caldwell was elected as part of the Mulroney sweep that year. However, in 1988, Essex–Kent swung back to its Liberal tradition when Jerry Pickard, a high school teacher and local politician, capitalized on local anxieties concerning the Free Trade Agreement (FTA) and won handily.

Pickard campaigned to hold the riding for the Liberals in 1993. He was confronted by four other candidates. The Tory nomination was won by Kevin Charles Flood, a grain elevator manager from Kingsville. Wayne Abbott, a construction supplier from Tilbury ran for the Reform Party. The NDP ran Mike Darnell, a union representative from Leamington. The Natural Law Party was represented locally by Lester Newby, a researcher from Brampton.

As with the other ridings which line the north shore of Lake Erie, the issues in Essex–Kent were the anticipated impact which GATT and NAFTA would likely have on agriculture and the plight of area manufacturing. In addition, the local campaign centred on the abortion debate and broken Progressive Conservative promises. Pickard, an outspoken anti-abortionist, was the only Liberal in the environs of Windsor to be endorsed by a local anti-abortion group and indeed has taken every opportunity since his election in 1988 to vote against abortion in the House of Commons. Broken promises probably hurt the Tory chances in 1993. During the 1988 election campaign, Jim Caldwell, the then-incumbent PC member, announced a $1.5 million federal grant to build a small boat marina in Wheatley, Ontario. A the time, the announcement was somewhat controversial, since the project had not been subject to the customary feasibility study. However, following the election and the Conservatives' loss of the seat, progress on the project only got as far as the erection of a massive sign announcing the marina and the federal grant which made it possible. Reform had high hopes for this riding. After all, the local town of Blenheim was the site of the first major tax protests in Ontario. In 1991 the town 'ceded' from Canada to protest the GST and taxes in general.

In the end, Reform's relatively poor showing (a very distant second) was somewhat surprising. It is possible that Reform candidate Wayne Abbott's open advocacy of the more neo-liberal elements of Reform's agriculture platform (the abolition of all marketing boards, total free trade, etc.) diminished his appeal. The Liberals' Pickard returned once again to the House by winning almost two-thirds of the vote and a 44% margin of victory over the second-place Reform Party.

Member of Parliament: Jerry Pickard; **Party**: Liberal; **Occupation**: Teacher; **Education**: MEd; **Age**: 54 (Nov. 14, 1940); **Year first elected to the House of Commons**: 1988

35020 Essex–Kent

A: Political Profile
i) Voting Behaviour

	% 1993	% 1988	Change 1988-93
Conservative	13.4	32.3	-18.9
Liberal	62.1	49.4	12.7
NDP	5.7	18.4	-12.7
Reform	18.1	0	18.1
Other	0.6	0	0.6

% Turnout	63.6	Total Ballots (#)	35625
Rejected Ballots (#)	262	% Margin of Victory	44
Rural Polls, 1988 (#)	149	Urban Polls, 1988 (#)	48
% Yes - 1992	32.7	% No - 1992	66.9

ii) Campaign Financing

	# of Donations	Total $ Value	% of Limit Spent
Conservative	138	39050	68.6*
Liberal	190	43253	75.4
NDP	39	22302	38.8
Reform	86	16915	33.4
Other	0	0	

B: Ethno-Linguistic Profile

% English Home Language	91.1	% French Home Language	0.7
% Official Bilingual	6.5	% Other Home Language	8.2
% Catholics	36.2	% Protestants	56.2
% Aboriginal Peoples	0.2	% Immigrants	17

C: Socio-Economic Profile

Average Family Income $	50534	Median Family Income $	45268
% Low Income Families	9.5	Average Home Price $	120414
% Home Owners	76.2	% Unemployment	8.4
% Labour Force Participation	68.7	% Managerial-Administrative	9.8
% Self-Employed	12.1	% University Degrees	5.9
% Movers	39.3		

D: Industrial Profile

% Manufacturing	23.8	% Service Sector	10.5
% Agriculture	13.6	% Mining	0.3
% Forestry	0	% Fishing	1
% Government Services	4.6	% Business Services	2.3

E: Homogeneity Measures

Ethnic Diversity Index	0.31	Religious Homogeneity Index	0.43
Sectoral Concentration Index	0.33	Income Disparity Index	10.4

F: Physical Setting Characteristics

Total Population	79894	Area (km²)	1912
Population Density (pop/km²)	41.8		

* Tentative value, due to the existence of unpaid campaign expenses.

Essex–Windsor

Constituency Number: 35021

Essex–Windsor is an L-shaped riding that stretches from the western tip of Lake Erie, north along the Detroit River (with the US bordering on the other side) on the west of the riding, to the southern shores of Lake St Clair in the north. This urban/suburban/rural riding is the wealthiest in the Windsor area and the fastest growing. The diversity of environments means both key issues from across the whole region — the fates of the manufacturing base and of agriculture — were important. However, manufacturing, which accounts for over 31% of the constituency's jobs (the second highest proportion in Ontario), dominates the local economy. The riding is proud of its strong tradition in the labour and union movement.

The constituency was formed in 1972, and was represented for 22 years by the former Liberal minister of agriculture, Eugene Whelan (some speculated that he might return to contest the seat again in 1993). Whelan's retirement in 1984 saw the riding change over to the NDP. Winning in 1984, and again in 1988 by a narrow margin, was Steven Langdon, a former economics professor, from Amherstburg. Once the NDP finance critic, Langdon (a former journalist, NDP leadership contender, and Carleton economics professor) was fired by NDP leader Audrey McLaughlin for publicly criticizing the economic policy of the Ontario NDP government. In a public letter, Langdon accused NDP premier Bob Rae of selling out the social democratic-labour movement with his government's 'social contract' legislation.

Confronting Langdon in the 1993 campaign were six challengers, and it seemed clear from virtually the outset of the campaign that Langdon would be in for a tough fight. Rather than returning to Eugene Whelan, the Liberals turned to his daughter to carry their banner. Susan Whelan is a corporate and commercial lawyer from Amherstburg. Throughout the campaign Whelan tried to distance herself from the 'guy in a green stetson' image of her father and generally followed the national Liberal platform. Local Liberals were hoping that Whelan would draw enough from the riding's agricultural sector to overcome Langdon's traditional appeal to the riding's union members. A self-employed contractor, John Larsen won the local nomination for the Reform Party, but was not expected to be a strong factor in the race. The Tories, who have never been strong in this riding, nominated Brian Payne, a 25-year-old sales manager. Three other minor party candidates also contested the seat, but registered no impact on election day.

Langdon had not only to run against the opposition but against his own party as well. During the election his campaign tried to avoid using the NDP label or party name and even adopted different sign colours. Instead, Langdon asked the riding to re-elect him so that he could 'return to Ottawa to stop the Mexican trade deal'. He also tried to capitalize on the closure of the Wyeth Pharmaceutical and Green Giant plants which left the area after they received grants from the Tory government to upgrade its operations in Quebec. Bob White (President of the Canadian Labour Congress, founding president of the Canadian Auto Workers) spent some time in the Windsor area and strongly urged all unionized workers to vote NDP. Although Langdon's 27.7% finish was the NDP's best in Ontario, it was far behind Whelan's 55%. Payne's paltry 3.3% finish was the Tories' lowest performance in the province.

Member of Parliament: Susan Whelan; **Party**: Liberal; **Occupation**: Lawyer; **Education**: LL.B; **Year first elected to the House of Commons**: 1993

35021 Essex–Windsor

A: Political Profile
i) Voting Behaviour

	% 1993	% 1988	Change 1988-93
Conservative	3.3	14.3	-11
Liberal	55.1	41.3	13.8
NDP	27.7	44.1	-16.4
Reform	13.2	0	13.2
Other	0.8	0.2	0.6

% Turnout	66.9	Total Ballots (#)	45997
Rejected Ballots (#)	272	% Margin of Victory	27.4
Rural Polls, 1988 (#)	107	Urban Polls, 1988 (#)	76
% Yes - 1992	33.2	% No - 1992	66.5

ii) Campaign Financing

	# of Donations	Total $ Value	% of Limit Spent
Conservative	28	16214	27.6
Liberal	224	78040	85.1
NDP	338	64157	91.7
Reform	62	16285	33.6
Other	6	2021	

B: Ethno-Linguistic Profile

% English Home Language	90.9	% French Home Language	2.7
% Official Bilingual	14.1	% Other Home Language	6.5
% Catholics	59.7	% Protestants	30
% Aboriginal Peoples	0.2	% Immigrants	16.8

C: Socio-Economic Profile

Average Family Income $	58541	Median Family Income $	53013
% Low Income Families	7.7	Average Home Price $	147847
% Home Owners	78.9	% Unemployment	9.9
% Labour Force Participation	69.5	% Managerial-Administrative	10
% Self-Employed	6.9	% University Degrees	8.4
% Movers	41.1		

D: Industrial Profile

% Manufacturing	31.1	% Service Sector	11.7
% Agriculture	2.6	% Mining	0.4
% Forestry	0	% Fishing	0
% Government Services	4.3	% Business Services	3.2

E: Homogeneity Measures

Ethnic Diversity Index	0.24	Religious Homogeneity Index	0.45
Sectoral Concentration Index	0.4	Income Disparity Index	9.4

F: Physical Setting Characteristics

Total Population	95162	Area (km²)	934
Population Density (pop/km²)	101.9		

Etobicoke Centre

Constituency Number: 35022

Etobicoke Centre is an upmarket, primarily residential riding in the western suburbs of Toronto. Average family incomes, at almost $80,000, are the third highest in the province. It is home to one of the province's most residentially-stable populations: the riding has the lowest proportion of families moving within the five-year period 1986-1991, and the third-lowest proportion reporting having moved in 1990-1991. Residents are well-educated (the riding is in the top ten in terms of university graduates) and in 1993, Etobicoke Centre led the province in voter turnout.

As the *Globe and Mail* pointed out during the campaign, Etobicoke Centre is an attractive seat for aspiring cabinet ministers — six MPs, including outgoing incumbent Conservative Michael Wilson, have been cabinet ministers in the past 33 years. Wilson himself was former Minister of Finance and Minister of International Trade under Brian Mulroney when he retired. He was succeeded by Royal Bank of Canada executive Charles Donley, who surprised many when he defeated Etobicoke mayor Bruce Sinclair to win the Tory nomination. Sinclair had prevailed over Donley in the 1991 mayoral election. Also running for the Conservative nomination was Norm Matusiak, a former deputy crown attorney and a tax revolt crusader. For his part, Donley described himself as a 'rough parallel to Wilson'. Given the unpopularity of the outgoing federal government, and of Wilson in particular (he was widely held to be personally responsible for the GST and the Tory failure to control the debt, and supported the Bank of Canada's controversial strong dollar policy), one would have thought Donley would have found a better way to introduce himself to his prospective and extremely dissatisfied upper middle-class constituents.

Also contesting the seat in 1993 was a strong local Reform organization which boasted 500, mostly ex-Conservative, members. Winning their nomination was Charles McLeod, an actuary. Liberal challenger Allan Rock was one of Chrétien's 'star' candidates, (one of Ontario's most well-known attorneys and the Treasurer of the Law Society of Upper Canada, the organization governing legal practice in the province) and presented a credible alternative to Donley. In appointing Rock, Chrétien may have avoided a thorny problem in that the local Liberal riding association had been the site of some mobilization efforts by an anti-abortion faction called 'Liberals for Life'. In early 1992, this group's representatives had claimed to have signed up 340 new members. Udayan Rege, a professor, ran for the NDP, and five other candidates represented minor parties. Of these, only Janice Tait, a psychotherapist running for the National Party, managed to win more than 1% of the poll on election day.

The story in the 1993 result is a familiar one for many Ontario constituencies. Conservative support collapsed; those neo-conservative former Tory voters probably defected to Reform, while the more pragmatic PC voters were probably attracted to Rock. The NDP, never strong in this area, registered its fourth-lowest finish in the province. Benefiting from all this was Rock, who won easily. In the aftermath of the election, Rock continued the tradition of cabinet representation for Etobicoke Centre by being named Minister of Justice and Attorney-General for Canada.

Member of Parliament: Allan Rock; **Party**: Liberal; **Occupation**: Lawyer; **Education**: LL.B; **Age**: 47 (Aug. 30, 1947); **Year first elected to the House of Commons**: 1993

35022 Etobicoke Centre

A: Political Profile
i) Voting Behaviour

	% 1993	% 1988	Change 1988-93
Conservative	19.5	48.4	-28.9
Liberal	54.4	40.5	13.9
NDP	2.2	9.6	-7.4
Reform	22.1	0	22.1
Other	1.9	1.5	0.4

% Turnout	76.2	Total Ballots (#)	47644
Rejected Ballots (#)	284	% Margin of Victory	32.3
Rural Polls, 1988 (#)	0	Urban Polls, 1988 (#)	202
% Yes - 1992	60.9	% No - 1992	38.5

ii) Campaign Financing

	# of Donations	Total $ Value	% of Limit Spent
Conservative	197	31145	90.5
Liberal	71	74654	96.9
NDP	112	22779	34.7
Reform	124	45799	61.5
Other	38	11747	

B: Ethno-Linguistic Profile

% English Home Language	83.7	% French Home Language	0.2
% Official Bilingual	8.9	% Other Home Language	16.1
% Catholics	39.4	% Protestants	42.7
% Aboriginal Peoples	0.1	% Immigrants	32.5

C: Socio-Economic Profile

Average Family Income $	79376	Median Family Income $	64433
% Low Income Families	9.5	Average Home Price $	338843
% Home Owners	65.3	% Unemployment	7
% Labour Force Participation	66.4	% Managerial-Administrative	21.3
% Self-Employed	10	% University Degrees	21.5
% Movers	32.6		

D: Industrial Profile

% Manufacturing	16.7	% Service Sector	8
% Agriculture	0.3	% Mining	0.2
% Forestry	0.1	% Fishing	0
% Government Services	6.2	% Business Services	9.8

E: Homogeneity Measures

Ethnic Diversity Index	0.19	Religious Homogeneity Index	0.35
Sectoral Concentration Index	0.47	Income Disparity Index	18.8

F: Physical Setting Characteristics

Total Population	87244	Area (km²)	31
Population Density (pop/km²)	2814.3		

Etobicoke–Lakeshore

Constituency Number: 35023

The southernmost of the three Etobicoke ridings, Etobicoke–Lakeshore fronts Lake Ontario to the west of Toronto. The northern section of the constituency is primarily residential, while the south is both residential and industrial/commercial.

Lakeshore was the only riding not to field a Liberal candidate on election day in 1988. The candidate who won the nomination suffered a heart-attack before election day, and it was too late in the campaign for a replacement to have been named. The vacuum caused by this unfortunate situation gave a distinctive quality to the result. In the end, the Conservative incumbent Patrick Boyer, an author and lawyer, narrowly held off a strong challenge from the NDP (his margin of victory was 1.8%).

In the summer of 1993 Boyer lost in his bid to replace Mulroney as leader of the Progressive Conservative Party, and then turned around to start his defence of his own seat. Coming in to the campaign, his outlook did not appear to be as grim as those facing other Tory candidates in Metro. In fact, he had created some separation between himself and the disastrous Conservative campaign when he quickly and publicly demanded the resignation of whoever authorized the release of the ill-fated Tory ads that focused on Chrétien's facial disfigurement. Facing Boyer in 1993 for the Liberals was Jean Augustine, an elementary school principal with a string of high profile public service credits. One of only two female Liberal candidates (along with Maria Minna in Beaches–Woodbine) in all of Metro, as another of Chrétien's 'star' candidates, Augustine's nomination created some controversy and ill-will within the local Liberal association. Reform candidate, manufacturing consultant Ken Anstruther from Mississauga, did not share the high profile of his Liberal and Tory opponents. Karen Ridley, an executive assistant, ran for the NDP. Rounding out the ballot were five other minor party candidates, but collectively they accounted for only 3.2% of the vote on election day.

This riding was hit hard by the simultaneous impact of the Free Trade Agreement, the strong dollar policy of the Bank of Canada, and the recession. The industrial base, which gave employment to the many working-class residents of the riding, was badly hurt in the early 1990s. Among the major industrial employers that closed shop in the early 1990s were Goodyear Tire and Rubber, Continental Can, Arrowhead Metal, and Pittsburgh Paint.

In the end, hard times and the unpopularity of the outgoing Conservative administration were handicaps too great for Boyer to overcome. Boyer's 31% finish was good enough to place him second in Lakeshore, and to make his the second-best Tory finish in the province of Ontario. Reform managed to take about 8,700 votes and that, combined with the collapse of the local NDP campaign (a drop of 39.2% from the 1988 result), allowed Jean Augustine to take the riding.

Member of Parliament: Jean Augustine; **Party**: Liberal; **Occupation**: Elementary school principal; **Education**: MEd; **Age**: 57 (Sept. 9, 1937); **Year first elected to the House of Commons**: 1993

35023 Etobicoke–Lakeshore

A: Political Profile

i) Voting Behaviour

	% 1993	% 1988	Change 1988-93
Conservative	31	46	-15
Liberal	42.1	0	42.1
NDP	5	44.2	-39.2
Reform	18.8	0	18.8
Other	3.2	9.7	-6.5

% Turnout	67.7	Total Ballots (#)	46674
Rejected Ballots (#)	463	% Margin of Victory	11.1
Rural Polls, 1988 (#)	0	Urban Polls, 1988 (#)	181
% Yes - 1992	53.9	% No - 1992	45.5

ii) Campaign Financing

	# of Donations	Total $ Value	% of Limit Spent
Conservative	262	41408	86.6
Liberal	221	44638	59.6
NDP	84	25015	33.3
Reform	121	26041	49
Other	16	2128	

B: Ethno-Linguistic Profile

% English Home Language	79.2	% French Home Language	0.3
% Official Bilingual	6.9	% Other Home Language	20.5
% Catholics	45.4	% Protestants	35.3
% Aboriginal Peoples	0.4	% Immigrants	35.5

C: Socio-Economic Profile

Average Family Income $	56405	Median Family Income $	50726
% Low Income Families	15.5	Average Home Price $	260827
% Home Owners	51.9	% Unemployment	8.9
% Labour Force Participation	66.7	% Managerial-Administrative	15.1
% Self-Employed	6.9	% University Degrees	14
% Movers	42.2		

D: Industrial Profile

% Manufacturing	20.1	% Service Sector	9.8
% Agriculture	0.4	% Mining	0.2
% Forestry	0.1	% Fishing	0.1
% Government Services	5.6	% Business Services	9

E: Homogeneity Measures

Ethnic Diversity Index	0.19	Religious Homogeneity Index	0.35
Sectoral Concentration Index	0.45	Income Disparity Index	10.1

F: Physical Setting Characteristics

Total Population	96592	Area (km²)	40
Population Density (pop/km²)	2414.8		

Etobicoke North

Constituency Number: 35024

Isolated from the rest of Metro by the Humber River to the east and a particularly broad stretch of Eglinton Ave W. and Highway 401 to the south, Etobicoke North is a corner of Metro that few outsiders visit except to get to the Toronto airport. A quick drive along Dixon Road, a nice stretch of single family dwellings followed by a stretch of high-rise condominiums, would not reveal anything untoward to the casual observer. But these condominiums are the site of some of the nastiest racial tensions in Metro. These high-rises have essentially become the centre of a Metro Somali community that did not exist five years ago, and many of the previously established residents are having to make an adjustment. The tensions are exacerbated by property relations. Most of the established residents own their units; most of the Somalis rent them from absentee landlords (mostly small speculators who got caught by the recession).

The riding is home to a diverse array of light industrial, service, and commercial enterprises. Politically, it is traditional Liberal ground, but in the Mulroney sweep in 1984, it joined over 200 other constituencies nationwide in electing Tory Members. In 1988, however, Etobicoke North voters elected Roy MacLaren, a former diplomat and magazine publisher (*Canadian Business*), who had originally been elected in the riding in 1979. He was re-elected in 1980 and served in Trudeau's cabinet prior to his defeat in 1984.

MacLaren defended the riding for the Grits against eight challengers. Reform, whose commitment to lower immigrant and refugee intake played to a sympathetic audience in this riding, ran Joe Peschisolido, a lawyer. The Tories offered Jane MacLaren, a manager, while Carmela Sasso, a legislative assistant, ran for the NDP. The five minor party candidates had a negligible impact on the race.

MacLaren easily held the seat with a more than 40% margin of victory over the runner-up Reform candidate. Following his election, MacLaren was named minister for international trade in the Liberal government.

Member of Parliament: Roy MacLaren; **Party**: Liberal; **Occupation**: Publisher; **Education**: MA, Cambridge University; **Age**: 60 (Oct. 26, 1934); **Year first elected to the House of Commons**: 1979

35024 Etobicoke North

A: Political Profile
i) Voting Behaviour

	% 1993	% 1988	Change 1988-93
Conservative	10.8	34.6	-23.8
Liberal	61.2	45.3	15.9
NDP	4	17.3	-13.3
Reform	20.8	0	20.8
Other	3.1	2.7	0.4

% Turnout	69.9	Total Ballots (#)	46425
Rejected Ballots (#)	506	% Margin of Victory	40.4
Rural Polls, 1988 (#)	0	Urban Polls, 1988 (#)	235
% Yes - 1992	52.6	% No - 1992	46.8

ii) Campaign Financing

	# of Donations	Total $ Value	% of Limit Spent
Conservative	83	30968	46.1
Liberal	122	59727	67.4
NDP	107	26982	38.5*
Reform	94	26344	55.5
Other	25	2302	

B: Ethno-Linguistic Profile

% English Home Language	76	% French Home Language	0.3
% Official Bilingual	5.3	% Other Home Language	23.7
% Catholics	43.3	% Protestants	32.8
% Aboriginal Peoples	0.2	% Immigrants	42.3

C: Socio-Economic Profile

Average Family Income $	55828	Median Family Income $	50838
% Low Income Families	16.3	Average Home Price $	254078
% Home Owners	59	% Unemployment	9.5
% Labour Force Participation	68	% Managerial-Administrative	12.4
% Self-Employed	7.1	% University Degrees	10.4
% Movers	41.2		

D: Industrial Profile

% Manufacturing	21.8	% Service Sector	10.1
% Agriculture	0.3	% Mining	0.1
% Forestry	0.1	% Fishing	0
% Government Services	4.4	% Business Services	7.5

E: Homogeneity Measures

Ethnic Diversity Index	0.18	Religious Homogeneity Index	0.32
Sectoral Concentration Index	0.42	Income Disparity Index	8.9

F: Physical Setting Characteristics

Total Population	103014	Area (km²)	52
Population Density (pop/km²)	1981		

*   Tentative value, due to the existence of unpaid campaign expenses.

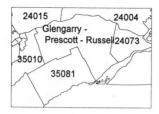

Glengarry–Prescott–Russell

Constituency Number: 35025

Glengarry–Prescott–Russell, the eastern tip of Ontario, is bounded in part by the provincial boundary with Quebec and by two rivers, the Ottawa and the St Lawrence. Over half of all residents use French as their home language, and over three-quarters are Catholics, making this riding the province's most francophone and Catholic constituency. Farming, food processing, and light manufacturing (especially clothing and furniture) are important to the riding's economy.

This is *bedrock* Liberal territory. Glengarry–Prescott–Russell was one of the few eastern Ontario ridings to buck the Mulroney sweep in 1984 as Don Boudria, a former federal civil servant, MPP, and Cumberland Township councillor won handily (with a more than 20% margin). Since then, the sometimes flamboyant (one of the Liberal 'rat-packers') and popular Boudria has cemented his hold on the seat. His 1988 victory was the Liberals' best in the entire country.

Opposing Boudria is not something to be undertaken lightly, yet five challengers emerged to contest the seat in 1993. France Somers, a registered nurse from Cumberland, ran for the Conservatives. Reform nominated Sam McCracken, a financial planner from Dalkeith. The NDP had put up only a token campaign in 1988, and in 1993 Pascal Villeneuve, a self-employed worker from Hawkesbury, accepted the party's nomination. Two minor party candidates each finished with less than 1% of the total vote.

As in many Canadian ridings, international trade formed the biggest opportunity and simultaneously the most serious danger for the economy of the riding. While the riding has fared better than neighbouring Stormont–Dundas in the aftermath of the FTA, fears remained about the impact the NAFTA and the GATT will have on local industry. Dairy farming dominates the agricultural sector and so concerns that a new GATT agreement would outlaw marketing boards was a serious issue in the riding. The PC government's approval of Canada Post Corporation's decision to close all rural post offices, as the postmasters retire, was also an issue. Incumbent Boudria promised a Liberal government would review each rural post-office on a case by case basis, but did not go so far as to promise to save every rural post office. 'I won't tell you that no community should lose its post office, but it is not reasonable to shut down every rural post office in Canada,' he said. Boudria also stressed the need to use environmental legislation to protect agricultural communities and economies. One point he made was that a carcinogenic gasoline additive, MMT, can be replaced by alcohol derived from corn. And in fact since MMT was banned in the United States, corn alcohol has been used as a substitute chemical-boosting demand for American corn.

Boudria continued to build on his already impressive local base. Taking 8 in every 10 votes in the riding, his 1993 win represented the Liberals' best finish in Ontario, its fourth best nationally, and the province's largest victory margin.

Member of Parliament: Don Boudria; **Party**: Liberal; **Occupation**: Purchasing agent; **Education**: University of Toronto and the University of Waterloo; **Age**: 49 (August 30, 1945); **Year first elected to the House of Commons**: 1984

35025 Glengarry–Prescott–Russell

A: Political Profile

i) Voting Behaviour

	% 1993	% 1988	Change 1988-93
Conservative	8.2	19.1	-10.9
Liberal	80.2	70.7	9.5
NDP	2.3	9.1	-6.8
Reform	8	0	8
Other	1.2	1.1	0.1

% Turnout	69.3	Total Ballots (#)	56362
Rejected Ballots (#)	547	% Margin of Victory	72
Rural Polls, 1988 (#)	173	Urban Polls, 1988 (#)	33
% Yes - 1992	63.7	% No - 1992	35.1

ii) Campaign Financing

	# of Donations	Total $ Value	% of Limit Spent
Conservative	70	26546	34.9
Liberal	55	59947	75.5
NDP	22	2125	1.8
Reform	29	5635	4.6
Other	0	0	

B: Ethno-Linguistic Profile

% English Home Language	42.7	% French Home Language	56.2
% Official Bilingual	56	% Other Home Language	1.1
% Catholics	75.8	% Protestants	19.2
% Aboriginal Peoples	0.8	% Immigrants	5

C: Socio-Economic Profile

Average Family Income $	51584	Median Family Income $	46624
% Low Income Families	8.5	Average Home Price $	119653
% Home Owners	77.6	% Unemployment	6.7
% Labour Force Participation	69.5	% Managerial-Administrative	13
% Self-Employed	12.6	% University Degrees	7.4
% Movers	43.3		

D: Industrial Profile

% Manufacturing	12.9	% Service Sector	10.5
% Agriculture	7.9	% Mining	0.2
% Forestry	0.2	% Fishing	0
% Government Services	11.9	% Business Services	4.3

E: Homogeneity Measures

Ethnic Diversity Index	0.56	Religious Homogeneity Index	0.59
Sectoral Concentration Index	0.36	Income Disparity Index	9.6

F: Physical Setting Characteristics

Total Population	99809	Area (km²)	3737
Population Density (pop/km²)	26.7		

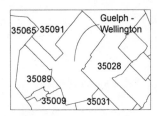

Guelph–Wellington

Constituency Number: 35026

Although the Y-shaped riding of Guelph–Wellington is in the middle of Canada's agricultural heartland, it is primarily an urban riding, composed of the city of Guelph and its surrounding suburbs. The city lies about 100 kilometres west of Toronto, close enough to put it within commuting distance for some. The riding's largest employers are manufacturing (including General Electric, ITT, Imperial Tobacco, and Fiberglas Canada) and educational services (the city is home to the University of Guelph, the Ontario Ministry of Colleges and Universities' central application centre, and the Ontario Veterinary College). Whereas people of English descent have traditionally dominated the riding's populace, the proportion of immigrants (particularly, Italians) has increased in recent decades. Guelph has not been an exception to the general decline in manufacturing which has swept southwestern Ontario, though its role as an education and governmental service centre for the region, and the province in general, has cushioned the recession's impact. However, voters were still anxious given the Ontario government's restraint program.

Voters in this riding have a reputation for fickleness. Since 1974, when Tory incumbent Alf Hays retired after 17 years of service, the area has been represented by four different Members, two each from the Liberals and Conservatives. With the resignation of incumbent Tory Science Minister Bill Winegard, 12 candidates stepped forward to contest the election. Within Liberal ranks there was a split when former Liberal MP Frank Maine, a professional engineer, lost the party's nomination to Brenda Chamberlain, an executive director of the Guelph–Wellington Career Education Council from Elora. Maine claimed that he was forced out by the riding association executive who wanted a woman candidate, and he stood as an independent candidate. Reform managed to field a 'star' candidate in ex-CFL great Gerry Organ. Now a pastor with a Toronto church, Organ said he chose to stand as a Reform candidate because he felt current taxation and social policies discouraged the traditional family and were hurtful to young Canadians trying to make a start in life. Alex Michalos, a philosophy and social science professor at the University of Guelph, ran again for the NDP (he had carried the party's banner in 1988 also). The only other candidate to win more than 1% of the poll on election day was the National Party's Maggie Laidlaw, a lab supervisor and nutritionist.

It would perhaps be too simplistic to say that the Reform/PC split on the right handed this riding to the Liberals (as Maine, running as an independent, bled some of the Liberal strength). Nevertheless, Chamberlain's victory, winning 39.2% of the poll, was among the party's 10 lowest totals in the province for the 1993 election. One right-of-centre candidate would likely have won this riding.

Member of Parliament: Brenda Kay Chamberlain; **Party**: Liberal; **Occupation**: Executive director; **Education**: High school; **Age**: 42 (April 9, 1952); **Year first elected to the House of Commons**: 1993

35026 Guelph–Wellington

A: Political Profile
i) Voting Behaviour

	% 1993	% 1988	Change 1988-93
Conservative	20.7	43.2	-22.5
Liberal	39.2	31.9	7.3
NDP	4.7	19.5	-14.8
Reform	24.9	0	24.9
Other	10.5	5.3	5.2

% Turnout	67.2	Total Ballots (#)	62663
Rejected Ballots (#)	583	% Margin of Victory	14.3
Rural Polls, 1988 (#)	48	Urban Polls, 1988 (#)	167
% Yes - 1992	53.5	% No - 1992	45.6

ii) Campaign Financing

	# of Donations	Total $ Value	% of Limit Spent
Conservative	228	54958	85.7
Liberal	237	34100	63.5
NDP	143	28994	40.1
Reform	199	44158	67.6
Other	155	41412	

B: Ethno-Linguistic Profile

% English Home Language	94.2	% French Home Language	0.6
% Official Bilingual	8.1	% Other Home Language	5.3
% Catholics	30.7	% Protestants	51.5
% Aboriginal Peoples	0.3	% Immigrants	18.7

C: Socio-Economic Profile

Average Family Income $	58660	Median Family Income $	52314
% Low Income Families	10	Average Home Price $	208673
% Home Owners	65.2	% Unemployment	7
% Labour Force Participation	73.2	% Managerial-Administrative	12.6
% Self-Employed	8.5	% University Degrees	15.9
% Movers	51		

D: Industrial Profile

% Manufacturing	23.2	% Service Sector	10.5
% Agriculture	3.5	% Mining	0.2
% Forestry	0.1	% Fishing	0
% Government Services	5.6	% Business Services	5.3

E: Homogeneity Measures

Ethnic Diversity Index	0.3	Religious Homogeneity Index	0.37
Sectoral Concentration Index	0.38	Income Disparity Index	10.8

F: Physical Setting Characteristics

Total Population	115075	Area (km²)	1036
Population Density (pop/km²)	111.1		

Haldimand–Norfolk

Constituency Number: 35027

This constituency on the northern edge of Lake Erie has a mix of agriculture (the province's 7th most agricultural riding) and manufacturing. Tobacco farming is particularly important in the region, and some fishing employment is found in coastal communities. Average family incomes are about $6,000 below the norm for Ontario ridings.

Predominantly anglophone and Protestant, Haldimand–Norfolk has a relatively 'traditional' electorate. An element of this traditionalism includes strong religious and moral convictions. Haldimand–Norfolk was one of the handful of ridings that in the 1988 election saw the Christian Heritage Party make significant inroads (winning almost 4,000 votes) and affect the local outcome. In this respect, the CHP was anticipating the role of many Reform candidates in 1993. Much of the CHP support probably came at the expense of the long-time Conservative incumbent, Bud Bradley, who had represented the seat since 1979. Bradley lost the seat in 1988 to the Liberals' Bob Speller, a former assistant to Sheila Copps, provincial civil servant, and a consultant, by just over 200 votes.

Four candidates challenged Speller in the 1993 campaign. Ken Gilpin, a mechanical technician from Simcoe, attempted to incorporate and expand upon the CHP's support base for the Reform Party. Like his counterpart in the riding of Burlington, Gilpin did his party some damage, locally and elsewhere in the province, by using 'feminazi' to describe his opponents, in this case, the head of the county women's shelter, in a letter that was later obtained by his Liberal opponent. Jack Cronkwright, a consultant from Simcoe, ran for the Tories. Herman Plas, a crane operator from Waterford, ran for the NDP, while Ross Bateman, a teacher from Langton, ran for the National Party.

The recession bit hard into the area's industries and international trade (GATT and the NAFTA) was creating great uncertainty for the riding's farmers. Nonetheless, not being a member of the incumbent governing party, Speller was not held responsible for these, and he was returned to Ottawa with a comfortable 30% margin.

Member of Parliament: Robert Speller; **Party**: Liberal; **Occupation**: Consultant; **Education**: MA, York University; **Age**: 38 (Feb. 29, 1956); **Year first elected to the House of Commons**: 1988

35027 Haldimand–Norfolk

A: Political Profile
i) Voting Behaviour

	% 1993	% 1988	Change 1988-93
Conservative	16.2	37.6	-21.4
Liberal	53.8	38	15.8
NDP	3.7	15.1	-11.4
Reform	23.5	0	23.5
Other	2.8	9.3	-6.5

% Turnout	66	Total Ballots (#)	45319
Rejected Ballots (#)	353	% Margin of Victory	30.3
Rural Polls, 1988 (#)	153	Urban Polls, 1988 (#)	44
% Yes - 1992	43.5	% No - 1992	55.8

ii) Campaign Financing

	# of Donations	Total $ Value	% of Limit Spent
Conservative	150	28665	61*
Liberal	226	45064	68
NDP	69	22614	23.4
Reform	84	25841	34.2
Other	18	7756	

B: Ethno-Linguistic Profile

% English Home Language	97.4	% French Home Language	0.2
% Official Bilingual	4	% Other Home Language	2.4
% Catholics	21.7	% Protestants	65.6
% Aboriginal Peoples	2	% Immigrants	11.6

C: Socio-Economic Profile

Average Family Income $	49788	Median Family Income $	45274
% Low Income Families	8	Average Home Price $	144045
% Home Owners	76.8	% Unemployment	7.2
% Labour Force Participation	68.5	% Managerial-Administrative	9.8
% Self-Employed	12.7	% University Degrees	5.8
% Movers	41.3		

D: Industrial Profile

% Manufacturing	16.6	% Service Sector	10.8
% Agriculture	12.7	% Mining	0.7
% Forestry	0.1	% Fishing	0.3
% Government Services	5.3	% Business Services	3.4

E: Homogeneity Measures

Ethnic Diversity Index	0.36	Religious Homogeneity Index	0.48
Sectoral Concentration Index	0.33	Income Disparity Index	9.1

F: Physical Setting Characteristics

Total Population	90246	Area (km^2)	2566
Population Density (pop/km^2)	35.2		

* Tentative value, due to the existence of unpaid campaign expenses.

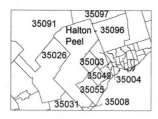

Halton–Peel

Constituency Number: 35028

This mixed rural-urban riding wraps around the western edge of Peel Region, taking in parts of this region and the centre of Halton Region, just west of metropolitan Toronto. It is home to a large Chrysler plant and 21% of the population is employed in manufacturing. However, this does not necessarily mean it is a blue-collar riding. With 18% of the workforce in managerial/administrative occupations, the riding ranks among the province's top 15 most white-collar. It is in the top ten in terms of average family incomes, and only 4.4% of families are categorized as 'low income'. Many workers commute to Toronto or Hamilton.

In many ways this heavy commuter population probably made Halton-Peel a natural Reform riding, in that it was perhaps suffering from the 'boiling point' syndrome. The real estate boom which southern Ontario experienced in the late 1980s drove many commuters further out from urban areas and led to a house building explosion in this part of Ontario. When the economic slump hit, many young families found themselves in deep financial water and were unable to get out as their homes were difficult to sell in the context of the recession. Throw in a high unemployment rate and ever rising taxation (including the GST and the Tory reduction in benefits to middle-class families) and you have the makings of a middle-class revolt against traditional conservatives similar to that American Kevin Phillips described in *Boiling Point*, his book about the defeat of George Bush and the Republican Party.

Crime and violence against women and children was an issue in this riding. One of the girls allegedly murdered by Paul Teale, Leslie Mahaffey, lived in the riding. The slain girl's mother has become an active participant in the campaign to impose greater restrictions on pornographic materials and products marketing violence and in campaigns against violent crime in general.

Defending his 1988 victory in the riding for the Tories was Garth Turner, a former business journalist prior to his parliamentary career. Turner had been named as Revenue Minister in Kim Campbell's short-lived Tory government. Running for the Liberals was Julian Reed, a former MPP, farmer, and artistic performer from Norval. The Reform Party ran Dick MacDuffee, an owner of a manufacturing company from Palgrave. Norma Peterson, an executive assistant from Fergus, offered for the NDP. Three other minor party candidates, none of whom managed even 1% of the poll in 1993, rounded out the ballot.

The division of conservative voters between Reform and the Tories handed this riding to the Liberals. With a combined total of about 35,000 votes, one right-of-centre candidate standing unopposed might well have kept the Liberals, who only won about 22,000 votes, from taking this riding. In this regard, Garth Turner (a seasoned ex-journalist who should have known better) may have shot himself in the foot, and contributed to his party's spectacular demise in 1993. Turner warned Canadians that the Tory bastion in Quebec (and hence, his whole party) was in danger. In an off-the-cuff comment Turner told Quebec Tories that the country was more important than their party and that if their Liberal opponents looked better placed to stop the BQ they should vote for them. While it is impossible to know how much this comment hurt the party's and Turner's own fortunes, it seems plausible to assume that they did some damage to each.

Member of Parliament: Julian Reed; **Party**: Liberal; **Occupation**: Actor; **Education**: Diploma in Agriculture, Ontario College of Agriculture (Guelph); **Age**: 58 (Jan. 27, 1936); **Year first elected to the House of Commons**: 1993

35028 Halton–Peel

A: Political Profile

i) Voting Behaviour

	% 1993	% 1988	Change 1988-93
Conservative	30.5	54.6	-24.1
Liberal	37	31.6	5.4
NDP	2.4	13	-10.6
Reform	28	0	28
Other	2.1	0.9	1.2

% Turnout	70.4	Total Ballots (#)	60600
Rejected Ballots (#)	397	% Margin of Victory	6.5
Rural Polls, 1988 (#)	75	Urban Polls, 1988 (#)	142
% Yes - 1992	57.3	% No - 1992	42.2

ii) Campaign Financing

	# of Donations	Total $ Value	% of Limit Spent
Conservative	127	31812	79.3
Liberal	114	38640	57.3
NDP	47	12180	8.9
Reform	104	39949	61.6
Other	20	8079	

B: Ethno-Linguistic Profile

% English Home Language	95.6	% French Home Language	0.5
% Official Bilingual	8.2	% Other Home Language	3.9
% Catholics	28.4	% Protestants	55.2
% Aboriginal Peoples	0.2	% Immigrants	19.8

C: Socio-Economic Profile

Average Family Income $	72505	Median Family Income $	64342
% Low Income Families	4.4	Average Home Price $	273907
% Home Owners	84.7	% Unemployment	5.9
% Labour Force Participation	77.2	% Managerial-Administrative	17.9
% Self-Employed	10.4	% University Degrees	13.4
% Movers	47.5		

D: Industrial Profile

% Manufacturing	21	% Service Sector	9
% Agriculture	3.2	% Mining	0.4
% Forestry	0.1	% Fishing	0
% Government Services	5.8	% Business Services	6.4

E: Homogeneity Measures

Ethnic Diversity Index	0.3	Religious Homogeneity Index	0.4
Sectoral Concentration Index	0.38	Income Disparity Index	11.3

F: Physical Setting Characteristics

Total Population	114670	Area (km²)	1337
Population Density (pop/km²)	85.8		

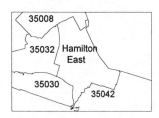

Hamilton East

Constituency Number: 35029

Hamilton East extends along the western shore of Lake Ontario and takes in most of the downtown section of the city of Hamilton. Most obvious to the observer passing through the riding on the Queen Elizabeth Way (QEW) is the smoking hulk of Stelco Steel on the waterfront of Hamilton Harbour. While the local economy is more diversified than the image of Hamilton as a steel city would lead you to believe, Hamilton East remains one of Canada's most heavily industrialized and blue-collar ridings. The recession exposed this area to a severe bout of job losses, and it has the province's second highest rate of unemployment. However by the time votes were actually cast, there were signs the economy was recovering, including the first quarterly profit in a number of years at Stelco and the retention of a number of employees who were initially hired solely as summer replacements. The concentration of manufacturing jobs ranks the riding fourth in the province; it has the lowest concentration of white-collar workers, and the lowest proportion of residents who are university graduates. Average family incomes are the second lowest among Ontario ridings.

This riding has had two MPs since 1962, both Liberals and both very powerful. From 1962 to 1984 it was represented by John Munro and since then by Sheila Copps. A former journalist and MPP, Copps entered politics with a clear advantage over her rivals. The daughter of a long-time Hamilton mayor, the late Vic Copps, she has been immersed in politics and the issues of this riding since birth. A candidate for leadership in the party, Copps is outspoken and flamboyant. A member of the Liberals' 'rat-pack' during the party's opposition years, her fluency in three languages (English, French, and Italian) make her a particularly attractive candidate for a party that traditionally appeals to ethnic groups. Only a scandal that directly impugns her personal honesty is likely ever to bring about her defeat here.

The Reform candidate during the 1993 campaign, John Stuart, a 45-year-old general contractor, said 'I think I'm facing the biggest challenge in the country. I'd rather run against Prime Minister Campbell than Sheila Copps.' The Tories ran Brian Joseph Bobolo, a registered nurse. His candidacy was hurt by spillovers from the Tory public relations disaster surrounding Toronto's Pearson Airport. In the contract signed by the Tories was a clause prohibiting the government of Canada from investing in the renovation, upgrading, or expansion of any rival air passenger handling facilities within 75 km of Pearson until volume reached 33 million passengers at Pearson (volume was 21 million at election date). What this meant was that the government had no intention of fostering the growth of Hamilton's Mount Hope Airport, one of the most under-used in Canada. With a capacity to handle 1.5 to 2 million air passenger trips a year, the facility only serves slightly more than 53,000. On the other hand, area Liberals in a joint presentation to the Chamber of Commerce promised an integrated development plan to make the Mount Hope Airport the main alternative to Pearson in Southern Ontario. Instead of adding new runways at Pearson they recommended creating passenger linkages between the two airports, including rail lines and an improved highway link. These linkages would also better connect the Hamilton Wentworth Region to Metro and of course create the kind of jobs Chrétien's infrastructure plan envisioned.

Wayne Marston, a telephone tester, ran for the NDP. He was joined by two independent and three minor party candidates, none of whom had any impact on the outcome. In the end, Copps surprised no one by holding the seat with a sizeable 50% margin over her closest rival.

Member of Parliament: Sheila M. Copps; **Party**: Liberal; **Occupation**: Deputy Prime Minister of Canada and Minister of the Environment; **Education**: BA, University of Western Ontario; **Age:** 44 (Nov. 27, 1952); **Year first elected to the House of Commons**: 1984

35029 Hamilton East

A: Political Profile

i) Voting Behaviour

	% 1993	% 1988	Change 1988-93
Conservative	6.8	21.4	-14.6
Liberal	67.3	49.8	17.5
NDP	6.6	28	-21.4
Reform	17	0	17
Other	2.2	0.7	1.5

% Turnout	62	Total Ballots (#)	34597
Rejected Ballots (#)	422	% Margin of Victory	50.3
Rural Polls, 1988 (#)	0	Urban Polls, 1988 (#)	174
% Yes - 1992	42.8	% No - 1992	56.4

ii) Campaign Financing

	# of Donations	Total $ Value	% of Limit Spent
Conservative	13	4211	7.9
Liberal	350	136088	94.6
NDP	69	19533	36.1
Reform	32	8798	30.3*
Other	17	3932	

B: Ethno-Linguistic Profile

% English Home Language	85.9	% French Home Language	0.7
% Official Bilingual	4.9	% Other Home Language	13.5
% Catholics	39.4	% Protestants	40
% Aboriginal Peoples	1.2	% Immigrants	24.1

C: Socio-Economic Profile

Average Family Income $	41153	Median Family Income $	38350
% Low Income Families	24.1	Average Home Price $	134734
% Home Owners	60.6	% Unemployment	13.3
% Labour Force Participation	61.2	% Managerial-Administrative	6.7
% Self-Employed	3.8	% University Degrees	4.3
% Movers	43		

D: Industrial Profile

% Manufacturing	29.3	% Service Sector	12.3
% Agriculture	0.9	% Mining	0.2
% Forestry	0	% Fishing	0.1
% Government Services	3.7	% Business Services	3.9

E: Homogeneity Measures

Ethnic Diversity Index	0.23	Religious Homogeneity Index	0.34
Sectoral Concentration Index	0.4	Income Disparity Index	6.8

F: Physical Setting Characteristics

Total Population	81401	Area (km²)	41
Population Density (pop/km²)	1985.4		

* Tentative value, due to the existence of unpaid campaign expenses.

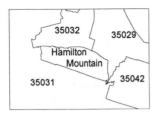

Hamilton Mountain

Constituency Number: 35030

Hamilton Mountain is a middle/lower middle class residential riding on the southwest side of Hamilton. Its northern border follows the Niagara Escarpment that bifurcates the city. Average family incomes are about $5,000 below the norm for provincial ridings, but the proportion of families classed as 'low income' is slightly below the provincial average. The area is unusual for urban Ontario in terms of the stability of its residential population; it has the second lowest proportion of families who have moved (whether in the last year, or in the last five years), and its rate of net population change between 1986 and 1991 was the fifth lowest of all provincial ridings.

Hamilton Mountain was held for the eight years ending in 1987 by Ian Deans of the NDP. Deans' resignation to become chair of the Federal Public Service Commission, and the subsequent by-election in July of 1987, saw Marion Dewar, a former mayor of Ottawa, retain the seat for the NDP. In 1988, however, the riding experienced a tight three-way race. Dewar lost by a mere 73 votes to the Liberal challenger, Beth Phinney. An educator and real estate representative, Phinney stressed her local roots in the 1988 campaign, criticizing the 'parachute' status of her NDP competitor.

In 1993, the NDP decided to make a strong run at regaining this riding, targeting it as a priority, and putting up Andrew Mackenzie, an electronics technologist who is the son of the NDP provincial labour minister and area MPP Bob Mackenzie. The younger Mackenzie is a seasoned political worker and union activist in his own right. The NDP provided Mackenzie with all the resources a top flight candidate usually gets, but the anti-NDP sentiment in Ontario was just too much to overcome. In the end, all those resources were essentially washed down the electoral drain and Mackenzie finished fourth. The Conservatives nominated Tamra Mann, a relatively low profile lawyer, and the Reform nomination went to a 23-year-old business lobbyist. The latter bitterly conceded defeat on election night by remarking: 'I guess the electors decided to give Phinney her super pension' (this term will qualify Phinney for the MPs' pension). Two minor party candidates rounded out the ballot, but had no significant effect on the outcome of the local race.

In addition to the national issues, voters in Hamilton Mountain were sensitive to the Conservative government's negotiations for the Pearson Airport (Toronto) sale, and its potentially negative implications for the future development of Hamilton's nearby Mount Hope Airport. Similarly, crime and sexual abuse was also a highly visible local issue, as a result of the enormous attention given to the Homolka/Teale arrests and trials. Phinney was able to hold the riding with a comfortable 35% victory margin over the second-place Reform candidate.

Member of Parliament: Beth Phinney; **Party**: Liberal; **Occupation**: Member of Parliament; **Education**: BA, McMaster University; **Age:** 56 (June 19, 1938); **Year first elected to the House of Commons**: 1988

35030 Hamilton Mountain

A: Political Profile
i) Voting Behaviour

	% 1993	% 1988	Change 1988-93
Conservative	11.5	30.5	-19
Liberal	57.3	32.9	24.4
NDP	7.6	32.8	-25.2
Reform	21.7	0	21.7
Other	1.9	3.8	-1.9

% Turnout	71.6	Total Ballots (#)	47973
Rejected Ballots (#)	464	% Margin of Victory	35.6
Rural Polls, 1988 (#)	0	Urban Polls, 1988 (#)	189
% Yes - 1992	46.5	% No - 1992	52.9

ii) Campaign Financing

	# of Donations	Total $ Value	% of Limit Spent
Conservative	131	23875	42.7
Liberal	102	42540	86.2
NDP	197	39203	56.9
Reform	92	30538	72.1
Other	33	5899	

B: Ethno-Linguistic Profile

% English Home Language	90.7	% French Home Language	0.4
% Official Bilingual	5.2	% Other Home Language	8.9
% Catholics	36.6	% Protestants	47.5
% Aboriginal Peoples	0.4	% Immigrants	24

C: Socio-Economic Profile

Average Family Income $	51125	Median Family Income $	47591
% Low Income Families	14.6	Average Home Price $	164800
% Home Owners	67.9	% Unemployment	8.4
% Labour Force Participation	63.3	% Managerial-Administrative	9.5
% Self-Employed	4.6	% University Degrees	7.7
% Movers	35.4		

D: Industrial Profile

% Manufacturing	22.4	% Service Sector	12.5
% Agriculture	0.5	% Mining	0.1
% Forestry	0.1	% Fishing	0
% Government Services	5.4	% Business Services	4.5

E: Homogeneity Measures

Ethnic Diversity Index	0.28	Religious Homogeneity Index	0.37
Sectoral Concentration Index	0.46	Income Disparity Index	6.9

F: Physical Setting Characteristics

Total Population	89662	Area (km²)	27
Population Density (pop/km²)	3320.8		

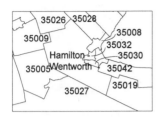

Hamilton–Wentworth

Constituency Number: 35031

The riding of Hamilton–Wentworth lies to the south and west of the city of Hamilton. Not long ago a rural riding, it now represents a rural/suburban mix in which less than 4% of the population work the land. Since 1986 population in the riding has grown by 28% (one of the top ten growth rates in the province for this period), mainly due to upper class suburban developments in Ancaster, Dundas, and Waterdown. Ancaster has one of Canada's highest average family income levels, bringing the riding average to $63,762, substantially above the norm for Ontario constituencies.

The retirement of 15-year veteran Tory Geoff Scott threw the 1993 campaign wide open. The race was made even more interesting by the fact that none of the seven candidates had ever held elected office before. In early October the campaign turned ugly when a large number of Conservative candidate Ray Johnson's signs were defaced with racist graffiti. Most disturbingly, the graffiti appeared in the Ancaster area where Johnson, an emeritus professor at McMaster University and chair of university athletics, has resided for more than half his life. A Hamilton-Wentworth Regional Police spokesperson noted that campaign vandalism is common and not usually not a high priority for police. However vandalism of this type, unseen in the region before, was of deep concern to the force.

The Liberals nominated John Bryden, a former journalist with the *Toronto Star*, while the NDP offered Rick McCall, an electrician. Meanwhile the Reform candidate, Mark Mullins, was desperate for electors to forget his predecessor as Reform candidate, Don Kennedy, who was dismissed by the Reform riding association when they discovered he had touched up his résumé with untruthful information. Mullins works as a staff member at McMaster University. Three minor party candidates rounded out the ballot, but none exceeded 1% of the poll on election day.

The general issues in this riding were the economy, the problem of violent crime, and the Hamilton airport. The Pearson airport deal negotiated by Mulroney's Conservatives included a clause prohibiting the government of Canada from investing in the renovation, upgrading, or expansion of any rival air passenger handling facilities within 75 km of Pearson. What this meant was that the government had no intention of fostering the growth of Hamilton's Mount Hope Airport, one of the most under-used in Canada. With a capacity to handle 1.5 to 2 million air passenger trips a year, the facility only serves slightly more than 53,000. The Canada-US air treaty allows only transborder service to Hamilton's airport (due to its proximity to Pearson) by aircraft with fewer than 20 seats. Hamilton business leaders saw the contract clause as a clear indication that further development of the Hamilton facility would not be a priority for the Campbell government. In fact, on a campaign stop Campbell's recommendation was that the civic backers investigate turning Mount Hope into a major air cargo centre. Area Liberals, in a joint presentation to the Chamber of Commerce, promised an integrated development plan for the Mount Hope Airport. The goal of this plan was to make Mount Hope the main alternative to Pearson in southern Ontario. Instead of adding new runways at Pearson they recommended creating passenger linkages between the two airports, including rail lines and an improved highway link. These linkages would also better connect the Hamilton Wentworth Region to Metro as well and of course create the kind of jobs the Liberals' infrastructure plan envisioned.

Taking the riding for the Liberals was Bryden, an expert on chemical and biological weapons, with a comfortable 20% margin of victory.

Member of Parliament: John Bryden; **Party**: Liberal; **Occupation**: Author and editor; **Education**: M.PH.; **Age**: 51 (July 15, 1943); **Year first elected to the House of Commons**: 1993

35031 Hamilton–Wentworth

A: Political Profile
i) Voting Behaviour

	% 1993	% 1988	Change 1988-93
Conservative	22.4	41.9	-19.5
Liberal	45.8	34	11.8
NDP	3.9	15.8	-11.9
Reform	25.5	0	25.5
Other	2.2	8.4	-6.2

% Turnout	72.3	Total Ballots (#)	65326
Rejected Ballots (#)	507	% Margin of Victory	20.3
Rural Polls, 1988 (#)	68	Urban Polls, 1988 (#)	172
% Yes - 1992	50.1	% No - 1992	49.3

ii) Campaign Financing

	# of Donations	Total $ Value	% of Limit Spent
Conservative	164	45805	99.2
Liberal	148	32991	49.9
NDP	73	17800	26
Reform	57	10770	19.9
Other	4	440	

B: Ethno-Linguistic Profile

% English Home Language	94.4	% French Home Language	0.2
% Official Bilingual	5.9	% Other Home Language	5.4
% Catholics	30.6	% Protestants	52
% Aboriginal Peoples	0.2	% Immigrants	20.6

C: Socio-Economic Profile

Average Family Income $	63762	Median Family Income $	56633
% Low Income Families	8.6	Average Home Price $	221026
% Home Owners	80.7	% Unemployment	6.9
% Labour Force Participation	72.9	% Managerial-Administrative	13.5
% Self-Employed	10.1	% University Degrees	13.3
% Movers	47		

D: Industrial Profile

% Manufacturing	18.3	% Service Sector	9.6
% Agriculture	3.8	% Mining	0.4
% Forestry	0.1	% Fishing	0
% Government Services	5.6	% Business Services	5.3

E: Homogeneity Measures

Ethnic Diversity Index	0.28	Religious Homogeneity Index	0.38
Sectoral Concentration Index	0.41	Income Disparity Index	11.2

F: Physical Setting Characteristics

Total Population	124854	Area (km²)	937
Population Density (pop/km²)	133.2		

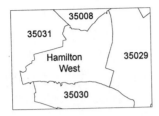

Hamilton West

Constituency Number: 35032

Hamilton West is an entirely urban riding in the city of Hamilton, with its northern borders provided by Lake Ontario and Hamilton Harbour, and its southern limit marked by the Niagara Escarpment. McMaster University is located in the riding and is a major economic actor. Housing ranges from some of Hamilton's most exclusive homes (though comparatively few own homes in this riding), to downtown apartment towers, to public housing projects.

Following a close race in 1988 Stan Keyes, a former broadcast journalist, took this seat from the incumbent Tory MP Peter Peterson, who had represented the area since 1984. In 1993 Peterson, a stockbroker, came back to try and reclaim the seat. Much like Peterson before him, Keyes had used his five-year term as MP to particularly good use in developing a reputation as a hard worker and good constituency MP. A former television journalist, Keyes also responded to a touchstone issue in this region (given the Homolka/Teale trials in connection with the Mahaffy, DeVilliers, and French homicides), that of violent crime. He sponsored a private members bill to amend the parole act so as to allow victims to have standing at parole application hearings.

Running for the Reform Party was George G. Mills, a business owner. The NDP ran Denise Giroux, a lawyer, but as elsewhere in the province, the unpopularity of the provincial NDP government handicapped her campaign. Three minor party candidates joined the campaign, but had little impact.

On election day, turnout was low at 58.4% (the second lowest in the province), but Keyes crushed the rest of the field with a 43% margin of victory.

Member of Parliament: Stan K. Keyes; **Party**: Liberal; **Occupation**: Television news journalist; **Education**: Mohawk College; **Age**: 41 (May 17, 1953); **Year first elected to the House of Commons**: 1988

35032 Hamilton West

A: Political Profile
i) Voting Behaviour

	% 1993	% 1988	Change 1988-93
Conservative	15	33.9	-18.9
Liberal	58.7	37.8	20.9
NDP	8.2	25.5	-17.3
Reform	15.2	0	15.2
Other	3	2.8	0.2

% Turnout	58.4	Total Ballots (#)	38934
Rejected Ballots (#)	417	% Margin of Victory	43.5
Rural Polls, 1988 (#)	0	Urban Polls, 1988 (#)	197
% Yes - 1992	50.9	% No - 1992	48.1

ii) Campaign Financing

	# of Donations	Total $ Value	% of Limit Spent
Conservative	48	43570	61.4
Liberal	106	57882	68.9
NDP	171	37491	49.3
Reform	150	18076	54
Other	7	2123	

B: Ethno-Linguistic Profile

% English Home Language	83.1	% French Home Language	0.7
% Official Bilingual	7.6	% Other Home Language	16.2
% Catholics	35.6	% Protestants	40
% Aboriginal Peoples	1.3	% Immigrants	27.3

C: Socio-Economic Profile

Average Family Income $	44071	Median Family Income $	37209
% Low Income Families	31	Average Home Price $	162055
% Home Owners	34.6	% Unemployment	12.6
% Labour Force Participation	61.6	% Managerial-Administrative	9.2
% Self-Employed	5.6	% University Degrees	14.6
% Movers	52		

D: Industrial Profile

% Manufacturing	18.5	% Service Sector	14.8
% Agriculture	1.2	% Mining	0.2
% Forestry	0	% Fishing	0
% Government Services	5.1	% Business Services	6.3

E: Homogeneity Measures

Ethnic Diversity Index	0.23	Religious Homogeneity Index	0.31
Sectoral Concentration Index	0.46	Income Disparity Index	15.6

F: Physical Setting Characteristics

Total Population	85796	Area (km²)	25
Population Density (pop/km²)	3431.8		

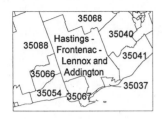

Hastings–Frontenac–Lennox and Addington

Constituency Number: 35033

Hastings–Frontenac–Lennox and Addington is a genuinely rural riding, sprawling across the northern sections of three counties in eastern Ontario. The riding's electorate is the most anglophone, and one of the most Protestant, in the province, and many families here have Loyalist roots. Napanee, a town west of Kingston located in the riding, joined with several others across Ontario in declaring itself to be an 'English only' community. This is not an affluent area. Average family incomes are substantially (approximately $10,000) below the norm for provincial ridings. Farming, and especially dairy farming, is concentrated in the southern portions of this large riding, while the northern areas are dominated by a variety of resource industries (mining, logging, etc.). There are also some light manufacturers (tires, furniture, metal fabrication, textiles) and correctional services are also important.

This is loyal Conservative country. The area's tradition of Tory representation extends back a century. Since 1979 the Conservative MP has been Bill Vankoughnet, a former administrator who himself has strong Loyalist ties. His 1988 re-election was a close one, however, and given the anti-Conservative tenor of the 1993 campaign, the riding seemed to be in danger of abandoning its partisan traditions. Vankoughnet did not help his re-election chances when he issued a misleading brochure that appeared to indicate that he had been endorsed by the Ontario Federation of Anglers and Hunters. The Federation makes no such endorsements and promptly issued a denial to the local media.

Challenging Vankoughnet for the Liberals was Larry McCormick, a retailer store owner, community activist and consultant from Camden. Stephen Ollerenshaw, an accountant from Marmora, ran under the Reform label. Betty Hay Lambeck, a library manager from Bancroft, ran for the NDP. Bob Hilson offered for the National Party, and two independent candidates rounded out the ballot. One, Ted 'Cheemo the Clown' Walczack added colour to the race. A retired professional engineer and manager at a Styrofoam plant, Walczack's campaign was managed by the editor of a local weekly newspaper. He promised to make kids come first and demonstrated this principle by campaigning in grease paint and a clown suit. On the campaign trail he regularly interrupted his campaigning to perform for children whenever they approached him on the hustings. In the end he finished sixth in the seven-candidate race.

The big issue in the election was the strained situation of local farmers and the impending NAFTA and GATT agreements with their possible ramifications for farm support programs. Other issues included the lack of opportunities for young people and their loss to urban centres. In the end, McCormick won the riding for the Liberals by a comfortable 27% margin.

Member of Parliament: Larry James Earl McCormick; **Party**: Liberal; **Occupation**: Small business owner and operator; **Education**: High school; **Age**: 54 (Jan. 4, 1940); **Year first elected to the House of Commons**: 1993

35033 Hastings–Frontenac–Lennox and Addington

A: Political Profile
i) Voting Behaviour

	% 1993	% 1988	Change 1988-93
Conservative	22.8	40	-17.2
Liberal	50.1	38	12.1
NDP	4.2	17.3	-13.1
Reform	18.4	0	18.4
Other	4.6	4.8	-0.2

% Turnout	67.7	Total Ballots (#)	48287
Rejected Ballots (#)	217	% Margin of Victory	27.3
Rural Polls, 1988 (#)	240	Urban Polls, 1988 (#)	0
% Yes - 1992	40.2	% No - 1992	59.7

ii) Campaign Financing

	# of Donations	Total $ Value	% of Limit Spent
Conservative	129	32186	77.1
Liberal	214	42497	79.4
NDP	91	12534	17.8*
Reform	171	16281	25.9
Other	41	6410	

B: Ethno-Linguistic Profile

% English Home Language	99.1	% French Home Language	0.3
% Official Bilingual	5	% Other Home Language	0.6
% Catholics	17.6	% Protestants	70.5
% Aboriginal Peoples	1	% Immigrants	6.8

C: Socio-Economic Profile

Average Family Income $	45444	Median Family Income $	40590
% Low Income Families	10.5	Average Home Price $	132728
% Home Owners	81	% Unemployment	9.5
% Labour Force Participation	64.2	% Managerial-Administrative	9.1
% Self-Employed	12.9	% University Degrees	6.6
% Movers	40.6		

D: Industrial Profile

% Manufacturing	13.3	% Service Sector	12.3
% Agriculture	5.7	% Mining	0.4
% Forestry	0.7	% Fishing	0.1
% Government Services	9.4	% Business Services	3.4

E: Homogeneity Measures

Ethnic Diversity Index	0.61	Religious Homogeneity Index	0.51
Sectoral Concentration Index	0.37	Income Disparity Index	10.7

F: Physical Setting Characteristics

Total Population	90831	Area (km²)	11978
Population Density (pop/km²)	7.6		

* Tentative value, due to the existence of unpaid campaign expenses.

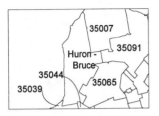

Huron–Bruce

Constituency Number: 35034

Huron–Bruce is a large rural riding that extends about 180 kilometres along the eastern shore of Lake Huron. Agriculture is an important part of the riding's economic base (the riding ranks fourth in terms of the proportion of the workforce employed in agriculture), with cash crops dominating Huron County and beef farming concentrated in Bruce County. The riding is heavily anglophone (and is the most Protestant riding in Ontario). If ever there was a riding ripe for environmental politics, one would assume it would be Huron–Bruce. The riding is naturally very beautiful, and is home to the Bruce Nuclear Power Development in Port Elgin, one of the largest nuclear facilities in Canada. The plant has received repeated poor reports from the federal regulators and is often shut down for safety-related concerns. Nevertheless environmental issues garnered little attention during the 1993 campaign, as local debate focused on which party would create jobs and secure the future of Canadian agriculture.

The Tories have held this riding continuously (except for one short break in the 1960s) since 1953. Since 1980, it has been represented in Parliament by Conservative MP Murray Cardiff, a third-generation cash crop and hog farmer from Ethel. However the 1993 election saw the incumbent Tory challenged by strong and locally popular Liberal and Reform candidates. Cardiff also had the unpopularity of his own party to overcome and, at times, he seemed to be running against his own party. For example, he admitted that paying off the deficit in five years (as PC leader Kim Campbell had proposed) was probably unrealistic as government revenue had fallen too severely during the recession and the country was in no shape to withstand higher taxation. He also likened cutting social programs to 'backing out on an insurance policy'. His proposed solution was more efficiency in government and better policies (such as improved preventive health care rather than curative care).

Challenging Cardiff under the Liberal banner was Paul Steckle, from Zurich, Ontario, a farmer and heavy equipment dealer with a long record of service in local politics. In such a traditional, rural Ontario environment, it is perhaps not surprising that the local Liberal's campaigning often seemed to be encroaching on the policy grounds staked out by the Reform Party's platform. At one all-candidates meeting Steckle said his own issue priorities if elected would be government waste, high taxes, and the deficit. However, he added that his purpose in tackling these issues was to secure the future of our social programs. Reform ran Len Lobb, a farm equipment salesman from Clinton. The NDP once again ran Tony McQuail, a livestock farmer from Lucknow (he had run unsuccessfully in the riding in 1988). Henry Zekveld, a farmer from Clifford, ran for the Christian Heritage Party, taking 1.6% of the poll. Two minor party candidates each won less than 1% of the vote.

On election day, the Reform/Tory split on the centre/right of the political spectrum allowed the Liberals to claim this riding.

Member of Parliament: Paul Steckle; **Party**: Liberal; **Occupation**: Farmer; **Year first elected to the House of Commons**: 1993

35034 Huron–Bruce

A: Political Profile

i) Voting Behaviour

	% 1993	% 1988	Change 1988-93
Conservative	28	42.6	-14.6
Liberal	44.1	35.3	8.8
NDP	4.2	16.5	-12.3
Reform	21.1	0	21.1
Other	2.7	5.6	-2.9

% Turnout	72.5	Total Ballots (#)	49829
Rejected Ballots (#)	307	% Margin of Victory	16.1
Rural Polls, 1988 (#)	156	Urban Polls, 1988 (#)	44
% Yes - 1992	52.2	% No - 1992	47.4

ii) Campaign Financing

	# of Donations	Total $ Value	% of Limit Spent
Conservative	111	47454	76.4*
Liberal	162	33965	67.1
NDP	102	24530	29.1
Reform	162	28543	62
Other	29	4625	

B: Ethno-Linguistic Profile

% English Home Language	98	% French Home Language	0.2
% Official Bilingual	4	% Other Home Language	1.7
% Catholics	18.4	% Protestants	72.7
% Aboriginal Peoples	0.3	% Immigrants	8.8

C: Socio-Economic Profile

Average Family Income $	50482	Median Family Income $	43730
% Low Income Families	8	Average Home Price $	126467
% Home Owners	77.3	% Unemployment	6.2
% Labour Force Participation	67.7	% Managerial-Administrative	9.8
% Self-Employed	16.3	% University Degrees	7.1
% Movers	39.2		

D: Industrial Profile

% Manufacturing	12.1	% Service Sector	11.8
% Agriculture	14.1	% Mining	1
% Forestry	0.2	% Fishing	0.1
% Government Services	4.8	% Business Services	2.3

E: Homogeneity Measures

Ethnic Diversity Index	0.47	Religious Homogeneity Index	0.55
Sectoral Concentration Index	0.34	Income Disparity Index	13.4

F: Physical Setting Characteristics

Total Population	94731	Area (km²)	5109
Population Density (pop/km²)	18.5		

* Tentative value, due to the existence of unpaid campaign expenses.

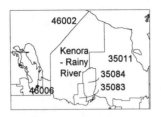

Kenora–Rainy River

Constituency Number: 35035

Located in Ontario's north, Kenora–Rainy River is the province's second largest riding in terms of its landmass, and the fifth largest in the country. The enormous territory defined by the riding's boundaries is rugged, forest-covered, and sparsely populated. There are 51 reservations in Kenora–Rainy River, and with just under a third of its residents members of Canada's First Nations, it ranks highest on this measure in Ontario. As with most northern Ontario ridings, resource industries dominate the constituency's economy (pulp and paper and mining are particularly important). The three major population centres in the riding, Kenora, Dryden, and Fort Frances, all have pulp and paper mills. The Red Lake district is known as Canada's most productive gold mining area.

Prior to 1984, the area traditionally returned Liberals to Ottawa. Liberal John Reid represented the riding for 19 years, but was replaced in 1984 by John Parry for the NDP. In 1988, the riding returned to its Liberal tradition, however, having been won in a tight three-way race by Bob Nault. Nault, a former railroad conductor from Keewatin, defended the riding in the 1993 campaign.

Challenging Nault in 1993 for the Reform Party was Mel Fisher, a professional engineer from Dryden. The NDP was represented locally by Peter Kirby, a lawyer from Kenora. George Hainsworth, a consultant from Kanata, ran for the Conservatives. A minor party and an independent candidate ran with little success in 1993. In the end, Nault benefited from the fragmentation of his opposition, and extended his 1988 victory margin from 3.5% to 44.2%.

Member of Parliament: Robert Daniel Nault; **Party**: Liberal; **Occupation**: Railroad conductor; **Education**: University of Alberta and University of Winnipeg; **Age**: 39 (Nov. 9, 1955); **Year first elected to the House of Commons**: 1988

35035 Kenora–Rainy River

A: Political Profile
i) Voting Behaviour

	% 1993	% 1988	Change 1988-93
Conservative	6	21.6	-15.6
Liberal	64.8	38.3	26.5
NDP	6.4	34.8	-28.4
Reform	20.6	0	20.6
Other	2.3	5.4	-3.1

% Turnout	63.8	Total Ballots (#)	34718
Rejected Ballots (#)	159	% Margin of Victory	44.2
Rural Polls, 1988 (#)	143	Urban Polls, 1988 (#)	59
% Yes - 1992	32.2	% No - 1992	67.2

ii) Campaign Financing

	# of Donations	Total $ Value	% of Limit Spent
Conservative	76	12684	27.2*
Liberal	266	58244	76.9*
NDP	106	16785	21.8
Reform	167	39137	58.3
Other	14	3832	

B: Ethno-Linguistic Profile

% English Home Language	88	% French Home Language	0.6
% Official Bilingual	5.7	% Other Home Language	11.4
% Catholics	27.7	% Protestants	55.2
% Aboriginal Peoples	31.3	% Immigrants	7.8

C: Socio-Economic Profile

Average Family Income $	48614	Median Family Income $	44758
% Low Income Families	8.6	Average Home Price $	96281
% Home Owners	66.5	% Unemployment	8
% Labour Force Participation	67	% Managerial-Administrative	10.4
% Self-Employed	9.2	% University Degrees	6.5
% Movers	42.5		

D: Industrial Profile

% Manufacturing	10.8	% Service Sector	15.9
% Agriculture	1.8	% Mining	3.8
% Forestry	4.6	% Fishing	0.2
% Government Services	14.5	% Business Services	1.8

E: Homogeneity Measures

Ethnic Diversity Index	0.22	Religious Homogeneity Index	0.4
Sectoral Concentration Index	0.39	Income Disparity Index	7.9

F: Physical Setting Characteristics

Total Population	74771	Area (km²)	307560
Population Density (pop/km²)	0.2		

* Tentative value, due to the existence of unpaid campaign expenses.

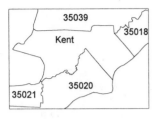

Kent

Constituency Number: 35036

Kent is a mixed rural and urban riding that spans peninsular southwestern Ontario between Lake Ontario and Lake St Clair. It comprises virtually all of the county of Kent, apart from its southwestern section. Roughly half of its residents live in Chatham, a city of about 40,000. Chatham served as one of the northern terminuses of the Underground Railroad that brought fugitive slaves to freedom in Canada. Descendants of these individuals constitute a significant part of the riding's population. The economy around Chatham is dominated by a diverse array of light industries. Farming is important in the rest of the riding.

This riding is perhaps typical of the entire southwestern Ontario region. Hit hard by plant closings, downsizings and layoffs, many workers are streaming back to the local community college to get the skills they are told they need to compete in the new labour market. Farmers are worried about the impact international trade talks and the geo-political economy will have on the prices their crops will earn. They watched with concern as nearby yet another processing plant closed (Green Giant in Tecumseh, Windsor–St Clair riding). On the other hand, the county's welfare role has been in gradual decline since 1992 and it appears that the economy was on the mend at election time in 1993. However, Kent voters were among the province's least enthusiastic in terms of their support level for the Charlottetown Accord in the 1992 constitutional referendum.

The riding has changed hands several times in recent elections. It shifted from Liberal to Conservative hands in 1984 as part of the Mulroney sweep in that election. In 1988, however, it went Liberal again, being won by Rex Crawford, a farmer and former warden of Kent county and vice president of the National Farmers Union.

Crawford defended his seat again in 1993 against five challengers. Reform had high hopes for the riding, based on the strong performance (1,942 votes) by the Christian Heritage Party candidate in 1988. It nominated Arnold Broeders, a teacher and businessman from Chatham. Tom Suitor, a farmer from Chatham, represented the Tories. Aaron G. DeMeester, a quality control inspector from Chatham, ran for the NDP. Two minor party candidates had negligible impact on the campaign.

As elsewhere in the province, the 1993 campaign focused on the economy. One related local issue in Kent concerned the 'importation' of subsidized prairie grains for use as stock feed, a practice that hurt the prices farmers received for their own crops destined for this use. In the end, the Reform challenge fell considerably short and Crawford was able to extend his hold on the riding for the Liberals.

Member of Parliament: Rex Crawford; **Party**: Liberal; **Occupation**: Municipal politician; **Education**: Michigan State University and St Clair College; **Age**: 62 (Feb. 25, 1932); **Year first elected to the House of Commons**: 1988

35036 Kent

A: Political Profile
i) Voting Behaviour

	% 1993	% 1988	Change 1988-93
Conservative	13.8	35	-21.2
Liberal	63.8	40	23.8
NDP	3.8	20.1	-16.3
Reform	15.5	0	15.5
Other	3.2	4.9	-1.7

% Turnout	62.6	Total Ballots (#)	36588
Rejected Ballots (#)	250	% Margin of Victory	48.3
Rural Polls, 1988 (#)	66	Urban Polls, 1988 (#)	102
% Yes - 1992	37.6	% No - 1992	62

ii) Campaign Financing

	# of Donations	Total $ Value	% of Limit Spent
Conservative	105	27096	46.6*
Liberal	194	23180	48.5
NDP	41	13778	20
Reform	74	18204	43.3
Other	18	2466	

B: Ethno-Linguistic Profile

% English Home Language	95	% French Home Language	1.4
% Official Bilingual	7.1	% Other Home Language	3.6
% Catholics	36.6	% Protestants	54
% Aboriginal Peoples	3.9	% Immigrants	10.9

C: Socio-Economic Profile

Average Family Income $	47200	Median Family Income $	42669
% Low Income Families	13.1	Average Home Price $	104558
% Home Owners	66.7	% Unemployment	9.6
% Labour Force Participation	68.2	% Managerial-Administrative	10.2
% Self-Employed	10	% University Degrees	6.7
% Movers	42		

D: Industrial Profile

% Manufacturing	24.5	% Service Sector	12.1
% Agriculture	8.4	% Mining	0.6
% Forestry	0	% Fishing	0
% Government Services	5.4	% Business Services	2.7

E: Homogeneity Measures

Ethnic Diversity Index	0.31	Religious Homogeneity Index	0.42
Sectoral Concentration Index	0.36	Income Disparity Index	9.6

F: Physical Setting Characteristics

Total Population	83344	Area (km²)	1644
Population Density (pop/km²)	50.7		

* Tentative value, due to the existence of unpaid campaign expenses.

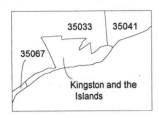

35033   35041

35067

Kingston and the
Islands

Kingston and the Islands

Constituency Number: 35037

Located at the head of the St Lawrence River, this eastern Ontario riding is centred upon the historic city of Kingston (former capital of the province of Canada). In addition, it includes several sparsely populated islands in Lake Ontario and the St. Lawrence. The city has a large public sector. Queen's University, the Royal Military College, the armed forces, and the penitentiary service (there are three federal prisons in the constituency) are the largest public sector employers. Alcan, Dupont, and Northern Telecom are large private sector employers in the riding.

Popular Tory MP and former cabinet minister Flora MacDonald held the seat for 16 years, ending with her narrow defeat at the hands of Peter Milliken, a lawyer, in 1988. Milliken faced six challengers in the 1993 campaign. Barry Gordon, a real estate broker and auctioneer, ran for the Conservatives. His campaign was not helped when the provincial Conservative leader predicted a Liberal majority government four days before the federal vote, during an interview preceding a dinner sponsored by the Tory riding association. Sean McAdam, a university student, ran for the Reform Party. The NDP nominated Mary Ann Higgs, a lawyer, who like Gordon also had to rise above her colleagues in her provincial party. The local MPP Gord Wilson (NDP) admitted that his government's restraint package had annoyed many of the provincial employees, university workers and health care workers who make up a substantial chunk of the riding's electorate. He acknowledged that this crisis of faith in the NDP could hurt the party's federal chances in the riding. Three minor party candidates rounded out the ballot.

The big issues here, as in many other communities, were jobs and the economy, including anxiety over NAFTA and the GATT. However, if crime and criminal justice was going to be an issue anywhere, most pundits predicted it would be in Kingston and the Islands, which is home to a handful of prisons including some of the nastiest in the country. In this community tougher crime laws mean not only safer streets but jobs as well. But few local candidates would dare campaign against 'law and order' and it was not an issue of importance in the campaign. A local spokesperson for the John Howard Society (a prisoners' advocacy and support group for parolees) noted that: 'Anxiety may be running high these days among Canadians, but we're more likely to be anxious about losing our jobs than being attacked by a paroled sex offender.' In addition, large federal property holdings in the area (the prisons, the Royal Military College, CFB Kingston, etc.) made the issue of the Grant-In-Lieu of Taxation an issue in this riding (at least among local government leaders).

In the end, Milliken romped to an easy victory, taking 56.5% of the poll.

Member of Parliament: Peter Andrew Stewart Milliken; **Party**: Liberal; **Occupation**: Lawyer; **Education**: LL.B; **Age**: 48 (Nov. 12, 1946); **Year first elected to the House of Commons**: 1988

35037 Kingston and the Islands

A: Political Profile

i) Voting Behaviour

	% 1993	% 1988	Change 1988-93
Conservative	19.1	35.9	-16.8
Liberal	56.5	40.6	15.9
NDP	7.1	20.1	-13
Reform	12.5	0	12.5
Other	5	3.4	1.6

% Turnout	60.6	Total Ballots (#)	57709
Rejected Ballots (#)	369	% Margin of Victory	37.4
Rural Polls, 1988 (#)	26	Urban Polls, 1988 (#)	230
% Yes - 1992	53.4	% No - 1992	46.1

ii) Campaign Financing

	# of Donations	Total $ Value	% of Limit Spent
Conservative	268	45592	82.9
Liberal	395	57089	70.2
NDP	173	29191	35.2
Reform	232	34653	49.4
Other	52	8794	

B: Ethno-Linguistic Profile

% English Home Language	94.6	% French Home Language	1.6
% Official Bilingual	11.8	% Other Home Language	3.8
% Catholics	31.7	% Protestants	52.4
% Aboriginal Peoples	0.6	% Immigrants	14.5

C: Socio-Economic Profile

Average Family Income $	54301	Median Family Income $	47891
% Low Income Families	14.9	Average Home Price $	166422
% Home Owners	53.9	% Unemployment	7.7
% Labour Force Participation	69.4	% Managerial-Administrative	11.1
% Self-Employed	7.2	% University Degrees	18
% Movers	55.6		

D: Industrial Profile

% Manufacturing	7.7	% Service Sector	19.6
% Agriculture	0.9	% Mining	0.2
% Forestry	0.1	% Fishing	0
% Government Services	14.8	% Business Services	4.6

E: Homogeneity Measures

Ethnic Diversity Index	0.42	Religious Homogeneity Index	0.37
Sectoral Concentration Index	0.57	Income Disparity Index	11.8

F: Physical Setting Characteristics

Total Population	106373	Area (km²)	785
Population Density (pop/km²)	135.5		

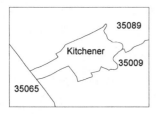

Kitchener

Constituency Number: 35038

Kitchener is a southern Ontario riding that takes in most of the city of the same name. A diversified local economy is based on a variety of light manufacturing and financial industries. Many of these industries originated in skills brought by the waves of German settlers who made the area their home in the nineteenth and early twentieth centuries (including a brewery which later became Labatt's). Rubber and tire manufactures, electrical appliance manufacturing, and two universities (Wilfrid Laurier and Waterloo) contribute to an extremely varied economic base that prospered during the boom of the 1980s, but fell back in the recession that led up to the 1993 election. Today, almost 15,500 residents are of German ancestry, and almost 9,000 speak the language.

In the past, Kitchener has mirrored the national vote at every election since 1958 (except 1963). Incumbent Conservative John Reimer, a former educator, first won the riding in 1979, lost it in 1980, regained it in 1984. In 1988, Reimer fended off a tough challenge from Liberal opponent John English, a history professor at the University of Waterloo and former editor of the *Canadian Historical Review*. Reg Gosse, a businessman who is credited by many for bringing Reform to Ontario, and denigrated by others as a racist, ran under the Reform banner. Ian MacFarlane, an occupational health and safety coordinator, ran for the NDP, while two minor party and one independent candidate ran with little effect in 1993.

From the very start of the campaign Reimer said he was fearful that the Reform candidate would steal enough votes to allow the Liberals to slip up the middle. Consequently, he spent much of his campaign trying to convince constituents that he could be more of a Reformer than the official Reform candidate. For example, Reimer said people should be forced to take any job that comes along or have their welfare support cut off. Nevertheless, Reimer ran directly into one of those situations Reform leader Preston Manning loves to deride, when Liberal challenger John English accused Reimer of abusing his Member's mailing privileges. Reimer had his MP's constituency newsletter (householder) prepared before the election and delivered it to Canada Post with orders not to mail it until the election writ was issued. This is indeed legal, but probably not good politics in this era of skeptical voters and easily impeachable virtue.

The big issue in Kitchener was of course the economy and the fate of the region's manufacturing sector. Big plant closings, such as the shut-down of a tire factory after the merger of Uniroyal and B.F. Goodrich, have racked the local economy for three years. The local press estimates the recession to have cost Kitchener approximately 6,000 jobs and 40 manufacturing plants. As well, the rollercoaster ride financial institutions took in the early 1990s sent shockwaves through the economy via restructuring drives at the area's insurance company head offices. Beyond this the most divisive issue in the riding was immigration and multiculturalism. Essentially John English and the NDP candidate, Ian MacFarlane, took supportive positions, while Gosse and Reimer took anti-immigration positions, though Reimer's stance was a bit more complex. He came down in favour of current immigration levels but was concerned that multicultural funding was being used for 'feel-good' cultural projects rather than necessary services to help new Canadians get settled and involved in their adopted communities. *Kitchener Waterloo Record* columnist Luisa D'Amato wrote a column titled 'Reformers Make Easy Targets for Racism Charges'. Her article dissected Gosse's (and Waterloo riding Reform candidate Mike Conolly's) views on the topic of immigration, showing where their cases were in error and their figures and statistics plain fabrications. Her conclusion, that the area Reform candidates were either incompetent or 'closet racists', generated a number of letters to the editor.

In the end Reimer did indeed lose to Liberal candidate John English on a split right-of-centre vote. The riding's bell-wether status had survived another election.

Member of Parliament: John Richard English; **Party**: Liberal; **Occupation**: Professor; **Education**: PhD; **Age**: 49 (January 26, 1945); **Year first elected to the House of Commons**: 1993

35038 Kitchener

A: Political Profile

i) Voting Behaviour

	% 1993	% 1988	Change 1988-93
Conservative	19.8	41.8	-22
Liberal	50.5	36.1	14.4
NDP	4.5	21.6	-17.1
Reform	23.2	0	23.2
Other	2	0.6	1.4

% Turnout	66.9	Total Ballots (#)	53131
Rejected Ballots (#)	437	% Margin of Victory	27.3
Rural Polls, 1988 (#)	0	Urban Polls, 1988 (#)	240
% Yes - 1992	48.8	% No - 1992	50.6

ii) Campaign Financing

	# of Donations	Total $ Value	% of Limit Spent
Conservative	115	27102	89.4
Liberal	261	76127	89.4
NDP	44	7984	7.9
Reform	123	28867	45.4
Other	44	12526	

B: Ethno-Linguistic Profile

% English Home Language	88.6	% French Home Language	0.3
% Official Bilingual	6.5	% Other Home Language	11.1
% Catholics	35.7	% Protestants	48.1
% Aboriginal Peoples	0.5	% Immigrants	23.5

C: Socio-Economic Profile

Average Family Income $	51996	Median Family Income $	47793
% Low Income Families	12.5	Average Home Price $	164662
% Home Owners	57.4	% Unemployment	9.3
% Labour Force Participation	71.7	% Managerial-Administrative	11.6
% Self-Employed	6.2	% University Degrees	10.1
% Movers	50.9		

D: Industrial Profile

% Manufacturing	26.4	% Service Sector	11.9
% Agriculture	0.5	% Mining	0
% Forestry	0.1	% Fishing	0
% Government Services	4.4	% Business Services	4.6

E: Homogeneity Measures

Ethnic Diversity Index	0.23	Religious Homogeneity Index	0.36
Sectoral Concentration Index	0.4	Income Disparity Index	8.1

F: Physical Setting Characteristics

Total Population	110950	Area (km^2)	49
Population Density (pop/km^2)	2264.3		

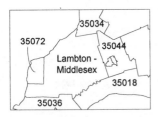

Lambton–Middlesex

Constituency Number: 35039

In this predominantly rural riding that surrounds the city of Sarnia in southwestern Ontario, diverse farming activities (beef cattle, hog farming and cash cropping, especially corn, wheat and soybeans) dominate economic activity. In fact, the riding has the highest proportion of its workforce employed in agriculture of any constituency in the province. However, many residents in the Lambton portion of the riding work in the Chemical Valley along the St Clair River. The recession put paid to the furniture industry centred on Strathroy, Ontario, making industrial jobs a local issue in the riding in the 1993 campaign.

The riding was created in the re-distribution of 1976 and until 1988 it seemed to be following national trends, see-sawing back and forth between the Liberals and the Conservatives. However, in 1988 Liberal Ralph Ferguson ended this tradition by winning the riding after a close race. With the departure of Ralph Ferguson prior to the 1993 campaign, the Liberals stayed close to home and nominated one of his constituency workers, registered nurse and long-time party and community activist Rose-Marie Ur, as his replacement. Challenging her for the seat for the Conservatives was David Crone, a businessman from Komoka. Randy Dayman, an electrician from Camlachie, carried the Reform banner. Following up a strong (2,467-vote) debut in 1988 that probably was crucial in the Liberal victory at that time, the Christian Heritage Party ran a vigorous campaign behind Ken Willis, an upholsterer from Wardsville. This time, however, the CHP would probably hurt Reform most of all. The NDP, which has traditionally found this difficult terrain, nominated Jamie Hamilton, a family support worker from Parkhill. Two other minor party and one independent candidate rounded out the ballot in 1993.

National party platforms and leaders' images dominated the campaign even more than is normally the case as none of the candidates had a particularly strong local reputation. Lambton–Middlesex candidates also had to deal with the Stoney Point Nation-Department of Defence dispute. During World War II the Department of Defence used the War Powers Act to expropriate the land of the Stoney Point Nation to create Camp Ipperwash. The First People have since been compensated for the land but they have never given up their demand that the land be returned to them and that they be issued an apology for the way they were treated during the War. It appears that the expropriation was not thoughtfully carried out and many people found themselves without adequate provision or shelter as winter approached, with the consequent onset of illnesses and loss of life. With the base declared more or less surplus before the election, it appeared they would get the land back, but the issue was not to be easily settled. With the return of the lands stalled, the Stoney Point people decided to use the election as an opportunity to gain attention for their cause. Their efforts took two approaches, a march on Ottawa and regular attendance at Lambton–Middlessex and other neighbouring ridings all-candidates meetings. They also tried to put questions to the party leaders as they toured the region, succeeding in the case of Prime Minister Campbell, who promised to have an official review the negotiation and report back to her.

While Rose-Marie Ur did not exactly sweep the riding, she did win by a comfortable margin, topping the combined Reform/PC total vote. This returns Lambton-Middlesex to its conventional position of acting as a bell-wether riding.

Member of Parliament: Rose-Marie Margaret Ur; **Party**: Liberal; **Occupation**: Farmer and constituency assistant; **Education**: Registered Nursing Assistant; **Age**: 48 (July 28, 1946); **Year first elected to the House of Commons**: 1993

35039 Lambton–Middlesex

A: Political Profile
i) Voting Behaviour

	% 1993	% 1988	Change 1988-93
Conservative	22.5	40.4	-17.9
Liberal	48.6	41.5	7.1
NDP	3.6	12.1	-8.5
Reform	19.4	0	19.4
Other	5.9	5.9	0

% Turnout	70.8	Total Ballots (#)	42001
Rejected Ballots (#)	225	% Margin of Victory	26.1
Rural Polls, 1988 (#)	168	Urban Polls, 1988 (#)	22
% Yes - 1992	44.8	% No - 1992	54.7

ii) Campaign Financing

	# of Donations	Total $ Value	% of Limit Spent
Conservative	103	31790	95.7
Liberal	307	50636	76.8
NDP	41	8281	16.4
Reform	74	19683	31
Other	115	20413	

B: Ethno-Linguistic Profile

% English Home Language	97	% French Home Language	0.3
% Official Bilingual	4.1	% Other Home Language	2.7
% Catholics	24.2	% Protestants	66.8
% Aboriginal Peoples	0.7	% Immigrants	12

C: Socio-Economic Profile

Average Family Income $	54622	Median Family Income $	48645
% Low Income Families	6.7	Average Home Price $	140992
% Home Owners	81.1	% Unemployment	6.4
% Labour Force Participation	71.4	% Managerial-Administrative	11.7
% Self-Employed	16.5	% University Degrees	7
% Movers	39		

D: Industrial Profile

% Manufacturing	15.7	% Service Sector	9.8
% Agriculture	16.1	% Mining	0.7
% Forestry	0.2	% Fishing	0
% Government Services	4.4	% Business Services	2.9

E: Homogeneity Measures

Ethnic Diversity Index	0.43	Religious Homogeneity Index	0.49
Sectoral Concentration Index	0.33	Income Disparity Index	10.9

F: Physical Setting Characteristics

Total Population	80663	Area (km^2)	4392
Population Density (pop/km^2)	18.4		

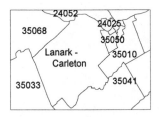

Lanark–Carleton

Constituency Number: 35040

Lanark-Carleton is an eastern Ontario riding that contains the western Ottawa suburb of Kanata, the small towns of Carleton Place, Perth, Smiths Falls and quite a lot of farm land as well. Public servants constitute an important portion of the local electorate; the riding ranks eighth on the measure of government service employment in Ontario. Otherwise, the economy is a diverse mix of light industrial, farming, and service industries.

Until 1993 the riding was the political fiefdom of six-time Conservative veteran Paul Dick, a lawyer who was appointed Minister of Supply and Services and Public Works in the short-lived Kim Campbell government. The issues that preoccupied the rest of the Ottawa-Carleton region were magnified in the riding because Dick was the only government incumbent in the whole region. Every group that had a disagreement with the government targeted Dick during the election campaign. Business groups, such as the Ottawa Board of Trade, aggressively pushed for approval of new air routes to connect Ottawa directly to major American business centres. Dick eventually won some ground on this front (12 days before the election). Just before election day Dick also managed to secure a federal grant for the new Ottawa hockey arena which is being built in the eastern part of the riding. However, civil servants, upset with the Campbell government's plans to reduce the civil service, also had Dick in their sights. Finally, the recent recession, free trade, and an over-valued Canadian dollar played havoc in the small towns of the riding, such as Perth, which were once thriving centres of light industry and consumer product manufacturing. These developments made unemployment an issue in the riding.

Challenging Dick for the Liberals was Ian Murray, a director of government relations for Northern Telecom from Carp. Earlier reports speculating that former agriculture minister (in a Trudeau administration) Eugene Whelan might offer for the Liberals were not borne out in the 1993 campaign. Dick was also under the gun from the right of the political spectrum. It appears the Reform Party targeted the riding as one of those traditionally conservative suburban-rural ridings that, totally disillusioned with the Tories, were potential bastions of Reform support. It nominated Ron MacDonald, a consultant from Kanata. During the campaign Reform leader Preston Manning held a rally in Smiths Falls (in the south of the riding) which was attended by 300 people, mostly former Conservative supporters. Judie McSkimmings, a conference coordinator from Kanata, carried the NDP banner in this traditionally infertile ground. Five minor party candidates attracted only a handful of votes.

In the end Dick and MacDonald evenly split the right of centre vote, but their combined total still fell a couple of thousand votes short of Liberal candidate Ian Murray's total.

Member of Parliament: Ian Munro Murray; **Party**: Liberal; **Occupation**: Researcher and lobbyist; **Education**: BA (History); **Age**: 43 (May 7, 1951); **Year first elected to the House of Commons**: 1993

35040 Lanark–Carleton

A: Political Profile

i) Voting Behaviour

	% 1993	% 1988	Change 1988-93
Conservative	23.6	48	-24.4
Liberal	49.4	35.6	13.8
NDP	2.4	14.7	-12.3
Reform	22.2	0	22.2
Other	2.4	1.7	0.7

% Turnout	72.7	Total Ballots (#)	71112
Rejected Ballots (#)	279	% Margin of Victory	25.8
Rural Polls, 1988 (#)	142	Urban Polls, 1988 (#)	107
% Yes - 1992	50.1	% No - 1992	49.5

ii) Campaign Financing

	# of Donations	Total $ Value	% of Limit Spent
Conservative	255	98015	96.1
Liberal	232	36043	70.6*
NDP	42	9664	7.1
Reform	236	33730	54.7
Other	46	11181	

B: Ethno-Linguistic Profile

% English Home Language	96.7	% French Home Language	1.4
% Official Bilingual	17.3	% Other Home Language	1.9
% Catholics	29.8	% Protestants	55.3
% Aboriginal Peoples	0.6	% Immigrants	10.9

C: Socio-Economic Profile

Average Family Income $	61806	Median Family Income $	57409
% Low Income Families	6	Average Home Price $	155659
% Home Owners	80	% Unemployment	5.9
% Labour Force Participation	73.7	% Managerial-Administrative	17.4
% Self-Employed	10.2	% University Degrees	16.1
% Movers	51		

D: Industrial Profile

% Manufacturing	13.2	% Service Sector	9.5
% Agriculture	3.3	% Mining	0.2
% Forestry	0.1	% Fishing	0
% Government Services	15.1	% Business Services	9.4

E: Homogeneity Measures

Ethnic Diversity Index	0.48	Religious Homogeneity Index	0.4
Sectoral Concentration Index	0.43	Income Disparity Index	7.1

F: Physical Setting Characteristics

Total Population	122945	Area (km²)	4292
Population Density (pop/km²)	28.6		

* Tentative value, due to the existence of unpaid campaign expenses.

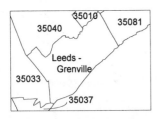

Leeds–Grenville

Constituency Number: 35041

Leeds–Grenville follows the St Lawrence River in eastern Ontario, and incorporates the two counties that give the riding its name. It is primarily a rural riding, but it also includes such riverside communities as Gananoque, Brockville, and Prescott and takes in the famous 'Thousand Islands' district. Farming, tourism, and light manufacturing industry dominate the riding's diversified economy. Brockville, a historic town and the largest population centre in the riding, is home to a variety of pharmaceutical, electrical/electronic, and chemical industries.

The riding changed partisan hands in 1988. It had elected Conservative members since 1968, and was represented by Tom Cossitt from 1972 until his death in 1982. His wife, Jennifer, took over as the riding's MP in a by-election in 1982, and retained the seat in 1984. In 1988, however, she was defeated by Jim Jordan, a retired administrator in the separate schools system who had narrowly missed being elected in a provincial election that preceded the federal one. Jordan's 1988 campaign emphasized the potentially negative local effects of the Free Trade Agreement, a particular concern in this border constituency.

To challenge Jordan in 1993, the Tories nominated Sandra Lawn, a consultant and teacher from Prescott. The Reform Party ran Paul West, a computer consultant also from Prescott. Mary Ann Greenwood, a homemaker from Brockville, ran for the NDP. Four minor party candidates ran also but failed to have an appreciable effect on the outcome.

The key issue in this riding was jobs and economic issues. Even though it had not been hit as hard as other parts of eastern Ontario, people were still concerned about the future. Jim Jordan, a grandfather of ten, repeated his victory in 1993, this time by choosing to campaign against Brian Mulroney. 'I am going to do my darndest for the next five weeks to make sure you don't forget him,' Jordan told the audience at an all-candidates meeting in Brockville. While the Conservatives managed one of their ten best finishes in the province here (and the NDP registered its worst) Jordan's message apparently got through, as he won with over 50% of the poll.

Member of Parliament: Jim Jordan; **Party**: Liberal; **Occupation**: Director of Education; **Education**: MSc; **Age**: 66 (Sept. 2, 1928); **Year first elected to the House of Commons**: 1988

35041 Leeds–Grenville

A: Political Profile

i) Voting Behaviour

	% 1993	% 1988	Change 1988-93
Conservative	26.9	38.9	-12
Liberal	52.6	43.4	9.2
NDP	2	11.1	-9.1
Reform	16	0	16
Other	2.5	6.6	-4.1

% Turnout	72.1	Total Ballots (#)	50791
Rejected Ballots (#)	252	% Margin of Victory	25.7
Rural Polls, 1988 (#)	143	Urban Polls, 1988 (#)	91
% Yes - 1992	41	% No - 1992	58.6

ii) Campaign Financing

	# of Donations	Total $ Value	% of Limit Spent
Conservative	305	69289	93
Liberal	158	43316	85.4
NDP	22	9655	12*
Reform	63	10081	14.2
Other	17	2692	

B: Ethno-Linguistic Profile

% English Home Language	98.5	% French Home Language	0.6
% Official Bilingual	7.9	% Other Home Language	0.9
% Catholics	22.6	% Protestants	66.7
% Aboriginal Peoples	0.4	% Immigrants	8.9

C: Socio-Economic Profile

Average Family Income $	48787	Median Family Income $	44069
% Low Income Families	9.4	Average Home Price $	124958
% Home Owners	73.6	% Unemployment	6.5
% Labour Force Participation	66	% Managerial-Administrative	11.9
% Self-Employed	10.3	% University Degrees	8.3
% Movers	43		

D: Industrial Profile

% Manufacturing	18.2	% Service Sector	12.6
% Agriculture	5.1	% Mining	0.2
% Forestry	0.2	% Fishing	0
% Government Services	9.1	% Business Services	4.1

E: Homogeneity Measures

Ethnic Diversity Index	0.57	Religious Homogeneity Index	0.49
Sectoral Concentration Index	0.4	Income Disparity Index	9.7

F: Physical Setting Characteristics

Total Population	90235	Area (km²)	3758
Population Density (pop/km²)	24		

* Tentative value, due to the existence of unpaid campaign expenses.

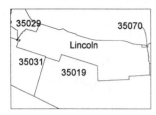

Lincoln

Constituency Number: 35042

The riding of Lincoln extends around the shore of Lake Ontario on the Niagara Peninsula, south of Hamilton. It includes a mixture of urban and rural areas. On the western end of the riding is some heavy and light industrial spillover from the city of Hamilton (the riding ranks among the top ten in the province on manufacturing employment), whereas the east is dominated by the agricultural production (especially grape and fruit growing) for which the region is famous. The recession caused serious dislocation among the manufacturers of Stoney Creek and trade liberalizations (especially the Free Trade Agreement) were blamed for lowering the fruit prices earned by the riding's orchards. Cross-border shopping and smuggling were also matters of concern to local retailers.

For more than the past 40 years, the riding has had the reputation of swinging with the national result and 1993 was to be no exception. It was taken as part of the 1984 Mulroney sweep for the Conservatives by Shirley Martin. Martin, who served briefly as a Tory cabinet minister prior to the 1988 election, narrowly held the riding (about a 400-vote margin) against a strong Liberal challenge by veteran MP John Munro at that time. With the Christian Heritage Party also registering a strong showing in the 1988 campaign (winning 2,700 votes), and in light of the unpopularity of the outgoing Conservative government, the Tories' prospects for holding this riding in 1993 looked bleak.

Jim Merritt, businessman with a school bus company from Grimsby, was the unfortunate person who had to defend the Tory record in the wake of Martin's retirement. One issue that did play well for the Tories locally was their proposal to purchase helicopters for national defence. In a reminder that not everyone opposed the Tories' plans to buy a large number of new naval helicopters, local aerospace firm Fleet Industries said it was re-evaluating its expansion plans in the light of the serious controversy the purchase had aroused. A spokesperson said that a Liberal victory would mean the cancellation of the firm's expansion plans. The Liberals' nomination race was acrimonious. Former senior Liberal cabinet minister John Munro withdrew from the race in April 1993 claiming that the party brass favoured Tony Valeri, an insurance consultant and realtor from Stoney Creek. Munro claimed that the Liberal organizers leaked the cutoff date for signing up new members to Valeri. Munro joined with would-be Liberal candidate Peter Li Preti (York Centre) in launching a court challenge to the national Liberal practice of allowing the party leader to nominate a candidate. This had no effect on the local race, however, as Valeri carried the Liberal banner in the campaign. Reform put up a credible candidate in Andy Sweck, a 39-year-old Stelco supervisor. Sweck kicked off the campaign with style, cutting the red ribbon on his campaign office door (actually a two by four) with a chainsaw with which he promised to cut government spending if elected. Peter Cassidy, a lawyer from Hamilton, ran for the NDP. Two minor party and one independent candidates rounded out the ballot, but had little impact.

Violent crime and the safety of women and children were constantly in the news in this riding due to the Teale and Homolka trials. The trial of Paul Teale accused in the murder of Mahaffy and French was just beginning as the election writ fell and that of his wife Karla Homolka in nearby St Catharines had just ended a couple of months before the writ. Homolka's trial caused controversy in that she was allowed to plead guilty to manslaughter only and was sentenced to just 12 years. The reason this plea was allowed were kept secret by a court ban on the publication of any further information about her trial.

In the end, after a heavy turnout, the Liberal candidate, Tony Valeri won by a comfortable margin over Sweck and even out-paced the combined Conservative/Reform total.

Member of Parliament: Tony Valeri; **Party**: Liberal; **Occupation**: Businessperson; **Education**: BA; **Age**: 37 (Aug. 11, 1957); **Year first elected to the House of Commons**: 1993

35042 Lincoln

A: Political Profile
i) Voting Behaviour

	% 1993	% 1988	Change 1988-93
Conservative	15.7	38.6	-22.9
Liberal	52.2	37.7	14.5
NDP	3.9	17.5	-13.6
Reform	25.7	0	25.7
Other	2.5	6.2	-3.7

% Turnout	72.1	Total Ballots (#)	56200
Rejected Ballots (#)	544	% Margin of Victory	26.5
Rural Polls, 1988 (#)	0	Urban Polls, 1988 (#)	194
% Yes - 1992	46.4	% No - 1992	53

ii) Campaign Financing

	# of Donations	Total $ Value	% of Limit Spent
Conservative	110	35492	70.3
Liberal	202	62531	79.2
NDP	66	18769	27.7
Reform	148	28850	59.5
Other	15	3780	

B: Ethno-Linguistic Profile

% English Home Language	89.8	% French Home Language	0.3
% Official Bilingual	4.7	% Other Home Language	9.9
% Catholics	39.5	% Protestants	44.3
% Aboriginal Peoples	0.3	% Immigrants	23.6

C: Socio-Economic Profile

Average Family Income $	55701	Median Family Income $	50985
% Low Income Families	10.8	Average Home Price $	195523
% Home Owners	74.4	% Unemployment	8.8
% Labour Force Participation	69.7	% Managerial-Administrative	12.4
% Self-Employed	7.7	% University Degrees	8.2
% Movers	42.9		

D: Industrial Profile

% Manufacturing	26.3	% Service Sector	10.1
% Agriculture	3.8	% Mining	0.1
% Forestry	0.1	% Fishing	0
% Government Services	4.4	% Business Services	4.3

E: Homogeneity Measures

Ethnic Diversity Index	0.24	Religious Homogeneity Index	0.36
Sectoral Concentration Index	0.38	Income Disparity Index	8.5

F: Physical Setting Characteristics

Total Population	105621	Area (km²)	343
Population Density (pop/km²)	307.9		

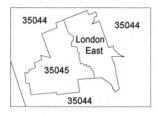

35044

35044

London East

35045

35044

London East

Constituency Number: 35043

London East is a typical urban melting pot of cultures and economic activities. The population is one of the most restless in the province, with the riding ranking in the top ten in terms of residential mobility, whether this is measured over a one-year or a five-year period. As with most urban ridings in this region, London East has seen its share of job losses, business closings and public sector cut-backs. In particular, London East lost a valuable economic driver when the federal government closed the Canadian Forces Base in the riding. Residents in the riding joined with others in the city in being shocked when the Northern Telecom factory in neighbouring London West was closed. Even though the factory was profitable and had a sizeable order book (workers often did overtime), the company chose it for closure. What made the closing worse for the Conservatives was that it took place in the riding of International Trade Minister Tom Hockin (London West). Doubtless some voters would wonder what a backbench Tory MP might be able to do to keep jobs in the riding if a minister was unsuccessful in this respect. It seemed to confirm people's worst fears about the Conservatives, that they really did not care how many unemployed people there were in Canada. A campaign visit in late September by Prime Minister Campbell unfortunately appeared to confirm this view. As one person who heard her speak in the city noted: 'They [jobs] were last on PM Kim Campbell's issues list, behind taxes, the deficit, inflation and trade.'

London East has traditionally been Liberal, having been represented for the party in Ottawa for most of the 1968-1984 period by Charles Turner. After Turner's appointment to the Senate, Jim Jepson took the seat in 1984 for the Tories as part of Mulroney's 211-seat sweep of the country that year. The 1988 contest was tightly contested, but Joe Fontana, an insurance broker and veteran of a decade of local politics, won the seat back for the Liberals by a narrow 102-vote margin. Rob Alder, an epidemiologist, won the Tory nomination in 1993, while Paul Cheng, a consultant in the oil and gas industry, stood for the Reform Party. Reform was hoping for a big breakthrough in the London area. Preston Manning's visit to the city in the last week of the campaign saw 2,000 people pay to attend a Reform rally. Alfredo Marroquin, a director with Global House, ran for the NDP. Five minor party candidates rounded out the ballot, but had negligible impact on the outcome.

International politics became a local issue in this riding when incumbent Liberal MP Joe Fontana demanded the deportation of the wife and family of Somali warlord Mohamed Farrah Aidid who had somehow come to live in London and were collecting welfare support. None of the other candidates seemed as aggressive on the issue as Fontana, arguing that there should be inquiries; if she had broken any laws, then deportation should be considered. In the end Fontana easily retained his seat with a 37% margin of victory.

Member of Parliament: Joseph Frank Fontana; **Party**: Liberal; **Occupation**: Businessperson; **Education**: University of Waterloo and University of Western Ontario; **Age**: 44 (Jan. 13, 1950); **Year first elected to the House of Commons**: 1988

35043 London East

A: Political Profile
i) Voting Behaviour

	% 1993	% 1988	Change 1988-93
Conservative	18.2	37.5	-19.3
Liberal	55.8	37.7	18.1
NDP	5.2	24.4	-19.2
Reform	17.2	0	17.2
Other	3.6	0.4	3.2

% Turnout	58.9	Total Ballots (#)	51076
Rejected Ballots (#)	424	% Margin of Victory	37.6
Rural Polls, 1988 (#)	0	Urban Polls, 1988 (#)	219
% Yes - 1992	52.3	% No - 1992	47.2

ii) Campaign Financing

	# of Donations	Total $ Value	% of Limit Spent
Conservative	263	50495	91.9
Liberal	137	43106	72.5
NDP	70	12510	11.6
Reform	154	36267	46.8
Other	24	4031	

B: Ethno-Linguistic Profile

% English Home Language	90.9	% French Home Language	0.3
% Official Bilingual	6.8	% Other Home Language	8.8
% Catholics	29.2	% Protestants	49.3
% Aboriginal Peoples	1.4	% Immigrants	20.3

C: Socio-Economic Profile

Average Family Income $	50102	Median Family Income $	42812
% Low Income Families	20	Average Home Price $	159097
% Home Owners	47.1	% Unemployment	10.5
% Labour Force Participation	69.2	% Managerial-Administrative	11.6
% Self-Employed	6.3	% University Degrees	14.8
% Movers	57.8		

D: Industrial Profile

% Manufacturing	14.7	% Service Sector	14.7
% Agriculture	1	% Mining	0.1
% Forestry	0.1	% Fishing	0
% Government Services	5.6	% Business Services	5.8

E: Homogeneity Measures

Ethnic Diversity Index	0.34	Religious Homogeneity Index	0.35
Sectoral Concentration Index	0.5	Income Disparity Index	14.6

F: Physical Setting Characteristics

Total Population	106359	Area (km²)	45
Population Density (pop/km²)	2363.5		

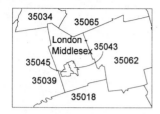

London–Middlesex

Constituency Number: 35044

London–Middlesex is a unique doughnut-shaped riding that totally surrounds the two central London ridings (London East and London West). This constituency offers a bit of everything: cities, suburbs and genuine rural areas. It includes some employees from the concentration of industries in east London, and some heavily populated areas in the city's south. Residents are slightly less affluent than the Ontario norm, with average family incomes falling approximately $4,000 below the corresponding provincial figure. As elsewhere in the province, jobs were the central concern of the local electorate in 1993. In this respect all of the London–Middlesex voters were shocked when the Northern Telecom factory in neighbouring London West was closed. Even though the factory was profitable and had a sizeable order book (workers often did overtime) the company chose it for closure. The work could simply be done even cheaper and with more profit at other Northern Telecom factories. The closure was part of a world-wide company restructuring which saw the departure of the company's CEO and followed in the wake of Northern Telecom's posting one of the largest yearly losses in Canadian corporate history.

The riding has changed partisan hands often since its creation in the late 1970s, and until 1988, the electorate had the distinction of never returning an incumbent MP for a second term. This pattern was broken in 1988, however, when Tory Terry Clifford managed to hold on to the seat by the slimmest of margins (in fact, only eight votes separated Clifford from the second-place Liberal challenger, making this the closest race in the country for that election). Sensing the tide turning against the Conservatives, Clifford resigned prior to the 1993 campaign. The absence of an incumbent, and the closeness of the 1988 race, called forth a strong slate of candidates. Clifford was replaced by Tory candidate Ed Holder, a group benefits worker. Pat O'Brien, a high school teacher, community activist, and local politician, won the Liberal nomination. The Reform party nomination went to Mark Simpson, a horticultural services worker from Komoka. Reform was hoping for a big breakthrough in the London area. Preston Manning's visit to the city in the last week of the campaign saw 2,000 people pay to attend a Reform rally. Carolyn Davies, a nurse practitioner, ran for the NDP. Six minor parties ran candidates in the 1993 campaign, including three students (one of whom, Sven Briggs, was an 18-year-old high school student, running for the Greens).

None of the minor party candidates had any appreciable impact on the outcome, and the race surprised many in not even being competitive. On election day, the riding voted overwhelmingly for O'Brien and the Liberal Party.

Member of Parliament: Patrick W. O'Brien; **Party**: Liberal; **Occupation**: Teacher; **Education**: MEd, University of Western Ontario; **Age**: 46 (Jan. 13, 1948); **Year first elected to the House of Commons**: 1993

35044 London–Middlesex

A: Political Profile
i) Voting Behaviour

	% 1993	% 1988	Change 1988-93
Conservative	18.1	38.3	-20.2
Liberal	53.9	38.3	15.6
NDP	5.3	23	-17.7
Reform	19.4	0	19.4
Other	3.4	0.4	3

% Turnout	65.8	Total Ballots (#)	50925
Rejected Ballots (#)	372	% Margin of Victory	34.5
Rural Polls, 1988 (#)	54	Urban Polls, 1988 (#)	130
% Yes - 1992	46.3	% No - 1992	53.3

ii) Campaign Financing

	# of Donations	Total $ Value	% of Limit Spent
Conservative	85	38270	98.3*
Liberal	200	43082	73.9
NDP	73	17553	15.7
Reform	76	18272	30.4
Other	65	6794	

B: Ethno-Linguistic Profile

% English Home Language	92.5	% French Home Language	0.2
% Official Bilingual	5.1	% Other Home Language	7.3
% Catholics	30.5	% Protestants	52.4
% Aboriginal Peoples	0.5	% Immigrants	19.2

C: Socio-Economic Profile

Average Family Income $	52433	Median Family Income $	47872
% Low Income Families	11.3	Average Home Price $	153273
% Home Owners	68.8	% Unemployment	7.7
% Labour Force Participation	75.2	% Managerial-Administrative	11.6
% Self-Employed	8	% University Degrees	7.8
% Movers	52		

D: Industrial Profile

% Manufacturing	18.2	% Service Sector	12.6
% Agriculture	3.8	% Mining	0.1
% Forestry	0	% Fishing	0
% Government Services	4.6	% Business Services	4.2

E: Homogeneity Measures

Ethnic Diversity Index	0.35	Religious Homogeneity Index	0.38
Sectoral Concentration Index	0.42	Income Disparity Index	8.7

F: Physical Setting Characteristics

Total Population	110996	Area (km²)	1208
Population Density (pop/km²)	91.9		

* Tentative value, due to the existence of unpaid campaign expenses.

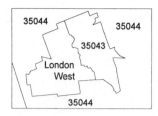

London West

Constituency Number: 35045

London West is a heavily residential urban riding that takes in part of the city of London's downtown core. One sixth of the landmass of the city of London is devoted to park and open space land, and several of the largest parks are located in this constituency. London West is the most affluent of the three London seats; average family incomes are about $6,000 higher than the norm for ridings in the province. It is home to the University of Western Ontario. Students comprise a relatively large proportion of the riding's residents, and the university is an important force in the riding's economy. Like other London constituencies, the electorate in London West is primarily of English background. Employment is concentrated in diverse manufacturing, financial, and other services.

Like the other two London ridings, London West's electorate was shocked when the Northern Telecom factory in the riding was closed. The story was front page news in the *London Free Press*. Even though the factory was profitable and had a sizeable order book (workers often did overtime) the work could simply be done even cheaper and with more profit at other Northern Telecom factories. Though Northern Telecom officials refused to comment on where specifically work would be relocated, it appeared that much was re-assigned to the company's plants in the USA and non-unionized plants in Western Canada. The closure was part of a world-wide company restructuring which saw the departure of the company's CEO and Northern Telecom's posting one of the largest yearly losses in Canadian corporate history. The closing scotched London Mayor Chip Martin's plans to build an educational-industrial centre of excellence in the field of computers and communications, based on a partnership of the city, the University of Western Ontario, and Northern Telecom. London West's MP at the time was Tom Hockin, a former political scientist and Minister for International Trade. Overall, the affair seemed to confirm people's worst fears about the outgoing Tory administration, namely that they really did not care about how many unemployed people there were in Canada. A campaign visit by Prime Minister Campbell unfortunately appeared to confirm this view. One person who heard her speak noted: 'They [jobs] were last on PM Kim Campbell's issues list, behind taxes, the deficit, inflation and trade.'

As with all other Progressive Conservative cabinet ministers, Hockin's riding was targeted by the Public Service Alliance of Canada for priority defeat. However, local PSAC members chose not to endorse any one of his challengers. The union's 1,200 members in the greater London area decided to concentrate their local election kitty of about $4,000 on defeating Hockin. It is uncertain what impact the large number of University of Western Ontario students resident in the riding had on Hockin's fate. However, the announced closing of the University's School of Journalism just before the start of the campaign possibly drove home to them the tenuous state of funding for post-secondary education (a shared federal-provincial responsibility).

Hockin, who had represented the riding since 1984, faced ten challengers in 1993. The Liberals nominated Susan Barnes, a lawyer who is active in a number of local and national organizations. Reform nominated Todd Christensen, a lawyer, and had high hopes for a strong showing in the area. Preston Manning's visit to the city in the last week of the campaign drew about 2,000 people, each paying $5 to $10, to a noon-time Reform rally. The NDP ran Margaret Hoff, a university professor. Six minor party candidates stood for election, along with one independent, but none had any appreciable impact on the outcome.

On election night, Barnes was declared the winner by a 25% victory margin over second-place Tom Hockin.

Member of Parliament: Susan Barnes; **Party**: Liberal; **Occupation**: Lawyer; **Education**: LL.B; **Age**: 42 (Sept. 8, 1952); **Year first elected to the House of Commons**: 1993

35045 London West

A: Political Profile
i) Voting Behaviour

	% 1993	% 1988	Change 1988-93
Conservative	23.6	45.7	-22.1
Liberal	48.3	37.5	10.8
NDP	4	16.1	-12.1
Reform	20.1	0	20.1
Other	4.2	0.7	3.5

% Turnout	69.3	Total Ballots (#)	64804
Rejected Ballots (#)	465	% Margin of Victory	24.7
Rural Polls, 1988 (#)	0	Urban Polls, 1988 (#)	233
% Yes - 1992	55.8	% No - 1992	43.8

ii) Campaign Financing

	# of Donations	Total $ Value	% of Limit Spent
Conservative	316	71564	92.3
Liberal	221	69161	93.1
NDP	123	29195	25.3
Reform	158	46965	52.7
Other	67	9699	

B: Ethno-Linguistic Profile

% English Home Language	94.4	% French Home Language	0.3
% Official Bilingual	7.9	% Other Home Language	5.3
% Catholics	26	% Protestants	54.7
% Aboriginal Peoples	0.8	% Immigrants	19

C: Socio-Economic Profile

Average Family Income $	62232	Median Family Income $	53312
% Low Income Families	12	Average Home Price $	180586
% Home Owners	53.7	% Unemployment	7.2
% Labour Force Participation	68.9	% Managerial-Administrative	15
% Self-Employed	8.1	% University Degrees	20.3
% Movers	52.6		

D: Industrial Profile

% Manufacturing	11.5	% Service Sector	11.5
% Agriculture	0.7	% Mining	0.1
% Forestry	0.1	% Fishing	0
% Government Services	5.3	% Business Services	6.3

E: Homogeneity Measures

Ethnic Diversity Index	0.38	Religious Homogeneity Index	0.39
Sectoral Concentration Index	0.55	Income Disparity Index	14.3

F: Physical Setting Characteristics

Total Population	113959	Area (km²)	57
Population Density (pop/km²)	1999.3		

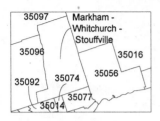

Markham–Whitchurch–Stouffville

Constituency Number: 35046

Markham–Whitchurch–Stouffville is a riding in transition. Once predominantly rural, the rapid growth of the metropolitan Toronto area meant that in little more than a decade it has become an urban riding. Among the longer term residents there are mixed feelings towards the newcomers. Development has meant enormous increases in their property values but also has robbed the area of its small town aura. Adding to the tension is the fact that many of the newcomers are Asian. The Chinese community in the riding has grown to over 20,000 in little more than a decade. Typical of the attitude is one ex-social worker who handled offender rehabilitation in the area. This person told the *Toronto Star* that over 80 per cent of her clients were 'imported from Asia'. However, the percentage of riding residents who are immigrants (37%) is not particularly high compared to other ridings in and around Metro Toronto. The riding is one of Ontario's most affluent and white-collar.

In this part of the world the economy is measured by housing prices and at the start of the election these were down from their pre-crash peaks by nearly 50% in some areas, leaving many homeowners with mortgages larger than the value of their homes (i.e., with unrenewable mortgages and unsaleable homes). The area has a large number of Chinese-Canadian small business owners. Many had become disenchanted with the Tories and entered the election uncommitted. Despite the controversy over the immigration and multiculturalism policy of the Reform Party, and the outright racism of one or two of its Metro area candidates, Reform was expected to do well in this riding.

The economy was not providing a sound environment for Tory incumbent and long-time party organizer Bill Attewell to run for re-election. A former trust company vice-president, Attewell had previously represented the riding of Don Valley East until boundary revisions prior to the 1988 election substantially altered that district and prompted him to move and run for re-election in Markham. He won handily in 1988, building up a margin of 14,700 votes over second-place finisher Liberal Jag Bhaduria, a management consultant and community activist. Bhaduria was back in 1993, however, to mount a challenge to Attewell. Also taking aim at the vulnerable Attewell were six other candidates. Joe Sherren, a business consultant from Stouffville ran for the Reform Party. The NDP nominated Markham resident Jack Grant, a company chairman. Three minor party and one independent candidate also ran, but did not attract much support.

Bhaduria's efforts paid off, and he won easily, with a 21% margin of victory. Curiously, the main story in this riding occurred after the election. In the early winter of 1994 MP Jag Bhaduria was expelled from the Liberal caucus. Liberal leader and PM Jean Chrétien decided that Bhaduria had presented misleading information about his career and credentials on his election material, claiming to be a law school graduate when in fact he was not. For his part, Bhaduria claimed that he put the letters 'int' after the degree title to indicate that the degree was incomplete and that the whole thing was a conspiracy to unseat him. However, according to the Liberal media guide, the biography which Bhaduria and his campaign team themselves submitted to the national office describes him as 'a lawyer who founded the east end legal assistance clinic'. He did not resign but rather has continued to sit as an independent member. Having an independent for an MP is not a new phenomenon here. In 1984, Tony Roman, a long-time mayor of Markham, won election as an independent Member.

Member of Parliament: Jag Bhaduria; **Party**: Independent Liberal; **Occupation**: Management consultant; **Education**: MSc (Physics); **Age**: 54; **Year first elected to the House of Commons**: 1993

35046 Markham–Whitchurch–Stouffville

A: Political Profile
i) Voting Behaviour

	% 1993	% 1988	Change 1988-93
Conservative	25.5	53.1	-27.6
Liberal	46.5	31.8	14.7
NDP	2.2	9	-6.8
Reform	23.2	0	23.2
Other	2.6	6.1	-3.5

% Turnout	70.2	Total Ballots (#)	77763
Rejected Ballots (#)	545	% Margin of Victory	21
Rural Polls, 1988 (#)	0	Urban Polls, 1988 (#)	260
% Yes - 1992	60.9	% No - 1992	38.5

ii) Campaign Financing

	# of Donations	Total $ Value	% of Limit Spent
Conservative	170	85345	92.3
Liberal	262	63332	81.4
NDP	39	8038	8.6
Reform	113	27746	33.2
Other	48	12012	

B: Ethno-Linguistic Profile

% English Home Language	81.9	% French Home Language	0.4
% Official Bilingual	7.9	% Other Home Language	17.7
% Catholics	27.4	% Protestants	37.2
% Aboriginal Peoples	0.1	% Immigrants	37.3

C: Socio-Economic Profile

Average Family Income $	78839	Median Family Income $	67730
% Low Income Families	7	Average Home Price $	343168
% Home Owners	83.4	% Unemployment	6.4
% Labour Force Participation	76	% Managerial-Administrative	21.4
% Self-Employed	12.6	% University Degrees	20.9
% Movers	53.5		

D: Industrial Profile

% Manufacturing	15.4	% Service Sector	8.2
% Agriculture	1.2	% Mining	0.2
% Forestry	0	% Fishing	0
% Government Services	4.7	% Business Services	11

E: Homogeneity Measures

Ethnic Diversity Index	0.19	Religious Homogeneity Index	0.28
Sectoral Concentration Index	0.48	Income Disparity Index	14.1

F: Physical Setting Characteristics

Total Population	172168	Area (km²)	424
Population Density (pop/km²)	406.1		

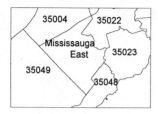

Mississauga East

Constituency Number: 35047

Mississauga East is a diversified riding in the city of Mississauga (named for the area's original inhabitants, the Mississauga, a band of the Ojibwa), a western suburb of Toronto. In fact, this riding is described has been described as a 'slice of suburbia'. It has a reasonable distribution of offices and light industry and is just across the highway from Pearson International Airport. The airport produced two worries in this riding. First, Transport Canada's long-standing desire to build a new north-south runway raised local concerns, and these were exacerbated by the way the department handled the privatization of Terminals 1 and 2, both of which seemed to indicate that residents' interests were not being attended to by the department. Approximately 43% of residents are classed as immigrants, with the highest concentrations coming from Italy, Portugal, Croatia, and China.

Mississauga East went from Liberal to Conservative as part of Mulroney's sweeping Conservative victory in 1984, but shifted back to the Liberals in the 1988 election. Winning the riding for the Grits was Albina Guarnieri, a management consultant and former aide to Toronto mayor Art Eggleton. Guarnieri's nomination as the Liberal candidate in the riding for the 1988 election was overturned because of irregularities in the voting, but she survived a second nomination process, and went on to win the seat in that election. Challenging Guarnieri in 1993 for the Conservatives was Car DeFaria, a lawyer, and the Reform Party nominated Peter Zathey, a computer analyst. John Jackson, a teacher, ran for the NDP, and was joined by two minor party and one independent candidate in not having much impact on the election outcome.

The usual concerns dominated the election, the economy, jobs, and good government. These conspired against the Conservative candidate. Liberal MP Albina Guarnieri, herself an immigrant from Italy, easily increased the approximately 2,092-vote plurality she won in 1988 into an absolute majority in 1993.

Member of Parliament: Albina Guarnieri; **Party**: Liberal; **Occupation**: Businesswoman; **Education**: MA, McGill University; **Age**: 41 (June 23, 1953); **Year first elected to the House of Commons**: 1988

35047 Mississauga East

A: Political Profile
i) Voting Behaviour

	% 1993	% 1988	Change 1988-93
Conservative	12.8	41.5	-28.7
Liberal	63.8	45.6	18.2
NDP	2.7	11.2	-8.5
Reform	18.8	0	18.8
Other	1.8	1.7	0.1

% Turnout	65.8	Total Ballots (#)	50755
Rejected Ballots (#)	369	% Margin of Victory	45
Rural Polls, 1988 (#)	0	Urban Polls, 1988 (#)	213
% Yes - 1992	54.4	% No - 1992	45.1

ii) Campaign Financing

	# of Donations	Total $ Value	% of Limit Spent
Conservative	81	23684	71.4
Liberal	60	41974	80.5
NDP	19	1605	11.5
Reform	123	18762	30
Other	16	2589	

B: Ethno-Linguistic Profile

% English Home Language	74.6	% French Home Language	0.6
% Official Bilingual	6.9	% Other Home Language	24.8
% Catholics	48.4	% Protestants	28.9
% Aboriginal Peoples	0.2	% Immigrants	43.2

C: Socio-Economic Profile

Average Family Income $	58065	Median Family Income $	52997
% Low Income Families	13	Average Home Price $	231169
% Home Owners	52.4	% Unemployment	8.8
% Labour Force Participation	75	% Managerial-Administrative	14.6
% Self-Employed	6.4	% University Degrees	13.1
% Movers	51		

D: Industrial Profile

% Manufacturing	21.7	% Service Sector	10.2
% Agriculture	0.3	% Mining	0.1
% Forestry	0	% Fishing	0
% Government Services	5	% Business Services	8

E: Homogeneity Measures

Ethnic Diversity Index	0.16	Religious Homogeneity Index	0.34
Sectoral Concentration Index	0.42	Income Disparity Index	8.7

F: Physical Setting Characteristics

Total Population	121584	Area (km²)	49
Population Density (pop/km²)	2481.3		

Mississauga South

Constituency Number: 35048

Mississauga South is a thin riding that extends along the shore of Lake Ontario between Etobicoke and Oakville, to the south of the City of Mississauga's two other parliamentary constituencies. It contains some of the most desirable residential areas in the city, and average home values are among the province's highest. Although the electorate is one of Ontario's ten most affluent (average family incomes are about $15,000 higher than the provincial norm), it had been hit by the recession. The economy is strong on professional (research and development) and industrial jobs.

This riding and its predecessors (before the 1976 redistribution) have a strong Tory tradition. Don Blenkarn, the outspoken Tory backbencher and chair of the House Finance Committee, had represented it since the 1970s. In the last two elections he won an outright majority of the votes. In any other election this might have been considered a safe Tory seat. However in 1993 the collapse of the NDP (meaning a unified vote on the left-of-centre) and the emergence of a powerful neo-conservative rival (meaning a split right-of-centre vote) put every Tory seat up for grabs and Blenkarn's was no exception. The dire economic straits at campaign time were symbolized in this riding by de-industrialization, entrepreneurial, professional and personal bankruptcies, and declining home prices. It was these types of ridings that the Reform Party was specifically looking for in Ontario. Blenkarn himself had been the target of a 'scurrilous mail' campaign between October 1991 and February 1992. Over this period, twenty letters that were deemed to contain 'obscene and racially hateful' material had been sent to his constituency office by a Mississauga man. The culprit was arrested and charged.

The Liberal candidate, Paul Szabo, a chartered accountant and community activist, faced Blenkarn for the third time in this election (although he had not run in the 1988 election). The Reform candidate was John Veenstra, an area realtor. Lili V. Weemen, a secretary from St Catharines, ran unsuccessfully for the NDP (registering the party's second lowest performance in the province). Four minor party and one independent candidate also contested the seat with little success.

In the middle of the campaign Blenkarn admitted that if he lost only 10% of his vote to Reform, and if the NDP's 10% went Liberal, he would be defeated. On election day he lost much more than 10%, plummeting to third place in the final total, with the Liberals taking a comfortable plurality over the split right-of-centre votes between the Reform and PC parties.

Member of Parliament: Paul John Mark Szabo; **Party:** Liberal; **Occupation:** Accountant; **Education:** MBA; **Age:** 46 (May 10, 1948); **Year first elected to the House of Commons:** 1993

35048 Mississauga South

A: Political Profile
i) Voting Behaviour

	% 1993	% 1988	Change 1988-93
Conservative	23.4	51.9	-28.5
Liberal	46.6	34.7	11.9
NDP	2.1	12	-9.9
Reform	25.1	0	25.1
Other	2.8	1.5	1.3

% Turnout	70.4	Total Ballots (#)	46445
Rejected Ballots (#)	343	% Margin of Victory	21.5
Rural Polls, 1988 (#)	0	Urban Polls, 1988 (#)	179
% Yes - 1992	56.9	% No - 1992	42.4

ii) Campaign Financing

	# of Donations	Total $ Value	% of Limit Spent
Conservative	159	36757	93.9
Liberal	66	34113	62.9
NDP	16	5652	5.8
Reform	144	47039	61.8
Other	32	8773	

B: Ethno-Linguistic Profile

% English Home Language	88.7	% French Home Language	0.6
% Official Bilingual	8.5	% Other Home Language	10.8
% Catholics	38	% Protestants	43.9
% Aboriginal Peoples	0.3	% Immigrants	29.1

C: Socio-Economic Profile

Average Family Income $	72560	Median Family Income $	61955
% Low Income Families	9.5	Average Home Price $	286564
% Home Owners	68.2	% Unemployment	7.4
% Labour Force Participation	73.2	% Managerial-Administrative	18
% Self-Employed	9.3	% University Degrees	16.5
% Movers	41.7		

D: Industrial Profile

% Manufacturing	18.7	% Service Sector	8.5
% Agriculture	0.6	% Mining	0.4
% Forestry	0.1	% Fishing	0
% Government Services	4.7	% Business Services	9.6

E: Homogeneity Measures

Ethnic Diversity Index	0.22	Religious Homogeneity Index	0.35
Sectoral Concentration Index	0.44	Income Disparity Index	14.6

F: Physical Setting Characteristics

Total Population	96208	Area (km²)	54
Population Density (pop/km²)	1781.6		

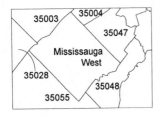

Mississauga West

Constituency Number: 35049

Ontario's fast-growing and second most populous riding, Mississauga West is located between the constituencies of Brampton and Mississauga South in the western suburbs of Metropolitan Toronto. Rapid growth has contributed to making this riding's electorate one of the most residentially mobile in the province. The local economy is dominated by light industrial, service, and commercial employers.

The riding has exhibited a slight tendency to swing between the two traditional major parties. Bob Horner swept to power in the Mulroney landslide of 1984, defeating the Liberal incumbent Doug Fisher. Horner held the seat with about a 7% margin over the Liberal challenger in 1988. A veterinarian and ex-RCMP officer, he might be best remembered by Canadian teenagers for his one-person campaign against rock and roll 'head shops': he was the moving force behind a criminal code amendment to prohibit the sale of drug paraphernalia and 'how to grow cannabis' books. In any other election this might not necessarily have been considered a 'safe' seat but certainly it would have been deemed an expected win by the Tories. However, the collapse of the NDP and the emergence of Reform (meaning a solid vote to the left of the Tories and a split vote on their own side of centre) put every single Conservative candidate in Ontario in jeopardy. Mississauga West was the type of riding that the Reform Party was specifically targeting in Ontario. If the economy was not necessarily going to help the incumbent Horner, the Pearson Airport Deal seemed likely to hurt him in 1993.

The Liberals experienced a tightly contested nomination race that saw the local membership numbers swell to over 15,000 in November 1992. It took five ballots and eight hours for the nomination meeting to select Carolyn Parrish, a secondary school teacher, freelance writer, community activist, and former chair of the Peel Regional School Board, as the Liberal candidate. Following her nomination, Parrish criticized the practice of having 'instant members' eligible to vote in nomination meetings. The spectacle was described as the largest nomination meeting in Canadian history. The Reform party selected Mississauga businessman and consultant Charles Corn. Paul Simon, a business agent who had unsuccessfully contested the seat in 1988, ran again for the NDP. Four minor party candidates also stood for election, though none of them won more than .5% of the vote.

According to the press, the race here had been expected to be close (just before voting day it was identified by the *Toronto Star* as one of the fifty 'tight races' to watch). However, in the end these expectations were unmet. Mississauga West turned into a rout and Parrish won easily.

Member of Parliament: Carolyn Parrish; **Party**: Liberal; **Occupation**: Teacher and writer, chairperson of public school board; **Education**: BEd; **Age**: 48 (1946); **Year first elected to the House of Commons**: 1993

35049 Mississauga West

A: Political Profile
i) Voting Behaviour

	% 1993	% 1988	Change 1988-93
Conservative	19.4	48.2	-28.8
Liberal	55.9	41.5	14.4
NDP	2.3	9.7	-7.4
Reform	21.1	0	21.1
Other	1.3	0.7	0.6

% Turnout	67.1	Total Ballots (#)	96468
Rejected Ballots (#)	589	% Margin of Victory	34.8
Rural Polls, 1988 (#)	0	Urban Polls, 1988 (#)	267
% Yes - 1992	58	% No - 1992	41.5

ii) Campaign Financing

	# of Donations	Total $ Value	% of Limit Spent
Conservative	80	50504	97.6
Liberal	148	82060	96.5
NDP	74	12337	12.8
Reform	157	26393	37.5
Other	13	4732	

B: Ethno-Linguistic Profile

% English Home Language	82.2	% French Home Language	0.7
% Official Bilingual	8.3	% Other Home Language	17.1
% Catholics	43.7	% Protestants	32.3
% Aboriginal Peoples	0.1	% Immigrants	37.9

C: Socio-Economic Profile

Average Family Income $	64948	Median Family Income $	60919
% Low Income Families	9.4	Average Home Price $	255065
% Home Owners	71.2	% Unemployment	7
% Labour Force Participation	79.2	% Managerial-Administrative	18.7
% Self-Employed	7.6	% University Degrees	17.1
% Movers	67.3		

D: Industrial Profile

% Manufacturing	19.5	% Service Sector	9.1
% Agriculture	0.4	% Mining	0.2
% Forestry	0	% Fishing	0
% Government Services	5.2	% Business Services	8.7

E: Homogeneity Measures

Ethnic Diversity Index	0.17	Religious Homogeneity Index	0.32
Sectoral Concentration Index	0.45	Income Disparity Index	6.2

F: Physical Setting Characteristics

Total Population	209706	Area (km²)	128
Population Density (pop/km²)	1638.3		

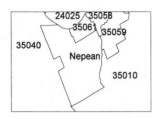

Nepean

Constituency Number: 35050

The suburban riding of Nepean is located to the west of the city of Ottawa in eastern Ontario. The area has grown extensively over the past couple of decades. The growth has generally been orderly, however, and the city of Nepean was named in 1988 by *Chatelaine* magazine as 'one of the ten best places to live in Canada'. The riding ranks among the top ten in the province in terms of average family incomes, university graduates, white-collar employees, and public service workers (although on the latter, the riding ranks behind several other Ottawa area ridings). Many are employed by the high technology industries that populate the western suburbs of Ottawa–Carleton.

Prior to 1988, the Nepean area had been solid Conservative territory. Since Confederation, only three Liberals had represented voters living here. 1988 saw the fourth Liberal, Beryl Gaffney, a former civil servant and Nepean city councillor, returned to the House of Commons.

Gaffney was challenged by nine candidates in 1993. Donna Hicks, a businesswoman, ran for the Conservatives, while the Reform nomination went to Gus Klovan, a local realtor. Nizam Siddiqui, a municipal civil servant, ran for the NDP. The remaining six candidates were running for minor parties, and none of them had any significant impact on the campaign.

After a heavy turnout (the province's third highest), Gaffney held on to the riding for the Liberals with an enormous majority of almost 15,500 votes.

Member of Parliament: Beryl Gaffney; **Party**: Liberal; **Occupation**: Advisor; **Education**: Prince of Wales College, P.E.I.; **Age**: 64 (April 1, 1930); **Year first elected to the House of Commons**: 1988

35050 Nepean

A: Political Profile
i) Voting Behaviour

	% 1993	% 1988	Change 1988-93
Conservative	17.8	41.5	-23.7
Liberal	59.6	47.2	12.4
NDP	3.4	10.8	-7.4
Reform	16.1	0	16.1
Other	3.1	0.5	2.6

% Turnout	74.5	Total Ballots (#)	61047
Rejected Ballots (#)	341	% Margin of Victory	41.8
Rural Polls, 1988 (#)	0	Urban Polls, 1988 (#)	189
% Yes - 1992	55.3	% No - 1992	44.3

ii) Campaign Financing

	# of Donations	Total $ Value	% of Limit Spent
Conservative	247	53207	81.5
Liberal	263	49548	90.8
NDP	85	19360	26.9
Reform	115	26636	43.6
Other	9	5846	

B: Ethno-Linguistic Profile

% English Home Language	89.8	% French Home Language	2.3
% Official Bilingual	26.9	% Other Home Language	7.9
% Catholics	40	% Protestants	39
% Aboriginal Peoples	0.4	% Immigrants	19.7

C: Socio-Economic Profile

Average Family Income $	69686	Median Family Income $	63549
% Low Income Families	8.6	Average Home Price $	185281
% Home Owners	64.6	% Unemployment	6.2
% Labour Force Participation	76.7	% Managerial-Administrative	19.8
% Self-Employed	7	% University Degrees	23.6
% Movers	53.4		

D: Industrial Profile

% Manufacturing	6.9	% Service Sector	10.5
% Agriculture	0.5	% Mining	0.1
% Forestry	0.1	% Fishing	0
% Government Services	20.8	% Business Services	11.2

E: Homogeneity Measures

Ethnic Diversity Index	0.26	Religious Homogeneity Index	0.33
Sectoral Concentration Index	0.53	Income Disparity Index	8.8

F: Physical Setting Characteristics

Total Population	107627	Area (km²)	134
Population Density (pop/km²)	803.2		

Niagara Falls

Constituency Number: 35051

Niagara Falls, Canada's traditional 'honeymoon capital', is a border city, located across the Niagara River from its counterpart, Niagara Falls, New York. An estimated 12 to 14 million visitors arrive each year to see the spectacular falls that give the city, a tourist centre since the mid-1800s, and the riding its name. Nearby Niagara-on-the-Lake, a scenic lakeside town also located in the riding, annually hosts a popular 'Shaw Festival' that also attracts visitors to the area. In addition to commercial and service employment, fruit farming and hydro-electric power generation are major economic forces in the riding.

Ontario's recession hit the area reasonably hard. The St Catharines–Niagara census municipal area had the distinction of running up Canada's highest unemployment rate in the month before the 1993 federal election. What was more ominous at election time was that the rate continued to rise and, with the anticipated closing of a St Catharines GM factory (which was later sold to a subcontractor instead), the rate seemed poised to go higher still. Since 1988 over 8,000 manufacturing jobs left the area, and many blamed the Canada-US free trade agreement (FTA) for this situation. The Conservative government's strong dollar policy (plus the initial shock of the GST) encouraged many tourists to stay on the US side in Niagara Falls, New York. It also encouraged a lot of tourists heading south to wait that extra kilometre to buy gasoline and many residents to cross-border shop (and of course to smuggle). Local fruit growers and vintners were still upset over the FTA and the downward impact they believed it was having on fruit and wine prices.

The area has elected both Conservative and Liberal members, one of the latter being Judy LaMarsh. The local electorate's concerns tended to work against the Tory incumbent, Rob Nicholson, a lawyer who had first won the riding in 1984. Seven challengers emerged to contest the seat in 1993. For the second time, the Liberals nominated Gary Pillitteri, a fruit farmer, vintner (member of the Grape Growers' Marketing Board), and alderman from Niagara-on-the-Lake. The Reform Party ran Mel Grunstein, a professional engineer, and the NDP was represented by Steve Leonard who was unemployed at the time of the campaign. Four other minor party candidates had no impact on the outcome.

On election night, Pillitteri's supporters were content with the almost 10,000-vote margin that separated the Liberal from his closest challenger, Reform's Grunstein.

Member of Parliament: Gary O.V. Pillitteri; **Party**: Liberal; **Occupation**: Viticulturalist; **Education**: High school; **Age**: 58 (March 1, 1936); **Year first elected to the House of Commons**: 1993

35051 Niagara Falls

A: Political Profile
i) Voting Behaviour

	% 1993	% 1988	Change 1988-93
Conservative	22.2	39.5	-17.3
Liberal	47.1	35	12.1
NDP	3.4	21.3	-17.9
Reform	25	0	25
Other	2.4	4.2	-1.8

% Turnout	66.8	Total Ballots (#)	44148
Rejected Ballots (#)	484	% Margin of Victory	22.1
Rural Polls, 1988 (#)	15	Urban Polls, 1988 (#)	163
% Yes - 1992	38.9	% No - 1992	60.6

ii) Campaign Financing

	# of Donations	Total $ Value	% of Limit Spent
Conservative	193	59236	97.3
Liberal	230	45772	84.2
NDP	29	8230	12.1
Reform	100	18260	47
Other	12	1611	

B: Ethno-Linguistic Profile

% English Home Language	93	% French Home Language	0.9
% Official Bilingual	6.9	% Other Home Language	6.1
% Catholics	38.4	% Protestants	48.3
% Aboriginal Peoples	0.3	% Immigrants	20.4

C: Socio-Economic Profile

Average Family Income $	48392	Median Family Income $	43485
% Low Income Families	13.5	Average Home Price $	156690
% Home Owners	72.5	% Unemployment	10
% Labour Force Participation	65.4	% Managerial-Administrative	11
% Self-Employed	8.6	% University Degrees	8.1
% Movers	40.9		

D: Industrial Profile

% Manufacturing	18.9	% Service Sector	16.8
% Agriculture	3	% Mining	0.2
% Forestry	0.2	% Fishing	0
% Government Services	6.8	% Business Services	4.3

E: Homogeneity Measures

Ethnic Diversity Index	0.27	Religious Homogeneity Index	0.38
Sectoral Concentration Index	0.42	Income Disparity Index	10.1

F: Physical Setting Characteristics

Total Population	88344	Area (km²)	366
Population Density (pop/km²)	241.4		

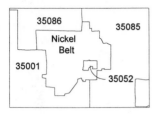

Nickel Belt

Constituency Number: 35052

Nickel Belt is a doughnut-shaped riding that completely surrounds the city of Sudbury in northern Ontario. Although the constituency includes some of the southernmost parts of the city of Sudbury, it is overwhelmingly rural. This riding's name says it all. Mining is king in Nickel Belt; the riding ranks second in the province in terms of the proportion of the workforce employed in this sector. While relatively few residents are immigrants, francophones are relatively numerous in this area (the riding ranks in the top ten on the measure of French home-language use).

Nickel Belt has long been an NDP stronghold and its representative since 1972, John Rodriguez, a former grade school principal, had always been a popular MP. However, this election showed how much the party has drifted apart from its traditional supporters. Quoting one journalist: 'Many feel [the NDP] has lost touch with its grass roots at both the federal level, where many see the party being overrun by a group of social activists and feminists and at the provincial level where Bob Rae is seen to have broken the sacred law of trade union honour by unilaterally changing contracts.' Rodriguez's strategy was to distance himself from his unpopular party and campaign as John Rodriguez, your neighbour, nice guy and 'Nickel Belt, through and through', rather than as John Rodriguez, NDP MP.

As military strategists say, there was a window of opportunity in Nickel Belt and it was up to the other parties to prove they were best capable of taking advantage of it. Given the Tories' unpopularity and their lack of local roots, strong candidates did not present themselves in abundance. They nominated a 23-year-old university student, Ian Munro, who was not even raised in the area. Janice Weitzel, a supply teacher from Garson, running for the Reform Party, probably had her support limited in this heavily francophone riding by her party's pledge to scrap the Official Languages Act and curtail bilingual federal service to a 'where necessary only' basis. For their part, the Liberals nominated Raymond Bonin, a university professor, ex-city councillor and community activist.

Crime and violence were big issues in this riding. On October 7, 1993 what started as a routine traffic violation ended with the murder of Sudbury Police Constable Joe MacDonald. The killers were two career criminals, one of whom was seriously wounded in the shoot-out. MacDonald was a recruiting poster police officer: university educated, an ex-collegiate athlete and family man, his two hobbies were coaching high school football and working with under-privileged children. After the murder of MacDonald all candidates re-iterated their belief that the criminal justice system was too slack.

The voting was heavily Liberal on election day. Speculation in advance of the election suggested that Reform's Weitzel was likely to take more votes from Roderiguez than from the Conservatives, thereby helping Bonin. This scenario seemed to play out and Bonin won with a crushing 15,000-vote margin over the veteran MP Roderiguez. Still, the latter's 23.1% of the vote was enough to qualify this as the NDP's fourth best finish in the province in 1993.

Member of Parliament: Raymond Bonin; **Party**: Liberal; **Occupation**: Professor; **Education**: BA (Political Science); **Age**: 52 (Nov. 20, 1942); **Year first elected to the House of Commons**: 1993

35052 Nickel Belt

A: Political Profile

i) Voting Behaviour

	% 1993	% 1988	Change 1988-93
Conservative	5.4	20.7	-15.3
Liberal	57.2	23.6	33.6
NDP	23.1	44.7	-21.6
Reform	12.7	0	12.7
Other	1.6	11	-9.4

% Turnout	70.7	Total Ballots (#)	44456
Rejected Ballots (#)	329	% Margin of Victory	34.1
Rural Polls, 1988 (#)	51	Urban Polls, 1988 (#)	115
% Yes - 1992	39	% No - 1992	60.5

ii) Campaign Financing

	# of Donations	Total $ Value	% of Limit Spent
Conservative	15	5900	8.7
Liberal	210	36256	77.7*
NDP	229	38020	95.3*
Reform	32	5535	7.5
Other	10	2100	

B: Ethno-Linguistic Profile

% English Home Language	74.6	% French Home Language	23.8
% Official Bilingual	41.2	% Other Home Language	1.5
% Catholics	64	% Protestants	27.9
% Aboriginal Peoples	1.5	% Immigrants	5.6

C: Socio-Economic Profile

Average Family Income $	55728	Median Family Income $	51574
% Low Income Families	9.5	Average Home Price $	118616
% Home Owners	79.1	% Unemployment	8.3
% Labour Force Participation	66.7	% Managerial-Administrative	9.5
% Self-Employed	6.3	% University Degrees	7.3
% Movers	42.3		

D: Industrial Profile

% Manufacturing	7.9	% Service Sector	11.3
% Agriculture	0.6	% Mining	12.7
% Forestry	0.3	% Fishing	0
% Government Services	10.9	% Business Services	2.4

E: Homogeneity Measures

Ethnic Diversity Index	0.36	Religious Homogeneity Index	0.49
Sectoral Concentration Index	0.37	Income Disparity Index	7.5

F: Physical Setting Characteristics

Total Population	81015	Area (km²)	3592
Population Density (pop/km²)	22.6		

* Tentative value, due to the existence of unpaid campaign expenses.

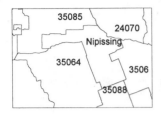

35085
24070
Nipissing
35064
3506
35088

Nipissing

Constituency Number: 35053

The riding of Nipissing serves as a transportation hub for northern Ontario. Rail lines and highways from south and east merge in North Bay (the largest community in the riding) and begin their long run around Lakes Huron and Superior here. North Bay, located along the old fur trade route, is called the Gateway to the North. The city has a large military base and is also the home base of the Ontario Northland Railway, which provides rail service southward to Toronto and northward to Moosonee on James Bay. Consequently, the fate of the provincially owned Ontario Northland Railroad was a major election concern in 1993. The line runs on tracks owned by CN, which the federally-owned railroad would dearly love to abandon. The fact that the Progressive Conservative government supported CN's position surely did not win it many friends here. Neither did the spending cuts in the defence area, which created uncertainty concerning CFB North Bay. Most of Nipissing's population is of English origin, but the riding also ranks among the top ten for French home-language use and Catholicism.

Other railroad problems also plagued Nipissing during the election. Specifically, CN and CP proposed amalgamating their tracks in the riding. While locals acknowledged that a consolidation was probably necessary, they were not very excited over the terms. Specifically, the new consolidation would increase rail traffic over a large number of level crossings. Some felt that this could hinder emergency services in the city as North Bay as it could lead to trains idling over a large number of level crossings in the heart of the city.

It could be said that in Northern Ontario old MPs do not die, and they do not fade away either; instead they go home and plot their comebacks. Illustrating this, witness the successful return of Ron Irwin in the Sault and the unsuccessful bid for a return waged by Moe Mantha in this riding (Mantha had won the seat in 1984). The ex-hockey player, golf course owner and flamboyant showman could not accept his 1988 loss to Liberal Bob Wood by the heart-breaking margin of 485 votes and came back for the Tories to challenge Wood again in 1993. Mantha felt that he lost in 1988 because of the division caused by the Free Trade Agreement and some dislike for Brian Mulroney.

Wood, a former radio broadcaster from North Bay, ended Mantha's comeback hopes, though, by winning the riding with a massive majority. His personal life, and the challenges he confronted, obviously struck a chord with the local electorate. In the early 1980s he went bankrupt, his marriage broke up, and he became a single parent. Consequently, when his constituents came to seek help during the recession he could advise them not from the book but from his own experience on how to put their lives back together. Arthur James Campbell, a labourer from Nipissing who is leader of Communications, Energy and Paperworkers' Union Local 870, ran for the NDP. The Local had been on strike for four years at the start of the election campaign against Nordfibre Ltd. However, Campbell collected only 1,300 votes for the NDP. The Reform candidate, Geraldine Lightfoot, a seminar leader from North Bay, had to fend off charges during the election campaign that her party was racist and anti-francophone. Two minor party candidates managed to combine for fewer than 300 votes.

Member of Parliament: Bob Wood; **Party**: Liberal; **Occupation**: Broadcaster; **Education:** High school; **Age**: 54 (March 11, 1940); **Year first elected to the House of Commons**: 1988

35053 Nipissing

A: Political Profile
i) Voting Behaviour

	% 1993	% 1988	Change 1988-93
Conservative	16.3	39.8	-23.5
Liberal	62.8	41.1	21.7
NDP	3.3	17.2	-13.9
Reform	16.9	0	16.9
Other	0.7	1.9	-1.2

% Turnout	66.6	Total Ballots (#)	40775
Rejected Ballots (#)	329	% Margin of Victory	45.9
Rural Polls, 1988 (#)	60	Urban Polls, 1988 (#)	114
% Yes - 1992	44.3	% No - 1992	55

ii) Campaign Financing

	# of Donations	Total $ Value	% of Limit Spent
Conservative	87	24788	60.3
Liberal	187	49664	97.6
NDP	30	9672	13.8
Reform	148	27438	45.2
Other	2	600	

B: Ethno-Linguistic Profile

% English Home Language	82	% French Home Language	16.9
% Official Bilingual	33.9	% Other Home Language	1.1
% Catholics	55.5	% Protestants	35.3
% Aboriginal Peoples	3.4	% Immigrants	5.1

C: Socio-Economic Profile

Average Family Income $	46573	Median Family Income $	41611
% Low Income Families	15.5	Average Home Price $	127144
% Home Owners	62.9	% Unemployment	9.5
% Labour Force Participation	63.7	% Managerial-Administrative	11
% Self-Employed	7.3	% University Degrees	7.9
% Movers	50		

D: Industrial Profile

% Manufacturing	8.1	% Service Sector	17.1
% Agriculture	1	% Mining	0.8
% Forestry	0.7	% Fishing	0.1
% Government Services	13.2	% Business Services	3.5

E: Homogeneity Measures

Ethnic Diversity Index	0.35	Religious Homogeneity Index	0.42
Sectoral Concentration Index	0.5	Income Disparity Index	10.7

F: Physical Setting Characteristics

Total Population	77920	Area (km²)	8207
Population Density (pop/km²)	9.5		

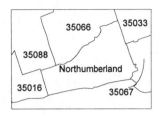

35066   35033

35088

Northumberland

35016   35067

Northumberland

Constituency Number: 35054

The riding of Northumberland stretches along the north shore of Lake Ontario between Port Hope and Trenton, south of the city of Peterborough. An area of heavy Loyalist settlement in the late 18th and early 19th centuries, the riding electorate is still one of Ontario's most anglophone and Protestant. While many live in the small communities like Cobourg, Brighton, and Campbellford, the riding is primarily rural. Agricultural jobs account for 5% of the workforce, while manufacturing jobs in a variety of light industries provide employment for more than one in five workers in the riding. Families in the riding on average earn about $7,000 less than the provincial average.

The area has strong Tory traditions. For 24 years, ending in his retirement prior to the 1988 election, the district was represented in parliament by George Hees. The open seat generated a close race in 1988 - in fact, a judicial recount was necessary before Liberal candidate Christine Stewart was declared a winner by a margin of 28 votes. Stewart, a resident of Roseneath, had to defend her seat in 1993 against seven challengers. The Tories ran Reg Jewell, a local funeral home director from Trenton, the same candidate whom Stewart nosed out for the seat in 1988. Gord Johnston, a self-employed businessman from Bewdley, ran for the Reform Party. Diana Stewart, a school trustee from Codrington, carried the NDP's banner. Four minor party candidates also stood for election, but none won even 1% of the vote on election day.

Unsurprisingly, Stewart increased her margin of victory substantially in 1993, and out-polled the Conservative/Reform candidates combined in her comfortable win.

Member of Parliament: Christine Susan Stewart; **Party:** Liberal; **Occupation:** Nurse; **Education:** BSc. (Nursing), University of Toronto; **Age:** 53 (Jan. 1, 1941); **Year first elected to the House of Commons:** 1988

35054 Northumberland

A: Political Profile
i) Voting Behaviour

	% 1993	% 1988	Change 1988-93
Conservative	21.1	41.1	-20
Liberal	49.5	41.1	8.4
NDP	3.4	14.4	-11
Reform	23.8	0	23.8
Other	2.1	3.5	-1.4

% Turnout	68.7	Total Ballots (#)	48749
Rejected Ballots (#)	336	% Margin of Victory	25.7
Rural Polls, 1988 (#)	111	Urban Polls, 1988 (#)	94
% Yes - 1992	45.3	% No - 1992	54.1

ii) Campaign Financing

	# of Donations	Total $ Value	% of Limit Spent
Conservative	141	20280	63.8
Liberal	176	37096	76.6
NDP	59	7005	8.9
Reform	56	29579	32.3
Other	14	4763	

B: Ethno-Linguistic Profile

% English Home Language	98.1	% French Home Language	0.6
% Official Bilingual	6.5	% Other Home Language	1.3
% Catholics	20.8	% Protestants	66.4
% Aboriginal Peoples	1.1	% Immigrants	10.5

C: Socio-Economic Profile

Average Family Income $	49732	Median Family Income $	45348
% Low Income Families	9.5	Average Home Price $	158525
% Home Owners	71.9	% Unemployment	8.4
% Labour Force Participation	66	% Managerial-Administrative	11.4
% Self-Employed	10.3	% University Degrees	6.6
% Movers	49.3		

D: Industrial Profile

% Manufacturing	21.5	% Service Sector	13.5
% Agriculture	5.1	% Mining	0.4
% Forestry	0.1	% Fishing	0.1
% Government Services	9.4	% Business Services	3.9

E: Homogeneity Measures

Ethnic Diversity Index	0.45	Religious Homogeneity Index	0.48
Sectoral Concentration Index	0.35	Income Disparity Index	8.8

F: Physical Setting Characteristics

Total Population	95132	Area (km²)	2226
Population Density (pop/km²)	42.7		

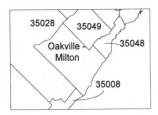

Oakville–Milton

Constituency Number: 35055

Oakville–Milton is one of metro Toronto's affluent outer suburban ridings, located on the shores of Lake Ontario about midway between Toronto and Hamilton. There is some manufacturing (the riding is home to a large Ford Motor plant that was built here after the Second World War), retailing and service employment in the community, but in many ways this is a bedroom community with a large segment of the population commuting to the other end of the train lines and highways that lead east to Metro Toronto and Mississauga. Residents in Oakville–Milton are white collar and affluent. The riding ranks third in Ontario in terms of its concentration of managers and administrators in the workforce. Average family incomes are over $20,000 higher than the provincial norm, giving the riding the fifth highest rank on this measure in Ontario. The unemployment rate at census time (1991) was the province's third lowest.

Conservative Otto Jelinek represented this riding for 14 years, for most of them as a cabinet minister. In many ridings the resignation of a sitting MP leaves his or her party in the lurch, hunting for a suitable candidate. Fortunately, following the departure of their four-term incumbent, the Tories had an attractive candidate on hand, Ann Mulvale, the Mayor of Oakville. Mulvale won her last mayoralty contest by acclamation. Nevertheless, even she could not save the party in this riding.

This is specifically the type of riding that the Reform Party wished to concentrate on in Ontario. However, the Reform Party badly mismanaged their opportunity. At first they nominated well respected Dr Allan Summerville as their candidate. However, Summerville resigned the candidacy after the local riding association selected David Andrus as its campaign manager. Andrus was expelled from the Don Valley West association following the nomination of former Conservative MP John Gamble, who alleged-edly has links to white supremacists. Dr Summerville, an African-Canadian, publicly denied that Andrus' selection led to his own resignation. However, in the same breath he gave a talk on how hard it is for a conservative party to screen out undesirable elements that wish to infiltrate it. Summerville was replaced by Richard Malboeuf, a businessman who caused some controversy within Reform Party ranks by arguing that the party had to change one of its foundational policies and recognize the existence of two founding nations in Canada if the party wished to expand into Quebec (as Preston Manning had announced). Willie Lambert, a bus driver from Oakville, ran for the NDP. A minor party and independent candidate rounded out the 1993 ballot.

The beneficiary of local Reform incompetence was Liberal candidate Bonnie Brown, Hamilton Mountain MP Beth Phinney's special assistant. A former Oakville councillor, Brown had unsuccessfully competed for the seat against Jelinek in 1988. Despite Mulvale's winning one of her party's top ten finishes on election day, Brown won with a comfortable plurality.

Member of Parliament: Bonnie Brown; **Party:** Liberal; **Occupation:** Social worker and teacher; **Year first elected to the House of Commons:** 1993

35055 Oakville–Milton

A: Political Profile
i) Voting Behaviour

	% 1993	% 1988	Change 1988-93
Conservative	26.2	54	-27.8
Liberal	46.6	35.1	11.5
NDP	2.2	8.7	-6.5
Reform	23.7	0	23.7
Other	1.3	2.2	-0.9

% Turnout	73.3	Total Ballots (#)	73782
Rejected Ballots (#)	497	% Margin of Victory	20.4
Rural Polls, 1988 (#)	0	Urban Polls, 1988 (#)	264
% Yes - 1992	59.4	% No - 1992	40.1

ii) Campaign Financing

	# of Donations	Total $ Value	% of Limit Spent
Conservative	433	77569	79.6
Liberal	262	41265	62
NDP	24	4425	3
Reform	132	41397	60.7
Other	8	1190	

B: Ethno-Linguistic Profile

% English Home Language	92.5	% French Home Language	0.6
% Official Bilingual	10.4	% Other Home Language	6.8
% Catholics	34.2	% Protestants	48.2
% Aboriginal Peoples	0.1	% Immigrants	25.7

C: Socio-Economic Profile

Average Family Income $	78689	Median Family Income $	68770
% Low Income Families	6.5	Average Home Price $	277657
% Home Owners	75.8	% Unemployment	5.5
% Labour Force Participation	75.5	% Managerial-Administrative	22.3
% Self-Employed	9.1	% University Degrees	19.1
% Movers	52.3		

D: Industrial Profile

% Manufacturing	18.1	% Service Sector	10
% Agriculture	0.9	% Mining	0.5
% Forestry	0.1	% Fishing	0
% Government Services	5.5	% Business Services	9.2

E: Homogeneity Measures

Ethnic Diversity Index	0.26	Religious Homogeneity Index	0.36
Sectoral Concentration Index	0.46	Income Disparity Index	12.6

F: Physical Setting Characteristics

Total Population	140013	Area (km²)	268
Population Density (pop/km²)	522.4		

Ontario

Constituency Number: 35056

This outer suburban Toronto riding is one of the fastest growing in Canada. Located east of Scarborough along Lake Ontario's shores, it is home to the Ontario Hydro Pickering Power Plant. The rapid population growth in recent years had resulted in the riding being home to the third highest population, and the third highest number of electors, of ridings in the province. The local economy is relatively diverse. Small manufacturing industries, especially automotive and aircraft parts, and commercial activities figure prominently in the riding's economy. When built, the Pickering nuclear plant was located in a relatively small community, but now suburban sprawl has brought several thousand homes to its very gates. This gives ecological/environmental issues a special salience here. However, in 1993 the economy pushed virtually all other issues to the margins of the political agenda. Just prior to the election, area welfare roles were up by almost 20% from the level of 1991 (at the start of the recession).

While every other riding in Metro and the Golden Horseshoe argued about Pearson International Airport, Ontario played out its own little airport drama. Nearly twenty years ago the federal government decided to build a second Toronto airport in the north of the riding and went about buying land; the land it could not buy, it expropriated. The government then cancelled the Pickering Airport project, deciding instead to expand Pearson (then called Malton) Airport. Just before the election of 1993 the federal government decided to return this vast area to private use and announced a tendering process. The previous owners (mostly farmers) argued it was unfair of the federal government to expropriate their land, hold it for nearly two decades, and then sell it back to private holders at a profit. They felt that they should have been given the chance to re-purchase their land at the price they were forced to accept when the land was expropriated. Meanwhile the province also objected. The Ontario Municipal and Environment ministries were concerned that A-1 farmland was about to be turned over to developers, just at a time when they were advocating a reduced tendency towards suburban sprawl and higher densities in already developed areas. The Municipal Affairs Minister issued a public warning to all potential bidders not to bother to attempt to purchase the land unless they planned to farm it, because that would be the only land use permitted once it left federal hands (excluding the small patches zoned for other uses such as local commerce), at least until a proper land-use plan was developed. The Ministry of the Environment also wanted to acquire certain valley lots to complete the Rouge River Conservation Area.

This was exactly the type of riding Reform strategists felt they could win. When Preston Manning visited the Metro area in the last week of the campaign, he held a rally here that drew an audience of over 4,000 people, each of whom paid $5 to hear his speech. The party nominated Don Sullivan, an administrator and former policeman. The Liberals ran Dan McTeague, a young public relations officer who had previously been a policy advisor to the provincial Housing Minister during David Peterson's government, from Ajax. Running for the NDP was secondary school teacher Lynn Jacklin. Six minor party candidates, and one independent, also offered in 1993.

In 1988, René Soetens, a former sales manager for a steel company and councillor in Ajax, had won this riding for the Conservatives with a comfortable 12,000 vote margin. This time (like every other Tory in Ontario) he faced a nightmare scenario: the collapse of the NDP had produced a unified challenge to his left and the birth of Reform had created a newly credible alternative to his right. Throw in the basic unpopularity of the government he had supported for five years and it is not surprising that he finished a distant third (by about 10,000 votes) behind Reformer Don Sullivan and the winner, Liberal Dan McTeague.

Member of Parliament: Dan McTeague; **Party**: Liberal; **Occupation**: Policy aide; **Education**: MA; **Year first elected to the House of Commons**: 1993

35056 Ontario

A: Political Profile
i) Voting Behaviour

	% 1993	% 1988	Change 1988-93
Conservative	18.9	48.9	-30
Liberal	43.4	32.3	11.1
NDP	3.1	17.8	-14.7
Reform	31.5	0	31.5
Other	3.4	0.9	2.5

% Turnout	70.4	Total Ballots (#)	89933
Rejected Ballots (#)	702	% Margin of Victory	11.9
Rural Polls, 1988 (#)	0	Urban Polls, 1988 (#)	272
% Yes - 1992	53.1	% No - 1992	46.5

ii) Campaign Financing

	# of Donations	Total $ Value	% of Limit Spent
Conservative	163	53770	89.7
Liberal	144	37542	37.3*
NDP	57	20860	18.4
Reform	135	24171	40.1
Other	24	7964	

B: Ethno-Linguistic Profile

% English Home Language	95.1	% French Home Language	0.6
% Official Bilingual	6.8	% Other Home Language	4.2
% Catholics	31.8	% Protestants	48.1
% Aboriginal Peoples	0.2	% Immigrants	23.2

C: Socio-Economic Profile

Average Family Income $	66036	Median Family Income $	63218
% Low Income Families	7	Average Home Price $	223027
% Home Owners	80.3	% Unemployment	6.5
% Labour Force Participation	77.9	% Managerial-Administrative	17.3
% Self-Employed	6.8	% University Degrees	12.1
% Movers	60.7		

D: Industrial Profile

% Manufacturing	17.7	% Service Sector	9.1
% Agriculture	0.8	% Mining	0.2
% Forestry	0	% Fishing	0
% Government Services	6.9	% Business Services	7.4

E: Homogeneity Measures

Ethnic Diversity Index	0.25	Religious Homogeneity Index	0.35
Sectoral Concentration Index	0.41	Income Disparity Index	4.3

F: Physical Setting Characteristics

Total Population	183160	Area (km²)	361
Population Density (pop/km²)	507.4		

* Tentative value, due to the existence of unpaid campaign expenses.

Oshawa

Constituency Number: 35057

The riding of Oshawa is located on the shore of Lake Ontario, approximately 60 kilometres east of Toronto. This is about as blue-collar a community as one is likely to find in Canada. It ranks fifth lowest in terms of the proportion of university graduates among Ontario ridings and is among the top ten in manufacturing employment. Its heart is the sprawling GM factory that employs over 18,000 workers. Understandably, voters in this riding were concerned when GM announced that it had lost $5.3 billion worldwide in 1991, the company's largest annual loss ever. Earlier years were kinder to GM and to the local economy, however. This factory was the site of one of the most important trade union victories in Canadian history. In 1937 the autoworkers succeeded in forcing GM to accept a union in its Canadian subsidiary in spite of a provincial government pledged to crush the workers, which organized a special police force to suppress them.

The strong union tradition has made the riding one of the safest NDP seats in the country. The party's long-time federal leader Ed Broadbent represented the riding between 1968 and 1990, but resigned to head an international human rights organization in Montreal. The riding was retained by the NDP in a by-election held January 2nd, 1990, by popular former MPP Michael Breaugh. There were clear signals early in the 1993 campaign, however, that the NDP's fortunes were on the downturn. In particular, in October the Canadian Auto Workers Local 222 (GM Oshawa) voted to sever its links to the provincial NDP. The members of the local wanted to register their objection to the Rae government's arbitrary re-writing of collective agreements with public sector employees and also some of its social justice policies which to many in the membership seemed to go far beyond fair and equal treatment. Discontented NDP voters were unlikely to find the Conservatives an attractive option in 1993. Many regard the FTA and NAFTA as having gutted the Auto Pact. Under the Auto Pact the big three US manufacturers were pledged to build one vehicle in Canada for every one they sold. Under FTA and NAFTA they merely have to meet a standard for 'North American Content'. So far the big Oshawa GM factory has managed to compete on price and quality, but since 1989 there is no longer a legal reason why GM must manufacture any vehicles whatsoever in Canada, and several other GM Canada plants have already been cut back.

Perhaps sensing the opportunity that these developments produced, eight candidates sought to displace the NDP incumbent in 1993. The local Tory candidate, Linda Dionne, a regional councillor, mismanaged her chances. In her prepared statements to the press, she wrote that Oshawa should elect her because it was time the city had a government member rather than an opposition one. Given the strong national anti-Tory tide, such a platform was unlikely to be effective, at least as a vote-winner for herself. Arguably, however, the electors of Oshawa took her advice and gave the Liberal candidate, local entrepreneur (owner of a sanitation firm) and community activist Ivan Grose, the seat. Finishing second in one of the ten tightest races in the province, was Reform candidate Andrew Davies, a computer automation specialist. Five minor party candidates contested the seat. When the dust settled on election eve, Breaugh had finished fourth.

Member of Parliament: Ivan Grose; **Party**: Liberal; **Occupation**: Small business owner; **Education**: Grade 11; **Age**: 66; **Year first elected to the House of Commons**: 1993

35057 Oshawa

A: Political Profile
i) Voting Behaviour

	% 1993	% 1988	Change 1988-93
Conservative	15	33.8	-18.8
Liberal	38.3	20.5	17.8
NDP	14.9	44.3	-29.4
Reform	28.9	0	28.9
Other	2.9	1.4	1.5

% Turnout	61.3	Total Ballots (#)	41298
Rejected Ballots (#)	405	% Margin of Victory	9.4
Rural Polls, 1988 (#)	0	Urban Polls, 1988 (#)	158
% Yes - 1992	46.7	% No - 1992	52.8

ii) Campaign Financing

	# of Donations	Total $ Value	% of Limit Spent
Conservative	110	33892	56
Liberal	93	23638	40
NDP	133	41296	82.7
Reform	74	21276	45.9
Other	25	2554	

B: Ethno-Linguistic Profile

% English Home Language	93.4	% French Home Language	1.2
% Official Bilingual	6.3	% Other Home Language	5.4
% Catholics	30.7	% Protestants	50.4
% Aboriginal Peoples	0.8	% Immigrants	16.9

C: Socio-Economic Profile

Average Family Income $	51773	Median Family Income $	50312
% Low Income Families	13.5	Average Home Price $	163945
% Home Owners	63.8	% Unemployment	9.6
% Labour Force Participation	69.2	% Managerial-Administrative	9.3
% Self-Employed	4	% University Degrees	5.5
% Movers	50.1		

D: Industrial Profile

% Manufacturing	27.7	% Service Sector	11.7
% Agriculture	0.6	% Mining	0.1
% Forestry	0	% Fishing	0
% Government Services	6.3	% Business Services	5.3

E: Homogeneity Measures

Ethnic Diversity Index	0.3	Religious Homogeneity Index	0.37
Sectoral Concentration Index	0.4	Income Disparity Index	2.8

F: Physical Setting Characteristics

Total Population	95278	Area (km^2)	47
Population Density (pop/km^2)	2027.2		

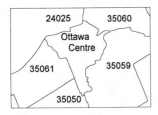

Ottawa Centre

Constituency Number: 35058

Ottawa Centre, the city's downtown riding, contains the seat of the federal government. Consequently, perhaps even more than other Ottawa constituencies, the public sector is always an issue in this riding both as an employer and as a source of trade (the riding ranks third in the province in terms of government service employment). An economically and ethnically diverse riding, its western edge is home to a large East Asian community. The combination of a large number of civil servants and the presence of Carleton University in the riding make for a very affluent and well educated electorate (over a third are university graduates, giving the riding the third highest concentration of university graduates in Ontario). Average income is the highest in the Ottawa-Carleton area. A large student and professional population always makes social and environmental issues hot topics in Ottawa Centre. Residents are among the province's most residentially mobile (the riding ranks third lowest in terms of home ownership, and has the highest proportion of any riding reporting a move in the year before the last census).

Incumbent Liberal MP Mac Harb barely squeaked out a victory to defeat NDP MP Mike Cassidy in 1988. Since then, Harb has developed a reputation as a 'populist constituency politician', and is generally believed to have worked hard representing constituent concerns. He has had a varied career that includes stints working in a pizzeria and driving cabs. In fact, as MP he organized a GST protest by hundreds of cabbies on Parliament Hill. In 1993, however, many were uncertain if he would keep his seat in the face of a stiff challenge from NDP candidate Marion Dewar, a former three-term Ottawa Mayor (one who actually managed to regularly balance the municipal budget) and past president of the NDP. Dewar had represented the Hamilton Mountain riding in the House of Commons after winning a by-election there in 1987. She narrowly lost the seat (by a 74-vote margin) in the 1988 election. After that loss Dewar returned to Ottawa and assumed the responsibility of executive director of the Canadian Council on Children and Youth. Her return to Ottawa lifted the spirits of local NDP activists; she was nominated by acclamation at a meeting that raised $15 thousand for her campaign.

However, it is likely that civil service hostility to the Ontario NDP government of Premier Bob Rae (who enacted legislation to make civil service collective agreements null and void and was also alleged to have betrayed many other 'progressive causes') reflected negatively on Dewar's campaign. In finishing second on election night, Dewar secured the NDP's fifth best finish in the province. Those looking for a truly unique approach to politics could have voted for Dr Neil Paterson who stood for the Natural Law Party in the riding and is that party's national leader. While his 44-page tabloid size householder was certainly the most impressive piece of candidate literature distributed during the election, Paterson finished a distant seventh (with 352 votes). Len Tucker, a federal civil servant, ran for the Reform Party, while Ian Lee, a Carleton University business professor, won the Tory nomination. Lee, a self-described 'red Tory', was critical of many Tory policies dealing with the civil service. Three other minor party candidates, and one independent, offered, but failed to have any significant impact on the outcome. In the end Harb, a former engineer with Northern Telecom, community college teacher, and city councillor, comfortably won re-election.

Member of Parliament: Mac Harb; **Party**: Liberal; **Occupation**: Engineer; **Education**: M.Eng, University of Ottawa; **Age**: 40 (Nov. 10, 1954); **Year first elected to the House of Commons**: 1988

35058 Ottawa Centre

A: Political Profile
i) Voting Behaviour

	% 1993		% 1988	Change 1988-93
Conservative	12.3		26.5	-14.2
Liberal	51.9		36.5	15.4
NDP	22.5		34.9	-12.4
Reform	9.4		0	9.4
Other	4.1		2.1	2

% Turnout	66.1	Total Ballots (#)	50394
Rejected Ballots (#)	385	% Margin of Victory	29.4
Rural Polls, 1988 (#)	0	Urban Polls, 1988 (#)	201
% Yes - 1992	58.1	% No - 1992	41

ii) Campaign Financing

	# of Donations	Total $ Value	% of Limit Spent
Conservative	119	33936	59.1
Liberal	110	53019	85.3
NDP	539	55292	90.3
Reform	72	19789	26.1
Other	18	47691	

B: Ethno-Linguistic Profile

% English Home Language	82.2	% French Home Language	7.7
% Official Bilingual	37.1	% Other Home Language	10.1
% Catholics	40.5	% Protestants	31
% Aboriginal Peoples	0.9	% Immigrants	21.6

C: Socio-Economic Profile

Average Family Income $	63499	Median Family Income $	53251
% Low Income Families	22.8	Average Home Price $	209029
% Home Owners	33.8	% Unemployment	7.9
% Labour Force Participation	72.7	% Managerial-Administrative	18.7
% Self-Employed	8.7	% University Degrees	34.2
% Movers	58.6		

D: Industrial Profile

% Manufacturing	4.5	% Service Sector	13.6
% Agriculture	0.3	% Mining	0
% Forestry	0.2	% Fishing	0
% Government Services	25.4	% Business Services	12.6

E: Homogeneity Measures

Ethnic Diversity Index	0.22	Religious Homogeneity Index	0.3
Sectoral Concentration Index	0.58	Income Disparity Index	16.1

F: Physical Setting Characteristics

Total Population	83755	Area (km²)	27
Population Density (pop/km²)	3102		

Ottawa South

Constituency Number: 35059

A new constituency in 1988, Ottawa South extends along the southern edge of Canada's capital city, and it includes the airport. Like other area constitutencies, the government is a major economic player: fully one quarter of the riding's workforce are employed in the government service sector. Residents are above average in family income, and in comparative terms, relatively white-collar. The riding belies its suburban image in being the most ethnically diverse riding in the region; 22.5% of the residents in this riding were born outside Canada (though of course new Canadians represent a somewhat smaller portion of the actual electors). Consequently, immigration issues take on a considerable importance here in regard both to numbers and to the way immigrants are received by Canadian society. As with other Ottawa area ridings, the state of the public sector in an era of governmental restraint was an important issue in the riding. Reflecting this disquiet, Conservative candidates would face an uphill struggle here.

The riding was won in 1988 by John Manley, a tax lawyer and professor (University of Ottawa) who formerly directed the Ottawa-Carleton Development Corporation and had been chair of the Ottawa Board of Trade (the youngest to have held the latter office). In 1993 he had to defend his seat against seven challengers. The Reform Party nominated Dough Walkinshaw, a consulting engineer. The Conservatives nominated Joe Anton, an auditor with Revenue Canada, who beat out a challenge from the mayor of Kanata at a July meeting of about 1,000 party members. The NDP offered Ursule Critoph, an economist. Four minor party candidates ran but failed to register much impact.

Manley was returned for a second term, having piled up a crushing 60% margin over his Reform opponent.

Member of Parliament: John Paul Manley; **Party**: Liberal; **Occupation**: Lawyer; **Education**: LL.B, University of Ottawa; **Age**: 44 (Jan. 5, 1950); **Year first elected to the House of Commons**: 1988

35059 Ottawa South

A: Political Profile
i) Voting Behaviour

	% 1993	% 1988	Change 1988-93
Conservative	12.6	35.1	-22.5
Liberal	65.9	50.8	15.1
NDP	3.9	13.5	-9.6
Reform	14.5	0	14.5
Other	3.2	0.6	2.6

% Turnout	71.5	Total Ballots (#)	55585
Rejected Ballots (#)	247	% Margin of Victory	51.4
Rural Polls, 1988 (#)	0	Urban Polls, 1988 (#)	209
% Yes - 1992	56.4	% No - 1992	43

ii) Campaign Financing

	# of Donations	Total $ Value	% of Limit Spent
Conservative	80	18730	80.6*
Liberal	405	116684	76.3
NDP	131	39876	46.3*
Reform	224	46281	48.9
Other	16	7341	

B: Ethno-Linguistic Profile

% English Home Language	76.9	% French Home Language	10.6
% Official Bilingual	35	% Other Home Language	12.5
% Catholics	47.4	% Protestants	32.2
% Aboriginal Peoples	0.6	% Immigrants	22.5

C: Socio-Economic Profile

Average Family Income $	60510	Median Family Income $	54023
% Low Income Families	19.5	Average Home Price $	177423
% Home Owners	48.2	% Unemployment	7.5
% Labour Force Participation	68.5	% Managerial-Administrative	17.4
% Self-Employed	7.3	% University Degrees	20.9
% Movers	54		

D: Industrial Profile

% Manufacturing	4.6	% Service Sector	15.9
% Agriculture	0.4	% Mining	0.1
% Forestry	0.1	% Fishing	0
% Government Services	25.2	% Business Services	9.3

E: Homogeneity Measures

Ethnic Diversity Index	0.21	Religious Homogeneity Index	0.35
Sectoral Concentration Index	0.58	Income Disparity Index	10.7

F: Physical Setting Characteristics

Total Population	102882	Area (km²)	65
Population Density (pop/km²)	1582.8		

* Tentative value, due to the existence of unpaid campaign expenses.

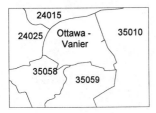

Ottawa–Vanier

Constituency Number: 35060

Ottawa–Vanier is one of the most diverse ridings imaginable, containing people from all walks of life and from income groups as diverse as those who inhabit the men's shelter at the edge of the riding and the Prime Minister's and Leader of the Official Opposition's residences. In between are the denizens of the student ghetto in Sandy Hill, the 'yuppies' of New Edinburgh, and many working class neighbourhoods. The state of the civil service is a key issue here both in terms of direct employment and as a customer base for the stores and restaurants who line the riding's main streets and the Byward Market area in the northwest corner of Ottawa–Vanier. With CFB Ottawa (North) located in the riding, defence spending is also a consideration. For lower income voters the outgoing Tory government's cutbacks to such programs as Mothers' Allowance (replaced with the child tax credit) and changes to Old Age insurance, and of course the GST have hit hard as has the tough labour market. A large francophone population (over a third report using French as home language) also makes bilingualism a serious issue here. The City of Vanier is the heart of Ottawa's francophone community. The University of Ottawa, also located in the riding, is Ontario's only officially bilingual university.

Bridges over the Ottawa River took on a new salience during the election campaign when a joint municipal, provincial, and federal committee received a consultants' report recommending that the best site for a new bridge linking Western Quebec to the 417 super highway was at an area on the eastern edge of the riding. Incumbent Liberal MP Jean Robert Gauthier advocated a ring road and bridge system that would totally bypass the built-up urban areas on both sides of the river. The current arrangement brings large numbers of trucks into Ottawa–Vanier as they make a 4 km run through downtown Ottawa on their way from the 417 to the bridge at the foot of Cumberland Street.

Gauthier, a chiropractor and long-time advocate of Franco-Ontarian rights, is as close to a life member of the House of Commons as anybody is likely to get since the death of Stanley Knowles. The 1993 election marked his seventh consecutive victory in the riding and his margin of victory was more than 20,000 votes. The *Ottawa Sun* may not have been exaggerating when it referred to Ottawa–Vanier as the safest Liberal seat in the entire country. En route to his victory, however, Gauthier confronted nine challengers. The Tories were represented by Marie-Christine Lemire, while Reform nominated parent therapist Sam Dancey. The NDP ran Willie Dunn, a filmmaker. Five minor party and one independent candidate rounded out the ballot.

Member of Parliament: Jean-Robert Gauthier; **Party**: Liberal; **Occupation**: Chiropractor; **Education**: Chiropractic College of Toronto; **Age**: 65 (Oct. 22, 1929); **Year first elected to the House of Commons**: 1972

35060 Ottawa–Vanier

A: Political Profile
i) Voting Behaviour

	% 1993	% 1988	Change 1988-93
Conservative	10.5	23.2	-12.7
Liberal	70.5	59.2	11.3
NDP	6.5	16	-9.5
Reform	7.9	0	7.9
Other	4.6	1.6	3

% Turnout	62.4	Total Ballots (#)	49081
Rejected Ballots (#)	517	% Margin of Victory	60
Rural Polls, 1988 (#)	0	Urban Polls, 1988 (#)	188
% Yes - 1992	61.7	% No - 1992	37.5

ii) Campaign Financing

	# of Donations	Total $ Value	% of Limit Spent
Conservative	24	25566	36.5
Liberal	305	51435	71.5
NDP	87	19355	26.2
Reform	30	10048	15
Other	25	4523	

B: Ethno-Linguistic Profile

% English Home Language	57.1	% French Home Language	34
% Official Bilingual	53.4	% Other Home Language	8.9
% Catholics	61.8	% Protestants	20.2
% Aboriginal Peoples	1.7	% Immigrants	16.8

C: Socio-Economic Profile

Average Family Income $	55955	Median Family Income $	45435
% Low Income Families	24	Average Home Price $	190270
% Home Owners	31.1	% Unemployment	9.6
% Labour Force Participation	68.7	% Managerial-Administrative	15.7
% Self-Employed	6.6	% University Degrees	20.9
% Movers	58.8		

D: Industrial Profile

% Manufacturing	3.9	% Service Sector	16.6
% Agriculture	0.5	% Mining	0
% Forestry	0.1	% Fishing	0
% Government Services	27	% Business Services	8.2

E: Homogeneity Measures

Ethnic Diversity Index	0.29	Religious Homogeneity Index	0.43
Sectoral Concentration Index	0.55	Income Disparity Index	18.8

F: Physical Setting Characteristics

Total Population	91286	Area (km²)	35
Population Density (pop/km²)	2608.2		

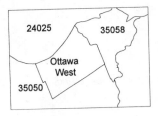

Ottawa West

Constituency Number: 35061

Ottawa West follows the Ottawa River to the border of the city of Nepean. Average family incomes in the riding are about at the provincial norm, and the riding is distinctly less affluent and white-collar than its counterparts in the city. Though still high in comparison to most Ontario ridings, government service employment is lower in this riding than others in Canada's capital city. As with Ottawa–Vanier on the east of the city, bridges are perhaps a bigger issue here than in most ridings given the riding's long stretch of river front. Residents in the Britannia neighbourhood in the riding mounted a stiff fight to insure that the planners rejected the option of building the new bridge at the foot of their community. One local note of interest, NDP candidate Norman Bobbitt's storefront campaign office was rented from Nepean Liberal MP Beryl Gaffney's husband.

The riding has never returned Conservative members to the House in consecutive elections since its creation in 1933. In 1988, Liberal Maureen Catterall, a former high school teacher and high profile Ottawa alderman (she had run unsuccessfully for Ottawa mayor in 1985), had succeeded in taking the seat from Tory incumbent David Daubney. Of course, 1993 was an unlikely year for a Liberal incumbent to be unseated. However, nine candidates lined up to make the attempt. Nancy Munro-Parry, a community advocate, won the Tory nomination. Reform was represented by Peter Boddy, a commercial property appraiser, while the NDP offered Bobbitt, an engineer. Bobbitt, a former member of the now-defunct Canadian Aviation Safety Board, created a stir in July 1993 by writing a public letter to NDP leader Audrey McLaughlin in which he urged her to disown the provincial NDP government of Bob Rae. In the letter he also took exception to the long-standing NDP policy of targeting ridings for concentrated campaign effort. Six minor party candidates also ran but had negligible effect on the outcome, which saw Catterall pile up a 22,000-vote majority over second-place Boddy.

Member of Parliament: Marlene Catterall; **Party**: Liberal; **Occupation**: Teacher; **Education**: BA, Carleton University; **Age**: 55 (March 1, 1939); **Year first elected to the House of Commons**: 1988

35061 Ottawa West

A: Political Profile
i) Voting Behaviour

	% 1993	% 1988	Change 1988-93
Conservative	14.1	38.6	-24.5
Liberal	63.4	49.6	13.8
NDP	4.1	11.2	-7.1
Reform	14.2	0	14.2
Other	4.3	0.6	3.7

% Turnout	70.3	Total Ballots (#)	45192
Rejected Ballots (#)	336	% Margin of Victory	49.2
Rural Polls, 1988 (#)	0	Urban Polls, 1988 (#)	203
% Yes - 1992	54.4	% No - 1992	45.1

ii) Campaign Financing

	# of Donations	Total $ Value	% of Limit Spent
Conservative	91	36772	79.6
Liberal	229	34674	81.8
NDP	54	27600	32.9
Reform	74	27140	44.5
Other	59	7937	

B: Ethno-Linguistic Profile

% English Home Language	87.7	% French Home Language	4
% Official Bilingual	25.7	% Other Home Language	8.4
% Catholics	38.6	% Protestants	40.1
% Aboriginal Peoples	0.6	% Immigrants	19.5

C: Socio-Economic Profile

Average Family Income $	56942	Median Family Income $	50014
% Low Income Families	18.8	Average Home Price $	167918
% Home Owners	43.1	% Unemployment	8.3
% Labour Force Participation	63.6	% Managerial-Administrative	16.1
% Self-Employed	7.4	% University Degrees	19.2
% Movers	49.2		

D: Industrial Profile

% Manufacturing	7	% Service Sector	13.4
% Agriculture	0.3	% Mining	0.1
% Forestry	0.1	% Fishing	0
% Government Services	21	% Business Services	11.3

E: Homogeneity Measures

Ethnic Diversity Index	0.27	Religious Homogeneity Index	0.32
Sectoral Concentration Index	0.54	Income Disparity Index	12.2

F: Physical Setting Characteristics

Total Population	79694	Area (km²)	25
Population Density (pop/km²)	3187.8		

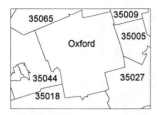

Oxford

Constituency Number: 35062

The riding of Oxford is located in southwestern Ontario, between the cities of Hamilton and London. The riding is nearly evenly split between urban and rural polling districts. The only major population centres are Woodstock in the centre of the riding, Tillsonburg in the south, and Ingersoll in the west. The area defined by the riding's boundaries is rich agricultural land, and the riding ranks among the province's top ten in terms of agricultural employment. Dairy, grain, fruit and tobacco farming are all important to the riding's economy. Ingersoll was the birthplace of the Canadian Dairyman's Association in 1867. Light manufacturing, notably of agricultural implements, also accounts for some of the area's employment. Oxford's residents are heavily anglophone and Protestant.

Since 1953 Oxford has had only two MPs, both Tories. But after 20 years Bruce Halliday retired and, given the unpopularity of the government, a close race was predicted in 1993. This riding has been seriously affected by the decline of manufacturing in the region. The most glaring example is perhaps the closing of the Trail Mobile plant in Ingersoll. The plant was closed and 300 put out of work when the owners chose to concentrate production in a sister plant in Arkansas. The situation has gone past people debating the pros and cons of free trade in this riding, according to one union activist. All they really care about now is what will you do to get me a job or help me keep the one I've got. 'There's a lot of posturing by politicians about . . . free trade. I don't think people care any more. They just want a job.'

Hoping to hold the riding for the Conservatives was George Klosler, a businessperson from Mount Elgin. Klosler, a political novice, campaigned against the traditional practice of using lawn signs as political advertising, claiming that this posed environmental problems. The Reform Party ran John Mohr, a salesman from Tavistock, while John Finlay, a retired school superintendent from Tavistock, contested the seat for the Grits. The NDP also offered a sales person, Martin Donlevy from Woodstock. Four minor party and one independent candidates also fought in the 1993 campaign.

The Liberals managed a to win a 7,000 vote margin of victory in this riding, in large measure due to a Reform-Tory vote split among the right-of-centre electors: Finlay's vote total was less than the combined Reform-Conservative candidates.

Member of Parliament: John Baird Finlay; **Party**: Liberal; **Occupation**: Teacher; **Education**: MEd; **Age**: 65 (Jan. 29, 1929); **Year first elected to the House of Commons**: 1993

35062 Oxford

A: Political Profile
i) Voting Behaviour

	% 1993	% 1988	Change 1988-93
Conservative	22.7	39.8	-17.1
Liberal	41.1	37	4.1
NDP	5	16	-11
Reform	26.5	0	26.5
Other	4.9	7.3	-2.4

% Turnout	68	Total Ballots (#)	48179
Rejected Ballots (#)	353	% Margin of Victory	14.6
Rural Polls, 1988 (#)	112	Urban Polls, 1988 (#)	102
% Yes - 1992	48.7	% No - 1992	50.8

ii) Campaign Financing

	# of Donations	Total $ Value	% of Limit Spent
Conservative	255	37853	98
Liberal	263	40644	48
NDP	23	17954	26.9
Reform	216	48243	87.2
Other	59	8879	

B: Ethno-Linguistic Profile

% English Home Language	96.4	% French Home Language	0.3
% Official Bilingual	4.2	% Other Home Language	3.3
% Catholics	18.8	% Protestants	68.9
% Aboriginal Peoples	0.3	% Immigrants	11.9

C: Socio-Economic Profile

Average Family Income $	51883	Median Family Income $	45544
% Low Income Families	8.8	Average Home Price $	144332
% Home Owners	70.8	% Unemployment	7
% Labour Force Participation	69.9	% Managerial-Administrative	11
% Self-Employed	12.6	% University Degrees	5.8
% Movers	43.9		

D: Industrial Profile

% Manufacturing	24.7	% Service Sector	9.8
% Agriculture	13.2	% Mining	0.2
% Forestry	0.1	% Fishing	0
% Government Services	4	% Business Services	2.8

E: Homogeneity Measures

Ethnic Diversity Index	0.43	Religious Homogeneity Index	0.51
Sectoral Concentration Index	0.33	Income Disparity Index	12.2

F: Physical Setting Characteristics

Total Population	98600	Area (km²)	2330
Population Density (pop/km²)	42.3		

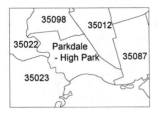

Parkdale–High Park

Constituency Number: 35063

Parkdale–High Park is a densely populated urban riding situated along the shore of Lake Ontario in the west end of the City of Toronto. This riding has a broad mixture of income levels and ethnic communities, including the heart of Metro's Polish Canadian community and a large Baltic contingent as well. This makes immigration a serious issue in the riding. This policy probably alienated an important number from the Conservatives in a riding where one in nine speak Polish as their first language and English is the home language in less than three-quarters of the riding's homes. This riding contains a considerable number of low income residents (17.8% of all families). Crime and mental health are often major issues as increasing police crackdowns in the nearby core of the city during the 1980s have forced increasing numbers of drug traffickers and prostitutes out towards Parkdale. The riding is home to many halfway homes for offenders on supervised release and for the mentally ill, and many residents are not so much NIMBYs (Not in My Back Yards) but NOMMBYs (No More in My Back Yards). However, in this election no one paid them much heed; the economy took full attention.

In 1984, the riding went Tory in the Mulroney sweep of that year, but in 1988, after a close-fought race, Jesse Flis, a former school principal and area MP (1979 and 1980), won the riding with a 3,200 vote victory margin for the Liberals. This was the third election in which Flis had contested the seat against Tory Andrew Witer. In 1993, Flis faced ten opponents. Running for the Tories this time around was Don Baker, a businessman from Etobicoke. Lee Primeau, a minister from Mississauga, won the Reform Party's nomination, while David Miller, a lawyer, ran for the NDP. Six minor party candidates, and one independent, rounded out the ballot.

Flis extended his victory in 1993 to almost 16,000 votes, easily retaining the riding for the Liberals.

Member of Parliament: Jesse Philip Flis; **Party**: Liberal; **Occupation**: Educator; **Education**: MEd, Ontario Institute for Studies in Education; **Age**: 61 (Nov. 15, 1933); **Year first elected to the House of Commons**: 1979

35063 Parkdale–High Park

A: Political Profile
i) Voting Behaviour

	% 1993	% 1988	Change 1988-93
Conservative	13.8	36.4	-22.6
Liberal	54.4	43.5	10.9
NDP	9.4	17.7	-8.3
Reform	16.2	0	16.2
Other	6.4	2.4	4

% Turnout	66.4	Total Ballots (#)	41547
Rejected Ballots (#)	416	% Margin of Victory	38.2
Rural Polls, 1988 (#)	0	Urban Polls, 1988 (#)	182
% Yes - 1992	57.5	% No - 1992	41.6

ii) Campaign Financing

	# of Donations	Total $ Value	% of Limit Spent
Conservative	147	38971	63.2
Liberal	232	52430	78.6
NDP	176	29810	44.8
Reform	179	19466	42.3
Other	25	5974	

B: Ethno-Linguistic Profile

% English Home Language	71.9	% French Home Language	0.5
% Official Bilingual	10.2	% Other Home Language	27.6
% Catholics	41.9	% Protestants	26.8
% Aboriginal Peoples	0.4	% Immigrants ·	42.3

C: Socio-Economic Profile

Average Family Income $	55600	Median Family Income $	46377
% Low Income Families	22.1	Average Home Price $	291867
% Home Owners	36.6	% Unemployment	10.3
% Labour Force Participation	68.5	% Managerial-Administrative	15.9
% Self-Employed	8.6	% University Degrees	23.1
% Movers	49.7		

D: Industrial Profile

% Manufacturing	15.1	% Service Sector	11.7
% Agriculture	0.2	% Mining	0.1
% Forestry	0.1	% Fishing	0
% Government Services	6.8	% Business Services	11.7

E: Homogeneity Measures

Ethnic Diversity Index	0.17	Religious Homogeneity Index	0.29
Sectoral Concentration Index	0.51	Income Disparity Index	16.6

F: Physical Setting Characteristics

Total Population	96464	Area (km²)	15
Population Density (pop/km²)	6430.9		

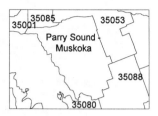

Parry Sound–Muskoka

Constituency Number: 35064

This large northern Ontario riding borders on the shores of both Georgian Bay and Lake Nipissing, about 200 kilometres north of Toronto. Once a logging town, Parry Sound has become a thriving tourist centre for the Thirty Thousand Islands vacation area around Georgian Bay. To the east, Muskoka, with its numerous lakes, granite rock formations, and maple and pine forests, has become virtually synonymous with 'cottage country' in Upper Canada. Ontario's popular Algonquin Park, a 7,600 hectare expanse of wilderness, is yet another tourist attraction for the region. The riding's year-round population is relatively anglophone, Protestant, and poor (the riding ranks fifth lowest in Ontario in terms of average family incomes).

Stan Darling represented this riding for the Tories for over 21 years (since 1972), and before him, the riding was held by the Tories since 1957. Darling, who was 83 in 1993 (making him the oldest living MP), decided to step down. Darling was known as a 'good constituency man', and he was noted for his work in pressuring the Mulroney government to sign an accord with the United States on acid rain (something it did in 1991). Darling's reaction to the 1988 redrawing of his constituency boundaries was typically colourful. Complaining that he had lost 'three full townships. That's 10,000 wolves, 35 deer and maybe 10 votes, the way I count it.'

In his place, the Conservatives nominated Terry Clarke, a former Mayor of Huntsville and a high school principal. Clarke more or less defended the Mulroney record, finding fault only with the government's delivery on its promises. He admitted, however, that Mulroney was perhaps not very good at explaining to Canadians why policies such as the GST were actually beneficial for Canadians. Having responsibility for the recession and the strong dollar policy pursued by the Mulroney government hurt this area severely, and handicapped Clarke's bid to hold the seat. The strong dollar kept foreigners away and encouraged many Canadians who traditionally summer in the area to finally take that foreign trip. The heavy interest rates that the strong dollar policy mandated also made the capital investments tourism requires harder to achieve and many family hotel mortgages difficult to meet. Therefore, this riding, like most others in Canada, had sensible reasons not to vote Progressive Conservative this time. Reform was doubtless expecting to capitalize on this discontent in a predominantly Conservative area.

Liberal contender Andy Mitchell, a bank manager from Gravenhurst and former president of the Northern Ontario Chamber of Commerce, presented the Liberal 'Red Book' platform more or less by rote, but added one or two innovations to adapt it to local conditions. Specifically he stressed his own personal experience as a banker helping to meet the needs of small business, the need to better co-ordinate local, provincial and federal efforts to promote the region as a tourism destination, and the area's potential for retirement living developments. The Reform candidate Jim Newman, a realtor and entrepreneur, closely adhered to the party line, stressing Reform's deficit-cutting zeal and its commitment to listening to constituents. However, local press reports noted that at one town hall meeting many came away disillusioned after talking to Newman, sensing that the high priority given to reducing the deficit might adversely affect the riding's economy. The NDP ran Shirley Davy, a sales broker from Pointe au Baril Station. Three minor party candidates and one independent also ran in 1993.

In 1988 the Progressive Conservatives won this riding by a margin of 4,846 votes over the Liberals. The collapse of the NDP in 1993 (its vote dropped 21%) and Reform's inroads into traditional Tory voters enabled the Liberals to romp to a 7,000 vote victory over second place Reform

Member of Parliament: Andrew Mitchell; **Party**: Liberal; **Occupation**: Bank manager; **Year first elected to the House of Commons**: 1993

35064 Parry Sound–Muskoka

A: Political Profile
i) Voting Behaviour

	% 1993	% 1988	Change 1988-93
Conservative	20.6	43.2	-22.6
Liberal	44.2	31.1	13.1
NDP	4.7	25.7	-21
Reform	28.2	0	28.2
Other	2.4	0	2.4

% Turnout	69.1	Total Ballots (#)	46408
Rejected Ballots (#)	215	% Margin of Victory	16
Rural Polls, 1988 (#)	173	Urban Polls, 1988 (#)	46
% Yes - 1992	44.6	% No - 1992	54.9

ii) Campaign Financing

	# of Donations	Total $ Value	% of Limit Spent
Conservative	152	34600	78.4
Liberal	127	20555	58.9*
NDP	49	17063	37.6
Reform	203	40274	54.4*
Other	8	740	

B: Ethno-Linguistic Profile

% English Home Language	98.4	% French Home Language	0.3
% Official Bilingual	5.9	% Other Home Language	1.2
% Catholics	17.1	% Protestants	66.9
% Aboriginal Peoples	2.3	% Immigrants	8

C: Socio-Economic Profile

Average Family Income $	43962	Median Family Income $	38094
% Low Income Families	11.1	Average Home Price $	158494
% Home Owners	79.4	% Unemployment	8.6
% Labour Force Participation	61.6	% Managerial-Administrative	10.7
% Self-Employed	14.7	% University Degrees	7
% Movers	44.8		

D: Industrial Profile

% Manufacturing	9.8	% Service Sector	13.9
% Agriculture	1.8	% Mining	0.4
% Forestry	0.5	% Fishing	0.1
% Government Services	7.7	% Business Services	3.2

E: Homogeneity Measures

Ethnic Diversity Index	0.5	Religious Homogeneity Index	0.48
Sectoral Concentration Index	0.45	Income Disparity Index	13.3

F: Physical Setting Characteristics

Total Population	86424	Area (km²)	15290
Population Density (pop/km²)	5.7		

* Tentative value, due to the existence of unpaid campaign expenses.

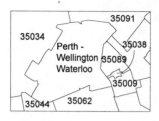

Perth–Wellington–Waterloo

Constituency Number: 35065

This riding, newly created in 1988, is located in southwestern Ontario just to the west of the cities of Kitchener-Waterloo. Located in the heart of 'traditional' rural and small-town Ontario, the so-called 'bible belt', it contains some of the most productive agricultural land in the province, concentrated in dairy and cash crop farming. The riding ranks second in the province in terms of the proportion of the workforce employed in agriculture. It has the smallest proportion of service sector workers of any riding in the province, and has the second highest proportion of Protestants and self-employed workers. The major centre of population is in Stratford (at an elevation of 364 metres, the highest city in the province), home to a mixture of light manufacturing and the famous Stratford Festival, founded in 1953.

The new riding of Perth–Wellington–Waterloo included much traditional Tory territory. Almost three-quarters of the new riding came from the old constituency of Perth that had returned Conservatives to Ottawa since 1953. With this background, the 1988 result was not surprising. It saw Tory Harry Brightwell, a former veterinarian who was first elected to the Commons in 1984, win re-election, but with a margin of victory of less than a thousand votes. This margin, given the low popularity of the government and the rise of Reform, hardly instilled confidence in the Tory camp as 1993 approached. In fact, the confidence in the campaign had shifted to the Liberals. Brightwell himself also became something of a campaign issue when some Tories reportedly told a *London Free Press* reporter that they had wanted him to retire.

Confronting Brightwell were seven challengers. The Liberals ran John Richardson, a self-employed resident of Stratford who had retired from a job as superintendent of schools. Jeff Gerber, a high school teacher from Shakespeare, ran for the Reform Party, and the NDP nominated Stephanie Levesque, a constituency assistant living in Stratford. Four minor party candidates also ran in 1993, but with little success.

This race centred on 'pocketbook issues' and the economy. Abortion and other non-economic issues that figured prominently in 1988 were not even on the radar screen in the contest. In the case of farmers, this included the international trade scene, GATT and NAFTA. The area's hog farmers, in particular, resented the failure of the United States to lower a countervailing duty which farmers felt reflected subsidies they no longer receive from the Canadian and Ontario governments .

As in many other area ridings which were once held by the Tories, right-of-centre voters in Perth–Wellington–Waterloo pretty much evenly split their votes between the Reform and Conservative parties, allowing a Liberal to slide up the middle.

Member of Parliament: John Richardson; **Party**: Liberal; **Occupation**: Teacher; **Education**: MEd; **Year first elected to the House of Commons**: 1993

35065 Perth–Wellington–Waterloo

A: Political Profile
i) Voting Behaviour

	% 1993	% 1988	Change 1988-93
Conservative	23.3	39.1	-15.8
Liberal	43.3	37	6.3
NDP	4.1	19	-14.9
Reform	26.2	0	26.2
Other	3.1	4.9	-1.8

% Turnout	66.3	Total Ballots (#)	46786
Rejected Ballots (#)	263	% Margin of Victory	17.1
Rural Polls, 1988 (#)	126	Urban Polls, 1988 (#)	85
% Yes - 1992	54	% No - 1992	45.5

ii) Campaign Financing

	# of Donations	Total $ Value	% of Limit Spent
Conservative	299	30140	70.5
Liberal	192	31431	70.4
NDP	69	19195	24.5
Reform	153	30748	34.8
Other	63	8715	

B: Ethno-Linguistic Profile

% English Home Language	93.6	% French Home Language	0.1
% Official Bilingual	3.7	% Other Home Language	6.3
% Catholics	18.6	% Protestants	72.4
% Aboriginal Peoples	0.2	% Immigrants	9.2

C: Socio-Economic Profile

Average Family Income $	53429	Median Family Income $	47278
% Low Income Families	8	Average Home Price $	160366
% Home Owners	74.4	% Unemployment	4.9
% Labour Force Participation	72.7	% Managerial-Administrative	11.5
% Self-Employed	16.5	% University Degrees	6.8
% Movers	39.3		

D: Industrial Profile

% Manufacturing	22.2	% Service Sector	9.4
% Agriculture	15.9	% Mining	0.1
% Forestry	0.1	% Fishing	0
% Government Services	3.4	% Business Services	2.1

E: Homogeneity Measures

Ethnic Diversity Index	0.37	Religious Homogeneity Index	0.55
Sectoral Concentration Index	0.32	Income Disparity Index	11.5

F: Physical Setting Characteristics

Total Population	99563	Area (km²)	3313
Population Density (pop/km²)	30.1		

Peterborough

Constituency Number: 35066

The riding of Peterborough takes in the city of the same name - located on the Otonabee River about 40 kilometres north of Lake Ontario and 110 kilometres northeast of Toronto - and its rural environs. The area, part of the Kawarthas (from 'kawatha', or 'bright waters and happy lands') is one of considerable beauty, and tourism and seasonal cottagers are important to the riding's economy. Early development of hydro-electric power along the Trent-Severn Waterway system attracted considerable manufacturing to the area. In addition, agricultural employment and Trent University are significant economic forces. The city of Peterborough is celebrated for its demographic 'averageness' - it has long had the reputation of being a bell-wether riding in federal and provincial politics, and is a favourite site for market researchers. In 1979, for example, the federal government used the city as a test-case for the introduction of metric conversion, four years before making it mandatory for the rest of the country.

In recent years, the riding has repeatedly gone Conservative, and has been represented since 1979 by William Domm, a former businessman and radio broadcaster. However, Domm's margin of victory was substantially reduced in 1988, and the riding looked vulnerable for the Tories coming into the 1993 campaign. Reform's growth was in part responsible for Tory concerns leading up to the election. In early 1992, Mulroney swept through Peterborough on a pre-election, campaign-like visit in which he vigorously defended his government's record, and attacked the Reform alternative.

The local economy was the dominant concern in the 1993 campaign. Layoffs at General Electric, a large employer in the riding, and double-digit unemployment in the lead-up to the campaign were driving people out of the area in search of jobs.

Domm faced five challengers in 1993. The Liberals had finished second in 1988, and in 1993 they nominated Peter Adams, a professor at Trent University in Peterborough. Reform ran Len Bagman, a building contractor from Peterborough, and the NDP offered Merv Richards, a constituency assistant who failed to continue the party's local advance in this election. Two minor party candidates also offered. In the end, Adams more than doubled his nearest opponent's vote total, and piled up a comfortable 20% margin of victory.

Member of Parliament: Peter Adams; **Party**: Liberal; **Occupation**: Professor; **Education**: PhD, McGill University; **Age**: 58 (April 17, 1936); **Year first elected to the House of Commons**: 1993

35066 Peterborough

A: Political Profile

i) Voting Behaviour

	% 1993	% 1988	Change 1988-93
Conservative	20.1	40.9	-20.8
Liberal	47.6	30.3	17.3
NDP	5.3	27.5	-22.2
Reform	23.2	0	23.2
Other	3.8	1.3	2.5

% Turnout	68.9	Total Ballots (#)	58244
Rejected Ballots (#)	314	% Margin of Victory	24.4
Rural Polls, 1988 (#)	96	Urban Polls, 1988 (#)	156
% Yes - 1992	42.1	% No - 1992	57.5

ii) Campaign Financing

	# of Donations	Total $ Value	% of Limit Spent
Conservative	170	43194	90.1
Liberal	302	60144	81.7
NDP	176	39067	46.7
Reform	169	35784	56
Other	37	4345	

B: Ethno-Linguistic Profile

% English Home Language	98.2	% French Home Language	0.3
% Official Bilingual	5.9	% Other Home Language	1.5
% Catholics	24.4	% Protestants	62.6
% Aboriginal Peoples	2	% Immigrants	9

C: Socio-Economic Profile

Average Family Income $	48618	Median Family Income $	42699
% Low Income Families	13.5	Average Home Price $	161797
% Home Owners	70	% Unemployment	8.5
% Labour Force Participation	63.3	% Managerial-Administrative	10.7
% Self-Employed	10.3	% University Degrees	9.2
% Movers	47.4		

D: Industrial Profile

% Manufacturing	15.3	% Service Sector	12.6
% Agriculture	3	% Mining	0.6
% Forestry	0.1	% Fishing	0.1
% Government Services	5.2	% Business Services	4.8

E: Homogeneity Measures

Ethnic Diversity Index	0.51	Religious Homogeneity Index	0.45
Sectoral Concentration Index	0.43	Income Disparity Index	12.2

F: Physical Setting Characteristics

Total Population	107289	Area (km²)	2118
Population Density (pop/km²)	50.7		

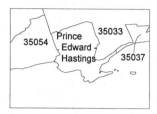

Prince Edward–Hastings

Constituency Number: 35067

Prince Edward–Hastings extends northwards from the shores of Lake Ontario, between Trenton and Kingston. It is almost bifurcated by the Bay of Quinte, an arm of Lake Ontario (Prince Edward county is Ontario's largest island). The riding is predominantly rural, with the major population concentrations being in the towns of Belleville and Picton. Agriculture and light manufacturing dominate the riding's economy. Sandy beaches, quiet coves, and good fishing have long attracted tourists to the riding's coastal areas. Many residents in the area trace their lineages to Loyalist settlers, and the area is heavily anglophone and Protestant.

In a riding where many farmers were worried about the impact that NAFTA will have on Canadian agriculture, Tory candidate Jim Hughes (who is a farmer from Picton) was the only candidate to endorse the FTA and NAFTA without qualification. The Reform candidate, Marjorie Foster, a travel consultant from Belleville, agreed with Liberal incumbent Lyle Vanclief that the FTA needed tighter rules to make the deal advantageous to the riding's voters. The NDP does not traditionally do well in this environment, and in 1993 it was represented locally by Jim Martin, a retailer from Kingston. Martin was a last-minute substitute for their original candidate, Adam Fisher. Fisher was disqualified by the NDP national head-quarters after a local newspaper raised questions about the authenticity of some of the past employment listed by him on his résumé. Three minor party candidates also contested the seat. In this heavily rural riding, it is not surprising that all four major candidates supported continued federal involvement in farm price support programs. However, the Reform candidate also noted that the new GATT deal might make marketing boards and agricultural tariffs a thing of the past, necessitating the use of other methods.

In the end, Vanclief, an agrologist from Ameliasburg, held the seat easily for the Liberals, piling up a 30% margin.

Member of Parliament: Lyle Vanclief; **Party**: Liberal; **Occupation**: Agrologist; **Education**: BSc (Agriculture), University of Guelph; **Age**: 51 (Sept. 19, 1943); **Year first elected to the House of Commons**: 1988

35067 Prince Edward–Hastings

A: Political Profile

i) Voting Behaviour

	% 1993	% 1988	Change 1988-93
Conservative	17.8	36.2	-18.4
Liberal	57.1	43.1	14
NDP	2.8	14.5	-11.7
Reform	19.4	0	19.4
Other	3	6.2	-3.2

% Turnout	64.8	Total Ballots (#)	46666
Rejected Ballots (#)	272	% Margin of Victory	37.7
Rural Polls, 1988 (#)	126	Urban Polls, 1988 (#)	83
% Yes - 1992	44.8	% No - 1992	54.8

ii) Campaign Financing

	# of Donations	Total $ Value	% of Limit Spent
Conservative	162	30704	76
Liberal	352	53586	86.2
NDP	32	9132	11.1*
Reform	161	21278	39.8
Other	68	12398	

B: Ethno-Linguistic Profile

% English Home Language	97.5	% French Home Language	1.1
% Official Bilingual	6.5	% Other Home Language	1.4
% Catholics	22.5	% Protestants	66.8
% Aboriginal Peoples	1.1	% Immigrants	8.3

C: Socio-Economic Profile

Average Family Income $	49227	Median Family Income $	43493
% Low Income Families	11.4	Average Home Price $	153132
% Home Owners	66.9	% Unemployment	8.5
% Labour Force Participation	65.5	% Managerial-Administrative	11.7
% Self-Employed	10.2	% University Degrees	7.6
% Movers	44.8		

D: Industrial Profile

% Manufacturing	15.9	% Service Sector	15.8
% Agriculture	4.2	% Mining	0.1
% Forestry	0.1	% Fishing	0.1
% Government Services	11	% Business Services	3.4

E: Homogeneity Measures

Ethnic Diversity Index	0.53	Religious Homogeneity Index	0.49
Sectoral Concentration Index	0.41	Income Disparity Index	11.6

F: Physical Setting Characteristics

Total Population	92417	Area (km²)	2203
Population Density (pop/km²)	42		

*   Tentative value, due to the existence of unpaid campaign expenses.

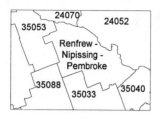

Renfrew–Nipissing–Pembroke

Constituency Number: 35068

The riding of Renfrew–Nipissing–Pembroke sprawls over 12,000 square kilometres along the Ottawa River northwest of the city of Ottawa. The riding's economy is dominated by the public sector, with the massive Canadian Forces Base in Petawawa (until recently home to the controversial Airborne Regiment among other units) and Atomic Energy of Canada in Deep River. Resource industries and tourism are also significant economic forces. Overall, the riding's residents are not affluent - average family incomes are about $10,000 less than the norm for ridings in the province. Consequently the Mulroney government's restraint program sparked concerns here and Kim Campbell's promise to contract out for even more services and privatize anything possible continued unease about the Tories in this riding.

Len Hopkins has represented this riding and its predecessor ridings since 1965. The former teacher had not always had an easy time in winning, however; in 1984, a recount was necessary to establish his victory margin at 38 votes. Hopkins had narrowly survived a challenge to his candidacy in the 1988 campaign, and his re-selection as Liberal candidate in 1993 was controversial. Hopkins called a nomination meeting on June 1st, 1992 - the first day permissible under Liberal Party rules - in the hopes of avoiding controversy. However, the tactic upset the local Liberal riding association, and a 'grassroots committee' vowed to work against Hopkins' re-election campaign. Subsequently, his candidacy was formally challenged by Hector Clouthier, a local businessman who had made unflattering public statements about First Nations people. The controversy was resolved when Liberal leader Jean Chrétien exercised his prerogative and named Hopkins as the Liberal candidate in the riding. After this decision by Chrétien, Clouthier decided to run as an independent. At first there was widespread discussion as to whether or not this would hurt Hopkins' chances of celebrating 30 years in office.

Challenging Hopkins for the Conservatives was Milton Stevenson, a farmer from Renfrew. The Reform Party nominated Edward Pinnell, an engineer from Arnprior. Barbara Clarke, a Pembroke administrator, ran for the NDP, and was joined on the ballot by two other minor party candidates (who between them won less than 300 votes).

As elsewhere unemployment and the economy were the top issues and this could not help the Conservatives. In the end Clouthier's independent challenge, while it succeeded in making him the runner-up with the largest proportion of any riding vote going to 'other candidates', did not even serve as speed bump on the road to Hopkins' re-election as he gathered just over 50% of all votes cast.

Member of Parliament: Leonard Donald Hopkins; **Party**: Liberal; **Occupation**: Teacher and vice-principal; **Education**: Queen's University; **Age**: 64 (June 12, 1930); **Year first elected to the House of Commons**: 1965

35068 Renfrew–Nipissing–Pembroke

A: Political Profile
i) Voting Behaviour

	% 1993	% 1988	Change 1988-93
Conservative	13.8	32.1	-18.3
Liberal	50.6	54.3	-3.7
NDP	2.7	12.5	-9.8
Reform	12.2	0	12.2
Other	20.8	1.1	19.7

% Turnout	73.3	Total Ballots (#)	51055
Rejected Ballots (#)	160	% Margin of Victory	29.8
Rural Polls, 1988 (#)	122	Urban Polls, 1988 (#)	84
% Yes - 1992	41.3	% No - 1992	58.3

ii) Campaign Financing

	# of Donations	Total $ Value	% of Limit Spent
Conservative	265	52366	81.5
Liberal	120	29852	63.3
NDP	117	20455	28.7*
Reform	183	27372	38.4
Other	310	65718	

B: Ethno-Linguistic Profile

% English Home Language	96.6	% French Home Language	2.1
% Official Bilingual	10.8	% Other Home Language	1.3
% Catholics	44.6	% Protestants	48.5
% Aboriginal Peoples	0.7	% Immigrants	5.6

C: Socio-Economic Profile

Average Family Income $	45396	Median Family Income $	40480
% Low Income Families	10.8	Average Home Price $	101044
% Home Owners	72.2	% Unemployment	8.5
% Labour Force Participation	64.2	% Managerial-Administrative	9
% Self-Employed	10.1	% University Degrees	7
% Movers	40.5		

D: Industrial Profile

% Manufacturing	13.4	% Service Sector	18.8
% Agriculture	4	% Mining	0.3
% Forestry	1.4	% Fishing	0
% Government Services	15.4	% Business Services	7.1

E: Homogeneity Measures

Ethnic Diversity Index	0.32	Religious Homogeneity Index	0.43
Sectoral Concentration Index	0.4	Income Disparity Index	10.8

F: Physical Setting Characteristics

Total Population	93066	Area (km²)	12392
Population Density (pop/km²)	7.5		

* Tentative value, due to the existence of unpaid campaign expenses.

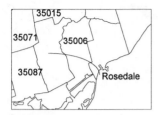

Rosedale

Constituency Number: 35069

This riding is an enormous contradiction. It contains some of the wealthiest and the poorest neighbourhoods in Canada (it ranks 94th highest among Ontario ridings in terms of *average* family income, but only 59th in terms of *median* family incomes). In the north end of the riding the latest edition of *Who's Who in Canada* is probably as useful as a phone or street directory. In the south end of the riding one can find the worst public housing developments, homeless shelters, and public hostels for the indigent in Metro. Housing is expensive, but the riding ranks lowest in the province in terms of the proportion of home owners. The stores around Bloor Street between Yonge and University Avenue are the most exclusive in Canada and those around Parliament and Queen feature names such as Bargain Harold's. The riding also contains some student housing around Ryerson Polytechnical University and the eastern fringe of University of Toronto (St Michael's and Victoria College residences). It is also home to the so-called 'Gay Ghetto' centred in the high-rise communities around Church, Jarvis, and Wellesley Streets. In addition, it is home to the few remaining residents of Toronto Island. Given the generally lower turnout among lower socio-economic groups (and as a whole, Rosedale ranked 6th lowest in Ontario on turnout in 1993), it is conventional wisdom that the riding is won or lost north of Bloor Street.

Although the riding had been held by Tories since 1978, it is hardly a safe Conservative seat. In 1988, a judicial recount was required to give former Conservative cabinet minister David MacDonald (a United Church minister and development aid worker) the victory with an 80 vote margin. MacDonald, who had originally represented a riding from Prince Edward Island (Egmont) for 16 years between 1965 and 1980, had earned a reputation as a 'red Tory'. Following his 1980 defeat, MacDonald went on to become Canada's ambassador to Ethiopia. His winning Rosedale in 1988 enabled the Conservatives to hold the seat, since MacDonald was replacing the popular Tory Cabinet Minister and former Toronto Mayor David Crombie. Given the closeness of the 1988 contest, it is not surprising that the runner-up, Liberal Bill Graham, a lawyer and professor of international trade at the University of Toronto, chose to run again in 1993. Graham had campaigned for the seat in each election since 1984. The *Globe and Mail* described Graham's credentials as those of the ideal Liberal candidate; bilingual, having studied in France and taught in Quebec, worked in a Toronto law firm and helped to form the international organization 'Doctors Without Borders', while simultaneously holding directorates in several large companies. Graham's nomination ended the Liberal's courting of Pat Lavelle, a former senior civil servant in David Peterson's provincial administration, and a potential star candidate, who was reported to be interested in running for the Liberals in the riding.

Also contesting the seat for the NDP was Jack Layton, a city councillor representing the central part of the riding and a veteran of a decade of Toronto city politics. A strong Reform insurgency, catering to the authentic neo-conservatives who previously voted Tory because there was no one even further to the right, was spearheaded by candidate Daniel Jovkovic, a manufacturer from Mississauga. Five minor party candidates and one independent also contested the seat.

After his several efforts, Graham's persistence paid off and he coasted to a comfortable victory for the Liberals. Doubtless Reform's strong showing, with 12.7% of the poll, cost the incumbent some votes, but his own government cost him even more; the combined Tory/Reform vote fell well short of Graham's total.

Member of Parliament: William Graham; **Party**: Liberal; **Occupation**: Lawyer and professor; **Education**: Doctorate; **Age**: 55 (March 17, 1939); **Year first elected to the House of Commons**: 1993

35069 Rosedale

A: Political Profile

i) Voting Behaviour

	% 1993		% 1988	Change 1988-93
Conservative	21.7		41.4	-19.7
Liberal	50		41.2	8.8
NDP	10.7		15.1	-4.4
Reform	12.7		0	12.7
Other	5		2.4	2.6

% Turnout	61.7	Total Ballots (#)	55928
Rejected Ballots (#)	491	% Margin of Victory	28.3
Rural Polls, 1988 (#)	0	Urban Polls, 1988 (#)	226
% Yes - 1992	59.2	% No - 1992	39.8

ii) Campaign Financing

	# of Donations	Total $ Value	% of Limit Spent
Conservative	230	47931	98.8
Liberal	178	38860	87.6
NDP	384	58945	72.7*
Reform	97	23127	40.5
Other	31	46663	

B: Ethno-Linguistic Profile

% English Home Language	81.5	% French Home Language	1
% Official Bilingual	15.7	% Other Home Language	17.5
% Catholics	26.8	% Protestants	35
% Aboriginal Peoples	0.5	% Immigrants	35.6

C: Socio-Economic Profile

Average Family Income $	77225	Median Family Income $	48952
% Low Income Families	27.1	Average Home Price $	419452
% Home Owners	20.6	% Unemployment	9.3
% Labour Force Participation	72.4	% Managerial-Administrative	22
% Self-Employed	11.8	% University Degrees	32.9
% Movers	57.3		

D: Industrial Profile

% Manufacturing	8.7	% Service Sector	11.3
% Agriculture	0.1	% Mining	0.3
% Forestry	0.1	% Fishing	0
% Government Services	6.9	% Business Services	16.4

E: Homogeneity Measures

Ethnic Diversity Index	0.19	Religious Homogeneity Index	0.27
Sectoral Concentration Index	0.66	Income Disparity Index	36.6

F: Physical Setting Characteristics

Total Population	118380	Area (km²)	26
Population Density (pop/km²)	4553.1		

* Tentative value, due to the existence of unpaid campaign expenses.

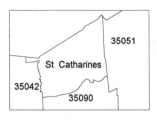

35051

St Catharines

35042

35090

St Catharines

Constituency Number: 35070

Located on the northeast portion of the Niagara Peninsula, the riding of St Catharines is centred on the city for which the district is named. Situated on the fruit belt of the peninsula adjacent to the Welland Ship Canal, 19 kilometres from the American border, the United States looms large in the consciousness of the residents of this riding. The riding's economy is comprised of a variety of light manufacturing, commercial, and service industries. Brock University is also located in the riding. The riding is characterized by lower than average levels of socio-economic affluence; for example, average family incomes run about $6,000 below the norm for ridings in the province.

The economy and 'law and order' were concerns in the 1993 campaign. The St Catharines-Niagara census municipal area had the distinction of running up Canada's highest unemployment rate in the month before the 1993 Federal election. What was more ominous was that the rate was rising, not falling, and with the anticipated closing of a St Catharines GM factory (which was later sold to a subcontractor instead) the rate was set to go higher still. Since 1988 over 8,000 manufacturing jobs left the area, many blamed the Canada-US free trade agreement for this situation. Proximity to the United States means that cross-border shopping and smuggling hurt the retail sector of the local economy. These were encouraged by the Conservative government's strong dollar policy and the initial shock of the GST. Each of these Conservative government policies (the FTA/NAFTA, the strong dollar, and the GST) was perceived to have caused hardship in this riding. Tory incumbent Ken Atkinson, a former lawyer who replaced the retiring Conservative Member Joe Reid and won a reasonably tight 3,500 vote majority in 1988, was widely expected to be in trouble in the 1993 campaign. The debacle of the Tories' national campaign did nothing to comfort the party's local activists.

Five challengers emerged to confront Atkinson. The Reform Party ran Rob Hesp, a businessperson, who was expected to benefit from the local sensitivity to the violent crime problem. Leading up to election day, in fact, some expected Hesp to win the seat. The trial of Paul Teale, accused in the murder of two teenage girls, Leslie Mahaffy and Kristen French, was just beginning as the election writ fell and that of his wife Karla Homolka had just ended just a couple of months before the writ. Homolka's trial caused controversy in that she was allowed to plead guilty to only manslaughter (and was sentenced to just 12 years). The reasons this plea was allowed were kept secret by a court ban on the publication of any further information about her trial. Running for the Liberals was Walt Lastewka, a plant manager with General Motors, and community activist. Jane Hughes, a teacher, ran for the NDP. Two minor party candidates rounded out the slate.

In the end, Lastewka won almost 50% of all votes cast, enough to give him a comfortable margin over the second-place finisher, the Reform's Hesp.

Member of Parliament: Walt Lastewka; **Party**: Liberal; **Occupation**: Manager; **Education**: University of Western Ontario Executive Program; **Age**: 54; **Year first elected to the House of Commons**: 1993

35070 St Catharines

A: Political Profile
i) Voting Behaviour

	% 1993	% 1988	Change 1988-93
Conservative	15.3	40.7	-25.4
Liberal	49	33.3	15.7
NDP	5.7	25.5	-19.8
Reform	28.7	0	28.7
Other	1.4	0.5	0.9

% Turnout	68.4	Total Ballots (#)	49223
Rejected Ballots (#)	383	% Margin of Victory	20.3
Rural Polls, 1988 (#)	0	Urban Polls, 1988 (#)	196
% Yes - 1992	39.7	% No - 1992	59.8

ii) Campaign Financing

	# of Donations	Total $ Value	% of Limit Spent
Conservative	123	26988	68.8
Liberal	151	56330	85.2
NDP	114	14073	18.6
Reform	185	35079	54
Other	36	4587	

B: Ethno-Linguistic Profile

% English Home Language	92.3	% French Home Language	0.9
% Official Bilingual	6.5	% Other Home Language	6.8
% Catholics	33.7	% Protestants	52.8
% Aboriginal Peoples	0.5	% Immigrants	21.9

C: Socio-Economic Profile

Average Family Income $	50708	Median Family Income $	45536
% Low Income Families	14.1	Average Home Price $	153073
% Home Owners	64.8	% Unemployment	10
% Labour Force Participation	64	% Managerial-Administrative	10.7
% Self-Employed	6.5	% University Degrees	9
% Movers	45.1		

D: Industrial Profile

% Manufacturing	19.9	% Service Sector	13.3
% Agriculture	2.5	% Mining	0.1
% Forestry	0.3	% Fishing	0
% Government Services	5.3	% Business Services	5.5

E: Homogeneity Measures

Ethnic Diversity Index	0.27	Religious Homogeneity Index	0.39
Sectoral Concentration Index	0.42	Income Disparity Index	10.2

F: Physical Setting Characteristics

Total Population	96438	Area (km^2)	63
Population Density (pop/km^2)	1530.8		

St Paul's

Constituency Number: 35071

St Paul's is a downtown Toronto riding of enormous contrasts, though not to the extent of its neighbour Rosedale. It has a mix of affluent and poor, although on balance the former are more numerous. Average family incomes, at over $100,000, are the highest in Ontario and its median family income rank second highest. However, more than Rosedale, St Paul's has a sizeable middle-class home-owning population that is white-collar and well educated. It is home to the highest concentration of university graduates in the province, and the second highest concentration of managers and administrators. There is considerable ethnic diversity in the riding. Many immigrant families live in the modest bungalows in the City of York in the riding's north, while there are significant Caribbean and African Canadian communities in the neighbourhood around St Clair Avenue West and Vaughan Road.

St Paul's is a classic swing riding, voting for the overall winning party in every general election since 1957. The 1988 campaign was an interesting one. Substantial redistribution prior to that election resulted in two incumbents running against one another (Liberal Aideen Nicholson and Tory Barbara MacDougall). The campaign was closely fought, but MacDougall won a 3,500 vote victory. When Barbara McDougall announced her retirement the riding became the site of a serious nomination battle. Larry Grossman, a one-time provincial Tory leader, was rumoured to be considering running for the Tory nomination and reportedly had Kim Campbell's support. However, he ran into local opposition, and withdrew before the race really started. The remaining two major candidates each had strong access to media and each spent considerable sums to secure what most thought (at least early in the campaign) was a winnable Conservative seat. Seeking the Tory nomination was Dan Iannucci, founder of MTV Canada, who made a point of his living in the riding, unlike the eventual nomination winner, Isabel Bassett, socialite and wife of media heir John Bassett. Bassett enjoyed a high profile from her broadcast journalism career (she is a producer at CFTO, a local television station), her extensive community work, presidency of the Canadian Club, and co-chairing the James Robinson Johnston Chair in Black Canadian Studies at Dalhousie University. The Liberal challenger, Barry Campbell, is no social outcast either. A lawyer with a prestigious downtown Toronto firm, Campbell is active as a volunteer for the Canadian Jewish Congress, an activist on housing and AIDS issues, and has worked for the International Monetary Fund in Washington. Paul Chaplin, a retiree, ran for the Reform Party, while David Jacobs, a lawyer, offered for the NDP. Seven minor party candidates and one independent also offered in 1993.

Jewish voters were likely turned off by the outgoing Conservative government's seemingly hesitant response to the scandal in the Airborne Regiment. When the government discovered members of the unit had clear racist convictions and one had been videotaped participating in neo-nazi meetings, the Canadian Jewish Congress demanded a zero tolerance policy on racists in the armed forces, arguing that the requirements of national security demanded their exclusion from the military, even if they had recanted (as was formerly the case with communists). The government, not only failed to act until about four months after the scandal broke, it also failed to answer the Canadian Jewish Congress' letter or meet with its leaders until after an official announcement of policy was made. Many of the organization's movers and shakers call St Paul's home. Over one quarter of the riding's residents are Jewish (the third highest proportion among Ontario ridings) and the riding is home to three of Metro's largest synagogues. Similarly, the image of the racism of some Reform candidates and activists probably hurt this party in St Paul's.

In the end, St. Paul's continued its record of anticipating the national result in electing Campbell for the Liberals with well over 50% of the local vote.

Member of Parliament: Barry Campbell; **Party**: Liberal; **Occupation**: Lawyer; **Education**: LL.M; **Age**: 44 (June 15, 1950); **Year first elected to the House of Commons**: 1993

35071 St Paul's

A: Political Profile
i) Voting Behaviour

	% 1993	% 1988	Change 1988-93
Conservative	24.4	47.5	-23.1
Liberal	54.3	40.8	13.5
NDP	5.2	10	-4.8
Reform	11.2	0	11.2
Other	4.9	1.6	3.3

% Turnout	69.7	Total Ballots (#)	51548
Rejected Ballots (#)	397	% Margin of Victory	29.9
Rural Polls, 1988 (#)	0	Urban Polls, 1988 (#)	193
% Yes - 1992	66.4	% No - 1992	32.8

ii) Campaign Financing

	# of Donations	Total $ Value	% of Limit Spent
Conservative	454	102191	99.4
Liberal	159	60674	88.7
NDP	99	11113	20.6
Reform	63	18807	32.7*
Other	119	52479	

B: Ethno-Linguistic Profile

% English Home Language	88.2	% French Home Language	0.5
% Official Bilingual	16.2	% Other Home Language	11.3
% Catholics	24.4	% Protestants	33.9
% Aboriginal Peoples	0.2	% Immigrants	29.1

C: Socio-Economic Profile

Average Family Income $	107631	Median Family Income $	73344
% Low Income Families	13	Average Home Price $	470248
% Home Owners	42.1	% Unemployment	6.7
% Labour Force Participation	72.7	% Managerial-Administrative	23.2
% Self-Employed	15.9	% University Degrees	38.7
% Movers	45.8		

D: Industrial Profile

% Manufacturing	8.4	% Service Sector	9.5
% Agriculture	0.2	% Mining	0.2
% Forestry	0.2	% Fishing	0
% Government Services	5.8	% Business Services	18.2

E: Homogeneity Measures

Ethnic Diversity Index	0.22	Religious Homogeneity Index	0.3
Sectoral Concentration Index	0.67	Income Disparity Index	31.9

F: Physical Setting Characteristics

Total Population	100660	Area (km²)	16
Population Density (pop/km²)	6291.3		

* Tentative value, due to the existence of unpaid campaign expenses.

35039

Sarnia -
Lambton

Sarnia–Lambton

Constituency Number: 35072

Sarnia–Lambton extends along the St Clair River that serves as the Canadian-American boundary to the south of Lake Huron. Proximity to the United States has made Sarnia a major link in Canada's international trade, with the Bluewater Bridge across the St Clair River and the CN rail tunnel to the US located in the city. It is also a major manufacturing and processing centre, especially in the petrochemical industry (the city is the southern terminus of a pipeline from Alberta). The area surrounding the city of Sarnia and in the Lambton polls of the riding is rich agricultural land.

Sarnia–Lambton is a bell-wether riding; only once since 1962 has it failed to vote for the party which wins the mandate to govern. The 1988 election saw the Conservative incumbent, former businessman and sales and account executive Ken James, re-elected. True to its bell-wether form, however, the riding was to go Liberal in 1993. Running for the Liberals was Roger Gallaway, a lawyer and former mayor of Point Edward. The Reform Party nominated Bruce Brogden, a property management worker. Julie Foley, a social worker and veteran of the previous two campaigns, ran again for the NDP, which could not expect to win the seat in light of the province-wide and national difficulties in the party's campaign. Moreover, the area only once elected a member from other than one of the two traditional major parties, and that was a one-term CCF member elected 40 years ago. Two minor party and two independent candidates rounded out the ballot.

Economic concerns dominated the local campaign here, as elsewhere in the province. Even though James could claim a reasonable record of bringing jobs and infrastructure funding to the riding (a new Coast Guard facility, Bluewater Bridge improvements, Community Futures grants for over 800 jobs, a Pollution Research Centre, harbour improvements and the new CN Rail tunnel, which will allow double stack-containers to pass under the river, theoretically boosting manufacturing in the area), the national anti-Tory tide was too much for him to overcome. Native Rights issues also played a role in this campaign as the Stoney Point Nation took their fight to regain their land from the Department of National Defence (see Lambton–Middlesex) to the voters. They started their walk on Ottawa in Sarnia with a kick-off rally and considerable media attention. Sarnia–Lambton was also one of the ridings adjacent to Lambton–Middlesex, where native spokespeople asked questions on the issue at all-candidates meetings. When Prime Minister Campbell visited the riding native leaders publicly questioned her on the issue.

Gallaway, the Liberal candidate, won handily after the ballots were counted, amassing over twice the votes of his nearest competitor, the incumbent James.

Member of Parliament: Roger John Gallaway; **Party**: Liberal; **Occupation**: Lawyer; **Education**: LL.B; **Age**: 46 (May 23, 1948); **Year first elected to the House of Commons**: 1993

35072 Sarnia–Lambton

A: Political Profile
i) Voting Behaviour

	% 1993	% 1988	Change 1988-93
Conservative	22.6	45	-22.4
Liberal	47.6	31.8	15.8
NDP	6.2	22.2	-16
Reform	21.2	0	21.2
Other	2.4	1	1.4

% Turnout	68.4	Total Ballots (#)	43070
Rejected Ballots (#)	327	% Margin of Victory	25
Rural Polls, 1988 (#)	16	Urban Polls, 1988 (#)	150
% Yes - 1992	44.3	% No - 1992	55.3

ii) Campaign Financing

	# of Donations	Total $ Value	% of Limit Spent
Conservative	306	64682	104.1
Liberal	213	52680	70.2
NDP	101	18230	23.4
Reform	163	52040	73.3
Other	172	10135	

B: Ethno-Linguistic Profile

% English Home Language	96.3	% French Home Language	0.9
% Official Bilingual	7.2	% Other Home Language	2.7
% Catholics	31.1	% Protestants	55.8
% Aboriginal Peoples	1.7	% Immigrants	14.7

C: Socio-Economic Profile

Average Family Income $	56708	Median Family Income $	52134
% Low Income Families	12	Average Home Price $	134289
% Home Owners	68.7	% Unemployment	9.3
% Labour Force Participation	66.7	% Managerial-Administrative	10.7
% Self-Employed	6.1	% University Degrees	9.5
% Movers	47.6		

D: Industrial Profile

% Manufacturing	20.9	% Service Sector	13.6
% Agriculture	1.5	% Mining	1.3
% Forestry	0	% Fishing	0.1
% Government Services	4.2	% Business Services	4.4

E: Homogeneity Measures

Ethnic Diversity Index	0.4	Religious Homogeneity Index	0.41
Sectoral Concentration Index	0.43	Income Disparity Index	8.1

F: Physical Setting Characteristics

Total Population	87870	Area (km²)	510
Population Density (pop/km²)	172.3		

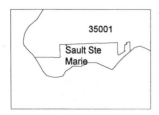

35001

Sault Ste
Marie

Sault Ste Marie

Constituency Number: 35073

This northern Ontario urban riding stretches along the St Mary's River, the international boundary between Canada and the United States. The city itself has benefited from its central location in east-west transportation routes. Just across the river from a city of the same name in the United States, 'the Soo' has grown around the industries of steelmaking (Algoma Steel is, after Hamilton, Canada's leading steel-producing area) and pulp and paper production. Like many ridings in the province's north, Sault Ste Marie has suffered in the recession of the 1990s, and before. Average family incomes run almost $10,000 below the norm for provincial ridings, and unemployment here is one of the ten highest rates.

The riding has changed partisan stripe four times in the previous four elections. Most recently, the NDP's Steve Butland succeeded in wresting the riding from the Tory incumbent and Solicitor-General James Kelleher in 1988. Butland, a former school teacher and principal, knew he was up against a stiff challenge from the start of his 1993 campaign, however, as a result both of Bob Rae's unpopularity and of the national NDP campaign's shortcomings. In the first all-candidates meeting of the campaign he asked the voters of the riding to consider if the Liberals would have intervened to save Algoma Steel and Saint Mary's Paper, or whether they would move a major government office to the region as the Ontario NDP government had done when they relocated Ontario's Lottery Corporation to the area. However, one must wonder if it was a sensible strategy when every poll indicated your party may not even win enough seats to qualify as an official party in the House of Commons, and when it seems the Rae administration is likely to be a one-term phenomenon. Despite these activities, the party did not appear to be much more popular locally than elsewhere in the province.

The major issues were similar to those affecting the neighbouring riding of Algoma: the impact of Free Trade and NAFTA on the region's heavy manufacturing; the refusal of the Mulroney government to repair the Sault canal system, routing traffic through the American locks; forestry and the ability of the forestry industry to export hassle free to the United States and Europe. Meanwhile cross-border shopping (in Michigan) and smuggling, induced by tax differentials and the Mulroney-Bank of Canada strong dollar policy, dented the sales receipts of local retailers. During the campaign Liberal leader Jean Chrétien pointed to the damaged Sault canal and said repairing it was the type of infrastructure project that the Liberals had in mind when they announced their plan for a national infrastructure project. The Liberal candidate, Ron Irwin, a former university lecturer in government and business relations and mayor of Sault Ste Marie, had represented the riding in Ottawa between 1980 and 1984. While Butland and Irwin debated which party could bring the most federal funding to the Sault, Conservative candidate Gerry Nori, a lawyer, decided to campaign on the promise of opposing official bilingualism (except where numbers warrant). It should be remembered that at the height of the constitutional debates over Meech Lake and the Charlottetown Accord the Sault City Council declared the city officially unilingual. Nori's view is incidentally the Reform position on the issue and that alone describes the trouble that he and Reformer Paul Matheswon, a retail automotive shop owner, had: there was not enough room on the right side of the political spectrum for both of them in this most pragmatic of all ridings. Two minor party candidates ran in the 1993 campaign, with no serious effect on the electoral outcome.

Butland, who only managed to win last time by slightly more than 1000 votes dropped to second but it was a distant second, nearly 13,000 votes behind the Liberal winner, Ron Irwin.

Member of Parliament: Ron Irwin; **Party**: Liberal; **Occupation**: Lawyer; **Education**: LL.B; **Age**: 58 (Oct. 29, 1936); **Year first elected to the House of Commons**: 1980 (re-elected 1993)

35073 Sault Ste Marie

A: Political Profile
i) Voting Behaviour

	% 1993	% 1988	Change 1988-93
Conservative	7.8	32.7	-24.9
Liberal	53	32	21
NDP	22.2	35.3	-13.1
Reform	16.3	0	16.3
Other	0.9	0	0.9

% Turnout	71.6	Total Ballots (#)	40768
Rejected Ballots (#)	309	% Margin of Victory	30.8
Rural Polls, 1988 (#)	0	Urban Polls, 1988 (#)	165
% Yes - 1992	28	% No - 1992	71.7

ii) Campaign Financing

	# of Donations	Total $ Value	% of Limit Spent
Conservative	271	54140	82.9
Liberal	240	50142	66.4
NDP	287	32102	91.3
Reform	138	26416	63.6
Other	11	795	

B: Ethno-Linguistic Profile

% English Home Language	93.7	% French Home Language	1.4
% Official Bilingual	10	% Other Home Language	4.9
% Catholics	47.3	% Protestants	41.9
% Aboriginal Peoples	2.9	% Immigrants	12.6

C: Socio-Economic Profile

Average Family Income $	46453	Median Family Income $	41679
% Low Income Families	16.8	Average Home Price $	115013
% Home Owners	65.8	% Unemployment	11.5
% Labour Force Participation	62.7	% Managerial-Administrative	9.7
% Self-Employed	5.2	% University Degrees	8.9
% Movers	41.2		

D: Industrial Profile

% Manufacturing	20.1	% Service Sector	15.1
% Agriculture	0.5	% Mining	0.4
% Forestry	0.5	% Fishing	0.1
% Government Services	8.1	% Business Services	3.8

E: Homogeneity Measures

Ethnic Diversity Index	0.26	Religious Homogeneity Index	0.4
Sectoral Concentration Index	0.46	Income Disparity Index	10.3

F: Physical Setting Characteristics

Total Population	76781	Area (km²)	132
Population Density (pop/km²)	581.7		

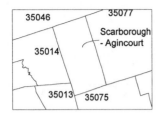

Scarborough–Agincourt

Constituency Number: 35074

Scarborough Agincourt is located in the northwestern corner of the suburban Metro Toronto city of Scarborough. The riding is a home to many commuters. Its economic base is diverse, comprised of a variety of commercial, service, and manufacturing industries. Most of these have been adversely affected by the recession of the 1990s. One teacher expressed the popular desperation in the riding when she asked how she was to motivate her students to learn when their parents both have good educations and are both unemployed. Scarborough is home to a sizeable immigrant community, concentrated particularly in its Agincourt and Rouge River ridings. In Agincourt, over half of all residents are immigrants, giving this the fourth highest proportion of immigrants in the province. The largest group of immigrants, numbering over 23,000, are from China. Only just over two-thirds of families report using English as their home language.

In this environment, the ethnic media is important and that probably hurt the Conservatives and the Reform Party, whose positions on immigration and multiculturalism caused many concern. Law and order issues also played prominently in the local campaign. The Conservative candidate, a consultant and former police sergeant Ben Eng, tried to capitalize on a fear of crime spreading into the riding and especially that crime caused by illegal immigrants and false refugee claimants. His message, that it was primarily Asians who were the victims of crimes committed by illegal Asian immigrants and false refugee claimants, struck a responsive cord in the riding's rapidly developing Chinese Canadian community, but his plan to 'get tough' on immigrants also raised concerns that Eng, one of the few Chinese Canadians ever to serve on the Metro Police force, might have been playing into the hands of racists.

The old York–Scarborough riding, from which Agincourt was drawn, was known to be a swing riding. McCrossan won the seat in 1979, but was defeated in 1980, only to be re-elected in 1984 and defeated again in 1988. Such a volatile electorate holds little comfort for an incumbent.

The Liberal incumbent, Jim Karygiannis, also had a law and order agenda, specifically a pledge to continue his campaign to stiffen the penalties contained in the Young Offenders Act. A Greek-born industrial engineer turned shoe-store owner, Karygiannis was first elected in 1988 (after an unsuccessful attempt to win provincial office in the 1987 election, and after surviving the opposition from the Liberal backrooms to his nomination as the riding's federal candidate) with a narrow 860 vote margin. In addition to Eng's challenge, Karygiannis faced seven other contestants in 1993. Cyril Gibb ran for the Reform Party, while Joe José Perez, a mechanical engineer, won the NDP's nomination. Three minor party candidates, and two independents, also ran but none won even 1% of the poll on election day.

Karygiannis won easily, taking almost 60% of the vote.

Member of Parliament: Jim Karygiannis; **Party**: Liberal; **Occupation**: Industrial engineer; **Education**: BSc, University of Toronto; **Age**: 39 (May 2, 1955); **Year first elected to the House of Commons**: 1988

35074 Scarborough–Agincourt

A: Political Profile

i) Voting Behaviour

	% 1993	% 1988	Change 1988-93
Conservative	21.3	42.4	-21.1
Liberal	59.7	44.3	15.4
NDP	2.3	11.6	-9.3
Reform	14.6	0	14.6
Other	2.2	1.8	0.4

% Turnout	67.4	Total Ballots (#)	41718
Rejected Ballots (#)	345	% Margin of Victory	38.4
Rural Polls, 1988 (#)	0	Urban Polls, 1988 (#)	174
% Yes - 1992	58.4	% No - 1992	41

ii) Campaign Financing

	# of Donations	Total $ Value	% of Limit Spent
Conservative	61	17869	62.8
Liberal	130	46851	90
NDP	11	8870	6
Reform	47	15994	26.5*
Other	20	4287	

B: Ethno-Linguistic Profile

% English Home Language	65	% French Home Language	0.6
% Official Bilingual	6.5	% Other Home Language	34.3
% Catholics	27.5	% Protestants	32.7
% Aboriginal Peoples	0	% Immigrants	51.6

C: Socio-Economic Profile

Average Family Income $	55145	Median Family Income $	49864
% Low Income Families	19.1	Average Home Price $	248547
% Home Owners	59.1	% Unemployment	9
% Labour Force Participation	66.5	% Managerial-Administrative	16.2
% Self-Employed	7.5	% University Degrees	14.9
% Movers	49.2		

D: Industrial Profile

% Manufacturing	17.8	% Service Sector	10.1
% Agriculture	0.3	% Mining	0.2
% Forestry	0	% Fishing	0
% Government Services	4.9	% Business Services	10.5

E: Homogeneity Measures

Ethnic Diversity Index	0.2	Religious Homogeneity Index	0.26
Sectoral Concentration Index	0.47	Income Disparity Index	9.6

F: Physical Setting Characteristics

Total Population	101283	Area (km²)	23
Population Density (pop/km²)	4403.6		

* Tentative value, due to the existence of unpaid campaign expenses.

Scarborough Centre

Constituency Number: 35075

Scarborough Centre, as the name suggests, is bordered on three sides by Scarborough ridings, and to the west by the constituency of Don Valley East. It is a middle/lower middle-class suburban riding that contains both single-family and apartment dwellings. Scarborough Centre families earn on average about $4,000 below the norm for provincial ridings. Over a fifth of residents are employed in manufacturing industries, the highest proportion of the five Scarborough ridings.

Politically, Scarborough ridings tend to swing with the national tide and Centre is no exception. Created in 1979, it elected a Conservative, but went Liberal in 1980. Pauline Browes, a former educator, took the seat from the Liberals in 1984, and held it in 1988. In keeping with the pattern, Centre went back to the Liberals in 1993.

Unemployment, poverty and crime were all perceived to be rising in the riding as in all other parts of Metro. As the election approached, economic conditions were just starting to turn around. However, it would have been impossible to convince the people in this riding, or the neighbouring riding of Scarborough West, that times were getting better. Not when General Motors closed its Scarborough van plant just before the election writ was dropped, sending 3,000 people on to unemployment insurance and cutting business for countless local suppliers and service companies. Most of the workers blamed the Free Trade Agreement for the closing and that meant blaming the Conservative administration, and its local representative, Conservative incumbent Browes.

Perhaps sensing electoral blood, nine candidates challenged Browes in 1993. The Liberal candidate was John Cannis, a human resources (management) consultant. Cannis claimed Royal Trust as a client, and this loosely implicated him in a controversy in the campaign. Royal Trust became insolvent in 1993 and its branch network was sold off to the Royal Bank of Canada at an enormous loss to its large and small owners (though its managers came away from the deal in better shape after a complicated and controversial settlement). Running for Reform was John Pope, an advertising executive from Willowdale. Guy Hunter, a law student, ran for the NDP. Five minor party candidates and one independent also contested the seat, but none was successful in taking even 1% of the vote.

Cannis won with a crushing majority and Browes was relegated to a close third, a few votes behind Reform candidate John Pope.

Member of Parliament: John Cannis; **Party**: Liberal; **Occupation**: Human resource consultant; **Year first elected to the House of Commons**: 1993

35075 Scarborough Centre

A: Political Profile
i) Voting Behaviour

	% 1993	% 1988	Change 1988-93
Conservative	20.3	40.6	-20.3
Liberal	52.5	39.7	12.8
NDP	4	18.9	-14.9
Reform	21	0	21
Other	2.4	0.8	1.6

% Turnout	68.2	Total Ballots (#)	40517
Rejected Ballots (#)	359	% Margin of Victory	31.5
Rural Polls, 1988 (#)	0	Urban Polls, 1988 (#)	165
% Yes - 1992	52.2	% No - 1992	47.2

ii) Campaign Financing

	# of Donations	Total $ Value	% of Limit Spent
Conservative	268	71866	80
Liberal	86	48715	84.4
NDP	106	30723	45.7
Reform	90	19215	31.4
Other	42	8451	

B: Ethno-Linguistic Profile

% English Home Language	81	% French Home Language	0.5
% Official Bilingual	4.9	% Other Home Language	18.5
% Catholics	30.6	% Protestants	39.4
% Aboriginal Peoples	0.2	% Immigrants	38.1

C: Socio-Economic Profile

Average Family Income $	52314	Median Family Income $	48506
% Low Income Families	16	Average Home Price $	226773
% Home Owners	56.9	% Unemployment	9.4
% Labour Force Participation	68.5	% Managerial-Administrative	11.8
% Self-Employed	5.3	% University Degrees	9.3
% Movers	38.3		

D: Industrial Profile

% Manufacturing	20.7	% Service Sector	11
% Agriculture	0.2	% Mining	0.1
% Forestry	0	% Fishing	0
% Government Services	5.8	% Business Services	8.2

E: Homogeneity Measures

Ethnic Diversity Index	0.18	Religious Homogeneity Index	0.29
Sectoral Concentration Index	0.42	Income Disparity Index	7.3

F: Physical Setting Characteristics

Total Population	88409	Area (km²)	25
Population Density (pop/km²)	3536.4		

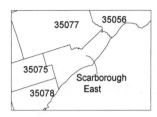

Scarborough East

Constituency Number: 35076

Scarborough East is a lakeshore suburban riding in the easternmost corner of the Metro Toronto region. With average family incomes slightly higher than the provincial norm, Scarborough East is Scarborough's most affluent constituency. Manufacturing, commercial and service activities dominate the riding's economy. Like other metro ridings, the economic recession of the early 1990s had hit home-owners particularly hard, and the recovery was not sufficiently advanced at election time to have assuaged local discontent.

Prior to 1979, the area was considered Liberal territory. Since then, however, the area has been held by the Tories. Incumbent Bob Hicks, a former principal of a Scarborough school, won the riding for the Tories in 1984. His retirement prior to the 1993 election, coupled with the misfortunes of the national Conservatives, opened up the local race.

Nine candidates vied for the seat in 1993. The Liberals nominated Doug Peters, a high profile economist and vice-president of the Toronto-Dominion Bank. Peters, a star candidate, had been wooed by the national Liberals who see in him a potential future Minister of Finance. However, the Liberal nomination became a battleground for pro-choice and pro-life forces within the Liberal Party. Peters had to hold off a determined challenge for the Grits' nomination from the national co-ordinator of the 'Liberals for Life' faction, Dan McCash. At the time, McCash, a 45-year-old computer systems specialist, was appealing two convictions for assault arising out a 1987 protest outside Dr Henry Morganthaler's abortion clinic. Reform ran Randall Flint, an insurance loss control inspector. Replacing Hicks for the Tories was D'Arcy Keene, a health management consultant. The NDP nominated Doug Ottenbreit, a constituency liaison officer. Five other minor party candidates campaigned, but none succeeded in winning even 1% of the poll.

Peters' credentials as an economist and banker were attractive in a campaign that turned heavily on pocketbook issues of the economy. In addition, Scarborough East includes much of the prosperous Scarborough Bluffs area, and isolated Guildwood was obsessed by crime for many years due to the numerous crimes of the 'Scarborough Rapist' (who police finally apprehended in the year before the election).

In the end, Peters almost doubled the vote of his nearest competitor, and succeeded in taking just over 50% of the total vote.

Member of Parliament: Douglas Dennison Peters; **Party**: Liberal; **Occupation**: Economist; **Education**: PhD; **Age**: 64 (March 3, 1950); **Year first elected to the House of Commons**: 1993

35076 Scarborough East

A: Political Profile
i) Voting Behaviour

	% 1993	% 1988	Change 1988-93
Conservative	16.6	43.3	-26.7
Liberal	50.5	39	11.5
NDP	3.8	16.4	-12.6
Reform	25.9	0	25.9
Other	3.1	1.4	1.7

% Turnout	68	Total Ballots (#)	40105
Rejected Ballots (#)	401	% Margin of Victory	24.6
Rural Polls, 1988 (#)	0	Urban Polls, 1988 (#)	165
% Yes - 1992	53.6	% No - 1992	45.9

ii) Campaign Financing

	# of Donations	Total $ Value	% of Limit Spent
Conservative	180	35954	58.7*
Liberal	57	47334	99
NDP	41	17272	25.7
Reform	67	14867	42.5
Other	6	2195	

B: Ethno-Linguistic Profile

% English Home Language	84.8	% French Home Language	0.3
% Official Bilingual	5.7	% Other Home Language	14.9
% Catholics	30.1	% Protestants	42.8
% Aboriginal Peoples	0.3	% Immigrants	35.1

C: Socio-Economic Profile

Average Family Income $	59098	Median Family Income $	52697
% Low Income Families	17.3	Average Home Price $	248844
% Home Owners	58.8	% Unemployment	9.8
% Labour Force Participation	69.9	% Managerial-Administrative	15.3
% Self-Employed	7	% University Degrees	11.5
% Movers	43.2		

D: Industrial Profile

% Manufacturing	18.7	% Service Sector	10
% Agriculture	0.2	% Mining	0.2
% Forestry	0.1	% Fishing	0
% Government Services	6.6	% Business Services	8.7

E: Homogeneity Measures

Ethnic Diversity Index	0.19	Religious Homogeneity Index	0.31
Sectoral Concentration Index	0.42	Income Disparity Index	10.8

F: Physical Setting Characteristics

Total Population	92713	Area (km²)	32
Population Density (pop/km²)	2897.3		

* Tentative value, due to the existence of unpaid campaign expenses.

Scarborough–Rouge River

Constituency Number: 35077

$\mathbf{T}$he largest of Scarborough's five constituencies, Rouge River is located in the northeast corner of the city, on the easternmost fringe of the Metro Toronto area. This riding consists of low and middle income neighbourhoods and has Scarborough's heaviest immigrant concentration; 52% of the riding's population are foreign born. About 35,000 residents are originally from Asia. The economic base is a diverse combination of light manufacturing and commercial/service industries.

Rouge River was a new riding in 1988 and it bucked the national tide in going Liberal that year. Rookie Liberal Derek Lee, a lawyer and former policy advisor to the provincial housing minister, had to survive a tight five-way nomination fight in 1988 before going on to win the riding with an almost 10% margin of victory.

As one of Jean Chrétien's star candidates, Lee had to survive the controversy that this status created for him within the Rouge River Liberal riding association. The riding association claimed that the nomination process had been artificially truncated by Chrétien's naming Lee as the candidate. One potential challenger to Lee had apparently been working for over a year to sign up Liberal Party members to support his challenge. The national Liberal organization responded that the potential candidate had been forewarned that Lee might be designated by Chrétien as the local candidate. While the practice of assigning star candidates to particular ridings is allowed by the Liberal Party's constitution, arguably it threatens the morale of many local party associations who feel that it infringes on their local democratic rights.

In the end, Lee had to defend his seat in 1993, and faced eight challengers. Reform was represented by Les Saunders, a businessman. Paul Ng, a director of operations for a data centre, ran for the Tories. Benn Orrin, a professor, ran for the NDP. An independent and four minor party candidates rounded out the ballot.

As elsewhere in Toronto, and indeed the province, economic issues dominated the campaign. However, the riding's large immigrant population gave the issues of multiculturalism and immigration a heightened salience. Discussing the immigration backlash, the incumbent MP found a new way to flay the Conservatives. Lee seemed to indicate that the Tory immigration policy was acceptable in its outline but, given all the other deceits perpetrated by the Mulroney government, he added 'There is a real lack of confidence in the present government's policies.'

Lee cruised to an easy victory with an absolute majority. If there was a surprise it was the second place showing of Reform in this immigrant-dominated riding.

Member of Parliament: Derek Lee; **Party**: Liberal; **Occupation**: Lawyer; **Education**: LL.B, Osgoode Hall Law School; **Age**: 46 (Oct. 2, 1948); **Year first elected to the House of Commons**: 1988

35077 Scarborough–Rouge River

A: Political Profile

i) Voting Behaviour

	% 1993	% 1988	Change 1988-93
Conservative	11.7	37.6	-25.9
Liberal	66.1	47.1	19
NDP	2.8	13.6	-10.8
Reform	16.8	0	16.8
Other	2.6	1.7	0.9

% Turnout	65.3	Total Ballots (#)	51740
Rejected Ballots (#)	532	% Margin of Victory	49.3
Rural Polls, 1988 (#)	0	Urban Polls, 1988 (#)	201
% Yes - 1992	55.4	% No - 1992	44

ii) Campaign Financing

	# of Donations	Total $ Value	% of Limit Spent
Conservative	22	23386	90.6
Liberal	121	37750	64.4
NDP	41	25966	38.1*
Reform	147	40012	43.6
Other	78	9089	

B: Ethno-Linguistic Profile

% English Home Language	70.7	% French Home Language	0.4
% Official Bilingual	5.3	% Other Home Language	28.9
% Catholics	31.6	% Protestants	31
% Aboriginal Peoples	0.2	% Immigrants	52.3

C: Socio-Economic Profile

Average Family Income $	55961	Median Family Income $	53025
% Low Income Families	14.9	Average Home Price $	248285
% Home Owners	67.7	% Unemployment	8.9
% Labour Force Participation	73.7	% Managerial-Administrative	15
% Self-Employed	6.1	% University Degrees	15
% Movers	58.6		

D: Industrial Profile

% Manufacturing	18.6	% Service Sector	9.8
% Agriculture	0.2	% Mining	0.1
% Forestry	0	% Fishing	0
% Government Services	5.3	% Business Services	9.4

E: Homogeneity Measures

Ethnic Diversity Index	0.21	Religious Homogeneity Index	0.27
Sectoral Concentration Index	0.47	Income Disparity Index	5.2

F: Physical Setting Characteristics

Total Population	147981	Area (km²)	79
Population Density (pop/km²)	1873.2		

* Tentative value, due to the existence of unpaid campaign expenses.

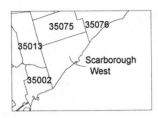

Scarborough West

Constituency Number: 35078

Scarborough West is a blue-collar suburban riding comprised of a diversity of housing, socio-economic, and ethnic backgrounds. It has the lowest average family income of Scarborough's five ridings and falls well below the norm for provincial ridings on this measure also. The constituency has a solid industrial base, concentrated along the rail lines that curve through the riding.

The constituency has the reputation of being a bell-wether riding that is unkind to its incumbents. Prior to 1988, the three traditional major parties have represented the area at one time or another following the riding's creation in 1966, the Liberals three times, the Conservatives twice, and the NDP once. The Liberals won the seat in a tight race in the last election, returning Tom Wappel, a lawyer who was active in the pro-life (including the 'Liberals for Life') movement. 1993 was to suspend the riding's anti-incumbent record, with Wappel sharing in his party's province-wide sweep.

The campaign was dominated by economic issues. Concerns over employment were heightened here, as in neighbouring Scarborough Centre, when General Motors closed its Scarborough van plant just before the election writ was dropped, sending 3,000 people on unemployment insurance and cutting business for countless local suppliers and service companies. Most of the workers blamed the Free Trade Agreement for the closing and that meant blaming the local Tory candidate (and former incumbent), Reg Stackhouse. Stackhouse is a professor who had represented the riding between 1984 and 1988. Six other candidates challenged for the seat in 1993. Aubrey Millard, a teacher, ran a strong campaign for the Reform Party, and Steve Thomas, a fund-raiser, won the NDP's nomination. Four minor party candidates also ran, but with negligible impact on the outcome.

The riding shaped up pretty much as expected: Wappel coasted to an easy re-election, Reform candidate Aubrey Millard came in second and Tory Reg Stackhouse finished third.

Member of Parliament: Thomas Wappel; **Party**: Liberal; **Occupation**: Lawyer; **Education**: LL.B, Queen's University; **Age**: 44 (Feb. 9, 1950); **Year first elected to the House of Commons**: 1988

35078 Scarborough West

A: Political Profile
i) Voting Behaviour

	% 1993	% 1988	Change 1988-93
Conservative	14.5	35.7	-21.2
Liberal	54.4	36.8	17.6
NDP	7.1	26.4	-19.3
Reform	21.2	0	21.2
Other	2.8	1.1	1.7

% Turnout	64.2	Total Ballots (#)	39536
Rejected Ballots (#)	346	% Margin of Victory	33.2
Rural Polls, 1988 (#)	0	Urban Polls, 1988 (#)	185
% Yes - 1992	49.8	% No - 1992	49.6

ii) Campaign Financing

	# of Donations	Total $ Value	% of Limit Spent
Conservative	177	57707	79.7
Liberal	296	45963	66.3
NDP	124	49290	71.9
Reform	92	16673	32.7*
Other	39	1795	

B: Ethno-Linguistic Profile

% English Home Language	81.7	% French Home Language	0.4
% Official Bilingual	4.9	% Other Home Language	17.9
% Catholics	29.4	% Protestants	39.8
% Aboriginal Peoples	0.3	% Immigrants	35.2

C: Socio-Economic Profile

Average Family Income $	49738	Median Family Income $	44975
% Low Income Families	20.1	Average Home Price $	224908
% Home Owners	49.9	% Unemployment	9.1
% Labour Force Participation	66.5	% Managerial-Administrative	12.9
% Self-Employed	6.5	% University Degrees	10.4
% Movers	43.7		

D: Industrial Profile

% Manufacturing	17.5	% Service Sector	11.6
% Agriculture	0.2	% Mining	0.1
% Forestry	0.1	% Fishing	0
% Government Services	6.3	% Business Services	8.8

E: Homogeneity Measures

Ethnic Diversity Index	0.19	Religious Homogeneity Index	0.29
Sectoral Concentration Index	0.45	Income Disparity Index	9.6

F: Physical Setting Characteristics

Total Population	94212	Area (km²)	28
Population Density (pop/km²)	3364.7		

* Tentative value, due to the existence of unpaid campaign expenses.

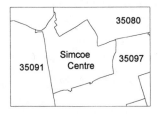

Simcoe Centre

Constituency Number: 35079

Centred on the city of Barrie on the western shore of Lake Simcoe, about 100 kilometres north of the city of Toronto, Simcoe Centre has the distinction of being the only riding in Ontario not won by the Liberals in 1993. MP Ed Harper is also the only Reformer east of the prairies. Simcoe Centre has a diversified economy. The area is a popular summer vacation destination, and in the winter ice fishing is also popular, making tourism an important economic factor. Dairy, poultry, grain and tobacco farming are also important. In the constituency's population centre, Barrie, light manufacturing (principally automotive, brewing, textiles and electronics) and commercial and service activities are also significant. Honda has an automotive plant in Alliston.

The riding has been solidly Conservative for over 40 years. The tradition was upheld in 1988 when the first-time Tory candidate Edna Anderson won the contest with a comfortable 12% margin. Anderson, who had previously worked in real estate and as a partner in her husband's construction agency, decided to make her first term in Parliament also her last. Replacing her as Conservative candidate in 1993 was Doug Jagges, a chartered accountant. Reform's Ed Harper was a former businessman and alderman from Barrie. Reform had made the area one of its early bases for growth, following its 1991 decision to campaign outside the west. The favourable response the party obtained was clearly unsettling to the Conservatives. In early 1992, Brian Mulroney made a pre-election campaign-like sweep to three Tory ridings where Reform was growing, with the purpose of defending his government's record. One of these three areas was Barrie, which was to host a rally later in the year for Preston Manning. The NDP nominated Pat Peters, a provincial government employee from Toronto. Four minor party and two independent candidates rounded out the ballot.

During the campaign two particularly grisly murders were perpetrated in the otherwise sleepy town. In one case a taxi driver was robbed and killed, in the other a local lay religious leader was murdered in his home. Reform's emphasis on law and order, stiffer sentences and a referendum on bringing back the death penalty probably had a particular appeal in this riding where the murder rate was, until recently, described in cases per decade rather than per year.

In the end, the local race was very tight. Ed Harper beat out Liberal candidate and Barrie mayor Janice Laking by only 182 votes. This was the second tightest margin of victory in the province.

Member of Parliament: Edward D. Harper; **Party**: Reform; **Occupation**: Businessman; **Age**: 63 (April 9, 1931); **Year first elected to the House of Commons**: 1993

35079 Simcoe Centre

A: Political Profile
i) Voting Behaviour

	% 1993	% 1988	Change 1988-93
Conservative	17.4	45.4	-28
Liberal	37.6	33.3	4.3
NDP	2.8	16.2	-13.4
Reform	37.9	0	37.9
Other	4.4	5.2	-0.8

% Turnout	66.7	Total Ballots (#)	67589
Rejected Ballots (#)	467	% Margin of Victory	4.7
Rural Polls, 1988 (#)	116	Urban Polls, 1988 (#)	130
% Yes - 1992	43.8	% No - 1992	55.3

ii) Campaign Financing

	# of Donations	Total $ Value	% of Limit Spent
Conservative	221	31262	53.3*
Liberal	179	43131	87.6
NDP	74	21364	22.5
Reform	341	52143	89.4
Other	58	18748	

B: Ethno-Linguistic Profile

% English Home Language	96.8	% French Home Language	1.4
% Official Bilingual	7.1	% Other Home Language	1.8
% Catholics	25	% Protestants	59.5
% Aboriginal Peoples	0.5	% Immigrants	12.2

C: Socio-Economic Profile

Average Family Income $	53857	Median Family Income $	49869
% Low Income Families	9	Average Home Price $	183590
% Home Owners	71	% Unemployment	8
% Labour Force Participation	71.7	% Managerial-Administrative	11.9
% Self-Employed	9.3	% University Degrees	8.4
% Movers	58		

D: Industrial Profile

% Manufacturing	17	% Service Sector	14.6
% Agriculture	2.4	% Mining	0.1
% Forestry	0.1	% Fishing	0
% Government Services	10.9	% Business Services	4.8

E: Homogeneity Measures

Ethnic Diversity Index	0.37	Religious Homogeneity Index	0.43
Sectoral Concentration Index	0.4	Income Disparity Index	7.4

F: Physical Setting Characteristics

Total Population	125380	Area (km²)	1374
Population Density (pop/km²)	91.3		

* Tentative value, due to the existence of unpaid campaign expenses.

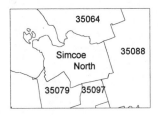

Simcoe North

Constituency Number: 35080

Simcoe North stretches between Lake Simcoe and Georgian Bay in the 'near north' of Ontario. Split almost evenly between urban and rural polls, the only larger towns in the riding are Midland and Orillia. The latter will be familiar to readers of Stephen Leacock's *Sunshine Sketches of a Little Town*, since it served as the backdrop for the town of 'Mariposa' in that humorous work. The area's economy depends heavily on tourism, but farming and light manufacturing (the auto parts manufacturer TRW is located in the riding) are also important.

Doug Lewis has held Simcoe North for 14 years and the riding has not sent anyone but Tories to Ottawa since Diefenbaker's time (1957). The former Minister of Public Security and the Solicitor General for Canada was the senior Tory in Mulroney's cabinet, and as such became something of a lightning rod for discontent with the outgoing Conservative administration. For example, when Lewis went to Toronto to explain the benefits of the Pearson Airport deal he was shouted down and heckled out of the press conference not by a street crowd but a group of municipal councillors, and even the reporters were openly critical of the deal. Many people thought that if Reform were to make a breakthrough into Ontario it would be here rather than in neighbouring Simcoe Centre (where it eventually won its only seat in Ontario). In 1990 Reform held its first major rally in central Canada here in Orillia, when 1,000 people gathered to hear Preston Manning speak. The perceived seriousness of Reform's threat to Lewis is apparent from the fact that the Tories began campaigning vigorously against Reform at least a year before the election had been called.

Lewis faced six opponents in the 1993 campaign. Reform's hopes were pinned on Ray Lyons, a 39-year-old manufacturing supervisor. It is possible that the early success of the Reform Party here and the propensity of the party to attract extremist elements scared voters away from Reform once they actually had their ballots in their hands. This unfortunate ability to attract extremists on the part of Reform was shown in two manners. First there were the number of unsavoury characters who stood or tried to stand as Reform candidates in the federal election in and around Toronto. The most notorious was John Beck (York Centre) who was actually removed by leader Preston Manning. Secondly there were the large number of racists and hate mongers who flocked to the Reform banner as simple supporters. One queried Mr Manning in an Orillia meeting 'on the immigration policies and the people that are coming in and raping our societies and raping our monies and taking from us, the Canadian people, what we don't have any more?' This question drew applause from the assembled crowd. Mr Manning's reply was disapproving but only mildly critical, urging people 'to be a little careful about generalizing on a subject'.

The Liberal nominee was Penetanguishene municipal lawyer and local activist Paul Devillers. Marsha Mitzak, a policy advisor, ran for the NDP. Three minor party candidates also competed in the campaign.

This was one more riding where neither Reform or the Progressive Conservatives could totally dominate on the right. By splitting the vote, the Liberals were able to slide up the middle with a moderate plurality.

Member of Parliament: Paul Devillers; **Party:** Liberal; **Occupation:** Lawyer; **Education:** LL.B; **Year first elected to the House of Commons:** 1993

35080 Simcoe North

A: Political Profile
i) Voting Behaviour

	% 1993	% 1988	Change 1988-93
Conservative	23.1	44	-20.9
Liberal	40.6	37.8	2.8
NDP	3.4	18.1	-14.7
Reform	30.7	0	30.7
Other	2.1	0	2.1

% Turnout	70.8	Total Ballots (#)	57283
Rejected Ballots (#)	360	% Margin of Victory	9.9
Rural Polls, 1988 (#)	122	Urban Polls, 1988 (#)	102
% Yes - 1992	42.4	% No - 1992	56.6

ii) Campaign Financing

	# of Donations	Total $ Value	% of Limit Spent
Conservative	367	53758	85.8
Liberal	196	33336	98.8
NDP	55	17108	36.8*
Reform	206	49243	72.7
Other	31	4773	

B: Ethno-Linguistic Profile

% English Home Language	97.1	% French Home Language	1.3
% Official Bilingual	8.7	% Other Home Language	1.6
% Catholics	29.5	% Protestants	57
% Aboriginal Peoples	2	% Immigrants	9.3

C: Socio-Economic Profile

Average Family Income $	49557	Median Family Income $	44123
% Low Income Families	9.3	Average Home Price $	181169
% Home Owners	75.8	% Unemployment	8.9
% Labour Force Participation	65.5	% Managerial-Administrative	11.3
% Self-Employed	11.3	% University Degrees	6.7
% Movers	47.1		

D: Industrial Profile

% Manufacturing	18.3	% Service Sector	11.4
% Agriculture	3.2	% Mining	0.5
% Forestry	0.2	% Fishing	0
% Government Services	7.9	% Business Services	3.3

E: Homogeneity Measures

Ethnic Diversity Index	0.39	Religious Homogeneity Index	0.41
Sectoral Concentration Index	0.41	Income Disparity Index	11

F: Physical Setting Characteristics

Total Population	103132	Area (km²)	2966
Population Density (pop/km²)	34.8		

* Tentative value, due to the existence of unpaid campaign expenses.

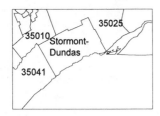

Stormont–Dundas

Constituency Number: 35081

The riding of Stormont–Dundas is a mixture of urban and rural regions of eastern Ontario that stretches south from the city of Cornwall along the north shore of the St Lawrence River. While the city of Cornwall in the southeast corner of the riding was originally a Loyalist settlement, just under a quarter of the riding's residents are of French ethnic origin, and about 14% report using French as their home language. Many of these francophones are concentrated in the eastern section of the city of Cornwall. The riding's economy is dominated by farming and light manufacturing. Petrochemical, paper, and textile manufacturing are found in the city of Cornwall.

The riding has a mixed partisan history. It joined with much of the country in electing a Tory in 1984, but the last election saw the Liberals win a relatively comfortable victory with a 17% margin. Bob Kilger, a businessman and former NHL hockey referee and coach of the Cornwall Royals junior hockey club was expected by most to run successfully for a second term for the Liberals in 1993.

He faced six challengers in the campaign. Leslie Ault, a lawyer from Winchester, won the Tory nomination. Annette Turner, a teacher from South Mountain, ran for Reform, and David Moss, a teacher from Long Sault stood for the NDP. Three minor party candidates rounded out the ballot.

It is the southern boundary of the riding, the St Lawrence River, that defines one of Stormont–Dundas's most serious problems, smuggling. The city of Cornwall was in the centre of the cigarette smuggling crisis. During the first half of the election the crisis was so severe that the mayor of Cornwall was placed in protective police custody due to a number of death threats after he ordered Cornwall city police to increase their intradiction efforts. During the campaign the mayor made a public appeal to the federal public safety minister to increase the RCMP presence in his community to help combat the illicit trade. Complicating the problem is the riding's other major problem, unemployment. In the city of Cornwall approximately 40% of households were in receipt of some sort of governmental benefit or another during the election campaign. For many smuggling is the only source of income available outside of government support. Over 20 major industrial employers have shut down operations in the riding in the last two years.

When the ballots were counted, Kilger had piled up an almost 20,000 vote margin of victory, taking over two-thirds of all votes.

Member of Parliament: Robert (Bob) Kilger; **Party:** Liberal; **Occupation:** Businessperson; **Education:** High school; **Age:** 50 (June 29, 1944); **Year first elected to the House of Commons:** 1988

35081 Stormont–Dundas

A: Political Profile
i) Voting Behaviour

	% 1993	% 1988	Change 1988-93
Conservative	17.6	29.3	-11.7
Liberal	63.4	46	17.4
NDP	2.7	12.7	-10
Reform	13.8	0	13.8
Other	2.6	12	-9.4

% Turnout	68	Total Ballots (#)	43023
Rejected Ballots (#)	309	% Margin of Victory	45.8
Rural Polls, 1988 (#)	87	Urban Polls, 1988 (#)	110
% Yes - 1992	46.4	% No - 1992	53.2

ii) Campaign Financing

	# of Donations	Total $ Value	% of Limit Spent
Conservative	177	30903	93.2
Liberal	189	30615	73.5
NDP	26	3585	3.9*
Reform	155	16639	27.9
Other	29	3958	

B: Ethno-Linguistic Profile

% English Home Language	84.9	% French Home Language	13.7
% Official Bilingual	34.8	% Other Home Language	1.4
% Catholics	54	% Protestants	39.2
% Aboriginal Peoples	0.5	% Immigrants	6.5

C: Socio-Economic Profile

Average Family Income $	45888	Median Family Income $	40633
% Low Income Families	14.5	Average Home Price $	103819
% Home Owners	67.4	% Unemployment	8.4
% Labour Force Participation	65.2	% Managerial-Administrative	10.5
% Self-Employed	10.8	% University Degrees	5.9
% Movers	44.4		

D: Industrial Profile

% Manufacturing	19.3	% Service Sector	11.7
% Agriculture	6.5	% Mining	0.2
% Forestry	0.6	% Fishing	0
% Government Services	8.3	% Business Services	3.6

E: Homogeneity Measures

Ethnic Diversity Index	0.36	Religious Homogeneity Index	0.44
Sectoral Concentration Index	0.36	Income Disparity Index	11.5

F: Physical Setting Characteristics

Total Population	85195	Area (km²)	2130
Population Density (pop/km²)	40		

* Tentative value, due to the existence of unpaid campaign expenses.

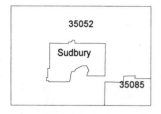

Sudbury

Constituency Number: 35082

The riding of Sudbury is an urban seat about 400 kilometres north of Toronto in northern Ontario which is entirely surrounded by one neighbouring constituency, Nickel Belt. Sudbury is the heart of the nickel mining industry (it is the largest single source of nickel in the world, and it also is Canada's largest producer of copper) along with the area in the riding of Nickel Belt. Indeed, the name Sudbury is closely associated in the minds of many Canadians with the names of two mineral resource companies - Inco (the International Nickel Company) and Falconbridge Nickel Mines. The riding's central location as the 'gateway to the north' has meant that it is becoming increasingly important as a transportation and public and private sector service centre. However, the community's heart is still in the mines and nickel smelters even if every year retail trade and services (such as health care) grab an increasing share of total labour market. Laurentian University is located in this riding. The workforce of Sudbury has been an important player in the emergence of the labour movement in Canada.

Since the riding's creation in 1947 it has returned Liberal MPs with one brief exception in a by-election in 1967 (when an NDP candidate won). More than the Free Trade Agreement and the NAFTA, it was the outgoing Conservative administration's strong dollar policy that hurt nickel exports and led to some tough years in Sudbury. The recession made those years even worse. Consequently, the Progressive Conservatives were not anticipated to be a strong force here in the 1993 election. The substantial French Canadian minority in the riding also augured ill for the Reform Party, whose vow to scrap the official languages act and replace it with a 'where necessary only' program, raised eyebrows in French Canadian communities coast to coast including here and in the neighbouring Nickel Belt. Crime and violence were also issues in this riding. On October 7, 1993 a routine traffic violation ended with the murder of Sudbury Police Constable Joe MacDonald. The killers were two career criminals, one of whom was seriously wounded in the shoot out. MacDonald was a recruiting-poster police officer: university educated, an ex-collegiate athlete and family man, his two hobbies were coaching high school football and working with under-privileged children. After the murder of MacDonald all candidates reiterated their belief that the criminal justice system was too lenient on offenders.

Winning the riding for the Liberals in 1988 was Diane Marleau, an accountant and veteran of municipal politics. She confronted eight challengers in the 1993 campaign. The Reform party ran Mike Smith, a sales manager from Verner. Winning the Conservative nomination was Maurice Lamoureaux, a real estate agent. The NDP candidate Rosemarie Blenkinsop, an unemployed worker, had to counter the same problems faced by MP John Rodriguez in neighbouring Nickel Belt, an overall perception that the party was too extreme in social policy and too conservative with regard to labour law and its treatment of public sector workers, of whom there are many in the Sudbury area. Three minor party and two independent candidates rounded out the 1993 ballot.

As expected, on election day Diane Marleau piled up a comfortable victory margin of more than 22,000 votes for the Liberals.

Member of Parliament: Diane Marleau; **Party:** Liberal; **Occupation:** Administrator; **Education:** BA, Laurentian University; **Age:** 51 (June 21, 1943); **Year first elected to the House of Commons:** 1988

35082 Sudbury

A: Political Profile

i) Voting Behaviour

	% 1993	% 1988	Change 1988-93
Conservative	8.7	22	-13.3
Liberal	66.1	42	24.1
NDP	8.7	27.8	-19.1
Reform	13.7	0	13.7
Other	2.9	8.2	-5.3

% Turnout	65.4	Total Ballots (#)	42677
Rejected Ballots (#)	379	% Margin of Victory	52.4
Rural Polls, 1988 (#)	0	Urban Polls, 1988 (#)	176
% Yes - 1992	38.9	% No - 1992	60.6

ii) Campaign Financing

	# of Donations	Total $ Value	% of Limit Spent
Conservative	224	32791	64
Liberal	231	61894	67.2
NDP	114	21696	66.3
Reform	55	11169	14.8
Other	36	5514	

B: Ethno-Linguistic Profile

% English Home Language	79.7	% French Home Language	15.7
% Official Bilingual	34.5	% Other Home Language	4.6
% Catholics	65.3	% Protestants	25.6
% Aboriginal Peoples	2.9	% Immigrants	10.4

C: Socio-Economic Profile

Average Family Income $	52822	Median Family Income $	47496
% Low Income Families	17.5	Average Home Price $	125963
% Home Owners	52	% Unemployment	9
% Labour Force Participation	63.8	% Managerial-Administrative	10.4
% Self-Employed	5.4	% University Degrees	10.3
% Movers	46.8		

D: Industrial Profile

% Manufacturing	7.6	% Service Sector	14.2
% Agriculture	0.3	% Mining	7.5
% Forestry	0.3	% Fishing	0
% Government Services	9.3	% Business Services	4.1

E: Homogeneity Measures

Ethnic Diversity Index	0.26	Religious Homogeneity Index	0.48
Sectoral Concentration Index	0.45	Income Disparity Index	10.1

F: Physical Setting Characteristics

Total Population	80925	Area (km²)	121
Population Density (pop/km²)	668.8		

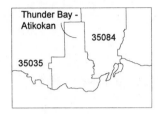

Thunder Bay–Atikokan

Constituency Number: 35083

Thunder Bay–Atikokan is a northern Ontario riding based on the western portion of the city of Thunder Bay, and extending south to the international border with Minnesota, and west to the township of Atikokan. The city of Thunder Bay, formed in 1970 from the amalgamation of the cities of Fort William and Port Arthur, is the western terminus in Canada of the St Lawrence Seaway. This strategic location has made the Port of Thunder Bay one of the largest grain-handling ports in the world. In addition to these transportation related industries, the riding's economy is dominated by resource extraction and processing industries (mining, forestry, pulp and paper) together with some manufacturing.

The NDP's incumbent, Iain Angus, has represented the riding since 1984. In 1993, however, Angus was destined to become yet another Ontario NDP MP to be defeated by a combination of his party's unpopularity and a division in the social democratic-labour union forces in his riding. While Angus received the traditional endorsement from the Thunder Bay District Labour Council, it was not a whole-hearted one. The large local of the Service Employees Union insisted that its own endorsement would be reserved for candidates who emulated Stephen Langdon (NDP MP Windsor–Essex) in publicly denouncing the public service wage cuts imposed by Ontario NDP premier Bob Rae. The riding's electorate had registered their discontent in the 1992 constitutional referendum, registering the lowest 'yes' vote in the province.

Confronting Angus in the 1993 campaign for the Liberals was Stan Dromisky, a retired university professor who had run a close second to Angus in the 1988 campaign. Reform nominated Colyne Gibbons, a retired administrator, while the Conservatives ran Tony Stehmann, a retail consultant.

With the Canadian-American border forming the southern boundary of this riding, smuggling, cross-border shopping, the strong Canadian dollar policy of the Mulroney government and the tax differential between Canada and the US (which was heightened by the GST), all impacted heavily on the riding. So serious was the cross-border shopping problem that the weekly *Thunder Bay Post* felt it had a moral obligation not to accept advertising from American retailers. Liberal Stan Dromisky also stuck pretty much to the plan laid out by his party, explain how the promises of the 'Red Book' would solve local problems, such as the need to improve Thunder Bay's harbour. Iain Angus meanwhile pointed to his record of achievements in spite of his opposition status, including airport improvements, a number of renovation contracts for federal buildings and the improvement in the Northern Health Travel Grants he helped bring about in cooperation with the provincial NDP government. At the start of the campaign Angus also won an award for a battle he lost. In September, Transport 2000 recognized him for his efforts to convince VIA rail to restore passenger rail service to the Lakehead.

All this aside, Angus could not overcome the division in his forces and the general national sentiment for the Liberals as the surest way to remove the Tory government, losing to his Liberal challenger by over 13,000 votes.

Member of Parliament: Stanley Dromisky; **Party:** Liberal; **Occupation:** Professor (emeritus); **Education:** PhD, University of Florida; **Age:** 63; **Year first elected to the House of Commons:** 1993

35083 Thunder Bay–Atikokan

A: Political Profile

i) Voting Behaviour

	% 1993	% 1988	Change 1988-93
Conservative	8.2	31.3	-23.1
Liberal	57.3	32.7	24.6
NDP	19	35.9	-16.9
Reform	15.6	0	15.6
Other	0	0.2	-0.2

% Turnout	68.1	Total Ballots (#)	34834
Rejected Ballots (#)	254	% Margin of Victory	38.3
Rural Polls, 1988 (#)	31	Urban Polls, 1988 (#)	120
% Yes - 1992	27.9	% No - 1992	71.6

ii) Campaign Financing

	# of Donations	Total $ Value	% of Limit Spent
Conservative	197	52013	79
Liberal	304	51634	81.3
NDP	231	59898	86.7
Reform	115	28698	51.9
Other	0	0	

B: Ethno-Linguistic Profile

% English Home Language	95.6	% French Home Language	0.9
% Official Bilingual	6.3	% Other Home Language	3.5
% Catholics	39.8	% Protestants	47.3
% Aboriginal Peoples	6.4	% Immigrants	10.2

C: Socio-Economic Profile

Average Family Income $	53087	Median Family Income $	48680
% Low Income Families	11.5	Average Home Price $	108214
% Home Owners	72.2	% Unemployment	10.1
% Labour Force Participation	67.2	% Managerial-Administrative	10.8
% Self-Employed	6.2	% University Degrees	7.6
% Movers	41.1		

D: Industrial Profile

% Manufacturing	12.6	% Service Sector	13.9
% Agriculture	1.1	% Mining	0.7
% Forestry	2.1	% Fishing	0
% Government Services	11	% Business Services	3.5

E: Homogeneity Measures

Ethnic Diversity Index	0.21	Religious Homogeneity Index	0.38
Sectoral Concentration Index	0.44	Income Disparity Index	8.3

F: Physical Setting Characteristics

Total Population	68169	Area (km²)	24413
Population Density (pop/km²)	2.8		

Thunder Bay–Nipigon

Constituency Number: 35084

This large northern riding extends northward from the city of Thunder Bay on the western shores of Lake Superior. The riding is dominated by the city of Thunder Bay, one of the world's largest grain ports. Forestry and pulp and paper are important to the riding's economy, as is Lakehead University and Confederation College, both of which are located in this district.

After decades of Liberal domination (including a long stint of representation by C.D. Howe), NDP MP Ernie Epp took the seat in 1984. In 1988, however, the riding returned to its traditions by electing Joe Comuzzi, a lawyer and former car dealer. The NDP's candidate, David Ramsay, a social worker from Kaministiquia, like his counterpart in neighbouring Thunder Bay–Atikokan was hurt by the less-than-enthusiastic endorsement from the Thunder Bay District Labour Council. The large local of the Service Employees Union insisted that its own endorsement would be reserved for candidates who emulated Stephen Langdon (NDP MP Windsor–Essex) in publicly denouncing the public service wage cuts imposed by Ontario NDP premier Bob Rae. With the Canada-US border forming the southern boundary of the neighbouring riding of Thunder Bay–Atikokan, smuggling, cross-border shopping, the strong Canadian dollar policy of the Mulroney government and the tax differential between Canada and the US (which was heightened by the GST), all impacted heavily on this riding. So serious was the cross-border shopping problem that the weekly *Thunder Bay Post* felt it had a moral obligation not to accept advertising from American retailers.

These issues and the high unemployment rate gave electors little reason to vote for the Tory candidate. The Tory candidate, educator Marlene Hogarth, arguably gave voters a few more. In one of her advertisements she criticized Liberal MP Joe Comuzzi for voting in favour of the Meech Lake Accord and the Charlottetown Agreement. While this might have played well in a riding that registered one of the lowest approval rates for the agreement in Ontario, the fact that these agreements were negotiated by a Conservative government was probably not lost on voters. In another advertisement Hogarth blamed Comuzzi for the high unemployment in the riding and his failure to obtain federal funds for the riding. However, many voters would likely blame the Conservative party for both of these problems rather than their opposition MP. The local Reform candidate was Bob Reynolds, a water treatment plant operator from Neebing. Two minor party candidates collected a little more than 500 votes between them.

On election day, Liberal MP Joe Comuzzi's re-election was assured by a crushing 60% margin over the second place Reform candidate.

Member of Parliament: Joe Comuzzi; **Party:** Liberal; **Occupation:** Lawyer; **Education:** LL.B, University of Windsor; **Age:** 61 (April 5, 1933); **Year first elected to the House of Commons:** 1988

35084 Thunder Bay–Nipigon

A: Political Profile

i) Voting Behaviour

	% 1993	% 1988	Change 1988-93
Conservative	9.6	25.6	-16
Liberal	65.1	40.2	24.9
NDP	9	34.1	-25.1
Reform	14.9	0	14.9
Other	1.4	0	1.4

% Turnout	67.7	Total Ballots (#)	37589
Rejected Ballots (#)	270	% Margin of Victory	50.2
Rural Polls, 1988 (#)	42	Urban Polls, 1988 (#)	106
% Yes - 1992	31.7	% No - 1992	67.6

ii) Campaign Financing

	# of Donations	Total $ Value	% of Limit Spent
Conservative	176	51298	83.3
Liberal	219	46388	96.4
NDP	186	43339	56.3
Reform	89	17167	25.3
Other	8	1521	

B: Ethno-Linguistic Profile

% English Home Language	92.1	% French Home Language	1.1
% Official Bilingual	6.9	% Other Home Language	6.8
% Catholics	39.6	% Protestants	46.8
% Aboriginal Peoples	5.3	% Immigrants	14.5

C: Socio-Economic Profile

Average Family Income $	55628	Median Family Income $	49920
% Low Income Families	12.3	Average Home Price $	119035
% Home Owners	67.9	% Unemployment	9.5
% Labour Force Participation	67.4	% Managerial-Administrative	11.3
% Self-Employed	6.5	% University Degrees	10.6
% Movers	42		

D: Industrial Profile

% Manufacturing	13.1	% Service Sector	12.8
% Agriculture	1.1	% Mining	0.9
% Forestry	2.2	% Fishing	0.1
% Government Services	10.3	% Business Services	3.8

E: Homogeneity Measures

Ethnic Diversity Index	0.18	Religious Homogeneity Index	0.38
Sectoral Concentration Index	0.44	Income Disparity Index	10.3

F: Physical Setting Characteristics

Total Population	72602	Area (km²)	44150
Population Density (pop/km²)	1.6		

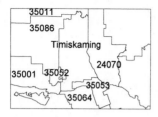

Timiskaming–French River

Constituency Number: 35085

This huge, primarily rural riding that borders Quebec in northern Ontario includes the depressed gold mining centre of Kirkland Lake. In addition to the latter town, population is also concentrated in the 'tri-towns' of Cobalt, New Liskeard, and Haileybury. The rugged Canadian shield gives the riding a rich resource base from which to draw. Forestry, mining, and tourism dominate the riding's economy. Timiskaming–French River is one of the poorest and one of the most francophone and Catholic constituencies in the province. In terms of its 1991 population, it is also the province's smallest district.

As with most mining centres the Progressive Conservative government's reduction in the tax advantages that accrue to those who invest in the shares of resource exploration companies (so-called 'flow through' shares) was a major bone of contention here. Especially galling to locals was the fact that many companies which had earned profits in the area were not re-investing in Kirkland Lake but rather in Chile and elsewhere abroad.

The Progressive Conservatives replaced their retiring MP John MacDougall with Bob Mantha, son of former Nipissing MP Moe Mantha, and a North Bay golf club manager and entrepreneur. The Liberals nominated Ben Serré, a bilingual businessman from Verner. Serré had narrowly lost to MacDougall in the 1988 campaign. NDP candidate Bob Yee, a miner from Kirkland Lake, promised taxation changes to make mining in Canada more attractive to domestic mining companies. Reform Candidate Dan Louie based his campaign on the position that a Reform government would give Northern Ontario a fairer deal. He specifically pointed to the disparity in federal aid available to Northern Ontario communities as opposed to that available to similar communities on the other side of the Quebec border, which forms the eastern boundary of this riding. According to his figures, the federal government spent only $15 million annually on development in Northern Ontario but over $231 million in Northern Quebec. Louie, a businessman from Kirkland Lake, probably alienated the francophones in the area by advocating his party's policy of scrapping the official languages act and reducing bilingual service to an 'as population dictates' basis. An independent and a minor party candidate also campaigned, but drew little support.

As in neighbouring Nipissing, the fate of the Ontario Northland Railroad (provincially owned and based in North Bay) was a major election concern. The line runs on tracks owned by CN, which the federally owned railroad would prefer to abandon. The fact that the Progressive Conservative government supported the railroad's position surely did not win it many friends here. This time Serré cruised to an easy victory, with the nearest candidate over 10,000 votes behind his total.

Member of Parliament: Benoit Serré; **Party**: Liberal; **Occupation**: Teacher; **Age**: 43 (April 7, 1951); **Year first elected to the House of Commons**: 1993

35085 Timiskaming–French River

A: Political Profile
i) Voting Behaviour

	% 1993	% 1988	Change 1988-93
Conservative	15.5	36.6	-21.1
Liberal	59.8	33.5	26.3
NDP	8.8	25.5	-16.7
Reform	13.3	0	13.3
Other	2.7	4.5	-1.8

% Turnout	68.6	Total Ballots (#)	29419
Rejected Ballots (#)	221	% Margin of Victory	44.3
Rural Polls, 1988 (#)	107	Urban Polls, 1988 (#)	50
% Yes - 1992	42.9	% No - 1992	56.4

ii) Campaign Financing

	# of Donations	Total $ Value	% of Limit Spent
Conservative	120	82319	94.9
Liberal	150	38088	93.9
NDP	69	30796	39.2
Reform	69	17249	17.2
Other	27	7944	

B: Ethno-Linguistic Profile

% English Home Language	73.1	% French Home Language	25.8
% Official Bilingual	37.8	% Other Home Language	1
% Catholics	54.3	% Protestants	36.1
% Aboriginal Peoples	1.6	% Immigrants	4.6

C: Socio-Economic Profile

Average Family Income $	43013	Median Family Income $	37263
% Low Income Families	15.4	Average Home Price $	79744
% Home Owners	73.8	% Unemployment	11.1
% Labour Force Participation	60.2	% Managerial-Administrative	9.2
% Self-Employed	10.2	% University Degrees	5.2
% Movers	38		

D: Industrial Profile

% Manufacturing	9.2	% Service Sector	12.5
% Agriculture	5	% Mining	7.2
% Forestry	2.3	% Fishing	0.1
% Government Services	8.7	% Business Services	3

E: Homogeneity Measures

Ethnic Diversity Index	0.38	Religious Homogeneity Index	0.43
Sectoral Concentration Index	0.35	Income Disparity Index	13.4

F: Physical Setting Characteristics

Total Population	57057	Area (km²)	32466
Population Density (pop/km²)	1.8		

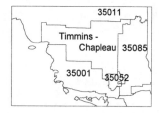

Timmins–Chapleau

Constituency Number: 35086

Timmins–Chapleau, Ontario's third largest riding, is located to the north of Sudbury, and stretches from Wawa in the west to Iroquois Falls in the northeast. Incorporated as a city in 1971, Timmins has the distinction of being the second largest city, covering 3212 square kilometres, in North America! As with other 'Canadian Shield' ridings in Ontario's north, resource industries dominate the local economy. It has the province's highest concentration of employment in mining industries, and as noted below, issues surrounding the financial health of this industry figured in the 1993 campaign. This is the heart of Ontario's hunting culture (especially moose and deer) and the strong dollar policy of the Mulroney government did some serious damage to the area's tourism industry, encouraging foreign hunters (mainly Americans) to stay home.

This riding was suffering from a great deal of discontentment. In 1984 the governing Progressive Conservatives took the seat and the electors felt slighted and ignored as their locally popular MP Aurel Gervais languished on Mulroney's crowded backbench. In 1988 the riding went NDP and Cid Samson, a former president of Local 7580 of the United Steelworkers, and a workers' advisor, was equally competent but as an opposition member he was equally lacking in power. Local press commentary suggested that there was considerable support for the kinds of major reforms to Canada's system of representative democracy being advanced by the Reform Party. However, this was the only riding in Ontario not to nominate a Reform candidate.

Not surprisingly, as with many of the Northern Ontario constituencies, a major issue here was the Conservative government's decision to curtail the tax advantages accruing to those who invest in mineral exploration companies (so-called 'flow through' shares). Both the Liberals and the NDP won wide support from community leaders in the riding for their public statements that their parties would restore the taxation savings formerly available through this type of investment. In the NDP's case, the announcement was made by national leader Audrey MacLaughlin. In the case of the Liberals the pronouncement was made by local candidate Peter Thalheimer, a barrister and solicitor who had run a close second to Samson in 1988. If anyone doubted that this was official Liberal policy they were re-assured when deputy Liberal leader Sheila Copps reiterated the promise at a local rally. John Murphy, a railroad supervisor, ran for the Tories. Two minor party challengers and one independent candiate also appeared on the ballot in 1993.

NDP incumbent Cid Samson was not helped by the unpopularity of the provincial NDP government of Bob Rae and found himself (like most federal NDPers in the province) spending much of his campaign energy reminding everyone that he was their federal rather than their provincial candidate. On the other hand Samson (whether he liked it or not) was official endorsed by Campaign Life's Timmins chapter as 'Pro-Life Candidate'. Federal NDP policy is that all candidates must be Pro-Choice, a policy Samson has tried numerous means to skirt while not overtly disobeying.

Last time Samson only won this riding by 1,275 votes. As voting day approached, Samson was reportedly baffled by the NDP's poor showing in national opinion polls, and confident that he was running a much stronger local campaign. While his 27% was well above his party's provincial or national average, and good enough to make his the NDP's third best finish in Ontario, it fell far short of the Liberals' 55.5%.

Member of Parliament: Peter Thalheimer; **Party:** Liberal; **Occupation:** Lawyer; **Education:** LL.B;
Year first elected to the House of Commons: 1993

35086 Timmins–Chapleau

A: Political Profile
i) Voting Behaviour

	% 1993	% 1988	Change 1988-93
Conservative	14.2	30.8	-16.6
Liberal	55.5	32.6	22.9
NDP	26.7	36.6	-9.9
Reform	0	0	0
Other	3.6	0	3.6

% Turnout	65.4	Total Ballots (#)	31096
Rejected Ballots (#)	296	% Margin of Victory	28.8
Rural Polls, 1988 (#)	65	Urban Polls, 1988 (#)	100
% Yes - 1992	42	% No - 1992	57.5

ii) Campaign Financing

	# of Donations	Total $ Value	% of Limit Spent
Conservative	68	36869	43.5
Liberal	152	71106	93.4
NDP	144	40953	53
Reform	0	0	0
Other	20	6496	

B: Ethno-Linguistic Profile

% English Home Language	69.6	% French Home Language	28.2
% Official Bilingual	44.6	% Other Home Language	2.2
% Catholics	66.3	% Protestants	25.7
% Aboriginal Peoples	2.8	% Immigrants	6

C: Socio-Economic Profile

Average Family Income $	50070	Median Family Income $	45860
% Low Income Families	13.9	Average Home Price $	102258
% Home Owners	66.3	% Unemployment	10.1
% Labour Force Participation	65.9	% Managerial-Administrative	8.4
% Self-Employed	5.8	% University Degrees	6.2
% Movers	46.6		

D: Industrial Profile

% Manufacturing	10	% Service Sector	13.1
% Agriculture	0.7	% Mining	14.9
% Forestry	3.1	% Fishing	0
% Government Services	7.5	% Business Services	2.8

E: Homogeneity Measures

Ethnic Diversity Index	0.38	Religious Homogeneity Index	0.5
Sectoral Concentration Index	0.34	Income Disparity Index	8.4

F: Physical Setting Characteristics

Total Population	65504	Area (km^2)	46730
Population Density (pop/km^2)	1.4		

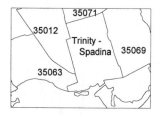

Trinity–Spadina

Constituency Number: 35087

This is a downtown Toronto riding that stretches from the Lake Ontario shores to the CN line north of Bloor Street West. It contains Chinatown, part of the upscale 'Annex' neighbourhood, and such landmarks as the University of Toronto and Queen's Park. The west of the constituency is primarily working class and heavily ethnic (Italian and Portuguese). The riding is home to a diverse array of commercial, service and small businesses, and the city's garment industry. The boundaries define a socio-economically diverse, but generally lower income, electorate. Average family incomes are about $6,000 below the norm for ridings in the province, but half of the riding's families earn less than $40,000 (the seventh lowest in the province). The riding's garment industry is notorious for exploiting an underclass of primarily immigrant workers in sweatshops, or who do piece-work sewing at home. This riding and parts of Scarborough have benefited substantially from the brain and entrepreneurial drain prompted by the political crisis in Hong Kong and other parts of South East Asia such as Vietnam. This same inflow (as with all other previous ones) has spurred a backlash among some previously established inhabitants who relate the inflow to their own lack of opportunity and crime rates.

Strong community support work and an activist relationship with the representatives of organized labour in the riding helped New Democrat Dan Heap maintain his seat for 13 years. Heap stole the riding in a by-election in 1981, after the sitting MP Peter Stollery was appointed to the Senate, ostensibly to clear the way for the election of Jim Coutts, then principal advisor to Pierre Trudeau, to the House of Commons. With Heap's retirement announcement in late 1991, holding the seat became a high priority for the NDP's campaign. Winnie Ng, a garment workers' union organizer and community activist (she helped found the Coalition of Visible Minority Women) inherited a good base to build from. However she also inherited the lacklustre federal campaign provided by the NDP's central office and an activist community disheartened by the restraint legislation imposed by an NDP government at nearby Queen's Park.

The open seat attracted nine other candidates. Returning to contest the seat for the Liberals was Tony Ianno, a young backroom worker, former policy advisor to David Peterson, and small businessperson, who had narrowly lost to Heap in the 1988 election. Ianno had built up an effective party machine centred on the riding's Italian community, and utilized this to his advantage in taking the Liberal nomination away from one of their 'star' candidates, John Roberts. Rumours that Art Eggleton would run here, or that even Jim Coutts himself would return to contest the Liberal nomination again, a rumour he heatedly denied, proved to be false. The Tories nominated Lee Monaco, a real estate lawyer whose roots were also in the riding's Italian community. However, the party was not expected to be particularly competitive in 1993. Peter Loftus, a retired businessperson, secured the Reform Party's nomination. This riding was unfriendly territory for the party, however, and members of the 'Toronto Coalition Against Racism' held an anti-hate rally outside Loftus' headquarters. Six other minor party candidates also competed in 1993, and collectively attracted a couple of thousand votes.

In the end Ng could not overcome the handicaps that came attached to her party label and she lost the riding to Ianno and the Liberals. Her 27.3% finish, however, was the NDP's second best performance in Ontario (after Steven Langdon's in Essex–Windsor).

Member of Parliament: Tony Ianno; **Party**: Liberal; **Occupation**: Businessperson; **Education**: BSc; **Age**: 37 (Jan. 2, 1957); **Year first elected to the House of Commons**: 1993

35087 Trinity–Spadina

A: Political Profile
i) Voting Behaviour

	% 1993	% 1988	Change 1988-93
Conservative	8.1	21.3	-13.2
Liberal	51	37.4	13.6
NDP	27.3	38.5	-11.2
Reform	7.8	0	7.8
Other	5.8	2.8	3

% Turnout	62	Total Ballots (#)	40800
Rejected Ballots (#)	623	% Margin of Victory	23.7
Rural Polls, 1988 (#)	0	Urban Polls, 1988 (#)	158
% Yes - 1992	58.1	% No - 1992	40.3

ii) Campaign Financing

	# of Donations	Total $ Value	% of Limit Spent
Conservative	130	31834	49.3
Liberal	115	43846	70.4
NDP	796	94712	96
Reform	30	18349	32.7*
Other	27	6834	

B: Ethno-Linguistic Profile

% English Home Language	59.9	% French Home Language	0.6
% Official Bilingual	12.5	% Other Home Language	39.5
% Catholics	41.1	% Protestants	17.9
% Aboriginal Peoples	0.2	% Immigrants	47.4

C: Socio-Economic Profile

Average Family Income $	50727	Median Family Income $	39873
% Low Income Families	26.1	Average Home Price $	302032
% Home Owners	35.2	% Unemployment	10.9
% Labour Force Participation	69.9	% Managerial-Administrative	13.2
% Self-Employed	10	% University Degrees	24.9
% Movers	52.2		

D: Industrial Profile

% Manufacturing	12	% Service Sector	15.6
% Agriculture	0.2	% Mining	0.1
% Forestry	0.1	% Fishing	0
% Government Services	6	% Business Services	11.4

E: Homogeneity Measures

Ethnic Diversity Index	0.24	Religious Homogeneity Index	0.29
Sectoral Concentration Index	0.55	Income Disparity Index	21.4

F: Physical Setting Characteristics

Total Population	97286	Area (km²)	16
Population Density (pop/km²)	6080.4		

*   Tentative value, due to the existence of unpaid campaign expenses.

Victoria–Haliburton

Constituency Number: 35088

Victoria–Haliburton is a large riding in the central portion of eastern Ontario. Primarily rural and village in character, the only population centre in Victoria–Haliburton is the Town of Lindsay. This town, located in the south of the constituency, about 90 minutes northeast of Toronto, is home to about 17,500. Numerous lakes and streams make the area popular with tourists. The area is heavily anglophone (the riding ranks among Ontario's lowest in terms of the proportion of francophones and Catholics).

Politics runs conservative in this part of small-town Ontario. The seat has returned Conservative members since 1945. Bill Scott, the incumbent, had represented the area for 28 years, giving him the second-longest record of service in the House of Commons, behind the Liberals' Herb Gray (Windsor West). Those local would-be Tory candidates, whose hopes for Scott's retirement in 1988 to open up the normally safe seat were dashed, were not disappointed this time around, as Scott stepped down. Unfortunately for them, the situation for the party in 1993 was hardly as propitious as it had been in 1988. In the end Lorne Chester, a lawyer from Lindsay, won the Tory nomination.

Challenging for the open seat were eight other candidates. The Liberals nominated John O'Reilly, a real estate broker from Lindsay. The Reform Party was set to make inroads into traditional Tory votes, and nominated Barry Devolin, a realtor from Dysart. Dennis Drainville, an Anglican clergyman, ran a strong campaign as an independent candidate. Cathy Vainio, a substitute teacher from Omemee, ran again for the New Democrats, after having finished third in the riding in 1988. Four minor parties rounded out the ballot in 1993.

On election eve, O'Reilly benefited from the split of former Conservative support among the Reform, Independent (Drainville), and Tory candidates. His total vote, while enough to give him the plurality, was the second lowest for the Liberals in Ontario.

Member of Parliament: John Francis O'Reilly; **Party**: Liberal; **Occupation**: Real estate broker; **Education**: High school; **Age**: 54 (Aug. 4, 1940); **Year first elected to the House of Commons**: 1993

35088 Victoria–Haliburton

A: Political Profile
i) Voting Behaviour

	% 1993	% 1988	Change 1988-93
Conservative	22.2	46.8	-24.6
Liberal	36.7	34.8	1.9
NDP	3.7	17.2	-13.5
Reform	28.5	0	28.5
Other	8.9	1.1	7.8

% Turnout	70.2	Total Ballots (#)	56142
Rejected Ballots (#)	310	% Margin of Victory	8.2
Rural Polls, 1988 (#)	182	Urban Polls, 1988 (#)	34
% Yes - 1992	44.3	% No - 1992	55.2

ii) Campaign Financing

	# of Donations	Total $ Value	% of Limit Spent
Conservative	154	63694	91.8
Liberal	192	25692	43.6
NDP	22	8618	16.2
Reform	245	45846	82
Other	101	45832	

B: Ethno-Linguistic Profile

% English Home Language	99	% French Home Language	0.1
% Official Bilingual	4	% Other Home Language	0.9
% Catholics	15.2	% Protestants	70.4
% Aboriginal Peoples	0.5	% Immigrants	9.3

C: Socio-Economic Profile

Average Family Income $	46487	Median Family Income $	40792
% Low Income Families	9	Average Home Price $	172779
% Home Owners	81.9	% Unemployment	9
% Labour Force Participation	62	% Managerial-Administrative	10.6
% Self-Employed	15.4	% University Degrees	5.9
% Movers	45.8		

D: Industrial Profile

% Manufacturing	16	% Service Sector	11
% Agriculture	6.4	% Mining	0.7
% Forestry	0.3	% Fishing	0.1
% Government Services	5.4	% Business Services	3.4

E: Homogeneity Measures

Ethnic Diversity Index	0.51	Religious Homogeneity Index	0.52
Sectoral Concentration Index	0.37	Income Disparity Index	12.3

F: Physical Setting Characteristics

Total Population	101513	Area (km²)	10426
Population Density (pop/km²)	9.7		

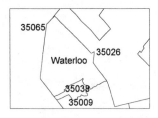

Waterloo

Constituency Number: 35089

The riding of Waterloo comprises all of the city of that name, part of its larger 'twin city' Kitchener, and some of the outlying rural areas. The city of Waterloo is a community of two parts. Savaged by the recession, many Waterloo area manufacturing establishments either downsized or closed completely. On the other hand the city is becoming known as a major node in the worldwide network of computer software development. Centred on the University of Waterloo and a handful of major producers such as Watcom, the area is recognized as a hotbed for innovation and quality. This is becoming so increasingly the case that many companies who do the bulk of their manufacturing and design elsewhere locate their customer services and head office functions in Waterloo so as to have the cachet of a Waterloo address. The area was first settled by Mennonites, and later Germans. Today, almost 10% of the residents report having Germanic ethnic origins, and German is spoken by 11,400 residents.

Since its creation in 1979, Conservative Walter McLean, a former Presbyterian minister, has represented the riding. McLean's retirement opened the way for Lynne Woolstencroft, a community college professor, to secure the Tory nomination. The Liberals nominated Andrew Telegdi, a social worker and local politician. The NDP nominated Scott Piatkowski, a housing co-operative coordinator who had finished third in the 1988 contest. Some commentary during the campaign suggested that the NDP was likely to suffer from tactical voting on the part of some of its former supporters as they might vote Liberal to ensure that neither the Tory nor the Reform candidate be elected. One such defector was local labour leader and city councillor Brian Strickland, but doubtless he was joined by others no longer willing to vote NDP due to the behaviour of the NDP Ontario government. Mike Connolly, a semi-retired worker who won the Reform Party nomination, got caught up in a controversy over the party's alleged racist tendencies (as in the neighbouring riding of Kitchener). The *Kitchener Waterloo Record* got in on the debate when columnist Luisa D'Amato wrote a column titled 'Reformers Make Easy Targets for Racism Charges'. In the article the columnist performed a point-by-point destruction of comments made by Waterloo Reform candidate Connolly and the party's Kitchener candidate Reg Gosse on the topic of immigration, showing where their cases were in error and their figures and statistics plain fabrications. Her conclusion, that the area Reform candidates were either incompetent or 'closet racists', generated a number of letters to the editor. Three minor party candidates and an independent rounded out the ballot.

On October 25th, a Reform/Tory split of the right-of-centre vote allowed the Liberals to claim this seat with a 10,000 vote margin.

Member of Parliament: Andrew Telegdi; **Party**: Liberal; **Occupation**: Municipal politician; **Education**: BA; **Year first elected to the House of Commons**: 1993

35089 Waterloo

A: Political Profile
i) Voting Behaviour

	% 1993	% 1988	Change 1988-93
Conservative	24.2	45.1	-20.9
Liberal	42.1	36.3	5.8
NDP	4.5	17.4	-12.9
Reform	25.5	0	25.5
Other	3.5	1.1	2.4

% Turnout	63.4	Total Ballots (#)	62888
Rejected Ballots (#)	556	% Margin of Victory	16.6
Rural Polls, 1988 (#)	19	Urban Polls, 1988 (#)	220
% Yes - 1992	55.1	% No - 1992	44.4

ii) Campaign Financing

	# of Donations	Total $ Value	% of Limit Spent
Conservative	187	33744	84.7*
Liberal	112	65890	88.5
NDP	65	11985	11.9
Reform	141	16572	43
Other	63	9812	

B: Ethno-Linguistic Profile

% English Home Language	90.1	% French Home Language	0.4
% Official Bilingual	8.2	% Other Home Language	9.5
% Catholics	28.1	% Protestants	54.2
% Aboriginal Peoples	0.2	% Immigrants	18.7

C: Socio-Economic Profile

Average Family Income $	60302	Median Family Income $	51133
% Low Income Families	11.3	Average Home Price $	191260
% Home Owners	60.5	% Unemployment	7.9
% Labour Force Participation	72.9	% Managerial-Administrative	12.9
% Self-Employed	8.9	% University Degrees	17.7
% Movers	52.5		

D: Industrial Profile

% Manufacturing	20.7	% Service Sector	10.6
% Agriculture	2.7	% Mining	0.1
% Forestry	0.1	% Fishing	0
% Government Services	4.2	% Business Services	6.1

E: Homogeneity Measures

Ethnic Diversity Index	0.24	Religious Homogeneity Index	0.39
Sectoral Concentration Index	0.39	Income Disparity Index	15.2

F: Physical Setting Characteristics

Total Population	120008	Area (km²)	421
Population Density (pop/km²)	285.1		

* Tentative value, due to the existence of unpaid campaign expenses.

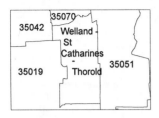

Welland–St Catharines–Thorold

Constituency Number: 35090

Welland–St Catharines–Thorold is a heavily industrial, primarily urban constituency located on the Niagara Peninsula. Many residents are blue-collar workers, and average family incomes are well below the provincial average. There are also important agricultural producers in the riding. There is a small francophone enclave here, with almost 4% of residents reporting French as their home language. This riding's manufacturing base was hard hit during the recession and many blamed its decline on the Canada-US free trade agreement. Close to the US border, cross-border shopping and smuggling, encouraged by the Conservative government's strong dollar policy and the initial shock of the GST, helped deplete the sections of the economy not impacted by the de-industrialization of the region.

In the past two federal elections this riding has produced close three-way races. In 1984 Welland–St Catharines–Thorold went Tory, electing Allan Pietz. However, in 1988 Gilbert Parent, a former MP who had represented the riding of St Catharines between 1974 and 1984, before Mulroney's sweep of that year, took it for the Liberals. The NDP currently holds its provincial counterpart.

Parent defended his seat against six challengers in 1993. The Reform Party was represented by Don Johnstone, a consultant from Welland. The Tories nominated Terry St Amand, a restaurateur from Thorold. The NDP was represented by Rob Dobrucki, a housing consultant from Welland. Three minor party candidates also ran in the campaign.

Here as elsewhere, the economy and the Conservatives' record in government were the dominant issues in the 1993 campaign. These concerns were joined, however, by the issues of crime and violence against women and children. The trial of Paul Teale accused in the murder of two teenage girls, Leslie Mahaffy and Kirsten French, was just beginning as the election writ fell and that of his wife Karla Homolka had ended just a couple of months before the writ. Homolka's trial caused controversy in that she was allowed to plead guilty to only manslaughter and sentenced to just 12 years; the reasons this plea was allowed were kept secret by a court ban on the publication of any further information about her trial. Consequently, the following events caused a greater disturbance in this part of Ontario than they likely would have in any other part of Canada.

In 1993 saw an unambiguous and unquestionable Liberal victory scored by Gilbert Parent. In January 1994 he was elected Speaker of the House of Commons.

Member of Parliament: Gilbert Parent; **Party**: Liberal; **Occupation**: Educator; **Education**: MEd, State University of New York; **Age**: 59 (July 25, 1935); **Year first elected to the House of Commons**: 1974

35090 Welland–St Catharines–Thorold

A: Political Profile
i) Voting Behaviour

	% 1993	% 1988	Change 1988-93
Conservative	11.6	34.5	-22.9
Liberal	54	37.9	16.1
NDP	7.9	26.8	-18.9
Reform	25.2	0	25.2
Other	1.4	0.8	0.6

% Turnout	65.5	Total Ballots (#)	47795
Rejected Ballots (#)	491	% Margin of Victory	28.8
Rural Polls, 1988 (#)	10	Urban Polls, 1988 (#)	180
% Yes - 1992	41	% No - 1992	58.4

ii) Campaign Financing

	# of Donations	Total $ Value	% of Limit Spent
Conservative	141	57811	90.4
Liberal	134	39275	79.1
NDP	156	24959	34.5
Reform	170	27890	49.1
Other	1	490	

B: Ethno-Linguistic Profile

% English Home Language	91.5	% French Home Language	3.9
% Official Bilingual	11.6	% Other Home Language	4.6
% Catholics	44.4	% Protestants	44.3
% Aboriginal Peoples	0.6	% Immigrants	16

C: Socio-Economic Profile

Average Family Income $	49482	Median Family Income $	45079
% Low Income Families	13.5	Average Home Price $	141565
% Home Owners	70.3	% Unemployment	9.9
% Labour Force Participation	63.6	% Managerial-Administrative	9.5
% Self-Employed	6.3	% University Degrees	7.9
% Movers	43.2		

D: Industrial Profile

% Manufacturing	23.2	% Service Sector	13.7
% Agriculture	1.6	% Mining	0.3
% Forestry	0.4	% Fishing	0
% Government Services	5.2	% Business Services	4.2

E: Homogeneity Measures

Ethnic Diversity Index	0.25	Religious Homogeneity Index	0.39
Sectoral Concentration Index	0.42	Income Disparity Index	8.9

F: Physical Setting Characteristics

Total Population	92012	Area (km²)	187
Population Density (pop/km²)	492		

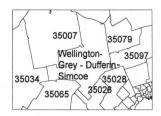

Wellington–Grey–Dufferin–Simcoe

Constituency Number: 35091

This sprawling, oddly shaped riding extends from just north of the city of Guelph to the shores of Georgian Bay. The heartland of the constituency is the small-town and rural areas dominated by family farms specializing in beef, hog, and dairy production. East of Orangeville, around Caledon Hills, however, is an area of million-dollar estates, horse farms, and 'rural chic'. The riding's north, near Collingwood and Wasaga Beach, is an important tourist area with skiing and beach activities. Some commuters to the Metro area reside in the easternmost sections of the riding. Industry is also important to the local economy, and approximately 17% of the riding's workforce is employed in manufacturing. The area is heavily anglophone and Protestant.

The area is both small and large 'c' conservative territory. The Tories have monopolized federal elections in the area since at least 1953, and Conservative cabinet minister Perrin Beatty had represented the area in Ottawa since 1972. While the race was expected to be tight in 1993, many expected him to be one of the Tory's last best hopes for retaining his seat. 'If Perrin Beatty is defeated on October 25th, Prime Minister Kim Campbell might as well go before the television cameras, concede defeat, wish the winner luck, and go to bed.' So prophetically opined the *Kitchener-Waterloo Record* eleven days before the 1993 vote.

Facing Beatty in 1993 were four challengers. The Liberals nominated Murray Calder, a poultry producer and welder from Egremont. The Reform Party ran Bob Greenland, a self-employed worker form Stayner. Dan Heffernan, a staff officer from Angus, ran for the NDP, and Sara Francis, a student from Guelph, offered for the Greens.

The Liberals campaigned on the line that Perrin Beatty is personally responsible for the bad government of the Mulroney years. As a senior cabinet minister 'He voted for all the Mulroney initiatives that have got us into all this trouble.' The local press covering the race noted that the candidates offered the voters a clear choice. A Liberal and an NDP candidate for whom jobs were priority number one and a Tory cabinet minister and a Reform challenger who were most concerned with the deficit and appeared to be in slash-and-burn mode. This riding showed signs of a new trend in modern Canadian politics, 'Ontario first' voters. In the past regional development was not a major issue in Ontario. This election Ontario voters began to ask why there was money for job creation everywhere but Ontario. In this riding it was a constituent who asked Beatty how he could stand there and say the government was too broke to help create jobs in his riding while millions of federal dollars were being poured into the Hibernia scheme in Newfoundland.

In the end, those predicting a close race were vindicated (the margin of victory was the province's narrowest). Beatty registered the Tories' best showing in Ontario. However, a strong Reform performance drew votes away from the Conservative incumbent, thereby allowing the Liberals to win the riding (despite the fact that this was their lowest proportion of the total vote in the province!).

Member of Parliament: Murray Calder; **Party**: Liberal; **Occupation**: Farmer; **Age**: 43 (Jan. 15, 1951); **Year first elected to the House of Commons**: 1993

35091   Wellington–Grey–Dufferin–Simcoe

A: Political Profile
i) Voting Behaviour

	% 1993	% 1988	Change 1988-93
Conservative	32.7	50.9	-18.2
Liberal	35.8	30.2	5.6
NDP	3.5	15.1	-11.6
Reform	27	0	27
Other	1	3.7	-2.7

% Turnout	69.1	Total Ballots (#)	57345
Rejected Ballots (#)	322	% Margin of Victory	3.1
Rural Polls, 1988 (#)	163	Urban Polls, 1988 (#)	78
% Yes - 1992	48.7	% No - 1992	50.6

ii) Campaign Financing

	# of Donations	Total $ Value	% of Limit Spent
Conservative	251	64947	95.9
Liberal	145	40635	65
NDP	65	19059	31.3
Reform	166	28402	46.9
Other	0	0	

B: Ethno-Linguistic Profile

% English Home Language	98	% French Home Language	0.2
% Official Bilingual	4.7	% Other Home Language	1.8
% Catholics	16.2	% Protestants	68.4
% Aboriginal Peoples	0.2	% Immigrants	11.2

C: Socio-Economic Profile

Average Family Income $	52931	Median Family Income $	47299
% Low Income Families	8	Average Home Price $	180713
% Home Owners	76	% Unemployment	8
% Labour Force Participation	71	% Managerial-Administrative	11.9
% Self-Employed	14.3	% University Degrees	7.6
% Movers	49		

D: Industrial Profile

% Manufacturing	17.6	% Service Sector	10
% Agriculture	8.9	% Mining	0.6
% Forestry	0.1	% Fishing	0.1
% Government Services	5.3	% Business Services	3.6

E: Homogeneity Measures

Ethnic Diversity Index	0.42	Religious Homogeneity Index	0.5
Sectoral Concentration Index	0.35	Income Disparity Index	10.6

F: Physical Setting Characteristics

Total Population	112778	Area (km²)	4247
Population Density (pop/km²)	26.6		

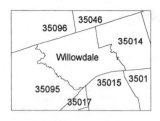

Willowdale

Constituency Number: 35092

The riding of Willowdale includes part of the city of North York north of Highway 401 in Metro Toronto, and is bounded on the east and west by branches of the Don River. The area is heavily residential, but there are diverse light manufacturing, service, and commercial establishments located in the riding. With roughly 45% of residents being immigrants, Willowdale ranks among the top ten Ontario ridings on this measure. It has the highest concentration of Jewish voters of any constituency in Canada, with 26% of the riding population claiming this faith on the last Census.

This riding has recently see-sawed back and forth between Liberal Jim Peterson, a tax lawyer, businessman, and brother of former Ontario Premier David Peterson, and Tory John Oostrom, an economist, consultant, and Dutch Catholic. Ideologically, Peterson is known as a moderate, while Oostrom offered a more conservative position on such issues as capital punishment, pornography, immigration, and abortion. Peterson lost his seat in 1984 to Oostrom, won it back in 1988 and faced him again in 1993. While attention naturally centred on the Oostrom-Peterson rematch, inroads by Reform were complicating the battle. Many predicted a close race.

Unfortunately for Oostrom, an open feud developed between the Canadian Jewish Congress and the Conservative government. When it became publicly known that members of the Airborne Regiment had clear racist convictions and one had been videotaped participating in neo-Nazi meetings (and even had links to the terrorist attack on an Alberta broadcaster), the Canadian Jewish Congress demanded a zero tolerance policy on racists in the Armed Forces, arguing that the requirements of national security demanded their exclusion from the military, even if they had recanted (as was formerly the case with communists). The government not only failed to act until about four months after the scandal broke, but it also failed to answer the Canadian Jewish Congress's letter or meet with its leaders until after an official announcement of policy was made. Meanwhile Oostrom must have been sincerely hoping that the good electors of Willowdale had not quite forgotten Patti Starr. Patti Starr was a prominent member of the National Council of Jewish Women, who was convicted of a number of offences under tax and election laws for making improper political donations to provincial and federal Liberal incumbents and candidates. Part of the scandal revolved around a subsidized apartment building erected by the National Council of Jewish Women. Starr used funds from the building (some of which was government funding) to make the improper contributions. Unfortunately for Jim Peterson he was one of the lucky recipients of her support; he had to return a tidy sum to the organization and offer a number of apologies, promising to be more careful to insure that contributions were more correctly scrutinized in the future. The speed with which Peterson announced he had received an improper contribution and refunded the cash confirmed for many that he was an innocent bystander in the whole affair.

In the end the collapse of the Tory vote was more complete than most had anticipated, and the inroads of Reform less substantial than many expected. This enabled Jim Peterson to win handily with a massive 21,000 vote majority.

Member of Parliament: James Scott Peterson; **Party**: Liberal; **Occupation**: Lawyer and law professor; **Education**: Doctor of Common Law, University of Paris; **Age**: 53 (July 30, 1941); **Year first elected to the House of Commons**: 1980

35092 Willowdale

A: Political Profile
i) Voting Behaviour

	% 1993	% 1988	Change 1988-93
Conservative	16.8	43.4	-26.6
Liberal	61.3	47	14.3
NDP	3.6	8.8	-5.2
Reform	15.2	0	15.2
Other	3.1	0.8	2.3

% Turnout	69.8	Total Ballots (#)	47117
Rejected Ballots (#)	397	% Margin of Victory	44.5
Rural Polls, 1988 (#)	0	Urban Polls, 1988 (#)	222
% Yes - 1992	62.5	% No - 1992	36.9

ii) Campaign Financing

	# of Donations	Total $ Value	% of Limit Spent
Conservative	109	28947	91.1*
Liberal	285	69507	80.6
NDP	57	10511	12
Reform	60	15964	23.9
Other	51	6439	

B: Ethno-Linguistic Profile

% English Home Language	74.1	% French Home Language	0.6
% Official Bilingual	9.1	% Other Home Language	25.3
% Catholics	22	% Protestants	30.9
% Aboriginal Peoples	0.2	% Immigrants	44.7

C: Socio-Economic Profile

Average Family Income $	66916	Median Family Income $	55862
% Low Income Families	16.1	Average Home Price $	323270
% Home Owners	52.5	% Unemployment	8.3
% Labour Force Participation	65	% Managerial-Administrative	18.5
% Self-Employed	12.1	% University Degrees	23.2
% Movers	46.2		

D: Industrial Profile

% Manufacturing	12.9	% Service Sector	8.9
% Agriculture	0.4	% Mining	0.2
% Forestry	0.1	% Fishing	0
% Government Services	5.9	% Business Services	11.8

E: Homogeneity Measures

Ethnic Diversity Index	0.23	Religious Homogeneity Index	0.33
Sectoral Concentration Index	0.52	Income Disparity Index	16.5

F: Physical Setting Characteristics

Total Population	100739	Area (km²)	28
Population Density (pop/km²)	3597.8		

* Tentative value, due to the existence of unpaid campaign expenses.

Windsor–Lake St Clair

Constituency Number: 35093

This mixed urban/suburban southwestern Ontario riding lies along the shores of the Fleming Channel of the Detroit River across from the city of Detroit, and Lake St Clair. Manufacturing, and more precisely, automobile manufacturing is king here - all of the 'Big Three' auto companies (GM, Ford, and Chrysler) have operations in the riding. These and their spinoff industries give Windsor–Lake St Clair the fifth highest proportion of its workforce (about 30%) employed in this sector of all Ontario ridings. While auto sales were picking up before the election, other areas of employment in the riding were still suffering from the recession. Just before the election, for example, the closure of the Pillsbury-Green Giant corn processing plant in suburban Tecumseh cost the riding 100 full-time and 500 part-time jobs. To make matters worse, it was determined that the company was moving the work to a factory it had recently modernized using a government grant in the province of Quebec.

Winning the riding (once the personal fiefdom of Paul Martin Sr, when it was called Windsor–Walkerville) in 1988 was the NDP's Howard McCurdy. A former microbiology professor at the University of Windsor, and Windsor city councillor, McCurdy had previously represented the riding of Windsor–Walkerville between 1984 and 1988. His margin of victory in 1988 was only 7.2%, and the emergence of three strong challengers in the 1993 campaign let many to expect that this would be one of the closest contests in the whole country. Running for the Liberals again in 1993 was Shaughnessy Cohen, an outspoken and aggressive lawyer who had to survive a tight nomination fight. She had run second to McCurdy in the 1988 election. Tom Porter, a lawyer and popular long-time city councillor, ran for the Progressive Conservatives. The Windsor area does not normally elect Conservatives, however, and Porter was not widely expected to win. Greg Novini, a business manager, ran for the Reform Party.

Perhaps because of the anticipated close nature of the race dirty tricks were at an all-time high in this race. Tory workers produced ex-Liberal 'workers' who claimed that Grit candidate Shaughnessy Cohen was not the same warm and polite person in private that she was in public. The Liberals claimed that the NDP sent spies to volunteer as workers for them to infiltrate their headquarters and, in the wildest incident of all, a defeated Liberal provincial parliament candidate and now Tecumseh town solicitor pressed charges against McCurdy for keeping an unduly noisy dog in violation of town by-law #1552!

Bob White (President of the Canadian Labour Congress, founding president of the Canadian Auto Workers, and local hero) spent some time in the Windsor area and strongly urged all unionized workers to vote NDP. In the end the race was not close after all and Cohen easily won the riding.

Member of Parliament: Shaughnessy Cohen; **Party**: Liberal; **Occupation**: Lawyer and teacher; **Education**: LL.B; **Age**: 46 (1948); **Year first elected to the House of Commons**: 1993

35093 Windsor–Lake St Clair

A: Political Profile
i) Voting Behaviour

	% 1993	% 1988	Change 1988-93
Conservative	11.1	19.4	-8.3
Liberal	55.6	37.2	18.4
NDP	21.9	43.4	-21.5
Reform	10.1	0	10.1
Other	1.4	0	1.4

% Turnout	64.3	Total Ballots (#)	41646
Rejected Ballots (#)	352	% Margin of Victory	33.7
Rural Polls, 1988 (#)	0	Urban Polls, 1988 (#)	168
% Yes - 1992	36	% No - 1992	63.6

ii) Campaign Financing

	# of Donations	Total $ Value	% of Limit Spent
Conservative	254	61457	88.2*
Liberal	107	34106	58.3
NDP	159	41186	67.5
Reform	47	7306	12.6
Other	3	1035	

B: Ethno-Linguistic Profile

% English Home Language	90.2	% French Home Language	1.6
% Official Bilingual	9.9	% Other Home Language	8.2
% Catholics	54.9	% Protestants	32.4
% Aboriginal Peoples	0.5	% Immigrants	19.7

C: Socio-Economic Profile

Average Family Income $	53685	Median Family Income $	47021
% Low Income Families	13.4	Average Home Price $	121757
% Home Owners	71.3	% Unemployment	12.5
% Labour Force Participation	63.7	% Managerial-Administrative	10.1
% Self-Employed	5.4	% University Degrees	10.8
% Movers	42.5		

D: Industrial Profile

% Manufacturing	29.3	% Service Sector	13.2
% Agriculture	0.5	% Mining	0.1
% Forestry	0	% Fishing	0
% Government Services	4.6	% Business Services	4.9

E: Homogeneity Measures

Ethnic Diversity Index	0.22	Religious Homogeneity Index	0.41
Sectoral Concentration Index	0.43	Income Disparity Index	12.4

F: Physical Setting Characteristics

Total Population	89079	Area (km²)	45
Population Density (pop/km²)	1979.5		

* Tentative value, due to the existence of unpaid campaign expenses.

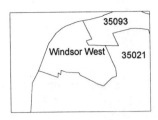

35093

Windsor West   35021

Windsor West

Constituency Number: 35094

Windsor West is an urban constituency, located across the Detroit River from the city of Detroit. It extends to encompass most of downtown Windsor. It combines a mix of older and new residential areas. Manufacturing, primarily concentrated in automobiles, is the primary employer, although St Clair College and the University of Windsor are both found in the riding. The riding has a significant immigrant (and primarily Italian) community, and the workforce is heavily unionized.

There was not much doubt that Gray would win and not much less that he would win handily in 1993. The economy was the issue and, given that there was a Tory government in power when it collapsed, the voters in Windsor West did not have much reason not to return Gray. 'Herb Gray is well entrenched. He's well respected. There's probably not a household in Windsor West which ... hasn't benefited from calling Gray's office.' What makes this assessment remarkable is that it comes from Gray's Progressive Conservative opponent! Imagine what Liberal supporters think of their long-standing MP (he has the longest record of service of any current Member), first elected in 1962 and returned every election since. While hardly describable as a colourful figure, Gray has earned the reputation of being an ardent economic nationalist. As such, he has been a fierce critic of the Free Trade Agreement between Canada and the United States. In 1972 he authored a landmark study on foreign ownership in Canada that was instrumental in the establishment of the Foreign Investment Review Agency, or FIRA.

Despite the unfavourable odds, a full slate of challengers emerged to take on Gray. The Conservative opponent quoted above was Dan Friesen, an executive director. Running for the Reform Party was Brett Skinner, a customs inspector, and the NDP ran Emily Carasco, a university professor. Four minor party candidates, and one independent, also campaigned for the seat.

In the end, October 25th brought no surprises to Windsor West. Herb Gray was returned for another term with a crushing margin of almost 24,000 votes, making this the Liberal's fourth best finish in the province.

Member of Parliament: Herbert E. Gray; **Party**: Liberal; **Occupation**: Lawyer; **Education**: LL.B, Osgoode Hall Law School; **Age**: 63 (May 25, 1931); **Year first elected to the House of Commons**: 1962

35094 Windsor West

A: Political Profile

i) Voting Behaviour

	% 1993	% 1988	Change 1988-93
Conservative	4.6	14.5	-9.9
Liberal	72.8	56.2	16.6
NDP	9.2	28.7	-19.5
Reform	11.4	0	11.4
Other	2.2	0.6	1.6

% Turnout	57.2	Total Ballots (#)	39275
Rejected Ballots (#)	321	% Margin of Victory	61.4
Rural Polls, 1988 (#)	0	Urban Polls, 1988 (#)	227
% Yes - 1992	36.6	% No - 1992	62.8

ii) Campaign Financing

	# of Donations	Total $ Value	% of Limit Spent
Conservative	23	12055	18.3
Liberal	218	60457	73.3
NDP	129	47258	67.6
Reform	65	22991	27.6
Other	23	2295	

B: Ethno-Linguistic Profile

% English Home Language	86.5	% French Home Language	0.8
% Official Bilingual	8.3	% Other Home Language	12.8
% Catholics	50.9	% Protestants	31.5
% Aboriginal Peoples	0.3	% Immigrants	23.7

C: Socio-Economic Profile

Average Family Income $	47569	Median Family Income $	41925
% Low Income Families	22.3	Average Home Price $	114633
% Home Owners	57.4	% Unemployment	12.8
% Labour Force Participation	60.7	% Managerial-Administrative	9.4
% Self-Employed	5.5	% University Degrees	11.2
% Movers	41.9		

D: Industrial Profile

% Manufacturing	23.6	% Service Sector	15.6
% Agriculture	0.6	% Mining	0.2
% Forestry	0.1	% Fishing	0
% Government Services	5	% Business Services	5.2

E: Homogeneity Measures

Ethnic Diversity Index	0.2	Religious Homogeneity Index	0.36
Sectoral Concentration Index	0.43	Income Disparity Index	11.9

F: Physical Setting Characteristics

Total Population	91199	Area (km²)	69
Population Density (pop/km²)	1321.7		

York Centre

Constituency Number: 35095

This large north Toronto riding lies sandwiched between Highway 401 on the south and Steeles Avenue West, and between Bathurst on the east and Jane on the west, in the city of North York. The riding itself is typically urban. Almost half of its residents are immigrants (over 25,000 are of Italian ethnic origin, and over 24,000 still speak the language). Commercial, service, and light manufacturing enterprises dot the riding. Its most distinguishing characteristic is CFB Toronto and Downsview Airport with its tenant, the DeHavilland division of Canadair/Bombardier, Metro Toronto's largest single industrial employer. The campus of York University occupies the northwest corner of the riding.

York Centre is the Liberals' safest seat in the Metro area, having returned Grits to Ottawa since the 1960s. Since 1974, Bob Kaplan, a lawyer and former cabinet minister under Pierre Trudeau, had held the seat. His death opened the seat up in 1993, however, and the candidates seeking to replace Kaplan initiated some shocks in the local campaign. The first shock in the riding came when Jean Chrétien announced he was installing Art Eggleton, an accountant and former mayor of Toronto, as the Liberal candidate in the riding. Eggleton had been the longest-serving Toronto mayor, and his former aide, Peter Donolo, is Chrétien's communications director. However, as in other instances when 'star candidates' are nominated by the national leadership, some would-be candidates are disappointed. In York Centre, Peter Li Preti, a psychologist and North York City councillor, was very upset by Chrétien's move, as he was planning to contest the nomination. Instead of bowing out, Li Preti filed suit against the party (along with John Munro) and chose to run as an Independent Liberal. Assigning this label to himself was, of course, illegal, unless he could find 49 other candidates, lawfully nominate them via petitions of constituents to field an official party, and then convince Elections Canada that 'Independent Liberal' does not violate the exclusive rights that the Liberal Party of Canada has to the name Liberal. Eggleton sought and won an injunction ordering Li Preti to cover up the word Liberal on all of his signs.

The second set of candidate-induced shocks were set off by Reformer John Beck who made statements about immigrants and Jews that were so extreme that Preston Manning and his senior advisors demanded Beck's resignation from the party within two hours of hearing of them. Manning arrived at York University to give a speech at the prestigious Osgoode Hall Law School and instead of discussing policy he spent the afternoon listening to tape recordings of an interview Beck gave to the student-run *York Excalibur* newspaper in which Beck, a limousine driver, said that immigrants 'bring death and destruction'. Later, Beck was quoted in the *Toronto Star* as saying 'I feel we have lost control of our country... It seems to be predominantly Jewish people who are running this country.' Manning won some praise for dispatching Beck quickly but the whole incident left many across Metro wondering if Beck was one misguided individual or typical of the Reform Party as a whole. Despite his having to withdraw, Beck's name stayed on the ballot and he attracted 5.5% of the poll. This was a major set-back for the Reform Party. The outlook was made even worse in that it happened in a riding which boasts a roadway called Raul Wallenberg Drive: the main entry for Metro Toronto's Earl Bales Park meanders past a monument to the millions killed in the Holocaust.

Also running in the 1993 campaign were George Tsiolis, a law student, who ran for the Tories and Israel Ellis, a self-employed worker who ran for the NDP. Six minor party candidates also offered in the campaign. After all the excitement the election of Eggleton, in a cakewalk, and his appointment to the cabinet as President of the Treasury Board and Minister Responsible for Infrastructure were something of an anti-climax.

Member of Parliament: Arthur C. Eggleton; **Party**: Liberal; **Occupation:** Accountant; **Age:** 51 (September 28, 1943); **Year first elected to the House of Commons:** 1993

35095 York Centre

A: Political Profile
i) Voting Behaviour

	% 1993	% 1988	Change 1988-93
Conservative	6.9	22.4	-15.5
Liberal	69.7	60.5	9.2
NDP	4	15.4	-11.4
Reform	5.5	0	5.5
Other	14	1.7	12.3

% Turnout	65.4	Total Ballots (#)	39459
Rejected Ballots (#)	508	% Margin of Victory	55.7
Rural Polls, 1988 (#)	0	Urban Polls, 1988 (#)	171
% Yes - 1992	54.2	% No - 1992	44.8

ii) Campaign Financing

	# of Donations	Total $ Value	% of Limit Spent
Conservative	129	33525	60*
Liberal	129	48209	86.7
NDP	60	10545	15.3
Reform	16	3485	5.1*
Other	72	32124	

B: Ethno-Linguistic Profile

% English Home Language	67.7	% French Home Language	0.5
% Official Bilingual	6.5	% Other Home Language	31.8
% Catholics	48.1	% Protestants	18.8
% Aboriginal Peoples	0.3	% Immigrants	47.8

C: Socio-Economic Profile

Average Family Income $	56000	Median Family Income $	44777
% Low Income Families	20.3	Average Home Price $	279128
% Home Owners	46.5	% Unemployment	10.5
% Labour Force Participation	66.7	% Managerial-Administrative	11.1
% Self-Employed	7.3	% University Degrees	11.5
% Movers	38.6		

D: Industrial Profile

% Manufacturing	18.3	% Service Sector	12.5
% Agriculture	0.2	% Mining	0.1
% Forestry	0	% Fishing	0
% Government Services	6.4	% Business Services	7.5

E: Homogeneity Measures

Ethnic Diversity Index	0.25	Religious Homogeneity Index	0.36
Sectoral Concentration Index	0.42	Income Disparity Index	20

F: Physical Setting Characteristics

Total Population	92322	Area (km²)	37
Population Density (pop/km²)	2495.2		

* Tentative value, due to the existence of unpaid campaign expenses.

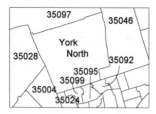

York North

Constituency Number: 35096

York North is a sprawling, partly urban riding on the northern fringe of Metropolitan Toronto. The riding takes in most of York Region, Canada's fastest growing Regional Municipality. A consequence of growth is that this is Canada's most populous riding, with 233,302 inhabitants. It has a split personality, typically suburban in the southern and eastern reaches, and downright aristocratic in the northwest. In the southern and eastern part of the riding, its boundary with neighbouring Metro Toronto is often indistinguishable. The boundary runs between equally attractive subdivisions and purposeful industrial estates and strip malls on either side of Steeles Avenue West. This part of the riding is essentially a piece of Metro outside Metro. It includes a number of ethnic communities that have drifted further north until they have finally left the Metro area altogether. Most notable in this regard is the sizeable Jewish population centred on Bathurst Street and the fairly prosperous Italian community in Woodbridge. On the other hand, the northwest of this riding is the seat of the Canadian gentry. Thoroughbred stud farms, show jumping rings and exquisite cars are hallmarks of this part of the riding. This is the Tory heartland in Canada.

A new riding in 1988, the election was so close that a judicial recount was ordered, thereby initiating a bizarre process whereby the riding was passed back and forth several times between two would-be MPs. Conservative Michael O'Brien was declared the winner on election night 1988 with a 58 vote margin. However, this ruling was subsequently overturned and the Liberal Maurizio Bevilacqua, a former aide to Sergio Marchi in York West and president of the York University student union, was given the seat. This decision was overturned after a second judicial recount, and O'Brien was again declared the winner. O'Brien actually sat as MP for the riding for 55 days, before this result was eventually overturned and Bevilacqua given the role of MP for a short period. Finally, the Ontario Supreme Court ordered that a by-election be held on December 16, 1990, at which time Bevilacqua was elected outright.

If Reform had any hope in this riding, the campaign of Heather Sinclair, a trustee from Aurora, was effectively torpedoed by John Beck (their candidate in neighbouring York Centre). Beck stepped right over the edge by claiming immigrants bring 'death and destruction to Canada' and by making other clearly racist and anti-Semitic comments. To his credit, when Preston Manning heard of the remarks he secured the candidate's resignation within two hours. The Jewish community in the Metro Toronto area tends to lean Liberal. This election the PCs and the Reform Party gave Jewish voters strong reason to not just lean Liberal but to actually flee to their local Liberal candidates.

The inability of the Tories to cut the deficit and the generally weak state of the economy united both halves of this riding in a general concern that the Tories may have lost their way intellectually and economically. Their candidate in 1993 was Dario D'Angela, a chartered accountant. Peter M.A. DeVita, a professional engineer, ran for the NDP. Three minor parties fielded candidates in the campaign also.

In essence the emergence of Reform locally guaranteed Bevilacqua's re-election by cutting into the traditional Tory support base. This time Bevilacqua was returned with a mountainous 50,000 vote margin.

Member of Parliament: Maurizio Bevilacqua; **Party**: Liberal; **Occupation**: Consultant; **Education**: BA, Bethune College; **Age**: 34 (June 1, 1960); **Year first elected to the House of Commons**: 1988

35096 York North

A: Political Profile
i) Voting Behaviour

	% 1993		% 1988	Change 1988-93
Conservative	13.7		42.6	-28.9
Liberal	63.3		42.7	20.6
NDP	2.7		13.2	-10.5
Reform	17.8		0	17.8
Other	2.5		1.5	1

% Turnout	70.1	Total Ballots (#)		114117
Rejected Ballots (#)	1105	% Margin of Victory		45.5
Rural Polls, 1988 (#)	40	Urban Polls, 1988 (#)		331
% Yes - 1992	57.5	% No - 1992		41.8

ii) Campaign Financing

	# of Donations	Total $ Value	% of Limit Spent
Conservative	225	110122	77*
Liberal	90	70902	87.2
NDP	49	11554	7.4
Reform	125	27563	37.5
Other	15	3405	

B: Ethno-Linguistic Profile

% English Home Language	82.9	% French Home Language	0.3
% Official Bilingual	7.6	% Other Home Language	16.9
% Catholics	44.7	% Protestants	26.1
% Aboriginal Peoples	0.1	% Immigrants	34.9

C: Socio-Economic Profile

Average Family Income $	75531	Median Family Income $	65536
% Low Income Families	7.7	Average Home Price $	347381
% Home Owners	82.9	% Unemployment	6.7
% Labour Force Participation	76	% Managerial-Administrative	20.1
% Self-Employed	13.5	% University Degrees	17.6
% Movers	58.7		

D: Industrial Profile

% Manufacturing	15.3	% Service Sector	8.7
% Agriculture	0.8	% Mining	0.2
% Forestry	0.1	% Fishing	0
% Government Services	4.6	% Business Services	8.8

E: Homogeneity Measures

Ethnic Diversity Index	0.25	Religious Homogeneity Index	0.33
Sectoral Concentration Index	0.45	Income Disparity Index	13.2

F: Physical Setting Characteristics

Total Population	233302	Area (km²)	627
Population Density (pop/km²)	372.1		

* Tentative value, due to the existence of unpaid campaign expenses.

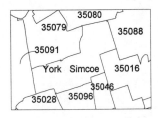

York Simcoe

Constituency Number: 35097

The furthest north of the Metro dependencies, York Simcoe is a mixed urban/suburban/rural riding which includes urban Newmarket (which has fast become a Metro suburb) and other more rural townships. The thick black soil of the Holland Marsh around the southern tip of Lake Simcoe, that forms one of the most important agricultural regions in Ontario, and the Marsh serves as Metro Toronto's market garden. Created by re-distribution in 1988 the predecessors of this riding had a strong Tory tradition. It is one of the most rapidly growing constituencies in the province, and it is now one of the top ten in terms of population size.

In 1988, Tory John Cole, a local optometrist and Newmarket councillor, beat his Liberal challenger, millionaire auto parts magnate Frank Stronach (the driving force behind the Magna manufacturing empire) by nearly 7,000 votes. It is possible that the riding had had enough of millionaire MPs. Former Tory cabinet minister Sinclair Stevens had represented a past incarnation of this riding, until his nomination papers were vetoed by Brian Mulroney in the lead-up to the 1988 election. This followed a series of conflict-of-interest violations and the public inquiry into his affairs. This time the Liberals chose a more traditional candidate, Karen Kraft Sloan. Sloan, an adult educator and freelance policy consultant, headed a group that fought to keep the area off the list of possible sites for a future regional dump and waste management facility. Paul Pivato, a public relations manager at Magna, was the Reform candidate, while Steve Pliakes, a property manager from Newmarket, ran for the NDP. Four minor party candidates also stood for election in 1993.

A good candidate, a tired government, and the Reform challenge which siphoned off the more right wing of the Tory supporters, spelled a victory for Sloan and the Liberals. It was hardly an easy win, however, as she only bested Pivato by about 4,000 votes.

Member of Parliament: Karen Kraft Sloan; **Party**: Liberal; **Occupation**: Public policy consultant; **Education**: MES; **Age**: 42 (April 4, 1952); **Year first elected to the House of Commons**: 1993

35097 York Simcoe

A: Political Profile
i) Voting Behaviour

	% 1993	% 1988	Change 1988-93
Conservative	23.3	47.2	-23.9
Liberal	38.9	35.1	3.8
NDP	2.5	13.2	-10.7
Reform	32.2	0	32.2
Other	3.1	4.5	-1.4

% Turnout	69.9	Total Ballots (#)	69706
Rejected Ballots (#)	514	% Margin of Victory	6.7
Rural Polls, 1988 (#)	149	Urban Polls, 1988 (#)	108
% Yes - 1992	49.9	% No - 1992	49.4

ii) Campaign Financing

	# of Donations	Total $ Value	% of Limit Spent
Conservative	145	37261	72.4
Liberal	58	28511	69.3
NDP	32	11133	14.6
Reform	141	27296	37.1
Other	121	24139	

B: Ethno-Linguistic Profile

% English Home Language	96	% French Home Language	0.3
% Official Bilingual	6.2	% Other Home Language	3.7
% Catholics	26.4	% Protestants	54.8
% Aboriginal Peoples	0.5	% Immigrants	16.5

C: Socio-Economic Profile

Average Family Income $	62725	Median Family Income $	58483
% Low Income Families	7	Average Home Price $	241387
% Home Owners	80.6	% Unemployment	5.9
% Labour Force Participation	75.2	% Managerial-Administrative	15.5
% Self-Employed	11.3	% University Degrees	10.5
% Movers	54.1		

D: Industrial Profile

% Manufacturing	16.5	% Service Sector	9.3
% Agriculture	4	% Mining	0.3
% Forestry	0.2	% Fishing	0
% Government Services	6.5	% Business Services	6.2

E: Homogeneity Measures

Ethnic Diversity Index	0.31	Religious Homogeneity Index	0.39
Sectoral Concentration Index	0.4	Income Disparity Index	6.8

F: Physical Setting Characteristics

Total Population	136082	Area (km²)	1725
Population Density (pop/km²)	78.9		

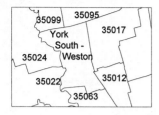

York South–Weston

Constituency Number: 35098

$\mathbf{Y}$ork South–Weston is a working class, heavily ethnic (with an especially large Italian community, it is among the ten most heavily immigrant ridings in the province), urban riding in Metropolitan Toronto. Its boundaries incorporate parts of the cities of Toronto, North York, and York. Average family incomes are more than $10,000 below the provincial norm, making this one of the ten least affluent ridings in the province. The Weston area of Toronto has had a tough couple of years. Industry has been abandoning the area and stores have been closing up and down Weston Road. At the south end of the riding the Ontario Stock Yard faced its last roundup at the end of 1993. The meat packing industry was being 'rationalized' virtually out of existence. In many ways it is understandable: most of the factories were old and hedged in by residential neighbourhoods on all sides. Businessmen, faced with the necessity of concentrating operations in large plants, might have found other, less constrained environments with greater growth potential more appealing.

York South–Weston is a long-time Liberal seat. Since 1984, it has been represented in Parliament by John Nunziata, a lawyer and former alderman for the city of York. Nunziata was a charter member of the Liberal 'rat pack' which regularly exposed and mercilessly attacked those in the Mulroney cabinet who demonstrated lapsed ethics or poor judgement. The 'rat pack' claimed the political scalps of many of them. Drawing on this background, Nunziata had a field day with the controversial 'Pearson Airport' privatization deal announced by the Tories before the election campaign. Nunziata's margin of victory in 1988 was a comfortable 30%.

Nunziata faced a full slate of 10 challengers in the 1993 campaign. Kathleen Crone, a florist, ran for the Reform Party. The Tories nominated Tony Figliano, a consultant, while the NDP was represented by Sil Salvaterra, an articling law student. Five minor party candidates and two independents rounded out the crowded ballot.

In sum the residents of York South–Weston had little reason to support the government and doubtless the unease concerning the Reform Party's policies on immigration and multiculturalism may have handicapped Crone's local appeal. The result, a Liberal landslide, with an almost 20,000 vote margin separating Nunziata from Crone's second place finish.

Member of Parliament: John V. Nunziata; **Party**: Liberal; **Occupation**: Lawyer; **Education**: LL.B, Osgoode Hall Law School; **Age**: 39 (Jan. 4, 1955); **Year first elected to the House of Commons**: 1984

35098 York South–Weston

A: Political Profile
i) Voting Behaviour

	% 1993	% 1988	Change 1988-93
Conservative	7	21.6	-14.6
Liberal	70.1	53.7	16.4
NDP	5.5	23.1	-17.6
Reform	14.8	0	14.8
Other	2.7	1.6	1.1

% Turnout	65.8	Total Ballots (#)	36317
Rejected Ballots (#)	450	% Margin of Victory	55.3
Rural Polls, 1988 (#)	0	Urban Polls, 1988 (#)	156
% Yes - 1992	50.6	% No - 1992	48.6

ii) Campaign Financing

	# of Donations	Total $ Value	% of Limit Spent
Conservative	41	16767	28.4*
Liberal	120	54895	67.1
NDP	128	21927	37.8
Reform	55	20485	48.9
Other	8	2531	

B: Ethno-Linguistic Profile

% English Home Language	70.2	% French Home Language	0.4
% Official Bilingual	5	% Other Home Language	29.5
% Catholics	46.1	% Protestants	30
% Aboriginal Peoples	0.3	% Immigrants	45.6

C: Socio-Economic Profile

Average Family Income $	45057	Median Family Income $	40759
% Low Income Families	25	Average Home Price $	232430
% Home Owners	42.8	% Unemployment	12.4
% Labour Force Participation	66.4	% Managerial-Administrative	10.2
% Self-Employed	6.5	% University Degrees	8.3
% Movers	44.9		

D: Industrial Profile

% Manufacturing	21.5	% Service Sector	12.7
% Agriculture	0.3	% Mining	0.1
% Forestry	0.1	% Fishing	0
% Government Services	4.9	% Business Services	5.9

E: Homogeneity Measures

Ethnic Diversity Index	0.19	Religious Homogeneity Index	0.33
Sectoral Concentration Index	0.42	Income Disparity Index	9.5

F: Physical Setting Characteristics

Total Population	97861	Area (km²)	22
Population Density (pop/km²)	4448.2		

* Tentative value, due to the existence of unpaid campaign expenses.

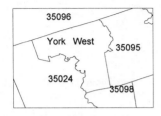

York West

Constituency Number: 35099

York West is located in the northwest corner of Metropolitan Toronto. taking in pieces of the cities of Etobicoke and York. This riding is home to a good many factories, most small and family-owned. A heavily ethnic riding (54% are foreign born, the second highest proportion in the province, after Davenport) and 20% identify themselves as of Italian ancestry. As with neighbouring York Centre, this riding has a mixture of very nice and very unpleasant sections, but most residents are well below other Ontarians in terms of family income. On average, incomes run almost $15,000 below the provincial standard, making this one of the province's ten poorest ridings. The workforce is disproportionately blue-collar, and one of the most heavily employed in the manufacturing sector in the province. The riding also has the highest rate of unemployment among constituencies in the province and the proportion of managers and administrators in the riding is one of the province's lowest.

The description above defines a Liberal bastion. Since 1962 this area has returned Liberal Members to Ottawa. In 1984, rookie MP Sergio Marchi, an Argentina-born former alderman of North York, gave the Liberals one of their few victories, in the face of Mulroney's sweep in the election. He was able to extend his margin of victory to over 40% in the 1988 election, making his victory one of the Liberal's best finishes in the country that year. Marchi has built a strong local reputation for constituency work and helping people caught up in red tape. A member of the so-called Liberal 'rat-pack' that kept pressure on the first Mulroney government, Marchi was given a key role in the party's election readiness committee. No one seriously felt that Marchi was in danger in 1993.

Six challengers emerged to compete against Marchi. Bruce Castleman, a law clerk, ran for the Reform Party, and Marguerite Bebluk, a teacher, won the Tory nomination. Roseanne Giulietti, a lawyer, offered for the NDP. Three minor party candidates rounded out the ballot.

In the end, Marchi remained firmly in control of the seat, obtaining the Liberal's second best result in the province by winning a 22,000 vote margin (almost 70% more than his nearest competitor, Reform's Castleman). Following the election, his efforts were rewarded by being named Minister for Citizenship and Immigration.

Member of Parliament: Sergio Marchi; **Party**: Liberal; **Occupation**: Federal politician; **Education**: BA (Hons.), York University; **Age**: 38 (May 12, 1956); **Year first elected to the House of Commons**: 1984

35099 York West

A: Political Profile
i) Voting Behaviour

	% 1993	% 1988	Change 1988-93
Conservative	4.7	19.1	-14.4
Liberal	79.8	59.6	20.2
NDP	3.4	18.2	-14.8
Reform	10.6	0	10.6
Other	1.5	3.1	-1.6

% Turnout	63.9	Total Ballots (#)	32135
Rejected Ballots (#)	322	% Margin of Victory	69.2
Rural Polls, 1988 (#)	0	Urban Polls, 1988 (#)	142
% Yes - 1992	50	% No - 1992	49

ii) Campaign Financing

	# of Donations	Total $ Value	% of Limit Spent
Conservative	12	15193	25.8
Liberal	101	45570	85
NDP	23	2825	2
Reform	34	3882	5.2
Other	1	273	

B: Ethno-Linguistic Profile

% English Home Language	60.5	% French Home Language	0.2
% Official Bilingual	3.8	% Other Home Language	39.3
% Catholics	47.3	% Protestants	24.1
% Aboriginal Peoples	0.1	% Immigrants	53.8

C: Socio-Economic Profile

Average Family Income $	42463	Median Family Income $	38515
% Low Income Families	25.6	Average Home Price $	228941
% Home Owners	41.2	% Unemployment	14.6
% Labour Force Participation	69.5	% Managerial-Administrative	8
% Self-Employed	4.6	% University Degrees	5.7
% Movers	46.9		

D: Industrial Profile

% Manufacturing	30	% Service Sector	11.3
% Agriculture	0.3	% Mining	0
% Forestry	0.1	% Fishing	0
% Government Services	3.3	% Business Services	5.3

E: Homogeneity Measures

Ethnic Diversity Index	0.22	Religious Homogeneity Index	0.34
Sectoral Concentration Index	0.39	Income Disparity Index	9.3

F: Physical Setting Characteristics

Total Population	105254	Area (km^2)	28
Population Density (pop/km^2)	3759.1		

THE MIDWEST:
MANITOBA-SASKATCHEWAN

The Midwest:

Manitoba–Saskatchewan Regional Overview

$\mathbf{M}$anitoba and Saskatchewan are Canada's Midwest, two prairie provinces wedged between the larger, richer provinces of Ontario to the east and Alberta to the west. Usually lumped into a four-province West (with Alberta and British Columbia) or a three-province Prairies (with Alberta), the latter regional groupings have become increasingly strained and irrelevant, an artifact of Canadian history: a West-in-formation was institutionalized in the Canadian Senate (where the new region was accorded 24 Senators, giving it equal representation to Ontario, Quebec and the Maritimes), whereas the vast prairie imposed its own geographic and economic unity on settlers, further cemented and mythologized in the political struggles of Prairie grain growers against 'eastern' domination. By the 1990s, however, such legacies seem of little import compared to the economic and political differences that now divide the region along the Alberta-Saskatchewan border.

In Confederation's fiscal terminology, Manitoba and Saskatchewan are clearly in the 'have-not' camp of seven Canadian provinces, with their western neighbours Alberta and British Columbia on the other side of an ever-widening fiscal gap, the beneficiaries of higher long-term economic and population growth rates. This has left the governments and residents of Manitoba and Saskatchewan much more reliant on Ottawa's financial support and redistributive role. In addition to the equalization payments that their governments receive, on average individual Midwesterners depend upon transfer payments for between 14 and 14.5% of their income, about the same as Quebeckers. Alberta is a large net contributor to the equalization scheme, while Albertans themselves receive an average 9.6% of their income from government transfers.

The effects of urbanization, population growth, and diversification away from the agrarian economy have been an especially glaring difference separating Alberta and Saskatchewan, with the latter suffering population decline in the 1980s, its agriculural economy crippled by the global subsidies war between grain-exporting countries. Alberta, on the other hand, always less dependent on agriculture, has prospered atop its oil and gas wealth and a generally more diversified economic base. Manitoba's economy historically has been more diversified, comprised of southern agriculture, northern resources, and the urban manufacturing and service-based economy of Winnepeg. For this reason the negative effect of the farm crisis has been less dramatic than for Saskatchewan, which remains heavily reliant upon the agricultural sector.

In demographic terms, Manitoba and Saskatchewan have about the same proportion of Aboriginals in their populations, around 11.2% (more than double the next closest province). This made Aboriginals a factor in several ridings in each province. Manitoba's immigrant population (12.1% of constituency population, on average) also made this group a factor in electoral outcomes, especially compared to Saskatchewan (with a 5.7% average). Even so, Manitoba's historic role as the West's most cosmopolitan province clearly has given way to the more dynamic societies of Alberta and British Columbia, where the immigrant share of constituency populations now stands at an average 14.2% and 21.1% respectively.

These fiscal and economic differences underlie the Midwest provinces' different orientation toward Ottawa, but they have also contributed to distinctly different party systems and political cultures. At the provincial level, both Manitoba and Saskatchewan have had New Democrat governments, whereas Alberta has always shunned socialism in favour of right-wing populist alternatives. This difference in the electoral politics of Alberta versus the Midwest has been evident at the federal level as well, and was especially so in the 1984, 1988 and 1993 federal elections. Saskatchewan divided its vote between New Democrats and Conservatives in 1984 and 1988 and between Liberals (5), New Democrats (5), and Reformers (4) in

1993. Manitoba divided its vote between Conservatives and New Democrats in 1984, three ways in 1988 (with the Liberals making gains against Conservatives and New Democrats), and gave the Liberals a near-landslide in 1993 (12 Liberals, 1 New Democrat, 1 Reformer). In total, the Midwest elected 17 Liberals, 6 New Democrats, and 5 Reformers in 1993. On the other hand, in the last three elections Alberta gave two landslide victories to the Conservative Party (1984, 1988) and one to the Reform Party. In 1993, Albertans elected 22 Reformers and only 4 Liberals.

The 1988 election in the Midwest was for the most part a single issue election which polarized the vote between the pro- and anti-free trade forces, with the Conservatives benefiting from the Liberal-NDP splitting of the anti-vote. This allowed the Tories to maintain most of their seats in the agriculture-dominated ridings of rural Manitoba and Saskatchewan, while giving way to either the Liberals (in Manitoba) or the NDP (in Saskatchewan) in the urban areas. In Manitoba, the Liberals, building on the resurgence of the provincial Liberal Party, went from one Winnipeg seat to five, their best showing in twenty years. This left the NDP holding on to just one of its traditional Winnipeg seats, as well as the northern riding of Churchill. Besides free trade, a major campaign issue was the CF-18 affair, involving a 1986 federal government decision to award a major aerospace contract to a Quebec-based firm over a Manitoba competitor, despite the latter's lower and technically superior bid. In Saskatchewan, the pattern was similar, with five Conservative incumbents going down to defeat, leaving intact four Tory-held agricultural ridings. From the outset, opposition to free trade was greater in Saskatchewan than anywhere else, and the stronger of the anti-free trade forces in the province - the New Democrats - drew sustenance from that. Other contributing factors to the outcome were the unpopularity of the provincial Conservative government and the issue of federal agricultural subsidies and drought aid.

The 1993 election results had no major issue such as free trade determining the outcome, but clearly there was widespread anti-government sentiment and a much higher propensity on the part of voters to register a political protest against the status quo. The outcome gives the partisan complexion of the Midwest a dramatically different hue: with two-thirds of the region's seats, the once-scorned Liberals are now the dominant party, with the remaining third shared between the decimated New Democrats and the surging Reformers. There was still an urban-rural cleavage evident in the results, with all five Reformers elected in rural ridings, though this divide was less prominent than in 1988. Nonetheless, different political dynamics were at work in the rural and urban areas of the region, with farm Tories forced to move to the right in response to the rise of Reform, and city Tories forced to move to the centre to counter surging Liberal support. Neither tactic was sufficient to save a single Tory seat: support levels for Reform in rural ridings, where insufficient to actually push a Reformer into office, merely splintered the vote on the right and helped to elect Liberals in previously unfriendly territory. In the cities, a rising tide of Liberalism and entrenched pockets of New Democratic Party support left little space for centrist Tory appeals; alternatively, Tory rearguard actions on the right against local Reform candidates merely guaranteed the relegation of both to political obscurity.

There was a diverse range of factors contributing to the collapse of the once-dominant Conservative Party, most of which were national: the long recession that preceded the election, the dramatically-worsening deficit situation, the spending cuts that were likely to get deeper, the failed attempts at constitutional reform. The Tory attempt to escape this legacy, and the visceral voter dislike of their former national leader, fell flat along with their new leader's highly-publicized departure in style and substance from the Mulroney years. The party's botched national campaign only served to deepen the widespread cynicism and alienation of voters. Added to this was the bleak agricultural scene caused by the worst grain crisis since the 1930s. In Saskatchewan, it was estimated that 35% of farmers were in danger of losing their farms, despite $5 billion in farm aid since 1988.

The other big loser in 1993 was the NDP, which lost half its seats in the Midwest region. For the most part, the issues it chose to focus on - the threat to social programs and the deleterious effects of free trade - remained peripheral concerns to the majority of voters who had the economy and the deficit on their minds. Even more of a difficulty perhaps, in a year of voter protest, was that the party had come to be perceived as part of the status quo, and therefore as part of the problem. The anti-government vote flowed to the Liberals, and the protest vote to the Reform Party. The lone NDP seat in Manitoba - Bill Blaikie in Winnipeg–Transcona - was retained by the barest of margins, in the closest contest in Canada. Other high-profile candidates whom the Party hoped would recapture some traditional left-wing Winnipeg seats were unable to stem the Liberal tide. In Saskatchewan, the party squeaked out a few wins in some close three- and four-party vote splits, and otherwise benefited from strong local party organizations and the presence of a still-popular provincial NDP government. Still, the loss of Lorne Nystrom in Yorkton–Melville was a major blow to the party: MP since 1968, bilingual, high-profile, and a likely candidate for the party's leadership, Nystrom's defeat at the hands of Reformer Garry Breitkreuz was highly symbolic of the party's fortunes in this election.

The Liberals, of course, were the big winners in the Midwest. With only one seat in the region in 1984, and five in 1988, the Party was actually fighting a quarter-century or more of political marginality in the region's politics. This history made its 1993 breakthrough all the more dramatic, finally giving the Liberals significant caucus representation west of Ontario and rightful claim to the title of national party. With a natural populist for a leader, and a safe, centrist policy stance that promised a modest, balanced approach of job creation and deficit reduction, the Liberals gathered in the votes of the disaffected who had become disgusted with the Tories, but were still repelled or wary of the latest of Alberta's right-wing populist alternatives. Buoyed in the region by polls predicting a national Liberal victory and a badly fading NDP, the Liberals were beneficiaries of a political opportunity structure that was clearly in their favour. In the wake of this Liberal triumph, two Midwest appointees were named to the new federal cabinet: Lloyd Axworthy from Winnipeg South-Centre was handed the enormous responsibilities and budget attached to the Human Resources and Labour ministry, while Ralph Goodale from Regina–Wascana was made Agriculture Minister.

The Reform Party did not make their hoped-for breakthrough in the Midwest, though they did establish a secure beach-head. This repeats an historical pattern whereby Alberta-spawned populist parties fail to catch fire the other two Prairie provinces, instead spreading westward into British Columbia. Some of the party's policies, such as the gradual removal of agricultural subsidies, were not winners for the party, though it did gain support for its tough line on crime and punishment, as well as its call for more constituent control over MPs. With the region's Conservatives flat on their backs politically speaking, Reform's future prospects will depend upon the performance of the Liberals in office, in particular with regard to Reform's key issues of deficit reduction and the question of Quebec's place within Canada.

Thanks to the proliferation of fringe parties in 1993, there were significantly more candidates running than in previous elections. One result was significantly more women candidates in the field: 27 of 108 in Manitoba and 16 of 93 in Saskatchewan. This did not translate, however, into a higher ratio of female MPs. Only two of the twenty-eight seats went to women (one each in Manitoba and Saskatchewan), a dismal 7% of the region's representatives compared to a national share of 18%.

Manitoba Results, 1988 & 1993 Elections, 1992 Referendum

	1988 Election			1993 Election	
	% Vote	Seats	1992	% Vote	Seats
Conservatives	36.9	7		11.9	0
Liberals	36.5	5		45.0	12
NDP	21.3	2		16.7	1
Reform	3.3	0		22.4	1
Other/Indep.	2.0	0		4.0	0
Turnout	74.7	–		68.7	–
% Yes (1992)			38.4		
% No (1992)			61.6		

Saskatchewan Results, 1988 & 1993 Elections, 1992 Referendum

	1988 Election			1993 Election	
	% Vote	Seats	1992	% Vote	Seats
Conservatives	36.4	4		11.3	0
Liberals	18.2	0		32.1	5
NDP	44.2	10		26.6	5
Reform	0.7	0		27.2	4
Other/Indep.	0.5	0		2.8	0
Turnout	77.8	–		69.4	–
% Yes (1992)			44.7		
% No (1992)			55.3		

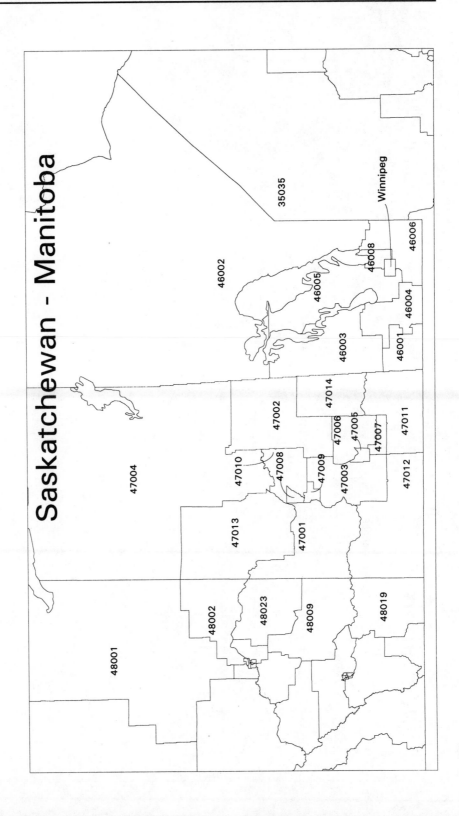

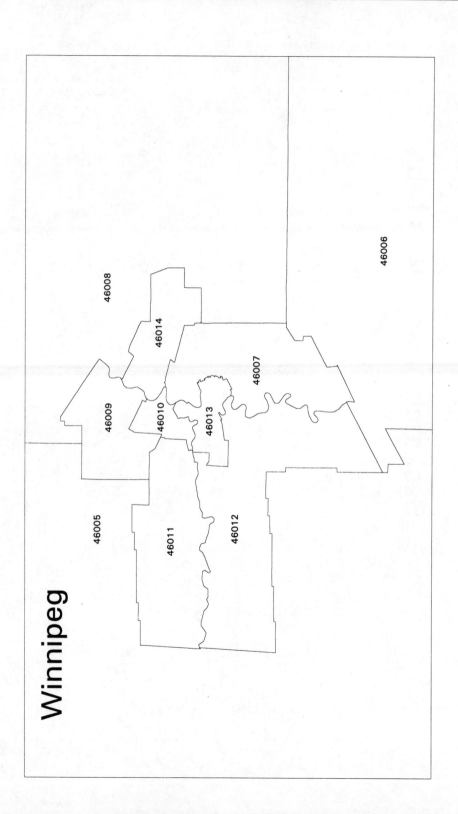

Winnipeg

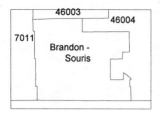

Brandon–Souris

Constituency Number: 46001

A strongly protestant riding in the southwest corner of Manitoba, Brandon–Souris has an economy based on agriculture and services. Largely unaffected by redistribution, Brandon–Souris continues to be evenly split between rural and urban voters, the latter concentrated in Brandon, a city of about 40,000 and the home of Brandon University. The riding also includes the towns of Killarney and Virden.

This riding has been bedrock Conservative for 42 years, having been first captured by Walter Dinsdale in 1951 and held until his death in 1982. In the subsequent by-election voters chose Brandon University history professor Lee Clark as Dinsdale's heir, and re-elected him in the general election of 1984. It is worth noting that the distant second place finisher to Clark in 1984 was neither the NDP nor the Liberal candidate, but the right-wing Confederation of Regions (CoR) candidate. The incumbent Clark, who for a time served as Chairman of the House of Commons Agriculture Committee and in 1987 was appointed Parliamentary Secretary to the Minister of Agriculture, was opposed in 1988 by Liberal David Campbell and NDP candidate David Serle, as well as a number of minor party candidates. The prospects of one of these - the CoR party - were somewhat reduced by internal feuding which saw their 1984 candidate in Brandon–Souris switch allegiances to yet another western protest party, the newly formed Reform Party of Canada. In any event, the main challenge to Clark in 1988 came from the Liberals who doubled their share of the popular vote to over 30%.

In 1993, there were pre-election indications that continued Conservative domination of the riding was threatened by surging support for the Reform Party and the improved prospects of a rejuvenated Liberal Party. With no Conservative incumbent running (Clark did not re-offer), a nomination battle ensued with farmer Larry Maguire defeating provincial Health Minister Jim McCrae. The other main contestants for the seat were the Mayor of Virden, Glen MacKinnon, for the Liberals, Brandon city councillor Ross Martin for the NDP, and dentist Ed Agnew for Reform. There were also four fringe party candidates: Eldon Obach for the National Party, Robert Roberts for Natural Law, Abe Neufeld for Christian Heritage, and George Armstrong for the Canada Party.

In an election campaign dealing with the national issues of health care, job creation, education, and deficit reduction, support for the Conservatives slipped and a two-party race ensued between the Liberal and Reform candidates. The election result gave the Liberal MacKinnon a close 1,005 vote margin over Reformer Agnew (33% to 30.4%). The Conservative vote held up enough to give their candidate third place with 22.4% of the vote, a relatively strong showing which may have deprived the Reform Party of victory. The NDP finished a distant fourth with 11.9% of the vote.

Member of Parliament: William Glen McKinnon; **Party:** Liberal; **Occupation:** Principal; **Education:** BEd, Brandon University; **Age:** 57 (Dec. 16, 1937); **Year first elected to the House of Commons:** 1993

46001 Brandon–Souris

A: Political Profile
i) Voting Behaviour

	% 1993	% 1988	Change 1988-93
Conservative	22.4	46.8	-24.4
Liberal	33	30.7	2.3
NDP	11.9	13.5	-1.6
Reform	30.4	4.2	26.2
Other	2.3	4.8	-2.5

% Turnout	68.7	Total Ballots (#)	36885
Rejected Ballots (#)	128	% Margin of Victory	2.6
Rural Polls, 1988 (#)	74	Urban Polls, 1988 (#)	73
% Yes - 1992	39.8	% No - 1992	59.9

ii) Campaign Financing

	# of Donations	Total $ Value	% of Limit Spent
Conservative	300	36966	92.1
Liberal	231	39240	60.5
NDP	2	17041	24.2
Reform	158	28090	56.3
Other	31	11645	

B: Ethno-Linguistic Profile

% English Home Language	97.2	% French Home Language	0.5
% Official Bilingual	5	% Other Home Language	2.3
% Catholics	17.3	% Protestants	69.3
% Aboriginal Peoples	7.6	% Immigrants	6

C: Socio-Economic Profile

Average Family Income $	40256	Median Family Income $	35968
% Low Income Families	18.8	Average Home Price $	67716
% Home Owners	67.4	% Unemployment	6.2
% Labour Force Participation	68	% Managerial-Administrative	8.5
% Self-Employed	16.1	% University Degrees	7.6
% Movers	41.4		

D: Industrial Profile

% Manufacturing	5.2	% Service Sector	17.7
% Agriculture	15.6	% Mining	0.6
% Forestry	0.2	% Fishing	0
% Government Services	10.6	% Business Services	2

E: Homogeneity Measures

Ethnic Diversity Index	0.36	Religious Homogeneity Index	0.51
Sectoral Concentration Index	0.45	Income Disparity Index	10.7

F: Physical Setting Characteristics

Total Population	72113	Area (km²)	14030
Population Density (pop/km²)	5.1		

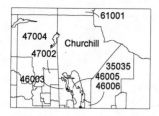

Churchill

Constituency Number: 46002

An immense Manitoba constituency that includes the towns of Flin Flon, The Pas, Thompson, and Leaf Rapids, Churchill has the second largest land mass of any federal riding in Canada. It is dotted with reserves, and the Aboriginal population comprises about 63% of the constituency and 43% of the electorate (the second highest percentage in Canada after Nunatsiaq). This makes the native vote important to all parties, though voter turnout in native communities has traditionally been lower than in other parts of the riding. Mining and government services are the big employers, but logging and fishing are also more important here than anywhere else in Manitoba. At around 15%, unemployment is second highest in the province. Churchill had the biggest 'No' vote in the province in the 1992 Referendum, despite national Aboriginal leaders' support for the deal.

Historically, this constituency has been strong NDP territory, both provincially and federally. In 1988 the incumbent MP for Churchill, New Democrat and former teacher Rod Murphy, won his fourth term of office. He did so with well-organized support from union locals in mining centres such as Flin Flon and Lynn Lake, as well as in The Pas. The Liberals made a strong bid for native support by fielding Chief Rodney Spence of the Nelson House Indian Band as their candidate. Nonetheless, Murphy won quite easily, outpolling the combined totals of his Conservative and Liberal rivals on his way to registering one of the biggest NDP victories anywhere in Canada.

At the outset of the campaign in 1993, local pundits said the race was too close to call. The incumbent Murphy again faced a Liberal opponent who was Aboriginal, this time well-known Elijah Harper, the former provincial NDP MLA who in 1990 blocked passage of the Meech Lake Accord. Lawyer and former RCMP officer Don Knight contested for the Progressive Conservatives, bus driver Wally Daudrich for Reform, and native prospector Charles Settee for the National Party. The issues in the campaign were both national and local. Job creation, health and social services gained the attention of the candidates, but so did more local concerns such as native rights and the future of the Hudson Bay rail line and the port of Churchill. Though Murphy had good relations with native groups, Harper won the endorsement of the largest native organization in the constituency. The likelihood of a federal Liberal government also helped Harper with voters seeking greater influence in Ottawa.

The election was a two-party affair, with the Liberal Harper sidelining incumbent NDP MP Murphy by a 47% to 36.9% margin. The Conservatives and Reform Party finished a distant third and fourth with 10.3% and 9.6% respectively.

Member of Parliament: Elijah Harper; **Party:** Liberal; **Occupation:** Analyst and native administrator; **Education:** University of Manitoba; **Year first elected to the House of Commons:** 1993

46002 Churchill

A: Political Profile

i) Voting Behaviour

	% 1993	% 1988	Change 1988-93
Conservative	10.3	20.5	-10.2
Liberal	40.7	23.1	17.6
NDP	36.9	56.4	-19.5
Reform	9.6	0	9.6
Other	2.5	0	2.5

% Turnout	54.1	Total Ballots (#)	23835
Rejected Ballots (#)	123	% Margin of Victory	3.8
Rural Polls, 1988 (#)	106	Urban Polls, 1988 (#)	60
% Yes - 1992	29.3	% No - 1992	70.4

ii) Campaign Financing

	# of Donations	Total $ Value	% of Limit Spent
Conservative	114	21624	34.7
Liberal	67	47892	51.3*
NDP	6	31389	46.4
Reform	9	2871	4.2
Other	6	23866	

B: Ethno-Linguistic Profile

% English Home Language	72	% French Home Language	0.2
% Official Bilingual	3.7	% Other Home Language	27.8
% Catholics	34.2	% Protestants	53.1
% Aboriginal Peoples	63.9	% Immigrants	3.6

C: Socio-Economic Profile

Average Family Income $	44596	Median Family Income $	39451
% Low Income Families	16.8	Average Home Price $	63943
% Home Owners	46.6	% Unemployment	15
% Labour Force Participation	64	% Managerial-Administrative	7.7
% Self-Employed	5.1	% University Degrees	5.5
% Movers	49.8		

D: Industrial Profile

% Manufacturing	5.1	% Service Sector	15.4
% Agriculture	0.6	% Mining	14.8
% Forestry	1.7	% Fishing	1.4
% Government Services	16	% Business Services	1.4

E: Homogeneity Measures

Ethnic Diversity Index	0.44	Religious Homogeneity Index	0.41
Sectoral Concentration Index	0.35	Income Disparity Index	11.5

F: Physical Setting Characteristics

Total Population	67949	Area (km²)	480460
Population Density (pop/km²)	0.1		

* Tentative value, due to the existence of unpaid campaign expenses.

Dauphin–Swan River

Constituency Number: 46003

A large, rural constituency covering west-central Manitoba, Dauphin–Swan River has the second lowest average income in the province and the fifth lowest in the country, creating a level of dependence on government transfer payments (at 22%) that is second in Manitoba only to Winnipeg North Centre. The riding's economy is mainly dependent upon agriculture, which is supplemented by mining. The riding is notable for having the lowest level of employment in business services anywhere in the country. Aboriginals make up more than one-fifth of the riding's population, tenth highest in Canada.

Dauphin–Swan River has traditionally been a swing riding between the Conservatives and the NDP, with the Liberals as third-place finishers. In recent elections, voter discontent has been manifested in growing support for protest parties. Changes brought about by redistribution in 1988 incorporated a sizeable chunk of the former Tory stronghold of Portage–Marquette, providing the Conservatives with a distinct advantage within the redrawn boundaries. In 1984, the Conservative candidate in Dauphin–Swan River, pharmacist Brian White, stole the seat from the NDP. In 1988, White was re-elected, though the Tory vote declined somewhat despite the favourable boundary changes. The NDP improved marginally on their 1984 performance, and the Liberals somewhat more so, while minor party candidates in the riding, eclipsed by the free trade battle waged by the major parties, fared poorly.

In 1993, the incumbent White did not re-offer, and was replaced as the Conservative candidate by farmer Bill Galloway. The Liberals ran farmer Marlene Cowling, the NDP the school principal Stan Struthers, and the Reform Party businessman Dale Brown. Farmer Tony Riley ran for the Canada Party. Agriculture and its future was addressed by all the candidates in this mainly agricultural riding. Other campaign issues of note were health care, education, the deficit, and rural postal services.

Though the Tory candidate warned traditional supporters not to vote Reform and thereby split the conservative vote, that is more or less what happened on election night. The Liberal Cowling narrowly defeated the Reform candidate by fewer than a thousand votes, winning with only 31.7% of the vote to 29.5% for Reformer Brown. The NDP finished third with 22.2% of the ballot and the Conservatives fourth with 15.8%. Cowling's victory was the only one for a woman candidate in Manitoba and the first Liberal win in the riding since the 1940s.

Member of Parliament: Marlene Cowling; **Party:** Liberal; **Occupation:** Farmer; **Education:** Technical Training Winnipeg; **Age:** 53 (Aug. 26, 1941); **Year first elected to the House of Commons:** 1993

46003 Dauphin–Swan River

A: Political Profile

i) Voting Behaviour

	% 1993	% 1988	Change 1988-93
Conservative	15.8	41.4	-25.6
Liberal	31.7	19.6	12.1
NDP	22.2	33.4	-11.2
Reform	29.5	3.4	26.1
Other	0.8	2.2	-1.4

% Turnout	72.4	Total Ballots (#)	33535
Rejected Ballots (#)	131	% Margin of Victory	2.2
Rural Polls, 1988 (#)	196	Urban Polls, 1988 (#)	23
% Yes - 1992	31.6	% No - 1992	68.1

ii) Campaign Financing

	# of Donations	Total $ Value	% of Limit Spent
Conservative	257	34313	100
Liberal	175	27387	34.9
NDP	2	42554	80.3
Reform	177	43626	47.8
Other	8	775	

B: Ethno-Linguistic Profile

% English Home Language	91.5	% French Home Language	1.2
% Official Bilingual	6.2	% Other Home Language	7.4
% Catholics	35.2	% Protestants	50.8
% Aboriginal Peoples	21.1	% Immigrants	4.1

C: Socio-Economic Profile

Average Family Income $	34388	Median Family Income $	28412
% Low Income Families	22.1	Average Home Price $	47548
% Home Owners	75.6	% Unemployment	6.7
% Labour Force Participation	60.8	% Managerial-Administrative	8.6
% Self-Employed	28.2	% University Degrees	4.8
% Movers	28.4		

D: Industrial Profile

% Manufacturing	2.9	% Service Sector	12
% Agriculture	30.6	% Mining	1.2
% Forestry	1	% Fishing	0.5
% Government Services	8	% Business Services	0.8

E: Homogeneity Measures

Ethnic Diversity Index	0.23	Religious Homogeneity Index	0.38
Sectoral Concentration Index	0.39	Income Disparity Index	17.4

F: Physical Setting Characteristics

Total Population	64555	Area (km²)	47260
Population Density (pop/km²)	1.4		

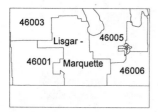

Lisgar–Marquette

Constituency Number: 46004

This south-central Manitoba riding, the most agricultural in Manitoba (fifth so in Canada), has a prosperous and diversified agricultural base as the mainstay of its economy, in addition to ranching and small business. It boasts the lowest unemployment rate in the country at around 3.5%. The most Protestant riding in Manitoba (fourth in Canada), it features a large Mennonite population, with some 12,000 constituents listing their mother tongue as German. There are a number of towns in the constituency, including Morden, Winkler, Carman, Minnedosa, and Neepawa.

Lisgar–Marquette was created in 1988 as an amalgamation of two ridings held by Progressive Conservative MPs. A bedrock Tory constituency since the Diefenbaker sweep of 1958, in 1984 both the NDP and Liberal candidates lost their election deposits as the right-wing Confederation of Regions Party (CoR) came in second to the Conservatives. While the CoR was displaced by the Reform Party as the fringe party of choice in 1988, once again a minor party was expected to outpoll both the main opposition parties. In the event, however, the vote for minor party candidates declined sharply, while the Liberals made a dramatic improvement, rising from a dismal 12% of the popular vote to 22%, and a second place finish. The victor in 1988, Charlie Mayer, a farmer first elected in 1979 and at the time of the election the Minister of State for Grains and Oilseeds, took advantage of the decline in support for the right-wing fringe parties vote to increase his already substantial plurality.

Incumbent PC Charlie Mayer was again running in 1993, this time as Minister of Agriculture, against six challengers. Retired accountant Grant Johnson ran for the Liberals, semi-retired farmer Jake Hoeppner for the Reform Party, and United Church minister Leslie King for the NDP. Minor party hopefuls were Martin Dewitt for Christian Heritage, Larry Jeffers for the National Party, and Roy Lyall for the Canada Party. Mayer, involved with the making of agricultural policy since the mid-1980s, was in trouble from the outset of the campaign with farmers in the southern part of the riding unhappy with these policies. The main beneficiary was the Reform Party's candidate, Hoeppner.

The election result was a major upset, with Mayer's vote total declining by almost 10,000 votes, the margin of his victory in 1988. Reformer Hoeppner easily took the constituency with 41% of the ballot, far ahead of Liberal Grant Johnson's 26.8%. Mayer's 24% tally was good enough for third. The NDP finished a distant fourth with 5.5%.

Member of Parliament: Jake E. Hoeppner; **Party:** Reform; **Occupation:** Farmer; **Age:** 59 (Feb. 1, 1936); **Year first elected to the House of Commons:** 1993

46004 Lisgar-Marquette

A: Political Profile

i) Voting Behaviour

	% 1993	% 1988	Change 1988-93
Conservative	24	53.9	-29.9
Liberal	26.8	22.1	4.7
NDP	5.5	6.8	-1.3
Reform	41	8.7	32.3
Other	2.7	8.4	-5.7

% Turnout	69.8	Total Ballots (#)	32705
Rejected Ballots (#)	78	% Margin of Victory	16.9
Rural Polls, 1988 (#)	191	Urban Polls, 1988 (#)	0
% Yes - 1992	39.6	% No - 1992	60.1

ii) Campaign Financing

	# of Donations	Total $ Value	% of Limit Spent
Conservative	116	24057	45.9*
Liberal	138	28790	46.1
NDP	3	4762	4.1
Reform	147	34892	64.9
Other	38	6220	

B: Ethno-Linguistic Profile

% English Home Language	87.1	% French Home Language	2.1
% Official Bilingual	6.2	% Other Home Language	10.9
% Catholics	14.4	% Protestants	77.7
% Aboriginal Peoples	1.6	% Immigrants	7

C: Socio-Economic Profile

Average Family Income $	38428	Median Family Income $	32099
% Low Income Families	15.1	Average Home Price $	57700
% Home Owners	79.9	% Unemployment	3.6
% Labour Force Participation	66.2	% Managerial-Administrative	7.8
% Self-Employed	25.2	% University Degrees	5.3
% Movers	29.3		

D: Industrial Profile

% Manufacturing	8.5	% Service Sector	12.1
% Agriculture	33	% Mining	0.3
% Forestry	0.2	% Fishing	0
% Government Services	4.2	% Business Services	1.2

E: Homogeneity Measures

Ethnic Diversity Index	0.3	Religious Homogeneity Index	0.61
Sectoral Concentration Index	0.37	Income Disparity Index	16.5

F: Physical Setting Characteristics

Total Population	66752	Area (km²)	20190
Population Density (pop/km²)	3.3		

* Tentative value, due to the existence of unpaid campaign expenses.

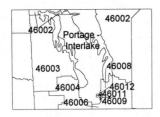

Portage–Interlake

Constituency Number: 46005

A largely rural riding covering the interlake district of central Manitoba west and north of Winnipeg, and including Portage la Prairie (the province's third largest town), Stonewall, and Gimli, Portage–Interlake was created in 1988 out of portions of the old ridings of Lisgar, Portage–Marquette, and Selkirk–Interlake. Ethnically diverse and with a large Aboriginal population (about 16%), the riding has an economic base dominated by agriculture and food processing. Government services are also an important employer.

The southern part of the riding, where most of the population resides, traditionally has been a strong bastion of Conservative support, while the northern area, with 11 Indian reserves and about 20% of the population, historically favoured the NDP. In 1984, Conservative Felix Holtmann won by a comfortable margin over his chief opponents, while fringe parties captured about 20% of the vote. In 1988, the incumbent, a former hog farmer, was again victorious, retaining the seat with a somewhat diminished plurality. The most significant change in this election, however, was the dramatic revival of Liberal fortunes in the riding concomitant with declining NDP and minor party support.

In 1993, Holtmann faced not only a revived Liberal Party, but competition for his traditional electorate from the Reform candidate as well. The Liberals fielded an impressive candidate in local Liberal constituency president Dr John Gerrard, a children's cancer specialist. The other major contenders were businessman Don Sawatsky for the Reform Party and nurse and union rep Connie Gretsinger for the NDP. Minor party candidates included Mel Christian for the National Party, Gary Schwartz for Natural Law, Dennis Rice, Libertarian, and Hans Kjear, Canada Party.

With the conservative vote divided between Holtmann and Reformer Sawatsky, the Liberal Gerrard was able to score an easy victory. Gerrard amassed almost 5,000 votes more than the Reform candidate, taking 40.7% of the ballot to Sawatsky's 27.5%. Holtmann managed to hang on to 19.7% of the vote, while the NDP's Gretsinger finished a distant fourth with 8.5%.

Member of Parliament: John Gerrard; **Party:** Liberal; **Occupation:** Medical doctor; **Education:** BM, BCh, DM (Medicine), McGill University; **Age:** 47 (Oct. 13, 1947); **Year first elected to the House of Commons:** 1993

46005 Portage–Interlake

A: Political Profile

i) Voting Behaviour

	% 1993	% 1988	Change 1988-93
Conservative	19.7	38.7	-19
Liberal	40.7	30.2	10.5
NDP	8.5	18.6	-10.1
Reform	27.5	11.8	15.7
Other	3.6	0.7	2.9

% Turnout	69.1	Total Ballots (#)	35780
Rejected Ballots (#)	119	% Margin of Victory	13.2
Rural Polls, 1988 (#)	159	Urban Polls, 1988 (#)	27
% Yes - 1992	33.3	% No - 1992	66.2

ii) Campaign Financing

	# of Donations	Total $ Value	% of Limit Spent
Conservative	190	43045	104
Liberal	295	50853	74.3
NDP	2	7263	10.7
Reform	253	29054	61.4
Other	9	10687	

B: Ethno-Linguistic Profile

% English Home Language	90.5	% French Home Language	2.5
% Official Bilingual	8.1	% Other Home Language	7
% Catholics	23.6	% Protestants	61.5
% Aboriginal Peoples	16.1	% Immigrants	4.9

C: Socio-Economic Profile

Average Family Income $	41691	Median Family Income $	37579
% Low Income Families	13.6	Average Home Price $	73548
% Home Owners	76	% Unemployment	6.2
% Labour Force Participation	68.9	% Managerial-Administrative	9.1
% Self-Employed	18.9	% University Degrees	5.4
% Movers	36.1		

D: Industrial Profile

% Manufacturing	7	% Service Sector	13.6
% Agriculture	22.2	% Mining	0.4
% Forestry	0.2	% Fishing	1.2
% Government Services	11.1	% Business Services	1.9

E: Homogeneity Measures

Ethnic Diversity Index	0.19	Religious Homogeneity Index	0.43
Sectoral Concentration Index	0.35	Income Disparity Index	9.9

F: Physical Setting Characteristics

Total Population	72051	Area (km²)	58960
Population Density (pop/km²)	1.2		

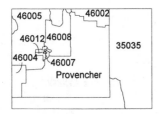

Provencher

Constituency Number: 46006

Stretching south and east of Winnipeg and covering the extreme southeast corner of Manitoba bordering Ontario and the United States, this rural, agricultural riding has an economic base in agriculture, manufacturing, business services, and mining. Almost 10% of the riding's residents are French-speaking and almost one-fifth are bilingual, second to St Boniface in Manitoba. The riding includes the towns of Steinbach and Altona.

In the 1870s this was the home constituency of Métis leader Louis Riel. Since then Provencher's French character has given way to English-speaking migrants from Ontario. Mennonites of Dutch-German ancestry now constitute the constituency's single largest ethnic group. In 1968, the riding went Conservative. In 1972, Provencher constituents elected teacher Jake Epp as their parliamentary representative. Epp went on to become a senior cabinet minister in both the Clark and Mulroney governments. His voter support was particularly strong in Steinbach, where one-third of the riding's constituents live and where Epp was regarded as a native son. In 1988, the election outcome was seen by most observers to be another easy victory for Epp, with the NDP putting up only a token campaign and the minor parties posing no threat to the incumbent. Liberal candidate and former teacher Wes Penner, however, waged a vigorous campaign which succeeded doubling the party's share of the vote and gaining the party a respectable second place finish.

In 1993, after 21 years in federal politics, Epp decided not to re-offer. With Epp's large personal following no longer a factor, the contest in Provencher opened up considerably. Absent from the riding for most of the campaign, Epp did little to aid his Tory successor, Kelly Clark. Preliminary polls in the riding indicated that with Epp gone, the election would be fought primarily between the Liberal and Reform candidates. The Liberals ran 37-year-old David Iftody, while the Reform Party, harbouring big hopes for Provencher, ran Dean Whiteway, Conservative MP for Selkirk in the 1970s. While Reform was well-organized in the riding and its campaign impressive, Whiteway did encounter some resistance to the party's positions on Quebec and the language question from the riding's significant francophone community. A fly in the ointment for the Liberals was that their candidate in 1988, Wes Penner, was running in 1993 for the National Party. The other candidates were Martha Wiebe Owen for the New Democrats, Corinne Ayotte for Natural Law, and Ted Bezan for the Canada Party.

With 44% of the vote, the election result gave the Liberal Iftody a clear 2,700 vote win over his nearest competitor, Reformer Whiteway, who collected 36.8%. The Conservative candidate Clark finished a distant third with 10.3% of the vote, a huge decline of 45% from Epp's total in 1988. The NDP managed just 5% of the ballot for a fourth place finish.

Member of Parliament: David Iftody; **Party:** Liberal; **Occupation:** Consultant; **Education:** MPA, Carleton University; **Year first elected to the House of Commons:** 1993

46006 Provencher

A: Political Profile

i) Voting Behaviour

	% 1993	% 1988	Change 1988-93
Conservative	10.3	55.5	-45.2
Liberal	44	32.5	11.5
NDP	5	7.3	-2.3
Reform	36.8	3.6	33.2
Other	3.9	1	2.9

% Turnout	69.5	Total Ballots (#)	36729
Rejected Ballots (#)	126	% Margin of Victory	7.2
Rural Polls, 1988 (#)	168	Urban Polls, 1988 (#)	0
% Yes - 1992	42.6	% No - 1992	57

ii) Campaign Financing

	# of Donations	Total $ Value	% of Limit Spent
Conservative	174	43276	81.6
Liberal	143	46621	71
NDP	3	7127	12.3
Reform	136	36984	83.6
Other	3	1060	

B: Ethno-Linguistic Profile

% English Home Language	80.2	% French Home Language	9.7
% Official Bilingual	18.3	% Other Home Language	10.1
% Catholics	29.9	% Protestants	60.7
% Aboriginal Peoples	4.4	% Immigrants	8

C: Socio-Economic Profile

Average Family Income $	43606	Median Family Income $	37914
% Low Income Families	10.9	Average Home Price $	74719
% Home Owners	80.3	% Unemployment	6
% Labour Force Participation	68.4	% Managerial-Administrative	8.6
% Self-Employed	17.4	% University Degrees	5.9
% Movers	35.3		

D: Industrial Profile

% Manufacturing	12.3	% Service Sector	11.7
% Agriculture	17.7	% Mining	1.1
% Forestry	1.1	% Fishing	0
% Government Services	5.1	% Business Services	3.7

E: Homogeneity Measures

Ethnic Diversity Index	0.31	Religious Homogeneity Index	0.46
Sectoral Concentration Index	0.33	Income Disparity Index	13.1

F: Physical Setting Characteristics

Total Population	76271	Area (km²)	22270
Population Density (pop/km²)	3.4		

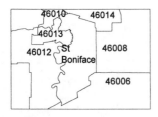

St Boniface

Constituency Number: 46007

A prosperous, urban middle-class constituency in metropolitan Winnipeg, St Boniface has an economic base of manufacturing, government and business services, with a hospital, university, and Royal Canadian Mint in addition to railway yards, packing industries, an oil refinery, and an industrial park. A multicultural riding, it is also the most francophone and Catholic riding in the West. It has a long history of support for the Liberal Party.

Only three times since 1924 - in the Diefenbaker sweep of 1958, in a 1978 by-election, and in the 1984 Mulroney sweep - has St Boniface opted for a Conservative rather than a Liberal. Leo Duguay, a school principal, was elected in the latter election. The question in 1988 was, could the Liberals rebound from their dismal 1984 performance to re-capture their traditional support base in the constituency? Trying to do this for the Liberals was Ron Duhamel, a University of Manitoba professor and former deputy minister of education. The election result in 1988 saw Duhamel take more than 50% of the vote to defeat the Conservative incumbent and return the constituency to its traditional Liberal allegiance.

In 1993, the incumbent Duhamel's personal popularity combined with his formidable constituency organization gave him an almost insurmountable advantage. An early poll gave him 63% support amongst voters. His opponents, therefore, faced an uphill struggle to woo committed Liberal voters their way. Seven challengers lined up against Duhamel, six of them women: Alison Anderson for the Reform Party, Barbara Thompson for the Conservatives, Pauline Dupont for the NDP, Marcelle Marion for the National Party, Ginette Robert for Natural Law, Don Dumesnil for the Canada Party, and Sharon Segal, Marxist-Leninist. There were no specifically local issues of note in the campaign, which revolved around national issues of jobs, health, education, and the deficit.

The election result provided no surprises, with Duhamel easily retaining his seat. The preliminary poll of 63% support for the Liberal incumbent was eerily close to the 63.4% he actually won. The Reform Party was a distant second with 16.8%, while the Conservative candidate shaded the NDP for third place with 7.2%.

Member of Parliament: Ronald J. Duhamel; **Party:** Liberal; **Occupation:** Educator; **Education:** PhD, University of Toronto; **Year first elected to the House of Commons:** 1988

46007 St Boniface

A: Political Profile
i) Voting Behaviour

	% 1993		% 1988	Change 1988-93
Conservative	7.2		33.6	-26.4
Liberal	63.4		51.5	11.9
NDP	7.1		10.7	-3.6
Reform	16.8		2.7	14.1
Other	5.5		1.4	4.1

% Turnout	72.3	Total Ballots (#)	47638
Rejected Ballots (#)	221	% Margin of Victory	46.6
Rural Polls, 1988 (#)	0	Urban Polls, 1988 (#)	185
% Yes - 1992	44.7	% No - 1992	54.9

ii) Campaign Financing

	# of Donations	Total $ Value	% of Limit Spent
Conservative	15	13800	19.3*
Liberal	310	46454	87.7
NDP	1	3738	2.9
Reform	80	8970	14.6
Other	64	11470	

B: Ethno-Linguistic Profile

% English Home Language	85.7	% French Home Language	10.4
% Official Bilingual	23.7	% Other Home Language	3.9
% Catholics	45.6	% Protestants	36.8
% Aboriginal Peoples	2.6	% Immigrants	11.8

C: Socio-Economic Profile

Average Family Income $	51991	Median Family Income $	48295
% Low Income Families	15.5	Average Home Price $	100454
% Home Owners	65.9	% Unemployment	7
% Labour Force Participation	71.7	% Managerial-Administrative	12.7
% Self-Employed	6.4	% University Degrees	13.8
% Movers	48.3		

D: Industrial Profile

% Manufacturing	9.7	% Service Sector	12.8
% Agriculture	0.7	% Mining	0.2
% Forestry	0.1	% Fishing	0
% Government Services	9.2	% Business Services	4.6

E: Homogeneity Measures

Ethnic Diversity Index	0.2	Religious Homogeneity Index	0.36
Sectoral Concentration Index	0.55	Income Disparity Index	7.1

F: Physical Setting Characteristics

Total Population	88376	Area (km²)	106
Population Density (pop/km²)	833.7		

* Tentative value, due to the existence of unpaid campaign expenses.

Selkirk–Red River

Constituency Number: 46008

Selkirk is a half-urban, half-rural riding stretching from northeast Winnipeg to Lake Winnipeg and encompassing a portion of the city in addition to suburbs, towns, a large rural area, and a reserve. Close to being the average Manitoba constituency on most indices, it has a fairly diverse economic base including agriculture and manufacturing, as well as business and government services. Selkirk had the highest voter turnout in Manitoba in the 1993 election.

A new constituency in 1988 without an incumbent, this was the riding in which the former NDP Premier of Manitoba, Howard Pawley, chose to run as a candidate. The likely outcome of Pawley's bid to switch from the provincial to federal arena was made difficult for observers to predict by the fact that the new riding had pockets of strong Tory as well as strong NDP support. As well, questions were raised by the loss of Pawley's former provincial seat in Selkirk to the resurgent Liberals just seven months previously. The Tories ran electrical contractor David Bjornson and hoped the Liberals and NDP would effectively split the anti-free trade vote. All three major party candidates agreed that the election result, which gave the PC candidate Bjornson a 4,000 vote plurality, was largely due to a siphoning off of NDP support to the Liberals.

In 1993, the incumbent Bjornson faced seven challengers, one of them the son of a former Premier and Governor-General. Jason Schreyer, son of Ed Schreyer, was contesting for the NDP, and early indications gave him the advantage. The other major candidates were Ron Fewchuck, former reeve of a local municipality, for the Liberals and Terry Lewis, director of an educational consulting firm, for the Reform Party. Two fringe party candidates also ran: Jim Slobodzian for the National Party and Eric Truijen for Christian Heritage. Health care, infrastructure renewal, jobs, and agriculture were the main issues of the campaign. As the early frontrunner and the beneficiary of 'royal family' treatment by the media, the 26-year-old Schreyer's youth and inexperience was questioned by his opponents. Later in the campaign, he was subjected to further criticism when it was made known that he had an unpaid fine for driving while his licence was suspended.

The election result gave the Liberal candidate Fewchuck, with 32.9% of the ballot, a comfortable 3,500 vote margin over New Democrat Schreyer, who with 25.7% of the vote finished in a near dead-heat with Reformer Lewis, just 103 votes behind. The incumbent Bjornson won only 11.7% of the vote to place a distant fourth.

Member of Parliament: Ron Fewchuk; **Party:** Liberal; **Occupation:** Small businessman; **Education:** Gonor Secondary School; **Age:** 53 (Oct. 28, 1941); **Year first elected to the House of Commons:** 1993

46008 Selkirk–Red River

A: Political Profile

i) Voting Behaviour

	% 1993	% 1988	Change 1988-93
Conservative	11.7	38.2	-26.5
Liberal	32.9	26.7	6.2
NDP	25.7	29.8	-4.1
Reform	25.5	1.3	24.2
Other	4.3	4.1	0.2

% Turnout	75.7	Total Ballots (#)	48832
Rejected Ballots (#)	155	% Margin of Victory	7.2
Rural Polls, 1988 (#)	104	Urban Polls, 1988 (#)	88
% Yes - 1992	34	% No - 1992	65.7

ii) Campaign Financing

	# of Donations	Total $ Value	% of Limit Spent
Conservative	97	30203	77.6
Liberal	40	34647	58.9
NDP	10	35440	97.6
Reform	176	40115	59.6
Other	48	21059	

B: Ethno-Linguistic Profile

% English Home Language	94.6	% French Home Language	0.2
% Official Bilingual	5.8	% Other Home Language	5.2
% Catholics	28.5	% Protestants	54.6
% Aboriginal Peoples	3.6	% Immigrants	12.3

C: Socio-Economic Profile

Average Family Income $	51356	Median Family Income $	47985
% Low Income Families	10.5	Average Home Price $	111071
% Home Owners	76.3	% Unemployment	7
% Labour Force Participation	70.5	% Managerial-Administrative	11
% Self-Employed	10.5	% University Degrees	8.7
% Movers	38		

D: Industrial Profile

% Manufacturing	12.2	% Service Sector	12.2
% Agriculture	4.6	% Mining	0.7
% Forestry	0.1	% Fishing	0.2
% Government Services	9.1	% Business Services	3.6

E: Homogeneity Measures

Ethnic Diversity Index	0.23	Religious Homogeneity Index	0.39
Sectoral Concentration Index	0.43	Income Disparity Index	6.6

F: Physical Setting Characteristics

Total Population	86201	Area (km²)	4130
Population Density (pop/km²)	20.9		

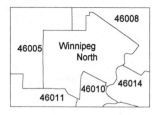

Winnipeg North

Constituency Number: 46009

Many of Winnipeg North's residents work in manufacturing industries, as well as construction, retail, government services, and health care. About one-quarter of its population are immigrants. While the riding has an average family income around the average for Manitoba, it also has a relatively high unemployment rate (third in the province).

Like Winnipeg North Centre, this riding had been one of the country's safest CCF-NDP seats, having elected the candidates of other parties only twice between 1924 and 1988. Prior to 1988, incumbent MP David Orlikow had represented the riding in Parliament since 1962. But Orlikow in 1988 was 70 years of age, by his own admission running in his last election, and for the first time having some trouble recruiting volunteers for his campaign. While Orlikow professed his belief that the NDP's hold on Winnipeg North was not seriously threatened by a resurgent Liberal Party in the province, the Liberals did succeed in wresting four of five seats in the north end of Winnipeg from the NDP in the April, 1988 provincial election. Running against Orlikow for the Liberals was Rey Pagtakhan, a medical doctor who 20 years earlier had emigrated from the Philippines. His appeal in the middle-class and Asian sections of the riding led to a doubling of the Liberal vote and a 1800 vote victory over Orlikow.

In 1993, the Liberal incumbent Pagtakhan sought re-election against seven challengers. His primary opponent, the NDP's Judy Wasylycia-Leis, was a well-known, popular and articulate provincial MLA and former cabinet minister who quit provincial politics to run federally. She made health care the sole issue of her campaign. In what was primarily a two-party race, the Conservatives ran Lyn Filbert and the Reform Party Mike Weins. The four fringe candidates were Anna Polonyi for the National Party, Joe Lynch for the Canada Party, Fred Pappetti for Natural Law, and Mary Stanley, Independent.

Despite the best efforts of the NDP, who had targeted Winnipeg North and North Centre in 1993, Liberal incumbent Rey Pagtaghan considerably increased his 1988 vote to score an easy victory over Wasylycia-Leis. Pagtaghan won 51.3% of the vote to the NDP candidate's 31.7%. The Reform Party was a distant third with 9.6% and the Conservatives a dismal fourth with 4.6%, a result which ranked as their worst in Manitoba (just ahead of North Centre) and their eighth-worst in Canada.

Member of Parliament: Rey Pagtakhan; **Party:** Liberal; **Occupation:** Doctor; **Education:** MD, Washington University; **Age:** 60 (Jan. 7, 1935); **Year first elected to the House of Commons:** 1988

46009 Winnipeg North

A: Political Profile
i) Voting Behaviour

	% 1993	% 1988	Change 1988-93
Conservative	4.6	24.6	-20
Liberal	51.3	38.3	13
NDP	31.7	34.2	-2.5
Reform	9.6	1.9	7.7
Other	2.9	1	1.9

% Turnout	68.3	Total Ballots (#)	43589
Rejected Ballots (#)	249	% Margin of Victory	19.6
Rural Polls, 1988 (#)	0	Urban Polls, 1988 (#)	173
% Yes - 1992	31.7	% No - 1992	67.8

ii) Campaign Financing

	# of Donations	Total $ Value	% of Limit Spent
Conservative	15	5695	17.1*
Liberal	146	50585	82.5
NDP	8	43215	91.7
Reform	13	1045	1.1
Other	6	10304	

B: Ethno-Linguistic Profile

% English Home Language	85.4	% French Home Language	0.2
% Official Bilingual	5.3	% Other Home Language	14.4
% Catholics	41.8	% Protestants	29.9
% Aboriginal Peoples	5.2	% Immigrants	25

C: Socio-Economic Profile

Average Family Income $	44191	Median Family Income $	41176
% Low Income Families	20.1	Average Home Price $	86403
% Home Owners	70.5	% Unemployment	9.4
% Labour Force Participation	68.7	% Managerial-Administrative	7.4
% Self-Employed	5.4	% University Degrees	8.4
% Movers	46		

D: Industrial Profile

% Manufacturing	19.4	% Service Sector	14
% Agriculture	0.3	% Mining	0.1
% Forestry	0	% Fishing	0
% Government Services	6.8	% Business Services	3.6

E: Homogeneity Measures

Ethnic Diversity Index	0.17	Religious Homogeneity Index	0.3
Sectoral Concentration Index	0.46	Income Disparity Index	6.8

F: Physical Setting Characteristics

Total Population	93586	Area (km²)	64
Population Density (pop/km²)	1462.3		

* Tentative value, due to the existence of unpaid campaign expenses.

Winnipeg North Centre

Constituency Number: 46010

With 30% of its constituents immigrants to Canada (the highest percentage in Manitoba) and 20% Aboriginal, this inner city and north-end riding has a polyglot population that ranks as the poorest in Canada in terms of average family income. The riding has an economic base that is heavily dependent on manufacturing. However, these jobs are insufficient for its workforce, who suffer an official unemployment rate (around 17%) and a level of dependence on government transfers that is the highest in the West. With the most single-parent families, lowest level of home ownership, and highest mobility in the province, Winnipeg North Centre is a classic case of the urban core riding, no longer exclusively working class but instead increasingly home to the socially and economically marginalized.

From 1921 to 1988, this was the most receptive riding in Canada to a left-wing political message. For the first 20 years of its existence it belonged to J.S. Woodsworth, the first leader of the NDP's forerunner, the CCF. It then became the home constituency of legendary parliamentarian Stanley Knowles who retained it for almost 40 years. Upon Knowles' retirement in 1984, it was won by the NDP's Cyril Keeper, whose foster-mother was former NDP Premier and Governor-General Ed Shreyer's mother. Keeper had moved over in 1984 from Winnipeg St James where he had first won election in 1980.

Despite the riding's long history of support for the NDP and its forerunners, the Liberals had reason to think that their chances in Winnipeg North Centre in 1988 were good. In the April, 1988 provincial election, three of four NDP seats encompassed by the federal riding had fallen to the Grits. And redistribution had significantly altered the riding's boundaries, turning it into a mixed bag of residential neighbourhoods, ranging from the upscale houses of Wolseley and Armstrong Point to the rundown low-rent hotels on north Main Street. The Liberal candidate, 41-year-old University of Winnipeg political scientist David Walker, concentrated on wooing the ethnic vote with the backing of community leaders from the Vietnamese, Portuguese, Philippino, and Chinese communities. The strategy and hard work paid off: Walker won the 1988 election by 1,500 votes over the incumbent Keeper, one of two stunning upsets by Liberals in previously safe NDP seats in Winnipeg.

In 1993, the Liberal incumbent was out to prove that his 1988 victory was neither an aberration nor a fluke. He faced seven other candidates vying for his seat: Maureen Hemphill for the NDP, Reg Smith for the Reform Party, and Leslie Zegalski for the Progressive Conservatives were the major contenders. The four fringe candidates were Gene Domine for the National Party, Deborah Shelton for Natural Law, Clifford Besson for the Canada Party, and James Plewak, Independent.

Despite NDP targeting of the riding (party leader Audrey McLaughlin visited four times), Walker won re-election with an increased plurality by promising jobs and economic renewal. The NDP candidate admitted that a desire to get rid of the Conservative government had discouraged voters from supporting the NDP. Walker won 50.2% of the vote to the NDP's 32.2%. Reform was a distant third with 8.2%, while the Tory candidate managed only 4.7%, less than the total votes cast for fringe candidates.

Member of Parliament: David Walker; **Party:** Liberal; **Occupation:** Professor; **Education:** PhD, McMaster University; **Age:** 47 (Aug. 1, 1947); **Year first elected to the House of Commons:** 1988

46010 Winnipeg North Centre

A: Political Profile
i) Voting Behaviour

	% 1993	% 1988	Change 1988-93
Conservative	4.7	18.2	-13.5
Liberal	50.2	41.2	9
NDP	32.2	36	-3.8
Reform	8.2	1.4	6.8
Other	4.7	3.2	1.5

% Turnout	54.9	Total Ballots (#)	28003
Rejected Ballots (#)	285	% Margin of Victory	18
Rural Polls, 1988 (#)	0	Urban Polls, 1988 (#)	152
% Yes - 1992	32.4	% No - 1992	66.7

ii) Campaign Financing

	# of Donations	Total $ Value	% of Limit Spent
Conservative	48	19543	26
Liberal	223	49550	87.4
NDP	6	30228	92.8
Reform	14	4325	5.1
Other	29	10383	

B: Ethno-Linguistic Profile

% English Home Language	77.7	% French Home Language	0.4
% Official Bilingual	5.3	% Other Home Language	21.8
% Catholics	42.7	% Protestants	30.1
% Aboriginal Peoples	19.7	% Immigrants	29.4

C: Socio-Economic Profile

Average Family Income $	29657	Median Family Income $	25039
% Low Income Families	47.7	Average Home Price $	62101
% Home Owners	39	% Unemployment	17
% Labour Force Participation	57.7	% Managerial-Administrative	5.4
% Self-Employed	5	% University Degrees	8.2
% Movers	58.7		

D: Industrial Profile

% Manufacturing	21.3	% Service Sector	19.1
% Agriculture	0.6	% Mining	0.1
% Forestry	0.1	% Fishing	0.1
% Government Services	6.5	% Business Services	3.7

E: Homogeneity Measures

Ethnic Diversity Index	0.16	Religious Homogeneity Index	0.31
Sectoral Concentration Index	0.46	Income Disparity Index	15.6

F: Physical Setting Characteristics

Total Population	79569	Area (km²)	18
Population Density (pop/km²)	4420.5		

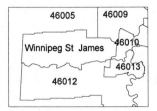

Winnipeg St James

Constituency Number: 46011

This riding is a microcosm of Winnipeg. Bordered on the south by the Assiniboine River, it stretches westward from the fringes of the downtown core through the blue-collar east end of St James, then through a mass of middle-class homes and past wealthy pockets to Headingly jail, where in 1993 prisoners could vote for the first time.

Adjusted to its new boundaries after redistribution, the 1984 results in this riding would have given the eventual winner of that election, Tory George Minaker, a much larger plurality in 1988. Such expectations, however, were shaken by the strong Liberal performance in the provincial ridings encompassed by St James in the 1988 provincial election, and by a local issue that fanned the flames of western alienation and provided the spark for the birth of the Reform Party. St James is home to Bristol Aerospace Ltd, which many Manitobans believed was victimized by the federal Tory government's decision in 1987 to award the lucrative CF-18 fighter contract to a Montreal firm instead of Bristol, despite the latter's lower bid and the technical superiority of its proposal. Continuing resentment over this decision was a factor in the 1988 election. Finally, the Liberals ran an aggressive campaign and a high-profile candidate in broadcaster John Harvard against a low-profile incumbent.

The election result in 1988 returned Winnipeg St James to the Liberals for the first time since the 'Trudeaumania' election of 1968. Harvard's 1,500 vote plurality was attributed by incumbent Tory Minaker to the collapse of the NDP vote in the riding occasioned by a consolidation of the anti-free trade vote behind the Liberal candidate.

In 1993, Harvard faced eight challengers for his seat. Teacher-turned-lawyer Dave Schioler carried the Tory banner and tried to turn the tables on the Liberal incumbent by portraying the Liberal Party's promise to cancel a multi-billion dollar military helicopter contract as a threat to the local aerospace industry. The issue, however, never caught fire with St James voters. More common was concern with jobs and the deficit, the latter an issue more favourable to the prospects of Reform Party candidate Peter Blumenschein, operator of a seniors' care home. The NDP fielded John Hutton, an advocate for the unemployed. Four fringe party candidates were also competing: Bjarne Aasland for the Canada Party, Ron Decter for Natural Law, Paul Reid for the National Party, and Glenn Michalchuk, Marxist-Leninist.

The final result awarded the Liberal Harvard 55% of the vote, more than 13,000 votes ahead of his nearest competitor, the Reform Party's Blumenschein, who took 21% of the vote. The Conservative candidate Schioler, despite an early nomination and an energetic, well-financed campaign, attracted only 13% of the vote, while the NDP's Hutton claimed only 6.6% of the ballot.

Member of Parliament: John Harvard; **Party:** Liberal; **Occupation:** Broadcaster; **Education:** High school; **Age:** 57 (June 4, 1938); **Year first elected to the House of Commons:** 1988

46011 Winnipeg St James

A: Political Profile
i) Voting Behaviour

	% 1993	% 1988	Change 1988-93
Conservative	13	40.8	-27.8
Liberal	55	44.8	10.2
NDP	6.6	10.2	-3.6
Reform	21	3.7	17.3
Other	4.8	0.5	4.3

% Turnout	70.8	Total Ballots (#)	39464
Rejected Ballots (#)	132	% Margin of Victory	34
Rural Polls, 1988 (#)	0	Urban Polls, 1988 (#)	165
% Yes - 1992	39.2	% No - 1992	60.4

ii) Campaign Financing

	# of Donations	Total $ Value	% of Limit Spent
Conservative	167	41727	72.6*
Liberal	171	21118	44.9
NDP	7	10354	16
Reform	75	12884	30.6
Other	38	22282	

B: Ethno-Linguistic Profile

% English Home Language	95.8	% French Home Language	0.6
% Official Bilingual	6.6	% Other Home Language	3.5
% Catholics	25.1	% Protestants	57
% Aboriginal Peoples	2	% Immigrants	12.7

C: Socio-Economic Profile

Average Family Income $	50979	Median Family Income $	46161
% Low Income Families	14.3	Average Home Price $	91100
% Home Owners	64	% Unemployment	6.7
% Labour Force Participation	67.7	% Managerial-Administrative	11.4
% Self-Employed	5.7	% University Degrees	10.6
% Movers	44.8		

D: Industrial Profile

% Manufacturing	11.5	% Service Sector	16.3
% Agriculture	0.6	% Mining	0.2
% Forestry	0.1	% Fishing	0
% Government Services	12.4	% Business Services	4.6

E: Homogeneity Measures

Ethnic Diversity Index	0.26	Religious Homogeneity Index	0.4
Sectoral Concentration Index	0.53	Income Disparity Index	9.5

F: Physical Setting Characteristics

Total Population	71627	Area (km²)	114
Population Density (pop/km²)	628.3		

* Tentative value, due to the existence of unpaid campaign expenses.

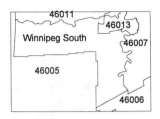

Winnipeg South

Constituency Number: 46012

Home to the University of Manitoba, this riding's residents are the wealthiest and best educated in Manitoba. The riding also registered the biggest 'Yes' vote in Manitoba in the 1992 referendum. Winnipeg South was created in 1988 out of the old ridings of Winnipeg Fort Gary and Winnipeg Assiniboine, the first a bastion of Liberal support which for years elected Liberal James Richardson and then Lloyd Axworthy to Parliament, the second renegade PC Dan MacKenzie's bailiwick. With Axworthy moving to Winnipeg South Centre in 1988 and MacKenzie retiring, Winnipeg South became the battleground in 1988 for two political newcomers: Dorothy Dobbie, the first woman president of the Winnipeg Chamber of Commerce, for the Conservatives and lawyer Allan Kaufman, executive assistant to Liberal justice critic Robert Kaplan, for the Liberals. In that campaign, concerns about free trade and resentment over the federal Tories' decision to award the CF-18 fighter contract to a Montreal firm instead of Winnipeg's own Bristol Aerospace took a toll on Conservative support in well-heeled and traditionally true-blue areas like Tuxedo (the provincial riding of Manitoba Premier Gary Filmon) and Charleswood. But Dobbie fervently defended the free trade agreement as 'a straight commercial agreement'. Her campaign was given a boost in its closing days by a visit to Winnipeg from Prime Minister Mulroney who hinted at a cabinet post for Dobbie should she be elected. On election night the traditional areas of Conservative support stayed firm, giving Dobbie a slim 677-vote margin over her Liberal opponent.

In 1993, Dobbie was an unpopular incumbent representing an unpopular party, and her re-election prospects were affected accordingly. Moreover, her slim plurality in 1988 was gained without any competition for the riding's conservative voters, whereas this time around she faced competition from the right-wing Reform Party. Running against Dobbie for the Liberals was Reg Alcock, who resigned as a provincial MLA to run federally. The Reform Party candidate was 36-year-old pastor Mark Hughes, who campaigned in the riding for almost a year before the election call. The NDP, never a force in this well-heeled riding, ran Rose Buss. Four fringe party candidates were also contesting: Shirley Loewen for the National Party, Bill Martens for the Canada Party, Rubin Kantorovich, Marxist-Leninist, and Richard Lepinsky, Natural Law. High taxes and the deficit were the primary concerns in some parts of the riding, jobs and the future of medicare in others.

Unlike 1988, the election result in 1993 was not close. Liberal Reg Alcock, with 49.6% of the vote, waltzed to victory with an 11,000 vote bulge over his nearest competitor, Reformer Mark Hughes, who took 28.3% of the ballot. Conservative Dorothy Dobbie finished with 12.3%. The NDP's Rose Buss, with 4.2%, finished fifth after National Party candidate Shirley Loewen, who won 216 more votes than Buss.

Member of Parliament: Reginald B. Alcock; **Party:** Liberal; **Occupation:** Consultant; **Education:** MPA, Harvard University; **Age:** 47 (April 16, 1948); **Year first elected to the House of Commons:** 1993

46012 Winnipeg South

A: Political Profile

i) Voting Behaviour

	% 1993	% 1988	Change 1988-93
Conservative	12.3	45.9	-33.6
Liberal	49.6	44.5	5.1
NDP	4.2	6.3	-2.1
Reform	28.3	2.9	25.4
Other	5.6	0.3	5.3

% Turnout	72.3	Total Ballots (#)	52532
Rejected Ballots (#)	214	% Margin of Victory	21.3
Rural Polls, 1988 (#)	0	Urban Polls, 1988 (#)	209
% Yes - 1992	46.9	% No - 1992	52.7

ii) Campaign Financing

	# of Donations	Total $ Value	% of Limit Spent
Conservative	250	48273	40.3*
Liberal	282	72903	68.3
NDP	1	2159	0.7
Reform	274	54742	86.1
Other	21	22763	

B: Ethno-Linguistic Profile

% English Home Language	93.3	% French Home Language	1
% Official Bilingual	11.4	% Other Home Language	5.6
% Catholics	24.1	% Protestants	52
% Aboriginal Peoples	1.5	% Immigrants	15.3

C: Socio-Economic Profile

Average Family Income $	64558	Median Family Income $	55651
% Low Income Families	13.5	Average Home Price $	126875
% Home Owners	69.5	% Unemployment	7
% Labour Force Participation	73.9	% Managerial-Administrative	15.5
% Self-Employed	8.6	% University Degrees	23.1
% Movers	50.4		

D: Industrial Profile

% Manufacturing	9.5	% Service Sector	12.9
% Agriculture	1	% Mining	0.1
% Forestry	0.2	% Fishing	0.1
% Government Services	9.2	% Business Services	5.4

E: Homogeneity Measures

Ethnic Diversity Index	0.2	Religious Homogeneity Index	0.36
Sectoral Concentration Index	0.55	Income Disparity Index	13.8

F: Physical Setting Characteristics

Total Population	93794	Area (km²)	194
Population Density (pop/km²)	483.5		

*   Tentative value, due to the existence of unpaid campaign expenses.

Winnipeg South Centre

Constituency Number: 46013

This well-to-do urban constituency has a diverse economy based primarily on the service sector - retail trades, business and government services, health care, and education. It also has a highly-educated population and a high average family income (second in Manitoba in both categories to Winnipeg South).

Winnipeg South Centre was created in 1988 primarily from the now defunct riding of Winnipeg Fort Gary represented by Liberal Lloyd Axworthy since 1979, with chunks of traditionally Liberal St Boniface and traditionally Conservative Winnipeg Assiniboine grafted onto it. The dominant influence on the election outcome in Winnipeg South Centre in 1988 was the popularity of Lloyd Axworthy, the former Liberal minister of transportation and their free trade critic. Having been Winnipeg's articulate spokesman and cabinet benefactor in Ottawa in the early 1980s, and a high-profile leadership hopeful on the opposition benches since 1984, Axworthy would probably have secured re-election on the basis of his personal popularity even if voter sympathies were running against the Liberal Party (as in 1984), but this most certainly was not the case in Winnipeg in 1988. On election night the voters in South Centre gave Axworthy a 14,000 vote margin over his nearest rival.

In 1993, Axworthy's popularity and personal following had not waned, making his opponents' prospects bleak. With 1,000 volunteers working for his re-election and a powerful local party machine, Axworthy himself was able to spend a good part of the campaign out of the riding helping other Liberal candidates. Still, eight candidates in addition to Axworthy were offering in South Centre. Lawyer Mike Radcliffe ran for the Conservatives, graduate student and former teacher Lloyd Penner for the NDP, and administrator Vern Hannah for the Reform Party. Bill Loewen, a chartered accountant and businessman who donated $4 million to the National Party of Canada, was also that party's candidate in South Centre. The other candidates were Ben Falawka for the Canada Party, Elizabeth Innes for Natural Law, Clancy Smith for the Libertarian Party, and Karen Taylor, Independent.

As expected, Axworthy was returned for a fifth time as an MP from Winnipeg, with his largest majority to date. With 61.4% of the vote, Axworthy's margin over the second-place Reform candidate was huge, with the latter gaining only 12.6% of the vote. Progressive Conservative Radcliffe took 9.3%, the NDP's Penner 8.3%, and the fringe party candidates 8.4%. The latter figure was the highest fringe party vote in Manitoba, most of it due to the National Party's Loewen, who finished just 526 votes back of Penner.

Member of Parliament: Lloyd Axworthy; **Party:** Liberal; **Occupation:** Professor; **Education:** PhD, Princeton University; **Age:** 55 (Dec. 21, 1939); **Year first elected to the House of Commons:** 1979

46013 Winnipeg South Centre

A: Political Profile
i) Voting Behaviour

	% 1993	% 1988	Change 1988-93
Conservative	9.3	28.9	-19.6
Liberal	61.4	58.4	3
NDP	8.3	10.3	-2
Reform	12.6	1.7	10.9
Other	8.4	0.6	7.8

% Turnout	67	Total Ballots (#)	42305
Rejected Ballots (#)	178	% Margin of Victory	48.8
Rural Polls, 1988 (#)	0	Urban Polls, 1988 (#)	155
% Yes - 1992	44.2	% No - 1992	55.2

ii) Campaign Financing

	# of Donations	Total $ Value	% of Limit Spent
Conservative	216	51760	75.5*
Liberal	533	107964	87.9
NDP	5	7042	7.7
Reform	74	11558	21
Other	20	30589	

B: Ethno-Linguistic Profile

% English Home Language	94.1	% French Home Language	1.2
% Official Bilingual	11.1	% Other Home Language	4.6
% Catholics	26.4	% Protestants	45.1
% Aboriginal Peoples	3.7	% Immigrants	15.7

C: Socio-Economic Profile

Average Family Income $	54012	Median Family Income $	44581
% Low Income Families	22.3	Average Home Price $	97380
% Home Owners	46.5	% Unemployment	8.9
% Labour Force Participation	66.5	% Managerial-Administrative	12.3
% Self-Employed	8.5	% University Degrees	21.8
% Movers	50.4		

D: Industrial Profile

% Manufacturing	8.8	% Service Sector	14.4
% Agriculture	0.5	% Mining	0.1
% Forestry	0.1	% Fishing	0
% Government Services	9.6	% Business Services	7.3

E: Homogeneity Measures

Ethnic Diversity Index	0.2	Religious Homogeneity Index	0.31
Sectoral Concentration Index	0.61	Income Disparity Index	17.5

F: Physical Setting Characteristics

Total Population	76651	Area (km²)	24
Population Density (pop/km²)	3193.8		

* Tentative value, due to the existence of unpaid campaign expenses.

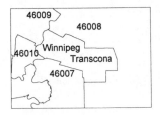

Winnipeg–Transcona

Constituency Number: 46014

Located in northeast Winnipeg, Transcona is a suburban, middle class, multi-ethnic riding 'built because of the railway'. Its main industries are the CNR, furniture and bus manufacturing, small business, food processing and lumberyards.

Comprised primarily of the old riding of Winnipeg–Birds Hill held since 1979 by United Church minister and NDP critic for external affairs Bill Blaikie, Transcona was left an even safer NDP seat as a result of redistribution, thanks to the addition of an area of traditionally strong NDP support that was formerly part of Winnipeg North Centre. Within the new constituency boundaries, Blaikie's 1984 majority would have been much greater. But as with all the Winnipeg ridings, a Liberal resurgence in 1988 was threatening the NDP incumbent. Still, despite a greatly improved Liberal performance that pushed the Conservatives into third spot in Transcona, NDP core support held firm, and incumbent Blaikie was returned to Parliament with a 4,000 vote plurality, the lone New Democrat in Winnipeg to have escaped the Liberal tide.

In 1993, Blaikie's re-election bid appeared to be in real trouble thanks to increasing voter volatility and a backlash against the status quo. With many voters angrily rejecting the Tories and lured by the prospect of having an MP on the winning side, Liberal Art Miki was threatening to end Blaikie's 14-year tenure as an MP. Miki, who worked as a high-school principal for 25 years in Transcona, gained national attention for his role in gaining redress from Ottawa for interning Japanese-Canadians during World War II. With a campaign bankrolled by countrywide donations by Japanese Canadians hoping to have the first MP elected from their community, Miki hoped to reap the benefits of strategic voting by former NDP supporters in the riding. For his part, Blaikie appealed to voters concerned about the future of health care and criticized Miki for living outside the riding.

Though Transcona quickly shaped up as a two-party race, the other major party candidates hoped to come up the middle after the Liberals and NDP had split the left-of-centre vote. The Conservatives ran 31-year-old Brett Eckstein, an aerospace consultant, while the Reform Party ran Helen Sterzer, a retired computer systems designer. A number of fringe party candidates were also offering: Geoff Danyluk for Natural Law, Marnie Johnson for the National Party, Ken Kalturnyk for the Marxist-Leninist Party, and Robert Scott for Christian Heritage.

By the smallest margin of victory in Canada, just 219 votes, Bill Blaikie was returned for the fifth time as MP for Transcona, this time as Manitoba's only elected New Democrat. It took a recount of ballots to determine that Blaikie had gathered 38.9% of the vote to Miki's 38.3%. The Reform candidate was a distant third with 14.1%, while the Tory candidate managed just 5.1%.

Member of Parliament: William Alexander Blaikie; **Party:** NDP; **Occupation:** Clergyman; **Education:** MDiv., Emmanuel College (Toronto School of Theology); **Age:** 44 (June 19, 1951); **Year first elected to the House of Commons:** 1979

46014 Winnipeg-Transcona

A: Political Profile

i) Voting Behaviour

	% 1993	% 1988	Change 1988-93
Conservative	5.1	25.6	-20.5
Liberal	38.3	31.9	6.4
NDP	38.9	41.1	-2.2
Reform	14.1	0	14.1
Other	3.7	1.4	2.3

% Turnout	70.1	Total Ballots (#)	41507
Rejected Ballots (#)	144	% Margin of Victory	0.6
Rural Polls, 1988 (#)	0	Urban Polls, 1988 (#)	168
% Yes - 1992	31	% No - 1992	68.6

ii) Campaign Financing

	# of Donations	Total $ Value	% of Limit Spent
Conservative	8	14423	24.7*
Liberal	658	59185	84.5
NDP	2	38407	61.3
Reform	56	7131	13.1
Other	67	20352	

B: Ethno-Linguistic Profile

% English Home Language	93.4	% French Home Language	0.4
% Official Bilingual	6.9	% Other Home Language	6.2
% Catholics	30.1	% Protestants	48.2
% Aboriginal Peoples	3.6	% Immigrants	14.1

C: Socio-Economic Profile

Average Family Income $	43995	Median Family Income $	41801
% Low Income Families	19.1	Average Home Price $	81923
% Home Owners	71.4	% Unemployment	8.4
% Labour Force Participation	68.5	% Managerial-Administrative	8.1
% Self-Employed	5	% University Degrees	6.3
% Movers	43.2		

D: Industrial Profile

% Manufacturing	15.8	% Service Sector	13.5
% Agriculture	0.4	% Mining	0.1
% Forestry	0.1	% Fishing	0
% Government Services	8.4	% Business Services	3.8

E: Homogeneity Measures

Ethnic Diversity Index	0.2	Religious Homogeneity Index	0.35
Sectoral Concentration Index	0.48	Income Disparity Index	5

F: Physical Setting Characteristics

Total Population	82447	Area (km²)	50
Population Density (pop/km²)	1648.9		

* Tentative value, due to the existence of unpaid campaign expenses.

Kindersley–Lloydminster

Constituency Number: 47001

Covering west-central Saskatchewan from the Saskatchewan-Alberta border to within six kilometres of Saskatoon, Kindersley–Lloydminster is a relatively prosperous rural riding that includes parched prairie, northern parkland and, around its major town of Lloydminster on the Alberta border, a piece of the western oil patch. With almost 38% of its workforce employed in agriculture, this riding is the second most agricultural in the country (after Swift Current). It also has the lowest level of service sector employment in Saskatchewan. Kindersley–Lloydminster also has the dubious distinction of suffering the greatest decline in riding population since 1988 (a distinction claimed by five Saskatchewan ridings out of the top six in Canada).

In 1988 the high-profile incumbent in the riding was Conservative Bill McKnight, a farmer first elected as MP for the area in 1979. At the time of the 1988 election he was the minister responsible for the Western Diversification Fund, as well as Indian and Northern Affairs. The main issue in the campaign was the free trade deal, particularly its likely impact on the farm economy. Agricultural policy was also important, with debate about the adequacy of government initiatives such as drought assistance and deficiency payments. The 1988 election results saw increases in voter support of 3-5% for each of the opposition parties, but still a comfortable margin of victory for McKnight over his nearest competitor, the NDP candidate. The Liberal and Reform candidates finished well back, though the latter, rancher Elwin Hermanson, gained a larger share of the popular vote than in any other Saskatchewan riding.

In 1993, the 40-year-old Hermanson was again contesting the seat, but this time around without an incumbent to defeat, as McKnight decided not to re-offer. In his stead the Conservatives were running former broadcaster and provincial MLA Jack Sandberg. Elizabeth Thomas was running for the NDP, Judy Setrakov for the Liberals, Rick Barsky for the National Party, and Emanuel Fahlman for the Canada Party. From the start of the campaign, the key question was how much of the Tory vote would leak to Reform and whether the NDP vote would hold. With Hermanson getting a sympathetic hearing from constituents, and with widespread discontent increasing the likelihood of a protest vote against 'politics as usual', the NDP focused its campaign attacks on Reform.

The NDP's concern was borne out by the election result. Reform candidate Hermanson was victorious over his Liberal counterpart by a comfortable margin of 40.5% to 27.8%. The Conservative vote hadn't leaked to Reform, it had flooded. With only 13.6% of the vote, the Tories finished fourth, suffering a decline in their vote of more than 31%. The NDP, down by 17% from 1988, finished third with 16.4% of the vote.

Member of Parliament: Elwin N. Hermanson; **Party:** Reform; **Occupation:** Farmer; **Age:** 42 (Aug. 22, 1952); **Year first elected to the House of Commons:** 1993

47001 Kindersley–Lloydminster

A: Political Profile

i) Voting Behaviour

	% 1993	% 1988	Change 1988-93
Conservative	13.6	45	-31.4
Liberal	27.8	15	12.8
NDP	16.4	33.4	-17
Reform	40.5	6.6	33.9
Other	1.7	0	1.7

% Turnout	72.2	Total Ballots (#)	30492
Rejected Ballots (#)	103	% Margin of Victory	14.4
Rural Polls, 1988 (#)	132	Urban Polls, 1988 (#)	11
% Yes - 1992	38.4	% No - 1992	61.3

ii) Campaign Financing

	# of Donations	Total $ Value	% of Limit Spent
Conservative	89	15205	75.7
Liberal	136	28648	39.4
NDP	11	44633	62.4
Reform	155	41044	52.6
Other	8	6000	

B: Ethno-Linguistic Profile

% English Home Language	97.5	% French Home Language	0.1
% Official Bilingual	2.2	% Other Home Language	2.5
% Catholics	27.4	% Protestants	60.8
% Aboriginal Peoples	2.5	% Immigrants	4.2

C: Socio-Economic Profile

Average Family Income $	42561	Median Family Income $	38215
% Low Income Families	14.3	Average Home Price $	58683
% Home Owners	78.1	% Unemployment	4.5
% Labour Force Participation	74	% Managerial-Administrative	9.4
% Self-Employed	29.4	% University Degrees	5.4
% Movers	30.4		

D: Industrial Profile

% Manufacturing	3.5	% Service Sector	10.5
% Agriculture	37.7	% Mining	5.1
% Forestry	0.1	% Fishing	0
% Government Services	2.8	% Business Services	1.4

E: Homogeneity Measures

Ethnic Diversity Index	0.28	Religious Homogeneity Index	0.45
Sectoral Concentration Index	0.41	Income Disparity Index	10.2

F: Physical Setting Characteristics

Total Population	63871	Area (km²)	42616
Population Density (pop/km²)	1.5		

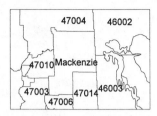

Mackenzie

Constituency Number: 47002

The poorest riding in Saskatchewan in terms of average family income and dependence on government transfers (ninth in Canada), Mackenzie, with 34% of its employment in agriculture, ranks along with Kindersley–Lloydminster and Swift Current–Maple Creek–Assiniboia as one of the most agricultural of ridings in Canada. Running north and east of Regina and Saskatoon to the Manitoba border, and taking in the communities of Wynyard, Nipawin, Tisdale and Melfort, the riding like other rural Saskatchewan ridings also ranked high on the list of constituencies suffering a population decline since 1988.

In 1988 redistribution turned this eastern Saskatchewan riding into a contest between two incumbents in what was likely to be a close race: within the new boundaries the 1984 vote amounted to a virtual dead heat between the Conservatives and New Democrats. Conservative MP and 62-year-old farmer Jack Scowen ran on his record as a constituency man and on the government's assistance package for drought relief; Vic Althouse, the NDP's 51-year-old agriculture critic and MP since 1980 for the suddenly defunct riding of Humboldt–Lake Centre, begged to disagree, and placed the free trade deal at the forefront of campaign issues. In the event, the NDP's Althouse handily defeated Scowen.

In 1993, Althouse was seeking re-election against five challengers: former provincial cabinet minister Sherwin Petersen for the Progressive Conservatives, three-time candidate and farmer Garfield Lutz for the Liberal Party, lawyer Brian Fitzpatrick for the Reform Party, businessman Ken Goudy for the Christian Heritage Party, and janitor and part-time farmer Tony Panas for the Canada Party. The main issues in the campaign were unemployment, the deficit, and agricultural problems.

Election night was a nail-biter for Althouse, who scraped by with 31% of the vote for the return trip to Ottawa. In a classic three-way split, Reformer Fitzpatrick and Liberal Lutz finished neck-and-neck for second and third place respectively with around 27% of the vote each, while the Conservatives suffered a 24% drop in their vote to finish with 12.8%.

Member of Parliament: Victor F. Althouse; **Party:** NDP; **Occupation:** Farmer; **Education:** BA, University of Saskatchewan; **Age:** 58 (April 15, 1937); **Year first elected to the House of Commons:** 1980

47002 Mackenzie

A: Political Profile
i) Voting Behaviour

	% 1993	% 1988	Change 1988-93
Conservative	12.8	36.9	-24.1
Liberal	26.7	14.6	12.1
NDP	31.1	46.5	-15.4
Reform	27.1	2	25.1
Other	2.4	0	2.4

% Turnout	71.9	Total Ballots (#)	30376
Rejected Ballots (#)	67	% Margin of Victory	4
Rural Polls, 1988 (#)	153	Urban Polls, 1988 (#)	14
% Yes - 1992	40	% No - 1992	59.6

ii) Campaign Financing

	# of Donations	Total $ Value	% of Limit Spent
Conservative	167	17389	19.7*
Liberal	131	15376	24.9
NDP	4	56806	94.8
Reform	215	31670	46.5
Other	30	4365	

B: Ethno-Linguistic Profile

% English Home Language	94.5	% French Home Language	0.7
% Official Bilingual	3.5	% Other Home Language	4.7
% Catholics	24.6	% Protestants	61.2
% Aboriginal Peoples	11.7	% Immigrants	4.1

C: Socio-Economic Profile

Average Family Income $	36411	Median Family Income $	30457
% Low Income Families	17.8	Average Home Price $	46605
% Home Owners	78.2	% Unemployment	6.7
% Labour Force Participation	64.5	% Managerial-Administrative	8.7
% Self-Employed	28.6	% University Degrees	4.3
% Movers	25.3		

D: Industrial Profile

% Manufacturing	6.1	% Service Sector	11
% Agriculture	34.1	% Mining	1
% Forestry	0.6	% Fishing	0
% Government Services	5.7	% Business Services	1.3

E: Homogeneity Measures

Ethnic Diversity Index	0.19	Religious Homogeneity Index	0.43
Sectoral Concentration Index	0.36	Income Disparity Index	16.4

F: Physical Setting Characteristics

Total Population	60732	Area (km²)	46219
Population Density (pop/km²)	1.3		

* Tentative value, due to the existence of unpaid campaign expenses.

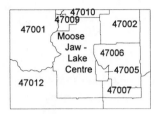

Moose Jaw–Lake Centre

Constituency Number: 47003

This south-central Saskatchewan riding which sits west of Regina is evenly split between urban and rural voters, with half the electorate located in the city of Moose Jaw (the only population centre with over 2000 inhabitants) and the other half in its agricultural hinterland. Agriculture is the riding's most important industry, complemented by a fairly large service sector. While redistribution after 1984 added potash mining communities to the northern section of the riding, this was offset by the extension of the southern boundary to include a number of small, drought-stricken, agriculture-based communities.

Won by the Conservative Bill Gottselig in 1984, the incumbent entered the 1988 contest as the only Saskatchewan MP on the Standing Committee on Agriculture. He agreed with his opponents that free trade and agricultural issues dominated the campaign, and attempted to counter NDP and Liberal arguments that medicare and the Canadian Wheat Board were being placed at risk by the agreement. Opposing Gottselig for the NDP was 35-year-old Moose Jaw lawyer and first-time candidate Rod Laporte. The election result gave the NDP's Laporte a slender margin of victory over Gottselig, with the Liberal candidate a distant third.

In 1993, the incumbent Laporte once again faced Gottselig who was vying to regain the seat for the Tories. Four additional challengers were contesting: 38-year-old farmer Allan Kerpan for the Reform Party, 25-year-old John Morris, an assistant to provincial Liberal leader Linda Haverstock, for the Liberals, Walton Eddy for the Canada Party, and Jack Heilman for Natural Law. With a volatile electorate that was manifestly disenchanted, this time around Laporte was less worried about Gottselig than the Reform candidate. Taking the blame for unpopular provincial NDP policies was also a problem for Laporte. Moreover, with the Liberals surging nationally, the prospect of an unpredictable three-way race loomed.

The 1993 result in Moose Jaw–Lake Centre was the closest in Saskatchewan and the second closest in Canada. With 30.3% of the vote, Kerpan took the seat for the Reform Party, 310 votes ahead of the incumbent Laporte with 29.4% (a 13% drop from 1988). Liberal candidate Morris was a close third with 27.2%, and former Tory MP Gottselig fourth with 12.2%.

Member of Parliament: Allan Kerpan; **Party:** Reform; **Occupation:** Farmer; **Education:** St Peter's College, Muenster; **Age:** 40 (Dec. 9, 1954); **Year first elected to the House of Commons:** 1993

47003 Moose Jaw–Lake Centre

A: Political Profile
i) Voting Behaviour

	% 1993	% 1988	Change 1988-93
Conservative	12.2	41.1	-28.9
Liberal	27.2	15.9	11.3
NDP	29.4	42.2	-12.8
Reform	30.3	0	30.3
Other	0.8	0.8	0

% Turnout	72.3	Total Ballots (#)	34489
Rejected Ballots (#)	102	% Margin of Victory	1.7
Rural Polls, 1988 (#)	91	Urban Polls, 1988 (#)	78
% Yes - 1992	44.7	% No - 1992	55

ii) Campaign Financing

	# of Donations	Total $ Value	% of Limit Spent
Conservative	109	44718	73.3
Liberal	90	19371	26.7
NDP	48	59984	85.5
Reform	142	20618	46.1
Other	1	255	

B: Ethno-Linguistic Profile

% English Home Language	98.1	% French Home Language	0.5
% Official Bilingual	4.6	% Other Home Language	1.3
% Catholics	24.4	% Protestants	64
% Aboriginal Peoples	1.2	% Immigrants	5.4

C: Socio-Economic Profile

Average Family Income $	42570	Median Family Income $	38013
% Low Income Families	16.3	Average Home Price $	58810
% Home Owners	72.5	% Unemployment	5.5
% Labour Force Participation	66.5	% Managerial-Administrative	8.3
% Self-Employed	21.8	% University Degrees	6.1
% Movers	36.5		

D: Industrial Profile

% Manufacturing	4.1	% Service Sector	15.9
% Agriculture	22.9	% Mining	2.4
% Forestry	0.1	% Fishing	0.1
% Government Services	9.3	% Business Services	1.5

E: Homogeneity Measures

Ethnic Diversity Index	0.28	Religious Homogeneity Index	0.47
Sectoral Concentration Index	0.41	Income Disparity Index	10.7

F: Physical Setting Characteristics

Total Population	65820	Area (km²)	26675
Population Density (pop/km²)	2.5		

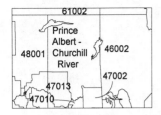

Prince Albert–Churchill River

Constituency Number: 47004

The eighth-largest riding in Canada, covering the northern half of the province of Saskatchewan, Prince Albert–Churchill River has the highest proportion of aboriginals in Saskatchewan (the second highest in Canada outside the North), accounting for 46.5% of the constituency. About half the riding's voters live in the city of Prince Albert, which is an important centre of government services for the north. Indeed, no other riding in the province has as much of its employment stemming from government services. Resource industries are the basis of the riding's economy, with agriculture, logging and mining all playing a part. The riding also suffers the highest unemployment rate in the province, at around 13%. In 1993, Prince Albert had the lowest voter turnout in Saskatchewan.

The riding was comprised of parts of three ridings prior to 1988, two of which were won by the Conservatives in 1984. The third, Prince Albert, had been represented for decades by former Conservative leader John Diefenbaker before his death in 1979, but was won by the NDP's Steve Hovdebo in a by-election that same year, and held through subsequent elections. In the 1988 election, the main contestants to represent the new constituency of Prince Albert–Churchill River were 66-year-old media personality J.J. Cennon for the Conservatives, and 40-year-old farmer and businessman Ray Funk for the NDP. Though the Liberals had finished second in 1984, they had trouble fielding a candidate, and had to recruit from outside the riding. Cennon was touted for being an Order of Canada receipient and Prince Albert 'Citizen of the Year'; the NDP focused their campaign on the dangers of free trade. On election night the Conservatives' 'celebration of the man' approach had failed: the NDP's superior political organization and the local Liberal Party's organizational disarray contributed to a landslide victory for Funk, who raked in a vote total that comfortably exceeded all his opponents.

The 1993 election was a more complicated affair, with the incumbent Funk facing a reorganized and revived Liberal Party with a high-profile candidate: 34-year-old Gordon Kirkby, a lawyer and the mayor of Prince Albert. The Progressive Conservatives were running Joyce Middlebrook, the Reform Party Paul Meagher, the Canada Party Donald Kavanagh, and the Natural Law Party Brian Baker. In addition there were two Independents: native Rick Laliberte and Richard Potratz. The NDP and Liberal frontrunners ran similar campaigns, emphasizing job creation and promoting Native self-government. Kirkby's mayoralty record of progressive race relations served him well in courting the Aboriginal vote.

The election result ousted the NDP incumbent in favour of the Liberal challenger Kirkby by a margin of 38.6% to Funk's 30.3%, a decline of 26% from the latter's 1988 vote. Reformer Meagher finished a strong third with 19% of the vote, while the Conservative garnered a tiny 4.7%, the worst Tory showing in Saskatchewan and ninth worst in Canada.

Member of Parliament: Gordon Kirkby; **Party:** Liberal; **Occupation:** Lawyer; **Education:** LL.B, University of Saskatchewan; **Age:** 36 (Sept. 26, 1958); **Year first elected to the House of Commons:** 1993

47004 Prince Albert–Churchill River

A: Political Profile

i) Voting Behaviour

	% 1993		% 1988	Change 1988-93
Conservative	4.7		25.9	-21.2
Liberal	38.6		15.8	22.8
NDP	30.3		56.4	-26.1
Reform	19		1.5	17.5
Other	7.4		0.3	7.1

% Turnout	62.3	Total Ballots (#)		30197
Rejected Ballots (#)	150	% Margin of Victory		8.3
Rural Polls, 1988 (#)	87	Urban Polls, 1988 (#)		65
% Yes - 1992	40.3	% No - 1992		59.4

ii) Campaign Financing

	# of Donations	Total $ Value	% of Limit Spent
Conservative	94	17635	34.8
Liberal	193	43619	50.3*
NDP	46	54945	98.5
Reform	97	18452	25.4
Other	60	22922	

B: Ethno-Linguistic Profile

% English Home Language	82.6	% French Home Language	0.8
% Official Bilingual	5.7	% Other Home Language	16.6
% Catholics	42.5	% Protestants	45.9
% Aboriginal Peoples	46.6	% Immigrants	3.4

C: Socio-Economic Profile

Average Family Income $	39928	Median Family Income $	33958
% Low Income Families	25.1	Average Home Price $	66435
% Home Owners	59.8	% Unemployment	12.8
% Labour Force Participation	62.1	% Managerial-Administrative	8
% Self-Employed	10.6	% University Degrees	6.3
% Movers	44.7		

D: Industrial Profile

% Manufacturing	5.7	% Service Sector	17.1
% Agriculture	7.2	% Mining	3.1
% Forestry	2.1	% Fishing	0.5
% Government Services	13.7	% Business Services	2.6

E: Homogeneity Measures

Ethnic Diversity Index	0.28	Religious Homogeneity Index	0.39
Sectoral Concentration Index	0.4	Income Disparity Index	15

F: Physical Setting Characteristics

Total Population	73952	Area (km²)	312981
Population Density (pop/km²)	0.2		

* Tentative value, due to the existence of unpaid campaign expenses.

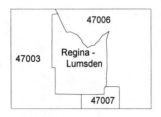

Regina–Lumsden

Constituency Number: 47005

An urban stronghold of the NDP, this riding encompasses the west end of Regina, farmland, and bedroom communities like Lumsden. In terms of population characteristics, there are working-class neighbourhoods near the core of the city, middle class suburbs, some farmers and a sizeable native population (about 11%). The economy of the constituency is fairly prosperous and diverse, with manufacturing, government services, and managerial/administrative occupations, as well as some agriculture. The riding registered the largest population growth in the province since 1988.

Since 1968, Les Benjamin of the NDP represented this part of Saskatchewan, formerly known as Regina West. The 63-year-old Benjamin, former Provincial Secretary and Manager of the Saskatchewan NDP, served on the House of Commons Transport Committee. At the outset of the 1988 campaign, all of his opponents recognized the daunting nature of their task in unseating the incumbent, and appeared content to settle for a good showing. Both the Conservative and Liberal candidates attempted to win over Benjamin supporters by arguing that they could sit as MPs on the governing side of the House. Despite their best efforts, however, the NDP machine in Regina–Lumsden recorded the biggest victory for any of their candidates anywhere in Canada, winning Benjamin 57.5% of the vote, 11,560 more than his closest contender.

In 1993, the 68-year-old Benjamin was not re-offering. In his stead a longtime provincial MLA, John Solomon, was the NDP standard-bearer with an organization the other candidates could only admire. Their hopes lay with a grumpy electorate that might reject casting their ballots yet again for the 'establishment' NDP candidate. There were five contenders in the hunt for this vote: Progressive Conservative Beattie Martin, Liberal Anita Bergman, Reformer Jerry Boychuk, the National Party's Nancy Penkala, and the Canada Party's Frederick King. While the NDP's Solomon was unlikely to benefit from being associated with unpopular provincial government policies like hospital closures, no other candidate was able to effectively focus public discontent.

The result was a close two-way race between the NDP and Liberals with Reform finishing a strong third. Solomon managed to keep 36% of Benjamin's big 1988 vote, enough to defeat a challenge from the Liberal Bergman, who attracted 33% of the ballot, and Reformer Boychuk, who got 21.3%. The Conservative Martin placed a distant fourth with 7.4%.

Member of Parliament: John Solomon; **Party:** NDP; **Occupation:** Small business owner and consultant; **Education:** BA, University of Manitoba; **Age:** 45 (May 23, 1950); **Year first elected to the House of Commons:** 1993

47005 Regina–Lumsden

A: Political Profile
i) Voting Behaviour

	% 1993	% 1988	Change 1988-93
Conservative	7.4	26.5	-19.1
Liberal	33	15.6	17.4
NDP	35.9	57.6	-21.7
Reform	21.3	0	21.3
Other	2.4	0.4	2

% Turnout	66.5	Total Ballots (#)	36102
Rejected Ballots (#)	177	% Margin of Victory	2.9
Rural Polls, 1988 (#)	13	Urban Polls, 1988 (#)	137
% Yes - 1992	47.7	% No - 1992	51.9

ii) Campaign Financing

	# of Donations	Total $ Value	% of Limit Spent
Conservative	17	14101	42.6
Liberal	123	24073	47
NDP	3	54205	98.5
Reform	48	8726	14.4
Other	4	5210	

B: Ethno-Linguistic Profile

% English Home Language	97.8	% French Home Language	0.4
% Official Bilingual	4.7	% Other Home Language	1.8
% Catholics	32.5	% Protestants	51.4
% Aboriginal Peoples	10.8	% Immigrants	5.9

C: Socio-Economic Profile

Average Family Income $	47283	Median Family Income $	44762
% Low Income Families	15.9	Average Home Price $	76229
% Home Owners	72.5	% Unemployment	7.2
% Labour Force Participation	73.7	% Managerial-Administrative	10.7
% Self-Employed	7.4	% University Degrees	7.9
% Movers	47.1		

D: Industrial Profile

% Manufacturing	7.6	% Service Sector	15.7
% Agriculture	2.6	% Mining	0.5
% Forestry	0	% Fishing	0
% Government Services	11.2	% Business Services	4.5

E: Homogeneity Measures

Ethnic Diversity Index	0.2	Religious Homogeneity Index	0.38
Sectoral Concentration Index	0.53	Income Disparity Index	5.3

F: Physical Setting Characteristics

Total Population	78177	Area (km²)	1645
Population Density (pop/km²)	47.5		

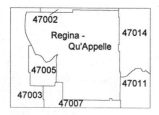

Regina–Qu'appelle

Constituency Number: 47006

Redistribution after 1984 doubled the size of the old Regina East riding to create Regina–Qu'appelle, a constituency now evenly divided between urban and rural voters. The new riding took in eight Indian reserves, and with aboriginals comprising 15.5% of the constituency's population, their vote became potentially important to electoral outcomes. The addition of rural expanses to the eastern portion of the riding also increased the importance of agriculture, with 15% of riding employment in that industry.

Since 1979, New Democrat Simon de Jong sat in Parliament representing the residents of Regina East. With 65% of the population of Regina East retained in the new riding of Regina–Qu'appelle, de Jong was clearly the favoured candidate in 1988. In the election itself, free trade was the main issue with the riding's urban dwellers, while in rural areas drought assistance and support for the family farm appeared to be paramount, though there were concerns about the impact free trade might have on the Canadian Wheat Board, marketing boards and stabilization programs. The performance of the provincial Conservative government was also cited by the NDP and Liberal candidates as a factor in voters' calculations. The election result gave the NDP's de Jong an impressive 54% of the vote and a substantially increased margin of victory over 1984.

In 1993, the incumbent de Jong's bid for a fifth straight victory was opposed by five other candidates: Tom Hull for the Conservatives, Kerry Gray for the Reform Party, Reina Sinclair for the Liberals, Joseph Thauberger for the Canada Party, and Jenny Watson for the National Party. With a core of longtime NDP voters, and a reputation for being a personable, hard-working MP who was sympathetic to the concerns of the riding's Aboriginal population, de Jong aimed to stem any ebb-tide away from the NDP to the Liberals or Reform.

Though de Jong's 1988 vote declined by almost 20% to 34.4%, he was able to prevail over a challenge from the Liberal Sinclair, who took 31.1% of the vote. The Reform candidate placed a strong third with 22.6%, relegating the Conservative to fourth with 10.1%.

Member of Parliament: Simon de Jong; **Party:** NDP; **Occupation:** Painter and restaurateur; **Education:** BA (Hons), University of Regina; **Age:** 53 (April 9, 1942); **Year first elected to the House of Commons:** 1979

47006 Regina–Qu'Appelle

A: Political Profile
i) Voting Behaviour

	% 1993	% 1988	Change 1988-93
Conservative	10.1	31.5	-21.4
Liberal	31.1	14.6	16.5
NDP	34.4	54	-19.6
Reform	22.6	0	22.6
Other	1.8	0	1.8

% Turnout	67.6	Total Ballots (#)	32546
Rejected Ballots (#)	114	% Margin of Victory	3.3
Rural Polls, 1988 (#)	84	Urban Polls, 1988 (#)	66
% Yes - 1992	45	% No - 1992	54.6

ii) Campaign Financing

	# of Donations	Total $ Value	% of Limit Spent
Conservative	62	20521	30.5
Liberal	54	15053	30
NDP	5	58729	80.8*
Reform	78	13629	21.6
Other	4	5642	

B: Ethno-Linguistic Profile

% English Home Language	97.2	% French Home Language	0.2
% Official Bilingual	3	% Other Home Language	2.7
% Catholics	37.5	% Protestants	48.5
% Aboriginal Peoples	15.6	% Immigrants	6.1

C: Socio-Economic Profile

Average Family Income $	41138	Median Family Income $	37260
% Low Income Families	17.3	Average Home Price $	65969
% Home Owners	71.6	% Unemployment	6.9
% Labour Force Participation	69.7	% Managerial-Administrative	9.7
% Self-Employed	16.4	% University Degrees	5.7
% Movers	38.1		

D: Industrial Profile

% Manufacturing	6.2	% Service Sector	14.1
% Agriculture	15.3	% Mining	0.6
% Forestry	0.1	% Fishing	0
% Government Services	8.4	% Business Services	3.4

E: Homogeneity Measures

Ethnic Diversity Index	0.19	Religious Homogeneity Index	0.38
Sectoral Concentration Index	0.4	Income Disparity Index	9.4

F: Physical Setting Characteristics

Total Population	69210	Area (km^2)	14088
Population Density (pop/km^2)	4.9		

* Tentative value, due to the existence of unpaid campaign expenses.

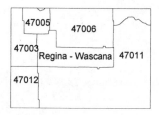

Regina–Wascana

Constituency Number: 47007

The wealthiest of Saskatchewan's 14 ridings, Regina–Wascana is comprised in large part of upper crust South Regina, though it also includes a portion of the downtown area and a number of small rural communities adjacent to Regina proper. The riding is also home to a large contingent of student residents who attend the University of Regina or the Institute of Applied Science. Regina–Wascana has the highest average income in the province, the highest home prices, the most holders of university degrees, the highest proportion of managers amongst its residents, as well as the highest proportion of service sector employment, including business and government services. With a well-heeled, highly educated population, the fact that the constituency was one of only two in Western Canada to say 'Yes' to the 1992 Charlottetown Accord shouldn't be too surprising.

In 1988, the Regina-Wascana contest received an intense amount of media coverage in Saskatchewan thanks to a tight three-way race. Former federal cabinet minister and provincial party leader Ralph Goodale for the Liberals had the higher profile, while Dickson Bailey, who was not well known to voters, was the standard-bearer for what had been the most widely supported party in the province. In former Regina Mayor Larry Schneider, the Tories had a star candidate with the longest and closest links to the majority of people in the riding. The final tally saw Schneider emerge as victor in an exceptionally close three-way race, as his Liberal and NDP opponents neatly split the opposition vote, allowing the PCs to sneak up the middle.

The 1993 election was something of a repeat of 1988, with the incumbent Schneider once again facing Ralph Goodale for the Liberals, this time along with seven other candidates: Donna Shire for the NDP, Andrew Jackson for the Reform Party, John Keen for the National Party, Walter Sigda for the Canada Party, Hugh Owens for Christian Heritage, Angus Hunt for Natural Law, and Barry Farr, Independent. Once again the election was expected to be close. Goodale, however, had the advantage of not being associated with any current government, federal or provincial, a distinct advantage with an electorate in an anti-government mood.

The election result bore this out. Goodale, with 44.2% of the vote, finished well ahead of the NDP's Shire who had 21.2%. The Conservative Schneider finished well back, tied for third with Reformer Andrew Jackson with 15.7%. It was the biggest margin of victory in Saskatchewan, and the highest Liberal vote in the province. Tellingly, Schneider's vote, which was barely enough to return him his deposit, was the best performance by a Conservative in the province.

Member of Parliament: Ralph Goodale; **Party:** Liberal; **Occupation:** Lawyer; **Education:** LL.B, University of Saskatchewan; **Age:** 45 (Oct. 5, 1949); **Year first elected to the House of Commons:** 1974

47007 Regina–Wascana

A: Political Profile
i) Voting Behaviour

	% 1993	% 1988	Change 1988-93
Conservative	15.7	34	-18.3
Liberal	44.2	32.8	11.4
NDP	21.2	32.9	-11.7
Reform	15.7	0	15.7
Other	3.1	0.3	2.8

% Turnout	74.3	Total Ballots (#)	44391
Rejected Ballots (#)	158	% Margin of Victory	23
Rural Polls, 1988 (#)	13	Urban Polls, 1988 (#)	155
% Yes - 1992	57.1	% No - 1992	42.6

ii) Campaign Financing

	# of Donations	Total $ Value	% of Limit Spent
Conservative	229	68464	99.3
Liberal	265	64808	93.7
NDP	8	50636	97.3
Reform	79	23165	31.9
Other	51	16757	

B: Ethno-Linguistic Profile

% English Home Language	95.6	% French Home Language	0.5
% Official Bilingual	7.6	% Other Home Language	4
% Catholics	33.8	% Protestants	47.8
% Aboriginal Peoples	3.2	% Immigrants	10.8

C: Socio-Economic Profile

Average Family Income $	62224	Median Family Income $	53404
% Low Income Families	14.4	Average Home Price $	93323
% Home Owners	60.9	% Unemployment	6.7
% Labour Force Participation	70	% Managerial-Administrative	16.5
% Self-Employed	10.5	% University Degrees	20.7
% Movers	48.7		

D: Industrial Profile

% Manufacturing	4.8	% Service Sector	11.7
% Agriculture	4.5	% Mining	1
% Forestry	0.1	% Fishing	0
% Government Services	11.7	% Business Services	6.8

E: Homogeneity Measures

Ethnic Diversity Index	0.2	Religious Homogeneity Index	0.35
Sectoral Concentration Index	0.57	Income Disparity Index	14.2

F: Physical Setting Characteristics

Total Population	75896	Area (km²)	3907
Population Density (pop/km²)	19.4		

Saskatoon–Clark's Crossing

Constituency Number: 47008

One of three Saskatoon ridings and geographically the smallest in Saskatchewan, this mainly urban constituency, which includes the downtown area of Saskatoon, includes some of the city's wealthiest and poorest residents. Its economy has a larger manufacturing component than any other Saskatchewan riding, complemented by a substantial service sector and managerial employment. Its population represents a broad income and ethnic mix, including a significant Mennonite population in adjacent rural areas.

Saskatoon–Clark's Crossing was created in 1988, derived principally from the former Saskatoon West riding which had been represented in Parliament since 1974 by Conservative Ray Hnatyshyn. Hnatyshyn, who went into the 1988 election as Minister of Justice, did not appear to be threatened by boundary changes, since a calculation of the 1984 vote within the new boundaries still suggested a strong majority in his favour.

Hnatyshyn's main opponent in 1988 was New Democrat Chris Axworthy, a political newcomer and University of Saskatchewan law professor. Axworthy claimed that free trade was 'the only issue' in the campaign, and he stressed the threat posed by the deal to farm marketing boards and medical and social programs. Hnatyshyn down-played the deal and emphasized the government's economic record, especially its western diversification and grain stabilization programs. The election result was regarded as a major upset, with the NDP's Axworthy winning by a comfortable margin. There was a consolation prize for Hnatyshyn, however: not long into his forced retirement he was named Canada's Governor General.

In 1993, the incumbent Axworthy faced seven opponents, three of them serious contenders: open-line radio host Roy Norris for the Liberals, businessman and city councillor Peter McCann for the Tories, and police officer Fred Wesolowski for the Reform Party. The fringe party candidates were Shawn Cawley for the Canada Party, Rhys Frostad for Christian Freedom, Henry Garman for the National Party, and Patrick Coulterman for Natural Law.

Axworthy had some advantages going into the election: he had earned himself a reputation as a hard worker during his term in Parliament, and provincial ridings in his constituency had gone NDP in the 1991 provincial election. By the same token, the popularity of the NDP provincial government had declined in the interim, and the federal NDP had bottomed out in the polls. As luck would have it, Axworthy's chief opponents in the election - Norris and Wesolowski - neatly divided the opposition vote between them, winning 28% each. This allowed Axworthy to scrape through with a mere 30.9% of the vote. McCann took fourth place for the Tories with 10.4%.

Member of Parliament: Chris Axworthy; **Party:** NDP; **Occupation:** Law professor; **Education:** LL.M, McGill University; **Age:** 48 (March 10, 1947); **Year first elected to the House of Commons:** 1988

47008 Saskatoon–Clark's Crossing

A: Political Profile
i) Voting Behaviour

	% 1993	% 1988	Change 1988-93
Conservative	10.4	35.8	-25.4
Liberal	28.2	15.8	12.4
NDP	30.9	47.9	-17
Reform	28	0	28
Other	2.6	0.5	2.1

% Turnout	65.7	Total Ballots (#)	39888
Rejected Ballots (#)	128	% Margin of Victory	2.7
Rural Polls, 1988 (#)	24	Urban Polls, 1988 (#)	145
% Yes - 1992	41.2	% No - 1992	58.4

ii) Campaign Financing

	# of Donations	Total $ Value	% of Limit Spent
Conservative	126	47230	72.8
Liberal	114	26815	49.1
NDP	4	62090	96.3
Reform	68	22067	35.9
Other	29	11158	

B: Ethno-Linguistic Profile

% English Home Language	95.1	% French Home Language	0.5
% Official Bilingual	5.4	% Other Home Language	4.4
% Catholics	28.9	% Protestants	55.1
% Aboriginal Peoples	8.2	% Immigrants	7.2

C: Socio-Economic Profile

Average Family Income $	46339	Median Family Income $	41729
% Low Income Families	19.3	Average Home Price $	82043
% Home Owners	61.7	% Unemployment	8.9
% Labour Force Participation	70.7	% Managerial-Administrative	10
% Self-Employed	10.2	% University Degrees	9.6
% Movers	49.6		

D: Industrial Profile

% Manufacturing	9.7	% Service Sector	16.2
% Agriculture	4.4	% Mining	1.7
% Forestry	0.2	% Fishing	0
% Government Services	5.8	% Business Services	4.5

E: Homogeneity Measures

Ethnic Diversity Index	0.19	Religious Homogeneity Index	0.4
Sectoral Concentration Index	0.49	Income Disparity Index	9.9

F: Physical Setting Characteristics

Total Population	85358	Area (km^2)	1454
Population Density (pop/km^2)	58.7		

Saskatoon–Dundurn

Constituency Number: 47009

A mainly urban riding derived chiefly from the old Saskatoon East and Saskatoon West ridings, Saskatoon–Dundurn is comprised for the most part of the upper-income and modest-income neighbourhoods of south Saskatoon, making it the second wealthiest riding in the province in terms of average family income. It has a diversified economic base that includes employment in business services, retail trades and other service industries, manufacturing, health and social services, construction, and in the rural portion of the riding, agriculture.

In 1988, the Conservatives and Liberals both fielded 33-year-old Saskatoon lawyers who attended law school together and were entering their first electoral contests: Grant Bryden for the PCs and Debra Ferguson, whose husband ran for the Liberals in the 1986 provincial election, for the Liberals. The NDP's Ron Fisher, a 54-year-old trade unionist, was a more experienced candidate, having run against and lost to Ray Hnatyshyn in 1984. Saskatoon–Dundurn was also contested by the leader of the Confederation of Regions Party, Elmer Knudson (a former Saskatoon resident), after a failed attempt to seek nomination in an Ontario riding. Fisher claimed victory for the NDP in that election, winning 48% of the vote.

In 1993, the incumbent Fisher faced eight opponents, three of whom could be labelled as contenders: lawyer Morris Bodnar for the Liberals, city councillor Donna Birkmaier for the Tories, and insurance salesman Eric Schenstead for the Reform Party. The other candidates were Kateri Hellman Pino for the National Party, Leon Laforge for Natural Law, Bob Lloyd for the Canada Party, Colleen Stanton for the Christian Freedom Party, and Independent Al Krieger.

The NDP's strongest support came from the less affluent parts of the riding, and it was this hardcore vote that the party hoped would suffice in the less hospitable electoral climate for incumbents in 1993. As things turned out, this core vote was smaller than expected. Liberal Morris Bodnar was elected with 35.3% of the vote, followed by the NDP's Fisher with 27.6%, a more than 20% decline from 1988. Reformer Schenstead was close behind with 24.7%. Birkmaier finished with 8.9% for the Tories.

Member of Parliament: Morris Bodnar; **Party:** Liberal; **Occupation:** Lawyer; **Education:** LL.B, University of Saskatchewan; **Age:** 46 (Sept. 4, 1948); **Year first elected to the House of Commons:** 1993

47009 Saskatoon–Dundurn

A: Political Profile
i) Voting Behaviour

	% 1993	% 1988	Change 1988-93
Conservative	8.9	31.7	-22.8
Liberal	35.3	19.2	16.1
NDP	27.6	48.1	-20.5
Reform	24.7	0	24.7
Other	3.4	1	2.4

% Turnout	67.2	Total Ballots (#)	41858
Rejected Ballots (#)	181	% Margin of Victory	7.7
Rural Polls, 1988 (#)	15	Urban Polls, 1988 (#)	166
% Yes - 1992	45.9	% No - 1992	53.8

ii) Campaign Financing

	# of Donations	Total $ Value	% of Limit Spent
Conservative	67	42495	60.7
Liberal	238	49782	69.3
NDP	13	50827	82.9
Reform	89	39967	38.5
Other	55	16892	

B: Ethno-Linguistic Profile

% English Home Language	95.5	% French Home Language	0.5
% Official Bilingual	6.1	% Other Home Language	4
% Catholics	32.7	% Protestants	49.3
% Aboriginal Peoples	7.1	% Immigrants	9.2

C: Socio-Economic Profile

Average Family Income $	48998	Median Family Income $	44118
% Low Income Families	19.6	Average Home Price $	87221
% Home Owners	61.6	% Unemployment	9.1
% Labour Force Participation	68.7	% Managerial-Administrative	10.2
% Self-Employed	9.5	% University Degrees	13.8
% Movers	50.1		

D: Industrial Profile

% Manufacturing	7.5	% Service Sector	15.6
% Agriculture	3.3	% Mining	2.6
% Forestry	0.3	% Fishing	0
% Government Services	7	% Business Services	5.3

E: Homogeneity Measures

Ethnic Diversity Index	0.18	Religious Homogeneity Index	0.36
Sectoral Concentration Index	0.5	Income Disparity Index	10

F: Physical Setting Characteristics

Total Population	81864	Area (km²)	1892
Population Density (pop/km²)	43.3		

Saskatoon–Humboldt

Constituency Number: 47010

A half-urban, half-rural riding, Saskatoon–Humboldt includes the area surrounding the University of Saskatchewan and much of its academic community, along with some of Saskatoon's high-technology and research industry. But it also includes the rolling mixed farmland northeast of Saskatoon and its rural communities, making agriculture an important industry in the riding.

A transposition of the 1984 vote left little to choose between the NDP and Conservatives within the boundaries of the new riding, with a slight advantage to the former. The Liberals garnered a respectable 24.4% of the vote in 1984 and previously had elected a federal cabinet minister from the area in the person of Otto Lang. In 1988 two incumbents whose ridings disappeared in redistribution contested the new riding: PC Don Ravis, a real estate developer first elected as the member for Saskatoon East in 1984, and former school superintendent and New Democrat Stan Hovdebo, a veteran MP for the riding of Prince Albert. The election result saw most of the anti-free trade vote gravitate to the NDP, which picked up votes at the Liberals' expense. This gave Hovdebo close to a 3000 vote margin over friend and committee-mate Ravis.

When the 1993 election was called, Hovdebo announced his retirement, leaving the riding without an incumbent. The NDP nominated lawyer and town councillor Barrett Halderman as its candidate. He faced six challengers for the NDP seat, three of whom at the outset of the election could have some expectation of prevailing: businessman and former naval officer Tom Gossen for the Conservatives, 38-year RCMP veteran Bob Head for the Reform Party, and Georgette Sheridan, who had worked on provincial leader Linda Haverstock's campaign team, for the Liberals. Sheridan was one of several women appointed as the Liberal candidate in their riding by Liberal leader Jean Chretien. There were also three fringe party candidates in the running: Dale Monson for Natural Law, Bryan Sandberg for Christian Freedom, and Larry Buhr for the National Party. Job creation, the deficit, and the health care system were the main issues in the campaign.

The election result no doubt cheered Sheridan in more than one sense. She became the first Liberal to represent the area since the 1970s; her election also helped to address the shortage of women MPs which Sheridan had bemoaned at the outset of the campaign. Taking 34.3% of the vote, an increase of almost 14% over 1988, Sheridan claimed the seat for the Liberals. The establishment parties in the riding - the NDP and Tories - both suffered precipitous drops in their support, finishing third and fourth with 22.9% and 9.4% respectively. Reformer Head finished a strong second with 29.8% of the vote.

Member of Parliament: Georgette Sheridan; **Party:** Liberal; **Occupation:** Lawyer and former teacher; **Education:** LL.B; **Age:** 43 (June 12, 1952); **Year first elected to the House of Commons:** 1993

47010 Saskatoon–Humboldt

A: Political Profile
i) Voting Behaviour

	% 1993	% 1988	Change 1988-93
Conservative	9.4	36.1	-26.7
Liberal	34.3	20.6	13.7
NDP	22.9	43.2	-20.3
Reform	29.8	0	29.8
Other	3.5	0	3.5

% Turnout	67.8	Total Ballots (#)	37594
Rejected Ballots (#)	208	% Margin of Victory	4.5
Rural Polls, 1988 (#)	119	Urban Polls, 1988 (#)	79
% Yes - 1992	48.4	% No - 1992	51.2

ii) Campaign Financing

	# of Donations	Total $ Value	% of Limit Spent
Conservative	124	42644	41.5
Liberal	85	35962	84.4
NDP	17	59873	96.3
Reform	158	29979	52.3
Other	25	9521	

B: Ethno-Linguistic Profile

% English Home Language	94.2	% French Home Language	2
% Official Bilingual	8.8	% Other Home Language	3.8
% Catholics	42.4	% Protestants	43.4
% Aboriginal Peoples	7.5	% Immigrants	6.4

C: Socio-Economic Profile

Average Family Income $	46005	Median Family Income $	40359
% Low Income Families	18.1	Average Home Price $	74611
% Home Owners	66.2	% Unemployment	7
% Labour Force Participation	71	% Managerial-Administrative	10
% Self-Employed	17.3	% University Degrees	16.3
% Movers	44.2		

D: Industrial Profile

% Manufacturing	5.4	% Service Sector	12.3
% Agriculture	16.2	% Mining	1.8
% Forestry	0.4	% Fishing	0
% Government Services	6.3	% Business Services	4.4

E: Homogeneity Measures

Ethnic Diversity Index	0.18	Religious Homogeneity Index	0.37
Sectoral Concentration Index	0.43	Income Disparity Index	12.3

F: Physical Setting Characteristics

Total Population	71080	Area (km²)	13660
Population Density (pop/km²)	5.2		

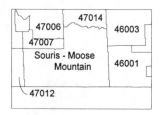

Souris–Moose Mountain

Constituency Number: 47011

This rural riding in the southeast corner of Saskatchewan borders on Manitoba and the United States and includes the towns of Weyburn, Estevan and Moosomin. Like the ridings of Kindersley–Lloydminster, Mackenzie, Swift Current and the Battlefords, Souris–Moose Mountain has an economic base heavily dependent upon agriculture, though the southeast oil patch is also an important employer. And like those other constituencies, it has been an area of bedrock Conservative support. These are the former stomping grounds of Alvin Hamilton, a prominent Conservative cabinet minister during the Diefenbaker years.

In 1988, Conservative Len Gustafson was running for a fourth straight term in the House of Commons. Parliamentary secretary to Prime Minister Brian Mulroney, his main opponents were geological consultant Jeff Sample for the NDP and farmer Mike Bauche for the Liberals. Unlike many other Saskatchewan ridings, free trade appeared to be less of an issue in the low-key Souris–Moose Mountain campaign, taking a back seat to the government's agricultural assistance and energy policies, and local concerns such as the Rafferty Dam project. The latter was lauded by Gustafson for its job creation and economic development potential and skewered by the NDP's Sample as poorly planned and environmentally unsound. Gustafson was able to coast to a comfortable majority, winning almost 47% of the popular vote.

In 1993, Gustafson was no longer a candidate, having accepted a Senate posting from his former boss, Brian Mulroney. Farmer and businessman Earl Silcox, former president of the PC party of Saskatchewan, was the new Tory candidate. He faced a high-profile Liberal opponent in Bernie Collins, a school administrator and former mayor of Estevan, who covered the riding with campaign ads and literature. The NDP fielded Caroline Saxon, a hairstylist and farmer, who hoped to retain the 30% vote garnered by the party in 1988 by focusing on concerns about the future of medicare. Yet a third major contender for the seat was businessman Doug Heimlick, who was running for the Reform Party. He hoped to capitalize on surging support for his party in a riding with the same blend of conservative politics, oil and gas, and agriculture that got Reform off the ground in Alberta. Three fringe candidates were also contesting: David Bouchard for the Canada Party, Independent Art Mainil, and David Davis, no affiliation.

In a close contest, Bernie Collins became the first Liberal elected in this area since the 1950s, winning by a narrow margin over Reformer Heimlick. The two were separated by less than 2% of the vote (32.4% to 30.7%). As elsewhere in Saskatchewan, the Conservatives and NDP suffered sharp declines in their vote share, with the NDP tumbling to 16.5% and the Tories to 15%.

Member of Parliament: A.B. (Bernie) Collins: **Party:** Liberal; **Occupation:** Educator and administrator; **Education:** MSc, Northern State College, South Dakota; **Age:** 60 (June 18, 1935); **Year first elected to the House of Commons:** 1993

47011 Souris–Moose Mountain

A: Political Profile
i) Voting Behaviour

	% 1993	% 1988	Change 1988-93
Conservative	15	46.8	-31.8
Liberal	32.4	19	13.4
NDP	16.5	32.5	-16
Reform	30.7	0	30.7
Other	5.5	1.8	3.7

% Turnout	71.5	Total Ballots (#)	33787
Rejected Ballots (#)	127	% Margin of Victory	3.8
Rural Polls, 1988 (#)	137	Urban Polls, 1988 (#)	44
% Yes - 1992	45.3	% No - 1992	54.3

ii) Campaign Financing

	# of Donations	Total $ Value	% of Limit Spent
Conservative	117	34242	59.9
Liberal	307	41603	63.2
NDP	23	36643	69.2
Reform	124	22178	37.7
Other	111	38470	

B: Ethno-Linguistic Profile

% English Home Language	99.1	% French Home Language	0.5
% Official Bilingual	3.9	% Other Home Language	0.5
% Catholics	28	% Protestants	63.5
% Aboriginal Peoples	6.4	% Immigrants	4.2

C: Socio-Economic Profile

Average Family Income $	43373	Median Family Income $	37506
% Low Income Families	14	Average Home Price $	56109
% Home Owners	76.6	% Unemployment	4.4
% Labour Force Participation	68	% Managerial-Administrative	9.1
% Self-Employed	25.9	% University Degrees	4.5
% Movers	29.2		

D: Industrial Profile

% Manufacturing	3	% Service Sector	10.8
% Agriculture	29.3	% Mining	6.8
% Forestry	0	% Fishing	0
% Government Services	4.7	% Business Services	2

E: Homogeneity Measures

Ethnic Diversity Index	0.26	Religious Homogeneity Index	0.47
Sectoral Concentration Index	0.39	Income Disparity Index	13.5

F: Physical Setting Characteristics

Total Population	66885	Area (km²)	33310
Population Density (pop/km²)	2		

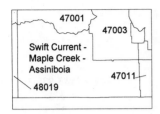

Swift Current–Maple Creek–Assiniboia

Constituency Number: 47012

The second largest in area in Saskatchewan, this rural riding covers the southwest corner of Saskatchewan bordering Alberta and the United States. With almost 39% of its employment in agriculture, it is the most agricultural of ridings in all of Canada. The ranch and farmland landscape is consistent throughout the riding, interrupted only by oil wells and the occasional farm service community, the major ones being Swift Current, Assiniboia, Maple Creek and Shaunavon. The most Protestant riding in Saskatchewan, it has the second lowest unemployment rate in Canada and ranks third in terms of population decline since the last census (with the Saskatchewan riding of Kindersley–Lloydminster ranking first).

The riding has a long Conservative tradition which continued when Swift Current lawyer Geoffrey Wilson inherited the seat in 1984 from former Conservative MP Frank Hamilton. In 1988, Wilson was opposed by first-time NDP candidate and farmer Laura Balas and Liberal candidate Paul Lewans, who appeared to hobble himself somewhat, especially in the riding's francophone communities, with some controversial remarks on bilingualism. The incumbent armed himself with the government's announcement of $850 million in drought assistance, an infusion of cash welcomed by the parched farmers of Swift Current–Maple Creek–Assiniboia. This proved sufficient to give the Conservative candidate a comfortable margin of victory in the election.

In 1993, voter alienation and distrust of politicians made the electorate more volatile and provided fertile ground for the Reform Party. The prospects of the incumbent Wilson being elected for a third time were dimmed as a result. The main threat to Wilson was his Reform opponent, geological consultant Lee Morrison. The NDP candidate was Lois Ross, a freelance journalist and small business owner. Lawyer Rob Heinrichs was offering for the Liberals. Shirley Wilson was the only fringe party candidate, running for the Natural Law Party.

The shift of Conservative supporters to the Reform Party was sufficient to elect Morrison with 34.9% of the vote, a narrow 2.5% margin over the Liberal Heinrichs. The NDP and Conservatives took the hit once again, dropping to 16.5% and 15.6% respectively.

Member of Parliament: Lee Glen Morrison; **Party:** Reform; **Occupation:** Farmer and geological engineer; **Education:** BEng. (Geology), University of Saskatchewan; **Age:** 63 (March 6, 1932); **Year first elected to the House of Commons:** 1993

47012 Swift Current–Maple Creek–Assiniboia

A: Political Profile

i) Voting Behaviour

	% 1993	% 1988	Change 1988-93
Conservative	15.6	44	-28.4
Liberal	32.4	22	10.4
NDP	16.5	32.7	-16.2
Reform	34.9	0	34.9
Other	0.7	1.3	-0.6

% Turnout	77.2	Total Ballots (#)	33035
Rejected Ballots (#)	105	% Margin of Victory	3.2
Rural Polls, 1988 (#)	115	Urban Polls, 1988 (#)	28
% Yes - 1992	43.7	% No - 1992	55.9

ii) Campaign Financing

	# of Donations	Total $ Value	% of Limit Spent
Conservative	147	28483	64.7
Liberal	160	27952	60
NDP	5	72426	96.5
Reform	221	37567	62.3
Other	1	500	

B: Ethno-Linguistic Profile

% English Home Language	94.6	% French Home Language	1.7
% Official Bilingual	7.2	% Other Home Language	3.7
% Catholics	24.7	% Protestants	64.3
% Aboriginal Peoples	1	% Immigrants	4.5

C: Socio-Economic Profile

Average Family Income $	41609	Median Family Income $	35531
% Low Income Families	16.1	Average Home Price $	54144
% Home Owners	78.2	% Unemployment	4
% Labour Force Participation	71.2	% Managerial-Administrative	9.6
% Self-Employed	31.1	% University Degrees	4.8
% Movers	28		

D: Industrial Profile

% Manufacturing	2.4	% Service Sector	11.1
% Agriculture	38.6	% Mining	2.8
% Forestry	0	% Fishing	0
% Government Services	4.3	% Business Services	1.3

E: Homogeneity Measures

Ethnic Diversity Index	0.26	Religious Homogeneity Index	0.47
Sectoral Concentration Index	0.41	Income Disparity Index	14.6

F: Physical Setting Characteristics

Total Population	62939	Area (km²)	59281
Population Density (pop/km²)	1.1		

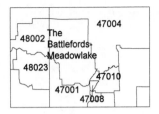

The Battlefords–Meadow Lake

Constituency Number: 47013

This rural riding runs northwest from Saskatoon to the Alberta border, and includes the communities of Battleford, North Battleford, and Meadow Lake. Agriculture is the basis of the riding's economy. Aboriginals account for 31% of the riding's population, second highest in the province after Prince Albert and sixth in Canada. The riding also has the second lowest average family income in Saskatchewan, tenth lowest in Canada.

The Battlefords has alternated between the NDP and the Conservatives, with Tory John Gormley taking the riding from the NDP's Doug Anguish in 1984 by a slim 344 votes. The re-drawing of constituency boundaries after 1984 left almost two-thirds of the voters living outside the riding's urban areas, a change which based on past voting behaviour aided the Conservative cause. Gormley was challenged in 1988 by journalist Len Taylor, parliamentary assistant to NDP MP Doug Anguish during his four years in Ottawa. Gormley, who served as chairman of the House of Commons committee on culture and broadcasting, made his staunch 'pro-life' position a major part of his re-election campaign. Like a number of other Saskatchewan Conservatives who went down to defeat in 1988, Gormley attributed Taylor's 900 vote victory to NDP 'scare tactics' on free trade. As in the previous election, the Liberal candidate finished a distant third.

Going into the 1993 campaign, the incumbent Taylor could take nothing for granted, since no sitting MP had been re-elected in The Battlefords since 1965. His opponents were farmer and small businessman Ken Cheveldayoff for the Conservatives, retired diplomat and second-time candidate Neil Currie for the Liberals, farmer Delon Bleakney for the Reform Party, retired businessman Peter Franklin for the Canada Party, and Leon Chretien, Independent. The 28-year-old Cheveldayoff emphasized the future of agriculture as the focal point of his election bid; Taylor emphasized his record in Parliament which he claimed illustrated his commitment to the riding; one of the main planks of Bleakney's platform was the need to reform Parliament and make politicians more accountable; Neil Currie reiterated his party's job-creation focus.

The election result was close, the second smallest margin of victory in Saskatchewan (next to Moosejaw) and the ninth smallest in Canada. Taylor prevailed in the end with a mere 31.2% of the vote, an 11.3% decline from 1988. The second place finisher was Reformer Bleakney at 28.9%, while the Liberal Currie took 23.5%. The Conservative Cheveldayoff lost his deposit, finishing fourth with only 13.4% of the vote.

Member of Parliament: Leonard William Taylor; **Party:** NDP; **Occupation:** Journalist; **Education:** BA, University of Saskatchewan; **Age:** 43 (Jan. 16, 1952); **Year first elected to the House of Commons:** 1988

47013 The Battlefords–Meadow Lake

A: Political Profile
i) Voting Behaviour

	% 1993	% 1988	Change 1988-93
Conservative	13.7	40.4	-26.7
Liberal	23.5	15.1	8.4
NDP	31.2	42.5	-11.3
Reform	28.9	1.4	27.5
Other	2.7	0.6	2.1

% Turnout	65.3	Total Ballots (#)	31429
Rejected Ballots (#)	140	% Margin of Victory	2.3
Rural Polls, 1988 (#)	134	Urban Polls, 1988 (#)	31
% Yes - 1992	36.4	% No - 1992	63.2

ii) Campaign Financing

	# of Donations	Total $ Value	% of Limit Spent
Conservative	197	50483	71.4*
Liberal	60	15179	28.8
NDP	17	51366	79
Reform	133	20306	39.3
Other	14	1160	

B: Ethno-Linguistic Profile

% English Home Language	90.9	% French Home Language	0.9
% Official Bilingual	5.8	% Other Home Language	8.2
% Catholics	40.5	% Protestants	45.8
% Aboriginal Peoples	31	% Immigrants	4.2

C: Socio-Economic Profile

Average Family Income $	36468	Median Family Income $	30495
% Low Income Families	20.3	Average Home Price $	58314
% Home Owners	70	% Unemployment	8.5
% Labour Force Participation	64.2	% Managerial-Administrative	8.9
% Self-Employed	23.7	% University Degrees	5.5
% Movers	34.7		

D: Industrial Profile

% Manufacturing	3.7	% Service Sector	11.9
% Agriculture	27.2	% Mining	1.5
% Forestry	1.1	% Fishing	0.1
% Government Services	7.9	% Business Services	1.7

E: Homogeneity Measures

Ethnic Diversity Index	0.2	Religious Homogeneity Index	0.38
Sectoral Concentration Index	0.37	Income Disparity Index	16.4

F: Physical Setting Characteristics

Total Population	70745	Area (km²)	58775
Population Density (pop/km²)	1.2		

* Tentative value, due to the existence of unpaid campaign expenses.

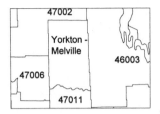

Yorkton–Melville

Constituency Number: 47014

This predominantly rural riding in the rolling parkland of east central Saskatchewan includes the towns of Esterhazy, Kamsack, Canora, Melville and Yorkton. Though it ranks near the bottom of the provincial scale in average household income and is second in dependence on government transfers, it also boasts the highest percentage of homeowners in the province. Its economic base is heavily dependent upon farming, with agriculture accounting for 30% of constituency employment. Potash mining is important in the southern part of the riding.

In 1968, the voters of Yorkton–Melville chose, in 21-year-old Lorne Nystrom, the youngest Canadian ever elected to the House of Commons. In 1988, the NDP energy and regional development critic was still representing this riding. His would-be giant-killers in the election of that year were both engaging in their first election campaign: for the Tories Virginia Battiste, a one-time member of the NDP who was labelled by her opponents as a one-issue candidate for her strong anti-abortion stand, and Liberal Robert Autumn, a 35-year-old employee of Yorkton's Holiday Inn. Though legendary Liberal agriculture minister Jimmy Gardiner had once represented the area, no Liberal had come close to being elected in over three decades. Nystrom had little trouble extending his string of consecutive election victories to seven, pushing his share of the popular vote over the 50% mark.

In 1993, Nystrom's 25-year streak of election wins was threatened by unfocused voter anger and a desire for change. His three opponents played on this, painting Nystrom as a professional politician who showed up in the riding only to get elected. The three contenders for Nystrom's job were school teacher Garry Breitkreuz for the Reform Party, former mayor of Melville Jim Walters for the Liberals, and Bob Reitenbach for the Conservatives.

The electorate's desire for change in 1993 and an anti-incumbent mood finally brought to an end one of the longest strings of election victories recorded by any sitting MP. A 22% decline in Nystrom's vote combined with the collapse of the Conservative vote produced a victory for Reformer Breitkreuz, who won with 32.7% of the vote. With 29.2%, Nystrom couldn't even claim second place, losing that distinction by a tiny margin to his Liberal opponent. The Tory standard-bearer finished a dismal fourth with 8.7% of the vote.

Member of Parliament: Garry Breitkreuz; **Party:** Reform; **Occupation:** Teacher; **Education:** BEd, University of Saskatchewan; **Age:** 49 (Oct. 21, 1945); **Year first elected to the House of Commons:** 1993

47014 Yorkton–Melville

A: Political Profile
i) Voting Behaviour

	% 1993	% 1988	Change 1988-93
Conservative	8.7	34.6	-25.9
Liberal	29.4	14.2	15.2
NDP	29.2	51.1	-21.9
Reform	32.7	0	32.7
Other	0	0	0

% Turnout	72.8	Total Ballots (#)	32571
Rejected Ballots (#)	123	% Margin of Victory	3.3
Rural Polls, 1988 (#)	129	Urban Polls, 1988 (#)	53
% Yes - 1992	40.9	% No - 1992	58.7

ii) Campaign Financing

	# of Donations	Total $ Value	% of Limit Spent
Conservative	153	32145	52.6
Liberal	138	20535	34.3
NDP	1	53068	94.3
Reform	246	42501	51.4
Other	0	0	

B: Ethno-Linguistic Profile

% English Home Language	96.8	% French Home Language	0
% Official Bilingual	2.3	% Other Home Language	3.2
% Catholics	31.6	% Protestants	52.7
% Aboriginal Peoples	5.1	% Immigrants	4.2

C: Socio-Economic Profile

Average Family Income $	38265	Median Family Income $	31903
% Low Income Families	17.1	Average Home Price $	55012
% Home Owners	78.9	% Unemployment	5.7
% Labour Force Participation	63.1	% Managerial-Administrative	8.5
% Self-Employed	25.9	% University Degrees	4.2
% Movers	27.1		

D: Industrial Profile

% Manufacturing	3.4	% Service Sector	11.7
% Agriculture	29.6	% Mining	3.7
% Forestry	0.2	% Fishing	0
% Government Services	4.7	% Business Services	1.6

E: Homogeneity Measures

Ethnic Diversity Index	0.26	Religious Homogeneity Index	0.38
Sectoral Concentration Index	0.39	Income Disparity Index	16.6

F: Physical Setting Characteristics

Total Population	62399	Area (km²)	22440
Population Density (pop/km²)	2.8		

ALBERTA

Alberta

Provincial Overview

Alberta is Canada's fourth largest province. That is true in terms of population: 2,545,553 residents at the 1991 census, 9.3% of the total population of the country. It is also true in physical terms: 661,188 sq. km, 6.7% of Canada. The province is also overwhelmingly urban (approximately 80% in 1991), in spite of a self portrayal as Canada's 'true west', home of cowboys, stampedes, and oil rigs. If British Columbia is too apt to be described externally, it might be argued that Albertans are overly inclined to define themselves. That definition - for example, of life on the open range - is seldom true, certainly for eight in ten of the residents of the province, but it is not unimportant in terms of the provincial culture, psyche and politics.

A majority of the population in the province live in its two largest cities: Edmonton, the capital, and Calgary, the economic centre. The population of the six Calgary constituencies is 709,796, 27.9% of the provincial population; 616,750 reside in the six Edmonton ridings, 24.3% of the total for all of Alberta. When suburban St Albert is added to Edmonton, 28% of the populace are accounted for; the two metropolitan areas together total 55.9% of all provincial residents. With three other large urban centres, Red Deer (population: 103,400), between the two major cities, and Lethbridge (100,127) and Medicine Hat (91,034), both south and east of Calgary, more than two-thirds (67.4%) of Alberta's population reside in these five cities. That still leaves ten (of twenty-six) constituencies with 828,841 residents to represent the Dallas North image so important to the Alberta tourism industry.

In terms of its politics, Alberta has been described as a one-party democratic state. Both provincially and federally, there has been a tendency to decide on which party should govern and then virtually all constituencies in the province elect only members of that party for long periods in office. That was the case provincially: Liberals governed over three terms, from 1905 to 1921; then United Farmers, also for three terms, from 1921 to 1935. In 1935, William Aberhart took Social Credit to power. He stayed as Premier until 1943, succeeded by current Reform Party leader Preston Manning's father, Ernest Manning, Social Credit Premier from 1943 to 1968; Harry Strom concluded the last three years of Social Credit governments (1968 - 1971), ending thirty-six years of one-party government in the province. In each of these eras, not only did the governing party spend a considerable time in office, during their terms they held overwhelming majorities in the provincial legislature; once defeated, they did not return to govern. In 1971, Peter Lougheed managed another dramatic turnover, taking the provincial Progressive Conservatives to power and keeping them there through the mid 1980s, when he was succeeded by Don Getty, and subsequently by current Premier Ralph Klein. Just at the point that the Conservatives looked like they might go the way of all previous governments of Alberta (at the end of Don Getty's brief term), Klein re-invigorated the party with a radical right-wing agenda. That has allowed the Conservatives to extend their turn as government, now closing in on a quarter century.

Federally, the pattern repeats itself: in four elections following World War One, Albertans sent a majority of Progressives to Ottawa; in 1935, at the same time that Social Credit was becoming the new governing party provincially, the province's voters elected a majority of its MPs from the Social Credit Party. That was repeated in 1940, 1945, 1949, 1953 and 1957. On six occasions in a row, one party dominated in the province's federal politics. With the 1958 Diefenbaker Conservative landslide, Albertans made another switch: though Social Credit continued in power provincially for another thirteen years, federal electoral politics in the province came to be dominated by the Progressive Conservatives. And as with earlier party eras provincially, federal Liberals and then Socreds fell off the electoral calendar following their period of electoral success - a success initiated as the challenger to the previous one-party dominance, followed by their own turn in office provincially or in an Albertan majority federally. Between 1958 and 1993 - a run of eleven federal elections - the Conservatives dominated federal politics in the province. The pattern of dominance included huge local majorities for the party - amongst the largest in the country; in 1984, for example, over two-thirds (68.8%) of Albertans voted Progressive Conservative. In the 1979 and 1980 Canadian general elections, the figure was just under two-thirds (65.6% and 64.9% respectively) for federal Tories in the province.

In economic terms, Alberta, particularly with its energy wealth, has been one of the country's three 'have' provinces. That 'have' status divides it from its other two prairie neighbours; so do essential features of the makeup of the provincial economy. Average family incomes, for example, at $51,576 are third highest in Canada, behind the other two 'have' provinces, Ontario and British Columbia. Average house prices are also third highest of all provinces, though just ahead of fourth-placed Quebec. Almost two-thirds of Albertans (65.9%) own their own homes. Negative economic indicators also put the province in the 'have' category: on unemployment, Alberta ranks second lowest in Canada (7.6%); only agricultural Saskatchewan was lower. And on percentage of provincial income dependent on income transfer payments to individuals, the province was lowest in the country - at 9.6%, a full point below Ontario and almost two per cent below British Columbia.

The manufacturing sector in the province is quite small - at 7.4%, the second lowest in the country. Agriculture continues to be important: only Saskatchewan (at over 19%), Manitoba (with 9%) and P.E.I. (just 0.3% ahead at 8.3%) had higher levels of provincial employment in this sector. It is in the energy and mining sector that Alberta performs best: with one provincial exception, this sector of the economy in Alberta is more than double (at 5.8%) the level of anywhere else in Canada. From early oil finds at Leduc, just south of Edmonton, to tar sands, heavy oil, and natural gas, energy has come to be a dominant player in the total economy of the province. Head offices have moved, especially to Calgary, with their share of service sector jobs. Services now make up 46.7% of all employment in Alberta; that places the province sixth in the shift to a tertiary economy. The continuing high dependence on primary resource exploitation is the largest single factor here. The rate of provincial education, tied closely to tertiary transitions, was another indicator of this shift: only the three 'have' provinces had more than one in ten of their residents with completed university degrees. Alberta had the second highest levels of education of any province: 11.2% with a university degree. The province also placed third in provincial standings on proportion of managerial/administrative work (with 11.1%).

The self-dependent 'do it yourself' ethos of the old west found expression in two categories: (i) Alberta had the second highest level of self-employment in the country; only Saskatchewan, where agriculture accounts for almost 20% of the economy (more than double any other province), ranked higher. (ii) The rate of government services in Alberta (7.5%) was also fourth lowest, virtually at the same levels as Quebec (7.2%) and Saskatchewan (7.4%). The restlessness of the new west was demonstrated in mobility patterns: only in B.C. (the highest) and Alberta did more than half the provincial population move over the five years between 1986 and 1991.

In terms of provincial demography, this was partly a factor of immigration: Alberta had the third highest level of immigrants (14.2%) in the country; only Ontario and British Columbia were higher. The strength of the local economy was obviously a large explanatory feature here. The province ranked in the middle on English home-language use (92.5%); it was fourth lowest in French use at home. When English and French are combined, Alberta is fourth lowest; this was a combination of significant numbers of immigrants, often concentrated within the metropolitan centres, and also a feature of a large Aboriginal community - at 5.1%, the third biggest in Canada. When religion is considered, some of these demographic patterns are repeated: for example, accompanying low French home-language rates, Catholics made up just one-quarter (26.5%) of the provincial population, the second lowest level of Catholic affiliation in Canada. While Protestantism in Alberta was about in the middle of the provincial tables, Alberta was second lowest in levels of religious affiliation overall. Fully one-quarter of Albertans reported no religion in the 1991 census; only British Columbia, its Pacific neighbour, was less religious.

In 1993, Alberta went through its own electoral revolution. This was certainly part of a larger political sea-change across the country, but in Alberta it was total: two parties with no representation in 1988 replaced two others, one which had held over 96% of all Parliamentary seats from the province. The dominance of Progressive Conservatives in Alberta federally after 1958 was impressive. Down through 1988, they managed to collect an absolute majority of votes in the province; in 1979 and 1980, they took all twenty-one seats, and in 1984, they collected 25 of 26 parliamentary seats for the party. The Tories' decline (to 51.8%) in 1988 signalled the possibility of a shift; the roots of that shift began several elections before. Elsewhere on the political spectrum in Alberta, patterns of support had already begun to alter in the late 1970s: in 1979, for example, while the Tories won just under two-thirds of the vote, Liberals were solidly in second place (with 22.1% support). Support for Alberta New Democrats hovered around one in ten in the population. In total, these three major parties captured 97.6% of all federal votes in the province, leaving 2.4% for minor parties and independents. In 1980, this pattern virtually repeated itself: Conservatives held about 65%, down 0.7%; Liberals were up 0.1% to 22.2% overall; and New Democrats increased their support 0.4% to 10.3%. The three party share was down slightly (0.2%), leaving 2.6% for 'others'.

In the 1984 Canadian general election, two things happened politically: minor party votes almost doubled - to 4.5%; and New Democrats replaced Liberals as the second place party federally in the province - 14% to 12.7% respectively, though neither party won any seats; they were all won again by Conservatives, whose voter support rose 3.9%. That NDP-Liberal Party reversal continued in 1988: both increased their share of the total vote slightly - with New Democrats at 17.4% and Grits at 13.7%. Out of that more than 31% share of the votes, only one NDP seat, its first in provincial history, was won: Edmonton East. The Progressive Conservatives won 25 of the (now) 26 ridings in 1988; they saw their voter support fall 17% from the previous general election, however. Most importantly, the 1988 election reflected a dramatic increase in 'other' party voting: over 17% of Alberta's voters - the same figure as the Tory drop - chose a party or candidate other than one of the 'old three'. The largest share of this went to Reform, emerging as the new voice of old western discontent. In 1988, Reform placed second in nine constituencies: three Calgary ridings (North, Southwest and West), Red Deer, Wetaskiwin, Wild Rose and Yellowhead; in Crowfoot and Macleod, they received more than 30% support from local voters. Only the New Democrats, with eleven second place finishes, had more. The Liberals picked up five of the other six (the Tories were second in Edmonton East). Reform also displaced the NDP or Liberals for third place in seven other ridings: Calgary Centre and Southeast, Edmonton Strathcona, Elk Island, Lethbridge, Peace River and Vegreville. New Democrats took an equal number of third place standings; Liberals had nine. In total, Reform place second or third in sixteen of the twenty-six Alberta federal ridings in the 1988 General Election with 15.4% of the votes in the province.

In 1993, Reform more than tripled its previous vote - to 52.3%. It took every riding where it had placed second or third in 1988, plus a half dozen others. The Liberals, improving their vote to just over one-quarter of all cast, managed to take four seats - all in Edmonton: East from the NDP, and Northwest, North and Southeast from the Tories. The Conservative vote collapsed everywhere; they were left with a mere shell of 14.6% support. That was still far better than the 4.1% left to the New Democrats - a drop of more than 13%. The NDP in Alberta were left with fewer votes than the 'other minor' parties (minus Reform) and independents: these won 6.5% of all votes cast.

The key issues in 1993 were largely defined by the ascendant right wing in Alberta: these included traditional grievances such as Senate Reform and no special constitutional deals for Quebec. Alberta had not voted as overwhelmingly 'No' on the Charlottetown Accord constitutional reform package as its neighbour British Columbia, but with one exception ridings had voted negatively in 1992, and Calgary Southeast's 'Yes' vote was a slim 50.5% in favour. Except for four Edmonton and four Calgary constituencies, the other eighteen ridings' referendum votes were between 60.1% and 71.3% No. The other campaign issues stemmed from a strong sense of frustration at 'the Ottawa syndrome': where Albertans voted with a message only to perceive their MPs becoming more beholden to party discipline than provincial representation. This was felt the case on the constitution; it was certainly the case with the Goods and Services Tax. The GST and the failure of Senate reform were important. Increasingly, the other Reform messages on the deficit/debt and law and order came to have electoral play as well; in certain races, local land claim/self-government issues raised by aboriginal peoples were a factor, but these were limited. The array of issues before the electorate in Alberta in 1993 was certainly broader than the free trade mantra of 1988. Other parties emphasized jobs, economic improvement and sustaining social programs; with the exception of Edmonton, these were largely drowned in a right-wing wave of Reform protest.

Amongst 'other' parties, the dominant grouping in Alberta in the 1993 general election was the National Party: it ran candidates in nineteen of the twenty-six races. In fifteen of these ridings, the National Party candidate placed fifth and in one it was sixth. In the other three it did better, with two fourth place finishes, ahead of the NDP in Lethbridge and St Albert; and in Edmonton Northwest, National Party leader Mel Hurtig took third spot with 12.8%, ahead of the Conservatives and the NDP. Natural Law, because of its capacity to fund candidacies, was the next most successful party: it had eleven sixth place finishes, and two fifth spot showings; NLP tended to do better when there were fewer minor party candidates to run against. The Greens had one fifth spot and four sixth places; that was slightly better than Christian Heritage, with three sixth placings and a fifth in Medicine Hat.

On incumbency in Alberta, the 1993 general election was deadly: only two MPs were returned - one only by changing party affiliation from Conservative to Liberal, the other a Reform MP elected first in a 1989 by-election; many sitting Members had seen the political wall writing in 1988 and during the referendum in 1992, and had chosen retirement to defeat. In 1988, sixteen sitting Members of Parliament had sought re-election; fifteen had been successful. All were Conservatives. In 1993, ten sitting Conservatives did not seek re-election: in nine cases, these seats were taken by Reform; the Liberals won in Edmonton North. One New Democratic MP and twelve Progressive Conservatives, including several Cabinet Ministers, ran again and were defeated. The New Democrat lost to a Liberal. One sitting Tory MP ran as an independent and lost and another Conservative, David Kilgour, crossed to the Liberals after being kicked out of the Tory caucus, and held his seat. Kilgour was one of two Alberta MPs to return to Parliament after the 1993 election. The only sitting Reform MP from 1988, Deborah Grey, from Beaver River, held her seat. Clearly, the hint of change indicated in 1988 came to pass. The remaining question is whether the Alberta tradition of long incumbency followed by almost complete dismissal will re-establish itself. There is every indication that in Alberta at least, the next federal election will be equally kind to Reform.

Alberta had not been a province with any tradition of supporting women running for federal office. In the 1984 general election, fourteen women had won one of the three major party nominations - just over 22% of those available; only one woman was elected to Parliament in 1984. In 1988, just seventeen candidates for the four largest parties were women: seven New Democrats, six Liberals and just one Conservative; Reform had nominated three. Two women were elected in that general election - Bobbie Sparrow (in Calgary Southwest) and Louise Feltham (in Wild Rose). In 1989, Deborah Grey became the third Alberta woman sitting in the House of Commons, after her by-election win in Beaver River. In 1993, forty-five women ran for Parliament: ten of these were for Natural Law; all lost their deposits. Six were for the National Party; each was defeated. And there were seven other minor party or independents: a total of 23 from the 'other' category, with no prospect of election. Of the twenty-two women running for one of the four main parties in 1993, half won nominations as New Democrats - again with some hope but little chance of election. The Conservatives nominated just three women of its twenty-six candidates; two were incumbents, and all three lost. The Liberals selected four women (15.4% of their total); two were elected: Judy Bethel, in Edmonton East and Anne McLennan, in Edmonton Northwest. Reform also nominated just four women in 1993, but three were returned to the House of Commons: incumbent Deborah Grey, from Beaver River, Diane Ablonczy, from Calgary North and Jan Brown, from Calgary Southeast. That represented a more than doubling of the number of women representing Alberta - from two to five, but still just 19.2% of the representative places available. In six Alberta constituencies in 1993, it was possible to attend all-candidate meetings without seeing any women candidates; in several others, only as a minor party representative or independent. If being a woman interested in federal politics in Alberta in 1988 held out limited promise of success, then 1993 could be categorized as reflecting a small step toward more gender equity in the politics on the province. It was not more than that.

1993 represented the end of one era in Alberta federal politics - one dominated for thirty-five years by Progressive Conservatives. It also heralded the potential beginning of a new Party hegemony - in the form of the Reform Party. The election of Reform to 85% of the seats in the province (for its 52.3% share of the vote) certainly represented a new beginning. The re-emergence of federal Liberals from Alberta in the Canadian Parliament was more a reflection of electoral system vagaries than of the fact there were no Liberals in the province over the past couple of decades. Liberal support in Alberta in 1993 was less than 3% above party support in 1979 and 1980. In this instance, it just produced four MPs. Reform's dominance in Alberta in 1993, coupled with the party's capturing of 75% of the parliamentary seats in British Columbia, may be reflecting the drift in Canadian politics away from traditional four-regional analysis. If so, the Canadian general election of 1993 may have defined a new Midwest and Cordilleran explanation of politics in Canada's four 'western' provinces.

Alberta Results, 1988 & 1993 Elections, 1992 Referendum

	1988 Election			1993 Election	
	% Vote	Seats	1992	% Vote	Seats
Conservatives	51.8	25		14.6	0
Liberals	13.7	0		25.1	4
NDP	17.4	1		4.1	0
Reform	15.4	0		52.3	22
Other/Indep.	1.7	0		3.9	0
Turnout	75.0	–		67.7	–
% Yes (1992)			39.8		
% No (1992)			60.2		

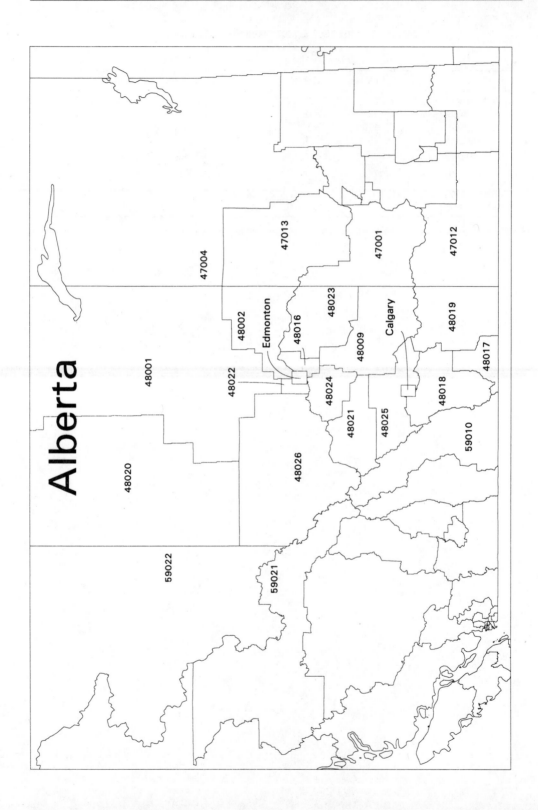

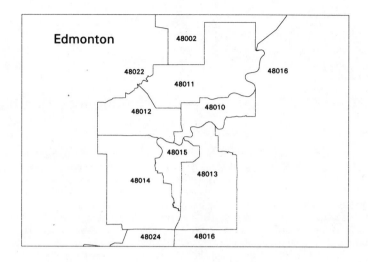

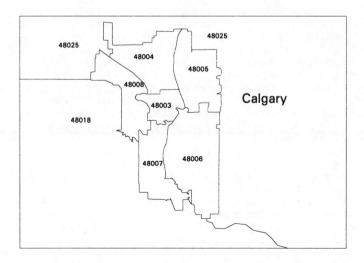

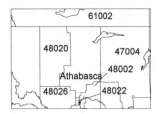

Athabasca

Constituency Number: 48001

Athabasca is the largest federal riding in the province of Alberta (area 196,260 sq. km); it is the thirteenth largest Canadian constituency. It is in the extreme northeast corner of the province, its boundaries on two sides the Northwest Territories and Saskatchewan; it includes part of Lake Athabasca and the large Wood Buffalo National Park which extends into NWT. Its population of 80,261 is the fifth smallest in Alberta; the largest urban community is the energy centre of Fort McMurray near the Saskatchewan border and there are smaller towns such as High Prairie, near Lesser Slave Lake. The percentage of immigrants (8.4%) is low, and of citizens high (96.9%). There is a fair level of language diversity: 7.1% are officially bilingual, and almost another per cent use French as their home language; English is spoken in just over nine in ten (91.2%) of the riding homes. Aboriginal peoples make up 22.6% of all area residents - the provincial norm is 5.1%: this includes the Lubicon Lake band, just north of High Prairie. The Lubicons have had a long-standing and high profile dispute with federal and provincial governments over land claims. The vast majority of riding residents are Protestant (41.9%) or Catholic (39.3%).

The local economy is heavily dependent on resource extraction: energy/mining (with 20.4% of all jobs) is the largest riding employer; indeed the level of mining/energy activity in Athabasca is the highest in all of Canada. There is also a large agricultural component: 8.4% of all work is farm-related. Local manufacturing (4.1%), related to resource and agricultural needs, and a forestry segment (1.6% of work) represent smaller elements of area economic activity. The service sector - in a riding where about half of the polls were rural - provided almost four in ten of local employment, 6.9% for governments and 2.1% in business. 11.3% of all work was through self employment, and 8.4% of all jobs were managerial or administrative. The local education rate for university degrees - at 7.0% - was more than four points below the average for all of Alberta. The unemployment rate locally - at 9% - was above Alberta's average of 7.6%, but income support from government transfers in the area was almost two points below the provincial norm. Two thirds of the residents (67.8%) owned their own homes, whose value was $30,000 lower that that for the province as a whole. Average family incomes in the riding at $53,476 were almost $2,000 above the provincial average.

Politically, the riding had been represented by Conservative Jack Shields since 1980. In 1984, Shields took 68.2% of all local votes; the local NDP were second with 17.4% and the Liberals at 11.5%. In the 1988 contest, even though the Conservative vote fell 15.4%, Shields still managed to take more than half of all votes (52.8%). The NDP were again in second place, this time with 27.3%. The local Liberals stayed fairly static - at 12.3%. In 1988, Reform managed 5.5% support in Athabasca; two other minor candidates won 2.1%. In the subsequent constitutional referendum, two thirds of the local voters were on the 'No' side.

In 1993, Conservative Shields sought a fourth term; as in 1988, he was challenged by five candidates: this time Natural Law and Green representatives, as well as Liberal, NDP and Reform. Reform selected David Chatters, a farmer from Jarvie, north of Edmonton; the Liberal candidate was Lawrence Courtereille, an administrator from Fort MacKay. Ian Thorn, who had placed second behind Shields in the 1988 election was again nominated by the NDP. Thorn, from Fort McMurray, was a union officer in Athabasca's energy sector. Harvey Scott, a farmer and teacher from Athabasca was the Green candidate. He managed 312 votes - 1% - when the 1993 votes were counted. The Natural Law representative had 0.6%. Four-time MP Jack Shields placed third, a drop of 33.6% to 19.2%. Reform's Dave Chatters won the riding, increasing the party vote to 47.1%. The NDP vote also slipped significantly, down 19.7%, to a fourth place low of 7.6%. The local Liberal vote for Lawrence Courtereille was up 12.3% - almost one-quarter (24.6%) support and second place. Voter turnout was low - at 59.6% the fifth lowest in the province and over five points below the provincial turnout.

Member of Parliament: David Chatters; **Party:** Reform; **Occupation:** Farmer; **Education:** High school; Age: 47 (1946); **Year first elected to the House of Commons:** 1993

48001 Athabasca

A: Political Profile

i) Voting Behaviour

	% 1993	% 1988	Change 1988-93
Conservative	19.2	52.8	-33.6
Liberal	24.6	12.3	12.3
NDP	7.6	27.3	-19.7
Reform	47.1	5.5	41.6
Other	1.6	2.1	-0.5

% Turnout	59.6	Total Ballots (#)	32695
Rejected Ballots (#)	81	% Margin of Victory	24.1
Rural Polls, 1988 (#)	94	Urban Polls, 1988 (#)	73
% Yes - 1992	33.8	% No - 1992	66

ii) Campaign Financing

	# of Donations	Total $ Value	% of Limit Spent
Conservative	202	47219	99.2
Liberal	29	24560	37.8
NDP	5	21858	38.6*
Reform	192	60801	62.2
Other	12	1325	

B: Ethno-Linguistic Profile

% English Home Language	91.2	% French Home Language	0.9
% Official Bilingual	7.1	% Other Home Language	7.9
% Catholics	39.3	% Protestants	41.9
% Aboriginal Peoples	22.6	% Immigrants	8.4

C: Socio-Economic Profile

Average Family Income $	53476	Median Family Income $	47588
% Low Income Families	14.9	Average Home Price $	80806
% Home Owners	67.8	% Unemployment	9
% Labour Force Participation	73	% Managerial-Administrative	8.4
% Self-Employed	11.3	% University Degrees	7
% Movers	52.3		

D: Industrial Profile

% Manufacturing	4.1	% Service Sector	12.5
% Agriculture	8.4	% Mining	20.4
% Forestry	1.6	% Fishing	0.1
% Government Services	6.9	% Business Services	2.1

E: Homogeneity Measures

Ethnic Diversity Index	0.2	Religious Homogeneity Index	0.35
Sectoral Concentration Index	0.34	Income Disparity Index	11

F: Physical Setting Characteristics

Total Population	80261	Area (km^2)	196260
Population Density (pop/km^2)	0.4		

* Tentative value, due to the existence of unpaid campaign expenses.

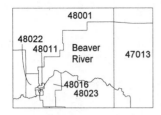

Beaver River

Constituency Number: 48002

Beaver River was a new constituency in the 1988 election. It includes parts of Athabaska, the abolished Pembina riding, and Vegreville. It cuts across the province from the Saskatchewan border to Edmonton, covering 28,530 sq. km, and includes the St Paul and Bonnyville areas. The large military base and community of Cold Lake (notable for cruise missile testing), near the Saskatchewan boundary is the only large centre in the riding. The local population of 72,738 is the second smallest in the province; most of the polls in the riding are rural. The constituency is quite diverse: the level of immigrants is small (5.7%) and of citizenship high (97.4%), and while British make up the largest local ethnic group, aboriginal peoples contribute 15.3% of the riding's residents. There is a large French community - 13.1% are officially bilingual and 4% use French as their home language, both well above the norms for the province of Alberta. Catholics outnumber Protestants (40.2% to 38.5%), and there is a large Jewish community (7.2%). The other significant ethnic group locally is Ukrainian.

While service employment makes up almost half of all jobs, much of that is in support of agricultural production (13.8%) and mining/energy activity (6.1%). Near the Saskatchewan border heavy oil production is significant. There is a small manufacturing sector (at 3.9%, the third lowest rate in the country), and a smaller business services component. The governmental segment of the economy provides 19.6% of all employment (fifteenth highest in Canada), much of it because of the military base at Cold Lake. Self-employment is at 16%, almost 4% higher than in the whole province; almost 8% are managers or administrators. The local educational standing is well below the provincial rate; 6% hold university degrees. Unemployment is just a half point above the provincial average, but income from government transfers is a point and a half above the norm. Family incomes average $44,764, over $6,000 below the Alberta average, but home ownership (of houses whose average value is $27,000 below the provincial norm) was high - at 71%, more that five per cent above that for Alberta.

As a new constituency, Beaver River had no incumbent in 1988 and the Conservative elected in the general election, John Dahmer, died five days after winning the local seat. In the ensuing March 13, 1989 by-election, Reform's first MP was elected. Deborah Grey had contested the 1988 election for Reform and placed fourth with 13.3%. Local Liberals had just edged out the NDP (21% to 20.9%). In the 1989 by-election Reform had significantly outdistanced its rivals, winning 48% of the votes in a four-way race. In the 1992 referendum on the Charlottetown Accord, Beaver River voted 70.3% 'No'.

With the 1993 general election, Beaver River had a high profile Reform candidate, Deborah Grey. Her own record in Parliament, defence review, environmental issues, immigration, jobs, the economy and the debt/deficit, dominated the debates. Grey faced five challengers: the Liberals nominated Michael Zackarko, a St Paul farmer; David Broda, a realtor from Redwater, who had represented the Conservatives in the 1989 by-election, was re-nominated; Eugene Houle, a management consultant from Saddle Lake, was the NDP selection. Natural Law and an Independent rounded out the field. The 1993 result in Beaver River included an increase in Deborah Grey's support; she won the seat with 58% of the votes, the ninth highest Reform vote in the country. The Tories, whose vote had fallen from 44% in 1988 to 30% at the by-election, just four months later, saw a further decline of over seventeen points: Dave Broda won just 12.6% of the votes and third place. Local Liberal Mike Zackarko was second, up slightly from 1988 to 24.7%. The NDP's Eugene House managed only 3.4%, not much ahead of Guy German, an Edmonton student and the Natural Law candidate (at 1%). The NDP fall between the two general elections was 17.5%. The Independent managed 94 votes. Local turnout was 66.9%, more than a point above the provincial vote norm.

Member of Parliament: Deborah Grey; **Party;** Reform; **Occupation:** Teacher; **Education:** BA, BEd, University of Alberta; **Age:** 41 (July 1, 1952); **Year first elected to the House of Commons:** 1989 (by-election)

48002 Beaver River

A: Political Profile
i) Voting Behaviour

	% 1993	% 1988	Change 1988-93
Conservative	12.6	44.3	-31.7
Liberal	24.7	21	3.7
NDP	3.4	20.9	-17.5
Reform	58	13.4	44.6
Other	1.3	0.4	0.9

% Turnout	66.9	Total Ballots (#)	30670
Rejected Ballots (#)	111	% Margin of Victory	34.6
Rural Polls, 1988 (#)	146	Urban Polls, 1988 (#)	22
% Yes - 1992	29.6	% No - 1992	70.3

ii) Campaign Financing

	# of Donations	Total $ Value	% of Limit Spent
Conservative	74	30657	44.1*
Liberal	23	12361	21.8
NDP	2	2229	1
Reform	141	51190	54.7
Other	0	0	

B: Ethno-Linguistic Profile

% English Home Language	93.2	% French Home Language	4
% Official Bilingual	13.1	% Other Home Language	2.8
% Catholics	40.2	% Protestants	38.5
% Aboriginal Peoples	15.3	% Immigrants	5.7

C: Socio-Economic Profile

Average Family Income $	44764	Median Family Income $	40813
% Low Income Families	14.6	Average Home Price $	83287
% Home Owners	71	% Unemployment	8.1
% Labour Force Participation	72.7	% Managerial-Administrative	7.9
% Self-Employed	16	% University Degrees	6
% Movers	43.6		

D: Industrial Profile

% Manufacturing	3.9	% Service Sector	18.7
% Agriculture	13.8	% Mining	6.1
% Forestry	1.1	% Fishing	0.2
% Government Services	19.6	% Business Services	1.9

E: Homogeneity Measures

Ethnic Diversity Index	0.17	Religious Homogeneity Index	0.33
Sectoral Concentration Index	0.36	Income Disparity Index	8.8

F: Physical Setting Characteristics

Total Population	72738	Area (km²)	28530
Population Density (pop/km²)	2.5		

---

*   Tentative value, due to the existence of unpaid campaign expenses.

Calgary Centre

Constituency Number: 48003

Calgary Centre has a population of 103,779. It represents the urban core of Calgary. Its population is highly mobile, with the highest rate of movers in one year in the country (and the second highest number of people moving over a five year period). The local populace is a mixture of British, German, Chinese, French and Ukrainian; 21.5% are immigrants, 88.7% citizens and nine in ten (90.5%) speak English at home. The riding has a significant aboriginal community (2.0%). Almost seven in ten are Protestant (43.3%) or Catholic (24.5%) and almost 6% are Jewish. Over one-quarter declared no religion.

The constituency is centre to much of the management of provincial oil and other resource exploitation companies: 56.2% of all jobs are tertiary, with 13.0% in management or administration; business services make up 12.0% of all jobs (eighth highest in the country), with a further 5.0% in the government sector. Self-employment rates are low (8.6%). Energy and Mining account for 7.6% of all jobs and local manufacturing another 6.8%. Average family incomes ($53,294) are just under $2,000 above the provincial average; house prices are almost $48,000 above the Alberta norm and only 30.1% own their own homes, the second lowest number of homeowners in all of Canada. Area unemployment - at 9.1% - is a point and a half above that across the whole province, but income support levels - at 9.2% - is just under the Alberta rate. The educational attainment in Calgary Centre is over nine points above that for all of the province for university degrees (20.5%).

Historically, Calgary Centre has been a strong Tory seat. Doug Harkness won the seat in 1968, having switched from Calgary North. The riding returned Conservative front-bencher Harvie Andre first in 1972. He was re-elected in 1974, 1979 and 1980. In 1984, Andre took just under two-thirds of the vote (64.9%), well ahead of the Liberals, with 17%, and the NDP, with 14.2%. In the 1988 general election, Andre, now a Cabinet Minister, was returned for the sixth time. Despite a vote drop of over 10%, he held the seat with 53.7%. The second place NDP had only 20%. Reform had more votes than the Liberals - 12.4% to 11.7%. In the referendum of 1992, the constituency split evenly - 49.5% 'Yes' and 50.2% 'No'.

In 1993, Harvie Andre decided to retire. His replacement was lawyer Sean O'Neil. O'Neil faced six others seeking to win the seat: Jim Silye, a former Calgary Stampeder defensive back and businessman won the Reform Party nod; retired oilman Bob Blair ran for the Liberals; Calgary Centre NDP selected lawyer Catherine McCreary again (she had run second to Andre in 1988); Peter Huff, an arts administrator represented the National Party; four other minor party candidates rounded out the field. The debt, smaller government and law and order were popular local issues. Reform's Jim Silye won the election with 45.1% of all votes. Bob Blair was second, the Liberal vote up over 18%. Both the Tory and NDP votes collapsed: the Conservatives held third place but fell almost 39%; the NDP lost almost 16%, leaving them at 4.3%. The National Party was just behind the NDP, with 3.5%. Greens, Natural Law, Canada Party and Marxist-Leninists shared 2.1% in that order. Voter turnout was the third lowest in the country, at 57.9%.

Member of Parliament: Jim Silye; **Party:** Reform; **Occupation:** Businessperson; **Education:** BA, University of Ottawa; **Age:** 47 (March 28, 1946); **Year first elected to the House of Commons:** 1993

48003 Calgary Centre

A: Political Profile
i) Voting Behaviour

	% 1993	% 1988	Change 1988-93
Conservative	14.9	53.7	-38.8
Liberal	30.2	11.7	18.5
NDP	4.3	20	-15.7
Reform	45.1	12.4	32.7
Other	5.6	2.1	3.5

% Turnout	57.9	Total Ballots (#)	50319
Rejected Ballots (#)	182	% Margin of Victory	20.5
Rural Polls, 1988 (#)	0	Urban Polls, 1988 (#)	204
% Yes - 1992	49.5	% No - 1992	50.2

ii) Campaign Financing

	# of Donations	Total $ Value	% of Limit Spent
Conservative	356	54090	81.1
Liberal	162	45504	86
NDP	5	19696	25.2
Reform	143	95844	90.9
Other	36	7067	

B: Ethno-Linguistic Profile

% English Home Language	90.5	% French Home Language	0.4
% Official Bilingual	8.9	% Other Home Language	9.1
% Catholics	24.5	% Protestants	43.3
% Aboriginal Peoples	2	% Immigrants	21.5

C: Socio-Economic Profile

Average Family Income $	53294	Median Family Income $	40574
% Low Income Families	28.6	Average Home Price $	158061
% Home Owners	30.1	% Unemployment	9.1
% Labour Force Participation	74	% Managerial-Administrative	13
% Self-Employed	8.6	% University Degrees	20.5
% Movers	67.6		

D: Industrial Profile

% Manufacturing	6.8	% Service Sector	15
% Agriculture	0.7	% Mining	7.6
% Forestry	0.1	% Fishing	0
% Government Services	5	% Business Services	12

E: Homogeneity Measures

Ethnic Diversity Index	0.21	Religious Homogeneity Index	0.31
Sectoral Concentration Index	0.53	Income Disparity Index	23.9

F: Physical Setting Characteristics

Total Population	103779	Area (km²)	36
Population Density (pop/km²)	2882.8		

Calgary North

Constituency Number: 48004

Calgary North remains the city's most populous constituency (128,566) and one of the largest in Canada; it is an area of single family homes for the British, Chinese and Germans that make up a large part of the riding. Over two in ten (21.7%) of the residents are immigrants; nine in ten speak English at home. Over seven per cent are officially bilingual. Its population is well educated - over two in ten with university degrees compared with 11.2% across the province. Seven in ten are Protestant (46.6%) or Catholic (24.8%); almost six per cent (5.9%) are Jewish. Average home prices are more than $37,000 above the provincial norm, but almost seven in ten (68.5%) own their own homes. Family incomes are $9,000 above the Alberta average.

The local economy has a significant small business base, though with 9.2% employed in the energy/ mining sector, it is twelfth highest in Canada in that category. There is also a manufacturing sector which produces more than 7% of local jobs. The majority of local work is service oriented: with almost one in ten in business services and 5.3% with government. Almost 9% are self-employed. Local unemployment is just below the provincial rate; income transfer payments are more than three points below the norm for Alberta.

The history of Calgary North is closely associated with the Conservatives: Douglas Harkness, first elected to Parliament in 1945, represented Calgary North from the time it was established, winning the 1953 election and being continuously re-elected through the 1965 general election. (In 1968, Harkness, a Diefenbaker Cabinet Minister, ran and won in Calgary Centre.) PC Eldon Woolliams took over the seat in 1968 and held it through to the 1980 general election. In 1984, the local Conservative vote was 73.3%. In the 1988 election, there was no incumbent; the Tory MP had resigned, citing boredom with Parliament. Al Johnson, the Conservative candidate, held the seat with almost 58% of the votes; as a harbinger of future change, the Reform Party placed second with 16.2%, several points ahead of the Liberals (at 13% and the NDP at 12.5%). On the subsequent referendum the riding was fairly evenly split, with 'No' winning 51.2% of the local votes.

In 1993, issues like strengthening the Young Offender Act, job creation - and whether it should be a government activity at all, Canadian Airlines survival, and the GST all stood out locally. So did the low profile of Al Johnson, the Tory MP. Johnson faced seven other contenders: they included former Western Canada Concept supporter, Calgary lawyer, and Reform Party co-founder Diane Ablonczy; former oil consultant James Maxim, laid off by PetroCan in a downsizing, won the Liberal nod. Andrea Garnier, a local archivist was the NDP candidate; Mike Schubert represented the National Party. Two other minor parties and an Independent also ran. The result was a solid Reform victory: Diane Ablonczy won 52.5% of the votes. Incumbent Tory Al Johnson fell over 42% to third place, with 15.4%. James Maxim doubled the local Liberal vote, taking second place with more than one-quarter of the electorate's support. The NDP vote fell over 10%, leaving Andrea Garnier just 0.4% ahead of Mike Schubert of the National Party. The other 1.4% of the votes was shared by a Green, Natural Law and Independent in that order. Local turnout was over three points above the average for the province.

Member of Parliament: Diane Ablonczy; **Party:** Reform; **Occupation:** Lawyer; **Education:** BEd, LL.B, University of Calgary; **Age:** 44 (1949); **Year first elected to the House of Commons:** 1993

48004 Calgary North

A: Political Profile
i) Voting Behaviour

	% 1993	% 1988	Change 1988-93
Conservative	15.4	57.7	-42.3
Liberal	26.4	13	13.4
NDP	2.4	12.5	-10.1
Reform	52.5	16.2	36.3
Other	3.4	0.5	2.9

% Turnout	68.8	Total Ballots (#)	67848
Rejected Ballots (#)	145	% Margin of Victory	29.5
Rural Polls, 1988 (#)	0	Urban Polls, 1988 (#)	244
% Yes - 1992	48.6	% No - 1992	51.2

ii) Campaign Financing

	# of Donations	Total $ Value	% of Limit Spent
Conservative	141	34618	94.6
Liberal	180	49301	68.7
NDP	2	3937	2.1
Reform	469	68860	88.3
Other	31	2249	

B: Ethno-Linguistic Profile

% English Home Language	90.1	% French Home Language	0.4
% Official Bilingual	7.1	% Other Home Language	9.5
% Catholics	24.8	% Protestants	46.6
% Aboriginal Peoples	0.9	% Immigrants	21.7

C: Socio-Economic Profile

Average Family Income $	60720	Median Family Income $	53764
% Low Income Families	14.6	Average Home Price $	147415
% Home Owners	68.5	% Unemployment	7.5
% Labour Force Participation	75	% Managerial-Administrative	14.1
% Self-Employed	8.7	% University Degrees	20
% Movers	57.8		

D: Industrial Profile

% Manufacturing	7.1	% Service Sector	11.6
% Agriculture	0.7	% Mining	9.2
% Forestry	0.1	% Fishing	0
% Government Services	5.3	% Business Services	9.5

E: Homogeneity Measures

Ethnic Diversity Index	0.21	Religious Homogeneity Index	0.34
Sectoral Concentration Index	0.45	Income Disparity Index	11.5

F: Physical Setting Characteristics

Total Population	128566	Area (km²)	95
Population Density (pop/km²)	1353.3		

Calgary Northeast

Constituency Number: 48005

Calgary Northeast is a working-class, multicultural constituency of 124,290, the third largest population in a federal riding in the province. It was created largely from the Calgary East riding. Its population is a mixture of British, German, Chinese and South Asian - 26% of the riding are immigrants. One in ten area residents are non-citizens. English home-language use is low, at under 84%; official bilingualism is close to 5%. Less than two-thirds of the residents are Catholic or Protestant. A large Jewish community (11.9%) makes Northeast Calgary its home.

The local economic base is industrial and manufacturing: over 12% of all jobs. More than four in ten of other jobs are service sector based: almost 7% in business services and just under 5% governmental. 9% of area jobs are managerial or administrative. There is also a segment of local employment attached to the energy/mining industry (4.2%). Educational levels in the constituency are below the average for the province by almost five per cent. Area unemployment is a point and a half above the rate for the province, but government income transfer levels are more than two and a half points below the provincial norm. Average family incomes are low for the metropolitan area, $6,000 below the Alberta average; area home prices are just $1,000 more than across the province. There is a relatively high home ownership rate (over two thirds) despite other below-average economic indicators.

Politically, maverick Conservative MP Alex Kindy represented the area. He had won the 1984 election with almost sixty per cent of the voters' support. In 1988, Kindy ran again in the revised constituency. He was opposed by six other aspirants. Kindy's 1984 spread had been almost 36%. In the 1988 general election, Kindy dropped 5% but still took an absolute majority of local votes. In second, third and fourth place - all within a couple of per cent of each other - were the Liberals (with 16.2%), the New Democrats (at 15.5%) and the local Reform candidate (with 13%). The other two candidates shared 0.6%. Kindy continued his 'opposition' to many of the key policy positions of the Mulroney Conservative government - on Canada Post, on language policy, and on the Goods and Services Tax. When he voted against the GST, the Calgary Northeast member was expelled from the Tory caucus. He continued to sit as an Independent, calling many of his former colleagues 'trained seals'. The 1992 constitutional referendum saw over six in ten local voters vote 'No'.

In the 1993 general election, the constituency was faced with an incumbent now running as an Independent. Kindy, a physician, confronted a Progressive Conservative candidate, David Aftergood, a restaurant owner. Aftergood had served as an assistant to several Conservative cabinet ministers; part of his campaign was against 'absentee' candidates who did not live in the riding, like Kindy and the Liberal representative, lawyer Colin MacDonald. Apart from living outside the riding, MacDonald had survived a bitter nomination fight that saw 13 local riding executive members resign, despite his endorsement by two Liberal premiers and other party brass. Reform nominated Art Hanger, a 22-year veteran of the Calgary police force whose primary platform was 'law and order'. NDP candidate Ken Richmond had run in five previous provincial elections and had placed third in the 1988 federal contest. His campaign theme was unemployment. Ray McLeod, a freelance writer/photographer was the National Party candidate; Natural Law and a Green rounded out the slate. Without outspoken Kindy, the Conservative vote fell almost 44%. The Conservatives managed some satisfaction when they outpointed Kindy 11.3% to 6.8%. Art Hanger and Reform took the seat with a 12% margin (44.4%) over Liberal Colin MacDonald (at 32.3%). The NDP vote also dropped - by almost 13% - leaving them just one point ahead of the National Party in the riding. Natural Law outdistanced the Greens 0.4% to 0.3%. Voter turnout was 58.5%, fourth lowest in Alberta in 1993.

Member of Parliament: Art Hanger; **Party:** Reform; **Occupation:** Police officer; **Education:** University of Calgary; **Age:** 50 (Feb. 19, 1943); **Year first elected to the House of Commons:** 1993

48005 Calgary Northeast

A: Political Profile

i) Voting Behaviour

	% 1993	% 1988	Change 1988-93
Conservative	11.3	54.7	-43.4
Liberal	32.3	16.2	16.1
NDP	2.8	15.5	-12.7
Reform	44.4	13	31.4
Other	9.3	0.6	8.7

% Turnout	58.5	Total Ballots (#)	46616
Rejected Ballots (#)	166	% Margin of Victory	21.4
Rural Polls, 1988 (#)	0	Urban Polls, 1988 (#)	196
% Yes - 1992	38.2	% No - 1992	61.5

ii) Campaign Financing

	# of Donations	Total $ Value	% of Limit Spent
Conservative	57	66705	82*
Liberal	345	73295	90.4
NDP	5	33485	51.3
Reform	93	31531	53.5
Other	133	37288	

B: Ethno-Linguistic Profile

% English Home Language	83.9	% French Home Language	0.4
% Official Bilingual	4.8	% Other Home Language	15.7
% Catholics	27.3	% Protestants	38.8
% Aboriginal Peoples	1.8	% Immigrants	26

C: Socio-Economic Profile

Average Family Income $	45447	Median Family Income $	43633
% Low Income Families	19.8	Average Home Price $	111400
% Home Owners	68	% Unemployment	9.1
% Labour Force Participation	78.4	% Managerial-Administrative	8.9
% Self-Employed	7.1	% University Degrees	6.5
% Movers	59.2		

D: Industrial Profile

% Manufacturing	12.1	% Service Sector	15.7
% Agriculture	0.6	% Mining	4.2
% Forestry	0.1	% Fishing	0
% Government Services	4.5	% Business Services	6.9

E: Homogeneity Measures

Ethnic Diversity Index	0.18	Religious Homogeneity Index	0.29
Sectoral Concentration Index	0.49	Income Disparity Index	4

F: Physical Setting Characteristics

Total Population	124290	Area (km²)	94
Population Density (pop/km²)	1322.2		

* Tentative value, due to the existence of unpaid campaign expenses.

Calgary Southeast

Constituency Number: 48006

Calgary Southeast was created in 1986 out of two very different ridings: the working-class East constituency and the wealthier South district (there was also a very small section of Bow River). It is the largest riding in Calgary geographically (162 sq. km), and the fourth largest in the province in population (119,738). Its population is British in the first instance, with sizeable French, German, Ukrainian and Chinese communities; almost two per cent are aboriginal peoples. Just under twenty per cent (18.7%) are immigrants and English is spoken in more than nine out of ten (91.3%) local homes; almost 6% of the population are bilingual. Just under three-quarters of the population is either Protestant (46.1%) or Catholic (26.0%); almost 6% are Jewish.

The local economy is a mixture of manufacturing (11.5% - the constituency is divided by Calgary's Industrial Park), small business (business services account for 8% of all local jobs), and other service sector work: almost 45% work in the tertiary sector generally, with just under 5% working for government, a very low rate compared to the province as a whole. Almost thirteen per cent are managers or administrators and over eight per cent are self-employed. There is also a noticeable element of local employment who work in the energy/mining sector (5.6%). Average family incomes are over $5,000 above the provincial rate, but local house prices are more than $22,000 above the average for Alberta. They are far from the most expensive in the metropolitan region, however, and more than seven in ten own their own.

As a new constituency, there was no incumbent; in 1988, former Peter Lougheed executive assistant and Brian Mulroney advisor Lee Richardson won the seat with more than six in ten of the local votes. Richardson had had to overcome criticism that he lived in Ottawa (he was originally from Calgary) and that he was parachuted into the new riding. There was also local criticism of how he had avoided bankruptcy while working for the Premier in 1981. In the 1988 election, the local NDP (represented by a former provincial vice president) were just ahead of both Reform (who captured third place with 12.8%) and the local Liberals (at 10.2%). Local Rhinos won more votes than either CoR or Social Credit.

At the 1993 election call, Tory incumbent Lee Richardson sought a second term against six contenders. The Reform Party nominated Jan Brown, a self-employed Calgary business management consultant who emphasized Reform's economic program. National Energy Board Engineer Quoi Nguyen was the Liberal Party standard-bearer; the NDP was represented by University of Calgary environmental studies student Neale Smith, who saw jobs and the environment as the key issues. Information analyst Jocelyne Wandler was the candidate for the National Party, and there was also a Natural Law and a Canada Party representative. The vote counting produced another Reform victory in Alberta. First-timer Jan Brown won almost sixty per cent of all votes, an increase from 1988 for Reform of 47% and the eighth highest Reform return in the country. Tory incumbent Lee Richardson managed second place, but saw his vote fall almost 43%, just slightly less than the Reform gain. The Liberal campaign, centred on 'standing up for the people', was hurt by the disclosure that its candidate, Quoi Nguyen, was facing outstanding criminal charges of assault and forcible confinement from an incident the previous summer. The Liberal vote in the riding was the tenth lowest in all of Canada The local NDP vote also dropped - down almost ten per cent from 1988; that left Neale Smith with just 3.4%, not far ahead of the local National Party representative, Jocelyne Wandler, at 2%. Natural Law outpointed Canada Party 443 votes to 148 for the last 1.1% of the riding votes. Voter turnout was right at the provincial rate (65.1%).

Member of Parliament: Jan Brown; **Party:** Reform; **Occupation:** Business management consultant; **Education:** BEd, MA, University of British Columbia, University of Calgary; **Age:** 46 (June 23, 1947); **Year first elected to the House of Commons:** 1993

48006 Calgary Southeast

A: Political Profile
i) Voting Behaviour

	% 1993	% 1988	Change 1988-93
Conservative	20.1	62.7	-42.6
Liberal	13.6	10.2	3.4
NDP	3.4	13.2	-9.8
Reform	59.9	12.8	47.1
Other	3.1	1.1	2

% Turnout	65.1	Total Ballots (#)	56255
Rejected Ballots (#)	172	% Margin of Victory	42.9
Rural Polls, 1988 (#)	0	Urban Polls, 1988 (#)	213
% Yes - 1992	43.4	% No - 1992	56.4

ii) Campaign Financing

	# of Donations	Total $ Value	% of Limit Spent
Conservative	204	84842	78.2
Liberal	20	14131	19.9
NDP	4	2897	1.4
Reform	116	68134	55.7
Other	6	266	

B: Ethno-Linguistic Profile

% English Home Language	91.3	% French Home Language	0.5
% Official Bilingual	5.8	% Other Home Language	8.2
% Catholics	26	% Protestants	46.1
% Aboriginal Peoples	1.7	% Immigrants	18.7

C: Socio-Economic Profile

Average Family Income $	57179	Median Family Income $	50936
% Low Income Families	17.1	Average Home Price $	133099
% Home Owners	70.9	% Unemployment	8.4
% Labour Force Participation	77	% Managerial-Administrative	12.5
% Self-Employed	8.1	% University Degrees	11.3
% Movers	57		

D: Industrial Profile

% Manufacturing	11.5	% Service Sector	13.1
% Agriculture	0.6	% Mining	5.6
% Forestry	0.1	% Fishing	0
% Government Services	4.4	% Business Services	8

E: Homogeneity Measures

Ethnic Diversity Index	0.22	Religious Homogeneity Index	0.33
Sectoral Concentration Index	0.47	Income Disparity Index	10.9

F: Physical Setting Characteristics

Total Population	119738	Area (km²)	162
Population Density (pop/km²)	739.1		

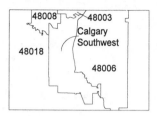

Calgary Southwest

Constituency Number: 48007

Calgary Southwest was created in 1986, but it is comprised of over 90% of the former Calgary South constituency. It is a largely affluent, professional area of the city. British make up the largest ethnic group in a population of 125,245, the second most populous in the province. Over eighteen per cent of the constituency is immigrant and a little more than seven per cent non-citizens, but more than 95% of the residents use English as their home language; almost 8% are bilingual. More than three-quarters are Protestant (49.7%) or Catholic (25.7%); just over 6% are Jewish. Nearly eighteen per cent of the residents are managers or administrators, and over half of all workers locally are in the service sector: ten per cent in business services and five per cent with government. Another ten per cent are self-employed. Seven per cent work in local manufacturing, and the energy/mining sector, with over nine per cent of area employment is fourteenth highest in Canada in this area. The education level - as measured by university degree completion - is right at the provincial average. Average family income ($69,640) is amongst the top fifteen in the country. Local income transfers are half the rate for the province as a whole, and area unemployment is a point below the Alberta overall rate. House prices are at $166,157, about $56,000 above the Alberta average; still almost 70% in the riding own their own dwellings.

Politically, south Calgary has been predominantly Conservative. As part of Calgary West it returned R.B. Bennett in 1925 and 1926, and acclaimed him in 1930. Bennett held the seat in 1935 while the Conservative Government was going down to defeat. Liberals won in 1940, but the area returned to the Conservatives in 1945, electing A.L. Smith. Tory Smith held the seat through the 1962 general election, with one exception (when another Tory held the seat). In the Pearson victory in 1963, Liberal cattleman/ businessman Harry Hayes took Calgary South. Hayes lost to the Conservatives in 1965 (by 115 votes), but another Liberal took the seat back in 1968. The Tories picked up the seat again in 1972, and held it in 1974. Another Conservative won again in 1979 and 1980. In 1984, Bobbie Sparrow, with business experience as a company president in 'the oilpatch', won Calgary South for the first time. She took more than 77% of all riding votes, leaving the Liberals just ahead of the local NDP. In Calgary Southwest in 1988, Sparrow, now Commons Energy, Mines and Resources Committee Chair, saw her vote shrink almost twelve points, still a sixth Tory victory in a row in the constituency and almost two-thirds of the local votes. Liberals again edged out the NDP, but for third place this time; Reform took second with 13.4% of the votes. In 1992, Calgary Southwest was the only constituency in Alberta - and only one of two in the West - to vote 'Yes' in the constitutional referendum. The margin was close, but 50.5% of the voters were positive about the Charlottetown Accord.

In the 1993 general election, Sparrow faced the local electorate for the third time as a Cabinet Minister - for Natural Resources - against management consultant and national Reform Party leader Preston Manning. Bill Richards, a local businessman for the Liberals, Catherine Rose, a Calgary chemist for the NDP, Lea Russell, a dental hygienist for the National Party, and Green and Natural Law Party representatives and two Independents rounded out the field. Alberta Premier Ralph Klein, whose own riding covers part of the federal district, campaigned on behalf of Sparrow, and a number of Klein 'insiders' worked on the Conservative campaign stressing the debt and the deficit, traditional Reform concerns. Manning ran on his 'New Canada' theme - one with 'equal' provinces, without debt or deficit, lower levels of business taxation and a much smaller public sector. When the votes were counted Reform Party Leader Preston Manning had won over 61%, the sixth highest level for Reform in the country. Conservative support had plummeted almost 47%. They were still in second place, however. The Liberals, up about five per cent, had third place, but with the second lowest Liberal result in all of Canada. The NDP, dropping 6.5%, were just 0.3% ahead of the local National Party candidate. The other four candidates shared 0.9% of the votes. Area turnout was more than 5% above the provincial average - at 70.8%, fourth highest in Alberta.

Member of Parliament: Preston Manning; **Party:** Reform; **Occupation:** Management consultant; **Education:** BA, University of Alberta; **Age:** 51 (June 10, 1942); **Year first elected to the House of Commons:** 1993

48007 Calgary Southwest

A: Political Profile
i) Voting Behaviour

	% 1993	% 1988	Change 1988-93
Conservative	18.6	65.2	-46.6
Liberal	16.3	11.5	4.8
NDP	1.6	8.1	-6.5
Reform	61.2	13.4	47.8
Other	2.2	1.8	0.4

% Turnout	70.8	Total Ballots (#)	68140
Rejected Ballots (#)	137	% Margin of Victory	44.8
Rural Polls, 1988 (#)	0	Urban Polls, 1988 (#)	223
% Yes - 1992	50.5	% No - 1992	49.2

ii) Campaign Financing

	# of Donations	Total $ Value	% of Limit Spent
Conservative	243	86770	93.1
Liberal	78	55011	90.9
NDP	3	7638	7.2
Reform	314	101462	89.3
Other	24	9341	

B: Ethno-Linguistic Profile

% English Home Language	95.3	% French Home Language	0.4
% Official Bilingual	7.9	% Other Home Language	4.3
% Catholics	25.7	% Protestants	49.7
% Aboriginal Peoples	0.6	% Immigrants	18.3

C: Socio-Economic Profile

Average Family Income $	69640	Median Family Income $	60069
% Low Income Families	11.4	Average Home Price $	166157
% Home Owners	69.9	% Unemployment	6.7
% Labour Force Participation	76.2	% Managerial-Administrative	17.6
% Self-Employed	9.8	% University Degrees	20.2
% Movers	57.2		

D: Industrial Profile

% Manufacturing	7.2	% Service Sector	11.3
% Agriculture	0.5	% Mining	9.1
% Forestry	0	% Fishing	0
% Government Services	5.1	% Business Services	10

E: Homogeneity Measures

Ethnic Diversity Index	0.24	Religious Homogeneity Index	0.35
Sectoral Concentration Index	0.47	Income Disparity Index	13.7

F: Physical Setting Characteristics

Total Population	125245	Area (km²)	79
Population Density (pop/km²)	1585.4		

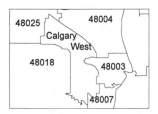

Calgary West

Constituency Number: 48008

Calgary West was left virtually untouched by the 1986 redistribution: 96% of the old constituency remained. It includes a suburban population of 108,178, second smallest of the Calgary seats. The riding includes the University of Calgary and Mount Royal College. It is substantially middle-class and white-collar. It is also largely British, but significant communities of German and Dutch, French, Chinese, Ukrainian and Italian also exist. Almost 8% of the population is bilingual; 94% speak English as their home language. Almost three-quarters are Protestant (49.2%) or Catholic (24.2%); there is a Jewish population of 5.2% of the population. Immigrants make up almost 18% of the riding.

The local economy reflects a class mix: it includes about 5% of all jobs in manufacturing. Almost 9% of jobs are in mining/energy related work, one of the highest rates in the country, but the majority of employment is tertiary, with more than one in ten employed in business services; almost the same number are self-employed and almost 8% work for government. Fourteen per cent are managers or administrators. Local education levels are high - over two in ten residents have university degrees; the provincial average is 11.2%. Average family income levels are more than $9,000 above the provincial rate; average house prices are over $40,000 above Alberta as a whole, but six in ten of the constituency are home-owners. Area unemployment (at 7.5%) and income transfer support (at 7.2%) are both below the pattern across the province as a whole.

The political traditions of the area are Conservative: as Calgary West, it returned Conservative Leader and Prime Minister R.B. Bennett four times between 1925 and 1935, then other Tories in every election (except 1940) up to 1963. They took the seat back in 1965, and have held it ever since. In 1979 Jim Hawkes, a University of Calgary social work professor won the area for the Conservatives. Hawkes, who was re-elected in 1980 and 1984, served as the Mulroney Government House Leader. In 1984, Hawkes won almost three-quarters of all votes, leaving the Liberals and NDP 'dead even'. In 1988, with free trade the central issue, the Conservative vote fell fifteen points, but that still left the incumbent with an overall majority (58.5%); local Liberals fell to third place but stayed ahead of the NDP. Reform, represented by Hawkes' former parliamentary assistant, university economics instructor Stephen Harper, was second with 16.6%.

In 1993, Hawkes sought a fifth term: he again confronted Reform's Stephen Harper, as well as six other contenders. Harper, a founding member of Reform, was helped by a $50,000 ad campaign by the National Citizens' Coalition targeting Hawkes for his support of Bill C-114, the proposed legislation to curtail third-party election spending. Harper stressed the failure of the Tories to deal with the deficit and debt. Liberal Karen Gainer, a local lawyer, was making her second run at Parliament. Rudy Rogers, an accounting consultant, was the NDP candidate. National, Natural Law, Green and Christian Heritage Party candidates represented the remainder of the 1993 slate. When the results were tallied, Stephen Harper had won Calgary West, with over half the total votes. Fourteen-year incumbent Jim Hawkes saw his vote support fall almost 43%; he was left in third place - with under 16% - behind Liberal Karen Gainer, who took over one-quarter of the riding's votes. The NDP - down almost ten per cent - was left just 0.2% ahead of Kathleen McNeil, a Mount Royal college student representing the National Party. Natural Law, Green and Christian Heritage shared the remaining 1.6% support in that order. Local turnout was 66.3% , a point above the provincial rate.

Member of Parliament: Stephen Harper; **Party:** Reform; **Occupation:** Economist; **Education:** BA, MA, University of Calgary; **Age:** 34 (1959); **Year first elected to the House of Commons:** 1993

48008 Calgary West

A: Political Profile

i) Voting Behaviour

	% 1993	% 1988	Change 1988-93
Conservative	15.7	58.5	-42.8
Liberal	26.5	12.6	13.9
NDP	2.1	11.6	-9.5
Reform	52.3	16.6	35.7
Other	3.5	0.7	2.8

% Turnout	66.3	Total Ballots (#)	57954
Rejected Ballots (#)	133	% Margin of Victory	29.3
Rural Polls, 1988 (#)	0	Urban Polls, 1988 (#)	203
% Yes - 1992	48.4	% No - 1992	51.4

ii) Campaign Financing

	# of Donations	Total $ Value	% of Limit Spent
Conservative	208	33518	87.3
Liberal	214	39689	58.9
NDP	3	1998	0.7
Reform	176	57659	72.1
Other	27	21624	

B: Ethno-Linguistic Profile

% English Home Language	94	% French Home Language	0.5
% Official Bilingual	7.7	% Other Home Language	5.6
% Catholics	24.2	% Protestants	49.2
% Aboriginal Peoples	1.8	% Immigrants	17.8

C: Socio-Economic Profile

Average Family Income $	60988	Median Family Income $	51300
% Low Income Families	17.3	Average Home Price $	150625
% Home Owners	59.6	% Unemployment	7.5
% Labour Force Participation	73.2	% Managerial-Administrative	13.9
% Self-Employed	9.8	% University Degrees	20.3
% Movers	56.7		

D: Industrial Profile

% Manufacturing	5	% Service Sector	14.7
% Agriculture	0.7	% Mining	8.6
% Forestry	0.2	% Fishing	0
% Government Services	7.7	% Business Services	10.1

E: Homogeneity Measures

Ethnic Diversity Index	0.22	Religious Homogeneity Index	0.34
Sectoral Concentration Index	0.49	Income Disparity Index	15.9

F: Physical Setting Characteristics

Total Population	108178	Area (km²)	79
Population Density (pop/km²)	1369.3		

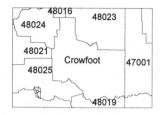

Crowfoot

Constituency Number: 48009

Crowfoot covers 37,700 sq. km of east-central Alberta, from Red Deer in the west to the Saskatchewan border, and from Camrose and the Battle River in the north to the Red Deer River above Medicine Hat in the south. Stettler and Camrose are the only two large centres, with smaller agricultural communities like Viking, Wainwright, Hanna, Drumheller and Coronation. A majority of its polls are rural, reflecting the farming nature of the local economy: well over one-quarter of all jobs (27.2%) are in agriculture, the ninth highest level in Canada, and many of the service jobs locally are in support of farming/ranching. Over one-quarter are self-employed in the constituency (the seventh highest rate in all of Canada) and ten per cent are managers or administrators. Government services add another 5.4% to the local economy, business services about half that. There is also an important mining sector - over 5% of all local jobs. Local manufacturing is the sixth lowest in the country. Unemployment is exceedingly low (4.9%), the ninth lowest level of any riding in Canada, but income support by government transfers is almost three points above the average for the province. The riding is predominantly British and 97% of all residents speak English as their home language; about two-thirds are Protestant. French home language is seventh lowest in all of Canada, though 2.4% reported being bilingual in the 1991 census. There are also German, Ukrainian, French and Dutch communities, though immigrants make up less than 7% of the populace. Average family incomes are below the provincial norm by more than $7,000, but three-quarters of the riding residents own their own homes; these homes are valued at $70,111, more than $40,000 less than the provincial average. The riding also has a fairly stable population; mobility rates are low. Educational levels locally are below the Alberta norm: just over 6% have degrees, almost five points below the level across the province.

Initially as the riding of Acadia, created in 1924 its residents have elected a Progressive (1925), United Farmers (1926 and 1930), Social Credit (1935 to 1957, V. Quelch), Conservative Jack Horner, from 1958 - through its change to Crowfoot - to 1974. Horner won the 1974 race by almost 15,000 votes. When Horner crossed the floor to sit as a Liberal, he lost the subsequent 1979 general election: Conservative Arnold Malone won the seat for the first time, taking 77.1% of all votes. In 1980, Malone again defeated Jack Horner, with a margin of just under 20,000 votes. Malone and the Conservatives held the seat in 1984, again with support of over 77% of the constituents. The 1988 results included a decline in Tory fortunes locally, but incumbent MP Malone held more than half the votes (53.7%) in the end; Reform representative Jack Ramsay, a former Independent Party of Alberta Leader and business consultant made a strong showing, taking 32.1% of the local votes. Liberals and New Democrats fell to single figures. In 1992, more than two-thirds of the riding voted 'No.'

In the 1993 general election, Reform's Jack Ramsay, a former RCMP officer and business consultant did not face an incumbent. MP Arnold Malone had resigned after heart surgery. In his place, the Conservatives selected Brian Heidecker, a grain and cattle farmer from Coronation. The Liberal candidate was Darryl Sandford, a Three Hills barber and California Bible Institute graduate with Central American aid experience; New Democrats nominated Berend Witling, a NAIT graduate, Edmonton steam engineer, and provincial party executive member. An Alberta Stock Exchange floor trader represented Natural Law and an Independent rounded out the field. The voters' choice was clear: Reform's Jack Ramsay took almost two-thirds of all votes, the highest vote percentage for Reform in the country; the Conservatives fell 36%, but held second place; Liberals were third (with one of their twelve lowest returns in 1993) and the NDP were down 5.3% to 2.4% overall. Natural Law and Canadian Economic Community Independent candidates shared the last 1%.

Member of Parliament: Jack Ramsay; **Party:** Reform; **Occupation:** Business consultant; **Education:** RCMP Training; **Age:** 56 (1937); **Year first elected to the House of Commons:** 1993

48009 Crowfoot

A: Political Profile
i) Voting Behaviour

	% 1993	% 1988	Change 1988-93
Conservative	18	53.7	-35.7
Liberal	12.6	6.6	6
NDP	2.4	7.7	-5.3
Reform	66	32.1	33.9
Other	1	0	1

% Turnout	71.3	Total Ballots (#)	35865
Rejected Ballots (#)	80	% Margin of Victory	49
Rural Polls, 1988 (#)	96	Urban Polls, 1988 (#)	53
% Yes - 1992	31.5	% No - 1992	68.2

ii) Campaign Financing

	# of Donations	Total $ Value	% of Limit Spent
Conservative	136	34772	99.2
Liberal	31	8743	13.6*
NDP	2	1267	0.4
Reform	149	43216	66.3
Other	3	249	

B: Ethno-Linguistic Profile

% English Home Language	97	% French Home Language	0.1
% Official Bilingual	2.4	% Other Home Language	3
% Catholics	18.6	% Protestants	65.7
% Aboriginal Peoples	1.1	% Immigrants	6.9

C: Socio-Economic Profile

Average Family Income $	44491	Median Family Income $	38599
% Low Income Families	13.6	Average Home Price $	70111
% Home Owners	75.4	% Unemployment	4.9
% Labour Force Participation	71.5	% Managerial-Administrative	9.8
% Self-Employed	25.5	% University Degrees	6.4
% Movers	37.8		

D: Industrial Profile

% Manufacturing	3.5	% Service Sector	11.1
% Agriculture	27.2	% Mining	5.2
% Forestry	0.1	% Fishing	0
% Government Services	5.4	% Business Services	2.1

E: Homogeneity Measures

Ethnic Diversity Index	0.26	Religious Homogeneity Index	0.47
Sectoral Concentration Index	0.37	Income Disparity Index	13.2

F: Physical Setting Characteristics

Total Population	69717	Area (km²)	37700
Population Density (pop/km²)	1.8		

* Tentative value, due to the existence of unpaid campaign expenses.

Edmonton East

Constituency Number: 48010

Edmonton East was altered in the 1986 redistribution: it retained the largely working-class, multicultural makeup of the old East constituency and added a third from the Edmonton North riding. Its population of 94,889 left it in the middle of federal constituencies in the province. It has a very high number of aboriginal peoples - eight per cent. Almost one-quarter (22.7%) of the voters are immigrants. One in ten are not citizens and English home-language use - at under 85% - is amongst the lowest levels in Alberta; more than 5% are bilingual. Catholics slightly outnumber Protestants, unusual in western Canada, and almost one in ten of the residents are Jewish.

Area unemployment is high for the province - five points above the overall rate; income transfer support is also high - at 14.4%, just under five points above the provincial rate. The working-class nature of the riding is further identified by average family incomes: they are at $39,118 more than $12,000 below the provincial average, unusually low for a metropolitan area. House prices in the constituency are $17,000 below the provincial average. This is unusual in a major metropolitan area. Just over four in ten (42.7%) managed to own their own homes. This low home ownership rate may be partly a product of population mobility as well: in Edmonton East, almost 28% moved over a one-year period, the sixth highest rate of population shift in all of Canada. Half of the local employment is in service work and a further one in ten worked in area manufacturing. Over eight per cent work for governmental organizations in the riding. Self-employment rates were low, as were managerial positions; education rates in the constituency were almost 5% below the provincial average (for attainment of a university degree).

Politically, Edmonton East was created in 1914, nine years after Alberta was granted provincial status. It returned a Progressive in 1921, a Conservative in 1925, and a Liberal in 1926. That pattern of loyalty continued through to 1953 - electing a Conservative, Social Credit, Liberal, Social Credit and Liberal between 1930 and 1949. In 1953 a Socred was elected; he was re-elected in 1957, the first MP re-elected (with the exception of 1908 and 1911) in Edmonton East. In the landslide Diefenbaker victory of 1958, Greek businessman William Storeyko won the seat from the Social Credit. He was re-elected in 1962, 1963, 1965, 1968, 1972, and 1974. In most elections Liberals were in second place, and Tory margins of victory were significant. In the 1979 general election, the seven-time Tory was replaced by Conservative Bill Yurko. He had twice the votes of the Liberals. Yurko won in 1980, again with double the votes of the Liberals. In 1984, internal Conservative squabbles saw incumbent Yurko running as an Independent, and stripping votes from the official Conservative candidate, Bill Lesick. Lesick still took the seat with just over half of all votes. In 1986 the NDP, normally third federally, took the equivalent provincial seat. In the 1988 general election, Ross Harris, a broadcaster and NDP research director 'stole the seat', defeating Lesick by a 1.7% margin. It was the first NDP victory in a federal election in the history of Alberta. In 1992, almost 64% locally voted 'No'.

In 1993, Harris faced Liberal Judy Bethel, a city councillor, former stock broker, and business owner; home economist Linda Robertson represented Reform (in 1988, Reform had taken 4.4% of the votes); Jim Musson, an Edmonton writer was National Party candidate, and Cor Labots, a former AGT engineer/technician, won the Christian Heritage nod; they had won 2% support locally the last time out. All local candidates except Reform emphasized jobs and the economy; for Reform the key issues were law and order and controls on government spending. Despite that general policy agreement, Harris lost his seat in 1993; he placed third, with 22.1%; the Liberal just edged out Reform - 33% to 32.6%, a difference of 115 votes. The Conservatives were left with just 7.4%; and the National Party with 2.9%. Christian Heritage, Natural Law, Green, Canada and an Independent shared 2% in that order.

Member of Parliament: Judy Bethel; **Party:** Liberal; **Occupation:** Stock broker/business owner; **Education:** BA, University of North Dakota; **Age:** 50 (1943); **Year first elected to the House of Commons:** 1993

48010 Edmonton East

A: Political Profile

i) Voting Behaviour

	% 1993	% 1988	Change 1988-93
Conservative	7.4	36.5	-29.1
Liberal	33	18.2	14.8
NDP	22.1	38.2	-16.1
Reform	32.6	4.4	28.2
Other	4.9	2.7	2.2

% Turnout	54	Total Ballots (#)	36364
Rejected Ballots (#)	193	% Margin of Victory	4.5
Rural Polls, 1988 (#)	0	Urban Polls, 1988 (#)	170
% Yes - 1992	36.1	% No - 1992	63.6

ii) Campaign Financing

	# of Donations	Total $ Value	% of Limit Spent
Conservative	108	33354	78.4
Liberal	88	36248	74.7
NDP	3	64842	82.2
Reform	94	38247	51.7
Other	68	15892	

B: Ethno-Linguistic Profile

% English Home Language	84.8	% French Home Language	0.5
% Official Bilingual	5.6	% Other Home Language	14.7
% Catholics	34.5	% Protestants	33.1
% Aboriginal Peoples	8	% Immigrants	22.7

C: Socio-Economic Profile

Average Family Income $	39118	Median Family Income $	34715
% Low Income Families	33.5	Average Home Price $	93106
% Home Owners	42.7	% Unemployment	12.6
% Labour Force Participation	66.9	% Managerial-Administrative	7.6
% Self-Employed	5.3	% University Degrees	6.8
% Movers	58.2		

D: Industrial Profile

% Manufacturing	10.3	% Service Sector	18.5
% Agriculture	1.2	% Mining	1.9
% Forestry	0.2	% Fishing	0.1
% Government Services	8.3	% Business Services	5.4

E: Homogeneity Measures

Ethnic Diversity Index	0.15	Religious Homogeneity Index	0.29
Sectoral Concentration Index	0.47	Income Disparity Index	11.3

F: Physical Setting Characteristics

Total Population	94889	Area (km²)	61
Population Density (pop/km²)	1555.6		

Edmonton North

Constituency Number: 48011

Edmonton North was created in the redistribution following the 1974 general election. It was subject to another (very small) redistribution again in 1986. A constituency of 116,650, it was the sixth most populous in Alberta. The largest ethnic group locally is British but there is a significant Ukrainian community and aboriginal peoples make up just under 3% of the local population. Catholics slightly outnumber Protestants, each making up a little more than one-third of the riding; almost 12% are Jewish. Over 22% of the residents are immigrants, and just under 9% non-citizens, so it is not surprising that just 86.5% of the area speak English as their home language; almost 6% are bilingual.

The local economy includes a sizeable light manufacturing sector - almost one in ten jobs; the service sector accounts for half of all local work, with 11.5% in government and just under 5% in business. Almost 9% are managers or administrators; and just under 7% self-employed. Average family wages are below the provincial average, by $4,000, and home prices by a little over $7,000. Two-thirds of all residents own their own homes. Area unemployment is about a point and a half above the norm provincially, but income support payments almost a point below. The riding's level of education (by university degrees) is below the average for Alberta by about 3%.

The riding has been Conservative since its establishment. Steve Paproski, first elected to the House of Commons in 1968 - in Edmonton Centre - and re-elected there in 1972 and 1974, won the new Edmonton North seat in the 1979 general election, with a margin of over 14,000 votes. Joe Clark appointed the Polish-born MP Minister of State for Fitness and Amateur Sport, and for Multiculturalism. In 1980, Paproski held the seat with a 12,000 margin; and though his vote fell in 1984, he still took more than half of all votes cast in 1984. The Conservative vote continued its slide in 1988, but Paproski won his seventh term with just under 40%, still 7% ahead of the local NDP. Liberal John Loney, a former Ontario Conservative MP (1963-68), placed third. Reform's vote was 5.5%. In 1992, more than six in ten voted 'No' on the Charlottetown Accord.

Just before the 1993 election, incumbent Paproski announced his retirement; he was replaced by 26-year-old management consultant and former Joe Clark assistant, Mitch Panciuk. Reform nominated Ron Mix, a construction contractor and video duplicating plant owner. John Loney, the Liberal defeated in 1988 was re-nominated; Lori Hall, a defeated local candidate and homemaker, was the NDP standard-bearer; Ed Agoto, a city engineering specialist, won the National Party nod; he, along with three others, rounded out the local slate. The NDP, Liberal, and National candidates emphasized jobs and the need for an economic recovery, Reform focused on 'getting our fiscal house in order'. When the results were in Liberal John Loney had just edged out Reform's Ron Mix - 39.5% to 39.1%. The Tory vote fell over 30% and the NDP's more than 25%. That left them in third and fourth place respectively. The National Party was just 2.5% behind the NDP at 4.4%. Natural Law, Canada and an Independent won 0.9% in that order.

Member of Parliament: John Loney; **Party:** Liberal; **Occupation:** Businessperson; **Education:** University of Toronto; **Age:** 66 (Feb. 23, 1929); **Year first elected to the House of Commons:** 1993

48011 Edmonton North

A: Political Profile
i) Voting Behaviour

	% 1993	% 1988	Change 1988-93
Conservative	9.3	40	-30.7
Liberal	39.5	19.5	20
NDP	6.9	32.8	-25.9
Reform	39.1	5.5	33.6
Other	5.3	2.2	3.1

% Turnout	62.8	Total Ballots (#)	49596
Rejected Ballots (#)	97	% Margin of Victory	4.9
Rural Polls, 1988 (#)	0	Urban Polls, 1988 (#)	215
% Yes - 1992	37.2	% No - 1992	62.7

ii) Campaign Financing

	# of Donations	Total $ Value	% of Limit Spent
Conservative	145	37986	57.1
Liberal	93	18037	33.8
NDP	4	21025	26.1*
Reform	126	26784	64.8
Other	60	17953	

B: Ethno-Linguistic Profile

% English Home Language	86.5	% French Home Language	0.5
% Official Bilingual	5.9	% Other Home Language	13
% Catholics	35.8	% Protestants	33.7
% Aboriginal Peoples	2.8	% Immigrants	22.3

C: Socio-Economic Profile

Average Family Income $	47260	Median Family Income $	45034
% Low Income Families	20.3	Average Home Price $	107628
% Home Owners	66.1	% Unemployment	9.1
% Labour Force Participation	74	% Managerial-Administrative	8.8
% Self-Employed	6.6	% University Degrees	6.9
% Movers	52.1		

D: Industrial Profile

% Manufacturing	9.2	% Service Sector	16.3
% Agriculture	0.7	% Mining	1.3
% Forestry	0.2	% Fishing	0
% Government Services	11.5	% Business Services	4.7

E: Homogeneity Measures

Ethnic Diversity Index	0.15	Religious Homogeneity Index	0.29
Sectoral Concentration Index	0.49	Income Disparity Index	4.7

F: Physical Setting Characteristics

Total Population	116650	Area (km²)	186
Population Density (pop/km²)	627.2		

---

* Tentative value, due to the existence of unpaid campaign expenses.

Edmonton Northwest

Constituency Number: 48012

Edmonton Northwest was carved out of five area ridings in 1986; two - working-class Edmonton East, with one quarter, and more affluent Edmonton West, with two-thirds - made up the majority of the new constituency. The larger portion from the north corner of west Edmonton was less wealthy than the southwest part of the city. That left a fairly ethnically diverse riding of 81,170, the fifth least populous in the province. British are the largest group, but significant French, German and Ukrainian populations and increasingly Chinese, Vietnamese and Italian groups, as well as over 5% aboriginal peoples, give a cultural mix to the constituency. Over 22% of the residents are immigrants, and 10% non-citizens. Seven percent are bilingual and just 87.5% speak English at home. The riding had the seventh highest level of 'other home language' in all of Canada. Four in ten are Protestant and three in ten Catholic; Jews add another 8.8% to the riding.

The local economy provides service to the heavy equipment of the oil and related industries. Almost 55% are in the service sector, with 7.5% in business, 8.4% with government, almost 8% self employed and 10% in management and administration. The economic standing of the constituency is also reflected in home incomes: at $43,282, the riding is more than $8,000 below the provincial average. House prices are were only slightly below the provincial norm so it was not surprising that home ownership locally was a low 32.5%, under half the rate for the province. Aside from lack of purchasing power, this was also a factor of mobility: Edmonton Northwest had the fourth highest rate in the country over one year and the tenth highest over a five year period. Unemployment - at 10.9%, more than three points above the norm and income transfer needs - also more than three points above Alberta as a whole, were equally contributing factors. The educational level was actually just above the provincial average however.

As a new constituency, the riding had little direct electoral history, though Edmonton North, West and East had been predominantly Conservative for a number of years. West Edmonton had been the sinecure of Tory Marcel Lambert for years; in 1984, Tory Murray Dorin ran and won. The Conservative vote was down but still almost 55% of all cast. In 1988, incumbent Dorin saw a further drop in the Tory vote - to 40.1%, but still held the seat with a margin of over 6%. The NDP was second with more than one-third of the local votes. Reform was fourth with 7.6% support. In the 1992 referendum, more than four in ten supported 'Yes'.

In 1993, Tory Murray Dorin sought a third term. He was unsuccessful; the Conservative vote fell over 30% to under ten per cent and fourth place. National Party leader, publisher Mel Hurtig was third with 12.8%; Reform candidate Richard Kyler, a small businessman, was second with 35.8%. Just twelve votes ahead was Liberal constitutional law university professor Anne McLellan. She won the seat. Stephanie Michaels of the NDP, an Alberta Treasury information officer on leave, managed only 4.8%. Like the Tories, almost 30% of the NDP votes disappeared. Natural Law, Green and an Independent shared 0.9% in that order. Local turnout was a low 57.3%.

Member of Parliament: Anne McLellan; **Party:** Liberal; **Occupation:** University law professor; **Education:** BA, LL.B, LL.M, University of London (King's College); **Age:** 43 (Aug. 31, 1950); **Year first elected to the House of Commons:** 1993

48012 Edmonton Northwest

A: Political Profile
i) Voting Behaviour

	% 1993	% 1988	Change 1988-93
Conservative	9.9	40.1	-30.2
Liberal	35.8	17.3	18.5
NDP	4.8	34	-29.2
Reform	35.8	7.6	28.2
Other	13.7	1	12.7

% Turnout	57.3	Total Ballots (#)	35295
Rejected Ballots (#)	100	% Margin of Victory	13.7
Rural Polls, 1988 (#)	0	Urban Polls, 1988 (#)	157
% Yes - 1992	41.7	% No - 1992	58

ii) Campaign Financing

	# of Donations	Total $ Value	% of Limit Spent
Conservative	120	30074	46.3*
Liberal	262	50972	78.7
NDP	4	22323	26.7
Reform	83	43811	96.5*
Other	129	70789	

B: Ethno-Linguistic Profile

% English Home Language	87.5	% French Home Language	0.7
% Official Bilingual	7.1	% Other Home Language	11.8
% Catholics	29.9	% Protestants	39.2
% Aboriginal Peoples	5.1	% Immigrants	22.2

C: Socio-Economic Profile

Average Family Income $	43282	Median Family Income $	36069
% Low Income Families	31.8	Average Home Price $	107483
% Home Owners	32.5	% Unemployment	10.9
% Labour Force Participation	67.7	% Managerial-Administrative	10.1
% Self-Employed	7.8	% University Degrees	11.5
% Movers	61.3		

D: Industrial Profile

% Manufacturing	7.5	% Service Sector	17
% Agriculture	0.6	% Mining	1.3
% Forestry	0.2	% Fishing	0
% Government Services	8.4	% Business Services	7.5

E: Homogeneity Measures

Ethnic Diversity Index	0.16	Religious Homogeneity Index	0.29
Sectoral Concentration Index	0.55	Income Disparity Index	16.7

F: Physical Setting Characteristics

Total Population	81170	Area (km²)	93
Population Density (pop/km²)	872.8		

---

*   Tentative value, due to the existence of unpaid campaign expenses.

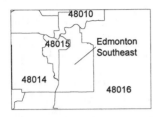

Edmonton Southeast

Constituency Number: 48013

Edmonton Southeast emerged almost entirely from the old Edmonton Strathcona constituency. Its borders - on two sides - are the city limits; in the north, the Saskatchewan River and the CNR line at the west. It has 112,939 residents, seventh largest population in the province. It contains an ethnic mix of British, Ukrainian and South Asian communities. It is a relatively affluent riding with a young population and growing families. Over 22% of the constituency are immigrants and over twelve per cent do not speak English at home, though almost seven per cent are bilingual. Over one and a half per cent of the riding are aboriginal peoples. 70% of the riding is either Protestant (43.5%) or Catholic (25.8%); almost 12% are Jewish.

Incomes in the riding are a little below the provincial average, but Southeast is second amongst Edmonton constituencies. House prices are right at the provincial average and two-thirds of the riding's residents own their own homes. University educational levels are just above the rate for the province. The local economy is more than half service-oriented, with a large manufacturing base (over 10%), much of it energy related. Over 8% work in government service and a slightly smaller number are self employed. Almost 11% are managers or administrators. Area unemployment is less than a point above the provincial rate and income support levels are two points below that for the province.

As Edmonton Strathcona, established in 1952, the area has elected a Liberal (1953), a Social Credit (1957), and after 1958 usually Progressive Conservatives: initially local lawyer Terry Nugent (1958, 1962, 1963, and 1965), then former alderman and economist Hu Harries for the Liberals (1968). Harries was defeated by Tory Doug Roche in 1972, by over 10,000 votes; Roche held the riding in 1974 but shifted to Edmonton South in 1979. Strathcona was held by a former crown prosecutor, David Kilgour of the Progressive Conservatives. Kilgour was a brother-in-law of Liberal John Turner; he was at times a Tory maverick. That perhaps kept him out of the Cabinets of both Joe Clark and Brian Mulroney, despite winning in 1980 and 1984. When Kilgour was asked to leave the Tory caucus over policy disagreements, he re-offered in 1988 in the new Edmonton Southeast constituency, covering much of his old territory. This time he had to face another Conservative nominee. He succeeded in winning the seat again despite his party differences, but subsequently broke with the Party over the GST. In 1992, just over 40% voted 'Yes' in the referendum.

In the 1993 general election, the popular incumbent ran as a Liberal. He faced seven other candidates. In 1988 Kilgour had taken 48.7% of the votes and had a margin of almost 28%; that was well down from his 1984 victory where the margin was just under 50%, but it was still comfortable. The issue of switching parties was not a large one, especially as the GST had been an important part of the break. Jobs, the economy and changes in parole and the criminal justice system stood out as local issues. David Kilgour was re-elected, for the fifth time; he had 46.2% of the votes, just two and a half points below his Tory total in the previous election; the Conservative vote, represented in the candidacy of John Kurian, a local lawyer, fell over 42%. They were left in third place with just 6.4%. That put them ahead of New Democrat Ken Ross, an unemployed physiotherapist, with just 4%. Ross just outdistanced Janet Blond, a teacher, for the National Party (with 2.9%). Aurell Royer, a local high school principal who emphasized the deficit came second with 39.7%; that was up considerably from 1988 when Reform took 10.7%. Natural Law, Green and Canada Party reps shared 0.9% in that order. Local voter turnout was at the provincial rate.

Member of Parliament: David Kilgour; **Party:** Liberal; **Occupation:** Lawyer; **Education:** BA, LL.B, University of Paris; **Age:** 52 (Feb. 18, 1941); **Year first elected to the House of Commons:** 1979

48013 Edmonton Southeast

A: Political Profile

i) Voting Behaviour

	% 1993	% 1988	Change 1988-93
Conservative	6.4	48.7	-42.3
Liberal	46.2	20.8	25.4
NDP	4	18.9	-14.9
Reform	39.7	10.7	29
Other	3.8	0.9	2.9

% Turnout	65.1	Total Ballots (#)	50211
Rejected Ballots (#)	103	% Margin of Victory	6.5
Rural Polls, 1988 (#)	0	Urban Polls, 1988 (#)	201
% Yes - 1992	40.4	% No - 1992	59.5

ii) Campaign Financing

	# of Donations	Total $ Value	% of Limit Spent
Conservative	105	33075	84.8*
Liberal	524	46808	43.9
NDP	3	17935	27.9*
Reform	109	41121	64.6
Other	15	2605	

B: Ethno-Linguistic Profile

% English Home Language	87.6	% French Home Language	1
% Official Bilingual	6.7	% Other Home Language	11.4
% Catholics	25.8	% Protestants	43.5
% Aboriginal Peoples	1.6	% Immigrants	22.1

C: Socio-Economic Profile

Average Family Income $	49644	Median Family Income $	47212
% Low Income Families	16.6	Average Home Price $	110739
% Home Owners	66.3	% Unemployment	8.3
% Labour Force Participation	75.7	% Managerial-Administrative	10.9
% Self-Employed	7.2	% University Degrees	11.9
% Movers	53.5		

D: Industrial Profile

% Manufacturing	11.3	% Service Sector	13.6
% Agriculture	0.6	% Mining	2
% Forestry	0.1	% Fishing	0
% Government Services	8.4	% Business Services	5.2

E: Homogeneity Measures

Ethnic Diversity Index	0.16	Religious Homogeneity Index	0.3
Sectoral Concentration Index	0.49	Income Disparity Index	4.9

F: Physical Setting Characteristics

Total Population	112939	Area (km²)	147
Population Density (pop/km²)	768.3		

* Tentative value, due to the existence of unpaid campaign expenses.

Edmonton Southwest

Constituency Number: 48014

Edmonton Southwest is the most affluent of the city's constituencies; it was created prior to the 1988 election out of almost equal parts of Edmonton South and Edmonton West. It is a mostly suburban riding of detached homes. Its ethnic makeup is, in the first instance, British, but there are also German and Ukrainian communities of note. Just under 20% are immigrants, though over nine in ten use English at home and 8.6% are bilingual. Seven in ten of the constituency are Protestant (43.3%) or Catholic (27.2%); over 9% are Jewish. It did have a highly mobile population - one of the highest in the country. The prosperity of the riding is reflected in several indices: average family incomes are almost $14,000 above the rate for the whole province; over six in ten (a little below the provincial average) own their own homes, but these houses are worth - on average - over $46,000 above the rate for all of Alberta. Area unemployment is slightly below the rate for the province and levels of governmental income support are over four points below the provincial rate. Educational levels in the constituency - as measured by university degrees - are 20.7%, compared to a provincial average of 11.2%. Over fifteen per cent of all jobs are administrative or managerial; over half are service sector, 7% in business and the same for government service. Slightly less than one in ten people are self employed. The local economy includes a small manufacturing component (6.3%) as well, but generally the riding is residential.

This wealthy corner of the city has been very safe territory for the Conservatives: as Edmonton West it had been Tory since 1957, with Marcel Lambert; as Edmonton South it had also been Conservative, with Doug Roche, first elected in 1968. He still held the riding in 1984. Then he was appointed Disarmament Ambassador. Jim Edwards, a local broadcaster, took over the seat after 1988. He served as chair of the House of Commons broadcasting committee and a term as Parliamentary Secretary to Communications and Western Economic Diversification. In 1988 he won over 53% of the local votes; the Liberals were second, over 34% behind, several points ahead of the NDP. Reform was not far behind, with 10.5%.

In 1993, incumbent Jim Edwards ran as President of the Treasury Board. As a Mulroney Cabinet Minister who had supported Kim Campbell's leadership bid, he had hoped for clear sailing locally. Local concerns fluctuated between jobs, social programs and the economy, the deficit and debt, and law and order/crime control. Edwards faced just six competitors: Reform nominated Ian McClelland, a local businessman (president and founder of Colourfast); the Liberals selected Betty MacFarlan, a small (property management) business owner; Colleen Glenn was the choice of the Southwest New Democrats: she was a former postal worker and union activist, now a consultant; Natural Law, a Canadian Economic Community Independent and a Marxist Leninist Independent also ran: the three of them shared 1.4% in that order. Incumbent Tory Cabinet Minister Jim Edwards saw the Conservative vote in the riding drop almost 38%; that left him in third place with just 16.1% support. Reform's Ian McClelland won the race taking 45.5% of the votes; Liberal Betty MacFarlan was second - with one-third of the votes. The local NDP vote also fell considerably - off over twelve points to just 3.7%. Local turnout was more than two points above the provincial turnout rate.

Member of Parliament: Ian McClelland; **Party:** Reform; **Occupation:** Businessperson; **Education:** College courses, NAIT; **Age:** 51 (June 22, 1942); **Year first elected to the House of Commons:** 1993

48014 Edmonton Southwest

A: Political Profile
i) Voting Behaviour

	% 1993	% 1988	Change 1988-93
Conservative	16.1	53.6	-37.5
Liberal	33.5	19.2	14.3
NDP	3.7	15.9	-12.2
Reform	45.5	10.5	35
Other	1.4	0.8	0.6

% Turnout	67.5	Total Ballots (#)	58626
Rejected Ballots (#)	144	% Margin of Victory	13.4
Rural Polls, 1988 (#)	0	Urban Polls, 1988 (#)	230
% Yes - 1992	46	% No - 1992	53.9

ii) Campaign Financing

	# of Donations	Total $ Value	% of Limit Spent
Conservative	244	86115	98.2
Liberal	115	21709	47.8
NDP	4	10561	9.9
Reform	256	46596	82.6
Other	16	2795	

B: Ethno-Linguistic Profile

% English Home Language	91.1	% French Home Language	0.8
% Official Bilingual	8.6	% Other Home Language	8.2
% Catholics	27.2	% Protestants	43.3
% Aboriginal Peoples	2.6	% Immigrants	19.8

C: Socio-Economic Profile

Average Family Income $	65097	Median Family Income $	53910
% Low Income Families	16.5	Average Home Price $	156686
% Home Owners	60.7	% Unemployment	7.5
% Labour Force Participation	75.7	% Managerial-Administrative	15.1
% Self-Employed	9.8	% University Degrees	20.7
% Movers	60		

D: Industrial Profile

% Manufacturing	6.3	% Service Sector	11.2
% Agriculture	0.6	% Mining	1.8
% Forestry	0.2	% Fishing	0
% Government Services	7.9	% Business Services	7.6

E: Homogeneity Measures

Ethnic Diversity Index	0.17	Religious Homogeneity Index	0.31
Sectoral Concentration Index	0.56	Income Disparity Index	17.2

F: Physical Setting Characteristics

Total Population	117758		180
Population Density (pop/km²)	654.2	Area (km²)	

Edmonton Strathcona

Constituency Number: 48015

Edmonton Strathcona was established with the 1952 redistribution. After 1957, with one exception, it elected Conservatives. Most of that constituency became Edmonton Southeast in 1986. Only one third of the old riding kept the name; to that was attached a two-thirds portion of Edmonton South, one of the wealthier areas of the city. The new riding has a population of 93,335, about mid-sized for the province. It is a mixture of British, the largest ethnic group, Germans and Ukrainians and others. Two in ten are immigrants and one in ten are not citizens; a similar percentage (10%) do not speak English as their home language, though over 11% are bilingual. About 70% are Catholic (24.5%) or Protestant (45.8%); over 6% are Jewish. The riding contains the University of Alberta, its largest employer; at 26.4% of the area residents with university degrees, the constituency is the tenth 'most educated' in the country.

The local economy is dependent on service sector/educational employment: most are in tertiary work, 8.8% with government and 7.4% in business; 7.6% are self-employed, and almost 12% are managers or administrators. The other source of employment is in light manufacturing - 7% of all local work. Area unemployment is just below the provincial rate, at 7.5%; income support by government transfers are a point and a half below the Alberta norm. Family incomes are a bit above the rate across the province - about $3500 over. Local house prices are $13,500 over the level in Alberta as a whole. The rate of movers, at almost 25% for a one year period, is fourteenth highest in all of Canada. There is a local home ownership rate of only 45.2% - over twenty points below the provincial average.

As Edmonton Strathcona, established in 1952, the area has elected Liberals (1953), Social Credit (1957) and, after 1958, with one exception, Progressive Conservatives: initially local lawyer Terry Nugent (1958, 1962, 1963 and 1965); then former alderman and economist Hu Harries for the Liberals (1968). Harries was defeated by Tory Doug Roche in 1972, by over 10,000 votes; Roche held the riding in 1974 but shifted to Edmonton South in 1979. Strathcona was then taken over by former crown prosecutor David Kilgour of the Progressive Conservatives. Despite winning in 1980 and 1984, Kilgour did not make it into the cabinets of Joe Clark in 1979 or Brian Mulroney after 1984. (Asked to leave the Tory caucus over policy disagreements, Kilgour re-offered in 1988 in the new Edmonton Southeast constituency; much of the old Strathcona was now in this new riding.) Scott Thorkelson, a former senior federal Conservative Government policy advisor, sought the nomination and won. He then defeated nine other aspirants to be the area MP. His vote total - certainly for Alberta, where most Conservative pluralities were absolute majorities - was a shaky 33.5%; New Democrats at 25.3% and Reform, with 22.2% weren't far behind. Local Liberals managed almost 18%. In the subsequent referendum the riding was fairly evenly split - just 50.9% voted for the 'No' side.

In 1993, incumbent Tory MP Thorkelson faced eight others. The Conservatives lost the seat; their vote fell over 22%, to third place. Reform's Hugh Hanrahan, a 46-year-old high school economics teacher who emphasized 'spending less' won with 39.3%. That was less than one point - 404 votes - ahead of Liberal lawyer Chris Peirce, in second place; Peirce had emphasized 'spending smarter' on job programs like apprenticeships. The local NDP vote fell here, as elsewhere, down over 20%, close to the Conservative decline. That left their candidate Rita Egan, project coordinator for the Edmonton Social Planning Council with just 5.1%. The National Party, represented by retired family counsellor Adrian Greenwood, were less than one point behind (with 4.3% support); the National Party locally had emphasized education, health care, banks and not being totally preoccupied with money. Greens, Natural Law, a Communist Independent, and the Canada Party shared 1.6% in that order. Voter turnout was just below the rate for all of Alberta.

Member of Parliament: Hugh Hanrahan; **Party:** Reform; **Occupation:** High school economics teacher; **Education:** MEd; **Age:** 46 (1947); **Year first elected to the House of Commons:** 1993

48015 Edmonton–Strathcona

A: Political Profile
i) Voting Behaviour

	% 1993	% 1988	Change 1988-93
Conservative	11.3	33.5	-22.2
Liberal	38.5	17.9	20.6
NDP	5.1	25.3	-20.2
Reform	39.3	22.2	17.1
Other	5.9	-3.3	9.2

% Turnout	64.9	Total Ballots (#)	49794
Rejected Ballots (#)	112	% Margin of Victory	6.7
Rural Polls, 1988 (#)	0	Urban Polls, 1988 (#)	221
% Yes - 1992	48.8	% No - 1992	50.9

ii) Campaign Financing

	# of Donations	Total $ Value	% of Limit Spent
Conservative	161	38153	80.8*
Liberal	206	53953	71.1
NDP	6	11200	13.7
Reform	223	36691	78.6
Other	48	10967	

B: Ethno-Linguistic Profile

% English Home Language	90.3	% French Home Language	1.4
% Official Bilingual	11.4	% Other Home Language	8.3
% Catholics	24.5	% Protestants	45.8
% Aboriginal Peoples	1.3	% Immigrants	20.1

C: Socio-Economic Profile

Average Family Income $	55151	Median Family Income $	47544
% Low Income Families	22.8	Average Home Price $	123817
% Home Owners	45.2	% Unemployment	7.5
% Labour Force Participation	72.2	% Managerial-Administrative	11.7
% Self-Employed	7.6	% University Degrees	26.4
% Movers	57.6		

D: Industrial Profile

% Manufacturing	7	% Service Sector	12.6
% Agriculture	0.7	% Mining	2
% Forestry	0.4	% Fishing	0
% Government Services	8.8	% Business Services	7.4

E: Homogeneity Measures

Ethnic Diversity Index	0.17	Religious Homogeneity Index	0.32
Sectoral Concentration Index	0.56	Income Disparity Index	13.8

F: Physical Setting Characteristics

Total Population	93335	Area (km²)	46
Population Density (pop/km²)	2029		

* Tentative value, due to the existence of unpaid campaign expenses.

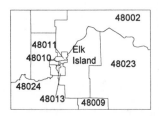

Elk Island

Constituency Number: 48016

Elk Island was a new constituency in 1986; its population of 86,839 was taken largely from the old Pembina riding, with smaller portions from Wetaskiwin and Vegreville. The riding covers over 4,000 sq. km just east of Edmonton's city limits and south and east of the North Saskatchewan River. It includes the smaller communities of Beaumont, Sherwood Park, Fort Saskatchewan and Bruderheim (two thirds of the residents live in these four communities), as well as Elk Island Park (whence the riding's name). British, Germans and Ukrainian ethnic groups predominate in the area, but there is a mixture of others. It is not a riding with a high aboriginal peoples population. English is the overwhelming choice in home language use (97.7%), though there is a relatively high (7.5%) rate of bilingualism. Eight in ten persons are Protestant (54.1%) or Catholic (26.8%); most of the rest declared no religion. It has the same level of residents with university degrees completed as does the province as a whole.

The area economy is tied to petrochemicals and agriculture, with most service sector employment tied to its support; so is area manufacturing, which produces just under 13% of all jobs. Farming provides about half of that, and there is a smaller component (3.2%) associated with the mining industry. Almost nine per cent of those in Elk Island work for government, and over 13% were managers or administrators. It has the 8th lowest rate of unemployment in Canada - at 5.2%, almost two and a half points below an already low provincial jobless rate. Only 6% received income support payments; that was more than three and a half points below the Alberta norm. The relative affluence of the area is reflected as well in family incomes: at $61,216, they are almost $10,000 above the rate for the whole province. House prices are over the provincial average by about $12,000 but almost 87% own their own dwellings; that is the third highest level of home ownership in all of Canada.

Pembina, which made up about 72% of the new constituency, was created after the general election of 1965. In 1968, the riding returned a Conservative MP; they have done so ever since. In 1972, a different Tory was elected and in 1974 a third, Peter Elzinga. He was re-elected in 1979, with a 22,000 vote margin over local Liberals; the NDP had less than half the Grit vote. Elzinga won a third term in 1980, repeating the result of 1979 with 20,000 more votes than the Liberal candidate. In 1984, the incumbent Tory's margin was 57%, this time over a New Democrat. In the 1988 election, in the new Elk Island riding, the Conservatives nominated educator Brian O'Kurley. He took almost half of the votes, more than double the NDP who were just ahead of Reform. Liberals were left in fourth place. Seeking a second term in the 1993 general election, the incumbent Tory faced criticism for his support for the GST; scrapping the GST, taxes, and the deficit seemed to be the predominant local issues. Reform nominated Ken Epp, a NAIT math instructor and Board Chair of Sherwood Park's Christian Academy; Epp's issues were 'controlling spending' and 'true representation'. Jean Boisvert, an AGT service manager was the Liberal choice: he called for controlling the deficit and job creation. Steve Jacobs, a Sherwood Park coin shop owner who felt the Tory record, especially its 'debt', was the key concern, was the NDP nominee; National Party candidate James Steinhubl called for job creation. Natural Law and a Canada Party candidate rounded out the field. In the end, the voters selected Ken Epp of the Reform Party, with 56% of all votes, eleventh highest Reform total in the country. The incumbent Tory MP fell almost 36% to third place. The Liberals took second, up over sixteen points, (to 25.3%). NDP support fell almost twenty per cent - to 2.8%; that was only 0.1% ahead of the National Party candidate. The others received 0.8%. Local turnout was highest in the province, at 73.5%, almost eight points above the Alberta rate.

Member of Parliament: Ken Epp; **Party:** Reform; **Occupation:** College instructor; **Education:** BSc, BEd; **Age:** 54 (1939); **Year first elected to the House of Commons:** 1993

48016 Elk Island

A: Political Profile

i) Voting Behaviour

	% 1993	% 1988	Change 1988-93
Conservative	12.5	48.2	-35.7
Liberal	25.3	9	16.3
NDP	2.8	22.4	-19.6
Reform	56	20.1	35.9
Other	3.5	0.3	3.2

% Turnout	73.5	Total Ballots (#)	45965
Rejected Ballots (#)	59	% Margin of Victory	34.2
Rural Polls, 1988 (#)	92	Urban Polls, 1988 (#)	88
% Yes - 1992	37.4	% No - 1992	62.3

ii) Campaign Financing

	# of Donations	Total $ Value	% of Limit Spent
Conservative	75	44979	79.7
Liberal	96	25963	42.4
NDP	29	2380	0.9
Reform	124	40760	52.4
Other	3	4950	

B: Ethno-Linguistic Profile

% English Home Language	97.7	% French Home Language	0.6
% Official Bilingual	7.5	% Other Home Language	1.6
% Catholics	26.8	% Protestants	54.1
% Aboriginal Peoples	0.9	% Immigrants	9.4

C: Socio-Economic Profile

Average Family Income $	61216	Median Family Income $	57769
% Low Income Families	6.5	Average Home Price $	122412
% Home Owners	86.8	% Unemployment	5.2
% Labour Force Participation	78.4	% Managerial-Administrative	13.6
% Self-Employed	11.9	% University Degrees	11.2
% Movers	45.5		

D: Industrial Profile

% Manufacturing	12.4	% Service Sector	10.6
% Agriculture	6	% Mining	3.2
% Forestry	0.2	% Fishing	0
% Government Services	8.8	% Business Services	4.3

E: Homogeneity Measures

Ethnic Diversity Index	0.23	Religious Homogeneity Index	0.39
Sectoral Concentration Index	0.39	Income Disparity Index	5.6

F: Physical Setting Characteristics

Total Population	86839	Area (km²)	4080
Population Density (pop/km²)	21.3		

48018   48019

Lethbridge

59010

Lethbridge

Constituency Number: 48017

Lethbridge is a 10,700 sq. km riding in southwestern Alberta, bordered on two sides by the United States and British Columbia. Its population of 100,127 is a mixture of British, German and Dutch ethnic communities. As Alberta's traditionalist/fundamentalist Bible Belt, over six in ten of its residents are Protestant, with large evangelical and Mormon populations. All but five per cent are citizens (immigrants make up 13% of the local population) and English is the home language in 93% of the cases. There is also a large number of aboriginal peoples - over one in ten, including the Blood Indian Reserve; local native issues, particularly over issues like the Oldman River dam, have been area hotspots.

The riding economy is split between agriculture (11.5% of all jobs) and manufacturing (8.3%) with related service work making up just under half of all employment, 8.4% with government and just over 3% in business. Area house prices are about $20,000 below the average for Alberta, and average family incomes in Lethbridge are over $5,000 less. Over two thirds (68.6%) of residents own their own homes. Ten per cent have university degrees, a point below Alberta as a whole. An equal number work as administrators or managers. Area unemployment is less than a per cent above the provincial rate, though income from government transfer payments to individuals is over 2.5% above.

Lethbridge elected Progressives in 1921 and 1925, then a United Farmer in 1926; in 1930, the first Conservative was elected. In 1935, J.H. Blackmore was elected for Social Credit; Blackmore had a political lock on the Lethbridge riding until he was defeated (trying for his seventh election) in the 1958 Conservative landslide by local Progressive Conservative Deane Gundlock, a farmer and former president of the Alberta Farmers Union. Gundlock held the seat in 1962, 1963, 1965, and 1968, each time with comfortable majorities. He was replaced by another Conservative, Ken Hurlburt, in 1972 and 1974. In 1979, the third Tory MP in a row was elected: Blaine Thacker, an area lawyer. Thacker held Lethbridge easily in 1980, 1984, and 1988. In the 1988 contest he took almost 59% of the votes, about 40% ahead of the second place Liberals. In that election, Christian Heritage, with significant Dutch Reform Church support (they spent almost 80% of that allowed under election expenses legislation, less than two per cent behind than the local Conservatives) managed 6.4% of the votes; Reform scored an almost equivalent level of local support. In the subsequent referendum on the Charlottetown Accord, the voters of Lethbridge were almost 61% on the 'No' side.

In 1993, the incumbent Conservative Member of Parliament did not seek a fourth term. In his place the local Progressive Conservatives selected Dean Lien, a Warner area farmer. Liberals nominated John W. McGee, a Lethbridge software designer. The Reform candidate was Lethbridge farmer Ray Speaker. Speaker, first elected as a Social Credit MLA in 1963, served as Minister in the governments of E.C. Manning and Manning's successor Harry Strom. Speaker continued to be elected to the Alberta legislature after the 1971 urban collapse of Social Credit and until after the complete demise of the party. By the early 1990s he had turned his attention to federal politics and Reform. The New Democrats named Doug Petherbridge, a retired university professor, as their standard-bearer. National Party candidate Carson Tannant, a Magrath businessman, and a Natural Law representative rounded out the local election slate. When the general election results were tallied, Reform's Ray Speaker had won over half (52.6%) of the votes in Lethbridge, the fifteenth best showing for Reform in the country. His closest rival was Liberal John McGee, who captured 25% of the votes. The Conservative vote fell over 43%, leaving their candidate with only 15% support. The NDP vote also fell - 7% - leaving them behind the National Party in the riding. National's Carson Tannant had 3.4% to the NDP's 2.8%; that left just 0.5 for Natural Law. Voter turnout in Lethbridge was 65.7%, just above the provincial rate.

Member of Parliament: Ray Speaker; **Party:** Reform; **Occupation:** Farmer/teacher; **Education:** BEd, MEd, University of Alberta; **Age** 57 (April 23, 1936); **Year first elected to the House of Commons:** 1993

48017 Lethbridge

A: Political Profile
i) Voting Behaviour

	% 1993	% 1988	Change 1988-93
Conservative	15.2	58.4	-43.2
Liberal	25.5	18.6	6.9
NDP	2.8	9.8	-7
Reform	52.6	6.8	45.8
Other	3.9	6.4	-2.5

% Turnout	65.7	Total Ballots (#)	46744
Rejected Ballots (#)	136	% Margin of Victory	31
Rural Polls, 1988 (#)	83	Urban Polls, 1988 (#)	125
% Yes - 1992	38.9	% No - 1992	60.8

ii) Campaign Financing

	# of Donations	Total $ Value	% of Limit Spent
Conservative	134	27565	65.3
Liberal	183	38907	61.3
NDP	4	11024	8.9
Reform	381	74921	85.8
Other	15	3571	

B: Ethno-Linguistic Profile

% English Home Language	93	% French Home Language	0.2
% Official Bilingual	4.2	% Other Home Language	6.8
% Catholics	22.4	% Protestants	61
% Aboriginal Peoples	10.2	% Immigrants	13

C: Socio-Economic Profile

Average Family Income $	46072	Median Family Income $	40784
% Low Income Families	15.6	Average Home Price $	90778
% Home Owners	68.6	% Unemployment	8.5
% Labour Force Participation	67.7	% Managerial-Administrative	10.6
% Self-Employed	11.7	% University Degrees	10
% Movers	46.9		

D: Industrial Profile

% Manufacturing	8.3	% Service Sector	14.9
% Agriculture	11.5	% Mining	0.8
% Forestry	0.1	% Fishing	0
% Government Services	8.4	% Business Services	3.4

E: Homogeneity Measures

Ethnic Diversity Index	0.22	Religious Homogeneity Index	0.43
Sectoral Concentration Index	0.41	Income Disparity Index	11.5

F: Physical Setting Characteristics

Total Population	100127	Area (km²)	10700
Population Density (pop/km²)	9.4		

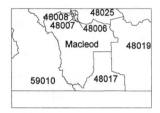

Macleod

Constituency Number: 48018

$\mathbf{M}$acleod was an old constituency dating from Alberta's entry as a Canadian province in 1905. It was altered in 1924 and eventually abolished in 1970. The 1986 redistribution re-created it - two thirds from Bow River and the rest from Lethbridge Foothills. Its small population of 73,304 (the fourth smallest federal riding in the province) is spread across more than 27,000 sq. km south and west of the City of Calgary; it includes no major urban centres (about three-quarters of the polls are rural), but there are small centres such as Fort Macleod, Coleman, Crowsnest Pass, High River and Pincher Creek. The area population includes a very high number of aboriginal peoples - over 12%, and the rest of the constituency is a mix of British, German and other ethnic groups. Fewer than 10% of the riding are immigrants, and almost 97% are citizens; English is the home language used 95% of the time. Over six in ten are Protestant; another 20%+ Catholic.

The riding's economy is primarily related to ranching and farming (at 18.5%, the thirteenth highest level in the country), with smaller segments in local manufacturing and mining (the latter in the southwest). Four in ten jobs are in a service sector, slightly more with government than in business services. Almost thirteen per cent were managers or administrators and over 20% were self-employed, the 12th highest rate in Canada. Income levels were healthy - over $1,500 above the average for all of Alberta. Home prices were about $9,000 over the provincial average, but over three-quarters of the local residents owned their own. Area educational levels were a little (under 2%) below provincial standards, but local unemployment - at 6.9%- and income transfer levels - at 10% - hovered around the norm for the whole province.

The early history of the old Macleod riding was Conservative and Liberal before World War I. After the war, it returned Progressives (1921 and 1925), the same MP as a United Farmer (in 1926 and 1930), then Social Credit for six elections (1935 to 1957). In 1958, the Conservatives returned Lawrence Kindt, a Nanton farmer; he was re-elected until 1965. After abolition of the seat, Tories continued to represent the area on each electoral occasion. When the seat was re-established for the 1988 election, Ken Hughes, a former special assistant on international trade to Joe Clark, with support from Deputy Prime Minister Don Mazankowski, won the Conservative nomination and the election. He had the support of over half the riding voters. Reform were a strong second place finisher in 1988, with 31.2%. In the subsequent referendum, almost two-thirds of the riding voters were on the 'No' side.

In 1993, Okotoks doctor Grant Hill was the Reform Party candidate; he and the incumbent MP, Ken Hughes, faced just four others. Liberal Roy Whitney, Chief of the Tsuu Tina Indian Nation, called for a more compassionate society. Susanne Abildgaard, a Nanton businessperson shared that view against 'the lack of social conscience' shown by the three main parties. A Green and a Natural Law completed the slate. Grant Hill took the riding with over 63% of the votes, the fifth highest Reform vote in the country. The Tories collapsed by 33% to 17.3% and second place; Liberals were less than a point behind. The NDP managed 1.9%, less than 1% above the other two minor parties combined. Turnout was 70.9%, third highest in the province.

Member of Parliament: Grant Hill; **Party:** Reform; **Occupation:** Physician-surgeon; **Education:** MD, University of Alberta; **Age:** 50 (Sept. 20 1943); **Year first elected to the House of Commons:** 1993

48018 Macleod

A: Political Profile
i) Voting Behaviour

	% 1993	% 1988	Change 1988-93
Conservative	17.3	50.5	-33.2
Liberal	16.5	9.4	7.1
NDP	1.9	8.6	-6.7
Reform	63.3	31.2	32.1
Other	1.1	0.2	0.9

% Turnout	70.9	Total Ballots (#)	37741
Rejected Ballots (#)	80	% Margin of Victory	47.1
Rural Polls, 1988 (#)	112	Urban Polls, 1988 (#)	40
% Yes - 1992	35.5	% No - 1992	64.3

ii) Campaign Financing

	# of Donations	Total $ Value	% of Limit Spent
Conservative	287	66548	91.4
Liberal	41	33840	94*
NDP	2	1418	0.5
Reform	229	66391	69
Other	5	364	

B: Ethno-Linguistic Profile

% English Home Language	95	% French Home Language	0.2
% Official Bilingual	3.7	% Other Home Language	4.8
% Catholics	20.6	% Protestants	60.6
% Aboriginal Peoples	12.2	% Immigrants	9.6

C: Socio-Economic Profile

Average Family Income $	53068	Median Family Income $	45138
% Low Income Families	11.4	Average Home Price $	119181
% Home Owners	75.4	% Unemployment	6.9
% Labour Force Participation	72	% Managerial-Administrative	12.7
% Self-Employed	20.1	% University Degrees	9.5
% Movers	45.1		

D: Industrial Profile

% Manufacturing	6.6	% Service Sector	11.8
% Agriculture	18.5	% Mining	5.8
% Forestry	0.4	% Fishing	0.1
% Government Services	6.6	% Business Services	4.5

E: Homogeneity Measures

Ethnic Diversity Index	0.25	Religious Homogeneity Index	0.43
Sectoral Concentration Index	0.35	Income Disparity Index	14.9

F: Physical Setting Characteristics

Total Population	73304	Area (km²)	27130
Population Density (pop/km²)	2.7		

* Tentative value, due to the existence of unpaid campaign expenses.

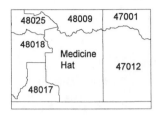

Medicine Hat

Constituency Number: 48019

Medicine Hat was one of Alberta's original constituencies. It was not affected by the 1986 redistribution. Its population of 91,034 is a mix of mostly British and German ethnic communities; they live in a 34,700 sq. km riding adjacent to the Saskatchewan border in the east and the U.S. boundary in the south. It is almost 85% Protestant (60.4%) or Catholic (23.9%) and over 95% speak English as their home language. The level of French home language use is the fifth lowest in Canada. Fewer than 10% of the residents were immigrants. There is also a small (1.5%) aboriginal peoples population in the riding.

The economy of the riding is heavily dependent on agriculture: it produces over 18% of all local jobs, the fourteenth highest level in the country. There is also a sizeable energy sector, largely built around natural gas production. Family incomes are below those for the province as a whole by about $6,000, but home prices in the constituency are $29,000 less that across Alberta; the level of local home ownership is 71%, almost 6% above the provincial norm. About four in ten jobs are in the service sector, three times as many with government as with business. Over 17% are self-employed and almost one in ten work as administrators or managers. The unemployment rate is a point and a half below the provincial rate of joblessness, though income assistance levels locally are more than one per cent above. Local education levels are low - about half the rate of university degree completion for Alberta.

Politically, Medicine Hat has been predominantly Social Credit or Conservative. Initially, it elected a Conservative (1908) and a Liberal (1911); in the Union Government of the First World War it returned A.L. Sifton. After another Conservative in 1921, it returned F.F. Gershaw for the Liberals from 1925 to 1945 (except electing a Social Credit in 1935). Social Credit held Medicine Hat from 1945 to 1957. A Conservative was elected in the sweep of 1958, but the riding returned former Social Credit MP Horace (Bud) Olson in 1962, and again in 1963 and 1965. In 1968 Olson was re-elected with a very small majority and sat as a Liberal: he was named Trudeau's first Minister of Agriculture. In 1972 the Minister lost to a Conservative. Olson lost again to the Tory incumbent in 1974. Tory Bert Hargrave made the riding a safe Conservative haven, winning again in 1979 and 1980, the latter with four times the vote of his main Liberal opponent. In 1984 a new Conservative MP was elected; he took over 75% of all riding votes. The incumbent, Bob Porter, held the seat in 1988, this time down but still with almost 59% support. The NDP took 15%, Liberals 12% and Reform 10.7%. In the 1992 referendum over 64% voted 'No' on the constitutional changes proposed.

In 1993, Bob Wyse received the PC nod: he was a former Social Credit MLA for the area in the early 1970s, who worked with seniors for the city of Medicine Hat. Five other candidates sought election to Parliament: Reform nominated Monte Solberg, a Brooks radio station general manager. Glenn Ennis, a Medicine Hat College political science instructor and Redcliff school trustee was the Liberals' choice; he had served as a facilitator for the Spicer Commission. Alan Hunt, a retired United Church minister and former psychologist, was the NDP candidate. Ivor Ottrey, an Anglican minister and president of the local Pro-Life movement was nominated by Christian Heritage. The final candidate was from the Canada Party - a grouping seeking to solve the recession by setting the bank reserve at 100% to remove the power of the banks. He received 0.6% and Rev. Ottrey 2.4%. The NDP were not much ahead, with 4.5%. The Conservative vote was 16.9%, a drop of 42%, leaving them in third place. The Liberals, at 20.9% took second place. Reform's Monte Solberg, on a ticket of deficit and crime fighting, won the day. His vote was 54.7%, just a little below where the Tory vote had been in the previous election. It was Reform's fourteenth best showing in the country. Local turnout was 63.9%, a point and a half below the turnout across the province.

Member of Parliament: Monte Solberg; **Party;** Reform; **Occupation:** Radio station manager; **Education:** High school completion/ 1 year university; **Age:** 35 (Sept. 17, 1958); **Year first elected to the House of Commons:** 1993

48019 Medicine Hat

A: Political Profile

i) Voting Behaviour

	% 1993	% 1988	Change 1988-93
Conservative	16.9	58.9	-42
Liberal	20.9	12.1	8.8
NDP	4.5	15.1	-10.6
Reform	54.7	10.8	43.9
Other	3	3.1	-0.1

% Turnout	63.9	Total Ballots (#)	41140
Rejected Ballots (#)	129	% Margin of Victory	36.8
Rural Polls, 1988 (#)	75	Urban Polls, 1988 (#)	138
% Yes - 1992	35.5	% No - 1992	64.2

ii) Campaign Financing

	# of Donations	Total $ Value	% of Limit Spent
Conservative	147	20720	47
Liberal	191	22970	31.3
NDP	12	23319	23.9
Reform	228	57878	77
Other	102	21422	

B: Ethno-Linguistic Profile

% English Home Language	95.2	% French Home Language	0.2
% Official Bilingual	3.1	% Other Home Language	4.6
% Catholics	23.9	% Protestants	60.4
% Aboriginal Peoples	1.5	% Immigrants	9.2

C: Socio-Economic Profile

Average Family Income $	45893	Median Family Income $	41175
% Low Income Families	14.6	Average Home Price $	81956
% Home Owners	71.1	% Unemployment	6.2
% Labour Force Participation	71	% Managerial-Administrative	9.8
% Self-Employed	17.1	% University Degrees	6
% Movers	45.4		

D: Industrial Profile

% Manufacturing	6.7	% Service Sector	13.4
% Agriculture	18.1	% Mining	6.5
% Forestry	0.2	% Fishing	0
% Government Services	6.8	% Business Services	2.1

E: Homogeneity Measures

Ethnic Diversity Index	0.29	Religious Homogeneity Index	0.43
Sectoral Concentration Index	0.37	Income Disparity Index	10.3

F: Physical Setting Characteristics

Total Population	91034	Area (km²)	34700
Population Density (pop/km²)	2.6		

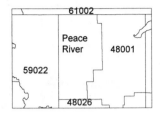

Peace River

Constituency Number: 48020

Peace River was originally established under redistribution in 1924. It covers an area of 148,330 sq. km (the fourteenth largest riding in Canada) in the extreme northwest corner of Alberta; two of its boundaries are British Columbia and the Northwest Territories. Its population of 106,962 is a mix of aboriginal peoples - 13% of the total population, British (the largest ethnic group), German and French. It has one of the lowest levels of immigrants (just over 6%) and a high level of citizenship (97.3%) but only 88.5% speak English as their home language; almost three per cent are French speakers, and over 8% are bilingual. Over one in three are Catholic; almost five in ten Protestant.

The area is half urban and half rural, with only Grande Prairie as a major population centre. The riding's economy is substantially dependent on agriculture: almost fifteen per cent of all local employment is directly dependent on farming and ranching. There are also mining (5.8%) and forestry (2.5%) components of the local economy; natural gas production also contributes to the economy. About four in ten workers are in a service sector that depends on these other primary sectors. So does a small manufacturing element. Seventeen per cent are self-employed and 9% are managers or administrators. The level of mobility is fairly low, just 19% having moved in the previous year. Income levels in the Peace River are below the provincial rate by between $5,000 and 6,000, but other local costs such as housing are also well below: average house prices are $73,257, about $37,000 below the provincial average. More than seven in ten own their own dwellings in Peace River. Area unemployment is just above the provincial rate; so are income transfer support payments. Local levels of education are relatively low, more than five points below the norm for Alberta as a whole.

The political history of the riding dates from the 1920s when it was split off from Edmonton West. Initially it elected a Progressive in 1925. D.M. Kennedy then won as a UFA candidate in 1926 and 1930. In 1935, Social Credit took the seat, but lost it to J.H. Sissons for the Liberals in 1940. In 1945, S.E. Low won the riding again for Social Credit; Low then held Peace River until the Diefenbaker sweep of 1958. In that election, Conservative Ged Baldwin, a lawyer, was elected; he served as Parliamentary Secretary to Prime Minister John Diefenbaker, as well as Chair of the Public Accounts Committee. Baldwin, who also served as Conservative House Leader, won every election in Peace River through until 1980 when he retired. His championing of the idea of Freedom of Information remains a model of backbench persistence. In 1980 Albert Cooper, a real estate and investment consultant, held the riding for the Conservatives. He was re-elected in 1984 and 1988, each time with more than half of all local votes, a pattern established by his predecessor. Local New Democrats took second place but were just ahead of Reform with 15.2%. In the 1992 constitutional referendum, Peace River split two-thirds 'No' - one-third 'Yes'.

In 1993, the electorate had a choice of six candidates, and no sitting MP: the Progressive Conservative candidate was Alan Tanaka, a senior administrator from High Level. He was challenged by Charlie Penson, a farmer from Sexsmith, the Reform Party nominee; the area Liberals selected Joshua Phillpotts, a parish priest and insurance agent from Edmonton. Grand Prairie social worker Jacqui Gaboury won the NDP nod; David Ridgeway, a Grand Prairie businessman was the candidate for the National Party. There was also a Natural Law candidate. Reformer Charlie Penson took over 60% of all votes, the seventh highest level of support for Reform in all of Canada. Liberal Joshua Phillpotts was second, up just slightly from the party result in 1988, but still the fifth lowest Grit vote in the country. The Conservatives, in third place, fell almost 40%; they were left at 14.4%, just behind the Liberals. That was considerably better than the NDP, down almost twelve points to 5.5%. The National's David Ridgeway scored more than half that (3.9%), leaving 0.6% for Natural Law. Voter turnout was 61.8%, fifth lowest in the province.

Member of Parliament: Charles Penson; **Party:** Reform; **Occupation:** Farmer; **Education:** High school; **Age:** 50 (Dec. 1, 1942); **Year first elected to the House of Commons:** 1993

48020 Peace River

A: Political Profile

i) Voting Behaviour

	% 1993	% 1988	Change 1988-93
Conservative	14.4	54.3	-39.9
Liberal	15.5	13.4	2.1
NDP	5.5	17.2	-11.7
Reform	60.2	15.2	45
Other	4.5	0	4.5

% Turnout	61.8	Total Ballots (#)	42880
Rejected Ballots (#)	105	% Margin of Victory	49.2
Rural Polls, 1988 (#)	205	Urban Polls, 1988 (#)	82
% Yes - 1992	33.7	% No - 1992	66

ii) Campaign Financing

	# of Donations	Total $ Value	% of Limit Spent
Conservative	89	35674	43.6*
Liberal	41	6984	12
NDP	10	20586	18.4
Reform	455	90322	88.2
Other	41	7109	

B: Ethno-Linguistic Profile

% English Home Language	88.5	% French Home Language	2.9
% Official Bilingual	8.3	% Other Home Language	8.6
% Catholics	30.1	% Protestants	48
% Aboriginal Peoples	13	% Immigrants	6.4

C: Socio-Economic Profile

Average Family Income $	45908	Median Family Income $	41505
% Low Income Families	14.5	Average Home Price $	73257
% Home Owners	70.3	% Unemployment	7.9
% Labour Force Participation	75	% Managerial-Administrative	9
% Self-Employed	17.4	% University Degrees	6.1
% Movers	46.7		

D: Industrial Profile

% Manufacturing	5.9	% Service Sector	12.2
% Agriculture	14.8	% Mining	5.8
% Forestry	2.5	% Fishing	0.1
% Government Services	6.8	% Business Services	2.3

E: Homogeneity Measures

Ethnic Diversity Index	0.18	Religious Homogeneity Index	0.36
Sectoral Concentration Index	0.36	Income Disparity Index	9.6

F: Physical Setting Characteristics

Total Population	106962	Area (km²)	148330
Population Density (pop/km²)	0.7		

* Tentative value, due to the existence of unpaid campaign expenses.

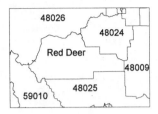

Red Deer

Constituency Number: 48021

Red Deer was established as a federal constituency in 1933. The 1986 redistribution added less than 5% from three surrounding ridings. This central Alberta constituency between Edmonton and Calgary (area: 22,010 sq. km) extends west to British Columbia and includes part of Banff National Park. Its population of 103,400 is predominantly British, with a large local German community. Aboriginal peoples add just over 3% to the area population; that is two per cent below the average across the province.

Economically, the area combines ranching and farming with an important energy and mining sector. Both provide over 7% of the jobs in the riding. A supporting manufacturing sector does likewise. With proximity to the National Park, there is a tourism element as well. Over four in ten work in services, 6.4% for governments, half that for business. Almost thirteen per cent are self-employed and over nine per cent are managers or administrators. The average family wage is below the provincial rate by about $3,500, but area house prices are also below the norm by $15,000. Almost two-thirds of all residents own their own homes. University education levels are well below the provincial rate - by over 4%. Unemployment in the constituency and levels of income support through government transfers are both right at the norm for Alberta as a whole.

The political history of the riding was dominated by Progressives/United Farmers in the 1920s and early 1930s. In 1935, the first election after a redistribution established a separate Red Deer riding, Social Credit took the seat. F.D. Shaw was elected in 1940 and held the seat for Social Credit until 1958. In the Diefenbaker sweep that year, a local Tory won; but in 1962, Robert Thompson, just elected leader of the National Social Credit Party, won the Red Deer Riding. Thompson held the seat for Social Credit in 1963, 1965, and 1968. In 1972, twice-defeated Tory farmer Gordon Towers won the seat for the Conservatives; he was re-elected in 1974. In both elections he defeated Thompson's Social Credit replacement, teacher Jim Keegstra. (Keegstra was later charged with teaching denial of the Holocaust at the Eckville high school. In both 1972 and 1974, he placed fourth.) Towers held the seat for the Tories again in 1979 and 1980. In 1984, he won his fifth term with almost 74% of Red Deer's votes. When he retired in 1988 Doug Fee, a local mayor, won the Tory nod. Fee took the seat, despite a drop of over 20% in Conservative support, with 53.3% of the votes. Reform was left in second place with 21.9% support, almost double either NDP (third) or Liberal (fourth) place results. In 1992, two-thirds of the Red Deer voters were opposed to the Charlottetown Accord.

Doug Fee sought a second term in 1993. The incumbent Tory met five challengers: Bob Mills, a Red Deer businessman ran on a platform of fiscal responsibility, criminal justice reform and sustainable development for Reform. Dobie To, a Red Deer restaurateur, won the Liberal nomination and emphasized economic growth and jobs; Karen McLaren, a pet groomer from Red Deer, was the NDP representative; she called for an end to fear - on social programs, on employment and the environment. Office manager Joan Hepburn was National Party candidate. There was also a representative of Natural Law. Fee's Conservative vote crashed 37% and he lost, left in second place less than three points ahead of the Liberals (13.5%). Bob Mills won the seat for Reform with 64.8%, one of the best Reform showings.

The NDP were at 2.7%, just 0.5% ahead of the National Party. Natural Law got the remaining 0.6%. Local turnout in Red Deer was right at the provincial average.

Member of Parliament: Bob Mills; **Party:** Reform; **Occupation:** Businessperson; **Education:** BSc, BEd, University of Saskatchewan; **Age:** 50 (July 28, 1943); **Year first elected to the House of Commons:** 1993

48021 Red Deer

A: Political Profile

i) Voting Behaviour

	% 1993	% 1988	Change 1988-93
Conservative	16.3	53.3	-37
Liberal	13.5	10.1	3.4
NDP	2.7	12.6	-9.9
Reform	64.8	21.1	43.7
Other	2.8	3	-0.2

% Turnout	65.1	Total Ballots (#)	49292
Rejected Ballots (#)	112	% Margin of Victory	51.3
Rural Polls, 1988 (#)	64	Urban Polls, 1988 (#)	126
% Yes - 1992	32.8	% No - 1992	67

ii) Campaign Financing

	# of Donations	Total $ Value	% of Limit Spent
Conservative	203	61902	91.9*
Liberal	76	19378	21.7
NDP	3	5236	2.5
Reform	117	78372	98.6
Other	43	3445	

B: Ethno-Linguistic Profile

% English Home Language	97.6	% French Home Language	0.2
% Official Bilingual	4.6	% Other Home Language	2.2
% Catholics	18	% Protestants	56.4
% Aboriginal Peoples	3.1	% Immigrants	7.8

C: Socio-Economic Profile

Average Family Income $	48039	Median Family Income $	42597
% Low Income Families	15.4	Average Home Price $	95380
% Home Owners	64.5	% Unemployment	7.7
% Labour Force Participation	74.5	% Managerial-Administrative	9.3
% Self-Employed	12.5	% University Degrees	7
% Movers	56.3		

D: Industrial Profile

% Manufacturing	7.2	% Service Sector	15.1
% Agriculture	7.8	% Mining	7.7
% Forestry	0.5	% Fishing	0
% Government Services	6.4	% Business Services	3.1

E: Homogeneity Measures

Ethnic Diversity Index	0.27	Religious Homogeneity Index	0.39
Sectoral Concentration Index	0.41	Income Disparity Index	11.3

F: Physical Setting Characteristics

Total Population	103400	Area (km²)	22010
Population Density (pop/km²)	4.7		

* Tentative value, due to the existence of unpaid campaign expenses.

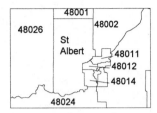

St Albert

Constituency Number: 48022

St Albert riding is centred on the municipality of the same name immediately to the northeast of Edmonton. Part of its eastern boundary is the Edmonton city limits; its southern border is the North Saskatchewan River. This suburban constituency covers an area totaling 2,440 sq. km and has a population of 95,605. It was created in 1986 out of the abolished Pembina riding (61%) and the 'continuing' Yellowhead constituency (39%). The riding's population is a mix of British (by far the largest ethnic group), German, French, Ukrainian, and Dutch communities; less than 10% are immigrants and less than 3% non-citizens. There is a high rate of bilingualism (almost 10%) but 97.6% speak English as their home language. Almost 5% of the constituents are from First Nations.

While many commute to Edmonton to work, St Albert is an affluent community: average family incomes are more than $8,000 above the provincial rate, and a sizeable 83.1% own their own homes, a provincial high, and the ninth highest rate of home ownership in Canada. The value of these houses is about $10,000 above the average cost in the province as a whole. Educational levels are average, and just under half work in the service sector, about 5% in business and double that for government. Almost 15% are administrators or managers and over 12% are self-employed. There is a small agricultural component to the riding, beyond the city. It provides work for about 4% of the riding. Employment in the oil industry provides about half that. Area unemployment is lower than the provincial rate, by more than a per cent and a half; government transfer levels of income support were also below the rate for all of Alberta, by 3.5%.

As a new constituency, its earlier representation was largely within Pembina. Conservative Peter Elzinga, a Sherwood Park farmer/rancher, represented that riding since 1974. Conservative Walter Van de Walle, a commercial farmer, won in a closely fought by-election in 1986. He held the constituency for the Tories in 1988, winning almost 47% of the votes and a margin of over 27% over his closest, NDP, rival. Reform were in fourth place, but with 13.9% of the votes. In the 1992 constitutional referendum, just over six in ten voters supported the 'No' side.

Just prior to the 1993 general election the incumbent Conservative member resigned, opening up an eight-way contest. The local Conservatives selected Jerry Manegre, a St Albert manager who campaigned on a platform of creating jobs, encouraging small business, and maintaining social programs. The Liberals nominated Jack Jeffrey, a chartered accountant from St Albert; his platform was 'the Tory record' and creating jobs. New Democrat Zahid Makhdoom, a social worker, emphasized poverty, health care, jobs, education and training. John Williams, a Morinville accountant, opened his campaign for Reform by announcing that he would not accept the MP's tax-free living allowance; crime and the deficit were his main preoccupations. Steven Powers, the National Party candidate, emphasized economic issues. Christian Heritage, Natural Law and an Independent (Canadian Economic Community) completed the local field.

The results of the 1993 general election in St Albert were a clear Reform victory: John Williams won the seat, with almost 51% of the votes. That was well ahead of the second place Liberals with 28.3%. The Progressive Conservative candidate saw the Tory vote drop almost 35%, leaving him in third place with just 12%. The local NDP vote in St Albert also collapsed - down almost 17%; that left them in fifth place, behind Steven Powers of the National Party: Powers had 4.5% of the votes, the NDP's Makhdoom just 2.9%. Christian Heritage, Natural Law and Independent (Canadian Economic Community) candidates shared the remaining 1.3% in that order. Voter turnout in St Albert was 70.7%, fifth highest in Alberta.

Member of Parliament: John Williams; **Party:** Reform; **Occupation:** Accountant; **Education:** CGA; **Age:** 47 (1946); **Year first elected to the House of Commons:** 1993

48022 St Albert

A: Political Profile
i) Voting Behaviour

	% 1993		% 1988	Change 1988-93
Conservative	12		46.7	-34.7
Liberal	28.3		16.7	11.6
NDP	2.9		19.6	-16.7
Reform	50.9		13.9	37
Other	5.8		3	2.8

% Turnout	70.7	Total Ballots (#)	49078
Rejected Ballots (#)	75	% Margin of Victory	28.4
Rural Polls, 1988 (#)	53	Urban Polls, 1988 (#)	126
% Yes - 1992	39.7	% No - 1992	60.1

ii) Campaign Financing

	# of Donations	Total $ Value	% of Limit Spent
Conservative	143	41610	52.8
Liberal	170	32220	48.6
NDP	11	9580	13
Reform	172	33512	76.8
Other	60	16378	

B: Ethno-Linguistic Profile

% English Home Language	97.6	% French Home Language	0.9
% Official Bilingual	9.4	% Other Home Language	1.5
% Catholics	33.4	% Protestants	47.1
% Aboriginal Peoples	4.6	% Immigrants	9.4

C: Socio-Economic Profile

Average Family Income $	59740	Median Family Income $	56390
% Low Income Families	7.4	Average Home Price $	119893
% Home Owners	83.1	% Unemployment	6
% Labour Force Participation	78.5	% Managerial-Administrative	14.7
% Self-Employed	12.1	% University Degrees	11.5
% Movers	50.2		

D: Industrial Profile

% Manufacturing	7	% Service Sector	10.5
% Agriculture	3.9	% Mining	2.2
% Forestry	0.2	% Fishing	0
% Government Services	9.3	% Business Services	4.9

E: Homogeneity Measures

Ethnic Diversity Index	0.21	Religious Homogeneity Index	0.36
Sectoral Concentration Index	0.45	Income Disparity Index	5.6

F: Physical Setting Characteristics

Total Population	95605	Area (km²)	2440
Population Density (pop/km²)	39.2		

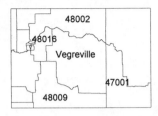

Vegreville

Constituency Number: 48023

Vegreville is a south-central Alberta constituency established originally in 1924. It covers an area of almost 28,000 sq. km, from the Saskatchewan border in the east; its northern boundary is the North Saskatchewan River. It has a population of 73,062, the third least populous federal riding in Alberta. Lloydminster, right at the Saskatchewan border, is the major population centre and an important part of the local economy with its oil. Other communities such as Wainwright, Vermilion and Vegreville are spread throughout the riding. British, Ukrainian and German communities are largest, with smaller French, Polish and aboriginal groups next. A low 5.6% are immigrants, and just over three per cent of the residents are non-citizens. Eighty per cent are Protestant (55.3%) or Catholic (26.4%); almost 6% are Jewish. The vast majority (almost 97%) speak English as their home language; a little over 3% are bilingual.

Agriculture is the most significant part of the economy: dairy and wheat farms predominate and farming contributes almost 27% of direct jobs in the local economy. One quarter of all workers are self-employed, the ninth highest level in Canada. Area manufacturing is amongst the lowest (9th) in the country. Only a third of employment is in services, about 6.5% with government. Vegreville's business service level (2%) is the lowest in all of Canada. Average family incomes are $6,000 lower than the provincial norm; area homes cost over $40,000 less. That helps explain a home ownership level of almost 77%, about twelve points above the provincial rate. University education in the riding is only half that for the whole province. The riding's unemployment rate, however is 4.7%, almost three per cent below the provincial rate, though government income transfer levels are two points above the Alberta norm.

Politically, the riding has elected Progressives/United Farmers (1925, 1926, 1930), Social Credit (1935, 1940, 1945), Liberals (J. Decore, in 1949 and 1953), Social Credit (again in 1957), then Progressive Conservatives (in 1958, 1962, 1963, and 1965). When Tory F.J.W. Fane retired in 1968, his place was taken by Don Mazankowski, a Vegreville businessman. 'Maz' held the seat in every election until 1993, usually with three to one majorities. He was Transport Minister in the Clark Government, then Minister of Multiple Portfolios in the Mulroney Governments, including the post of Deputy Prime Minister. In 1988, he won almost two-thirds of the riding votes, almost 50% ahead of his next rival. Reform placed third, with 9.9%.

In 1993, Mazankowski, like many Mulroney Tories, announced his resignation. Conservatives in the riding nominated Roger Lehr, a Wainwright businessman as his replacement. Lehr faced seven others: Leon Benoit, a Mannville farmer; Ed Wieclaw, a Vegreville Economic Development officer; Terry Zawalski, an Edmonton manager; Alex Ziniewicz, retired, for the National Party; two Independents, and a Natural Law representative. Lehr emphasized the good record of local representation by the Tories and the deficit. Benoit, nominated early, had spent two years contacting constituents with the traditional Reform message of restrained government. The Liberals argued that the deficit was a bogus issue, stressing a 'more balanced' approach. New Democrats emphasized jobs. In the end the Tory vote collapsed almost 43%, leaving them in second place with just 22.7% support. Reform's Leon Benoit was elected with 54.7%, and a 32% margin; Liberals were third and the NDP just managed to double the National Party vote of 1.6%, for fourth place. The 2.2% remaining was shared, by the two independents, and Natural Law. Turnout was 68.9%, sixth highest in the province.

Member of Parliament: Leon E. Benoit; **Party:** Reform; **Occupation:** Farmer/agricultural economist; **Education:** BSc, PAg, University of Alberta; **Age:** 43 (July 2, 1950); **Year first elected to the House of Commons:** 1993

48023 Vegreville

A: Political Profile

i) Voting Behaviour

	% 1993	% 1988	Change 1988-93
Conservative	22.7	65.3	-42.6
Liberal	15.6	7.8	7.8
NDP	3.3	16.1	-12.8
Reform	54.7	9.9	44.8
Other	3.8	1	2.8

% Turnout	68.9	Total Ballots (#)	36112
Rejected Ballots (#)	65	% Margin of Victory	35.8
Rural Polls, 1988 (#)	137	Urban Polls, 1988 (#)	33
% Yes - 1992	32.5	% No - 1992	67.3

ii) Campaign Financing

	# of Donations	Total $ Value	% of Limit Spent
Conservative	158	61251	79.5
Liberal	119	24590	39
NDP	4	5037	2.2
Reform	156	61438	64.6
Other	46	4472	

B: Ethno-Linguistic Profile

% English Home Language	96.4	% French Home Language	0.2
% Official Bilingual	3.3	% Other Home Language	3.4
% Catholics	26.4	% Protestants	55.3
% Aboriginal Peoples	1.2	% Immigrants	5.6

C: Socio-Economic Profile

Average Family Income $	45577	Median Family Income $	39410
% Low Income Families	13	Average Home Price $	70061
% Home Owners	76.9	% Unemployment	4.7
% Labour Force Participation	72.2	% Managerial-Administrative	9.7
% Self-Employed	24.7	% University Degrees	5.9
% Movers	36.1		

D: Industrial Profile

% Manufacturing	3.3	% Service Sector	11.3
% Agriculture	27	% Mining	5.9
% Forestry	0.1	% Fishing	0
% Government Services	6.5	% Business Services	2

E: Homogeneity Measures

Ethnic Diversity Index	0.25	Religious Homogeneity Index	0.38
Sectoral Concentration Index	0.37	Income Disparity Index	13.5

F: Physical Setting Characteristics

Total Population	73062	Area (km²)	27900
Population Density (pop/km²)	2.6		

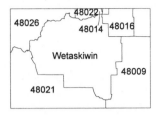

Wetaskiwin

Constituency Number: 48024

Wetaskiwin is a 12,600 sq. km riding whose northern boundary is the city of Edmonton and the North Saskatchewan River; part of its south boundary is the Red Deer River. It includes the oil town of Leduc, Wetaskiwin, as well as smaller centres like Lacombe and Ponoka. The local population of 84,514 is made up of British and Germans, with smaller French, Ukrainian and Dutch elements. The constituency is also home to the Hobbema and Pigeon Lake Indian bands: aboriginal peoples make up almost 5% of the local population. Immigrant levels are low (7.6%) and citizenship rates are high (96.1%); English is home language in over 98% of the riding, though almost 4% are bilingual. Protestantism is predominant (62.1%); Catholics add an additional 16.8%.

The local economy is agricultural and energy based: 17% of all work is in farming and a further 6.7% in energy/resources. Four in ten of the local population work in the service sector, almost 6% with government and about half that in business. Nine per cent are managers or administrators. Self-employment - at 19% - is the thirteenth highest in all of Canada. Three-quarters of all residents own their own homes; house values are about $25,000 below the rate for all the province. Average family incomes in Wetaskiwin are about $7,000 below the provincial average. Educational levels are over three per cent below the rate for all Alberta, but unemployment levels are a point and a half below the rate for the province; income transfer levels are about the same percentage above.

Politically, the constituency dates back to 1924. In the 1925 election it returned a Liberal; in 1926 and 1930 William Irvine was its MP; in 1935, N. Jacques won for Social Credit; he held the seat through to 1949, when another Social Credit MP (R. Thomas) was returned. Thomas won again in 1953 and 1957, but the seat went Conservative in the Diefenbaker rout of 1958. Dairy farmer Harry Moore won for the Conservatives in 1962 and kept the seat until 1972; in that election Tory Stan Schenberger won with a margin of about 14,000 votes. He kept the seat Conservative until 1988. In the 1988 election, lawyer Willie Littlechild, a businessman and legal counsel for area Indian bands, won the seat - a ninth straight victory for the Conservatives. Littlechild's vote was just over half of all cast. Indicative of changing support, however, a former Social credit Health Minister, running for Reform took second place, with 18.5% support. In the 1992 constitutional referendum on the Charlottetown Accord, Wetaskiwin voters voted 71.3% 'No'; their MP, a local Indian leader, had campaigned strongly for the 'Yes' side.

In 1993, Willie Littlechild did not seek another term. In his place Brian Rhiness, an agrologist with Alberta Agriculture, stood for the Conservatives; his platform emphasized 'bringing the deficit down to zero'. Doug Sirrs, a Wetaskiwin lawyer, was the Liberal nominee; he called for a continuing role for governments to regulate markets, to protect the environment, ensure competition and fairness. Dale Johnson, a Ponoka farmer, and former town councillor ran for Reform - calling for a balanced budget. Clifford Reid, a retired ironworker from Leduc, was the NDP standard-bearer; he called for a new infrastructure for economic growth. Canada Party and Natural Law candidates rounded out the slate locally. The results of the 1993 general election in Wetaskiwin included a solid Reform victory: over 63% voted for Dale Johnson, the fourth highest total for the Party in Canada. That represented a complete reversal for the Conservatives; their vote fell over 35%, and they ended up in third place, about two points behind the Liberals. Doug Sirrs of the Liberals received the support of 16.7% of the local voters. The NDP vote, in collapse across the province, was down more than ten points; that left them at 3.6%. The Canada Party and Natural Law shared the final 1.5% in that order. Voter turnout was just above the provincial average.

Member of Parliament: Dale Johnson; **Party:** Reform; **Occupation:** Farmer; **Age:** 52 (Nov. 14, 1941); **Year first elected to the House of Commons:** 1993

48024 Wetaskiwin

A: Political Profile

i) Voting Behaviour

	% 1993	% 1988	Change 1988-93
Conservative	14.8	50.2	-35.4
Liberal	16.7	8.4	8.3
NDP	3.6	14.3	-10.7
Reform	63.4	18.5	44.9
Other	1.5	8.6	-7.1

% Turnout	65.9	Total Ballots (#)	41403
Rejected Ballots (#)	71	% Margin of Victory	48.2
Rural Polls, 1988 (#)	106	Urban Polls, 1988 (#)	64
% Yes - 1992	28.5	% No - 1992	71.3

ii) Campaign Financing

	# of Donations	Total $ Value	% of Limit Spent
Conservative	93	19520	54.3
Liberal	121	28385	45.4
NDP	3	6304	6.8
Reform	229	64644	61
Other	0	0	

B: Ethno-Linguistic Profile

% English Home Language	98.2	% French Home Language	0.2
% Official Bilingual	3.7	% Other Home Language	1.6
% Catholics	16.8	% Protestants	62.1
% Aboriginal Peoples	4.6	% Immigrants	7.6

C: Socio-Economic Profile

Average Family Income $	44833	Median Family Income $	40118
% Low Income Families	13.8	Average Home Price $	84768
% Home Owners	75.5	% Unemployment	6.2
% Labour Force Participation	72.7	% Managerial-Administrative	9.1
% Self-Employed	19	% University Degrees	6.5
% Movers	45.1		

D: Industrial Profile

% Manufacturing	5.5	% Service Sector	12.1
% Agriculture	17	% Mining	6.7
% Forestry	0.2	% Fishing	0
% Government Services	5.9	% Business Services	2.8

E: Homogeneity Measures

Ethnic Diversity Index	0.24	Religious Homogeneity Index	0.44
Sectoral Concentration Index	0.38	Income Disparity Index	10.5

F: Physical Setting Characteristics

Total Population	84514	Area (km²)	12600
Population Density (pop/km²)	6.7		

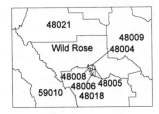

Wild Rose

Constituency Number: 48025

Wild Rose constituency was created in 1986. Its 92,092 residents 'emerged' primarily from Bow River (two-thirds) and Red Deer (one-third). The riding covers all the territory across the top of the city of Calgary, up through Airdrie and Carstairs to the town of Olds, as well as areas east toward Strathmore and west through Cochrane and Canmore to Banff, Lake Louise, and the B.C. border. These small communities are British in the first instance, with significant German, Ukrainian, Dutch and French ethnic elements throughout. Native peoples make up about 5% of the riding's residents. Over 95% speak English as their home language; almost 6% are bilingual. Immigrant levels are fairly low (under 9%); citizenship is almost 96%. Six in ten residents are Protestant; only 17.2% Catholic - more reported no religion.

The local economy includes a large tourism sector - with skiing and Banff and Lake Louise areas. There is also a large agricultural sector - almost 16% of all direct jobs, and a smaller mining and energy component. About 43% work in services, over 6% for government and over 4% for business; almost 12% are administrators or managers. Almost 19% are self-employed, in the top fifteen in Canada for that category. Average family wages for the riding are a little (less than $1,000) above the provincial norm; house prices are almost $18,000 more. Still, almost three-quarters (73.6%) of Wild Rose residents own their own homes. Area unemployment is quite low - at 5.5%, sixth lowest in all of Canada; government income transfer payments were also low in Wild Rose, at 8.3%, more than a per cent below the Alberta rate. University education levels in the riding were below the provincial norm but by less than 2%.

Politically, much of the area's history is tied to that of Bow River. That constituency was formed in 1914: it elected Progressives/United Farmers in five elections between 1917 and 1930; a single Social Credit MP in six elections between 1935 and 1957; Conservative Eldon Woolliams in 1958 and in four subsequent elections until 1968. Later it returned Gordon Taylor for the Conservatives, for example in 1979 and 1980. When the Wild Rose constituency was created prior to the 1988 election, there was no incumbent challenging for re-election. Louise Feltham, a Calgary businessperson, won the seat for the Conservatives. She took 48.2% of the votes, a margin of almost 15% over the Reform Party's Dale Brown, who won 33.4% and second place. In the 1992 referendum on the Charlottetown Accord, just under two-thirds of Wild Rose went 'No'.

In 1993, local concern over unemployment and crime jockeyed with the deficit and the GST on the electoral agenda. Incumbent Tory Louise Feltham sought a second term; she was challenged by eight other aspirants. Reform selected Myron Thompson, a retired teacher from Sundre; Roy Shellnutt, a Calgary lawyer, was the Liberal choice. Anne Wilson, a landscape gardner from Canmore represented the NDP; Stuart Hughes, a Calgary-based independent businessman won the National Party nod. Two Independents, a Green and a Natural Law candidate were the others running in Wild Rose. The Reform Party won the 1993 election locally: Myron Thompson took 63.8% of all votes, the third highest Reform victory in the country. The vote for the Conservative incumbent fell almost 33%, but she hung on to second place, a little over one per cent above the Liberals. The local NDP was fourth, but at 2.2%, just ahead of the National Party, with 1.7%. Michael Leslie, a waiter in Banff running as an Independent took, 1.2% of the votes. The Greens, Natural Law and a CoR/Independent shared the remaining 1.5% in that order. Turnout locally was 66.2% - a per cent above the Alberta rate.

Member of Parliament: Myron Thompson; **Party:** Reform; **Occupation:** Retired teacher; **Education:** BEd; **Age:** 57 (April 23, 1936); **Year first elected to the House of Commons:** 1993

48025 Wild Rose

A: Political Profile

i) Voting Behaviour

	% 1993	% 1988	Change 1988-93
Conservative	15.5	48.2	-32.7
Liberal	14.2	10.1	4.1
NDP	2.2	7.8	-5.6
Reform	63.8	33.4	30.4
Other	4.4	0.5	3.9

% Turnout	66.2	Total Ballots (#)	48734
Rejected Ballots (#)	125	% Margin of Victory	52.7
Rural Polls, 1988 (#)	163	Urban Polls, 1988 (#)	21
% Yes - 1992	34.7	% No - 1992	65

ii) Campaign Financing

	# of Donations	Total $ Value	% of Limit Spent
Conservative	122	39507	82.9
Liberal	67	15945	19.4*
NDP	5	4615	3.7
Reform	148	53192	66.3
Other	5	1049	

B: Ethno-Linguistic Profile

% English Home Language	95.2	% French Home Language	0.3
% Official Bilingual	5.8	% Other Home Language	4.4
% Catholics	17.2	% Protestants	60.6
% Aboriginal Peoples	5	% Immigrants	9

C: Socio-Economic Profile

Average Family Income $	52481	Median Family Income $	46515
% Low Income Families	10.4	Average Home Price $	128115
% Home Owners	73.6	% Unemployment	5.5
% Labour Force Participation	76.7	% Managerial-Administrative	11.7
% Self-Employed	18.7	% University Degrees	9.5
% Movers	51.5		

D: Industrial Profile

% Manufacturing	7.3	% Service Sector	13.9
% Agriculture	15.7	% Mining	5.4
% Forestry	0.3	% Fishing	0
% Government Services	6.2	% Business Services	4.3

E: Homogeneity Measures

Ethnic Diversity Index	0.28	Religious Homogeneity Index	0.43
Sectoral Concentration Index	0.37	Income Disparity Index	11.4

F: Physical Setting Characteristics

Total Population	92092	Area (km²)	23680
Population Density (pop/km²)	3.9		

---

*   Tentative value, due to the existence of unpaid campaign expenses.

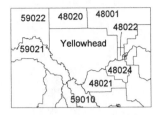

Yellowhead

Constituency Number: 48026

Yellowhead was created prior to the 1979 general election. It is a territory of 84,140 sq. km in the north and west part of the province, stretching from the Jasper Park boundary and British Columbia border in the west and along the Brazeau and North Saskatchewan Rivers toward Edmonton. It includes the Drayton Valley, as well as Edson, Hinton and Jasper on the old CNR transcontinental route; further north it also encompasses the communities of Grande Cache and Whitecourt. Its population of 89,361 is a mixture of British, German, Ukrainian, French and Dutch ethnic communities; over 6% of the residents are aboriginal peoples. Immigrants make up a little under 8% of the population; most (97.3%) are citizens. English is the predominant home language, used in over 97% of area homes; almost 6% are bilingual. Three-quarters of the riding's residents are Protestant or Catholic, with twice as many of the former as the latter.

The local economy includes tourism, especially around Jasper, agriculture (almost 11% of all area jobs), mining and energy (almost 14% of area employment, fifth highest level in the country) and local manufacturing (about 9% of local jobs). The area service sector produces a little under 36% of employment, with there being twice the opportunities in government compared to business. Over 15% are self-employed and under 8% are administrators/managers. Area educational levels are low, less than half the provincial average for university degree completion. Area family incomes are about $3,000 below the average for the province, but house prices are $29,000 below as well. As a result, almost 73% of riding residents own their own dwellings. Local unemployment is a little below the rate for all of Alberta; so are area income transfer support levels.

Politically, the area had been represented by Conservative Joe Clark. Clark had defeated an incumbent Liberal to win Rocky Mountain in 1972. He held the seat for the Conservatives in 1974. When redistribution created Yellowhead in 1979, Clark won the new constituency by a wide margin over his nearest (Liberal) opponent. As a result of that election, Joe Clark formed a Conservative Government. In 1980, when the Clark Government was defeated, Joe Clark held Yellowhead with a similarly wide majority. With the Mulroney victory in 1984, Clark's third Yellowhead riding victory involved just under three-quarters (73.7%) of all area votes; Clark was appointed Minister for External Affairs. The 1988 result involved a significant drop (over 29%) in Clark's voter support, but he still maintained the seat with a 16.6% margin. In that race, Reform Party Leader Preston Manning was his main challenger; Manning picked up 27.9% of the local votes. (In 1993, Manning was elected in Calgary Southwest.) In the subsequent constitutional referendum Yellowhead, the riding of the Minister for Constitutional Affairs, voted almost 70% 'No'.

In 1993, Joe Clark decided to resign, after more than twenty years in the House of Commons. His place was taken by Marilyn Stecyk, a former Clark political advisor from Jasper. Reform's candidate was Cliff Breitkreuz, an Onoway farmer; John Higgerty, a Hinton crown prosecutor won the Liberal nod; Joe Woytowich, a public relations consultant from Entwistle was the NDP candidate; Alex Mann, an oil rig mechanic from Parkland County was the representative of the National Party. Christian Heritage, Natural Law and an Independent were the remaining candidates on the Yellowhead ballot. The issues which dominated the campaign included law and order, jobs and the debt. The local voters in 1993 returned Cliff Breitkreuz of Reform to the House of Commons. He won the support of 55% of the voters; the Tory vote fell over 30%, leaving Marilyn Stecyk in third place; ahead of her was the Liberal standard-bearer, with 21.7% support. The NDP dropped 11%, ending up with 4.4%, not far ahead of the National Party, with 2.8%. Peter Piers, a Neerlandia farmer, won 1.1% for Christian Heritage. The remaining 1.1% was shared by Natural Law and the Independent in that order. Local turnout was a per cent and a half above the provincial rate.

Member of Parliament: Cliff Breitkreuz; **Party:** Reform; **Occupation:** Farmer; **Education:** BA, BEd, University of Alberta, University of Lethbridge; **Age:** 53 (Oct. 21, 1942); **Year first elected to the House of Commons:** 1993

48026 Yellowhead

A: Political Profile
i) Voting Behaviour

	% 1993	% 1988	Change 1988-93
Conservative	14	44.5	-30.5
Liberal	21.7	9.9	11.8
NDP	4.4	15.4	-11
Reform	55	27.9	27.1
Other	5	2.2	2.8

% Turnout	66.6	Total Ballots (#)	41534
Rejected Ballots (#)	129	% Margin of Victory	38.3
Rural Polls, 1988 (#)	148	Urban Polls, 1988 (#)	63
% Yes - 1992	30.2	% No - 1992	69.6

ii) Campaign Financing

	# of Donations	Total $ Value	% of Limit Spent
Conservative	96	48509	65.7*
Liberal	92	26673	48.5
NDP	0	0	0
Reform	200	44742	59.5
Other	53	16129	

B: Ethno-Linguistic Profile

% English Home Language	97.2	% French Home Language	0.8
% Official Bilingual	5.5	% Other Home Language	2
% Catholics	23.9	% Protestants	50.3
% Aboriginal Peoples	6.1	% Immigrants	7.8

C: Socio-Economic Profile

Average Family Income $	48586	Median Family Income $	46343
% Low Income Families	11.4	Average Home Price $	81281
% Home Owners	72.9	% Unemployment	7.5
% Labour Force Participation	75.2	% Managerial-Administrative	7.7
% Self-Employed	15.7	% University Degrees	5.4
% Movers	49.3		

D: Industrial Profile

% Manufacturing	8.6	% Service Sector	12.9
% Agriculture	10.8	% Mining	13.7
% Forestry	2.8	% Fishing	0
% Government Services	5.4	% Business Services	2.1

E: Homogeneity Measures

Ethnic Diversity Index	0.22	Religious Homogeneity Index	0.36
Sectoral Concentration Index	0.33	Income Disparity Index	4.6

F: Physical Setting Characteristics

Total Population	89361	Area (km²)	84140
Population Density (pop/km²)	1.1		

* Tentative value, due to the existence of unpaid campaign expenses.

BRITISH COLUMBIA

British Columbia

Provincial Overview

In October, 1993, British Columbia experienced a political transformation. Its usual pattern of sending Members to Parliament primarily from two parties, the Progressive Conservatives and the New Democrats, was overturned. Instead, two other parties predominated: Reform and the Liberals. Only a small remnant from the NDP remained, and the governing Progressive Conservative Party was annihilated. At least that would be the picture, if one were to concentrate only on the distribution of the thirty-two Parliamentary seats allocated to British Columbia in the October 25th, 1993, Canadian general election. Such perception would be less than true reality.

The province of British Columbia might be said to suffer from too many perceptions. Just as Mackenzie King once said that Canada suffered from too much geography, in the same way, external descriptors of British Columbia over-abound; most of them obscure almost as much as they elucidate. The province has been described as Lotusland; California North; Super, Natural; Ecotopia; Cascadia; Fantasyland; the Left Coast. It has been included in 'the West' and as Canada's 'Fifth Region'. It has been described as much for its politics as its topography, for its social setting as much as for its climate. In reality, British Columbia is different from any of these. It is certainly different, for example, than forming one coherent part of a single 'West'; and while it has much in common with its Pacific Northwest partner, Alberta, it has as much that divides it from its provincial neighbour, not least its politics.

In physical terms, British Columbia is separated into three geological regions: (i) the rain-forested (and now citied) Pacific Coast; (ii) the dry Interior Plateau (between the Coastal Mountains and the third region); and (iii) the Rocky Mountains. The nature of each region has had an impact on its economic and social development, and on the politics of the province. British Columbia is Canada's third largest province. That is the case geographically: it covers an area of 948,596 sq. km, 9.5% of Canada. Only Ontario - at 10.8% - and Quebec - at 15.5% - are larger in area. In terms of population: at the 1991 census, there were 3,282,061 people living in British Columbia, just over 12% of the total population of Canada. Only Ontario - with a population of 10,084,885, 37% of Canada - and Quebec - with 6,895,963 people, 25.3% of the country - are larger in population. The province is over 80% urban, yet that population lives in 151 municipalities that take up less than 1% of the total territory of the province. The majority of the province's residents - approximately two-thirds - reside in the fast-growing Vancouver-centred Lower Mainland, 'from Desolation to Hope', and the Victoria-centred Capital Regional District to Nanaimo/mid-Island area; together, this highly urbanized region within the province is referred to as the Georgia Basin. Most of the rest of the population are scattered about in communities where primary agricultural, forestry, mining, energy exploitation, and, sometimes, secondary manufacturing predominate. Given its climate, location, and terrain, however, service components such as tourism increasingly have come to represent a significant component of the provincial economy. Given its location as Canada's Pacific gateway, other manifestations of the tertiary economy - often in economic services - have come to predominate as well, despite the continuation of idyllic 'beer commercial' images of British Columbia as a land of woods and water.

In political terms, the province has most often been described as highly polarized. Certainly, the pattern of its early resource exploitation, and the links between political and economic leadership, especially in the forestry and mining sectors and through infrastructure investment by the province, helped produce a rough and tumble class-based politics which affected agenda setting and public policy choices. By the 1930s, these were finding reflection in electoral contests, provincially and federally. Some have referred to this link between province building and resource development in British Columbia as 'the Company Province'.

Whatever the patterns of capital accumulation (and not all agree that a singular class interpretation of B.C. politics is sufficient), the resources of the Pacific periphery were plentiful enough to produce one of the country's three consistent 'have' provinces. That economic growth and standing produced a population pull to B.C. from within the country as well as from outside. The shift from more rural and smaller communities, and from primary to tertiary economies began in the late 1930s: between 1939 and 1949, the provincial population grew by more than forty per cent and Gross Provincial Product more than three times. Even with that growth, the percentage of provincial residents concentrated in the Vancouver and Capital regions was still just forty-three per cent at the 1951 census. Within twenty-five years, this figure increased to over fifty-six per cent and since then these city-regions have expanded to represent fully two-thirds of the province.

The relative wealth of British Columbia compared with many of the other provinces may offer some clue as to why its politicians traditionally have played such a limited role in federal politics in Canada. Its provincial leaders have often been well known but just as often have been seen as eccentrics by those in Ottawa and beyond. Sir John A. Macdonald's term as Victoria MP in the 1870s or John Turner's Prime Ministerial interlude in the 1980s included, few Members of Parliament from B.C. have dominated the federal stage. Needing less from Ottawa and being far removed from the national capital and a governmental system seemingly dominated by the population heavyweights of central Canada, certainly contributed to a sense of political remoteness sometimes referred to as the 'over-the-mountain syndrome'. As one of few provinces contributing to equalization through Ottawa, this sense of difference may have been reinforced. Certainly when patterns of wealth are examined, the 'have' definition becomes apparent: average family incomes in British Columbia were the second highest amongst Canadian provinces - at $52,349, almost $800 ahead of neighbouring Alberta; only Ontario (with $56,162) was higher at the last national census. Average house prices - at $174,254 - were second only to Ontario again; almost 66% owned their own; and while that ownership rate was lower than many provinces, given price differences that in five cases were almost $100,000 less than B.C., a B.C. ownership rate about 10% lower was not that significant.

In terms of negative economic indicators, the 'have' quality continues: on the percentage of population dependent on income transfer support payments from government, for example, B.C. was third lowest - 11.43% of the income of residents of the province was in this form; only Alberta and Ontario had lower rates. Patterns of unemployment did not quite reflect the same status: B.C. - at 10.5% - was fifth ranked, behind Ontario and Alberta, but also with higher levels of those out of work than the 'have-not' western neighbours of Saskatchewan and Manitoba. When combined with average incomes, however, the seasonal nature of what have been well-paid jobs in resource-based work would appear to offset this unemployment rate as far as British Columbia is concerned. This is evident when industrial sectors are examined: only two provinces had over two per cent of their employment in forestry: B.C. was one of these, second highest, at 2.7%; six other provinces had higher levels of employment in agriculture. The shift to third wave economy was partly reflected in manufacturing versus service sector rates: manufacturing levels range from a low of 5.2% in Saskatchewan to 17.9% in Quebec; at 11.4% B.C. ranked sixth in this secondary category. While, comparatively, across Canada, all provincial economies are increasingly service-oriented (none is below 44%); yet in B.C., the tertiary economy is the highest of any province, 48.4%. The related educational component of tertiary development was reflected in the have vs have-not provincial differences as well: Ontario (with 12.3%), Alberta (at 11.2%) and B.C. (with 10.75%) were the only provinces where more than one in ten residents had completed a university degree.

In terms of demographic makeup, British Columbia had the lowest rate of French home-language use in the country, only about half the rate of Alberta though on a par with Newfoundland; in English home-language use, B.C. ranked in the middle of the pack (with 90.9%). When English and French language use is combined, British Columbia was third lowest (91.3%) behind Ontario and Manitoba. In Manitoba, with over eleven per cent of its population aboriginal peoples, this was reflective of First Peoples' home-language use. In B.C. it was more a feature of high levels of immigration, particularly from the Asia Pacific region. Aboriginal peoples certainly made up a significant portion of the provincial population (4.5%), but this was below Alberta, in third place, and well below the 11% plus in both Saskatchewan and Manitoba. In several constituencies, particularly in the north of the province, First Nations were sufficient in numbers to significantly affect 1993 electoral outcomes. Throughout the rest of British Columbia, however, immigrants, who make up more than two in ten (21.1%) of all residents in British Columbia (only Ontario with 22.4% was higher), were more politically influential in constituency voting contests. That is different than in most Canadian provinces - six of the ten - where immigration rates are well below one in ten. In many B.C. constituencies, especially in the Georgia Basin megalopolis, concentrations of distinct immigrant populations affected candidate choice and eventual electoral outcomes. In some constituencies - for example, Richmond and Vancouver South, or in Surrey - one ethnic community confronted another as democratic combatants. The contests that resulted, and the MPs that were elected in 1993 reflect this multicultural mix: of B.C.'s thirty-two MPs, there are representatives from Chinese, East Indian, German, West Indian, Italian, Scandinavian and British ethnic communities.

Religious patterns reflected some of the above characteristics as well: for example, not only was French home-language in B.C. the lowest in the country, so also were levels of Catholicism. Fewer than two in ten British Columbians (18.4%) were Catholic; Alberta was next lowest at 26.5%, but with one other exception (Manitoba: 29.9%); in all other provinces, more than three in ten of their residents were Catholic. British Columbia also ranked low in terms of number of Protestants amongst its residents: apart from Quebec and New Brunswick (both with high Catholic and French populations), only Ontario (with 44.6%) was below B.C. (and then only by a difference of 0.3%). In fact, the pattern of overall religious affiliation shifts downward from the East Coast to the West: more than nine in ten of all Atlantic Canadians indicated adherence to either Catholic or Protestant religions; the same was true in Quebec, though again Catholicism was higher here. In Ontario, the figure for these two major religious groupings was still more than eight in ten; that was the parallel pattern in Manitoba and Saskatchewan. By Alberta, the level of affiliation to any religion was down to just over three-quarters of the population; in British Columbia, it was below two-thirds: fully 36% of all residents in British Columbia declared no religion in the 1991 census.

Many of these demographic and economic differences played out in electoral politics in the province. The provincial party system was predominantly two-party from the beginning of the 1950s until the 1990s; the difference was that it was not the two main parties in the country as a whole. Instead of Conservatives and Liberals, Social Credit, led by W.A.C. Bennett, and then his son Bill, were in power continuously between 1952 and 1986, with the exception of 1972 to 1975, when the Dave Barrett-led New Democrats formed the government. The CCF and then its successor, the NDP, ran a consistent second in provincial elections, regularly scoring around 40% of the voters' support.. That pattern continued after 1986, when Bill Vander Zalm led a term of Social Credit government - their last. By the mid 1970s the Social Credit in B.C. had become a coalition party of old Socreds, Liberals, and Conservatives, forged to keep the NDP out of office. Vander Zalm's one 'faaan-taas-tic' term ended that, destroying Social Credit in the process. That allowed a Mike Harcourt-led New Democratic government to be elected in 1991. It also provided the opportunity for provincial Liberals to emerge as the Official Opposition, and it let remnant Socreds forge an alliance with a new provincial Reform Party and claim official party status in the legislature. A multi-party system had re-emerged in British Columbia politics in the mid 1990s.

Federally, the picture was different, but also by 1988 showed signs of transition and flux. Initially, in the post-W.W. II era, this was largely because the provincial Socreds avoided direct involvement at the federal level; that abandonment of active organizational involvement in national electoral politics occurred much earlier in B.C. than in Alberta, where Social Credit continued to run federal candidates long after. In national political contests in British Columbia, throughout the 1950s to 1980s, Tories and Liberals fought each other; they were regularly confronted by the NDP. The general result, certainly over the past twenty years, was for Conservatives and New Democrats to split the parliamentary spoils.

In 1979, for example, the Conservatives captured 44.3% of the vote and 67.9% of the seats (19 of 28); the NDP took 31.9% support, for 28.6% (8) of the seats. Liberals, with 23% of all votes cast, managed one seat (a 3.6% share of parliamentary seats). In 1980, the Liberal vote stayed virtually unchanged - at 22.2% - but they lost their one seat. All House of Commons seats were won by Progressive Conservatives or New Democrats: the Progressive Conservatives took 16 seats (57.1% of the total) for just 41.4% of the votes; the New Democrats, despite more votes - 42.9% of the total votes cast - managed only 12 seats, 42.9%. Under a proportional representation system, that would have been the total number of seats they should have received. In the 1984 Mulroney landslide, 53.4% of British Columbians voted against Conservatives; they still managed to win nineteen of the twenty-eight seats, more than two-thirds of those contested for their 46.6% support. The Liberal vote actually slipped in B.C. in the 1984 Canadian general election - to 16.4% - but the party still managed to win one seat in Parliament: John Turner's Vancouver Quadra victory. The voter support for New Democrats in 1984 fell to 35.1%, down 7.8% from 1980; however, the NDP lost one third of their seats in parliament, down four seats to eight. In none of these three elections did 'other party/independent' votes total up to more than 2%.

The vagaries of our plurality, first-past-the-post x-voting were demonstrated again in the 1988 general election. The New Democratic Party managed to increase its vote by only two per cent from the previous contest - up to 37%; for that small additional support, the party improved its parliamentary standing from eight seats to nineteen, an increase of more that 100%. The Conservatives saw their vote drop about 12% (to 34.4%) and their seats in Parliament from two-thirds of the B.C. total to 42.9%. Liberals increased their voter numbers to 21.3% in 1988; under a more proportional electoral system, they might have received between five and six seats. Instead, all they were able to do was hold on to the one (John Turner/Vancouver Quadra) they had won in 1984. The other factor emerging in 1988 federal election voting in British Columbia was the emergence of new party formations under the traditional 'other' party category. Total other party/independent voting in B.C. was 7.3% in 1988; almost 5% of that was for the new right wing Reform Party. That was enough to affect outcomes in seventeen of the thirty-two ridings. In six seats this negatively impacted on the results for incumbent Conservative MPs; in at least five races, it resulted in the election of five New Democrats. Still, in 1988 it was possible to talk of half the seats in the province being safe for either New Democrats or Conservatives. The transition started in 1988; the shift was further suggested in the 1992 constitutional referendum on the Charlottetown Accord: of all constituencies in Canada voting 'No', eleven of the top fifteen highest 'No' votes were in British Columbia.

In 1988, free trade dominated the electoral agenda in British Columbia. This was a natural feature of a province more dependent than any other on trade outside of that with the United States; it was also influenced by the extra local coverage accorded Liberal Party leader John Turner who represented a Vancouver constituency. The 65.6% not voting for the Conservatives in 1988, produced nineteen New Democrat and one Liberal M.P. The Tories still managed twelve B.C. seats. In 1993, the NDP campaign focus in British Columbia was on jobs, the residual negative effects of the expanded NAFTA agreement and protection of social programs. These increasingly did not resonate well with B.C. voters. As a result, the NDP lost seventeen of its nineteen seats and saw its vote drop by more than 100% - down to 15.5% and two seats (6.3% of those available in B.C.). That was still two per cent ahead of the Progressive Conservatives. The Conservatives had felt an initial perceived advantage in the fact that the new Prime Minister, Kim Campbell, was from Vancouver. However, Campbell's prior cheerleading for a sinking Mulroney ship - for example, the pushing of an unpopular GST and an unsupported Charlottetown Accord - together with the political cement shoes of her predecessor and a poorly orchestrated campaign of her own, were enough to send the Tories in B.C. into a tailspin. They ended up with just 13.5% support, losing every one of their twelve B.C. seats (from 1988), including the Prime Minister's and those of several of her Cabinet colleagues. B.C. Liberals saw their voter support increase in 1993; and while not dramatically - up less than 7% to 28.1% - they added five additional House of Commons seats to the Vancouver Quadra seat previously represented by Party leader John Turner, and won in the 1993 general election by constitutional law expert Ted McWhinney. Their six seats represented 18.8% of those available for their more than 28% share of the vote. The Party with the most dramatic breakthrough in British Columbia in 1993 was Reform. In 1988, Reform had managed just under 5% support; even when combined with other right-wing party totals (including Christian Heritage, Libertarian, Confederation of Regions, Western Party, Western Canada Concept separatists, Social Credit and Lyndon LaRouche's Commonwealth) the total was just 6.3% of the total provincial vote.

In 1993, running on a platform which emphasized the deficit and debt, the need for less government, law and order issues (such as toughening the Young Offenders Act, limitations on parole, stiffer sentencing, and more police) and limits on immigration, the Reform Party tapped into much of the residual frustration extant in the British Columbia electorate. Certainly in a 'have' province highly dependent on trade, opposition to trade deals had limited appeal, and the deficit won out over jobs, as a campaign issue, in a province where unemployment, while high, was far from the number one issue on peoples' minds. As a result, Reform climbed more than 30% in 1993: they won the support of 36.4% of the B.C. voters. For that one-third plus vote Reform received the electoral system bonus of 'double your seats': had seats been allocated proportionally, they would have received eleven or twelve House of Commons seats; instead Reform ended the 1993 election with twenty-four Members of Parliament elected from British Columbia. These were from all regions. In 1988, the NDP had taken all six Vancouver Island seats; in 1993, Reform won five (and the Liberals the other). In 1988, the seven interior ridings were split five for the NDP and two to the Progressive Conservatives; in 1993, Reform took six; only NDP incumbent Nelson Riis managed to hold on to his own Kamloops seat. In the three Northern constituencies in 1988, the NDP won two, just losing the third to a Conservative; in 1993, Reform won all three; and in the Vancouver centred Lower Mainland in 1988, of the sixteen seats, Conservatives won nine, New Democrats six and Liberals one; in 1993, Reform took ten, the Liberals five of their six B.C. seats, and New Democrat Svend Robinson held his Burnaby–Kingsway riding.

One feature of the 1993 vote, first notable in 1988, was the continuing presence of minor parties; in 1988, Reform was counted as part of this political phenomenon; combined, that represented the votes of 7.3% of all British Columbia voters. In 1993, a certain political testiness as well as some uncertainty as to where to park a vote during the uncertainty of a transitional election, resulted more than in the significant swing to the political right with Reform; it also produced the support of 6.5% of the B.C. electorate for candidates other than those seeking to represent the (now) four major parties outside of Quebec. That was almost as high as the 'protest vote' in 1988 with Reform. In British Columbia in 1993, over four per cent of this 'other party' vote (4.1%) went to the National Party. In twenty-eight of the thirty-two ridings in B.C., the National Party placed fifth; and in one constituency, Skeena, their candidate placed fourth ahead of one of the 'big four' representatives, a Conservative. Sixth spot was split between Christian Heritage with its fundamentalist moral agenda (10, plus 2 fifth place finishes), environmentally conscious Greens (10), the yogic flying Natural Law Party (8), right wing economic Libertarians (3) and one for the Canada Party. And while the gnus (with the 'g' pronounced) and a few others still provided a place for the disgruntled, eccentric, and anarchic, clearly the days when Rhinos were the fourth largest party in the country have given way to those with a much more serious political purpose: nationalist, fundamentalist Christian or right-wing economic. What that will mean for future elections is not certain; it will certainly produce more seriousness of purpose and less humorous in the Canadian electoral exercise.

Two other features of the Canadian general election of 1993 in British Columbia are of note: the first is in terms of incumbency. In 1988, sixteen of the twenty-eight incumbent Members of Parliament from 1984 were returned; only six lost, the rest deciding to retire. That was an incumbent return (vs. defeat) rate of 78.6%. In 1993, only two of thirty-two incumbents re-won their Parliamentary seats: both were New Democrats (Nelson Riis and Svend Robinson). In seven ridings, five in the Lower Mainland and two in the North, incumbents did not run again. In the other twenty-five seats, many of them previously considered safe by either the NDP or the Conservatives, incumbents lost their seats. In total, sixteen New Democrat M.P.s were voted out of office; seven Conservatives, including Cabinet Ministers such as Mary Collins, in Capilano–Howe Sound, and Tom Siddon, in Richmond, joined Prime Minister Kim Campbell (Vancouver Centre) in being defeated by the voters. Clearly, in 1993, incumbency was not a strong factor in British Columbia.

The other point of note was the political status of women in British Columbia in the Canadian general election: in 1988, it was reported that women had been somewhat more able to secure major party nominations than in 1984; for the 1984 election, Liberals had nominated eight, they had elected none; New Democrats nominated four and elected two; and the Conservatives had nominated two and elected both. In 1988, the NDP had nominated nine and elected four; the Conservatives selected six and saw two elected; and the Liberals had chosen six with none elected. That meant that 18.8% of the B.C. parliamentary seats were won by women in 1988. In 1993, (at least) seventy-five women contested the election for House of Commons' seats, from major and minor parties, and as independents. The NDP nominated nine women; all were defeated. The Progressive Conservatives also selected nine women as candidates; they too were defeated. Eight women ran for the Liberals in B.C. in 1993; two (Hedy Fry in Vancouver Centre and Anna Terrana in Vancouver East) were elected. In the process they defeated two women sitting as MPs. The Reform Party nominated only five women; their record of success was higher, though - four of the five (Daphne Jennings in Mission–Coquitlam, Sharon Hayes in Port Moody–Coquitlam, Margaret Bridgman in Surrey North and Val Meredith in Surrey–White Rock–South Langley) won, only one of them defeating another incumbent woman in the process. The end result was that while more women were nominated - 31 by the four largest parties (as well as eight by the fifth place National Party) - only six were elected in B.C. in 1993. That was the same 18.8% share as in the 1988 election.

For British Columbia, it is easy to describe the 1993 Canadian general election: it was one of significant change in parliamentary representational patterns, one that saw a new party emerge as politically dominant, with a continuing, not unimportant, presence of minor parties (largely with serious policy purpose), and one where, while the number of women seeking public office increased, women made no new inroads in elective terms; indeed many high profile women in Canadian politics left the political scene as a result of voter choices. In sum, in 1993, British Columbia was very much part of the most extraordinary election in Canadian history.

British Columbia Results, 1988 & 1993 Elections, 1992 Referendum

	1988 Election			1993 Election	
	% Vote	Seats	1992	% Vote	Seats
Conservatives	35.3	12		13.5	0
Liberals	20.4	1		28.1	6
NDP	37.0	19		15.5	2
Reform	4.9	0		36.4	24
Other/Indep.	2.4	–		6.5	0
Turnout	78.7	–		67.8	–
% Yes (1992)			31.7		
% No (1992)			68.3		

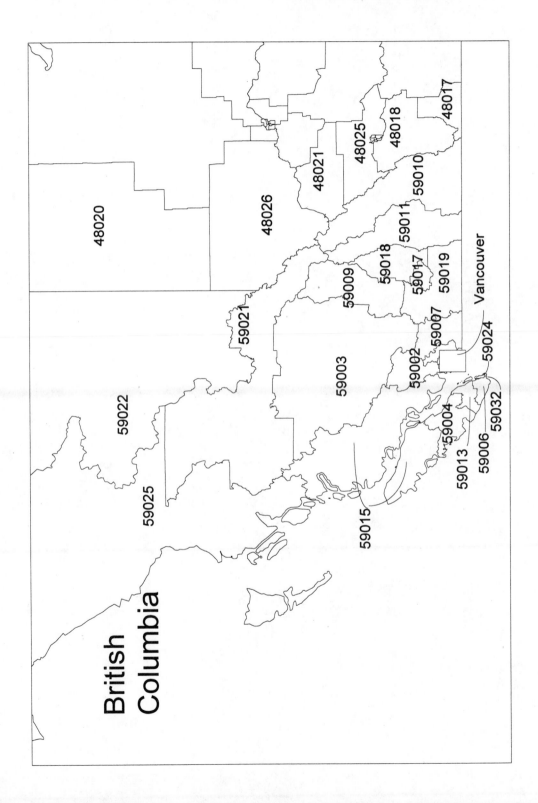

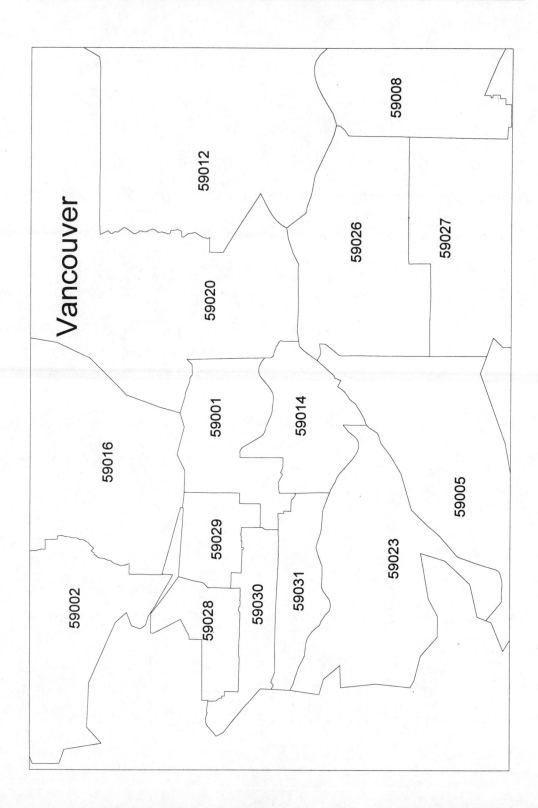

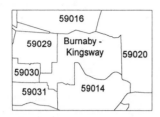

Burnaby–Kingsway

Constituency Number: 59001

Burnaby–Kingsway is an urban riding of 119,305 residents, sixth largest in the province. Three-quarters of the constituency is in Burnaby (all but the city's southern portion) immediately to the east of Vancouver; the rest of the riding is from the Kingsway portion of the disbanded (in 1986) Vancouver Kingsway seat of Ian Waddell (and much earlier, Grace MacInnis). The riding reflects an increasingly diversified demography (36.6% are immigrants), with a mixture of British, Italian and other Eastern and Western Europeans, Chinese and other South Asians; three-quarters speak English as their home language (though only 0.2% French, the lowest rate of French language use in all of Canada). The riding includes Simon Fraser University and the British Columbia Institute of Technology. Apart from these institutions, the local economy is significantly service oriented (4.9% governmental, 7.4% in business) or light manufacturing - 12.0%. Over 12% of the local population have university degrees; more that one in ten are 'managers' and a further 8.7% are self-employed; the average house price is just over one-quarter million dollars, second highest of all the Vancouver suburbs, and over half (56.6%) own their own homes; yet average family incomes ($51,651) are amongst the lowest in the region. The unemployment rate is 9.5%, slightly below the provincial average of 10.5%. While 56.9% are either Catholic or Protestant, and 11.11% Jewish, the largest 'religious' category in the riding in the 1991 census was 'non-religious' (32%).

The major Burnaby portion of the constituency has been represented by NDP MP Svend Robinson; first elected in 1979, at age 26, Robinson fought the 1988 general election as the first openly gay Member of Parliament; that issue, along with free trade, dominated the contest, with Robinson winning his fourth term and increasing his support to 43%. His nearest rivals emphasized 'family values' and received 30% (Conservative) and 22% (Liberal) respectively. During the 1992 Constitutional referendum, two-thirds of the constituency voted 'No'.

In the 1993 election, Robinson faced the local electorate with his party significantly down in the national polls, and with some controversy about his high profile on issues such as criticism of China's human rights record and subsequent 'expulsion' from China, his opposition to logging in Clayoquot Sound and his involvement in Sue Rodriguez' right to assisted suicide case. His ten opponents faced a hard working incumbent with an excellent record of constituency and community work, however. For Robinson, the major issues during the local campaign were jobs, the economy, health care, and education. Many of his opponents sought to make Robinson's 'personal' and 'maverick' style a key plank. A 'rightist' Liberal, Conservative and Reform candidates also placed considerable emphasis on the federal deficit.

The results included the re-election of Svend Robinson to a fifth term, but with his support reduced by nine points to 34.2%; that was still the second highest NDP vote in the province (and the seventh highest in Canada). Businessmen Liberal (and former Reform Party member) Kwangyul Peck (at 26.3% - up 4.1%) and Reform candidate John Carpay (at 25% - up 22%+) were second and third. Former National President of the PC Women's Federation, Adelle Haines saw local Conservative support shrink from 30% to 10%, perhaps partly reflective of her strong support for Kim Campbell. Amongst the six other candidates (National, Commonwealth, Libertarian, Natural Law, Marxist-Leninist and Independent) only 4.6% support was garnered (in that order) - up 0.1% from 1988 when (including Reform) four minor party candidates sought election. Local turnout was 66%, just below the (67.8%) average across the province.

Member of Parliament: Svend Robinson; **Party:** NDP; **Occupation:** Lawyer; **Education:** LL.B, London School of Economics; **Age:** 41 (March 4, 1952); **Year first elected to the House of Commons:** 1979

59001 Burnaby–Kingsway

A: Political Profile

i) Voting Behaviour

	% 1993	% 1988	Change 1988-93
Conservative	10	30	-20
Liberal	26.3	22.2	4.1
NDP	34.2	43.2	-9
Reform	25	2.7	22.3
Other	4.6	1.9	2.7

% Turnout	66	Total Ballots (#)	53928
Rejected Ballots (#)	416	% Margin of Victory	7.9
Rural Polls, 1988 (#)	0	Urban Polls, 1988 (#)	224
% Yes - 1992	33.2	% No - 1992	66.4

ii) Campaign Financing

	# of Donations	Total $ Value	% of Limit Spent
Conservative	58	21822	34.9
Liberal	80	38656	69*
NDP	53	79631	82.6
Reform	196	30407	46.7
Other	36	5650	

B: Ethno-Linguistic Profile

% English Home Language	75.8	% French Home Language	0.2
% Official Bilingual	5.3	% Other Home Language	24
% Catholics	25.2	% Protestants	31.7
% Aboriginal Peoples	1	% Immigrants	36.6

C: Socio-Economic Profile

Average Family Income $	51651	Median Family Income $	46566
% Low Income Families	18.8	Average Home Price $	250063
% Home Owners	56.6	% Unemployment	9.5
% Labour Force Participation	68.9	% Managerial-Administrative	10.1
% Self-Employed	8.7	% University Degrees	12.1
% Movers	53.5		

D: Industrial Profile

% Manufacturing	12	% Service Sector	13.2
% Agriculture	0.6	% Mining	0.3
% Forestry	0.4	% Fishing	0.3
% Government Services	4.9	% Business Services	7.4

E: Homogeneity Measures

Ethnic Diversity Index	0.22	Religious Homogeneity Index	0.27
Sectoral Concentration Index	0.5	Income Disparity Index	9.8

F: Physical Setting Characteristics

Total Population	119305	Area (km²)	63
Population Density (pop/km²)	1893.7		

* Tentative value, due to the existence of unpaid campaign expenses.

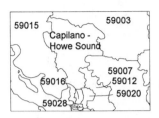

Capilano–Howe Sound

Constituency Number: 59002

Capilano–Howe Sound has been described as 'the province's poshest riding'. Its 83,407 residents (fifth smallest in B.C.) live in homes which average $345,176, centred around one of Canada's wealthiest communities, West Vancouver and the resort community of Whistler; it also includes the resource towns of Squamish and Pemberton, where farming and resources dominate. A portion (20%) of the constituency is in the ranching Cariboo-Chilcotin region in the North. 71.6% of the constituents own their own homes, whose value averages $345,176, almost double the B.C. cost. Average family incomes are $82,310 (the highest in the province - and third highest in Canada) and the unemployment rate is just 7.2%, one of the lowest in the province. Almost one quarter (24.4%) have university degrees, second highest rate in the province - and fourteenth highest in Canada. In ethnic terms, the riding has the highest proportion of British (almost 55%) in the province, and 92.9% speak English at home, only 0.5% French. Almost 2% of the constituency are aboriginal peoples. Half of Capilano–Howe Sound (49.5%) is Protestant; 16% are Catholic (the second lowest level in B.C. and Canada) and over 6% Jewish. In economic terms, the affluent riding is reflected in its managerial/service components: 17.7% are managerial/administrative, highest in B.C., and 12.3% in business services (the second highest in B.C./seventh highest in Canada) and 5.05% governmental.

The riding covers over 9,000 sq. km, much of it in the sparsely populated northern Cariboo area. In 1984, Mary Collins replaced Conservative Ron Huntington when he chose not to run again. Huntington had defeated Liberal Cabinet Minister Jack Davis in 1974. Between 1949 and 1958 Liberal Cabinet Minister James Sinclair (better known as the father of Margaret Trudeau) had held the old Coast-Capilano riding. Since the 1974 election, however, the constituency has been solidly Conservative: Collins held the seat in 1988 with a margin of more than 17% over a Liberal. The Reform Party placed fourth (at 8.2%) behind the NDP (14.3%). In the 1988 race, Reform leader Preston Manning had helped local Conservatives by having to force the resignation of controversial right-wing columnist Doug Collins as the Reform party standard bearer. That alienated many potential Reformers who supported Doug Collins.

In 1993, Mary Collins ran as a Cabinet Minister for the first time, having held posts in Defence, Western Diversification, Status of Women and finally, Health. Like many Conservatives, she faced a serious Reform surge, led locally by Simon Fraser University economist and Fraser Institute author Herb Grubel. The Liberals had nominated former West Van School Board Chair Audrey Sojonsky. Seven other candidates, including the NDP, National, Green, Libertarian, Natural Law, Commonwealth, and one Independent, also sought election in Capilano–Howe Sound. Local issues which dominated the campaign included the economy - particularly debt and deficit for Reform (as well as some local controversy from statements by Reform's Herb Grubel about limiting immigration), job retraining for jobs lost in the forest industry, in tourism (Whistler's population had more than doubled in the 1986-91 census period), local infrastructure and - an unusual issue for a constituency of such affluence - legalization of marijuana. Local 'growers' in the Pemberton Valley helped promote this latter issue during the election.

When the 1993 votes were counted, Collins' Conservative total had shrunk over 29%. Herb Grubel had increased Reform's vote by just under 34% to 42% overall, enough to take the seat. The Liberal vote held (actually increasing 2.1% to 31.8%). The local NDP, never a threat to take the riding, saw their vote fall 11% to 3.3% of local support. The seven remaining candidates managed 5.2%, up from 1.2% (when Reform is excluded) from 1988. National Party candidate Doris Fuller, a retired teacher-librarian from Gibsons, was just 0.1% behind the NDP. Green representative Peggy Stortz, a West Van songwriter, managed 1%; the other four took the last 1%. Turnout fell from a high of 82.5% in 1988, to 73.6% in 1993, but this was still more than 5.5% above the provincial average.

Member of Parliament: Herb Grubel; **Party:** Reform; **Occupation:** University economics professor; **Education:** PhD, Yale University; **Age:** 59 (Feb. 26, 1934); **Year first elected to the House of Commons:** 1993

59002 Capilano–Howe Sound

A: Political Profile

i) Voting Behaviour

	% 1993	% 1988	Change 1988-93
Conservative	17.7	46.8	-29.1
Liberal	31.8	29.7	2.1
NDP	3.3	14.3	-11
Reform	42	8.2	33.8
Other	5.2	1.1	4.1

% Turnout	73.6	Total Ballots (#)	46055
Rejected Ballots (#)	145	% Margin of Victory	15.4
Rural Polls, 1988 (#)	42	Urban Polls, 1988 (#)	134
% Yes - 1992	40.6	% No - 1992	59.1

ii) Campaign Financing

	# of Donations	Total $ Value	% of Limit Spent
Conservative	121	86161	84
Liberal	224	74559	80.3
NDP	18	14853	9.2
Reform	202	53434	90.8
Other	41	5479	

B: Ethno-Linguistic Profile

% English Home Language	92.9	% French Home Language	0.5
% Official Bilingual	11	% Other Home Language	6.5
% Catholics	16.1	% Protestants	49.5
% Aboriginal Peoples	2	% Immigrants	26.6

C: Socio-Economic Profile

Average Family Income $	82310	Median Family Income $	64821
% Low Income Families	9.1	Average Home Price $	345176
% Home Owners	71.6	% Unemployment	7.2
% Labour Force Participation	68.4	% Managerial-Administrative	17.7
% Self-Employed	17.9	% University Degrees	24.4
% Movers	52.6		

D: Industrial Profile

% Manufacturing	6.6	% Service Sector	12.4
% Agriculture	0.7	% Mining	0.6
% Forestry	1.7	% Fishing	0.3
% Government Services	5	% Business Services	12.2

E: Homogeneity Measures

Ethnic Diversity Index	0.34	Religious Homogeneity Index	0.35
Sectoral Concentration Index	0.6	Income Disparity Index	21.2

F: Physical Setting Characteristics

Total Population	83407	Area (km²)	9605
Population Density (pop/km²)	8.7		

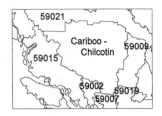

Cariboo–Chilcotin

Constituency Number: 59003

Cariboo–Chilcotin is the third largest constituency in British Columbia (101,076 sq. km), and one of the fifteen largest in the country. Situated to the north of Greater Vancouver's Capilano–Howe Sound and stretching across farming/grazing land in the central Interior of the province to Kamloops, it remains sparsely populated - only 72,605, third smallest in the province, and with a population density rate of 0.7 per sq. km. Its largest ethnic group is British and English is the home language for over 95% of the population, but it also contains the second highest concentration of aboriginal peoples in B.C., 16.3%, in 32 Bands spread throughout the constituency. The riding's population is concentrated around regional centres such as Williams Lake and Quesnel and its economy is primarily based on cattle ranching/farming and forestry (the second highest level in this category in B.C. and Canada), with some area mining. What local manufacturing there is, is mostly in support of these industries, as is its service sector employment. Unemployment is high (at 14.1%, one of two tied for second highest in the province), largely affected by a 'seasonal' economy. Average family incomes are $44,197 and over 12% of the local population, as in 1988, receive some form of government assistance. Over 12% of the population in Cariboo–Chilcotin have less than Grade 9 education. Still, 72.1% own their own homes; their average value is $76,258, amongst the lowest levels in the province.

In the 1988 Canadian general election, Dave Worthy took the seat with 36.7% of the votes, replacing three-term Tory Lorne Greenaway. Worthy, a forest products manager, saw a drop of over 20% in Conservative support in the riding. The local NDP were just 1% behind, with the Liberals trailing at 25.1%. Reform managed 1.7% in that election - more than the margin of victory for BC caucus chair Worthy and the Conservatives. The possibility of a subsequent upswing in Reform support was indicated in the 1992 Constitutional referendum: over seven in ten (71.4%) of the voters in Cariboo–Chilcotin voted 'No' on the Charlottetown Accord.

During the 1993 general election, Worthy was confronted by seven opponents: representatives from the National Party, Natural Law, Canada Party, and the Greens as well as local New Democratic President and businessperson Gillian MacDonald; Liberal Barry Nordin, a Quesnel local councillor and lawyer; and Reform hopeful Philip Mayfield, a Vancouver pastor for the United Church. In an election where the economy was central, local NDP fortunes suffered a complete collapse. Having missed taking the seat by one per cent in the previous election, their support plummeted 25.4% to 10.4%. Land use policies such as those affecting forestry, farming, and fishing, and how these might be affected by native land claims also played a large part in the local campaigns. The Conservative incumbent lost 14.4%.and ended up in third place. Much of both the 'losses' by local Conservatives and New Democrats went to Reform. Philip Mayfield, running for Parliament while on insured disability leave for stress from his job as a pastor for the United Church in Vancouver - a situation requiring an 'incapacity' to perform 'regular work'- seemed to receive little negative reaction locally even when this became known during the campaign. Mayfield won the riding for Reform with 36.4%, an increase of almost 35% from 1988. The Liberal vote actually increased 1.7%, leaving them in second place (at 26.8%). The other four candidates, which included two students, a band administrator and a logger/miner, received a total of 4.1% support. National's Richard Bennett, the Ashcroft band administrator won 1.7% and Canada Party candidate Bob Hampton from Likely, B.C., managed 1%. Turnout was 64.8%, three points below the provincial average.

Member of Parliament: Phillip Mayfield; **Party:** Reform; **Occupation:** Minister of religion; **Education:** BA, University of British Columbia; **Age:** 57 (1937); **Year first elected to the House of Commons:** 1993

59003 Cariboo–Chilcotin

A: Political Profile
i) Voting Behaviour

	% 1993	% 1988	Change 1988-93
Conservative	22.3	36.7	-14.4
Liberal	26.8	25.1	1.7
NDP	10.4	35.8	-25.4
Reform	36.4	1.7	34.7
Other	4.1	0.7	3.4

% Turnout	64.8	Total Ballots (#)	31712
Rejected Ballots (#)	125	% Margin of Victory	13.7
Rural Polls, 1988 (#)	126	Urban Polls, 1988 (#)	40
% Yes - 1992	28.2	% No - 1992	71.4

ii) Campaign Financing

	# of Donations	Total $ Value	% of Limit Spent
Conservative	155	44742	68.6
Liberal	0	0	0
NDP	33	40298	52.9
Reform	180	45285	67.1
Other	3	3597	

B: Ethno-Linguistic Profile

% English Home Language	95.2	% French Home Language	0.2
% Official Bilingual	4.4	% Other Home Language	4.5
% Catholics	19.7	% Protestants	41.6
% Aboriginal Peoples	16.3	% Immigrants	11.2

C: Socio-Economic Profile

Average Family Income $	44197	Median Family Income $	41453
% Low Income Families	13.8	Average Home Price $	76258
% Home Owners	72.1	% Unemployment	14.1
% Labour Force Participation	69.2	% Managerial-Administrative	7.3
% Self-Employed	12.9	% University Degrees	5.4
% Movers	49		

D: Industrial Profile

% Manufacturing	15.9	% Service Sector	14.8
% Agriculture	5.3	% Mining	2.1
% Forestry	8.2	% Fishing	0.2
% Government Services	6.3	% Business Services	2.3

E: Homogeneity Measures

Ethnic Diversity Index	0.24	Religious Homogeneity Index	0.33
Sectoral Concentration Index	0.32	Income Disparity Index	6.2

F: Physical Setting Characteristics

Total Population	72605	Area (km²)	101076
Population Density (pop/km²)	0.7		

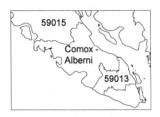

Comox–Alberni

Constituency Number: 59004

Comox-Alberni is one of six Vancouver Island constituencies, all six of which returned New Democrats to Parliament in 1988. With a population of 103,805 (over 13,167 sq. km), it stands at the mid point between largest and smallest ridings in B.C. The local economy has been undergoing a fundamental shift: challenges to forest resource use - in constituency 'hot spots' like Clayoquot Sound - and to mining, and uncertainty over a declining fishery and the impact of native fishing rights and land claim treaty negotiations, have all placed such issues high on the local and provincial agenda. Some, like local logging practices, have had national and international exposure. Despite this focus, the forestry sector still provides 6.6% of all direct jobs - the fifth highest level in B.C. and one of the (top 15) highest in the country. Most of the service sector operate in support of the area's traditional industries. Almost one in ten (9.2%) were employed locally in 'governmental' services and 12.9% were self-employed. Part of this latter employment was in a strong local tourism industry, much of it environmentally based. Given the economic uncertainty and seasonal nature of much of the work, it is not surprising that unemployment is at 12.1%, a couple of points above the provincial average; over 15% of the local population receive income assistance. 55.3% had moved between 1986 and 1991. Yet, just over three-quarters of the residents own their own homes (average value, $112,328 - more than $60,000 below the provincial norm); family incomes locally averaged $46,131 - more than $6,000 below the B.C. rate. Like other Island constituencies, British ethnicity was high - five of the six seats were 'tops' in this category (North Island was seventh) - as was English home-language use (97.3%). Protestantism was reported by almost half (49%) of the local population. Aboriginal peoples represented six per cent of the citizens in the riding, their aboriginal rights reflecting major questions throughout the region.

Historically, the Nanaimo–Cowichan portion of the riding had been Conservative (in the late 1940s with General George Pearkes and then Colin Cameron); by the late 1960s, it had switched to the New Democrats, and supported Tommy Douglas, national party leader, who held the seat between 1968 and 1974. The Comox–Alberni area - centre of pulp and paper processing - was CCF/NDP since 1953, only losing to Liberals in 1968 and 1974. With the Mulroney landslide of 1984, the seat went PC; it returned to the NDP in the 1988 election, to be represented by former provincial NDP Opposition Leader Bob Skelly: (Skelly's brother Ray, MLA, represented the adjacent North Island–Powell River riding). The NDP vote in 1988 was 42.8%, unchanged from 1984; that put them 14.5% ahead of the Conservatives. Hinting at political trouble for NDP/Conservative domination subsequently, the local Reform vote was 10%; Christian Heritage, another right-wing element, added 1% .

In 1993, incumbent New Democrat Skelly faced eight other challengers. These included candidates from the National Party (a fishing resort assistant manager), the Greens (a businessperson), the Canada Party (a bailiff), Natural Law (a homemaker/office manager), and a retired Independent. The Liberals nominated a Qualicum Beach consultant, Lonnie Hindle; the Conservatives, Mike Hicks, a Bamfield businessperson; and Reform, Bill Gilmour, a Nanoose Bay professional forester with 23 years experience working for MacMillan Bloedel. Gilmour had served two years (1986-88) on the Alberni School Board.

The outcome of the election in Comox–Alberni in 1993 involved a 26.2% drop in NDP fortunes and an 18.6% fall for the Tories. Bob Skelly was left in third place with only 16.6% support. The local Liberal vote actually increased 3.8% to 20.4% overall and second place. Reform support, at a respectable 10% in the previous contest, shot up to 42.2% and a win for Bill Gilmour. Ernest Daley, the National candidate, from Courtney, took 5.8%, less than 4% behind the NDP; Richard Porter, also from Courtney, managed 2.3% for the Green Party. Natural Law, an Independent, and the Canada Party shared the last 1.1%, in that order. Turnout was up three points above the provincial average.

Member of Parliament: Bill Gilmour; **Party:** Reform; **Occupation:** Forester; **Education:** BScF, University of British Columbia; **Age:** 50 (Dec. 29, 1942); **Year first elected to the House of Commons:** 1993

59004 Comox–Alberni

A: Political Profile
i) Voting Behaviour

	% 1993		% 1988	Change 1988-93
Conservative	9.7		28.3	-18.6
Liberal	20.4		16.6	3.8
NDP	16.6		42.8	-26.2
Reform	44.2		9.9	34.3
Other	9.2		2.3	6.9

% Turnout	70.8	Total Ballots (#)	56802
Rejected Ballots (#)	199	% Margin of Victory	33
Rural Polls, 1988 (#)	128	Urban Polls, 1988 (#)	96
% Yes - 1992	28.1	% No - 1992	71.5

ii) Campaign Financing

	# of Donations	Total $ Value	% of Limit Spent
Conservative	119	42439	67
Liberal	73	22563	35*
NDP	22	55162	57.9
Reform	458	65127	59.4
Other	67	12275	

B: Ethno-Linguistic Profile

% English Home Language	97.3	% French Home Language	0.7
% Official Bilingual	6	% Other Home Language	2
% Catholics	16.2	% Protestants	49
% Aboriginal Peoples	6	% Immigrants	14.7

C: Socio-Economic Profile

Average Family Income $	46131	Median Family Income $	41379
% Low Income Families	12.6	Average Home Price $	112328
% Home Owners	75.2	% Unemployment	12.1
% Labour Force Participation	61.1	% Managerial-Administrative	7
% Self-Employed	12.9	% University Degrees	6.6
% Movers	55.3		

D: Industrial Profile

% Manufacturing	11.6	% Service Sector	17.3
% Agriculture	2.4	% Mining	0.4
% Forestry	6.6	% Fishing	3.2
% Government Services	9.2	% Business Services	2.8

E: Homogeneity Measures

Ethnic Diversity Index	0.35	Religious Homogeneity Index	0.37
Sectoral Concentration Index	0.36	Income Disparity Index	10.3

F: Physical Setting Characteristics

Total Population	103805	Area (km²)	13167
Population Density (pop/km²)	7.9		

* Tentative value, due to the existence of unpaid campaign expenses.

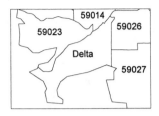

Delta

Constituency Number: 59005

Delta was a new constituency in 1988, encompassing the suburban Greater Vancouver municipality of Delta, south of Richmond (205 sq. km), including Tswassen and the BC Ferry terminal to Vancouver Island and the southern Gulf Islands. Its population of 92,629 has undergone considerable local controversy around the preservation of farm and wet lands over the past decade. This land use conflict had resulted in the longest land use planning hearings in Canadian history and resulted in a highly politicized electorate. The constituency was the second wealthiest in the province: average home prices were $207,648 and average family incomes $63,612, second only to Capilano–Howe Sound; over 80% of the residents owned their own homes, the highest rate of home ownership in British Columbia (as in 1988 when it was at 66.7%); more than 12% were managers/administrators (fourth highest in BC) and 11.1% had university degrees, just slightly above the level for B.C. as a whole. Unemployment in the riding, at 6.9%, is second lowest in the province; income transfers from government are also at a low 7.3%. Half the constituency is Protestant, 93.1% use English as the home language and British make up the largest ethnic group, followed by East Indians and Germans. Delta recorded the second lowest rate of French home-language use in B.C. The vast majority - over 72% of men (highest) and 64% of women (second highest) - commute outside the riding to work, making it a Vancouver bedroom suburb.

In 1988, redistribution left the new seat with no incumbent. The Conservative who won the riding was Stan Wilbee, a former alderman and local doctor. Wilbee proved to be a Conservative maverick, one of two breaking with the party on the referendum (71.3% voted 'No' in Delta) and a critic of Mulroney's party leadership, particularly during its final term, Wilbee's first. The PCs had taken the riding in 1988 with 44.3%, a margin of 15.2% over the second place New Democrats, who had run a 'farmland preservationist'. Local Liberals, placing third, received the support of 19.9% of the voters. Reform (at 4.5%) and Christian Heritage (with 1.8%) had helped erode Conservative support, which had been at 57.6% in the 1984 general election.

During the 1993 election, environmental protection of farm/wetlands, fishing issues, port development in the Fraser River (Delta is almost completely encompassed by the Gulf of Georgia and the arms of the Fraser River) and - one important local issue that Delta shared with neighbouring Richmond - the continuance of Canadian Airlines International, all dominated electoral discussions.

When the votes were cast, Reform, represented by John Cummins, a commercial salmon fisher and teacher, had won the race with 38.2% support (a jump of over 33%); the Tories, with incumbent MP Stan Wilbee (who had been courted by Reform party leader Preston Manning) fell to third place (at 21% - a drop of 23.3%); the Liberals, with freelance editor and local party secretary Karen Morgan as their candidate, picked up 10.6% extra support (for 30.5%) and took second place. The local NDP President, former school administrator/educational reseacher/writer Lloyd Macdonald, dropped as much as the Tories; the NDP vote fell 23.4% to 5.7%, not much more than double the total for National's John Waller, a research chemist (at 2.6%). Christian Heritage (with 0.7%), Natural Law (0.4%), Green (0.4%), Independents (0.2%, 0.1, 0.1) and Party of the Commonwealth (12 votes!) shared the remaining 1.9%. A total of twelve had contested the election. Voter turnout was 73.1%, second highest in the province (again behind Capilano–Howe Sound).

Member of Parliament: John Cummins; **Party:** Reform; **Occupation:** Teacher/fisher; **Education:** BA, MA, University of British Columbia; **Age:** 51 (March 12, 1942); **Year first elected to the House of Commons:** 1993

59005 Delta

A: Political Profile
i) Voting Behaviour

	% 1993	% 1988	Change 1988-93
Conservative	21	44.3	-23.3
Liberal	30.5	19.9	10.6
NDP	5.7	29.1	-23.4
Reform	38.2	4.5	33.7
Other	4.5	2.3	2.2

% Turnout	73.1	Total Ballots (#)	48036
Rejected Ballots (#)	164	% Margin of Victory	12.2
Rural Polls, 1988 (#)	0	Urban Polls, 1988 (#)	155
% Yes - 1992	28.5	% No - 1992	71.3

ii) Campaign Financing

	# of Donations	Total $ Value	% of Limit Spent
Conservative	75	54953	82.9
Liberal	111	44312	74.3
NDP	24	23040	34
Reform	147	42356	70.6
Other	68	23351	

B: Ethno-Linguistic Profile

% English Home Language	93.1	% French Home Language	0.2
% Official Bilingual	7	% Other Home Language	6.8
% Catholics	17.5	% Protestants	49.6
% Aboriginal Peoples	0.8	% Immigrants	21.7

C: Socio-Economic Profile

Average Family Income $	63612	Median Family Income $	58833
% Low Income Families	9	Average Home Price $	207648
% Home Owners	80.9	% Unemployment	6.9
% Labour Force Participation	73.4	% Managerial-Administrative	12.3
% Self-Employed	9.5	% University Degrees	11.1
% Movers	50.5		

D: Industrial Profile

% Manufacturing	12.3	% Service Sector	12.7
% Agriculture	1.6	% Mining	0.3
% Forestry	0.5	% Fishing	0.7
% Government Services	6	% Business Services	6.7

E: Homogeneity Measures

Ethnic Diversity Index	0.28	Religious Homogeneity Index	0.34
Sectoral Concentration Index	0.5	Income Disparity Index	7.5

F: Physical Setting Characteristics

Total Population	92629	Area (km²)	205
Population Density (pop/km²)	451.8		

Esquimalt–Juan de Fuca

Constituency Number: 59006

Esquimalt–Juan de Fuca (population 92,105) was created in 1988; two-thirds out of the Cowichan portion of the old Cowichan–Malahat–The Islands riding and the rest from the old Victoria suburb of Esquimalt (from the Esquimalt–Saanich constituency). British make up the largest ethnic grouping in the riding; this is also reflected in English home-language use (at 97.7%) and Protestantism (at 49.5%). Catholics number amongst the third lowest in either B.C. or Canada. The constituency also has German, Dutch and French residents in significant numbers - over 6% are either bilingual or French speakers; Aboriginal peoples represent 2.2% of the local population. Government employment (significantly based on the Esquimalt naval base and its provincial Capital Region status) is the highest in any B.C. constituency - at almost 20%. The total service sector for the riding economy is almost six in ten of all jobs; a further 10% are self-employed. 8.4% reported university degrees - up from 5.3% in 1986, but still almost 3% below the average for the province.. Unemployment - at 7.5% - is well below the provincial average (unlike in 1988), though public income transfers are at 13.5%, just over two points above. Still, over seven in ten of the residents own their homes, which have an average value of $145,608, almost $30,000 below the provincial average for dwellings; average family incomes are at $47,094, about $4,000 below the provincial norm. Over 20% of the riding 'moved' in the one year prior to the 1991 census, more than half (57.1%) in the previous five years.

Politically, the history of the Esquimalt-centred area has been NDP, though when 'connected' to other areas it also often returned Conservatives. In 1968, David Anderson won the seat (Esquimalt–Saanich) for the Liberals on the Trudeau coat-tails; he then resigned to lead the B.C. Liberals. This constituency returned to the Tories between 1972 and 1988, with Pat Crofton winning five times. In 1988, with redistribution, the NDP nominated former NDP Provincial premier, Dave Barrett. Barrett faced seven challengers and won with over half of all votes (50.9%) and a margin of 25.8% against the second place Conservatives (25.1%); the Liberals were third (with 12%). The local Reform candidate managed to get 10% support, leaving the Greens (at 1%) and others to share the final two per cent. As elsewhere, the 1988 contest was dominated by Free Trade issues.

The focus of the 1993 general election locally included uncertainty about Conservative defence cuts and the potential impact on the Esquimalt naval base (worth $300 million a year to the local economy) as well as Tory contracting-out of base civilian jobs; the NDP, as Barrett had been its 'frontman' on NAFTA, spent considerable time on the implications for jobs and the economy; the local Reform emphasis echoed the party refrain elsewhere on the deficit. In 1993, NDP incumbent MP Barrett was confronted by seven parliamentary hopefuls: these included Keith Martin, a 31-year-old GP/physician who had worked in African relief medicine, as candidate for Reform; Ross McKinnon, an area manager, for the Liberals; and Grace Holman, a Victoria bed-and-breakfast operator, for the Progressive Conservatives. There were also National, Natural Law, Canada Party and independent candidates. These four 'minor' candidates received 6.1% of the vote, not far below the local Conservatives (who received 9.9% support - a drop of 15.2%). Dan Whetung, the National Party candidate, and one of two Vancouver Island First Peoples candidates, managed 4.8% by making aboriginal issues part of the campaign. Dave Barrett, who had had the largest margin of victory in the province in 1988, saw his local support fall 23.7%. That left him in second place (at 27.2%) behind Reform's Keith Martin, who won the constituency with 35.3% support. The local Liberals increased their vote by almost 10%, placing third (at 21.5%). Local turnout was down more than ten per cent from 1988: only 65.8% of the constituents voted, two points below the provincial average.

Member of Parliament: Keith Martin; **Party:** Reform; **Occupation:** Physician; **Education:** BSc, MD, University of Toronto; **Age:** 33 (April 13, 1960); **Year first elected to the House of Commons:** 1993

59006 Esquimalt–Juan de Fuca

A: Political Profile
i) Voting Behaviour

	% 1993	% 1988	Change 1988-93
Conservative	9.9	25.1	-15.2
Liberal	21.5	12	9.5
NDP	27.2	50.9	-23.7
Reform	35.3	10.4	24.9
Other	6.1	1.6	4.5

% Turnout	65.8	Total Ballots (#)	46506
Rejected Ballots (#)	167	% Margin of Victory	14.2
Rural Polls, 1988 (#)	102	Urban Polls, 1988 (#)	78
% Yes - 1992	30.5	% No - 1992	69.3

ii) Campaign Financing

	# of Donations	Total $ Value	% of Limit Spent
Conservative	57	31798	47.5
Liberal	67	18996	39.9
NDP	49	74268	92.3
Reform	211	47858	49.4
Other	51	10043	

B: Ethno-Linguistic Profile

% English Home Language	97.7	% French Home Language	0.5
% Official Bilingual	5.9	% Other Home Language	1.8
% Catholics	16	% Protestants	49.5
% Aboriginal Peoples	2.2	% Immigrants	14.1

C: Socio-Economic Profile

Average Family Income $	47094	Median Family Income $	43890
% Low Income Families	11.9	Average Home Price $	145608
% Home Owners	70.1	% Unemployment	7.5
% Labour Force Participation	67.7	% Managerial-Administrative	7.6
% Self-Employed	10.2	% University Degrees	8.4
% Movers	57.1		

D: Industrial Profile

% Manufacturing	6.2	% Service Sector	20.3
% Agriculture	1.8	% Mining	0.2
% Forestry	1.7	% Fishing	0.9
% Government Services	19.8	% Business Services	4.8

E: Homogeneity Measures

Ethnic Diversity Index	0.41	Religious Homogeneity Index	0.37
Sectoral Concentration Index	0.49	Income Disparity Index	6.8

F: Physical Setting Characteristics

Total Population	92105	Area (km²)	2326
Population Density (pop/km²)	39.6		

Fraser Valley East

Constituency Number: 59007

Fraser Valley East is one half of B.C.'s 'Bible Belt'. Protestants (particularly evangelicals) make up 57.6% of the population, the highest numbers in B.C. A further 16.2% are Catholics, though this is the lowest level in all of Canada. The highest rates of German and Dutch ethnic background were found in Fraser Valley East, an 11,101 sq. km area of mostly farmland that includes the Valley centres of Chilliwack and Abbotsford. Farming and related business dominate the local economy: almost 7% are in direct agricultural employment, third highest in B.C.; a further 47.1% are in the service sector and 12.6% are self-employed. One in ten jobs are in governmental services, with a significant Corrections Canada and Canadian Forces Base Chilliwack component. There is a small (2.4%) forestry job sector. More than seven in ten residents are home owners (up from 50% in 1986); average home prices are $131,613, the lowest in all of the Lower Mainland region and more than $43,000 below the provincial average. Local unemployment is just below the provincial average, at 10%, though 14.2% also receive governmental income assistance, almost 3% above the B.C. rate. Average family incomes are at the low end of the provincial scale: $47,886. About six in ten men and one-third of women commute outside the constituency to work, many of them into metropolitan Vancouver. The riding also has a sizeable aboriginal community - 6.2% of the total population, spread along the Fraser River and throughout the riding.

The constituency 'contributed' a portion of itself to its Fraser Valley neighbour in the previous redistribution. Its population is 99,344. The riding had been represented by Social Credit in 1953 and 1957, lost to a Tory in the 1958 Diefenbaker landslide, re-won in 1962 and held in 1963 and 1965. Socred Alex Patterson ran again as a Conservative in 1972 and 1974 and retook the seat from the Liberal who had won in the 1968 Trudeau victory. Patterson held the seat for the Conservatives in 1979 and 1980, capping a career than involved eight electoral wins (and two defeats) for two different parties over more than thirty years. In 1984 Ross Belsher replaced the retiring Patterson. Belsher's political views - anti-gay, anti-abortion, pro-death penalty and harsher treatment of prisoners - reflected his fundamentalist evangelical church membership. He held the seat in the 1988 general election, though the Tory vote slipped more than 18%. The NDP was second, Liberals third. Reform was outdistanced by the local Christian Heritage Party candidate (9.4% to 3.1%), Christian Heritage's best showing in that election. In the subsequent referendum, the riding voted 73.2% 'No', the sixth highest 'No' in B.C., and one of the most negative in Canada.

Belsher served as Parliamentary Secretary in Transport and Fisheries and Oceans (including ACOA) and was briefly (1989-90) chair of the B.C. caucus. In 1993 he faced eight other candidates. Both Christian Heritage and Reform shared fundamentalist religious and political agendas with the Tory candidate. Belsher also faced Liberal Hal Singleton, a military engineer, with a 33-year career in the Canadian Armed Forces, and New Democrat Rollie Keith, a former paratroop officer/small businessman. Chuck Stahl, a construction company owner, who had toured Northern Ontario speaking against the Charlottetown Accord in 1992, was the Reform Party nominee. Stahl was also Reform's candidate liaison spokesperson for the Lower Mainland in 1993. The 'minor' candidates included Christian Heritage, National Party, Green, Natural Law, and Canada Party. When the 1993 votes were tallied, Reformer Stahl had won the seat with 45.9%, the Liberals were second (with 30.8%, an improvement of 9.6%). The Tories collapsed more than 25% to 13%, and the NDP did likewise, falling 22.7% to just over 5% support; that was just more than double the (2.3%) vote for the Christian Heritage candidate, Bill Boesterd. The National Party took 1.7%. The other three parties shared 1%, with the Greens beating out Natural Law and the Canada Party. Overall turnout was above the provincial average by a point and a half.

Member of Parliament: Chuck Strahl; **Party:** Reform; **Occupation:** Businessperson; **Education:** High school completion; **Age:** 36 (Feb. 25, 1957); **Year first elected to the House of Commons:** 1993

59007 Fraser Valley East

A: Political Profile
i) Voting Behaviour

	% 1993	% 1988	Change 1988-93
Conservative	13	38.8	-25.8
Liberal	30.8	21.2	9.6
NDP	5.3	28	-22.7
Reform	45.9	3.1	42.8
Other	5	8.9	-3.9

% Turnout	69.3	Total Ballots (#)	51321
Rejected Ballots (#)	149	% Margin of Victory	20.1
Rural Polls, 1988 (#)	193	Urban Polls, 1988 (#)	0
% Yes - 1992	26.6	% No - 1992	73.2

ii) Campaign Financing

	# of Donations	Total $ Value	% of Limit Spent
Conservative	108	46196	79.3*
Liberal	181	44478	79.1
NDP	82	33062	27.5
Reform	397	76832	93.7
Other	111	27821	

B: Ethno-Linguistic Profile

% English Home Language	96.7	% French Home Language	0.4
% Official Bilingual	4.8	% Other Home Language	2.9
% Catholics	16.2	% Protestants	57.6
% Aboriginal Peoples	6.2	% Immigrants	15.3

C: Socio-Economic Profile

Average Family Income $	47886	Median Family Income $	43001
% Low Income Families	12.9	Average Home Price $	131613
% Home Owners	71.7	% Unemployment	10
% Labour Force Participation	65.7	% Managerial-Administrative	8.5
% Self-Employed	12.6	% University Degrees	6.4
% Movers	58.4		

D: Industrial Profile

% Manufacturing	9.7	% Service Sector	17.7
% Agriculture	6.7	% Mining	0.3
% Forestry	2.4	% Fishing	0.2
% Government Services	10.3	% Business Services	2.9

E: Homogeneity Measures

Ethnic Diversity Index	0.28	Religious Homogeneity Index	0.41
Sectoral Concentration Index	0.39	Income Disparity Index	10.2

F: Physical Setting Characteristics

Total Population	99344	Area (km^2)	11101
Population Density (pop/km^2)	8.9		

---

* Tentative value, due to the existence of unpaid campaign expenses.

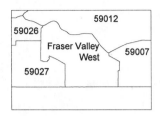

Fraser Valley West

Constituency Number: 59008

Fraser Valley West is the fourth most populous constituency in British Columbia (124,091). The local economy has been shifting from an agricultural base to more light manufacturing, service sector employment, and small business. Almost twelve per cent are self-employed, 41.4% work in the tertiary sector with 5.9% for government and 4.2% in business services; almost one in ten (9.9%) hold managerial/administrative positions and 6.8% have university degrees, just under 5% below the provincial educational level. Despite the development pressures (Fraser Valley West grew more than 30% between 1986 and 1991, the second fastest rate of growth in B.C.) direct agricultural employment still makes up 7.2% of the local economy, second highest in the province. Fraser Valley West remains a significant part of the province's Bible Belt: 56.2% of the residents are Protestant, a large element of which includes fundamentalist, evangelical denominations. The number of Catholics is tenth lowest in all of Canada; the religious pattern is reflected in the large Dutch and German populations in the riding (total immigrant population is 19.4%). The largest grouping of Mennonites in B.C. call Fraser Valley West home, though British elements continue to predominate. 92.2% speak English at home, only 0.2% French. Unemployment, at 8.8%, is a per cent and a half below the average for B.C., though almost fourteen per cent require governmental income assistance, about two and a half points above the norm. Family incomes (at $50,537) were at the lower end for the Lower Mainland, though home ownership was over seven in ten; house values averaged $166,998, with a significant number of homes built in the intervening half dozen years. That pace of development created a number of tensions: regionally, issues such as air quality and pressure for commuter rail and road link improvements stood out; locally, preservation of farmland versus housing - most of it not well attached to local employment, with over six in ten workers having to commute outside the constituency - were strong issues.

In political terms, the seat was held from 1968 to 1974 by New Democrat Mark Rose; Tory businessman/teacher and former Social Credit MLA Bob Wenman defeated Rose in 1974 and held the seat through the 1979, 1980, 1984, and 1988 elections with margins of victory of 24.5% in 1984 and 20.2% in 1988. In 1988, Reform and Christian Heritage (represented by John Van Woudenberg, its National leader) had taken 8.2% of the votes, with the Conservative vote falling 16.1%, and Reform was behind Christian Heritage 3.5% to 4.7%. The New Democrats were second with just over one-quarter of the local votes. The third-place Liberals had improved their standing by almost 8%. As with the overwhelming 'No' vote in adjacent Fraser Valley East, the 'No' vote in West in the 1992 referendum was 74.7%, the highest in B.C. and one of the highest in the country.

Just before the election call in 1993 Wenman resigned to take a United Nations posting, despite having already been acclaimed as Conservative candidate. The Tories replaced him with Langley lawyer Don Nundal. The New Democrats renominated consultant Lynn Fairall who had taken second place in the 1988 poll. The Liberals put forward forest product company president Peter Warkentin, publisher of a booklet entitled 'Eight Economic Policies for Canadians'. The new Reform candidate, Randy White, was a chartered accountant and labour negotiator, with a background in the RCAF, as Finance Director with Alberta Energy and a twelve-year career (1981-93) as Secretary-Treasurer/CEO of the Abbotsford School District. These four faced challenges from Christian Heritage (John Van Woudenberg again), National, Natural Law, Libertarian, and an Independent.

When the results were announced, the National Party's Robert Billyard had outdistanced the Christian Heritage (2.1% to 1.7%); the last three candidates shared one per cent. And Randy White had taken the seat for the Reform Party with almost half the votes, an improvement of over 45%. The Tory vote fell 34.4% and the local NDP dropped 20.4%. That left the Liberals up almost ten points at 29.5% and in second place. The turnout rate was just above the overall provincial average.

Member of Parliament: Randy White; **Party:** Reform; **Occupation:** Accountant; **Education:** CMA, University of Alberta, Extension; **Age:** 45 (Sept. 3, 1948); **Year first elected to the House of Commons:** 1993

59008 Fraser Valley West

A: Political Profile
i) Voting Behaviour

	% 1993	% 1988	Change 1988-93
Conservative	11.4	45.8	-34.4
Liberal	29.5	19.6	9.9
NDP	5.2	25.6	-20.4
Reform	49.1	3.5	45.6
Other	4.8	5.4	-0.6

% Turnout	68	Total Ballots (#)	62763
Rejected Ballots (#)	300	% Margin of Victory	24.4
Rural Polls, 1988 (#)	79	Urban Polls, 1988 (#)	146
% Yes - 1992	25	% No - 1992	74.7

ii) Campaign Financing

	# of Donations	Total $ Value	% of Limit Spent
Conservative	60	41104	88.8
Liberal	102	45746	90.2
NDP	32	23202	25
Reform	201	72909	78.3
Other	73	14718	

B: Ethno-Linguistic Profile

% English Home Language	92.2	% French Home Language	0.2
% Official Bilingual	4.8	% Other Home Language	7.6
% Catholics	13	% Protestants	56.2
% Aboriginal Peoples	1	% Immigrants	19.4

C: Socio-Economic Profile

Average Family Income $	50537	Median Family Income $	44995
% Low Income Families	12.9	Average Home Price $	166998
% Home Owners	71.8	% Unemployment	8.8
% Labour Force Participation	66.4	% Managerial-Administrative	9.9
% Self-Employed	11.7	% University Degrees	6.8
% Movers	62.7		

D: Industrial Profile

% Manufacturing	13.6	% Service Sector	13
% Agriculture	7.2	% Mining	0.2
% Forestry	0.6	% Fishing	0.2
% Government Services	5.9	% Business Services	4.2

E: Homogeneity Measures

Ethnic Diversity Index	0.26	Religious Homogeneity Index	0.39
Sectoral Concentration Index	0.38	Income Disparity Index	11

F: Physical Setting Characteristics

Total Population	124091	Area (km²)	420
Population Density (pop/km²)	295.5		

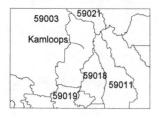

Kamloops

Constituency Number: 59009

Kamloops is a sprawling (25,972 sq. km) riding in central British Columbia. Three-quarters of the 87,144 residents (seventh smallest in the province) reside in the city of Kamloops, the only major urban centre in the constituency. Almost one-quarter of the area is British, and 97.3% speak English as their home language. French make up 1.5% of the local population, considerably fewer than aboriginal residents at 5.4% of the constituency. Three in ten indicate no religious affiliation, while almost half (46.4%) were Protestant and a further 20.9% Catholic. Seven in ten constituents own their homes (up from 53.7% in 1986); the average value of these is $86,936. More than 20% of the riding moved in the previous year. The local economy is diverse, with almost half in the service sector, 6.1% in government and 3.3% in business services. There are agricultural (2.7%) and forestry (3.4%) components, but more are employed in manufacturing (8.8%), and construction (7.0%). Eight per cent are managerial/administrative and seven per cent have university degrees (8.9% had less than grade nine). Unemployment ranges above the provincial average (at 12.8%) and 12.5% of the local population receive governmental income transfers, a point above also.

The riding was held between 1945 and 1963 by E. Davie Fulton, Diefenbaker's Justice Minister. After a brief fling as Provincial Conservative leader, Fulton took the seat again in 1965. He was defeated in 1968 (in Kamloops–Cariboo) by Len Marchand, the first Indian elected to the House of Commons. Marchand kept the seat in 1972 and 1974. The Conservatives re-took the seat (now Kamloops-Shuswap) in 1979, but lost to first-time NDPer and college social sciences instructor/chair Nelson Riis in 1980; Riis had served as a Kamloops alderman (1975-80) and as a school trustee (1978-80). In the 1984 election Riis held the seat with 55% of the votes; the Tories were second with 35.5%. Running as NDP house leader in 1988, Riis kept his margin at almost twenty per cent, though his total support fell to 52.3%. The Conservatives, again in second place, also dropped, to 32.4%. The Liberals picked up much of this slippage; local Reform received only 1.2%. In 1992, 63.5% of the area voted 'No' on constitutional change.

In 1993, Riis (now deputy Party Leader) began the campaign on a NAFTA and sale of water theme, a significant issue in the dry, agricultural central interior. He faced eight other opponents including Keith Raddatz, a local businessman for Reform, Frank Coldicott, a former teacher, Kamloops realtor, and past president of the local Conservatives, and Kevin Krueger, a city insurance claims manager. There were also representatives of the National Party, Natural Law (a Richmond businessman), Libertarians, a Canada Party candidate and an Independent businessman (from Burnaby). Apart from NAFTA and water sales to the United States, the economy was a significant local issue. All candidates challenging the incumbent confronted the local MP's popularity and national reputation.

When the 1993 results were counted, that local popularity was a factor. While most of his party colleagues were falling, Nelson Riis managed to hold the Kamloops seat (with 36.3% of the votes) though local party fortunes sagged 16%. Riis' vote support was the highest for the NDP in B.C., and the third highest in Canada. It was better than the Tories' performance: they fell 23.7% to fourth place (at 8.7%). Riis and the NDP edged out Reform, now in second place, with 26.8%. They in turn were not much ahead of the Liberals who received 24.3% support. The local turnout was just over a point above the average for B.C.

Member of Parliament: Nelson Riis; **Party:** New Democratic; **Occupation:** College geography instructor; **Education:** BEd, MA, University of British Columbia; **Age:** 51 (Jan. 10, 1942); **Year first elected to the House of Commons:** 1980

59009 Kamloops

A: Political Profile
i) Voting Behaviour

	% 1993	% 1988	Change 1988-93
Conservative	8.7	32.4	-23.7
Liberal	24.3	13.2	11.1
NDP	36.3	52.3	-16
Reform	26.8	1.2	25.6
Other	4	1	3

% Turnout	69.1	Total Ballots (#)	44439
Rejected Ballots (#)	169	% Margin of Victory	9.5
Rural Polls, 1988 (#)	67	Urban Polls, 1988 (#)	143
% Yes - 1992	36.3	% No - 1992	63.5

ii) Campaign Financing

	# of Donations	Total $ Value	% of Limit Spent
Conservative	83	63652	63.1
Liberal	104	43488	65.3
NDP	39	64183	87.4
Reform	237	38266	55
Other	54	10245	

B: Ethno-Linguistic Profile

% English Home Language	97.3	% French Home Language	0.3
% Official Bilingual	5.3	% Other Home Language	2.5
% Catholics	20.9	% Protestants	46.4
% Aboriginal Peoples	5.4	% Immigrants	11.4

C: Socio-Economic Profile

Average Family Income $	48607	Median Family Income $	45565
% Low Income Families	15.5	Average Home Price $	86936
% Home Owners	71	% Unemployment	12.8
% Labour Force Participation	68.7	% Managerial-Administrative	8
% Self-Employed	9.6	% University Degrees	7
% Movers	52.4		

D: Industrial Profile

% Manufacturing	8.8	% Service Sector	14.8
% Agriculture	2.7	% Mining	3.7
% Forestry	3.4	% Fishing	0.1
% Government Services	6.1	% Business Services	3.3

E: Homogeneity Measures

Ethnic Diversity Index	0.28	Religious Homogeneity Index	0.34
Sectoral Concentration Index	0.44	Income Disparity Index	6.3

F: Physical Setting Characteristics

Total Population	87144	Area (km^2)	25972
Population Density (pop/km^2)	3.4		

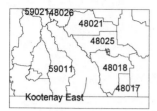

Kootenay East

Constituency Number: 59010

Kootenay East is a 45,310 sq. km riding bordered on two sides by Alberta and United States. It has closely reflected the fortunes on both New Democrats and Progressive Conservatives, often changing hands to coincide with broader electoral 'victories'. Its population of 70,562 is two-thirds rural and the second smallest in the province. It includes resort and mining towns like Kimberly, Golden, Fernie and Cranbrook. Dependence on mining (with employers like Cominco and employment at 11.4%) is the second highest in all of B.C., and one of the highest in Canada; similarly, forestry (at 5.1%) is sixth in ranking for the province, and one of the top fifteen across the whole country. Together, they make up the centre of the local economy; as a result, there has been a history of economic ups and downs depending on resource prices and trade. This is reflected in a population that actually shrank (-0.3%) between 1986 and 1991. Much work is in the service sector, generally related to resource extraction, and one in ten are self-employed. Unemployment is slightly above the provincial average (11%) and an equal number of residents (11.4%) need government income assistance. Still, almost three-quarters (74.6%) owned homes with a average value of $73,850, more than $100,000 below the average for the province; the average family income was $47,068. Almost twice as many residents had less than grade nine (10.0%) as had university degrees (5.6%). Just over seventy per cent declared themselves Protestant (48.4%) or Catholic (21.9%); 27.8% said they were non-religious. The largest ethnic group is British (just under 25%) with Germans (5.8%), aboriginal peoples (3.2%), Italians (2.6%), and French (2.4%) being the next largest communities. In 1992, over three-quarters of this riding voted 'No' in the constitutional referendum; that was the second highest 'No' vote in B.C. and the fourth highest in all of Canada.

Politically, the riding has returned Socreds (in 1953 and 1957), Conservatives (in 1958, 1962, 1963, and 1965), Liberals (as Okanagan–Kootenay) in 1968 and 1972, and Conservatives again in 1974; it then alternated Conservatives (in 1979 and 1984) and New Democrats (Sid Parker, a CPR train conductor and former Revelstoke mayor, in 1980 and 1988). In the 1988 general election, the NDP margin was a narrow 4.7%. Free trade and its impact was the key issue then. In that election, the Conservatives were second and Liberals third (at 12.1%), with Reform (at just over 4%) and Christian Heritage(at 2.14%) picking up enough votes to deny the Tories victory.

In 1993, New Democrat Sid Parker sought a third term; instead he saw his vote slip 28.7%, leaving him in third place, with just 14.5% local support. The seat was taken by Toronto-born electronics dealer/manager Jim Abbott of Reform. Reform improved their vote total by over 44%, to 48.4%. The Conservative vote fell by as much as the NDP (27.6%), leaving former RCAF officer and local college president Jake McInnis of the Conservatives in fourth place. Liberal Jim Wavrecan, a Cranbrook busdriver and businessman won second place with 22.5% support, up more than ten points. Candidates for the National (1.7%), Green (0.8%), Christian Heritage (0.6%), Natural Law (0.5%) and Canada (0.2%) rounded out the field; their total vote was 3.8%. Voter turnout was 2.5% above the average for BC.

Member of Parliament: Jim Abbott; **Party:** Reform; **Occupation:** Businessperson; **Education:** 1.5 years university; **Age:** 51 (Aug. 18, 1942); **Year first elected to the House of Commons:** 1993

59010 Kootenay East

A: Political Profile
i) Voting Behaviour

	% 1993	% 1988	Change 1988-93
Conservative	10.9	38.5	-27.6
Liberal	22.5	12.1	10.4
NDP	14.5	43.2	-28.7
Reform	48.4	4.1	44.3
Other	3.8	2.2	1.6

% Turnout	70.3	Total Ballots (#)	35369
Rejected Ballots (#)	159	% Margin of Victory	29.7
Rural Polls, 1988 (#)	112	Urban Polls, 1988 (#)	60
% Yes - 1992	24.5	% No - 1992	75.2

ii) Campaign Financing

	# of Donations	Total $ Value	% of Limit Spent
Conservative	92	47199	72.2
Liberal	44	22777	32.2
NDP	94	34292	34.2
Reform	394	63678	81.6
Other	29	4921	

B: Ethno-Linguistic Profile

% English Home Language	97.6	% French Home Language	0.3
% Official Bilingual	4.2	% Other Home Language	2.1
% Catholics	21.9	% Protestants	48.4
% Aboriginal Peoples	3.2	% Immigrants	12

C: Socio-Economic Profile

Average Family Income $	47068	Median Family Income $	43987
% Low Income Families	11.4	Average Home Price $	73850
% Home Owners	74.6	% Unemployment	11
% Labour Force Participation	66.7	% Managerial-Administrative	8.1
% Self-Employed	10.4	% University Degrees	5.6
% Movers	44.9		

D: Industrial Profile

% Manufacturing	9.1	% Service Sector	15.9
% Agriculture	2.9	% Mining	11.4
% Forestry	5.1	% Fishing	0
% Government Services	5.6	% Business Services	2

E: Homogeneity Measures

Ethnic Diversity Index	0.29	Religious Homogeneity Index	0.35
Sectoral Concentration Index	0.38	Income Disparity Index	6.5

F: Physical Setting Characteristics

Total Population	70562	Area (km²)	45310
Population Density (pop/km²)	1.6		

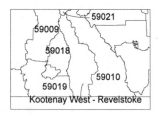

Kootenay West–Revelstoke

59021
59009
59018
59010
59019
Kootenay West - Revelstoke

Kootenay West–Revelstoke

Constituency Number: 59011

Kootenay West–Revelstoke has the smallest population of any constituency in B.C., 68,403. Taken together with its neighbour Kootenay East, the combined population of the Kootenays is 138,965; that is smaller than Surrey North, the largest riding in the province at 142,797. It is a mountainous area east of the Okanagan, bordering on its south with the U.S. It contains the centres of Trail, Revelstoke, Castlegar and Nelson, traditionally important in the extraction and processing of mineral and forest resources, and in related manufacturing. Forestry still accounts for 4.6% of direct jobs, mining another 3.1%; almost 45% are in service work and ten per cent are self-employed. Over 5% are governmental employees, though management and administration positions - at 6.9% - was the lowest level in B.C., and the second lowest in all of Canada. The local economy has shifted somewhat toward tourism and related industries such as movie making. Unemployment remains high (at 12.8%, more than 2% above the provincial rate) and governmental income support at 14%, also more than 2% above the B.C. norm. Despite this, 76.4% of the riding residents are homeowners, where homes average $79,948 in value, almost $100,000 below the across-B.C. value. The local mobility rate is very low: only 16.4% moved in the previous year and just 41% over the previous five. Average family incomes are $45,626. The largest ethnic block in Kootenay West–Revelstoke is British (22.1%) with large Italian (4.3%), German (4.1%) and French (2.4%) communities. Aboriginal population in the riding is small, less that 0.5%.

Politically, throughout the 1970s and 1980s, the riding was known as the Bob and Lyle Show. Between 1925 and 1940, Tories held the seat. From 1945 to 1968 CCF/NDP Bert Herridge represented the region. It was retained by the NDP between 1968 and 1974. In the 1974 election, Conservative Bob Briscoe narrowly won the seat. He held it in 1979, defeating New Democrat Lyle Kristiansen. In 1980, Kristiansen took the riding by 815 votes; he, in turn, lost it back to Tory Bob Briscoe by 744 votes, a margin of 2.2% in the 1984 general election. In 1988, facing each other for the fourth time, Kristiansen retook the redistributed riding, this time with a margin of 10.5%. Apart from his usual Conservative opponent, Kristiansen was challenged by a Liberal who took 15.6% and a mushroom-picking 'hermit' who ran for the Greens despite appeals from the NDP to stay out of what they foresaw as another close race. The local Greens took only 1.9%. The 1992 Referendum vote was strongly 'No', over seven in ten rejecting the Charlottetown Accord.

In 1993, neither Kristiansen nor Briscoe contested the election. The 'incumbent' New Democrats nominated Nelson staff representative Heather Suggitt; Reform proposed Castlegar realtor, alderman, and defeated mayoral candidate Jim Gouk. Gouk had also spent over twenty years as an air traffic controller with Transport Canada. The Liberal standard-bearer was Rossland doctor Barry Jenkins, who had run unsuccessfully in 1988. The Conservatives, regular seat-holders, nominated Nelson lawyer, former city solicitor, and Attorney General of Canada agent Blair Suffredine. Local issues such as airport expansion (at Nakusp) as well as national preoccupations such as jobs and the deficit ran throughout the campaign.

At the end of the 1993 general election, the five minor party candidates (National, Green, Christian Heritage, Natural Law, and Canada) took a respectable 12.6% of the vote. Local Green, Jack Ross took 2.3% and Bev Collins, National Party representative from Nelson, managed 8.5% support; that was only 0.4% behind the local Tories, who had sunk 27.1% to fourth place. The other traditional winner, the New Democrats, sank even further; their vote dropped 30.8% to 15.7% and third place. As was often the case throughout the province, Liberal support grew, here by 14.8% for a second place finish at 30.4%. Local turnout was over two points above the average for the province.

Member of Parliament: Jim Gouk; **Party:** Reform; **Occupation:** Realtor; **Education:** Douglas College; **Age:** 47 (April 15, 1946); **Year first elected to the House of Commons:** 1993

59011 Kootenay West–Revelstoke

A: Political Profile
i) Voting Behaviour

	% 1993	% 1988	Change 1988-93
Conservative	8.9	36	-27.1
Liberal	30.4	15.6	14.8
NDP	15.7	46.5	-30.8
Reform	32.5	0	32.5
Other	12.6	1.9	10.7

% Turnout	70.1	Total Ballots (#)	35136
Rejected Ballots (#)	176	% Margin of Victory	14.7
Rural Polls, 1988 (#)	97	Urban Polls, 1988 (#)	73
% Yes - 1992	28.9	% No - 1992	70.5

ii) Campaign Financing

	# of Donations	Total $ Value	% of Limit Spent
Conservative	86	25516	70.4
Liberal	146	30992	77.5*
NDP	159	43542	41.3*
Reform	250	44192	47.3
Other	108	16158	

B: Ethno-Linguistic Profile

% English Home Language	95.8	% French Home Language	0.2
% Official Bilingual	4.7	% Other Home Language	4
% Catholics	20.2	% Protestants	45.2
% Aboriginal Peoples	0.5	% Immigrants	11.9

C: Socio-Economic Profile

Average Family Income $	45626	Median Family Income $	43190
% Low Income Families	13	Average Home Price $	79948
% Home Owners	76.4	% Unemployment	12.8
% Labour Force Participation	64	% Managerial-Administrative	6.9
% Self-Employed	10.4	% University Degrees	7
% Movers	41		

D: Industrial Profile

% Manufacturing	15.7	% Service Sector	15.2
% Agriculture	1.3	% Mining	3.1
% Forestry	4.6	% Fishing	0.1
% Government Services	5.7	% Business Services	3.1

E: Homogeneity Measures

Ethnic Diversity Index	0.26	Religious Homogeneity Index	0.35
Sectoral Concentration Index	0.39	Income Disparity Index	5.3

F: Physical Setting Characteristics

Total Population	68403	Area (km²)	29942
Population Density (pop/km²)	2.3		

* Tentative value, due to the existence of unpaid campaign expenses.

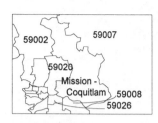

Mission–Coquitlam

Constituency Number: 59012

Mission–Coquitlam was a new constituency in 1988, carved out (69%) of the old Mission – Port Moody seat. With a population of 115, 375, it is the eighth largest riding in the province; local population grew by 27.8% in the five years between 1986 and 1991. Consisting of the north part of fast-growing Coquitlam (riding population growth between 1986 and 1991 was the fourth fastest in British Columbia) and the north shore of the Fraser River out to the lumber-processing centre Mission, it covers almost three thousand sq. km. The local population consists of 27% British, 4.8% German, 2.4% French and smaller groupings of Chinese, aboriginal peoples (1.9%), and Italians. The immigrant population is more that 16%. Almost one third report no religious affiliation, while just under half (46.7%) indicate Protestantism and 16.9% Catholic. Just under 4% are Jewish. English is used as the home language by more than 96% of the local population. An equal number - between 6% -7% - reported university degrees or less than grade nine in education. The Coquitlam area sustains manufacturing (13.7%) and service sector employment (at 43%), with 6.2% in government and 4.3% in business services; the more rural segments include agriculture (3.2%), forestry (1.1%) and smaller amounts of fishing and mining. A significant number of citizens (9.8%) were self-employed. Overall, the unemployment rate is somewhat below the provincial average (though at 9.3%, the third highest in the Lower Mainland for under 24s) and 11.2% of residents received some form of governmental income assistance. Average family incomes were $51,440. Over three-quarters (76.5%) owned homes with an average value of $165,114.

Politically, Mission–Port Moody was created in 1976. Mark Rose of the NDP, who had lost in the 1974 election in Fraser Valley West, won the new seat in 1979. He held it in 1980. Rose resigned in 1983 to run for the B.C. Legislature. In the ensuing by-election Tory Gerry St Germain picked up the seat. With boundary revisions prior to 1988, the new Mission–Coquitlam seat fell to the New Democrats' Joy Langan, a Pacific Press compositor and former provincial party president. Prime Minister Brian Mulroney had named St Germain to the Cabinet just prior to the election in hopes of helping hold the seat. That and the promise of commuter rail, a hot item in the eastern/valley portions of the Lower Mainland (over three-quarters of the riding's workers commute 'outside' to work), were not enough: Langan won with a plurality of almost 44%, a spread of over 4% over the Conservative. Reform placed fourth with 1.7% support. During the 1992 referendum, over three-quarters of the voters locally rejected 'Charlottetown'. The 'No' vote in Mission–Coquitlam was third highest in B.C., fifth highest in Canada.

In the general election of 1993, Langan and the NDP faced ten other candidates. A number of local issues predominated, among them commuter rail (still not in place), highway improvements, Fraser River cleanups and fishing, the aboriginal fishery, and dairy farming concerns around NAFTA and GATT. Mae Abbott, the local Liberal Party president, a former school trustee and city councillor, who was twice defeated - in 1984 and 1988 - was re-nominated. Maple Ridge reporter and former special assistant to Gerry St Germain, Sandy Macdougal, represented the Progressive Conservatives. Daphne Jennings, a teacher, won the Reform Party nod. The National Party candidate was Mike Shields, a Port Moody entrepreneur. There were also candidates from Christian Heritage, the Greens, Natural Law, Libertarians, and two independents. Shields and the National Party took 5% of the 1993 vote. The other minor party candidates won the support of only 2.9% of the constituency, with the Greens outperforming the Christian Heritage candidate. The 1993 election in Mission–Coquitlam was won by Daphne Jennings and Reform, improving their total to 36.7%. The Liberals improved their standing (by almost 14%) to second place and 26.9%. Both the Conservatives and the NDP, the most recent holders of the riding, lost 27% of the constituency's support; that left the NDP in third place and the Tories in fourth. Local turnout was 67.8%, exactly what it was for B.C. as a whole.

Member of Parliament: Daphne Jennings; **Party:** Reform; **Occupation:** Teacher; **Education:** BEd., University of British Columbia; **Age:** 54 (Jan. 26, 1939); **Year first elected to the House of Commons:** 1993

59012 Mission–Coquitlam

A: Political Profile
i) Voting Behaviour

	% 1993	% 1988	Change 1988-93
Conservative	11.7	39.5	-27.8
Liberal	26.9	13.1	13.8
NDP	16.8	43.8	-27
Reform	36.7	1.7	35
Other	7.9	2	5.9

% Turnout	67.8	Total Ballots (#)	55178
Rejected Ballots (#)	242	% Margin of Victory	17.7
Rural Polls, 1988 (#)	50	Urban Polls, 1988 (#)	146
% Yes - 1992	24.5	% No - 1992	75.2

ii) Campaign Financing

	# of Donations	Total $ Value	% of Limit Spent
Conservative	103	41840	66.4
Liberal	77	27962	53.4
NDP	82	56605	93.3*
Reform	158	35140	37.5
Other	74	27093	

B: Ethno-Linguistic Profile

% English Home Language	96	% French Home Language	0.3
% Official Bilingual	5.5	% Other Home Language	3.7
% Catholics	16.9	% Protestants	46.7
% Aboriginal Peoples	1.9	% Immigrants	16.1

C: Socio-Economic Profile

Average Family Income $	51440	Median Family Income $	47879
% Low Income Families	11.4	Average Home Price $	165114
% Home Owners	76.5	% Unemployment	9.3
% Labour Force Participation	71.2	% Managerial-Administrative	8.4
% Self-Employed	9.8	% University Degrees	6.1
% Movers	58.2		

D: Industrial Profile

% Manufacturing	13.7	% Service Sector	13.7
% Agriculture	3.2	% Mining	0.3
% Forestry	1.1	% Fishing	0.4
% Government Services	6.2	% Business Services	4.3

E: Homogeneity Measures

Ethnic Diversity Index	0.31	Religious Homogeneity Index	0.35
Sectoral Concentration Index	0.42	Income Disparity Index	6.9

F: Physical Setting Characteristics

Total Population	115375	Area (km²)	2973
Population Density (pop/km²)	38.8		

* Tentative value, due to the existence of unpaid campaign expenses.

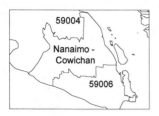

Nanaimo–Cowichan

Constituency Number: 59013

Nanaimo–Cowichan was a new constituency in 1988. Its population of 118,952 was the seventh highest in B.C. in 1991. The new riding contained major portions of the old Nanaimo–Alberni riding but dropped the NDP town of Alberni and added communities south of Nanaimo like Ladysmith and Duncan, the Cowichan portion of the old Cowichan–Malahat–The Islands with the Cowichan Indian Band, one of the country's largest. In 1988, it was almost half and half urban-rural, but it has been one of the fast-growth hot spots in the province over the past several years, growing almost 28%, third fastest in the province and one of the top four in growth in Canada. Historically, Nanaimo was one of the centres of coal mining in B.C. The mines, owned by the highly political Dunsmuir family, did much to shape labour response in the north portion of the constituency, even though the mines play a small part in the local economy today. Forestry and fishing are larger employers; pulp and paper mills are major employers, as is agriculture. Related manufacturing now provides many of the riding's jobs (12.8%). The majority of workers are now in tertiary employment. A high 11.3% are self-employed. The British make up over 30% of the constituency. The second largest grouping are aboriginal peoples (7%), with smaller German (3.3%) and French (2.2%) communities. Almost 97% speak English at home. A large segment are non-religious (33.8%); the only larger group are Protestants (at 46.7%). Catholics - at under 16% - ranked amongst the the lowest in a Canadian constituency; 3.6% of the constituency is Jewish. Seven per cent of the ridings residents have university degrees (the provincial average is 10.8%); slightly more (8.8%) had less than grade nine. Average family incomes were at $46,327 (about $6,000 below the average for B.C.) and the unemployment rate was a couple of points above the provincial average, at 12%. Sixteen per cent of the local population required governmental income assistance - over 4.5% above the norm; yet over seven in ten owned their homes - valued at $116,791 on average.

Politically, the area has been a supporter of New Democrats and Conservatives, depending on political fortunes and constituency boundaries. It elected the CCF in 1953 and 1957, Tories in the 1958 Diefenbaker landslide, then New Democrats in 1962, 1963, and 1965. When the Member of Parliament Colin Cameron died in 1968 and NDP leader Tommy Douglas lost his seat in the 1968 election, the area returned Douglas in a by-election. He held the seat in 1972 and 1974. The area returned another New Democrat in 1979 and 1980, but in 1984 Ted Schellenberg defeated the incumbent for the Conservatives in a close race. In the 1988 election Schellenberg faced former provincial Finance Minister and Nanaimo MLA Dave Stupich. Stupich and the NDP handily took the seat - with a margin of 14.8%. The Reform Party took six per cent, making inroads amongst a growing retired population; in 1991, almost 14% of the riding's residents were over 65. In 1992, 73% of Nanaimo-Cowichan voted 'No' in the constitutional referendum, one of the fifteen highest rejections in the country.

In the general election the following year, incumbent Stupich, facing criticism for the finances of a charitable organization with NDP links and with a provincial government which had alienated considerable union support over resource and land use issues on Vancouver Island, was strongly challenged. His voter support dropped 29.5% and he fell to third place. Reform, represented by retired Major General Bob Ringma, took the seat with 41.2% of the votes. That was almost 20% over the second place Liberals (at 22.5%) and their candidate realtor, Ron Cantelon. In fourth place was local business manager Bruce Wilbee for the Tories at 9.1% (Wilbee is the son of Delta Tory MP Stan Wilbee). The National Party candidate Larry Whaley, with another respectable showing, won 5.6% support. Natural Law and Libertarians 'outvoted' two independents, and the Canada Party came last; none received 1% of the local vote support. Turnout was a little below the provincial average.

Member of Parliament: Bob Ringma; **Party:** Reform; **Occupation:** retired (Major General) military officer; **Education:** 2 years university/5 years military and staff college; **Age:** 65 (June 30, 1928); **Year first elected to the House of Commons:** 1993

59013 Nanaimo–Cowichan

A: Political Profile

i) Voting Behaviour

	% 1993	% 1988	Change 1988-93
Conservative	9.1	34.3	-25.2
Liberal	22.5	9.4	13.1
NDP	19.6	49.1	-29.5
Reform	41.2	6	35.2
Other	7.6	1.2	6.4

% Turnout	67.1	Total Ballots (#)	61763
Rejected Ballots (#)	291	% Margin of Victory	26.3
Rural Polls, 1988 (#)	121	Urban Polls, 1988 (#)	117
% Yes - 1992	26.7	% No - 1992	73

ii) Campaign Financing

	# of Donations	Total $ Value	% of Limit Spent
Conservative	119	42102	56.4*
Liberal	151	31236	44.8
NDP	5	38440	57.8
Reform	484	58162	68.9
Other	115	21504	

B: Ethno-Linguistic Profile

% English Home Language	96.8	% French Home Language	0.3
% Official Bilingual	5.2	% Other Home Language	2.9
% Catholics	16	% Protestants	46.7
% Aboriginal Peoples	7	% Immigrants	14.6

C: Socio-Economic Profile

Average Family Income $	46327	Median Family Income $	42004
% Low Income Families	15.8	Average Home Price $	116791
% Home Owners	70.8	% Unemployment	12
% Labour Force Participation	62.5	% Managerial-Administrative	8
% Self-Employed	11.3	% University Degrees	7
% Movers	56.2		

D: Industrial Profile

% Manufacturing	12.8	% Service Sector	15.7
% Agriculture	1.7	% Mining	0.1
% Forestry	3.8	% Fishing	1.5
% Government Services	6	% Business Services	3.9

E: Homogeneity Measures

Ethnic Diversity Index	0.34	Religious Homogeneity Index	0.35
Sectoral Concentration Index	0.41	Income Disparity Index	9.3

F: Physical Setting Characteristics

Total Population	118952	Area (km²)	4272
Population Density (pop/km²)	27.8		

* Tentative value, due to the existence of unpaid campaign expenses.

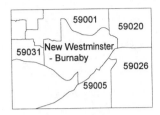

New Westminster–Burnaby

Constituency Number: 59014

New Westminster–Burnaby was created out of the New Westminster (B.C.'s oldest city) portion of the New Westminster–Coquitlam seat and the south portion of Burnaby (one of B.C.'s newest 'cities') in the 1986 redistribution. The riding has a population of 112,510, split between British (23.9%), Chinese (6.7%), German (4.1%), Italian (2.1%), French (1.8%) and other ethnic groups. It is 8.4% Jewish, 20.1% Catholic, and 41.8% Protestant. Over one-quarter (26.2%) of the constituency is made up of immigrants; 12% of the population use neither English or French as their home language. Home ownership is relatively low - 43.54%, perhaps not surprising with average house prices at $223,474, almost $50,000 above the overall provincial average, and affected by the extension of rapid transit into the municipality since 1986. Unemployment is at 10% (just below the provincial average) and a total of 13% receive some form of income assistance, a point and a half above the provincial norm. Average family income is $51,639, below the overall rate for the province. The local economy is very much part of the Greater Vancouver metropolis: almost half of all jobs are in services - over 7% in business and 5.5% in government. Almost one in ten (9.8%) jobs are managerial/administrative. The constituency had the sixth highest rate of movers over a one-year period; it also has the highest rate of seniors (one in six) within the Lower Mainland.

Politically, New Westminster has reflected its blue-collar background, but if, for example, part of Burnaby was attached to the north shore, or to Richmond/Delta, it elected Conservatives (e.g. Chuck Cook) or Liberals (e.g. Ray Perrault). As Burnaby, it has returned New Democrats: in 1979, 26-year-old Lawyer Svend Robinson beat out Simon Fraser University president and former (Liberal) Ontario MP Pauline Jewett for the local nomination. Robinson went on to win the seat. He defeated the same Conservative candidate in 1980 and increased his lead in 1984. The New West portion of the constituency was twinned with eastern neighbour Coquitlam in 1979. Here Pauline Jewett won the nomination for the NDP and took the seat. Like Robinson, Jewett held the seat with an increased New Democratic majority in 1980, and in 1984 took almost half the local votes (49.1%). The second place Conservative was fifteen points behind at 35.8%. In 1988 Jewitt's ill-health allowed Dawn Black, her constituency assistant, to contest the new riding that combined New West with south Burnaby. Svend Robinson decided to contest the new Burnaby–Kingsway seat. Black took the new riding in 1988 with a margin of 12.1% over the Progressive Conservatives. Local Reform won three per cent and Social Credit 1.3%.

In 1993, as her party's critic on women's issues, Black developed a strong reputation. As a private member, she sponsored a bill establishing Dec. 6th as a National Day of Remembrance and Action on Violence Against Women which passed Parliament; she also was central to changes to anti-stalking legislation. During her first term in office she spoke in Parliament over 400 times. Her 1993 opponents tried to tar her as a 'women's issues only' candidate. The Reform representative was Paul Forseth, a former probation officer and court counsellor with the provincial government; he stressed law and order and the economy. The Tories nominated Neil MacKay, a retired RCMP Inspector and local real estate developer. Leanore Copeland, a former teacher and publisher won the Liberal nod. National, Natural Law, Green, Libertarian, Commonwealth parties also nominated candidates and one Independent, an entertainer, ran.

The results of the 1993 general election included a Reform victory, but with only 29.3% of the votes. Just three points behind was the NDP incumbent, Dawn Black; her support had slipped 17.5%, much less than many B.C. New Democrats. The Conservative vote shrank more - 19.9% - leaving them in fourth place (with 11.6%). An 8.6% increase in local Liberal fortunes left Copeland in second place -at 27.9%, 1.8% above Black and the NDP. Of the other candidates, only the National Party achieved more that one per cent: Jeffrey Jewell, an engineering systems manager, received 3.2%. Natural Law, Green, Libertarian, an Independent and Commonwealth shared 2% in that order. Voter turnout was at 63.3%, third lowest in the province in 1993.

Member of Parliament: Paul Forseth; **Party:** Reform; **Occupation:** Probation officer/court counsellor; **Education:** BEd; **Age:** 47 (Dec. 14, 1946); **Year first elected to the House of Commons:** 1993

59014 New Westminster–Burnaby

A: Political Profile
i) Voting Behaviour

	% 1993	% 1988	Change 1988-93
Conservative	11.6	31.5	-19.9
Liberal	27.9	19.3	8.6
NDP	26.1	43.6	-17.5
Reform	29.3	3	26.3
Other	5.2	2.6	2.6

% Turnout	63.3	Total Ballots (#)	55797
Rejected Ballots (#)	359	% Margin of Victory	6.6
Rural Polls, 1988 (#)	0	Urban Polls, 1988 (#)	221
% Yes - 1992	31.4	% No - 1992	68.1

ii) Campaign Financing

	# of Donations	Total $ Value	% of Limit Spent
Conservative	103	31415	51.5
Liberal	92	33083	66.1*
NDP	44	89206	69.1
Reform	119	27503	31.4
Other	23	5168	

B: Ethno-Linguistic Profile

% English Home Language	87.8	% French Home Language	0.3
% Official Bilingual	5.3	% Other Home Language	11.9
% Catholics	20.1	% Protestants	41.8
% Aboriginal Peoples	0.9	% Immigrants	26.2

C: Socio-Economic Profile

Average Family Income $	51639	Median Family Income $	44992
% Low Income Families	20.8	Average Home Price $	223474
% Home Owners	43.5	% Unemployment	10
% Labour Force Participation	67	% Managerial-Administrative	9.8
% Self-Employed	7.5	% University Degrees	10.1
% Movers	59.4		

D: Industrial Profile

% Manufacturing	12.1	% Service Sector	13
% Agriculture	0.8	% Mining	0.2
% Forestry	0.4	% Fishing	0.2
% Government Services	5.5	% Business Services	7.1

E: Homogeneity Measures

Ethnic Diversity Index	0.22	Religious Homogeneity Index	0.3
Sectoral Concentration Index	0.5	Income Disparity Index	12.9

F: Physical Setting Characteristics

Total Population	112510	Area (km²)	56
Population Density (pop/km²)	2009.1		

* Tentative value, due to the existence of unpaid campaign expenses.

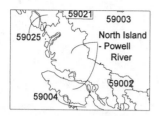

North Island–Powell River

Constituency Number: 59015

North Island–Powell River is a constituency covering the northern half of Vancouver Island and the adjacent mainland coast. It covers 83,711 sq. km, parts of it only accessible by air or water. With a population of 94,833, more than two-thirds of it 'rural', it stands near the middle of constituencies in B.C. in size. Many of the small towns, like Powell River, Ocean Falls, and Port Hardy are resource communities, heavily dependent on forestry and fishing (both these occupational categories were listed as the highest in B.C.; the forestry sector was also the highest in all of Canada) and to a lesser extent mining. In total these make up just under twenty per cent of all direct jobs in the area. Major employers include MacMillan Bloedel, Fletcher Challenge and Canadian Forest Products. The relatively small service sector is directly dependent on support for - or is supported by - these primary industries. At 12% unemployment is a point and a half above the provincial average and income transfers are also almost a point above the provincial norm; these are features of a work base that is seasonal. Yet over seven in ten (72.9% - up from 51.2% in 1986) own their own homes (the provincial norm is 65.7%); the average value of these is $108,440, well below the B.C. norm. Average family incomes were over $1,200 below the average for the province. The riding has one of the highest aboriginal populations in B.C. - at 12.2% (third highest in the province). Only residents with British roots (at 27.2%) were more plentiful; smaller German (3.4%), French (2.4%) and Italian (1.3%) communities were evident as well. Somewhat more (8.9% vs 7%) of the area residents had not completed grade nine schooling versus those with university degrees. There was a fairly high rate (35.6%) of non-religious affiliation; Protestants made up the largest religious grouping (46.7%).

The political history of the region reflected its primary industrial profile: in the 1950s it returned a CCF Member of Parliament (Tom Barnett) in 1953 and 1957. He lost to a Conservative in 1958, but retook the seat in 1962, held it in 1963 and 1965, lost by nine votes - to a Liberal - in 1968 (however, this election was declared invalid by the courts); in the ensuing by-election (1969) Barnett won again; he held the seat in 1972 but retired in 1974. In that election, a Liberal won the seat. In 1979, New Democrat Ray Skelly, a former millwright, corrections officer, and teacher, took the riding, with the Tories in second place. Skelly held the seat in 1980 (by 8462 votes), but had a closer victory (again over the Conservatives) in 1984. In the 1988 election, incumbent Skelly increased his support, taking more than half the local votes. Powell River alderman Michael Rabu was second for the Conservatives. Local Reform picked up just 1.7%. In the 1992 constitutional referendum, 72.2% voted 'No' - amongst the fifteen highest 'No' votes in the country.

The 1993 election was a very different contest: Skelly faced seven contenders and an electorate angry with provincial NDP land use decisions affecting resources and uncertainty over aboriginal land and fishing claims. The Conservatives had nominated Mark Von Schellwitz, a former research and special assistant to Vancouver Cabinet Minister Pat Carney. He had spent almost three years in the B.C. Regional Ministers' Office working on Western Economic Diversification. The Liberals put up Port Hardy telephone technician Al Huddlestan; Reform's candidate was John Duncan, a Campbell River forester. There were also National, Green, Natural Law, and Canada Party candidates. When the results were counted, Reform's John Duncan had won - with 39.3% support. The Liberals had moved to second place, picking up 9.5% in extra votes. Skelly, the NDP incumbent, dropped 35.2% to 16.8% and third place, just more than double the Tories; the Conservatives only managed to edge out the National Party's Mark Grenier, a Campbell River house painter, for fourth place (7.9% vs 7.4%); the local Green candidate, Michael Mascall, an economist, picked up 2.2% support. Natural Law and Canada Party reps shared the rest. Voter turnout was about average.

Member of Parliament: John Duncan; **Party:** Reform; **Occupation:** Forester; **Education:** BScF, University of British Columbia; **Age:** 44 (Dec. 19, 1948); **Year first elected to the House of Commons:** 1993

59015 North Island–Powell River

A: Political Profile
i) Voting Behaviour

	% 1993	% 1988	Change 1988-93
Conservative	7.9	24.4	-16.5
Liberal	25.6	16.1	9.5
NDP	16.8	52	-35.2
Reform	39.3	1.7	37.6
Other	10.5	5.8	4.7

% Turnout	68	Total Ballots (#)	46666
Rejected Ballots (#)	189	% Margin of Victory	24.2
Rural Polls, 1988 (#)	178	Urban Polls, 1988 (#)	71
% Yes - 1992	27.4	% No - 1992	72.2

ii) Campaign Financing

	# of Donations	Total $ Value	% of Limit Spent
Conservative	113	43502	65.1*
Liberal	100	33036	47.5
NDP	39	66796	88.8
Reform	251	61264	87.4
Other	125	12060	

B: Ethno-Linguistic Profile

% English Home Language	97.5	% French Home Language	0.4
% Official Bilingual	5.3	% Other Home Language	2.1
% Catholics	15.5	% Protestants	46.7
% Aboriginal Peoples	12.2	% Immigrants	13.2

C: Socio-Economic Profile

Average Family Income $	51074	Median Family Income $	47820
% Low Income Families	11.1	Average Home Price $	108440
% Home Owners	72.9	% Unemployment	12
% Labour Force Participation	68	% Managerial-Administrative	7
% Self-Employed	12.1	% University Degrees	7
% Movers	53.3		

D: Industrial Profile

% Manufacturing	16.7	% Service Sector	13.4
% Agriculture	0.8	% Mining	3
% Forestry	10.5	% Fishing	4.6
% Government Services	4.8	% Business Services	2.4

E: Homogeneity Measures

Ethnic Diversity Index	0.31	Religious Homogeneity Index	0.37
Sectoral Concentration Index	0.32	Income Disparity Index	6.4

F: Physical Setting Characteristics

Total Population	94833	Area (km²)	83711
Population Density (pop/km²)	1.1		

* Tentative value, due to the existence of unpaid campaign expenses.

North Vancouver

Constituency Number: 59016

North Vancouver was a new constituency in 1988. It 'dropped' North Burnaby and added one third of the more affluent Capilano riding to its west. Situated on Vancouver's North Shore, this constituency of 93,938 includes the British Properties, an expensive enclave below the mountains overlooking downtown Vancouver. The British remain the largest group - at 28.5% - though there are identifiable Chinese (3.5%) German (3.4%), aboriginal (2.1%), Italian (1.8%), and French (1.6%) communities. Over one-quarter (26.4%) are immigrants, and almost 11% are non-citizens; English is the home language for 92.4% of the residents. There is a large Jewish population - 7.2% - though Protestants make up the largest religious group (42.4%); more than three in ten residents reported no religion in the 1991 census. House prices in the constituency were $248,623, well above the provincial average of $174,254; as a result, only 59.3% owned homes (8th lowest rate in the province), below the provincial norm of 65.7%. Average family incomes for the province were $52,350; in North Vancouver they were $62,269, fourth highest in B.C. More than 56% of all jobs were in services, including 10.5% in business services and 5.6% in government. A high 14.7% of all jobs were managerial/administrative (the provincial average was 9.8%). And while just over 10% of the B.C. population had university degrees, almost seventeen per cent of this North Shore constituency had completed university. Only 3.6% had less than grade nine. The local unemployment rate - at 7.5% - was well below the 10.5% norm for B.C. and government income assistance rates - at 7.8% - was also below the 11.4% provincial mean. Rates of movement in and out of the community were about normal over the previous several years. Almost one in ten (9.6%) of the constituency was retired.

Given various boundary changes, the electoral history of the area has been varied: when North Vancouver was 'attached' to Burnaby, for example, in the 1950s and 1960s, it elected CCF in 1963, 1957, 1958, and 1962. It returned Tommy Douglas for the NDP in a 1962 by-election; Douglas held the seat in 1963 and 1965. Liberal Ray Perrault defeated Douglas in 1968 in what was then Burnaby–Seymour; in 1972 he in turn was defeated by a New Democrat. In 1974 the Liberals took the seat, but in 1979 broadcaster Chuck Cook won the seat for the Tories, defeating former provincial Liberal Leader Gordon Gibson. Cook defeated Gibson again in 1980. In 1984, former Liberal Cabinet Minister Iona Campagnola was defeated by Cook. In that race the New Democrats had 27.1% (to 27% for the Liberals). In the 1988 election, Cook won his fourth term with a ten point spread in votes. Here, the Liberals outdistanced the local New Democrats by more than 3%, their fourth best showing in the province. Reform had its best B.C. showing, managing almost 9% of the vote. In the 1992 referendum, almost one-third of North Vancouver voted 'Yes'. Maverick MP Chuck Cook died in February, 1993. He had opposed Charlottetown. In early September, as required by law, Prime Minister Kim Campbell called a by-election for December. That by-election was superseded by the general election in October, 1993.

In the 1993 election, the Conservatives, represented by Will McMartin, a former provincial Socred researcher and publisher of the magazine *BC Politics and Policy*, was only able to get 15.4% support - down 22.2% from Cook's last victory, to third place. McMartin had defeated Chuck Cook's son for the nomination. Ted White, owner of an office equipment leasing company, took 40% of the riding votes and victory for Reform. Liberal lawyer Mobina Jaffer was second with 31.5%; NDP lawyer Graeme Bowbrick picked up just 6.4% support - a fall of 17.5%, and only two points above National Party rep Dallas Collins, a hairstylist. Local Green, Anne Hansen, an environmental consultant, managed 1%; Natural Law, Libertarian, Commonwealth, and Independent Clarke Ashley each got less than 1% in that order; Independent Clarke Ashley, a former Conservative Yukon Justice Minister representing something called the Canadian Economic Community, placed 8th out of 10. At 72.5%, turnout was the fourth highest in the province.

Member of Parliament: Ted White; **Party:** Reform; **Occupation:** Businessperson; **Education:** Cert. in Electrical Engineering, Auckland University; **Age:** 44 (April 18, 1949); **Year first elected to the House of Commons:** 1993

59016 North Vancouver

A: Political Profile
i) Voting Behaviour

	% 1993	% 1988	Change 1988-93
Conservative	15.4	37.6	-22.2
Liberal	31.5	27.2	4.3
NDP	6.4	23.9	-17.5
Reform	40	8.9	31.1
Other	6.8	2.4	4.4

% Turnout	72.5	Total Ballots (#)	50783
Rejected Ballots (#)	209	% Margin of Victory	15.3
Rural Polls, 1988 (#)	0	Urban Polls, 1988 (#)	190
% Yes - 1992	32	% No - 1992	67.7

ii) Campaign Financing

	# of Donations	Total $ Value	% of Limit Spent
Conservative	135	50841	98.7
Liberal	100	67680	96.6
NDP	21	28179	35
Reform	226	45643	69.4
Other	48	17320	

B: Ethno-Linguistic Profile

% English Home Language	92.4	% French Home Language	0.3
% Official Bilingual	8.4	% Other Home Language	7.3
% Catholics	19.8	% Protestants	42.4
% Aboriginal Peoples	2.1	% Immigrants	26.4

C: Socio-Economic Profile

Average Family Income $	62269	Median Family Income $	55214
% Low Income Families	14.1	Average Home Price $	248623
% Home Owners	59.3	% Unemployment	7.5
% Labour Force Participation	73.9	% Managerial-Administrative	14.7
% Self-Employed	11.7	% University Degrees	16.8
% Movers	54.7		

D: Industrial Profile

% Manufacturing	8.1	% Service Sector	12.3
% Agriculture	0.4	% Mining	0.6
% Forestry	0.5	% Fishing	0.3
% Government Services	5.6	% Business Services	10.5

E: Homogeneity Measures

Ethnic Diversity Index	0.29	Religious Homogeneity Index	0.31
Sectoral Concentration Index	0.59	Income Disparity Index	11.3

F: Physical Setting Characteristics

Total Population	93938	Area (km²)	417
Population Density (pop/km²)	225.3		

Okanagan Centre

Constituency Number: 59017

Okanagan Centre was a new constituency in 1988, reflecting the fast-paced growth of this central interior region of the province. Its population is 111,846, centred in Kelowna, the only large city in the constituency. Half urban/half rural, Kelowna had been the base of the Bennett Social Credit dynasty for over thirty years, and the local economy remains centred on small business, fruit growing, some manufacturing (for example, Western Star Trucks) and related service work - just under 5% in both governmental and business services. The same percentage - 4.3% - are in direct agricultural jobs, but the fruit-growing industry has been hard hit in recent years, not least by development pressures. There is also a small forestry sector in the local economy. The local population is one quarter British, with a large (10.1%) German population. There are also French, aboriginal and Italian communities of some size. Immigrants make up almost 15% of the local population, though English home-language use is at 96.3%; over 72% of the residents are Protestant (51.6%) or Catholic (20.9%). Average family incomes are more than $6,000 below the provincial norm - at $46,029, but more (71.1%) own homes than the 65.7% norm for BC. These homes are valued at $135,417. Area unemployment is just under two points above the rate for the province and income transfers - at 16.6% - well above the 11.4% provincial average. That may explain the fact that over six in ten residents had moved in the previous five years - 5% above average for the province as a whole, and the fifth highest rate in B.C.. More that 16% of the residents are retired, an increasing feature of life in the Okanagan.

The political history of the area is fairly straightforward: as either Okanagan Boundary or Okanagan Kootenay, the general tendency was to return Conservatives to Parliament, occasionally breaking to support a local Liberal. Between 1958 and 1979, Okanagan Boundary was held by two Conservatives with only one exception - 1968, when a Liberal defeated the Tory incumbent. Okanagan Kootenay had returned Social Credit MPs in 1953 and 1957. Tories held the seat in 1958, 1962, 1963, and 1965. A Liberal won with Trudeau in 1968, and held the riding in 1972 but lost to a Conservative in 1974. The Tories held Okanagan Boundary in 1979, 1980 and 1984. In 1988, Kelowna alderman and realtor Al Horning won the new Okanagan Centre. His vote total was only 37%, a drop of more than 20% from 1984. Almost 14% of that drop went to local Reform candidate Werner Schmidt. The NDP were second and the Liberals third, just ahead of Reform. In 1992, 72.6% of the riding voted 'No', one of the top fifteen 'No' votes in the country.

In 1993, one of Kim Campbell's first campaign stops was the Okanagan. Local commentators suggested the Reform threat was real, not apparent. Incumbent MP Al Horning, running for a second term, faced eight challengers. When the votes were counted - in an election where local issues such as water quality and federal assistance to deal with increasing pollution were important - Horning was left in third place: 18.1% of the Conservative vote had disappeared. Most of it had gone to Reform, whose second time candidate Werner Schmidt, a former Alberta school trustee/superintendent, college vice president, management consultant and for two years (1973-75) leader of the Social Credit party of Alberta, won with 46.6% of the riding's support. The NDP, represented by Brian McIver, an insurance agent who had run federally in 1972 and provincially in 1979,and who had placed second to Horning in 1988, collapsed even more than the Tories - falling 23.3% to fourth place. Liberal school board chairman Murli Pendharker was left in second place, up over six points to 23.8%. Of the minor parties, only the National's Jack Davis, an artist, (at 1.6%) and the Green's David Hughes, an environmental consultant, (at 1%) were over one per cent in voter support. A Natural Law, Canada Party, and Independent shared 0.8% in that order to round out the count. Voter turnout was 70.6%, eighth highest in the province.

Member of Parliament: Werner Schmidt; **Party:** Reform; **Occupation:** Businessperson; **Education:** BEd, MEd; **Age:** 61 (Jan. 18, 1932); **Year first elected to the House of Commons:** 1993

59017 Okanagan Centre

A: Political Profile

i) Voting Behaviour

	% 1993	% 1988	Change 1988-93
Conservative	19.2	37.3	-18.1
Liberal	23.8	17.1	6.7
NDP	6.9	30.2	-23.3
Reform	46.6	14.5	32.1
Other	3.4	0.9	2.5

% Turnout	70.6	Total Ballots (#)	66111
Rejected Ballots (#)	257	% Margin of Victory	26.2
Rural Polls, 1988 (#)	105	Urban Polls, 1988 (#)	106
% Yes - 1992	27.1	% No - 1992	72.6

ii) Campaign Financing

	# of Donations	Total $ Value	% of Limit Spent
Conservative	127	66995	82.1
Liberal	143	26183	57.9
NDP	14	32005	41.2
Reform	321	51659	97.8
Other	28	4485	

B: Ethno-Linguistic Profile

% English Home Language	96.3	% French Home Language	0.5
% Official Bilingual	5.9	% Other Home Language	3.3
% Catholics	20.9	% Protestants	51.6
% Aboriginal Peoples	1.8	% Immigrants	14.9

C: Socio-Economic Profile

Average Family Income $	46029	Median Family Income $	39209
% Low Income Families	14.1	Average Home Price $	135417
% Home Owners	71.1	% Unemployment	12.3
% Labour Force Participation	61.8	% Managerial-Administrative	9.5
% Self-Employed	13.4	% University Degrees	7.2
% Movers	60.8		

D: Industrial Profile

% Manufacturing	9.9	% Service Sector	14.9
% Agriculture	4.3	% Mining	0.9
% Forestry	1.3	% Fishing	0.1
% Government Services	4.3	% Business Services	4.6

E: Homogeneity Measures

Ethnic Diversity Index	0.27	Religious Homogeneity Index	0.36
Sectoral Concentration Index	0.45	Income Disparity Index	14.8

F: Physical Setting Characteristics

Total Population	111846	Area (km²)	3169
Population Density (pop/km²)	35.3		

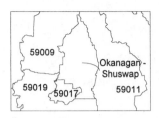

Okanagan–Shuswap

Constituency Number: 59018

Okanagan–Shuswap is the ninth smallest riding in B.C. in population (88,188), but covers an area of 13,780 sq. km. It is mostly rural: only two towns are over 2,000, Vernon being the best known centre. The largest ethnic group is British - over one-quarter - but there are sizeable German (7.6%), aboriginal (3.7%) and French (2.6%) populations. Over half (54.4%) are Protestant, 29.2% non-religious and 14.8 Catholic (amongst one of the 10 smallest Catholic populations in Canada - and amongst the 10 smallest in B.C.). Just over twelve per cent are immigrants, but English home-language use is at 97.4%. The local economy is agricultural (6.1% of direct jobs), forestry (4.7%, amongst the top 15 in Canada for this industry), some related manufacturing (13.3%) and related services with between three and four per cent in each of business and governmental services. Almost nine per cent are managers/administrators and almost 15% are self-employed; the provincial self-employment norm is 11.38%. Those with university degrees (6.1%) fall well below the 10.75 provincial norm. Average family incomes are almost $10,000 below the provincial average of $52,350; area unemployment is high - at 13.1%, more than two and a half points above that for B.C. as a whole. Income support, at a rate of 17.8%, is well above the provincial rate of 11.4%; yet three-quarters of the riding's residents own their own homes, whose average value is $106,254. The rate of movers over the previous five years was slightly below the average for B.C.

Historically, the region has tended to support Conservatives. The Shuswap region was once part of the Kamloops constituency: this area elected E. Davie Fulton between 1945 and 1968 - except when Fulton left federal politics briefly (1963-65) to lead the provincial Conservatives. In 1968 and 1972 Liberal Len Marchand, Canada's first Indian MP, represented the area. In 1979 a Conservative took this seat only to be defeated by current incumbent NDP (now Deputy Leader) Nelson Riis in 1980. In the Okanagan portion of the constituency, Conservatives and Liberals held the seat in the 1960s and 1970s. The Tories, having won the riding (Okanagan North) in 1979, held it in 1980 and 1984. In 1988, former teacher Lyle MacWilliam, defeated provincial MLA for the NDP, won the new Okanagan–Shuswap with 43.5% support. The Conservatives, with their vote down 12.2%, were left in second place. Reform managed 3.1%, The Liberals were third with 15.9% of the votes. Trade and economic issues dominated this campaign. In the 1992 referendum, 31.1% of the riding voted 'Yes'.

In 1993, the NDP's MacWilliam faced eight candidates vying for his parliamentary job. Reform had nominated Darrel Stinson, a local businessperson; the Liberals chose Brooke Jeffrey, a Vernon political scientist; the Progressive Conservative candidate was Alice Klim, a former small business manager, Vernon School District chair, and area Parks and Recreation Director. Don MacLennan, a Vernon engineer, was National Party representative. There were also Green, Natural Law, Canada Party candidates and one Independent. The electoral results saw 1.5% support for the Green, Natural Law, Canada Party and Independent hopefuls, in that order. MacLennan's National Party won 4.1% of the local votes. The Tory vote collapsed 26.3% to 9.9%, just over half the 18.4% Liberal result. Incumbent MacWilliam dropped 19.8% but held second place with 23.7% still supporting the local NDP. Reform's Darrel Stinson improved over 39 points to 42.4% and a seat representing Okanagan–Shuswap in Parliament. Voter turnout was just above the average for the province.

Member of Parliament: Darrel Stinson; **Party:** Reform; **Occupation:** Businessperson; **Education:** High school; **Age:** 48 (June, 1945); **Year first elected to the House of Commons:** 1993

59018 Okanagan–Shuswap

A: Political Profile
i) Voting Behaviour

	% 1993	% 1988	Change 1988-93
Conservative	9.9	36.2	-26.3
Liberal	18.4	15.9	2.5
NDP	23.7	43.5	-19.8
Reform	42.4	3.1	39.3
Other	5.6	1.4	4.2

% Turnout	68.2	Total Ballots (#)	49497
Rejected Ballots (#)	175	% Margin of Victory	24.3
Rural Polls, 1988 (#)	148	Urban Polls, 1988 (#)	54
% Yes - 1992	31.1	% No - 1992	68.5

ii) Campaign Financing

	# of Donations	Total $ Value	% of Limit Spent
Conservative	132	36216	56.5
Liberal	169	44053	78
NDP	57	66418	83.3
Reform	389	57760	94.5
Other	112	17173	

B: Ethno-Linguistic Profile

% English Home Language	97.4	% French Home Language	0.2
% Official Bilingual	4.6	% Other Home Language	2.3
% Catholics	14.8	% Protestants	54.4
% Aboriginal Peoples	3.7	% Immigrants	12.3

C: Socio-Economic Profile

Average Family Income $	42400	Median Family Income $	36318
% Low Income Families	13.5	Average Home Price $	106254
% Home Owners	74.5	% Unemployment	13.1
% Labour Force Participation	60.7	% Managerial-Administrative	8.7
% Self-Employed	14.5	% University Degrees	6.1
% Movers	53.5		

D: Industrial Profile

% Manufacturing	13.3	% Service Sector	13.4
% Agriculture	6.1	% Mining	0.5
% Forestry	4.7	% Fishing	0.1
% Government Services	3.9	% Business Services	3.4

E: Homogeneity Measures

Ethnic Diversity Index	0.29	Religious Homogeneity Index	0.39
Sectoral Concentration Index	0.38	Income Disparity Index	14.3

F: Physical Setting Characteristics

Total Population	88188	Area (km^2)	13780
Population Density (pop/km^2)	6.4		

Okanagan - Similkameen - Merritt

59009
59018
59003
59007
59017
59011

Okanagan–Similkameen–Merritt

Constituency Number: 59019

Okanagan–Similkameen–Merritt covers more than 24,000 sq. km of 'border country' along the 49th parallel, between B.C.'s Kootenays in the east and the Coast Mountains at the end of the Fraser Valley near Vancouver. It extends north into the cattle ranching of Merritt near Kamloops, to the southern end of Okanagan Lake and the Similkameen River area. It is fairly sparsely populated, the eighth smallest seat in B.C., with 87,726 residents spread throughout the riding and in the regional centres of Grand Forks, Merritt and Penticton. Almost 27% of the area population claim British roots, another 6.5% German; 52.2% are Protestant. Over 5% of the area residents are aboriginal peoples, 2.5% are French and 1% Italian. Immigrants make up 15.6% of the population in the riding, but English is home language for 95.6% of the residents. The local economy is very dependent on agriculture (9.3% of all direct employment), particularly in fruits, vineyards and, around Merritt, cattle production. Almost nine per cent of local jobs are managerial/administrative and almost six per cent are in government service; the local service sector, much of it agriculturally related, is 42.2% of all jobs. Almost 15% are self-employed. There is also a sizeable forestry sector - 3.4% of local employment, the largest employer locally being New Zealand multi-national Fletcher Challenge - and an important mining industry (2.4%) of work placements, particularly with Newmount Mines. Tourism has begun to grow as part of the local economy. At 12.5% the unemployment rate is two points above that for the province; governmental income support payments - at 19% - is over 7.5% above the B.C. average. However, almost 73% of area residents own their homes, over seven per cent above the provincial norm. Average home values are $102,467 and average family incomes are $41,128 - more than $11,000 below the average for the province as a whole.

The history of the region has been politically dominated by the Conservatives. As Okanagan Boundary, it returned PCs between 1958 and 1968. A Liberal won during the first Trudeau victory that year. In 1972 the Tories retook the riding and held it in 1974. In 1979, Conservative orchardist Fred King took the seat; he fought off NDP and Liberal challenges in 1980 and 1984. With redistribution in 1988, Osoyoos lawyer and former alderman Jack Whittaker beat King by a margin of 3.1% and took the seat for the NDP. The Liberals won 17.4% support, Reform 5.8%. In 1992, Okanagan–Similkameen–Merritt had the lowest 'Yes' vote in B.C., and one of the fifteen lowest in the country.

That indicated an upswing toward Reform that carried over into the 1993 general election. Reform nominated Jim Hart, a Summerland television account executive, with twenty years military/military reserve involvement. Sitting MP Jack Whittaker ran again for the NDP. The Liberals selected an Okanagan orchardist, Mike Reed. The Conservative candidate was Sue Irvine, a local vineyard owner, BC Marketing Board member and Vice Chair of the University of Victoria Board of Governors. Irvine had spent ten years on the Penticton School Board, including serving as Chair. These four faced four minor party aspirants - from the National, Green, Natural Law and Canada parties. National's Ken Noble, a writer/historian, won 2.4%, the Green's Harry Naegel, a horticultural contractor, 1%, and the other two the rest. The seat was taken by Reform's Jim Hart. With an NDP (-23.8%) and Conservative (-22.8%) collapse in support, Hart was left with 43.6% of all local votes. Some of that slippage went to the Liberals, Mike Reed capturing second place with 24.5% support. The local turnout was 71.8%, the fifth highest in the province.

Member of Parliament: Jim Hart; **Party:** Reform; **Occupation:** Account executive; **Education:** High school/broadcasting courses, Columbia Academy; **Age:** 38 (Oct. 30, 1955); **Year first elected to the House of Commons:** 1993

59019 Okanagan–Similkameen–Merritt

A: Political Profile
i) Voting Behaviour

	% 1993	% 1988	Change 1988-93
Conservative	12.7	35.5	-22.8
Liberal	24.5	17.4	7.1
NDP	14.8	38.6	-23.8
Reform	43.6	5.8	37.8
Other	4.5	2.6	1.9

% Turnout	71.8	Total Ballots (#)	48732
Rejected Ballots (#)	210	% Margin of Victory	23.6
Rural Polls, 1988 (#)	141	Urban Polls, 1988 (#)	71
% Yes - 1992	27.2	% No - 1992	72.4

ii) Campaign Financing

	# of Donations	Total $ Value	% of Limit Spent
Conservative	210	45333	72
Liberal	166	30104	34.5
NDP	21	63528	73.7
Reform	347	74065	94
Other	57	17813	

B: Ethno-Linguistic Profile

% English Home Language	95.6	% French Home Language	0.5
% Official Bilingual	5.2	% Other Home Language	3.9
% Catholics	18.4	% Protestants	52.2
% Aboriginal Peoples	5.1	% Immigrants	15.6

C: Socio-Economic Profile

Average Family Income $	41128	Median Family Income $	36002
% Low Income Families	13.9	Average Home Price $	102467
% Home Owners	72.8	% Unemployment	12.5
% Labour Force Participation	58	% Managerial-Administrative	8.8
% Self-Employed	14.8	% University Degrees	5.8
% Movers	53.7		

D: Industrial Profile

% Manufacturing	11	% Service Sector	16.4
% Agriculture	9.3	% Mining	2.4
% Forestry	3.4	% Fishing	0
% Government Services	6	% Business Services	2.2

E: Homogeneity Measures

Ethnic Diversity Index	0.27	Religious Homogeneity Index	0.37
Sectoral Concentration Index	0.38	Income Disparity Index	12.5

F: Physical Setting Characteristics

Total Population	87726	Area (km²)	24073
Population Density (pop/km²)	3.6		

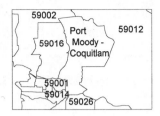

Port Moody–Coquitlam

Constituency Number: 59020

Port Moody–Coquitlam was a new constituency in 1988. It has a population of 114,524, tenth largest in B.C. Situated just east of Vancouver's neighbour Burnaby, it includes the city of Port Moody, the original western terminus of the CPR and parts of the city of Coquitlam and adjacent Port Coquitlam. The area was one of the fastest growing in the Vancouver-centred Lower Mainland. There are large Chinese (6.2%), German (3.9%), French (2.7%) and Italian (2.1%) communities, but the largest ethnic group remains British (24.3%). Immigrants made up 22.5% of all residents and English home-language use was just 91.7% (French home-language only added 0.5% to that total). Area home prices averaged $198,661, above the provincial average but low in the Lower Mainland. That allowed 68.8% of residents to own their own homes, three points above the average for B.C. Average family incomes in the area - at $59,125 - were well above the provincial norm and amongst the highest in Vancouver's suburbs. Only Capilano–Howe Sound, North Vancouver and Delta had higher incomes. More than seven in ten of all riding workers commute outside the constituency to work, making it increasingly, because of new development, a bedroom community. Local jobs and the economy are centred around manufacturing (11.7%), particularly in oil refining and rail yards. Almost half (48%) of all jobs are tertiary, with 7% in business services and 5.3% with governments. More than 12% of jobs are classified as managerial/administrative and 8.5% of work is through self employment. Local unemployment rates are below the provincial average (at 8.1%) as are government income support rates (also at 8.1%) Those with university degrees mirror the provincial norm; locally the percentage was 10.9%.

Politically, the New Westminster–Coquitlam riding was created in 1976. Pauline Jewett won the seat in 1979. The former Ontario Liberal MP and Simon Fraser University president held the seat in 1980 and 1984. Neighbouring Mission–Port Moody had elected NDP MP Mark Rose in 1979. He held it in 1980, resigned for the BC general election in 1983 and saw Tory Gerry St Germain win the seat in a by-election. St Germain kept the seat in 1984. When Ian Waddell's Vancouver–Kingsway seat was abolished for the 1988 election, the high profile NDP MP was selected to run in Port Moody–Coquitlam. He beat local alderman Mae Reid of the Conservatives by a comfortable 8% margin and returned to Parliament. Reform's share was just 3%. The Liberals had taken 15.5%. In 1992, local voters voted 30.5% 'Yes' on constitutional reform.

In the 1993 electoral contest, incumbent Ian Waddell faced nine challengers for his job. The Conservatives nominated Jim Allard, a local businessman who had run provincially and lost for Social Credit in Coquitlam in 1991. The Liberal candidate was lawyer Celso Boscariol, B.C. president of the federal Liberals. Reform's nominee was Sharon Hayes, a self-employed consultant. Businessman Mark Hemming represented the National Party. Natural Law, Green, Libertarian, Commonwealth parties and an Independent rounded out the slate. Reform's Sharon Hayes took the seat with 34% of the votes. Both Ian Waddell and the NDP, and the local Conservatives, saw their voter support slide 23% each. MP Waddell fell to third place - with 21.2% support. Liberal Boscariol increased 12.3% to second place; Jim Allard the Conservative was left with 12.8% and the National Party's Mark Hemming was at 2.6%. That left only 1.8% for the other candidates to share. Local turnout was a point and a half above the rate for the province as a whole.

Member of Parliament: Sharon Hayes; **Party:** Reform; **Occupation:** Homemaker/computer consultant; **Education:** BMath; **Age:** 45 (Jan. 15, 1948); **Year first elected to the House of Commons:** 1993

59020 Port Moody–Coquitlam

A: Political Profile
i) Voting Behaviour

	% 1993	% 1988	Change 1988-93
Conservative	12.8	36.2	-23.4
Liberal	27.8	15.5	12.3
NDP	21.2	44.2	-23
Reform	34	3	31
Other	4.4	1.2	3.2

% Turnout	69.5	Total Ballots (#)	59913
Rejected Ballots (#)	288	% Margin of Victory	10.6
Rural Polls, 1988 (#)	3	Urban Polls, 1988 (#)	203
% Yes - 1992	30.5	% No - 1992	69.2

ii) Campaign Financing

	# of Donations	Total $ Value	% of Limit Spent
Conservative	96	49135	72
Liberal	227	75832	88.2
NDP	42	49703	62.5
Reform	229	48941	66.2
Other	11	3790	

B: Ethno-Linguistic Profile

% English Home Language	91.7	% French Home Language	0.5
% Official Bilingual	7.6	% Other Home Language	7.9
% Catholics	22.4	% Protestants	41.7
% Aboriginal Peoples	0.7	% Immigrants	22.5

C: Socio-Economic Profile

Average Family Income $	59125	Median Family Income $	54110
% Low Income Families	13.8	Average Home Price $	198661
% Home Owners	68.8	% Unemployment	8.1
% Labour Force Participation	75	% Managerial-Administrative	12.5
% Self-Employed	8.5	% University Degrees	10.9
% Movers	59.7		

D: Industrial Profile

% Manufacturing	11.7	% Service Sector	12.3
% Agriculture	0.4	% Mining	0.3
% Forestry	0.4	% Fishing	0.2
% Government Services	5.3	% Business Services	7

E: Homogeneity Measures

Ethnic Diversity Index	0.23	Religious Homogeneity Index	0.31
Sectoral Concentration Index	0.5	Income Disparity Index	8.5

F: Physical Setting Characteristics

Total Population	114524	Area (km²)	678
Population Density (pop/km²)	168.9		

Prince George–Bulkley Valley

Constituency Number: 59021

Prince George–Bulkley Valley covers more than 100,000 sq. km, from the Alberta border in the east, across the middle of the province to the southern portion of the city of Prince George, on to Skeena and the Pacific Coast. The major population centre is part of the northern B.C. 'capital' of Prince George, but smaller towns such as Vanderhoof, Houston and Burns Lake also serve as local centres. There remain more rural than urban polls, however. Forestry is the largest sector of the local economy. It produces almost 8% of all direct jobs, the third highest rate of forest dependence in B.C. and in Canada. Firms like Canfor and Northwood Pulp and Timber employ large numbers of wood- and pulp and paper workers. Manufacturing (15.6%) is largely related to this industry and to a smaller (2.1%) local mining industry. A sizeable agricultural base (3%) exists as well; and almost one in ten work for themselves. The service sector is smaller than many constituencies in the province though higher than many on the governmental service sector side. Only 6% have university degrees; over 11% have less than grade nine. The local population is relatively young as well; only 4.8% have reached 65. More than two in ten of the local population (21.49%) are British; other ethnic communities include a large aboriginal population (11.5%) and a significant German community as the next most populous ethnic group (6.3%), followed by smaller French (2.7%) and Italian (1.2%) groupings. Still, 95.1% speak English at home. Despite an area unemployment rate (at 13.3%) almost three points above the provincial average, income transfers are below that across B.C. Over 70% of the locals own their homes; home values average $78,881, well below the average for the province.

Politically, the area has elected Liberals, Conservatives and New Democrats: in the 1968 election, a Liberal was returned in Prince George–Peace River; in 1972 and 1974 Conservative Frank Oberle was elected. In 1979 and 1980, Lorne McCuish of the Conservatives took the seat. McCuish defeated Brian Gardiner for the NDP in 1984; in 1988, when McCuish did not run again, Gardiner took the seat for the NDP with a six point margin, reversing a 14.6% Tory spread from the previous contest. Reform managed just 1.6% in 1988; the Liberals gained the support of almost one-quarter of the voters. In the 1992 Constitutional referendum, the riding had the fourth highest 'No' vote in the province; it was also in the top fifteen in Canada in rejecting the Charlottetown Accord.

In 1993, Brian Gardiner, a former Legislative Assistant to MP Jim Fulton, and an owner of a desktop publishing company in Prince George, was confronted by just six challengers: the Liberals nominated David Wilbur, a Prince George lawyer; Reform put forward a Prince George retiree, Dick Harris; and the Progressive Conservatives selected Colin Kinsley, a construction superintendent with B.C. Gas, and a Prince George city councillor who also served as Regional District Chair and as a Director with the Federation of Canadian Municipalities. Christian Heritage, Green, and Natural Law parties rounded out the ticket. Local campaign issues included the federal role in Alcan's Kemano Completion Project and its possible effects on the Nechako and Fraser river salmon runs; native land claim uncertainties; and the CNR rail link from Edmonton to Prince Rupert, through the riding. The results of the 1993 general election in Prince George–Bulkley Valley included election of a Reform MP: Dick Harris took 40.3% of all votes. Incumbent Brian Gardiner was second with 23.3% support, followed by the local Liberal, David Wilbur, just 1% behind; Kinsley of the Tories had 12.2%, a drop of 19.5% from 1988, and the local Christian Heritage candidate Bert Prins managed 1% of the votes. That left just 1.1% to be shared by the Greens and the Natural Law parties, in that order. Gardiner held second place despite a fall of 14.9% in NDP support. Voter turnout was the sixth lowest in the province, at 64.7%.

Member of Parliament: Dick Harris; **Party:** Reform; **Occupation:** retired self-employed businessperson; **Education:** High school; **Age:** 49 (Sept. 6, 1944); **Year first elected to the House of Commons:** 1993

59021 Prince George–Bulkley Valley

A: Political Profile
i) Voting Behaviour

	% 1993	% 1988	Change 1988-93
Conservative	12.2	31.7	-19.5
Liberal	22.3	24.9	-2.6
NDP	23.3	38.2	-14.9
Reform	40.3	1.6	38.7
Other	2.1	3.6	-1.5

% Turnout	64.7	Total Ballots (#)	36782
Rejected Ballots (#)	159	% Margin of Victory	19.1
Rural Polls, 1988 (#)	114	Urban Polls, 1988 (#)	89
% Yes - 1992	25.1	% No - 1992	74.6

ii) Campaign Financing

	# of Donations	Total $ Value	% of Limit Spent
Conservative	117	42882	67.6
Liberal	62	21646	48.2*
NDP	19	60334	87.2
Reform	257	70221	80.1
Other	13	3622	

B: Ethno-Linguistic Profile

% English Home Language	95.1	% French Home Language	0.4
% Official Bilingual	4.3	% Other Home Language	4.5
% Catholics	22.3	% Protestants	42.3
% Aboriginal Peoples	11.5	% Immigrants	12.7

C: Socio-Economic Profile

Average Family Income $	50445	Median Family Income $	47810
% Low Income Families	11.9	Average Home Price $	78881
% Home Owners	70.2	% Unemployment	13.3
% Labour Force Participation	73.7	% Managerial-Administrative	7.5
% Self-Employed	9.1	% University Degrees	6.2
% Movers	49.9		

D: Industrial Profile

% Manufacturing	15.6	% Service Sector	13.5
% Agriculture	3	% Mining	2.1
% Forestry	7.9	% Fishing	0.1
% Government Services	6.4	% Business Services	2.7

E: Homogeneity Measures

Ethnic Diversity Index	0.22	Religious Homogeneity Index	0.33
Sectoral Concentration Index	0.35	Income Disparity Index	5.2

F: Physical Setting Characteristics

Total Population	86829	Area (km²)	100525
Population Density (pop/km²)	0.9		

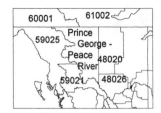

Prince George–Peace River

Constituency Number: 59022

Prince George–Peace River is one of the largest constituencies in Canada in size (215,513 sq. km); it is the second largest in B.C. It covers the whole of Northeastern B.C. from the Northwest Territories and Yukon in the north and Alberta's border in the east, down to the north portion of the city of Prince George. Its western boundary is the coastal constituency of Skeena. Resource towns like Fort St John, Dawson Creek, Tumbler Ridge and Mackenzie dot the riding. They are numerous enough that the constituency's 89,821 residents (10th smallest in B.C.) are almost as 'urban' as they are 'rural'. Many of the communities are single-industry resource based towns. The key economic sectors are mining (7.2%), forestry (4.6%), related service and manufacturing and a strong farming/ranching sector (5.4% of all jobs) centred in the Peace River district next to Alberta. The overall service sector is significant but smaller than many ridings: government services account for 5.3% of jobs, business services for another 2.7%. Almost 12% of the local workforce are self-employed; 8% are managers/administrators. The local population is twice as likely to have less than grade nine (11.3%) than to have a university degree (5.7%). It is also less British (21.7%) with sizeable aboriginal (9.4%), German (6.8%), and French (3.3%) populations. Under half (47.1%) were Protestant and more than three in ten were non-religious. Unemployment in this resource dependent constituency was a 1.5% above the provincial norm, but income assistance rates were more than two per cent below that for B.C. as a whole. Average wages ($51,328) were only $1,000 below the provincial average and house prices - at $72,632 - were over $100,000 less than the B.C. average; so it was not surprising that home ownership was just over the provincial average.

The 1966 redistribution created the riding. In 1968 it returned a Liberal MP; a local Social Credit candidate came second. In 1972, with strong support from the local German population Conservative Frank Oberle was elected. Oberle re-won the seat in 1974, 1979, and 1980; in the latter two contests the NDP was second. In the 1984 Mulroney victory Oberle was re-elected and appointed Minister of State for Science and Technology. The NDP were again second, almost 37% behind. In 1988 Minister Oberle won the seat for the sixth time but with a plurality that had shrunk almost 22%. The NDP remained second; however the Reform candidate took third - at 14.5%, almost three points above the Liberals. Infighting between Oberle and neighbouring Tory MP Lorne McCuish - over free trade, the softwood lumber dispute with the U.S. and federal aid to the local constituency - had hurt the local Conservative campaign. The local Tory problems compounded when, in 1992, the riding recorded the highest 'No' vote in B.C. (and one of the 15 highest in Canada) against the government and its Charlottetown Accord.

In 1993, the strong Reform vote in 1988 was multiplied: Jay Hill, the Taylor, B.C. farmer who placed third in 1988, won the seat; his support was 56.4%, the highest in B.C. and one of the best showings ('top 15') for Reform in all of Canada. The NDP, with second time candidate Alan Timberlake, a provincial Health Ministry manager in Prince George who had run for the Greens in the 1983 B.C. election, fell 22.3% to fourth place. The NDP were only 0.3% behind Dawson Creek businessman Ted Sandhu (at 11.3%) for the Conservatives, a drop of over 28%. Jacques Monlezum, a Dawson Creek service shop owner, took second place (with 19.5% support) for the Liberal Party. Natural Law, Christian Heritage, Commonwealth and an Independent shared 1.8%, none with more than 0.8% support. Turnout was more than four points below the provincial norm for B.C. in 1993, the fourth lowest in the province.

Member of Parliament: Jay Hill; **Party:** Reform; **Occupation:** Farmer; **Education:** High school completion; **Age:** 40 (Dec. 27, 1952); **Year first elected to the House of Commons:** 1993

59022 Prince George–Peace River

A: Political Profile
i) Voting Behaviour

	% 1993	% 1988	Change 1988-93
Conservative	11.3	39.6	-28.3
Liberal	19.5	11.9	7.6
NDP	11	33.3	-22.3
Reform	56.4	14.5	41.9
Other	1.8	0.7	1.1

% Turnout	63.5	Total Ballots (#)	37033
Rejected Ballots (#)	190	% Margin of Victory	38.7
Rural Polls, 1988 (#)	114	Urban Polls, 1988 (#)	92
% Yes - 1992	23.5	% No - 1992	76.2

ii) Campaign Financing

	# of Donations	Total $ Value	% of Limit Spent
Conservative	63	54041	62.9
Liberal	22	9929	16.2
NDP	41	46532	69.1
Reform	304	73982	89.9
Other	8	5735	

B: Ethno-Linguistic Profile

% English Home Language	97.1	% French Home Language	0.5
% Official Bilingual	5.1	% Other Home Language	2.3
% Catholics	21.1	% Protestants	47.1
% Aboriginal Peoples	9.4	% Immigrants	8.5

C: Socio-Economic Profile

Average Family Income $	51328	Median Family Income $	48098
% Low Income Families	12	Average Home Price $	72632
% Home Owners	65.8	% Unemployment	12.1
% Labour Force Participation	75	% Managerial-Administrative	8
% Self-Employed	11.5	% University Degrees	5.7
% Movers	53.6		

D: Industrial Profile

% Manufacturing	12.6	% Service Sector	12.8
% Agriculture	5.4	% Mining	7.2
% Forestry	4.6	% Fishing	0.1
% Government Services	5.3	% Business Services	2.7

E: Homogeneity Measures

Ethnic Diversity Index	0.23	Religious Homogeneity Index	0.35
Sectoral Concentration Index	0.32	Income Disparity Index	6.3

F: Physical Setting Characteristics

Total Population	89821	Area (km²)	215213
Population Density (pop/km²)	0.4		

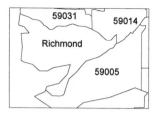

59031
59014
Richmond
59005

Richmond

Constituency Number: 59023

Richmond, Vancouver's southern neighbour, with a population of 126,624 is now the third most populous constituency in B.C. Surrounded by the arms of the Fraser River, and including Vancouver's International Airport, the constituency has been undergoing considerable growth and change. The local Chinese population (16.4%) is now challenging the ethnic British (21.5%) for largest group in the riding. German (at 3.9%) and French (at 1.4%), and smaller East Indian and Japanese groupings, also are important local communities. The Japanese centred in Steveston have been active in the local fishery for almost a century. Shedding a past that was largely based on farming, market gardens and fishing (though agriculture still employs 1% of all direct jobs), Richmond has become part of the metropolitan economy. It has pursued Asian investment with considerable success. Many new businesses cater primarily to the Asian population. The more cosmopolitan nature of the riding is reflected in other ways: English home language is a low 79.8%. Protestants make up only 38.6% of the population, Catholics, only another 19.4%. Over 12% of the riding is Jewish. 35.2% of all residents are immigrants and over 15% non-citizens. The unemployment rate of 7.4% is over three points below the norm for B.C. And only 7.5% of Richmond's population received government income assistance, almost four points below B.C.'s average. University education at 14.2% is above the provincial norm; so are managerial/administrative jobs; almost one in four of all jobs is service-sector, 7.8% in business and 4.4% with government. Average family salaries at $58,527 are more than $6,000 above the provincial average; home ownership - of houses priced between $50,000 and $60,000 above the provincial norm - was at 65%, the same as for the province as a whole.

Depending on boundaries, the area has returned P.C.s (in 1958), New Democrats (in 1962, 1963, and 1965) and Liberals (in 1968). As Burnaby–Richmond–Delta, it elected Conservative right-winger John Reynolds in 1972. He held the seat in 1974 but resigned in 1977. As Richmond–Delta, it elected Tom Siddon, a professional aerospace engineer, for the Conservatives. Siddon held his seat in 1979, 1980, and 1984, defeating a New Democrat handily each time. Mulroney appointed Siddon as Minister of State (Science and Technology) and then Fisheries and Oceans. In 1988, Tom Siddon's support dropped nine points, but he still held the riding with a 16.8% margin over the second place NDP. Liberals were third. Reform managed 3.3% in that election. Almost two-thirds of the riding voted 'No' in the 1992 constitutional referendum.

During the 1993 general election, the fate of Canadian Airline International, based in Richmond, was a hot issue locally; so was local farmland preservation, under heavy development pressure. Incumbent MP Siddon (now former Minister of Indian Affairs and Northern Development, running as Minister of Defence) faced eleven challengers. These included Clyde Vint, the B.C. president of the Christian Heritage Party. Raymond Chan, a research engineer, was nominated by the Liberals, after a bitter nomination fight pitting the Chinese community against the East Indian (bitterness eased when the losing candidate, Herb Dhaliwal, won the Vancouver South party nomination). Nick Loenen, a former alderman and Social Credit seatmate of Bill Vander Zalm, received the Reform Party nod; Sylvia Surette, a sales agent whose husband worked for Canadian Airlines, received the NDP nomination. National Green, Natural Law, Independent, Christian Heritage, Independent, Libertarian and Independent finished in that order. Only Fred Pawluk, a local small businessman, for the Green Party achieved more than 1% - his total was 3.9%. The rest totalled 3%. Raymond Chan took the seat for the Liberals, one of six in B.C. His margin was just over six per cent over Loenen and the Reform Party. Siddon's bid for a sixth term ended with a 25% collapse in his vote; he was left in third place with 19.1%; the NDP slide was almost as bad - 20.9%, leaving them with only 6.3%, less than double the local Green support. Area turnout was almost two points above the provincial rate.

Member of Parliament: Raymond Chan; **Party:** Liberal; **Occupation:** Research engineer; **Education:** BSc, University of British Columbia; **Age:** 42 (Oct. 21, 1951); **Year first elected to the House of Commons:** 1993

59023 Richmond

A: Political Profile

i) Voting Behaviour

	% 1993	% 1988	Change 1988-93
Conservative	19.1	44	-24.9
Liberal	37.1	22.8	14.3
NDP	6.3	27.2	-20.9
Reform	30.9	3.3	27.6
Other	6.9	2.6	4.3

% Turnout	69.7	Total Ballots (#)	58299
Rejected Ballots (#)	387	% Margin of Victory	6.2
Rural Polls, 1988 (#)	0	Urban Polls, 1988 (#)	229
% Yes - 1992	34.3	% No - 1992	65.4

ii) Campaign Financing

	# of Donations	Total $ Value	% of Limit Spent
Conservative	132	95755	96.7
Liberal	166	65941	84.2
NDP	35	31033	39.3*
Reform	188	45555	58.5
Other	86	21456	

B: Ethno-Linguistic Profile

% English Home Language	79.8	% French Home Language	0.4
% Official Bilingual	6.5	% Other Home Language	19.8
% Catholics	19.4	% Protestants	38.6
% Aboriginal Peoples	0.3	% Immigrants	35.2

C: Socio-Economic Profile

Average Family Income $	58527	Median Family Income $	51843
% Low Income Families	15.1	Average Home Price $	230450
% Home Owners	65.6	% Unemployment	7.4
% Labour Force Participation	71.5	% Managerial-Administrative	13.6
% Self-Employed	9.8	% University Degrees	14.2
% Movers	59.5		

D: Industrial Profile

% Manufacturing	10.9	% Service Sector	12.7
% Agriculture	1	% Mining	0.2
% Forestry	0.4	% Fishing	0.5
% Government Services	4.4	% Business Services	7.8

E: Homogeneity Measures

Ethnic Diversity Index	0.24	Religious Homogeneity Index	0.29
Sectoral Concentration Index	0.55	Income Disparity Index	11.4

F: Physical Setting Characteristics

Total Population	126624	Area (km²)	153
Population Density (pop/km²)	827.6		

* Tentative value, due to the existence of unpaid campaign expenses.

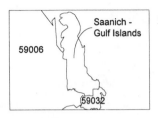

Saanich–Gulf Islands

Constituency Number: 59024

Saanich–Gulf Islands was a new constituency in 1988, consisting of the fast-growing Saanich peninsula including a north part of the city of Victoria, and the Gulf Islands, themselves under increasing development pressure and growth. With a population of 122,051, it is the fifth most populous riding in B.C., and the fastest growing on Vancouver Island. The riding is predominantly middle class. with a large seniors population. Over one third (34.4%) of the residents are British; Chinese (at 2.9%), Germans (at 2.9%), aboriginal peoples (at 2.2%) and French (at 1.5%) are the next most populous ethnic communities in the constituency. Immigrants comprise 21.1% of all residents, but English is the predominant home language (at 95.8%). Almost seven in ten of those in the riding are Protestant (53.4%) or Catholic (14.9%); that is one of the smallest percentage of Catholics in any B.C. (amongst ten lowest) or Canadian (in lowest fifteen) riding. 3.9% of the population was Jewish, while 27.8% reported no religion. Family income - at $55,801 - was highest in the region; home ownership - at over 77% - was also very high, even though average home prices were at $199,584 - $25,000 above the provincial average. The local economy is affected substantially by its proximity to the provincial capital: 13.3% of all jobs were with government; a majority of those working were in the service sector, including an additional 6% in business services. 12% of all workers were administrative/ managers. The local population included 15.4% with university degrees. Like Victoria, a considerable tourist business existed throughout the region as well. Unemployment (at 6.5%) was four points below the provincial rate; income support was almost at the 11.4% average for B.C. as a whole.

Politically, the area has returned Conservatives: General George Pearkes (in Nanaimo–Saanich) between 1945 and 1961. The Conservatives held the riding in the 1961 by-election and kept it in 1962, 1963, and 1965. Liberal David Anderson won in 1968, but left to become BC Liberal leader. In 1972, Conservative Donald Munro won the seat back for the Tories and held it in 1974, 1979, and 1980. In 1984, Munro was replaced by Pat Crofton. Like Munro, Conservative Crofton left the NDP in second place. In the 1988 general election, Crofton lost his seat because of a drop of 15.2% in Tory support. Most of this was taken by Bob Slavik of Reform; his 12.5% support left him in fourth place, but it allowed Lynn Hunter, an Island Oxfam coordinator, to win the seat for the NDP - with only 35.4% support and a 1.9% margin, the lowest in the region. In 1992, 62% of the riding voted 'No' in the referendum.

In 1993, the NDP MP Lynn Hunter faced seven other aspirants: Reform nominated Jack Frazer, a retired Air Force colonel with over 35 years experience in the military; the Conservatives selected Marilyn Loveless, a Victoria activity coordinator; Alex Phillips, a legal counsel from Sidney represented the Liberals; Lynn Hunter was re-nominated by the NDP. Judith Rayburn, a Victoria College instructor, was the National Party candidate. Jack Frazer improved considerably on Reform's 1988 showing: he received the support of 37.2% of the voters, and won the seat. The Liberals, up over eight points, was second with one-quarter of all votes cast. Both the Conservative vote (at -21.9%) and the NDP support (at -16.5%) collapsed. Hunter took third place with 18.9%; the Tory vote was 11.6%. Judith Rayburn won 5.4% for the National Party. Natural Law, an Independent and a Canada Party candidate shared 1.1% in that order. Turnout was 72.9%, third highest in the province during the General Election.

Member of Parliament: Jack Frazer; **Party:** Reform; **Occupation:** retired military officer; **Education:** Staff College/Officer Training; **Age:** 61 (Dec. 20, 1931); **Year first elected to the House of Commons:** 1993

59024 Saanich–Gulf Islands

A: Political Profile

i) Voting Behaviour

	% 1993	% 1988	Change 1988-93
Conservative	11.6	33.5	-21.9
Liberal	25.9	17.6	8.3
NDP	18.9	35.4	-16.5
Reform	37.2	12.5	24.7
Other	6.5	1	5.5

% Turnout	72.9	Total Ballots (#)	71416
Rejected Ballots (#)	247	% Margin of Victory	17.8
Rural Polls, 1988 (#)	73	Urban Polls, 1988 (#)	174
% Yes - 1992	37.6	% No - 1992	62

ii) Campaign Financing

	# of Donations	Total $ Value	% of Limit Spent
Conservative	170	54441	60.4
Liberal	80	21249	29.4
NDP	449	66243	83.5
Reform	278	80877	76.7
Other	102	17948	

B: Ethno-Linguistic Profile

% English Home Language	95.8	% French Home Language	0.3
% Official Bilingual	7.2	% Other Home Language	3.9
% Catholics	14.9	% Protestants	53.4
% Aboriginal Peoples	2.2	% Immigrants	21.1

C: Socio-Economic Profile

Average Family Income $	55801	Median Family Income $	49862
% Low Income Families	9.5	Average Home Price $	199584
% Home Owners	77.3	% Unemployment	6.5
% Labour Force Participation	64.2	% Managerial-Administrative	12
% Self-Employed	13.6	% University Degrees	15.4
% Movers	53.8		

D: Industrial Profile

% Manufacturing	5.1	% Service Sector	15.3
% Agriculture	2.1	% Mining	0.1
% Forestry	0.8	% Fishing	0.7
% Government Services	13.3	% Business Services	6.1

E: Homogeneity Measures

Ethnic Diversity Index	0.38	Religious Homogeneity Index	0.38
Sectoral Concentration Index	0.55	Income Disparity Index	10.6

F: Physical Setting Characteristics

Total Population	122051	Area (km^2)	1605
Population Density (pop/km^2)	76		

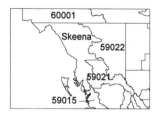

Skeena

Constituency Number: 59025

Skeena is the largest constituency in British Columbia in size - at 242,846 sq. km it is also one of the fifteen largest ridings in Canada. It boundaries are the Alaska Panhandle and Pacific Ocean (at the disputed Dixon Entrance), the Yukon, and Peace River area. Its population of 78,443 - fourth smallest in B.C. - is just under half 'urban', centred in Prince Rupert, Kitimat, Terrace and Smithers. Primary resource extraction is the basis of the local economy: the forestry sector is largest (7.3% of all direct jobs, the 4th highest level in B.C.); mining and fishing are both just at 2% each in providing jobs. Local manufacturing is high (18%) - the constituency is home to large corporations such as Alcan, Eurocan and Repap - and a strong service sector support much of this primary economic activity. Almost eight per cent of all workers were managers/administrative. There is also a high level of government work (9.4% of all jobs) in the region. Apart from a nine per cent self-employment rate, local agriculture also provides employment to 1.4% of the local workforce. Area unemployment is high - over 3.5% above the provincial rate, but income transfers were lower - at 9.3%. Income, due to high levels of unionized work, was more than $1000 above the B.C. rate, and two-thirds of all families owned their own homes, valued at just under $82,000, well below the overall average. The largest ethnic grouping were aboriginal peoples, at 28.7%, the highest level in B.C. (and one of the fifteen highest in Canada). British are the second highest - at 16.9%, with smaller German (4.2%), French (2.6%), and Italian (1%) communities. Almost 95% of the riding use English as their home language. Immigrants make up a low 13.7%, more than seven points below the provincial average.

The Skeena constituency was created in 1914: after W.W. One, it elected Liberals (1921, 1925, 1930, 1935, 1940) and, occasionally, Conservatives (1926). In 1945, with the industrialization of the region by primary producers/manufacturers, it returned a CCF Member of Parliament. The Liberals returned in 1949 and 1953, but between 1957 and 1972 the CCF/NDP had a political lock on the riding. Frank Howard was elected in each election. The NDP failed in 1974, Howard being defeated by Liberal Iona Campagnola. Campagnola served as Minister of State (Fitness and Amateur Sport) in the Trudeau government, but was defeated in 1979 by New Democrat Jim Fulton. Fulton was re-elected in 1980 and 1984, beating Liberals and Conservatives. In 1988, Fulton won his fourth term with 52.7% of all riding votes and a margin of 24.4% over the second place Conservative. Reform was fifth (with 0.9%) well behind Christian Heritage (at 3.6%) and the Liberals (with 14.6%) In the 1992 constitutional referendum, Skeena's 'No' vote - at 72.8% - was eighth highest in BC (and twelfth in 'No' votes in Canada).

In 1993, Jim Fulton decided not to run again; the New Democrats nominated Joe Barrett, a teacher and the son of former BC Premier and Esquimalt–Juan de Fuca MP Dave Barrett. Seven others also sought election: the Conservative nominated Danny Sheridan, a former realtor and Kitimat area Housing Society executive director; Reform's representative was Mike Scott, a former Kitimat construction company owner and consultant who had run unsuccessfully for alderman in 1988; the Liberal nominee was Rhoda Witherly, a manager from Prince Rupert. The election results produced a Reform win. Mike Scott took 37.9% of the votes; the Liberals' Rhoda Witherly was second with 24% - up almost ten points; Joe Barrett was third: the NDP support in the riding had slipped 32%. That left him at 20.7%. Isaac Sobol, a family physician from New Aiyansh, took fourth place, ahead of the Conservatives. Sobol, the National Party candidate, won 7.7% of the votes; Tory Danny Sheridan was at 6.8%. Christian Heritage's Louis Kwantes with 2%, the Greens with 0.6% and Natural Law with 0.5% completed the vote sharing in Skeena. Interesting, for an election with so much change, voter turnout was a low 62.9%, almost five points below that for B.C. as a whole and the second lowest level of voting in the province in 1993

Member of Parliament: Mike Scott; **Party:** Reform; **Occupation:** Businessperson; **Education:** High school; **Age:** 39 (April 18, 1954); **Year first elected to the House of Commons:** 1993

59025 Skeena

A: Political Profile

i) Voting Behaviour

	% 1993	% 1988	Change 1988-93
Conservative	6.8	28.3	-21.5
Liberal	24	14.6	9.4
NDP	20.7	52.7	-32
Reform	37.9	0.9	37
Other	10.8	3.6	7.2

% Turnout	62.9	Total Ballots (#)	31775
Rejected Ballots (#)	128	% Margin of Victory	24.7
Rural Polls, 1988 (#)	113	Urban Polls, 1988 (#)	76
% Yes - 1992	26.7	% No - 1992	72.8

ii) Campaign Financing

	# of Donations	Total $ Value	% of Limit Spent
Conservative	0**	0**	0**
Liberal	106	28764	51.8
NDP	31	55431	82.8
Reform	226	46362	87.6
Other	46	26266	

B: Ethno-Linguistic Profile

% English Home Language	94.2	% French Home Language	0.8
% Official Bilingual	5.7	% Other Home Language	5
% Catholics	19.9	% Protestants	48.9
% Aboriginal Peoples	28.7	% Immigrants	13.7

C: Socio-Economic Profile

Average Family Income $	53586	Median Family Income $	50172
% Low Income Families	10.8	Average Home Price $	81919
% Home Owners	66.6	% Unemployment	14.1
% Labour Force Participation	74.7	% Managerial-Administrative	7.6
% Self-Employed	8.8	% University Degrees	7.1
% Movers	53		

D: Industrial Profile

% Manufacturing	18	% Service Sector	14
% Agriculture	1.4	% Mining	1.9
% Forestry	7.3	% Fishing	2
% Government Services	9.4	% Business Services	2.7

E: Homogeneity Measures

Ethnic Diversity Index	0.21	Religious Homogeneity Index	0.35
Sectoral Concentration Index	0.32	Income Disparity Index	6.4

F: Physical Setting Characteristics

Total Population	78443	Area (km²)	242846
Population Density (pop/km²)	0.3		

** No return filed.

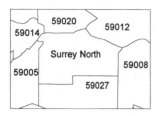

Surrey North

Constituency Number: 59026

Surrey North is the most populous constituency in British Columbia. Its 142,797 residents live in a 128 sq. km area and elect one Member of Parliament (138,968 voters in the Kootenays elect two). It is a new constituency formed for the 1988 election out of Surrey–White Rock–Delta (59%) and Fraser Valley West (41%). Its northern boundary is the Fraser River; on the east is Langley, a new Greater Vancouver suburb; on the west is the city of Delta. The farmland that was much of Surrey has been significantly developed (2.6% of all local jobs remain agricultural, however). Surrey now forms the southern/eastern terminus of Greater Vancouver's 'skytrain' rapid transit system. Change over the past twenty years has produced a host of big/inner city problems. The local RCMP detachment is the largest in the province. Early in the next century, Surrey will replace Vancouver as the largest city in the Lower Mainland. Much of the local population commutes out to work. The Fraser River provides one of the largest sectors of the economy. Shipping and Asia Pacific trade are significant elements. Related manufacturing (15.2%) is also important. Almost four in ten of local jobs are in services, just over 5% in government and just under 5% in business. Almost eight per cent are self-employed and 7.6% are managers or administrators. Reflective of the pace of local change, 26.5% of all residents moved in the previous year, the second highest in B.C. (and seventh highest rate in Canada) and 65.2% had moved in the previous five years, again the second highest rate of movers in B.C. (and the fifth highest rate in all of Canada between 1986 and 1991). Overall, Surrey North had the highest rate of population change in B.C. in the five years between the 1986 and 1991 census. It was the fifth highest rate of change in Canada. 21.7% of Surrey North is British; Germans (at 4.7%), Chinese (at 2.5%), and French (with 2.1%) make up the next largest ethnic communities in the riding. Over 1% of the constituency is made up of aboriginal peoples, and over one-quarter (26.5%) of the riding's residents are immigrants. The English home-language rate is just 84.8%. Protestants are the most populous (39%). Catholics (at 18%) just outnumber Jews (at 16.1%) in Surrey North; the riding is 25% non-religious. The rate of university degrees in Surrey North is low - at 6.1% (over 10% have less than grade nine.). Area unemployment is a couple of points above the provincial rate, and income support just over 1% above that for B.C. Still 63.2% own their own homes, average value $175,034, just above the B.C. average. Family incomes locally averaged $46,718, over $6,000 less than the B.C. average.

In the 1960s, the area - as part of a larger constituency - returned New Democrats. Barry Mather, elected in 1968, defeated former Social Credit leader Robert Thompson who ran as a Conservative in 1972. When Mather did not run in 1974, Tory Benno Friesen won. Friesen held the Surrey–White Rock seat in 1979. He defeated second place New Democrats in each election through 1988. The Fraser Valley portion generally elected Tories. Bob Wenman was elected in 1974 through until 1988. In 1988 New Democrat Jim Karpoff, a former alderman, was returned; he defeated a former Mayor, Don Ross for the Liberals; Ross was third behind Cliff Blair, a local realtor, for the PCs. Reform managed 2.3%. In the 1992 referendum Surrey North voted almost 74% 'No', fifth highest in B.C., seventh highest in Canada.

In 1993, Karpoff was faced with eight challengers: Cliff Blair ran again for the Conservatives; businessman Prem Vinning represented the Liberals; Margaret Bridgman, a nurse manager, was Reform's candidate. In the election, Karpoff's support dropped 19.9%; he fell to third place; the Tory vote also slipped 19%, leaving them in fourth spot, with 13.8%. Reform's Margaret Bridgman won the seat, with 36.9% support. In second place was Prem Vinning of the Liberals, with just over one-quarter of the local votes. Shirley Ann Stonier, of the National Party had 3.3% of the voters; Bill Stillwell, husband of National Christian Heritage Party Leader Heather Stillwell (a Surrey–White Rock–South Langley candidate) won 1.5% support. Natural Law, an Independent and a Commonwealth Party candidate shared the remaining 0.9% in that order. Turnout, at 63.3%, was the third lowest in the province.

Member of Parliament: Margaret Bridgman; **Party:** Reform; **Occupation:** Nurse manager; **Education:** RN; **Age:** 53 (1940); **Year first elected to the House of Commons:** 1993

59026 Surrey North

A: Political Profile
i) Voting Behaviour

	% 1993	% 1988	Change 1988-93
Conservative	13.8	32.8	-19
Liberal	26.4	24.9	1.5
NDP	17.1	37	-19.9
Reform	36.9	2.3	34.6
Other	5.7	3	2.7

% Turnout	63.3	Total Ballots (#)	60961
Rejected Ballots (#)	349	% Margin of Victory	16.2
Rural Polls, 1988 (#)	0	Urban Polls, 1988 (#)	208
% Yes - 1992	25.8	% No - 1992	73.9

ii) Campaign Financing

	# of Donations	Total $ Value	% of Limit Spent
Conservative	46	12485	70.2*
Liberal	273	51702	91.9
NDP	29	62980	57.3
Reform	106	20922	25.1
Other	76	20989	

B: Ethno-Linguistic Profile

% English Home Language	84.8	% French Home Language	0.2
% Official Bilingual	4.1	% Other Home Language	15.1
% Catholics	18	% Protestants	39
% Aboriginal Peoples	1	% Immigrants	26.5

C: Socio-Economic Profile

Average Family Income $	46718	Median Family Income $	43409
% Low Income Families	18.8	Average Home Price $	175034
% Home Owners	63.2	% Unemployment	12.4
% Labour Force Participation	70.7	% Managerial-Administrative	7.6
% Self-Employed	7.8	% University Degrees	6.1
% Movers	65.2		

D: Industrial Profile

% Manufacturing	15.2	% Service Sector	12.8
% Agriculture	2.6	% Mining	0.1
% Forestry	0.4	% Fishing	0.3
% Government Services	5.1	% Business Services	4.7

E: Homogeneity Measures

Ethnic Diversity Index	0.22	Religious Homogeneity Index	0.29
Sectoral Concentration Index	0.42	Income Disparity Index	7.1

F: Physical Setting Characteristics

Total Population	142797	Area (km²)	128
Population Density (pop/km²)	1115.6		

* Tentative value, due to the existence of unpaid campaign expenses.

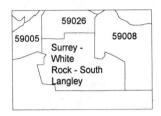

Surrey–White Rock–South Langley

Constituency Number: 59027

Surrey–White Rock– South Langley is Greater Vancouver's most southerly riding. With the U.S. border as its boundary, the riding stretches north and west through White Rock to Delta. In the east it includes part of Langley. It covers 292 sq. km and is the second most populous constituency in B.C., behind its North Surrey neighbour. With redistribution in 1986, North Delta was eliminated, but more Conservative Langley added. Population change at 31.4% was the second highest rate of change in B.C., and one of the highest in Canada, and the riding had the fourth highest rate of movers in the province over the five years 1986-1991. Two in ten of the area residents were immigrants; 29% of the riding is British, with sizeable German (3.1%), French (1.3%), and Chinese (1.3%) communities. Half of the constituency is Protestant; 6.2% Jewish, and only 16% Catholic, the eleventh smallest such community in B.C., and one of the smallest in the country. English home-language use is high, though, at 94.6%. One in ten residents have a university degree, and 12.3% are managers/ administrators. Almost fourteen per cent are self-employed. The local economy is light manufacturing (11.9%) and related service support: over four in ten of all jobs in the tertiary sector, with over 5% in both government and in business services. Reflecting the past agricultural significance of the area, 3.3% of all jobs locally continue to be agricultural. Unemployment is almost three points below the B.C. norm; governmental income support is at the provincial norm. Average income for families at $57,884 is more than $5,000 above the B.C. average, ninth in provincial ranking. Home ownership is high - at 77.4%, twelve points above that for B.C. as a whole, and the second highest rate in the province. Local house prices are a relatively high $215,586.

In the riding's political history Barry Mather, a *Vancouver Sun* humour columnist, was elected for the NDP five times between 1962 and 1974. Conservative Mennonite Benno Friesen was then returned five times - from 1974 to 1993. Both retired, rather than were beaten. In the adjacent Fraser Valley seat New Democrat Mark Rose won in both 1968 and 1972, but was defeated by Tory Bob Wenman in 1974. Wenman held the seat and its boundary variants until Benno Friesen took over the new Surrey–White Rock–Langley seat in 1968. In 1988, Friesen beat anti-racism campaigner New Democrat Charan Gill and Liberal Judy Higgenbottom. Reform's Val Meredith won 6.3% support. In 1992, seven in ten of the constituency voters said 'No' to the Charlottetown Accord.

In the 1993 election, with no incumbent, twelve candidates stepped forward. Several were high profile: Val Meredith, a former Stave Lake, Alberta mayor running for a second time for Reform, was a front runner; the Conservative Candidate Norm Blair, a B.C. Tel manager, had been a Director of the B.C. and local Chambers of Commerce; Heather Stillwell, National Party leader for Christian Heritage, ensured extra electoral coverage. The local NDP added its own presence by nominating Mota Singh Jheeta, a CNR accounts administrator, then having the local party executive resign claiming a last-minute 'packing' of the nomination meeting by the local East Indian community. The Liberal candidate was Gordon Hogg, White Rock's mayor since 1984. Local issues, including youth gangs and local violence, federal infra-structure support for sewage treatment, and Canadian Airlines support were obvious throughout the campaign. When the votes were counted, Reform's Val Meredith had won, with 44.1% support. The Liberal's Gordon Hogg, up 10.3% was second with 33.8% of the votes. The local PC vote fell 31.3% but Norm Blair managed third place ahead of a disorganized NDP: their candidate, Jheeta, took only 4.2%, a drop of over 20%; that left him just 0.9% above Carolyn Goertzen, a local counsellor, whose National Party vote total was 3.3%. Christian Heritage's Heather Stillwell got 1.2% support. The Greens, Natural Law, Marxist-Leninist, an Independent, Canada Party and Commonwealth candidates shared 1.3% of the votes, in that order. Turnout at 71.8% was fifth highest in B.C.

Member of Parliament: Val Meredith: **Party:** Reform; **Occupation:** Realtor; **Education:** 1 year University of Alberta; **Age:** 44 (April 22, 1949); **Year first elected to the House of Commons:** 1993

59027 Surrey–White Rock–South Langley

A: Political Profile
i) Voting Behaviour

	% 1993	% 1988	Change 1988-93
Conservative	12.2	43.5	-31.3
Liberal	33.8	23.5	10.3
NDP	4.2	24.3	-20.1
Reform	44.1	6.3	37.8
Other	5.8	2.4	3.4

% Turnout	71.8	Total Ballots (#)	73325
Rejected Ballots (#)	334	% Margin of Victory	16.1
Rural Polls, 1988 (#)	0	Urban Polls, 1988 (#)	224
% Yes - 1992	29.6	% No - 1992	70

ii) Campaign Financing

	# of Donations	Total $ Value	% of Limit Spent
Conservative	84	57220	77.7
Liberal	206	72021	96.8*
NDP	15	56516	74.1
Reform	428	69080	92.4
Other	158	25142	

B: Ethno-Linguistic Profile

% English Home Language	94.6	% French Home Language	0.2
% Official Bilingual	6.5	% Other Home Language	5.2
% Catholics	16	% Protestants	50.3
% Aboriginal Peoples	0.6	% Immigrants	20.5

C: Socio-Economic Profile

Average Family Income $	57884	Median Family Income $	51851
% Low Income Families	10.5	Average Home Price $	215586
% Home Owners	77.4	% Unemployment	7.7
% Labour Force Participation	66	% Managerial-Administrative	12.3
% Self-Employed	13.3	% University Degrees	10.1
% Movers	61.1		

D: Industrial Profile

% Manufacturing	11.9	% Service Sector	11.3
% Agriculture	3.3	% Mining	0.3
% Forestry	0.5	% Fishing	0.3
% Government Services	5.4	% Business Services	5.8

E: Homogeneity Measures

Ethnic Diversity Index	0.3	Religious Homogeneity Index	0.35
Sectoral Concentration Index	0.45	Income Disparity Index	10.4

F: Physical Setting Characteristics

Total Population	134816	Area (km²)	292
Population Density (pop/km²)	461.7		

* Tentative value, due to the existence of unpaid campaign expenses.

Vancouver Centre

Constituency Number: 59028

Vancouver Centre is the densely populated urban centre of Canada's third largest metropolis. Its population of 114,559 - within 35 sq. km - is a cosmopolitan mix of one-quarter British, 4.4% Chinese, 3.8% German, 2.7% French, 1.15% Italian and 0.94% aboriginal. Over one fourth (27.6%) are immigrants; English is home language for 91.4% (and French another 1%). Non-religious affiliates (at 36.3%) outnumber Protestants (at 35%) and Catholics (at 20.1%); Jews number 8.6%. A large gay and lesbian population has had a political impact locally, provincially and federally. The riding is well educated - the highest in the province - with almost 30% having university degrees (the seventh highest in Canada, and three times the provincial average); it is wealthy-average family incomes are at $61,186, $9,000 above the province's average; unemployment and income transfer dependence are below the provincial rates; it is mobile - the highest rate of movers in B.C. in either one or five years (the second highest or highest in Canada for the same categories); it is the most tertiary in employment - over two thirds are employed in the service sector; it also has the highest rate of workers in business services in the province - and the fifth highest in Canada. Another 5.3% are employed by government. Almost 15% are employed as managers or administrators; over eleven per cent are self-employed. Its house prices at $290,440 are $116,000 above the provincial average; that, and its mobility patterns, explain why it has the lowest rate of home ownership - 24.5% - in the province, and one of the lowest in the country.

Its political history is split between Conservatives and Liberals federally. In the 1950s it elected a Conservative; in 1962, 1963 and 1965, Liberal John Nicolson was MP; after he resigned to become B.C.'s Lieutenant Governor, lawyer Ron Basford, Vancouver Burrard MP in 1963 and 1965, won the seat in 1968. Basford served as Consumer and Corporate Affairs Minister, then Urban Affairs Minister; after he held Vancouver Centre in 1974, Basford was named Minister of National Revenue and then Justice Minister. When Basford resigned in 1979, Vancouver mayor Art Phillips ran and won, beating PC Pat Carney by 95 votes. In 1980, Carney defeated New Democrat Ron Johnson and Art Phillips and the Liberals. In 1984 Carney won with an eleven point spread over New Democrat Johanna den Hertog. Carney was subsequently Energy Minister, International Trade for the FTA negotiations and finally President of the Treasury Board. For health considerations Carney did not run in 1988. Former Vancouver School Board chair and city MLA Kim Campbell 'filled in' for the Conservatives and won over a second time effort by Johanna den Hertog and the NDP, by 269 votes - a margin of 0.4%. Reform managed 1.4%. Campbell served as Indian Affairs Minister of State, Justice Minister and Minister of Defence, before replacing Brian Mulroney as Prime Minister in June 1993. In the intervening referendum, just over half (53.7%) of Campbell's constituency voted 'No', despite a strong intervention by the Member for Vancouver Centre.

In 1993, with Kim Campbell running as Prime Minister, Vancouver Centre attracted a lot of interest; it also produced thirteen candidates. Apart from the incumbent, now Conservative Prime Minister, there was Betty Baxter, a former Canadian Olympic Volleyball coach and small business owner, a member of the riding executive and its Lesbian and Gay Caucus. Reform selected Ian Isbister, a local businessman; Hedy Fry, a Vancouver physician, was nominated by the Liberals. Thorston Ewald, a technical writer won the National Party nod. The defeat of the Campbell government nationally coincided with her own defeat in Vancouver Centre. Her vote decline was less dramatic than that of many B.C. Tories, only 12%, enough to leave her in second place, almost six points behind Liberal Hedy Fry (with 31.1% support). Reform's Isbister took third place with 17.4%, just ahead of the NDP; Betty Baxter won only 15.2%, a fall for the NDP of 21.6% from 1988. Thorsten Ewald's National Party candidacy won more that half the NDP total - 8%. The local Natural Law and Green candidates each won 1%; Christian Heritage, Libertarian, two Independents, the Commonwealth and one final independent shared 1.2% in that order. Turnout was low - 64.7%, three points below the provincial average, the sixth lowest rate in B.C. in 1993.

Member of Parliament: Hedy Fry; **Party:** Liberal; **Occupation:** Physician; **Education:** MD, Royal College of Surgeons (Dublin); **Age:** 52 (Aug. 6, 1941); **Year first elected to the House of Commons:** 1993

59028 Vancouver Centre

A: Political Profile

i) Voting Behaviour

	% 1993	% 1988	Change 1988-93
Conservative	25.2	37.2	-12
Liberal	31.1	22.8	8.3
NDP	15.2	36.8	-21.6
Reform	17.4	1.4	16
Other	11.2	1.8	9.4

% Turnout	64.7	Total Ballots (#)	65273
Rejected Ballots (#)	644	% Margin of Victory	5.9
Rural Polls, 1988 (#)	0	Urban Polls, 1988 (#)	231
% Yes - 1992	45.9	% No - 1992	53.7

ii) Campaign Financing

	# of Donations	Total $ Value	% of Limit Spent
Conservative	193	151616	78.1
Liberal	224	44134	77.9
NDP	115	71079	93.8
Reform	215	51356	62.9
Other	305	37833	

B: Ethno-Linguistic Profile

% English Home Language	91.4	% French Home Language	1
% Official Bilingual	14	% Other Home Language	7.6
% Catholics	20.1	% Protestants	35
% Aboriginal Peoples	0.9	% Immigrants	27.6

C: Socio-Economic Profile

Average Family Income $	61186	Median Family Income $	49038
% Low Income Families	23.1	Average Home Price $	290440
% Home Owners	24.5	% Unemployment	9.5
% Labour Force Participation	76.2	% Managerial-Administrative	14.5
% Self-Employed	11.5	% University Degrees	29.9
% Movers	68.8		

D: Industrial Profile

% Manufacturing	5.8	% Service Sector	14.5
% Agriculture	0.2	% Mining	0.7
% Forestry	0.5	% Fishing	0.2
% Government Services	5.3	% Business Services	13.6

E: Homogeneity Measures

Ethnic Diversity Index	0.24	Religious Homogeneity Index	0.29
Sectoral Concentration Index	0.67	Income Disparity Index	19.9

F: Physical Setting Characteristics

Total Population	114559	Area (km²)	35
Population Density (pop/km²)	3273.1		

59016

Vancouver
East

59028

59001

59030

Vancouver East

Constituency Number: 59029

Vancouver East is a working-class community, situated between Burnaby to the east and downtown Vancouver. Its population of 109,069 has been described as 'the poorest' in British Columbia; the constituency (just 30 sq. km) was also termed a 'safe bet for the NDP' just three weeks before the October 25th, 1993 general election. It is one of the few B.C. constituencies where British ethnic background does not predominate. Chinese account for almost one in three (28.6%) compared with 11.5% British; the local Chinatown is the second largest in North America. Italians contribute a further 6% to the local population. The area is also the centre of a large, mostly poor, aboriginal population: fully 4.7% of Vancouver East. Germans (at 1.7%) and French (with 1.6%) make up the other significant communities in the riding; there are still another 22.2% 'other' (including a growing Vietnamese community). In total, 44.4% were immigrants, the second highest rate in B.C.; only six in ten (61%) of the local population spoke English as their home language and less that one third were born in the province, the lowest rate in 1991. It was one of the few constituencies in the west where Catholics (at 24.9%) outnumbered Protestants (with 20.2%). Jews made up 12% of the riding; the largest religious category was 'non-religious': 42.9%. In economic terms, this 'poorest' description is apt: average family incomes for the area were $38,572; that was almost $14,000 below the average for the province and the lowest rate in the province. Unemployment was well above the city or provincial average: at 15.5%, the highest rate in the province; over two in ten of all residents received income assistance of some form. Local house prices, were $42,000 above the B.C. norm; that area poverty, and explained why under one third of all residents owned their own homes. One quarter of the population had moved in the previous year; just under six in ten in the previous five years. What jobs exist are predominantly service work; 6.24% in business and 4% in government services.

The constituency was created in 1933. It elected Angus McInnis of the CCF from 1935 until 1953, when McInnis switched to Vancouver Kingsway. CCF's Harold Winch took the riding in 1953 and held it for the CCF/NDP until 1972. In the 1974 election, local lawyer Art Lee took it for the Liberals, but in 1979 Margaret Mitchell, a former social worker and community organization director, retook the seat for the NDP. Mitchell defeated Lee again in 1980. In 1984 she won 52.1% of all local votes; the second place Liberals had 26.9%. In the 1988 general election Margaret Mitchell took Vancouver East for the fourth time, again capturing more than half of all votes, and with a 21.4% margin over the Liberals. Reform did not run a candidate. In the 1992 referendum vote, 62.5% of Mitchell's constituents voted 'No'.

In 1993 Mitchell faced Anna Terrana, executive director of the large local/regional Italian Cultural Centre. The Conservatives, traditional third place finishers, always with less than 25% of the votes, nominated Hong Kong-born Susan Tom, an area lawyer; Reform's candidate was notary public Joan Stewart. A large number of minor party, unofficial party and independent candidates (nine in all) rounded out the field. Local issues included immigration matters, not one that favoured Reform here, affordable housing and income support, area violence and prostitution, and Port of Vancouver development, little of the latter benefiting the local population. Margaret Mitchell hoped that her fourteen years of hard work and a high recognition factor would be enough. In the end it was not: Mitchell's vote slipped 20% - to 31.2%, still the third highest in B.C.and amongst the top 15 in the country. A six point addition to the Liberals left Anna Terrana (a Burnaby resident) as the new MP (with 36%). Reform (with 11.8%) managed to outdistance the Conservatives (at 8.8%). Bruce Wright of the National Party was not far behind, at 6.1%. The Libertarians (2%), Greens (1.4%) and Natural Law (1%) all received more that one per cent of the votes; four independents/unregistered party candidates (e.g. the Socialists) and a Marxist Leninist shared 1.8%, with the Marxist Leninist in the middle of that pack. Voter turnout in Vancouver East was the lowest in the province - at 57.8%, a full ten points below the average for B.C. in 1993.

Member of Parliament: Anna Terrana; **Party:** Liberal; **Occupation:** Executive director, non- profit sector; **Education:** Language Studies/Italy,U.K.; **Age:** 56 (March 31, 1937); **Year first elected to the House of Commons:** 1993

59029 Vancouver East

A: Political Profile
i) Voting Behaviour

	% 1993	% 1988	Change 1988-93
Conservative	8.8	15.9	-7.1
Liberal	36	29.8	6.2
NDP	31.2	51.2	-20
Reform	11.8	0	11.8
Other	12.3	3.1	9.2

% Turnout	57.8	Total Ballots (#)	40123
Rejected Ballots (#)	558	% Margin of Victory	4.8
Rural Polls, 1988 (#)	0	Urban Polls, 1988 (#)	155
% Yes - 1992	36.6	% No - 1992	62.5

ii) Campaign Financing

	# of Donations	Total $ Value	% of Limit Spent
Conservative	32	38931	77.4*
Liberal	173	46072	82.5
NDP	28	60635	85.6
Reform	23	4616	7.9
Other	88	22862	

B: Ethno-Linguistic Profile

% English Home Language	61	% French Home Language	0.3
% Official Bilingual	6.3	% Other Home Language	38.6
% Catholics	24.9	% Protestants	20.2
% Aboriginal Peoples	4.7	% Immigrants	44.4

C: Socio-Economic Profile

Average Family Income $	38572	Median Family Income $	33388
% Low Income Families	36.5	Average Home Price $	216872
% Home Owners	33	% Unemployment	15.5
% Labour Force Participation	64	% Managerial-Administrative	5.8
% Self-Employed	7.7	% University Degrees	10.3
% Movers	58.4		

D: Industrial Profile

% Manufacturing	14	% Service Sector	21.4
% Agriculture	0.5	% Mining	0.2
% Forestry	0.3	% Fishing	0.6
% Government Services	4	% Business Services	6.2

E: Homogeneity Measures

Ethnic Diversity Index	0.28	Religious Homogeneity Index	0.3
Sectoral Concentration Index	0.54	Income Disparity Index	13.4

F: Physical Setting Characteristics

Total Population	109069	Area (km²)	30
Population Density (pop/km²)	3635.6		

* Tentative value, due to the existence of unpaid campaign expenses.

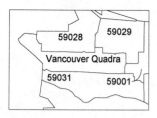

Vancouver Quadra

Constituency Number: 59030

Vancouver Quadra is a riding of 110,717 that includes affluent neighbourhoods like Kitsilano, Arbutus, Kerrisdale, and Point Grey. It also encompasses the University of British Columbia and the wealthy Endowment Lands. Redistribution in 1986 added 30% of the less affluent Vancouver Kingsway and 4% from Vancouver East. Its ethnic makeup reflects the changing nature of Vancouver and the influence of its Asian connections. Here, as elsewhere in the city, Chinese make up the largest ethnic group: fully 23.4% of the local population. The 'British' are second at 17.1%, followed by smaller German (2.7%), Italian (1.5%), and French (1.1%) communities. Over four in ten (41.1%) of the constituency is immigrant, though its rate of growth was low in the period between 1986 and 1991. Only seven in ten (71.1%) speak English as home language; almost 18% are not citizens. The largest religious group is Protestant (30.5%); Catholics (19.4%) just outnumber a large Jewish community (14.7%). Over one third (35.4%) claimed no religious affiliation. Over six in ten of all local jobs are in the service sector; almost 10% in business and another 4% in government. There is also a light manufacturing sector. The local unemployment rate is more than a point below the B.C. average; percentage of income transfers is also below that for the province as a whole. Average family incomes are above the norm by more than $10,000, but local house prices are more than double the average for B.C., at $374,923, the highest rate in the province; area affluence still allows almost six in ten residents (58.1%) to own their own homes. Over 12% of the local population is self-employed and 11.1% were managers/administrators. Almost one-quarter (24.3%) had university degrees, more than two and a half times the B.C. average.

Politically, the constituency was created in 1946. Between 1949 and 1962 it elected Progressive Conservative Howard Green. Liberal Grant Dechman held the constituency in 1963, 1965 and 1968. Conservative Bill Clarke took the riding in 1972, defeating the incumbent; he rewon it in 1974, 1979, and 1980. In the 1984 election Clarke faced new Prime Minister John Turner. Turner lost the government but won Vancouver Quadra - 40% to 25% over Clarke and the Tories. In 1988, Turner increased his margin, again over conservative Clarke, winning 44% of the votes. That election had added the Kingsway and East Vancouver portions to Quadra. Gerry Scott of the NDP was third with 21.4%. Reform managed 2% in that election. In the 1992 referendum, Vancouver Quadra voted 'No' by only a small margin - 54.7%.

In 1993, Quadra Liberals faced an electorate without incumbent John Turner. They turned to Simon Fraser University political science professor Edward McWhinney, an international law expert and former constitutional advisor to the federal and several provincial governments. McWhinney, understanding the changed nature of the riding, sought to produce a 'rainbow coalition'. Confronting him were twelve other aspirants. Reform had nominated Bill McArthur, a former Chief Coroner for B.C.; the Conservatives selected Geoff Chutter, a chartered accountant and owner of a park equipment company. The NDP candidate was Tommy Tao, a Vancouver lawyer. Teacher Willy Spat ran for the National Party and Alannah New-Small, a student, for the Greens. Seven other candidates also sought election. Issues such as health care and federal support for the UBC-based Triumph nuclear accelerator were important local considerations. The results were a victory for Ted McWhinney and the Liberals but the Liberal vote fell 4.5%. That was considerably better than the Conservatives with a drop of 13.1% or the NDP with slippage of 10.6%, to fourth place. Bill McArthur's Reform vote in 1993 was 22.2%, good for second place. The National Party's Willy Spat, a teacher, collected 6.5% and the Greens' Alannah New-Small, 1.2%. A Libertarian, Natural Law, Christian Heritage, two Independents, Marxist Leninist and Commonwealth candidates shared 2.6% collectively in that order, none above 1%. The local turnout was a point plus below the provincial vote.

Member of Parliament: Edward McWhinney, Q.C.; **Party:** Liberal; **Occupation:** University political science professor; **Education:** LLM, SJD; **Age:** 69 (1924); **Year first elected to the House of Commons:** 1993

59030 Vancouver Quadra

A: Political Profile
i) Voting Behaviour

	% 1993	% 1988	Change 1988-93
Conservative	17.4	30.5	-13.1
Liberal	39.5	44	-4.5
NDP	10.8	21.4	-10.6
Reform	22.2	2	20.2
Other	10.3	2.1	8.2

% Turnout	66.7	Total Ballots (#)	52027
Rejected Ballots (#)	416	% Margin of Victory	17.3
Rural Polls, 1988 (#)	0	Urban Polls, 1988 (#)	204
% Yes - 1992	44.8	% No - 1992	54.7

ii) Campaign Financing

	# of Donations	Total $ Value	% of Limit Spent
Conservative	234	51320	92.5*
Liberal	139	44605	70.5
NDP	16	51622	79
Reform	166	42153	81.2*
Other	111	30017	

B: Ethno-Linguistic Profile

% English Home Language	71.1	% French Home Language	0.4
% Official Bilingual	8.5	% Other Home Language	28.5
% Catholics	19.4	% Protestants	30.5
% Aboriginal Peoples	0.8	% Immigrants	41.1

C: Socio-Economic Profile

Average Family Income $	62960	Median Family Income $	48684
% Low Income Families	21	Average Home Price $	374923
% Home Owners	58.1	% Unemployment	9.3
% Labour Force Participation	66.5	% Managerial-Administrative	11.1
% Self-Employed	12.5	% University Degrees	24.3
% Movers	52.1		

D: Industrial Profile

% Manufacturing	9.7	% Service Sector	16.1
% Agriculture	0.6	% Mining	0.4
% Forestry	0.4	% Fishing	0.2
% Government Services	4	% Business Services	9.4

E: Homogeneity Measures

Ethnic Diversity Index	0.27	Religious Homogeneity Index	0.27
Sectoral Concentration Index	0.62	Income Disparity Index	22.7

F: Physical Setting Characteristics

Total Population	110717	Area (km²)	42
Population Density (pop/km²)	2636.1		

* Tentative value, due to the existence of unpaid campaign expenses.

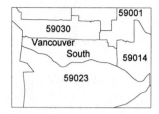

59001
59030
Vancouver
South
59014
59023

Vancouver South

Constituency Number: 59031

Vancouver South stretches from the Fraser River in the south up to Vancouver's 41st Avenue. Half of the riding is 'east of Main', the traditional dividing line between working-class East Vancouver and the affluent 'west'. Its population of 114,031 is a mixture of Chinese (28.6%), British (14.6%), East Indian (11%), German (2.6%) and aboriginal peoples, especially the Musqueam Indian Band (1.1%). Another 16% are classified as 'other'. Immigrants make up almost half (46.5%), the highest level of any constituency in B.C. and one of the highest rates in Canada. It also had the highest rate of non-citizens in B.C. and one of the highest in Canada. In Vancouver South there are more Jews (18.9%) than Catholics (17.9%); both are outnumbered by the 31.9% Protestants and 31.3% with no religious affiliation. Fewer than two-thirds (64.7%) speak English as their home language; 6.3% were bilingual. It contains the largest seniors population (one in six) in Greater Vancouver. The local economy is primarily service and manufacturing: 8.5% in business services and 4.5% with government. Almost 12% are self-employed and over 11% are managers or administrators. The local unemployment and income transfer rates were both at least a point below the B.C. averages. Family incomes were $6,500 above the provincial rate, at $58,871. Average home prices were $358,423, more than double the average B.C. price for a home. Still 55.1% owned their own homes and 17.9% of all residents had a university degree.

Established in 1914 the constituency returned Conservatives between 1917 and 1926. In 1930 Lib-Lab Angus McInnis was first elected. McInnis ran in Vancouver East in 1935 and the seat returned to the Tories with the election of Howard Green and was held by the Conservatives in 1940 and 1945. In 1949 Green ran in Vancouver Quadra and Liberal Arthur Laing won the seat. In 1953 and 1957 it was held by two other Liberals. In 1958 Arthur Laing ran again, won, and held Vancouver South until his Senate appointment in 1972. In 1968, Laing defeated Vancouver lawyer John Fraser a Conservative. Fraser took the seat vacated by the incumbent in 1972, defeating Liberal Gordon Gibson. Fraser almost tripled his margin over Gibson in 1974 and in 1979 served as Postmaster General and Minister of the Environment in Joe Clark's short-lived Government. In 1980 he again defeated a second place Liberal. In 1984, with the NDP in second place with 26% of the votes, Fraser won half of the riding's support. Brian Mulroney appointed him Minister of Fisheries and Oceans. Following the so-called 'tuna affair', Fraser resigned from cabinet. Just over a year later, he was elected House Speaker. Fraser ran as Speaker in 1988 and was re-elected with a 13.4% margin over the second placed Liberal. Reform picked up 2.1%. In the 1992 constitutional referendum, more than four in ten area voters supported the 'Yes' side.

In the 1993 general election, Vancouver South found itself without its six-time elected MP and House Speaker: John Fraser had retired. Ethnic politics played large in the jockeying for position during nominations in the riding. The Liberal candidate, East Indian businessman Herb Dhaliwal from Richmond, had lost a nomination battle in his own home riding to Raymond Chan. One of Chan's Richmond Liberal delegates, Kin Wong Wan, a Vancouver dentist won the nomination of the Vancouver South Conservatives after signing up 2,000 new members, defeating Geoff Chutter, who had strong East Indian community support. Chutter subsequently won the Tory nod in Vancouver Quadra. The Liberals also faced an Independent Liberal initially ruled ineligible because of an outstanding suit against him by the Law Society of B.C. Reform's candidate was Gordon Shreeve, a local Baptist minister. Cameron Ward, a lawyer, represented the Nationals. The election count produced a Liberal win: Herb Dhaliwal took 35.6% of the votes, just over ten points ahead of Reform's Shreeve. Wan managed 23.5% for the Conservatives, a drop of 18.7%; John Mate, an environmental consultant, saw the NDP vote fall 16.3%, him with just 7.5%, only three points above Ward of the National Party. A local Libertarian won 1.2%; all other candidates - a Green, Natural Law, three Independents, a Marxist Leninist and another independent had less that 1% each. Voter turnout was 65.9%, almost two points below the B.C. average.

Member of Parliament: Herb Dhaliwal; **Party:** Liberal; **Occupation:** Businessperson; **Education:** BComm., University of British Columbia; **Age:** 41 (Dec. 12, 1952); **Year first elected to the House of Commons:** 1993

59031 Vancouver South

A: Political Profile

i) Voting Behaviour

	% 1993	% 1988	Change 1988-93
Conservative	23.5	42.2	-18.7
Liberal	35.6	28.8	6.8
NDP	7.5	23.8	-16.3
Reform	25.4	2.1	23.3
Other	8	3.1	4.9

% Turnout	65.9	Total Ballots (#)	48824
Rejected Ballots (#)	487	% Margin of Victory	10.2
Rural Polls, 1988 (#)	0	Urban Polls, 1988 (#)	214
% Yes - 1992	40.5	% No - 1992	59.2

ii) Campaign Financing

	# of Donations	Total $ Value	% of Limit Spent
Conservative	192	104403	91.2
Liberal	423	77665	96.6
NDP	18	22791	36.6
Reform	237	51494	75.7
Other	90	58410	

B: Ethno-Linguistic Profile

% English Home Language	64.7	% French Home Language	0.3
% Official Bilingual	6.3	% Other Home Language	35
% Catholics	17.9	% Protestants	31.9
% Aboriginal Peoples	1.1	% Immigrants	46.5

C: Socio-Economic Profile

Average Family Income $	58871	Median Family Income $	46172
% Low Income Families	19.6	Average Home Price $	358423
% Home Owners	55.1	% Unemployment	9.5
% Labour Force Participation	64.2	% Managerial-Administrative	11.1
% Self-Employed	11.6	% University Degrees	17.9
% Movers	53		

D: Industrial Profile

% Manufacturing	10.9	% Service Sector	15.7
% Agriculture	1.4	% Mining	0.3
% Forestry	0.4	% Fishing	0.3
% Government Services	4.5	% Business Services	8.5

E: Homogeneity Measures

Ethnic Diversity Index	0.28	Religious Homogeneity Index	0.27
Sectoral Concentration Index	0.56	Income Disparity Index	21.6

F: Physical Setting Characteristics

Total Population	114031	Area (km²)	39
Population Density (pop/km²)	2923.9		

59024

59006   Victoria

Victoria

Constituency Number: 59032

Victoria is British Columbia's capital. Its population of 101,012 is predominantly British: 35.12%, compared with smaller German (2.5%), Chinese (2.6%), French (2%), and aboriginal peoples (1.8%) communities. Half of the constituents (49.6%) are Protestant, almost one third (31.3%) non-religious, 15.4% Catholic and 3.7% Jewish. Immigrants make up over two in ten in the riding (21.5%) but almost 96% of all residents speak English as their home language. The constituency includes the City of Victoria, a small portion of Saanich (including the University of Victoria) to the north, and the affluent municipality of Oak Bay, locally referred to as the Tweed Curtain, to the east. As the provincial capital, the governmental service sector is quite large: over fifteen per cent of all jobs are with government, and half that amount in business services. Overall, at 67.4%, Victoria has the second highest level of tertiary economy in B.C. and one of the highest in Canada. Over eleven per cent of all jobs are administrative or managerial. The riding also has a high rate of mobility: the third highest rate of people who had moved during one year in B.C., and again one of Canada's highest. Its manufacturing sector was the smallest in B.C. and second smallest in Canada as a whole. Average family incomes were just above the norm for the province, at $53,155; local house prices were $25,000 above the overall provincial rate. Well under half - 44% - owned their homes. And while local unemployment was over a point below the provincial rate, income transfers were several points above the provincial norm, at 15.7%.

The Victoria constituency was first established in 1872, as B.C. joined Confederation. It was a dual seat until 1903, electing Sir John A. Macdonald in 1878. In 1924, it was re-established and between 1925 and 1935, it elected Tories. In 1936 and again in 1937, by-elections returned a Conservative and a Liberal. Liberals held the seat from then until 1953. In the 1957 election, Conservative A.D. Phillips was elected MP. He held the seat in the 1958 and 1962 elections. The Liberals won the seat with the Pearson election in 1963. Incumbent Liberal David Groos took Victoria again in 1965 and 1968. In 1972, former school trustee Allan McKinnon won the constituency for the Conservatives, defeating the Liberal Member and won again in 1974 and 1979. In the latter election, McKinnon defeated Gretchen Brewin of the NDP. (Brewin subsequently became Victoria mayor, and is currently area MLA.) Joe Clark appointed the Victoria MP Minister of National Defence and Veterans Affairs. In 1980 McKinnon held the seat against the NDP, and in 1984 defeated John Brewin, former provincial NDP President and son of long-serving Toronto NDP MP Andy Brewin, 48% to 38%. In the 1988 general election, incumbent McKinnon did not run. John Brewin won the riding for the NDP, virtually reversing the margin over the Tories from his defeat in 1984. Liberals were third with 21.4%; Reform had a strong showing with over 8% overall. In the 1992 referendum on the Charlottetown Accord, just slightly more than half (55.9%) voted 'No'.

In 1993, John Brewin and the NDP faced a strong challenge from both Reform and the Liberals. Former MP (1968-1972, Esquimalt–Saanich) and former provincial MLA/Party leader David Anderson won the Liberal nomination. Patrick Hunt, a former submarine officer, Nova Scotian Conservative MLA (Hants East, 1978-1981) and a marketing manager, was the Reform Party choice. The Conservatives selected Faith Collins, a University of Victoria program administrator and Oak Bay councillor. University lecturer Cecilia Mavrow was the National Party representative. There were seven other minor party/ independent candidates. David Anderson won the 1993 election, with an improvement of 15.8% in party fortunes; John Brewin placed third after a slip in popularity of 23.9%. Patrick Hunt took second place for Reform with 27.6%, ten points behind the Liberals. Faith Collins and the Tories saw a 19.5% drop, leaving only 10.4% of the votes. That was only a little more than three per cent above Cecelia Mavrow for the National Party; the local Green candidate, Donna Morton, won support from 2% of the voters. Natural Law, Libertarian, an Independent, Canada Party, and two other independents shared, in that order, 1.7% of the total votes. Local turnout was 64%, sixth lowest in B.C. in 1993.

Member of Parliament: David Anderson; **Party**: Liberal; **Occupation**: Lawyer/environmental consultant; **Education**: LL.B; **Age**: 56 (Aug. 16, 1937); **Year first elected to the House of Commons**: 1968

59032 Victoria

A: Political Profile
i) Voting Behaviour

	% 1993	% 1988	Change 1988-93
Conservative	10.4	29.9	-19.5
Liberal	37.2	21.4	15.8
NDP	14.1	38	-23.9
Reform	27.6	8.4	19.2
Other	10.7	2.3	8.4

% Turnout	64	Total Ballots (#)	58269
Rejected Ballots (#)	332	% Margin of Victory	9.6
Rural Polls, 1988 (#)	0	Urban Polls, 1988 (#)	204
% Yes - 1992	43.6	% No - 1992	55.9

ii) Campaign Financing

	# of Donations	Total $ Value	% of Limit Spent
Conservative	121	56317	82.7*
Liberal	284	62335	85.8
NDP	13	63175	79.6
Reform	299	68776	96.9
Other	134	26055	

B: Ethno-Linguistic Profile

% English Home Language	95.8	% French Home Language	0.5
% Official Bilingual	9.4	% Other Home Language	3.8
% Catholics	15.4	% Protestants	49.6
% Aboriginal Peoples	1.7	% Immigrants	21.5

C: Socio-Economic Profile

Average Family Income $	53155	Median Family Income $	42224
% Low Income Families	19.3	Average Home Price $	199708
% Home Owners	43.9	% Unemployment	9.1
% Labour Force Participation	60.2	% Managerial-Administrative	11.1
% Self-Employed	11	% University Degrees	19
% Movers	57.5		

D: Industrial Profile

% Manufacturing	3.9	% Service Sector	18.6
% Agriculture	0.4	% Mining	0.1
% Forestry	0.9	% Fishing	0.4
% Government Services	15.1	% Business Services	7.3

E: Homogeneity Measures

Ethnic Diversity Index	0.42	Religious Homogeneity Index	0.35
Sectoral Concentration Index	0.62	Income Disparity Index	20.6

F: Physical Setting Characteristics

Total Population	101012	Area (km²)	45
Population Density (pop/km²)	2244.7		

* Tentative value, due to the existence of unpaid campaign expenses.

THE NORTH

The North

Territorial Overview

The Canadian North is different: it is different in size - 3,862,199 sq. km, thirty-nine per cent of the total area of Canada; the two Northwest Territories' ridings are the largest in all of Canada, Yukon is sixth in size. It is different in population: 85,466, including the two least populous constituencies in the country, as well as a third that ranks seventh smallest. It is different culturally: only two provinces, Manitoba and Saskatchewan, have more than one in ten of their populace with aboriginal backgrounds; in Canada's North, more than half (56.8%) of the population are aboriginal peoples. That means multi-lingual legislative debates; it means English or French home-language use in fewer than three-quarters of the homes in the North; it means a home ownership rate of just over one-third (36.55%), more than twenty per cent behind the next lowest province; it means one of the lowest levels of declared religious affiliation in the country (only B.C. and Alberta are lower). It means the highest rate of movers in the country: almost two-thirds (64.8%) had moved in the previous five years; that was almost ten per cent above the next most mobile provinces, B.C. and Alberta. It is different economically: fewer than two per cent of its people are involved in manufacturing, for example; only two provinces - Saskatchewan (at 5.2%) and Alberta (at 7.4%) - had less than 10% of their economy in manufacturing. The North also had the lowest rate of agricultural production in the country (only Newfoundland came close), and the second highest level of energy and mining activity.

Its population was amongst the best educated in Canada: fourth (at 10% with university degrees), behind Ontario, Alberta and British Columbia. The region also had the second highest average annual family income level (though the northern cost of living is also high) and the lowest levels of income by government transfers (8.4%), more than a point below Alberta, next lowest in this category. Its unemployment rate, however, is third only to Newfoundland and New Brunswick, just ahead of P.E.I. and Nova Scotia. The region does have the largest number of managers/administrators in the country (15.6%), though, almost two and a half points ahead of second-placed Ontario. This is largely a by-product of the high level of government services in the region. It is different constitutionally and in terms of governance: the region is organized as 'territories' rather than provinces, and though there have been reforms over the past decades away from the federally-appointed 'Commissioner' model, to legislative and executive structures resembling their southern Canadian provincial neighbours, the territories' more limited constitutional standing has an impact across an array of items, from participation in First Ministers' Meetings and full fiscal responsibility to control over resources and levels of government services. In Atlantic Canada, levels of government services are the highest in the country: Newfoundland, at 12.5%, is highest amongst Canadian provinces, PEI (11.9%), Nova Scotia (11.2%) and New Brunswick (at 9.7%) are next; in the North, just under three in ten jobs are with government (28.6%), almost two and a half times the rate anywhere else in Canada.

Having said all that, it is also essential to point out that the North is not monolithic: as the individual constituency profiles which follow attest, there are significant differences between Yukon and NWT, and equally important differences within the Northwest Territories between Western Arctic and Nunatsiaq. So, for example, there are real differences between the levels of aboriginal peoples across the three Northern constituencies, but while Nunatsiaq is overwhelmingly the highest in this category, Western Arctic remains third in Canada, and Yukon, eighth, still constituting a difference between 'north of 60' in Canada and the south.

Politically, author Peter Clancy has suggested that there is a striking similarity in the definition of key issues and in the pattern of the conflict between the North and the rest of Canada; it is at the level of outcomes that significant differences emerge. Certainly in the 1988 Canadian general election, the issue of free trade animated the North as it did the south; the difference was that this was mitigated by a range of local issues distinct from most southern Canada's concerns. In 1984, the Progressive Conservatives had won all three parliamentary seats in the North, consistent with the Mulroney landslide elsewhere in the country; that meant holding Yukon and Western Arctic and taking Nunatsiaq, a seat the New Democratic Party had won in 1979. Subsequently, when long-serving Conservative Deputy Prime Minister Eric Neilsen resigned in Yukon over a year ahead of the 1988 general election, that territory's by-election returned New Democrat Audrey McLaughlin.

The free trade focus of the 1988 election had a negative impact on the Tories' northern political fortunes; so did the reaction of the large number of aboriginal peoples to the Meech Lake Accord of 1987. The exclusion of outstanding aboriginal constitutional reform concerns and uncertainty over the effects on northern issues, such as living allowance subsidies, resulted in the election of two native Members of Parliament (one a Dene, the other an Inuk) for the Liberals in the Northwest Territories; in Yukon, Audrey McLaughlin held the seat she had won in the by-election the year before. In 1993, there were an array of issues: some of these - such as on law and order, jobs or the deficit - mirrored pan-Canadian concerns; but again, these usually involved a northern prism. On justice issues, for example, constitutional matters related to self-government and settlement of land claims intruded to add an aboriginal component to matters such as crime and punishment. Calls for a distinct native justice system were part of the campaign. After the failure of the Charlottetown Accord, the Territories were perhaps the only region in the country where constitutional matters were front and centre in 1993. Two of the three ridings had voted 'Yes' in the 1992 referendum: Nunatsiaq (74.7%) and Western Arctic (51.2%); Yukon's 'Yes' vote had been almost 44%. Just over a week before the October 25th, 1993 election day, Jean Chrétien had unveiled a New Partnership With Aboriginal Peoples comprehensive reform package in a campaign visit to the North: the campaign promise included self-government and self-sufficiency as its central components, the gradual winding down of the Department of Indian Affairs, increases in skills and training assistance, and expediting land claims settlements. Liberal leader Chrétien, a former Minister of Indian Affairs and Northern Development, emphasized that the policy had been developed in consultation with aboriginal peoples. Apart from the settlement of long-standing aboriginal questions, the other campaign issue that predominated in the North in 1993, was the economy and jobs. In a region where unemployment was high, and much work seasonal, the issue of jobs and economic performance clearly predominated over the Reform Party's preoccupation with deficits and the debt. In that, the North was closer to other constituencies throughout much of the rest of Canada.

The politics of the North is not quite the same as in the rest of the country, however. Yukon, with a much smaller percentage of aboriginal peoples (26.7%, vs. 88.5% in Nunatsiaq and 55.3% in Western Arctic), has developed a party system not unlike other Canadian provinces. As in NWT, however, the territorial assembly - and government - ensure that aboriginal matters form part of the permanent political agenda. The differences between the North and the rest of Canada are most noticeable in the governance of the Northwest Territories. Here normal party affiliations are absent. The executive (a Government Leader and Cabinet) which functions like provincial Cabinets elsewhere is chosen from - and by - the Members of the Legislative Assembly. These MLAs run and are elected in twenty-four constituencies as Independents. As Clancy has demonstrated, a system of consociational democracy, allowing Dene, Innu, Métis and 'White' communities to move beyond coexistence to effective territorial governance, is what permits this NWT model to function.

One spillover of such differences into federal politics in the North, is the relative closeness of vote splits, voter turnout and party turnover patterns: in general, voter turnout in the North is lower than the national norm. In 1993, that was the case in NWT: 67.5% of the voters in Nunatsiaq and 60.1% in Western Arctic cast ballots; the Canadian average was 69.6%. In Yukon, slightly more actually voted in 1993 (70.4%), perhaps a product of a national party leader, the NDP's Audrey McLaughlin, running in the riding. Party vote splits are often close as well and, as a result, party turnover rates are high in the Territories: in the four general elections between 1979 and 1988, the two federal ridings in the Northwest Territories had been represented by all three main political parties in the country. In 1984, the vote split between the winner in Nunatsiaq (a Conservative) and third place (a New Democrat) was 266 votes. The second place Liberals were within this difference. In 1988, the three winners' margins were larger. In the 1993 general election, all three northern incumbent MPs were returned with substantial margins: almost fifty per cent for the two returning Liberals in NWT and twenty per cent for the New Democratic Party in Yukon.

Two other brief points could be added: (i) two of the three MPs elected in 1993 in the North were women; four of the fifteen candidates for all parties (26.66%) were women as well. (ii) in Party terms, Reform ran candidates in only two of the ridings - Yukon and Western Arctic: both received 13.1% and 14.1% support. No minor parties - or Reform- ran in Nunatsiaq; minor parties contesting the election elsewhere in the region included a Green, a National, a Natural Law, and a Christian Heritage: the Green and the National Party did better.

In sum, the politics of the North includes commonalities with the rest of Canada; however, understanding how these commonalities play out in the northern Territories requires an understanding of the differences.

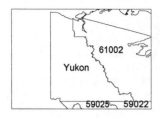

Yukon

Constituency Number: 60001

Yukon is both a Territory (area 455,400 sq. km, the sixth largest riding in Canada) and a constituency (population 27,797). Its main population centre, Whitehorse, is the capital. Whitehorse contains more than half the territory's population, with smaller centres such as Dawson City, Carcross, and Teslin. The largest ethnic group is British, but Yukon also contains the eighth largest aboriginal population in the country: over one-quarter (26.7%) of the local population. There are smaller German, French, and other communities, but immigrants make up only one in ten of the Yukon populace. English is the home language for 97.1%, but almost one in ten (9.2%) is bilingual and 1.3% speak French at home. Protestants make up the largest religious community (43%); Catholics are at 20.2% and Jews 2.5%. Over one-third (34.2%) claim no religion. The local economy is highly service oriented with almost one-quarter (23.6%) employed by government; the business sector is much smaller - with just 4.1% in business services. Almost 16% of all employment is as a manager or administrator. The other large sector of Yukon's economy is mining: 5.9% of the territory's jobs are in this field. Local mining at centres such as Faro have been subject to downturns with significant impact on the whole economy of the region. There is a small local manufacturing sector as well, providing 2.2% of all jobs, one of the lowest rates in Canada. Unemployment is somewhat above national standards (11.5%), but below rates in Atlantic Canada and Quebec; income transfer levels are lower than anywhere else in the country - at 8.2%. Average family incomes -at $56,034 - are higher than anywhere in Canada, except Ontario (they trail Ontario by $128), though the northern cost of living more than makes up for the difference. House prices average a 'modest' $95,973, which puts Yukon below only Ontario, British Columbia, Alberta and Quebec in that category; the home ownership rate of 57.6% puts the territory just ahead of Quebec for the low rate in the country. Yukon has the sixth highest rate of 'movers' over a five year period, and the tenth highest over one year. The territory's education rate is high (12.5% with university degrees) - only Ontario *as a whole* compares.

Politically, the Conservatives - or at least its Yukon MP Eric Neilsen - dominated the territory for thirty years. First elected in the Diefenbaker landslide - as one of the 208 of 265 seats - in 1958, Neilsen served in various ministerial capacities, including, under Brian Mulroney, Deputy Prime Minister. In his last election, his tenth victory, Neilsen's Conservative vote was well over half of all cast (57%). His closest rivals were at 21.4% (a Liberal) and 16.4% (a New Democrat). By the end of this thirty-year Conservative era, there were signs of political shifts: for example, the territory had elected its first NDP Government. When Neilsen resigned more than a year before the general election, Audrey McLaughlin, a former social worker and consultant, won the by-election. McLaughlin held the seat at the subsequent general election , taking 51.4% of the territory's votes. The Conservatives dropped more than twenty-one points - to 35.3%. Liberal voters also were fewer in 1988. Reform did not run a local candidate, but Christian Heritage did. He won 2% support. In the 1992, constitutional referendum 56% voted for the 'No' side.

In 1993 Audrey McLaughlin, now leader of the national NDP faced five candidates. The Liberals nominated Don Branigan, a Whitehorse doctor; the Progressive Conservatives selected a local business-man, Al Kapty; Reform's candidate in Yukon was a farmer, from Charlie Lake, B.C., near Fort St John; the National Party aspirant was Robert Olson, a Carcross businessman; the Christian Heritage representa-tive was Geoffrey Capp, a Yukon clerk. The final vote tally gave Capp 61 votes, 0.4% of the total. The Nationals received 2.1%. Although seeing national support for her Party drop significantly, Audrey McLaughlin held her Yukon seat handily, with only an 8% decline to 43.3%. Local Liberals were second: Don Branigan took 23.3% support, second place, twenty points behind the NDP. The Conservatives took more votes than Reform (17.8% to 13.1%) in 1993. Voter turnout at 70.4% was high.

Member of Parliament: Audrey McLaughlin; **Party:** New Democratic; **Occupation:** Businessperson; **Education:** BA, MSW, University of Toronto; **Age:** 56 (Nov. 7, 1936); **Year first elected to the House of Commons:** 1987 (by-election)

60001 Yukon

A: Political Profile
i) Voting Behaviour

	% 1993	% 1988	Change 1988-93
Conservative	17.8	35.3	-17.5
Liberal	23.3	11.3	12
NDP	43.3	51.4	-8.1
Reform	13.1	0	13.1
Other	2.5	2	0.5

% Turnout	70.4	Total Ballots (#)	14471
Rejected Ballots (#)	46	% Margin of Victory	20
Rural Polls, 1988 (#)	45	Urban Polls, 1988 (#)	29
% Yes - 1992	43.4	% No - 1992	56.1

ii) Campaign Financing

	# of Donations	Total $ Value	% of Limit Spent
Conservative	139	46266	93.5
Liberal	45	35977	61.8
NDP	154	30403	82.4
Reform	47	13390	32.2
Other	14	2773	

B: Ethno-Linguistic Profile

% English Home Language	97.1	% French Home Language	1.3
% Official Bilingual	9.2	% Other Home Language	1.6
% Catholics	20.2	% Protestants	43
% Aboriginal Peoples	26.7	% Immigrants	10.7

C: Socio-Economic Profile

Average Family Income $	56034	Median Family Income $	53127
% Low Income Families	0	Average Home Price $	95973
% Home Owners	57.6	% Unemployment	11.5
% Labour Force Participation	81.5	% Managerial-Administrative	15.9
% Self-Employed	10.7	% University Degrees	12.5
% Movers	64.6		

D: Industrial Profile

% Manufacturing	2.2	% Service Sector	13
% Agriculture	0.9	% Mining	5.9
% Forestry	0.9	% Fishing	0.3
% Government Services	23.6	% Business Services	4.1

E: Homogeneity Measures

Ethnic Diversity Index	0.24	Religious Homogeneity Index	0.34
Sectoral Concentration Index	0.42	Income Disparity Index	5.2

F: Physical Setting Characteristics

Total Population	27797	Area (km²)	455400
Population Density (pop/km²)	0.1		

Nunatsiaq

Constituency Number: 61001

Nunatsiaq is the largest constituency in Canada. It covers 3,433,165 sq. km across three time zones. It extends from the northern pole and Arctic islands to the northern borders of Labrador, Quebec, Ontario and Manitoba. Its population of 22,943 is the smallest of any constituency in the country. With only one town with a population of over 2,000, the population density is very dispersed. In Nunatsiaq, the highest percentage of aboriginal peoples in Canada live across a vast territory from Tuktoyaktuk to the Davis Strait: 88.5% of the local population. Neither English - at 35.4% home use - nor French - at 1.3% home use, make up the majority language in Nunatsiaq. The rest of the population speak any one of the other four official languages represented in the territorial assembly. The riding has one of the lowest rates of immigrants (1.9%) and the highest levels of citizens (99.2%) in Canada. Seven in ten of the residents in the constituency are Protestant; one-quarter are Catholic. Non-religious residents number only 3.9%. The local economy is made up substantially of services - over three in ten workers (31.9%) are employed by governments, the highest rate in the country; only 1.6% in business services. Mining (at 4.1%), fishing (at 2.1%), local manufacturing (at 1.2%, one of the lowest rates in Canada), and traditional hunting and trapping make up much of the rest of the local economy. The unemployment rate has lowered in recent years, but at 18.8% still ranks amongst the fifteen highest in Canada; only Newfoundland as a whole ranks higher. Yet income from governmental transfers is comparable with neighbouring provinces, lower than some - at 10.7%. Average family incomes ($42,643) are considerably lower than its Yukon neighbour; and average home prices are high ($136,920); that might help explain the level of home ownership in Nunatsiaq: only 9.6% of residents own their homes. Despite a house price disparity, other factors are involved here. In Yukon, the rate is almost 58%; in Western Arctic it is almost 43%.

Politically Nunatsiaq was created when NWT was given two seats in Parliament in 1976. The sitting Tory MP, elected in 1984 with just 32.5%, had quit politics after one term. In 1984, the Liberals placed second with 29%, just 3.5% behind the winning Conservative; the NDP was third with 28.6%; even the Independent vote was almost one in ten of those cast in the riding. In 1988, the vote margins were again small: in this election the Liberal candidate took 39.9% support. He was Jack Iyerak Anawak, a seasoned Inuit politician from Rankin Inlet. The New Democrats, with Peter Kusugak, an Inuit manager with the federal Department of Indian and Northern Affairs, were second with 33.2%, just 6.7% behind. The Conservatives won 22.9% of the votes; a local Independent took the remaining 4%. In the 1992 constitutional referendum, Nunatsiaq voted overwhelmingly 'Yes', reflecting the aboriginal component in the constitutional package: three-quarters voted 'Yes', the tenth highest positive vote in Canada.

In 1993, Liberal incumbent Jack Iyerak Anawak faced only two challengers. The Conservatives nominated an Iqaluit policy advisor, Leena Evic-Twerdin; the NDP put forward Mike Illnik, a maintenance coordinator from Arviat. Running as an incumbent, and well known in the local Inuit and wider community was obviously an advantage in 1993. Jack Anawak took seven in ten of all votes (6,685 votes, a total of 69.8%); the Conservative vote in Nunatsiaq held (dropping only 2.3%) leaving the Tory candidate, Leena Evic-Twerdin in second place with 20.6%. The NDP vote fell significantly (almost 24%) to leave the local party with just 9.7% support in the riding. Voter turnout was just over two points below the Canadian average.

Member of Parliament: Jack Iyerak Anawak; **Party:** Liberal; **Occupation:** Businessperson; **Education:** Western Canada Co-op College; **Age:** 43 (Sept. 26, 1950); **Year first elected to the House of Commons:** 1988

61001 Nunatsiaq

A: Political Profile
i) Voting Behaviour

	% 1993	% 1988	Change 1988-93
Conservative	20.6	22.9	-2.3
Liberal	69.8	39.9	29.9
NDP	9.7	33.2	-23.5
Reform	0	0	0
Other	0	4	-4

% Turnout	67.5	Total Ballots (#)	9697
Rejected Ballots (#)	118	% Margin of Victory	49.2
Rural Polls, 1988 (#)	76	Urban Polls, 1988 (#)	0
% Yes - 1992	74.7	% No - 1992	24.3

ii) Campaign Financing

	# of Donations	Total $ Value	% of Limit Spent
Conservative	57	44850	68.5
Liberal	47	42935	35
NDP	13	13058	5.5
Reform	0	0	0
Other	0	0	

B: Ethno-Linguistic Profile

% English Home Language	35.4	% French Home Language	1.3
% Official Bilingual	3.5	% Other Home Language	63.3
% Catholics	24.9	% Protestants	70.6
% Aboriginal Peoples	88.5	% Immigrants	1.9

C: Socio-Economic Profile

Average Family Income $	42643	Median Family Income $	34223
% Low Income Families	0	Average Home Price $	136920
% Home Owners	9.6	% Unemployment	18.8
% Labour Force Participation	63.7	% Managerial-Administrative	12.9
% Self-Employed	5.6	% University Degrees	5.9
% Movers	62.3		

D: Industrial Profile

% Manufacturing	1.2	% Service Sector	15.3
% Agriculture	0.2	% Mining	4.1
% Forestry	0	% Fishing	2.1
% Government Services	31.9	% Business Services	1.6

E: Homogeneity Measures

Ethnic Diversity Index	0.79	Religious Homogeneity Index	0.56
Sectoral Concentration Index	0.47	Income Disparity Index	19.7

F: Physical Setting Characteristics

Total Population	22943	Area (km^2)	3433165
Population Density (pop/km^2)	0		

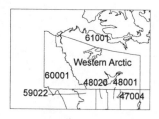

Western Arctic

Constituency Number: 61002

Western Arctic is the second largest riding in Canada, covering 1,138,844 sq. km, and the eighth smallest in population (34,706). It extends from the Beaufort Sea to Alberta and Saskatchewan's northern borders, and from Yukon to Nunatsiaq. It includes the territorial capital, Yellowknife, and smaller centres like Hay River, Fort Smith, Fort Simpson, Rae, Inuvik, and Norman Wells. More than half (55.3%) of the population are aboriginal peoples, from a variety of first peoples backgrounds. Smaller British, French and German communities, particularly in the larger centres, also exist. Almost nine in ten (88%) of the riding residents speak English at home; just under 1% speak French. Most of the rest speak one of several native languages as there are few immigrants (6.8%). The Canadian citizenship rate in Western Arctic is 94%. At variance from its other NWT neighbour, 46.9% of the constituents are Catholic, more than ten per cent above the level of Protestant affiliation. Non-religious rates are also higher than in Nunatsiaq: 14.9%. Services dominate the local economy: three in ten, the second highest rate in the country, are employed by government. The self-employed make up 7.1% of the local workforce, business services another 3.7%. Much of this service work is in support of mining (at 5.6% of the local economy) and tourism, a growing sector. Unemployment is around the Canadian average (10.8%) and considerably below the 18.8% in Nunatsiaq. Rates of government income transfers are quite low, about half that of the other NWT constituency. Average family incomes are also much higher - over $20,000 more than in Nunatsiaq, at $63,320. Home prices are actually lower, helping to explain the higher rates of ownership: over four in ten (42.5%) of Western Arctic residents own their homes. The rate is still low by countrywide standards, but Western Arctic has one of the highest rates of population mobility in Canada: 30% moved over a one year period, third highest in Canada; over two-thirds moved over a five year period, again third highest in the country. The level of education in the riding - 11.7% have completed a university degree - is high.

The riding had been created in 1976 when NWT was split in two for Parlimentary elections. Conservative David Nickerson, a former Minister of Health and Social Services in NWT took the seat in the 1979 election, beating a Liberal. The Conservative victory came with 35.2% support locally. In the 1980 election, Nickerson beat the local NDP but by only 19 votes. He was returned in 1984 with 46% of the votes; the NDP had 28.1% and the Liberals 25.9% in a straight three-way race. The incumbent Tory sought a fourth term in 1988, but Liberal Ethel Blondin, a former territorial deputy minister and a Dene, picked up most of the 17.4% slide in local Conservative fortunes, winning support from 42.4% of the riding. Two local well known independents won just under 4%. In the 1992 referendum, a small majority (51.2%) voted in favour of the Charlottetown Accord.

In 1993, Blondin-Andrew faced Reform, Progressive Conservative, New Democrat, Green and Natural Law challengers. National issues such as the future of health care and social programs, jobs and training, the deficit and the GST, and the young Offender Act were important to local electors; so were land claims, adequate funding for the Western Arctic after the split in the Northwest Territories, and highways (such as in the Mackenzie Valley and north of Yellowknife). In the 1993 election Blondin-Andrew won 62.5% of the Western Arctic vote. Mansell Grey, a Hay River roofing contractor and the father of Alberta Reform MP Deborah Grey, put local Reform in second place with just 14.1%. One point behind was Martin Hanly, a territorial civil servant (Municipal and Community Affairs) on leave to fight the election for the Conservatives. New Democrat Bill Schram, president of the union representing Royal Oak miners, emphasized the need for laws protecting women and children, and anti-scab work legislation. He received half the Tory tally, 6.3%. Chris O'Brien, a writer/photographer, of the Greens - with 2.3% and Lynn Taylor, a Yellowknife librarian, representing Natural Law finished the balloting with 1.5%. Western Arctic's general election turnout was low, 60.1%, over 9% below the rate across Canada.

Member of Parliament: Ethel Blondin-Andrew; **Party:** Liberal; **Occupation:** Public servant; **Education:** BEd, University of Alberta; **Age:** 42 (March 25, 1951); **Year first elected to the House of Commons:** 1988

62002 Western Arctic

A: Political Profile
i) Voting Behaviour

	% 1993	% 1988	Change 1988-93
Conservative	13.3	28.6	-15.3
Liberal	62.5	42.4	20.1
NDP	6.3	25.1	-18.8
Reform	14.1	0	14.1
Other	3.8	3.9	-0.1

% Turnout	60.1	Total Ballots (#)	14265
Rejected Ballots (#)	71	% Margin of Victory	48.4
Rural Polls, 1988 (#)	57	Urban Polls, 1988 (#)	26
% Yes - 1992	51.2	% No - 1992	48.3

ii) Campaign Financing

	# of Donations	Total $ Value	% of Limit Spent
Conservative	99	35926	74.7*
Liberal	147	69465	92.8
NDP	0**	0**	0**
Reform	20	4190	5.1
Other	19	5030	

B: Ethno-Linguistic Profile

% English Home Language	88	% French Home Language	1
% Official Bilingual	7.8	% Other Home Language	11
% Catholics	46.9	% Protestants	36.3
% Aboriginal Peoples	55.3	% Immigrants	6.8

C: Socio-Economic Profile

Average Family Income $	63320	Median Family Income $	59055
% Low Income Families	0	Average Home Price $	109356
% Home Owners	42.5	% Unemployment	10.8
% Labour Force Participation	78.5	% Managerial-Administrative	18
% Self-Employed	7.1	% University Degrees	11.7
% Movers	67.5		

D: Industrial Profile

% Manufacturing	1.4	% Service Sector	14.4
% Agriculture	0.2	% Mining	5.6
% Forestry	0.9	% Fishing	1.1
% Government Services	30.4	% Business Services	3.7

E: Homogeneity Measures

Ethnic Diversity Index	0.36	Religious Homogeneity Index	0.37
Sectoral Concentration Index	0.46	Income Disparity Index	6.7

F: Physical Setting Characteristics

Total Population	34706	Area (km²)	1138844
Population Density (pop/km²)	0		

* Tentative value, due to the existence of unpaid campaign expenses.
** No return filed.

APPENDICES

Appendix One

Alphabetical List of Constituencies

Constituency Name	Identification Number	Province
Abitibi	24001	Quebec
Acadie-Bathurst (formerly Gloucester)	13005	New Brunswick
Ahuntsic	24002	Quebec
Algoma	35001	Ontario
Anjou–Rivière-des-Prairies	24003	Quebec
Annapolis Valley–Hants	12001	Nova Scotia
Argenteuil–Papineau	24004	Quebec
Athabasca	48001	Alberta
Beaches–Woodbine	35002	Ontario
Beauce	24005	Quebec
Beauharnois–Salaberry	24006	Quebec
Beauport–Montmorency–Orléans (formerly Montmorency–Orléans)	24046	Quebec
Beauséjour	13001	New Brunswick
Beaver River	48002	Alberta
Bellechasse	24007	Quebec
Berthier–Montcalm	24008	Quebec
Blainville–Deux-Montagnes	24009	Quebec
Bonaventure–Îles-de-la-Madeleine	24010	Quebec
Bonavista–Trinity–Conception	10001	Newfoundland
Bourassa	24011	Quebec
Brampton	35003	Ontario
Brampton–Gore–Malton (formerly Brampton–Malton)	35004	Ontario
Brandon–Souris	46001	Manitoba
Brant	35005	Ontario
Broadview–Greenwood	35006	Ontario
Brome–Missisquoi	24012	Quebec
Bruce–Grey	35007	Ontario
Burin–St George's	10002	Newfoundland
Burlington	35008	Ontario
Burnaby–Kingsway	59001	British Columbia
Calgary Centre	48003	Alberta
Calgary North	48004	Alberta
Calgary Northeast	48005	Alberta
Calgary Southeast	48006	Alberta
Calgary Southwest	48007	Alberta
Calgary West	48008	Alberta
Cambridge	35009	Ontario
Cape Breton Highlands–Canso	12003	Nova Scotia

Constituency Name	Identification Number	Province
Cape Breton–East Richmond	12002	Nova Scotia
Cape Breton–The Sydneys	12004	Nova Scotia
Capilano–Howe Sound	59002	British Columbia
Cardigan	11001	Prince Edward Island
Cariboo–Chilcotin	59003	British Columbia
Carleton–Charlotte	13002	New Brunswick
Carleton–Gloucester	35010	Ontario
Central Nova	12005	Nova Scotia
Châteauguay	24018	Quebec
Chambly	24013	Quebec
Champlain	24014	Quebec
Charlesbourg	24016	Quebec
Charlevoix	24017	Quebec
Chicoutimi	24019	Quebec
Churchill	46002	Manitoba
Cochrane–Superior	35011	Ontario
Comox–Alberni	59004	British Columbia
·Crowfoot	48009	Alberta
Cumberland–Colchester	12006	Nova Scotia
Dartmouth	12007	Nova Scotia
Dauphin–Swan River	46003	Manitoba
Davenport	35012	Ontario
Delta	59005	British Columbia
Don Valley East	35013	Ontario
Don Valley North	35014	Ontario
Don Valley West	35015	Ontario
Drummond	24020	Quebec
Durham	35016	Ontario
Edmonton East	48010	Alberta
Edmonton North	48011	Alberta
Edmonton Northwest	48012	Alberta
Edmonton Southeast	48013	Alberta
Edmonton Southwest	48014	Alberta
Edmonton–Strathcona	48015	Alberta
Eglinton–Lawrence	35017	Ontario
Egmont	11002	Prince Edward Island
Elgin–Norfolk (formerly Elgin)	35018	Ontario
Elk Island	48016	Alberta
Erie	35019	Ontario
Esquimalt–Juan de Fuca	59006	British Columbia
Essex–Kent	35020	Ontario
Essex–Windsor	35021	Ontario
Etobicoke Centre	35022	Ontario
Etobicoke–Lakeshore	35023	Ontario
Etobicoke North	35024	Ontario
Fraser Valley East	59007	British Columbia
Fraser Valley West	59008	British Columbia

Constituency Name	Identification Number	Province
Fredericton–York-Sunbury (formerly Fredericton)	13003	New Brunswick
Frontenac	24022	Quebec
Fundy–Royal	13004	New Brunswick
Gander–Grand Falls	10003	Newfoundland
Gaspé	24023	Quebec
Gatineau–La Lièvre (formerly Chapleau)	24015	Quebec
Glengarry–Prescott–Russell	35025	Ontario
Guelph–Wellington	35026	Ontario
Haldimand–Norfolk	35027	Ontario
Halifax	12008	Nova Scotia
Halifax West	12009	Nova Scotia
Halton–Peel	35028	Ontario
Hamilton East	35029	Ontario
Hamilton Mountain	35030	Ontario
Hamilton–Wentworth	35031	Ontario
Hamilton West	35032	Ontario
Hastings–Frontenac–Lennox and Addington	35033	Ontario
Hillsborough	11003	Prince Edward Island
Hochelaga–Maisonneuve	24024	Quebec
Hull–Aylmer	24025	Quebec
Humber–St Barbe–Baie Verte	10004	Newfoundland
Huron–Bruce	35034	Ontario
Joliette	24026	Quebec
Jonquière	24027	Quebec
Kamloops	59009	British Columbia
Kamouraska–Rivière-du-Loup	24028	Quebec
Kenora–Rainy River	35035	Ontario
Kent	35036	Ontario
Kindersley–Lloydminster	47001	Saskatchewan
Kingston and the Islands	35037	Ontario
Kitchener	35038	Ontario
Kootenay East	59010	British Columbia
Kootenay West–Revelstoke	59011	British Columbia
La Prairie	24032	Quebec
Labrador	10005	Newfoundland
Lac-Saint-Jean	24030	Quebec
Lachine–Lac-Saint-Louis	24029	Quebec
Lambton–Middlesex	35039	Ontario
Lanark–Carleton	35040	Ontario
LaSalle– Émard	24033	Quebec
Laurentides	24034	Quebec
Laurier–Sainte-Marie	24035	Quebec
Laval Centre (formerly Laval des Rapides)	24037	Quebec
Laval Est (formerly Duvernay)	24021	Quebec
Laval Ouest (formerly Laval)	24036	Quebec

Constituency Name	Identification Number	Province
Leeds–Grenville	35041	Ontario
Lethbridge	48017	Alberta
Lévis	24038	Quebec
Lincoln	35042	Ontario
Lisgar–Marquette	46004	Manitoba
London East	35043	Ontario
London–Middlesex	35044	Ontario
London West	35045	Ontario
Longueuil	24039	Quebec
Lotbinière	24040	Quebec
Louis-Hébert	24041	Quebec
Mackenzie	47002	Saskatchewan
Macleod	48018	Alberta
Madawaska–Victoria	13006	New Brunswick
Malpeque	11004	Prince Edward Island
Manicouagan	24042	Quebec
Markham–Whitchurch–Stouffville (formerly Markham)	35046	Ontario
Matapédia–Matane	24043	Ontario
Medicine Hat	48019	Alberta
Mégantic–Compton–Stanstead	24044	Quebec
Mercier	24045	Quebec
Miramichi	13007	New Brunswick
Mission–Coquitlam	59012	British Columbia
Mississauga East	35047	Ontario
Mississauga South	35048	Ontario
Mississauga West	35049	Ontario
Moncton	13008	New Brunswick
Mont-Royal	24047	Quebec
Moose Jaw–Lake Centre	47003	Saskatchewan
Nanaimo–Cowichan	59013	British Columbia
Nepean	35050	Ontario
New Westminster–Burnaby	59014	British Columbia
Niagara Falls	35051	Ontario
Nickel Belt	35052	Ontario
Nipissing	35053	Ontario
North Island–Powell River	59015	British Columbia
North Vancouver	59016	British Columbia
Northumberland	35054	Ontario
Notre-Dame-de-Grâce	24048	Quebec
Nunatsiaq	61001	Northwest Territories
Oakville–Milton	35055	Ontario
Okanagan Centre	59017	British Columbia
Okanagan–Shuswap	59018	British Columbia
Okanagan–Similkameen–Merritt	59019	British Columbia
Ontario	35056	Ontario
Oshawa	35057	Ontario

Constituency Name	Identification Number	Province
Ottawa Centre	35058	Ontario
Ottawa South	35059	Ontario
Ottawa–Vanier	35060	Ontario
Ottawa West	35061	Ontario
Outremont	24049	Quebec
Oxford	35062	Ontario
Papineau–Saint-Michel	24050	Quebec
Parkdale–High Park	35063	Ontario
Parry Sound–Muskoka	35064	Ontario
Peace River	48020	Alberta
Perth–Wellington–Waterloo	35065	Ontario
Peterborough	35066	Ontario
Pierrefonds–Dollard	24051	Quebec
Pontiac–Gatineau–Labelle	24052	Quebec
Port Moody–Coquitlam	59020	British Columbia
Portage–Interlake	46005	Manitoba
Portneuf	24053	Quebec
Prince Albert–Churchill River	47004	Saskatchewan
Prince Edward–Hastings	35067	Ontario
Prince George–Bulkley Valley	59021	British Columbia
Prince George–Peace River	59022	British Columbia
Provencher	46006	Manitoba
Québec (formerly Langelier)	24031	Quebec
Québec-Est	24054	Quebec
Red Deer	48021	Alberta
Regina–Lumsden	47005	Saskatchewan
Regina–Qu'Appelle	47006	Saskatchewan
Regina–Wascana	47007	Saskatchewan
Renfrew–Nipissing–Pembroke (formerly Renfrew)	35068	Ontario
Restigouche–Chaleur (formerly Restigouche)	13009	New Brunswick
Richelieu	24055	Quebec
Richmond	59023	British Columbia
Richmond–Wolfe	24056	Quebec
Rimouski–Témiscouata	24057	Quebec
Roberval	24058	Quebec
Rosedale	35069	Ontario
Rosemont	24059	Quebec
Saanich–Gulf Islands	59024	British Columbia
St Albert	48022	Alberta
St Boniface	46007	Manitoba
St Catharines	35070	Ontario
Saint-Denis	24060	Quebec
Saint-Henri–Westmount	24061	Quebec
Saint-Hubert	24062	Quebec
Saint-Hyacinthe–Bagot	24063	Quebec

Constituency Name	Identification Number	Province
Saint-Jean	24064	Quebec
Saint John	13010	New Brunswick
St John's East	10006	Newfoundland
St John's West	10007	Newfoundland
Saint-Laurent	24065	Quebec
Saint-Léonard–Cartierville (formerly Saint-Léonard)	24066	Quebec
Saint-Maurice	24067	Quebec
St Paul's	35071	Ontario
Sarnia–Lambton	35072	Ontario
Saskatoon–Clark's Crossing	47008	Saskatchewan
Saskatoon–Dundurn	47009	Saskatchewan
Saskatoon–Humboldt	47010	Saskatchewan
Sault Ste Marie	35073	Ontario
Scarborough–Agincourt	35074	Ontario
Scarborough Centre	35075	Ontario
Scarborough East	35076	Ontario
Scarborough–Rouge River	35077	Ontario
Scarborough West	35078	Ontario
Selkirk–Red River (formerly Selkirk)	46008	Manitoba
Shefford	24068	Quebec
Sherbrooke	24069	Quebec
Simcoe Centre	35079	Ontario
Simcoe North	35080	Ontario
Skeena	59025	British Columbia
Souris–Moose Mountain	47011	Saskatchewan
South Shore	12010	Nova Scotia
South West Nova	12011	Nova Scotia
Stormont–Dundas	35081	Ontario
Sudbury	35082	Ontario
Surrey North	59026	British Columbia
Surrey–White Rock–South Langley (formerly Surrey–White Rock)	59027	British Columbia
Swift Current–Maple Creek–Assiniboia	47012	Saskatchewan
Témiscamingue	24070	Quebec
Terrebonne	24071	Quebec
The Battlefords–Meadow Lake	47013	Saskatchewan
Thunder Bay–Atikokan	35083	Ontario
Thunder Bay–Nipigon	35084	Ontario
Timiskaming	35085	Ontario
Timmins–Chapleau	35086	Ontario
Trinity–Spadina	35087	Ontario
Trois-Rivières	24072	Quebec
Vancouver Centre	59028	British Columbia
Vancouver East	59029	British Columbia
Vancouver Quadra	59030	British Columbia

Constituency Name	Identification Number	Province
Vancouver South	59031	British Columbia
Vaudreuil	24073	Quebec
Vegreville	48023	Alberta
Verchères	24074	Quebec
Verdun–Saint-Paul	24075	Quebec
Victoria	59032	British Columbia
Victoria–Haliburton	35088	Ontario
Waterloo	35089	Ontario
Welland–St Catharines–Thorold	35090	Ontario
Wellington–Grey–Dufferin–Simcoe	35091	Ontario
Western Arctic	61002	Northwest Territories
Wetaskiwin	48024	Alberta
Wild Rose	48025	Alberta
Willowdale	35092	Ontario
Windsor– St Clair (formerly Windsor–Lake St Clair)	35093	Ontario
Windsor West	35094	Ontario
Winnipeg North	46009	Manitoba
Winnipeg North Centre	46010	Manitoba
Winnipeg St James	46011	Manitoba
Winnipeg South	46012	Manitoba
Winnipeg South Centre	46013	Manitoba
Winnipeg Transcona	46014	Manitoba
Yellowhead	48026	Alberta
York Centre	35095	Ontario
York North	35096	Ontario
York–Simcoe	35097	Ontario
York South–Weston	35098	Ontario
York West	35099	Ontario
Yorkton–Melville	47014	Saskatchewan
Yukon	60001	Yukon Territory

Appendix Two

List of Candidates

Abbreviations

Abol.	Abolitionist Party of Canada
BQ	Bloc Québécois
CEC	Canadian Economic Community
CHP	Christian Heritage Party of Canada
CP	Canada Party
CPR	Canadian Party for Renewal
CRWP	Confederation of Regions Western Party
Com'lth	Party for the Commonwealth of Canada
Comm.	Communist Party of Canada
FP	Freedom Party of Canada
GP	The Green Party of Canada
Ind.	Independent
Lib.	Liberal Party of Canada
Libert.	Libertarian Party of Canada
M-L	Marxist-Leninist Party of Canada
MR	Reform of the monetary law
NDP	New Democratic Party of Canada
NLP	Natural Law Party of Canada
Nil	No affiliation (not sponsored by a registered political party)
Nat.	National Party of Canada
OC	Option Canada Party
PC	Progressive Conservative Party of Canada
PNQ	Parti Nationaliste du Quebec
RP	Reform Party of Canada
Rhino	Parti Rhinoceros
SC	Social Credit Party of Canada

Members Elected in 1993 in Bold

Aalto, Brian (Com'lth/Rep./Rep./Com'lth) Thunder Bay–Nipigon, Ontario
Aasland, Bjarne (CP) Winnipeg St James, Manitoba
Abbott, Jim (RP/PR) Kootenay East/Kootenay-Est, B.C./C. B.
Abbott, Wayne (RP/PR) Essex–Kent, Ontario
Abildgaard, Susanne (NDP/NPD) Macleod, Alberta (Female)
Ablonczy, Diane (RP/PR) Calgary North/Calgary-Nord, Alberta (Female)
Adams, Peter (Lib.) Peterborough, Ontario
Adams, Robert (CHP/PHC) Saint Henri–Westmount, Montreal
Adams, Scott (Ind.) Vancouver Centre/Vancouver-Centre, B.C./C. B.
Adams, Trevor L. (Nil) Okanagan Centre/Okanagan-Centre, B.C./C. B.
Adomeit, Karl (NDP/NPD) Louis-Hebért, Quebec

Aftergood, David (PC/P-C) Calgary Northeast/Calgary-Nord-Est, Alberta
Agnew, Edward George (RP/PR) Brandon–Souris, Manitoba
Agoto, Ed (Nat.) Edmonton North/Edmonton-Nord, Alberta
Ajemian, John (Com'lth/Rep./Rep./Com'lth) Laval West/Laval-Ouest, Montreal
Akoum, Mohamed (NDP/NPD) La Prairie, Quebec
Alain, Claude K. (Nat.) Saint-Hubert, Quebec
Albert, Lionel (Nil) Pierrefonds–Dollard, Montreal
Alcock, Reg (Lib.) Winnipeg South/Winnipeg-Sud, Manitoba
Alder, Rob (PC/P-C) London East/London-Est, Ontario
Alexander, Rick (NLP/PLN) Huron–Bruce, Ontario
Allard, Jim (PC/P-C) Port Moody–Coquitlam, B.C./C.-B.
Allison, Gordon E. (NDP/NPD) Miramichi, N.B./N.-B.
Allmand, Warren (Lib.) Notre-Dame-de-Grâce, Montreal
Althouse, Vic (NDP/NPD) Mackenzie, Saskatchewan
Alvarez-Toye, Michael (GP/PV) Calgary North/Calgary-Nord, Alberta
Amarica, George (NLP/PLN) LaSalle–Emard, Montreal
Amos, Bill (NLP/PLN) Niagara Falls, Ontario
Amos, Laureen (NLP/PLN) Welland–St Catharines–Thorold, Ontario (Female)
Amyot, Guy (BQ) Lachine–Lac-Saint-Louis, Montreal
Anawak, Jack Iyerak (Lib.) Nunatsiaq, N.W.T./T.N.-O.
Anderson, Alison (RP/PR) St Boniface/Saint Boniface, Manitoba (Female)
Anderson, Annie (NLP/PLN) Calgary Centre/Calgary-Centre, Alberta (Female)
Anderson, David (Lib.) Victoria, B.C./C.-B.
Anderson, Doug (Ind.) Ontario, Ontario
Anderson, Ralph (Nat.) Nepean, Ontario
Anderson, Roy (NLP/PLN) Northumberland, Ontario
Angus, Iain (NDP/NPD) Thunder Bay–Atikokan, Ontario
Anstruther, Ken (RP/PR) Etobicoke–Lakeshore, Toronto
Anton, Joe (PC/P-C) Ottawa South/Ottawa-Sud, Ontario
Appleman, Joe (CHP/PHC) Northumberland, Ontario
Apostol, William-John (Abol.) Mercier, Montreal
Ardis, Jack (Nat.) Bramalea–Gore–Malton, Ontario
Arkelian, John (Nat.) Oshawa, Ontario
Armour, Randy (Abol.) York Centre/York-Centre, Toronto
Armstrong, George H. (CP) Brandon–Souris, Manitoba
Arnold, Ken (NLP/PLN) Red Deer, Alberta
Arseneault, Guy (Lib.) Restigouche–Chaleur, N.B./N.-B.
Ashdown, Clayoquot Keith (Nil) Ottawa Centre/Ottawa-Centre, Ontario
Ashick, Ernie (Nil) Nickel Belt, Ontario
Ashley, Audrey (Nil) Capilano–Howe Sound, B.C./C.-B. (Female)
Ashley, Clarke L. (Nil) North Vancouver, B.C./C.-B.
Ashmore, Anita (Nil) Crowfoot, Alberta (Female)
Ashmore, Kevin (Nil) Edmonton Southwest/Edmonton-Sud-Ouest, Alberta
Askin, Margaret (M-L) Calgary Centre/Calgary-Centre, Alberta (Female)
Assad, Mark (Lib.) Gatineau-La Lièvre, Quebec
Assadourian, Sarkis (Lib.) Don Valley North/Don Valley-Nord, Toronto
Asselin, Gérard (BQ) Charlevoix, Quebec
Aston, Alan (RP/PR) Bruce–Grey, Ontario
Atkinson, Ken (PC/P-C) St Catharines, Ontario

Atkinson, Sarah (GP/PV) Windsor West/Windsor-Ouest, Ontario (Female)
Attewell, Bill (PC/P-C) Markham–Whitchurch-Stouffville, Ontario
Audain, Tunya (Libert.) Vancouver Centre/Vancouver-Centre, B.C./C.-B. (Female)
Audy, Michel (NLP/PLN) Charlesbourg, Quebec
August, Arnold (M-L) Saint-Henri–Westmount, Montreal
Augustine, Jean (Lib.) Etobicoke Lakeshore, Toronto (Female)
Ault, Leslie (PC/P-C) Stormont–Dundas, Ontario (Female)
Averes, Gerry (CP) Elk Island, Alberta
Axworthy, Chris (NDP/NPD) Saskatoon–Clark's Crossing, Saskatchewan
Axworthy, Lloyd (Lib.) Winnipeg South Centre/Winnipeg-Sud-Centre, Manitoba
Ayling, William Robert (NLP/PLN) Port Moody–Coquitlam, B.C./C. B.
Aylwin, Pierre (Com'l/Rep./Rep./Com'lth) Mercier, Montreal
Ayotte, Celyne (Abol.) Témiscamingue, Quebec (Female)
Ayotte, Corrine (NLP/PLN) Provencher, Manitoba (Female)
Bachand, Claude (BQ) Saint-Jean, Quebec
Baghjajian, Aida (PC/P-C) Saint-Denis, Montreal (Female)
Bailie, A. David H. (NDP/NPD) Beauséjour, N.B./N.-B.
Bains, Hardial (M-L) Ottawa Centre/Ottawa-Centre, Ontario
Baker, Brian (Nat.) Prince Albert–Churchill River/Prince-Albert–Churchill River, Saskatchewan
Baker, Don (P.C./P. C.) Parkdale–High Park, Toronto
Baker, George (Lib.) Gander–Grand Falls, Nfld/T.-N.
Baker, Holly (Nat.) Leeds–Grenville, Ontario (Female)
Baker, Ross (Ind.) Hastings–Frontenac–Lennox and Addington, Ontario
Bakopanos, Eleni (Lib.) Saint Denis, Montreal (Female)
Bangma, Len (RP/PR) Peterborough, Ontario
Banks, Don (RP/PR) Cochrane–Superior/Cochrane–Superieur, Ontario
Bannister, James George (Nat.) Beauséjour, N.B./N.-B.
Barbeau, Bill (NDP/NPD) Carleton–Charlotte, N.B./N.-B.
Barker, Paul (Libert.) Trinity–Spadina, Toronto
Barlett, Bill (Ind.) Burlington, Ontario
Barnes, Sue (Lib.) London West/London Ouest, Ontario (Female)
Baronikian, Haig (Libert.) Parkdale–High Park, Toronto
Barrett, Dave (NDP/NPD) Esquimalt–Juan de Fuca, B.C./C.-B.
Barrett, Joe (NDP/NPD) Skeena, B.C./C.-B.
Barrett, Richard (Libert.) Mississauga South/Mississauga-Sud, Ontario
Barron, J. Leonard (RP/PR) St John's East/St John's-Est, Nfld/T.-N.
Barsky, Rick (Nat.) Kindersley–Lloydminster, Saskatchewan
Barteau, Bill (NDP/NPD) Carleton–Charlotte, N.B./N.-B.
Bassett, Isabel (PC/P-C) St Paul's, Toronto (Female)
Bateman, Ross (Nat.) Haldimand–Norfolk, Ontario
Bauer, Sandra, (NDP/NPD) Capilano–Howe Sound, B.C./C.-B. (Female)
Baux, Marylise (NLP/PLN) Verdun–Saint-Paul, Montreal (Female)
Baxter, Betty (NDP/NPD) Vancouver Centre/Vancouver-Centre, B.C./C. B. (Female)
Bay, Michael (GP/PV) Mississauga West/Mississauga-Ouest, Ontario
Beatty, Perrin (PC/P-C) Wellington–Grey–Dufferin–Simcoe, Ontario
Beaubien, Denise (Abol.) Laval East/Laval-Est, Montreal (Female)
Beaudin, Jean-Marc (GP/PV) Verdun–Saint-Paul, Montreal
Beaudoin, André (NLP/PLN) Papineau–Saint-Michel, Montreal
Beaudoin, Kim (BQ) Verdun–Saint-Paul, Montreal (Female)

Beaumier, Colleen (Lib.) Brampton, Ontario (Female)
Beaumont, Tilton (Nil) Timmins–Chapleau, Ontario
Beauregard, Stephane (Com'l/Rep./Rep./Com'lth) Châteauguay, Quebec
Beausoleil, Michèle (NLP/PLN) Shefford, Quebec (Female)
Beaver, Wanda (NLP/PLN) Parkdale–High Park, Toronto (Female)
Bebluk, Marguerite (PC/P-C) York West/York Ouest, Toronto (Female)
Bechler, Hilda (Nat.) Kootenay East/Kootenay-Est, B.C./C.-B. (Female)
Beck, John (RP/PR) York Centre/York Centre, Toronto
Beck, Steven R. (NLP/PLN) Okanagan–Similkameen–Merritt, B.C./C.-B.
Bedard, Jean Paul (M-L) York West/York-Ouest, Toronto
Beecroft, Richard (NLP/PLN) Leeds–Grenville, Ontario
Begley, Bracken (Abol.) Lanark–Carleton, Ontario
Beifuss, Michael (NLP/PLN) Mississauga West/Mississauga-Ouest, Ontario
Bélair, Danièle (NLP/PLN) Gatineau-La Lièvre, Quebec (Female)
Bélair, Reginald (Lib.) Cochrane–Superior/Cochrane–Superieur, Ontario
Bélanger, Anne (NLP/PLN) Timiskaming–French River, Ontario (Female)
Bélanger, Karl (NDP/NPD) Jonquière, Quebec
Belanger, Louise J. (Com'lth/Rep./Rep./Com'lth) Surrey North/Surrey-Nord, B.C./C.-B. (Female)
Bélanger, Madeleine (Lib.) Berthier–Montcalm, Quebec (Female)
Bélanger, Normand (Com 'lth/Rep./Rep./Com'lth) Saint-Henri–Westmount, Montreal
Bélanger, Steve (Com'lth/Rep./Rep./Com'lth) Hochelaga–Maisonneuve, Montreal
Belisle, Fernand (Abol.) Saint-Denis, Montreal
Bélisle, Richard (BQ) La Prairie, Quebec
Bellehumeur, Michel (BQ) Berthier–Montcalm, Quebec
Bellemare, Eugene (Lib.) Carleton–Gloucester, Ontario
Belsher, Ross (PC/P-C) Fraser Valley East/Fraser Valley-Est, B.C./C.-B.
Belzile, Richard (NDP/NPD) LaSalle–Émard, Montreal
Benn, Orrin O. (NDP/NPD) Scarborough–Rouge River, Toronto
Bennett, Richard Lawrence (Nat.) Cariboo–Chilcotin, B.C./C.-B.
Bennett, Rose (GP/PV) Mission–Coquitlam, B.C./C.-B. (Female)
Benoît, Jacqueline (NLP/PLN) Mégantic–Compton–Stanstead, Quebec (Female)
Benoit, Leon E. (RP/PR) Végréville/Vegreville, Alberta
Berger, David (Lib.) Saint Henri–Westmount, Montreal
Bergeron, Daniel (NLP/PLN) Outremont, Montreal
Bergeron, Pierre (NLP/PLN) Laurier–Sainte-Marie, Montreal
Bergeron, Stéphane (BQ) Verchères, Quebec
Bergman, Anita (Lib.) Regina–Lumsden, Saskatchewan (Female)
Bergson, Sheldon (Nat.) Markham–Whitchurch–Stouffville, Ontario
Bernard, Junior (NDP/NPD) Cape Breton Highlands–Canso/Cap-Breton Highlands–Canso, N.S./N-E.
Berner, Ferdinand (NDP/NPD) Drummond, Quebec
Berner, Geoffrey (GP/PV) Port Moody–Coquitlam, B.C./C.-B.
Bernier, Gilles (Ind.) Beauce, Quebec
Bernier, Maurice (BQ) Mégantic–Compton–Stanstead, Quebec
Bernier, Yvan (BQ) Gaspé, Quebec
Bertrand, Robert (Lib.) Pontiac—Gatineau—Labelle, Quebec
Bessette, Ronald (NLP/PLN) Lachine–Lac-Saint-Louis, Montreal
Besson, Cliff (CP) Winnipeg North Centre/Winnipeg Nord Centre, Manitoba
Bethel, Judy (Lib.) Edmonton East/Edmonton Est, Alberta (Female)
Bevan-Baker, Peter Stewart (GP/PV) Leeds–Grenville, Ontario

Bevilacqua, Maurizio (Lib.) York North/York-Nord, Ontario
Bezan, Ted (CP) Provencher, Manitoba
Bezanson, Allan H. (M. L.) Vancouver South/Vancouver Sud, B.C./C.-B.
Bhaduria, Jag (Lib.) Markham–Whitchurch–Stouffville, Ontario
Bharmal, Ayesha F. (Abol.) Windsor–St Clair/Windsor–Sainte-Claire, Ontario (Female)
Bianco, Marc (CHP/PHC) Halton–Peel, Ontario
Biega, Stephen A. (Nat.) Parkdale–High Park, Toronto
Bigge, Ryan (Nil) Delta, B.C./C.-B.
Biggs, Sven (GP/PV) London–Middlesex, Ontario
Bigras, Gilles (NLP/PLN) Halifax, N.S./N.-E.
Billyard, Robert J. (Nat.) Fraser Valley West/Fraser Valley Ouest, B.C./C.-B.
Binda, Ken (RP/PR) Carleton–Gloucester, Ontario
Bird, J.W. Bud (PC/P-C) Fredericton–York-Sunbury, N.B./N.-B.
Birkmaier, Donna L. (PC/P-C) Saskatoon–Dundurn, Saskatchewan (Female)
Biron, Michel (Lib.) Richelieu, Quebec
Biron, Normand (Lib.) Anjou–Rivière-des-Prairies, Montreal
Bissonnette, Marco (Abol.) Mégantic–Compton–Stanstead, Quebec
Bjornson, David (PC/P-C) Selkirk–Red River, Manitoba
Black, Dawn (NDP/NPD) New Westminster–Burnaby, B.C./C.-B.(Female)
Blackburn, Jean Pierre (PC/P-C) Jonquière, Quebec
Blaikie, Bill (NDP/NPD) Winnipeg Transcona, Manitoba
Blain, Norm (PC./PC) Surrey–White Rock–South Langley, B.C./C.-B.
Blair, Bob (Lib.) Calgary Centre/Calgary-Centre, Alberta
Blair, Cliff (PC/P-C) Surrey North/Surrey-Nord, B.C./C.-B.
Blais, Lucie (Lib.) Abitibi, Quebec (Female)
Blais, Pierre (PC/P-C) Bellechasse, Quebec
Blaquière, Jean (CHP/PHC) Verchères, Quebec
Blatter, Rick (Libert.) Laval West/Laval-Ouest, Montreal
Bleakney, Delon (RP/PR) The Battlefords–Meadow Lake, Saskatchewan
Blenkarn, Don (PC/P-C) Mississauga South/Mississauga-Sud, Ontario
Blenkinsop, Rosemarie (NDP/NPD) Sudbury, Ontario (Female)
Blond, Janet (Nat.) Edmonton Southeast/Edmonton-Sud-Est, Alberta (Female)
Blondin, Pierrette (NLP/PLN) Glengarry–Prescott–Russell, Ontario (Female)
Blondin–Andrew, Ethel (Lib.) Western Arctic, N.W.T./T.N.-O.(Female)
Blonski, Brian (Abol.) Broadview–Greenwood, Toronto
Blumenschein, Peter (RP/PR) Winnipeg St James, Manitoba
Bobbitt, Norman (NDP/NPD) Ottawa West/Ottawa Ouest, Ontario
Bobolo, Brian Joseph (PC/P-C) Hamilton East/Hamilton-Est, Ontario
Boddy, Christopher (Abol.) Oshawa, Ontario
Boddy, Peter (RP/PR) Ottawa West/Ottawa-Ouest, Ontario
Bodnar, Morris (Lib.) Saskatoon–Dundurn, Saskatchewan
Boesterd, Bill (CHP/PHC) Fraser Valley East/Fraser Valley-Est, B.C./C.-B.
Boikoff, Lucille (Com'lth/Rep./Rep./Com'lth) Vancouver Centre/Vancouver-Centre,
    B.C./C.-B.(Female)
Bois, Hélène (NDP/NPD) Kamouraska–Rivière-du-Loup, Quebec (Female)
Boisvert, Jean (Lib.) Elk Island, Alberta
Bonin, Ray (Lib.) Nickel Belt, Ontario
Bonner, Tim (CHP/PHC) Mission–Coquitlam, B.C./C.-B.
Boscariol, Celso (Lib.) Port Moody–Coquitlam, B.C./C.-B.

Bosley, John (PC/P-C) Don Valley West/Don Valley-Ouest, Toronto
Bouchard, David (CP) Souris–Moose Mountain, Saskatchewan
Bouchard, Lucien (BQ) Lac-Saint-Jean, Quebec
Bouchard, Roger (NLP/PLN) Ottawa–Vanier, Ontario
Boucher, Daniel (BQ) Papineau–Saint-Michel, Montreal
Boudreau, Bernard (Lib.) Drummond, Quebec
Boudreau Pedersen, Mae (CHP/PHC) Beauséjour, N.B./N.-B.(Female)
Boudria, Don (Lib.) Glengary–Prescott–Russell, Ontario
Bourgault, Lise (PC/P-C) Argenteuil–Papineau, Quebec(Female)
Bourke, Shannon M. (NLP/PLN) Sarnia–Lambton, Ontario (Female)
Bourque, Francine (NDP/NPD) Hull–Aylmer, Quebec (Female)
Bourque, Jeannine (PC/P-C) Beauce, Quebec (Female)
Bourque, Pierre (Lib.) Rosemont, Montreal
Boutilier, Sam (PC/P-C) Cape Breton–East Richmond/Cap-Breton–Richmond-Est, N.S./N.-E.
Boutin, Guy (BQ) Sherbrooke, Quebec
Bowbrick, Graeme (NDP/NPD) North Vancouver, B.C./C.-B.
Bowman, Joseph (NDP/NPD) Frontenac, Quebec
Boyce, Joe (Nil) Saint John, N.B./N.-B.
Boychuk, Jerry (RP/PR) Regina–Lumsden, Saskatchewan
Boyer, Patrick (PC/P-C) Etobicoke–Lakeshore, Toronto
Boylan, Charles (ML) Surrey–White Rock–South Langley, B.C./C.-B.
Boyle, Andy (Nat.) Stormont–Dundas, Ontario
Boytinck, Walter (Libert.) Vancouver Quadra, B.C./C.-B.
Bradburn, Tom (Libert.) Guelph–Wellington, Ontario
Braini, Joe (Nat.) Don Valley East/Don Valley-Est, Toronto
Branigan, Don (Lib.) Yukon, Y.T./T.Y.
Braovac, Marko (Com'lth/Rep./Rep./Com'lth) Nepean, Ontario
Brassard, Henri-Paul (P.C.) Roberval, Quebec
Brassard, Sophie (Com'lth/Rep.) Laurier–Sainte-Marie, Montreal (Female)
Breaugh, Mike (NDP/NPD) Oshawa, Ontario
Bregaint, Bernard (NLP/PLN) Algoma, Ontario
Breitkreuz, Cliff (RP/PR) Yellowhead, Alberta
Breitkreuz, Garry (RP/PR) Yorkton–Melville, Saskatchewan
Breton, Jean-Guy (BQ) Beauce, Quebec
Brett, Charlie (PC/P-C) Bonavista–Trinity–Conception, Nfld/T.-N.
Brewer, Eric J. (Abol.) Scarborough–Rouge River, Toronto
Brewer, Gary George (Abol.) York–Simcoe, Ontario
Brewin, John (NDP/NPD) Victoria, B.C./C.-B.
Bridgman, Margaret (RP/PR) Surrey North/Surrey Nord, B.C./C. B.(Female)
Brien, Pierre (BQ) Témiscamingue, Quebec
Brien, Pierre (Lib.) Blainville–Deux-Montagnes, Quebec
Bright, Harry (NLP/PLN) Oakville–Milton, Ontario
Brightwell, Harry (PC/P-C) Perth–Wellington–Waterloo, Ontario
Brinders, Gerald Lionel (CHP/PHC) Kootenay East/Kootenay-Est, B.C./C.-B.
Brink, James (Nil) Hamilton East/Hamilton-Est, Ontario
Brisson, Jean Serge (Libert.) Glengarry–Prescott–Russell, Ontario
Broad, Gayle Erma (NDP/NPD) Algoma, Ontario (Female)
Brochu, Jacques (Com'lth/Rep./Rep./Com'lth) Louis-Hébert, Quebec
Broda, Dave (PC/P-C) Beaver River, Alberta

Broeders, Arnold (RP/PR) Kent, Ontario
Brogden, Bruce (RP/PR) Sarnia–Lambton, Ontario
Brooke, Alan M. (NLP/PLN) Vancouver Quadra, B.C./C.-B.
Brooke, Estelle Rachel (NLP/PLN) Fraser Valley East/Fraser Valley-Est, B.C./C.-B. (Female)
Brosseau, Claude (Com'lth/Rep./Rep./Com'lth) Lachine–Lac-Saint-Louis, Montreal
Brouillet, Claire (Lib.) Terrebonne, Quebec (Female)
Brousseau, Margo (Lib.) Louis-Hébert, Quebec (Female)
Browes, Pauline (PC-P-C) Scarborough Centre/Scarborough-Centre, Toronto (Female)
Brown, Bonnie (Lib.) Oakville–Milton, Ontario (Female)
Brown, Cliff (NLP/PLN) Nanaimo–Cowichan/Nanaimo–Cowichan, B.C./C.-B.
Brown, Dale (RP/PR) Dauphin–Swan River, Manitoba
Brown, Jan (RP/PR) Calgary Southeast/Calgary-Sud-Est, Alberta (Female)
Brown, Shirley (NDP/NPD) Saint John, N.B./N.-B. (Female)
Brown, Thomas (Nil) Kamloops, B.C./C.-B.
Bruinsma, Durk T. (CHP/PHC) Durham, Ontario
Brunelle, Claude (M-L) Saint-Léonard, Montreal
Brunet, Gilles (Nat.) Etobicoke–Lakeshore, Toronto
Bruns, Hermann (GP/PV) Okanagan–Shuswap, B.C./C.-B.
Brushett, Dianne (Lib.) Cumberland–Colchester, N.S./-N.-E. (Female)
Bryden, John (Lib.) Hamilton–Wentworth, Ontario
Buckingham, Bob (NDP/NPD) St John's East/St John's-Est, Nfld/T-.N.
Bugmann, Ida (NLP/PLN) Calgary Southwest/Calgary-Sud-Ouest, Alberta (Female)
Buhr, Larry (Nat.) Saskatoon–Humboldt, Saskatchewan
Burello, Albina (Nat.) Mississauga South/Mississauga-Sud, Ontario (Female)
Burton, Cindy A. (Abol.) Nickel Belt, Ontario (Female)
Busch, Craig (Nat.) Simcoe Centre/Simcoe-Centre, Ontario
Buss, Rose (NDP/NPD) Winnipeg South/Winnipeg-Sud, Manitoba (Female)
Butland, Steve (NDP/NPD) Sault Ste Marie, Ontario
Buzik, Joan (NLP/PLN) Delta, B.C./C.-B. (Female)
Bylsma, David W. (CHP/PHC) St Catharines, Ontario
Cabott, Mae (Lib.) Mission–Coquitlam, B.C./C.-B. (Female)
Caccia, Charles (Lib.) Davenport, Toronto
Cafe, Loucas (NLP/PLN) Scarborough–Rouge River, Toronto
Calder, Murray (Lib.) Wellington–Grey–Dufferin–Simcoe, Ontario
Caldwell, Rhyon (Nil) Victoria, B.C./C.-B.
Callender, Sandy (NLP/PLN) Peterborough, Ontario (Female)
Callender, Travis (NLP/PLN) Lambton–Middlesex, Ontario
Cameron, John Frederick (Nat.) Beaches–Woodbine, Toronto
Cameron, Peter (NLP/PLN) Hillsborough, P.E.I./ Î-.P.-E.
Cameron, William Alexander (NLP/PLN) Capilano–Howe Sound, B.C./C.-B.
Campbell, Arthur James (NDP/NPD) Nipissing, Ontario
Campbell, Barry (Lib.) St Paul's, Toronto
Campbell, Dorothy (Nat.) Don Valley West/Don Valley-Ouest, Toronto (Female)
Campbell, Gordon (Nil) Okanagan–Shuswap, B.C./C.-B.
Campbell, Ian (NLP/PLN) Stormont–Dundas, Ontario
Campbell, Judith (Nil) Richmond, B.C./C.-B. (Female)
Campbell, Ken (Nil) Oakville–Milton, Ontario
Campbell, Kim (PC/P-C) Vancouver Centre/Vancouver-Centre, B.C./C.-B. (Female)
Candel, Sol (GP/PV) Calgary Southwest/Calgary-Sud-Ouest, Alberta

Cannavino, Tony (Nil) Hull–Aylmer, Quebec

Canning, A.R. Art (Ind.) Halifax, N.S./N.-E.

Cannis, John (Lib.) Scarborough Centre/Scarborough-Centre, Toronto

Cantelon, Ron (Lib.) Nanaimo–Cowichan/Nanaimo–Cowichan, B.C./C. B.

Canuel, Rene (BQ) Matapédia–Matane, Quebec

Caouette, Martine (NDP/NPD) Sherbrooke, Quebec (Female)

Capp, Geoffrey (CHP/PHC) Yukon, Y.T./T.Y.

Carasco, Emily (NDP/NPD) Windsor West/Windsor-Ouest, Ontario (Female)

Cardiff, Murray (P. C ./P. -C.) Huron–Bruce, Ontario

Cariou, Kimball (Nil) Vancouver East/Vancouver-Est, B.C./C.-B.

Carli, Giampaolo (Com'l/Rep./Rep./Com'lth) LaSalle–Émard, Montreal

Carlisle, Robert (Abol.) Saint-Henri–Westmount, Montreal

Caron, Andre (BQ) Jonquière, Quebec

Caron, Jean-Pierre (Lib.) Trois-Rivières, Quebec

Carpay, John (RP/PR) Burnaby–Kingsway, B.C./C.-B.

Carpentier, Audrey (NDP/NPD) Charlevoix, Quebec (Female)

Carrier, Carole (Abol.) Lévis, Quebec (Female)

Carson, John K. (Ind.) Simcoe Centre/Simcoe-Centre, Ontario

Carter, Gene (Abol.) Simcoe Centre/Simcoe-Centre, Ontario

Carter, Phillip Scott (RP/PR) York South–Weston/York-Sud–Weston, Toronto

Carter, Roger (M-L) Don Valley East/Don Valley-Est, Toronto

Carver, Ken (CP) Selkirk–Red River, Manitoba

Casey, Bill (PC/P-C) Cumberland–Colchester, N.S./N.-E.

Cassidy, Peter (NDP/NPD) Lincoln, Ontario

Castleman, Bruce A. (RP/PR) York West/York-Ouest, Toronto

Catterall, Marlene (Lib.) Ottawa West/Ottawa-Ouest, Ontario (Female)

Cauchon, Denis (NLP/PLN) Laval East/Laval-Est, Montreal

Cauchon, Martin (Lib.) Outremont, Montreal

Cawley, Shawn (CP) Saskatoon–Clark's Crossing, Saskatchewan

Cecil-Smith, Bill (Nat.) London East/London-Est, Ontario

Cerigo, Jean (NLP/PLN) Saint-Hubert, Quebec

Chadwick, Harry (PC/P-C) Bramalea–Gore–Malton, Ontario

Chalifoux, Benoît (Com'lth/Rep./Rep./Com'lth) Saint-Denis, Montreal

Chamberlain, Brenda (Lib.) Guelph–Wellington, Ontario (Female)

Chamberland, Luc (NDP/NPD) Saint-Hyacinthe–Bagot, Quebec

Chamlian, Haytoug (Nil) Ahuntsic, Montreal

Champagne, Andrée (PC/P-C) Saint-Hyacinthe–Bagot, Quebec (Female)

Champagne, Michel (PC/P-C) Champlain, Quebec

Chan, Raymond (Lib.) Richmond, B.C./C.-B.

Chandler, Craig (RP/PR) Hamilton Mountain, Ontario

Chaplin, Paul (RP/PR) St Paul's, Toronto

Charest, Jean J. (PC/P-C) Sherbrooke, Quebec

Charette, Michael John (Nil) Mississauga South/Mississauga-Sud, Ontario

Charland, Danielle (NLP/PLN) Québec, Quebec (Female)

Charland, Marlène (NLP/PLN) Saint-Léonard, Montreal (Female)

Charlebois, Gisèle (NDP/NPD) Papineau–Saint Michel, Montreal (Female)

Charles, Glenford (Com'lth/Rep./Rep./Com'lth) Pierrefonds–Dollard, Montreal

Charles, Robert (Com'lth/Rep./Rep./Com'lth) Vaudreuil, Montreal

Chartrand, Guy (Lib.) Longueuil, Quebec

Chase, Mark Alan (Libert.) Nanaimo–Cowichan/Nanaimo–Cowichan, B.C./C.-B.
Chatters, Dave (RP/PR) Athabasca, Alberta
Cheng, Paul (RP/PR) London East/London-Est, Ontario
Chenier, Pierre (M-L) Beaches–Woodbine, Toronto
Chenier, Pierre (PC/P-C) Hull–Aylmer, Quebec
Chester, Lorne Edward (PC/P-C) Victoria–Haliburton, Ontario
Cheveldayoff, Ken (PC/P-C) The Battlefords–Meadow Lake, Saskatchewan
Chiasson, Brian (CHP/PHC) Oshawa, Ontario
Chiquette, Benoît (Lib.) Verchères, Quebec
Chislett, Paul H. (Nat.) Sudbury, Ontario
Chitty, Steve (GP/PV) Surrey–White Rock–South Langley, B.C./C.-B.
Choquette, Maryse (NDP/NPD) Trois-Rivières, Quebec (Female)
Chouerv, Christian (Com'lth/Rep./Rep./Com'lth) Terrebonne, Quebec
Chouinard, Normand (M-L) Laurier–Sainte-Marie, Montreal
Chrétien, Jean (Lib.) Saint-Maurice, Quebec
Chrétien, Jean-Guy (BQ) Frontenac, Quebec
Chretien, Leon W. (Nil) The Battlefords–Meadow Lake, Saskatchewan
Christian, Mel (Nat.) Portage–Interlake, Manitoba
Christiansen, Billie (Nil) Sudbury, Ontario (Female)
Christensen, Todd (RP/PR) London West/London-Ouest, Ontario
Christin, Yves Marie (NDP/NPD) Vaudreuil, Montreal
Chutter, Geoff (PC/P-C) Vancouver Quadra, B.C./C.-B.
Cimon, Éric (BQ) LaSalle–Émard, Montreal
Clancy, Mary (Lib.) Halifax, N.S./N.-E. (Female)
Clark, Kelly (PC/P-C) Provencher, Manitoba
Clark, Shelley Ann (Nat.) Carleton–Gloucester, Ontario (Female)
Clarke, Barbara (NDP/NPD) Renfrew–Nipissing–Pembroke, Ontario (Female)
Clarke, John (Libert.) Vancouver South/Vancouver-Sud, B.C./C.-B.
Clarke, Terry (PC/P-C) Parry Sound–Muskoka, Ontario
Clews, Stephen (Nil) Mission–Coquitlam, B.C./C.-B.
Clouthier, Hec (Ind.) Renfrew–Nipissing–Pembroke, Ontario
Cloutier, Louise (NDP/NPD) Abitibi, Quebec (Female)
Cobbold, Peter (RP/PR) Don Valley North/Don Valley-Nord, Toronto
Coderre, Denis, (Lib.) Bourassa, Montreal
Cohen, Shaughnessy (Lib.) Windsor–St Clair/Windsor–Sainte-Claire, Ontario (Female)
Coldicott, Frank (PC/P-C) Kamloops, B.C./C.-B.
Cole, Denise (PC/P-C) Beaches–Woodbine, Toronto (Female)
Cole, John (PC/P-C) York–Simcoe, Ontario
Collenette, David (Lib.) Don Valley East/Don Valley-Est, Toronto
Collins, Bernie (Lib.) Souris–Moose Mountain, Saskatchewan
Collins, Bev (Nat.) Kootenay West–Revelstoke/Kootenay-Ouest–Revelstoke, B.C./C.-B. (Female)
Collins, Faith (PC/P-C) Victoria, B.C./C.-B.(Female)
Collins, Mary (PC/P-C) Capilano–Howe Sound, B.C./C.-B. (Female)
Collis, Dallas (Nat.) North Vancouver, B.C./C.-B.
Collrin, Christopher B. (NLP/PLN) Saint John, N.B./N.-B.
Compagnat, Jocelyn (PC/P-C) Shefford, Quebec
Comuzzi, Joe (Lib.) Thunder Bay–Nipigon, Ontario
Conn, Charles (RP/PR) Mississauga West/Mississauga-Ouest, Ontario
Connell, Mark (NDP/NPD) Fundy–Royal, N.B./N.-B.

Connolly, Mike (RP/PR) Waterloo, Ontario
Conrad, Jim (Ind.) St Paul's, Toronto
Cooke, Bradford (NLP/PLN) North Vancouver, B.C./C.-B.
Coon, Michael (NLP/PLN) Victoria, B.C./C.-B.
Cooper, Ron (Nat.) Cambridge, Ontario
Copeland, Leanore (Lib.) New Westminster–Burnaby, B.C./C.-B. (Female)
Copps, Sheila (Lib.) Hamilton East/Hamilton-Est, Ontario (Female)
Corbeil, Jean (PC/P-C) Anjou–Rivière-des-Prairies, Montreal
Corbett, Bob (PC/P-C) Fundy–Royal, N.B./N.-B.
Corriveau, Brian (Nat.) Pontiac–Gatineau–Labelle, Quebec
Costisella, Marie-Therese (Com'lth/Rep./Rep./Com'lth) Ottawa Centre/Ottawa-Centre, Ontario (Female)
Côté, François (NDP/NPD) Chambly, Quebec
Côté, Yvon (PC/P-C) Richmond–Wolfe, Quebec
Coulombe, Sylvain M. (Abol.) Outremont, Montreal
Coulter, Carol Anne (NLP/PLN) Scarborough East/Scarborough-Est, Toronto (Female)
Coulterman, Patrick James (NLP/PLN) Saskatoon–Clark's Crossing, Saskatchewan
Courtoreille, Lawrence (Lib.) Athabasca, Alberta
Cousineau, Yvan (Abol.) Verdun–Saint-Paul, Montreal
Couto, Elaine (Nil) Hamilton West/Hamilton-Ouest, Ontario (Female)
Couture, Clément (PC/P-C) Saint-Jean, Quebec
Couture, Miville (NLP/PLN) Bourassa, Montreal
Cowan, John (Nat.) Niagara Falls, Ontario
Cowan, R. Kent (Libert.) Victoria, B.C./C. B.
Cowhig, John (NLP/PLN) Vancouver Centre/Vancouver Centre, B.C./C.-B.
Cowling, Marlene (Lib.) Dauphin—Swan River, Manitoba (Female)
Cox, Hill (Libert.) Halton–Peel, Ontario
Crane, Dolores Dodi (NDP/NPD) Hillsborough, P.E.I./Î-P.-E. (Female)
Crawford, Rex (Lib.) Kent, Ontario
Créte, Paul (BQ) Kamouraska—Rivière-du-Loup, Quebec
Crewson, Adrian Earl (Nil) Mississauga East/Mississauga-Est, Ontario
Critoph, Ursule (NDP/NPD) Ottawa South/Ottawa-Sud, Ontario (Female)
Crone, David (PC/P-C) Lambton–Middlesex, Ontario
Crone, Kathleen (RP/PR) York South–Weston/York-Sud–Weston, Toronto (Female)
Cronkwright, Jack (PC/P-C) Haldimand–Norfolk, Ontario
Croteau, Réal (NLP/PLN) Berthier–Montcalm, Quebec
Cruise, Robert (M.L.) Windsor West/Windsor-Ouest, Ontario
Culbert, Harold (Lib.) Carleton–Charlotte, N.B./N.-B.
Culbert, Jeff (GP/PV) London East/London-Est, Ontario
Cummins, John (RP/PR) Delta, B.C./C.-B.
Curran, Michael Patrick (Nat.) Mississauga East/Mississauga-Est, Ontario
Currie, John Ernest (Nil) Victoria, B.C./C.-B.
Currie, Neil (Lib.) The Battlefords–Meadow Lake, Saskatchewan
Dahlby, Lewis C. (Libert.) Fraser Valley West/Fraser Valley-Ouest, B.C./C.-B.
Dakin, Geoff (Com'l/Rep./Rep./Com'lth) New Westminster–Burnaby, B.C./C.-B.
Daley, Ernest (Nat.) Comox–Alberni, B.C./C.-B.
Dalla Valle, Giancarlo (Com'lth/Rep./Rep./Com'lth) Surrey–White Rock–South Langley, B.C./C.-B.
Dalphond-Guiral, Madeleine (BQ) Laval Centre/Laval-Centre, Montreal (Female)
D'Amours, Guy (NDP/NPD) Mercier, Montreal
Dance, George (Libert.) Scarborough Centre/Scarborough-Centre, Toronto

Dancey, Sam (RP/PR) Ottawa–Vanier, Ontario
Dandenault, Christine (M-L) Hochelaga–Maisonneuve, Montreal (Female)
D'Andrea, David (NDP/NPD) Saint-Léonard, Montreal
Daneault, Pauline B. (PC/P-C) Saint-Maurice, Quebec (Female)
Danelon, Emanuele (Nat.) Etobicoke North/Etobicoke-Nord, Toronto
D'Angela, Dario (PC/P-C) York North/York-Nord, Ontario
Danyluk, Calvin (NLP/PLN) Skeena, B.C./C.-B.
Danyluk, Geoff (NLP/PLN) Winnipeg Transcona, Manitoba
D'Aoust, P.A. (Abol.) Papineau–Saint-Michel, Montreal
Darisse, Helene Ann (NLP/PLN) Oshawa, Ontario (Female)
Darnell, Mike (NDP/NPD) Essex–Kent, Ontario
Da Silva, Paulo (Com'lth/Rep./Rep./Com'lth) Richelieu, Quebec
d'Audibert-Garcien, Yann Patrice (Abol.) Rosedale, Toronto
Daudrich, Wally (RP/PR) Churchill, Manitoba
Daviault, Michel (BQ) Ahuntsic, Montreal
David, Guy (Com'lth/Rep./Rep./Com'lth) Saint-Jean, Quebec
Davies, Andrew (RP/PR) Oshawa, Ontario
Davies, Bill (NLP/PLN) Bramalea–Gore–Malton, Ontario
Davies, Carolyn (NDP/NPD) London–Middlesex, Ontario (Female)
Davis, David (Nil) Souris–Moose Mountain, Saskatchewan
Davis, Jack (Nat.) Okanagan Centre/Okanagan-Centre, B.C./C.-B.
Davy, Shirley (NDP/NPD) Parry Sound–Muskoka, Ontario (Female)
Dawson-Bernard, Doris (Lib.) Beauport–Montmorency–Orléans, Quebec (Female)
Day, Richard (NLP/PLN) St Albert/Saint-Albert, Alberta
Dayman, Randy (RP/PR) Lambton–Middlesex, Ontario
Deacon, Matt (NLP/PLN) Mission–Coquitlam, B.C./C.-B.
Deans, Ashley James (NLP/PLN) Trinity–Spadina, Toronto
Debien, Maud (BQ) Laval East/Laval Est, Montreal (Female)
De Billy, Andre (NDP/NPD) Champlain, Quebec
de Billy, Jean-Pierre (NDP/NPD) Berthier–Montcalm, Quebec
DeBlois, Charles (PC/P-C) Beauport–Montmorency–Orleans, Quebec
Decarie, Yves (NLP/PLN) Brome–Missisquoi, Quebec
De Chantal, Gilles (NDP/NPD) Joliette, Quebec
Decter, Larry (NLP/PLN) Windsor West/Windsor-Ouest, Ontario
Decter, Ron (NLP/PLN) Winnipeg St James, Manitoba
DeFaria, Carl (PC/P-C) Mississauga East/Mississauga-Est, Ontario
Deguire, Grégoire (NLP/PLN) Témiscamingue, Quebec
de Jong, Frank (GP/PV) Ottawa–Vanier, Ontario
de Jong, Simon (NDP/NPD) Regina–Qu'Appelle, Saskatchewan
Dekraker, Bob A. (CHP/PHC) Elgin–Norfolk, Ontario
Deland-Gervais, Christiane (Com'lth/Rep./Rep./Com'lth) Ahuntsic, Montreal (Female)
Della Noce Vincent (PC/P-C) Laval East/Laval-Est, Montreal
Demaine, Shirley (Nat.) Notre-Dame-de-Grâce, Montreal (Female)
De Meester, Aaron G. (NDP/NPD) Kent, Ontario
Denis, François-Michel (Nil) Rimouski–Témiscouata, Quebec
De Pontbriand, Carmen (PC/P-C) Papineau–Saint-Michel, Montreal (Female)
De Santis, Joe (Nat.) Laval Centre/Laval-Centre, Montreal
De Savoye, Pierre (BQ) Portneuf, Quebec
Desbiens, Robert (Lib.) Laurier–Sainte-Marie, Montreal

Deschambault, Delbert (Lib.) Saint-Jean, Quebec

Deschamps, Fernand (M-L) Trinity–Spadina, Toronto

Des Champs, Robert (NDP/NPD) Saint-Maurice, Quebec

Deschênes, Sylvain (Com'lth/Rep./Rep./Com'lth) Saint-Léonard, Montreal

Desforges, Jacques (Lib.) Argenteuil–Papineau, Quebec

Desgagnés, André (Lib.) Charlevoix, Quebec

Deshaies, Bernard (BQ) Abitibi, Quebec

Desjardins, Gabriel (PC/P-C) Témiscamingue, Quebec

Desmeules, Majella (NDP/NPD) Québec, Quebec (Female)

Des Roches, Nicole (NDP/NPD) Pontiac–Gatineau–Labelle, Quebec (Female)

Destroismaisons, Michel (Com'l/Rep./Rep./Com'lth) Laval Centre/Laval-Centre, Montreal

Dettweiler, Allan (Libert.) Huron–Bruce, Ontario

DeVillers, Paul (Lib.) Simcoe North/Simcoe-Nord, Ontario

Devita, Peter M.A. (NDP/NPD) York North/York-Nord, Ontario

Devolin, Barry (RP/PR) Victoria–Haliburton, Ontario

DeVries, Ken (CHP/PHC) London West/London-Ouest, Ontario

Dewar, Marion (NDP/NPD) Ottawa Centre/Ottawa-Centre, Ontario (Female)

Dewit, Martin (CHP/PHC) Lisgar–Marquette, Manitoba

Dhaliwal, Herb (Lib.) Vancouver South/Vancouver-Sud, B.C./C.-B.

Dhillon, Amarjit (M-L) Brampton, Ontario

Di Carlo, Anna (Nil) Guelph–Wellington, Ontario (Female)

Dick, Paul (PC/P-C) Lanark–Carleton, Ontario

Dickie, Neil C. (NLP/PLN) Fredericton–York-Sunbury, N.B./N.-B.

Di Felice, Antonio (Nil) Etobicoke North/Etobicoke-Nord, Toronto

Di Genova, Umberto (BQ) Saint-Léonard, Montreal

Dingwall, David (Lib.) Cape Breton–East Richmond/Cap-Breton–Richmond-Est, N.S./N.-E.

Dingwall, Keith (RP/PR) Cape Breton–The Sydneys/ Cap-Breton–The Sydneys, N.S./N.-E.

Dionne, Linda (PC/P-C) Oshawa, Ontario (Female)

Discepola, Nick (Lib.) Vaudreuil, Montreal

Di Tomaso, Nick (PC/P-C) Lachine–Lac-Saint-Louis, Montreal

Dobbie, Dorothy (PC/P-C) Winnipeg South/Winnipeg-Sud, Manitoba (Female)

Dobrucki, Rob (NDP/NPD) Welland–St Catharines–Thorold, Ontario

Dodier, Yvon (NLP/PLN) Laval Centre/Laval-Centre, Montreal

Dods, Jeffrey (NLP/PLN) Mississauga South/Mississauga-Sud, Ontario

Doherty, John (NDP/NPD) Davenport, Toronto

Doiron, Alain (GP/PV) Carleton–Gloucester, Ontario

Dolby, Brian (Nat.) Lincoln, Ontario

Domine, Gene (Nat.) Winnipeg North Centre/Winnipeg-Nord-Centre, Manitoba

Domm, Bill (PC/P-C) Peterborough, Ontario

Domm, Richard (GP/PV) Quebec, Quebec

Donahue, A. James (Nat.) South Shore, N.S./N.-E.

Donderi, Don (Nil) Notre-Dame-de-Grâce, Montreal

Donley, Charles (PC/P-C) Etobicoke Centre/Etobicoke-Centre, Toronto

Donlevy, Martin (NDP/NPD) Oxford, Ontario

Donohue, Jim (RP/PR) Halifax West/Halifax-Ouest, N.S./N.-E.

Doram, Dale (NLP/PLN) Wild Rose, Alberta

Doram, Maureen (NLP/PLN) Calgary Southeast/Calgary-Sud-Est, Alberta (Female)

Dorin, Murray (PC/P-C) Edmonton Northwest/Edmonton-Nord-Ouest, Alberta

D'Orsay, Alan (Libert.) Etobicoke–Lakeshore, Toronto

Doucet, Kevin (Abol.) St Catharines, Ontario
Doucet, Leonard (Abol.) Welland–St Catharines–Thorold, Ontario
Dougherty, Mabel E. (PC/P-C) Brant, Ontario (Female)
Doyle, Martin (Nat.) Victoria–Haliburton, Ontario
Doyle, Paul D. (RP/PR) Miramichi, N.B./N.-B.
Drabkin, Neil (PC/P-C) Mount Royal/Mont Royal, Montreal
Drainville, Dennis (Ind.) Victoria–Haliburton, Ontario
Drapeau, Jean G. (NDP/NPD) Argenteuil–Papineau, Quebec
Dreben, Jeffrey Ian (NLP/PLN) Erie, Ontario
Dromisky, Stan (Lib.) Thunder Bay–Atikokan, Ontario
Dubé, Antoine (BQ) Lévis, Quebec
Dube, Linda (NLP/PLN) York Centre/York-Centre, Toronto (Female)
Dubinsky, Mike (NLP/PLN) Willowdale, Toronto
Dubois, Linda (Abol.) Hull–Aylmer, Quebec (Female)
Dubuc, Marc (NDP/NPD) Beauharnois–Salaberry, Quebec
Duceppe, Gilles (BQ) Laurier–Saint-Marie, Montreal
Duchesnay, Georges (Com'lth/Rep./Rep./Com'lth) Mount Royal/Mont-Royal, Montreal
Duda, Felix (Com'lth/Rep./Rep./Com'lth) York South–Weston/York-Sud–Weston, Toronto
Dufour, Normand (NLP/PLN) Jonquière, Quebec
Dugré, Michel (Nil) Laurier–Sainte-Marie, Montreal
Duhamel, Ronald J. (Lib.) St Boniface/Saint-Boniface, Manitoba
Duke, Louis (CHP/PHC) Sarnia–Lambton, Ontario
Dumas, Gaetan (Lib.) Richmond–Wolfe, Quebec
Dumas, Guillaume (BQ) Mount Royal/Mont-Royal, Montreal
Dumas, Maurice (BQ) Argenteuil–Papineau, Quebec
Dumesnil, Don (CP) St. Boniface/Saint-Boniface, Manitoba
Dumville, Basil Brian (NDP/NPD) Egmont, P.E.I./Î-.P.-E.
Duncan, John (RP/PR) North Island–Powell River, B.C./C.-B.
Dunn, Willie (NDP/NPD) Ottawa–Vanier, Ontario
Duplessis, Suzanne (PC/PC) Louis-Hébert, Quebec (Female)
Dupont, Pauline (NDP/NPD) St Boniface/Saint-Boniface, Manitoba (Female)
Dupuy, Michel (Lib.) Laval West/Laval-Ouest, Montreal
Easter, Wayne (Lib.) Malpeque/Malpèque, P.E.I./Î.-P.-E.
Eckstein, Brett (PC/P-C) Winnipeg Transcona, Manitoba
Eddy, Walton (CP) Moose Jaw–Lake Centre, Saskatchewan
Ede, Robert (Libert.) York North/York-Nord, Ontario
Eder, Ernst (GP/PV) Edmonton East/Edmonton-Est, Alberta
Edge, Randall (Libert.) Kamloops, B.C./C.-B.
Edmison, Ken (RP/PR) Brant, Ontario
Edwards, Bobby-Joe (Abol.) Simcoe North/Simcoe-Nord, Ontario
Edwards, Jim (PC/P-C) Edmonton Southwest/Edmonton-Sud-Ouest, Alberta
Egan, Croft (CP) Fraser Valley East/Fraser Valley-Est, B.C./C.-B.
Egan, Rita (NDP/NPD) Edmonton–Strathcona, Alberta (Female)
Eggleton, Art (Lib.) York Centre/York-Centre, Toronto
Elbourne, Ann (NDP/NPD) Saint-Henri–Westmount, Montreal (Female)
Elbourne, Frances (NDP/NPD) Verchères, Quebec (Female)
Elliot, John Kenneth (Nil) Sarnia–Lambton, Ontario
Ellis, Israel (NDP/NPD) York Centre/York-Centre, Toronto
Ellis, Ralph (Nat.) Hamilton–Wentworth, Ontario

Emms, Bill (GP/PV) Bramalea–Gore–Malton, Ontario
Eng, Ben (PC/P-C) Scarborough–Agincourt, Toronto
English, John (Lib.) Kitchener, Ontario
Ennis, Glenn (Lib.) Medicine Hat, Alberta
Enserink, Jack (CHP/PHC) Annapolis Valley–Hants, N.S./N.-E.
Epp, Ken (RP/PR) Elk Island, Alberta
Erbs, John V. (RP/PR) Saint John, N.B./N.-B.
Ethier, Carl (NDP/NPD) Richelieu, Quebec
Evans, Chris (NLP/PLN) Sault Ste Marie, Ontario
Evic-Twerdin, Leena (PC/P-C) Nunatsiaq, N.W.T./T.N.-O. (Female)
Ewald, Thorsten, (Nat.) Vancouver Centre/Vancouver-Centre, B.C./C.-B.
Ewart, Peter (M-L) London–Middlesex, Ontario
Eyolfson, Greg (CP) Kootenay West–Revelstoke/Kootenay-Ouest–Revelstoke, B.C./C.-B.
Faguy, Allan (NLP/PLN) Saint-Henri–Westmount, Montreal
Fahlman, Emanuel (CP) Kindersley–Lloydminster, Saskatchewan
Fairall, Lynn (NDP/NPD) Fraser Valley West/Fraser Valley-Ouest, B.C./C.-B. (Female)
Faithful, Don Philip (Ind.) Waterloo, Ontario
Falardeau, Denise (PC/P-C) Lac-Saint-Jean, Quebec (Female)
Falardeau, Jérôme P. (PC/P-C) Gatineau-La Lièvre, Quebec
Falk, Rod (NLP/PLN) Elgin–Norfolk, Ontario
Fannon, Jim (GP/PV) Welland–St. Catharines–Thorold, Ontario
Farquharson, Larry (Nat.) Lambton–Middlesex, Ontario
Farr, Barry James (Ind.) Regina–Wascana, Saskatchewan
Farr, John (Ind.) Parry Sound–Muskoka, Ontario
Fee, Doug (PC/P-C) Red Deer, Alberta
Feltham, Louise (PC/P-C) Wild Rose, Alberta (Female)
Fennell, Susan (PC/P-C) Brampton, Ontario (Female)
Ferland, Marc (PC/P-C) Portneuf, Quebec
Fernandez, Ernst (Abol.) Québec, Quebec
Fewchuk, Ron (Lib.) Selkirk–Red River, Manitoba
Figliano, Tony (PC/P-C) York South–Weston/York-Sud–Weston, Toronto
Figueroa, Miguel (Nil) Parkdale–High Park, Toronto
Filbert, Lynn (PC/P-C) Winnipeg North/Winnipeg-Nord, Manitoba (Female)
Fillion, Gilbert (BQ) Chicoutimi, Quebec
Finestone, Sheila (Lib.) Mount Royal/Mont Royal, Montreal (Female)
Finkelstein, Ruby (NLP/PLN) Pierrefonds–Dollard, Montreal (Female)
Finlay, John (Lib.) Oxford, Ontario
Finlay, Katherine (NLP/PLN) Kitchener, Ontario (Female)
Fisher, Katherine Emilia (NLP/PLN) Vegreville/Végréville, Alberta (Female)
Fisher, Mel (RP/PR) Kenora–Rainy River, Ontario
Fisher, Ron (NDP/NPD) Saskatoon–Dundurn, Saskatchewan
Fitzpatrick, Brian Maurice (RP/PR) Mackenzie, Saskatchewan
Flannery, D'Arcy James (Libert.) Mission–Coquitlam, B.C./C.-B.
Fletcher, Ronald (Nat.) York–Simcoe, Ontario
Flint, Randall (RP/PR) Scarborough East/Scarborough-Est, Toronto
Flis, Jesse (Lib.) Parkdale–High Park, Toronto
Flood, Kevin Charles (PC/P-C) Essex–Kent, Ontario
Florence, Darlene (RP/PR) Bramalea–Gore–Malton, Ontario (Female)
Folco, Raymonde (Lib.) Laval East/Laval-Est, Montreal

Foley, Julie (NDP/NPD) Sarnia–Lambton, Ontario (Female)

Folk, Dorothy (Com'l/Rep./Rep./Com'lth) Prince George–Peace River, B.C./C.-B. (Female)

Fong, Robert (Libert.) New Westminster–Burnaby, B.C./C.-B.

Fontaine, Daniel (Nat.) Burnaby–Kingsway, B.C./C. B.

Fontana, Joe (Lib.) London East/London-Est, Ontario

Ford, Neal (Libert.) Vaudreuil, Montreal

Formoe, Tim (CP) Edmonton North/Edmonton-Nord, Alberta

Forseth, Paul E. (RP/PR) New Westminster–Burnaby, B.C./C.-B.

Fortier, Bruno (PC/P-C) Laval Centre/Laval-Centre, Montreal

Fortin, Guymond (Lib.) Laval Centre/Laval-Centre, Montreal

Fortin, Suzanne (NDP/NPD) Beauport–Montmorency–Orléans, Quebec (Female)

Foss, Claire (CP) Okanagan–Shuswap, B.C./C.-B.

Foss, V. Anne (CP) Victoria, B.C./C.-B. (Female)

Foster, Dwayne (Abol.) Mississauga West/Mississauga-Ouest, Ontario

Foster, Garry, (NLP/PLN) Simcoe North/Simcoe-Nord, Ontario

Foster, John (Nat.) Ottawa Centre/Ottawa-Centre, Ontario

Foster, Judith (Abol.) London West/London-Ouest, Ontario (Female)

Foster, Kenneth R. (Ind.) Comox–Alberni, B.C./C.-B.

Foster, Marjorie (RP/PR) Prince Edward–Hastings, Ontario (Female)

Foster, Marva (Abol.) London–Middlesex, Ontario (Female)

Foster, Wayne (NLP/PLN) York North/York-Nord, Ontario

Fournier, Angeline (Lib.) Saint-Hubert, Quebec (Female)

Fournier, Jules (BQ) Gatineau–La Lièvre, Quebec

Fraleigh, Paul (Com'lth/Rep./Rep./Com'lth) North Vancouver, B.C./C.-B.

Francis, Don (GP/PV) Calgary West/Calgary-Ouest, Alberta

Francis, Sara (GP/PV) Wellington–Grey–Dufferin–Simcoe, Ontario (Female)

Francis, Simon C. (GP/PV) Guelph–Wellington, Ontario

Franklin, Peter (CP) The Battlefords–Meadow Lake, Saskatchewan

Frappier, Lorraine (PC/P-C) Richelieu, Quebec (Female)

Fraser, Colby (Nil) Fundy–Royal, N.B./N.-B.

Fraser, Doreen (Nil) Fredericton–York-Sunbury, N.B./N.-B.(Female)

Frazer, Jack (RP/PR) Saanich–Gulf Islands/Saanich–Les Îles-du-Golfe, B.C./C.-B.

Fredeen, Donalda (NLP/PLN) Beaches–Woodbine, Toronto (Female)

Fredeen, Fred (NLP/PLN) Don Valley East/Don Valley-Est, Toronto

Frenette, Georges (Lib.) Chicoutimi, Quebec

Friesen, Dan (PC/P-C) Windsor West/Windsor-Ouest, Ontario

Fritz, Randy (NLP/PLN) Wetaskiwin, Alberta

Frostad, Rhys (Nil) Saskatoon–Clark's Crossing, Saskatchewan

Fry, Hedy (Lib.) Vancouver Centre/Vancouver-Centre, B.C./C.-B. (Female)

Fulawka, Ben J. (CP) Winnipeg South Central\Winnipeg-Sud-Centre, Manitoba

Fuller, Doris (Nat.) Capilano–Howe Sound, B.C./C.-B. (Female)

Funk, Raymond John (NDP/NPD) Prince Albert–Churchill River/Prince-Albert–Churchill River, Saskatchewan

Fusco, Rolando (Abol.) Ahuntsic, Montreal

Fusco, Mauro (Abol.) Saint-Léonard, Montreal

Fyfe, Karen (NDP/NPD) Malpeque/Malpéque, P.E.I./Î.-P.-E. (Female)

Gaboury, Jacquie (NDP/NPD) Peace River, Alberta (Female)

Gabriel, Miel S.R. (Ind.) Calgary Southwest/Calgary-Sud-Ouest, Alberta

Gaffney, Beryl (Lib.) Nepean, Ontario (Female)

Gagliano, Alfonso (Lib.) Saint-Léonard, Montreal
Gagne, Eddy (NLP/PLN) Laval West/Laval-Ouest, Montreal
Gagnon, Christiane (BQ) Québec, Quebec (Female)
Gagnon, Henri (Abol.) Québec-Est, Quebec
Gagnon, Jean-Marc (Lib.) Lévis, Quebec
Gagnon, Patrick (Lib.) Bonaventure—Îles-de-la-Madeleine, Quebec
Gainer, Karen (Lib.) Calgary West/Calgary-Ouest, Alberta (Female)
Gallant, Kim (NDP/NPD) Acadie–Bathurst, N.B./N.-B. (Female)
Gallant, Paul A. (PC/P-C) Burin–St George's/Burin–Saint-Georges, Nfld/T.-N.
Gallaway, Roger (Lib.) Sarnia–Lambton, Ontario
Galloway, Bill (PC/P-C) Dauphin–Swan River, Manitoba
Gardiner, Brian (NDP/NPD) Prince George–Bulkley Valley, B.C./C.-B.
Garfinkle, Harry (GP/PV) Edmonton–Strathcona, Alberta
Garman, Henry (Nat.) Saskatoon–Clark's Crossing, Saskatchewan
Garnier, Andrea (NDP/NPD) Calgary North/Calgary-Nord, Alberta (Female)
Garrity, Jim (GP/PV) Bruce–Grey, Ontario
Gass, Judith (PC/P-C) Dartmouth, N.S./N.-E. (Female)
Gatley, Jeanne (M-L) Eglinton–Lawrence, Toronto (Female)
Gauthier, Alain (Com'lth/Rep./Rep./Com'lth) La Prairie, Quebec
Gauthier, Jean-Robert (Lib.) Ottawa–Vanier, Ontario
Gauthier, Luce-Andrée (PC/P-C) Acadie–Bathurst, N.B./N.-B. (Female)
Gauthier, Maurice (Lib.) Matapédia–Matane, Quebec
Gauthier, Michel (BQ) Roberval, Quebec
Gauthier, Pierre (NLP/PLN) Matapédia–Matane, Quebec
Geddes, Paul A. (Libert.) Port Moody–Coquitlam, B.C./C.-B.
Gee, Keith (CHP/PHC) Delta, B.C./C.-B.
Gelfand, Rig (NLP/PLN) Okanagan–Shuswap, B.C./C.-B.
George, Clem (NDP/NPD) Bonavista–Trinity–Conception, Nfld/T.-N.
Gerber, Jeff (RP/PR) Perth–Wellington–Waterloo, Ontario
Germain, Guy C. (NLP/PLN) Beaver River, Alberta
Gerrard, Jon (Lib.) Portage–Interlake, Manitoba
Gershuny, David (M-L) St Paul's, Toronto
Gerstenberger, Rolf (M-L) Hamilton East/Hamilton-Est, Ontario
Gervais, Gilles (Com'lth/Rep./Rep./Com'lth) Laurentides, Quebec
Gibb, Cyril (RP/PR) Scarborough–Agincourt, Toronto
Gibbons, Colyne (RP/PR) Thunder Bay–Atikokan, Ontario (Female)
Gibbons, Linda Dale (Nil) Rosedale, Toronto (Female)
Gibeau, Marie (PC/P-C) Bourassa, Montreal (Female)
Giguère, Alain (NDP/NPD) Roberval, Quebec
Gilbert, Patrick (NLP/PLN) Cape Breton–East Richmond/Cap-Breton–Richmond-Est, N.S./N.-E.
Gill, Aurelien (Lib.) Roberval, Quebec
Gillen, Teresa (NLP/PLN) Cariboo–Chilcotin, B.C./C.-B. (Female)
Gillrie, Steven (CP) Fredericton–York-Sunbury, N.B./N.-B.
Gilmour, Bill (RP/PR) Comox–Alberni, B.C./C.-B.
Gilpin, Ken (RP/PR) Haldimand–Norfolk, Ontario
Girard, Noël (Lib.) Lac-Saint-Jean, Quebec
Giroux, Denise (NDP/NPD) Hamilton West/Hamilton-Ouest, Ontario (Female)
Gitterman, Manuel (M-L) Broadview–Greenwood, Toronto
Giulietti, Rosanne (NDP/NPD) York West/York-Ouest, Toronto (Female)

Glenn, B.H. Bud (Nil) Beaver River, Alberta
Glenn, Colleen (NDP/NPD) Edmonton Southwest/Edmonton-Sud-Ouest, Alberta (Female)
Glover, David (Nat.) Scarborough East/Scarborough-Est, Toronto
Goddard, Gilles (PC/P-C) Mégantic–Compton–Stanstead, Quebec
Godfrey, John (Lib.) Don Valley West/Don Valley-Ouest, Toronto
Godin, Maurice (BQ) Châteauguay, Quebec
Godlewski, Mario (Nat.) St Paul's, Toronto
Goertzen, Carolyn Dorothy (Nat.) Surrey–White Rock–South Langley, B.C./C.-B. (Female)
Gogan, Greg (Nat.) Scarborough West/Scarborough-Ouest, Toronto
Goldstein, Shelley (Nat.) Willowdale, Toronto (Female)
Goldstick, Danny Red (Nil) York South–Weston/York-Sud–Weston, Toronto
Goodale, Ralph (Lib.) Regina–Wascana, Saskatchewan
Goodman, David (NLP/PLN) London–Middlesex, Ontario
Gordon, Barry (PC/P-C) Kingston and the Islands/Kingston et les Îles, Ontario
Gordon, David (NLP/PLN) Scarborough Centre/Scarborough Centre, Toronto
Gormley, Bernard (NLP/PLN) Halifax West/Halifax Ouest, N.S./N. E.
Gosse, Reg (RP/PR) Kitchener, Ontario
Gossen, Tom (PC/P-C) Saskatoon–Humboldt, Saskatchewan
Gottselig, Bill (PC/P-C) Moose Jaw–Lake Centre, Saskatchewan
Goudy, Ken (CHP/PHC) Mackenzie, Saskatchewan
Gouin, Richard Lionel (Abol.) Sudbury, Ontario
Gouk, Jim (RP/PR) Kootenay West–Revelstoke/Kootenay-Ouest–Revelstoke, B.C./C.-B.
Graham, Bill (Lib.) Rosedale, Toronto
Grant, Jack (NDP/NPD) Markham–Whitchurch–Stouffville, Ontario
Gravel, Alain (NDP/NPD) Laurier–Sainte-Marie, Montreal
Gravel, Pierre (Lib.) Beauce, Quebec
Gray, Darryl L. (PC/P-C) Bonaventure–Îles-de-la-Madeleine, Quebec
Gray, Herb (Lib.) Windsor West/Windsor-Ouest, Ontario
Gray, Kerry (RP/PR) Regina–Qu'Appelle, Saskatchewan
Grayson, Carolyn (NLP/PLN) New Westminster Burnaby, B.C./C.-B. (Female)
Grayson, David (NLP/PLN) Vancouver East/Vancouver-Est, B.C./C.-B.
Green, Michael (Abol.) Scarborough–Agincourt, Toronto
Greene, Barbara (PC/P-C) Don Valley North/Don Valley-Nord, Toronto (Female)
Greene, David M. (CP) Wetaskiwin, Alberta
Greene, Steve (RP/PR) Halifax, N.S./N.-E.
Greenland, Bob (RP/PR) Wellington–Grey–Dufferin–Simcoe, Ontario
Greenwood, Adrian (Nat.) Edmonton–Strathcona, Alberta
Greenwood, Mary Ann (NDP/NPD) Leeds–Grenville, Ontario (Female)
Gregory, John (NLP/PLN) Simcoe Centre/Simcoe-Centre, Ontario
Greig, David (M-L) Etobicoke North/Etobicoke-Nord, Toronto
Grenier, Mark A. (Nat.) North Island–Powell River, B.C./C.-B.
Gretsinger, Connie (NDP/NPD) Portage–Interlake, Manitoba (Female)
Grey, Deborah (RP/PR) Beaver River, Alberta (Female)
Grey, Mansell C. (RP/PR) Western Arctic, N.W.T./T.N.-O.
Grose, Ivan (Lib.) Oshawa, Ontario
Grubel, Herb (RP/PR) Capilano–Howe Sound, B.C./C.-B.
Grunstein, Mel (RP/PR) Niagara Falls, Ontario
Guarnieri, Albina (Lib.) Mississauga East/Mississauga–Est, Ontario (Female)
Guay, Monique (BQ) Laurentides, Quebec (Female)

Gubbels, Alex E. (Ind.) Lambton–Middlesex, Ontario
Guernon, Jean-René (GP/PV) Frontenac, Quebec
Guest, Andy (NLP/PLN) Saanich–Gulf Islands/Saanich–Les Îles-du-Golfe, B.C./C. B.
Guest, Russell (NLP/PLN) Parry Sound–Muskoka, Ontario
Guilbault, Jean-Guy (PC/P-C) Drummond, Quebec
Guimond, Michel (BQ) Beauport–Montmorency–Orléans, Quebec
Guimond, Raymond (Abol.) Louis-Hébert, Quebec
Gunn, John Freddie (CHP/PHC) Malpeque/Malpeque, P.E.I./Î.-P.-E.
Gushnowski, Michael (CP) Edmonton Southeast/Edmonton-Sud-Est, Alberta
Guy, Gérard (PC/P-C) Charlevoix, Quebec
Ha, Tom (CP) London West/London-Ouest, Ontario
Habkirk, Bob (NDP/NPD) Elgin–Norfolk, Ontario
Hache, Val (Com'lth/Rep./Rep./Com'lth) Ontario, Ontario
Hachem, Amin (BQ) Saint Laurent–Cartierville, Montreal
Haika, Frank (NLP/PLN) Calgary West/Calgary–Ouest, Alberta
Haines, Adele (PC/P–C) Burnaby–Kingsway, B.C./C.-B. (Female)
Hainsworth, George (PC/P-C) Kenora–Rainy River, Ontario
Haldeman, Jerry (Ind.) Richmond, B.C./C.-B.
Halderman, Barrett (NDP/NPD) Saskatoon–Humboldt, Saskatchewan
Hall, Lori (NDP/NPD) Edmonton North/Edmonton Nord, Alberta (Female)
Hall, Phyllis (NLP/PLN) Cumberland–Colchester, N.S./N.-E. (Female)
Halpern, George (GP/PV) Hull–Aylmer, Quebec
Hamelin, Alcide (Abol.) Nipissing, Ontario
Hamilton, Ian (PC/P-C) Beauséjour, N.B./N.-B.
Hamilton, Jamie (NDP/NPD) Lambton–Middlesex, Ontario
Hampton, Bob (CP) Cariboo–Chilcotin, B.C./C.-B.
Hanger, Art (RP/PR) Calgary Northeast/Calgary-Nord-Est, Alberta
Hanke, Ralph (Libert.) Bruce–Grey, Ontario
Hanly, Martin (PC/P-C) Western Arctic, N.W.T./T.N.-O.
Hannah, Vern A. (RP/PR) Winnipeg South Centre/ Winnipeg-Sud-Centre, Manitoba
Hanrahan, Hugh (RP/PR) Edmonton–Strathcona, Alberta
Hansen, Arne B. (GP/PV) North Vancouver, B.C./C.-B.
Hansen, Bruce (NLP/PLN) Calgary North/Calgary-Nord, Alberta
Hansen, Gloria (NLP/PLN) Macleod, Alberta (Female)
Harb, Mac (Lib.) Ottawa Centre/Ottawa-Centre, Ontario
Harper, Ed (RP/PR) Simcoe Centre/Simcoe-Centre, Ontario
Harper, Elijah (Lib.) Churchill, Manitoba
Harper, Stephen (RP/PR) Calgary West/Calgary-Ouest, Alberta
Harris, Dick (RP/PR) Prince George–Bulkley Valley, B.C./C.-B.
Harris, Jim (GP/PV) St Paul's, Toronto
Hart, Jim (RP/PR) Okanagan–Similkameen–Merritt, B.C./C.-B.
Harvard, John (Lib.) Winnipeg St James, Manitoba
Harvey, André (PC/P-C) Chicoutimi, Quebec
Harvey, Guy (NLP/PLN) St John's West/St John's-Ouest, Nfld/T.-N.
Harvey, Laurent (Nat.) Berthier–Montcalm, Quebec
Harvey, Ross (NDP/NPD) Edmonton East/Edmonton-Est, Alberta
Harvey, Stephen (GP/PV) Windsor–St. Clair/Windsor–Sainte-Claire, Ontario
Haver, Lelannd (CP) Kootenay East/Kootenay-Est, B.C./C.-B.
Hawkes, Jim (PC/P-C) Calgary West/Calgary-Ouest, Alberta

Hawkins, Mark (NLP/PLN) London West/London-Ouest, Ontario
Hawkins, Paul (M.-L.) Essex– Windsor, Ontario
Hawley, Robert Arthur (NDP/NPD) Cape Breton–The Sydneys/Cap-Breton–The Sydneys, N.S./N.-E.
Hayes, Sharon (RP/PR) Port Moody–Coquitlam, B.C./C.-B. (Female)
Haze, Leanne (GP/PV) Beaches–Woodbine, Toronto (Female)
Hea, James M. (NLP/PLN) Carleton–Gloucester, Ontario
Head, Bob (RP/PR) Saskatoon–Humboldt, Saskatchewan
Hearn, Loyola (PC/P-C) St John's West/St John's-Ouest, Nfld/T.-N.
Heather, Larry (CHP/PHC) Calgary West/Calgary-Ouest, Alberta·
Hebert, Eric (NDP/NPD) Manicouagan, Quebec
Heffernan, Dan (NDP/NPD) Wellington–Grey–Dufferin–Simcoe, Ontario
Heidecker, Brian (PC/P-C) Crowfoot, Alberta
Heilman, Jack (NLP/PLN) Moose Jaw–Lake Centre, Saskatchewan
Heimlick, Doug (RP/PR) Souris–Moose Mountain, Saskatchewan
Heinrichs, Rob (Lib.) Swift Current–Maple Creek–Assiniboia, Saskatchewan
Hemming, Mark (Nat.) Port Moody–Coquitlam, B.C./C.-B.
Hemphill, Maureen (NDP/NPD) Winnipeg North Centre/Winnipeg-Nord-Centre, Manitoba (Female)
Henning, Doug (NLP/PLN) Rosedale, Toronto
Hepburn, Joan (Nat.) Red Deer, Alberta (Female)
Hepworth, Gael (NDP/NPD) Eglinton–Lawrence, Toronto (Female)
Hérivault, Jean-Louis (BQ) Outremont, Montreal
Hermanson, Elwin (RP/PR) Kindersley–Lloydminster, Saskatchewan
Héroux, Gilles (Lib.) Témiscamingue, Quebec
Héroux, Hélène (M-L) Rosemont, Montreal (Female)
Hervieux-Payette, Céline (Lib.) Ahuntsic, Montreal (Female)
Hesp, Rob (RP/PR) St Catharines, Ontario
Hetherington, David (NLP/PLN) Victoria–Haliburton, Ontario
Hickey, Bonnie (Lib.) St John's East/St John's-Est, Nfld/T.-N. (Female)
Hicks, Donna (PC/P-C) Nepean, Ontario (Female)
Hicks, Mike (PC/P-C) Comox Alberni, B.C./C.-B.
Higgerty, John (Lib.) Yellowhead, Alberta
Higgs, Mary Ann (NDP/NPD) Kingston and the Islands/Kingston et les Îles, Ontario (Female)
Hill, Grant (RP/PR) Macleod, Alberta
Hill, Jay (RP/PR) Prince George–Peace River, B.C./C.B.
Hill, Jim (NLP/PLN) London East/London-Est, Ontario
Hill, Wayne (Nat.) Thunder Bay–Nipigon, Ontario
Hilson, Bob (Nat.) Hastings–Frontenac–Lennox and Addington, Ontario
Hindle, Lonnie W. (Lib.) Comox–Alberni, B.C./C.-B.
Hinz, Gunter (Nat.) Hamilton Mountain, Ontario
Hird, Cathy (NDP/NPD) Bruce–Grey, Ontario (Female)
Hislop, Bruce (NLP/PLN) Davenport, Toronto
Hobson, Joy Ann (Nat.) Saint John, N.B./N.-B. (Female)
Hockin, Tom (PC/P-C) London West/London-Ouest, Ontario
Hoeppner, Jake E. (RP/PR) Lisgar–Marquette, Manitoba
Hoff, Lorne (NLP/PLN) Elk Island, Alberta
Hoff, Margaret (NDP/NPD) London West/London-Ouest, Ontario (Female)
Hoff, Peter (Nat.) Calgary Centre/Calgary-Centre, Alberta
Hogarth, Marlene (PC/P-C) Thunder Bay–Nipigon, Ontario (Female)
Hogg, Gordon J. (Lib.) Surrey–White Rock–South Langley, B.C./C.-B.

Hogue, Jean Pierre (PC/P-C) Outremont, Montreal
Holden, Elizabeth (NDP/NPD) Gatineau–La Lièvre, Quebec (Female)
Holder, Ed (PC/P-C) London–Middlesex, Ontario
Holman, Grace (PC/P-C) Esquimalt–Juan de Fuca, B.C./C.-B.(Female)
Holtmann, Felix (PC/P-C) Portage–Interlake, Manitoba
Hones, Peter, (Nil) York South–Weston/York-Sud–Weston, Toronto
Honsey, Gordon E. (RP/PR) Don Valley East/Don Valley-Est, Toronto
Hope, Peter (CP) Calgary Southeast/Calgary-Sud-Est, Alberta
Hopkins, Jack (CP) Medicine Hat, Alberta
Hopkins, Len (Lib.) Renfrew–Nipissing–Pembroke, Ontario
Horgan, Gerard W. (Nat.) Central Nova, N.S./N.-E.
Horner, Bob (PC/P-C) Mississauga West/Mississauga-Ouest, Ontario
Horning, Al (PC/P-C) Okanagan Centre/Okanagan-Centre, B.C./C.-B.
Hough, Jim (NDP/NPD) Burlington, Ontario
Houle, Eugene (NDP/NPD) Beaver River, Alberta
Houle, Patricia (NDP/NPD) Laurentides, Quebec (Female)
Houle, Stéphane (NDP/NPD) Laval East/Laval-Est, Montreal
Howe, Marty (NLP/PLN) Kent, Ontario
Howell, David (Nat.) London–Middlesex, Ontario
Hubbard, Charles (Lib.) Miramichi, N.B./N.-B.
Huddlestan, Al (Lib.) North Island–Powell River, B.C./C.-B.
Hudson, Kevan (GP/PV) Richmond, B.C./C.-B.
Hughes, David (GP/PV) Okanagan Centre/Okanagan-Centre, B.C./C.-B.
Hughes, Jane (NDP/NPD) St Catharines, Ontario (Female)
Hughes, Jim (PC/P-C) Prince Edward–Hastings, Ontario
Hughes, Ken (PC/P-C) Macleod, Alberta
Hughes, Mark (RP/PR) Winnipeg South/Winnipeg-Sud, Manitoba
Hughes, Stuart (Nat.) Wild Rose, Alberta
Hull, Tom (PC/P-C) Regina–Qu'Appelle, Saskatchewan
Hunt, Allan (NDP/NPD) Medicine Hat, Alberta
Hunt, C. Angus (NLP/PLN) Regina–Wascana, Saskatchewan
Hunt, Daniel (Libert.) Etobicoke North/Etobicoke-Nord, Toronto
Hunt, Patrick (RP/PR) Victoria, B.C./C.-B.
Hunter, Guy (NDP/NPD) Scarborough Centre/Scarborough-Centre, Toronto
Hunter, Leslie (GP/PV) Rosedale, Toronto (Female)
Hunter, Lynn (NDP/NPD) Saanich–Gulf Islands/Saanich–Les Îles-du-Golfe, B.C./C.B. (Female)
Hurtig, Mel (Nat.) Edmonton Northwest/Edmonton-Nord-Ouest, Alberta
Hurvid, Judy (GP/PV) Durham, Ontario (Female)
Huschka Sprague, Rita (Libert.) Waterloo, Ontario (Female)
Hustvedt, Eric (NDP/NPD) South Shore, N.S./N.-E.
Hutchinson, Sean (NDP/NPD) Brome–Missisquoi, Quebec
Hutton, John (NDP/NPD) Winnipeg St James, Manitoba
Hyman, Bob (NLP/PLN) Broadview–Greenwood, Toronto
Hyodo, Eleanor Toshiko (NLP/PLN) Brant, Ontario (Female)
Ianno, Tony (Lib.) Trinity–Spadina, Toronto
Iftody, David (Lib.) Provencher, Manitoba
Illnik, Mike (NDP/NPD) Nunatsiaq, N.W.T./T.N.-O.
Imrie, Alan (Nil) Vancouver East/Vancouver-Est, B.C./C.-B.
Innes, Elizabeth (NLP/PLN) Winnipeg South Centre/Winnipeg-Sud-Centre, Manitoba (Female)

Irvine, Sue (PC/P-C) Okanagan–Similkameen–Merritt, B.C./C.-B. (Female)
Irwin, Ron (Lib.) Sault Ste Marie, Ontario
Isabelle, Manon Charleen (NLP/PLN) Nipissing, Ontario (Female)
Isbister, Ian (RP/PR) Vancouver Centre/Vancouver Centre, B.C./C.-B.
Jack, Barbara (NDP/NPD) Cumberland–Colchester, N.S./N.-E. (Female)
Jacklin, Lynn (NDP/NPD) Ontario, Ontario (Female)
Jackman, Bruce (CP) Calgary Centre/Calgary-Centre, Alberta
Jackman, J.G. Joseph (Com'l/Rep./Rep./Com'lth) Vancouver Quadra, B.C./C.-B.
Jackson, Andrew (RP/PR) Regina–Wascana, Saskatchewan
Jackson, Brian (NLP/PLN) Nepean, Ontario
Jackson, Don (NLP/PLN) Etobicoke–Lakeshore, Toronto
Jackson, Geraldine (NLP/PLN) Mississauga East/Mississauga-Est, Ontario (Female)
Jackson, John (NDP/NPD) Mississauga East/Mississauga-Est, Ontario
Jackson, Ovid L. (Lib.) Bruce–Grey, Ontario
Jackson, R. W. (Nil) Nanaimo–Cowichan/Nanaimo–Cowichan, B.C./C.-B.
Jacob, Jean-Marc (BQ) Charlesbourg, Quebec
Jacobs, David (NDP/NPD) St Paul's, Toronto
Jacobs, Steve (NDP/NPD) Elk Island, Alberta
Jacques, Carole (Nil) Mercier, Montreal (Female)
Jacques, James (Nil) Edmonton East/Edmonton-Est, Alberta
Jaffer, Mobina (Lib.) North Vancouver, B.C./C.-B. (Female)
Jaggard, Robert (Nil) Hamilton East/Hamilton-Est, Ontario
Jagges, Doug (PC/P-C) Simcoe Centre/Simcoe-Centre, Ontario
Jakubcak, Michael (RP/PR) Davenport, Toronto
Jalbert, Marie D. (NDP/NPD) Lac-Saint-Jean, Quebec (Female)
Jam, Jean-Guy (Lib.) Frontenac, Quebec
James, Ken (PC/P-C) Sarnia–Lambton, Ontario
James, Lois Jean (GP/PV) Scarborough East/Scarborough-Est, Toronto (Female)
Jasich, Anthony (Libert.) North Vancouver, B.C./C.-B.
Jeffers, Larry (Nat.) Lisgar–Marquette, Manitoba
Jeffery, Jack (Lib.) St Albert/Saint-Albert, Alberta
Jeffrey, Brooke (Lib.) Okanagan–Shuswap, B.C./C.-B. (Female)
Jenkins, Garry (Lib.) Kootenay West–Revelstoke/ Kootenay-Ouest–Revelstoke, B.C./C.-B.
Jennings, Daphne (RP/PR) Mission–Coquitlam, B.C./C.-B. (Female)
Jerome, Valerie (GP/PV) Vancouver South/Vancouver-Sud, B.C./C.-B. (Female)
Jewell, P. Jeffery (Nat.) New Westminster–Burnaby, B.C./C.-B.
Jewell, Reg (PC/P-C) Northumberland, Ontario
Jheeta, Mota Singh (NDP/NPD) Surrey–White Rock–South Langley, B.C./C.-B.
Johns, Stephen, (GP/PV) Lanark–Carleton, Ontario
Johnsen, Paula (NLP/PLN) Edmonton East/Edmonton-Est, Alberta (Female)
Johnsen, Ric (NLP/PLN) Edmonton Northwest/Edmonton-Nord-Ouest, Alberta
Johnson, Al (PC/P-C) Calgary North/Calgary-Nord, Alberta
Johnson, Grant (Lib.) Lisgar–Marquette, Manitoba
Johnson, Oran K. (CP) Edmonton–Strathcona, Alberta
Johnson, Ray (PC/P-C) Hamilton–Wentworth, Ontario
Johnston, Dale (RP/PR) Wetaskiwin, Alberta
Johnston, Diane (M-L) York Centre/York-Centre, Toronto (Female)
Johnston, Gord (RP/PR) Northumberland, Ontario
Johnston, Marnie (Nat.) Winnipeg Transcona, Manitoba (Female)

Johnstone, Don (RP/PR) Welland–St Catharines–Thorold, Ontario
Jolicoeur, Daniel (NLP/PLN) Nickel Belt, Ontario
Joncas, Jean Luc (PC/P-C) Matapédia–Matane, Quebec
Jones, Alan (GP/PV) York Centre/York-Centre, Toronto
Jones, Lynn (NDP/NPD) Halifax, N.S./N.-E. (Female)
Jordan, Jim (Lib.) Leeds–Grenville, Ontario
Jourdenais, Fernand (PC/P-C) La Prairie, Quebec
Journeau, Jim (Abol.) Parry Sound–Muskoka, Ontario
Jovkovic, Daniel (RP/PR) Rosedale, Toronto
Joyce, Marion Velma (Abol.) St Paul's, Toronto (Female)
Judge, Kirby (Nat.) Halifax West/Halifax–Ouest, N.S./N.-E.
Judson, Baird (CHP/PHC) Hillsborough, P.E.I./Î.-P.-E.
Julien, Linda (Lib.) Beauharnois–Salaberry, Quebec (Female)
Juneau, Gaston (NDP/NPD) Charlesbourg, Quebec
Kalevar, Chai (Nat.) Scarborough–Rouge River, Toronto
Kallos, Catherine (NDP/NPD) Outremont, Montreal (Female)
Kalturnyk, Ken (M-L) Winnipeg Transcona, Manitoba
Kantorovich, Rubin (M-L) Winnipeg South/Winnipeg-Sud, Manitoba
Kapty, Al (PC/P-C) Yukon, Y.T./T.Y.
Karpoff, Jim (NDP/NPD) Surrey North/Surrey-Nord, B.C./C.-B.
Karringten, Braden (Nil) Surrey North/Surrey Nord, B.C./C.-B.
Karygiannis, Jim (Lib.) Scarborough–Agincourt, Toronto
Kasiurak, Ivan W. (Ind.) London West/London-Ouest, Ontario
Kasvand, Tonis (Abol.) Nepean, Ontario
Kavanagh, Donald (CP) Prince Albert–Churchill River/ Prince-Albert–Churchill River, Saskatchewan
Kayler, Richard (RP/PR) Edmonton Northwest/Edmonton-Nord-Ouest, Alberta
Kealey, Glen Emmett Patrick (Ind.) Pontiac–Gatineau–Labelle, Quebec
Keen, John (Nat.) Regina–Wascana, Saskatchewan
Keene, D'Arcy (PC/P-C) Scarborough East/Scarborough-Est, Toronto
Keith, Rollie (NDP/NPD) Fraser Valley East/Fraser Valley-Est, B.C./C.-B.
Kelembet, Roma (Libert.) York South–Weston/York-Sud–Weston, Toronto (Female)
Kelly, Terry (Nil) Beaches–Woodbine, Toronto
Kendall, Richard Kirkman (Libert.) Blainville–Deux-Montagnes, Quebec
Kennedy, Billy (Nat.) Cape Breton–East Richmond/Cap-Breton–Richmond-Est, N.S./N.-E.
Kennedy, Tom J. (Abol.) Carleton–Gloucester, Ontario
Kenny, David (Libert.) Scarborough–Rouge River, Toronto
Kerpan, Allan (RP/PR) Moose Jaw–Lake Centre, Saskatchewan
Kestein, Ben (Nat.) York North/York-Nord, Ontario
Keyes, Stan (Lib.) Hamilton West/Hamilton-Ouest, Ontario
Khalsa, Sat K. Singh (GP/PV) Davenport, Toronto
Khan, Golam (Com'lth/Rep./Rep./Com'lth) Verdun–Saint-Paul, Montreal
Kiers, Alfred (CHP/PHC) Erie, Ontario
Kilger, Bob (Lib.) Stormont–Dundas, Ontario
Kilgour, David (Lib.) Edmonton Southeast/Edmonton-Sud-Est, Alberta
Kindy, Alex (Nil) Calgary Northeast/Calgary-Nord-Est, Alberta
King, Dan (GP/PV) Don Valley West/Don Valley-Ouest, Toronto
King, Frederick B. (CP) Regina–Lumsden, Saskatchewan
King, Leslie (NDP/NPD) Lisgar–Marquette, Manitoba (Female)
King, Lindsay George (Abol.) Don Valley North/Don Valley–Nord, Toronto

Kinsley, Colin J. (PC/P-C) Prince George–Bulkley Valley, B.C./C.-B.
Kinzel, Cliff (NLP/PLN) Lethbridge, Alberta
Kinzel, Ria (NLP/PLN) Edmonton North/Edmonton-Nord, Alberta (Female)
Kirby, Peter (NDP/NPD) Kenora–Rainy River, Ontario
Kiriaka, Peter (CP) Edmonton East/Edmonton-Est, Alberta
Kirkby, Gordon (Lib.) Prince Albert–Churchill River/Prince-Albert–Churchill River, Saskatchewan
Kisby, Richard Steven (GP/PV) Fraser Valley East/ Fraser Valley-Est, B.C./C.-B.
Kjear, Hans C. (CP) Portage–Interlake, Manitoba
Klim, Alice (PC/P-C) Okanagan–Shuswap, B.C./C.-B. (Female)
Klonowski, W. Vladimir (GP/PV) Halifax, N.S./N.-E.
Klosler, George (PC/P-C) Oxford, Ontario
Klovan, Gus (RP/PR) Nepean, Ontario
Knight, Barry (NDP/NPD) Labrador, Nfld/T. N.
Knight, Don (PC/P-C) Churchill, Manitoba
Knight, Ian (CHP/PHC) York–Simcoe, Ontario
Knight, Victor (Nat.) Kent, Ontario
Knoll, Leonard (Libert.) Ottawa West/Ottawa-Ouest, Ontario
Knutson, Gar (Lib.) Elgin–Norfolk, Ontario
Kos, Nevenka (Com'lth/Rep./Rep./Com'lth) Delta, B.C./C.-B.(Female)
Kosman, Christine (Nat.) Prince Edward–Hastings, Ontario (Female)
Kouri, Joan (Lib.) Brome–Missisquoi, Quebec (Female)
Koury, Allan (PC/P-C) Hochelaga–Maisonneuve, Montreal
Kovacs, Kevin (PC/P-C) Edmonton East/Edmonton-Est, Alberta
Kozaroff, George S. (Libert.) Ontario, Ontario
Kraft Sloan, Karen (Lib.) York–Simcoe, Ontario (Female)
Krieger, Al (Ind.) Saskatoon–Dundurn, Saskatchewan
Kropfel, Ursula (NLP/PLN) Burlington, Ontario (Female)
Krueger, Kevin (Lib.) Kamloops, B.C./C.-B.
Kruis, Herman (Nat.) Brant, Ontario
Kruschel, Linda (Abol.) Eglinton–Lawrence, Toronto (Female)
Kryn, Ted (CHP/PHC) Waterloo, Ontario
Kuegle, Mike (PC/P-C) Burlington, Ontario
Kurian, John (PC/P-C) Edmonton Southeast/Edmonton-Sud-Est, Alberta
Kurmis, Helmut (Libert.) Brant, Ontario
Kutney, Patrick (Nat.) Trinity–Spadina, Toronto
Kwantes, Louis Luke (CHP/PHC) Skeena, B.C./C.-B.
Labots, Cor (CHP/PHC) Edmonton East/Edmonton-Est, Alberta
Lachapelle, Serge (M-L) Papineau–Saint-Michel, Montreal
Lacoste, Gérald (PC/P-C) Mercier, Montreal
Lacroix, Marc (NLP/PLN) Ahuntsic, Montreal
Lafford, Earl (NLP/PLN) Cape Breton Highlands–Canso/Cap-Breton Highlands–Canso, N.S./N.E.
Laforge, Leon (NLP/PLN) Saskatoon–Dundurn, Saskatchewan
Lafortune, Serge (M-L) Ottawa–Vanier, Ontario
Laidlaw, Maggie (Nat.) Guelph–Wellington, Ontario (Female)
Lajeunesse, Jean Paul (NDP/NPD) Cochrane–Superior/Cochrane–Superieur, Ontario
Lakhanpal, Pulkesh (NLP/PLN) Central Nova, N.S./N.-E.
Laking, Janice (Lib.) Simcoe Centre/Simcoe-Centre, Ontario (Female)
Laliberte, Rick V. (Nil) Prince Albert–Churchill River/Prince-Albert–Churchill River, Saskatchewan
Lalonde, Francine (BQ) Mercier, Montreal (Female)

Lam, Steven (Ind.) Scarborough Centre/Scarborough-Centre, Toronto
Lamarre, Roger (NDP/NPD) Rosemont, Montreal
Lambeck, Betty Hay (NDP/NPD) Hastings–Frontenac–Lennox and Addington, Ontario (Female)
Lambert, Willie (NDP/NPD) Oakville–Milton, Ontario
Lamey, Jack (RP/PR) Fredericton–York-Sunbury, N.B./N.-B.
Lamey, Joanne (NDP/NPD) Cape Breton–East Richmond/Cap-Breton–Richmond-Est, N.S./N.E. (Female)
Lamont, Scott Chisholm (GP/PV) Wild Rose, Alberta
Lamothe, Siggi (NLP/PLN) Prince Edward–Hastings, Ontario (Female)
Lamothe, Stan (NLP/PLN) Ottawa West/Ottawa-Ouest, Ontario
Lamoureux, Maurice (PC/P-C) Sudbury, Ontario
Lanctôt, Monique (Com'l/Rep./Rep./Com'lth) Saint-Laurent–Cartierville, Montreal (Female)
Landers, Pat (Lib.) Saint John, N.B./N.-B. (Female)
Landry, Jean (BQ) Lotbinière, Quebec
Landry, Monique (PC/P-C) Blainville–Deux-Montagnes, Quebec (Female)
Landry, Reginald (Com'lth/Rep./Rep./Com'lth) Stormont–Dundas, Ontario
Langan, Joy (NDP/NPD) Mission–Coquitlam, B.C./C.-B. (Female)
Langdon, Steven (NDP/NPD) Essex–Windsor, Ontario
Langlois, Charles (PC/P-C) Manicouagan, Quebec
Langlois, François (BQ) Bellechasse, Quebec
Lanier, Tom (NLP/PLN) Perth–Wellington–Waterloo, Ontario
Lanigan, Martin (Nat.) Rosedale, Toronto
Lapeyrouse, Kathleen (NLP/PLN) Comox–Alberni, B.C./C.-B. (Female)
Lapointe, Lucien (Abol.) Bourassa, Montreal
Lapointe, Stéphane (Ind.) Saint-Denis, Montreal
Laporte, Rod (NDP/NPD) Moose Jaw–Lake Centre, Saskatchewan
Larmand, Micheal Paul (NLP/PLN) Durham, Ontario
Larrivée, Gaby (PC/P-C) Joliette, Quebec
Larsen, John (RP/PR) Essex–Windsor, Ontario
Lastewka, Walt (Lib.) St Catharines, Ontario
Laurent, Raymond (NDP/NPD) Bourassa, Montreal
Laurin, René (BQ) Joliette, Quebec
Lauwn, Richard (NLP/PLN) Hochelaga–Maisonneuve, Montreal
Lavigne, Laurent (BQ) Beauharnois–Salaberry, Quebec
Lavigne, Raymond (Lib.) Verdun–Saint-Paul, Montreal
Lavoie, Rita (Lib.) Manicouagan, Quebec (Female)
Law, Kurtis (Nat.) Mount Royal/Mont-Royal, Montreal
Lawn, Sandra (PC/P-C) Leeds–Grenville, Ontario (Female)
Laycox, Scott (GP/PV) Ontario, Ontario
Layton, Jack (NDP/NPD) Rosedale, Toronto
Lea, Chris (GP/PV) Trinity–Spadina, Toronto
Lebel, Ghislain (BQ) Chambly, Quebec
Le Blanc, Bernadette (PC/P-C) Moncton, N.B./N.-B. (Female)
LeBlanc, Francis (Lib.) Cape Breton Highlands–Canso/Cap-Breton Highlands–Canso, N.S./N.-E.
LeBlanc, Kelly Ann (Abol.) Etobicoke Centre/Etobicoke-Centre, Toronto (Female)
Leblanc, Nic (BQ) Longueuil, Quebec
Leblanc, Nicole (M-L) Gatineau–La-Lièvre, Quebec (Female)
Leclerc, Robert (NDP/NPD) Bellechasse, Quebec
Ledgister, Paul (NDP/NPD) Bramalea–Gore–Malton, Ontario

Ledoux, Claude (NDP/NPD) Verdun–Saint-Paul, Montreal
Ledoux, Richard (PC/P-C) Longueuil, Quebec
Leduc, François (PC/P-C) Verchères, Quebec
Leduc, Michel (BQ) Laval West/Laval-Ouest, Montreal
Lee, Derek (Lib.) Scarborough–Rouge River, Toronto
Lee, Ian R. (PC/P-C) Ottawa Centre/Ottawa-Centre, Ontario
Lee, Jess P. (Nil) New Westminster–Burnaby, B.C./C.-B.
Lefebvre, Ben (NLP/PLN) Timmins–Chapleau, Ontario
Lefebvre, Rejean (BQ) Champlain, Quebec
Lefebvre, Rejean (Lib.) Joliette, Quebec
Leffler, Ken (RP/PR) Algoma, Ontario
Legacey, Jamie (GP/PV) Brant, Ontario
Légaré, Roger (Lib.) Shefford, Quebec
Légaré-St-Cyr, Linda (NLP/PLN) Blainville–Deux-Montagnes, Quebec (Female)
Léger, Jules (Lib.) Hochelaga–Maisonneuve, Montreal
Legere, Isaac J. (CHP/PHC) Moncton, N.B./N.-B.
Leggat, Peter (NLP/PLN) Oxford, Ontario
Lehr, Roger (PC/P-C) Vegreville/Végréville, Alberta
Lejeune, Nelson (Abol.) Charlesbourg, Quebec
Lemieux, Eric (Lib.) Bellechasse, Quebec
Lemire, Marie Christine (PC/P-C) Ottawa–Vanier, Ontario (Female)
Lenard, Neall (CP) Nanaimo–Cowichan/Nanaimo–Cowichan, B.C./C.-B.
Leonard, Steve (NDP/NPD) Niagara Falls, Ontario
Lepine, Dany (Com'lth/Rep./Rep./Com'lth) Longueuil, Quebec
Lépine, François (Com'lth/Rep./Rep./Com'lth) Laval East/Laval-Est, Montreal
Lepinsky, Richard (NLP/PLN) Winnipeg South/Winnipeg-Sud, Manitoba
Leroux, Gaston (BQ) Richmond–Wolfe, Quebec
Leroux, Jean H. (BQ) Shefford, Quebec
Lesage, Jean (PC/P-C) Saint-Hubert, Quebec
Le Sieur, Jacques (PC/P-C) Lotbinière, Quebec
Leslie, Michael (Ind.) Wild Rose, Alberta
Lesosky, Louis J. (Nil) Esquimalt–Juan de Fuca, B.C./C.-B.
Léveillé, Serge (PC/P-C) Lévis, Quebec
Lévesque, Stéphane (Com'lth/Rep./Rep./Com'lth) Rosemont, Montreal
Levesque, Stephanie (NDP/NPD) Perth–Wellington–Waterloo, Ontario (Female)
Lewis, Doug (PC/P-C) Simcoe North/Simcoe-Nord, Ontario
Lewis, Terry (RP/PR) Selkirk–Red River, Manitoba
Lien, Dean (PC/P-C) Lethbridge, Alberta
Lightfoot, Geraldine (RP/PR) Nipissing, Ontario (Female)
Limoges, Michel (GP/PV) Gaspé, Quebec
Lincoln, Clifford (Lib.) Lachine–Lac-Saint-Louis, Montreal
Lipke, Bruno (Com'lth/Rep./Rep./Com'lth) Saint-Hubert, Quebec
Li Preti, Peter (Ind.) York Centre/York-Centre, Toronto
Livingston, Alan J. (NLP/PLN) Crowfoot, Alberta
Lloyd, Bob (CP) Saskatoon–Dundurn, Saskatchewan
Lobb, Len (RP/PR) Huron–Bruce, Ontario
Locas, Ronald, (Nat.) Timmins–Chapleau, Ontario
Loeb, Kurt (Nat.) York Centre/York-Centre, Toronto
Loenen, Nick (RP/PR) Richmond, B.C./C.-B.

Loewen, Bill (Nat.) Winnipeg South Centre/Winnipeg-Sud-Centre, Manitoba
Loewen, Shirley (Nat.) Winnipeg South/Winnipeg-Sud, Manitoba (Female)
Loftus, Peter (RP/PR) Trinity–Spadina, Toronto
Logan, Dan (Nil) Vancouver South/Vancouver Sud, B.C./C.-B.
Loignon, Micheline (Abol.) Beauport–Montmorency–Orléans, Quebec (Female)
Loiselle, Gilles (PC/P-C) Québec, Quebec
Loney, John (Lib.) Edmonton North/Edmonton-Nord, Alberta
Long, John H. (CP) Guelph–Wellington, Ontario
Longpré, Alain (NLP/PLN) Saint-Jean, Quebec
Loper, Janice Waud (NDP/NPD) Don Valley East/Don Valley-Est, Toronto (Female)
Lopez, Ricardo (PC/P-C) Châteauguay, Quebec
Lord, Alain Edouard (NLP/PLN) Saint-Denis, Montreal
Lorimier, Renée-Claude (NDP/NPD) Terrebonne, Quebec (Female)
Loubier, Denis (Abol.) Shefford, Quebec
Loubier, Yvan (BQ) Saint-Hyacinthe–Bagot, Quebec
Louie, Dan (RP/PR) Timiskaming–French River, Ontario
Loveless, Marilyn (PC/P-C) Saanich–Gulf Islands/Saanich–Les Îles-du-Golfe, B.C./C.-B. (Female)
Lovett, Marlene (PC/P-C) Cape Breton–The Sydneys/Cap-Breton–The Sydneys, N.S./N.-E. (Female)
Lowe, Darren (CHP/PHC) Vancouver Centre/Vancouver-Centre, B.C./C.-B.
Lu, David (NDP/NPD) Don Valley North/Don Valley-Nord, Toronto
Ludlam, Janet (Nil) Vancouver Quadra, B.C./C.-B. (Female)
Lund, Bob (RP/PR) Erie, Ontario
Lutz, Garfield (Lib.) Mackenzie, Saskatchewan
Ly, Mai (Abol.) Elgin–Norfolk, Ontario (Female)
Lyall, Roy (CP) Lisgar–Marquette, Manitoba
Lynch, Joe (CP) Winnipeg North/Winnipeg-Nord, Manitoba
Lyons, Ray (RP/PR) Simcoe North/Simcoe-Nord, Ontario
MacAulay, Lawrence (Lib.) Cardigan, P.E.I./Î.-P.-E.
MacDonald, Colin (Lib.) Calgary Northeast/Calgary-Nord-Est, Alberta
MacDonald, David (PC/P-C) Rosedale, Toronto
MacDonald, Gillian (NDP/NPD) Cariboo–Chilcotin, B.C./C.-B. (Female)
Macdonald, Lloyd (NDP/NPD) Delta, B.C./C.-B.
MacDonald, Ron (Lib.) Dartmouth, N.S./N.-E.
MacDonald, Ron (RP/PR) Lanark–Carleton, Ontario
MacDonald, Wilbur (PC/P-C) Cardigan, P.E.I./Î.-P.-E.
Macdougall, A.M. Sandy (PC/P-C) Mission–Coquitlam, B.C./C.-B.
MacDuffee, Dick (RP/PR) Halton–Peel, Ontario
MacFarlan, Betty (Lib.) Edmonton Southwest/Edmonton-Sud-Ouest, Alberta (Female)
MacFarlane, Ian (NDP/NPD) Kitchener, Ontario
MacFarlane, John (NDP/NPD) Portneuf, Quebec
MacIntosh, Bruce N. (PC/P-C) Restigouche–Chaleur, N.B./N.-B.
MacKay, Neil (PC/P-C) New Westminster Burnaby, B.C./C.-B.
Mackenzie, Andrew (NDP/NPD) Hamilton Mountain, Ontario
MacKenzie, Hugh (NDP/NPD) Central Nova, N.S./N.-E.
Mackenzie, Pauline (NDP/NPD) Fredericton–York-Sunbury, N.B./N.-B. (Female)
MacKinnon, Howard (RP/PR) Central Nova, N.S./N.-E.
MacKinnon, Lewis (PC/P-C) Cape Breton Highlands–Canso/Cap-Breton Highlands–Canso, N.S./N.E.
Mackintosh, Brian (Libert.) Nepean, Ontario
MacLaren, Jane (PC/P-C) Etobicoke North/Etobicoke-Nord, Toronto (Female)

MacLaren, Roy (Lib.) Etobicoke North/Etobicoke-Nord, Toronto
MacLellan, Russell (Lib.) Cape Breton-The Sydneys/Cap-Breton–The Sydneys, N.S./N.-E.
MacLennan, Don (Nat.) Okanagan–Shuswap, B.C./C.-B.
MacLeod, Jim (GP/PV) Scarborough West/Scarborough-Ouest, Toronto
MacNeil, Cyril G. (Nat.) Laval West/Laval-Ouest, Montreal
Macrisopoulos, Panagiotis (M-L) Saint-Denis, Montreal
MacWilliam, Lyle (NDP/NPD) Okanagan–Shuswap, B.C./C. B.
Maguire, Larry (PC/P-C) Brandon–Souris, Manitoba
Maheu, Shirley (Lib.) Saint-Laurent–Cartierville, Montreal (Female)
Maine, Frank (Nil) Guelph–Wellington, Ontario
Mainil, Art (Ind.) Souris–Moose Mountain, Saskatchewan
Mair, David (PC/P-C) Algoma, Ontario
Makhdoom, Zahid (NDP/NPD) St Albert/Saint-Albert, Alberta
Malboeuf, Richard (RP/PR) Oakville–Milton, Ontario
Malenfant, Pierre-Paul (Nil) Kamouraska–Rivière-du-Loup, Quebec
Malhi, Gurbax (Lib.) Bramalea–Gore–Malton, Ontario
Maloney, John (Lib.) Erie, Ontario
Maltais, Laurent (NLP/PLN) Restigouche–Chaleur, N.B./N.-B.
Mandala, Zamba (NDP/NPD) Anjou–Rivière-des-Prairies, Montreal
Mangat, Jas (Ind.) Vancouver South/Vancouver-Sud, B.C./C.-B.
Manegre, Jerry (PC/P-C) St Albert/Saint-Albert, Alberta
Manley, John (Lib.) Ottawa South/Ottawa-Sud, Ontario
Mann, Alex S. (Nat.) Yellowhead, Alberta
Mann, Tamra (PC/P-C) Hamilton Mountain, Ontario
Manning, Preston (RP/PR) Calgary Southwest/Calgary-Sud-Ouest, Alberta
Mansour, Issam (Nil) Vancouver South/Vancouver-Sud, B.C./C.-B.
Mantha, Bob (PC/P-C) Timiskaming–French River, Ontario
Mantha, Moe (PC/P-C) Nipissing, Ontario
Marchand, Cynthia (NLP/PLN) Lincoln, Ontario (Female)
Marchand, Jean-Paul (BQ) Québec-Est, Quebec
Marchi, Sergio (Lib.) York West/York-Ouest, Toronto
Marin, Charles-Eugène (PC/P-C) Gaspé, Quebec
Marion, Marcelle (Nat.) St Boniface/Saint-Boniface, Manitoba (Female)
Maris, Nicholas (Com'lth/Rep./Rep./Com'lth) Verchères, Quebec
Marjot, Marcel (Com'lth/Rep./Rep./Com'lth) Chambly, Quebec
Marleau, Diane (Lib.) Sudbury, Ontario (Female)
Marois, Anne Marie (NLP/PLN) Richmond–Wolfe, Quebec (Female)
Maron, Mary (NDP/NPD) Willowdale, Toronto (Female)
Marroquin, Alfredo (NDP/NPD) London East/London Est, Ontario
Marsden, Wayne (Libert.) Vancouver East/Vancouver-Est, B.C./C.-B.
Marshall, John (Nat.) Parry Sound–Muskoka, Ontario
Marshall, Terry M. (CHP/PHC) Kingston and the Islands/Kingston et les Îles, Ontario
Marston, Wayne (NDP/NPD) Hamilton East/Hamilton Est, Ontario
Martel, Emilien (Abol.) Laval Centre/Laval-Centre, Montreal
Martens, Bill (CP) Winnipeg South/Winnipeg-Sud, Manitoba
Martin, André (PC/P-C) Verdun–Saint-Paul, Montreal
Martin, Beattie (PC/P-C) Regina–Lumsden, Saskatchewan
Martin, Jim (NDP/NPD) Prince Edward–Hastings, Ontario
Martin, Keith (RP/PR) Esquimalt–Juan de Fuca, B.C./C.-B.

Martin, Parise (NDP/NPD) Madawaska–Victoria, N.B./N.-B.
Martin, Paul (Lib.) LaSalle–Émard, Montreal
Martin, Robert (Abol.) Trinity–Spadina, Toronto
Martin, Ross C. (NDP/NPD) Brandon–Souris, Manitoba
Martinez, Sergio (NDP/NPD) Longueuil, Quebec
Marwick, Stuart (Nat.) Bruce–Grey, Ontario
Mascall, Michael (GP/PV) North Island–Powell River, B.C./C.-B.
Mason, Louis E. (RP/PR) South West Nova, N.S./N.-E.
Massand, D. Le Sheik (Nil) Verdun–Saint-Paul, Montreal
Massé, Marcel (Lib.) Hull–Aylmer, Quebec
Mate, John (NDP/NPD) Vancouver South/Vancouver-Sud, B.C./C.-B.
Matheson, Joel (PC/P-C) Halifax West/Halifax Ouest, N.S./N.-E.
Mathewson, Paul (RP/PR) Sault Ste Marie, Ontario
Matiowsky, Rebecca (GP/PV) Calgary Centre/Calgary-Centre, Alberta (Female)
Matté, Rene (Nil) Portneuf, Quebec
Matthews, Ken (NLP/PLN) Mount Royal/Mont-Royal, Montreal
Matthiasson, Anne (RP/PR) South Shore, N.S./N.-E. (Female)
Mavrow, Cecilia (Nat.) Victoria, B.C./C.-B. (Female)
Maxim, James (Lib.) Calgary North/Calgary-Nord, Alberta
Maxwell, John E. (Ind.) Bramalea–Gore–Malton, Ontario
Mayer, Charlie (P.C./P. C.) Lisgar–Marquette, Manitoba
Mayer, Robert (NLP/PLN) Hull–Aylmer, Quebec
Mayfield, Philip William (RP/PR) Cariboo–Chilcotin, B.C./C.-B.
Mazerolle, Denis A. (Abol.) Scarborough Centre/Scarborough-Centre, Toronto
Mazerolle, Michael (Abol.) Don Valley East/Don Valley-Est, Toronto
McAdam, Sean (RP/PR) Kingston and the Islands/Kingston et les Îles, Ontario
McArthur, Bill (RP/PR) Vancouver Quadra, B.C./C.-B.
McBain, Bill (NDP/NPD) Cambridge, Ontario
McBride, Anne C. (Ind.) Scarborough–Agincourt, Toronto (Female)
McBurney, John Bruce (GP/PV) Niagara Falls, Ontario
McCabe, Michael (Abol.) Etobicoke–Lakeshore, Toronto
McCall, Rick (NDP/NPD) Hamilton–Wentworth, Ontario
McCallum, Robert (Ind.) Calgary North/Calgary-Nord, Alberta
McCann, Peter (PC/P-C) Saskatoon–Clark's Crossing, Saskatchewan
McCarthy, Don (NLP/PLN) Esquimalt–Juan de Fuca, B.C./C.-B.
McClelland Ian (RP/PR) Edmonton Southwest/Edmonton-Sud-Ouest, Alberta
McClement, Kathy (NLP/PLN) Richmond, B.C./C.-B. (Female)
McCooey, Mark (NLP/PLN) Kamloops, B.C./C.-B.
McCormick, April I. (Nil) Kenora–Rainy River, Ontario (Female)
McCormick, Larry (Lib.) Hastings–Frontenac–Lennox and Addington, Ontario
McCracken, Sam (RP/PR) Glengarry–Prescott–Russell, Ontario
McCreary, Catherine (NDP/NPD) Calgary Centre/Calgary-Centre, Alberta (Female)
McCreath, Peter L. (PC/P-C) South Shore, N.S./N. E.
McCurdy, Howard (NDP/NPD) Windsor–St Clair/Windsor–Sainte-Claire, Ontario
McDonald, Ernie (RP/PR) Brampton, Ontario
McDonald, Lynn (NDP/NPD) Broadview–Greenwood, Toronto (Female)
McGee, John William (Lib.) Lethbridge, Alberta
McGuire, Joe (Lib.) Egmont, P.E.I./Î.-P.-E
McInnis, Jake (PC/P-C) Kootenay East/Kootenay Est, B.C./C.-B.

McIntosh, Jim (Libert.) Scarborough East/Scarborough-Est, Toronto
McIver, Bryan (NDP/NPD) Okanagan Centre/Okanagan-Centre, B.C./C.-B.
McKellar, Therese (PC/P-C) Carleton–Gloucester, Ontario (Female)
McKenzie, Jewel (Abol.) Willowdale, Toronto (Female)
McKiel, Dan (RP/PR) Fundy–Royal, N.B./N.-B.
McKinnon, Glen (Lib.) Brandon–Souris, Manitoba
McKinnon, Ross (Lib.) Esquimalt–Juan de Fuca, B.C./C.-B.
McKoy, Robert (NDP/NPD) Matapédia–Matane, Quebec
Mc Laren Karen (NDP/NPD) Red Deer, Alberta (Female)
McLaughlin, Audrey (NDP/NPD) Yukon, Y.T./T.Y. (Female)
McLean, Steve (CHP/PHC) Cumberland–Colchester, N.S./N. E.
McLeod, Charles (RP/PR) Etobicoke Centre/Etobicoke-Centre, Toronto
McLeod, Ray (Nat.) Calgary Northeast/Calgary-Nord-Est, Alberta
McLellan, Anne (Lib.) Edmonton Northwest/Edmonton-Nord-Ouest, Alberta (Female)
McMartin, Will (PC/P-C) North Vancouver, B.C./C.-B.
McMenemy, Rob (Nat.) Ontario, Ontario
McMillan, Tom (PC/P-C) Hillsborough, P.E.I./Î.-P.-E.
McNeil, Kathleen (Nat.) Calgary West/Calgary-Ouest, Alberta (Female)
McPherson, J.J. (Nat.) Verdun–Saint-Paul, Montreal
McQuail, Tony (NDP/NPD) Huron–Bruce, Ontario
McSkimmings, Judie (NDP/NPD) Lanark–Carleton, Ontario (Female)
McSween, Marie Andrée (PC/P-C) Beauharnois–Salaberry, Quebec (Female)
McTeague, Dan (Lib.) Ontario, Ontario
McWhinney, Ted (Lib.) Vancouver Quadra, B.C./C.-B.
Meadowcroft, Keith (Nil) Beaches–Woodbine, Toronto
Meagher, J. Paul (RP/PR) Prince Albert–Churchill River/Prince-Albert–Churchill River, Saskatchewan
Medjedovic, Ljiljana (Abol.) York West/York-Ouest, Toronto (Female)
Mehling, Peter Ewart (GP/PV) Skeena, B.C./C.-B.
Meindl, Poldi (Ind.) Burnaby–Kingsway, B.C./C.-B.
Melvin, Wayne A. (NLP/PLN) North Island–Powell River, B.C./C.-B.
Ménard, Réal (BQ) Hochelaga–Maisonneuve, Montreal
Mercier, Paul (BQ) Blainville–Deux-Montagnes, Quebec
Meredith, Val (RP/PR) Surrey–White Rock–South Langley, B.C./C.-B. (Female)
Merriam, John (RP/PR) Annapolis Valley–Hants, N.S./N.-E.
Merritt, Jim (PC/P-C) Lincoln, Ontario
Meschino, Mark (Libert.) Don Valley East/Don Valley-Est, Toronto
Methot, Ann-Marie (Com'lth/Rep./Rep./Com'lth) Oshawa, Ontario (Female)
Meyers, Frank (RP/PR) Broadview–Greenwood, Toronto
Michaelchuk, Dennis Ronald (NLP/PLN) Yellowhead, Alberta
Michaels, Stephanie (NDP/NPD) Edmonton Northwest/Edmonton-Nord-Ouest, Alberta (Female)
Michalchuk, Glenn (M.-L.) Winnipeg St James, Manitoba
Michalos, Alex (NDP/NPD) Guelph–Wellington, Ontario
Middlebrook, Joyce (PC/P-C) Prince Albert–Churchill River/Prince-Albert–Churchill River, Saskatchewan (Female)
Mifflin, Fred J. (Lib.) Bonavista–Trinity–Conception, Nfld/T.-N.
Miki, Art (Lib.) Winnipeg Transcona, Manitoba
Milkovich, Mike (Com'lth/Rep./Rep./Com'lth) Burnaby–Kingsway, B.C./C.-B.
Millard, Aubrey (RP/PR) Scarborough West/Scarborough-Ouest, Toronto
Miller, David (NDP/NPD) Parkdale–High Park, Toronto

Milliken, Peter (Lib.) Kingston and the Islands/Kingston et les Îles, Ontario
Millman, Isabel (NLP/PLN) Hamilton Mountain, Ontario (Female)
Mills, Avard (NLP/PLN) Cape Breton–The Sydneys/Cap-Breton–The Sydneys, N.S./N.-E.
Mills, Bob (RP/PR) Red Deer, Alberta
Mills, Dennis (Lib.) Broadview–Greenwood, Toronto
Mills, George G. (RP/PR) Hamilton West/Hamilton-Ouest, Ontario
Minna, Maria (Lib.) Beaches–Woodbine, Toronto (Female)
Mitchell, Andy (Lib.) Parry Sound–Muskoka, Ontario
Mitchell, David W. (NLP/PLN) Guelph–Wellington, Ontario
Mitchell, Margaret (NDP/NPD) Vancouver East/Vancouver-Est, B.C./C.-B. (Female)
Mitchell, Stéphanie (NDP/NPD) Québec-Est, Quebec (Female)
Mitchell, Thomas (NLP/PLN) Cambridge, Ontario
Mitton, Frantz-Albert (Com'lth/Rep./Rep./Com'lth) Anjou–Rivière-des-Prairies, Montreal
Mitzak, Marsha (NDP/NPD) Simcoe North/Simcoe-Nord, Ontario (Female)
Mix, Ron (RP/PR) Edmonton North/Edmonton-Nord, Alberta
Mockford, Steve (Nat.) Annapolis Valley–Hants, N.S./N.-E.
Mohamed, Gulam (Ind.) Scarborough–Rouge River, Toronto
Mohr, John (RP/PR) Oxford, Ontario
Monaco, Lee (PC/P-C) Trinity–Spadina, Toronto (Female)
Moniatowicz, Stephanie (NLP/PLN) Windsor–St Clair/Windsor–Sainte-Claire, Ontario (Female)
Monlezun, Jacques (Lib.) Prince George–Peace River, B.C./C.-B.
Monson, Dale L. (NLP/PLN) Saskatoon–Humboldt, Saskatchewan
Monson, Marc (PC/P-C) Eglinton–Lawrence, Toronto
Monteith, Ken (PC/P-C) Elgin–Norfolk, Ontario
Montpetit, Pierre (NLP/PLN) La Prairie, Quebec
Moore, Barry (P.C./P.C.) Pontiac–Gatineau–Labelle, Quebec
Moore, Christine (NDP/NPD) Chicoutimi, Quebec (Female)
Moore, George (Ind.) Oxford, Ontario
Morgan, Karen (Lib.) Delta, B.C./C.-B. (Female)
Morgan, Owen (Nat.) Hamilton West/Harnilton-Ouest, Ontario
Moriarty, Cindy (NDP/NPD) Carleton–Gloucester, Ontario (Female)
Morin, Jean (PC/P-C) Rimouski–Témiscouata, Quebec
Morningstar, Ken (Nil) Lincoln, Ontario
Morris, Gerard (NLP/PLN) Ontario, Ontario
Morris, John (Lib.) Moose Jaw–Lake Centre, Saskatchewan
Morris, John (NDP/NPD) Brampton, Ontario
Morrison, Bill (NLP/PLN) Scarborough–Agincourt, Toronto
Morrison, Lee (RP/PR) Swift Current–Maple Creek–Assiniboia, Saskatchewan
Morrissette, Pauline G. (Abol.) Ottawa Centre/Ottawa-Centre, Ontario (Female)
Morrow, Valerie (Nil) Vegreville/Végréville, Alberta (Female)
Morton, Alfred (Abol.) Scarborough West/Scarborough-Ouest, Toronto
Morton, Donna (GP/PV) Victoria, B.C./C.-B. (Female)
Morton, Peggy (M-L) Edmonton Southwest/Edmonton-Sud-Ouest, Alberta (Female)
Moss, David (NDP/NPD) Stormont–Dundas, Ontario
Mullins, Mark (RP/PR) Hamilton–Wentworth, Ontario
Mulvale, Ann (P.C./P.-C.) Oakville–Milton, Ontario (Female)
Munday, Marion (CP) Kamloops, B.C./C.-B. (Female)
Munro, Ian (PC/P-C) Nickel Belt, Ontario
Munro Parry, Nancy (PC/P-C) Ottawa West/Ottawa-Ouest, Ontario (Female)

Murphy, Everett (NLP/PLN) Etobicoke Centre/Etobicoke-Centre, Toronto
Murphy, Gregg (NLP/PLN) South West Nova, N.S./N.-E.
Murphy, John (Lib.) Annapolis Valley Hants, N.S./N.-E.
Murphy, John (PC/P-C) Timmins–Chapleau, Ontario
Murphy, Peter (PC/P-C) Miramichi, N.B./N.-B.
Murphy, Rod (NDP/NPD) Churchill, Manitoba
Murray, Ian (Lib.) Lanark–Carleton, Ontario
Murray, Janice (M-L) Etobicoke Centre/Etobicoke-Centre, Toronto (Female)
Musson, Jim (Nat.) Edmonton East/Edmonton Est, Alberta
Nadeau, Derek (NLP/PLN) Surrey–White Rock–South Langley, B.C./C.-B.
Nadeau, Jean–Claude (PC/P-C) Frontenac, Quebec
Nadeau, Michel (NLP/PLN) Louis-Hébert, Quebec
Naegel, Harry (GP/PV) Okanagan–Similkameen–Merritt, B.C./C.-B.
Nagle, Conan (Nil) Fraser Valley West/Fraser Valley-Ouest, B.C./C.-B.
Naud, Réal (PC/P-C) Berthier–Montcalm, Quebec
Nault, Robert D. (Lib.) Kenora–Rainy River, Ontario
Naylor, Eugene (Lib.) Mégantic–Compton–Stanstead, Quebec
Naylor, Karen (Nil) Winnipeg South Centre/Winnipeg-Sud-Centre, Manitoba (Female)
Neufeld, Abe (CHP/PHC) Brandon–Souris, Manitoba
Newby, Lester (NLP/PLN) Essex–Kent, Ontario
Newby, Maxim (NLP/PLN) Brampton, Ontario
Newman, Jim (RP/PR) Parry Sound–Muskoka, Ontario
New-Small, Alannah (GP/PV) Vancouver Quadra, B.C./C.-B. (Female)
Ng, Alex En Hwa (NDP/NPD) Rimouski–Témiscouata, Quebec
Ng, Paul (PC/P-C) Scarborough–Rouge River, Toronto
Ng, Winnie (NDP/NPD) Trinity–Spadina, Toronto (Female)
Nguyen, Quoi (Lib.) Calgary Southeast/Calgary-Sud-Est, Alberta
Nicholson, Rob (PC/P-C) Niagara Falls, Ontario
Nigro, Carlo (Libert.) Burnaby–Kingsway, B.C./C.-B.
Noble, Ken (Nat.) Okanagan–Similkameen–Merritt, B.C./C.-B.
Noel, Leona (Nat.) Northumberland, Ontario (Female)
Norcross, Norm (GP/PV) Calgary Northeast/Calgary-Nord-Est, Alberta
Nord, Bruce (Nat.) Scarborough–Agincourt, Toronto
Nordin, Barry Lorne (Lib.) Cariboo–Chilcotin, B.C./C.-B.
Nori, Gerry (PC/P-C) Sault Ste Marie, Ontario
Normandeau, Normand (Com'lth/Rep./Rep./Com'lth) Papineau–Saint-Michel, Montreal
Norris, Roy (Lib.) Saskatoon–Clark's Crossing, Saskatchewan
Northrup, Julie (M-L) Etobicoke–Lakeshore, Toronto (Female)
Noseworthy, Mark (NDP/NPD) Burin–St George's/Burin–Saint-Georges, Nfld/T.-N.
Novini, Greg (RP/PR) Windsor–St Clair/Windsor–Sainte-Claire, Ontario
Nowlan, Pat (Ind.) Annapolis Valley–Hants, N.S./N.-E.
Nundal, Donald Lyle (PC/P-C) Fraser Valley West/Fraser Valley-Ouest, B.C./C.-B.
Nunez, Osvaldo (BQ) Bourassa, Montreal
Nunziata, John (Lib.) York South–Weston/York-Sud-Weston, Toronto
Nuthall, Peter (Nil) Vancouver Centre/Vancouver-Centre, B.C./C.-B.
Nystrom, Lorne (NDP/NPD) Yorkton–Melville, Saskatchewan
Obach, Eldon (Nat.) Brandon–Souris, Manitoba
O'Brien, Chris (GP/PV) Western Arctic, N.W.T./T.N. -O.
O'Brien, Pat (Lib.) London–Middlesex, Ontario

O'Dell, Doug (Nil) Lambton–Middlesex, Ontario
O'Donnell, Dorothy Jean (M-L) Vancouver Quadra, B.C./C.-B. (Female)
Offley, Will (Nil) Vancouver East/Vancouver-Est, B.C./C.-B.
O'Keeffe, Stew (PC/P-C) Bruce–Grey, Ontario
O'Kurley, Brian (PC/P-C) Elk Island, Alberta
Olito, Charles (CP) Victoria–Haliburton, Ontario
Olito, Mike (Ind.) Winnipeg South/Winnipeg-Sud, Manitoba
Oliver, Alisen (CP) Esquimalt–Juan de Fuca, B.C./C.-B. (Female)
Ollerenshaw, Stephen (RP/PR) Hastings–Frontenac–Lennox and Addington, Ontario
Olson, Robert L. (Nat.) Yukon, Y.T./T.Y.
O'Neil, Sean (PC/P-C) Calgary Centre/Calgary-Centre, Alberta
Oostrom, John (PC/P-C) Willowdale, Toronto
Opacic, George (Nat.) Essex–Windsor, Ontario
Openshaw, Ronald Edwin (NLP/PLN) Moncton, N.B./N.-B.
Opmeer, Walter (CHP/PHC) Vancouver Quadra, B.C./C.-B.
Opzoomer, René de Cotret (BQ) Pierrefonds–Dollard, Montreal
Organ, Gerry (RP/PR) Guelph–Wellington, Ontario
O'Reilly, John (Lib.) Victoria–Haliburton, Ontario
O'Rourke, Margaret Ann (PC/P-C) Humber–St Barbe–Baie Verte/Humber–Sainte-Barbe–Baie Verte,
    Nfld/T.-N. (Female)
Ottenbreit, Doug (NDP/NPD) Scarborough East/Scarborough-Est, Toronto
Ottrey, Ivor (CHP/PHC) Medicine Hat, Alberta
Ouellet, André (Lib.) Papineau—Saint-Michel, Montreal
Ouellet, Gilbert (BQ) Notre-Dame-de-Grâce, Montreal
Owen, Ted (Nat.) Perth–Wellington–Waterloo, Ontario
Owens, Hugh (CHP/PHC) Regina–Wascana, Saskatchewan
Pabbies, Prince (NLP/PLN) Vancouver South/Vancouver-Sud, B.C./C.-B.
Pagtakhan, Rey D. (Lib.) Winnipeg North/Winnipeg-Nord, Manitoba
Palmer, Joe (G.P. /P.V.) Ottawa South/Ottawa-Sud, Ontano
Panas, Tony (CP) Mackenzie, Saskatchewan
Panciuk, Mitch (PC/P-C) Edmonton North/Edmonton-Nord, Alberta
Panet-Raymond, Josée (NDP/NPD) Saint-Denis, Montreal (Female)
Paolini, Claudio (NLP/PLN) York West/York-Ouest, Toronto
Papadakis, John (PC/P-C) Broadview–Greenwood, Toronto
Papadopoulos, Chris (Nat.) Kingston and the Islands/Kingston et les Îles, Ontario
Papadopoulos, Dean (Abol.) Markham–Whitchurch Stouffville, Ontario
Papetti, Federico (NLP/PLN) Winnipeg North/Winnipeg-Nord, Manitoba
Papetti, Rose Marie (NLP/PLN) Selkirk Red River, Manitoba (Female)
Paquet, Pierre Paul (NLP/PLN) Québec-Est, Quebec
Paré, Philippe (BQ) Louis-Hébert, Quebec
Parent, Gilbert (Lib.) Welland–St. Catharines–Thorold, Ontario
Parent, Muriel J. (PC/P-C) Cochrane–Superior/Cochrane–Superieur, Ontario (Female)
Parker, Ronald J.D. (NLP/PLN) Ottawa South/Ottawa-Sud, Ontario
Parker, Sid (NDP/NPD) Kootenay East/Kootenay-Est, B.C./C.-B.
Parrish, Carolyn (Lib.) Mississauga West/Mississauga--Ouest, Ontario (Female)
Parsons, Les (Ind.) Vegreville/Végréville, Alberta
Paterson, Neil Laughlin (NLP/PLN) Ottawa Centre/Ottawa-Centre, Ontario
Patriquin, Brian (Nat.) Halton–Peel, Ontario
Patry, Bernard (Lib.) Pierrefonds–Dollard, Montreal

Patterson, Dave (Nat.) Hillsborough, P.E.I./Î.P.–E.
Pawluk, Fred (Nat.) Richmond, B.C./C.-B.
Payne, Brian (PC/P-C) Essex–Windsor, Ontario
Payne, Jean (Lib.) St. John's West/St. John's-Ouest, Nfld/T.-N. (Female)
Paynter, Farlie (CP) Surrey–White Rock–South Langley, B.C./C.-B.
Pearson, Kerry Daniel (Libert.) Richmond, B.C./C.-B.
Peck, Kwangyul (Lib.) Burnaby–Kingsway, B.C./C.-B.
Pederson, Douglas Bruce (Ind.) Yellowhead, Alberta
Peirce, Chris (Lib.) Edmonton–Strathcona, Alberta
Pelchat, Gilles (BQ) Saint-Denis, Montreal
Pelletier, Jean (Lib.) Québec, Quebec
Pelletier, Jean Paul (Lib.) Sherbrooke, Quebec
Péloquin, Gaston (BQ) Brome–Missisquoi, Quebec
Péloquin, Jean Guy (Abol.) Brôme–Missisquoi, Quebec
Péloquin, Marc-Andre (NDP/NPD) Richmond–Wolfe, Quebec
Pendharkar, Murli G. (Lib.) Okanagan Centre/Okanagan-Centre, B.C./C.-B.
Penkala, Nancy (Nat.) Regina–Lumsden, Saskatchewan (Female)
Penner, Lloyd (NDP/NPD) Winnipeg South Centre/Winnipeg-Sud-Centre, Manitoba
Penner, Rudy (CHP/PHC) St Albert/Saint-Albert, Alberta
Penner, Wes (Nat.) Provencher, Manitoba
Pennington, Susan Lylliane (Abol.) Davenport, Ontario (Female)
Pennington, Thomas Earl (Abol.) Parkdale–High Park, Toronto
Penson, Charlie (RP/PR) Peace River, Alberta
Penwarden, Lesley (NDP/NPD) Erie, Ontario (Female)
Pepper, Bob (NLP/PLN) Don Valley West/Don Valley–Ouest, Toronto
Pepper, Marilyn (NLP/PLN) Etobicoke North/Etobicoke-Nord, Toronto (Female)
Perez, Alain (PC/P-C) Saint-Henri–Westmount, Montreal
Perez, Joe Jose (NDP/NPD) Scarborough–Agincourt, Toronto
Peric, Janko (Lib.) Cambridge, Ontario
Perigny, Roger (NLP/PLN) Trois-Rivières, Quebec
Peschisolido, Joe (RP/PR) Etobicoke North/Etobicoke-Nord, Toronto
Peters, Doug (Lib.) Scarborough East/Scarborough-Est, Toronto
Peters, Pat (NDP/NPD) Simcoe Centre/Simcoe-Centre, Ontario (Female)
Petersen, Reg (RP/PR) Cambridge, Ontario
Petersen, Sherwin (PC/P-C) Mackenzie, Saskatchewan
Peterson, Jim (Lib.) Willowdale, Toronto
Peterson, Norma (NDP/NPD) Halton–Peel, Ontario (Female)
Peterson, Peter (PC/P-C) Hamilton West/Hamilton-Ouest, Ontario
Petherbridge, Doug (NDP/NPD) Lethbridge, Alberta
Phelan, Reg (NDP/NPD) Cardigan, P.E.I./Î.-P.-E.
Philips, John (Ind.) Notre-Dame-de-Grâce, Montreal
Phillips, Alan (NLP/PLN) Prince George–Bulkley Valley, B.C./C.-B.
Phillips, Alex (Lib.) Saanich–Gulf Islands/Saanich–Les Îles-du-Golfe, B.C./C.-B.
Phillips, Charles (Nat.) Halifax, N.S./N.-E.
Phillpotts, Joshua (Lib.) Peace River, Alberta
Phinney, Beth (Lib.) Hamilton Mountain, Ontario (Female)
Piatkowski, Scott (NDP/NPD) Waterloo, Ontario
Picard, Michael (CHP/PHC) Cambridge, Ontario
Picard, Pauline (BQ) Drummond, Quebec (Female)

Pickard, Jerry (Lib.) Essex–Kent, Ontario
Pickell, Guy (Nil) Winnipeg St James, Manitoba
Piercey, G. Wayne (PC/P-C) Labrador, Nfld/T.-N.
Piers, Peter (CHP/PHC) Yellowhead, Alberta
Pillitteri, Gary (Lib.) Niagara Falls, Ontario
Pilon, Louise (Nat.) Saint-Henri–Westmount, Montreal (Female)
Pinnell, Edward (RP/PR) Renfrew–Nipissing–Pembroke, Ontario
Pino, Kateri Hellman (Nat.) Saskatoon–Dundurn, Saskatchewan (Female)
Piquette-Bédard, Madelaine (Abol.) Saint-Laurent-Cartierville, Montreal (Female)
Pivato, Paul (RP/PR) York–Simcoe, Ontario
Plamondon, Louis (BQ) Richelieu, Quebec
Plamondon, Paulin (Lib.) Portneuf, Quebec (Female)
Plas, Herman (NDP/NPD) Haldimand–Norfolk, Ontario
Plewak, James (Nil) Winnipeg North Centre/Winnipeg-Nord-Centre, Manitoba
Pliakes, Steve (NDP/NPD) York–Simcoe, Ontario
Plourde, André (PC/P-C) Kamouraska–Rivière-du-Loup, Quebec
Plumb, Al (CP) London East/London-Est, Ontario
Poirier, Francine (NDP/NPD) Saint Laurent–Cartierville, Montreal (Female)
Poirier, Germaine (NDP/NPD) Bonaventure–Îles-de-la-Madeleine, Quebec (Female)
Pokonzie, Ed (Ind.) Sudbury, Ontario
Polansky, Harry (Nil) Mount Royal/Mont-Royal, Montreal
Pollett, Harry (RP/PR) Cape Breton–East Richmond/Cap-Breton–Richmond-Est, N.S./N.-E.
Polonyi, Anna (Nat.) Winnipeg North/Winnipeg-Nord, Manitoba (Female)
Pomerleau, Roger (BQ) Anjou–Rivière-des Prairies, Montreal
Popat, Imtiaz (GP/PV) Vancouver Centre/Vancouver Centre, B.C./C. B.
Pope, Ernie (Nat.) Fraser Valley East/Fraser Valley Est, B.C./C. B.
Pope, John (RP/PR) Scarborough Centre/Scarborough Centre, Toronto
Pope, Julian (RP/PR) Don Valley West/Don Valley Ouest, Toronto
Pope, Rose (Abol.) Windsor West/Windsor Ouest, Ontario (Female)
Pope, W.H. Harry (Nat.) Durham, Ontario
Porter, Richard (GP/PV) Comox–Alberni, B.C./C.-B.
Porter, Stephen R. (NLP/PLN) Markham–Whitchurch–Stouffville, Ontario
Porter, Tom (PC/P-C) Windsor–St. Clair/Windsor–Sainte-Claire, Ontario
Potratz, Richard Arthur (Nil) Prince Albert–Churchill River/Prince-Albert–Churchill River, Saskatchewan
Powers, Steven (Nat.) St. Albert/Saint-Albert, Alberta
Préfontaine, Richard (PC/P-C) Vaudreuil, Montreal
Prendergast, Hugh (RP/PR) Beaches–Woodbine, Toronto
Primeau, Lee (RP/PR) Parkdale–High Park, Toronto
Prins, Bert (CHP/PHC) Prince George–Bulkley Valley, B.C./C.-B.
Proud, George (Lib.) Hillsborough, P.E.I./Î.-P.-E.
Proulx, Luc (NDP/NPD) Châteauguay, Quebec
Provencher, Michael (Lib.) Lotbinière, Quebec
Prust, Steve R. (Libert.) Northumberland, Ontario
Purcell, Sherelanne (Nat.) Davenport, Toronto (Female)
Quaid, Maeve (PC/P-C) Notre-Dame-de-Grâce, Montreal (Female)
Quance, Anthony F. (NLP/PLN) Surrey North/Surrey-Nord, B.C./C.-B.
Quance, Daphne (NLP/PLN) Renfrew–Nipissing–Pembroke, Ontario (Female)
Quesnel, Harold Anthony (Com'lth/Rep./Rep./Com'lth) Bourassa, Montreal
Quigley, Nancie (NDP/NPD) Restigouche–Chaleur, N.B./N.-B. (Female)

Quinn, Douglas (Libert.) York Centre/York-Centre, Toronto
Qureshi, Afsun (NDP/NPD) Laval Centre/Laval-Centre, Montreal (Female)
Radcliffe, Mike (PC/P-C) Winnipeg South Centre/Winnipeg-Sud-Centre, Manitoba
Raddatz, Keith (RP/PR) Kamloops, B.C./C.-B.
Radermaker, Claude (BQ) Pontiac–Gatineau–Labelle, Quebec
Rahn, Bryan John (Nat.) Oxford, Ontario
Ramolla, Hugh (RP/PR) Burlington, Ontario
Ramsay, David (NDP/NPD) Thunder Bay–Nipigon, Ontario
Ramsay, Jack (RP/PR) Crowfoot, Alberta
Ramsay, Mike (Ind.) Simcoe Centre/Simcoe-Centre, Ontario
Rankin, Darrell T. (Nil) Calgary Southwest/Calgary-Sud-Ouest, Alberta
Rankin, Naomi (Nil) Edmonton–Strathcona, Alberta (Female)
Rashid, Mamunor (Com'l/Rep./Rep./Com'lth) Outremont, Montreal
Rassenberg, Rita (NLP/PLN) Hamilton West/Hamilton-Ouest, Ontario (Female)
Ray, Gisèle (Com'l/Rep./Rep./Com'lth) Blainville–Deux-Montagnes, Quebec (Female)
Rayburn, Judith (Nat.) Saanich–Gulf Islands/Saanich–Les Îles-du-Golfe, B.C./C.-B. (Female)
Rayment, Michael (NLP/PLN) St John's East/St John's-Est, Nfld/T.-N.
Raymond, Gilles (NLP/PLN) Anjou–Rivière-des-Prairies, Montreal
Redway, Alan (PC/P-C) Don Valley East/Don Valley-Est, Toronto
Reed, Julian (Lib.) Halton–Peel, Ontario
Reed, Mike (Lib.) Okanagan–Similkameen–Merritt, B.C./C.-B.
Regan, Geoff (Lib.) Halifax West/Halifax-Ouest, N.S./N.-E.
Rege, Udayan (NDP/NPD) Etobicoke Centre/Etobicoke-Centre, Toronto
Reid, André (Lib.) Rimouski–Témiscouata, Quebec
Reid, Clifford (NDP/NPD) Wetaskiwin, Alberta
Reid, Murray (Abol.) Renfrew–Nipissing–Pembroke, Ontario
Reid, Paul (Nat.) Winnipeg St James, Manitoba
Reid, Ross (PC/P-C) St John's East/St John's-Est, Nfld/T.-N.
Reimer, John (PC/P-C) Kitchener, Ontario
Reitenbach, Bob (PC/P-C) Yorkton–Melville, Saskatchewan
Renaud, Marie-France (NDP/NPD) Lévis, Quebec (Female)
Renaud, Michel (Lib.) Charlesbourg, Quebec
Rendell, Michael (NLP/PLN) Burin–St George's/Burin–Saint-Georges, Nfld/T.-N.
Rennie, Donald Stuart (GP/PV) Cariboo–Chilcotin, B.C./C.-B.
Reynolds, Bob (RP/PR) Thunder Bay–Nipigon, Ontario
Rhiness, Brian (PC/P-C) Wetaskiwin, Alberta
Ricard, Guy (PC/P-C) Laval West/Laval-Ouest, Montreal
Rice, Dennis (Libert.) Portage–Interlake, Manitoba
Richards, Bill (Lib.) Calgary Southwest/Calgary-Sud-Ouest, Alberta
Richards, Merv (NDP/NPD) Peterborough, Ontario
Richardson, Christine M. (Abol.) Leeds–Grenville, Ontario (Female)
Richardson, E. Chum (Ind.) Mission–Coquitlam, B.C./C.-B.
Richardson, John (Lib.) Perth–Wellington–Waterloo, Ontario
Richardson, Lee (PC/P-C) Calgary Southeast/Calgary-Sud-Est, Alberta
Richardson, Sheila (NDP/NPD) Halifax West/Halifax-Ouest, N.S./N.-E. (Female)
Richmond, Ken (NDP/NPD) Calgary Northeast/Calgary-Nord-Est, Alberta
Rideout, George S. (Lib.) Moncton, N.B./N.-B.
Rideout, Tom G. (PC/P-C) Gander–Grand Falls, Nfld/T.-N.
Rideout-Erais, Catherine J. (NDP/NPD) Pierrefonds–Dollard, Montreal (Female)

Ridgeway, David (Nat.) Peace River, Alberta
Ridley, Karen (NDP/NPD) Etobicoke–Lakeshore, Toronto (Female)
Riendeau, Hélène (Lib.) Saint-Hyacinthe–Bagot, Quebec (Female)
Riley, Tony (CP) Dauphin–Swan River, Manitoba
Rimek, Steve (Ind.) Halifax, N.S./N.-E.
Ringma, Bob (RP/PR) Nanaimo–Cowichan/Nanaimo–Cowichan, B.C./C.-B.
Ringuette-Maltais, Pierrette (Lib.) Madawaska–Victoria, N.B./N.-B.(Female)
Rioux, Jean-Paul (NDP/NPD) Blainville–Deux-Montagnes, Quebec
Riis, Nelson (NDP/NPD) Kamloops, B.C./C.-B.
Robbins, Bill (Nat.) Erie, Ontario
Robert, Ginette (NLP/PLN) St Boniface/Saint-Boniface, Manitoba (Female)
Roberts, Britt (NLP/PLN) Lanark–Carleton, Ontario
Roberts, Greg W. (NLP/PLN) York South–Weston/York-Sud–Weston, Toronto
Roberts, Ian (NLP/PLN) York–Simcoe, Ontario
Roberts, Robert (NLP/PLN) Brandon–Souris, Manitoba
Robertson, Heather (M-L) York South–Weston/York-Sud–Weston, Toronto (Female)
Robertson, Linda (RP/PR) Edmonton East/Edmonton-Est, Alberta (Female)
Robertson, Richard (NLP/PLN) South Shore, N.S./N.-E.
Robichaud, Fernand (Lib.) Beauséjour, N.B./N.-B.
Robins, Ron (NLP/PLN) Scarborough West/Scarborough-Ouest, Toronto
Robinson, Michael (Abol.) Lachine–Lac-Saint-Louis, Montreal
Robinson, Svend J. (NDP/NPD) Burnaby–Kingsway, B.C./C.-B.
Robitaille, André-Pierre (NDP/NPD) Lotbinière, Quebec
Robitaille, Jean-Marc (PC/P-C) Terrebonne, Quebec
Rocan, Roger (Ind.) Victoria, B.C./C.-B.
Rochefort, Nathalie (NDP/NPD) Saint-Hubert, Quebec (Female)
Rocheleau, Gilles (BQ) Hull–Aylmer, Quebec
Rocheleau, Michel (M-L) Outremont, Montreal
Rocheleau, Yves (BQ) Trois-Rivières, Quebec
Rochette, Gilles (NLP/PLN) Beauport–Montmorency–Orléans, Quebec
Rock, Allan (Lib.) Etobicoke Centre/Etobicoke-Centre, Toronto
Rodriguez, John (NDP/NPD) Nickel Belt, Ontario
Roess, Henry A. (Nat.) Sault Ste Marie, Ontario
Rogers, Rudy (NDP/NPD) Calgary West/Calgary-Ouest, Alberta
Roldan, Carlos (Nat.) Pierrefonds–Dollard, Montreal
Rolind, Arleigh (CP) Saanich–Gulf Islands/Saanich–Les Îles-du-Golfe, B.C./C.B. (Female)
Romain, Eugenia (BQ) Saint-Henri–Westmount, Montreal (Female)
Romaine, Todd E. (GP/PV) New Westminster–Burnaby, B.C./C.-B.
Rompkey, Bill (Lib.) Labrador, Nfld/T.-N.
Rompré, Claude (BQ) Saint-Maurice, Quebec
Roper, Mark Edward Anderson (Nil) Saint-Henri–Westmount, Montreal
Rose, Catherine (NDP/NPD) Calgary Southwest/Calgary-Sud-Ouest, Alberta (Female)
Ross, Jack (GP/PV) Kootenay West–Revelstoke/Kootenay-Ouest–Revelstoke, B.C./C.-B.
Ross, Ken (NDP/NPD) Edmonton Southeast/Edmonton-Sud-Est, Alberta
Ross, Lois (NDP/NPD) Swift Current–Maple Creek–Assiniboia, Saskatchewan (Female)
Ross, Robert Walter (Nil) Vancouver South/Vancouver-Sud, B.C./C.-B.
Ross, Wilmot F. (CP) Miramichi, N.B./N.-B.
Roussel, Gilles (NLP/PLN) Rimouski–Témiscouata, Quebec
Routhier, Yvan (PC/P-C) Laurier–Sainte-Marie, Montreal

Rowe, Barbara (Libert.) Lanark–Carleton, Ontario (Female)
Rowe, Harold (Nat.) Kenora–Rainy River, Ontario
Rowe, Hugh (Libert.) Pierrefonds–Dollard, Montreal
Rowley, Elizabeth (Nil) Broadview–Greenwood, Toronto (Female)
Roy, Françoise (M-L) Hull–Aylmer, Quebec (Female)
Roy, Gilles (NLP/PLN) Joliette, Quebec
Roy, Marc (NLP/PLN) Rosemont, Montreal
Roy, Michèle (NLP/PLN) Kootenay West–Revelstoke/Kootenay-Ouest–Revelstoke, B.C./C.-B. (Female)
Roy, Richard (GP/PV) Parkdale–High Park, Toronto
Roy-Arcelin, Nicole (PC/P-C) Ahuntsic, Montreal (Female)
Royer, Aurell (RP/PR) Edmonton Southeast/Edmonton-Sud-Est, Alberta
Royer, Robert (NLP/PLN) Portneuf, Quebec
Rubacha, Jacques (Nat.) Lanark–Carleton, Ontario
Rubin, Deborah (NLP/PLN) Burnaby–Kingsway, B.C./C.-B. (Female)
Runkle, John (NLP/PLN) Annapolis Valley–Hants, N.S./N.-E.
Russell, Lea (Nat.) Calgary Southwest/Calgary-Sud-Ouest, Alberta (Female)
Rutchinski, Steve (M-L) Rosedale, Ontario
Rybka Becker, Lucy (NDP/NPD) Durham, Ontario (Female)
Saada, Jacques (Lib.) La Prairie, Quebec
Sackville, Cathie (Nil) Port Moody–Coquitlam, B.C./C.-B. (Female)
Saint-Pierre, Michel (BQ) Bonaventure–Îles-de-la-Madeleine, Quebec
Salmi, Brian Godzilla Gnu (Nil) Vancouver Centre/Vancouver-Centre, B.C./C.-B.
Salsberg, Tom (GP/PV) Willowdale, Toronto
Salvaterra, Sil (NDP/NPD) York South–Weston/York-Sud–Weston, Toronto
Sams, Delton (Lib.) Gaspé, Quebec
Samson, Camil (Lib.) Québec-Est, Quebec
Samson, Cid (NDP/NPD) Timmins–Chapleau, Ontario
Samson, René (NDP/NPD) Ahuntsic, Montreal
Samuel, Margaret (PC/P-C) Davenport, Toronto (Female)
Samuels, Raymond (Nat.) Ottawa–Vanier, Ontario
Sandberg, Bryan (Nil) Saskatoon–Humboldt, Saskatchewan
Sandberg, J. S. Jack (PC/P-C) Kindersley–Lloydminster, Saskatchewan
Sandford, Darryl (Lib.) Crowfoot, Alberta
Sandhu, Ted (PC/P-C) Prince George–Peace River, B.C./C.-B.
Sanfacon, Guy (Nat.) Québec-Est, Quebec
Sanna, Marielle (NDP/NPD) Shefford, Quebec (Female)
Sargent, Kaye (Libert.) Oxford, Ontario (Female)
Sasso, Carmela (NDP/NPD) Etobicoke North/Etobicoke-Nord, Toronto (Female)
Saunders, Les (RP/PR) Scarborough–Rouge River, Toronto
Sauvageau, Benoît (BQ) Terrebonne, Quebec
Savard, Gilles (Lib.) Jonquière, Quebec
Sawatsky, Don (RP/PR) Portage–Interlake, Manitoba
Saxon, Caroline (NDP/NPD) Souris–Moose Mountain, Saskatchewan (Female)
Scarff, Terry (NLP/PLN) Fraser Valley West/Fraser Valley Ouest, B.C./C.-B.
Scalzo, Rudolph (Ind.) Saint-Henri–Westmount, Montreal
Schell, Ed (GP/PV) Edmonton Southeast/Edmonton-Sud-Est, Alberta
Schenstead, Eric Eugene (RP/PR) Saskatoon–Dundurn, Saskatchewan
Schiebel, Pat (CHP/PHC) Kitchener, Ontario (Female)
Schilling, Jean (Nat.) Scarborough Centre/Scarborough-Centre, Toronto (Female)

Schioler, Dave (PC/P-C) Winnipeg St. James, Manitoba
Schmidt, Werner (RP/PR) Okanagan Centre/Okanagan-Centre, B.C./C.-B.
Schneider, Larry (PC/P-C) Regina–Wascana, Saskatchewan
Schram, Bill (NDP/NPD) Western Arctic, N.W.T./T.N.-O.
Schreyer, Jason E. (NDP/NPD) Selkirk–Red River, Manitoba
Schubert, Mike (Nat.) Calgary North/Calgary-Nord, Alberta
Schwartz, Gary (NLP/PLN) Portage–Interlake, Manitoba
Scott, Andy (Lib.) Fredericton–York-Sunbury, N.B./N.-B.
Scott, Bill (PC/P-C) Guelph–Wellington, Ontario
Scott, Harvey A. (GP/PV) Athabasca, Alberta
Scott, Mike (RP/PR) Skeena, B.C./C.-B.
Scott, Robert (CHP/PHC) Winnipeg Transcona, Manitoba
Seed, Barbara (M-L) Davenport, Toronto (Female)
Seed, Tony (M-L) Halifax, N.S./N.-E.
Segal, Sharon (M-L) St Boniface/Saint-Boniface, Manitoba (Female)
Séguin, Edmond (Nat.) Brome–Missisquoi, Quebec
Sehgal, Arun D. (CP) London–Middlesex, Ontario
Senécal, Johanne (PC/P-C) LaSalle–Émard, Montreal (Female)
Serre, Ben (Lib.) Timiskaming–French River, Ontario
Setrakov, Judy (Lib.) Kindersley–Lloydminster, Saskatchewan (Female)
Settee, Charles (Nat.) Churchill, Manitoba
Shah, Kamal (Com'l/Rep./Rep./Com'lth) Ottawa West/Ottawa-Ouest, Ontario
Shapka, Maury (NLP/PLN) Edmonton–Strathcona, Alberta
Shapka, Roger (NLP/PLN) Athabasca, Alberta
Shapka, Roni (NLP/PLN) Peace River, Alberta (Female)
Shaw, Bill (Nil) Lachine–Lac-Saint-Louis, Montreal
Shaw, David (NLP/PLN) Sudbury, Ontario
Shelford, Richard (NLP/PLN) Edmonton Southeast/Edmonton-Sud-Est, Alberta
Shelley, Richard (Nat.) Carleton–Charlotte, N.B./N.-B.
Shellnut, Roy (Lib.) Wild Rose, Alberta
Shelton, Deborah (NLP/PLN) Winnipeg North Centre/Winnipeg-Nord-Centre, Manitoba (Female)
Shepherd, Alex (Lib.) Durham, Ontario
Sheridan, Danny (PC/P-C) Skeena, B.C./C.-B.
Sheridan, Georgette (Lib.) Saskatoon–Humboldt, Saskatchewan (Female)
Sherren, Joe (RP/PR) Markham–Whitchurch–Stouffville, Ontario
Shields, Jack (PC/P-C) Athabasca, Alberta
Shields, Mike (Nat.) Mission–Coquitlam, B.C./C.-B.
Shire, Donna (NDP/NPD) Regina–Wascana, Saskatchewan (Female)
Shiroka, Alexander (Com'lth/Rep./Rep./Com'lth) Notre-Dame-de-Grâce, Montreal
Shirreff, George (Nat.) Ottawa South/Ottawa-Sud, Ontario
Shreeve, Gordon (RP/PR) Vancouver South/Vancouver Sud, B.C./C.-B.
Siddiqui, Nizam (NDP/NPD) Nepean, Ontario
Siddon, Tom (PC/P-C) Richmond, B.C./C.-B.
Sigda, Walter P. (CP) Regina–Wascana, Saskatchewan
Silcox, Earl (PC/P-C) Souris–Moose Mountain, Saskatchewan
Silye, Jim (RP/PR) Calgary Centre/Calgary-Centre, Alberta
Sim, Barbara A. (Nat.) Broadview–Greenwood, Toronto (Female)
Simard, Christian (NLP/PLN) Saint-Maurice, Quebec
Simard, Martine (NDP/NPD) Mégantic–Compton–Stanstead, Quebec (Female)

Simmons, Roger (Lib.) Burin–St George's/Burin–Saint Georges, Nfld/T.-N.
Simon, Éric E. (NLP/PLN) Vaudreuil, Montreal
Simon, Paul (NDP/NPD) Mississauga West/Mississauga-Ouest, Ontario
Simpson, Mark (RP/PR) London–Middlesex, Ontario
Simpson, Pat (NLP/PLN) Edmonton Southwest/Edmonton-Sud-Ouest, Alberta
Sinclair, Heather (RP/PR) York North/York-Nord, Ontario (Female)
Sinclair, Norm (NLP/PLN) Hamilton–Wentworth, Ontario
Sinclair, Reina (Lib.) Regina–Qu'Appelle, Saskatchewan (Female)
Singh, Gurdev (M-L) Mississauga West/Mississauga-Ouest, Ontario
Singh, Roopnarine (Nat.) Saint-Laurent–Cartierville, Montreal
Singleton, Hal (Lib.) Fraser Valley East/Fraser Valley-Est, B.C./C.-B.
Sirrs, Doug (Lib.) Wetaskiwin, Alberta
Skelly, Bob (NDP/NPD) Comox–Alberni, B.C./C.-B.
Skelly, Raymond (NDP/NPD) North Island–Powell River, B.C./C.-B.
Skinner, Brett (RP/PR) Windsor West/Windsor Ouest, Ontario
Skoke, Roseanne (Lib.) Central Nova, N.S./N.-E. (Female)
Slobodzian, Jim (Nat.) Selkirk–Red River, Manitoba
Smith, Clancy (Libert.) Winnipeg South Centre/Winnipeg-Sud-Centre, Manitoba
Smith, Elizabeth (Com'lth/Rep./Rep./Com'lth) Port Moody–Coquitlam, B.C./C.-B. (Female)
Smith, Michael C. (NDP/NPD) Brant, Ontario
Smith, Mike (RP/PR) Sudbury, Ontario
Smith, Neale (NDP/NPD) Calgary Southeast/Calgary-Sud-Est, Alberta
Smith, Owen (Ind.) Willowdale, Toronto
Smith, Reg (RP/PR) Winnipeg North Centre/Winnipeg-Nord-Centre, Manitoba
Smith, Rhonda (GP/PV) Kootenay East/Kootenay-Est, B.C./C.-B. (Female)
Smith, Warren (GP/PV) Macleod, Alberta
Smuda, Guenther Heinrich (CP) Comox–Alberni, B.C./C.-B.
Smyth, Ian (RP/PR) Durham, Ontario
Snow, Gerard (NDP/NPD) Moncton, N.B./N.-B.
Snow, Judith A. (Nil) Don Valley West/Don Valley-Ouest, Toronto (Female)
Sobeski, Pat (PC/P-C) Cambridge, Ontario
Sobol, Isaac (Nat.) Skeena, B.C./C.-B.
Soetens, Rene (PC/P-C) Ontario, Ontario
Sojonky, Audrey (Lib.) Capilano–Howe Sound, B.C./C.-B. (Female)
Solberg, Monte (RP/PR) Medicine Hat, Alberta
Solomon, John (NDP/NPD) Regina–Lumsden, Saskatchewan
Somers, France (PC/P-C) Glengarry–Prescott–Russell, Ontario (Female)
Sommer, Bill (Nat.) Hamilton East/Hamilton-Est, Ontario
Soper, Linda (NDP/NPD) Humber–St Barbe–Baie Verte/Humber–Sainte-Barbe–Baie Verte, Nfld/
    T.-N. (Female)
Sparling, William J. (NLP/PLN) Don Valley North/Don Valley-Nord, Toronto
Sparrow, Bobbie (PC/P-C) Calgary Southwest/Calgary-Sud-Ouest, Alberta (Female)
Spat, W.J. Willy (Nat.) Vancouver Quadra, B.C./C.-B.
Speaker, Ray (RP/PR) Lethbridge, Alberta
Speller, Bob (Lib.) Haldimand–Norfolk, Ontario
Spikings, Kimberly C. (RP/PR) Madawaska–Victoria N.B./N.-B. (Female)
Sproule, Brian (M-L) Vancouver East/Vancouver-Est, B.C./C.-B.
Square-Briggs, John Edgar (Nil) Richmond, B.C./C.-B.
Stackhouse, Reg (PC/P-C) Scarborough West/Scarborough-Ouest, Toronto

St. Amand, Terry (PC/P-C) Welland–St Catharines–Thorold, Ontario
Stanley, Mary (Nil) Winnipeg North/Winnipeg-Nord, Manitoba (Female)
Stanton, Colleen (Nil) Saskatoon–Dundurn, Saskatchewan (Female)
Staples, Audrey (RP/PR) Cumberland–Colchester, N.S./N.-E. (Female)
Staples, Garth E. (PC/P-C) Malpeque/Malpèque, P.E.I./Î.-P.-E.
Start, Julie (Abol.) Ottawa West/Ottawa-Ouest, Ontario (Female)
St. Denis, Brent (Lib.) Algoma, Ontario
Steckle, Paul (Lib.) Huron–Bruce, Ontario
Stecyk, Marilyn (PC/P-C) Yellowhead, Alberta (Female)
Steedman, Eric Wilson (NDP/NPD) Gaspé, Quebec
Stehmann, Tony (PC/P-C) Thunder Bay–Atikokan, Ontario
Steinhubl, James Keith (Nat.) Elk Island, Alberta
Stelpstra, Doug (Nil) Brant, Ontario
Stenhouse, Rick (Libert.) St Paul's, Toronto
Steptoe, Bill (Ind.) Windsor West/Windsor-Ouest, Ontario
Sterzer, Helen (RP/PR) Winnipeg Transcona, Manitoba (Female)
Stevenson, Milton (PC/P-C) Renfrew–Nipissing–Pembroke, Ontario
Stevenson, Ross (PC/P-C) Durham, Ontario
Stewart, Basil L. (PC/P-C) Egmont, P.E.I./Î.-P.-E.
Stewart, Brian (Nat.) Simcoe North/Simcoe-Nord, Ontario
Stewart, Christine (Lib.) Northumberland, Ontario (Female)
Stewart, Diana (NDP/NPD) Northumberland, Ontario (Female)
Stewart, James (Nat.) Mégantic–Compton–Stanstead, Quebec
Stewart, Jane (Lib.) Brant, Ontario (Female)
Stewart, Joan (RP/PR) Vancouver East/Vancouver-Est, B.C./C.-B. (Female)
Stewart, John (RP/PR) Hamilton East/Hamilton-Est, Ontario
Stiles, Jeremy (GP/PV) Malpeque/Malpèque, P.E.I./Î.-P.-E.
Stilwell, Bill (CHP/PHC) Surrey North/Surrey-Nord, B.C./C.-B.
Stilwell, Heather (CHP/PHC) Surrey–White Rock–South Langley, B.C./C.-B. (Female)
Stinson, Darrel (RP/PR) Okanagan–Shuswap, B.C./C.-B.
St-Julien, Guy (PC/P-C) Abitibi, Quebec
St-Laurent, Bernard (BQ) Manicouagan, Quebec
Stonier, Shirley Ann (Nat.) Surrey North/Surrey-Nord, B.C./C.-B. (Female)
Stortz, Peggy (GP/PV) Capilano–Howe Sound, B.C./C.-B.(Female)
Strahl, Chuck (RP/PR) Fraser Valley East/Fraser Valley-Est, B.C./C.-B.
Strang, Dave (Nil) Wild Rose, Alberta
Strasser, Heidi (GP/PV) London West/London-Ouest, Ontario (Female)
Streatch, Ken (PC/P-C) Central Nova, N.S./N.-E.
Strikwerda, Hans (CHP/PHC) Oxford, Ontario
Stroo, Faye (CP) Okanagan Centre/Okanagan-Centre, B.C./C.-B. (Female)
Struthers, Stan (NDP/NPD) Dauphin–Swan River, Manitoba
Stupich, David (NDP/NPD) Nanaimo–Cowichan/Nanaimo–Cowichan, B.C./C.-B.
Suffredine, Blair (PC/P-C) Kootenay West–Revelstoke/Kootenay-Ouest–Revelstoke, B.C./C.-B.
Suggitt, Heather (NDP/NPD) Kootenay West–Revelstoke/Kootenay-Ouest–Revelstoke, B.C./C.-B.
   (Female)
Suitor, Tom (PC/P-C) Kent, Ontario
Sullivan, Dagmar (M-L) Mississauga South/Mississauga-Sud, Ontario (Female)
Sullivan, Don (RP/PR) Ontario, Ontario
Sumbal, Iqbal (M-L) Bramalea–Gore–Malton, Ontario

Surette, Sylvia (NDP/NPD) Richmond, B.C./C.-B. (Female)
Swan, Roger (GP/PV) Edmonton Northwest/Edmonton-Nord-Ouest, Alberta
Swartz, Leonard (NDP/NPD) Don Valley West/Don Valley-Ouest, Toronto
Sweck, Andy (RP/PR) Lincoln, Ontario
Switzer, Dave (CHP/PHC) Prince Edward–Hastings, Ontario
Sykes, Leslie G. (CP) Okanagan–Similkameen–Merritt, B.C./C.-B.
Szabo, Paul (Lib.) Mississauga South/Mississauga-Sud, Ontario
Tadros, Magda (Lib.) Mercier, Montreal (Female)
Tait, Andrew (Abol.) Guelph–Wellington, Ontario
Tait, Janice (Nat.) Etobicoke Centre/Etobicoke-Centre, Toronto (Female)
Talbot, David (Ind.) Ottawa–Vanier, Ontario
Tanaka, Alan Y. (PC/P-C) Peace River, Alberta
Tannant, Carson (Nat.) Lethbridge, Alberta
Tannock, Archie (Nil) Prince George–Peace River, B.C./C.-B.
Tao, Tommy (NDP/NPD) Vancouver Quadra, B.C./C.-B.
Tarback, Joel (Libert.) Kitchener, Ontario
Tardif, Monique B. (PC/P-C) Charlesbourg, Quebec (Female)
Tardif-Provencher, Marcella (NDP/NPD) Laval West/Laval-Ouest, Montreal (Female)
Tarleton, Sid (Com'lth/Rep./Rep./Com'lth) London East/London-Est, Ontario
Tataryn, Bill (CP) Winnipeg Transcona, Manitoba
Taves, Ruth Anne (NLP/PLN) Kootenay East/Kootenay-Est, B.C./C.-B. (Female)
Tayler, Carollyne (Nil) Delta, B.C./C. B. (Female)
Taylor, Len (NDP/NPD) The Battlefords-Meadow Lake, Saskatchewan
Taylor, Lynn (NLP/PLN) Western Arctic, N.W.T./T.N.-O. (Female)
Teigeler, Jutta (NDP/NPD) Saint-Jean, Quebec (Female)
Telegdi, Andrew (Lib.) Waterloo, Ontario
Terfry, Dick (NDP/NPD) Annapolis Valley–Hants, N.S./N.-E.
Terrana, Anna (Lib.) Vancouver East/Vancouver-Est, B.C./C.-B. (Female)
Thakore, Sp. (Ind.) Scarborough–Agincourt, Toronto
Thalheimer, Peter (Lib.) Timmins–Chapleau, Ontario
Thauberger, Joseph A. (CP) Regina–Qu'Appelle, Saskatchewan
Theriault, Joseph (M-L) Burnaby–Kingsway, B.C./C.-B.
Thibault, Yvon Joseph (PC/P-C) South West Nova, N.S./N.-E.
Thiessen, Rhonda (Nil) Surrey–White Rock–South Langley, B.C./C.-B. (Female)
Thomas, Elizabeth (NDP/NPD) Kindersley–Lloydminster, Saskatchewan (Female)
Thomas, Steve (NDP/NPD) Scarborough West/Scarborough-Ouest, Toronto
Thompson, Barbara (PC/P-C) St Boniface/Saint-Boniface, Manitoba (Female)
Thompson, Frank (GP/PV) Ottawa Centre/Ottawa-Centre, Ontario
Thompson, Greg (PC/P-C) Carleton–Charlotte, N.B./N.-B.
Thompson, Judy (CHP/PHC) Carleton–Gloucester, Ontario (Female)
Thompson, Myron (RP/PR) Wild Rose, Alberta
Thorkelson, Scott (PC/P-C) Edmonton–Strathcona, Alberta
Thorn, Ian (NDP/NPD) Athabasca, Alberta
Timberlake, Alan (NDP/NPD) Prince George–Peace River, B.C./C.-B.
Tirmizi, Zahid H. (Abol.) Beaches–Woodbine, Toronto
Tisseyre, Michelle (Lib.) Laurentides, Quebec (Female)
To, Dobie (Lib.) Red Deer, Alberta
Tober, Bruce (Nil) Nanaimo–Cowichan/Nanaimo–Cowichan, B.C./C.-B.
Tobin, Brian (Lib.) Humber–St Barbe–Baie Verte/Humber–Sainte-Barbe–Baie Verte, Nfld/T.-N.

Tobin, Lynn (NLP/PLN) Bonavista–Trinity–Conception, Nfld/T.-N. (Female)
Tom, Susan (PC/P-C) Vancouver East/Vancouver-Est, B.C./C.-B.(Female)
Tomassi, Tony (PC/P-C) Saint-Léonard, Montreal
Tomlins, Ann Marie (CHP/PHC) Simcoe Centre/Simcoe-Centre, Ontario (Female)
Tomlinson, Bill (Libert.) Capilano–Howe Sound, B.C./C.-B.
Tompkins, A.B. Short (RP/PR) Yukon, Y.T./T.Y.
Toombs, Bruce (NDP/N.P.D) Notre-Dame-de-Grâce, Montreal
Torres, Jose (NLP/PLN) Saint Laurent–Cartierville, Montreal
Torsney, Paddy (Lib.) Burlington, Ontario (Female)
Tremblay, Benoît (BQ) Rosemont, Montreal
Tremblay, France (M-L) Scarborough Centre/Scarborough-Centre, Toronto (Female)
Tremblay, Hélène (PC/P-C) Chambly, Quebec (Female)
Tremblay, Jean-Sebastien (Com'lth/Rep./Rep./Com'lth) Hamilton East/Hamilton-Est, Ontario
Tremblay, Marcel R. (PC/P-C) Québec-Est, Quebec
Tremblay, Maurice (Lib.) Kamouraska–Rivière-du-Loup, Quebec
Tremblay, Suzanne (BQ) Rimouski–Témiscouata, Quebec (Female)
Tremblett, Bob (CHP/PHC) St John's East/St John's-Est, Nfld/T.-N.
Trépanier, Jean-Guy (Abol.) Sherbrooke, Quebec
Trépanier, Serge (NLP/PLN) Sherbrooke, Quebec
Tromp, John (GP/PV) Laurier–Sainte-Marie, Montreal
Truijen, Eric (CHP/PHC) Selkirk–Red River, Manitoba
Tsiolis, George (PC/P-C) York Centre/York-Centre, Toronto
Turbide, Mario (BQ) Vaudreuil, Montreal
Tucker, Dana (RP/PR) St John's West/St John's-Ouest, Nfld/T.-N. (Female)
Tucker, Len (RP/PR) Ottawa Centre/Ottawa-Centre, Ontario
Turgeon, Yvon (M-L) Mississauga East/Mississauga-Est, Ontario
Turmel, Jean C. (Abol.) Frontenac, Quebec
Turmel, Therese (Abol.) LaSalle–Émard, Montreal (Female)
Turner, Annette (RP/PR) Stormont–Dundas, Ontario (Female)
Turner, Garth (PC/P-C) Halton–Peel, Ontario
Turner, James Peter (CP) North Island–Powell River, B.C./C.-B.
Twose, Mike (Com'lth/Rep./Rep./Com'lth) St Paul's, Toronto
Tylor, Byrun F. (Nil) Burnaby–Kingsway, B.C./C.-B.
Udvarhely, Val (NDP/NPD) Lachine–Lac-Saint-Louis, Montreal
Ulan, Orest (RP/PR) Dartmouth, N.S./N.-E.
Ur, Rose Marie (Lib.) Lambton–Middlesex, Ontario (Female)
Vachon, Andre (M-L) Parkdale–High Park, Toronto
Vachon, Paul (NDP/NPD) Hochelaga–Maisonneuve, Montreal
Vainio, Cathy (NDP/NPD) Victoria–Haliburton, Ontario (Female)
Valaskakis, Kimon (Lib.) Châteauguay, Quebec
Valcourt, Bernard (PC/P-C) Madawaska–Victoria, N.B./N.-B.
Valeri, Tony (Lib.) Lincoln, Ontario
Vallee, Jennifer (Nil) St Albert/Saint-Albert, Alberta (Female)
Vallee, Robert (Nil) Edmonton North/Edmonton-Nord, Alberta
Van Berkel, Henry (RP/PR) Cape Breton Highlands–Canso/Cap-Breton Highlands–Canso, N.S./N.-E.
Vanclief, Lyle (Lib.) Prince Edward–Hastings, Ontario
Van Den Enden, Rien (CHP/PHC) Hamilton–Wentworth, Ontario
Vander Heide, Sid (CHP/PHC) Perth–Wellington–Waterloo, Ontario
Van Der Veen, John (RP/PR) Elgin–Norfolk, Ontario

Van der Woude, John (CHP/PHC) Prince George–Peace River, B.C./C.-B.

van Holst, Michael (Nat.) London West/London-Ouest, Ontario

Vankoughnet, Bill (PC/P-C) Hastings–Frontenac–Lennox and Addington, Ontario

Van Iterson, Andrew (GP/PV) Nepean, Ontario

Van Tuinen, Charles C. (RP/PR) Eglinton–Lawrence, Toronto

Vanwoudenberg, Edward John (CHP/PHC) Fraser Valley West/ Fraser Valley-Ouest, B.C./C.-B.

Van Wyck, Morgan (GP/PV) Ottawa West/Ottawa-Ouest, Ontario

Varma, Neeraj (NLP/PLN) Calgary Northeast/Calgary-Nord-Est, Alberta

Vaudrin, Georges (Abol.) Laval West/Laval-Ouest, Montreal

Vaughan, Jim (PC/P-C) Halifax, N.S./N.-E.

Veenstra, John (RP/PR) Mississauga South/Mississauga-Sud, Ontario

Veillette, Michel (Lib.) Champlain, Quebec

Venne, Pierrette (BQ) Saint-Hubert, Quebec (Female)

Venuto, Nunzio (Libert.) Davenport, Toronto

Verran, Harry (Lib.) South West Nova, N.S./N.-E.

Vetter, Bill (Nat.) St John's East/St John's-Est, Nfld/T.-N.

Viau, Claude (NLP/PLN) Dartmouth, N.S./N.-E.

Vien, Jacques (PC/P-C) Laurentides, Quebec

Vienneau, Marie (Abol.) Mount Royal/Mont-Royal, Montreal (Female)

Villeneuve, Pascal (NDP/NPD) Glengarry–Prescott–Russell, Ontario

Villiard, Jean-Claude (Lib.) Chambly, Quebec

Vincelette, Francine (PC/P-C) Brome–Missisquoi, Quebec (Female)

Vincent, Pauline (PC/P-C) Rosemont, Montreal (Female)

Vincent, Pierre H. (PC/P-C) Trois-Rivières, Quebec

Vinning, Prem S. (Lib.) Surrey North/Surrey-Nord, B.C./C.-B.

Vint, Clyde E. (CHP/PHC) Richmond, B.C./C.-B.

Volpe, Joseph (Lib.) Eglinton–Lawrence, Toronto

Von Schellwitz, Mark (PC/P-C) North Island–Powell River, B.C./C.-B.

Vouloumanos, Tom (NDP/NPD) Beauce, Quebec

Waddell, Ian (NDP/NPD) Port Moody–Coquitlam, B.C./C.-B.

Wagman, Bryan (GP/PV) Delta, B.C./C.-B.

Walczak, T. Cheemo The Clown (Ind.) Hastings–Frontenac–Lennox and Addington, Ontario

Waldman, Louise (M-L) Ottawa South/Ottawa-Sud, Ontario (Female)

Walker, David (Lib.) Winnipeg North Centre/Winnipeg-Nord-Centre, Manitoba

Walker, Douglas (NLP/PLN) Okanagan Centre/Okanagan-Centre, B.C./C.-B.

Walker, Robert (NLP/PLN) Prince George–Peace River, B.C./C.-B.

Walkinshaw, Doug (RP/PR) Ottawa South/Ottawa-Sud, Ontario

Waller, John (Nat.) Delta, B.C./C.-B.

Walsh, Sharon (NDP/NPD) St John's West/St John's-Ouest, Nfld/T.-N. (Female)

Walters, Jim (Lib.) Yorkton–Melville, Saskatchewan

Wan, K. K. (PC/P-C) Vancouver South/Vancouver-Sud, B.C./C.-B.

Wandler, Jocelyne (Nat.) Calgary Southeast/Calgary-Sud-Est, Alberta (Female)

Wang, Paul (Nil) Markham–Whitchurch–Stouffville, Ontario

Wappel, Tom (Lib.) Scarborough West/Scarborough-Ouest, Toronto

Ward, Cameron (Nat.) Vancouver South/Vancouver-Sud, B.C./C.-B.

Ward, C.R. Bob (Ind.) Saanich–Gulf Islands/Saanich–Les Îles-du-Golfe, B.C./C.-B.

Warkentin, Peter (Lib.) Fraser Valley West/Fraser Valley-Ouest, B.C./C.-B.

Wasylycia-Leis, Judy (NDP/NPD) Winnipeg North/Winnipeg-Nord, Manitoba (Female)

Waterhouse, Donald (CHP/PHC) Victoria–Haliburton, Ontario

Watson, Bill (Nat.) Burlington, Ontario
Watson, Blaine P. (NLP/PLN) Waterloo, Ontario
Watson, Jenny (Nat.) Regina–Qu'Appelle, Saskatchewan (Female)
Wavrecan, Jim S. (Lib.) Kootenay East/Kootenay-Est, B.C./C.-B.
Wayne, Elsie (PC/P-C) Saint John, N.B./N.-B. (Female)
Webb, Jim (CP) Saint John, N.B./N.–B.
Weberg, Debbie (NLP/PLN) Eglinton–Lawrence, Toronto (Female)
Weberg, Rick C. (NLP/PLN) St Paul's, Toronto
Weemen, Lili V. (NDP/NPD) Mississauga South/Mississauga-Sud, Ontario (Female)
Weiner, Gerry (PC/P-C) Pierrefonds–Dollard, Montreal
Weiner, Mark (PC/P-C) Saint-Laurent–Cartierville, Montreal
Weitzel, Janice (RP/PR) Nickel Belt, Ontario (Female)
Welbourn, Gerry (RP/PR) Willowdale, Toronto
Wells, Derek (Lib.) South Shore, N.S./N.-E.
Werbowski, Michael Richard (NDP/NPD) Mount Royal/Mont-Royal, Montreal
Wertheimer, Earl (Libert.) Notre-Dame-de-Grâce, Montreal
Wesolowski, Frederick (RP/PR) Saskatoon–Clark's Crossing, Saskatchewan
West, Paul (RP/PR) Leeds–Grenville, Ontario
Whalen, Dennis (NDP/NPD) Gander–Grand Falls, Nfld/T.-N.
Whaley, Larry (Nat.) Nanaimo–Cowichan/Nanaimo–Cowichan, B.C./C.-B.
Whelan, Susan (Lib.) Essex–Windsor, Ontario (Female)
Whetung, Dan W. (Nat.) Esquimalt–Juan de Fuca, B.C./C.-B.
White, Jim (PC/P-C) Annapolis Valley–Hants, N.S./N.-E.
White, Kelly Elizabeth (GP/PV) Vancouver East/Vancouver-Est, B.C./C.-B. (Female)
White, Nolan (NLP/PLN) Gander–Grand Falls, Nfld/T.-N.
White, Randy (RP/PR) Fraser Valley West/Fraser Valley-Ouest, B.C./C.-B.
White, Steven Edward (Abol.) Ottawa–Vanier, Ontario
White, Ted (RP/PR) North Vancouver, B.C./C.-B.
Whiteway, Dean Waldon (RP/PR) Provencher, Manitoba
Whitman, Gary (Nil) Timiskaming–French River, Ontario
Whitney, Roy (Lib.) Macleod, Alberta
Whittaker, Jack (NDP/NPD) Okanagan–Similkameen–Merritt, B.C./C.-B.
Whitty, Freeman T. (RP/PR) Hillsborough, P.E.I./Î.-P.-E.
Wiebe, Jim (Libert.) Lachine–Lac-Saint-Louis, Montreal
Wiebe Owen, Martha (NDP/NPD) Provencher, Manitoba (Female)
Wieclaw, Ed (Lib.) Vegreville/Végréville, Alberta
Wiens, Mike (RP/PR) Winnipeg North/Winnipeg-Nord, Manitoba
Wightman, Gary (Nil) Brome–Missisquoi, Quebec
Wilbee, Bruce (PC/P-C) Nanaimo–Cowichan/Nanaimo–Cowichan, B.C./C.-B.
Wilbee, Stan (PC/P-C) Delta, B.C./C.-B.
Wilbur, David Stephen (Lib.) Prince George–Bulkley Valley, B.C./C.-B.
Williams, Cliff (Nat.) Dartmouth, N.S./N.-E.
Williams, John (RP/PR) St Albert/Saint-Albert, Alberta
Willis, Ken (CHP/PHC) Lambton–Middlesex, Ontario
Wilson, Anne (NDP/NPD) Wild Rose, Alberta (Female)
Wilson, Bradd (PC/P-C) Erie, Ontario
Wilson, Bryce (Nat.) Ottawa West/Ottawa-Ouest, Ontario
Wilson, Chris (NLP/PLN) Kingston and the Islands/ Kingston et les Îles, Ontario
Wilson, Geoff (PC/P-C) Swift Current–Maple Creek–Assiniboia, Saskatchewan

Wilson, Michael E. (NLP/PLN) Notre-Dame-de-Grâce, Montreal
Wilson, Shirley (NLP/PLN) Swift Current–Maple Creek–Assiniboia, Saskatchewan (Female)
Wilson, Stephen (Abol.) Don Valley West/Don Valley-Ouest, Toronto
Wilting, Berend J. (NDP/NPD) Crowfoot, Alberta
Windeyer, Michael (Abol.) Notre-Dame-de-Grâce, Montreal
Winters, Stan (CHP/PHC) London–Middlesex, Ontario
Wiseman, Herb (Nat.) Peterborough, Ontario
Witherly, Rhoda (Lib.) Skeena, B.C./C.-B. (Female)
Witzsche, Rolf A.F. (Com'lth/Rep./Rep./Com'lth) Capilano–Howe Sound, B.C./C.-B.
Wiwchar, Ted (Abol.) Niagara Falls, Ontario
Wolfe, Benjamin Brian (Ind.) Delta, B.C./C. B.
Wolter, John (NLP/PLN) Bruce–Grey, Ontario
Wood, Bob (Lib.) Nipissing, Ontario
Woods, Brian (Nat.) Nickel Belt, Ontario
Woods, Peter (Abol.) Ontario, Ontario
Woodwortht Clyde (RP/PR) Moncton, N.B./N.-B.
Woodyard, Dale (M-L) Windsor–St Clair/Windsor–Sainte-Claire, Ontario
Woolstencroft, Lynne (PC/P-C) Waterloo, Ontario (Female)
Worthington, James Norton (Abol.) Scarborough East/Scarborough-Est, Toronto
Worthy, Dave (PC/P-C) Cariboo–Chilcotin, B.C./C.-B.
Woytowich, Joe (NDP/NPD) Yellowhead, Alberta
Wright, Bruce Frank (Nat.) Vancouver East/Vancouver-Est, B.C./C.-B.
Wunderlich, Kathrine (Nat.) Kamloops, B.C./C.-B. (Female)
Wyborn, Greg (RP/PR) Carleton–Charlotte, N.B./N.-B.
Wyse, Bill (PC/P-C) Medicine Hat, Alberta
Yee, Steve (NDP/NPD) Timiskaming–French River, Ontario
York, Roman (Ind.) Vancouver Quadra, B.C./C.-B.
Young, Douglas (Lib.) Acadie–Bathurst, N.B./N.-B.
Young, Joe (Nil) Vancouver East/Vancouver-Est, B.C./C.-B.
Young, Neil (NDP/NPD) Beaches–Woodbine, Ontario
Yundt, Joe (Libert.) Perth Wellington–Waterloo, Ontario
Zacharias, Brian (CHP/PHC) Kootenay West–Revelstoke/Kootenay Ouest–Revelstoke, B.C./C. B.
Zacharko, Michael J. (Lib.) Beaver River, Alberta
Zammuto, Rick (GP/PV) Prince George–Bulkley Valley, B.C./C.-B.
Zathey, Peter (RP/PR) Mississauga East/Mississauga-Est, Ontario
Zavitz, Peter (NDP/NPD) South West Nova, N.S./N.-E.
Zawalski, Terry (NDP/NPD) Vegreville/Vegreville, Alberta
Zed, Paul (Lib.) Fundy–Royal, N.B./N.-B.
Zeeper, Heide (Nil) Edmonton Northwest/Edmonton-Nord-Ouest, Alberta (Female)
Zegalski, Leslie (PC/P-C) Winnipeg North Centre/Winnipeg-Nord-Centre, Manitoba (Female)
Zekveld, Henry (CHP/PHC) Huron–Bruce, Ontario
Zelenietz, Marty (NDP/NPD) Dartmouth, N.S./N.-E.
Ziniewicz, Alex (Nat.) Vegreville/Végréville, Alberta
Zmak, Joseph (Com'lth/Rep./Rep./Com'lth) Etobicoke Centre/Etobicoke-Centre, Toronto
Zugaj, Vlado (Com'lth/Rep./Rep./Com'lth) Essex–Windsor, Ontario

Appendix Three

Summary Definition of Measures Reported on Data Grids, Sources and Descriptive Statistics (National Means)

A) Political Profile
  i) *Voting Behaviour*

  1993 Voting Percentages reflect proportion of total valid votes (i.e., total votes minus rejected ballots) cast in the riding.
  All 1993 electoral data taken from Elections Canada, *Official Voting Results: Thirty-Fifth General Election, 1993; Synopsis*, Ottawa: Chief Electoral Officer, Catalogue Number SE1-1/1-1993, 1993.

  1988 Voting Percentages reflect proportion of total valid votes (i.e., total votes minus rejected ballots) cast in the riding.
  All 1988 electoral data taken from Elections Canada, *Report of the Chief Electoral Officer, Thirty-Fourth General Election, Appendices (Revised)*, Ottawa: Elections Canada, Catalogue Number SE 1-1/1988-1-4, 1988.

  The *% Margin of Victory* represents the difference in the percentages of the vote obtained by the top two parties/candidates in the 1993 election (winner's % vote - runner-up's % vote).

  Referendum voting was administered in all parts of Canada *except* Quebec by Elections Canada.
  The referendum results were obtained from Elections Canada, *Referendum 92: Official Voting Results; Synopsis*, Ottawa: Chief Electoral Officer, Catalogue Number SE 1-8/1-1992, 1992.

  The province of Quebec administered its own constitutional referendum in 1992. Official results were released on the basis of the 125 provincial electoral districts. Unofficial results for referendum voting in Quebec, aggregated at the federal constituency level, were obtained from *La Presse*.

  ii) *Campaign Financing*

  % of Allowable Limit Spent is the proportion of the maximum allowable election expenses declared by parties. The allowable maximum varies from riding to riding, according to a formula that takes into account: (a) the number of eligible electors in each riding; (b) an indexing factor that is published each election year by Elections Canada; and (c) adjustments for geographic density and deviation from the national average of eligible electors.

Local candidates may spend:

(a) $1.00 per elector for the first 15,000 eligible electors;
       0.50 per elector for the next 10,000 eligible electors;
       0.25 per elector for all remaining eligible electors.
(b)   1993 indexing factor of 1.908 (multiply total from (a) by this amount)
(c)   adjust for geographic density if population density is less than 10 people per square kilometre, add $0.15 times the number of square kilometres in the riding;
(d)   adjust for deviation in size of electorate if number of electors is less than national average, add 1/2 of the difference to the actual number of electors in the riding.

All campaign expenditure data is taken from Elections Canada, *Contributions and Expenses of Registered Political Parties and Candidates: Thirty-Fifth General Election, 1993*, Ottawa: Chief Electoral Officer of Canada, Catalogue Number SE1-7/ 1993, 1993.

B) Ethno-Linguistic/Socio-Economic/Industrial Profiles

% English Home Language, % French Home Language, % Other Home Language, all refer to the proportion of residents who report these as the language normally spoken at home. Unlike 1986, the additional instruction for respondents reporting more than one language being used at home to specify which language was used most often was dropped in 1991.

% Official Bilingual indicates the proportion of residents who are able (by their own assessment) to carry on a conversation in either of Canada's official languages (English and French).

% Catholic and *% Protestant* refer to the proportion of residents affiliating with each religion.

% Aboriginal Peoples refers to the proportion of residents whose ethnic origins are with Canada's native peoples. It is important to note that in the 1991 census (as in the 1986 sample census), census enumeration was not permitted on some Indian reserves, was interrupted, or was undertaken late. For these reasons, the figures for this measure should be treated as rough approximations only. For a full discussion, readers should consult the definitional notes in the census publication cited below.

% Immigrants refers to the proportion of residents who were not born in Canada.

$ Average Family Income refers to the weighted mean total income, from all sources, of all members of census households, in dollars, for 1990.

$ Median Family Income is that dollar amount of total 1990 family income from all sources that divides the total number of census households into two groups of equal size, i.e., the first half have family incomes above the median family income value, the second half have family incomes below the median family income value.

% Low Income Families is the proportion of all families whose income in 1990 fell below a certain threshold. This threshold varies according to the size of families, national family expenditure data (from 1986), and the area of residence (primarily reflecting differences in population size). Threshold values are determined by Statistics Canada. A table summarizing these thresholds can be found in the census publication cited below.

% Home Owners refers to the proportion of all households in a riding who are one family households owning/buying their dwelling.

% Unemployment refers to the unemployed labour force expressed as a percentage of the total labour force in a riding for the reference week (the week prior to enumeration, 4 June 1991). The total labour force includes persons 15 years of age and older, excluding institutional residents.

% Labour Force Participation refers to the total labour force (those employed and unemployed in the reference week prior to enumeration, 4 June 1991) expressed as a percentage of the total population aged 15 years and older, excluding institutional residents.

% Managerial-Administrative refers to the proportion of all employed males and females 15 years of age and older who hold 'managerial, administrative, or related occupations', according to Statistics Canada's 1980 Standard Occupational Classification.

% Self-Employed refers to the proportion of all employed males and females who are either incorporated or non-incorporated self-employed workers.

% University Degrees refers to the proportion of a riding's total population aged 15 years and older who have received a university/college degree.

% Movers refers to the proportion of residents who, on census day, were living in a different dwelling than the one they occupied five years earlier (1986).

% Manufacturing refers to the proportion of a riding's total work force in industry who are employed in manufacturing industries, as classified by the Standard Industrial Classification (1980).

% Service Sector refers to the proportion of all employed males and females who work in service industries, as classified by the Standard Occupational Classification (1980).

% Agriculture refers to the proportion of a riding's total work force in industry who are employed in agriculture and related service industries, as classified by the Standard Industrial Classification (1980).

% Mining refers to the proportion of a riding's total work force in industry who are employed in mining (including milling), quarrying and oil well industries, as classified by the Standard Industrial Classification (1980).

% Forestry refers to the proportion of a riding's total work force in industry who are employed in logging and forestry and related industries, as classified by the Standard Industrial Classification (1980).

% Fishing refers to the proportion of a riding's total work force in industry who are employed in fishing and trapping industries, as classified by the Standard Industrial Classification (1980).

% Government Services refers to the proportion of a riding's total work force in industry who are employed in government service industries, as classified by the Standard Industrial Classification (1980).

% Business Services refers to the proportion of a riding's total work force in industry who are employed in business service industries, as classified by the Standard Industrial Classification (1980).

All census data are derived from electronic census files obtained from Statistics Canada.

Most data, and a more detailed discussion of the operational meaning of census categories, are available in paper format in Statistics Canada, *Census 91: Profile of Federal Electoral Districts - Parts A & B*, Ottawa: Statistics Canada, Catalogue Numbers 93-335 and 93-336, September 1992 and July 1993.

C) Homogeneity Measures

Ethnic Diversity Index is a Herfindahl index calculated using data for 'ethnic origins' of residents. Ten general ethnic origins were utilized in the calculation: British; French; Aboriginal; Canadian; Black; Asian (Chinese, Vietnamese, Filipino, Japanese, Korean); Scandinavian (Danish, Swedish, Norwegian, Finnish); Other West European (Greek, Portuguese, Spanish, Italian, German, Dutch); East European (Polish, Yugoslav, Croatian, Hungarian, Ukrainian) and Other (Jewish, Lebanese, East Indian, Other). Mathematically, the Ethnic Diversity Index (EDI) is defined as:

$$EDI = \sum_{i=1}^{n} (E_i)^2$$

where E_i is ethnic group i's proportion of the total population in the district and $n = 10$ ethnic groups. If all ten ethnic groups (defined in terms of ethnic origins) are of equal size in a riding, then the EDI would be equal to 1/10 or .10. Ridings dominated by one ethnic group will be associated with EDI measures approximating 1.

Religious Homogeneity Index is a Herfindahl index calculated using the distribution of religious affiliations in ridings with ten religions/religious denominations. The component religious groups are: Catholic; Protestant; Other Christian religions; Jew; Islam; Buddhist; Hindu; Sikh; other religions; no religious affiliations. Mathematically, the Religious Homogeneity Index (RHI) is defined as:

$$RHI = \sum_{i=1}^{n} (R_i)^2$$

where R_i is religion i's membership as a proportion of all residents in the riding, and $n = 10$ religions. If all ten religious groups were of equal size in a riding, RHI would be equal to 1/10 (or .10). Ridings dominated by a single religious group would be associated with RHI values approaching 1.0.

Sectoral Concentration Index is a Herfindahl index calculated using the distribution of employment in ridings across 17 industrial classes, as classified by the Standard Industrial Classification (1980). The component classes are: agricultural employment; business services; accommodation services; construction; educational services; fishing; government services; logging and forest industries; manufacturing; mining; health services; other services; real estate; retail services; transportation; wholesale; communication and utilities. Mathematically, the Sectoral Concentration Index (SCI) is defined as:

$$SCI = \sum_{i=1}^{n} (S_i)^2$$

where S_i is sector i's proportion of total employment in the riding, and $n = 17$ sectors. If all seventeen employment sectors were of equal size in a riding, SCI would be equal to 1/17 or approximately .06. Ridings dominated by a single employment sector would be associated with SCI values approaching 1.0.

Income Disparity Index is a percentage measure of the ratio of median to average family incomes in a riding. It is calculated as:

IDI = {(average-median family incomes)/average family incomes} * 100

If average and median family incomes were identical in a riding, IDI would equal 0. The larger the IDI, the greater the disparity between median and average incomes, and the greater the wealth gap among families within a riding.

Means/Standard Deviations for Statistical Measures

Measure	Mean	StdDev	N
Political Profile			
% Conservative Vote, 1993	16.07	8.01	295
% Conservative Vote, 1988	42.40	12.04	295
% Change, PC, 1988-1993	-26.33	11.53	295
% Liberal Vote, 1993	42.20	17.21	295
% Liberal Vote, 1988	32.19	13.47	295
% Change, Lib., 1988-1993	10.01	9.07	295
% NDP Vote, 1993	7.55	8.75	295
% NDP Vote, 1988	20.83	12.67	295
% Change, NDP, 1988-1993	-13.28	7.36	295
% Bloc Québécois, 1993	12.45	22.55	295
% Reform Vote, 1993	18.28	17.00	295
% Reform Vote, 1988	2.09	5.32	295
% Change, Reform, 1988-1993	16.19	13.69	295
% Other/Minor Vote, 1993	3.50	3.80	295
% Other/Minor Vote, 1988	2.50	2.53	295
% Change, Minor/Oth., 1988-1993	1.00	4.52	295
% Turnout, 1993	69.61	6.24	295
# Rejected Ballots, 1993	664.63	736.61	295
Total # of Votes, 1993	46995.63	13604.96	295
% Victory Margin, 1993	28.06	17.07	295
# Rural Polling Districts	64.91	66.64	295
# Urban Polling Districts	131.29	73.56	295
% Yes Vote, 1992 Referendum	45.09	12.58	295
% No Vote, 1992 Referendum	54.54	12.68	295
Campaign Spending			
# of Donations, Conservatives, 1993	122.80	82.19	295
$ Total Donations, Conservatives, 1993	40213.83	20715.05	295
% Of Limit Spent, Conservatives, 1993	71.47	21.92	295
# of Donations, Liberals, 1993	150.54	94.69	295
$ Total Donations, Liberals, 1993	43745.45	20065.04	295
% Of Limit Spent, Liberals, 1993	68.34	21.23	295
# of Donations, NDP, 1993	49.99	84.39	295
$ Total Donations, NDP, 1993	19600.11	20545.27	295
% Of Limit Spent, NDP, 1993	27.34	30.61	295
# of Donations, Reform/BQ, 1993	188.24	156.69	295
$ Total Donations, Reform/BQ, 1993	30656.64	19921.53	295
% Of Limit Spent, Reform/BQ, 1993	48.07	26.94	295
# of Donations, Other/Minor, 1993	33.95	47.88	295
$ Total Donations, Other/Minor, 1993	8762.90	11917.18	295

Measure	Mean	Std Dev	N
Ethno-Linguistic Profile			
% English, Home Language, 1991	68.38	36.54	295
% French, Home Language, 1991	24.11	37.64	295
% Bilingual (English & French), 1991	16.09	15.89	295
% Other Home Languages, 1991	7.52	9.50	295
% Catholic, 1991	46.50	27.51	295
% Protestant, 1991	36.56	21.94	295
% Aboriginal Peoples, 1991	3.50	8.83	295
% Immigrants, 1991	14.42	12.81	295
Socio-Economic Profile			
$ Average Family Income, 1991	50103.94	10498.40	295
$ Median Family Income, 1991	44262.47	8466.70	295
% Low Income Families, 1991	15.91	6.84	295
$ Average Home Value, 1991	137769.43	77929.23	295
% Home Owners, 1991	63.99	15.80	295
Unemployment Rate, 1991	10.73	4.72	295
Labour Force Participation Rate, 1991	67.33	5.45	295
% Managers & Administrators, 1991	11.59	3.59	295
% Self-Employed, 1991	9.91	4.62	295
% University Degrees, 1991	10.65	6.52	295
% Movers, 1986-1993	45.30	9.81	295
Industrial Profile			
% Manufacturing Sector Employment, 1991	14.40	6.81	295
% Service Sector Jobs, 1991	13.06	2.47	295
% Agricultural Sector Employment, 1991	4.28	6.74	295
% Mining Sector Employment, 1991	1.60	3.10	295
% Forestry Sector Employment, 1991	0.93	1.63	295
% Fishing Sector Employment, 1991	0.50	1.46	295
% Government Services Employment, 1991	18.08	4.95	295
% Business Services Employment, 1991	5.08	3.11	295
Homogeneity Measures			
Ethnic Origins Herfindahl Index, 1991	0.43	0.25	295
Religious Diversity Herfindahl Index, 1991	0.49	0.20	295
Sectoral Concentration Herfindahl Index, 1991	0.43	0.08	295
% Income Diversity Index, 1991	11.35	5.01	295
Physical Setting Characteristics			
Total Population, 1991	92531.73	24900.88	295
Population Density (sq. km)	1075.65	1864.34	295
Area (square kilometres)	36868.98	220654.39	295

Appendix Four

ELECTION '93 CAMPAIGN CALENDAR

Federal Leaders:

Kim Campbell: Progressive Conservative Party
Jean Chrétien: Liberal Party
Audrey McLaughlin: New Democratic Party
Lucien Bouchard: Bloc Québécois
Preston Manning: Reform Party
Mel Hurtig: National Party

September 11:

Campbell: Visits Quebec City, touring a shopping centre and joining a round-table discussion at the Laval Women's Centre.
Chrétien: Attends Paul Martin's nomination meeting in Montreal; visits shopping mall in Longueuil.
McLaughlin: Spends day on Vancouver Island; visits Nanaimo, Duncan and Victoria.
Bouchard: Holds official campaign kickoff in Montreal.
Manning: Visits Fredericton and Halifax.
Hurtig: Visits Edmonton.

September 12:

Campbell: Visits Montreal.
Chrétien: Visits Winnipeg for appearance on CBC Radio and brunch with area Liberal MPs; visits Granville Island and has supper in Vancouver.
McLaughlin: Joins NDP candidate Betty Baxter in Vancouver, and campaigns with Premier Harcourt.
Bouchard: Goes to Alma for meetings, leads rally in Jonquière.
Manning: Visits Regina.
Hurtig: Continues visit to Edmonton.

September 13:

Campbell: No public appearances.
Chrétien: Visits Marco Polo restaurant in Edmonton; visits Atrium Building of the Innovation Place Research Park; travels to Ottawa.
McLaughlin: Visits school and does radio show in Edmonton; visits with local NDP candidates.
Bouchard: Lunches with BQ candidates in Hull, tapes a Newsworld interview in Ottawa and a radio interview in Gatineau; delivers speech in Hull in evening.
Manning: Does Vancouver radio show with Rafe Mair in the morning, lunches with supporters at the Star of the Sea community hall, flies to Calgary in afternoon.
Hurtig: Continues visit to Edmonton.

September 14:

Campbell: Leaves Ottawa for Kelowna, overnights in Vernon.
Chrétien: No official appearances.
McLaughlin: Spends day in Regina: does CKRW interview, delivers a statement on health care before mainstreeting with local MPs; meets with aboriginal leaders.
Bouchard: Addresses college students in Longueuil; travels to Sherbrooke for rally marking the official filing of nomination papers for two local BQ candidates.
Manning: Attends several events in Calgary. Appears on CBC Newsworld in the evening.
Hurtig: Continues visit to Edmonton.

September 15:

Campbell: Conducts radio interview and visits mill in Kelowna; visits Penticton and Cranbrook en route to Calgary.
Chrétien: Unveils party platform in Ottawa.
McLaughlin: Delivers speeches in Montreal and Halifax.
Bouchard: Speaks to students at University of Montreal, followed by question-and-answer session.
Manning: Takes part in debate at Western Canada High School in Calgary.
Hurtig: Campaigns in his Edmonton riding and appears in court to try to secure a voice for his party in television debates.

September 16:

Campbell: Meets with editorial board of the *Calgary Herald*; speaks to Calgary Chamber of Commerce; stops in Strathmore en route to a barbecue at High River; travels to Regina.
Chrétien: Tours central Ontario, stopping in Woodbridge, Barrie, Orillia and Peterborough.
McLaughlin: Addresses Atlantic fishery crisis in Halifax; takes part in round-table discussion on health in Saint John; travels to Hamilton.
Bouchard: Speaks to students at University of Quebec in Montreal, followed by reception at Ste Thérèse City Hall.
Manning: Makes breakfast appearance in Victoria; campaigns throughout Vancouver Island.
Hurtig: Gives several interviews in Edmonton, followed by a town hall meeting at Grant MacEwan Community College.

September 17:

Campbell: Delivers speech in Regina; lunch visit to Keystone Agricultural Centre in Brandon; holds 'electronic round table' with regional media before flying to Halifax.
Chrétien: Breakfast meeting in Trenton; visits dairy farm in Napanee, visits Kingston and Brockville.
McLaughlin: Tours plants in Hamilton which have been closed since F.T.A. took effect.
Bouchard: Visits Montreal, touring an arts centre and taping a Radio-Québec interview.
Manning: Breakfasts at the Penticton Trade and Convention Centre and makes appearances in Kelowna; holds town hall meeting with students from neighbouring communities.
Hurtig: Holds press conference in Winnipeg on National Party's taxation policies before returning to Edmonton.

September 18:

Campbell: Attends football game at St Mary's University in Halifax; tours Gagetown County fairgrounds and attends a reception at St Stephen High School before leaving for Saint John.
Chrétien: Visits local candidates in Montreal, Fabreville, Laval and St-Jérôme.
McLaughlin: No public events.
Bouchard: Visits seniors' home in Alma and potato farm in St-Ambroise; conducts evening rally in Alma.
Manning: Mainstreets in Calgary and attends barbecue at the Hungarian Cultural Centre.
Hurtig: Campaigns in Edmonton and appears on local open-line radio show.

September 19:

Campbell: Attends a New Brunswick Political Caucus meeting before flying to Ottawa.
Chrétien: Visits St-Tite Western festival; lunch meeting in Quebec City; delivers speech in Charlesbourg.
McLaughlin: Visits with local candidates at a farm south of Vanscoy, Sask.; appears on CBC radio.
Bouchard: No official activities.
Manning: Tapes CBC Town Hall meeting in Toronto.
Hurtig: Campaigns in Edmonton and appears on CBC radio.

September 20:

Campbell: No official activities.
Chrétien: Visits Corner Brook and Stephenville, NF; flies to Edmunston, NB.
McLaughlin: Delivers speech at University of Saskatoon.
Bouchard: Addresses joint meeting of the Canadian Club of Toronto and the Empire Club of Canada; interviewed by Lloyd Robertson of CTV and meets with editorial board of the *Toronto Star*.
Manning: Visits Peterborough, Lindsay and Orillia.
Hurtig: Campaigns in Vancouver, meeting local candidates, touring area ridings and appearing on CKNW radio.

September 21:

Campbell: Visits community centre in Wiarton, Ont.; attends opening ceremonies of the International Plowing Match in Walkerton; goes to Karaoke Night at Canterbury Inn in Sarnia.
Chrétien: Campaigns in Edmunston and Grand Falls; tours the Thomas Equipment Plant in Fredericton; visits a literacy class.
McLaughlin: Campaigns in Kelowna, Vernon and Kamloops.
Bouchard: Visits Ville-Marie for radio interview and reception at city hall; speaks to students and mining executives in Rouyn-Noranda; visits Val d'Or for mine tour and dinner with BQ supporters.
Manning: Visits Georgian College in Barrie; flies to Calgary.
Hurtig: Campaigns in Edmonton and Toronto.

September 22:

Campbell: Visits Strathroy and London for speeches; attends community reception at the New Sarum Diner in St Thomas; flies to Montreal.

Chrétien: No public events.

McLaughlin: Delivers speech and campaigns in Kamloops.

Bouchard: Visits printing shop in Chicoutimi; speaks to students at the University of Quebec in Chicoutimi; visits Abitibi-Price mill in Alma.

Manning: Appears at all-candidates forum in Calgary; lunches at the 400 Club and appears on CHQR radio; flies to Winnipeg.

Hurtig: Appears in Toronto for news conference on free trade; flies to Edmonton.

September 23:

Campbell: Campaigns in Montreal, visiting École nationale d'aérotechnique in St Hubert and ATS Aérospatiale Inc. in St Bruno; attends reception in Drummondville.

Chrétien: Campaigns in Vancouver.

McLaughlin: Delivers speech and appears on local radio in Prince George; appears at all-candidates forum in Whitehorse.

Bouchard: Visits with local BQ candidates in Sept-Îles, Manicouagan and Baie-Comeau; tours a smelter and holds a rally in the latter.

Manning: Breakfasts at Carman Community Centre in Carman; mainstreets in Portage La Prairie; appears on open-line radio show in Brandon; hosts town hall meeting in Dauphin.

Hurtig: Appears on Edmonton open-line show; appears in court in support of his case against the CBC; holds a media reception in his home.

September 24:

Campbell: Campaigns in Montreal, being interviewed on CKAC radio and on Télé-Métropole television; flies to Vancouver.

Chrétien: Tours Lester B. Pearson High School in Calgary; tours Ron and Nancy Perrault's farm near Grand Coulee, Sask.; does television interview in Regina.

McLaughlin: Visits a day-care centre in Whitehorse; holds a media reception in her living room; campaigns in Faro, Carcross, Teslin and Haines Junction.

Bouchard: Visits the Gaspé region, meeting fishermen in Newport and touring a factory in Chandler before greeting party workers in Sainte-Anne-des-Monts; meets with regional municipal officials in Rimouski.

Manning: Breakfasts at Legion Hall in Yorkton, Sask.; visits Weyburn and speaks at Moose Jaw town hall.

Hurtig: Appears on Calgary radio phone-in show; gives interviews in Edmonton.

September 25:

Campbell: No public events.

Chrétien: Visits Franco-Ontarian Club in Timmins, and Sudbury Centre Mall; appears on Sudbury open-line radio show; flies to North Bay.

McLaughlin: Campaigns in her Yukon riding.

Bouchard: Continues visit to the Gaspé, meeting loggers, business people and residents in Rimouski, Kamouraska, and Riviérè-du-Loup.

Manning: Breakfasts in Medicine Hat and mainstreets in Brooks, Alta.; travels to Calgary.
Hurtig: Visits Westmount Shopping Centre in Edmonton; goes door-to-door in his riding.

September 26:

Campbell: Campaigns in Vancouver.
Chrétien: Breakfasts at the Armenian Community Centre in Toronto; attends round-table meeting with small businesspeople in Scarborough; meets area Liberal candidates for lunch.
McLaughlin: Speaks to the Manitoba Federation of Labour in Winnipeg; attends a ceremony to commemorate the 1930s famine in the Ukraine; attends a reception held by provincial NDP.
Bouchard: Continues visit to the Gaspé.
Manning: Attends rally in Red Deer; appears on CBC Radio.
Hurtig: Attends afternoon meeting in Calgary.

September 27:

Campbell: Appears on Rafe Mair radio show in Vancouver; meets high school students at Marriott Senior Secondary School; campaigns in the Surrey – White Rock riding.
Chrétien: Meets with Montreal mayor Jean Doré; tours downtown food bank; attends rally with local candidates in Dorval.
McLaughlin: Campaigns in the Winnipeg North riding; appears on CBC open-line radio show.
Bouchard: No public events.
Manning: Campaigns in Calgary, giving breakfast speech, meeting with seniors, and attending town hall meeting.
Hurtig: Campaigns in the Edmonton Northwest riding.

September 28:

Campbell: Talks with Peter Gzowski on CBC Radio in Toronto; speaks to the PC Business Association; attends a reception at the Ontario Science Centre.
Chrétien: Visits a nutrition counselling centre; attends the Liberals' annual Confederation Dinner in Toronto.
McLaughlin: Visits the Omega restaurant in Oshawa; meets supporters in Peterborough; attends fund-raising dinner for Winnie Ng at the Jade Garden Restaurant in Toronto.
Bouchard: Meets with mayor and council in Waterloo; attends a reception at Sherbrooke city hall and delivers speech to the Chamber of Commerce.
Manning: Attends all-candidates meeting in Calgary; talks with university students at Beta Sigma Phi sorority; travels to Courtenay, B.C.
Hurtig: Visits the Oliver Child Care Centre in Edmonton; takes part in all-candidates meeting; speaks at the Elks Lodge.

September 29:

Campbell: Speaks to United Nations General Assembly in New York.
Chrétien: Visits the Victoria day care centre in Toronto; attends the Maple Leaf fund-raising dinner in Ottawa.

McLaughlin: Delivers speech in London; attends rally at the Caboto Club in Windsor.

Bouchard: Visits Technoler Inc. in Danville; tours Teinturiers Élite Inc. in Drummondville; attends rally with local BQ candidate in Trois-Rivières.

Manning: Holds town hall meetings in Courtenay and Nanaimo; travels to Vancouver.

Hurtig: Attends small business breakfast in Richmond; attends town hall meeting at Kerrisdale Community Centre; meets with candidates in Vancouver South and Skeena ridings.

September 30:

Campbell: No public events.

Chrétien: No public events.

McLaughlin: Holds news conference on medicare in Windsor; attends rally in Cambridge; speaks at a reception in Toronto.

Bouchard: Conducts radio interview in Trois-Rivières; attends a rally at Shawinigan CEGEP.

Manning: Mainstreets in North Vancouver; releases criminal justice reform plans at press conference in downtown Vancouver; flies to Toronto.

Hurtig: Campaigns in Campbell River; delivers speech in Courtenay; campaigns in Nanaimo and Victoria.

October 1:

Campbell: Prepares for debates in Ottawa.

Chrétien: Prepares for debates in Ottawa.

McLaughlin: Prepares for debates in Ottawa.

Bouchard: Tours Scott Paper Plant in Montreal; holds news conference at Joliette city hall; meets with students at Joliette CEGEP.

Manning: Appears on CTV Television; addresses the Empire Club in Toronto; prepares for debates in Ottawa.

Hurtig: Speaks to students at Edmonton's Holy Trinity High School; campaigns in his riding.

October 2:

Campbell: Prepares for debates in Ottawa.

Chrétien: Prepares for debates in Ottawa.

McLaughlin: Prepares for debates in Ottawa.

Bouchard: Prepares for debates.

Manning: Holds town hall meeting in Smiths Falls; travels to Ottawa to prepare for debate.

Hurtig: Campaigns at Strathcona Farmers' Market in Edmonton.

October 3:

Campbell: Participates in televised French-language debate.

Chrétien: Participates in televised French-language debate.

McLaughlin: Participates in televised French-language debate.

Bouchard: Participates in televised French-language debate.

Manning: Participates in televised French-language debate.

Hurtig: Campaigns in Edmonton.

October 4:

Campbell: Participates in televised English-language debate.
Chrétien: Participates in televised English-language debate.
McLaughlin: Participates in televised English-language debate.
Bouchard: Participates in televised English-language debate.
Manning: Participates in televised English-language debate.
Hurtig: Monitors debate from *Ottawa Citizen* office.

October 5:

Campbell: Visits Trois-Rivières, Ste-Marthe-du-Cap-de-la-Madeleine and Repentigny, and Bathurst, N.B.
Chrétien: Campaigns in Toronto and Montreal.
McLaughlin: No public events.
Bouchard: Visits veterinary college in St-Hyacinthe; meets party workers in Quebec City; interviewed by
    Radio-Canada.
Manning: Breakfasts with media in Ottawa; visits the Austin Nixon seniors home and holds town hall
    meeting at the Clinton Ford school in Calgary.
Hurtig: Campaigns in Toronto.

October 6:

Campbell: Visits Beresford, Newcastle, Charlottetown; flies to St John's.
Chrétien: Visits a vegetable farm in St-Clotilde; speaks in Granby, Brossard and Outremont.
McLaughlin: Holds forum on medicare in Timmins; speaks to supporters at the Port Arthur Labour Assoc.
    in Thunder Bay.
Bouchard: Speaks to students at Laval University; visits St-Augustin and Lac Delage.
Manning: Holds town hall meeting in Whitecourt, Alberta; holds rally in Lloydminster.
Hurtig: Campaigns in Edmonton.

October 7:

Campbell: Speaks to St John's Board of Trade and does radio interview in St John's; flies to Toronto.
Chrétien: Attends forum at the Helena Seniors Centre; tours a growers' co-op in Winfield; attends a
    multicultural round-table in Richmond.
McLaughlin: Speaks on medicare to an International Woodworkers of America convention in Saskatoon;
    tours an environmental technology plant and speaks to supporters.
Bouchard: Attends Chamber of Commerce luncheon in Quebec City; tours bicycle factory and attends
    rally in St-Georges-de-Beauce.
Manning: Conducts radio interviews and delivers a speech to the Prince George Chamber of Commerce;
    speaks at a town hall meeting in Quesnel.
Hurtig: Campaigns in Edmonton; appears on CBC television.

October 8:

Campbell: Appears on open-line radio show in Toronto; attends a community reception in St Catharines;
    visits Fort Erie and Niagara Falls.

Chrétien: Visits Saskatoon and Winnipeg.

McLaughlin: Speaks at a Women's Equality Breakfast in Burnaby; tours the Vancouver Aboriginal Friendship Centre; appears on a radio show.

Bouchard: Meets with editorial board of *Le Soleil*; meets workers at MIL Davie Shipbuilding in Lévis; meets supporters in Plessisville.

Manning: Conducts town-hall meeting in Chilliwack; attends rally in Abbotsford; flies to Calgary.

Hurtig: Holds press conference in Edmonton; speaks to Rotary Club and attends a barbecue in Edmonton.

October 9:

Campbell: Visits Stony Creek Ont., and attends the Rockton World Fair.

Chrétien: Speaks and tours canal locks in Sault Ste Marie.

McLaughlin: Visits Prince Albert, Melfort, Regina and Moose Jaw.

Bouchard: Tapes interviews.

Manning: Visits Calgary Southwest Mall.

Hurtig: Visits Nelson, Kamloops and Vernon, B.C.

October 10:

Campbell: Visits Vancouver.

Chrétien: Visits Toronto for television interview and other events.

McLaughlin: Visits Toronto and Ottawa.

Bouchard: Visits the Saguenay region of Quebec, meeting supporters in Canton, Tremblay and St-David-de-Falardeau.

Manning: Rest day.

Hurtig: Campaigns in Edmonton.

October 11:

Campbell: Visits Richmond, Red Deer and Edmonton.

Chrétien: No official appearances.

McLaughlin: No official appearances.

Bouchard: No official appearances.

Manning: Attends Thanksgiving brunch in Calgary; flies to Toronto.

Hurtig: Campaigns in Edmonton.

October 12:

Campbell: Visits Horizon Village and LaZerte High School in Edmonton; travels to Saskatoon.

Chrétien: Visits Ontario, stopping in Welland, St Catharines, Niagara-on-the-Lake and Hamilton.

McLaughlin: Tours a group health centre in Sault Ste Marie; appears on MuchMusic.

Bouchard: Meets with the editorial board of *La Presse*; tours hospital in Saint-Jérôme; visits Repentigny and Terrebonne; returns to Montreal.

Manning: Attends town hall meetings in Cambridge and Sarnia.

Hurtig: Appears on CBC Radio Edmonton; speaks at the University of Alberta.

October 13:

Campbell: Campaigns in Rosetown and Battleford, Sask.; flies to Toronto.
Chrétien: Visits Guelph, Kitchener and Acton; attends fund-raising event in Trois-Rivières.
McLaughlin: Appears on CTV; attends rally in Chambly, Que.
Bouchard: Appears in Radio-Canada interview; visits Chicoutimi, Roberval and Saint-Félicien.
Manning: Campaigns in Toronto and Edmonton.
Hurtig: Addresses Winnipeg Chamber of Commerce.

October 14:

Campbell: Attends reception in Toronto; attends luncheon in Rosedale; appears at reception for John
   Bosley, Conservative candidate for Don Valley West.
Chrétien: Visits Grand-Mère; travels to Shawinigan for mainstreeting, an open-line radio interview, and a
   visit to a tire-retreading plant; tours a window-manufacturing plant in St-Boniface.
McLaughlin: Visits Winnipeg plant which was closed after Conservative drug-patent bill was passed, and
   speaks on generic drugs; attends all-candidates meeting in Whitehorse.
Bouchard: Conducts radio interview in Quebec City; meets ethnic leaders in Montreal.
Manning: Attends breakfast meeting in Edmonton; conducts town hall meeting in Vegreville; attends an
   all-candidates forum at the Calgary Jewish Centre.
Hurtig: Meets students at York University; tapes an appearance on 'Royal Canadian Air Farce'; attends a
   rally at the Metro Toronto Convention Centre.

October 15:

Campbell: Campaigns in Montreal and Quebec City.
Chrétien: Visits Saint John, Falmouth and Lunenburg; travels to Prince Edward Island.
McLaughlin: Attends an all-candidates meeting in Whitehorse; mainstreets on Main Street, Whitehorse;
   meets with supporters in Prince Rupert.
Bouchard: Meets with the editorial board of *Le Devoir*; tours the Pointe-St-Charles district of Montreal;
   conducts television interviews on TVA and CBC.
Manning: Attends breakfast meeting in Airdrie, Alta.; visits Wetaskiwin, Drumheller and Calgary.
Hurtig: Campaigns in Toronto; appears on CBC Radio Halifax.

October 16:

Campbell: Tours Quebec, stopping in Montmagny, Victoriaville and Montreal.
Chrétien: Breakfasts in Sarnia; tours a farm in Mandaumin; delivers speeches in Chatham and Windsor.
McLaughlin: Attends a health-care forum in Edmonton.
Bouchard: Visits Montreal and Anjou; meets with ethnic groups in Laval.
Manning: Campaigns in his Calgary Southwest riding.
Hurtig: Visits Orillia and Barrie; attends several events in Metro Toronto.

October 17:

Campbell: No details available.
Chrétien: Appears with local candidates in Thunder Bay.

McLaughlin: Holds a news conference on tax loopholes in Brandon, Man.; speaks to supporters at a seniors' centre in Dauphin.

Bouchard: Speaks to supporters in Metabetchouan, Alma and La Baie.

Manning: Tapes a town hall meeting in Toronto for the CBC.

Hurtig: Tapes a town hall meeting in Toronto for the CBC.

October 18:

Campbell: Visits Orillia and Toronto; appears on MuchMusic.

Chrétien: Attends campaign breakfast in Yellowknife; speaks at the Italian Cultural Centre in Vancouver; meets supporters in the Victoria Airport and in the Calgary Airport.

McLaughlin: Holds a Q&A session with students at Margaret Barbour Collegiate school; meets with the Assembly of Manitoba Chiefs; flies to Toronto.

Bouchard: Meets with the editorial board of the *Journal de Montréal*; conducts interviews on radio and on 'MusiquePlus'; attends an evening rally.

Manning: Attends evening rally at Prince Andrew High School in Halifax.

Hurtig: Addresses the Empire Club in Toronto.

October 19:

Campbell: Breakfasts at the Old Mill restaurant in Toronto; attends a reception in Oakville; attends reception at the Polish Community Centre in Burlington; attends reception in Dundas.

Chrétien: Appears at a Liberal breakfast in Edmonton; appears at a Liberal luncheon in Prince Albert; attends rally in Winnipeg.

McLaughlin: Appears on CBC Radio's 'Morningside' in Toronto; appears on several open-line radio shows in Toronto; flies to Vancouver.

Bouchard: Visits the Ahuntsic riding in Montreal.

Manning: Attends rally at Tudor Hall in Ottawa; holds rally at the Metro East Trade Centre in Pickering.

Hurtig: Attends breakfast meeting in Montreal; holds evening rally in Vancouver.

October 20:

Campbell: Breakfasts in Guelph; delivers speech in Kitchener; visits Cambridge and continues to a reception at Wonderland Gardens in London.

Chrétien: Appears on CTV's 'Canada AM'; conducts other television interviews.

McLaughlin: Appears on radio show in Vancouver; speaks to students at the University of British Columbia; flies to Winnipeg.

Bouchard: Campaigns in Gatineau, Masson-Angers and Vaudreuil.

Manning: Holds a rally in London; attends a rally at the Keystone Centre in Brandon, Man.

Hurtig: Campaigns in Edmonton.

October 21:

Campbell: Conducts radio interview in London; attends receptions in Woodstock, Brampton and Don Mills.

Chrétien: Meets Canadair executives, tours their Montreal plant; leads rally at Palais des Congrès.

McLaughlin: Speaks to students at the Sisler High School in Winnipeg; meets supporters at Elmwood High School in Winnipeg.

Bouchard: Tapes interview with Radio-Canada; meets BQ candidates in Trois-Rivières; joins Corinne Côté-Lévesque at launching of René Lévesque journalism prizes, University of Quebec in Montreal.

Manning: Speaks to Calgary Chamber of Commerce; holds evening rally in Saskatoon.

Hurtig: Tours a food bank in Edmonton.

October 22:

Campbell: Appears on CTV's 'Canada AM' in Toronto; addresses the Empire and Canadian Clubs; attends an evening reception in Winnipeg.

Chrétien: Appears on CBC's 'Prime Time News' in Toronto; visits Mississauga, Burlington and Trinity-Spadina in Toronto; appears on MuchMusic.

McLaughlin: Meets with Premier Roy Romanow and visits the Pioneer Senior Citizens Home; speaks to supporters at the Saskatchewan Centre of the Arts.

Bouchard: Wraps up campaign with a press conference in Montreal.

Manning: Holds a rally at Royal Athletic Park in Victoria; attends rally at the University of Alberta.

Hurtig: Campaigns in Edmonton.

October 23:

Campbell: Visits Regina, Medicine Hat, Williams Lake, Victoria, and Vancouver.

Chrétien: Visits Toronto and Shawinigan.

McLaughlin: Visits Watson Lake, Yukon.

Bouchard: No official appearances.

Manning: Holds a rally in Red Deer; visits Vancouver.

Hurtig: Campaigns in Edmonton.

October 24:

Campbell: Awaits election results in Vancouver.

Chrétien: Awaits election results in Shawinigan.

McLaughlin: Awaits election results in Whitehorse.

Bouchard: Awaits election results in Alma.

Manning: Flies to Kelowna for a rally; holds rally at the Stampede Corral in Calgary.

Hurtig: Campaigns in Edmonton.

October 25:

Election day.

Appendix Five

Rankings of Federal Ridings by Selected Variables

15 Largest/Smallest Ridings by Physical Area

Largest
Nunatsiaq (NWT)
Western Arctic (NWT)
Abitibi (PQ)
Churchill (MB)
Manicouagan (PQ)
Yukon (YT)
Cochrane–Superior (ON)
Prince Albert–Churchill River (SK)
Labrador (NF)
Kenora–Rainy River (ON)
Skeena (BC)
Prince George–Peace River (BC)
Athabasca (AB)
Peace River (AB)
Caribou–Chilcotin (BC)

Smallest
Rosemont (PQ)
Saint-Denis (PQ)
Davenport (ON)
Papineau–Saint-Michel (PQ)
Bourassa (PQ)
Outremont (PQ)
Beaches–Woodbine (ON)
Hochelega–Maisonneuve (PQ)
Notre-Dame-de-Grâce (PQ)
Parkdale–High Park (ON)
Saint-Henri–Westmount (PQ)
Saint-Léonard (PQ)
St Paul's (ON)
Trinity–Spadina (ON)
Ahuntsic (PQ)

15 Largest/Smallest Ridings by Population, 1991

Largest
York North (ON)
Mississauga West (ON)
Ontario (ON)
Markham–Whitchurch–Stouffville (ON)
Brampton (ON)
Terrebonne (PQ)
Scarborough–Rouge River (ON)
Blainville–Deux-Montagnes (PQ)
Surrey North (BC)
Oakville–Milton (ON)
York Simcoe (ON)
Surrey–White Rock–South Langley (BC)
Carleton–Gloucester (ON)
Gatineau–La Lièvre (PQ)
Calgary North (AB)

Smallest
Nunatsiaq (NWT)
Yukon (YT)
Cardigan (PEI)
Labrador (NF)
Malpeque (PEI)
Hillsborough (PEI)
Egmont (PEI)
Western Arctic (NWT)
Bonaventure–Îles de la Madeleine (PQ)
Restigouche–Chaleur (NB)
Gaspé (PQ)
Miramichi (NB)
Timiskaming (ON)
Madawaska–Victoria (NB
Manicouagan (PQ)

15 Largest/Smallest Ridings by Population Change, 1986-91

Largest
York North (ON)
Mississauga West (ON)
Ontario (ON)
Brampton (ON)
Surrey North (BC)
Markham–Whitchurch–Stouffville (ON)
Fraser Valley West (BC)
Surrey–White Rock–South Langley (BC)
Carleton–Gloucester (ON)
York Simcoe (ON)
Simcoe Centre (ON)
Durham (ON)
Hamilton–Wentworth (ON)
Terrebonne (PQ)
Mission–Coquitlam (BC)

Smallest
Kindersley–Lloydminster (SK)
Gaspé (PQ)
Swift Current–Maple Creek–Assiniboia (SK)
Mackenzie (SK)
Yorkton–Melville (SK)
Souris–Moose Mountain (SK)
Rosemont (PQ)
Burin–St George's (NF)
Matapédia–Matane (PQ)
Bourassa (PQ)
Moose Jaw–Lake Centre (SK)
Papineau–Saint-Michel (PQ)
Winnipeg-St James (MB)
Saint-Léonard (PQ)
Algoma (ON)

15 Largest/Smallest Ridings by Number of Electors, 1993

Largest
York North (ON)
Mississauga West (ON)
Ontario (ON)
Terrebonne (PQ)
Markham–Whitchurch–Stouffville (ON)
Blainville–Deux-Montagnes (PQ)
Brampton (ON)
Surrey–White Rock (BC)
Carleton–Gloucester (ON)
Simcoe Centre (ON)
Vancouver Centre (BC)
Oakville–Milton (ON)
York–Simcoe (ON)
Waterloo (ON)
Calgary North (AB)

Smallest
Nunatsiaq (NWT)
Labrador (NF)
Yukon (YT)
Cardigan (PEI)
Malpeque (PEI)
Western Arctic (NWT)
Egmont (PEI)
Hillsborough (PEI)
Bonaventure–Îles-de-la-Madeleine (PQ)
Manicouagan (PQ)
Restigouche–Chaleur (NB)
Mackenzie (SK)
Kindersley–Lloydminster (SK)
Gaspé (PQ)
Davenport (ON)

15 Highest/Lowest Ridings by Population Density (pop/km²), 1991

Highest
Rosedale (ON)
Davenport (ON)
Saint-Denis (PQ)
Outremont (PQ)
Papineau–Saint-Michel (PQ)
Bourassa (PQ)
Parkdale–High Park (ON)
Beaches–Woodbine (ON)
St Paul's (ON)
Trinity–Spadina (ON)
Saint-Léonard (PQ)
Saint-Henri–Westmount (PQ)
Hochelaga–Maisonneuve (PQ)
Ahuntsic (PQ)
Notre-Dame-de-Grâce (PQ)

Lowest
Nunatsiaq (NWT)
Western Arctic (NWT)
Yukon (YT)
Labrador (NF)
Manicouagan (PQ)
Churchill (MB)
Abitibi (PQ)
Cochrane–Superior (ON)
Prince Albert–Churchill River (SK)
Kenora–Rainy River (ON)
Skeena (BC)
Athabasca (AB)
Prince George–Bulkley Valley (BC)
Cariboo–Chilcotin (BC)
Peace River (AB)

15 Highest/Lowest Ridings Voting 'Yes' in the 1992 Referendum

Highest
Mont-Royal (PQ)
Acadie–Bathurst (NB)
Madawaska-Victoria (NB)
Notre-Dame-de-Grâce (PQ)
Pierrefonds–Dollard (PQ)
Saint-Laurent–Cartierville (PQ)
Hillsborough (PEI)
Restigouche–Chaleur (NB)
Egmont (PEI)
Nunatsiaq (NWT)
Fraser Valley West (BC)
Beauséjour (NB)
Lachine–Lac-Saint-Louis (PQ)
Malpeque (PEI)
Saint-Henri–Westmount (PQ)

Lowest
Athabasca (AB)
Jonquière (PQ)
Lac-Saint-Jean (PQ)
Prince George–Peace River (BC)
Kootenay East (BC)
Mission–Coquitlam (BC)
Prince George–Bulkley Valley (BC)
Surrey North (BC)
Fraser Valley East (BC)
Nanaimo–Cowichan (BC)
Chicoutimi (PQ)
Skeena (BC)
Terrebonne (PQ)
Okanagan Centre (BC)
Okanagan–Similkameen–Merritt (BC)

15 Highest/Lowest Ridings Voting 'No' in the 1992 Referendum

Highest
Jonquière (PQ)
Lac-Saint-Jean (PQ)
Prince George–Peace River (BC)
Kootenay East (BC)
Mission–Coquitlam (BC)
Prince George–Bulkley Valley (BC)
Surrey North (BC)
Chicoutimi (PQ)
Fraser Valley East (PQ)
Nanaimo–Cowichan (BC)
Terrebonne (PQ)
Skeena (BC)
Okanagan Centre (BC)
Okanagan–Similkameen–Merritt (BC)
North Island–Powell River (BC)

Lowest
Mount Royal (PQ)
Acadie–Bathurst (NB)
Madawaska–Victoria (NB)
Notre-Dame-de-Grâce (PQ)
Restigouche–Chaleur (NB)
Hillsborough (PEI)
Pierrefonds–Dollard (PQ)
Saint-Laurent–Cartierville (PQ)
Egmont (PEI)
Nunatsiaq (NWT)
Beauséjour (NB)
Fraser Valley West (BC)
Lachine–Lac-Saint-Louis (PQ)
Malpeque (PEI)
Saint-Henri–Westmount (PQ)

15 Highest/Lowest Ridings by Turnout in the 1992 Referendum

Highest
Ahuntsic (PQ)
Verchères (PQ)
Lachine–Lac-Saint-Louis (PQ)
Vaudreuil (PQ)
Laval Centre (PQ)
La Prairie (PQ)
Laval West (PQ)
Saint-Jean (PQ)
Chambly (PQ)
Saint-Léonard (PQ)
Terrebonne (PQ)
Mont-Royal (PQ)
Saint-Hubert (PQ)
Charlesbourg (PQ)
Pierrefonds–Dollard (PQ)

Lowest
Gander–Grand Falls (NF)
Bonavista–Trinity–Conception (NF)
Burin–St George's (NF)
Labrador (NF)
Humber–St Barbe–Baie Verte (NF)
Churchill (MB)
Winnipeg North Centre (MB)
Edmonton East (AB)
St John's East (NF)
St John's West (NF)
South Shore (NS)
York West (ON)
Kenora–Rainy River (ON)
Prince Albert–Churchill River (SK)
Davenport (ON)

15 Highest/Lowest Liberal Finishes, 1993

Highest	Lowest
Mont-Royal (PQ)	Sherbrooke (PQ)
Humber–St Barbe–Baie Verte (NF)	Chicoutimi (PQ)
Burin–St George's (NF)	Jonquière (PQ)
Glengarry–Prescott–Russell (ON)	Crowfoot (AB)
York West (ON)	Red Deer (AB)
Cape Breton–East Richmond (NS)	Calgary Southeast (AB)
Gander–Grand Falls (NF)	Wild Rose (AB)
Labrador (NF)	Lac-Saint-Jean (PQ)
Beauséjour (NB)	Beauport–Montmorency–Orléans (PQ)
Cape Breton–The Sydneys (NS)	Beauce (PQ)
Bonavista–Trinity–Conception (NF)	Peace River (AB)
Davenport (ON)	Vegreville (AB)
Windsor West (ON)	Abitibi (PQ)
Cochrane–Superior (ON)	Calgary Southwest (AB)
Eglinton–Lawrence (ON)	Joliette (PQ)

15 Highest/Lowest Bloc Qubecois Finishes, 1993*

Highest	Lowest
Lac-Saint-Jean (PQ)	Mont-Royal (PQ)
Terrebonne (PQ)	Notre-Dame-de-Grâce (PQ)
Jonquière (PQ)	Pierrefonds–Dollard (PQ)
Verchères (PQ)	Saint-Laurent–Cartierville (PQ)
Richelieu (PQ)	Saint-Henri–Westmount (PQ)
Joliette (PQ)	Lachine–Lac-Saint-Louis (PQ)
Longueuil (PQ)	Hull–Aylmer (PQ)
Chicoutimi (PQ)	Saint-Léonard (PQ)
Rosemont (PQ)	Lasalle–Émard (PQ)
Charlevoix (PQ)	Bonaventure–Îles-de-la-Madeleine (PQ)
Laurier–Sainte-Marie (PQ)	Pontiac–Gatineau–Labelle (PQ)
Lévis (PQ)	Charlesbourg (PQ)
Hochelaga–Maisonneuve (PQ)	Beauce (PQ)
Berthier–Montcalm (PQ)	Saint-Denis (PQ)
Laurentides (PQ)	Outremont (PQ)

* Only includes Quebec ridings, since the BQ did not offer candidates outside the province.

15 Highest/Lowest Reform Party Finishes, 1993

Highest
Crowfoot (AB)
Red Deer (AB)
Wild Rose (AB)
Wetaskawin (AB)
Macleod (AB)
Calgary Southwest (AB)
Peace River (AB)
Calgary Southeast (AB)
Beaver River (AB)
Prince George–Peace River (BC)
Elk Island (AB)
Yellowhead (AB)
Vegreville (AB)
Medicine Hat (AB)
Lethbridge (AB)

Lowest
Bonavista–Trinity–Conception (NF)
Burin–St George's (NF)
Gander–Grand Falls (NF)
Humber–St Barbe–Baie Verte (NF)
Labrador (NF)
Cardigan (PEI)
Egmont (PEI)
Malpeque (PEI)
Beauséjour (NB)
Acadie–Bathurst (NB)
Restigouche–Chaleur (NB)
Timmins–Chapleau (ON)
Nunatsiaq (NWT)
St John's West (NF)
Madawaska–Victoria (NB)

15 Highest/Lowest NDP Finishes, 1993

Highest
Yukon (YT)
Winnipeg Transcona (MB)
Churchill (MB)
Kamloops (BC)
Regina–Lumsden (SK)
Regina–Qu'Appelle (SK)
Burnaby–Kingsway (BC)
Winnipeg North Centre (MB)
Winnipeg North (MB)
The Battlefords–Meadow Lake (SK)
Vancouver East (BC)
Mackenzie (SK)
Saskatoon–Clark's Crossing (SK)
Prince Albert–Churchill River (SK)
Moose Jaw–Lake Centre (SK)

Lowest
Témiscamingue (PQ)
Saint-Maurice (PQ)
Gaspé (PQ)
Beauce (PQ)
Matapédia–Matane (PQ)
Richelieu (PQ)
Sherbrooke (PQ)
Trois-Rivières (PQ)
Champlain (PQ)
Rimouski–Témiscouata (PQ)
Saint-Jean (PQ)
Berthier–Montcalm (PQ)
Frontenac (PQ)
Blainville–Deux-Montagnes (PQ)
Laval East (PQ)

15 Highest/Lowest Progressive Conservative Finishes, 1993

Highest
Sherbrooke (PQ)
Madawaska–Victoria (NB)
Saint John (NB)
St John's East (NF)
Carleton–Charlotte (NB)
Bellechasse (PQ)
Egmont (PEI)
St John's West (NF)
Cumberland–Colchester (NS)
Cardigan (PEI)
Wellington–Grey–Dufferin–Simcoe (ON)
South Shore (NS)
Central Nova (NS)
Malpeque (PEI)
Etobicoke–Lakeshore (ON)

Lowest
Essex–Windsor (ON)
Saint-Maurice (PQ)
Mercier (PQ)
Papineau–Saint-Michel (PQ)
Davenport (ON)
Lasalle–Émard (PQ)
Windsor West (ON)
Winnipeg North (MB)
Prince Albert–Churchill River (SK)
Winnipeg North Centre (MB)
York West (ON)
Winnipeg Transcona (MB)
Laurier–Sainte-Marie (PQ)
Saint-Denis (PQ)
Rosemont (PQ)

Best Minor Party and Independent Finishes, 1993

Beauce (PQ)
Annapolis Valley–Hants (NS)
Renfrew–Nipissing–Pembroke (ON)
Mercier (PQ)
Beaches–Woodbine (ON)
York Centre (ON)
Edmonton Northwest (AB)
St John (NB)
Kootenay West–Revelstoke (BC)
Vancouver East (BC)
Vancouver Centre (BC)
Skeena (BC)
Hull–Aylmer (PQ)
Victoria (BC)

15 Safest/Most Marginal Liberal Victories, 1993

Safest	Most Marginal
Mont-Royal (PQ)	St John's South East (NF)
Glengarry–Prescott–Russell (ON)	Dauphin–Swan River (MB)
Cape Breton–East Richmond (NS)	Verdun–Saint-Paul (PQ)
York West (ON)	Carleton–Charlotte (NB)
Humber–St Barbe–Baie Verte (NF)	Brandon–Souris (MB)
Davenport (ON)	Madawaska–Victoria (NB)
Cape Breton–The Sydneys (NS)	Wellington–Grey–Dufferin–Simcoe (ON)
Burin–St George's (NF)	Laval West (PQ)
Cochrane–Superior (ON)	Churchill (MB)
Windsor West (ON)	Souris–Moose Mountain (SK)
Beauséjour (NB)	Saskatoon–Humboldt (SK)
Eglinton–Lawrence (ON)	Edmonton East (AB)
Ottawa–Vanier (ON)	Vancouver East (BC)
Gander–Grand Falls (NF)	Edmonton North (AB)
Labrador (NF)	Cambridge (ON)

15 Safest/Most Marginal Bloc Victories, 1993

Safest	Most Marginal
Lac-Saint-Jean (PQ)	Bourassa (PQ)
Mercier (PQ)	La Prairie (PQ)
Joliette (PQ)	Anjou–Rivière-des-Prairies (PQ)
Terrebonne (PQ)	Bellechasse (PQ)
Jonquière (PQ)	Ahuntsic (PQ)
Verchères (PQ)	Brôme–Missisquoi (PQ)
Richelieu (PQ)	Abitibi (PQ)
Charlevoix (PQ)	Gaspé (PQ)
Laurier–Sainte-Marie (PQ)	Mégantic–Compton–Stanstead (PQ)
Longueuil (PQ)	Argenteuil–Papineau (PQ)
Lévis (PQ)	Beauharnois–Salaberry (PQ)
Chicoutimi (PQ)	Champlain (PQ)
Roberval (PQ)	Lotbinière (PQ)
Hochelaga–Maisonneuve (PQ)	Laval Centre (PQ)
Charlesbourg (PQ)	Matapédia–Matane (PQ)

15 Safest/Most Marginal Reform Victories, 1993

Safest	Most Marginal
Wild Rose (AB)	Moose Jaw–Lake Centre (SK)
Red Deer (AB)	Swift Current–Maple Creek–Assiniboia (SK)
Peace River (AB)	Yorkton–Melville (SK)
Crowfoot (AB)	Simcoe Centre (ON)
Wetaskiwin (AB)	New Westminster–Burnaby (BC)
Macleod (AB)	Edmonton–Strathcona (AB)
Calgary Southwest (AB)	Port Moody–Coquitlam (BC)
Calgary Southeast (AB)	Delta (BC)
Prince George–Peace River (BC)	Edmonton Southwest (AB)
Yellowhead (AB)	Cariboo–Chicotin (BC)
Medicine Hat (AB)	Esquimalt–Juan de Fuca (BC)
Vegreville (AB)	Kindersley–Lloydminster (SK)
Beaver River (AB)	Kootenay West–Revelstoke (BC)
Elk Island (AB)	North Vancouver (BC)
Comox–Alberni (BC)	Capilano–Howe Sound (BC)

15 Highest/Lowest Turnout Rates, 1993

Highest	Lowest
Lachine–Lac-Saint-Louis (PQ)	Gander–Grand Falls (NF)
La Prairie (PQ)	Bonavista–Trinity–Conception (NF)
Saint-Maurice (PQ)	Edmonton East (AB)
Laval East (PQ)	Churchill (MB)
Chambly (PQ)	Burin–St George's (NF)
Verchères (PQ)	Winnipeg North Centre (MB)
Vaudreuil (PQ)	St John's East (NF)
Lasalle–Émard (PQ)	Labrador (NF)
Ahuntsic (PQ)	Humber–St Barbe–Baie Verte (NF)
Richelieu (PQ)	Windsor West (ON)
Saint-Hubert (PQ)	Edmonton Northwest (AB)
Saint-Jean (PQ)	St John's West (NF)
Pierrefonds–Dollard (PQ)	Vancouver East (BC)
Mont-Royal (PQ)	Calgary Centre (AB)
Notre-Dame-de-Grâce (PQ)	Hamilton West (ON)

15 Highest/Lowest Victory Margins, 1993

Highest
Mont-Royal (PQ)
Glengarry–Prescott–Russell (ON)
Cape Breton–East Richmond (NS)
York West (ON)
Humber–St Barbe–Baie Verte (NF)
Davenport (ON)
Cape Breton–The Sydneys (NS)
Burin–St George's (NF)
Cochrane–Superior (ON)
Beauce (PQ)
Windsor West (ON)
Lac-Saint-Jean (PQ)
Beauséjour (NB)
Eglinton–Lawrence (ON)
Ottawa–Vanier (ON)

Lowest
Winnipeg Transcona (MB)
Moose Jaw–Lake Centre (SK)
Bourassa (PQ)
St John's East (NF)
Dauphin–Swan River (MB)
La Prairie (PQ)
Anjou–Rivière-des-Prairies (PQ)
Verdun–Saint-Paul (PQ)
The Battlefords–Meadow Lake (SK)
Carleton–Charlotte (NB)
Brandon–Souris (MB)
Saskatoon–Clark's Crossing (SK)
Bellechasse (PQ)
Regina–Lumsden (SK)
Madawaska–Victoria (NB)

15 Highest/Lowest Ridings by English Home Language, 1991

Highest
Bonavista–Trinity–Conception (NF)
Humber–St Barbe–Baie Verte (NF)
Gander–Grand Falls (NF)
Cardigan (PEI)
St John's West (NF)
South Shore (NS)
Burin–St George's (NF)
Cumberland–Colchester (NS)
Central Nova (NS)
Malpeque (PEI)
St John's East (NF)
Souris–Moose Mountain (SK)
Hastings–Frontenac–Lennox–Addington (ON)
Victoria–Haliburton (ON)
Carleton–Charlotte (NB)

Lowest
Kamouraska–Rivière-du-Loup (PQ)
Rimouski–Témiscouata (PQ)
Bellechasse (PQ)
Lac-Saint-Jean (PQ)
Charlevoix (PQ)
Matapédia–Matane (PQ)
Beauce (PQ)
Roberval (PQ)
Lotbinière (PQ)
Saint-Hyacinthe–Bagot (PQ)
Beauport–Montmorency–Orléans (PQ)
Lévis (PQ)
Champlain (PQ)
Saint-Maurice (PQ)
Québec-Est (PQ)

15 Highest/Lowest Ridings by French Home Language, 1991

Highest

Kamouraska–Rivière-du-Loup (PQ)
Rimouski–Témiscouata (PQ)
Bellechasse (PQ)
Lac-Saint-Jean (PQ)
Matapédia–Matane (PQ)
Beauce (PQ)
Lotbinière (PQ)
Saint-Hyacinthe–Bagot (PQ)
Saint-Maurice (PQ)
Beauport–Montmorency–Orléans (PQ)
Lévis (PQ)
Jonquière (PQ)
Chicoutimi (PQ)
Richelieu (PQ)
Joliette (PQ)

Lowest

Bonavista–Trinity–Conception (NF)
Yorkton–Melville (SK)
Humber–St Barbe–Baie Verte (NF)
Bruce–Grey (ON)
St John's West (NF)
Kindersley–Lloydminster (SK)
Perth–Wellington–Waterloo (ON)
Gander–Grand Falls (NF)
Crowfoot (AB)
Victoria–Haliburton (ON)
Medicine Hat (AB)
Surrey North (BC)
Wellington–Grey–Dufferin–Simcoe (ON)
Delta (BC)
Burnaby–Kingsway (BC)

15 Highest/Lowest Ridings by Percentage of 'Other' Home Languages, 1991

Highest

Nunatsiaq (NWT)
Davenport (ON)
Trinity–Spadina (ON)
York West (ON)
Saint-Denis (PQ)
Vancouver East (BC)
Vancouver South (BC)
Scarborough–Agincourt (ON)
York Centre (ON)
Eglinton–Lawrence (ON)
Broadview–Greenwood (ON)
York South–Weston (ON)
Scarborough–Rouge River (ON)
Don Valley North (ON)
Vancouver Quadra (BC)

Lowest

Gaspé (PQ)
Lac-Saint-Jean (PQ)
Matapédia–Matane (PQ)
Bonavista–Trinity–Conception (NF)
Egmont (PEI)
Bellechasse (PQ)
Beauce (PQ)
Rimouski–Témiscouata (PQ)
Restigouche–Chaleur (NB)
Burin–St George's (NF)
Kamouraska–Rivière-du-Loup (PQ)
Saint-Maurice (PQ)
Acadie–Bathurst (NB)
Gander–Grand Falls (NF)
Cardigan (PEI)

15 Highest/Lowest Ridings by Percentage of Bilingual (English & French) Speakers, 1991

Highest
Hull–Aylmer (PQ)
Saint-Henri–Westmount (PQ)
Pierrefonds–Dollard (PQ)
Lachine–Lac-Saint-Louis (PQ)
Outremont (PQ)
Beauséjour (NB)
Notre-Dame-de-Grâce (PQ)
La Prairie (PQ)
Gatineau–La Lièvre (PQ)
Saint-Laurent–Cartierville (PQ)
Glengarry–Prescott–Russell (ON)
Mount Royal (PQ)
Vaudreuil (PQ)
Ahuntsic (PQ)
Ottawa-Vanier (ON)

Lowest
Bonavista–Trinity–Conception (NF)
Gander–Grand Falls (NF)
Kindersley–Lloydminster (SK)
Humber–St Barbe–Baie Verte (NF)
Yorkton–Melville (SK)
Crowfoot (AB)
Regina–Qu'Appelle (SK)
Medicine Hat (AB)
Burin–St George's (NF)
Vegreville (AB)
Cape Breton–The Sydneys (NS)
Mackenzie (SK)
Nunatsiaq (NWT)
St John's West (NF)
Wetaskiwin (AB)

Highest/Lowest Ridings by Roman Catholic Population, 1991

Highest
Jonquière (PQ)
Kamouraska–Rivière-du-Loup (PQ)
Charlevoix (PQ)
Lac-Saint-Jean (PQ)
Bellechasse (PQ)
Roberval (PQ)
Beauce (PQ)
Frontenac (PQ)
Lotbinière (PQ)
Richelieu (PQ)
Chicoutimi (PQ)
Matapédia–Matane (PQ)
Champlain (PQ)
Beauport–Montmorency–Orléans (PQ)
Rimouski–Témiscouata (PQ)

Lowest
South Shore (NS)
Fraser Valley West (BC)
Lisgar–Marquette (MB)
Okanagan–Shuswap (BC)
Saanich–Gulf Islands (BC)
Victoria–Haliburton (ON)
Victoria (BC)
North Island–Powell River (BC)
Bonavista–Trinity–Conception (NF)
Nanaimo–Cowichan (BC)
Surrey–White Rock–South Langley (BC)
Carleton–Charlotte (NB)
Esquimalt–Juan de Fuca (BC)
Capilano–Howe Sound (BC)
Fraser Valley East (BC)

15 Highest/Lowest Ridings by Protestant Population, 1991

Highest	Lowest
Bonavista–Trinity–Conception (NF)	Kamouraska–Rivière-du-Loup (PQ)
Gander–Grand Falls (NF)	Charlevoix (PQ)
South Shore (NS)	Jonquière (PQ)
Lisgar–Marquette (MB)	Lac-Saint-Jean (PQ)
Carleton–Charlotte (NB)	Bellechasse (PQ)
Cumberland–Colchester (NS)	Beauport–Montmorency–Orléans (PQ)
Huron–Bruce (ON)	Chicoutimi (PQ)
Perth–Wellington–Waterloo (ON)	Québec Est (PQ)
Humber–St Barbe–Baie Verte (NF)	Rimouski–Témiscouata (PQ)
Annapolis Valley–Hants (NS)	Richelieu (PQ)
Bruce–Grey (ON)	Portneuf (PQ)
Nunatsiaq (NWT)	Trois-Rivières (PQ)
Hastings–Frontenac–Lennox–Addington (ON)	Québec (PQ)
Victoria–Haliburton (ON)	Charlesbourg (PQ)
Brandon–Souris (MB)	Beauce (PQ)

15 Highest/Lowest Ridings by Jewish Population, 1991

Highest	Lowest
Mont-Royal (PQ)	Lac-Saint-Jean (PQ)
Willowdale (ON)	Bonavista–Trinity–Conception (NF)
Saint-Laurent–Cartierville (PQ)	Kamouraska–Rivière-du-Loup (PQ)
Don Valley North (ON)	Acadie–Bathurst (NB)
St Paul's (ON)	Restigouche–Chaleur (NB)
Outremont (PQ)	Témiscamingue (PQ)
York Centre (ON)	Gaspé (PQ)
Saint-Denis (PQ)	Burin–St George's (NF)
Eglinton–Lawrence (ON)	Roberval (PQ)
Broadview–Greenwood (ON)	Frontenac (PQ)
Pierrefonds–Dollard (PQ)	Bonaventure–Îles de la Madeleine (PQ
Markham–Whitchurch–Stouffville (ON)	Beauport–Montmorency–Orléans (PQ)
Mississauga East (ON)	Saint-Maurice (PQ)
Don Valley East (ON)	Richmond–Wolfe (PQ)
Don Valley West (ON)	Lotbinière (PQ)

15 Highest/Lowest Ridings by Immigrants as a Percentage of Population, 1991

Highest	Lowest
Davenport (ON)	Matapédia–Matane (PQ)
York West (ON)	Gaspé (PQ)
Scarborough–Rouge River (ON)	Lac-Saint-Jean (PQ)
Scarborough–Agincourt (ON)	Roberval (PQ)
York Centre (ON)	Bonaventure–Îles-de-la-Madeine (PQ)
Don Valley North (ON)	Bellechasse (PQ)
Trinity–Spadina (ON)	Kamouraska–Rivière-du-Loup (PQ)
Vancouver South (BC)	Charlevoix (PQ)
Eglinton–Lawrence (ON)	Bonavista–Trinity–Conception (NF)
York South–Weston (ON)	Jonquière (PQ)
Willowdale (ON)	Burin–St George's (NF)
Vancouver East (BC)	Rimouski–Témiscouata (PQ)
Mississauga East (ON)	Saint-Maurice (PQ)
Don Valley East (ON)	Chicoutimi (PQ)
Etobicoke North (ON)	Beauce (PQ)

15 Highest/Lowest Ridings by Aboriginal Population[1], 1991

Highest	Lowest
Nunatsiaq (NWT)	Scarborough–Agincourt (ON)
Churchill (MB)	Bonavista–Trinity–Conception (NF)
Western Arctic (NWT)	York North (ON)
Prince Albert–Churchill River (SK)	Etobicoke Centre (ON)
Kenora–Rainy River (ON)	Don Valley North (ON)
The Battlefords–Meadow Lake (SK)	St John's West (NF)
Skeena (BC)	Markham–Whitchurch–Stouffville (ON)
Yukon (YT)	Oakville–Milton (ON)
Athabaska (AB)	Mont-Royal (PQ)
Dauphin–Swan River (MB)	Pierrefonds–Dollard (PQ)
Cochrane–Superior (ON)	York West (ON)
Winnipeg North Centre (MB)	Mississauga West (ON)
Labrador (NF)	Kamouraska–Rivière-du-Loup (PQ)
Abitibi (PQ)	St John's East (NF)
Caribou–Chilcotin (BC)	Don Valley East (ON)

[1] See cautionary note on the definition of this measure in Appendix Three.

15 Highest/Lowest Ridings by Average Family Income, 1991

Highest
St Paul's (ON)
Don Valley West (ON)
Capilano–Howe Sound (BC)
Etobicoke Centre (ON)
Markham–Whitchurch–Stouffville (ON)
Saint-Henri–Westmount (PQ)
Oakville-Milton (ON)
Rosedale (ON)
York North (ON)
Mississauga South (ON)
Halton–Peel (ON)
Carleton–Gloucester (ON)
Mount Royal (PQ)
Nepean (ON)
Calgary Southwest (AB)

Lowest
Winnipeg North Centre (MB)
Saint-Denis (PQ)
Bonavista–Trinity–Conception (NF)
Papineau–Saint-Michel (PQ)
Burin–St George's (NF)
Dauphin–Swan River (MB)
Gaspé (PQ)
Acadie–Bathurst (NB)
Mackenzie (SK)
The Battlefords–Meadow Lake (SK)
Matapédia–Matane (PQ)
Gander–Grand Falls (NF)
Madawaska–Victoria (NB)
Laurier–Sainte-Marie (PQ)
Hochelaga–Maisonneuve (PQ)

15 Highest/Lowest Ridings by Median Family Income, 1991

Highest
Don Valley West (ON)
St Paul's (ON)
Oakville–Milton (ON)
Markham–Whitchurch–Stouffville (ON)
Carleton–Gloucester (ON)
York North (ON)
Capilano–Howe Sound (BC)
Etobicoke Centre (ON)
Halton–Peel (ON)
Nepean (ON)
Ontario (ON)
Mississauga South (ON)
Mississauga West (ON)
Calgary Southwest (AB)
Western Arctic (NWT)

Lowest
Winnipeg North Centre (MB)
Dauphin–Swan River (MB)
Saint-Denis (PQ)
Laurier–Sainte-Marie (PQ)
Bonavista–Trinity–Conception (NF)
Papineau–Saint-Michel (PQ)
Burin–St George's (NF)
Gaspé (PQ)
Mackenzie (SK)
The Battlefords–Meadow Lake (SK)
Acadie–Bathurst (NB)
Gander–Grand Falls (NF)
Matapédia–Matane (PQ)
Yorkton–Melville (SK)
Quebec (PQ)

15 Highest/Lowest Percentage of Low Income Families, 1991

Highest
Winnipeg North Centre (MB)
Laurier–Sainte-Marie (PQ)
Saint-Denis (PQ)
Papineau–Saint-Michel (PQ)
Hochelaga–Maisonneuve (PQ)
Quebec (PQ)
Vancouver East (BC)
Verdun–Saint-Paul (PQ)
Rosemont (PQ)
Edmonton East (AB)
Bourassa (PQ)
Hamilton West (ON)
Calgary Centre (AB)
Saint-Laurent–Cartierville (PQ)
Davenport (ON)

Lowest
Yukon (YT)
Nunatsiaq (NWT)
Western Arctic (NWT)
Halton–Peel (ON)
Lanark–Carleton (ON)
Carleton–Gloucester (ON)
Durham (ON)
Oakville–Milton (ON)
Elk Island (AB)
Lambton–Middlesex (ON)
Markham–Whitchurch–Stouffville (ON)
Ontario (ON)
York–Simcoe (ON)
St Albert (AB)
Verchères (PQ)

15 Highest/Lowest Ridings by Percentage of Income in Government Transfers, 1991

Highest
Bonavista–Trinity–Conception (NF)
Gaspé (PQ)
Burin–St George's (NF)
Bonaventure–Îles de la Madeleine (PQ)
Acadie–Bathurst (NB)
Gander–Grand Falls (NF)
Matapédia–Matane (PQ)
Cape Breton–East Richmond (NS)
Egmont (PEI)
Humber–St Barbe–Baie Verte (NF)
Cape Breton–The Sydneys (NS)
Miramichi (NB)
Cardigan (PEI)
Winnipeg North Centre (MB)
Beauséjour (NB)

Lowest
Markham–Whitchurch–Stouffville (ON)
Mississauga West (ON)
Carleton–Gloucester (ON)
Don Valley West (ON)
Halton–Peel (ON)
Oakville–Milton (ON)
St Paul's (ON)
York North (ON)
Ontario (ON)
Calgary Southwest (AB)
Nepean (ON)
Western Arctic (NWT)
Scarborough–Rouge River (ON)
Elk Island (AB)
Brampton (ON)

15 Highest/Lowest Ridings Ranked by Average Home Value

Highest
Don Valley West (ON)
St Paul's (ON)
Rosedale (ON)
Vancouver Quadra (BC)
Vancouver South (BC)
York North (ON)
Capilano–Howe Sound (BC)
Markham–Whitchurch–Stouffville (ON)
Etobicoke-Centre (ON)
Saint-Henri–Westmount (PQ)
Willowdale (ON)
Trinity–Spadina (ON)
Parkdale–High Park (ON)
Mont-Royal (PQ)
Eglinton–Lawrence (ON)

Lowest
Labrador (NF)
Mackenzie (SK)
Dauphin–Swan River (MB)
Burin–St George's (NF)
Bonavista–Trinity–Conception (NF)
Matapédia–Matane (PQ)
Gaspé (PQ)
Gander–Grand Falls (NF)
Swift Current–Maple Creek–Assiniboia (SK)
Cape Breton–East Richmond (NS)
Bonaventure–Îles-de-la-Madeleine (PQ)
Yorkton–Melville (SK)
Manicouagan (PQ)
Souris–Moose Mountain (SK)
Humber–St Barbe–Baie Verte (NF)

15 Highest/Lowest Ridings by Home Ownership, 1991

Highest
Bonavista–Trinity–Conception (NF)
Malpeque (PEI)
Elk Island (AB)
Fundy–Royal (NB)
Cardigan (PEI)
Halton–Peel (ON)
Burin–St George's (NF)
Markham–Whitchurch–Stouffville (ON)
St Albert (AB)
York North (ON)
Carleton–Charlotte (NB)
South Shore (NS)
Humber–St Barbe–Baie Verte (NF)
Beauséjour (NB)
Cape Breton Highlands–Canso (NS)

Lowest
Nunatsiaq (NWT)
Laurier–Sainte-Marie (PQ)
Hochelaga–Maisonneuve (PQ)
Rosedale (ON)
Saint-Henri–Westmount (PQ)
Rosemont (PQ)
Quebec (PQ)
Outremont (PQ)
Saint-Denis (PQ)
Vancouver Centre (BC)
Verdun–Saint-Paul (PQ)
Papineau–Saint-Michel (PQ)
Bourassa (PQ)
Calgary Centre (AB)
Notre-Dame-de-Grâce (PQ)

15 Highest/Lowest Ridings by Unemployment, 1991

Highest
Bonavista–Trinity–Conception (NF)
Burin–St George's (NF)
Gander–Grand Falls (NF)
Humber–St Barbe–Baie Verte (NF)
Gaspé (PQ)
Miramichi (NB)
Acadie–Bathurst (NB)
Labrador (NF)
Bonaventure–Îles de la Madeleine (PQ)
Restigouche–Chaleur (NB)
St John's West (NF)
Cape Breton–The Sydneys (NS)
Cape Breton–East Richmond (NS)
Matapédia–Matane (PQ)
Nunatsiaq (NWT)

Lowest
Lisgar–Marquette (MB)
Swift Current–Maple Creek–Assiniboia (SK)
Souris–Moose Mountain (SK)
Kindersley–Lloydminster (SK)
Vegreville (AB)
Perth–Wellington–Waterloo (ON)
Crowfoot (AB)
Elk Island (AB)
Carleton–Gloucester (ON)
Wild Rose (AB)
Oakville–Milton (ON)
Moose Jaw–Lake Centre (SK)
Don Valley West (ON)
Yorkton–Melville (SK)
Halton–Peel (ON)

15 Highest/Lowest Ridings by Labour Force Participation, 1991

Highest
Yukon (YK)
Carleton–Gloucester (ON)
Mississauga West (ON)
Western Arctic (NWT)
St Albert (AB)
Elk Island (AB)
Calgary Northeast (AB)
Brampton (ON)
Ontario (ON)
Halton–Peel (ON)
Calgary Southeast (AB)
Wild Rose (AB)
Nepean (ON)
Bramalea–Gore–Malton (ON)
Vancouver Centre (BC)

Lowest
Cape Breton–East Richmond (NS)
Saint-Maurice (PQ)
Cape Breton–The Sydneys (NS)
Bonavista–Trinity–Conception (NF)
Gaspé (PQ)
Matapédia—Matane (PQ)
Quebec (PQ)
Gander–Grand Falls (PQ)
Burin–St Georgeís (NF)
Hochelaga–Maisonneuve (PQ)
Winnipeg North Centre (MB)
Okanagan–Similkameen–Merritt (BC)
Papineau–Saint-Michel (PQ)
South Shore (NS)
Bellechasse (PQ)

15 Highest/Lowest Ridings by Employment as Managers and Administrators, 1991

Highest	Lowest
Don Valley West (ON)	Burin–St George's (NF)
St Paul's (ON)	Winnipeg North Centre (MB)
Oakville–Milton (ON)	Bonavista–Trinity–Conception (NF)
Rosedale (ON)	Vancouver East (BC)
Markham–Whitchurch–Stouffville (ON)	Egmont (PEI)
Etobicoke Centre (ON)	Hamilton East (ON)
Carleton–Gloucester (ON)	Cape Breton–East Richmond (NS)
La Prairie (PQ)	Miramichi (NB)
York North (ON)	Gander–Grand Falls (NF)
Nepean (ON)	Acadie–Bathurst (NB)
Saint-Henri–Westmount (PQ)	Cochrane–Superior (ON)
Mont-Royal (PQ)	South West Nova (NS)
Don Valley North (ON)	Humber–St Barbe–Baie Verte (NF)
Lachine–Lac-Saint-Louis (PQ)	Kootenay West–Revelstoke (BC)
Louis-Hébert (PQ)	South Shore (NS)

15 Highest/Lowest Ridings by Percentage Self-Employed, 1991

Highest	Lowest
Swift Current–Maple Creek–Assiniboia (SK)	Hamilton East (ON)
Kindersley–Lloydminster (SK)	Oshawa (ON)
Mackenzie (SK)	St John (NB)
Dauphin–Swan River (MB)	Labrador (NF)
Yorkton–Melville (SK)	Mercier (PQ)
Souris–Moose Mountain (SK)	Hamilton Mountain (ON)
Crowfoot (AB)	York West (ON)
Lisgar–Marquette (MB)	Dartmouth (NS)
Vegreville (AB)	Papineau–Saint-Michel (PQ)
The Battlefords–Meadow Lake (SK)	Jonquière (PQ)
Moose Jaw–Lake Centre (SK)	Winnipeg Transcona (MB)
Macleod (AB)	Winnipeg North Centre (MB)
Wetaskawin (AB)	Sault Ste Marie (ON)
Portage–Interlake (MB)	Hochelaga–Maisonneuve (PQ)
Wild Rose (AB)	Lasalle–Émard (PQ)

15 Highest/Lowest Ridings by Residents with University Degrees, 1991

Highest
St Paul's (ON)
Don Valley West (ON)
Ottawa Centre (ON)
Saint-Henri–Westmount (PQ)
Rosedale (ON)
Outremont (PQ)
Vancouver Centre (BC)
Louis-Hébert (PQ)
Notre-Dame-de-Grâce (PQ)
Edmonton Strathcona (AB)
Mont-Royal (PQ)
Trinity–Spadina (ON)
Halifax (NS)
Capilano–Howe Sound (BC)
Vancouver Quadra (BC)

Lowest
Berthier–Montcalm (PQ)
Bonavista–Trinity–Conception (NF)
Burin–St George's (NF)
Gaspé (PQ)
Bellechasse (PQ)
Yorkton–Melville (SK)
Mackenzie (SK)
Hamilton East (ON)
Matapédia–Matane (PQ)
Gander–Grand Falls (NF)
Beauce (PQ)
Souris–Moose Mountain (SK)
Frontenac (PQ)
Dauphin–Swan River (MB)
Charlevoix (PQ)

15 Highest/Lowest Ridings by Residential Mobility, 1990-91 (One year)

Highest
Calgary Centre (AB)
Vancouver Centre (BC)
Western Arctic (NWT)
Edmonton Northwest (AB)
Winnipeg North Centre (MB)
Edmonton East (AB)
Surrey North (BC)
Ottawa Centre (ON)
Laurier–Sainte-Marie (PQ
Yukon (YT)
Victoria (BC)
Ottawa–Vanier (ON)
Edmonton Southwest (AB)
Edmonton–Strathcona (AB)
Nunatsiaq (NWT)

Lowest
Bellechasse (PQ)
Cardigan (PEI)
Bonavista–Trinity–Conception (NF)
Beauce (PQ)
Beauséjour (NB)
Frontenac (PQ)
Cape Breton-Highlands–Canso (NS)
Acadie–Bathurst (NB)
Burin–St George's (NF)
Kamouraska–Rivière-du-Loup (PQ)
Gaspé (PQ)
Cape Breton–East Richmond (NS)
Carleton–Charlotte (NB)
Bonaventure–Îles de la Madeleine (PQ)
Miramichi (NB)

15 Highest/Lowest Ridings by Residential Mobility, 1986-91 (Five years)

Highest
Vancouver Centre (BC)
Calgary Centre (AB)
Western Arctic (NWT)
Mississauga West (ON)
Surrey North (BC)
Yukon (YT)
Fraser Valley West (BC)
Nunatsiaq (NWT)
Laurier–Sainte-Marie (PQ)
Edmonton Northwest (AB)
Surrey–White Rock–South Langley (BC)
Okanagan Centre (BC)
Ontario (ON)
Edmonton Southwest (AB)
Brampton (ON)

Lowest
Bonavista–Trinity–Conception (NF)
Burin–St George's (NF)
Cape Breton Highlands–Canso (NS)
Humber–St Barbe–Baie Verte (NF)
Bellechasse (PQ)
Cardigan (PEI)
Acadie–Bathurst (NB)
Bonaventure–Îles de la Madeleine (PQ)
Gaspé (PQ)
Beauséjour (NB)
Mackenzie (SK)
Cape Breton–East Richmond (NS)
Gander–Grand Falls (NF)
Miramichi (NB)
Beauce (PQ)

15 Highest/Lowest Ridings by Employment in Manufacturing, 1991

Highest
Shefford (PQ)
Cambridge (ON)
Essex–Windsor (ON)
York West (ON)
Windsor–St Clair (ON)
Hamilton East (ON)
Saint-Denis (PQ)
Oshawa (ON)
Mégantic–Compton–Stanstead (PQ)
Beauce (PQ)
Papineau–Saint-Michel (PQ)
Bramalea–Gore–Malton (ON)
Brôme–Missisquoi (PQ)
Drummondville (PQ)
Kitchener (ON)

Lowest
Nunatsiaq (NWT)
Western Arctic (NWT)
Yukon (YT)
Swift Current–Maple Creek– Assiniboia (SK)
Dauphin–Swan River (MB)
Souris–Moose Mountain (SK)
Vegreville (AB)
Yorkton–Melville (SK)
Kindersley–Lloydminster (SK)
Crowfoot (AB)
Labrador (NF)
The Battlefords–Meadow Lake (SK)
Beaver River (AB)
Victoria (BC)
Ottawa–Vanier (ON)

15 Highest/Lowest Ridings by Service Sector Employment, 1991

Highest
Vancouver East (BC)
Esquimalt–Juan de Fuca (BC)
Dartmouth (NS)
Kingston and the Islands (ON)
Winnipeg North Centre (MB)
Fredericton–York-Sunbury (NB)
Renfrew–Nipissing–Pembroke (ON)
Beaver River (AB)
Victoria (BC)
Edmonton East (AB)
Quebec (PQ)
Brandon–Souris (MB)
Fraser Valley East (BC)
Davenport (ON)
Comox–Alberni (BC)

Lowest
Don Valley West (ON)
Etobicoke Centre (ON)
Markham–Whitchurch–Stouffville (ON)
Mississauga South (ON)
York North (ON)
Willowdale (ON)
Brampton (ON)
Halton–Peel (ON)
Mississauga West (ON)
Ontario (ON)
York–Simcoe (ON)
Perth–Wellington–Waterloo (ON)
Lanark–Carleton (ON)
Lachine–Lac-St-Louis (PQ)
St Paul's (ON)

15 Highest/Lowest Ridings by Employment in Agriculture, 1991

Highest
Swift Current–Maple Creek–Assiniboia (SK)
Kindersley–Lloydminster (SK)
Mackenzie (SK)
Lisgar–Marquette (MB)
Dauphin–Swan River (MB)
Yorkton–Melville (SK)
Souris–Moose Mountain (SK)
The Battlefords–Meadow Lake (SK)
Crowfoot (AB)
Vegreville (AB)
Moose Jaw–Lake Centre (SK)
Portage–Interlake (MB)
Macleod (AB)
Medicine Hat (AB)
Provencher (MB)

Lowest
Manicouagan (PQ)
Halifax (NS)
Mount Royal (PQ)
Papineau–Saint-Michel (PQ)
Rosedale (ON)
Scarborough East (ON)
Saint-Léonard (PQ)
Scarborough Centre (ON)
Labrador (NF)
Scarborough–Rouge River (ON)
Nunatsiaq (NWT)
Scarborough West (ON)
Lasalle–Émard (PQ)
Western Arctic (NWT)
York Centre (ON)

15 Highest/Lowest Ridings by Employment in Mining, 1991

Highest
Athabasca (AB)
Labrador (NF)
Timmins–Chapleau (ON)
Churchill (MB)
Yellowhead (AB)
Manicouagan (PQ)
Nickel Belt (ON)
Kootenay East (BC)
Abitibi (PQ)
Algoma (ON)
Témiscamingue (PQ)
Calgary North (AB)
Calgary Southwest (AB)
Calgary West (AB)
Cape Breton–East Richmond (NS)

Lowest
Kitchener (ON)
Rosemont (PQ)
Mount Royal (PQ)
Papineau–Saint-Michel (PQ)
Ottawa Centre (ON)
Ottawa–Vanier (ON)
Ahuntsic (PQ)
Sherbrooke (PQ)
Outremont (PQ)
York West (ON)
Saint-Denis (PQ)
Saint-Hubert (PQ)
Prince Edward–Hastings (ON)
Hillsborough (PEI)
Oshawa (ON)

15 Highest/Lowest Ridings by Employment in Forest Industries, 1991

Highest
North Island–Powell River (BC)
Cariboo–Chilcotin (BC)
Prince George–Bulkley Valley (BC)
Roberval (PQ)
Skeena (BC)
Miramichi (NB)
Comox–Alberni (BC)
Cochrane–Superior (ON)
Madawaska–Victoria (NB)
Pontiac–Gatineau–Labelle (PQ)
Kootenay East (BC)
Cape Breton-Highlands–Canso (NS)
Matapédia–Matane (PQ)
Okanagan–Shuswap (BC)
Kenora–Rainy River (ON)

Lowest
Nunatsiaq (NWT)
Papineau–Saint-Michel (PQ)
Saint-Denis (PQ)
Saint-Léonard (PQ)
Sarnia–Lambton (ON)
Bramalea–Gore–Malton (ON)
Laval West (PQ)
Scarborough Centre (ON)
Mississauga West (ON)
Windsor–St Clair (ON)
Kent (ON)
Laval Centre (PQ)
Ontario (ON)
Swift Current–Maple Creek–Assiniboia (SK)
York Centre (ON)

15 Ridings with the Highest Employment in the Fishing Industry, 1991

Cardigan (PEI)
Egmont (PEI)
Humber–St Barbe–Baie Verte (NF)
South Shore (NS)
Burin–St George's (NF)
South West Nova (NS)
Bonavista–Trinity–Conception (NF)
Gander–Grand Falls (NF)
Acadie–Bathurst (NB)
Bonaventure–Îles-de la Madeleine (PQ)
North Island–Powell River (BC)
Cape Breton Highlands–Canso (NS)
Labrador (NF)
Gaspé (PQ)
Cape Breton–The Sydneys (NS)

15 Highest/Lowest Ridings by Employment in Government Services, 1991

Highest	Lowest
Nunatsiaq (NWT)	Mont-Royal (PQ)
Western Arctic (NWT)	Kindersley–Lloydminster (SK)
Carleton–Gloucester (ON)	Pierrefonds–Dollard (PQ)
Ottawa–Vanier (ON)	York West (ON)
Hull–Aylmer (PQ)	Beauce (PQ)
Ottawa Centre (ON)	Frontenac (PQ)
Ottawa South (ON)	Perth–Wellington–Waterloo (ON)
Yukon (YT)	Shefford (PQ)
Fredericton–York-Sunbury (NB)	Beauharnois–Salaberry (PQ)
Gatineau–La Lièvre (PQ)	Notre-Dame-de-Grâce (PQ)
Ottawa West (ON)	Hamilton East (ON)
Dartmouth (NS)	Lotbinière (PQ)
Nepean (ON)	Drummondville (PQ)
Esquimalt–Juan de Fuca (BC)	Saint-Laurent (PQ)
Beaver River (AB)	Berthier–Montcalm (PQ)

15 Highest/Lowest Ridings by Percentage of Employment in Business Services, 1991

Highest
St Paul's (ON)
York North (ON)
Eglinton–Lawrence (ON)
Etobicoke–Lakeshore (ON)
Oakville–Milton (ON)
Ottawa South (ON)
Vancouver Quadra (BC)
Lanark–Carleton (ON)
Scarborough–Rouge River (ON)
Calgary North (AB)
Mississauga South (ON)
Verdun–Saint Paul (PQ)
Etobicoke Centre (ON)
La Prairie (PQ)
Calgary Southwest (AB)

Lowest
Dauphin–Swan River (MB)
Burin–St George's (NF)
Cochrane–Superior (ON)
Lisgar–Marquette (MB)
Egmont (PEI)
Madawaska–Victoria (NB)
Mackenzie (SK)
Swift Current–Maple Creek–Assiniboia (SK)
Cardigan (PEI)
Kindersley–Lloydminster (SK)
Bonavista–Trinity–Conception (NF)
Labrador (NF)
Churchill (MB)
Humber–St Barbe–Baie Verte (NF)
Gaspé (PQ)

15 Most/Least Homogeneous Ridings in Terms of Ethnic Origins, 1991

Most
Bonavista–Trinity–Conception (NF)
Kamouraska–Rivière-du-Loup (PQ)
Bellechasse (PQ)
Gander–Grand Falls (NF)
Beauce (PQ)
Rimouski–Témiscouata (PQ)
Lotbinière (PQ)
Matapédia–Matane (PQ)
Lac-Saint-Jean (PQ)
St John's West (NF)
St-Maurice (PQ)
Beauport–Montmorency–Orléans (PQ)
Frontenac (PQ)
Richelieu (PQ)
Lévis (PQ)

Least
Edmonton East (AB)
Edmonton North (AB)
Edmonton Southeast (AB)
Winnipeg North Centre (MB)
Mississauga East (ON)
Parkdale–High Park (ON)
Edmonton Southwest (AB)
Winnipeg North (MB)
Beaver River (AB)
Edmonton–Strathcona (AB)
Saskatchewan–Dundurn (SK)
Calgary Northeast (AB)
Don Valley East (ON)
Peace River (AB)
Saskatchewan–Humboldt (SK)

15 Most/Least Religiously Homogeneous Ridings, 1991

Most Homogeneous
Jonquière (PQ)
Lac-St-Jean (PQ)
Charlevoix (PQ)
Chicoutimi (PQ)
Roberval (PQ)
Bellechasse (PQ)
Kamouraska–Riviére-du-Loup (PQ)
Champlain (PQ)
Rimouski–Témiscouata (PQ)
Matapédia–Matane (PQ)
Beauce (PQ)
Lotbinière (PQ)
Richelieu (PQ)
Portneuf (PQ)
Charlesbourg (PQ)

Least Homogeneous
Broadview–Greenwood (ON)
Scarborough–Agincourt (ON)
Vancouver South (BC)
Rosedale (ON)
Don Valley North (ON)
Vancouver–Quadra (BC)
Scarborough–Rouge River (ON)
Burnaby–Kingsway (BC)
Beaches–Woodbine (ON)
Markham–Whitchurch–Stouffville (ON)
Don Valley East (ON)
Edmonton North (AB)
Edmonton East (AB)
Scarborough West (ON)
Richmond (BC)

15 Highest/Lowest Disparity in Distribution of Family Incomes, 1991

Most
St-Henri–Westmount (PQ)
Rosedale (ON)
St Paul's (ON)
Outremont (PQ)
Don Valley West (ON)
Mont-Royal (PQ)
Calgary Centre (AB)
Vancouver–Quadra (BC)
Laurier–Ste-Marie (PQ)
Vancouver South (BC)
Trinity–Spadina (ON)
Capilano–Howe Sound (BC)
Eglinton–Lawrence (ON)
Victoria (BC)
York Centre (ON)

Least
Labrador (NF)
Oshawa (ON)
Châteauguay (PQ)
Calgary Northeast (AB)
St-Hubert (PQ)
Ontario (ON)
Beauport–Montmorency–Orléans (PQ)
Yellowhead (AB)
Edmonton North (AB)
Edmonton Southeast (AB)
Winnipeg–Transcona (MB)
Bramalea–Gore–Malton (ON)
Yukon (YT)
Prince George–Bulkley Valley (BC)
Scarborough–Rouge River (ON)

15 Most/Least Homogeneous Ridings in Terms of Employment Sectors, 1991

Most	**Least**
Vancouver Centre (BC)	Burin–St George's (NF)
St Paul's (ON)	Bonavista–Trinity–Conception (NF)
Rosedale (ON)	Cardigan (PEI)
Halifax (NS)	Beauce (PQ)
Don Valley West (ON)	Acadie–Bathurst (NB)
Quebec (PQ)	Mégantic–Compton–Stanstead (PQ)
Vancouver Quadra (BC)	Carleton–Charlotte (NB)
Victoria (BC)	Skeena (BC)
Louis-Hébert (PQ)	Miramichi (NB)
Winnipeg South Centre (MB)	Perth–Wellington–Waterloo (ON)
Capilano–Howe Sound (BC)	Lotbinière (PQ)
Laurier–Sainte-Marie (PQ)	North Island–Powell River (BC)
Outremont (PQ)	Humber–St Barbe–Baie Verte (NF)
North Vancouver (BC)	Egmont (PEI)
Hillsborough (PEI)	South Shore (NS)

Appendix Six

Standing of the Parties in the House of Commons
at Dissolution, following the 1993 Election, and at May 1st, 1995
(Seats in the House of Commons)

	Dissolution[a]	1993 Election	May 1st, 1995[b]
Liberal Party	80	177	177
Bloc Québécois Party	8	54	53
Reform Party	1	52	52
New Democratic Party	44	9	9
Progressive Conservative Party	157	2	2
Independent/Other	10	1	2

[a] September 1993. Three seats (Shefford, PQ; Malpeque, PEI; and North Vancouver, BC) were vacant at dissolution.

[b] Figures obtained from Elections Canada.

By-Election Results: February 13, 1995

	Brome-Missisquoi 24012	Saint-Henri–Westmount 24061	Ottawa–Vanier 35060
% Liberal	51.0	75.9	60.1
% Conservative	3.3	3.3	9.6
% NDP	1.0	1.8	6.3
% Bloc Québécois	42.2	14.1	n/a
% Reform	1.4	2.8	20.3
% Other	1.2	2.2	3.7
% Turnout	64.3	31.6	30.5
Total ballots	37,679	16,797	20,044
Member of Parliament	Denis Paradis, Liberal Party	Lucienne Robillard, Liberal Party	Mauril Bélanger, Liberal Party

Source: Elections Canada, *The February 1995 By-Elections: Another Step Forward: Report of the Chief Electoral Officer of Canada*, Ottawa: Chief Electoral Officer of Canada, Catalogue No. SE 1-2/1995, 1995.